MW00417189

"Habermas's argument from evidential near-death experiences and a likely afterlife to resurrection appearances of some sort is a useful addition to the literature."

—**Dale C. Allison Jr.**, Richard J. Dearborn Professor of New Testament Studies, Princeton Theological Seminary

"In volume 1 of this four-volume series, Gary Habermas has already produced a masterful defense of the resurrection of Jesus with his comprehensive collection of evidence. In volume 2, he responds to all the major and quite a few minor alternative explanations for the resurrection with grace and truth with level-headed reason. No doubt there will continue to be critics who simply ignore or casually skim and brush off this *opus giganticum*, and there will be those who follow them. Anyone wishing to *credibly* defend a skeptical position, however, will have to engage and then refute this work in considerable detail. I do not currently see how this would be possible."

—**Craig L. Blomberg**, distinguished professor emeritus of New Testament, Denver Seminary

"This book presents a monumental scholarly debate on the validity of vision for the resurrection of Jesus in Western Christianity."

—**John Dominic Crossan**, emeritus professor of biblical studies, DePaul University

"This second volume of Habermas's magisterial treatment of Jesus's resurrection thoroughly and persuasively engages objections, applies relentless logic, and challenges critics to be evenhanded in their evaluations. This series confirms Habermas's status as the leading voice among an increasing number of eminent scholars openly affirming the strong evidence for Jesus's resurrection."

—**Craig S. Keener**, F. M. and Ada Thompson Professor of Biblical Studies, Asbury Theological Seminary

"Gary Habermas has made it his main mission in his scholarly work to focus on the resurrection of Jesus and its importance. After many decades of hard work and detailed scholarship, he is now producing a four-volume series that is and will be, to my knowledge, the most detailed treatment of this crucial subject in Christian history. While the first volume deals at length with the reality and factuality of Jesus's resurrection from many angles, this second volume deals with the attempts ancient and modern to refute the idea that the historical Jesus was raised bodily from death in Jerusalem in antiquity. This volume deals with both ancient and modern attempts to deny the reality of miracles in general and the reality of Jesus's bodily resurrection in particular. This is a resource that every Christian college and seminary library should have on its shelf because it promises to be the most complete and compelling treatment of this subject available."

—**Ben Witherington III**, Amos Professor of New Testament for Doctoral Studies, Asbury Theological Seminary

"Professor Gary Habermas has made studying the resurrection of Jesus Christ his life's work. Probably no one else on the planet has researched or documented the relevant arguments in greater detail."

—**Peter Williams**, principal, Tyndale House, Cambridge, United Kingdom

On the Resurrection:

Vol. 2 REFUTATIONS

On the Resurrection:

REFUTATIONS

Vol. 2

—

GARY R. HABERMAS

B&H
ACADEMIC
BRENTWOOD, TENNESSEE

On the Resurrection, volume 2: *Refutations*
Copyright © 2024 by Gary Habermas

Published by B&H Academic®
Brentwood, Tennessee
All rights reserved.

ISBN: 978-1-0877-7862-4

Dewey Decimal Classification: 232.97
Subject Heading: JESUS CHRIST--PASSION WEEK \ JESUS CHRIST--
RESURRECTION \ JESUS CHRIST--APPEARANCES

Printed in China

29 28 27 26 25 24 RRD 1 2 3 4 5 6 7 8 9 10

CONTENTS

ANCIENT SOURCES
ABBREVIATION LIST

Babylonian Talmud

    b. *Gittin*   *Babylonian Gittin*

Early Jewish Writings

11Q19	Temple Scroll (Dead Sea Scrolls)
2 Macc.	*2 Maccabees*
3 Macc.	*3 Maccabees*
Josephus	
Ag. Ap.	*Against Apion*
Ant.	*Jewish Antiquities*
J.W.	*Jewish War*
Life	*Life*
Lam. Rab.	*Lamentations Rabbah*
Philo	
Embassy	*Embassy to Gaius*
Flacc.	*Against Flaccus*
Spec.	*On the Special Laws*
Tob.	*Tobit*
Wis.	*Wisdom of Solomon*

Greco-Roman Writings

Aristotle

    Rhet.   *Rhetoric*

Cassius Dio

    Hist. rom.   *History of Rome*

Cicero

    Fat.   *Concerning Fate*

    Phil.   *Phillipics*

Horace

    Ep.   *Letters*

Iamblichus

    Bab.   *Babylonica*

Juvenal

    Sat.   *Satires*

Lucian

    Peregr.   *Death of Peregrinus*

Ovid

    Fast.   *Fasti*

    Metam.   *Metamorphoses*

Plautus

    Poen.   *Poenulus*

Philostratus

    Vit. Apoll.   *Life of Apollonius*

Pliny the Younger

    Ep.   *Letters*

Plutarch

    Cleom.   *Life of Cleomenes*

    Per.   *Pericles*

Seneca

    Dial.   *Dialogues*

Suetonius

    Aug.   *Augustus*

    Cal.   *Gaius Caligula*

    Claud.   *Claudius*

    Dom.   *Domitian*

    Galb.   *Galba*

Jul.	*Julius*
Tib.	*Tiberius*
Tit.	*Titus*
Vesp.	*Vespasian*

Tacitus

Ann.	*Annals*
Hist.	*Historiae*

Valerius Maximus

De fact.	*De factis*

Early Christian Writings

1 Clem.	*1 Clement*
Acts Andr.	*Acts of Andrew*
Ap. John	*Apocryphon of John*

Aristides

Apol.	*The Apology of Aristides*
Barn.	*Epistle of Barnabas*
Did.	*Didache*

Eusebius

Hist. eccl.	*Ecclesiastical History*
Gos. Pet.	*Gospel of Peter*
Gos. Thom.	*Gospel of Thomas*
Gos. Truth	*Gospel of Truth*

Ignatius (Ign.)

Eph.	*To the Ephesians*
Magn.	*To the Magnesians*
Phld.	*To the Philadelphians*
Pol.	*To Polycarp*
Rom.	*To the Romans*
Smyrn.	*To the Smyrnaeans*
Trall.	*To the Trallians*

Ireneaus

Haer.	*Against Heresies*

Jerome

Vir. ill.	*On Illustrious Men*

Justin
    1 Apol.   *First Apology*
    2 Apol.   *Second Apology*
    Dial.   *Dialogue with Trypho*
Origen
    Cels.   *Against Celsus*
Polycarp (Pol.)
    Phil.   *To the Philippians*
Quintilian
    Decl.   *Declamations*
Sulpicius Severus
    Chr.   *Chronicle*
Tertullian
    Apol.   *Apology*
    Spect.   *On Spectacles*
Treat. Res.   *Treatise on the Resurrection*

Later Sources
QS   *Quran Surah*

INTRODUCTION: REFUTATIONS

In volume 1 of this study, I made a detailed positive case for the resurrection of Jesus. Obviously, rejoinders to the resurrection facts have been in existence virtually as long as the resurrection data have been proclaimed. In the pages of the Gospels alone, it was suggested that Jesus's dead body might be stolen by the disciples (Matt 27:62–66) or perhaps had already been moved by the gardener (John 20:13–16). Pilate wondered that Jesus had died so quickly and checked out the news with the centurion (Mark 15:43–45). The disciples thought that the women who had returned from the empty tomb were spreading tall tales (Luke 24:11). When the disciples saw Jesus, they thought that he might be a spirit or ghost of some sort (Luke 24:36–40). Ironically, three of these five issues were expressed by believers, perhaps signaling the hint that people on both sides of the aisle can doubt.

Over the centuries the challenges to belief in Jesus's resurrection have grown in variety and number as well as in sophistication, being declared in debates, university lectures, and elsewhere. On the heels of these questions, equally refined and complex defenses have appeared as well. In the field of religious studies, it seems that few subjects have received this much attention.

Among the pro-resurrection volumes that address the naturalistic and other alternative theses, twenty pages of attention is fairly lengthy. Thus, Michael Licona's nearly 200 pages on this topic are definitely exemplary, particularly as he works carefully through the details of six major challenges.[1] Licona's text drew much praise for the quality of the entire work, not to mention his attention to the more skeptical analyses. The coauthored work between Licona and me tallied slightly fewer than 100 pages on alternative challenges, counting the applicable endnotes.[2] By such standards, some may judge this present volume to be a case of overkill, though it is the companion to the larger first volume of evidence, and thus a much smaller treatment might be considered inappropriate by comparison. Nonetheless, the hope is that the details here will encourage further evaluation and discussion, regardless of the readers' perspectives.

In volume 1, I acknowledged and saluted my research assistants who helped extraordinarily throughout various stages of this huge, multiyear research project. Since the first volume, Dr. Ben Shaw has continued to interact with this work on nearly a daily basis, and I would once again like to acknowledge his very special and ongoing commitment to this project. His insights have been profound.

---

[1] Michael R. Licona, *The Resurrection of Jesus: A New Historiographical Approach* (Downers Grove, IL: InterVarsity Academic, 2010), 465–610.

[2] Gary R. Habermas and Michael R. Licona, *The Case for the Resurrection of Jesus* (Grand Rapids: Kregel, 2004).

1

Second-Century Challenges to the
Death and Resurrection of Jesus

In the previous volume, it has been argued from a variety of angles that Jesus was indeed a figure of human history, with his existence being corroborated in several different ways from varying sources. For example, dozens of reported facts can be gleaned from more than a dozen non-Christian writers, though many of these references are brief, in addition to many Christian writers (from both canonical as well as quite early noncanonical texts) along with some helpful archaeological artifacts.[1]

---

[1] Regarding the input from archaeology in the twentieth century and on into this present century, many details may be found in a large number of worthwhile sources, written from liberal and conservative perspectives as well as those in between. Some of these discoveries open the door to more general background information, while a few of them contribute more directly to the possibility of greater knowledge concerning the historical Jesus and related data. For starters, these sources on the value of archaeology for historical Jesus studies include William M. Ramsay, *Luke the Physician, and Other Studies in the History of Religion* (London: Hodder & Stoughton, 1908); William Foxwell Albright, *From the Stone Age to Christianity: Monotheism and the Historical Process* (Baltimore: Johns Hopkins University Press, 1946), particularly chap. 6, sec. D; Millar Burrows, *What Mean These Stones? The Significance of Archaeology for Biblical Studies* (New Haven, CT: American Schools of Oriental Research, 1941); A. N. Sherwin-White, *Roman Society and Roman Law in the New Testament* (Oxford: Oxford University Press, 1963); Joseph P. Free with Howard F. Vos, *Archaeology and Bible History*, rev. ed. (Grand Rapids: Zondervan, 1992),

With such a widespread amalgamation of sources, it is rather amazing and quite difficult to understand how Jesus's existence can be denied, though even as atheist New
Testament specialist Bart Ehrman states, this attitude is in large part due to the vast
majority of these doubts being expressed by individuals who are not trained in any of
the relevant research areas.[2]

Volume 1 of this study was largely concerned with the data that can be drawn
from the canonical New Testament texts, with special emphasis on passages located
in Paul's Epistles, the Gospels, and Acts.[3] These books are by far the oldest sources
for Jesus and represent the most crucial resources ever since the earliest church.
This chapter addresses the next generation of writings about Jesus that the majority of specialist scholars usually date after the canonical texts, though there are
discussions about the composition dates for a few of them. These later sources were
also about Jesus, though they often depicted quite different themes and emphases. These postcanonical writings will be divided into Tier 1 and Tier 2 layers for

---

esp. chaps. 26–29; Jonathan L. Reed, *Archaeology and the Galilean Jesus: A Re-examination
of the Evidence* (Harrisburg, PA: Trinity Press International, 2000); John Dominic Crossan,
The Historical Jesus: The Life of a Mediterranean Jewish Peasant (New York: HarperCollins,
1991); Geza Vermes, *Jesus in His Jewish Context* (Minneapolis: Fortress, 2003); N. T. Wright,
The New Testament and the People of God, vol. 1 of *Christian Origins and the Question of God*
(Minneapolis: Fortress, 1992); Craig S. Keener, *The Historical Jesus of the Gospels* (Grand
Rapids: Eerdmans, 2009), see chap. 13 and 179–83 in particular; F. F. Bruce, *Jesus and
Christian Origins outside the New Testament* (Grand Rapids: Eerdmans, 1974), esp. chap. 11;
R. T. France, *The Evidence for Jesus* (Downers Grove, IL: InterVarsity, 1986), esp. chap. 4;
Gary R. Habermas, *The Historical Jesus: Ancient Evidence for the Life of Christ* (Joplin, MO:
College Press, 1996), see chap. 8. For several more-specialized archaeological studies related
to the specific themes of this overall study, see V. Tzaferis, "Jewish Tombs at and near Giv'at
ha-Mivtar," *Israel Exploration Journal* 20 (1970): 18–32; Vassilios Tzaferis, "Crucifixion—
The Archaeological Evidence," *Biblical Archaeological Review* 11 (1985): 44–53; N. Haas,
"Anthropological Observations on the Skeletal Remains from Giv'at ha-Mivtar," *Israel
Exploration Journal* 20 (1970): 38–59; Joseph Zias and Eliezer Sekeles, "The Crucified
Man from Giv'at ha-Mivtar: A Reappraisal," *Israel Exploration Journal* 35 (1985): 22–27;
Joe Zias and James H. Charlesworth, "Crucifixion: Archaeology, Jesus, and the Dead Sea
Scrolls," in *Jesus and the Dead Sea Scrolls*, ed. James H. Charlesworth (New York: Doubleday,
1992), 273–89; Martin Hengel, *Crucifixion in the Ancient World and the Folly of the Message
of the Cross*, trans. John Bowden (Philadelphia: Fortress, 1977).

[2] Bart D. Ehrman, *Did Jesus Exist? The Historical Argument for Jesus of Nazareth* (New
York: HarperCollins, 2012), 2, 17, 20–23, 167, 194–96, 268.

[3] These sources include the exceptionally early and valuable creedal traditions found
almost solely in the epistles that are usually thought by scholars to have their roots in the
30s or slightly thereafter.

clearer reference. It is difficult to be precise in every case, but the Tier 1 category will be composed of texts usually thought to have been composed from about AD 100 to just before 150, while Tier 2 will include later writings that are usually dated from 150 to roughly 200.

Since only writings with themes chiefly revolving around Jesus and Christianity are considered in each of these two tiers, neither historical writings that simply mention Jesus once or twice (such as Josephus or Tacitus) nor the Jewish Mishnah are included in this chapter.[4] Thus, exempting the earlier canonical references treated in volume 1, the sources for Jesus being treated here were mostly composed between 100 and 200 years after Jesus's crucifixion.[5]

Speaking generally, the earliest wave of *serious challenges* to the general canonical period largely began somewhat later, after the beginning of what has been identified above as the Tier 1 sources.[6] For the purposes at hand in this chapter, the facts of Jesus's crucifixion and resurrection were especially unchallenged.[7]

---

[4] For reference, the most helpful pagan sources were from the Tier 1 period here (though Josephus is dated a little before AD 100), with the Mishnah being composed at the close of Tier 2 (about 200). It might be noted that with a few considerations, there is some slight overlap with volume 1 of this study, chiefly in the chapter concerning the historicity of Jesus, where a few passages from Tier 1 texts are considered with regard to what they may have contributed strictly regarding Jesus's life. Those references were more specifically topical and more of a historical nature, including sources that mentioned Jesus sparsely, rather than the general overviews in this discussion.

[5] In his own studies, for example, Ehrman includes in his primary grouping of texts for the historical Jesus those that were in existence within 100 years after Jesus's crucifixion (i.e., from approximately AD 30–130). This collection by Ehrman corresponds roughly to what is being termed the canonical sources composed before Tier 1. See Ehrman, *Did Jesus Exist?*, 97; Bart D. Ehrman, *The New Testament: A Historical Introduction to the Early Christian Writings* (Oxford: Oxford University Press, 2000), 44, 197.

[6] The term "serious" is important here. No one is asserting that there were no disputes whatsoever in the earliest canonical period. New Testament texts like Romans 14 and 1 Corinthians 15, among many other similar passages, should alone put an end to the sort of thinking that questions disputes in the early era. But as addressed below, the term "serious" does not apply to matters concerning which enjoyable dialogues are the focus of the three- and four-views books that even conservatives enjoying reading today. Thus, "serious challenges" are taken here to address matters such as attacks on the Christian gospel of the deity, death, and resurrection of Jesus, or other areas commonly termed the fundamental doctrines of Christianity.

[7] Accounts such as Matthew's story of the priests bribing the guards at the tomb to report that Jesus's disciples stole his dead body and presumably lying later about his appearances are of course examples defending the orthodox accounts rather than any sort of disputed themes among believers.

At any rate, the major challenges to orthodoxy largely started arriving on the scene quite late in the first century. The challengers sometimes even started rival movements featuring their own house churches and variations in theology. Within a couple of decades after the earliest Tier 1 sources, there were several objections that were pushing back, mostly beginning around AD 120 or 130.

At least the early challenges consisted chiefly of persons and groups that mostly acknowledged the more fundamental points of the Christian message—such as the deity, death, and resurrection of Jesus—but objected, sometimes strenuously, to more outlying beliefs, perhaps like eating meat offered to idols, or espoused particular versions of church government and hierarchy, and so on. Yet, probably due to their vehemence at various points, the earliest critics still often triggered the perception that they were actually enemies of the emerging Christian message or rejected the salvation of everyone else on the "other side" when, by today's standards, they may have been roughly the equivalent of different denominations who shared a similar core message!

By the middle of the second century, however, the next wave of critics consisted largely of "professional" non-Christian philosophers and others who held far more critical positions altogether, attacking the Christian message as a whole, often from the center out. In this they were significantly different from the earlier wave of critics.

Examples here would include Justin Martyr's Trypho the Jew (whether or not he is considered to be an actual person), whose objections are found in Justin's *Dialogue with Trypho* (written about AD 150–160). Origen's antagonist Celsus wrote his famous critical work (now lost), titled *On the True Doctrine*, about 170–185.[8] This work probably launched the most famous early attack against the Christianity of that day. Some would add Marcion to this group, too, writing a little earlier than Justin at about 140, but he definitely was not as vitriolic as were Trypho and Celsus. Writing in the late third century, Porphyry is sometimes thought to be an even more trenchant critic of Christianity than the others mentioned here, but to consider his ideas would move the discussion too far away from the date of the crucifixion (well over 200 years later) to be really helpful in discussing the early criticisms against Christianity.[9]

---

[8] This was the same time that Origen was born, and he wrote his famous apologetic work *Contra Celsum* against Celsus a half century later.

[9] Jeremiah J. Johnston states that Porphyry was "akin to modern-day 'New Atheists.'" See Johnston, *The Resurrection of Jesus in the Gospel of Peter: A Tradition-Historical Study of the Akhmim Fragment* (London: Bloomsbury, 2016), 143.

This chapter begins by viewing some of the diversity that very skeptical scholars like to think may have existed in the mid-first century, occurring during what has been termed here the canonical period before Tier 1. This has been a huge topic for discussion and debate in recent decades. Afterward, two other waves of criticism will be considered—both the milder canonical critiques from as early as approximately AD 85 or 90 until just before the time of Marcion in 140, and then on to some representative stronger attacks on Christianity after that time, starting with Marcion and then moving later into the Tier 2 category. The goal of this chapter is to track these second-century challenges to Jesus's death and resurrection. Detailed critiques of these views will be reserved until the later chapters that address other similar attacks on these same doctrines.

First-Century AD Diversity?

This has been one of the most intriguing topics in historical Jesus research, and one where liberal and conservative lines of demarcation are often more than obvious. More specifically, it is an area where very skeptical scholars exhibit quite divergent views from moderates, conservatives, and even from a number of liberal thinkers. It is also the area where some of the largest clashes have occurred between these researchers, though the conflict seems to have died down somewhat from where it has been. Like everyday political clashes, the interpretations of the data are often the most strained and stretched of all, since so much may ride on the outcomes of these discussions!

In recent decades, it has become apparent that a number of more skeptical commentators yearn to find alternate Christianities (and especially alternate Christologies) lurking among the teachings of the earliest church. The bottom line is often that finding such gems would then both ground the ideas themselves as well as point to a smorgasbord of equally authoritative options among which the early Christians (as well as Christians today) might choose without fear of being condemned for not taking a particular option that someone else may wish to foist upon them. The goal might be to argue that first-century Christianity was tolerant and diverse, thereby providing a paradigm for today. But a key to making these moves is to redate what are usually thought of as second-century writings to a much earlier time, often very far back into the first century. After all, this recent thesis depends on having options that rivaled the dates of the earlier canonical texts as well as the sources behind them.

As a result, quite steadily over recent decades, certain writings that are most commonly dated to the mid-second century or even later by a consensus of scholars

have started being dated in more radical publications back into the first century—
sometimes almost 100 years earlier than previously dated.[10] The reasons for these
moves regularly seem to be rather arbitrary, too, as pointed out by other critical
scholars. But what findings, specifically, have changed in the actual research? What
are the real reasons that justify the shift to sometimes much earlier dates for these
writings? Far too seldom are strong and careful arguments provided.

Another crucial and common move is maintaining that while a text may indeed
be dated to the same time generally held by most other scholars, manuscript versions
or portions of the text in question should now be dated many decades earlier. Often,
these smaller, presumably earlier slices of a text always contain the key ideas that
critics need most in order to make their arguments. This second option is capable of
garnering almost all the needed results of the initial move.

The German Liberal Religionsgeschichtliche Schule

Vestiges of these teachings occurred more frequently in the late nineteenth century with
the emergence of the German liberal school of thought known as the *religionsgeschichtliche
Schule* (history of religion school) movement. However, there was not as much emphasis
at that time on securing hard data for the various sources that were employed, since
these dates were largely unavailable. Since ascertainable dates were often impossible to
obtain, there was often no clear way to decipher the very specific claims that these critics
were making. They could have been, and sometimes were, citing sources that originated
long after the Christian sources, all the time thinking that those sources predated the
Christian materials. Therefore, in these accounts a plethora of unrelated persons, myths,
and amazing stories were often lumped together in unscholarly ways, sometimes one
after the other, as if there were almost automatic causal connections between them and
the Christian sources, with the former texts inspiring the latter ones.[11]

---

[10] As strange as it may seem, the atheist New Testament scholar Bart Ehrman dates
the *Gospel of Thomas* to about AD 120 (*New Testament*, 44), which is within the range of
dates chosen by evangelical New Testament scholar Darrell L. Bock in *The Missing Gospels:
Unearthing the Truth behind Alternative Christianities* (Nashville: Nelson, 2006), esp. the
chart on 219, cf. also 7, 59–65.

[11] The most influential volume that taught some of these ideas was probably anthro-
pologist James George Frazer's well-known study, *The Golden Bough: A Study in Comparative
Religion* (New York: Macmillan, 1890). The best-known scholar who applied this thesis to the
New Testament was most likely Wilhelm Bousset's 1913 work, *Kyrios Christos: A History of the*

This practice may be the most apparent in one of Otto Pfleiderer's works, where he compiled verses from the New Testament along with example after example from ancient mythology.[12] But as mentioned, the required dating of many pagan texts here was unknown or not provided. For example, the repeated citing of Buddha's writings, teachings, and actions were treated in a straightforward way (as in "Buddha taught" or "Buddha said") without knowing or divulging that the texts in question had often been written literally hundreds of years after Buddha's actual teachings or the events in his life.[13] So how would anyone trust for sure that Buddha taught these things? Examples such as these could certainly be multiplied in the publications of the *religionsgeschichtliche Schule*.

Defenses of the Gospel of Thomas

Unlike the end of the nineteenth century however, the dates of these ancient materials are known far better today. But this does not impede the presence of huge amounts of recent debate over these issues. For instance, the *Gospel of Thomas* (discovered in Nag Hammadi in 1945) is one of the major "prizes" in these discussions, especially regarding the role it plays surrounding the early theological diversity pertaining to the first few decades after Jesus's crucifixion. The Jesus Seminar is the chief group of scholars that favors dating the *Gospel of Thomas* to the first century AD, often before the composition of any of the Synoptic Gospels. In group votes,

---

Belief in Christ from the Beginnings of Christianity to Irenaeus, trans. John E. Steely (Nashville: Abingdon, 1970). Another influential scholar was Ernst Troeltsch, "The Significance of Jesus for Faith," in Troeltsch, *The Christian Faith*, trans. Garrett E. Paul (Minneapolis: Fortress, 1991), 87–100 (originally published in 1925); Troeltsch, "The Significance of the Historical Existence of Jesus for Faith (1911)," in *Ernst Troeltsch: Writings on Theology and Religion*, ed. and trans. Robert Morgan and Michael Pye (Atlanta: Knox, 1977), 182–207.

[12] Otto Pfleiderer, *The Early Christian Conception of Christ: Its Significance and Value in the History of Religion* (London: Williams & Norgate, 1905), as in chaps. 2 and 4.

[13] Pfleiderer, 51–53, 65–68, 154–55. Compare Buddhist scholar Edward Conze, trans. and ed., *Buddhist Scriptures* (London: Penguin, 1959), 11–12, 34, on the disparity of dates between the reports of the early church and the documents that report them versus the huge temporal distances between Buddha's teachings and actions and the sources regarding his words and exploits. More recent though very similar evaluations of Buddha's sources is supplied by Paul Gwynne, *Buddha, Jesus and Muhammad: A Comparative Study* (West Sussex, UK: Wiley-Blackwell, 2014), 1–6, 18–19; and Thich Nhat Hanh, *The Heart of the Buddha's Teaching: Transforming Suffering into Peace, Joy, and Liberation* (Chatsworth, CA: Random House Harmony, 1999), 13.

the *Gospel of Thomas* was placed by the Seminar at about AD 50–60, though some (even key) individuals in the Jesus Seminar opted for dates a few decades later.[14]

A few non-Jesus Seminar members have agreed on this general date too. Helmut Koester tends to place the *Gospel of Thomas* in the first century, but not later than the early second century.[15] One of the most critical scholars, Burton Mack, reports regarding the original Greek version "that scholars now date [*Thomas*] to the last quarter of the first century." However, he does not even refer here to the *majority* position that places the book much later![16]

Often, the major reason for dating the *Gospel of Thomas* so early is that this writing with its 114 sayings seems closely related to the form of the Q text, which is also a sayings document. This plus the presence of so many sayings that parallel Q (and Mark as well) leads to the inference that the *Gospel of Thomas* and Q date from about the same time.[17] Yet, most scholars think that this reason far from demonstrates this early dating thesis.

Though these moves to date the *Gospel of Thomas* to the first century are usually opposed, perhaps additional ideas may support these recent maneuvers to push back the date of the *Gospel of Thomas* from several decades to a century. One particular hypothetical idea that was initially floated almost a century ago has been noised about quite loudly ever since. It is now the most popular response in defense of an early date for the text, though it is not evidential in nature. It was claimed that in the mid-first century AD, the writings that were later adopted into the orthodox Christian canon were possibly circulated side by side with gnostic texts and other Gospels, all on fairly equal terms. From this multiplicity of diverse publications,

---

[14] Robert W. Funk, Roy W. Hoover, and the Jesus Seminar, *The Five Gospels: The Search for the Authentic Words of Jesus* (New York: Macmillan, 1993), 500–501, 548, plus charts on 18, 128; Robert W. Funk and the Jesus Seminar, *The Acts of Jesus: The Search for the Authentic Deeds of Jesus* (New York: HarperCollins, 1998), 555. For examples of those dating the *Gospel of Thomas* later, Stephen J. Patterson leans toward AD 70–80 in *The Gospel of Thomas and Jesus* (Salem, OR: Polebridge, 1993), 120. The date of 70–100 is also mentioned in Robert J. Miller, ed., *The Complete Gospels* (New York: HarperCollins, 1994), 303.

[15] Helmut Koester, *Introduction to the New Testament*, 2 vols. (Philadelphia: Fortress, 1982), 2:7, 152.

[16] Burton L. Mack, *The Lost Gospel: The Book of Q and Christian Origins* (New York: HarperCollins, 1993), 181.

[17] Funk, Hoover, and the Jesus Seminar, *Five Gospels*, 15, 548; Funk and the Jesus Seminar, *Acts of Jesus*, 555; Mack, *Lost Gospel*, 16, 26–27, 34–38, 177, 181, plus charts on 259 and 260–61.

the proto-orthodox movement emerged as the victor, but not necessarily because it taught the truth or because it was the original position of Jesus and his disciples. Rather, the orthodox members in the struggle took control of the situation by means of a political and social power grab, since they controlled the most influence and authority.

After the demise of German liberalism as a whole and the *religionsgeschichtliche Schule* movement in particular, the major work that served as a sort of fountainhead for this oft-repeated thesis was Walter Bauer's volume *Rechtgläubigkeit und Ketzerei im ältesten Christentum*.[18] An entire host of later publications took up a similar theme.[19] Raymond Brown noted some of the "increasing chorus of objections" that developed over against these emerging positions, such as their simplistic positions and especially that they never answered the major question of whether the orthodox views that "won" did so because they were more faithful to Jesus's teachings while the other positions were not.[20]

Scholarly Criticisms against the Early Dating of the Gospel of Thomas

However, the majority of contemporary scholars by far reject the early dating of the *Gospel of Thomas*, due specifically to the reasons supporting the later date. The current consensus position of scholars on the original date has moved somewhat earlier from where it was a few decades ago, but it is generally dated at somewhere between

---

[18] Walter Bauer, *Rechtgläubigkeit und Ketzerei im ältesten Christentum* (Tübingen: Mohr Siebeck, 1934). The English translation was published as *Orthodoxy and Heresy in Earliest Christianity*, ed. Robert Kraft and Gerhard Krodel, trans. Paul J. Achtemeier (Philadelphia: Fortress, 1971).

[19] Examples include Frederik Wisse, "The Use of Early Christian Literature as Evidence for Inner Diversity and Conflict," in *Nag Hammadi, Gnosticism, and Early Christianity*, ed. Charles Hedrick and Robert Hodgson (Peabody, MA: Hendrickson, 1986), 177–92; James M. Robinson, "On Bridging the Gulf from Q to the Gospel of Thomas (or Vice Versa)," in Hedrick and Hodgson, *Nag Hammadi*, 127–76; Helmut Koester, "Introduction to The Gospel of Thomas," in *The Nag Hammadi Library in English*, ed. James M. Robinson (New York: Harper & Row, 1977), 116; Elaine Pagels, *The Gnostic Gospels* (New York: Random House, 1979), xxii–xxiv, 12–13, 20, 29, 32, 56, 84–90, 112–14, 170–71, 177–81. A popular and older example is A. Powell Davies, *The Meaning of the Dead Sea Scrolls* (New York: New American Library, 1956), particularly 120.

[20] Raymond E. Brown, *The Churches the Apostles Left Behind* (Mahwah, NJ: Paulist, 1984), esp. 16–18.

the early to mid-second century AD.[21] The mainstream view also postulates that the *Gospel of Thomas* clearly borrowed from the existing canonical Gospels and possibly even the letters of John and Paul.[22]

Since a mid-second-century origin had been the more widely accepted range for both the *Gospel of Thomas* and many other significant texts of this general genre basically since their modern discovery, on exactly what additional grounds did the skeptics seemingly jump their date all the way back, in some cases, to approximately 100 years earlier while mentioning comparatively little evidence (and sometimes without any major confirmation at all)? Wright notes that many early *Thomas* dating problems often come in two species: naive and circular arguments. As examples of naive arguments, Wright cites John Dominic Crossan taking at face value the origin of the *Gospel of Thomas*'s own testimony according to saying 12, or Helmut Koester citing and accepting traditions regarding Matthew's Gospel from the *Gospel of Thomas*'s teaching.[23]

Another naive comment, this time from Mack, is found in his statement of gushing appreciation that the *Gospel of Thomas* "contains a truly amazing collection of the

---

[21] For this second-century date for the *Gospel of Thomas*, including a number of good arguments for these conclusions, see James D. G. Dunn, *Jesus Remembered*, vol. 1 of *Christianity in the Making* (Grand Rapids: Eerdmans, 2003), 58–59, 161–65; John P. Meier, *A Marginal Jew: Rethinking the Historical Jesus*, 5 vols., Anchor Bible Reference Library (New York: Doubleday, 1994), 2:333. See N. T. Wright, *New Testament and the People of God*, 436, for some historical perspective on this question. See also Keener, *Historical Jesus*, 54–57; Bock, *Missing Gospels*, esp. 61–63 where Bock surveys a number of recent scholars on the general date for *Thomas*; Craig L. Blomberg, *The Historical Reliability of the Gospels* (Downers Grove, IL: InterVarsity, 1987), 210–11.

[22] That most scholars also think the *Gospel of Thomas* borrowed at least from the Synoptic Gospels is noted by Dunn, *Jesus Remembered*, 162, 165, cf. 59; Meier, *Marginal Jew*, 1:124–39, 2:332–33, 476–77n106; F. L. Cross and E. A. Livingstone, *The Oxford Dictionary of the Christian Church* (Oxford: Oxford University Press, 1974), 1370; Craig Evans, "Jesus and the Gnostic Literature," *Biblica* 62 (1981): 406–12; Keener, *Historical Jesus*, 54–55; Bock, *Missing Gospels*, 61; Craig Blomberg, "Tradition and Redaction in the Parables of the Gospel of Thomas," *Gospel Perspectives: The Jesus Tradition outside the Gospel*, ed. David Wenham and Craig Blomberg (Sheffield: JSOT Press, 1984), 177–205; France, *Evidence for Jesus*, 75–78; cf. Paul Rhodes Eddy and Gregory A. Boyd, *The Jesus Legend: A Case for the Historical Reliability of the Synoptic Jesus Tradition* (Grand Rapids: Baker Academic, 2007), 228n72 (in this footnote, following C. M. Tuckett, Eddy and Boyd even make the point that the direction in 1 Cor 2:9 // *Gos. Thom.* 17 seems to favor the *Gospel of Thomas* borrowing from Paul).

[23] Wright, *New Testament and the People of God*, 439n72.

sayings of Jesus."[24] Here again, Mack's hypercritical attitudes toward the dating of the canonical Gospel sayings are contrasted with his treatment of the often less than orthodox teachings in the noncanonical texts, which are simply and naively praised and accepted virtually at face value.[25] But this regularly seems to be the way that much criticism proceeds. Rarely if ever are any of the nonorthodox sayings exposed to anything near the same textual intensity.

In the circular argument category, Wright places the opinions of another Jesus Seminar member, John Kloppenborg, with Helmut Koester in their comparisons and interactions between the canonical Gospels, the *Gospel of Thomas*, and Q. Sometimes the Q sayings are placed in the early strata of that document because they are thought to be similar to certain sayings to the *Gospel of Thomas*, and the *Gospel of Thomas* teachings may be called early when some of its sayings are similar to those in Q.[26] A similar example occurs when Mack claims that the *Gospel of Thomas* is shown to be early because its text parallels Q[1] (the hypothetical division of Q into parts, largely supporting the previous views of the critics). Mack utterly takes Q's writing and its layers for granted, failing to provide the provenance for this document, not to mention he engages in the *highly* controversial dividing of Q into strata![27]

It does not even seem to occur to Mack that though a number of passages in Q and the *Gospel of Thomas* may parallel each other in various ways, this by absolutely no means requires that they date from the same time! Could it not be the case that a source like the *Gospel of Thomas* could have borrowed from a first-century source like Q and still have been written in the second century or even later? This happens repeatedly in ancient history. For example, the apostolic fathers, such as Clement,

---

[24] Mack, *Lost Gospel*, 181. For other "kid-gloves" treatments of some Q sayings, see 86, 132, as well as an example of the informal logical faux pas of Mack's genetic fallacy on 215.

[25] Such as his late dating of the Synoptic Gospels plus Acts, even placing the compositions of Luke and Acts at about AD 120. See Mack, *Lost Gospel*, 178, 183, 186, chart on 259. All the while Mack backs the dating of the *Gospel of Thomas* into the first century, favoring a main date of about 90 though with aspects extending back to 65 (see the chart on 259). These are simply incredible and unacceptable switches and flip-arounds without the necessary arguments in support. But such is the attitudinal nature of much radical criticism at present. Other naive arguments from Mack occur when he compares Q and the Synoptic Gospels with regard to their miracle accounts, of course with more out-of-the-mainstream and unsupported criticisms of the Gospel texts; see *Lost Gospel*, 18, 22, 246.

[26] Wright, *New Testament and the People of God*, 439n72.

[27] Mack, *Lost Gospel*, 181.

Ignatius, and Polycarp, widely cite unattributed words that also appear in Paul's Epistles, but this does not mean that the works of these writers date to the 50s just like Paul's writings.

In fact, another hint that Mack is mistaken in his *Gospel of Thomas* and Q early dating comparisons is that, as Wright notes, the former was never mentioned in the ancient literature until Hippolytus and Origen do so in the third century.[28] But if the *Gospel of Thomas* is dated to the mid-first century AD like the canonical Gospels, and if it was as important and influential a book as some critics claim, at least for its own followers, then why would it take over a century and a half to find it cited? Given this fact, it makes more sense that the third-century citations were due to a second-century appearance of the *Gospel of Thomas*.

Besides these more head-to-head arguments, there is also the other major issue mentioned above, namely: what drastic change has caused some radical critics to move the date of the *Gospel of Thomas* 100 years earlier so quickly? This seems strongly to point to other factors. It would be an understatement to conclude that the current, very deep-seated desire to locate diversity in the theology of the earliest first-century Christian communities is presently a driving force. For whatever reasons, these scholars long for other christological options to have been available for the earliest Christians, seemingly to quell ideas like the notion that proto-orthodox, first-century Christology maintained that there was only one way to God and that Jesus was the messenger. Those who reject and even deny that this was the original teaching of Jesus and his followers need to produce *data* evidencing that this was not the original teaching and that other options were also originally taught by these same teachers. The *Gospel of Thomas* has been the most popular source for a different angle on the early Christian message, but the reasons do not line up with the strength of the claims.

Those who might conclude that the significance of such a "diversity message" has been emphasized too strongly here, or that it is not such a central concern today in critical circles that it would actually trump and even overpower scholarship, might consider the following recommendation in the pages of a recently released book by Andreas J. Köstenberger and Michael J. Kruger entitled *The Heresy of Orthodoxy*.[29]

---

[28] Wright, *New Testament and the People of God*, 436.

[29] Andreas J. Köstenberger and Michael J. Kruger, *The Heresy of Orthodoxy: How Contemporary Culture's Fascination with Diversity Has Reshaped Our Understanding of Early Christianity* (Wheaton, IL: Crossway, 2010).

In a rather exceptionally scornful response regarding early dating of the *Gospel of Thomas*, well-known scholar D. A. Carson quips brilliantly:

> In the beginning was Diversity. And the Diversity was with God, and the Diversity was God. Without Diversity was nothing made that was made. And it came to pass that nasty old "orthodox" people narrowed down Diversity and finally squeezed it out, dismissing it as heresy. But in the fullness of time (which is, of course, our time), Diversity rose up and smote orthodoxy hip and thigh. Now, praise be, the only heresy is orthodoxy. As widely and as unthinkingly accepted as this reconstruction is, it is historical nonsense: the emperor has no clothes.

This comment is followed by Carson's final line, thanking the two authors of the book for "patiently, carefully, and politely exposing this shameful nakedness for what it is."[30]

It is absolutely crucial to remember here too that the question at hand is *not* whether today's scholars would actually *prefer* diversity and toleration over a single, uniform, and rather exclusive message. Rather, the question in view is which position was taught by Jesus and his disciples. *That* is the subject that is being debated here—the main historical issue. But in attempting to decipher this latter question, some have allowed the common and contemporary issues of diversity and tolerance to assume the leading roles and have permitted the horses to pull the cart instead of asking the straightforward historical questions that they actually claim to be seeking. It *must* be remembered too that if the original teaching of Jesus and his disciples had been diversity and toleration, *that message* is most likely what moderates and conservatives would be proclaiming as the main idea.

What makes these recent radical moves even more frustrating and so disappointingly hypocritical is that the Jesus Seminar, representing the largest group of scholars pushing in this direction, has taken great pains to make many statements that clearly cloud the issues. For example, they have warned repeatedly against any sort of prejudice and its potential detrimental role in research, heavily criticizing other groups that they find offensive.[31] Yet, they also claim to be "neutral

---

[30] Carson's recommendation appears in the front pages of the volume by Köstenberger and Kruger.

[31] Funk, Hoover, and the Jesus Seminar, *Five Gospels*, 5–6, 24, include just a few of the examples.

observers" (!) in their work.[32] Most amusingly, they warn about discovering a Jesus in our own research who looks too much like ourselves![33] But then, in their seeming prejudgments, they attempt to rule out by fiat (perhaps because they do not have the *evidence* on their side to do otherwise?) the apparently despised positions that bother them so much.[34]

Back to Carson, Köstenberger, and Kruger: if they are correct in their own assessments of these topics, then there is a decided lack of evidence here for touting any of the gnostic or proto-gnostic writings and taking them from the second century back into the first century. It appears to be more like the earlier-mentioned, much-desired thesis in search of support. As such, it may be more like the maxim that if someone states something enough times, even without confirming data (as here), not only will it be believed, but the supporting "evidence" will appear soon enough. Yet, these three scholars are far from the only ones who think that there is a dearth of evidence for the early dating of the *Gospel of Thomas*.

Other recommendations issued by major scholars regarding the work by Köstenberger and Kruger were also forthcoming. Nicolas Perrin warned that the historical evidence fails to favor this recent view and instead supports the rival orthodox view. Daniel Wallace advised against giving in to "the siren song of postmodern relativism and tolerance." D. Jeffrey Bingham referred to the diversity and toleration thesis as one that "long ago should have been buried."[35]

Still other prominent New Testament specialists have chimed in similarly. Referring repeatedly to what he prefers to call the "Q-and-*Thomas* thesis," Wright asserts regarding Mack's version of the hypothesis in particular that there is "no real evidence for it whatsoever." Rather, it is all "an exercise in creative imagination. We just do not have the evidence to be able to postulate with any hope of accuracy." Then he includes Koester along with Mack and notes that they are so sure of their views in spite of their doing so "without any basis in actual evidence."[36] Then Wright adds

---

[32] Funk, Hoover, and the Jesus Seminar, 34.

[33] Funk, Hoover, and the Jesus Seminar, 5, but see also 28, 33, and so on.

[34] Funk, Hoover, and the Jesus Seminar, 16, 24–25, 32–33.

[35] Along with Carson's recommendation above, these comments also appear in the front pages of Köstenberger and Kruger, *Heresy of Orthodoxy*, as do additional remarks of a similar nature from New Testament scholars Charles Hill, Darrell Bock, and Paul Trebilco.

[36] N. T. Wright, *Jesus and the Victory of God*, vol. 2 of *Christian Origins and the Question of God* (Minneapolis: Fortress, 1996), 40, including n57.

that since Mack's thesis is a historical one, it needs to be judged on those grounds. But "by those canons, it fails."[37]

It is plainly the case that for Wright, perhaps the chief criticism of the "Q-and-*Thomas* thesis" remains a straightforward one: it clearly lacks any noteworthy evidence from which the hypothesis might be investigated and evaluated. As Wright summarizes some major issues regarding Mack's thesis, "It does not do justice to the data: it chops up texts with cheerful abandon and relocates them all over the place, radically misreading first-century Judaism and completely marginalizing the theology and religion of Paul—which is the one body of literature we not only actually possess but which we know for certain was produced within thirty years of the crucifixion."[38]

Elaine Pagels's volume *The Gnostic Gospels* is another example of scholarship that makes some similar claims supposing the idea that the proto-orthodox Gospels and the proto-gnostic Gospels simply circulated together, welcoming readers to espouse many of these radically different beliefs basically as they chose to do so.[39] But many reviewers responded to her work by pointing out, similarly to the scholars above, that the facts indicate that these two groups of writings simply were *not* on equal footing. That the canonical Gospels certainly appear to have been written decades earlier or even more is at least a preliminary indication that these four writings could possibly also be more authoritative.

O. C. Edwards has agreed with these latter critical comments. Speaking in particular of Pagels's thesis, he asserts: "It is precisely as history that I find her work most unsatisfactory. Nowhere, for instance, does she give the impression that the basic picture of Jesus given in the New Testament gospels did not arise contemporaneously with the Gnostic portrait, but antedated it by at least half a century. As historical reconstructions there is no way that the two can claim equal credentials."[40] Eminent New Testament scholar Joseph A. Fitzmyer responded in similar fashion: "Time and time again, [Pagels] is blind to the fact that she is ignoring a good century of Christian existence in which those 'Gnostic Christians' were simply not around."[41]

---

[37] Wright, 43.

[38] Wright, 43.

[39] Pagels, *Gnostic Gospels*, xxiii.

[40] O. C. Edwards, "A Surprising View of Gnosticism," *New Review of Books and Religion* (May 1980): 27.

[41] Joseph A. Fitzmyer, "The Gnostic Gospels according to Pagels," *America* (February 16, 1980): 123.

This straightforward indictment is certainly brief and directed to the same general point as the others. Another prominent participant in these dialogues who even appreciates some of Pagels's work, Pheme Perkins, still asserts that "Pagels either knows or cares too little about the theological diversity and development of 'orthodox' Christian theology in the first three centuries to be fair to its defenders in their debates with the gnostics. She is frequently taken in by the stock rhetorical polemics of both sides, mistaking rhetoric for fact."[42]

Edwards also charges that Pagels's text is plagued by a reductionism for which no evidence is provided beyond only her own words.[43] Perkins summarizes her critique this way: "The whole is so flawed by hasty generalization, over-interpretation of texts to fit a pre-determined scheme, and lack of sympathetic balance that this reviewer found herself constantly wishing that the whole could have been redone with more care."[44] Other issues raised regarding Pagels's thesis include her popularizing methodology; her constant imposition of modern political, sociological, and psychological factors on ancient philosophical and theological questions where they do not belong; and the apparent frustration with the lack of her desired support for woman's rights not being found in the gnostic sources.[45]

Overall, Brown judges regarding the *Gospel of Thomas* that "we learn not a single verifiable new fact about Jesus's ministry and only a few new sayings that might plausibly have been his."[46] Fitzmyer agrees but is even stronger in his assertions: "The Coptic texts of Nag Hammadi tell us little that is new. . . . It has been mystifying, indeed, why serious scholars continue to talk about the pertinence of this material to the study of the New Testament."[47] Several unifying theses occur repeatedly.

---

[42] Pheme Perkins, "Popularizing the Past," *Commonweal* (November 9, 1979): 634–35.

[43] Edwards, "Surprising View of Gnosticism," 7.

[44] Perkins, "Popularizing the Past," 635.

[45] For these many details among others, see Raymond E. Brown, "The Christians Who Lost Out," *New York Times Book Review* (January 20, 1980): 3; Kathleen McVey, "Gnosticism, Feminism, and Elaine Pagels," *Theology Today* 37 (1981): 498, 501; Edwards, "Surprising View of Gnosticism," 7; Fitzmyer, "Gnostic Gospels according to Pagels," 122; Perkins, "Popularizing the Past," 635.

[46] Brown, "Christians Who Lost Out," 3, though again, the chief issue is not whether there is much of value in the *Gospel of Thomas* but rather its historical provenance. Interestingly, Bock agrees with Brown on the possible presence of some authentic sayings of Jesus in *Thomas*; see Bock, *Missing Gospels*, 7, 61, 63.

[47] Fitzmyer, "Gnostic Gospels according to Pagels," 122–23.

The combined theses of the more radical scholars such as Pagels, Koester, Funk, Mack, and Robinson, along with some other members of the Jesus Seminar, have failed to convince the vast majority of their scholarly colleagues across the spectrum of views. But again, this point must not be missed here: it is decidedly *not* the influential scholarly names lining up against these gnostic theories, but the absence of any solid, determining evidence that favors these positions in any clear sense. The arguments against the skeptics have continued to mount, while a great many of their critics unite in remarking that their theses were bereft of the necessary supporting data, as seen above. As William Farmer comments, "We can only conclude that a hypothesis is being set forth for which there is very little evidence." As a result, and reminiscent of Wright's earlier "creative imagination" statement, Farmer concludes that when the *Gospel of Thomas* and Q are handled in the manner of their supporters, then the result is only revealed as "a grand vision . . . a romance."[48]

So as the dust settles from the scholarly debate chiefly on the *Gospel of Thomas*, there remain convincing and even dominant reasons for dating it as a second-century document, like other, similar writings that are most commonly dated to the mid-second century. This is the consensus position according to a dominant number of commentators, including moderate, conservative, and even some liberal scholars.[49] In fact, in probably the most scholarly volume on the *Gospel of Thomas* to date (over 700 pages in length), Simon Gathercole also decides for a second-century date. In this in-depth study, Gathercole argues for the *Gospel of Thomas*'s dependence on at least two canonical Gospels along with other New Testament books. Other scholarly volumes have consistently drawn the same or similar conclusions.[50]

---

[48] William R. Farmer, "The Church's Stake in the Question of 'Q,'" *Perkins School of Theology Journal* 39 (1986): 12, 14. Farmer's full-length treatise on this topic was one of the first scholarly whistle-blowing efforts here: *The Synoptic Problem: A Critical Analysis* (London: Macmillan, 1964).

[49] Strange as it may seem, even Bart D. Ehrman dates the *Gospel of Thomas* to about AD 130 in Ehrman, *The New Testament: A Historical Introduction to the Early Christian Writings*, 2nd ed. (Oxford: Oxford University Press, 2000), 44. This 130 date is within the range of dates chosen by evangelical New Testament scholar Darrell Bock, *Missing Gospels*, 7, 59–65! An agnostic skeptic who makes helpful comments in this regard was the late Maurice Casey, *Jesus: Evidence and Argument or Mythicist Myths?* (London: Bloomsbury, 2014), esp. 18, cf. also 52, 59. Cf. also Wright, *Jesus and the Victory of God*, 41.

[50] Simon Gathercole, *The Gospel of Thomas: Introduction and Commentary* (Leiden: Brill, 2014); see also Gathercole, *The Composition of the Gospel of Thomas: Original Language and Influences*, Society for New Testament Studies Monograph Series 151 (Cambridge:

As mentioned, these consensus critical views rest on a plethora of intricate studies leading to closely argued positions and conclusions. Unlike the first-century *Gospel of Thomas* option held by the Jesus Seminar and a comparatively small number of other scholars, several arguments have already been mentioned here in favor of the second-century position. These include the *Gospel of Thomas*'s seeming knowledge of and reliance upon two (and perhaps even all three) of the Synoptic Gospels plus other New Testament books.[51] Further, some of the ideas in the *Gospel of Thomas* along with similar proto-gnostic ideas were absent during the first two or three decades after the crucifixion, but with the same ideas being quite similar to other writings from the mid-second century onward.[52] Moreover, it has already been mentioned that the *Gospel of Thomas* is never quoted or cited in the early literature until the third century.[53] These last arguments are quite damaging to the early dating thesis.

The scholarly citations above contained more than just the final evaluative verdicts themselves. Beyond the latter critiques just mentioned, there were also at least five more specific critiques that need to be unpacked and addressed by the skeptics. One recurring theme from among the respondents above was that the proto-orthodox texts were simply much earlier, up to a half century or more. Another argument that strongly favors the priority of the canonical texts is that these writings have much stronger and more solid claims to being dated earlier. Moreover, the canonical works were more authoritative in that they had much closer connections to

---

Cambridge University Press, 2014); Mark Goodacre, *Thomas and the Gospels: The Case for Thomas's Familiarity with the Synoptics* (Grand Rapids: Eerdmans, 2014), who dates the *Gospel of Thomas* at about AD 140 (171). All three of these texts also opt in detail for the *Gospel of Thomas*'s dependence on Matthew and Luke, along with other New Testament books.

[51] John Meier makes an amazing statement here. He states that he can show the likelihood of this reliance of the *Gospel of Thomas* on Matthew and Luke based only on just four key passages: sayings 54, 68, 69a, and 69b. See Meier, *Marginal Jew*, 2:333. Goodacre spends an entire chapter on *Gos. Thom.* 79 because he considers the case for dependency on Luke to be so strong here; see chap. 6 of *Thomas and the Gospels*. Most of all, Gathercole develops his argument for the dependence of the *Gospel of Thomas* in over 100 pages alone in his comparatively short volume on this text; see chaps. 6–11 in *Composition of the Gospel of Thomas*.

[52] This question has been discussed at length throughout this chapter with the conclusion being that the *Gospel of Thomas* is most likely a mid-second-century composition. Appropriate sources are listed throughout, such as Nicholas Perrin, *The Judas Gospel* (Downers Grove, IL: InterVarsity, 2006), 24.

[53] Wright, *New Testament and the People of God*, 436.

Jesus's apostles.[54] Further, the New Testament canon was decided much earlier than normally thought (without the pro-gnostic writings, perhaps arguing that they were not yet widely known, as already mentioned). Last, the centrality of Jesus's death and resurrection (see below on this), admitted by virtually all critical scholars, also argues in the direction of the canonical texts over the dissenting direction preferred by the proto-gnostic works.[55]

One last absolutely crucial item must be mentioned here. *Even if* it were the case that the *Gospel of Thomas* belonged back in the mid-first century, this does not at all disprove or challenge the historical events of Jesus's death and resurrection. The reason for this conclusion is quite straightforward: the *Gospel of Thomas* does not dispute either event, but the text teaches or implies both events several times. Jesus's death is predicted, implied, or mentioned (*Gos. Thom.* 12, 55, 65), as is the resurrection and exaltation of Jesus (*Gos. Thom.* prologue, 59, 66, 71, 111).[56] These events are hinted at in ways that seem to indicate that knowledge of the Gospel narratives lies behind the mere mentions of items such as Jesus having to depart from his disciples (*Gos. Thom.* 12) or Jesus's teaching that his hearers should take up their crosses and follow him (*Gos. Thom.* 55). In particular, the parable of the master's son being killed (*Gos. Thom.* 65; cf. Mark 12:1–12) especially points in this direction of further behind-the-scenes teachings of Jesus's death.

The very next saying notes that the stone that was rejected by builders became the cornerstone (*Gos. Thom.* 66), thereby pointing to Jesus being exalted after his death. In *Gos. Thom.* 71, Jesus appears to be saying that while he will be raised and exalted (as per *Gos. Thom.* 66), it will not be his physical body that will be raised. So while the *mode* of Jesus's appearances presumably might have been a matter for

---

[54] For just a few examples, there are the early creeds in 1 Cor 11:23–25; 15:3–7, among many others, plus other passages such as Gal 1:18–24; 2:1–10, each of these being drawn from what Ehrman (as well as virtually all other critical scholars) terms the "undisputed Pauline epistles." See Ehrman, *New Testament*, 262, 290, cf. 44. Luke 1:1–4 and the Acts sermon summaries (the latter found chiefly in Acts 1–5, 10, 13, and 17) also must be given their critical scholarly due, with Ehrman dating at least some of the latter to just one to two years after the crucifixion in *Did Jesus Exist?*, 109–13, 140–41, 172, 232, 261–62!

[55] The defense and explication of these last four arguments would take us far beyond the present scope of the above topic. However, for the details, see the sources in footnotes 33–41 above, plus the interested reader may consult volume 1 of this study. For a briefer look, see Habermas, *Historical Jesus*, particularly 106–18.

[56] The meaning of Jesus being called "the living Jesus" (prologue) or "the Living One" (59, 111, cf. 52b) in the *Gospel of Thomas* is discussed later in this chapter.

dispute between the *Gospel of Thomas* and other Christians, had the former spelled out these views further, there would not be a disagreement over the *fact* that Jesus had actually been raised from the dead.[57]

The Q Document and Resurrection Teachings

The other presumed document that is so often paired with the *Gospel of Thomas*, in that both consist of a list of sayings of Jesus, is the so-called Q document, taken from the German term *Quelle* (Source). Whether or not there actually was such a document is of no concern here, though it has never been discovered in whole or in part. Q is referred to as the document that stands behind the sayings of Jesus in Matthew and Luke that are not found in Mark. That is also how it will be referred to here. The overall question pertains to whether or not Q contributes to or subtracts from the teaching of Jesus's resurrection.

For the record, there is more dispute today about the existence of an actual Q document than at any other time in this century.[58] A second issue concerns whether Q can be subdivided into layers or editions, three of which are most prominently

---

[57] Gregory J. Riley, *Resurrection Reconsidered: Thomas and John in Controversy* (Minneapolis: Fortress, 1995), esp. 177–79. Regarding the relevance of discussing the date for the *Gospel of Thomas*, Riley is one of the researchers who holds to the first-century date and considers the *Gospel of Thomas* to be earlier than the canonical Gospels. As such, Reilly mentions its nonphysical view of resurrection and that it may be both earlier and more authoritative than the later bodily version found in the Gospels (66, 178–79). For example, in *Gos. Thom.* 71, Jesus states that no one will raise his body, presumably because while he definitely will be raised from the dead in a spiritual body, perhaps like that which was witnessed by the apostle Paul in Jesus's appearances described in Acts 9, 22, and 26, his *physical body* will never be raised (178). Riley takes the old position on 1 Corinthians 15 that Paul (like the *Gospel of Thomas*) also taught that Jesus was raised and appeared in a spiritual body (88–90, 96, 177–79). Incidentally, Riley crucially considers the pre-Pauline creed in 1 Cor 15:3–5 to be the very earliest of the known resurrection appearance texts (65).

[58] For a list of a few of the critical scholars who either advocate or lean toward other alternatives besides Markan priority or the existence of Q, see William R. Farmer, "Preface: Order Out of Chaos," *The Perkins School of Theology Journal* 40 (1987): 1–6. For a number of more recent studies questioning the existence of Q by quite prominent scholars, see Mark Goodacre, *The Case against Q: Studies in Markan Priority and the Synoptic Problem* (London: T&T Clark, 2002); Mark Goodacre and Nicholas Perrin, eds., *Questioning Q: A Collection of Essays* (London: SPCK, 2005). For a helpful summary of arguments for and against theses such as the priority of Mark and the existence of Q, see David Barrett Peabody, "In Retrospect and Prospect," *The Perkins School of Theology Journal* 40 (1987): 9–16.

discussed. On the first question, Marcus Borg reports that probably 90 percent of recent scholars accept its existence, so it is a very popular thesis.[59] However, he realizes that many scholars have trouble with the claim that Q can be accurately divided into layers.[60]

Pertaining to the date of the Q document, the *terminus ad quem* would have to be locked in before the composition of Matthew, which employed this text and is usually placed by critical scholars at about AD 80. For these researchers, Q would have to have been in existence by perhaps AD 50–60. For those who date Matthew's authorship some twenty years earlier (a popular but not predominant date), then Q would have to date much earlier still. The Jesus Seminar dates Q to about 50–60.[61]

Here again, it must be remembered that, like the *Gospel of Thomas*, Q is by no means a problem for Christianity. That should be even more obvious in this case, given that since there are no manuscript copies of Q, what is known to be in the hypothetical text is held in common with Matthew and Luke, and that is hardly troublesome in that it is already part of the canon.

The Q texts used in Matthew and Luke cite miracles and exorcisms by Jesus.[62] Another Q passage records the Jewish leader's question about receiving a sign, which precipitated Jesus's comment concerning the sign of Jonah along with a rebuke.[63] The reproach was probably given due to Jesus's sense earlier in the same context that the leaders would not have believed even if they had personally seen an appearance from someone who had been raised from the dead, similar to Jesus's comment in Luke 16:30–31. After all, when Jesus healed a possessed man not long before, the Pharisees responded that Jesus did so by the power of Beelzebul (or Beelzebub; Matt 12:22–24;

---

[59] Marcus J. Borg, *The Lost Gospel Q: The Original Sayings of Jesus*, ed. Mark Powelson and Ray Riegert (Berkeley, CA: Ulysses, 1996), 15.

[60] Borg, *Lost Gospel Q*, 16.

[61] Funk, Hoover, and the Jesus Seminar, *Five Gospels*, 18, 128.

[62] Miracles are reported in QS 15 and QS 16, and an exorcism is found in QS 28, according to Mack's reckoning of the Q passages (corresponding to Q 23, Q 24, and Q 37, respectively, in Borg's accounting).

[63] Both Matthew and Luke also report the request for a miracle that was answered by Jesus, who offered the coming sign of Jonah (QS 32 Mack; Q 41 Borg). However, the words regarding the three days and nights in the great fish as recorded in Matt 12:38–40 were deleted in both of these textual renditions of the Q sayings, probably since they are absent from the passage in Luke. One question, however, concerns whether the words implying Jesus's resurrection in Matthew were incorrectly left out of Mack's and Borg's critical texts.

Luke 11:14–15), rather than admitting a miracle from God. What would keep the leaders from responding similarly again?

Most likely, even without Luke including the portion of the comment on the Son of Man spending three days and nights in the heart of the earth, there are several reasons why the Q reference here seems most likely to be referring to Jesus's resurrection. As I. Howard Marshall has crucially remarked, the word picture would conjure up for Jewish ears the notion of Jonah's "miraculous deliverance from death."[64] Further, the similar text later in Luke 16:30–31 points in this direction by mentioning the resurrection as well. Last, Matthew may be even closer to the original Q reading, with Luke simply deleting a few words. At the very least, this was clearly Matthew's personal interpretation of this text's meaning.[65]

Needless to say, on the surface at least, these reports of miracles and an exorcism probably pointing to Jesus's resurrection in Q hardly militates against anything in the New Testament. This is especially the case with the last point in particular, assuming it is concluded that Q was affirming Jesus's resurrection. By virtue of the three days and nights reference, Matthew has "unpacked" what he considered to be the obvious meaning here.

Brief Excursus: Are Jesus's Death and Resurrection Central in the *Gospel of Thomas* and Q?

Before leaving the topics of the *Gospel of Thomas* and Q, an important side theme needs to be mentioned. The discussion of the *Gospel of Thomas* above may indicate that Jesus's death and resurrection may potentially be more prominent than is often thought. It has been noted that the *Gospel of Thomas* may mention or imply the death of Jesus at least three times and the resurrection about five times. Further and more crucially, what about the many commentators who think that "the living Jesus" in the *Gospel of Thomas* prologue (or "the Living One" of *Gos. Thom.* 59, 111, cf. 52b)

---

[64] I. Howard Marshall, *Commentary on Luke*, New International Greek Testament Commentary (Grand Rapids: Eerdmans, 1978), 485.

[65] Much scholarly research has been done on this question, including PhD dissertations. Examples include Simon Siu Chun Chow, "The Sign of Jonah Reconsidered: A Study of its Meaning in the Gospel Traditions" (PhD diss., Uppsala Universitet, 1995); Titus Oluwafidipe Oluwafemi, "Jesus' Resurrection as the Ultimate 'Sign' of His Messianic Authority (A Special Reference Study of the Jonah-Sign in Matthew-Luke and the Temple-Sign in John)," (PhD diss., Baylor University, 1979).

either is or could possibly be the resurrected, currently living Jesus?[66] If they correctly decipher the *Gospel of Thomas*'s meaning here, then arguably the entire book can be crafted from the standpoint of this opening text, meaning that the resurrection of Jesus marks the very center of the *Gospel of Thomas* as well, since the resurrected and living Jesus would be the source and purveyor of the book's wisdom. Robert M. Grant suggests that the opening text may be precisely why the *Gospel of Thomas* devotes comparatively little attention to Jesus's life and death.[67]

The question regarding Q appears to be even more straightforward. The Q text is incomplete; thus, scholars do not possess these actual sayings in their entirety. Basically, only the portions that appear in both Matthew and Luke but not in Mark can be evaluated for sure. Given that fact, how can it possibly be known how the document begins and ends, or the content of the additional material? The text's overall

---

[66] This list would include a number of relevant researchers. James M. Robinson thinks it is possible that, like the *Gospel of Thomas*, the entire perspective of Q also may be that of the living Jesus ("Jesus from Easter to Valentinus," *Journal of Biblical Literature* 101 [1982]: 23–24). Robinson adds that a theme not being as prominent as some might think does not mean that the communities were unaware of those teachings (Robinson, "The Sayings of Jesus: Q," *Drew Gateway* [1983]: 32). The Jesus Seminar even judged that the Jesus who speaks in the prologue to the *Gospel of Thomas* may possibly be that of the resurrected Jesus (Funk, Hoover, and the Jesus Seminar, *Five Gospels*, 398). Borg indicates a possible though rather strange position that the *Gospel of Thomas* may depict the living Jesus, regardless of whether or not the *Gospel of Thomas* community knew about the resurrection (Borg, "Thinking about Easter," *Bible Review* 10 [1994]: 49). Speaking more of Q but also with some relevance to the *Gospel of Thomas*, Meier remarks that concluding that the Q group had no "knowledge of or interest in Jesus' death and resurrection is simply not verified by the data at our disposal." See John P. Meier, "Dividing Lines in Jesus Research Today: Through Dialectical Negation to a Positive Sketch," *Interpretation* 50 (1996): 59. Similar to Meier, N. T. Wright thinks that simply not enough is known about Q (or the *Gospel of Thomas* for that matter) to remark dogmatically concerning the specific content regarding these sorts of questions; see *Jesus and the Victory of God*, 41–43. Gerald O'Collins cites Raymond Brown, who criticizes the confidence of those who think that they possess and understand the entire knowledge of the Q community simply by reconstructing Q; see O'Collins, *Interpreting the Resurrection* (Mahweh, NJ: Paulist, 1988), 18. Pheme Perkins notes about Q (and the *Gospel of Thomas* should be added here as well) that "there is no element of early Christian belief in Jesus of Nazareth that is not marked by the 'resurrection.'" See Perkins, "The Resurrection of Jesus of Nazareth," in *Studying the Historical Jesus: Evaluations of the State of Current Research*, ed. Bruce Chilton and Craig A. Evans (Leiden: Brill, 1994), 442.

[67] Robert M. Grant, *Gnosticism and Early Christianity*, rev. ed. (New York: Harper & Row, 1966), 183–84.

theme and purpose are unknown, except to record various sayings of Jesus. So how
can the content of the remaining portions of Q be ascertained by guessing?

The comments in the notes above concerning James Robinson and other
scholars could be helpful here. If the living Jesus (especially if he is resurrected)
begins and frames the *Gospel of Thomas*, Q, and any other possible sayings texts,
whether or not they were composed during the same period, then this could provide some potential answers regarding these questions as to why the resurrection
may be less prominent.[68]

Working further in the direction of the brief survey above, there are a few key
texts in Q that *do* speak of Jesus's miracles, an exorcism, and the "sign of the prophet
Jonah" and its probable reference to both Jesus's death and resurrection. So, while
there are not enough data to answer just how much more of a role these supernatural
topics may have played in this collection, it is unknown whether they were further
encouraged, avoided, or denied. In the absence of all these potential questions, it
seems virtually impossible to ascertain whether the death and resurrection of Jesus
were central themes in Q. That certainly could be the case, but it cannot be asserted
with confidence.

Thus, when various commentators make their seemingly offhanded remarks
(sometimes even appearing to hope or wish that this were the case) that Jesus's death
and resurrection are not central in the *Gospel of Thomas* and Q, upon what are such
comments based? If all anyone knew was that the *Gospel of Thomas* begins with what
may purportedly be the words of the living Jesus and that the Q material is likely to
be only a portion of these teachings of Jesus, these facts alone should keep anyone
from being secure in their comments that Jesus's death and resurrection are not central in these sources. Therefore, based on these known factors alone, it would appear
that such doubts regarding these two sources amount to whistling in the dark—it is
simply unknown at present. Regardless, these subjects were not absent from Q and
the *Gospel of Thomas*. As stated by New Testament specialist Reginald H. Fuller concerning Q, "So although the Q material does not contain the kerygma of the resurrection it presupposes it all the way through."[69]

Another suggested potential first-century source often accepted by recent critical
scholars should be mentioned here too. Often called the Miracles Source, it seems

---

[68] Robinson, "Jesus from Easter to Valentinus," 23–24.

[69] Reginald H. Fuller, *The Foundations of New Testament Christology* (New York:
Scribner's Sons, 1965), 143.

to have been employed at least in the Gospels of John and Mark and is usually dated to about the same time as Q: in the 50s, according to the Jesus Seminar. Though there are other ways to explain the data, the usually cited evidence for the presence of this source is that John states that changing water to wine in 2:11 was Jesus's first public miracle, while later identifying Jesus's healing of the official's son as his second miracle (4:54).[70] Further, Crossan notes that the total of seven miracle stories in John 2–9 have Markan parallels in the same order (chiefly in Mark 2, 6, 8).[71] Many contemporary scholars conclude that John and perhaps Mark were thus employing a previously tabulated list of Jesus's miracles.

None of the sources dated to approximately AD 100 conflict with the canonical New Testament teachings regarding the facticity of Jesus's death and resurrection. Rather, these events were known and affirmed during this period. Alternate *interpretations* occurred here or there, as with the *Gospel of Thomas* possibly holding the view that Jesus appeared with glorified, nonbodily manifestations (even when the early-dating option is accepted, which seems most likely to be mistaken, as just argued in detail). But there were no assured factual denials or challenges to the historical events of the death and resurrection during this early time.

The other question posed in this section was answered in the affirmative, namely, that there were certainly a number of items over which there was a diversity of views in this early New Testament period—in theological, ethical, political, and social areas. The New Testament itself is a witness to this conclusion, as Romans 14 sets forth clearly. Paul did not just choose some "ho-hum" areas of discussion in this passage either. He raises questions concerning two of the toughest issues of all in the early church—a theological argument drawn from the Ten Commandments regarding the specific day on which believers should worship and the ethical issue of eating meat that had been offered to idols. Of course, even more diversity of views exists between believers today. But in this earliest period, the historical facts of Jesus's death by crucifixion and his resurrection were not the targets of the disputes.[72]

---

[70] Funk, Hoover, and the Jesus Seminar, *Five Gospels*, 16–18; Funk and the Jesus Seminar, *Acts of Jesus*, 388–89, while questioning its existence at least somewhat (389).

[71] Crossan, *Historical Jesus*, 429.

[72] As mentioned previously, views regarding the *mode* of Jesus's resurrection appearances would sometimes arise later without rejecting the occurrence itself. As Wright asserts, the bodily appearance "meaning is constant throughout the ancient world, until we come to a new coinage in the second century." See Wright, *The Resurrection of the Son of God*, vol. 3

Diversity in the Tier 1 Texts (AD 100–150)

By the close of the earlier canonical period, there were differences of opinion within the early church, though none that denied major doctrines or historical events.[73] However, this minor diversity grew steadily in the decades ahead.

At the Close of the Canonical Period

In an intriguing volume that emerged chiefly from the Sprunt Lectures given at Union Theological Seminary in Richmond, Virginia, in January 1980, New Testament specialist Raymond Brown developed a thesis regarding the Christian diversity of beliefs that occurred after the death of the apostles during the last third of the first century.[74] For Brown, orthodox theology extended back to Jesus, whose teachings were the very center of Christian doctrine, especially regarding the belief in Jesus's death and resurrection.[75]

At the close of the canonical period, a number of noticeable differences began to emerge. Noting chiefly the exception of Paul's "undisputed letters," Brown states that most of the remainder of the New Testament books were written during this "sub-apostolic" window. He then proceeds to summarize these differences according to the communities represented by groups of New Testament books, such as the Pastoral Epistles, Colossians and Ephesians, Luke-Acts, the Petrine Epistles, the Johannine tradition including the Epistles, and Matthew. However, the differences that he notes between these communities are usually remarkably small and not fundamental.

For example, for Brown the Pastoral Epistles hold different views on the place of women in the church.[76] Colossians and Ephesians reveal contrasts regarding ecclesiology and especially different perspectives on Judaism.[77] Luke-Acts diverges from

---

of *Christian Origins and the Question of God* (Minneapolis: Fortress, 2003), esp. 31 for this quotation, also 547, 550–51.

[73] Depending somewhat on whether the *Gospel of Thomas* is early (which was rejected here).

[74] Brown, *Churches the Apostles Left Behind*, 146.

[75] Brown, 86, 147–48n201. Brown cites Reginald Fuller as also agreeing especially on the last point regarding the center of the orthodox message; R. H. Fuller, "New Testament Trajectories and Biblical Authority," in *Studia Evangelica VII*, ed. Elizabeth A. Livingstone (Berlin: Akademie Verlag, 1982), 189–99.

[76] Brown, *Churches the Apostles Left Behind*, 20–21, 31–46.

[77] Brown, 21, 47–60.

Ephesians and Colossians on concepts of the church and perhaps on the nature of fellowship.[78] Johannine Christology is the highest among the Gospels, being the only Gospel teaching of preexistence, again according to Brown. Also, John's realized eschatology is contrasted with the more traditional, futuristic eschatologies.[79] The writer of Hebrews has a very high Christology, like John and Paul, and shares some other similarities with Paul too, but with a totally different style. Hebrews also places more emphasis on various aspects of Jesus's true humanity as well as gives a "radical critique" to the "Israelite cult" of Judaism.[80] Brown also comments on 1 Peter (on which he takes what he terms the majority view that it was written by a Petrine disciple), James, Matthew, and Mark, emphasizing each of their distinctives.[81]

In conclusion, Brown pronounces that "we have found a remarkable sub-apostolic variety of thought" in the last third of the first century. Then he adds, "By the time of the death of the apostles, the churches were already breaking away from much of what previously constituted authority in Judaism."[82]

Therefore, Brown thinks that there are two mistaken extreme positions to avoid here. He objects to both the conservative view that holds that everything existed in perfect harmony at the end of the first century, as well as the liberal view that sometimes postulates that most items were in flux almost with a theological smorgasbord from which to choose. Brown argues that "no one can show" that these first-century churches actually broke *koinōnia* or communion over the competing ideas that existed from time to time. The bottom line is that "we would make a bad mistake not to recognize that a strong insistence on sound doctrine is both a NT idea and a strength in the Christian picture."[83]

The main issue with Brown's reconstruction seems to be that for many scholars on both sides of the conservative-liberal spectrum, to utilize the word "diversity" for

---

[78] Brown, 21–22, 61–74.

[79] Brown, 22–24, 84–101. On the point pertaining to John and preexistence, Simon Gathercole wrote *The Pre-Existent Son: Recovering the Christologies of Matthew, Mark, and Luke* (Grand Rapids: Eerdmans, 2006) since Brown's death, arguing quite persuasively and in much detail that each of the Synoptic Gospels also teaches the preexistence of Jesus in a variety of ways. If Gathercole is correct here, this would make a more then noteworthy difference to Brown's thesis at this point.

[80] Brown, *Churches the Apostles Left Behind*, 25–26.

[81] Brown, 25–29, 124–45.

[82] Brown, 29–30.

[83] Brown, 146–50, quotation on 149.

the sorts of differences that Brown describes in this book is simply not a fair usage of that term. It sometimes conveys the sense of "discovering" conflict or even serious differences where there is actually very little. As commented earlier in this chapter, the differences that Brown describes all seem like quite normal differentiations of the milder sort. To use the earlier analogy, these differences that existed appear to be more like the contents of the multiple-views books that are currently so popular with modern Christian readers. In fact, many of the actual issues at the close of the first century do not even seem as major as many of those contrasted in these multiple-view books of today!

In other words, the differences cited above by Brown seem to involve Christian communities that hold the same or very similar underlying doctrine, especially in the theological center, with largely outlying differences in noncrucial areas. These kinds of differences seem more like the sorts of disagreements that might exist between two churches in the same town without believers missing a beat between congregations. For example, few of these differences in certain lesser subjects should ruffle many feathers today. Thus, if this is the extent of much of the diversity that was present by AD 110 or 120, the overall view would indeed appear to be more monolithic in nature—the sorts of beliefs that cause even believers to shrug their shoulders and keep walking!

However, by the early decades of the second century some of the dividing points led to much more diversity. Perhaps even as soon as the late first century, some more serious kinds of multiplicity began to emerge. One such example is the *Gospel of the Hebrews*, which is no longer fully extant though parts of it appear in patristic citations and in a few fragments. Crossan dates this writing to the 50s in Egypt, though without producing any arguments for that date. He comments that the *Gospel of the Hebrews* accepted "the preexistence, advent, sayings, and resurrection appearances of Jesus as the incarnation of the divine wisdom."[84]

On the other hand, in a more technical treatment, Philipp Vielhauer and Georg Strecker date the same work well over a half century later, to the first portion of the second century.[85] According to Koester, the content and style of this *Gospel* were similar to the Synoptic Gospels, and "this work contains a resurrection story in which

---

[84] Crossan, *Historical Jesus*, 428–29.

[85] Philipp Vielhauer and Georg Strecker, "Jewish Christian Gospels," in *New Testament Apocrypha*, ed. Wilhelm Schneemelcher, trans. Robert McLachlan Wilson, 2 vols. (Philadelphia: Westminster John Knox, 1991), 1:177–78.

Jesus appeared to his brother James and broke bread with him."[86] Whether Crossan or Vielhauer and Strecker are closer to being correct about the date, the testimony in the *Gospel of the Hebrews* would still be in an early enough position to provide some possibly important details about Jesus's postresurrection visit to his brother James, which is not described in the New Testament.

On the one hand, though so little is known regarding it, the *Gospel of the Hebrews* is often (generally) viewed and treated well among Christian writers, both in the second century and onward. However, some negative comments also appear here and there, often surrounding the overall topic that the *Gospel of the Hebrews* is actually proto-gnostic in nature and seems to have denied certain key doctrines from that theological angle. This entire plethora of potential issues is apparent though difficult to decipher, especially when there is no real document to pick up and study. The differences in the two dates make a huge difference as well.

Regarding a small group of other so-called Hebrew Gospels, the *Gospel of the Nazareans* may have been written in Aramaic as a translation of part or all of the Gospel of Matthew. The *Gospel of the Ebionites* was another member of this group of texts, with the distinction that it may have combined the three Synoptic Gospels into a fuller account of Jesus's life. Regarding these works, there are differences of opinion as to whether Jesus was viewed strictly from the Jewish perspective as a prophet and the Messiah but not as born of a virgin or as deity. Of these more Jewish writings, the *Gospel of the Ebionites* may possibly have been the most opposed to certain Christian doctrines.

These often similarly grouped "Hebrew Gospels" viewed Christianity through Jewish lenses and were in circulation during the second century.[87] But Crossan lists the *Gospel of the Nazareans* and the *Gospel of the Ebionites* as not being written until about the midpoint of the second century or a little later than the *Gospel of the Hebrews*.[88]

The situation here is further complicated by a number of difficult factors. To start, commentators' statements regarding these texts are occasionally divergent and conflict with one another, probably due largely to the absence of much or even most

---

[86] Koester, *Introduction to the New Testament*, 2:223–24.

[87] Vielhauer and Strecker also agree in listing and treating these "Hebrew Gospels" as the *Gospel of the Nazareans*, the *Gospel of the Ebionites*, and the *Gospel of the Hebrews*.

[88] Crossan, *Historical Jesus*, 433. In spite of the likely differences in dates between these three Hebrew Gospels, they were grouped here together due to some of their similarities of outlook and content.

of the information from texts that are missing. It also depends on the particular distinctions and deductions the researcher makes, including questions concerning whether the same book is being addressed, since the original, proper names are not known with regard to one or two of these texts. The writings are sometimes identified by different titles, with quite divergent dates being assigned to the same writing and with large percentages of missing manuscripts and manuscript portions (such as having *no* extant manuscripts of the *Gospel of the Hebrews* beyond several tiny bits).[89] As a result, apparent commentator confusion should hardly be a surprise but rather expected.

Due to issues like these, having at least identified some texts and addressed the subject briefly, this will be the extent of any further attempts to parse out the historical specifics of these mentions of the "Hebrew Gospels." Suffice it to say, however, that there were probably some early gnostic overtones here, such as the extent and various ways in which Jesus was thought to actually have possessed a human body. Then there were the Jewish writings with implications such as whether Jesus was actually divine in some sense or rather just a Jewish prophet. At these points, larger and more crucial theological differences were emerging.

Marcion

Living around the close of the early Tier 1 period, Marcion was probably the most influential of the postcanonical critical figures.[90] Though he had been raised in a family that held orthodox Christian beliefs, he developed an intriguing combination of views that would have placed him in between the outlooks of the Hebrew Gospels just surveyed, which he would have opposed in large part, and early proto-gnostic

---

[89] Discussing a number of the intricacies involved in these subjects are Vielhauer and Strecker, "Jewish Christian Gospels," 134–78; Ron Cameron, ed., *The Other Gospels: Non-Canonical Gospel Texts* (Louisville: Westminster John Knox, 1982), 83–86, 97–106; Crossan, *Historical Jesus*, 428–29; Koester, *Introduction to the New Testament*, 2:223–24; Ehrman, *New Testament*, 180–82, cf. 170–78, 256–59; D. A. Carson, Douglas J. Moo, and Leon Morris, *An Introduction to the New Testament* (Grand Rapids: Zondervan, 1992), 71; Bruce, *Jesus and Christian Origins*, 99–109; Bock, *Missing Gospels*, 218–19.

[90] It is sometimes said that Adolf von Harnack's work on Marcion is the foremost study ever written here; see Adolf von Harnack, *Marcion: Das Evangelium vom fremden Gott. Eine Monographie zur Geschichte der Grundlegung der katholischen Kirche* (Leipzig: Hinrichs, 1921). English translation in von Harnack, *Marcion: The Gospel of the Alien God*, trans. John E. Steely and Lyle D. Bierma (Eugene, OR: Wipf & Stock, 2007).

positions of the docetic variety, though without going all the way over to their later positions. He was excommunicated from the church for his views in 144.[91]

Marcion concluded that the Being who created the world and was depicted in the Old Testament was neither the righteous nor the redeemer "high" God of the universe. Though none of his writings are extant, he reportedly concluded in his work *Antitheses* that this creator who had chosen the Jews as his people was capricious and performed evil acts, including being self-contradictory. On the other hand, Jesus was not born as a child but simply appeared on the first-century scene (which would seem to eliminate the virgin birth as well), ministered, appeared to be human (but was not), appeared to have suffered and died on the cross (but did not actually die), and later appeared once again to his followers. Paul was a hero to Marcion, restoring the original gospel that Jesus's disciples tended to drag back in the direction of Judaism, especially legalism.

Marcion's standard is often said to be the first effort to set forth a New Testament canon.[92] It consisted of an edited version of Luke's Gospel (expunging Luke's first two chapters due to Jesus not being born in a human body, for example) along with ten of Paul's Epistles (but even here with some editing, and with the Pastoral Epistles being exempted), all of them fashioned according to Marcion's theological preferences. It was thought that various interpolations had crept into these texts angled toward Jewish perspectives. Therefore, Marcion had to ensure that these writings remained "pure," hence the need for his editing. It is true that groupings of New Testament books such as the Gospels, Acts, and Paul's Epistles had at least generally been recognized as Scripture for some time before Marcion.[93] But at the least, Marcion's efforts probably spurred forward several of the serious orthodox attempts to arrive at an official or semiofficial canon, such

---

[91] Most of this information on Marcion is commonly known. Further details may be found in Larry W. Hurtado, *Lord Jesus Christ: Devotion to Jesus in Earliest Christianity* (Grand Rapids: Eerdmans, 2003), 549–58; F. F. Bruce, *The Canon of Scripture* (Downers Grove, IL: InterVarsity, 1988), esp. 134–44; Koester, *Introduction to the New Testament*, 1:99; 2:8–10, 307–8, 328–34; Ehrman, *New Testament*, 3–6, 11, 89, 170–82; Donald Guthrie, *New Testament Introduction*, rev. ed. (Leicester: InterVarsity, 1990), 126–27, 609–11, 986–88.

[92] This depends, for example, on when the Muratorian Canon is dated. Surprisingly, though often placed a few decades after Marcion at about 180, Koester notes that some scholars date the Muratorian Canon up to a century earlier than that! See Koester, *Introduction to the New Testament*, 2:11.

[93] For some details, see Habermas, *Historical Jesus*, 108–14.

as the efforts that were exerted by the likes of Irenaeus, Tatian, and probably the Muratorian Canon itself.

Specifically regarding the central doctrine of the death and resurrection of Jesus, again, Marcion's Jesus never truly had a human body or really died, thus he was not strictly raised *from the dead*. Marcion did not question Jesus's appearances per se, agreeing that Jesus was seen by his followers after the crucifixion event had occurred, though the latter did not result in Jesus's death. So, Jesus not actually dying was a major factor for the church, denying the soteriological aspect of that event on the New Testament view. Further, though it is difficult to be exact without having his writings before us, the extent to which Marcion leaned toward gnostic views may also have had a bearing on his view of whether Jesus truly appeared bodily to his followers. In the latter case, though the appearances actually occurred, their form and interpretation also differed substantially.[94] At the very least, in Marcion's case, Jesus's "appearances" that were not preceded by his death were not *resurrection* appearances at all![95]

To summarize this section, the canonical texts (up to approximately AD 100) saw very few if any serious disagreements among each other in what might be called central, fundamental areas of Christian theology. As argued by Brown, fellowship and communion were not broken over the differences. Early Tier 1 texts more or

---

[94] Especially Riley, *Resurrection Reconsidered*, 65 in the context of 58–68; Koester, *Introduction to the New Testament*, 2:331.

[95] This double problem with Marcion's denial of the death and resurrection of Jesus needs to be differentiated from a different issue that is often raised in some circles in contemporary theological discussions. It must be noted very carefully that there is no effort or desire whatsoever in this study to minimize Jesus's bodily resurrection and appearances, which are clearly affirmed. This doctrine is crucially important and is clearly the New Testament position, as mentioned throughout these volumes and particularly emphasized in volume 4. Yet the contrast is sometimes made between those who hold that Jesus *actually* died, rose, and appeared bodily and those who hold that Jesus *actually* died, rose, and appeared in a glorified, spiritual body (perhaps like the type of body that some think Paul saw in Acts 9, 22, 26 on the way to Damascus). If it is helpful to describe it this way, the difference here is in *how bodily* Jesus's appearances were in each of these positions. Both views embrace the facts of Jesus's literal death, resurrection, and appearances. The truth and facticity of Jesus's resurrection appearances is held in both positions, with the bottom line being Jesus's appearance in a resurrection body, even if in the latter case Paul's description of "spiritual body" is used. These views may differ, which is an important matter vis-à-vis the New Testament teaching, though it appears that both views are clearly pro-resurrection positions, unlike Marcion's.

less followed the lead of the canonical writings without major theological issues. But beginning approximately with the writings produced around 140, the serious questioning intensified in several of these fundamental areas, particularly between the beliefs that proto-gnostics or gnostics held over against the ones held by the proto-orthodox or orthodox believers. These included questions of whether Jesus was actually a human being and had an actual body, the virgin birth, if it was Jesus himself who died at the event of the crucifixion, and if Jesus rose bodily from the dead, if indeed he was crucified. These crucial subjects were working their way to confrontation in the church.

Diversity in the Tier 2 Texts (AD 150–200)

It was noted earlier that some historical Jesus researchers continue to examine sources dated past the AD 150 mark, approximately 120 years after Jesus's crucifixion. They variously also include sources such as Lucian, Celsus, a few later gnostic writers, or even the Jewish Mishnah. Due to the importance of some of these writings, viewing some of the historical objections to Christianity during this period up to about 180 or so may be helpful. Again, the Mishnah, for example, will not be included due to its late date, even with its earlier traditions.[96] Nor will Lucian, who was treated in volume 1 of this study, and who freely and heartily criticized the believers in his day for being gullible, without really leveling any historical complaints. Celsus, who did offer very serious objections, will occupy most of the space in this section.

The Gospel of Peter

A fragment of this writing was the first noncanonical gospel to be discovered. It was found in Egypt just six miles from the site of the Nag Hammadi gnostic texts by French archaeologist Urbain Bouriant in the mid-1880s.[97] The text was divided into

---

[96] The implication in the Mishnah that Jesus's mother Mary was not a virgin seems similar to Celsus's criticisms that are discussed below.

[97] See M. R. James, ed. and trans., *The Apocryphal New Testament* (Oxford: Clarendon, 1924), 90, who listed the *Gospel of Peter*'s discovery date as 1884. In a recent evaluation, Jeremiah J. Johnston, "The Gospel of Peter: The Importance of a North African Discovery," *Sapientia Logos* 3 (2011): 183–215, placed the date of discovery as 1886–1887. A popular discussion is found in the blog by J. Warner Wallace, "Why Shouldn't We Trust the Non-canonical Gospels

fourteen chapters of sixty total verses. This particular fragment is dated much later than the presumed original date of the work and may point to its popularity in the church, though this is undetermined. The original composition is generally placed in the second century AD, often in the latter half of this period, though occasionally dated earlier. One of the chief reasons for this particular date is the mention of the writing by Bishop Serapion of Antioch (199–211) and an even later citation by Eusebius (*Hist. eccl.* 3.3.2; 6.12). The possibility of an earlier pre-Serapion existence for the text has not been established.

A potential question is whether this present text is totally or substantially the same *Gospel of Peter* as the one known to these ancient Christian writers. At least until more manuscripts are found for comparison, scholars seem satisfied that they represent the same text. At any rate, the obvious benefit from the discovery is any value that may be derived from the text itself. Rather understandably, the authorship is never assigned to the apostle Peter, in spite of this identification (*Gos. Pet.* 15.60).

Another area of scholarly interest concerns whether any material from this Gospel manifests gnostic influences. Researchers often assert that it exhibits docetic tendencies, though N. T. Wright denies the presence of gnostic teachings.[98] Those who support the former view, such as Bishop Serapion, point to items such as Jesus apparently feeling no pain during his crucifixion (*Gos. Pet.* 4.11), the difficulty in determining if Jesus had died before his exit from the cross since "he was taken up" in his final moments (5.19), and the lack of bodily appearances.

Regarding the appearances, however, a wounded Jesus was viewed by many onlookers as he was assisted out of the tomb (*Gos. Pet.* 10.39–42) and the fragmented account of a fishing scene at the very end of the story (15.58–60) is reminiscent of the disciples in John 21, just before seeing the resurrected Jesus. Further, the lack of other appearances is less significant due to the missing beginning and ending of the fragment, hence the question of additional appearances is somewhat open. Serapion, Jerome, and Pope Gelasius all condemned the writing.

Many have also mentioned certain anti-Jewish sentiments in the fragment, such as Pilate being exonerated while Herod and the Jews are blamed for Jesus's crucifixion and death. The text opens with Herod and the Jews being unwilling to wash their

---

Attributed to Peter?," *Cold Case Christianity*, March 23, 2018, https://coldcasechristianity.com/writings/why-shouldnt-we-trust-the-non-canonical-gospels-attributed-to-peter/.

[98] Wright, *Resurrection of the Son of God*, 595.

hands of the situation, and Herod condemning Jesus to death instead of Pilate (*Gos. Pet.* 1.1–2). Though less weighty due to the matter of silence, there are also no references to Old Testament precedent. After the crucifixion, the Jews were sorrowful and conceded that Jesus was righteous (7.25; 8.28–29).

The question of the *Gospel of Peter*'s sources and their dates is an area of pointed scholarly dispute, one that potentially has a bearing on issues regarding early Christian proclamation. Johnston points out that it is chiefly the Jesus Seminar proponents and related scholars who argue the highly controversial idea that the *Gospel of Peter* is "the oldest independent source for the passion narrative" in the Gospels![99] For John Dominic Crossan, for example, it is the conjectural "Cross Gospel" that is the proposed source thought to reside within *Peter*.[100]

M. R. James asserted that the *Gospel of Peter* drew from all four of the canonical Gospels, though this is not heard as frequently today.[101] Raymond Brown pointed out that while there is an independent story about the soldiers at Jesus's tomb in *Gos. Pet.* 8.28–11.49, the *Gospel of Peter* obviously knows Matthew's account of the guards at the tomb, including details like the sealing of the burial stone and the soldiers being forbidden to speak about what happened. But the guards were not paid as in Matthew.[102] It could be added that the fishing scene in the final paragraph of the *Gospel of Peter* is fairly similar to the one in John 21:1–3 as well.

This information is crucial, for if Brown is correct that the *Gospel of Peter* used and hence was written after Matthew, according to the predominant critical dating, then at a bare minimum that would place the *Gospel of Peter* no earlier than the very end of the first century or into the second century. It would also date the *Gospel of Peter* post-Mark and probably post-Luke or even John, especially given the fishing scene.

Further, Johnston lists several traits that point to a second- or even a third-century date, including such later elements as the regular use of the "Lord's Day," the lack of knowledge of Jewish customs, blaming the Jews for Jesus's death, multiplying the number of resurrection witnesses at the tomb, the mythical-sounding and gigantic size of the angels and an even taller Jesus, the descent into hell, and the talking cross.

---

[99] Johnston, "Gospel of Peter," 209.

[100] Crossan, *The Cross That Spoke: The Origins of the Passion Narrative* (New York: HarperCollins, 1988).

[101] James, *Apocryphal New Testament*, 90.

[102] Raymond E. Brown, *The Death of the Messiah: From Gethsemane to the Grave* (New York: Doubleday, 1994), 1287, 1301, 1305–7; cf. Johnston, "Gospel of Peter," 209.

To this summary may be added that the *Gospel of Peter* names the crucifixion centurion as Petronius (8.31). Accordingly, J. K. Elliott states that the general scholarly conclusion is that the *Gospel of Peter* "is secondary to, and dependent on, the accounts of the passion in the canonical gospels."[103]

The *Gospel of Peter* fragment begins with Jesus's sentencing without prior details of a potential religious or political trial. Herod takes the lead in the proceedings and sentences Jesus to die. Jesus is crowned with thorns, beaten, and crucified between two other men, with a sign placed overhead proclaiming him as the King of Israel (3.6–4.12). Jesus's oppressors gamble for his garments, and one of the other crucified men defends him. But Jesus's ankles are not broken so that he suffers more than the others (4.12–14). Jesus calls out to his Father ("My power, my power") before "he was taken up" (5.19). After the temple veil is torn in two and an earthquake occurs, Joseph takes Jesus's body and buries it (5.20–6.22).

Next, the Jewish leaders beseech Pilate to provide a Roman guard for Jesus's tomb, which is granted. The centurion Petronius and a group of soldiers seal the stone covering the tomb with seven seals and set up camp nearby (8.29–33). A multitude of people come to the tomb and, along with the soldiers, watch as "a great light" accompanies two shining men as they come down from heaven and enter the tomb after the stone rolls away by itself (9.34–10.38).

The soldiers and the chief priests, who are also present, all witness these events. The two men who entered the tomb return, supporting a third man. The heads of the first two rise up to heaven, though the head of the third person who was supported as he emerged from the tomb rises above the heavens. The men are followed by a cross that also appears from the tomb. A voice from heaven asks the cross if it had preached to the dead, and the cross answers affirmatively (10.38–42). The men at the tomb then go to Pilate and tell him what they saw. Pilate charges the soldiers not to tell anyone (11.43–49).

Next, early on the first day of the week, Mary Magdalene and other women come to the tomb to complete the burial process. Concerned about the size of the stone in front of the tomb, they arrive and find the tomb open and the stone rolled away. A young man in dazzling clothing sitting inside the tomb informs them that Jesus

---

[103] For Johnston's comment and quotation, see "Gospel of Peter," 209–10, 212. For J. K. Elliott's research, see *The Apocryphal New Testament: A Collection of Apocryphal Christian Literature in an English Translation Based on M. R. James* (Oxford: Clarendon, 1993), 151.

has risen from the dead and has already left the tomb. Frightened, they ran away (12.50–13.57).

The fragment ends at this point after a final comment concerning the twelve disciples (three of whom are singled out and mentioned by name: Peter, Andrew, and Levi), who were grieving over their recent loss. Apparently, they left Jerusalem to return home and heard nothing from the women, so the men decide to go fishing. But the manuscript breaks off mid-sentence (14.58–60) and it is unknown what else may have been included in the original text, such as whether or not Jesus appeared to his followers and, if so, what form the appearances may have taken.

Commentators have noted that the extant portion of the *Gospel of Peter* fragment is largely in harmony with that of the canonical Gospels, including Jesus's condemnation to death for no specific crime, the crown of thorns and beating, the crucifixion between two other men, and the "King of the Jews" sign, among other shared features. As Johnston states, *Peter* exhibits "a greater resonance with the canonical gospels than it does when compared with the wider spectrum of extra-canonical writings."[104] However, some of the reports featured in the *Gospel of Peter* differ from the canonical Gospels as well, such as Herod issuing Jesus's chief condemnation, the massive angels, and the talking cross, among several other features. Overall, the familiar elements in the *Gospel of Peter* outnumber the surprises, though some of those "wonders" are rather substantial. Johnston sums up these features here as "a walking and talking cross, conspiratorial cover-ups and pay-offs, graphic polymorphic anatomical changes, hostile witnesses with specific sensory details, and an increased attention upon the miraculous."[105]

Additionally, depending on how the verses are counted, the resurrection narrative in the *Gospel of Peter* is one of the longest among early church texts. It is also the only account where the witnesses actually watch as the resurrection event unfolds before them, with Jesus being accompanied by the angels as they exit the tomb.

Regarding the question of historicity, the *Gospel of Peter* is not a very exceptional minefield. In a few cases, it may just possibly add its voice as an independent source. For the minority of scholars who date the text early, such as the Jesus Seminar, it could possibly date back to the late first century.[106] Ehrman dates the *Gospel of Peter* somewhat later, at about 120, though in both cases it is still rejected

---

[104] Johnston "Gospel of Peter," 207; cf. Wallace, "Non-canonical Gospels."

[105] Johnston "Gospel of Peter," 207.

[106] Funk and the Jesus Seminar, *Acts of Jesus*, 553.

as an important text.[107] The Jesus Seminar asserts, "The Gospel of Peter depicts a mythical Jesus."[108]

The *Gospel of Peter* continues to be an intriguing source, but very seldom has much historical importance attached to it. The extreme cases of mythical accretion, such as the three giants, the cross that speaks as it emerges from the tomb, and so on, along with the possibility that the story could have grown even more substantially over the many decades from its earliest form, are all important problems. Gnostic hints along with potential anti-Jewish sentiment and apparent borrowing from perhaps all four canonical Gospels are also complications. The most serious issues are the questions pertaining to the absence of any early or other historical provenance along with the dates of such earlier sources. In short, confirming data, especially for the more unique aspects of the *Gospel of Peter*, are seriously lacking. As such, it provides no challenges to the many early records of Jesus's death and resurrection appearances, such as those presented in the first volume of this study.

The Gospel of Judas

The unaware reader could be forgiven for taking at face value the overly bombastic news that broke in 2004—acting as if a recent find, the *Gospel of Judas*, would utterly change the direction of Christianity forever.[109] Written around AD 150, this writing portrayed the apostle Judas as the hero of the events at the end of Jesus's life, which closes with the abrupt ending of Judas turning Jesus over to the Jewish authorities.[110] It might be thought that, without this action by Judas as the initiator of the final events in Jesus's life, Jesus may never have been crucified and raised from the dead!

So was Judas a bit of a gospel facilitator? Throughout this Gospel, Judas is the hero, for he alone worships the Creator (the gnostic god) while the other apostles (and apparently the whole of orthodox theology) are under judgment for thinking Jehovah in the Old Testament *is* the same creator. Judas is thus superior to all the others.

Perrin notes three inferences found in the *Gospel of Judas*. The book teaches the docetic version of Gnosticism, where Jesus himself does not really have a physical

---

[107] Ehrman, *New Testament*, 44.
[108] Funk and the Jesus Seminar, *Acts of Jesus*, 451.
[109] For a few examples, see Perrin, *Judas Gospel*, 3–4, 31.
[110] Perrin, 13.

body but is clothed with one. Jesus tells Judas twice, "You will exceed all of them, for you will sacrifice the man that clothes me."[111] Further, like Marcion above, the *Gospel of Judas* is anti-Jewish and vehemently opposes the identification or even the closeness of Judaism and Christianity. Finally, the *Gospel of Judas* is highly individualistic—it has "so little interest in ethics or community life."[112]

Is there any historical value to the *Gospel of Judas*? As perhaps the most prominent of all the gnostic authorities, James M. Robinson reported in his own evaluation of the situation regarding *Judas*, "One will find that it does not shed light on what happened during Jesus's trip to Jerusalem . . . but rather will shed light on a second century Gnostic sect." As Robinson implied, the sensationalists were hoping for more than that. However, this Gospel is simply too late to be historically helpful.[113] Perrin notes that there is very little of any use for historians in the *Gospel of Judas*, adding that "the historical distance between the time of composition and the setting of its subject matter makes any claim of authenticity difficult to sustain."[114]

To be sure, the *Gospel of Judas* clearly portrays Jesus as teaching a number of very strange-sounding, secret gnostic doctrines. It also alters surrounding historical circumstances pertaining chiefly to Jesus's betrayal. Moreover, different interpretations are provided throughout the scenes, such as reversing the canonical order of the Gospels by casting Judas as the hero.

But the overall view of Jesus in the *Gospel of Judas* is positive, beginning with Jesus being a marvelous miracle worker. Herbert Krosney states that the *Gospel of Judas* "was written by someone who revered Jesus. He communicates that adoration with fervor and good humor." Further, Jesus appears more joyous in *Judas* than in the canonical Gospels. Nonetheless, *Judas* ends with Judas taking the offered money from the Jewish leaders and turning Jesus over to them.[115] Even with these different

---

[111] Rodolphe Kasser, Marvin Meyer, and Gregor Wurst with François Gaudard, eds., *The Gospel of Judas* (Washington, DC: The National Geographic Society, 2006), 4, 43.

[112] Perrin, *Judas Gospel*, 19–23.

[113] James M. Robinson, *The Secrets of Judas: The Story of the Misunderstood Disciple and His Lost Gospel* (New York: HarperCollins, 2006), 183.

[114] Perrin, *Judas Gospel*, 24–25, for the quotation, cf. 25.

[115] Kasser et al., *Gospel of Judas*. See esp. the portions of the translation under the headings "The Earthly Ministry of Jesus" and "Conclusion: Judas Betrays Jesus." Besides the sometimes-raving newspaper articles, another popular treatment of *Judas* is the volume by Herbert Krosney, *The Lost Gospel: The Quest for the Gospel of Judas Iscariot*

scenes, teachings, and interpretations, there is no effort to deny the historicity of Jesus's "betrayal." There the *Gospel of Judas* ends.

While Jesus's immaterial spirit did not die by crucifixion or any other way, the event of death by crucifixion that followed Judas's betrayal is implied regarding the

---

(Washington, DC: The National Geographic Society, 2006). The above quotation from Krosney is from 278.

As an example of the explosive, overblown comments about *Judas*, the Coptic translator of the *Gospel of Judas*, Professor Rodolphe Kasser, claims in the prologue of his volume that "it is certainly one of the greatest discoveries of this century" (9). But just years after the publication of Krosney's book, the *Gospel of Judas* is rarely even mentioned, except perhaps in a very few specific, scholarly circumstances. Further, never do scholars hold either that it was written by Judas Iscariot or that it is an essentially historical or otherwise accurate work. Yet, near the end of Krosney's volume, it is commented: "Because the Gospel of Judas was written in the century that followed Jesus' life, it is a startling text that provides fresh insight into early Christianity and its varied movements" (279). In this context, it is very difficult to understand the use and meaning of words such as "startling text," "fresh insight," and especially "early Christianity," at least with any literal meaning, given the true nature of this writing apart from any sensational hype. Note too that Krosney, a few pages before, begins another sentence regarding *Judas* with these words: "The codex, written during the very heart of the early Christian era." In particular, how is "early" to be understood here when the author also tells his readers that *Judas* was written during the next century *after* Jesus? (279; cf. Perrin, *Judas Gospel*, 4). Given this late date, it is difficult to ascertain how the codex could possibly provide any "fresh insight" into "Christianity." This is especially true since the codex is supposed to apply Gnostic Christianity from over a century later, which is entirely too late to provide any new considerations.

To make matters worse, Ehrman also refers to the *Gospel of Judas* as "ancient" in his foreword to Krosney, *Lost Gospel*, xvii, and elsewhere he refers to books written in the second century as "early" (*New Testament*, 2). Some skeptics might complain that the second century is indeed "early" and "ancient" when compared to all the later centuries. But what is so strange about these sorts of comments is that some of these same scholars would probably hesitate seriously to call any of the Synoptic Gospels early or ancient, and this would much more rarely be the case with John, even though the Fourth Gospel was written more than a half century before *Judas*! Remember too that Ehrman only counts the first 100 years of sources for the historical Jesus in his book *Did Jesus Exist?* (e.g., 56, 171, 290–91, cf. 140–41). But when it favors the second-century gnostic works, critical scholars frequently seem to want to point the conversation in a different direction, raising the rhetoric on behalf of these clearly later and nonhistorical writings. It is this difference that further illustrates the comments above on the double standard used with the canonical works (especially the Gospels) over against the gnostic writings, seemingly hoping to raise the standard of diversity of the available sources.

male body that "clothed" Jesus.[116] Moreover, Jesus perhaps "appeared" afterward to his followers, though without his dying first. Krosney states it well: "The Gospel of Judas offers an alternative narrative, but does not challenge the bases of Christian faith."[117] Later, Krosney comments that Judas "does not directly criticize or contradict the canonical gospels."[118] However, one might fairly wonder how Jesus, by not actually dying by crucifixion himself, fails to question one of "the bases of Christian faith"!

Many other gnostic writings appeared after the ones that were viewed in this chapter and in the earlier treatment on historical sources for the existence of the historical Jesus in volume 1 of this study. While not valueless, they are really too late to help researchers understand what can be known about either Jesus's life or the more formative criticisms of orthodox Christian beliefs.[119]

Celsus

R. Joseph Hoffmann remarks that before Celsus's time, moral critiques of Christians were more common than philosophical attacks simply because a solid body of canonical texts was not yet available to the critics.[120] Hoffmann adds that theological questions were also raised quite early, some of them even being obviously derived from the pages of what became the New Testament. Theological challenges for believers to

---

[116] Kasser et al., *Gospel of Judas*, 4, 43.

[117] Krosney, *Lost Gospel*, 279.

[118] Krosney, 295.

[119] Using the convenient chart provided by Darrell Bock in *Missing Gospels*, 218–19, a few of the more important works (for various reasons), along with Bock's suggested dates, are as follows. First, surveyed and used in the volume 1 chapter on the existence of Jesus: the *Gospel of Thomas* (late first to early second century); the *Gospel of Truth* (mid-second century); *Treatise on Resurrection* (also called the *Letter to Rheginos*; late second century); the *Apocryphon of John* (mid-second to early third century). Regarding the *Gospel of Peter* just mentioned in this chapter, Bock suggests a mid-second-century date. Works that are often or generally thought to simply be too late to include for historical purposes include the *Gospel of Mary Magdalene*; the *Gospel of Philip*; the *Apocryphon of James*; the *Gospel of Thomas the Contender*; and the *Valentinian Exposition*. Each of these writings, except for the *Gospel of Peter*, is available in Robinson, *Nag Hammadi Library*, cited earlier.

[120] R. Joseph Hoffmann, "General Introduction" to Celsus, *On the True Doctrine: A Discourse against the Christians*, trans. R. Joseph Hoffmann (Oxford: Oxford University Press, 1987), 24.

address included the delay of Jesus's return and Christians who left the faith during times of persecution, along with ethical questions about the early believers.[121]

The moral aberrations of believers added numerous other problems of their own. Even in the New Testament Epistles, overlapping issues were charged and addressed, such as factions and infighting, cliquishness, gluttony, jealousy over spiritual gifts, libertinism, antinomianism, pleasure seeking, drunkenness, an entire cartel of sexual sins, lying, sorcery, and illicit cultic practices.[122]

Later, non-Christians also began noticing believers who practiced what they considered to be unacceptable behaviors, though some of these reports plainly turned out to be due to false rumors, misinterpretations, and even outright lies. These widespread reports included Christians sacrificing or eating their children, sexual debaucheries, murder, treason, drinking blood, or that believers were really cannibals or even atheists! Hoffmann reports that most of these charges were "based almost certainly on casual impressions and heresay."[123]

Later Christian scholars who defended the Christians or answered specific charges included Justin Martyr, Ignatius, Tertullian, and Clement of Alexandria. However, Justin, Tertullian, and Epiphanius also knew of Christian groups who did engage in detestable behavior.[124] Surprisingly, given his several negative comments regarding believers taken from the same passage, Pliny the Younger seems to defend the Christian practice of the Eucharist in his area of Bithynia.[125]

The Greek philosopher Celsus wrote his famous attack on Christians, *On the True Doctrine*, between 170 and 185. He concentrated less on the Christians' perceived moral lapses and more on theological, historical, and philosophical problems. Though Celsus's entire writing is lost, scholars conclude that his chief areas of attack may be retrieved from Origen's careful critique *Contra Celsum*, written in the next century. In his text, Celsus raises a large number of objections to Christianity, many of which are subpoints of several major themes. Hoffmann notes, "As a rule, the pagan critics of the later second century, Celsus included, are critics of Christian credulity, not of Christian

---

[121] Hoffmann, "General Introduction," 9–13.

[122] Similarly, Hoffmann, 13–16, mentioning a few New Testament texts, such as Rom 8:12–13; 1 Cor 5:1; 11–15; Jude v. 11, to which many other texts could be appended.

[123] Hoffmann, 25.

[124] Hoffmann, 16–25.

[125] See *Ep.* 97 in Pliny the Younger, *Letters*, trans. William Melmoth, rev. by F. C. T. Bosanquet (New York: Collier & Son, 1909), 404–6. Emperor Trajan's reply appears in the next letter (*Ep.* 98).

creeds."[126] Though perhaps the general rule, however, a number of Celsus's criticisms were concerned with matters of Christian doctrine, including historical issues.

It might be mentioned initially that Celsus sometimes mistakenly attributes particular beliefs to Christians that they did not hold, though it is possible that some believers in his time did believe one or more of these.[127] On the other hand, perhaps Celsus purposely or even mockingly attributed certain "silly" positions to Christians in order to make them appear even more senseless or preposterous. For example, stated in his own words, Celsus charged that Christians would preach like this: "Let no one educated, no one wise, no one sensible draw near. For these abilities are thought by us to be evils. But as for anyone ignorant, anyone stupid, anyone uneducated, anyone childish, let him come boldly."[128] Closely related is this thought by Celsus: "Christian teachers are only happy with stupid pupils—indeed scout about for the slow-witted."[129] Hopefully, these comments do not even need to be addressed.[130]

Regarding his other charges against Christians, Celsus speaks out against the biblical prophets as well as Jesus being incorrect in their predictive pronouncements.[131] Further, Celsus thinks there are many discrepancies in the Bible.[132] Also, one of Celsus's most common criticisms, sometimes mentioned rather forcefully, is that Christians did not want their followers to ask questions and did not want to give any evidence for what they believed. "Just believe" was their motto, reports Celsus.[133]

Four other critiques in particular demand a little more attention. First, Celsus was one of Jesus's many detractors over the centuries, beginning with the Jewish leaders

---

[126] Hoffmann, "General Introduction," 28–30.

[127] In quoting or citing Celsus's words here, Hoffmann's edition is being followed where particular passage references are not used. Thus, only a page number will be provided.

[128] Celsus, *On the True Doctrine*, 72–73.

[129] Celsus, 75.

[130] Here are a few more of Celsus's erroneous comments from *On the True Doctrine*: Christians agree that there are seven heavens and the way of the soul is through the planets (95). Many self-styled Christian prophets call themselves God, the Son of God, or the Holy Spirit (106)! Christians worship the Son of Man and claim that he is mightier than the almighty God (117). One does wonder on the last point how someone can be mightier than an almighty Being?

[131] Celsus, 58–59, 119–21.

[132] Celsus, 64, 68, 90. Hoffmann notes that for Celsus, the inconsistencies and discrepancies were "fatal" to Christianity; see his "General Introduction," 36, 39, 137n108, 141n161.

[133] Celsus, *On the True Doctrine*, 54, 72–76. Hoffmann also mentions in his introduction Celsus's attacks on Christians in these areas; see "General Introduction," 27–29, 128n5.

in the canonical Gospels themselves, who charged that Jesus was a magician and a sorcerer.[134] Jesus's reply to these Jewish leaders indicated that they had committed the blasphemy of the Holy Spirit (Mark 3:28–30). Celsus states that Jesus learned these secrets in Egypt, where he went in order to take a job as a workman.[135]

Second, Celsus declared more than once that Jesus's mother, Mary, was by no means a virgin, since she was made pregnant via a Roman soldier named Panthera. Here Celsus repeats a comment that has shown up in a number of places, especially in later Jewish polemical material. As a result, Mary's husband drove her away as an adulteress.[136] Celsus adds that old Greek myths also reported a "divine birth" to various heroes.[137]

Third, on many occasions, Celsus compares Christianity to pagan personages and religions. He asks repeatedly, Why should Christians boast about this or that teaching, miracle, prophecy, and so on when pagans also exhibit these along with other supernatural manifestations such as soothsaying and producing apparitions? The pagans even hold corresponding doctrines that are similar to those of Jews and Christians, making the latter just one tradition among many. Of course, Celsus adds, Christians will reject all of the pagan occurrences out of hand but assume that theirs

---

[134] Celsus adds other items on this subject, including that these pagan sorcerers also did miracles: "They drive away demons, conquer diseases of all kinds, and make the dead heroes of the past appear" (*On the True Doctrine*, 59–60). Is it thought that Celsus *really* believed these pagan miracles that he seems to report here rather straightforwardly? Apparently not, since he refers to them as legends (67). He also claims, equally incredibly, that Christians claimed they gained power by "pronouncing the names of demons" or via magic and incantations (53, 98), in spite of the extremely strong historic Christian stance taken against anything whatsoever that was even remotely related to demonic or occultic material. Some of these comments cause one to wonder about Celsus's own sources, or whether he had much accurate information at all. As mentioned elsewhere regarding many other critics, while data on early Christianity is examined with scrupulous attention, Celsus sometimes seems like he required very little information at all other than any old comment from an unbeliever that either favored the pagan reports or disfavored Christian teachings, miracle claims, and so on before he repeated the material.

[135] Celsus, *On the True Doctrine*, 53–54, 57, 59–60, 64–69, 98–99. Hoffmann provides additional details on these particular critiques by Celsus (36, 129–30, 140), which were also common fare for the Jewish leaders in Jesus's day. A prominent work a few decades ago was Morton Smith's *Jesus the Magician: A Renowned Historian Reveals How Jesus Was Viewed by People of His Time* (New York: HarperCollins, 1978).

[136] Celsus, *On the True Doctrine*, 57–58. Hoffmann relates that the name "Panthera" may be a play on the Greek term for virgin (*parthenos*) in Matt 1:23 (129n14).

[137] Celsus, *On the True Doctrine*, 59, also 54.

are all true. Moreover, pagans have suffered willingly too. So, what are the claimed differences all about? However, it appears that some sleight of hand is going on here by Celsus, and it should be recognized on its own grounds.[138]

Fourth, Celsus makes numerous observations with reference to Jesus's resurrection. For instance, he levels his well-known comment regarding this event being based on the hallucinations of a hysterical woman and maybe one other (unnamed) person.[139] The comment might appear rather odd, because Celsus would know that there were more than two resurrection witnesses. But as Hoffmann notes, he was probably just talking about the scene at the tomb in the Gospel of John; though even if so, the apostle John was also reportedly Peter's companion on that occasion, which is not mentioned by Celsus.[140]

---

[138] Celsus, 54–55, 59–60, 67, 69, 95, 106, 112–16. It is quite curious here that Celsus admits his own view that these pagan personages themselves or their so-called supernatural accomplishments are all legends (67) and that he belittles their religious followers, calling them "sniveling" and "gullible" (54). Yet on the other hand, he also knows that Jesus really lived in history and that Christians offer actual historical evidence for some of Jesus's supernatural events, unlike the pagan legends. After all, like the Jewish leaders of Jesus's time who accused Jesus of doing his miracles by the power of Satan, Celsus admits the actual occurrence of Jesus's miraculous events, at least in some supernatural sense. Given these data, it is unclear whether Celsus simply does not recognize the difference in quality between the Christian and the pagan cases or if he indeed *does* recognize the contrast but is not "showing his hand" in order to put his best-sounding foot forward on behalf of his admittedly legendary pagan counterargument. Doubtless, these disparities do indeed produce a huge discontinuity between the two systems, explaining why the Christians that Celsus criticizes actually believe the way they do. The major and immediate question surely is *not* whether each side makes similar *claims*, and anyone who misses this point may have taken Celsus's diversionary bait. Rather, the issue concerns who can show that their claims are *correct*. For if, based on evidential aspects, the Christian perspective is correct while the pagan alternative is incorrect, then the presence of comparative *claims* hardly matters. The Christian doctrines could very well follow, whereas the pagan doctrines would not be true (especially given Celsus's view that these are illegitimate anyway) on account of the incongruity of the respective supernatural occurrences. Further, it would then be no wonder that Christians, who could ascertain the same thing that Celsus could, would accept neither the pagan accounts nor their doctrines, but would accept both in the case that their Christian examples were evidenced. So when Celsus admonishes Christians to "follow reason as a guide before accepting any belief" and to test doctrine (54), it sounds as if the Christians were already doing precisely that, whereas Celsus is the one who has not done so. In such cases, the tables seem to have turned here.

[139] Celsus, 67–68.

[140] Celsus, 132n49.

Celsus takes quite a negative view of the resurrection. He proclaims that Christians worship a mere man who stayed dead. But if Jesus were ever dead, then how could he be immortal?[141] Further, even if Jesus predicted his resurrection, as Christians claimed, many pagans experienced similar experiences as well.[142]

Overall, Celsus clearly took a very dim view of Christianity, questioning it on numerous fronts. Most of his complaints studied here had to do with the supernatural claims made by Christians, which he rejected. These would include subjects like Jesus's virgin birth, miracles, prophecies (as well as those prophecies cited by Christians from the Old Testament), and, of course, Jesus's resurrection. For Celsus, the presence of contradictions and inconsistencies in any of these accounts always constituted an important critique, and he thought there were many of them.[143]

In most cases, Celsus was quite fond of comparing Christian claims to supernatural beliefs from among the pagans, which he apparently rejected anyway. But as pointed out above, these claims alone, no matter on whose side they may fall, far from settle the crucial issues. So, one's case is not made just by trading claims for and against a proposition. Anyone can make claims, but which ones, if any, are most likely true—or, in this case, historical? Celsus would even agree that subjects such as those discussed here have far more to do with the strength of the evidence. So, if only one position turns out to be correct, it can hardly be opposed by flaunting more *claims* of a contrary sort.

Conclusion

As Ehrman crucially states more than once, the diversity of theological views really develops in the second century rather than in the first: "Virtually, the only Christian writings that can be reliably dated to the first century are found in the New Testament itself."[144] On the other hand, "most of the noncanonical Gospels are legendary and late, dating from the second to the eighth centuries."[145] Then in a blow to the radical scholars who want to move *Thomas* and other proto-gnostic books to the mid-first century or so, Ehrman asserts, "We have nothing to suggest that the beliefs embraced by later Gnostic Christians were present in first-century rural Palestine."[146]

[141] Celsus, 62, 65, 69, 115.
[142] Celsus, 54, 60, 66–67, 71–72; cf. Hoffmann's comments on 132nn42–48.
[143] Again, as explained by Hoffmann in his "General Introduction," 36.
[144] Ehrman, *New Testament*, 2.
[145] Ehrman, 198.
[146] Ehrman, *Did Jesus Exist?*, 290.

In this chapter the subject of early challenges to the death and resurrection appearances of Jesus were treated, and the overall study produced positive results with regard to this subject. From AD 30 until perhaps 140—that is, later in the Tier 1 category—a few examples of diverse views in nonfundamental areas of general Christian theology were observed. But no denials of either of these two crucial gospel events were witnessed during this time.[147] Excluding Celsus at the very end of this time period, the only aberrations surrounded proto-gnostic or gnostic doctrine, which we have discussed in a little detail. As Perrin notes, more developed gnostic thought does not emerge until the mid-second century. Further, "as far as we know, the historical accuracy of the four Gospels was never questioned" until the same time.[148]

Approximately AD 140 or perhaps somewhat later, there were a few proto-gnostic or gnostic texts that mentioned, assumed, or accepted the crucifixion, though Jesus himself was thought to have actually escaped that death on the cross. But this view was not due to any historical evidence. Rather, it was a concept that functioned strictly for theological reasons, since it was often believed among these gnostics that Jesus never really had a physical body in the first place and could not really die. So, this less-than-physical doctrine was not motivated by any historical evidence but by former doctrinal commitments. As Perrin reminds us, "*Both* sides would have agreed that their respective claims cannot simultaneously hold true. The claims . . . are fundamentally at odds with each other."[149]

What was the *practical* value of such gnostic and semi-gnostic beliefs? As pointed out above, it certainly seemed that everyone in the canonical Gospels who contacted Jesus thought he had a physical body—he walked, talked, ate, drank, touched others, and was touched throughout his life. So, for all practical purposes, this gnostic position was not grounded in any substantial data or evidence. It is difficult to say exactly,

---

[147] As commented several times, this depends on when the *Gospel of Thomas* was written and what view this writing took on the nature and form of Jesus's appearances. The conclusion here was to place the *Gospel of Thomas* at about AD 140–160, with the majority of scholars, and while a less than bodily appearance view *may* be the *Gospel of Thomas's* position, the latter seems difficult to prove from the sayings alone. But again, even taking a different view on the *form* of Jesus's resurrection body does not mean that the *Gospel of Thomas* necessarily denied Jesus's resurrection appearances if it were taught that Jesus truly did appear to his followers, which, again, cannot really be determined in this case.

[148] Perrin, *Judas Gospel*, 24, 28–29, with the quotation on 28–29.

[149] Perrin, 26 (emphasis added).

but if not by the midpoint of the second century, certainly these positions were proclaimed within just a few decades after this time.

For the same theological reasons, there were a couple of accounts from this general time or a little later where it was hinted that Jesus truly *did appear* to his disciples
and others after whatever happened to him or to someone else on the cross (or just
before it), though he still may not have had a physical body during these appearances.
But again, as just explained, this disembodied position was held due to prior doctrinal
beliefs, *not* because this is where the data were located. Hence, as before, this was a
rather ungrounded and trivialized position held on faith alone. As will be seen later,
the view was mistaken as well.

One reason this is known is because Jesus apparently looked to everyone present
precisely as if he possessed a physical body. After all, he had been observed and treated
by everyone throughout his entire public ministry as if his body were real. He occupied
time and space, traveled by foot, talked, and ate. Significantly, he touched others, and
when they touched him, their hands did not pass straight through him. The canonical
Gospels do not refer to Jesus as a phantom. So without any indications to the contrary
from the physical world, it is difficult to draw anything but a theological distinction here.

In an extended argument reaching literally hundreds of pages in length, N. T.
Wright argues similarly and in great depth that the change in belief among some
Christians from bodily to nonbodily appearances (chiefly as held by the gnostics)
did not come until somewhere between the late second century and the writings of
Tertullian (died c. 220). From the crucifixion until this time, at least a century and a
half, the Christian view was that the use of Greek terms like *anastasis*, *egeirō*, and their
cognates indicated that the appearances of Jesus were bodily in nature.[150] This would
be very close to the findings here.

One of the easily missed points made repeatedly by Wright on this subject is
that "there is no difference between pagans, Jews and Christians." Thus, *whenever*
and by *whomever* these terms were used, a bodily situation after death was being discussed, though pagans almost always despised this bodily afterlife option. The point
is *not* that pagans and others rejected the existence of any other disembodied afterlife

---

[150] Wright, *Resurrection of the Son of God*, 31, 83–84, 534–52, esp. 547–52; Wright,
"Opening Statement," in *The Resurrection of Jesus: John Dominic Crossan and N. T. Wright
in Dialogue*, ed. Robert B. Stewart (Minneapolis: Fortress, 2006), 19; Wright, *Surprised
by Hope: Rethinking Heaven, the Resurrection, and the Mission of the Church* (New York:
HarperCollins, 2008), 42.

manifestations such as ghosts or spirits, for they could always have used Greek terms like *pneuma* for those entities. Rather, it was the case that, when the particular words *anastasis*, *egeirō*, and their cognates were used, these specific terms referred only to bodily afterlife events.[151] So if nonbodily entities were being discussed, different terms were employed.

Writing approximately at the same time as the gnostic movement just mentioned, Celsus's *On the True Doctrine* denied Jesus's historical resurrection appearances altogether, whether bodily or not. It was written a long way from the events of AD 30 (in the category termed Tier 2, dating from about 150–200). But here the resurrection event was rejected outright, with Celsus's critique coming at the end of the outlying period of time for this study of the historical Jesus. But at approximately 130–50 years after the crucifixion, Celsus's critique had already reached the extremes of the historical parameters in terms of assisting with the historical goals here. As indicated in the earlier survey of the historical Jesus in volume 1 of this study, a number of scholars think that such a time gap is too far away from the crucifixion to be of any real historical value anyway. That is why this text moves from the second century here to the eighteenth century in chapter 2, where alternative challenges to Jesus's resurrection grow more sophisticated. Regardless, it appears to have taken a few decades longer, until the time of Celsus, for perhaps the earliest writing to have rejected outright this historical event.[152]

---

[151] Wright, *Resurrection of the Son of God*, esp. 31, but cf. also 35, 38, 62–64.

[152] It should be mentioned once again that few specific refutations, especially of Celsus's charges, were addressed in detail in this chapter since naturalistic and other objections are precisely the theme of this entire second volume. As a result, much more sophisticated forms of these issues will be entertained and critiqued elsewhere in this volume.

2

Hume 1: The Argument against Miracles

Without much doubt, David Hume (1711–1776) has exercised more influence on subsequent discussions of the question of miracles than any other thinker, placing his weight on the negative side of these considerations. Hume's essay "Of Miracles" (1748) has been so influential that one can hardly even deal with this question in a scholarly manner at all without at least mentioning his work, if not discussing and evaluating it in detail.[1]

Some Background

The importance of Hume's relatively short essay has been reflected by its enormous effect on contemporary theology and philosophy, as noted by influential critics. For example, prominent nineteenth-century German liberal scholar David Strauss cited Hume's essay as the reason for considering the miracle question to be settled. Such supernatural events could not be understood as transgressing the laws of nature.[2]

---

[1] "Of Miracles" is section 10 of David Hume's famous work *An Enquiry concerning Human Understanding*. It has also been published many times as a stand-alone essay, such as in anthologies.

[2] David Friedrich Strauss, *A New Life of Jesus*, 2nd ed., 2 vols. (London: Williams & Norgate, 1879), 1:199–201.

Columbia University philosopher John Herman Randall attested that critical thought ever since the appearance of the essay "Of Miracles" had largely followed "the great philosopher Hume," who "demolished" arguments from miracles. Hume devastated the miracles argument so thoroughly "that intelligent men have rarely questioned it since."[3] Since that time, liberals as a whole have also rejected the existence of events that interfere with the laws of nature. Natural explanations such as human error, imagination, and legend make much better sense, leaving only faith or mysticism as the bases for religious belief.[4]

Even conservative theologian Wilbur M. Smith admitted that Hume's treatise, while actually being quite brief, comprised the strongest retort ever presented against the belief in miracles. As a result, it "soon took its place as the most powerful argument ever raised against belief in the miracles of Christ, and for that matter, in all miracles."[5] By common consent, it would certainly appear that Hume is an excellent example of the scholarly rejection of the belief in any sort of miracle, including the resurrection of Jesus. The popularity and repute of his essay among still other scholars further reflects this choice.[6]

Hume's contribution to the question of miracles came just after the heyday of English deism, a notoriously difficult movement to date specifically. According to the late prominent historian from Columbia University, Peter Gay, deism may be described as reaching from the 1690s with John Toland's *Christianity Not Mysterious*, which began the debate, to Conyers Middleton's *Free Inquiry* published at the end of the 1740s.[7]

---

[3] John Herman Randall Jr., *The Making of the Modern Mind: A Survey of the Intellectual Background of the Present Age*, rev. ed. (Boston: Houghton Mifflin, 1940), 292–93.

[4] Randall, 294, 553–54.

[5] Wilbur M. Smith, *The Supernaturalness of Christ: Can We Still Believe in It?* (Boston: Wilde, 1940), 142.

[6] For a brief overview and overall discussion of Hume and his essay, as well as a critique and a survey of some of the critical scholars who followed Hume and similar approaches in rejecting miracles, see chaps. 5–6 of the published dissertation of Gary R. Habermas, *Risen Indeed: A Historical Investigation into the Resurrection of Jesus* (Bellingham, WA: Lexham Academic, 2021), esp. 112–15 on Hume's influence on other scholars.

[7] Peter Gay, "Toward an Interpretation," in *Deism: An Anthology*, ed. Peter Gay (Princeton: Van Nostrand, 1968), 9. For more on the interplay between deism and Hume, see the dated but still excellent treatment by Gay, *The Enlightenment, An Interpretation: The Rise of Modern Paganism* (New York: Knopf, 1966), 374–419. According to Owen C. Thomas and many others, deism began with the views of Herbert of Cherbury (*De Veritate*,

Deistic trends were intrinsically in agreement with similar proclivities across the water in French and German circles, though the continental representatives were more sophisticated due to the presence of greater scholarship among their numbers. The chief method was rationalistic in nature. Nonetheless, a lack of known or accomplished scholars did not slow the deists from attacking traditional Christian dogmas as being unreasonable. Quite radical for their times, the deists expressed chiefly rational doubts regarding traditional views of revelation and religious authority, opposing especially any ideas of miracles and the supernatural.

Most overviews today treat the deists (and others of their ilk) as being out of their intellectual depths and ill prepared for serious scholarly debate, yet still having influence, especially among lay Christians tired of various aspects of the professional church, such as its perceived failures. The result, as Gay notes, is "Deism, then, produced a great debate, and a debate the deists were bound to lose: the opposing side engrossed most of the talent." Gay then lists among some of the prominent adversaries of deism the likes of true intellectuals such as Joseph Butler, Alexander Pope, Jonathan Edwards, and even another skeptic, David Hume.[8]

It may seem strange to some that Hume should be numbered among these prominent scholars who critiqued ideas such as those of the deists, since their mutual dislike of supernatural revelatory claims, as with prophecy and miracles, would contribute to their being more united. However, Hume's ideas opposed those of the deists at more than one juncture. Epistemically, Hume thought that experience, not reason, was the chief criterion by which to obtain knowledge. Although experience was definitely not infallible, ideas were still judged according to its standards. The crux of Hume's polemic against miracles, then, would come from a different angle than from the more rational approaches of the deists. Finally, Hume disliked sloppy

---

1624) more than a half century before Toland's work; see Owen Thomas, ed., *Attitudes toward the Other Religions: Some Christian Interpretations* (New York: Harper & Row, 1969), 30. Gay labels Herbert of Cherbury as a precursor to deism instead of its founder; see *Deism*, 30.

[8] Gay, "Toward an Interpretation," 10. For other examples, compare Albert Schweitzer, *The Quest of the Historical Jesus: A Critical Study of Its Progress from Reimarus to Wrede*, trans. W. Montgomery (New York: Macmillan, 1968), 38–39; Frederick Copleston, *A History of Philosophy*, vol. 5, *Modern Philosophy: The British Philosophers*, part 1, *Hobbes to Paley* (Garden City, NY: Image, 1964), 174–77; Colin Brown, *Philosophy and the Christian Faith: A Historical Sketch from the Middle Ages to the Present Day* (Downers Grove, IL: InterVarsity, 1968), 76–81.

thinking wherever he came across it, and as we have said, the deists were not exactly known for their philosophical rigor![9]

David Hume's Argument against Miracles

Several pages into his essay "Of Miracles," Hume reaches a crucial stretch in his thinking.[10] He argues:

> A miracle is a violation of the laws of nature; and as a firm and unalterable experience has established these laws, the proof against a miracle, from the very nature of the fact, is as entire as any argument from experience can possibly be imagined. . . . Nothing is esteemed a miracle, if it ever happen [*sic*] in the common course of nature. . . . But it is a miracle, that a dead man should come to life; because that has never been observed in any age or country. There must, therefore, be a uniform experience against every miraculous event, otherwise the event would not merit that appellation. And as a uniform experience amounts to a proof, there is here a direct and full *proof*, from the nature of the fact, against the existence of any miracle.[11]

At the close of this paragraph, a footnote tidies up Hume's definition of miracles. It reads: "A miracle may be accurately defined, *a transgression of a law of nature by a particular volition of the Deity, or by the interposition of some invisible agent*" (211). Some clarifications then follow.[12]

---

[9] Some may treat as a parallel the historical Jesus studies of today, where even very critical scholars rarely give even an ounce of credence to those more radical writers who are usually not trained in relevant fields and who often even deny Jesus's existence. The point is that, for a variety of potential reasons, not all critics operate on the same page with each other. By comparison, Bart D. Ehrman's trenchant critique of the "Jesus Mythicists" may provide somewhat of a parallel here; see Ehrman, *Did Jesus Exist? The Historical Argument for Jesus of Nazareth* (New York: HarperCollins, 2012), 2–3, 16–34, for examples.

[10] This occurs in the well-known last two paragraphs, just before the end of part 1.

[11] See part 1 of Hume, "Of Miracles," 210–12. The quotations and other references to Hume's essay in this chapter are taken from the edition in *Hume on Religion*, ed. Richard Wollheim (London: Collins, 1963), 205–29. Hereafter in this chapter, page numbers for "Of Miracles" will appear in-text.

[12] Rather than specifying aspects of his previous definition, some commentators think that Hume is actually offering two definitions here.

Following directly in the very next and last paragraph of this same section, Hume continues:

> The plain consequence is (and it is a general maxim worthy of our attention), "That no testimony is sufficient to establish a miracle, unless the testimony be of such a kind, that its falsehood would be more miraculous, than the fact, which it endeavors to establish. . . . When anyone tells me, that he saw a dead man restored to life, I immediately consider with myself, whether it be more probable, that this person should either deceive or be deceived, or that the fact, which he relates, should really have happened. I weigh the one miracle against the other; and according to the superiority, which I discover, I pronounce my decision, and always reject the greater miracle. (211–12)

Few paragraphs in the philosophy of religion have engendered more dispute, clarification, and various sorts of explanations than have these last two from Hume's pen. Hume is convinced that "uniform" human experiences somehow stand against all miraculous events (defined as events that violate or transgress nature's laws) and that these uniform experiences in some sense comprise a proof against miracles' occurrence.

Moreover, Hume thinks that human testimony seemingly cannot reverse this conclusion since the likelihood of some species of deceit will always be more probable. The lone exception here occurs when the only other option is when all the available possibilities are miraculous, in which case he states that he will still always opt for the lesser miracle. Hume adds that the definition of a miracle also requires that such events be brought about by the will of God or another invisible agent, so the event must be caused by some supernatural power or other such agency.

For Hume, then, part 1 of his essay ends by arguing that the experience of the laws of nature and their uniform quality favor miracles being rejected alongside the more likely possibility of human deception or error. This may be Hume's central assertion: "When anyone tells me, that he saw a dead man restored to life, I immediately consider with myself, whether it be more probable, that this person should either deceive or be deceived, or that the fact, which he relates, should really have happened" (212).

Hume begins part 2 of his essay by adding four additional supportive considerations against the belief in miracles, which are often taken to be a posteriori observations. First, there are no historical accounts of miracles that are attested by "a sufficient number of men, of such unquestioned good-sense, education, and learning, as to secure us against all delusion in themselves" (212).

This is a rather incredible constraint to achieve. Hume requires witnesses with such "unquestioned" integrity and other qualities that they are proficient and capable enough to "secure us against all delusion." Is that even possible? How literally should these requirements be applied? Apparently, no one should be able to raise any questions about these witnesses with regard to their character, sense, education, and observational abilities. Further, how is it to be absolutely guaranteed that any witnesses will be able to ensure against all possible error? Then, would all skeptical evaluators have to agree across the board that every one of these qualities had been fulfilled? Have these characteristics ever been true of anyone (212)?

Hume's second assertion is more varied and is composed of several related thoughts. Trustworthy and probable data tend to be the "most usual" or normal reports and "we ought to give the preference to such as are founded on the greatest number of past observations." These sorts of cautions should help us guard against "forged miracles, and prophecies, and supernatural events" that come especially from those who exhibit a "strong propensity" for extraordinary and marvelous reports. There is simply too much passion where people are inclined to speak of extraordinary experiences of one sort or another, even to the point of fabricating the miraculous when it is known to be false in order to spread strange, wonderful, and attention-getting religious truths.

Actually, if not indiscriminately overapplied, this second caution offers some decent comments on the reporting of supernatural tales. It would be difficult to deny that most events are the usual, normal, and most common sorts that follow similar occurrences from the past. Further, it is troublesome to come across these examples of religious enthusiasm or exaggerated reports, most especially when the embellishment can readily be detected. When the report comes close to or includes actual fabrication, this is the most troublesome aspect of all, particularly if it is known that some of these reports are false while still being propagated. Hume even allows for the possibility of "greater evidence" potentially coming into play in the confirmation process (212–15).

Third, miraculous events are often "observed chiefly to abound among ignorant and barbarous nations." Hume makes the further point, "*It is strange . . . that such prodigious events never happen in our days.* But it is nothing strange, I hope, that men should lie in all ages" (215). Two of the prominent thoughts here are that miracles tend to happen almost totally, or at least predominantly, among unschooled peoples, plus the further idea that "lies" figure more commonly into the regular course of events. The observation regarding the seeming absence of many supernatural reports in the present day and in the most advanced countries is a common one and is worth contemplating. But to what extent does it question the existence of miracles altogether?[13]

In fact, as a number of specific studies have pointed out in detail, thousands of claimed healing events have reportedly also taken place in the modern world in answer to prayer, and in other religious contexts, and in the most modern, civilized, and educated parts of the world as well. Moreover, it is only in these advanced societies where confirmatory empirical testing is potentially available, such as is the case with pre- and post-CT scans, MRIs, and X-rays. These procedures are certainly capable of verifying or disproving many of these claims. Furthermore, it has been claimed regularly that these events have occurred exceptionally often. But that is a matter for the next chapter. If nothing substantive shows up from such tests, then Hume may be thought to be vindicated. But what is to be concluded if, after close studies, such confirmation actually *does* exist? It might appear then as if Hume simply repeating this third point may fail to rule out this testimony.

Fourth, Hume postulates that the miraculous events from one religion destroy the probability that those of another faith are also true, and vice versa. Further, this loss of the miracle claims also destroys the "rival systems" of belief in each religion too. As a result, supernatural accounts in different religions nullify each other as well as the remainder of their claims and teachings. Once the dust clears, the apparent idea is that all such occurrences and belief systems are effectively eliminated in the process (217–21).

This fourth critique may quite likely be the most dubious of Hume's four additional arguments against the occurrence of miracles, for it does not take account of an entire host of other options. In short, too many other possibilities exist. Hume maintains "that it is impossible the religions of ancient Rome, of Turkey, of Siam, and of China should, all of them, be established on any solid foundation" (217). But if the vast majority of religious miracle claims are "pretended," as Hume states in this context—or if they are indeed "lies" as he states a couple of times earlier—how could it be the case that such false reports could even come close to nullifying the existence of confirmed data such as documented healings, for example, if such were discovered?

---

[13] This initial accusation appears to clearly commit the informal genetic fallacy as well, but that is another matter for later comments.

Or what if miracles in more than one religious system were actually quite compatible with other faiths? Or what if all miracles were compatible with each other? Or yet again, what if only one religious system was superior or true? It does not appear that Hume's critique comes close to nullifying different miracle claims or the religious systems themselves, as he claims.

In circumstances such as these last examples illustrate, the canceling of claims, events, and doctrines by others of a similar nature need not apply at all, hence the unconvincing nature of Hume's last challenge. If all "miracles" are simply false anyway, as Hume would like to believe, then that is the bottom line, but *not* because he simply states this. On the other hand, if there are a combination of true and false miracle claims, or ones that are compatible with others, this point is simply wrongheaded for more than one reason.

Hume argues that it is more probable that when considered alongside realities such as human delusion, pretense, and lies, perhaps among others, the experience favoring the uniformity of nature's laws is more reliable than human miracle claims. Therefore, miracle claims that are contrary to the laws of nature ought to be rejected. Since each case of miracle comes against a greater species of experiential data on the other side from the laws of nature, these occurrences are rejected as a whole (222–26).

Hume concludes the matter: "Upon the whole, then, it appears, that no testimony for any kind of miracle has ever amounted to a probability, much less to a proof." Then he continues, "Therefore we may establish it as a maxim, that no human testimony can have such force as to prove a miracle, and make it a just foundation for any such system of religion" (222–23). An important note here, however, is that Hume does not really speak disparagingly of God or any deity and was not trying to disprove the existence of God with such an argument (211n3, 224). It will be mentioned below that a number of scholars today argue that Hume was actually a deist of sorts.

Though there are other interpretations that will be examined, Hume's general argument appears at least to be fairly clear. Hume often repeats these major arguments as well as some of the additional points, and they seem to be the crux of his influential essay. Nonetheless, scholars have differed in opinion on how he constructed his argument, his overall theme, how the parts fit together, and how the whole should be interpreted. The resulting difference has grown more intense during the past few decades in particular. But these ideas may be fashioned variously, in more than one manner, even by careful scholars.

Other Recent Humean Nuances

Gregory Bock has summarized five different interpretations of Hume's essay, which he thinks includes the possible four interpretations:

(1) No miracle has ever happened.

(2) There is never enough justification for our believing that a miracle has occurred.

(3) Point 2 plus the addition of believing such a notion based on human testimony.

(4) Point 3 plus the addition of there being no sufficient argument that could then allow the miracle to serve as a basis for the truth of additional religious beliefs.

There could also be a combination of the four responses listed here.[14]

While such a list may helpfully assist in organizing some of the Hume interpretations, the views of what specifics this major philosopher actually taught on this subject may remain quite complicated, often where the differences between the choices exhibit only slight nuances. A few of the possibilities here, especially considering what could fall into option 5 above, may provide helpful insight into this matter. For Bock, following R. M. Burns, the classical view of Hume's argument held the dominant position for the first 200 years after its appearance.[15] This view postulated that no amount of evidence would ever be sufficient to establish a reasonable belief in miracles. This interpretation was standard and favored by skeptical philosophers like John Stuart Mill and T. H. Huxley.[16]

However, prominent Hume interpreter and philosophical skeptic Antony Flew challenged this traditional inclination in a 1959 journal article, arguing that Hume had not attempted a head-on challenge with the purpose of absolutely ruling out the belief in miracles a priori or to otherwise treat them as impossible events. Rather, Hume was somewhat more nuanced and did not provide some "insuperable bulwark" against the belief in miracles, as held by the traditional view, but was rather just

---

[14] Gregory L. Bock, "Understanding David Hume's Argument against Miracles: Establishing a Religion on the Testimony of a Miracle," *Philosophia Christi* 12 (2010): 372–91.

[15] R. M. Burns, *The Great Debate on Miracles: From Joseph Glanville to David Hume* (Lewisburg, PA: Bucknell University Press, 1981), 142–43.

[16] Bock, "Understanding David Hume's Argument," 378.

"checking" the growth of arguments that favored miracles by pointing out that to contend for such events was more difficult than that and that it invoked "a conflict in the evidence."[17]

Another recognized Hume scholar, Robert J. Fogelin, argued against these views as being Hume's position. Explaining that "Antony Flew stands virtually alone in challenging the traditional interpretation" of Hume, Fogelin contended against the other views here, supporting the idea that "Hume does present an a priori argument against the existence of miracles."[18]

While Bock favors his option 4 listed above,[19] philosopher and miracles specialist Robert A. Larmer challenged this selection, asserting that Bock's understanding of Hume's essay "has little to recommend it" from Hume's own text. For Larmer, Hume's main point "is to demonstrate that one could never have epistemological justification for accepting the testimonial evidence for a miracle, and this remains the dominant line of argument throughout."[20] However, Hume still intermixed some

---

[17] Antony Flew first published this interpretation of Hume's essay in his journal article, "Hume's Check," *Philosophical Quarterly* 9 (1959): esp. 3–4. Flew developed the argument further in his chapter "Miracles and Methodology," in Antony Flew, *Hume's Philosophy of Belief: A Study of His First Inquiry* (London: Routledge & Kegan Paul, 1961). Flew's quotations above were taken from 174, 176–77 of this volume. In our many discussions as well as three friendly debates on the question of miracles and the resurrection of Jesus, Tony Flew frequently made this point that Hume only held that miracles were quite unlikely events, not that they were absolutely ruled out or otherwise impossible. Tony also held that view himself.

[18] Robert J. Fogelin, "What Hume Actually Said about Miracles," *Hume Studies* 16 (1990): 81–87, esp. 81–82. Later, Fogelin followed up these thoughts with his volume *A Defense of Hume on Miracles* (Princeton: Princeton University Press, 2003).

[19] Bock, "Understanding David Hume's Argument," 374, 385–86, 391.

[20] The quotations are from Robert Larmer, "Misunderstanding Hume's Argument against Miracles: A Response to Gregory L. Bock," *Philosophia Christi* 13 (2011): 161 and 163, respectively. Quite intriguingly, Larmer further clarifies that Hume was quite well aware of efforts by two of his early antagonists, Philip Shelton and George Campbell, who challenged his thesis against miracles. In spite of this, Hume had actually recommended Shelton's work to the publisher and accepted an opportunity to respond to Campbell. Yet, though Shelton and Campbell each argued basically for what has been identified above as the traditional view, like Larmer, Hume never corrected their impressions of his argument or retorted that they were mistaken in how they characterized his work. While this may hint a bit of an argument from silence, it must be remembered that Hume was responding to both these critiques of his own essay, and it might be expected that he should have commented regarding something as serious as an opponent misunderstanding the nature of his

additional ideas too.[21] Bock responded that Larmer's option fit well into his delineation of option 3, but that it didn't account well for the strongest emphasis that Hume employed near the close of the essay. Bock still favored what he considered to be a charitable reading of Hume that involved a unified argument.[22]

The issue of Hume's exact argumentative structure in "Of Miracles" of course will not be solved here, especially in the sense of discovering an exact and proper interpretation of Hume's essay that pleases almost everyone. That remains an issue for doctoral dissertations. Hume specialists have argued the finer nuances for a few decades. But we have hopefully laid enough groundwork and strategic principles alike to have at least a fair idea of what Hume was attempting to accomplish. With so many ideas in the offing, it is necessary to respond to the overall family of Humean views, mentioning nuances where they may be helpful. Along the way, specific points may be directed more to one interpretation than to another, but these certainly remain scholarly options nonetheless. Even if Hume ultimately did not hold certain of these perspectives, some of his many commentators no doubt did so, still making this a useful study.[23]

Many of the preliminary responses so far point in the same direction: sooner or later, to determine if supernatural events have actually occurred, all the available data must be investigated. Mere speculation, faith alone, quoting texts from holy books, references to skeptical platitudes, and a priori dismissals will not indicate the answers

---

own treatment, should that have been the case. For this additional thought, see also chaps. 2–3 in Robert A. Larmer, *The Legitimacy of Miracle* (Lanham, MD: Lexington, 2014), specifically 60–61.

One other matter might be noted here just briefly. Fogelin intriguingly makes it sound as if Flew basically was almost by himself in holding his counterview of Hume's essay over against the traditional interpretation, though that is not the only possible meaning. See Fogelin, "What Hume Actually Said," 81. Yet Larmer states that since Flew's challenge to the traditional view, "commentators have increasingly tended to argue" in favor of Flew's position; see Larmer, *Legitimacy of Miracle*, 53. However, it must be acknowledged that the different perspectives between Fogelin and Larmer may have something to do with the intervening years between their two publications.

[21] Larmer, "Misunderstanding Hume's Argument," 155–63, emphasizing 155, 161–63. As an aside, Larmer makes the intriguing though minority move of arguing that since there is no necessity for miracles to break the laws of nature, this thereby renders Hume's argument in part 1 of his essay not only "deeply flawed" but also "irrelevant to the issue" (72).

[22] Gregory L. Bock, "Hume and Religious Miracles: A Reply to Robert Larmer," *Philosophia Christi* 13 (2011): 165–68, particularly 165, 167–68.

[23] The next chapter unpacks at least a few of the many additional positions.

for which we are searching. There is simply no substitute for viewing the claimed evidence for miracle claims on the one hand, along with responsible alternative explanations on the other, in order to ascertain which are more strongly attested.

This approach is therefore largely based, once again, on the subject of experiential testimony. After all, this support is claimed for both sides of the argument here. The various lines of data that *favor* miracle claims must be pitted against considerations that argue *against* them, such as the uniformity of nature, alternative nonmiraculous scenarios, and so forth. But before moving forward with the investigation in this study, we must ascertain in both this chapter as well as the next one whether there are other issues with either Hume's argument or the other scholars who have more or less followed him.

Some General Critiques of Hume's Essay

In his groundbreaking 1748 essay, Hume hit a number of topics that resounded with at least some of his readers, perhaps especially regarding the four a posteriori accusations against the belief in miracles that he recounts in part 2. For example, the assumption of proclaimed falsehoods and lies concerning miracle claims, exaggerations and bragging, the desire for attention, less-than-stellar witnesses with little education ("ignorant and barbarous nations" as Hume referred to them), such events always being reported in countries or locations other than that of the person speaking—all seem to have engendered some votes in his favor, especially with the religious skeptics such as those who may have appreciated the English deistic critiques.

However, major problems with Hume's approach to miracles also began to come to light after only a short interval, similar to what occurred in answer to several theological writings during the heyday of the nineteenth-century German criticism of miracles. Stanley Tweyman asserts that "few essays in the history of philosophy have attracted so much attention and criticism. Scholars and clerics have, ever since the essay first appeared, sought to understand what precisely Hume holds on the topic of the credibility and reality of miracles, and, at least as many, have attempted to show that his argument (which they think they understand) is defective."[24]

---

[24] Stanley Tweyman, "Introduction," in *Hume on Miracles*, ed. Stanley Tweyman (Bristol, UK: Thoemmes, 1996), ix–x.

However, from the mid-eighteenth to the nineteenth centuries, "Hume had few supporters."[25] One of Hume's only enthusiasts, Joseph Mazzini Wheeler, mentioned a host of his detractors by name in 1882. Then Wheeler humorously quipped after completing the list of names: "and a shoal of ministerial minnows sailing in the wake of these theological Tritons, have felt it incumbent upon them to refute the 'sophisms' of the sceptic Hume."[26]

Were the first impressions and critiques of David Hume's essay correct in their own return accusations? Was he understood properly? Were there similarities between these initial critiques and later ones? The answers to these questions will depend largely on how Hume was interpreted, as already noted. Here we will mention several major criticisms aimed at Hume's polemic.

Initially, Hume was probably blamed most frequently for committing a myriad of logical fallacies in his essay, often in different combinations. He was charged with improperly defining both the nature of miracles as well as ignoring the evidence for and against them, or with displaying an entire host of logical errors in the process. As Bock remarks of the more traditional interpretations, they typically charge "that Hume is either begging the question or being 'obscure.'"[27]

To repeat, Hume stated, "A miracle is a violation of the laws of nature; and as a firm and unalterable experience has established these laws, the proof against a miracle, from the very nature of the fact, is as entire as any argument from experience can possibly by imagined." So miracles are defined as violating nature's laws, and the totality of "firm and unalterable," not to mention "uniform experience" (just a few lines later), indicates that these laws cannot be interfered with or broken (210–11).

As per Bock's statement above regarding the most common varieties of critique, many commentators thought that they gained a further insight into Hume's reasoning process from this same paragraph. Perhaps thinking of the claims regarding Jesus, which would of course be well known in his society, Hume spoke generally of the resurrection of a dead individual, then promptly informed his readers, "But it is a miracle, that a dead man should come to life; because that has never been observed in

---

[25] Tweyman "Introduction," x. For a discussion on a contemporary collapse of Hume's arguments, see Timothy J. McGrew, "Of Miracles," in *The Nature Miracles of Jesus: Problems, Perspectives, and Prospects*, ed. Graham H. Twelftree (Eugene, OR: Cascade, 2017), 152–73.

[26] Joseph Mazzini Wheeler, "Introduction to Hume's Essay on Miracles," in Tweyman, *Hume on Miracles*, 155.

[27] Bock, "Understanding David Hume's Argument," 391, cf. also 378, 380–82 for further details.

any age or country." In the next sentence, he continued full speed ahead, still without producing any evidence to the contrary: "There must, therefore, be a uniform experience against every miraculous event, otherwise the event would not merit that appellation." Not slowing down for even a moment, Hume next informed his readers that, "as a uniform experience amounts to a proof, there is here a direct and full *proof*, from the nature of the fact, against the existence of any miracle" (210–11).

Almost immediately after the publication of Hume's essay, many researchers began raising several key questions. Since Hume's position is apparently taken both before, and in spite of, any potential testimony to the contrary, if this is not an a priori dismissal of the claimed data, then what is it? Where's the necessary examination of the facts? Though making a clear comment against a resurrection, Hume did not produce a speck of evidence specifically against the resurrection of Jesus occurring. Nor did he examine what, even in his own time, were arguments for Jesus's resurrection.

Thus, Hume's critics questioned what they interpreted as reasoning fallacies, objecting to the way he set up the problem from the outset. The complaints were numerous. Hume appeared to be allowing his definition and other straightforward assertions to do the heavy lifting for him. Then significantly, he failed to entertain any historical or other investigations featuring an impartial look at the facts. Rather, his very definition ruled out miracles a priori because of what seemed to be arbitrary and unproven assumptions on his part. His definition even asserted that the totality of human experience rested against the miracle when such a statement was anything but proven. There definitely were miracle claims that included experiential testimony, some perhaps with attending medical witnesses, but these were brushed aside by Hume due to the assumed superiority of alternate varieties of experience of nature's laws. But how could Hume know if the assertions made by supernaturalists were true apart from an investigation of the facts?

Therefore, it is often claimed that Hume's approach served as a textbook example of circular reasoning or begging the question. Dead men are assumed never to rise because that's just the way nature is; thus, all experience must stand against such as an event. This is a mere *assumption* against any experience to the contrary that may be produced in favor of miracle claims.[28] The evidence for miracles is simply and conveniently eliminated. But such moves in inductive matters can only properly be

---

[28] Further, given the recent empirical data favoring perhaps hundreds of extraordinary miracle-like events occurring today (as discussed later), this cannot provide much hope that Hume's eighteenth-century denials and assertions held much weight on the evidential front.

made *after* an investigation of the evidence. Thus, Hume assumes that which he must demonstrate, though he clearly has not done so.

C. S. Lewis agreed on the nature of these problems, recognizing this weakness and developing them into a trenchant criticism of Hume's position. Lewis relates, "Now of course we must agree with Hume that if there is absolutely 'uniform experience' against miracles, if in other words they have never happened, why then they never have. Unfortunately, we know the experience against them to be uniform only if we know that all reports of them are false. And we can know all the reports to be false only if we know already that miracles have never occurred. In fact, we are arguing in a circle."[29] Lewis has clearly noted these problems here, some of the same ones that bothered other thinkers as well. Hume can only claim that all experience affirms his view if he has first ascertained that all other experience is false. But since he has not investigated the evidence potentially favoring other positions, he can only state that they are false by assuming that miracles cannot occur. As Lewis seems to conclude fairly, Hume is reasoning circularly.

Again, it is C. S. Lewis who points out yet another example of circular reasoning in "Of Miracles." For Hume, the two questions, "Do miracles occur" and "Is the course of nature absolutely uniform?" are one and the same but simply asked from a different angle. But "by sleight of hand" Hume answers yes to the second question and then utilizes that response in answering no to the first question of whether miracles occur. The real issue that he endeavors to address is never really dealt with at all. So we still cannot be sure whether or not miracles have occurred. Thus, Hume "gets the answer to one form of the question by assuming the answer to another form of the same question."[30] Once again Lewis appears to have uncovered an example of circular reasoning in Hume.

The point is that it should go without saying that one cannot disallow miracles simply by defining them so that they cannot occur. Circular definitions are clearly unsatisfactory. But Hume does appear to define miracles as impossible in light of the experience that testifies to the existence of laws in nature. This is done without any real investigation to determine if the purported experience on behalf of miracle claims can establish their validity. As Lewis explains, Hume must somehow know this latter experience to be false, and he can only know that is so by assuming that miracles cannot occur in the first place.

---

[29] C. S. Lewis, *Miracles: A Preliminary Study* (New York: Macmillan, 1960), 102.
[30] Lewis, 103.

It may be that one agrees with Hume's conclusions that nature does rule out miracles. But the point here is that one cannot simply define or assume this to be the case, or arrange the "facts" in an arbitrary way, in order to proclaim that this assumption has been supported. As prominent philosopher Richard Swinburne points out, questions concerning whether or not an event occurred are a matter of historical rather than philosophical debate.[31]

But we have seen Bock's disagreement that this is the case. This strict interpretation of Hume "is based on a literal reading."[32] But it must be asked in return: is there something antecedently mistaken about such a way to read a text? Bock opts for taking a "weaker empirical sense" for some of Hume's language.[33] But does this also not sound a bit like special pleading in light of the text?

Perhaps this is why David Johnson argues that "Hume apparently begs the question." Then, just a few pages later, he states similarly, "Hume's own argument either obviously begs the question or becomes obscure."[34] Johnson goes on to ask in the same context, What are we supposed to do with witnesses who claim otherwise? This is an inductive issue for us to solve. As he ends his book, Johnson states his own conclusion: "Thus it has always seemed to me that the most persuasive argument for theism is the historical argument—the argument from miracles."[35]

Early Critiques of Hume's Essay

Most of the various issues mentioned so far in this initial critique were actually raised fairly soon after the appearance of Hume's essay. Stanley Tweyman's volume mentioned above is an invaluable collection of more than a dozen essays written concerning Hume's argument (chiefly in opposition against it), beginning just three years following its initial publication through 1882. These authors tended to take the more traditional interpretation of Hume's argument as outlined above.

---

[31] Richard Swinburne, *The Concept of Miracle* (London: Macmillan, 1970), esp. 15, 17. Most of this volume was republished in Richard Swinburne, *Miracles* (New York: Macmillan, 1981), see chaps. 1, 8, and 13.

[32] Bock, "Understanding David Hume's Argument," 380.

[33] Bock, 382–83.

[34] David Johnson, *Hume, Holism, and Miracles* (Ithaca: Cornell University Press, 1999), 18, 21.

[35] Johnson, 99–100.

The most common complaints centered on the need for evidence to back up Hume's claims. These authors charged that Hume failed to produce actual evidential arguments in favor of his position, but rather simply stated his points while leaving them as seemingly based on his own authority. Also, he failed to answer any specific contrary evidence that had been put forward against his approach, including evidential suggestions regarding data that stood against his presentation. In spite of needing evidence against others in order to make his critiques, he produced none.[36]

For instance, William Adams stated straightforwardly that "tho' the author is pleased to pronounce [miracles] impossible, he hath offered no argument (and, indeed, none can possible [*sic*] be offered): against the *credibility* of it, the experience which he pleads is no argument at all."[37] Adams concluded the matter quite powerfully: "The surest way not to believe [miracles] is not to examine them."[38]

Moreover, it was also charged frequently that Hume committed many logical errors in his essay, invalidating his entire approach.[39] Further, the question was posed concerning what Hume would do if evidence were actually produced in favor of

---

[36] Several of these examples from Tweyman are among the earliest of the replies to Hume's essay (some of which are extracted from the original publications). For these responses, see Thomas Rutherford, "The Credibility of Miracles Defended against the Author of Philosophical Essays" (1751), in Tweyman, *Hume on Miracles*, 26–28, 33; Anthony Ellys, "Remarks on Mr. Hume's Essay concerning Miracles" (1753), in Tweyman, *Hume on Miracles*, 85; Samuel Vince, "Remarks on Mr. Hume's Principles and Reasoning, in his 'Essay on Miracles'" (1809), in Tweyman, *Hume on Miracles*, 99, 106–7; plus several anonymous review essays: "The Credibility of Miracles Defended against the Author of Philosophical Essays, in a Discourse Delivered at the Primary Visitation of the Bishop of Ely, in St. Michael's, Cambridge," *The Monthly Review* 5 (1751): 37; "An Essay on Mr. Hume's Essay on Miracles," *The Monthly Review* 6 (1752): 65; "A Review of George Campbell's Dissertation on Miracles: Containing an Examination of the Principles Advanced by David Hume, Esq; in an Essay on Miracles," *The Monthly Review* 26 (1762): 88. Regarding some of these authors' names, see James Fieser's reviews "Hume on Miracles," and "Hume on Natural Religion (Review)," *Hume Studies* 24 (1998): 195–200.

[37] William Adams, "An Essay on Mr. Hume's Essay on Miracles" (1752), in Tweyman, *Hume on Miracles*, 47.

[38] Adams, 63.

[39] Anonymous, "Conclusion of the Account of Price's Dissertations on Providence," *Monthly Review* 36 (1767): 91, 97; Vince, "Remarks on Mr. Hume's Principles," 99, 104; Rutherford, "Credibility of Miracles," 28.

miracles.[40] Then, as if to help Hume compose an even stronger argument, Rutherford attempted to recast Hume's argument in a couple of other forms, just to ascertain "whether your conclusion will succeed better," but then followed his own alternate suggestions with further refutations![41]

The similarity of these complaints from over 200 years ago to the present is rather instructive. It seems that, regarding the traditional interpretations of Hume's essay, this initial critique regarding the need for evidence both in favor of his position as well as addressing concerns raised by others was quite widespread. As mentioned already, even Hume himself did not object to this viewpoint, though it appears to have devastated his efforts.

Seven Critiques of Hume's Miracles Essay

This first set of problems with regard to Hume's essay is certainly a major one. Initially, Hume's logical blunders from the outset, consisting of several circular and a priori moves, limit severely the value of his essay in terms of the possibility of dismissing miracles by these means. As mentioned above, Hume can only know that there is uniform experience against all miracles if he has investigated all of the serious claims in their favor. Apart from that, which he has neglected completely and even ignored, he can only know that all experience opposes miracles by ruling that they cannot happen in the first place—clearly a circular move.[42]

---

[40] Adams, "Hume's Essay on Miracles," 46–47.

[41] Rutherford, "Credibility of Miracles," 28–30.

[42] In particular, taking the traditional interpretation of Hume's essay "Of Miracles," this philosopher's logical problems usually consist of both defining and arguing circularly (especially while defining a miracle) and begging the question by using unproved and unsupported assumptions (particularly in reference to the assumed absolute authority of the laws of nature and the negligible value of any experience of miracles). True, in Hume's long, entire series of fallacious comments (usually located in part 1 of the essay), many of his assertions are repeated in different words, causing them to appear to be more numerous than they are by a strict count. The sheer volume of Hume's unsupported assertions is just amazing. Lining up a couple of these statements by fiat, Hume asserts that human experience is allied *uniformly* against all miraculous events, and as such, these events cannot occur. Therefore, all reliable experience on their behalf will indeed coincide with these conditions since the opposite has already been defined forcefully as an impossibility.

Continuing, Hume even defines this "uniform experience" so that, if all of this is not the case, then the miraculous event "would not merit that appellation." So then, unless all human experience automatically stands against miraculous testimony, the event cannot

A second issue may be equally problematic for Hume. This concerns the evidential place that should be given to experience for the laws of nature. Hume is no doubt correct that nature behaves according to certain laws. After all, how can abnormalities like miracles be identified apart from recognizing that nature has a normal pattern? But Hume asserts that the existence of these laws is absolutely confirmed by experience, and that is sufficient to disprove all experience of miracles (210–12, 221, 223).

At this point there are many scholars who would disagree with Hume, and the outcry has only grown louder in the past few decades. Even if nature behaves according to laws, this does not for a moment dictate that occasional exceptions or even abnormalities cannot occur. If these laws regulate the daily workings of nature, then

---

even be referred to as a miracle! Then Hume insists next that the sum of these statements constitutes "a direct and full *proof*" (his emphasis) against any brand of miraculous event. Then the term "proof" is repeated three more times in the exact same sentence in order to make the point entirely clear. From this he states next that, "no testimony is sufficient to establish a miracle." Incredibly, a condition follows here—the only exception to the previous rule is if the denial or falsehood of the miracle would turn out to be more miraculous than the original event itself! But in that case Hume still imposes another rule: we are "always to reject the greater miracle." Where did this statement come from? And why is this the case other than, once again, by the authority of the statement alone? These are some of the chief prohibitions imposed against miracles from the very beginning.

Talk about piling up a contrived list of problems! All of this is done without stating any contrary evidence against or conducting a factual investigation of some miracle claims, as called for by his critics. The burden of the second (uniformity of experience) rests upon the solidity of the first (experience of nature), which has not at all been evidenced, let alone "proven." The moment an event becomes designated as a miracle, Hume determines that it was to be snuffed out of existence arbitrarily. But one can "demonstrate" anything if definitions are allowed to be all-inclusive and contain the conclusion to be proven as a given. Therefore, it certainly appears that Hume's "proof" against miracles fails, and for several reasons here. It indeed relies on the previously given circular definition of a miracle and constitutes a solid example of circular reasoning throughout. It is easier now to see why so many scholars have objected to various aspects of Hume's rejection of miracles. This even applies to some who agree with him on the general issue of miracles. He assumes here that which he wishes to prove, but which he has not investigated.

These arguments alone, if accurate, are enough to invalidate Hume's entire thesis against miracles. We could also "prove" that miraculous events *do* occur by definition and by accepting all experience in favor of miracles, while rejecting any experience for the laws of nature in these specific instances. Then it could be concluded that all other experience must agree with this. To do so would of course prove nothing. But it could be couched in a logical form that is very similar to Hume's argument. However, many more points of critique still remain to be made with regard to Hume's work on miracles.

they describe what will happen if the system is left to itself. But these laws cannot dictate the possible results of more powerful interferences from the outside, whether natural or supernatural. We are not addressing in this chapter whether supernatural influence has actually occurred—after all, that is the subject of this entire study. Rather, the concern here is that Hume is simply begging the question once again when he assumes that the experience for the laws of nature is superior to experience (*if* established) for the miraculous.

Here is why: the very experience of possible miracles, which Hume dismisses as nonexistent or as inferior, if established, would *actually overrule* the supposedly stronger experience for the laws of nature! This is because a true miracle, even according to Hume, would involve a supernatural intervention into nature, and if such intervention occurred, it would show that the laws of nature *could* be temporarily suspended. Thus, accredited experience for a miracle would actually be shown to be *superior* at the precise intersection of that *particular* convergence point. If the laws of nature were in effect "overpowered" at that moment, these laws could not stop it from occurring. After all, the laws of nature describe rather than prescribe what can occur.

It must be noted very carefully, once again, that we are not in this chapter somehow investigating to see if a miraculous event happened. Neither are we attempting to somehow smuggle such occurrences in through the back door or anything of the sort. Similarly, it is unnecessary to prove the existence of God or a supernatural agent of any sort. Only the *possibility* of such interaction need be postulated here. We are raising a more basic point that if it is even *possible* that God or a supernatural world existed, Hume would have to be open to such events, since the laws of nature would not be the ultimate authority.

So, here's the chief point we are making: by failing to investigate sufficiently any *even potentially* credible experience in favor of miraculous events, Hume cannot employ the laws of nature as an absolute rule that cannot ever be broken. In other words, how does Hume possibly know, *apart from detailed checking*, whether one or more laws already have been temporarily set aside by a superior force? Therefore, to simply keep asserting the strength or uniform experience of nature's laws simply exacerbates the empty, a priori ring of Hume's declarations.

C. S. Lewis aims a similar, potent criticism at Hume: "Probabilities of the kind that Hume is concerned with hold inside the framework of an assumed Uniformity of Nature. When the question of miracles is raised we are asking about the validity or perfection of the frame itself. No study of probabilities inside a given frame can ever tell us how probable it is that the frame itself can be violated."[43] In other words, Lewis charged that Hume was simply answering a question from *within* the framework of his own assumed view of a completely uniform nature, when in reality we should be asking whether the entire framework itself could potentially be *temporarily suspended by a stronger force*. Thus, Hume is concerned exclusively with things that might or might not obtain within a system when he should rather be concerned with what may transpire from outside this restricted area by a superior power. Is it possible that this current system of nature, as trustworthy as it might be in and of itself, could be interrupted from the outside (as with a miracle)?[44]

A couple of decades before Lewis, Cornell University philosopher Edwin Burtt leveled a similar criticism at Hume. Burtt contended that Hume failed to account for the position that God might not only exist, but that he could act in nature anytime he chose to do so, simply because these laws were part of his own creation. Nonetheless, this possibility would not upset the system—rather, the same law would remain in place both before and after the event.[45]

Hence, the question of possible experience for miracles at this point is indispensable. If such were discovered to be the case, it would indicate that any applicable laws of nature indeed could be temporarily *suspended or superseded*, thus making the empirical claims in favor of the miracle *dominant* over the empirical claims for nature's laws *at that precise moment*. Even though on other occasions the law would still apply, both before and after, it would clearly outweigh the laws at that particular juncture.

Hence the charges immediately after his essay were correct. By refusing to investigate such miracle claims, Hume thereby rejected virtually out of hand the exact evidence that would be needed to disrupt his assumptions and indicate that a miracle had probably happened. But he insisted on working only within the presumed framework of the laws of nature, without taking any account whatsoever of possible interferences from the outside due to the exertion of yet more powerful forces.

---

[43] Lewis, *Miracles*, 103.

[44] Rather incredibly, it has become fairly popular of late to recognize that Hume was most likely a deist of some sort (see the mention of this below). If Hume held that God exists or if he was even open to that idea, this potential critique should make his position even more open to this critique, not less so.

[45] Edwin A. Burtt, *Types of Religious Philosophy* (New York: Harper & Row, 1939), 213n5.

This criticism also provides an additional window on Hume's informal logical errors that were mentioned initially, such as formulating a circular definition
and begging the question with regard to the presumed importance of natural laws.
Unfortunately for Hume, his errors are not only improperly lodged at the very heart
of his polemic as the foundation of his position, but they constitute his chief reasons
for disallowing any such events or even the need to study the data. The repetition of
these informal fallacies may have served as potential impediments to another path
which, if Hume had taken it, could have unraveled his entire thesis.

A number of these previous details as well as similar aspects regarding miracles
potentially being able to supersede nature's laws were also made frequently in several of the very earliest essays in Tweyman's work. This critique actually figured quite
prominently in this volume of philosophical analyses of Hume's essay on miracles. For
instance, after referring to Hume's argument, Rutherford brilliantly asserted: "But such
an experience will never prove, that no events . . . can be brought about by the interposition of him, who established these laws, and can over-rule them." He continued,
"The force of an argument, deduced from experience, can extend no farther." Thus,
Hume's argument "can be no proof at all, in respect of a power superior to nature."[46]

Referring to Hume's example of iron floating in the air, Adams commented that
even a man can cause iron or lead objects to fly through the air or to be suspended in
water by his own human power exerted against nature.[47] Likewise, Adams asserted
that Hume had never answered the question or provided an argument against the
potential ability of some invisible agent to perform an event of this sort in nature
by exerting a greater power on particular occasions.[48] Adams later concluded the

---

[46] As noted by Rutherford in "Credibility of Miracles," 26–27.

[47] Like Adams's iron example, it may be added today along these same lines of thought
that humans can, by their own power, even send spacecraft through and far beyond earth's
gravity and out into the far reaches of our solar system. While the spacecraft did not, strictly
speaking, "break" a law of nature at all, they overcame or superseded what in Hume's day
would never have been thought possible. Furthermore, such spacecraft were powered by a
stronger force than nature's laws, though these were not supernatural forces at all. What's
more, the laws were still firmly in place both before as well as after the spacecraft passed
through, with absolutely no ill effects. If there were a God with certain attributes who chose
to act in nature by a still stronger power, why should this be deemed an impossibility, with
the laws of nature returning to their normal course immediately afterward? How could
Hume disallow this argument?

[48] Adams, "Hume's Essay on Miracles," 46–47, where Adams also used the word
"frame," just as Lewis did in talking about the same problem (Lewis, *Miracles*, 103).

matter rather nicely and succinctly: "Against the interposition of such superior power, experience, as we have seen, can determine nothing."[49]

Somerville concluded his essay like this: "The Supreme Being is the author of the laws of nature; that as it is by his power that these laws operate, so he must have the power of suspending or altering them when he sees meet . . . it might have been expected that the Supreme Being would have interfered, and suspended or altered the laws of nature, to prove that it came from him." Then Somerville continues with this last point, also against Hume's case, that these miracles were "wrought in support of revelation, particularly of the gospel."[50] From the context, this may have been a reference to Hume's additional argument that miracles could not support matters of doctrine.

Three of the anonymous authors in Tweyman also made remarks along similar lines.[51] One unidentified writer stated concisely, "Miracles, if at all, are effects of an extraordinary power upon extraordinary occasions: consequently, common experience can determine nothing concerning them."[52] Another commented that the events in nature were "established by an intelligent Being in the constitution of nature."[53] Discussing the idea of Hume's use of the "firm and invariable experience" against miracles as derived from the laws of nature, yet another author summarized Rutherford's argument that such an approach is incapable of ever proving "that no events . . . can be brought about by the immediate interposition of him who established these laws, and can over-rule them."[54]

This second critique is actually quite straightforward and absolutely devastating because it actually bypasses the chief argument being made in Hume's essay. The argument there was offered from *inside of nature* and concerned either the strength of nature's laws—Hume referred to them as "the most established laws of nature" (221) and "the usual course of nature" (223), or to the "firm and unalterable

---

[49] Adams, 53.

[50] James Somerville, "Remarks on an Article in the Edinburgh Review, in which the Doctrine of Hume on Miracles Is Maintained," in Tweyman, *Hume on Miracles*, 128–29.

[51] Once again, see Fieser's reviews "Hume on Miracles" and "Hume on Natural Religion (Review)" mentioned above.

[52] Anonymous, "An Essay on Mr. Hume's Essay on Miracles," in Tweyman, *Hume on Miracles*, 66.

[53] Anonymous, "Conclusion of the Account of Price's Dissertations on Providence," in Tweyman, *Hume on Miracles*, 95, in a continuation of note 3 on page 94.

[54] Anonymous, "Credibility of Miracles," 35.

experience" or "uniform experience" that in turn confirms these laws (210–11). Hume's assertion is that these were sufficient to offset actions by a more powerful force. However, *it really does not matter* how complete or how powerful either the laws or the experience behind them are since it makes no practical difference! The force of these twin considerations holds only if they are the most powerful entities in existence, where no other more powerful forces are operating. What if we arbitrarily projected that these laws plus the experience of them were ten times greater than they actually are, but yet the force that birthed the miraculous event was infinite?

A crucial idea here is the understanding that sufficiently powerful historical evidence could, perhaps *only for a precise moment* at a very brief time, indicate that the laws of nature were either abrogated, superseded, nullified, overruled, set aside, or some other arrangement that allowed an occurrence *due to a superior power*. Afterward, these laws then returned to their normal operation. But *continuing* to talk about how strong, powerful, verified, inviolable, or impregnable these laws are and how incredible amounts of experience confirm them just plain misses the boat.

Thus, one of the chief arguments repeated throughout this study is that such potential evidence in favor of the *historical portion* of credible miracle claims (just the part that can be examined with historical tools) must be investigated in order to ascertain whether or not any such qualifying events may ever have happened. Since Hume failed to do so, he would be unable to declare that these laws could never be abrogated. Therefore, there is no substitute for research here—such an examination cannot be avoided in spite of Hume's oft-repeated protestations to the contrary.

However, many skeptics will pose an obvious question at this juncture. An editorial remark in Tweyman's volume noted that atheists might be unaffected by this move, perhaps with their rejoinder being to prove God or the supernatural realm first.[55] Initially, it will be mentioned simply that these questions will be introduced and treated in much detail later in this study. But the middle of a chapter is not the place to begin such a book-length hiatus. Further, it has been mentioned that Hume himself is often thought to be some variety of deist. If so, he would have to answer if this Being could perform a miracle, even if that is not his view.

But a more relevant response here is more straightforward. The earlier point was that if it is even *possible* that such a being or force exists that is capable of producing

---

[55] Tweyman, *Hume on Miracles*, 128n7.

events in nature, especially if these occurrences appear to be manifestations that nature probably cannot perform on its own, Hume would *still* have to check out this possibility before issuing such a universal challenge. In other words, if miracles are even possible, Hume should not stand aloof and declare that such a scenario cannot obtain under any circumstance. That *would* sound like an a priori dismissal. Thus, just shouting concerning how strong the laws of nature are and how human experience confirms them just does not answer the question of the *possible* action of a stronger power.[56]

Asserting as Hume does that nature's laws as backed by experience can nullify all supernatural claims, he needs to back up that claim by showing that no such events have ever occurred.[57] He does say regularly and repeatedly that miracle claims most likely are due to false reporting and fakery, one's imagination, exaggeration, lies, and so on (206–8, 212–17, esp. 212). But skeptics assert regularly that believers must be prepared to answer alternative theses contrary to their own views, so why doesn't this apply to Hume? Or what if Hume attempted to counter a particular counterevent (or events) with all the natural avenues at his disposal and still did not produce the best counterargument?

Once again we have established the need for solid, experiential research into the available documents and information. Whether it is the theist who is arguing for miracles or other supernatural events, or naturalists who are arguing against these, there is just no substitute for checking out the claimed data potentially against one's position. Overarchingly, more static "umbrella" laws and principles of various sorts may have been helpful in Sir Isaac Newton's time (just a couple of decades before Hume's writing), or even still at some junctures today. But when it comes right down to the heart of the issue, we must ascertain the actual nature of these events. In keeping with Hume's own proclamations, the best data must rule here! As Hume famously pronounced, "A wise man, therefore, proportions his belief to the evidence" (206).

---

[56] Perhaps a sports illustration serves as a very simple example here. A proud head coach may announce that his team is the very best in the world, perhaps mentioning this or that player and asserting that they are simply unstoppable. But the team is probably not thereby challenging the world champions. To carry out this notion, Hume does not appear to be challenging Little League teams here. He's making as wide a proclamation as possible, offering the challenge to anyone. As such, he must be prepared to take on any challenge.

[57] To carry the sports analogy one step further, what if the head coach continued to proclaim loudly that no one anywhere could beat his team, but when challenged, he simply dodged the challenge every time?

The third major criticism of Hume's essay "Of Miracles" pertains to his four supportive, largely a posteriori arguments in part 2, which extend his case against miracles. While at least some of the thoughts there are certainly helpful cautions, none prohibits miracles singly or as a whole. Moreover, Hume then appears to mishandle an entire series of miracles that even he admits fulfills all four of these "conditions," thereby leaving the way open to the possibility that miracles may also fulfill them. The latter case in question concerns a series of reputed miracles performed among the Jansenist believers in eighteenth-century France. Hume's own investigation of these events engendered a very interesting final response indeed in light of his own four criteria.

Reviewing Hume's four subpoints briefly that functioned as backup considerations against the belief in miracles, the first one asserted that the witnesses to the miraculous events need to be "a sufficient number of men, of such unquestioned good-sense, education, and learning, as to secure us against all delusion in themselves" (212). It can be agreed that we need good witnesses, but requiring that they be virtually impervious to any sort of character flaw whatsoever is a rather incredible, self-defeating requirement, essentially cutting against any job on either side of the issue before us that requires good witnesses! Can anyone ever be absolutely sure that they are capable of insuring against *all possible error*? When has this ever applied to any witness? Hume's general idea is helpful, apart from the obvious exaggeration.

Hume's second assertion includes a number of somewhat-related requirements. He maintains that in the evaluation process, we ought to prefer details that are based on what might be called "normal" observations. Such a requirement would help us to guard against false claims of bogus miracles and prophecies, especially reported by those who exhibit a "strong propensity" for extraordinary and marvelous reports. The possibility of an extraordinary account is too alluring for some folks, raising the likelihood of fabrication of one sort or another, even when the account is known to be false. There can be little doubt that many eccentric, strange, and attention-getting religious truths often make headlines and talk shows apart from being characterized by solid credentials (212–15).

This second criterion is actually helpful as a generalized warning regarding super-natural accounts. As Hume notes, normal, everyday sorts of occurrences are the most common kinds, and these are the ones that are confirmed by the majority of good data. Further, it is troublesome when we are exposed to instances of religious exag-geration, most especially when we were also present, observed the event for ourselves, and can clearly recognize the embellishment. The most troublesome of all are those that seem to include actual fabrication.

Third, Hume asserts that miraculous events are often "observed chiefly to abound among ignorant and barbarous nations." Further, Hume asserts, "*It is strange . . . that such prodigious events never happen in our days.* But it is nothing strange, I hope, that men should lie in all ages" (215–17). So besides being poorly attested as a whole, miracles are claimed most of all to be reported in other societies where education is not strong to say the least. Once again, we also note the mention of lies here.

But Hume is correct in certain circumstances. Many have claimed that very few credible supernatural reports seem to be made in the present day and age, and when they are, they seem to appear in another location far away from us. We are simply never around when these reports occurred. To one degree or another, it is easy to identify with at least some of these complaints. They can indeed help with evaluations of miracle claims.

However, the major question before us is the extent to which these first three standards apply to all miracle claims. Are they of sufficient magnitude to cause us to doubt even a majority of these claims? For the most part, they serve more as cautionary warnings than as some sort of roadblock. So they may play the role of assisting us in making sure that we look before we leap, but there is no way that they simply rule out these seeming miraculous events.

However, taking these three criteria at face value, they simply cannot bear the weight of *eliminating* all miracle claims and relegating them to the trash heaps. To be straightforward, they simply lack that sort of rigor and insight, perhaps not because of Hume's lack of reasoning power but because the tools with which Hume had to work were just too dull. Further, this has become an even more daunting task, not a lesser one, in the twenty-first century. Actually, it could even be said in one respect that these three criteria may actually help to hone an even stronger case for supernatural events, in that they may assist in enhancing and sharpening the researcher's focus so that the weaker cases can hopefully be culled out and avoided. Thus, when truly impressive contemporary cases of miracle claims come to light, as we will mention below, they may arise with even more force.

It has already been pointed out above that Hume's fourth criterion was unlike the others. It was quite likely the most unconvincing, doubtful, and least helpful of his subpoints against the occurrence of miracles. Hume proposed that if the "pretended" miracles from one religion went "head-to-head" with those of other faiths, they would nullify or even destroy each other, along with the likelihood that any miracles were true. All told, the contrary teachings from each "rival system" of belief would also be destroyed and eliminated. As a result, supernatural accounts in the various religions nullify each other's occurrences, as do their claims and teachings. Once the dust settled, then, no religious systems would be left standing. Each was thought to be eradicated by the other (217–21).

But several misleading statements and inferences should be noticed here. Since Hume referred to these religions as being false anyway, perhaps just built on lies, how could false reports even come close to nullifying the possibility of true data? Or if Hume's point is that *all* miracle claims were false, has he at least attempted to show that (or how) this is the case? If he has not done so, then we are precisely back to the previous critique: how does Hume know that the various supernatural claims and reputedly miraculous events are untrue, unless he has checked them out first?

Or again, what if miracles in one religious system or in another region of the world are actually quite compatible with different beliefs? Incidentally, this need not only apply to different groups *within* a particular religion, such as Roman Catholicism, Greek Orthodoxy, or various Protestant groups. It could likewise apply *between* various systems of thought. For example, C. S. Lewis commented, "I do not think that it is the duty of a Christian apologist (as many sceptics suppose) to disprove all stories of the miraculous which fall outside the Christian records, nor of a Christian man to disbelieve them. I am in no way committed to the assertion that God has never worked miracles through and for Pagans or never permitted created supernatural beings to do so."[58] In the circumstances like the ones just mentioned, no canceling of religious teachings or events is necessitated or can be shown to be the case, hence indicating the unconvincing nature of Hume's fourth challenge. Even if all miracle claims were simply false anyway, as Hume would presumably prefer, then that is the bottom line—but *not* because of this last criterion. Further, how would Hume *know* that these claims were false? On the other hand, if there is a combination of true and false miracle claims, or ones that are compatible with others, or simply one true religion, then his fourth point is simply wrongheaded anyway.

---

[58] Lewis, *Miracles*, 132. A few examples from the Gospels may be helpful. We are told that as Jesus traveled from town to town, he frequently healed all the sick who came to him (as in Luke 6:19). These numbers included non-Jews from other nations (Mark 7:25–30; Luke 6:17–18; cf. Matt 8:5–13). We never read that Jesus refused to help any of the needy ones simply because they had not believed in him before this time! All alike were healed without discrimination. Further, it appears that the Pharisees were likewise casting out demons (Matt 12:27), so the practice was not reserved for Jesus or his disciples alone.

Before moving on from this present critique, an additional issue concerns Hume's own response to a series of reputed miracles that happened among the French Jansenists in the eighteenth century. Hume described the miraculous events in question as the "curing of the sick, giving hearing to the deaf, and sight to the blind" (220). How does Hume respond when even he admits that these events appear to have fulfilled his own requirements for at least his first three more experiential tests for such occurrences? Though fairly brief, Hume's own investigation of these events is the closest he comes in this essay to checking out the available historical evidence in favor of miracle claims. In fact, it seems that he is answering his own four questions by supplying the available data. Surprisingly, given his own criteria, Hume reached some seemingly strange and intriguing conclusions, as will be seen below. Many commentators have been left scratching their heads on this particular subject.

Hume's first criterion required reports from the most compelling witnesses with an "unquestioned" number of traits that would "secure us against all delusion" (212). But Hume actually admitted that the Jansenist events were "proved upon the spot, before judges of unquestioned integrity, attested by witnesses of credit and distinction" (220). In a lengthy endnote, Hume provided quite a long account of many very reputable persons from different walks of life who reportedly either witnessed the relevant evidence personally or examined some cases later. These witnesses included several physicians, twenty-two rectors, a well-known and respected police lieutenant, a duke, and even 120 other witnesses who were quite influential in Paris.[59] Hume even listed several famous scholars, like Pascal and Racine, who were apparently convinced of the miracles as well (226–29). It certainly appears that Hume went out of his way to make the point that there were an acceptable number of reputable witnesses here for the Jansenist events.

Hume's second criterion required witnesses that do not falsify, imagine, or even lie about potentially miraculous events. Yet, he allows that these Jansenist miracle reports had been investigated by the Jesuits and others who were enemies of these teachings. The group of antagonists included the same police lieutenant whose job was to expose or suppress the events in question, but he was unsuccessful. The Molinist party also attempted to discredit these occurrences but only ended up attributing the

---

[59] This number appears to be a rather obvious reference to the 120 witnesses in the early church who gathered in Jerusalem after Jesus ascended to heaven (Acts 1:15), perhaps signifying a similar new beginning for this Jansenist group in France.

miracles to "witchcraft and the devil," thereby admitting that they had actually happened. Moreover, the Molinists were reminded that this was the same response the Jews made to Jesus.

In another instance, the "queen-regent of France" wished to expose these miracles as well. So, she dispatched her personal physician to examine the claims, only to have him return as a Jansenist convert! An archbishop who "was an enemy to the Jansenists" would not get involved. However, none of those whose job it was to disprove these miraculous claims were able to uncover any "cheat" whatsoever (220, 226–29).

Concerning Hume's third criterion of miracles being reported "chiefly" from "among ignorant and barbarous nations," this likewise was not true in this case, as Hume admitted himself. In the Jansenist case, these events occurred not long before Hume's own day, "in a learned age, and on the most eminent theatre that is now in the world" (215, 220). This seems to cover his testimonial concerns regarding witnesses who did not understand science or the laws of nature. Once again, Hume recognized that the conditions stated in his own cautions did not pertain to these specific miracles in present-day France.

Hume's fourth criterion also fails to pose an adequate challenge here. Even if purported miracles in some religions were somehow capable of canceling, nullifying, or destroying those in other faiths (which is, once again, an exceptionally dubious assertion), the proper research procedure would be to first investigate instances of the relevant reports. If there were some examples better documented than others, perhaps like those in the French cases cited here, the stronger instances could hardly be abrogated just because "lesser" miracle claims were reported elsewhere, perhaps even hundreds of years after the events in question.

Thus, it would be far more reasonable to uphold those occurrences best evidenced by the historical facts. Quite curiously, Hume seemed to adopt a similar procedure himself. Just before his discussion of the Jansenist reports, he investigated what he considered to be a much "lesser" miracle claim, agreeing that it was a falsehood. Then, immediately afterward, Hume recognized that the Jansenist reports were far better attested. Yet he apparently had no immediate interest in attempting to rule out the Jansenist claims because of the lesser instance (219–20).

It was countered above that Hume's fourth challenge could have been more plausible if it were assumed that all miracle accounts were true, even equally so. This would make it more straightforward to locate some possible ideological conflicts. But since all such claims are plainly not factual, this situation produces a potential mix-and-match situation. How else can a solution be found apart from the research principle of investigating each case on its own merits? Certain well-attested events, should there be any, simply cannot be ruled out due to some other accounts that look very much like falsehoods. How else can the research be moved forward except by determining if any such occurrences obtained? Hume's fourth point is simply not applicable as a critique of miracle claims.

For reasons such as these, all four of Hume's additional criteria in part 2 of his essay do not succeed as valid critiques of any miracle claims, but especially not those in the Jansenist reports. None of these cautions have disproved the French testimonies. Actually, these four "prerequisites" for miracles have all been fulfilled in these cases, as Hume himself seems willing to admit. The following statement could be construed as Hume's acknowledgment of this concession. Speaking of the Jansenist claims, he summarizes, "What is more extraordinary; many of the miracles were immediately proved upon the spot, before judges of unquestioned integrity, attested by witnesses of credit and distinction, in a learned age, and on the most eminent theatre that is now in the world" (220).

So, Hume plainly allowed that there were actually a surplus of reputable witnesses of these Jansenist occurrences, including persons of sufficient integrity and unquestioned character (criterion one). That many of these witnesses were outright *enemies* of the Jansenist reports militates against their having lied to make the miracles appear plausible. Neither did they attempt to gossip and spread false reports, for it was their own desire to expose these facts. Many of those who checked out the data had a private interest in disproving these events. Even Hume admitted that the witnesses were reliable. All of this would seem to militate directly against charges like those of lying, forgery, overwrought imaginations, or the unscrupulous spreading of tales in order to entertain others (criterion two).

Additionally, these Jansenist reports were proclaimed to have occurred not in a distant land far away or decades after the events, but rather in an intellectual age in France, one of the clearly most educated and advanced countries of the world at that time (criterion three). The fourth criterion likewise cannot be employed here because we cannot rule out that well-attested events such as these may have been in an a priori manner, simply because the testimony favoring other similar wondrous events could perhaps have been documented very poorly. Judgment can only be made on the evidence at hand. Neither does Hume specifically assert that the fourth point applied to the Jansenist accounts.

It should be noted that the purpose here was definitely not to determine if any of the Jansenist miracles actually occurred or not. For our purposes, that is a totally moot point.[60] Rather, our goal was to determine how Hume reacted himself, when he even admitted that these miracle claims fulfilled his criteria. This conclusion would help further in determining the overall strength and internal consistency of his argument.

So, it appears to be quite clear that Hume thought the Jansenist miracles were well-attested cases. The human testimony favoring these occurrences was impressive, especially in view of the fact that the evidence apparently concerned supernatural claims. Thus it would be quite instructive to learn how Hume responded to the question of whether or not he considered that these were legitimate miraculous claims. But Hume could only conclude the following concerning these events: "Where shall we find such a number of circumstances, agreeing to the corroboration of one fact? *And what have we to oppose such a cloud of witnesses, but the absolute impossibility or miraculous nature of the events, which they relate? And this surely, in the eyes of all reasonable people, will alone be regarded as a sufficient refutation*" (220, emphasis added).

It appears that Hume's abrupt dismissal of the miraculous occurrences here was quite arbitrary. Even though he recognized and admitted that all of the available information added up to support a particular conclusion, it must all simply be dismissed because there are supernatural implications involved. Even if these were

---

[60] Tim and Lydia McGrew reported an admirable piece of sleuthing (in the section of their essay listed below that is aptly entitled "Knavery, Folly, and the Love of Wonder"), where they present the findings of several major researchers from Hume's own time who uncovered a large number of falsehoods in the Jansenist claims and literature. These charges included actual confessions regarding fabricated testimonies, the "healing" of people who were previously well, notarized documents that were later tampered with, and so on. But as McGrew and McGrew noted, it does not follow that all the claimed Jansenist healings were faked, just that the documented problems raised significant questions for a number of the accounts. Most incredibly, Hume was aware of these criticisms of the Jansenists published by those who critiqued his own work, though he never acknowledged the problems in successive editions of his essay "Of Miracles." These works included the writings of William Adams (1767), John Douglas (1757), and George Campbell (1762). The Tweyman-edited volume above includes a critique of Hume by Adams and an essay on Campbell's work. For further details, see Timothy McGrew and Lydia McGrew, "The Argument from Miracles: A Cumulative Case for the Resurrection of Jesus of Nazareth," in *The Blackwell Companion to Natural Theology*, ed. William Lane Craig and J. P. Moreland (Oxford: Wiley-Blackwell, 2009), 593–662.

among the most corroborated facts in all of human history, testimony, and experience, Hume apparently thought they must be rejected because miracles are impossible.

Especially if the traditional interpretation of Hume's essay is accepted, it may be difficult to discover a more blatant case from a well-established philosopher of what appears to be due to circular reasoning. When historical evidence on behalf of a miracle claim is believed to have been confirmed, why was the conclusion rejected anyway? Was it due to Hume's a priori conclusion that such events simply do not occur? This could have been the precise evidence Hume needed to be capable of demonstrating that miracles *do* in fact occur.

Other philosophers have agreed with these basic problems in Hume's essay and elsewhere, perhaps stemming from his treatment of the Jansenist accounts. Larmer asserted rather strongly, "Miracles seem ruled out by fiat. Either the event would have been a miracle, in which case it could not have occurred, or it occurred, in which case it could not be a miracle."[61] After citing the Jansenist example, Swinburne added: "Here the credibility of the witnesses in terms of their number, integrity, and education is dismissed, not as inadequate, but as irrelevant."[62]

One would just naturally assume that Hume was genuinely interested in exploring the possibility of miracles in an essay written on this topic. Rather, what emerges is the firmness of his belief that miracles never occur no matter what. No examination of the experience in their favor can ever establish that they probably do occur. Thus, it seems that Hume may have initially assumed from the outset that miracles could never occur, which was then followed by his subsequent disregard for any possible evidence on their behalf.[63]

---

[61] Larmer, *Legitimacy of Miracle*, 76n72.

[62] Swinburne, *Concept of Miracle*, 16.

[63] Of course, based on our comments above from the insightful essay by Tim and Lydia McGrew (see note 60), it could be postulated that Hume disregarded the Jansenist miracles without stating this because he had grown to distrust the details himself, perhaps based on the investigative reports that had been circulated in his time. If Hume knew of these doubts ahead of time, that may have removed some of the sting from his response. But this scenario still raises an additional conundrum. If Hume did in fact know that they were highly questionable events, why did he defend the Jansenist miracle claims in the first place? After all, he could have pointed out to his glee that these sorts of questions were exactly what is found when miracles are investigated! But without that knowledge, perhaps having to change his prior views and make the sort of appropriate changes in his beliefs that such evidence might require would be difficult indeed and may have led to the published response. This entire situation in his essay does in fact raise many questions.

Even if Hume did have reasons to distrust these Jansenist miracle reports, the charge that he apparently dismissed them arbitrarily even in the presence of this much evidence is disheartening. However, he made similar statements earlier in the essay unrelated to the Jansenist issue. After his apparently question-begging definition of miracles mentioned above, he again observed that "no testimony is sufficient to establish a miracle, unless the testimony be of such a kind, that its falsehood would be more miraculous, than the fact, which it endeavors to establish . . . always reject the greater miracle" (211–12). This is one of the strong points supporting the traditional interpretation of Hume's essay, which seems to assert that *no amount* of testimony is ever sufficient to establish an actual miracle. Even in cases where Hume's additional criteria were satisfied or inapplicable, he still held that miracles were impossible, or at least that they could never be established or believed. These statements have all the appearance of being unsupported assumptions. Miracles are rejected because they would be supernatural events, *regardless* of whatever amount of experience may support their historicity.

Even if Hume continued to rely on other conclusions (like miracle reports in other religions) to oppose miraculous events such as the Jansenist claims, that would seem to require some evidence from those *other* religious traditions. Further, he discredited the fact that the available evidence might be sufficient to establish Christian miracles even if no other miracles had over occurred. In fact, the latter cases might have been sufficient even to serve as the supreme examples of supernatural action, whatever the status of other such claims. After all, if an event has occurred, it is made no less real because there may exist other claims to similar occurrences.

One other matter should be added here as well. Hume's four additional criteria are objectionable in the first place quite apart from the miracles question. How much of our currently recognized knowledge of history could stand the same amount of scrutiny? That is, were the discipline of history to be viewed through the lens of Hume's glasses, how would it fare? For example, how much of our accepted world history is composed of events that were not attested by a goodly number of unquestionably intelligent and educated persons who were so trustworthy that the data they shared should be regarded as sufficient to rule out *all kinds* of honest mistakes, delusion, or even exaggeration? Some significant amounts of history may not conform to this rule.

Or again, how much history is prejudiced by the reporter standing to gain much by the acceptance of these events, such as Julius Caesar narrating his victories over the barbarians in Gaul? Surely many other events took place among "ignorant," "barbarous," and other backward nations (215)? Since Hume included at least portions of the Greek and Roman civilizations in this category, because they are some of the examples that he used in this section (212–15), should the historical accounts be doubted (or worse) during these periods? What about ancient Nineveh and Babylon, about which ancient historians seem not to have these sorts of issues?

One begins to note several potential problems involved in such an application of these four criteria to history. Yet, history is treated as a reputable and reliable tradition. As Richard Whately once so aptly wrote, the same methods that Hume employed to dismiss the miracles from the life of Jesus could also be employed to remove the unique elements from the life of Napoleon. As such, much of the past would be lost. Such reconstructing of history is correctly viewed as being highly problematic.[64]

But few scholars of his time should have known about historiography better than Hume himself. Later in his career he turned to the study of history, writing his successful multivolume work, *The History of England.*[65] Hume knew better than to attempt to apply his four subpoints to the composing of these volumes. Who could write history if they first had to ascertain that every witness must be "of such unquestioned good-sense, education, and learning, as to secure us against all delusion in themselves" (212)? True, Hume was discussing the issue of testimony on behalf of miracles, where there may be more deception than with normal historical events. But there is still enough prejudice in historical matters, where the historian would have to be quite careful, such as the cause of wars and strife or political causes. Also, as mentioned, Hume's point about ignorant and uncivilized peoples could have an even more tremendous effect on his writing of history. But there is no ruling out or total distrust of ancient events in his works, hence the issue of inconsistency appears again in Hume, whose skepticism did not show in his historical recording.

For reasons like these, this third major criticism of Hume's essay also appears to have hit its mark. Hume failed to do justice to potentially miraculous occurrences, even if they had attained credibility due to the weight of the experiential testimony in their favor. Therefore, it appears that we might be compelled to consider granting probable status to certain miracle claims if they best account for the available evidence.

---

[64] Richard Whately, *Historic Doubts Relative to Napoleon Bonaparte* (London: Hatchard, Piccadilly, 1819), 69–70. The 1819 edition was originally published anonymously, but later editions ascribe the work to Whately.

[65] David Hume, *The History of England*, 6 vols. (London: Gilbert and Revington, 1848).

88   REFUTATIONS

The fourth major criticism of Hume's essay is brief but hard hitting and aimed
at the sort of experience that might be encountered either for or against miracles.
Philosopher George Mavrodes argues concerning the nature of the inductive method
that "Hume's sample is just too small. . . . And so is your sample and mine." Granted,
a miracle may occur only rarely, so if one did, then the likelihood that Hume and his
friends would have experienced it is still small. The chief issue here is that Hume's
sample size is simply far from large enough to be statistically significant. Here is
Mavrodes's conclusion: "So Hume's own negative experience is irrelevant."[66]

One way to correct this need for further research would be to expand the search
for additional testimony both for and against miracle claims. However, among
other issues, Mavrodes charges that from Hume's perspective there is a very serious
problem with such a move. Once the inquiry is extended to a statistically significant
experiential group, reports of miracle claims will definitely result, even as seen in
recent surveys. These claims, of course, cannot be ignored simply because they do not
fit Hume's prior purposes or even if he thinks the accounts are simply false. But at any
rate, neither the results of Hume's argument that "uniform experience" is opposed to
all miracles nor what will occur when the testimony sample size grows to sufficient
numbers will confirm Hume's argument against miracles. Such conclusions will now
inevitably draw the discussion into the nitty-gritty of the evidence itself, and the
historical data favoring Jesus's resurrection will need to be viewed head-on.

So, there is a choice to be made in this matter. Mavrodes maintains that we must
choose between either utilizing a very small sampling of testimonies, which is much
too miniscule for any significant purposes, or expanding our sample size and thereby
encountering miracle claims. Where does this leave us, then? Mavrodes concludes:
"In any case, however, the project . . . provides no basis for assigning a low antecedent
probability to singular miracle claims, such as that of Jesus's resurrection."[67]

If Mavrodes is correct, Hume has violated the principles of inductive research
and sampling. The result is that Hume is not even close to establishing the nature of

[66] George I. Mavrodes, "David Hume and the Probability of Miracles," *International Journal for Philosophy of Religion* 43 (1998): 176–77. For some other pertinent thoughts on these issues by philosophers who generally oppose Hume's reasoning in these matters, compare Benjamin F. Armstrong Jr., "Hume on Miracles: Begging-the-Question against Believers," *History of Philosophy Quarterly* 9 (1992): 319, 327; John Earman, "Bayes, Hume, and Miracles," *Faith and Philosophy* 10 (1993): esp. 293, 305–6; Roy A. Sorensen, "Hume's Scepticism concerning Reports of Miracles," *Analysis* 43 (1983): 60.

[67] Mavrodes, "Probability of Miracles," 179–81.

his "uniform experience" claim in this matter. Of course, asking a few of his friends concerning their views on the subject does not do the job adequately. But to obtain an acceptably large sample size, miraculous testimonies will result.

The initial four critiques presented thus far with regard to Hume's essay "Of Miracles" have been on more substantial areas that, if they obtain, would arguably apply to crucial enough concepts that they would seriously disrupt if not disprove Hume's entire efforts even by themselves. The remaining three critiques below concern more or less subsidiary portions of his essay that may not be as well known. As such, even though these last contributions make both true and worthwhile points, the results will chiefly add to the overall force that should invalidate Hume's efforts altogether.

Fifth, Hume's repeated notion was that a miracle, by definition, necessarily involved the principle that these occurrences needed to violate, transgress, or otherwise break the laws of nature (210–11, 221, 223). Many scholars have objected to this notion for a number of reasons. Larmer makes the intriguing assertion that this is hardly a necessary feature of miraculous events. Rather, Larmer holds that God "thereby produces an event that nature would not have produced on its own but breaks no laws of nature."[68] As Larmer adds later: "Miracles, as events at least partially caused by the direct intervention of a supernatural agent in no way imply that the laws of nature are violated, since they describe not the operation of natural causes, but the operation of a supernatural cause."[69]

Lewis argues similarly here. He states: "It is therefore inaccurate to define a miracle as something that breaks the laws of Nature. It doesn't."[70] So a miracle is caused by God, but once it occurs, "its results follow according to Natural Law." After God inserts the event into the environment, "it is interlocked with all of Nature just like any other event." So it is intertwined with nature in its forward position, but with God in its past.[71] However, as Lewis helpfully states elsewhere, "*in the whole history of the universe the laws of Nature have never produced a single event. . . . The laws are the pattern to which events conform: the source of events must be sought elsewhere.*"[72]

---

[68] Larmer, *Legitimacy of Miracle*, 39.

[69] Larmer, 40.

[70] Lewis, *Miracles*, 59, cf. also 5, 46.

[71] Lewis, 59–60.

[72] C. S. Lewis, "The Laws of Nature," in *God in the Dock: Essays on Theology and Ethics*, ed. Walter Hooper (Grand Rapids: Eerdmans, 1970), 77–78.

By way of illustration, Larmer points out that a woman who is a virgin may have a fertilized egg implanted in her via a modern medical procedure. Even though she remains a virgin, she may still give birth to a healthy baby. Of course, no laws of nature have been broken in this instance. But is this case a miracle? Now consider, though by quite different means, that God could arguably create *ex nihilo* the conditions under which another virgin would also bear a child, but do so likewise in a manner that does not break the laws of nature. This case would involve a miracle due to God's interaction into the events.[73]

To sustain the argument that miracles do not break the laws of nature would be a very helpful step forward in this dialogue, providing more options for the theist. Larmer calls it "an even more fundamental objection than the ones we have mentioned." The consequence is that it "reveals that not only is Hume's argument of Part I deeply flawed, it is irrelevant to the issue." If miracles do not break nature's laws, then the result is that the "argument in Part I . . . cannot get started."[74]

The sixth critique of Hume's essay revolves around another matter of internal consistency. Hume is famous in the history of philosophy for his rejection of an assumed uniformity in nature. Yet in spite of his well-known positions on these matters, Hume still insisted on rejecting miracles because of the uniform human experience that presumed that the course of nature would continue exactly as it was currently perceived, not to mention the assumption that it had always continued in this manner at least back to biblical times. However, according to Hume, the truth is that we know only a rather trivial portion of nature and cannot even be sure that what we do know will continue to be the same in the future or that it has continued this way throughout the past.

Making this inconsistency all the more noticeable is that Hume himself recognized that we cannot accept cause and effect as a reliable concept, at least not in the sense of being demonstrably true.[75] This is especially evident in Hume's small follow-up volume, *An Abstract of a Treatise of Human Nature*, where he attempts to

---

[73] For a variety of other helpful considerations on the relationship between miracles and the laws of nature, see Larmer, *Legitimacy of Miracle*, 37–46, in particular. These illustrations above are found on 40 and 39 respectively and are similar to Lewis's examples from *Miracles*, 59–60.

[74] Larmer, *Legitimacy of Miracle*, 72.

[75] For David Hume's rejection of cause and effect, see the treatment in his work, *A Treatise of Human Nature*, ed. L. A. Selby-Bigge (Oxford: Clarendon, 1964), 73–78, esp. 76.

explain carefully why these notions cannot reasonably be accepted as being verified.[76] Though humans customarily expect an effect to follow what they take to be the cause, there are no reasonable, logical, or necessary grounds for this custom.[77]

But if Hume was truly convinced that there were no compelling reasons to accept the interaction of cause and effect, how did he know that uniform experience confirmed the laws of nature? Or what about the knowledge that the laws of nature were themselves uniform? How is it to be known that these laws were capable of providing insurance against the miraculous? Hume could not be so adamant that nature's laws in biblical times, for instance, ruled out miracles the same way he thought they did in the present. After all, the knowledge of this uniformity, which is so necessary for such assertions, cannot be determined.

In other words, Hume could not know that human experience of nature's laws ruled out miracles because he could not know from his vantage point and way of thinking that nature was truly uniform. This leaves out the additional problem that, all this time, he was inconsistent with his own statements and theses to the contrary. Strange indeed, but this never kept Hume the historian from pontificating historically on the lives and teachings of Alexander, Lucian, Vespasian, Livy, Tacitus, Plutarch, and Marcus Aurelius, among a host of other persons and events. What about all the information on the Jansenists that he recounted in "Of Miracles"?

This argument against Hume's consistency challenges his thesis against miracles, unless he wishes to retract his skeptical concepts regarding cause and effect, past human experience in particular, and nature's uniformity in the present. But if he will not relent on these matters, how could he have gained such dogmatic knowledge regarding the laws of nature? This purported interaction between uniform experience

---

[76] David Hume, *An Abstract of a Treatise of Human Nature*, ed. J. M. Keyes and P. Spaffa (Cambridge: Cambridge University Press, 1938). This brief volume was published anonymously and has often in the past been attributed to Hume's friend Adam Smith. However, editors Keyes and Spaffa in their 1938 introduction to this text presented convincing reasons for regarding the author as Hume himself. Since their argument, this has been the most widely held conclusion. On this discussion, see Mark G. Spencer, "Another 'Curious Legend' about Hume's *An Abstract of a Treatise of Human Nature*," *Hume Studies* 29 (2003): 89–99, particularly 89–90. In spite of Hume's contemporaries not being terribly impressed with his lack of assurance concerning cause and effect, Hume's challenge was taken up by Kant and others; see J. Bronowski and Bruce Mazlish, *The Western Intellectual Tradition from Leonardo to Hegel* (New York: Harper & Row, 1960), 474–75, primarily note 3.

[77] Hume, *Treatise of Human Nature*, 16.

and the reliability of nature's laws forms the very center of his polemic against miracles, as has been noted many times already.

That Hume felt free, given his earlier philosophical arguments, to use the same principles that he had rejected and chided others for using in order to rule out the occurrence of miracles is simply amazing. Hume argued that even if one could garner good evidence for a miracle, it would then be confronted by the greater "proof" drawn from this uniform conception of nature, meaning that the evidence for a miracle claim could never gain the upper ground here, due to the "superior" evidence with which it is confronted (211–12). Yet, given Hume's own critique, the imagined wall that supposedly confronts all miracle claims and stops them dead in their tracks seems like nothing but a Humean inconsistency.

Therefore, for Hume himself and anyone else who may hold his view of cause and effect, there is no wall of opposition to miracles based on a uniform, causal notion of nature's laws as backed by human experience. Thus, Hume's own objections to miracles at this point are themselves inconsistent as well as quite defective.

C. S. Lewis pointed out a similar problem with Hume's argument against miracles:

> The whole idea of Probability (as Hume understands it) depends on the principle of the Uniformity of Nature. . . . We observe many regularities in Nature. But of course all the observations that men have made or will make while the race lasts cover only a minute fraction of the events that actually go on. Our observations would therefore be of no use unless we felt sure that Nature when we are not watching her behaves in the same way as when we are: in other words, unless we believed in the Uniformity of Nature. Experience therefore cannot prove uniformity, because uniformity has to be assumed before experience proves anything. . . . The odd thing is that no man knew this better than Hume. His *Essay on Miracles* is quite inconsistent with the more radical, and honourable, scepticism of his main work.[78]

Lewis clearly recognized some of the same things that were just mentioned. Hume's entire argument depends on the uniformity of nature; yet, Hume elsewhere in his writings accepted similar arguments *against* the causality of nature.

Yet another problem here is that nature is observed and incorporated into human experience. But the whole of human experience accounts for only a small part of

---

[78] Lewis, *Miracles*, 102–3.

nature. To assert that nature acts completely uniformly with *no* interruptions from the outside (as Hume asserts) would be to know all of nature. This is once again a circular argument because, as Lewis points out well, one must assume uniformity in all of nature in order to say that we experience the same when the whole is unknown. It must be believed that the portion of nature that cannot be observed directly works precisely the same way as what is observed. In other words, one must already have assumed that nature is completely uniform and acting in a causal way even if the evidence indicates otherwise.

Lewis was not the only scholar to have recognized these same problems in Hume. Larmer agrees as well, naming both C. D. Broad and A. E. Taylor as raising similar criticisms, while Fred Wilson defended Hume's consistency.[79] For his part, Larmer concluded the matter: "It appears, therefore, that Hume should have either repudiated his explicitly stated position concerning induction and causality or else admitted that his conception of what is meant by a law of nature prohibited him from pressing his objection to belief in miracles."[80]

A seventh critique of Hume must be mentioned ever so briefly here and expanded later. Actually, as was remarked earlier in this chapter, there are perhaps even hundreds of well-evidenced cases of claimed supernatural events that have been reported in the modern world during the last few decades alone. In a number of these accounts, MRIs, X-rays, and CT and PET scans along with other means of measurable corroboration have been provided for comparison. It is a strange role reversal of Hume's third subpoint concerning "ignorant and barbarous nations" that in the advanced, scientific world of today is where these sorts of empirical confirmation are in fact available!

The sophisticated medical procedures and tests just mentioned are sometimes able either to verify or falsify many of these incredible medical claims. What happens to Hume's thesis if such confirmation in the modern world is a reality, actually

---

[79] For Larmer's view, see *Legitimacy of Miracle*, 61–66. Cf. also C. D. Broad, "Hume's Theory of the Credibility of Miracles," *Proceedings of the Aristotelian Society* 17 (1916–1917): 77–94; A. E. Taylor, "David Hume and the Miraculous," *Philosophical Studies*, ed. A. E. Taylor (London: Macmillan, 1934), 330–65. For Fred Wilson's defense of Hume, see Wilson, *Hume's Defense of Causal Inference* (Toronto: University of Toronto Press, 1997); Wilson, "The Logic of Probabilities in Hume's Argument against Miracles," *Hume Studies* 15 (1989): 255–75. Larmer's response to Wilson is found on 62–65 of *Legitimacy of Miracle*.

[80] Larmer, *Legitimacy of Miracle*, 65.

many times over, and is unexplainable in medical terms? Is the situation enhanced if the eyewitness circumstances occurred during the presence of religious practices such as prayer, worship, or Scripture reading? Simply reiterating the old mantra of the strength of nature's laws as backed by human experience may grow stagnant when faced with a long list of documented cases often confirmed by very different types of evidence.[81] In fact, regarding Craig Keener's two volumes of healing testimonies, Richard Bauckham appropriately quipped in terms of our present chapter: "So who's afraid of David Hume now?"[82]

These conclusions therefore stand in light of this knowledge. Hume's foundation for rejecting miracles is flawed in many places. One cannot reject a potential miraculous claim if it best fits the evidence simply because of an assumed uniformity in nature, especially if such uniformity has not been shown to exist first. Cause and effect of some variety seemingly would have to be in operation before Hume's arguments could even begin to be asserted, even though Hume appeared to think that this view of nature was mistaken. Thus, nothing is left but to abandon the very basis of his reasoning.

As before, the question once again concerns which data best fit the available evidence, indicating once again the need for an investigation of the facts. If a miracle claim in past history is found to offer the best explanation of the evidence, it can no longer be opposed in an a priori manner just because of the belief that these sorts of occurrences simply do not happen or because nature opposes such an event. On the other hand, neither can decisions be made in favor of a miracle without solid

---

[81] Perhaps the best resource currently available is the two-volume work by Craig S. Keener, *Miracles: The Credibility of the New Testament Accounts* (Grand Rapids: Baker Academic, 2011), including almost 1,500 total pages of testimony. Other resources include two by medical doctors: H. Richard Casdorph, *Real Miracles: Indisputable Evidence That God Heals* (Gainesville, FL: Bridge-Logos, 2003); Rex Gardner, *Healing Miracles: A Doctor Investigates* (London: Darton, Longman & Todd, 1986). Larmer investigated and included a few examples of his own in *Legitimacy of Miracle*, 197–206. Another simply remarkable volume both in terms of actually testing miracle claims and with the publisher involved is Candy Gunther Brown, *Testing Prayer: Science and Healing* (Cambridge: Harvard University Press, 2012).

[82] Bauckham's comment is found on the back of Keener's second volume. Ben Witherington also remarks in the same location that Keener "shows that whatever the merits of Hume's claim in his own day, it can hardly be maintained today. . . . We have here perhaps the best book ever written on miracles in this or any age. Highly recommended."

reasons for doing so. The bottom line is to at least be open to the occurrence of well-evidenced events.

A Brief Summary and Conclusion

Additional criticisms have also been leveled at Hume's essay "Of Miracles."[83] Many objections have been lodged against this work, and it has certainly been rejected for a variety of reasons. The trend in more recent philosophical studies appears to be

---

[83] A more positive aspect of Hume's philosophy is his heavy reliance on probabilistic reasoning in inductive matters, which is one of the chief convictions of modern thought but was not as common an emphasis in Hume's day. Hume's emphasis on probabilities can be seen in his volume *Essays, Literary, Moral, and Political* (London: Ward, Lock, and Bowden, n.d.), 341–43, as well as in "Of Miracles," 206–7, 213. In this sense, at least, Hume may even be seen as a forerunner to some more modern theses that also postulate the importance of probabilities in inductive matters. However, it was just mentioned above that Hume rejected the popular notions regarding cause and effect. In an age when it was popular to accept a more Newtonian view of the universe, including more mechanistic aspects, Hume insisted otherwise.

Another problem arises when trying to reconcile Hume's belief in a more open universe with his rejection of miracles. Hume does not allow the evidence to speak for itself, since any potential inductive evidence for miracles should not be ruled out a priori, especially while favoring problematic views of nature and its laws, as might be expected when one holds the above positions. Instead, Hume transgresses his own position in order to rule out miracles. He neither allows nor engages in the serious investigation of data that seem to indicate positive experience in favor of miraculous occurrences. Even in the cases when he appears to think that the evidence may be impressive (as with the Jansenist events), he tends to deviate from his own views elsewhere by retreating to positions that he had already dismissed.

So, the problem here continues to involve Hume's movement toward a more modern view of the universe in several senses, while remaining rather premodern and even inconsistent in his treatment of miracles. Hence, his treatment of miracle claims is one of the avenues that shows more signs of his premodern critical consciousness by resorting to what may be termed as more of a closed view of cause and effect with nature's workings. Thus there may be a reliance on probabilities, only to veer backwards in some of these less helpful areas. These internal inconsistencies as well as reverting to a more premodern consciousness are other areas to note. The chief question is not whether or not nature's laws exist, for of course they do. But what are these laws, and can they be temporarily suspended? Then again, as some like Lewis and Larmer have also suggested, perhaps some miracles do not transgress the laws of nature at all.

against Hume's effort as a means of ruling out miracles.[84] But these criticisms will have to suffice for now in our current treatment. If the critiques here are anywhere close to accurate, it certainly appears that Hume's effort is vulnerable in many places.

It appears that all seven of these major criticisms of Hume hit their mark in various respects, some in more crucial places than others. A brief summary may be helpful in closing. First, the dominant interpretations of his essay maintain that Hume is guilty of committing a series of informal logical errors, chiefly concerning his several circular and question-begging assertions regarding especially his definition of miracles and his unsupported assumptions concerning the negligible value of any experience of miracles, as well as the "uniform experience" against them.[85] He also fails by refusing to investigate any of these events when this very investigation could reveal an exception to his case.

Second, Hume never pauses to ascertain whether a superior supernatural force (as per his own definition involving God's action) could just temporarily have overridden, superseded, or otherwise bypassed nature's laws (without breaking them) in order to cause such an event in space and time. Further, an occurrence of this sort would have been due to just such superior power because it would indicate that, *at that very moment*, an exception to these laws may have occurred. Pinpointing the data,

---

[84] For some thoughtful examples, see Rodney D. Holder, "Hume on Miracles: Bayesian Interpretation, Multiple Testimony, and the Existence of God," *British Journal for the Philosophy of Science* 49 (1998): esp. 60–62; George N. Schlesinger, "Miracles and Probabilities," *Nous* 21 (1987): esp. 219, 230–32; Schlesinger, "The Credibility of Extraordinary Events," *Analysis* 51 (1991): 125; Armstrong, "Hume on Miracles," 319, 327; John Earman, *Hume's Abject Failure: The Argument against Miracles* (Oxford: Oxford University Press, 2000), especially the entire host of critiques found in part 1; Earman, "Bayes, Hume, and Miracles," esp. 293, 305–6; Sorensen, "Hume's Scepticism," 60; Stanley L. Jaki, *Physics and Miracles* (Front Royal, VA: Christendom, 1989), esp. 19–25, 32–33, 78–79, 92–93; Mavrodes, "Probability of Miracles," 176–77; Larmer, *Legitimacy of Miracle*, particularly chaps. 3–4. For rejoinders on behalf of Hume's basic ideas, see Antony Flew, *Hume's Philosophy of Belief*, esp. Flew's chapter, "Miracles and Methodology"; Fogelin, *Defense of Hume on Miracles*; and also Fogelin, "What Hume Actually Said," 81–87; Wilson, *Hume's Defense of Causal Inference*; Richard Otte, "Schlesinger and Miracles," *Faith and Philosophy* 10 (1993): esp. 93, 97.

[85] The full title of Armstrong's previously cited article states it well: "Hume on Miracles: Begging-the-Question against Believers." Even some scholars who did not take this strong of a position still thought that Hume had argued incorrectly, overemphasized the strength of his case, and made overly easy criticisms against miracles. An example was theologian William Hordern, *A Layman's Guide to Protestant Theology* (New York: Macmillan, 1956), 37.

time, and place may even produce the evidence of the superior force. If the evidence indicated that such an event *did* occur, then of course the question regarding whether it *could* occur has apparently been answered! But without an investigation, how would this ever be known? Hence it must be emphasized that even the *possibility* of such an event should provoke an examination in order to know whether or not an exception most likely happened.[86] If Hume believed in God's existence, this could simply make the critique more forceful.[87]

Third, Hume's four subpoints raised some thoughtful considerations and worthwhile cautions, yet they are insufficient in themselves to rule out miraculous events. These cautions serve more like warnings and pitfalls to be avoided. Moreover, even when Hume admitted that the miracle claims such as those of the eighteenth-century Jansenists were very well attested by human experience, Hume still rejected them for what appeared to be rather arbitrary reasons even after he admitted the high credibility of their attestation due simply to the impossibility of miraculous events. This should serve as an indication that while the four subpoints provide some restraint, even Hume did not consider them to be rock-solid edifices, for he seemed to base his rejection not on the possible cautions that could be made but on his prior circular argument in part 1 of his essay.

---

[86] Once again, it needs to be emphasized clearly that there is no sense in which "proving" God's existence or some such endeavor comes into play here. The chief point here is to raise the prior question that, if it is even *possible* that God or a supernatural reality existed, Hume would have to be open to such events transcending nature. But he has not really left this door open.

[87] As to the question of whether Hume was an atheist or some species of theist, there are different views. Earman suggests that Hume may have been a theist, "albeit of a vague and weak-kneed sort. He seems to have been convinced by the argument from design." If so, "Hume's inconsequential theism was combined with an abhorrence of organized religion." See Earman, *Hume's Abject Failure*, 4–5. Two other scholars who agree that Hume was a theist of some stripe are Jordan Howard Sobel, *Logic and Theism: Arguments for and against Beliefs in God* (Cambridge: Cambridge University Press, 2009), see sec. 7.5; and William Lad Sessions, *Hume's Dialogues: A Veneration for True Religion* (Bloomington: Indiana University Press, 2002). Gay takes what might be thought of as a more conventional view and identifies Hume with the skeptic Philo of his *Dialogues on Natural Religion*; see Gay, *Enlightenment*, 414–15. However, Gay also recounted the story told in a letter written by French philosopher Denis Diderot, who was present when Hume once asserted before a number of French scholars that he doubted that there were any real atheists in the world (400–401)! These comments by Earman and Gay are not necessarily exclusive.

Fourth, the portion of Hume's essay "Of Miracles" that dealt with human testimony and his claim that "uniform experience" opposed all miracle claims (211) was clearly falsified on inductive grounds. His human sample size was far too small to draw conclusions regarding all human experience, as he did.

But the problem here was that if Hume expanded his sample size to anything even approximately large enough to make such assertions, then he would definitely have encountered many miracle claims as well.[88] So his dilemma was this: keep his own sample size small and be able to draw virtually no conclusions of the sort that he drew, or increase his sample size and then be prepared to treat the influx of miracle claims. But what he surely could not do was keep his current strategy and still pontificate on what "uniform experience" is available.[89]

Fifth, some theists like Lewis and Larmer have argued that miracles would not necessarily have to break the laws of nature. This argument will not be repeated here, except to say that if such an argument follows, as Larmer states often, Hume's argument could never even get started.[90]

Sixth, Hume revealed further specific inconsistencies in that some of his most important reasons for rejecting miracles revolved around the principle that nature was uniform, as well as his rejection of the human ability to demonstrate with certainty the nature of cause and effect. Elsewhere Hume had also rejected that these ideas could be known. But if he was correct in abandoning the knowledge of nature's uniformity as well as cause and effect, then he may have forfeited some of the themes in his polemic against miracles. If so, the apex of his polemic against miracles might also fall.

Seventh, there is a growing case to be made today that hundreds of seeming miracle claims have been documented in medical literature and elsewhere. A number

---

[88] As pointed out in the collections of hundreds if not more than a thousand such claims above.

[89] Another related issue here is whether Hume's essay, especially in part 1, was meant to be an a priori or an a posteriori claim. If the former, was it intended to be an a priori *objection*, or an a priori *rejection*? (There is more than one view on this subject, and the issue will not be solved here, but these options are discussed in depth in the next chapter.) But if Hume was making an a priori claim, then this still brings up the question of how such a prior rejection of experience would fare against real evidence, a subject on which many theists have challenged him for over two centuries. If Hume is making an a posteriori claim, then he would be charged with producing alternative scenarios that would better explain the data on behalf of these miracle claims.

[90] Larmer, *Legitimacy of Miracle*, 4, 39–41, 46, 72.

of these examples are accompanied by intriguing and extensive pre- and post-healing medical documentation from MRIs, CT and PET scans, and X-rays. We cannot develop this critique any further here.[91] But suffice it to say that if any of these cases obtain, as well as the ensuing conclusions about supernatural involvement, especially in any significant numbers and variety, then Hume's thesis would appear to be in quite serious trouble from this critique alone.

These are not all the critiques that have been leveled against Hume's attack on the credibility of miraculous testimony. But this effort has attempted to highlight some of the more crucial ones which, if they were warranted, would probably disprove Hume's treatment of miracle claims. It was also argued above that several of these errors and improper conclusions in Hume's work were published and challenged almost immediately after the publication of his essay in 1748. Alexander Campbell even reported hearing from an eyewitness who told him that some of Hume's friends were teasing him about losing the miracles argument to George Campbell in the latter's essay entitled "Essay upon Miracles," to which Hume responded to those present that "the Scotch theologue had beaten him."[92]

However, it has been mentioned by scholars that the growing view in the Enlightenment was often to reject miracles, and under such conditions Hume's essay provided the needed authority for such a venture, even if a number of serious problems were present. On this view, Hume's essay fit the already-established critical conviction of the time.[93]

But Hume's polemic against miracles, while appearing to many to be a strong argument at the outset, failed when it was investigated more closely. Hume's essay simply had too many serious issues to serve as the model refutation of miracles, even

---

[91] This topic was discussed in more detail in volume 1 of this study, especially in concert with the well-established idea in recent historical Jesus studies that Jesus also produced healings.

[92] This incident is reported in Alexander Campbell, *Debate on the Evidences of Christianity, Containing an Examination of the Social System and All the Systems of Scepticism of Ancient and Modern Times, between Robert Owen and Alexander Campbell* (London: Groombridge, 1839), 246. (My thanks to Tim McGrew, who first alerted me to these developments along with sending me Campbell's volume.) Not to be confusing here, note that Alexander Campbell coauthored this debate with Robert Owen and that Campbell was speaking about George Campbell, who wrote the "Essay upon Miracles," which was credited with having beaten David Hume on this subject.

[93] Cf. Earman, *Hume's Abject Failure*, 71; Hordern, *Layman's Guide to Protestant Theology*, 37.

though it often has that reputation. Today the prevailing view seems to be that Hume was unsuccessful overall in his efforts in this essay and cannot therefore be cited in order to rule out miracle claims. As Larmer concludes regarding Hume's case: "His argument is deeply flawed, being vulnerable to charges that it reduces to absurdity by proving too much and begs the question of whether miracles actually occur by defining them out of existence."[94]

A more proper approach would have been to define miracles without any inherent statement as to the a priori possibility of their occurring, or without attempting to pile up the imagined case against them. Then it would have been possible to investigate the available claims in order to determine the strength of the argument.

So once again, the challenge is to investigate the evidence, wherever it leads, in order to better ascertain what may have occurred. Such an investigation of the data that makes such miracle claims is therefore among the chief needs, as has been concluded repeatedly in this chapter. In the specific case of Jesus's resurrection, evidential claims have been made since the beginning of church history, claiming testimony for the appearances of the risen Lord. These are among the major accounts that must be examined to ascertain if this event is the best explanation for the facts.

---

[94] Larmer, *Legitimacy of Miracle*, 71.

3

Hume 2: Reformulations of Hume

As discussed in the previous chapter, there has been widespread disagreement among scholars regarding how best to interpret the heart of David Hume's argument in his famous essay "Of Miracles" ever since it first appeared in 1748. This has especially been the case in recent times. Before then, especially in the initial decades after its publication, friend and foe alike usually took a fairly similar position, what might be identified as the "traditional" position on the matter. Interestingly enough, throughout much interaction, including with Hume himself, he did not dispute this interpretation, even speaking positively of other scholars. Strictly speaking, this atmosphere perhaps did not arise to much more than an argument from silence, though the amicable comments of many may hint at a shared understanding here. The more or less traditional interpretation has been the one taken here. Since then, however, other interpretations have arisen.

Regardless of how Hume's essay was interpreted in the past, this has not impeded a host of recent authors from developing their own arguments against miracles. Most frequently following in a Humean brand of the analytic philosophical tradition, these writers have developed a host of sometimes rather creative objections to the occurrence of these supernatural events.

However, it should not be assumed that every argument that juxtaposed miracles with the laws of nature was due only to Hume's influence. Even before Hume's essay, others, such as Benedict Spinoza and the English deists, made similar moves, from which it even appears in retrospect that Hume himself may have borrowed.[1] After Hume, many scholars made comments to the effect that ignorance of nature's laws accounted for much of the widespread belief in these miraculous events. To that extent, at least, Hume was not the first thinker to state some of these arguments, though he may be the best known among them.

It is not always clear what causes one particular work to be singled out for fame (or infamy) above other similar efforts. However, in Hume's case, several factors probably converged, including aspects such as these: his amalgamation of major and minor arguments in a single place, his more forceful debate style compared to those of some other contemporaries, along with fitting his critique to Enlightenment times. But Hume's reputation as perhaps the best known of the skeptical philosophers of his time certainly was another consideration in the acclaim that he received. This combination of factors probably accounted for the praise that Hume's essay received above the others, making this essay far and away the best known and most referenced work on this subject by supporters and opponents alike. That this is even the case more than 250 years later is simply astounding.

Having viewed Hume's essay in some detail in the previous chapter, the chief approach here will be to respond to many different objections to miracles categorically, grouping together similar complaints and working from more general to more specific replies. Within each classification, several different objections and nuances will be developed, many seemingly inspired by Hume's previous efforts. As mentioned,

---

[1] Benedict Spinoza, *The Chief Works of Benedict De Spinoza*, trans. R. H. M. Elwes, 2 vols. (New York: Dover, 1951), 1:87; also, Richard H. Popkin, "Some New Light on the Roots of Spinoza's Science of Bible Study," in *Spinoza and the Sciences*, ed. Marjorie Grene and Debra Nails (Dordrecht: Reidel, 1986), 171–88. For an example of the English deists, see Thomas Woolston, "A Defence of the Discourses on Miracles," in *Deism: An Anthology*, ed. Peter Gay (Princeton, NJ: Van Nostrand, 1968), 122–39. Woolston's "Six Discourses on the Miracles of our Saviour" were published between 1727 and 1729, about twenty years before Hume's essay. Gay notes elsewhere that the deists were known for two primary themes: the wickedness of priests and the claim that God would not break his own universal laws. See Peter Gay, *The Enlightenment: An Interpretation, The Rise of Modern Paganism* (New York: Knopf, 1966), 383–84. John Herman Randall Jr. likewise agreed, noting that the deist's central contention was that God would not violate nature's laws as they had been revealed so magnificently via the Newtonian discoveries. See Randall, *The Making of the Modern Mind: A Survey of the Intellectual Background of the Present Age*, rev. ed. (Boston: Houghton Mifflin, 1940), 291–93. As with Woolston's discourses, almost all of these additional deist efforts also predated Hume's essay.

most of these objections to miracles tend to be a priori in nature, though a few are a posteriori. Accordingly, most of the responses will also tend to be a priori, where the actual evidence or other specifics will seldom if ever be spelled out in this chapter, just as specifications of the criticisms were similarly not explicated. Rather, a general, a priori objection will most often engender a similar general, a priori response, including more than one potential comeback each in the process.

One last note of caution may be helpful here. Many readers may have been taught that a priori objections are illegitimate, so why are we presenting them here as serious queries? Actually, a priori *rejections* (before the facts) are often very poor responses. But a priori *objections* or questions that do not reject but only seek further clarification can actually be helpful, leading to progress in the exchange of ideas.

A Brief Word about New Atheist Approaches to Miracles

Some authors raise issues regarding the entire classification of miracles. Many of these objections tend to be quite general, though some do move on to more specific charges. This order of the categories is listed below. Many skeptical objections to miracles revolve around questions pertaining to the availability of sufficient evidence in order to establish the occurrence of these events. Frequent opposing claims in recent years, especially from among the so-called New Atheist authors, portray Christianity (and other religions too) rather naively as basically resting upon faith alone, bereft of any reason or evidence whatsoever, whereas atheism is viewed as almost a purely rational and scientific endeavor. These comments often seem to be made in a pejorative sense, almost as if it is hoped that repetitive comments to this effect will justify these claims and make them true, shaming believers in the process so that there may be no responses at all.[2]

---

[2] These exceptionally prominent themes are widely displayed, most prominently in New Atheist authors such as Sam Harris, *The End of Faith: Religion, Terror, and the Future of Reason* (New York: Norton, 2004), beginning with chapter 1, "Reason in Exile," regarding the unreasonable nature of religion. Harris's follow-up volume, *Letter to a Christian Nation* (New York: Knopf, 2006), emphasized throughout what he took to be Christianity's lack of evidence (6, 25, 33, 43, 49, 51–52, 64–65, 67, 87–91) as contrasted with atheism's exalted and superior positions (45–46, 51). Likewise, Christopher Hitchens complained regarding the faith-only stance of religious followers; see his work *God Is Not Great: How Religion Poisons Everything* (New York: Hachette, 2007), 150–51, 202–4. In *The God Delusion* (Boston: Houghton Mifflin, 2008), Richard Dawkins seems to propose that religion (referring in context to

Seemingly indicative of their penchant for bombastic statements that are often quite far from correct, well-known New Atheist neuroscientist Sam Harris proclaims, "In fact, every religion preaches the truth of propositions for which no evidence is even *conceivable*."[3] Inconceivable or not, virtually all of these New Atheist authors are well aware of some of the arguments put forward in favor of God's existence and, more specifically, for Christianity, including miracles.[4]

Christianity in particular) has at least some of its roots in psychological maladaptation (207–21). The side effects include irrationality (214, 219), ridiculous beliefs (207–8), and the all-pervasive importance of faith without any evidence (134 and throughout).

For a few rejoinders directed to these New Atheist works, showing that there are indeed strong arguments for theism in general and Christianity in particular, as well as devastating critiques against atheism, see John C. Lennox, *God's Undertaker: Has Science Buried God?* (Oxford: Lion Hudson, 2007); Alister McGrath and Joanna Collicutt McGrath, *The Dawkins Delusion? Atheist Fundamentalism and the Denial of the Divine* (Downers Grove, IL: InterVarsity, 2007); Alister McGrath, *Why God Won't Go Away: Is the New Atheism Running on Empty?* (Nashville: Nelson, 2010); Peter S. Williams, *A Sceptic's Guide to Atheism* (Milton Keynes: Paternoster, 2009); Dinesh D'Souza, *What's So Great about Christianity* (Washington, DC: Regnery, 2007). Rather incredibly, the McGrath and McGrath volume here includes a comment displayed on its front cover by well-known skeptical philosopher of science Michael Ruse and directed at Dawkins, which states, "*The God Delusion* makes me embarrassed to be an atheist, and the McGraths show why"! Other outstanding recommendations concerning the McGrath and McGrath text come from world-renowned scientists Francis Collins of the Human Genome Project and Harvard University astrophysicist Owen Gingerich.

[3] Harris, *End of Faith*, 23. Even if Harris is only referring here to *some* rather than all religious propositions, he fails to acknowledge that evidential considerations on behalf of religious notions even exist at all, which is in spite of his knowing otherwise that such religious defenses exist (as indicated by his sources immediately below).

[4] For several examples, Harris in *Letter to a Christian Nation* is aware of arguments that some believers propose from fulfilled prophecy (57–60); arguments against evolution, including the evidence of Intelligent Design (67–79); and from historical arguments, where he mentions Scripture and even Jesus's resurrection (64–67). Yet Harris seems either to be oblivious or at least unaware of scholarly Christian teachings contrary to his assertions that believers simply accept these arguments by faith, "without evidence" (67). Hitchens (in *God Is Not Great*) also mentions Christian arguments from miracles (141–45), including Jesus's resurrection appearances (135), and seems to treat these a little more fairly than does Harris, but ignores any strong points by believers. Dawkins (in *The God Delusion*) also at least mentions miracles and afterlife beliefs, as well as a lengthy section on what are often referred to as the related topics of cosmology, intelligent design, the anthropic principle, and irreducible complexity (35, 134, 137–138, 144–189, 208), but almost always served with a noticeable disdain. Yet, like the others here, Dawkins emphasizes throughout the

There is some truth to these atheist accusations, given that a fair number of everyday Christians and even a fair number of pastors at least seem to favor the faith route. Still, probably the majority of trained Christian scholars, especially among evangelicals, as well as a large swath of other believers do not couch their claims in terms like this and are usually aware of a host of evidential considerations for Christianity as well as their opponent's arguments, whether or not that is the path they choose to take.

---

role of faith in believers rather than any evidential considerations, almost as if believers simply never argue from that angle at all (134, 181). Life illustrations, stories, or examples (especially in Hitchens) that often make adherents to religion look naive are common, apparently to seal the diatribe, as if to represent the majority of those who espouse the Christian *faith*.

To be very clear here, it is *not* being charged in any way that because these New Atheist authors disagree with Christians, they are therefore deficient somehow. More positively for the skeptics, Hitchens does introduce David Hume's essay against miracles when discussing the subject, which is far from naive in itself (*God Is Not Great*, 241–45). So even if believers disagree with Hitchens, they ought to recognize that he is nonetheless attempting to craft a response rather than simply ignoring Christian claims. Of course, he can be critiqued for his weak defense of Hume.

But the chief point to be raised here is at least twofold. The New Atheists seem regularly to willingly ignore and seriously mischaracterize the Christian arguments, judging that they are based on faith alone, no matter how strong the data. It is this theme that seems to be at the very head of their list too, often making a parody of what Christians are really arguing, trying to make them appear foolish while the atheists (which they sometimes refer to as the "brights") are celebrated for their totally rational and scientific stances! The New Atheists who engage in such mischaracterizations deserve blame for this sort of behavior, especially when each of the best-known ones mentioned has debated evangelical scholars and the dialogues indicate that they have not done very well, even as judged by fellow atheists. In fact, the atheist "brights" seemed rather dulled by these public exercises. Further, with regard to their tactics, the New Atheists appear to share some kinship with the so-called mythicists, who seem willing to use any argument whatever, no matter how absolutely outlandish, in order to argue that Jesus never (or probably never) lived.

Both of these groups are also criticized regularly by other specialized critical scholars who very rarely support either of these radical positions, as indicated by the strong language such as that mentioned above from atheist philosopher of science Michael Ruse, which was aimed at Dawkins, in addition to the other top-notch scholarly recommendations of the same McGrath and McGrath volume. This indicates why the New Atheists generally tend to appeal to more popular audiences of untrained readers who also tend to exhibit similar strong feelings toward Christian beliefs, reveling in the nasty and often angry language.

But it is hardly fair to cite the easiest, simplest path of attacking other positions, whatever the views. After all, seemingly few atheists or other skeptics, including those just listed, would want their positions to be expressed, represented, or
defended in terms of the so-called village atheist or the "lunatic fringes" of their
own movements, such as with angry comments or letters to newspaper editors. The
real issue, after all, is where the arguments and data lie, and that is precisely what
we intend to pursue, in spite of where popular observations from nonscholars on
either side may reside.

Reviewing Hume and the Initial State
of the Evidence for Miracles

A few caveats will be mentioned at the outset. It often seems that these required
levels of confirmation as set by critics are so high that they could never possibly be
reached. It is as if, even in a case where a surprising number of positive considerations
have already been provided, the adequate level is always just a little higher and out
of reach. In short, the claim might even be meant to indicate that the evidence can
never achieve a sufficient amount, so that a miraculous conclusion could never be
reached. But it needs to be pointed out that greater evidence for miracle claims than
for normal events does not mean it is impossible for the appropriate amount to ever
be attained, for that amounts to an a priori rejection, as mentioned above.

We will not repeat from the last chapter each of the seven general responses
directed toward Hume's 1748 essay against miracles. But several of the critiques that
were raised there will also be quite relevant at various places in this chapter, at least in
edited or adapted form, as they apply to the many neo-Humean moves against belief
in miracles that followed in Hume's wake.

This chapter considers four categories of objections. The initial three consider
primarily *philosophical* questions: (1) whether there is sufficient evidence for miracle
claims; (2) if the characteristics of nature's laws may in any way be adjusted in order
to incorporate "supernatural events" as natural occurrences; and (3) if miracle claims
can ever be identified as supernatural acts of God. The fourth category involves
historical questions, primarily (4) whether there are any reasons of a historical
nature as to why miracle claims should be questioned chiefly on a priori grounds.
Again, these many issues have been raised by a host of recent commentators who
often more or less follow Hume's steps. We will note some of the many variations

among these four total categories as well, along with several problems with each of these charges.[5]

More than twenty different objections to miracle claims from all four categories will be entertained here, with almost all posed in an a priori manner. Theoretically, these protests raise issues that purport to present roadblocks to there ever being adequate evidence or other considerations in favor of miracles *before* the arguments are actually being presented. If these criticisms are later found to obtain, they could pose obstructions to the belief in supernatural events. Of course, good responses and evidences could later serve to move the situation in the opposite direction.

To repeat, since the objections are usually raised in an a priori manner, so the majority of the responses to the critics will be couched in that same jargon. In other words, neither critic nor defender will be trying to actually amass their data in this context. Just as the objections are raised only as potential roadblocks without data, the responses will be made in similar fashion. If the responses are found later to be stronger, they could pose sufficient rejoinders to those who deny the belief in the supernatural, helping to establish the positive case for religious belief and miracles in particular.

We will now survey a variety of more specific charges that skeptical scholars have aimed at religious beliefs in miracles, with each charge in the first category zeroing in on the question of there being sufficient evidence for the supernatural claims. An assortment of responses will be directed to each challenge, numbered consecutively throughout this category, all addressing a wide range of considerations and available evidence on behalf of miracle claims.

With these caveats in mind, it may be noticed that several of Hume's criticisms of miracles will appear again here, sometimes in a straightforward manner and often being adjusted in a similar manner but from other angles. Many of the critiques of Hume and defenses of miracles from the previous chapter will be spread out here as

---

[5] The consecutive numbering of these critiques will be continued throughout each of the four categorical objections to miracles, though the count will begin anew with each new category of challenges. Critiques that were already made and numbered earlier will still be listed again whenever applicable, but these repeats will not be numbered when the point being made is sufficiently close to the earlier one. Exceptions occur in cases where what appears to be a repeat point is actually extended further than the earlier version of the critique. This way, the reader should get a sense of the minimum number of the many different potential responses that might be made to each of these four total categories.

well, sometimes being repeated while addressing slightly different objections. Note that the first two comebacks below are review items that were already raised in the previous chapter, while the last three present what might be thought of as extensions of the seven critiques of Hume's essay.

Category 1: Is there enough evidence for miracles?

Challenge 1:1—Can a miracle occur if it is contrary to nature and its laws?

This initial critique is more general. Is there sufficient evidence to establish whether, contrary to some, there exists enough positive data on behalf of miracle claims to declare that these events have occurred in opposition to what is known of nature and its laws? Hume insisted that there is not enough unquestionable evidence favoring a miracle.[6] After all, as often repeated by skeptics, more evidence is needed to establish miracles than to determine ordinary events.[7]

Response 1

As mentioned in the previous chapter, perhaps most crucially, *strong evidence directed to a very specific point in time* could actually provide enough confirmation to conclude that, *at that precise moment and none other*, the normal course of nature may have been (or appeared to have been) temporarily set aside by a superior power. This or a similar critique has been raised many times since Hume first published his essay. But other skeptical scholars often make moves that do not allow for the possibility being described here.

It should also be recalled that the emphasis here was *definitely not* on either assuming or attempting to establish God's existence, which is actually not even part of this discussion. Neither is any actual evidence for a miracle on display in this context (or any other such item) any more than the critic has to prove her points at this juncture. Again, this a priori response is directed to an a priori objection, neither of which has so far provided the *actual arguments* in favor of the position in question.

---

[6] David Hume, "Of Miracles," in *Hume on Religion*, ed. Richard Wollheim (London: Collins, 1963), 205–29, especially the last two paragraphs in part 1 (210–12) and the first subpoint in part 2 (212).

[7] Antony Flew, "Miracles," in *The Encyclopedia of Philosophy*, ed. Paul Edwards (New York: Macmillan, 1967), 5:349.

Rather, the idea was that if such an intervention at that specific juncture were even *possible*, then Hume and other skeptics would need to be open to any potential evidence for such an option, which could only be ascertained by a careful investigation rather than by critical fiat.

The point of the response, then, is that the laws of nature could be uniform both before and after potential supernatural events. But evidence could indicate particular "hot spots" in history where another sort of occurrence altogether seems to have entered the natural order at that very moment, as indicated by the data.

This is what many theists are requesting here—that skeptics like Hume and others check out the possibilities by examining the evidence. For example, Dennis Jensen remarks that if the evidence is sufficient to indicate that particular events may have occurred, they ought not be rejected or sidestepped simply as "odd" occurrences.[8] There could be enough evidence to vindicate a miracle claim at that juncture and make it the best explanation of the known data on that particular occasion.

Response 2

Another devastating critique of David Hume's essay mentioned in the previous chapter is that of George Mavrodes and others.[9] The manner in which Hume's experiential argument for the laws of nature fails. His misguided attempt to rule out miracles begins with his misunderstanding of induction and his own lack of adequate sample size. Hume ascertained in the 1740s that "firm and unalterable experience has established these laws," evidence he later termed as "uniform experience."[10] How did Hume arrive at this "firm," "unalterable," and "uniform" evidence for nature's laws? If his experiential sample consisted of the views of his philosophical friends and perhaps a few others, or if they were simply generalized statements, then this sample was far too small to be accurately predictive.

---

[8] Dennis Jensen, "The Logic of Miracles," *Journal of the American Scientific Affiliation* 33 (1981): 150.

[9] See this second critique in detail in George I. Mavrodes, "David Hume and the Probability of Miracles," *International Journal for Philosophy of Religion* 43 (1998): 173–81; cf. Stanley L. Jaki, *Miracles and Physics* (Front Royal, VA: Christendom, 1989), 92–93. Antony Flew actually seems to agree that this or a similar critique relates to more than one aspect of Hume's notions of historiography and causality. See Flew, *Hume's Philosophy of Belief: A Study of the First Inquiry* (London: Routledge & Kegan Paul, 1961), 195, 204.

[10] Hume, "Of Miracles," 210–11.

But if the sample size had been greatly expanded to, say, at least hundreds of representative testimonies, then miracles would almost assuredly have been reported among these accounts as well, just as they are so recounted today. Either way, the very foundation for Hume's essay fails, for it most likely rests on faulty experimental groundwork. Therefore, in addition to his circular argument, what Hume most likely *does* evidence in this essay is not a successful argument against miracles but just poor research techniques. In terms of informal logic, Hume's thesis (or others that may be similar) presents an example of the fallacy of hasty generalization (more particularly, "insufficient or biased statistics").[11] In such a case, such a small study sample would have no probative force whatsoever in ruling out miracles.

Response 3

Moreover, as an extension of comments directed to Hume as well as to other skeptics who more or less agree with his general approach, these critiques are the sort that could potentially apply to almost anything—one can always demand more and more (and even more!) evidence. Yet, as German theologian Wolfhart Pannenberg responded wisely to then-atheist philosopher Antony Flew, demanding additional evidence for a miracle claim assumes that what has already been provided has been addressed adequately![12] However, in such a situation, to continue rejecting an occurrence in the presence of what could be sufficient evidence without responding adequately to that evidence amounts to an a priori rejection of the miraculous. Granted, as already noted, this evidence has not been discussed yet in this chapter, but Pannenberg's response may still be proposed as a preliminary caution that may become warranted by the data when they are given.

Response 4

Further, since historical facts are not self-interpreting, it would also be significant if additional evidences of other sorts were available in order to connect the resurrection

---

[11] Charles W. Kegley and Jacquelyn Ann Kegley, *Introduction to Logic* (Columbus, OH: Merrill, 1978), 138–39, 157; Irving M. Copi, *Introduction to Logic*, 7th ed. (New York: Macmillan, 1986), 100.

[12] Pannenberg's comment was made during a response to Flew following our initial debate on the subject of Jesus's resurrection. See Wolfhart Pannenberg's "Response to the Debate," in Gary R. Habermas and Antony G. N. Flew, *Did Jesus Rise from the Dead? The Resurrection Debate*, ed. Terry L. Miethe (San Francisco: Harper & Row, 1987), 128, cf. 134.

to an interpretive system that best explains the resurrection and other related occurrences. For instance, if Jesus's miracles and exorcisms were found to be consistent and integrated with his overall life, ethics, and other teachings, that would potentially also be significant in providing a worldview context for an occurrence such as his resurrection, as well as in contributing more structure and identification to the overall project. These as well as other additional considerations could serve as further evidential clues pointing beyond this natural world.[13]

Response 5

Related to the previous consideration of interpretive systems, it should also be mentioned that if a surprising amount of evidence does obtain on behalf of a particular miracle claim, the opposite consideration also needs to be considered. In the case that the only chief opposition to the claim is that such events simply do not ever occur, the particular opposition worldview that asserts such a stance should also be prepared to defend why it is superior and why this particular belief should be allowed to "trump" the data simply by its assertion. The compelling reasons on behalf of the competing worldview that proposed such a dismissal are also on display. No mere assertion of a competing view should be allowed to simply dismiss the presentation of data.

We will now survey a variety of more specific charges that skeptical scholars have aimed at religious beliefs in miracles, with each one zeroing in on the question of there being sufficient evidence for the supernatural claims. An assortment of responses will be directed to each challenge, numbered consecutively throughout this category—all addressing a wide range of considerations and available evidence on behalf of miracle claims.

Challenge 1:2—Is There Empirical Evidence for Miracles?

The next evidential challenge to the belief in miracles can come from more than one related direction. After the initial discussion above, perhaps some critical scholars will

---

[13] For examples, volume 1 of this study treats some of these suggestions here, such as the evidence for Jesus being a healer and an exorcist and, to a lesser extent, the nature of Jesus's key teachings, whether Jesus was unique among the major religious founders, or if he predicted his resurrection ahead of time. These last three topics are projected to be discussed in far more detail in volume 4.

understand that many believers think there are some strong and worthwhile considerations that can be brought to bear on the miracles discussion. But not satisfied with
merely *some* decent evidence, the ante may be raised to require a particular species of
evidence. Or perhaps another critical group altogether simply begins at this higher
threshold of data.

In discussions of this sort, *empirical* data is often or even generally preferred. The
idea is often that the scientific method, based on acquiring sense data as the preferred
species of evidence-gathering, yields the premier brand of knowable data. Very strict
forms of this challenge, such as those by Ayer's positivism or other requirements for
empirical evidence posed by scholars, are sometimes thought of as the only meaningful and hence admissible species of confirmation that could gain true knowledge
concerning the world.[14] While more general observations or comments of this nature
are still heard frequently in one guise or another, there are serious flaws in these sorts
of requirements.

Response 6

So, is there any possibility that *empirical* evidence exists for miracle claims? Actually,
it was not long before a number of strong critiques sidelined Ayer's stringent variety
of skepticism, and it became a rather short-lived philosophical option. Ayer himself
actually helped with the reconstruction of this view!

Philosopher David Elton Trueblood asserted one such prominent critique of
Ayer's requirement in a treatment entitled "The Self-Contradiction of Positivism."
In treating the logical positivist's variety of this charge (which is perhaps the
strongest of the major versions), Trueblood pointed out that the central decree
that requires employing empirical data is a rule that cannot be empirically verified itself. Trueblood closes the matter rather succinctly. He states, "In the light of
such analysis we have a right to conclude that logical positivism fails to undermine
religious belief, because it undermines itself in the effort."[15] Trueblood concluded,

---

[14] Such as observed in one well-known form decades ago by the famous analytical
philosophical challenge brought by A. J. Ayer, *Language, Truth, and Logic* (London: Dover,
1936), 5, 16, 19, 90, 101, plus chap. 1, "The Elimination of Metaphysics," particularly
35–37, 40.

[15] David Elton Trueblood, *Philosophy of Religion* (New York: Harper & Brothers, 1957),
195–99, with the quotation on page 199. At the time Trueblood was writing, unlike today,
logical positivism was still a live philosophical option (191). Observable from Trueblood's

"It must be a mere matter of taste, in which case we do not need to pay serious attention to it."[16]

In other words, Ayer's regulation that required the necessity of producing positive empirical data for meaningful knowledge had strangely neglected to provide any such scientific backup on behalf of this original initial claim itself on the necessity of empirical data. In short, the rule that required empirical information had no empirical reason on its own behalf. Therefore, Ayer's principle actually flunked its own test!

Just four years after the initial publication of A. J. Ayer's popular volume *Language, Truth, and Logic* in 1936, another prominent philosopher, Edgar Sheffield Brightman, also critiqued his position in detail. Like Trueblood, he pointed out that positivism was "a very popular view at the present time." Brightman offered a couple of criticisms, another of which was a common complaint, namely, that the same argument as employed by Ayer would also rule out our knowledge of history.[17]

Years later, after many other scholars also noted these and other problems with the verification principle as well as with other items involved in the attendant skeptical reasoning, the demise of logical positivism ensued. Renowned philosopher Alvin Plantinga still took another swipe at Ayer's principle by returning to the earlier criticism raised by Trueblood: "It seems impossible to state the so-called 'verifiability criterion' in a way which rules out theological and metaphysical statements without paying the same compliment to scientific and common-sense statements."[18]

Hence, there exists no reason for anyone to be obliged to follow the verification principle or its other strictures. There is no solid foundation on which this regulation can stand. In fact, nothing substantial backs up such a rule, hence there is absolutely no need to require the sort of empirical testing that it demands. It turns out to be merely an ungrounded or preferential assertion, and it has been recognized as such.

Moving forward to postmodern times, charges often still emerge regarding less strident claims that sense experience is the only admissible, justified sort of evidence or, at least, that it is the strongest variety of confirmation. For example, it

---

treatment, the critiques appeared fairly quickly after the appearance of Ayer's second edition in 1946.

[16] Trueblood, 196.

[17] Edgar S. Brightman, *A Philosophy of Religion* (New York: Prentice-Hall, 1940), 4–6, 143, 396–97, particularly note 7; the quotation is located on 396.

[18] See Alvin Plantinga, *God, Freedom, and Evil* (New York: Harper & Row, 1974), 66.

is asserted commonly that empirical testing and its results are the very backbone of modern science and hence should be emulated. But these statements are similarly not effective at all. The stronger accusation that empirical truth is the only allowable path to affirming claims makes virtually the same error as with the harder verification principle above. On what grounds is this challenge grounded? How could it be *shown* that empirical evidence is the *only* way to know something, or the *only* means of establishing truth? Not even science itself makes this claim, and scientific truth is often decided on other grounds, not to mention that this claim rules out certain types of science altogether. The latter category would include the many philosophical aspects of modern physics, geology, and many of the biological sciences.

The weaker claim that empirical data is the *best* species of evidence does not even need to be challenged, for it may in fact be the case. But this is a far cry from making the first claim above, that it is the only admissible type of evidence. After all, the *best* football team in the league is certainly not the *only* team in the league, and so it is with empirical evidence as well.

Response 7

Further, even if believers accepted this skeptical challenge by using only or primarily empirical sources to confirm some of their claims, the discipline of history still meets that standard, at least in the sense employed by the social sciences.[19] Thus, historical research would be admissible in the sense of relying on empirical research. In other words, historical data would be allowed similar to the way that psychological, sociological, or anthropological research might be utilized.

---

[19] As a reminder of the overview in volume 1 pertaining to whether or not history should be regarded as one of the scientific disciplines, this debate took place in western Europe and North America over many decades, beginning in the mid-nineteenth century and carrying well into the twentieth century. The general conclusion was that history should perhaps best be considered as among the second-order social sciences in the sense of presenting non-repeatable sense data. But history still relies on the accumulation of first-order information, such as eyewitness sources, interviews, and archaeological remains. A good "secular" example of this hands-on process can be found in Otto Eisenschiml and Ralph Newman, *Eyewitness: The Civil War as We Lived It* (New York: Grosset and Dunlap, 1956), which consists of the same such eyewitness sources, interviews, and archaeological relics of many sorts.

The value and force of this argument regarding the evidential use of historical research is even indicated by very skeptical, analytic philosophers themselves, who proposed these empirical tests in the first place as they freely employed these historical methods. The reasons for their lack of challenge on the rigors of history include not only the evidential aspects that these methods produced, but even the more practical truth that it is self-stultifying, if not self-contradictory, to reject history since scientific progress, for example, requires the knowledge of truthful historical precedent with its theories and experimentation. Hence, it is hardly surprising that quite skeptical analytic philosophers such as David Hume,[20] Bertrand Russell,[21] A. J. Ayer,[22] J. L. Mackie,[23] and Antony Flew,[24] among others, have each provided examples of the

---

[20] Throughout his essay "Of Miracles" (especially in part 2), Hume is pleased to pursue many of his own historical reflections on the past (as with the more specific Jansenist case discussed in the previous chapter, for example), or simply when referring to details in the lives of ancient persons such as Alexander, Vespasian, Lucian, Marcus Aurelius, or Muhammad; in ancient historians like Herodotus, Livy, Plutarch, Tacitus, and Suetonius; concerning ancient locations like the city of Athens or the Roman Empire; or concerning far-away locations such as Turkey or China. But what would truly be to miss the forest for the trees here would be to ignore that during David Hume's own life, his multivolume *The History of England*, 6 vols. (London: Gilbert and Revington, 1848), was most likely the best known of his works. Perhaps needless to say, though, Hume's historical publications are not pursued with the same amount of epistemic rigor as his philosophical works. For some specific details concerning ascertaining the occurrence of past events, see David Hume, *An Enquiry concerning Human Understanding*, sec. 5: "Sceptical Solution of These Doubts," ed. P. H. Nidditch, 3rd ed., ed. L. A. Selby-Bigge (Oxford: Clarenden, 1975). An analysis of the intriguing relation between Hume's philosophy and his history is provided by Nicholas Phillipson in *David Hume: The Philosopher as Historian*, rev. ed. (New Haven, CT: Yale University Press, 2012).

[21] Bertrand Russell, *The Problems of Philosophy* (Oxford: Clarendon, 1912); see his chapter entitled "Truth and Falsehood."

[22] In Alfred Jules Ayer's follow-up edition just ten years after the initial, 1936 publication of *Language, Truth, and Logic* (London: Victor Gollancz, 1946), Ayer admitted that his verification criterion was insufficient in itself to rule out metaphysical arguments (16). Further, he recognized the relevance and importance of investigating claimed historical events with regard to whether or not they occurred as well (esp. 19, but also 40, 101–2). Other relevant details include the initial concept of verification itself (5, 16), the differentiation of strong and weak versions (9), as well as exceptions (15).

[23] J. L. Mackie, *The Miracle of Theism: Arguments for and against the Existence of God* (Oxford: Clarendon, 1982), 22–29.

[24] Antony Flew, *God and Philosophy* (New York: Dell, 1966), particularly the variety of comments from both believing and unbelieving perspectives in chapter 7, "The

acceptance of historical investigation in order to ascertain which events did or did not occur.

The same could be stated regarding skeptical historians, including the precursors to contemporary postmodern trends. None of these scholars deny that we can still gain knowable historical facts through investigation. The data we possess are sufficient to arrive at key events.[25] Besides the philosophers just mentioned, many examples of skeptical historians could be cited here as well, including Wilhelm Dilthey,[26] Benedito Croce,[27] Ernst Troeltsch,[28] R. G. Collingwood,[29] Charles Beard,[30] and Carl Becker.[31] All of them also freely used methods of historical investigation in spite of their own skepticism.

Credentials of Revelation" under subsections 7.2–3, 9, 16, 22, and 26. Interestingly, Antony Flew's last edition of *God and Philosophy* (Amherst, NY: Prometheus, 2005) still contains the important comments, again both pro and con, in subsections 7.9, 15–17, 22, 25, and 28. This includes his comment to basically check out the claims of what has or has not occurred. It is especially in this latest edition that Flew's new introduction (9–17) notes some of the changes in current research that led him to what he termed a "conversion" from atheism to at least deism. Elsewhere, Flew makes a particular point of emphasizing Hume's appreciation of eyewitness testimony of past events and its ability to yield proof or probability; see Flew, *Hume's Philosophy of Belief*, 175.

[25] As noted by W. H. Walsh, "Can History Be Objective?," in *The Philosophy of History in Our Time: An Anthology*, ed. Hans Meyerhoff (Garden City, NY: Doubleday, 1959), 224.

[26] For the contrast between subjective and objective data, see Wilhelm Dilthey, "The Understanding of Other Persons and Their Life-Expressions," in *Theories of History: Readings from Classical and Contemporary Sources*, ed. Patrick Gardiner (New York: Free Press, 1959), 220–25. This essay, translated by J. J. Kuehl, was originally published in German in volume 7 of Dilthey, *Gesammelte Schriften* (Leipzig: Verlag von B. G. Teubner, 1927).

[27] Benedetto Croce, "History and Chronicle," in *History: Its Theory and Practice*, trans. Douglas Ainslee (New York: Harcourt, Brace and Company, 1921), 11–26; cited here from Meyerhoff, *Philosophy of History*, 47.

[28] Ernst Troeltsch, *The Christian Faith*, ed. Gertrud von le Fort, trans. Garrett E. Paul (Minneapolis: Fortress, 1991), 87–89.

[29] R. G. Collingwood, *The Idea of History* (Oxford: Oxford University Press, 1956), 228–49, cf. 252–62, 292–96.

[30] Charles A. Beard, "Written History as an Act of Faith," *American Historical Review* 39, no. 2 (1934): 219–31; cited here from Meyerhoff, *Philosophy of History*, 146–51.

[31] Like other scholars of this ilk, even though Becker is sympathetic to the notion of the subjectivity, especially of historical interpretations, he still acknowledges and even assumes the presence of much history. Carl L. Becker, *The Heavenly City of the Eighteenth-Century Philosophers* (New Haven: Yale University Press, 1932), 17–21, 28–31. Meyerhoff includes a different selection from Becker, "What Are Historical

Other skeptical thinkers could also be added to these lists, since the vast majority of even the more subjective-leaning idealistic historians agreed with this assessment regarding the knowledge of historical facts.[32] In fact, Meyerhoff even helpfully comments that each of these skeptical researchers combined some version of "historicism" with their idealism.[33] Earlier in volume 1 it was also observed that while even the major, contemporary postmodern historians may take different angles on these questions, they likewise do not deny the probable presence of particular historical facts.[34]

Two other considerations will be mentioned briefly below.

Response 8

Those who reject the historicity of Jesus's resurrection could further their positions by suggesting and defending a naturalistic alternative hypothesis contrary to the occurrence of this event, one that they consider capable of explaining all of the empirical data. But, strangely enough, comparatively few serious attempts have been produced in recent years, even from the best-established skeptical scholars, as we will see later in this volume.

Response 9

It is clearly the case that the Shroud of Turin could well turn out to be a counterfeit object of some unexplained variety. But even if this cloth is an actual archaeological artifact but simply not the burial cloth of Jesus, this sheet could still have wrapped

---

Facts?," *Western Political Quarterly* 8, no. 3 (1955): 327–40; see Meyerhoff, *Philosophy of History*, 132–37.

[32] Such as Karl Mannheim, "The Sociology of Knowledge," in Gardiner, *Theories of History*, 247–48. W. H. Walsh is a particularly balanced scholar, as seen in his essay, "The Limits of Scientific History," *Historical Studies* 3 (1961): 45–57; cited here from *Philosophical Analysis and History*, ed. William H. Dray (New York: Harper & Row, 1966), particularly 60–61, 68–71.

[33] See Meyerhoff, *Philosophy of History*, 36.

[34] Besides those historians mentioned in earlier chapters, another example would be the prominent French scholar Michel Foucault, *The Archaeology of Knowledge and the Discourse on Language*, trans. A. M. Sheridan Smith (New York: Pantheon, 1972), 149–56, including normal historical illustrations that assume the presence of historical material (162–65, 195).

the body of a crucified man, thereby providing some further repeatable, empirical evidence for at least the nature of death by crucifixion. But if this garment does turn out to be Jesus's actual burial cloth, more specific data of an empirical (as well as repeatable) variety closer to the scientific research model would provide a very crucial addition to the already existing data pertaining to the specific death and even the resurrection of Jesus.[35]

Challenge 1:3—Are Miracles Repeatable Events?

Another somewhat related line of questioning is to inquire whether evidence for miracle claims is repeatable as in the hard sciences. Yet, if these occurrences are un-repeatable, then how can they be interpreted?[36]

Initially, two earlier responses need to be repeated from the discussion above. First, this and the next objection both address miracles in terms more related to the hard sciences. But as has been explained both above as well as in much detail in volume 1 of this study, history is a social science rather than a hard science. So, for starters, these two challenges are, strictly speaking, out of place, sort of like comparing apples to oranges.[37] But these two subjects will still be addressed.

Second, as was likewise already explained, requiring empirical evidence as the only *sine qua non* test for miracle claims is a self-refuting move, since the requirement or rule itself fails to provide any empirical evidence on its own behalf. So how can the requirement of an empirical test simply trump the entire process when it fails to pass its own standard?

---

[35] For the current state of the scientific testing and evidence, see the encyclopedic overview by Mark Antonacci, *Test the Shroud: At the Atomic and Molecular Levels* (Brentwood, TN: Forefront, 2015). Cf. Antonacci's earlier book, *The Resurrection of the Shroud: New Scientific, Medical, and Archaeological Evidence* (New York: Evans, 2000); Mary and Alan Whanger, *The Shroud of Turin: Adventure in Discovery* (Franklin, TN: Providence House, 1998); Tristan Casabianca et al., "The Radiocarbon Dating of the Turin Shroud: New Evidence from Raw Data," *Archaeometry* 5 (2019): 1223–31; Tristan Casabianca, "The Shroud of Turin: A Historiographical Approach," *Heythrop Journal* 54 (2013): 414–23.

[36] Antony Flew offers this notion in the context of explaining Hume's position in his book *Hume's Philosophy of Belief*, 208; also Flew, "Miracles," 5:350; Flew, "Introduction" to David Hume, *Of Miracles* (La Salle, IL: Open Court, 1985), 19–23; George D. Chryssides, "Miracles and Agents," *Religious Studies* 11 (1975): 319–27.

[37] Cf. Richard Taylor, "Two Kinds of Explanation," in *Miracles*, ed. Richard Swinburne (New York: Macmillan, 1989), 103–13.

Similarly, the related charge to this initial empirical challenge is that miracles are not repeatable occurrences. However, to require repeatability as a test either for eventfulness or to provide an interpretation stumbles into the same problem. The rule itself that necessitates repeatability cannot be verified or otherwise shown to be necessary. Such a rule is hardly repeatable on its own grounds, and hence it fails miserably in its attempt to gain any compliance whatsoever on its own behalf. In other words, why should this requirement be allowed to set the pace for research when the very rule is nothing more than a command that is hanging out in unverified space? Where is the force behind a requirement that also flunks its own test? So, again, on what is this rule based?[38]

Response 10

What rule determines additionally that unrepeatable events cannot be interpreted? Are historians unable to give an adequate interpretation of Julius Caesar's victories over Gaul or to describe the tremendous importance of the British Magna Carta without repeating the original moments of each? Frankly, attaching this additional rider to the previous idea seems almost like a nonsequitous move, perhaps to make the objection appear to be more robust. Here is yet another requirement that turns out to be a mere assertion that also lacks repeatability or any other backup.

Further, individual skeptics as well as the dominant positions in scientific and other disciplines as a whole regularly allow significance for nonrepeated events. Hume admitted the possibility of onetime events, like total darkness.[39] In fact, Flew thought that this was a weakness in Hume's position.[40] Recent science has no objection to nonrepeatable singularities such as the Big Bang or the origin of initial life itself.[41] As just mentioned, historians have no problems arriving at meaningful interpretations of historical events in spite of a lack of repetition. Even though these

---

[38] This assessment will be counted as an extension of the earlier critique rather than as a new response. Hence, the criticism is not an addition to the consecutively numbered critiques.

[39] Hume, "Of Miracles," 223.

[40] Flew, "Introduction" to Hume, *Of Miracles*, 9.

[41] Similarly, see Norman L. Geisler, "Miracles and the Modern Mind," in *In Defense of Miracles: A Comprehensive Case for God's Action in History*, ed. Douglas Geivett and Gary R. Habermas (Downers Grove, IL: InterVarsity, 1997), 82–84.

examples are not miracles, they provide principles for recognizing the occurrence and meaning of onetime events.[42]

Response 11

This objection sounds suspiciously like an a priori rejection of miracle claims, something along the lines of: "If this event is not repeatable, then it does not count. But if it is repeatable, then it is obviously just a natural occurrence." By such reasoning, then, a miracle could be ruled out from the very outset, even *before* an investigation is conducted, regardless of *whether or not* it even happened![43]

Response 12

Even apart from repetition, we know enough about the laws of nature to explain that side of the equation. We likewise know what most likely would be an exception to these laws. As such, we may identify the potential miracle claim under such circumstances. If a particular event occurred, then it (obviously) happened. Not only can such an event not be ruled out simply because it is a one-time occurrence or otherwise unique, but uniqueness is often considered to be one possible sign of the miraculous in the first place.[44]

Response 13

We will need to return to the details of this subject below, but it is at least both relevant and possible that well-documented miraculous events may indeed occur today, perhaps even in abundance. Further, they may even be repeatable, at least in the sense of very similar occurrences happening in diverse settings with different people. Further study may discover these significant features.

---

[42] Jensen, "Logic of Miracles," 15.

[43] As pointed out at this juncture in the discussion by David Basinger and Randall Basinger, *Philosophy and Miracle: The Contemporary Debate* (Lewiston, NY: Mellen, 1986), 48–49.

[44] Cf. some similar ideas in Basinger and Basinger, 48–51. Cf. also Richard Swinburne, *The Concept of Miracle* (London: Macmillan, 1970), 26–27, 31; Swinburne, "Violation of a Law of Nature," in *Miracles*, ed. Richard Swinburne (New York: Macmillan, 1989), 78–81.

Additionally, whether the Shroud of Turin, mentioned earlier, is a nonmiraculous cloth that wrapped an unknown crucifixion victim—in which case much can still be learned about crucifixion—or it belonged to Jesus, it remains the most scientifically tested archaeological artifact in history. But in terms of this critique, virtually all of these tests are repeatable, thus also fulfilling the critique.

Challenge 1:4—Are Miracles Predictable Events?

Another challenge to the strength of the potential evidence for belief in miracles is this: if these occurrences followed nature's laws, they should be predictable. But if miracles are unlawful and unpredictable, then they are inexplicable. But if they are inexplicable, then they are neither verifiable nor falsifiable.[45]

This objection is beset by many complications to say the least. Two of the issues at the outset have already been raised above and will not be counted again. The first issue pertaining to this challenge is that it has not been shown that lawfulness in explanations or actions must obtain in the exact manner as stated by critics. But to identify or require predictability as a criterion that determines truth or meaning is itself without a basis. It remains yet another disguised requirement, such as those already seen above, that flunks its own criteria—it is a concocted rule without external support. Yet other propositions are supposed to comply to its make-believe rules.[46]

Second, this proposed challenge once again makes an unwarranted prior assumption that all law is natural. This is simply yet another hardly disguised form of what has already been encountered elsewhere in this chapter as an a priori rejection of miracles. But if God has indeed acted in history, miracles will be *super*natural by their very nature, as Hume even agreed in his famous definition of these occurrences.

Response 14

C. S. Lewis mentioned another relevant issue here. Miracles would be linked to God in their past history but then tied into the laws of nature in their forward

---

[45] Patrick Nowell-Smith, "Miracles," in *New Essays in Philosophical Theology*, ed. Antony Flew and Alasdair MacIntyre (New York: Macmillan, 1955), 248–49.

[46] Paul J. Dietl, "Of Miracles," in *Logical Analysis and Contemporary Theism*, ed. John Donnelly (New York: Fordham University Press, 1972), 244.

direction once they happened.[47] This skeptical objection would prefer to ignore all of this in an attempt to rule out these events simply by fiat. So, what, then, if miracles are not generally predictable and do not proceed according to natural law?[48] That's their very nature! Purtill notes that they would be free acts of God not unlike a presidential pardon.[49]

Response 15

Also, this objection commits the "either-or" fallacy of informal logic (also known variously as the "false dilemma," "black-white," or "all or nothing" fallacies) and does so in multiple places too. In such misconceptions, the options in a situation are "erroneously reduced to two" when there are other possibilities.[50]

Many examples of this "either-or" logical fallacy could be provided here from critics, such as the declarations made by one skeptical scholar after another that miracles are either lawful or unlawful, predictable or unpredictable, explicable or inexplicable, verifiable or unverifiable, including the further charge that we must investigate all of a miracle or none of it.[51] But additional options are clearly available in each of these cases—hence the repeated logical fallacies. Therefore, since a miracle would be a *super*natural occurrence due to our inability to investigate its originating direction with God, the observable direction may still be investigated. In other words, the effects of such actions in our world could be observed and often even measured.

In short, as supernatural events, miracles would *not* need to occur in the same ways that natural events happen. The prefix *super* should make it abundantly clear that something in addition to the "natural" portion would definitely be present here. That should be obvious, though these objections continually attempt to squeeze a square peg into a round hole.

---

[47] C. S. Lewis, *Miracles: A Preliminary Study* (New York: Macmillan, 1947), 60–63 (see 59–62 in the 1960 Macmillan edition).

[48] See Dietl, "Of Miracles," 245.

[49] Richard L. Purtill, "Proofs of Miracles and Miracles as Proofs," *Christian Scholar's Review* 6 (1976): 43.

[50] Kegley and Kegley, *Introduction to Logic*, 143, 157.

[51] Nowell-Smith, "Miracles," 253.

Response 16

Major exceptions that appear to transgress this requirement of prediction are noted regularly in the world. Numerous examples are even available. Historical events are rarely predictable, but they still operate by natural laws and very few scholars disregard history. Are there such things as free choices? If so, are these actions always verifiable according to these strictures, or is freedom even related to verification in such a manner? Additionally, occurrences studied in modern physics are not always predictable. In fact, perhaps this applies to even a majority of the phenomena studied in physics. So, is this branch of science unknowable or unverifiable according to this same charge?[52] If examples such as these from history and physics obtain without any apparent problems, why must miracle claims be any different? Or why must miracles measure up to a different standard?

Response 17

As with our earlier comment regarding empirical evidence in general, a Christian could always simply accept the criterion of predictability anyway, at least up to a certain point. Such a move could still help establish the case for Christian theism in spite of the lack of missing support on behalf of this criterion. To that end, if Jesus did indeed predict his resurrection beforehand, and if such is ascertainable by critical standards (as we argued in volume 1 and will do so again below), then the resurrection was both predictable and predicted. In such an instance, this criterion is *still* satisfied.

Challenge 1:5—Are the Scientifically Verifiable Laws of Nature Superior to Even Potential Historical Evidence on Behalf of Miracle Claims?

The chief idea here is that scientific data, as a type or species of evidence, is superior to historical evidence. After all, at least the hard sciences boast of repeatable claims along with stricter, more readily measurable criteria, which history cannot produce. In such cases, as per Hume's analogy of one "proof" confronting another "proof," when the experiential evidence favoring the laws of nature confronts the "proof" of

---

[52] See Werner Schaaffs, *Theology, Physics, and Miracles*, trans. Richard L. Renfield (Washington, DC: Canon, 1974), 44–47, 52–53.

historical testimony for miracle claims, the former is recognized as being the superior method. The argument is that the support for the laws of nature is sufficient to trump the weaker historical testimony.[53] An additional angle on this sort of objection is sometimes referred to as the issue of "dwindling probabilities," where historical arguments lose some force.[54]

---

[53] Hume, "Of Miracles," 211–12. This is another notion that Flew posits in agreement with Hume's examples in Flew, *Hume's Philosophy of Belief*, 207–8. Following Hume, Flew agreed elsewhere too, as in his article "Miracles," 5:349–50, and with his later essay, Antony Flew, "Neo-Humean Arguments about the Miraculous," in Geivett and Habermas, *In Defense of Miracles*, 50–51.

[54] Several examples from history, often consisting of innuendos and cognate arguments, bear on this issue. One well-known instance is the essay by Gotthold Lessing, "On the Proof of the Spirit and of Power," in *Lessing's Theological Writings*, trans. Henry Chadwick (London: Black, 1956), 51–56. Here Lessing charges that contemporary miracles and prophecies would be much more convincing than those same occasions from long ago since he had never witnessed the latter for himself, thus making much of the time difference and corresponding lack of recent eyewitness support (51–53).

In one of the intriguing moments that often arise in the history of ideas, Søren Kierkegaard responded to Lessing several decades later by opposing Lessing's perhaps tongue-in-cheek contrast of the benefits regarding present observation of supernatural events. Kierkegaard charged that *neither* contemporaneity *nor* historical evidence availed anything substantial with regard to the exercise of faith. See Søren Kierkegaard, *Concluding Unscientific Postscript*, trans. David Swenson (Princeton: Princeton University Press, 1968), 89, including note 2; also, Kierkegaard, *Philosophical Fragments or a Fragment of Philosophy*, trans. Howard V. Hong (Princeton: Princeton University Press, 1967), particularly 108. However, Kierkegaard also noted that Lessing probably did not actually believe the supernatural items anyway, in spite of his affirmation to the contrary (*Concluding Unscientific Postscript*, 88).

Jumping to the present by noting a recent, rigorous, and much more technical dialogue between two accomplished analytic Christian philosophers, only a few of the more relevant items will be pointed out here. At the turn of the new century, Alvin Plantinga published his magnum opus, *Warranted Christian Belief* (Oxford: Oxford University Press, 2000). In this text, he objected to certain evidentialist defenses of Christianity and argued that Christians do not need that sort of evidence in order to be assured of their faith (268–80). Throughout, Plantinga preferred the Reformed system of thought, constructed of self-attesting belief that relies primarily on special revelation and the internal witness of the Holy Spirit.

Plantinga's thesis was challenged by Christian philosopher Timothy McGrew. After a very rigorous critique of the finer points of analytic evidence-gathering, McGrew concluded with some fanfare that "Plantinga's critique of the historical argument is a failure—if not an abject failure, then at least a decisive one." See Timothy McGrew, "Has Plantinga Refuted the Historical Argument?," *Philosophia Christi* 6 (2004): 24. McGrew concluded by enumerating four strong conclusions that follow from his treatment (24–26).

Two vital issues that were addressed in detail in the previous chapter on Hume's essay on miracles as well as in the review at the outset of this chapter need to be revisited here briefly.[55] First, it was argued that one of the crucial matters in this entire discussion is *not* at all the one regarding the general strength of the laws of nature, but whether there was a God who was stronger than those laws. Think of it this way: why should anyone care about the evidence for nature's laws if there is a Creator God who is omnipotent and who chose to act in history? But rather than an ensuing discussion of God's existence, the crux of this critique was to assert that *if God even possibly existed*, the data in favor of these possible events would at least need to be examined because that information could potentially trump other considerations.

According to what has been termed here as the "frame argument," these laws of nature could be just as powerful as the critics assert and *still* be superseded by an even stronger power.[56] Thus, rather than asking how strong or well established these laws

---

McGrew's article led to a rejoinder from Alvin Plantinga, "Historical Arguments and Dwindling Probabilities: A Response to Timothy McGrew," *Philosophia Christi* 8 (2006): 7–22. After beginning with a genuinely impressive compliment and a few others throughout (7, 19–20), Plantinga leveled his own response. He posited that in his volume *Warranted Christian Belief*, he was not primarily attempting to critique or disallow historical arguments per se, as much as to postulate that they were not strictly necessary moves when the self-attestation of special revelation and the Holy Spirit were available. So then, if there were *also* strong historical arguments, then he was "delighted to discover that" and "I admire his [McGrew's] way of making the point" (20–21). Plantinga closed his essay with the words that this development "is a real step forward and contributes substantially to our understanding of historical arguments" (22).

McGrew's response (coauthored with his wife, Lydia) was to further clarify his argument. While he was pleased that Plantinga had come that far in his thinking, he was careful to point out that Plantinga's journal argument "*is* a retreat" from the position that he had taken in his book, which had indeed formerly supported the stronger conclusions. See McGrew and McGrew, "On the Historical Argument: A Rejoinder to Plantinga," *Philosophia Christi* 8 (2006): 37–38, chiefly 24. The McGrews then pressed forward to emphasize the need for careful research in order to ascertain which ancient historical events actually occurred, since there was no longer anything to stand in the way of such a study (31–32, 36, 38). The McGrews also briefly recount the conclusion to this matter in their essay "The Argument from Miracles: A Cumulative Case for the Resurrection of Jesus of Nazareth," in *The Blackwell Companion to Natural Theology*, ed. William Lane Craig and J. P. Moreland (West Sussex: Wiley-Blackwell, 2012), 644–50, esp. 650.

[55] Hence, they will not be renumbered here.

[56] Intriguingly, even Flew was aware of this argument, though he does not really comment on it except to call it a "tempting argument"! See Flew, "Introduction" to Hume, *Of Miracles*, 8; Flew, *God and Philosophy*, 154 (158 in the 2005 edition).

are, the more telling issue is whether the entire system (or "frame") can be temporarily superseded. Lewis said it this way: "No study of probabilities inside a given frame can ever tell us how probable it is that the frame itself can be violated."[57]

Here is the most crucial element of this countercritique: *if* a miracle actually occurred, it would actually be *superior* to these laws of nature, *but only at that precise moment*, and it would therefore take precedent over nature's laws at that juncture. The laws of nature are often thought to describe what generally hold in normal circumstances.[58] History can tell us if or when there was an apparent exception on a particular occasion. The available data on behalf of the miracle claim, then, could potentially indicate that the observed strength of nature's laws had been superseded *at that point*.[59]

The second matter is that even what may well be the *strongest* form of argumentation, as in the empirical sciences, is not thereby the *only* way to gain data. Solid facts as determined by physics cannot overrule or disprove historical events, such as Napoleon's defeat at Waterloo, as long as there is no contradiction that has to be decided. In this chapter, contradictory claims are being treated one at a time. But to give another example here, the "frame argument" just referred to above is an indication of how an actual miracle could at least potentially coexist with the laws of nature, each within

---

[57] See Lewis, *Miracles*, 106 (103 in the 1960 edition). Lewis also addressed the subject briefly in his excellent and thoughtful essay "The Laws of Nature," in *God in the Dock: Essays on Theology and Ethics*, ed. Walter Hooper (Grand Rapids: Eerdmans, 1970), 78. Recall too, as pointed out in the previous chapter, that both the concept as well as the use of the term "frame" itself were among the most popular denunciations raised in early critiques of Hume's essay from soon after its publication in 1748, as several writers comment in Stanley Tweyman, ed., *Hume on Miracles* (Bristol: Thoemmes, 1996). This argument is cited by authors Thomas Rutherford (27), William Adams (46–47, including using the word "frame"), William Rose (35–36, 66, 95), and James Somerville (128–29)—all writing between the years 1751 and 1767, except Somerville's slightly later essay in 1815.

[58] Swinburne, *Concept of Miracle*, 27–28; Swinburne, "Law of Nature," 80–81. In Lewis's essay "The Laws of Nature," he states that "*in the whole history of the universe, the laws of Nature have never produced a single event*" (77).

[59] Flew made some similar points about the "strength" of nature and her laws, such as: "Our only way of determining the capacities and the incapacities of Nature is to study what does in fact occur." See Flew, *God and Philosophy*, 153–54 (cited from 2005 edition). This statement would please many conservative defenders of miracles. It ought to be mentioned before leaving this point that the analogy of stronger and weaker scientific evidence is not always adequate. For instance, does a carefully and accurately weighed gram of paper clips rule out the strong likelihood of the Big Bang singularity?

their own domains. Thus, the question expressed in challenge 1:5 is a bit of a non sequitur unless one is choosing between contradictions, which is not the case here.[60]

Response 18

The notion that science by its very nature necessarily opposes miracles or that we are too modern to believe in these occurrences is a false dichotomy that must be abandoned. Famous comments such as those by German theologian Rudolf Bultmann may still be repeated: "It is impossible to use electric light and the wireless and to avail ourselves of modern medical and surgical discoveries, and at the same time to believe in the New Testament world of spirits and miracles." The same applies to Bultmann's lead comment on Jesus's resurrection: "But what of the resurrection? Is it not a mythical event pure and simple? Obviously, it is not an event of past history."[61]

Inductive studies require probabilistic conclusions. Openness even to supernatural events, miracles included, is needed. Science can no longer be used as a club that rules out miracles in an a priori manner.[62] Strictly speaking, science does not even answer the question of miracles. While science does not favor miracles, it does not forbid them either. So, we must beware of a priori dismissals of these or any events.

Response 19

The informal logical fallacy of division seems apparent in these objections here as well. In such cases, the fallacy occurs when a general law is applied to a specific case.[63]

---

[60] See the further explanation in response 18 directly below.

[61] Rudolf Bultmann, "New Testament and Mythology," in Bultmann et al., *Kerygma and Myth: A Theological Debate*, ed. Hans Werner Bartsch, trans. Reginald H. Fuller (New York: Harper & Row, 1961), with the quotations on 5 and 38, respectively.

[62] Three renowned physicists who constantly argued in their distinguished publications against these dogmatic theses of scientism were Sir John Polkinghorne (former professor of mathematical physics at Cambridge University), Stanley L. Jaki (former distinguished university professor at Seton Hall University, who delivered both the Fremantle Lectures at Oxford University and the Gifford Lectures at Edinburgh University), and Werner Schaaffs (professor of physics at Berlin Technical University). See Polkinghorne, *Quantum Physics and Theology: An Unexpected Kinship* (New Haven: Yale University Press, 2008); Jaki, *Miracles and Physics*; and Schaaffs, *Theology, Physics, and Miracles*, with the last two being cited above.

[63] Kegley and Kegley, *Introduction to Logic*, 151–52, 158; Copi, *Introduction to Logic*, 119–22.

Thus, whatever may be attributed generally to the sciences or to the individual sciences as a whole cannot necessarily be applied to separate topics or issues within these areas of study.

Response 20

While the resurrection argument indicates that miracles may be *possible*, additional worldview data can be introduced to show that the resurrection actually provides the best explanatory network into which to place the evidence for this event. Here event and interpretive structure could work together.[64]

Challenge 1:6—Is There a Dilemma or Even a Contradiction between There Being Strong Laws in Nature While Needing Real Exceptions to Them in the Case of Miracles?

It is charged, especially by Flew, that those who believe in miracles have the problem of needing to accept both the powerful laws of nature as well as actual exceptions to them. Without the former, miracles could not even be recognized as exceptions, hence Hume defining these events with relation to these laws. So, it is sometimes contended that there seems to be a contradiction here.[65]

Response 21

Proponents of miracles usually assert that there is no conflict whatsoever in having both adequate laws of nature along with real exceptions to them. There is no inherent problem here.[66] As David and Randall Basinger point out, counterinstances are

---

[64] For very specific details, see Gary R. Habermas, *The Risen Jesus and Future Hope* (Lanham, MD: Rowman & Littlefield, 2003), esp. chaps. 1–6.

[65] Flew, "Miracles," 5:347, 349, 352; Flew, "Neo-Humean Arguments," 49–50; Flew, "Introduction" to Hume, *Of Miracles*, 7–8; Flew, *God and Philosophy*, 148–49 (153 in 2005 edition); Flew, *Hume's Philosophy of Belief*, 202; Flew, "Miracle," in *A Dictionary of Philosophy*, rev. ed. (New York: St. Martin's, 1979), 234.

[66] Swinburne, "Law of Nature," 78–84; Swinburne, *Concept of Miracle*, 26–32; David Basinger, "Christian Theism and the Concept of Miracle," *Southern Journal of Philosophy* 18, no. 2 (1980): 139–40; McGrew and McGrew, "Argument from Miracles," 637–44, esp. 638, 641–42.

"perfectly compatible" with natural laws.[67] Even as a nonmiraculous illustration, space shuttles need to overcome the law of gravity and do so by a superior force, yet the laws are still operating before, during, and afterward.

Response 22

Evidence for a nonrepeatable event may indicate that such an occurrence may be a real exception to a properly operating law.[68] Some exceptional events may simply have adequate enough evidence to indicate that they occurred, and to deny this possibility would constitute an unwarranted rejection.[69]

Response 23

As C. S. Lewis explained, even though the cause of a miracle would be the hand of God, once it occurred, it would immediately be tied into the natural order, behaving from that time onward according to the normal laws. In Lewis's words, "Nature digests or assimilates this event with perfect ease."[70] So when the Gospels report that Jesus fed 5,000 people at once, seemingly with only some small loaves of bread and a very few fish, then everyone ate a normal meal as if a feast had just been prepared on the spot, no conflict exists here.

Response 24

This idea of a broken law would be more problematic with an outdated, Newtonian concept of natural law or something similar. However, the laws of nature are not unbreakable entities like some sort of crystal chalices that either impede or prevent events from happening. Rather, they may be viewed as statistical descriptions of what *generally* occurs.[71]

---

[67] Basinger and Basinger, *Philosophy and Miracle*, 13.

[68] Swinburne, "Law of Nature," 78–79; Swinburne, *Concept of Miracle*, 26–27.

[69] Dietl, "Of Miracles," 242–43.

[70] Lewis, *Miracles*, 60–63 (59–62 in the 1960 edition).

[71] Even Alastair McKinnon, who rejects the existence of miracles, makes this point in his essay, "'Miracle' and 'Paradox,'" *American Philosophical Quarterly* 4 (1967): 309. McKinnon's essay is also available in Swinburne, *Miracles*, 49–52. See Swinburne, "Introduction," and

Challenge 1:7—Do Miracles Violate the Principle of the Conservation of Energy?

For example, it is sometimes claimed that God's acting in the system of nature would introduce additional energy into the system, but that such a prospect would change the amount of energy which, according to scientific principles, should remain constant.[72] Many responses have been proposed to different aspects of the issue.

Response 25

One additional and thoughtful consideration is that miracles need not break or even impede the laws of nature at all. C. S. Lewis and Larmer provide the example of a female virgin having a fertilized egg implanted in her such that it leads to the birth of a baby nine months later, though she still remains a virgin. Likewise, God could do the implanting and never break one of his laws.[73] A potential natural example could be a *Voyager* space flight that appears to break the law of gravity, an event that is easily explained by the exertion of greater thrust as it leaves the earth's atmosphere, in a way like the frame objection mentioned above and elsewhere. But clearly, no natural law has been broken here, and in both instances nature carries on after the events.[74] For

---

"Laws of Nature," in *Miracles*, 3–4, 82–83, respectively; Swinburne, *Concept of Miracle*, 2–3, 30–32, respectively; Lewis, "Laws of Nature," 77.

[72] Though he strongly disputes this objection, Larmer still provides a detailed statement of it. See Robert A. Larmer, *The Legitimacy of Miracle* (Lanham, MD: Lexington, 2014), esp. 41–45, also 6, 51–52. One proponent listed by Larmer is William R. Stoeger, "Describing God's Action in the World in Light of Scientific Knowledge of Reality," in *Chaos and Complexity: Scientific Perspectives on Divine Action*, ed. Robert John Russell, Nancey Murphy, and Arthur R. Peacocke (Notre Dame: Notre Dame University Press, 1996), 244. Another proponent listed by Larmer is Evan Fales, *Divine Intervention: Metaphysical and Epistemological Puzzles* (New York: Routledge, 2010), 16, 98; Fales, "It Is Not Reasonable to Believe in Miracles," in *Debating Christian Theism*, ed. J. P. Moreland, Chad Meister, and Khaldoun A. Sweis (Oxford: Oxford University Press, 2013), 299–301.

[73] Lewis, *Miracles*, 60–61 (59 in the 1960 edition); Larmer, *Legitimacy of Miracle*, 39–40, 46.

[74] German physicist Werner Schaaffs also argues that no miracles break the laws of nature. See chap. 6 of Schaaffs, *Theology, Physics, and Miracles*, 27–30, cf. also 66. See also Schaaffs, *Christus und die physikalische Forschung* (Berghausen: Evangelisations-Verlag, 1969); Schaaffs, *Jesus, Meister der Natur* (Wuppertal: Brockhaus, 1971).

Lewis, miracles may interfere with nature, but we should not think of them as breaking nature's laws.[75]

Response 26

If the conservation of energy knows no exceptions, how do scientists explain the Big Bang? What about the deaths of some stars and the birth of new ones, black holes, or other such examples, for that matter? At the very least, the metaphysical form of the principle would appear to be at odds with certain known traits of the universe, providing serious issues for this scientific configuration. It seems as if too little is known about some of these particulars in the universe to answer such specifics.[76]

Response 27

For Fales and many others, the principle of conservation obtains in a closed universe.[77] But for Al Plantinga and many other scholars, God acting in our time-space world, along with other indications, indicate that the universe is open.[78] Hence there are more issues here that have to be addressed and detailed; miracles are far from a special concern.

Response 28

Larmer argues further that if there is strong evidence for miracles, then these data cannot be ruled out by the *scientific*, experimental evidence for the conservation of energy. Once again, this appears to be another apples-oranges application. Rather, it is the speculative *metaphysical* claims concerning this conservation principle that are the problem, even with the notion and the Big Bang itself. These are precisely the most difficult issues (as stated in response 26 immediately above), so the evidence for miracles will have to be disproven otherwise.[79]

---

[75] Lewis, *Miracles*, cf. 10, 47, 69 (5, 45–46, 59 in the 1960 edition).

[76] Larmer, *Legitimacy of Miracle*, 43.

[77] Fales, "It Is Not Reasonable," 299.

[78] Alvin Plantinga, *Where the Conflict Really Lies* (Oxford: Oxford University Press, 2011), 8–79, as cited by Larmer, *Legitimacy of Miracle*, 8–79. Cf. Schaaffs, *Theology, Physics, and Miracles*, 61–66.

[79] Larmer, *Legitimacy of Miracle*, esp. 42–46.

These more than two dozen responses were aimed at the first category of seven skeptical questions or objections to miracle claims, which were generally of the a priori sort. Each of these objections seemed to eventually pertain to whether or not there was adequate evidence in favor of the miracle claim. As explained at the outset, just as the criticisms are usually a priori, so are the responses. Therefore, very few evidential considerations were presented throughout either for the objections or for the miracle claims. Our focus so far, as in the rest of the chapter, has had to do with the conditions under which these occurrences may be impossible or possible.

Category 2: Questions concerning Accommodating Nature to a Miracle Claim

Continuing this same approach, the second of the four major categories mostly also consists of a priori objections to miracles. But rather than questioning the amount of evidence available on behalf of a potential miracle, as before, these challenges tend to ask whether a different configuration or view of nature's laws would help in denying these miracle claims.[80]

Challenge 2:1—Is there a difference between a miracle and a natural anomaly?

After all, strange things can and do happen.[81] So the skeptical strategy in each of the cases might be to "expand" the definition of the affected laws of nature in order to simply incorporate and explain seemingly miraculous events as natural occurrences.[82]

---

[80] It should be noted once again that the consecutive numbering of responses will be restarted at the beginning of each of the four categories, in order to provide a sense of the overall direction and strength of the available rejoinders vis-à-vis each species or group of objections.

[81] Nowell-Smith, "Miracles," 246; Basinger, "Christian Theism," 140.

[82] Hume, "Of Miracles," 212, 223; Nowell-Smith, "Miracles," 253; Antony Flew, "The Impossibility of the Miraculous," in *Hume's Philosophy of Religion: The Sixth James Montgomery Hester Seminar* (Winston-Salem: Wake Forest University Press, 1986), 22–23; Flew, *Hume's Philosophy of Belief*, 193, 199, 207; Flew, "Miracles," 5:349; Flew, *God and*

The chief idea behind these moves is apparently to note that since the totality of nature is not known, it is certainly possible that natural laws are more complicated than we previously thought, meaning that periodic expansions and reformulations of them are necessary. There are examples throughout history—such as the nature of eclipses during medieval times, tales of ice on lakes being explained in tropical areas where such had never been observed previously, and so on—where adjustments had to be made to our concepts of what is possible or impossible in nature. It is conceivable, even in modern times, that a different conception or angle on this or that law could place an event in an entirely new perspective. If nature's laws are expanded, perhaps these strange events could be recategorized as quite natural occurrences. But as with other objections to miracles from the natural side, the appropriateness of such natural explanations has likewise also been challenged by the defenders of miracles.

Before beginning the responses, an earlier point needs to be reiterated here. This response attempts to avoid one of the most crucial issues of all, namely, whether events that have occurred in space and time have actually *superseded* the laws of nature altogether, due to a greater power being exerted. If this were discovered to be the best explanation here, no amount of expanding the laws would help to produce the proper or accurate interpretation.[83]

Response 1

Perhaps more than with other critical responses entertained thus far, such a position certainly seems to be a textbook case not of an a priori *objection* but of an a priori *rejection* of miracles. The chief point here definitely seems to be that no matter how much evidence may be available on behalf of an event, the opponents have gone on record to interpret them in terms of natural occurrences if at all possible rather than to consider them as actual miracles.

Philosophy, 149–50, 155 (153, 159 in the 2005 edition); cf. Flew, "Introduction" to Hume, *Of Miracles*, 14–15; cf. also Basinger and Basinger, *Philosophy and Miracle*, 63–64.

[83] As per the "frame argument" of C. S. Lewis and others, which we have already explained in this and the previous chapter. See Lewis, *Miracles*, 106 (103 in the 1960 edition); Lewis, "Laws of Nature," 78. Note also the early critiques of Hume recorded in Tweyman, *Hume on Miracles*, with the specific articles already noted above.

Response 2

R. F. Holland charges that anomalies should not be considered the preferable explanations, even if the alternative is a miraculous occurrence. The evidence and explanation that best fit the situation at hand should be recognized and adopted. Holland
argues that miracle claims can be investigated like other events.[84]

Response 3

Swinburne helpfully suggests that miracles may exhibit certain characteristics that
indicate when they could actually be true interferences with the laws of nature rather
than simple anomalies to be somehow ignored. Such characteristics might include

- (1) being nonrepeatable events
- (2) being clearly counter to a known law of nature
- (3) being of a nature such that no known expansion of a law can explain the
      event naturally[85]

Response 4

As an extended example of the previous point (especially characteristic 3 listed above),
what can be concluded concerning nature's laws with regard to the resurrection of
Jesus? How would this move, as described above, help the critic's efforts? Would
the new, enlarged and expanded natural law hypothesize that dead men always stay
dead, unless their name is Jesus? The point here is that if Jesus were indeed the only
founder of a major world religion who is believed by his own followers to have been
raised literally from the dead,[86] and the relevant evidence for this event is impressive,

---

[84] Cf. R. F. Holland, "The Miraculous," in Donnelly, *Logical Analysis*, 225–32. (Holland's
essay is also included in Swinburne, *Miracles*, with this same argument on 56–66.) It was
originally published by the same name in the *American Philosophical Quarterly* 2 (1965):
43–51.

[85] Swinburne, "Law of Nature," 78–84; Swinburne, *Concept of Miracle*, 26–32; cf. also
Holland, "Miraculous," 232.

[86] For instance, see Stephen Neill, *Christian Faith and Other Faiths* (Downers Grove,
IL: InterVarsity, 1984), 284–87; cf. the earlier edition of this work, *Christian Faith and Other
Faiths: The Christian Dialogue with Other Religions*, 2nd ed. (Oxford: Oxford University
Press, 1970), 231–33.

can the new law regarding death be specifically crafted for his case alone? It would seem that virtually no one would think so! Continuing the a priori avoidance, some other path would clearly need to be taken by the critics in order to avoid this entire matter of Jesus's resurrection. It seems fair to say that this event alone would disprove this natural response. So, the critic is seemingly either pushed back to choose a viable naturalistic thesis or compelled to simply forget this second category altogether.

Response 5

Since it was argued in volume 1 of this study that historical events are not self-interpreting, it follows that additional worldview considerations are necessary to further identify the resurrection as a miracle performed by God in the context of the historical Jesus's life, death, and afterward. Such a worldview context could potentially provide the final indication that this event was not explainable as a freak occurrence or by expanding nature's laws. This is precisely because this move would indicate that the resurrection stood beyond the pale of nature itself due to its theistic context, as argued in volume 4 of this study.

Challenge 2:2—Can an event in nature be anything other than a natural event? [87]

This objection almost seems as if it is characterized by some sort of play on words. However, McKinnon apparently interprets the criticism in the strong sense of showing that true miracles are contradictory concepts. Since the laws of nature are descriptions of the way reality usually behaves rather than barriers to be transgressed, there are no such things as exceptions to them. [88]

A couple of additional issues are also applicable to this criticism that will not be numbered here since they were already utilized earlier within this second category of challenges. For example, Swinburne's characteristics of miracles (nonrepeatability, being counter to the laws of nature, along with the absence of a coherent explanation even if nature's laws were expanded) can still provide several important indications that an event is an actual counteroccurrence to nature. [89] Further, in McKinnon's

---

[87] McKinnon, "'Miracle' and 'Paradox,'" 309.
[88] McKinnon, "Miracle," in Swinburne, esp. 49–50.
[89] Swinburne, "Law of Nature," 78–84; see also Swinburne, *Concept of Miracle*, 26–32.

attempted reduction of the options here to just two, this objection appears to be another example of the "either-or" or "false dilemma" fallacy of informal logic already mentioned above, since there are certainly more than just these two alternatives.[90]

Response 6

Again, this position appears to have almost every earmark both of an *a priori rejection* of miracles as well as a circular argument that miracles never occur, for it seems to rule them out before the discussion ever gets started, regardless of the characteristics of the events in question. As Richard Purtill complains in his own critique, McKinnon tries "to cut off an interesting argument by definition."[91]

Response 7

For our purposes, of course, miracles *must* occur in nature if they are to happen at all. But simply because miracles may occur in nature, this would not somehow automatically baptize these events as normal, everyday circumstances. So this approach fails to answer the overarching causal question regarding the possible origins of Jesus's resurrection, which could still have come from God's hand and which nature could by no means produce. But as with recent arguments that favor signs of Intelligent Design, it will be argued later that Jesus's resurrection actually does manifest those sorts of otherworldly pointers.

Response 8

This question has only been pointed to hypothetically so far, but *if* this is a theistic universe, that would appear to be quite a strong prospective indication by itself that such a being could potentially produce miracles and has actually done so. Again, this is only a hypothetical a priori response, as are the vast majority of the critical questions, but it might be that if God exists, the resurrection would seem to be exactly the sort of event that only God could cause and would actually even *require* God's

---

[90] Kegley and Kegley, *Introduction to Logic*, 143, 157.

[91] Richard L. Purtill, "Defining Miracles," in Geivett and Habermas, *In Defense of Miracles*, 68.

attributes.[92] Actually, the existence of God plus the resurrection just might attract like magnets! But as has been mentioned throughout, no evidence is being produced by either side at this juncture.

Challenge 2:3—What if science discovers a naturalistic explanation in the future?[93]

It is often pointed out that the hallmark of science is discovery, including finding new explanations for previously unexplained phenomena. Tightening the point even further, David and Randall Basinger even prefer to include the words "permanently inexplicable" as part of their preferred definition and treatment of miracle.[94] Several counterpoints have been raised in response.

Response 9

Many or even most theories could be answered this way, including the theories of Galileo or Einstein. Granted, it is always possible that future scientific discoveries could definitely upset the scientific scene in a variety of ways. After all, it has happened frequently in the past. Yet that is not a sufficient reason to hold back from proclaiming something to be the case in the present, at least *until* that time. Without this ability to teach the current state of the data at present, human information would basically have to be continually couched in repeated, never-ending nuances, with expressions of the state of knowledge basically being held hostage. But we cannot simply suspend judgment on a majority of events and issues until adequate evidence is available upon which an informed decision may be made. For example, scientists did not fail to proclaim Newton's or Einstein's theses because they could be mistaken in the future.

---

[92] See W. David Beck, *Does God Exist? A History of Answers to the Question* (Downers Grove, IL: InterVarsity Academic, 2021); chap. 2 of Habermas, *Risen Jesus*.

[93] Malcolm L. Diamond, "Miracles," *Religious Studies* 9 (1973): 320–21; Nowell-Smith, "Miracles," 245–46, 251; Basinger, "Christian Theism," 140–41; Basinger and Basinger, *Philosophy and Miracle*, 15–16, 63–71.

[94] Basinger and Basinger, 15–23. David Basinger had already taken steps in this direction in "Christian Theism," 146–49.

Response 10

As Holland remarks, science regularly breaks new ground and will definitely add to our knowledge in many subjects. But it is a confusion to conclude that science regularly contradicts its well-established truths.[95]

Response 11

Swinburne makes the excellent point that even miracle claims are corrigible anyway, as is all scientific knowledge. It is all subject to future investigation.[96] So what keeps us from making the very best, probable decisions known to us at this present time? Besides, if a critical scholar issued a rejoinder sometime in the future, Christian scholars would be quick to respond to it anyway. Thus, it is very difficult to feel any force behind this objection, including Basinger's rider regarding permanent inexplicability. Believers would simply be doing what scholars in all of the inductive disciplines have done all along—do the best research possible and respond if and when new challenges occur.

Response 12

Some events (such as Jesus's resurrection) would seemingly never occur naturally, as far as we know.[97] While there have been obvious surprises through history, to assert the opposite in this case is to rely on tremendous improbabilities.[98] Few laws of nature seem more secure than the fact that fully dead men do not rise.[99] As was observed in the initial volume of this study, this event (1) is accompanied by very good evidence, (2) is without viable counterhypotheses (see also this volume), (3) has been well established for centuries, and (4) is also backed by strong worldview considerations.[100]

---

[95] Holland, "Miraculous," 231.

[96] Swinburne, "Law of Nature," 83–84; also, Swinburne, *Concept of Miracle*, 31–32.

[97] Jensen, "Logic of Miracles," 146.

[98] Purtill, "Proofs of Miracles," 48.

[99] Swinburne, "Law of Nature," 83–84; also, Swinburne, *Concept of Miracle*, 31–32.

[100] Many years ago, I arrived at a quite similar demarcation of what our surest facts might look like. See Gary R. Habermas, *The Historical Jesus: Ancient Evidence for the Life of Christ* (Joplin, MO: College Press, 1996), 263.

As we have already noted several times, worldview data provide an additional, excellent, and necessary framework for predominantly historical arguments. In other words, they fit together well. In sum, the overall case for the resurrection is best seen as being a *super*natural event with further considerations in its favor, completing the overall case.

A dozen different responses were directed at the three generally a priori challenges related to the second category of skeptical rejections of miracle claims, namely, to charges that the laws of nature themselves might somehow be adjusted or viewed differently in order to allow the status of seemingly miraculous events to instead be viewed as perhaps somewhat special but still natural occurrences. Each of these objections pertained to whether or not the miracle claim could be stated in terms that were unaffected by the suggestions concerning the laws of nature.

The third and final philosophical category of challenges to the belief in miraculous occurrences is that there are no distinguishing markers on these events that identify their origin.[101] In many ways, some of those in this group are the toughest questions of all. We are not so much concerned in this grouping with the actual evidence on behalf of miracles or with their relation to the laws of nature. Rather, the major focal point of these issues has to do with various worldview and epistemic aspects related to miracle claims. Since historical events need interpretive paradigms, as we have mentioned many times, some of these challenges inquire regarding what sorts of adjustments might have to be made in light of the search for a meaningful worldview structure for these events.

Category 3: Identifying an Event as an Act of God

Some scholars have considered this species of objection as perhaps the chief angle for theists to address. The main idea is that, even if a true miracle really occurred, it could never be known for sure that it was an event that was actually performed by God. Or again, how is God's potential activity in the world to be discovered? Several varieties of this objection will be considered here.

Challenge 3:1—How can any event ever be identified as an actual miracle?

Even if a true miracle really occurred, it could never be known for sure that it was an event that was actually performed by God. We do not possess the requisite tools to

---

[101] A fourth historical category of objections is also introduced later in this chapter.

recognize, measure, or identify the presence of a divine cause, even if a miracle was directly in front of us and it (metaphorically of course!) hit us right between the eyes.[102] In the words of Flew, "The crunch comes over the problem of identification."[103] Think of it this way: there are no such things as identification labels stuck on events that read, "Performed by God" or "Made in Heaven."

This objection does raise some tough and thoughtful questions. Another way to look at the "freak event of nature" objection in the previous category is this: unless we knew for sure that a divine author performed a particular event, what knowledge would allow us to assert that God did it, or that it was part of a particular heavenly plan? Somehow, we have to have a clear argument that connects the event to the hand of God—a sort of bridge between the occurrence and its cause. Many scholars have suggested a host of ways to engineer such a connecting path.

Response 1

Some scholars have attempted to construct evidential routes across the bridge. Various examples include Holland's suggestion that by studying the data as best we can, we may judge a miracle claim by the same criteria used in ascertaining the facticity of other historical events.[104] Geisler argues first from the existence of God to the reality of actual miracles performed by God.[105] Dietl proposes utilizing randomizing processes and predictions to recognize present-day miracles.[106]

Response 2

Other scholars have tried to build larger worldview connections across the bridge between miracle claims and the overall landscape. Even Basinger admits that a

---

[102] Nowell-Smith, "Miracles," 245–46, 251; Flew, "Miracles," 5:347; Flew, *God and Philosophy*, 144–45, 149–50 (150, 153–54 in the 2005 edition); Basinger, "Christian Theism," 139–49.

[103] Flew, *God and Philosophy*, 149 (153 in 2005 edition). Flew affirms this position on behalf of Hume too; see *Hume's Philosophy of Belief*, 202.

[104] Holland, Miraculous," 225–27.

[105] Norman L. Geisler, *Miracles and the Modern Mind: A Defense of Biblical Miracles* (Grand Rapids: Baker, 1992), esp. chaps. 5 and 11. For a more succinct case, see Geisler, "Miracles and the Modern Mind," in Geivett and Habermas, *In Defense of Miracles*, 73–85.

[106] Dietl, "On Miracles," 238.

miracle may be identified as "probable" if it fulfills a "divine action pattern." He then provides details as to what this might look like, though the conclusion is not epistemically certain.[107] Jensen emphasizes Jesus's predictions of his resurrection mixed with others of his special claims.[108] John W. Montgomery, Grace Jantzen, Douglas Erlandson, and Tan Tei Wei also suggest paths regarding linking miracle claims to a worldview scenario.[109]

Response 3

This project argues for the usefulness of both of these initial avenues. The first approach argues from God to the resurrection as a divine event since the occurrence actually requires God's attributes (termed the *prospective argument*). The second route combines a number of Jesus's claims and actions with his resurrection for further validation of his teachings, pointing back to the originating cause of this monumental event with God (termed the *retrospective argument*). It is argued that both of these bridges independently categorize the resurrection as an event performed by God, thus allowing for its identification as an actual miracle.[110] In many places in these four volumes, I argue for portions of this twofold approach, with the chief and most detailed treatment coming in volume 4.

Challenge 3:2—Isn't it circular to use the Bible to establish a miracle?

Believers cannot argue circularly from Scripture to indicate that Jesus's miracles occurred, and then use those miracles to argue back that Scripture is God's

---

[107] Basinger, "Christian Theism,"142–45; cf. Basinger and Basinger, *Philosophy and Miracle*, 89–90, 100.

[108] Jensen, "Logic of Miracles," 146–47.

[109] In a chapter section entitled "The Validation of the Christian World-View," John Warwick Montgomery maps out a six-step scenario for his bridge. See his *The Shape of the Past: A Christian Response to Secular Philosophies of History* (Minneapolis: Bethany, 1975), 138–45. This approach is mapped out more briefly in Montgomery, *Where Is History Going? Essays in Support of the Historical Truth of the Christian Revelation* (Grand Rapids: Zondervan, 1969), 35–36; Grace M. Jantzen, "Hume on Miracles, History, and Politics," *Christian Scholar's Review* 8 (1979): 325; Douglas K. Erlandson, "A New Look at Miracles," *Religious Studies* 13 (1977): 425; Tan Tei Wei, "Recent Discussions on Miracles," *Sophia* 11 (1972): 24.

[110] See chaps. 1–6 of Habermas, *Risen Jesus*, for the heart of the two arguments.

revelation.[111] As has been remarked often, other criteria are necessary to break this circular argument and judge when a miracle has occurred.

Flew thinks it is too frequently forgotten or even "ignored almost universally" that the second half of Hume's essay is particularly aimed at the charge that "a miracle can never be proved, so as to be the foundation of a system of religion."[112] It might also be added here that this concern often raised by Flew has been addressed elsewhere. Actually, Flew's critique here is freely acknowledged and admitted in some fashion by many if not most Christian philosophers and theologians. It is strange, however, that the particulars of this concern are almost never spelled out or detailed in these critiques beyond the comment itself. Of which *specific* transgressions are Christian arguments guilty?

Response 4

Independent arguments for the general reliability or trustworthiness of the Gospel texts, as well as more specific and perhaps even stronger approaches consisting of many defenses of specific, critically ascertained passages that may be used in building one's case, could break the circular nature of this argument and provide a stronger basis for using at least these individual texts to address the miracle accounts mentioned in them.[113]

---

[111] Flew makes this assertion concerning Hume's essay in Flew, *Hume's Philosophy of Belief*, 202. Note also that Flew himself agrees on this matter in Flew, "Miracles," 5:348–49.

[112] See the examples given in Flew, *Hume's Philosophy of Belief*, 173, 178, 181, 183, 188, 190, 193, 199.

[113] Defenses of specific New Testament passages can be found in individual journal articles and commentaries or in other specialized literature. For some examples of overview volumes on the general reliability of the Gospels or of the New Testament as a whole, see Richard Bauckham, *Jesus and the Eyewitnesses: The Gospels as Eyewitness Testimony*, 2nd ed. (Grand Rapids: Eerdmans, 2017); James D. G. Dunn, *Jesus Remembered*, vol. 1 of *Christianity in the Making* (Grand Rapids: Eerdmans, 2003); Birger Gerhardsson, *Reliability of the Gospel Tradition* (Grand Rapids: Baker Academic, 2001); Craig L. Blomberg, *The Historical Reliability of the New Testament: Countering the Challenges to Evangelical Christian Beliefs* (Nashville: B&H Academic, 2016); Steven B. Cowan and Terry L. Wilder, eds., *In Defense of the Bible: A Comprehensive Apologetic for the Authority of Scripture* (Nashville: B&H Academic, 2013); Michael R. Licona, *Why Are There Differences in the Gospels? What We Can Learn from Ancient Biography* (Oxford: Oxford University Press, 2017); Craig A. Evans, *Jesus and the Manuscripts: What We Can Learn from the Oldest Texts* (Peabody, MA: Hendrickson, 2021); Paul Barnett, *Is the New Testament Reliable? A Look at the New*

Response 5

The minimal facts approach primarily used in these volumes seeks to establish the resurrection of Jesus or other truths totally apart from the inspiration or even the reliability of Scripture, building upon a lesser number of well-established and almost unanimously accepted historical facts. By this argument, even an *unreliable* New Testament text would not impede a decisive argument that could ascertain the occurrence of the resurrection or other key events.[114]

Response 6

We have said and will continue to say often that the presence of broader worldview concerns beyond the empirical data itself also provides additional criteria for identifying certain events, such as Jesus's resurrection, as a miracle and moves beyond this conclusion to provide a grounding for Jesus's Christian theism as well. This challenge remains an a priori concern, so only this initial response has been provided. It will be dealt with at great length in later chapters. But for now, these responses seem more than sufficient to address the willingness to answer the concerns of Hume, Flew, and any others who share it, as well as to indicate directions that may be pursued.

Response 7

If some of the modern miracle claims are established among the dozens that are cited with confirmation, such a case would strengthen significantly the Christian theistic

---

Testament Evidence (Downers Grove, IL: InterVarsity, 1986); A. N. Sherwin-White, *Roman Society and Roman Law in the New Testament* (Oxford: Oxford University Press, 1963), esp. lecture 8; Gary R. Habermas, "Recent Perspectives on the Reliability of the Gospels," *Christian Research Journal* 28 (2005): 22–31. Although quite outdated, the old classic by F. F. Bruce is still valuable; see Bruce, *The New Testament Documents: Are They Reliable?* (Grand Rapids: Eerdmans, 1960). For a couple of the general works that treat particular textual issues, see Gleason L. Archer, *New International Encyclopedia of Bible Difficulties* (Grand Rapids: Zondervan, 1982); Norman L. Geisler and Thomas Howe, *When Critics Ask: A Popular Handbook on Bible Difficulties* (Wheaton, IL: Victor, 1992).

[114] For details on the method, see Gary R. Habermas, "The Minimal Facts Approach to the Resurrection of Jesus: The Role of Methodology as a Crucial Component in Establishing Historicity," *Southeastern Theological Review* 3 (2012): 15–26. For specifics on the factual argument itself, see chap. 1 of Habermas, *Risen Jesus*.

position. Further, such would be done totally apart from discussions over circular arguments concerning the use of the New Testament.

Challenge 3:3—Do the alleged miracles in other religions cancel one another?

Various religions and philosophical perspectives also claim their own miracles. These events would then presumably conflict with each other, even as the various teachings behind the events likewise conflict with one another. In this manner, the different traditions cancel out the others.

As Flew describes it, "[Hume] is urging that against any evidence for a miracle in any one religion must be offset all evidence for all miracles alleged in support of all the rest." However, slightly later, Flew adds a conditional caveat that these conflicts must occur under the right conditions: "For the fact, if it be a fact, that all religious systems are both mutually incompatible and committed to denying the occurrence of any miracles under auspices other than their own," it must be the case that they are truly contrary to each other, for it is at least possible that miracles in different systems could still be both recognized and accepted.[115]

Response 8

This objection was responded to at length in the prior chapter but will still be addressed here. This entire objection is severely misplaced for a variety of reasons. If scholars are correct that no other religions have credible evidence for their own miracle claims, especially in the form of both early and eyewitness testimony, then there is nothing with which to oppose the potential evidence for any Christian miracle claims. The latter, on the other hand, are both well evidenced and exceptionally early. For apart from reliable evidence for other religious miracles, there are only the mere claims themselves. If this is the case, then the lack of evidence for alternative miracle claims in other religions is hardly on the same footing as Christian miracle claims *if* the latter claims are evidenced, and so the former cannot truly oppose the latter on these grounds. After all, unsupported or poorly evidenced

---

[115] This is Hume's fourth subpoint in his essay "Of Miracles," part 2 (217–218); Flew, *Hume's Philosophy of Belief*, 180–181, with the quotations on 181; also, Nowell-Smith, "Miracles," in Flew and MacIntyre, eds., *New Essays in Philosophical Theology*, 245.

"miracles" cannot rule out the possibility of any verified or actual miracle claims, should these be the case.

Flew even appears to agree here. Continuing soon after his two quotations cited in the previous footnote, Flew explains that Hume's fourth subpoint assumes and even requires that there be "strong evidence for miracles under the auspices of at least two incompatible systems of revelation" and possibly even three such evidenced examples. Otherwise, there is no "clash" between the events in question and the critique fails to materialize.[116]

For example, ancient historian Edwin Yamauchi asserts that there are no rival non-Christian miracle claims that are early, non-legendary, reported in ancient sources, and attributed to the founders of other major religions or philosophies. Only Christianity includes this sort of data.[117] If Yamauchi's comment is correct, Christianity would have a huge head start here. Since historical evidence is almost always crucial to make a case for miracles, those belief systems that deny, disregard, or downplay history would certainly seem to be at a mighty disadvantage on this subject. But this neglect of historical matters is what we find even from non-Christian and skeptical commentators.[118] As stated so often, it is a matter of the evidence. But in historical terms, Christianity would seem to have no rivals here.

Especially in a comparative context, the use of evidence on more than one front is necessary. As eminent world religions expert Geoffrey Parrinder points out, "Whether a religion is true or false could, at best, only be decided after full study of

---

[116] Flew, *Hume's Philosophy of Belief*, 183.

[117] Edwin M. Yamauchi, *Jesus, Zoroaster, Buddha, Socrates, Muhammad*, rev. ed. (Downers Grove, IL: InterVarsity, 1972), 40, cf. 20.

[118] For a number of examples, see David Levinson, *Religion: A Cross-Cultural Dictionary* (Oxford: Oxford University Press, 1996); S. A. Nigosian, *World Religions: A Historical Approach*, 3rd ed. (Boston: Bedford St. Martin's, 2000); and esp. Edward Conze, trans. and ed., *Buddhist Scriptures* (London: Penguin, 1959), 11–12, 34; A. C. Bhaktivedanta Swami Prabhupāda, "Preface," in *Bhagavad-Gītā as It Is*, rev. ed. (Los Angeles: Bhaktivedanta Book Trust, 1983); Lao Tzu, *Tao Teh King: Interpreted as Nature and Intelligence*, ed. Archie J. Bahm, 2nd ed. (Albuquerque, NM: World, 1986); James E. Ketelaar, "The Non-modern Confronts the Modern: Dating the Buddha in Japan," *History and Theory* 45 (2006): 132–49; Nirad C. Chaudhuri, *Hinduism: A Religion to Live by* (Oxford: Oxford University Press, 1979); Robert Ernest Hume, "An Outline of the Philosophy of the Upanishads," in *The Thirteen Principal Upanishads Translated from the Sanskrit*, ed. Robert Ernest Hume, 2nd ed. (Oxford: Oxford University Press, 1931); John A. T. Robinson, *Truth Is Two-Eyed* (Philadelphia: Westminster, 1979).

all its doctrines and practices, and not by dogmatic assertion without examination. By this standard many theologians have failed in their duty to examine the evidence."[119] This is an approach that also will be treated in a later volume of this study.

Response 9

For the purposes of this critique, consider only the *unevidenced* religious views. As far as Hume's notion that the various teachings of different religions oppose each other, even in a case where there exists no strong evidence on behalf of any of the particular religious belief systems, Hume's critique still hardly applies. So if there are only different, ungrounded views clamoring for the spotlight, then this situation is definitely moot, as Parrinder notes. If the views under consideration are all equally fideistic, then such teachings are unable to "cancel" the truth of any other beliefs. But to reinsert response 8 here, if only a single religious system's miracles are backed by strong evidence while all the others are not, those holding to the latter unevidenced belief systems cannot protest, for they have no support for their doctrines or claims.

Response 10

Further, since historical events as a whole (including any potential miracle claims) are not self-interpreting, which miracles are linked more closely to worldview factors and other propositional claims? No other religion exceeds Christianity in this regard either.[120] For some examples, Jensen asks which miracle claims evidence greater power.[121] Jensen also proposes a moral test: Are evil or immoral ends claimed to be the purpose behind the events in question? Or does another option fit the data more closely?[122] Purtill points out that actual miracles in other belief systems can actually be compatible with the Christian message, such as still being caused by God (or other powers) and fulfilling God's own purposes. Hence, from this angle as well, there is once again no necessary reason why such events and teachings must be opposed to each other.[123]

---

[119] Geoffrey Parrinder, *Comparative Religion* (Westport, CT: Greenwood, 1962), 56.
[120] Purtill, "Proofs of Miracles," 47.
[121] Jensen, "Logic of Miracles," 151.
[122] Jensen, 151.
[123] Purtill, "Proofs of Miracles," 45.

Challenge 3:4—Can a single miracle establish a religious worldview?

Historical evidence alone for the miracle claim is too ambiguous—we need an interpretive system to accompany the event. Since miracles have never been shown to be probable, among other issues such as the ones pointed out in this chapter, they cannot establish a system of religion.[124]

Response 11

We have already seen that this charge is also fully and widely admitted by Christian apologists.[125] While Hume and Flew think that Christian scholars have not established the necessary arguments here, Christian scholars would object strongly to those assertions. To that end, different Christian researchers have proposed a variety of ways to anchor a miracle claim to just such an interpretive system. Swinburne and Geisler are two of the many who offer specific examples.[126] So nothing remains here except to develop just such a system, including the appropriate connections to the events in question. Amazingly, Flew apparently even admits more than once that if the theists can actually establish their claims here, then they could potentially ground and authenticate their revelatory system.[127]

Challenge 3:5—Isn't any naturalistic theory more likely than a miracle?

Some scholars say that *any* fact is more likely than a miracle. On this view, a naturalistic alternative theory is *always* more likely than a miraculous event such as Jesus's resurrection from the dead.[128]

---

[124] Hume, "Of Miracles," 222–23; Flew, "Miracles," 5:348, 353; Flew, *God and Philosophy*, 145, 152 (150, 156 in 2005 edition); Flew, *Hume's Philosophy of Religion*, 21.

[125] Jensen, "Logic of Miracles," 146–48; Holland, "Miraculous," 231; Purtill, "Proofs of Miracles," 44; Geisler, *Miracles and the Modern Mind*, chap. 5; Winfried Corduan, "Recognizing a Miracle," in Geivett and Habermas, *In Defense of Miracles*, 105–11.

[126] See especially Richard Swinburne, *The Coherence of Theism*, rev. ed. (Oxford: Clarendon, 1993); cf. also Swinburne, *The Existence of God*, rev. ed. (Oxford: Clarendon, 1991); Geisler, *Miracles and the Modern Mind*, chap. 5.

[127] Flew, *God and Philosophy*, 152 (156 in 2005 edition); also, Flew, "Head-to-Head: Habermas-Flew," in Habermas and Flew, *Resurrection Debate*, 49–50.

[128] This is probably the best way to take Hume's comments in "Of Miracles" that it is far more likely that the person reporting the miracle "should either deceive or be

Beginning with a couple of briefly stated though unnumbered repeat critiques, this objection surely appears to be a very thinly disguised a priori denial, whereby certain events are rejected without having their day in court. On this view, there is no need to study or even view the issue of the resurrection because the conclusion has been prejudged. That *any* natural theory, no matter how poor, is held to be more likely than the resurrection shows the degree and depth of this a priori rejection. It is naturalism that is additionally judged (and assumed) to be true here while theism is scoffed at, often also a priori, and this in spite of naturalism's severe lack of any positive arguments capable of indicating that it is true, along with many other signs to the contrary.[129]

Moreover, the frequently stated criticism already mentioned several times by a few commentators is that this naturalistic outlook at least needs to entertain the possibility that God could have acted in history by a superior authority since at that precise moment or moments that power may have been greater than nature's laws. This consideration almost by itself could change the discussion.

Response 12

It was mentioned earlier that critical scholars could always choose the naturalistic hypothesis that best supports their views. However, the alternative theses that have

---

deceived" (212), as well as his later, similar comment (226). Critical scholars such as Bart D. Ehrman repeat comments like this quite frequently; see Ehrman, *The New Testament: A Historical Introduction to the Early Christian Writings*, 2nd ed. (Oxford: Oxford University Press, 2000), 208–12, esp. 211–12; also, Ehrman, *How Jesus Became God: The Exaltation of a Jewish Preacher from Galilee* (New York: HarperCollins, 2014), 164–65.

[129] Naturalists, materialists, and other fellows should be asked what sorts of evidences indicate the probability of *their* view. For three very careful treatments of this subject, see Stephen E. Parrish, *Atheism? A Critical Analysis* (Eugene, OR: Wipf & Stock, 2019); Stewart Goetz and Charles Taliaferro, *Naturalism* (Grand Rapids: Eerdmans, 2008); J. P. Moreland, *Scientism and Secularism* (Wheaton, IL: Crossway, 2018). Infamous atheist/agnostic philosopher Bertrand Russell stated, "I do not pretend to be able to prove that there is no God. . . . The Christian God may exist" along with the other gods of Olympus, Egypt, or Babylon. See Russell, *Why I Am Not a Christian* (London: Allen & Unwin, 1957), 44. Russell also commented when asked about God, "I don't think it's certain that there is no such thing. . . . I can't prove they [the other gods too] don't. . . . I think they are a bare possibility." See the interview by Woodrow Wyatt in *Bertrand Russell Speaks His Mind* (New York: Avon, 1960), 20.

been proposed are usually so unlikely that scholarly critics will often refuse to choose one, even in a debate. Perhaps the desire is not to be "locked in a corner" by the refutations, including the idea that another thesis should have been chosen instead. These examples may reveal something crucial.

But critics may retort that, as bad as a particular naturalistic option may be, even the worst one is more likely to have occurred than a miracle, which is far less likely still—once again assuming naturalism. This chapter contains many retorts and several different lines of reasoning for each of the potential theses. Plus, it will be argued in later chapters of this volume that there is much evidence to be brought into the discussion to back up the resurrection, such as worthwhile arguments for God's existence; additional data from Jesus's personal ethics; the fact that even critical New Testament scholars almost always recognize that Jesus was a healer (see volume 1); the fact that Jesus most likely predicted his death, resurrection, and exaltation ahead of time; and contemporary medically documented miracle claims and near-death experiences, among others. God's actions could be shown to be the more likely cause at this point. Most of these topics are discussed throughout this study.

Challenge 3:6—How would a miracle worker be identified?

Given the necessary connection between a potentially miraculous event and the need for an accompanying interpretive system or worldview, should anyone who comes along and claims to perform a miracle or some odd, inexplicable event, and then also claims to be God, deserve to be called divine and perhaps even be worshiped?[130]

Response 13

Perhaps surprising to some, Jewish and Christian teachings do not deny the reality of similar scenarios (of course, minus the worship and claims to be God). There are many warnings throughout the Old and New Testaments to *expect* miracles, prophecies, exorcisms, or other strange phenomena produced by both believers and unbelievers, including some who would falsely claim to be the Messiah.

---

[130] Stephen J. Wykstra, "The Problem of Miracle in the Apologetic from History," *Journal of the American Scientific Affiliation* 30 (1978): 157; cf. also Jensen, "Logic of Miracles," 148.

The false prophets and teachers were to be distinguished from the true ones by whether the messages of the former agreed with those of the latter who had preceded them (Deut 13:1–5) or if they agreed with Jesus himself (Matt 24:4–5, 11). There was also an empirical test to administer as to whether the prophecies of the former really occurred as they had been predicted (Deut 18:20–22).

Other possible options also exist. These supernatural manifestations could consist of genuine acts of God among unbelievers, or they might be occultic, magical, or other counterfeit manifestations meant to deceive. These phenomena are reported in Scripture, including the episodes involving Abimelech, the Egyptian magicians before Moses, Balaam, Naaman, the witch of Endor, Nebuchadnezzar, Simon the sorcerer, and the unnamed slave girl who followed Paul and Barnabas. Strong and specific warnings are also issued against getting involved with supernatural teachings and phenomena that are not of God. But there is no need for Christians to think that they need to always deny these phenomena.

Response 14

It must be clarified that the subject here is that of someone performing one or more seemingly miraculous events rather than simply producing some interesting phenomena perhaps more likely in the category of magic, illusion, or anything else that appears to be initially unexplainable. These are much easier comparisons and should not count in the manner described in the challenge above.

Response 15

Does the person in question also make actual, serious claims to be God or divine? Without this second condition, there are definitely no grounds for a divine identification or for worship. Parallels to these direct claims to deity are much less plentiful in the historical religions.[131]

Response 16

If these events in question can be repeated under certain circumstances, the more appropriate response, as mentioned above, would be to count them as natural events.

---

[131] This last point is discussed in much detail in volume 3 of this study.

For instance, ESP (extrasensory perception) or bending spoons by touch has been duplicated. Researcher D. Scott Rogo contends that there are major differences between true miracles and phenomena like ESP, mind-over-matter tests, and so on, which can be repeated regularly.[132] As Swinburne notes, "But if we have good reason to believe that . . . similar events would occur in similar circumstances, then undoubtedly we have good reason to believe that the formulae which we previously believed to be the laws of nature were not in fact such laws."[133]

Response 17

Misses or mistakes such as incorrect prophecies, faked healings, or other similar phenomena would also count very heavily against these actions as well as the corresponding claims being made (see Deut 18:20–22). For example, it was reported that a survey of three popular astrologers indicated that the *best* score achieved among them was getting just twelve predictions correct in thirty attempts! The lowest score was only four hits out of thirty attempts![134] Another article reported that one of the very best-known astrologers in the world was incorrect about 35 percent of the time.[135] This is highly relevant information with regard to this question.

Response 18

Other helpful tests may also be applied in these cases. Jensen makes a number of very pertinent and helpful suggestions: often, overall "fitness" is lacking in these alternative accounts, a term that typically applies to the coherence of the scenario. For example, even if something noteworthy is more or less on record for an individual, perhaps the person fails in other regards, such as by exhibiting moral lapses. Moreover, these accounts are often not backed or accompanied by well-expressed or well-developed worldview systems.

Another issue might pertain to which miracle claims actually exhibit a *greater power*, as in the Old Testament cases of the prophets of Baal being trumped by Elijah

---

[132] D. Scott Rogo, *Parapsychology: A Century of Inquiry* (New York: Dell, 1975), 33–36.

[133] Swinburne, "Law of Nature," 79; Swinburne, *Concept of Miracle*, 26.

[134] No author, "Do You Believe in Astrology?," *Saturday Evening Post*, January/February 1974; reprinted in *The Reader's Digest*, May 1974, 211–16.

[135] Roy B. Zuck, "What's Wrong with Astrology?," *Moody Monthly* (November 1968), 40.

or the inability of Pharaoh's magicians to compete with Moses. Even beyond inquiring as to the greater power, *what sort* of power is being manifest? Or perhaps a moral
test is applicable to these cases? In such circumstances, the question might be what a
miracle or prophecy is supposed to signify or point toward. Does it lead to ungodly
scenarios such as killing those who disagree with the message, like the apocalyptic
vision in Rev 13:1–15 where miraculous signs are followed by the murder of all who
refuse to worship the person?[136]

Response 19

If every one of the pertinent conditions obtained, then the entire situation would have
to be reclarified and reevaluated much more carefully. But as the issue stands here, the
original challenge is far too hypothetical. Is there even a single, clear candidate for
this combination of necessary and crucial traits? If so, where are these straightforward
cases that have actually happened, as far as has been ascertained, rather than merely
supposed?

Response 20

As we have already noted, the Christian message is accompanied and surrounded by
the most sophisticated worldview scenario of all the world's religious messages.[137] It
will be argued in this study that Jesus's resurrection (complete with a new body) is
the most unique and nonreplicable miracle in human history, and that Jesus's claims
are also utterly unique. This combination of an entirely unique event, along with
an equally unique accompanying message, plus the accompanying worldview, is not
found anywhere else among the world's religions and philosophies.[138] In fact, nothing

---

[136] Jensen, "Logic of Miracles," 148, 151.

[137] For a different sort of argument indicating that no other worldview even comes
close to Christianity in terms of evidence and explanatory power, see Kenneth Samples,
Seven Truths That Changed the World: Discovering Christianity's Most Dangerous Ideas
(Grand Rapids: Baker, 2012). Cf. also J. N. D. Anderson, *Christianity and Comparative
Religion* (Downers Grove, IL: InterVarsity, 1970), particularly chaps. 2–4, or the updated
version by Anderson, *Christianity and World Religions: The Challenge of Pluralism* (Leicester:
InterVarsity, 1984).

[138] These are among the major points argued in the volumes in the previous footnote
by Samples and Anderson, among other major studies.

even comes close to it. If we are right, the result will be that Jesus's theistic worldview will be validated.[139]

Challenge 3:6—Why not prefer an alternative, "natural miracle" such as mass hallucinations rather than an actual time-space resurrection from the dead?[140]

As Wykstra states, "natural miracles" are always more likely to occur than the literal actions of God in history.[141] To this critical response, an excited believer might proclaim triumphantly, "But there's no such thing as mass hallucinations!"[142] But the astute skeptic who may have been waiting for just such a retort might respond, "Perhaps so, my friend, but real resurrections do not occur either!"

Response 21

This proposal appears to conceal a strong a priori dismissal, prejudice, or rejection of the miraculous. But there are additional notes here beyond other mentions of this critique elsewhere in this chapter. In the head-to-head comparison above, if a mass hallucination is always preferred, then a true miracle would probably never be entertained or admitted under any circumstances, since some similar option could always be proposed, hence the prejudice. In these discussions, miracles are always the very last option, and perhaps that should be so. But the point is that this critique assumes the truth of naturalism or a similar view. But as has been countered here, this supposition is far from established, especially in today's world of highly evidenced near-death experiences, for just one example.

---

[139] It must be remembered that the discussions here regarding both the objections to miracles as well as the potential responses have been carried out in an a priori manner, where neither side is required to produce its reasons or evidences as of yet.

[140] Though Hume did not state it exactly this way, it is quite reminiscent of his comments, such as in "Of Miracles," 212. Flew is probably most responsible for asking this creative question explicitly; see "Miracles," 5:346–53; cf. Jensen, "Logic of Miracles," 149.

[141] Wykstra, "Problem of Miracle," 154–63.

[142] By the way, Flew himself was willing to admit that mass hallucinations do not occur: "I have always understood that mass or collective hallucinations cannot really happen." See Habermas and Flew, *Resurrection Debate*, 86–87, cf. 52.

Response 22

Alternative, "natural miracles" are always the more likely option for anyone who assumes that naturalism is the proper worldview, as just noted. But if the God of Christian theism exists, the possibility of miracles would receive a huge "boost." In the latter case, miracles would not necessarily be rare at all—they might have occurred thousands of times throughout world history. As Flew even admits, given some key beliefs about God, "the occurrence of the resurrection does become enormously more likely."[143]

Thus, it needs to be determined which worldview is ultimately correct. Why do naturalists—who frequently just assume via their viewpoint that *virtually any event* is more likely than a miracle, as this challenge definitely does—not begin by first establishing their own naturalistic worldview? For a position that so often goes on the offensive against religious views, naturalists should also be challenged to supply well-evidenced reasons that establish their own perspective!

Response 23

Onetime natural miracles are one thing. However, *repeated* natural miracles, especially when each of the scenarios so strongly sidesteps the known data, are much less likely. A couple of examples may be helpful.

For starters, group hallucinations of any sort are opposed strongly by the psychological, medical, and other relevant evidence against such hypotheses, such as these phenomena never being clearly observed in the professional literature.[144] In the case of Jesus's disciples, further data militating against such hallucinations would include that these experiences occurred too many times before too many persons at distinctly

---

[143] Flew, in Habermas and Flew, 39, cf. also 3.

[144] Licensed clinical psychologist Gary Sibcy, PhD, attested in private correspondence (March 10, 2009): "I have surveyed the professional literature (peer-reviewed journal articles and books) written by psychologists, psychiatrists, and other relevant healthcare professionals during the past two decades and have yet to find a single documented case of a group hallucination, that is, an event for which more than one person purportedly shared in a visual or other sensory perception where there was clearly no external referent." Physician Joseph Bergeron discovered the same result in a comprehensive data base search of the Pubmed and American Psychological Association websites; see Gary R. Habermas, "The Resurrection of Jesus: A Clinical Review of Psychiatric Hypotheses for the Biblical Story of Easter," *Irish Theological Quarterly* 80 (2015): esp. 162.

different places and times. Additional evidence that favors the empty tomb is the failure to account for the disciples' lifelong transformations in the cases where that information is available, such as Saul the persecutor's "hallucination" and James the unbelieving brother of Jesus's "hallucination" when neither one desired to observe the risen Jesus, along with many other issues.[145]

All these many issues aside, perhaps the largest problem for the "natural miracle mass hallucination hypothesis" is that these group hallucinations would have to re-occur continually, every single time that Jesus appeared to a group of people.[146] Even though such events have arguably never occurred before or since, they would have happened several times here in just a very short time span.[147] Thus there is a giant conundrum here, something like this: "Perhaps the only time that mass hallucinations have ever occurred in history, as far as is known, they apparently occurred to the followers of Jesus, who just happened to be the most unique person who has ever lived! And in Jesus's case, these events occurred repeatedly!"

This sounds less like a *natural* miracle and more like a literal miracle! Rather than a natural miracle group hallucination hypothesis, this thesis is more like a natural miracle group hallucination, natural miracle group hallucination, natural miracle group hallucination (and so on) hypothesis! Whether a string of several one-of-a-kind natural hallucination miracles is rarer and more difficult to achieve than an actual resurrection would probably be answered differently according to the personal worldview issues raised above. But this indicates just some of the difficulties in applying this particular "natural miracle" to Jesus.

Second, consider the theory that Jesus's disciples stole his dead body out of the tomb and then lied about Jesus's appearances to them. Once again, several strands of strong evidence exist against such a natural hypothesis even in just

---

[145] These problems are detailed in both the appropriate chapters in volume 1 as well as in the applicable chapters in this volume, especially on hallucination hypotheses.

[146] For example, the exceptionally early creedal statement in 1 Cor 15:3–7 alone lists three such group sightings to "the Twelve," to the 500 at once, and to "all the apostles." The Gospels and Acts sermon summaries add other apparent group appearances to this list as well, such as the most critically recognized ones to the twelve disciples and to the women who went to the tomb.

[147] Even for those who tend to support the concept of group hallucinations, the exceptionally rare possible stories of this nature in recent history as contrasted with the number of well-attested group appearances of Jesus over such a brief time period form an incredibly enormous barrier by itself.

the cases that we know about, such as liars hardly being likely to become willing martyrs.[148] It is even quite possible that, like the group hallucinations, this scenario has perhaps never been observed before. Plus the disciples' extreme lifelong transformations; Paul the persecutor's conversion, which was totally removed from the disciples' cases, as was James the probable unbeliever's conversion; the lack of any records of disciples who recanted later; and so on, all make this an extremely unlikely situation.[149]

Again, however, as with the mass hallucinations, the major problems with the "natural miracle stolen body hypothesis" emerge at the weakest points of the thesis. The disciples living their lives and being utterly transformed by their very obvious lie that Jesus was raised from the dead and appeared later (the most difficult item in this thesis) would have to be repeated countless times. Basically, every time one of the perpetrators proclaimed the resurrection, which they knew to be faked, especially in the face of the perceived or actual threat of death, this hypothesis would have to be invoked. Thus, there would be *many dozens* of occasions for the view to go awry for the individual disciples. Like the previous example, we end up with something like this: "Perhaps the only time in history that we know a case where individuals willingly died for what they absolutely knew to be false, it happened to the disciples who had studied with Jesus, who was perhaps the most unique person who ever lived. Further, in this case, it happened very frequently—over and over again!"

Similarly, this is not so much a "stolen body followed by a huge lie in the face of certain and imminent death hypothesis" so much as it is "a stolen body followed by a huge lie in the face of certain and imminent death hypothesis, a stolen body followed by another huge lie in the face of certain and imminent death hypothesis, a stolen body followed by a huge lie in the face of certain and imminent death hypothesis, and so on," multiplied perhaps dozens and dozens of times. Yet again, this is so much

---

[148] Even Ehrman does not consider this view to be very likely in *How Jesus Became God*, 165.

[149] On the disciples dying or at least being willing to die for their faith, as well as the question of whether any of them recanted their faith later, see the revised PhD dissertation by Sean McDowell, *The Fate of the Apostles: Examining the Martyrdom Accounts of the Closest Followers of Jesus* (Surrey: Ashgate, 2015). On the disciples' willingness to die for their faith, see 14, 150–51, 243, 246, 256–57, 259–65. On the question of any apostles recanting, see 6, 8, 243, 259–65. See volume 1 of this study in the chapter on the disciples' transformations for other supporting sources.

more than a "*natural* miracle"! As before, different worldviews will differently assess each scenario as more or less likely, such as whether dozens or more of these natural examples are more miraculous than the actual resurrection itself.

The chief point regarding both examples mentioned here is that it is not a single group hallucination or a single case of a lying group versus an actual resurrection. It is a case of multiple natural events, none of which has perhaps ever been observed even once before, versus one real miracle. In the case of the previous "lying and dying" thesis, it may even be hundreds of natural cases to one miracle. As mentioned earlier, and as will be a separate argument below, when we consider the hundreds of evidenced near-death experiences (NDEs) that support the probability of an afterlife involving another dimension,[150] plus additional arguments, which of these options looks better? It appears that perhaps only the hardened view of "the natural position is my option and I'm sticking with it no matter what" remains. The evidence seems to have shifted. (In spite of the mention here, this will be a separate argument later.)

Response 24

Other apparently nonnatural considerations that indicate a different angle on the truth of Jesus's claims and teachings could also help show that the resurrection was not some sort of natural anomaly. For example, if Jesus healed people and predicted his death and resurrection along with making other unique claims, these would all serve as indications that are far more consistent with an actual resurrection than with some abnormality.[151]

Challenge 3:7—Antecedent Probability

Before examining any of the claimed evidence for miracles, it can be stated from the outset that purported miraculous events are so antecedently improbable, given what we know of nature and science, that *no* amount of evidence could ever surmount this level of unlikelihood.[152]

---

[150] See the first appendix in volume 1 for many NDE examples and details.

[151] See Habermas, *Risen Jesus*, chaps. 1–6.

[152] David Owen, "Hume versus Price on Miracles and Prior Probabilities," in Swinburne, *Miracles*, 115–32, esp. 126–29. Owen's article was published previously in the *Philosophical Quarterly* 37 (1987): 187–202.

Response 25

Scholars must be careful here that *a priori objections* or *questions*, which are fitting, do not slip into *a priori rejections*, which are illegitimate. We made this point at the outset of this chapter. The two positions can sometimes be very difficult to distinguish. Taking this critique somewhat further, in the context of mentioning the existence of the afterlife, even Flew asserted that Hume and Joseph Butler both agreed here: "Hume has argued that it is impossible to know a priori that anything must be or cannot be the cause of anything else." Rather, a posteriori investigations are required.[153] Yet, Flew also admitted that Hume failed at times regarding the application of this and similar matters to the study of miracles, where Hume exhibited some "momentary lapses" in part 1 of his essay.[154]

Response 26

The statistics for antecedent (or prior) probabilities, as in the computations for Bayes' Theorem, would have to be adjusted significantly on the notion of whether God did or did not exist, since in the former case it might even be expected that God might act supernaturally. This alone could move the overall case in the direction of a miracle, as both Flew and even Owen admitted.[155] In short, if there is a God who chooses to act, this would be a huge impetus to the occurrence of miraculous events.

Response 27

If near-death experiences or certain other arguments indicated the probability of at least a minimal notion of an afterlife, then this would be another factor that could also favor the computation of probabilities in the direction of miracle claims. In such a scenario, the *realm* in which a resurrection from the dead would most commonly be thought to exist, namely the afterlife, would probably be true. This would be a huge step toward there being other similar events from the same realm, as with Jesus's resurrection.[156]

---

[153] Flew, *Hume's Philosophy of Belief*, 168.

[154] Flew, 171, 173, quotation on 173.

[155] Flew, in Habermas and Flew, *Resurrection Debate*, esp. 39; Owen, "Hume versus Price," 132.

[156] As I have argued in several places, such as *Risen Jesus*, 60–62, 71; Gary R. Habermas, "Resurrection Appearances of Jesus as After-Death Communication: Response to Ken Vincent," *Journal of Near-Death Studies* 30 (2012): 149–58.

Response 28

If Jesus actually claimed to perform healings and exorcisms during his life, the general occasions of which are almost always conceded by contemporary critical scholars to be historical, then these might serve as actual examples of supernatural events. Perhaps the historical evidence is even stronger than critical scholars presume, and there are plenty of data to solve this issue by taking the historical route of an inference to the best explanation.[157]

Response 29

Especially if well-documented miracle claims actually occur today, this would obviously also affect the likelihood that miracles could possibly have happened years ago during Jesus's life.[158] Many cases describe intriguing situations and details where amazing corroboration is apparently available.[159]

Response 30

Concerning the chief miracle claim before us in these volumes, we need most centrally to address two key questions that can be answered by the historical information that we have presently. First, did Jesus die? And second, after his death, was Jesus seen again by his followers? The latter question is without reference to whether or not these sightings were supernatural events, but simply whether Jesus was actually seen in some form. Minus the supernatural element, both of these questions can be

---

[157] Regarding Jesus performing events such as these, see the massive treatments by John P. Meier in volume 2 of *A Marginal Jew: Mentor, Message, and Miracles*, 5 vols., Anchor Bible Reference Library (New York: Doubleday, 2001); Graham H. Twelftree, *Jesus the Miracle Worker: A Historical and Theological Study* (Downers Grove, IL: InterVarsity, 1999); Craig S. Keener, *Miracles: The Credibility of the New Testament Accounts*, 2 vols. (Grand Rapids: Baker Academic, 2011), esp. chap. 1 of vol. 1.

[158] See these contemporary discussions: H. Richard Casdorph, *The Miracles: A Medical Doctor Says Yes to Miracles* (Plainfield, NJ: Logos, 1976); Rex Gardner, *Healing Miracles: A Doctor Investigates* (London: Darton, Longman & Todd, 1986); Keener, *Miracles*.

[159] While some of the individuals in Casdorph and Gardner above are exemplary, Keener produces the most cases by far of both healing (see *Miracles*, 1:428, 431–32, 435, 440, 463, 491, 503; 2:680, 682n2, cf. the comments on 607) as well as apparent exorcisms (2:800, 815, 838–40, 843n381, 847, 851–52, cf. the comments on 784, 788, 856).

settled on straightforward inductive grounds (such as historical or medical information). Even agnostic New Testament scholar A. J. M. Wedderburn agrees with this
conclusion, as do many other critical scholars.[160]

As we already enumerated above, the value of the Shroud of Turin could be
immeasurable in this context. Granted, the entire subject has not yet been settled
scientifically, so this artifact cannot be tallied yet in the positive column. However,
enough studies have already been conducted to allow the conclusion that this cloth
is clearly an authentic archaeological artifact that could potentially tip the scales
decisively by producing empirical evidence of a repeatable variety that may solve
some of the most germane issues being discussed here.[161] This research would also
be another factor that could move the needle substantially in discussing our latest challenge here regarding the issue of antecedent probabilities as well as with
other questions.[162]

In sum, this third category of philosophical objections to miracle claims included
some challenging questions, to be sure. Most of these specific questions were concerned not so much with the actual evidence that may or may not be available on
behalf of individual miracle claims. Rather, this classification chiefly revolved around
how and why a particular occurrence could be said to have originated from God's
hand, drawing heavily from the tie-in between miracle claims and worldviews. In
this category alone, seven objections were raised and challenged by a total of thirty
counterresponses.

For those who accept the very familiar and influential definition of miracles
popularized by Hume and many others, or one like it, the link between God's actions
and miracles is a necessary connection, hence the import of this discussion.[163] Among

---

[160] A. J. M. Wedderburn, *Beyond Resurrection* (Peabody, MA: Hendrickson, 1999),
12–19, 21–23, 38–39.

[161] For just one of the dozens of authoritative and largely experimental results, see
"insider" scientific specialist and Jewish researcher Barrie M. Schwortz, "The History and
Current State of Modern Shroud Research," in *Raised on the Third Day: Defending the
Historicity of the Resurrection of Jesus, Essays in Honor of Dr. Gary R. Habermas* (Bellingham,
WA: Lexham, 2020), 201–24.

[162] See the sources on this subject already listed above.

[163] For highly influential philosophical treatments of this relation between God's
existence and the laws of nature, see Stephen T. Davis, "God's Actions," in Geivett and
Habermas, *In Defense of Miracles*, 163–77; William P. Alston, *Divine Nature and Human
Language: Essays in Philosophical Theology* (Ithaca: Cornell University Press, 1989), 81–102,
197–222; Alston, "How to Think about Divine Action," in *Divine Action: Studies Inspired by*

some two and a half dozen responses in this section are several hints to be explored later regarding where some of the tightest connections between God and historical events may lie.

Category 4: Historical A Priori Objections to Miracle Claims

The three categories of objections to miracles raised above were chiefly philosophical in nature, though these were often interspersed throughout with historical concerns and considerations as well. On the subject of whether miraculous events obtain, there is indeed much overlap between these two disciplines. As a result, many of the more historical a priori objections in this category also involve corollaries in the philosophical a priori section above, including similarities.

Challenge 4:1—Can historians comment on God or divine activity?

Historians cannot investigate miracles because they simply do not possess any tools that allow them to test for the presence of God or divine activity in the world. So, at least in principle, historians can only assume a natural methodology that deals straightforwardly with potential events and whether or not they occurred rather than with supernatural causation.[164]

---

the Philosophical Theology of Austin Farrer, ed. Brian Hebblethwaite and Edward Henderson (Edinburgh: T&T Clark, 1990), 51–70; Eleonore Stump and Norman Kretzmann, "Eternity," *Journal of Philosophy* 78 (1981): 429–58.

[164] Atheist New Testament specialist Bart D. Ehrman has been an outspoken advocate regarding the historian's inability to judge the truth or falsehood of miracle claims. He makes an epistemic move somewhat reminiscent of Hume as well as the third category of objections above, in that *even if* miracles had actually happened, "the historian cannot demonstrate it." He considers this to be an "insurmountable" issue in discussions of miracles. See Ehrman, *New Testament*, 208, cf. 210–12. Ehrman often repeats these and very similar claims, as in his other volumes such as *Jesus: Apocalyptic Prophet of the New Millennium* (Oxford: Oxford University Press, 1999), 227–30; *Did Jesus Exist? The Historical Argument for Jesus of Nazareth* (New York: HarperCollins, 2012), 315–17. In *How Jesus Became God*, Ehrman states clearly that the resurrection can neither be proven nor disproven by historical means (132, 143, 204). Defenses of *methodological* naturalism from a different perspective are also provided by Tor Egil Førland, "Acts of God, Miracles, and Scientific Explanation," *History and Theory* 47 (2008): 483–94; Førland, "Historiography without God: A Reply to Gregory," *History and Theory* 47 (2008): 520–32; Flew, *God and Philosophy*, 146–47.

Response 1

Even if it were agreed that historians do not possess the tools to judge whether or not God was the cause of a particular event, it would still seem to be undeniable that the *historical portions* of the miracle *claims* nonetheless *still* remain front and center in historical investigation. In other words, we have emphasized often that there are basically two sides to a miracle—the historical side (did some event happen in space and time?) and the philosophical side (the meaning of the event, including worldview questions of possible divine causation). These demarcations are readily apparent in the categories of challenges in this chapter.

So, while the latter, philosophical questions may indeed seem imposing to historians, since they are not within their field of expertise, historians are the *primary* scholars trained to answer the first portion of the question regarding the occurrence of an event, whatever that was. This would be precisely in the very center of their training.

For example, historians may inquire as to whether Jesus died by crucifixion by evaluating the available data. Ehrman is more than confident that historians qua historians can affirm this fact without any difficulty whatsoever.[165] Another skeptic, John Dominic Crossan, is equally positive of this truth, attesting of Jesus, "That he was crucified is as sure as anything historical can ever be." He states further that "the soldiers would have made certain Jesus was dead."[166]

The second question is likewise deemed to be a historical one. Without inquiring or deciding regarding the nature of the events in question, were Jesus's followers correct that they saw him alive again after his death by crucifixion, *whatever* the explanation? Again, agnostic New Testament scholar Wedderburn concedes that answering this question is a legitimate historical procedure.[167]

Based on the strength of the historical data, other scholars have answered yes to these questions. Prominent, self-identified liberal scholar E. P. Sanders goes even

---

[165] Ehrman declares, "That Jesus died by crucifixion is almost unanimously attested in our sources." See Ehrman, *Did Jesus Exist?*, 163. Similarly strong comments are addressed on 156–58, 163–64, 173, 291–92, 327–31.

[166] John Dominic Crossan, *Jesus: A Revolutionary Biography* (New York: HarperCollins, 1994), 145, 154, respectively. Similarly, Crossan asserts, "I take it absolutely for granted that Jesus was crucified under Pontius Pilate." See Crossan, *The Historical Jesus: The Life of a Mediterranean Jewish Peasant* (New York: HarperCollins, 1991), 372, cf. 375.

[167] As noted above, Wedderburn, *Beyond Resurrection*, 12–19, 21–23, 38–39.

further.[168] He begins his discussion of the historical Jesus's life by listing a number of consensus historical items upon which contemporary scholars almost uniformly agree. Some of these details may surprise today's readers who are unfamiliar with the recent scholarly terrain, such as the state of contemporary studies on Jesus's healings. Perhaps most astonishing of all, among the historical facts that Sanders lists as enjoying consensus critical agreement is that Jesus was actually seen by his followers in some form after his death by crucifixion.[169]

It would seem then that if the question of whether Jesus's postresurrection appearances were actually miraculous acts of God is bracketed, the other two questions regarding Jesus's death and his being seen afterward remain fully historical issues. After all, people die and people are seen regularly.[170] If Sanders is correct, both of these items are also affirmed by the majority of contemporary critical scholars. That even skeptics may affirm these occurrences, due to the strong reasons for doing so, at least gets the vital building blocks on the table.[171] After all, these are the questions being addressed here. On these absolutely crucial points, this bypasses the miracle question for historians. In fact, it appears that this response alone has the ability to offset and even nullify the first skeptical challenge of the historical variety.

Response 2

Although these are probably minority opinions, many noted historians have pointed out the congruence between religious and historical beliefs, in part because they are not enemies. Rather, religious beliefs may even be brought into the historical arena

---

[168] E. P. Sanders identifies himself as a liberal in his influential volume *Jesus and Judaism* (Philadelphia: Fortress, 1985), 334.

[169] E. P. Sanders, *The Historical Figure of Jesus* (London: Penguin, 1993), 6, 11, 13, 278, 280.

[170] Recall that the question of whether or not Jesus was resurrected from the dead via a miracle is not being discussed here.

[171] Among the most incredible comments in this regard is the statement by well-known skeptical scholar Dale Allison, who comments, "I think that the tomb was probably empty, although I am sure that the disciples saw Jesus after his death." See Dale C. Allison Jr., *Resurrecting Jesus: The Earliest Christian Tradition and Its Interpreters* (London: T&T Clark, 2005), 346. Allison makes a similar comment on 343–44. Similarly, Allison comments in his more recent, 2021 volume on Jesus's resurrection, "I believe that the disciples saw Jesus and that he saw them, and next Easter will find me in church." Dale C. Allison Jr., *The Resurrection of Jesus: Apologetics, Polemics, History* (New York: Bloomsbury, 2021), 3. This is an example of the widespread recognition on the part of critical scholars, as just recounted by Sanders.

and be investigated, as long as they are well-supported views.[172] It has already been argued here from the best historical data why this latter position is even held by a fair number of skeptical or liberal scholars such as Wedderburn, Allison, and Sanders, along with still others who will be pointed out elsewhere.

Response 3

Although the pursuit of this topic would take us far beyond the theme of this volume, it should at least be noted that without much question, methodological naturalism is the most influential underlying philosophical position in this discussion, even though it has many exceptionally serious issues of its own.[173] One of these problems has already been treated in detail here. The backdrop that grounds methodological naturalism—namely, metaphysical naturalism—is highly problematic and currently suffers from many major critiques. Some scholars have concluded that it has probably already been disproven. There are an entire host of topics that point in the direction of this demise, such as some specialized arguments for God's existence, an entire cadre of facets drawn from the Intelligent Design and Fine-Tuning scientific arguments, strongly evidential near-death experiences, Jesus's own miracles, modern documented miracle claims, a few successful double-blind prayer experiments, and the myriad strands of arguments for Jesus's resurrection.[174]

---

[172] Brad S. Gregory, "No Room for God? History, Science, Metaphysics, and the Study of Religion," *History and Theory* 47 (2008): 495–519; Jon Butler, "Theory and God in Gotham," *History and Theory* 45 (2006): 47–61; Mark S. Cladis, "Modernity *in* Religion: A Response to Constantin Fasolt's History and Religion in the Modern Age," *History and Theory* 45 (2006): 93–103; Montgomery, *Shape of the Past*, 138–45; William Wand, *Christianity: A Historical Religion?* (Valley Forge, PA: Judson, 1972), 29–31, 51, 59, 70–71, 84–85, 91–94, 122, 139–40; Paul Barnett, *The Birth of Christianity: The First Twenty Years* (Grand Rapids: Eerdmans, 2005), 6–8, 26, 55, 77, 106, 185–86. Cf. also Walsh, "Can History Be Objective?" in Meyerhoff, *Philosophy of History*, 218.

[173] For good overviews of these matters, see Goetz and Taliaferro, *Naturalism*, 7, 26, 32, 44, 50–51, 84–85, 90, 93, 117–122; Parrish, *Atheism?*, 27–33; Moreland, *Scientism and Secularism*, 49–84, 161–71. See also Robert A. Larmer, "The Many Inadequate Justifications of Methodological Naturalism," *Organon F* 26 (2019): 5–24; Tiddy Smith, "Methodological Naturalism and Its Misconceptions," *International Journal for Philosophy of Religion* 82 (2017): 321–36; Michael A. Cantrell, "Must a Scholar of Religion Be Methodologically Atheistic or Agnostic?," *Journal of the American Academy of Religion* 84 (2016): 373–400.

[174] For just a very few of the many treatments here, see Jerry L. Walls and Trent Dougherty, eds., *Two Dozen (or So) Arguments for God: The Plantinga Project* (Oxford:

If naturalism has already fallen, as some have hinted,[175] or will so in the future, it would seem that its methodological sister cannot be very far behind.[176] From another angle, if a supernatural reality actually exists, then there must be some way to integrate both it and the natural world into contemporary inductive research, especially since they would be integrated already in our everyday lives. These theoretical and practical concerns will be left to other, more qualified individuals. Just one side note might be mentioned at this point. If miracles have ever occurred throughout history, it would indeed be odd if they could still not even be investigated by those who hold a presumed methodological naturalism. In other words, miracles actually may have happened, even frequently, while naturalists simply pronounce that they cannot be considered or examined. As concluded earlier in this study, the only alternative is to investigate supernatural claims to ascertain the answers to these issues.

Response 4

Some authors have suggested that perhaps believers possess the capacity to gain additional insights into situations where God's presence may be detected.[177] This may be the case because these individuals may already be more attuned to supernatural reality due to a personal relationship, such as their regular seeking of the Lord, as with the spiritual disciplines. A related idea was even mentioned by prominent atheist philosopher J. L. Mackie, who remarked that someone "who is fortunate enough"

Oxford University Press, 2018); Stephen E. Parrish, *God and Necessity: A Defense of Classical Theism* (Lanham, MD: University Press of America, 1997); Donnelly, *Logical Analysis*; Stephen C. Meyer, *Signature in the Cell: DNA and the Evidence for Intelligent Design* (New York: HarperCollins, 2009); Gary R. Habermas, "Evidential Near-Death Experiences," in *The Blackwell Companion to Substance Dualism*, ed. Jonathan J. Loose, Angus J. L. Menuge, and J. P. Moreland (Oxford: Wiley-Blackwell, 2018), 227–44; Candy Gunther Brown, *Testing Prayer: Science and Healing* (Cambridge: Harvard University Press, 2012).

[175] For an exceptionally creative treatment of this subject, see David Brooks's op-ed article, "The Neural Buddhists," *New York Times*, May 13, 2008.

[176] J. P. Moreland, "Creation Science and Methodological Naturalism," in *Man and Creation: Perspectives on Science and Theology*, ed. Michael Bauman and Lissa Roche (Hillsdale, MI: Hillsdale College Press, 1993), 105–39; Moreland, *Christianity and the Nature of Science: A Philosophical Investigation* (Grand Rapids: Baker, 1989), particularly chap. 6.

[177] Such as Basinger, "Christian Theism," 148–49; Francis J. Beckwith, "History and Miracles," in Geivett and Habermas, *In Defense of Miracles*, 88–91.

to have carefully observed and noted an apparently miraculous occurrence "is no doubt rationally justified in taking it very seriously" while still entertaining natural explanations as well.[178]

Challenge 4:2—Is history too subjective and uncertain?

Historical investigations can never be totally objective, hence these studies are incapable of producing proof or totally demonstrating a thesis. Further, the constant presence of subjective elements entering the research process can keep the researcher from being sure of their historical results.[179]

Response 5

Sometimes it appears obvious that skeptical scholars attempt to go overboard in "loading up" the language and data against miracles. This is often done by utilizing exceptionally strong terms, such as "can never *prove*," "cannot *demonstrate*," "beyond all doubt," "without question," or "it is impossible."[180]

Going back some two-plus centuries, it was observed repeatedly in the previous chapter that Hume was a master of these techniques as well, as he insisted that "firm and unalterable experience," "uniform experience," and "a direct and full *proof*" opposed all miraculous claims.[181] On the other hand, Hume naturally considered that his own arguments amounted to an "entire proof," even opening his essay with the words, "I flatter myself, that I have discovered an argument . . . which . . . will . . . be an everlasting check to all kinds of superstitious delusion, and consequently, will be useful as long as the world endures."[182] In short, everything that the arguments from miracles were *not*, Hume's arguments *were*, without virtually any questions or evidential arguments in favor of his position. It appears to go without saying that such stilted language both "proves" nothing while raising the ire of one's opponents.

---

[178] Mackie, *Miracle of Theism*, 28.

[179] Ernest Nagel notes this problem and explains it, while still offering a corrective to it; see "The Logic of Historical Analysis," in Meyerhoff, *Philosophy of History*, 212–13, 215.

[180] Such as Ehrman, *Apocalyptic Prophet*, 227–30; cf. related ideas in Basinger and Basinger, *Philosophy and Miracle*, 15–18, 23, 59–71.

[181] Hume, "Of Miracles," 210–11.

[182] These last two quotations are found in Hume's "Of Miracles," 212, and in the introduction to part 1 (206), respectively.

Response 6

Some elements of subjectivity exist in all inductive research, including even the most technical scientific, medical, and historical studies. For this as well as other reasons, none of the research in any of the fields discussed in this chapter is capable of producing any full, final *proof* of its teachings. Further, this has already been acknowledged readily by theistic writers and has been stated many times in these volumes. But to leap ahead from a lack of proof in inductive matters like science and history to *some degree of subjectivity* is an unwarranted and unevidenced conclusion. The inductive disciplines such as science, medicine, and history have always had to move from probability to knowledge, and there is a significant agreement in these matters. Moreover, this critique would ultimately disprove science. Therefore, moving from a lack of proof to a charge of subjectivity in these areas can hardly nullify probable inductive theses or their conclusions.

So as just mentioned, this epistemic knife cuts both ways. Since the skeptic's research also utilizes historical, scientific, and other inductive conclusions, does it follow that she likewise includes subjective notions that similarly lack any species of strong evidence? Virtually no one would argue this way. There is no getting around the conclusion that, assuming inductive studies are being employed, probable factual arguments are the best on offer.

As many scholars have both remarked and acknowledged, subjectivity of more than one variety definitely may remain even in research. Armed with this knowledge, historians and others must be diligent, refuse to grow lazy, and be careful about their research so that these subjective and distorted features may be identified and removed as much as possible, making appropriate allowances for them.[183]

Response 7

Beckwith argues quite intriguingly that this critical position based on the subjectivity of our knowledge and lack of proof may also entail there being no ascertainable *bad* historical judgments. But this is simply absurd. For example, suppose that one historian argues the traditional view that a dictator *murdered* millions of people for a variety of twisted psychological reasons. However, a second historian argues that

---

[183] Nagel, "Logic of Historical Analysis," 215; and also Walsh, "Can History Be Objective?," 217.

this same dictator actually did so not because of his internal problems but because he loved the victims so much that he wanted them all to go to heaven much more quickly! Even compiling the relevant data to argue one view over the other requires historical research to yield a strong enough basis to make a probable decision.[184]

Response 8

In spite of potential subjective issues in historical research and the inability to absolutely *prove* one's conclusions, virtually no scholars deny that we can still gain knowable history through the normal channels of investigation. The available data are sufficient to gain this information.[185] Even historians such as Carl Becker who are sympathetic to this challenge and think that interpretations are more difficult to determine, still acknowledge the presence of much history.[186] Following Becker and others before him, the vast majority of even the skeptical, more subjective-leaning idealistic historians agree.[187]

Challenge 4:3—Do miracles have to be analogous to other events?

We can recognize historical events and their meanings from the past only if they have analogies in the present. This critique is most frequently attributed to the writings of nineteenth-century German liberal theologian Ernst Troeltsch and is known as the "argument from analogy." However, the idea (or perhaps hint) appeared at least 150 years earlier in Hume's essay "Of Miracles."[188]

---

[184] Beckwith, "History and Miracles," 89.

[185] Walsh, "Can History Be Objective?," 224.

[186] Becker, "What Are Historical Facts?," 132–35.

[187] The scholars and sources mentioned earlier in this chapter and elsewhere in this study (such as the chapter in volume 1 on postmodern history) will not be repeated again here, but a sample list of some of the skeptical researchers who would still agree with Becker on the possibility of knowing historical facts would include Hume, Dilthey, Croce, Troeltsch, Collingwood, Beard, Mannheim, Walsh, Russell, Ayer, Mackie, Flew, and Foucault. Meyerhoff's comment concerning even skeptics not denying the historical process itself is instructive in this regard (*Philosophy of History*, 36).

[188] Ernst Troeltsch, "Historical and Dogmatic Method in Theology," in *Religion in History: Ernst Troeltsch—Essays*, trans. James Luther Adams and Walter F. Bense (Edinburgh: T&T Clark, 1991), 11–32 (originally written in 1898); also reproduced in Gregory W. Dawes, ed., *The Historical Jesus Quest: Landmarks in the Search for the Jesus of*

Response 9

By what scientific, historical, psychological, or other authority is this absolute rule required? On what critical grounds is the analogical test itself established? Somewhat like the verification principle above, this appears to be another example of a critical assertion or test that simply hangs there in space but is an unproven assertion. If so, it is similarly self-refuting.

Response 10

All information was new at some time. Could these past data never be recognized, interpreted, and accepted at that time until there was a later analogy? But automatically disallowing older, historical, or other information—in this case, miracles—is both self-defeating (because past information often provides crucial information that is necessary for the present) and also amounts to an a priori rejection.

Response 11

This principle would seem to dispute a great many events or scientific discoveries of the past, even if they were established by proper inductive procedures. For example, what about singularities like the Big Bang? Does it have any true analogy in the present or will it ever? If not, could it still be held that it occurred in the past?

Response 12

As Frank Beckwith notes, this argument confuses the "consistency and continuity" expected of the past with what may be discovered by these methods. But there is no reason why the historical method cannot discover, inspect, or research a historical singularity.[189] The historical tools that have already been listed and discussed earlier in this study remain the same and can still be used to discover new data.

History, rev. ed. (Louisville: Westminster John Knox, 2000), esp. 32–39. See also Hume, "Of Miracles," part 2. A more recent version of this charge is mentioned by Antony Flew, "Introduction" to Hume, *Of Miracles*, 13, 18; also Flew, *God and Philosophy*, 146 (150 in the 2005 edition).

[189] Beckwith, "History and Miracles," 97.

Response 13

Past events often have enough evidence to establish their historicity on their own. In such cases, how can the unproven, rather random requirement of present analogies step in and rule out the data itself?

Response 14

Many healings were apparently performed by Jesus, as argued in great detail by careful scholars like John Meier, Graham Twelftree, and Craig Keener among many others. Further, these events are largely accepted in some capacity by contemporary scholars, including very skeptical ones. These would actually provide some analogical events of another sort from Jesus's own ministry.[190]

Response 15

What if true miracles have occurred throughout world history, including in the present? Then there actually *are* analogies for these potentially supernatural events, and this principle could be completely fulfilled.[191]

Response 16

The case of Jesus's resurrection has at least some continuity with evidence derived from contemporary studies of highly evidential near-death experiences (NDEs) and similar phenomena, such as substantiated postmortem apparitions, deathbed visions, and the like. While these cases do not correspond completely to the resurrection, the NDEs would still be quite helpful in indicating some major similarities regarding the existence of an afterlife, hence providing key analogies for life in another realm altogether.

---

[190] See the references above to the research presented in Meier's *A Marginal Jew*, Twelftree's *Jesus the Miracle Worker*, and volume 1 of Keener's *Miracles*.

[191] For literally thousands of details, see also the references above to the works by physicians Richard Casdorph (*The Miracles*) and Rex Gardner (*Healing Miracles*), as well as Keener's monumental two-volume work, *Miracles*, including many carefully documented examples.

Challenge 4:4—Aren't miracles just exaggerations told by gossips or by those in the ancient world?

People like to gossip, exaggerate, and even lie about miraculous or incredible events, and these stories quite often grow larger and even more farfetched in the multiple retellings. Additionally, miracles are thought by many to have occurred chiefly in ancient times among "ignorant and barbarous nations."[192] Such recurrent problems cast doubt on miracle reports.

Response 17

This objection is a very clear, textbook example of committing the genetic fallacy of informal logic. Even a correct explanation of an idea's origin does not somehow "whisk" away the actual event into nonexistence.[193] Ancient peoples had some correct beliefs too! So how do we know the difference between their true and false beliefs? Here once again, careful investigation is necessary.

Response 18

Hume's comment concerning "ignorant and barbarous nations" is also an ad hominem abusive fallacy of informal logic.[194] While making light of someone or criticizing him or her as a person may have advantages in some contexts, a formal argument is not one of them. There is no necessary connection between the characteristics of the person being criticized, whether true or false, and whether his or her argument is correct or incorrect, hence the fallacy.

Response 19

Hume introduced the case of the Jansenist miracles, providing some rather incredible evidence on behalf of their claims. Were these reports guilty of being reported

---

[192] Hume, "Of Miracles," part 2, objection 3. Flew notes that Hume meant these four subpoints *not* as offensive moves capable of disproving miracles or of providing "an insuperable bulwark" against them, but only "as a check" against their occurrence. See Flew, *Hume's Philosophy of Belief*, 174, 177.

[193] Copi, *Introduction to Logic*, 92.

[194] Copi, 92; Kegley and Kegley, *Introduction to Logic*, 127–28, 156–57.

only among "ignorant and barbarous nations"? Not at all, for almost as if Hume was addressing his own charges, he judged that these events were "attested by witnesses of credit and distinction, in a learned age, and on the most eminent theatre that is now in the world." Further, upon inspection, the Jansenists were found to have neither lied nor otherwise produced falsehoods. These were quite noteworthy compliments.

So, if the Jansenist miracle claims were supposedly exempted from these charges according to Hume, then how did he respond? Hume still dismissed these healing cases and other anomalies with a mere wave of his hand. He asked what more was needed here besides "the absolute impossibility or miraculous nature of the events, which they relate? And this surely, in the eyes of all reasonable people, will alone be regarded as a sufficient refutation."[195] Thus, it appeared that whether or not the critical conditions had been fulfilled by the available evidence, it ultimately made no appreciable difference. Miracles simply do not occur and that is enough. That is the extent of Hume's investigation.

Even Flew seemed to struggle mightily with Hume's treatment of the Jansenist cases, including Hume's long endnote that adds many relevant evidential details. Flew remarked of Hume's treatment, "It might seem that this must be inconsistent." Really? Incredibly, Flew then allowed that Hume's stance on the Jansenists could be consistent with part 1 of his essay, "which allows the theoretical possibility of establishing that a miraculous event has occurred" while still somehow rejecting it. Then Flew resorted to what appears to be an incredible ensemble of ad hoc special pleading comments, all to say that Hume should not be pushed too far in questioning his consistency![196] One wonders why not if, as it appears, Hume is simply mistaken here.

Response 20

This charge actually could be quite true, as it often is in antiquity, and yet it utterly fails to rule out every bit of ancient testimony. If so, then all or most of our earliest history could be in jeopardy. However, this problem fails to cause trained historians to give up on our knowledge regarding Alexander the Great or Julius Caesar, for example. As former Oxford University philosopher of history W. H. Walsh along with many other historians attest, in spite of these subjective factors we must allow for such errors and imprecisions and still ascertain what occurred, even in the far-off

---

[195] Hume, "Of Miracles," 220.
[196] Flew, *Hume's Philosophy of Belief*, 185–86.

past.[197] Similarly, historian Ernst Breisach reminds us that while ancient writers frequently engaged in artistic reworking of their material, contemporary scholars are still able to sort through the reports and distinguish historical truth from "the fanciful tale, willful distortion, and honest error" of the past.[198]

Response 21

While it is difficult to ascertain whether or not Flew meant the comment somewhat tongue-in-check, he remarked that Hume's third subpoint (or "check") makes it seem as if the witnesses to miracles "must also be completely detached and disinterested."[199] Of course, it has been commented throughout that a few witnesses may indeed fit this description for many historical observations, and yet they may still be fully capable of properly observing and getting the facts straight. Nonetheless, the question will be pursued later in this study as to whether any resurrection witnesses might still have failed in this or similar areas.

Response 22

It already has been argued in volume 1 of this study that the historical evidence for the resurrection of Jesus is superior and that this event can be demonstrated probabilistically *in spite of such challenges and cautions*, especially those regarding the nature of ancient texts. Further, it was proposed there that the minimal facts argument entirely abrogates this species of critique as well as others, in that it utilizes only those historical data where each fact is initially established by many other details. Incredibly, the entire list of these few minimal facts is supported by dozens of other factual considerations.

As a result of this factual basis, these individual pieces of data have even gained the endorsements of the vast majority of skeptical scholars who address them and affirm that there is plenty of information to assert that each of these facts is by far the best explanation of the findings. But it needs to be noted carefully, as we have pointed out already in a great amount of detail, that these historical facts are not true

---

[197] W. H. Walsh, *Philosophy of History: An Introduction* (New York: Harper & Brothers, 1960), 18–22, 100–103.

[198] Ernst Breisach, *Historiography: Ancient, Medieval, and Modern*, 2nd ed. (Chicago: University of Chicago Press, 1994), 56–72, 408.

[199] Flew, *Hume's Philosophy of Belief*, 177.

just because skeptical scholars assert them, but because multiple factual arguments support in detail each of these events. After all, the skeptics would hardly affirm the details without the evidence.

Challenge 4:5—Can postmodern considerations rule out supernatural occurrences?

Some postmodern studies indicate that all historical writing is relative in some sense, and that it often serves as a political power play to be used as a means to manipulate people and ideas. Beyond the historical data that are recorded, it is the resulting *interpretations* regarding the data that most trouble these postmodern writers.[200]

Response 23

For anyone to hold that all historical knowledge is relative is a self-contradictory notion, as even skeptical historians like Charles Beard have conceded. As Beard concluded concerning the matter: "If all historical conceptions are merely relative to passing events . . . then the conception of relativity is itself relative. When absolutes in history are rejected the absolutism of relativity is also rejected . . . the apostle of relativity will surely be executed by his own logic."[201] Many other scholars also agree with this general assessment.[202]

---

[200] Some of the major postmodern scholars include Jean-François Lyotard, "The Postmodern Condition," in *The Postmodern History Reader*, ed. Keith Jenkins (London: Routledge, 1997); Hayden White, *The Fiction of Narrative: Essays of History, Literature, and Theory, 1957–2007*, ed. Robert Doran (Baltimore: Johns Hopkins University Press, 2010); White, *The Content of the Form: Narrative Discourse and Historical Representation* (Baltimore: Johns Hopkins University Press, 1987); White, *Figural Realism: Studies in the Mimesis Effect* (Baltimore: Johns Hopkins University Press, 1999); White, "Historical Emplotment and the Problem of Truth," in Jenkins, *Postmodern History Reader*, 292–96; White, *Tropics of Discourse: Essays in Cultural Criticism* (Baltimore: John Hopkins University Press, 1978); Keith Jenkins, "Introduction: On Being Open about Our Closures," in Jenkins, *Postmodern History Reader*, 1–30; Jenkins, *On 'What is History?' From Carr and Elton to Rorty and White* (London: Routledge, 1995).

[201] Beard, "Written History," 147–48.

[202] Here and in the footnotes below, we will not repeat all the sources from our earlier chapter in volume 1 on "Historical Postmodernism," but a sample listing of some of the scholars who would agree at least generally with this first critique would include Peter

Response 24

This relativistic challenge is actually a nonsequitous accusation, an indication that its conclusion fails to follow from its premises. Even if some historical research were to exhibit all sorts of subjective issues involved with the writing of history, including history being written on manipulative grounds such as the ones mentioned here, this still tells us nothing about whether or not there may be good, trustworthy data that were still investigated and interpreted according to proper standards. As former Harvard University philosopher of history Morton White explains, "The mere fact that historians are biased is no argument against the existence of impersonal standards."[203] Many other researchers share White's view as well.[204]

Response 25

Relativistic historians too frequently apply their views to their own research in inconsistent manners. Contrary to their own conclusions, while these skeptics may view historical studies as unreliable in a host of ways, when it comes to *their own relativistic conclusions*, they are often alleged to be true, proper, and even objective!

Many examples were provided in our earlier volume 1 chapter, "Historical Postmodernism," such as Beard's general distrust of historical interpretations altogether, with the exception of his own rather novel views of the American Constitution—a subject concerning which he freely employed terms such as "coldly neutral" and "objective realities"![205] According to more than one scholar, the reason for Beard's issues here is that he never really recognized these problems in his own writings, hence the subjective and objective elements remained in tension with one another. In brief, Beard's relativism was inconsistent. White states it this way: "Beard's

---

Novick, Richard Evans, Brian Fay, Thomas Haskell, Perez Zagorin, Alan B. Spitzer, Stuart Kelly, John Tosh, Ben Meyer, and Scot McKnight.

[203] Morton White, in Walsh, "Can History Be Objective?," 194–95, quotation on 194. For a few related thoughts, see White's text, *Foundations of Historical Knowledge* (New York: Harper & Row, 1965), 229.

[204] These scholars include Ernest Nagel, C. Behan McCullagh, Chris Lorenz, and James Tabor, among many others. See chapter 3, "Historical Postmodernism" (55–88) in volume 1 of this study.

[205] These two descriptions are found in the introduction in Charles A. Beard, *An Economic Interpretation of the Constitution of the United States*, rev. ed. (New York: Macmillan, 1935), ix–x. See also Beard, "Written History," 149–50.

later philosophy of history seems most implausible. It is obscure and contradictory
. . . a lack of respect for logical rigor and clear thinking."[206]

Other examples of relativistic inconsistencies are not difficult to locate. Thomas
Haskell criticizes Lyotard for being critical of more objective historiography, only
to employ the latter techniques on other occasions. Haskell comments that Lyotard
"puts his representational pants on pretty much the same way the rest of us do." As a
result, there is very little to distinguish Lyotard's technique from those more objective approaches that he criticizes regularly. So Lyotard "seems in the end, in practice,
unable to escape it . . . he acts as if the past is real."[207]

Kelly argues that postmodern relativists often make much stronger claims than
their concepts would allow them as long as that move favors a position that they support. Kelly summarizes one of the main issues this way: "When the chips are down,
most appeal to some sort of objective reality to settle the matter, with such appeals
being seen as binding on all."[208] Yet, the implication is that when they argue against
positions with which they disagree, they take a much stricter view of their theory!

Other historians produce more examples of inconsistent relativists. Perez Zagorin
reports that Elizabeth Earmarth speaks often concerning past facts and then attempts
to defend her lack of skepticism in these instances.[209] Zagorin adds that postmodernist
authors regularly speak about the past as if they think that these examples represent
real facts and occurrences.[210] Speaking more forcefully, philosopher Brian Fay makes
the point that "most postmetaphysical metatheories implode because they utilize
what they deny is legitimate."[211] Evans agrees that postmodernism often combines
many "sometimes contradictory and conflicting ideas."[212]

---

[206] White, in Walsh, "Can History Be Objective?," 200; cf. also Breisach, *Historiography*,
333; along with Meyerhoff, *Philosophy of History*, 138.

[207] Thomas L. Haskell, "Objectivity Is Not Neutrality: Rhetoric vs. Practice in Peter
Novick's *That Noble Dream*," *History and Theory* 29 (1990): 155–56, as cited by Michael R.
Licona, *The Resurrection of Jesus: A New Historiographical Approach* (Downers Grove, IL:
InterVarsity Academic, 2010), 90–91.

[208] Stewart E. Kelly, *Truth Considered and Applied: Examining Postmodernism, History,
and Christian Faith* (Nashville: B&H Academic, 2011), 112. Kelly also notes that Goss and
Levitt similarly charge postmodernists with speaking with very similar assurances (227).

[209] Perez Zagorin, "History, the Referent, and Narrative: Reflections on Postmodernism
Now," *History and Theory* 38 (1999): 14, as cited by Licona, *Resurrection of Jesus*, 79–80.

[210] Zagorin, "History," 14.

[211] Brian Fay, "Nothing but History?," *History and Theory* 37 (1998): 84.

[212] Richard J. Evans, *In Defense of History* (New York: Norton, 1999), 222n6.

It may be wondered if this seemingly regular inconsistency among postmodern-ists is really a correctable error. It appears to be so common that, as realists often charge, perhaps they espouse a theory that looks challenging in theory but can hardly be applied either when making their own case or in arguing against other positions.

Response 26

Bias in historical reporting usually can be both recognized and corrected. This is one of the chief roles that historians are prepared to do, and it is often the result of dialogue among members of the scholarly community. As just one excellent example, Kelly points out how Hayden White modified his own skeptical view in light of new data regarding the nature of the Holocaust.[213]

As detailed in our earlier chapter, Breisach explains the progress here: "Generations of scholars have developed a historical methodology—testing, retest-ing, and absorbing elements from other disciplines—until by now it can act as a wall of defense against the fanciful tale, willful distortion, and honest error, as well as a sufficiently reliable instrument for truth-finding." After much application, then, bias and subjectivity fail to "doom historiography's ability to deliver useful results."[214] McCullagh adds the crucial conclusion that in spite of our never being able to dis-cover the complete picture of the past, our myriad of checks and balances allows us to evaluate our data.[215]

Kelly decides similarly, pointing out rather concisely that "bias is hardly incom-patible with objectivity properly understood."[216] The latter can coexist with the for-mer because "there are methodological tools, objective to a degree, which make it possible to make progress adjudicating such controversies."[217] While bias, selectiv-ity, and outright prejudice will all remain, "none of this needs to compromise the

---

[213] Kelly, *Truth Considered and Applied*, 199, 204. Other scholars, especially historians, likewise agree with this process. Further details are supplied by Walsh, *Philosophy of History*, 19; Nagel, "Logic of Historical Analysis," 210, 212–13; Breisach, *Historiography*, 408; C. Behan McCullagh, *The Truth of History* (London: Routledge, 1998), 38; cf. also Alan B. Spitzer's thoughtful text, *Historical Truth and Lies about the Past: Reflections on Dewey, Dreyfus, de Man, and Reagan* (Chapel Hill, NC: University of North Carolina Press, 1996).

[214] Breisach, *Historiography*, 408.

[215] McCullagh, *Truth of History*, 38.

[216] Kelly, *Truth Considered and Applied*, 204.

[217] Kelly, 215.

integrity, accuracy, or objectivity of what is written."[218] So, according to Kelly, "The historian must take care not to superimpose present concerns and issues onto a study of the past."[219] To be sure, it is easy to make all these assertions, but if Kelly is right, there is at least a potential path for scholars to trod. Probably even the majority of professional historians agree at least broadly with a process such as this.[220]

Response 27

The inductive procedures of applied historiography nevertheless yield knowable conclusions, as even relativist Charles Beard acknowledges: "He [the historian] likewise sees the doctrine of relativity crumble in the cold light of historical knowledge."[221] Many other major relativistic and postmodern historians and philosophers agree with Beard and regularly concede this point regarding the discoverability of real historical facts.[222] Virtually all non-postmodernist scholars also agree with the legitimacy of the historiographical process as well.[223]

---

[218] Kelly, 217.

[219] Kelly, 213.

[220] Spitzer's volume *Historical Truth and Lies* (especially the introduction) is a remarkable attempt to actually work through some of these issues in order to settle some of these historical disagreements. One of Spitzer's main contentions, as seen above, is that when crucial issues are at stake, even postmodernist thinkers regularly resort to processes that are similar to more objective methodologies and arguments that they have actually rejected elsewhere.

[221] Beard, "Written History," 148. Cf. also Beard's earlier comment in the same essay, where after noting that personal selection processes are involved too, he still affirms that it remains the case that "facts, multitudinous and beyond calculation are known" (141). As indicated here, no one denies the subjective biases, but that Beard realizes the facts still clearly remain is a crucial recognition.

[222] A list of some of the earlier precursors to contemporary postmodernists who agree here can be found in Habermas, *Historical Jesus*, 268–69n35. This list of skeptic scholars includes Wilhelm Dilthey, Benedetto Croce, Robin Collingwood, Charles Beard, and Carl Becker, to which Karl Mannheim ought also to be added (as in note 36 in Habermas, *Historical Jesus*). Another list of postmodern scholars who agree can be found in the chapter "History and Postmodernism" in volume 1 of this work as well as earlier in this volume. This group includes Jean-François Lyotard, Hayden White, Frank Ankersmit, and Keith Jenkins, among others.

[223] In addition to the skeptics just mentioned directly above, here are just a few of the additional researchers whose writings have been identified in this chapter and the earlier one ("Historical Postmodernism," volume 1) as holding to historical research:

Since this study chiefly deals with the question of miracles in general and the resurrection of Jesus in particular, it should also be pointed out that virtually no skeptical theologian or New Testament scholar, no matter how unconvinced, denies that the rules of historiography are indeed capable of discovering many historical facts regarding Jesus's life. This can also be extended to information concerning the earliest church as well.[224]

The ability to ascertain historical facts is the most significant critique of all with regard to this particular challenge, since the outcome is that data *can* be investigated and established. That such a wide array of scholars drawn from about every imaginable critical position agree with one another certainly does not *demonstrate* anything, but it does tend to indicate that it is the historical method, rather than scholarly agreement, that can indeed arrive at facts.

As McCullagh asserts rather remarkably, "I know of no practicing historians who admit that they cannot discover anything true about the past. They . . . do not deny that a lot of the basic facts they present are very probably true."[225] Indicative of this comment, three separate studies by philosopher Nicholas Rescher, historian George Marsden, and philosopher Stewart Kelly all reported after their own overviews of the field that the majority scholarly position definitely affirmed the existence of at least some historical facts.[226]

Ernest Nagel, John Dewey, Christopher Blake, William H. Dray, Isaiah Berlin, Morton White, W. H. Walsh, Bruce Mazlish, David Hacket Fischer, C. Behan McCullagh, Brian Fay, Thomas Haskell, Perez Zagorin, Alan B. Spitzer, Ernst Breisach, George Marsden, Nicholas Rescher, Mark Gilderhus, Stewart E. Kelly, Nancy Partner, Donald Akenson, John Tosh, and Carol Cleland.

[224] As with the previous notes above, the chapter "History and Postmodernism" in the previous volume also lists many theological and New Testament skeptics who agree that there are knowable facts concerning the historical Jesus. Many of these researchers are agnostics or atheists: Gerd Lüdemann, A. J. M. Wedderburn, James D. Tabor, Dale Allison, John A. T. Robinson, and E. P. Sanders. From other chapters on this study, we may add David Strauss, Ernest Renan, F. C. Baur, Albert Schweitzer, Otto Pfleiderer, Rudolf Bultmann, Norman Perrin, Willi Marxsen, Michael Goulder, Paul van Buren, William Hamilton, John Dominic Crossan, Marcus Borg, Robert Funk, Burton L. Mack, Roy W. Hoover, Robert J. Miller, Thomas Sheehan, Donald Cupitt, and John Shelby Spong.

[225] McCullagh, *Truth of History*, 15. In addition, McCullagh declares that philosophers of history will provide additional responses whenever other challenges are leveled at the veracity of historical facts.

[226] Nicholas Rescher, *Objectivity: The Obligations of Impersonal Reason* (Notre Dame: Notre Dame University Press, 1997), 199–200; George M. Marsden, "Christian Advocacy

Response 28

As to the prominent postmodern charge that facts may be less troubling than interpretations, McCullagh aims an absolutely crucial rejoinder: "An historical explanation
or interpretation is objective if it can be proved superior to alternative explanations *or
interpretations* according to commonly accepted criteria." Therefore, "when historians
compare different explanations *and interpretations* it becomes clear that they do have
criteria by which they judge them."[227] Hence it follows that each factual or inter-
pretational instance needs to be worked through carefully. But the vital point here
is that such a process is possible and viable precisely because there are agreed-upon
standards that are based on the data we possess.

Response 29

For those who are interested in surveys and overviews, the widespread notion among
scholars in the field regarding postmodernism is that it has convinced very few professional historians and is definitely a minority position.[228] Even prominent postmodernist Keith Jenkins admits this: "Protected by a continued adherence to common
sense empiricism, and realist notions of representation and truth, most historians—
and certainly most of those who might be termed 'academic' or professional 'proper'
historians—have been resistant to that postmodernism which has affected so many
of their colleagues in adjacent discourses."[229]

Nancy Partner offered this hard-hitting critique of the lack of postmodern
influence in historical circles: "It is my impression that the 'linguistic turn' was a
revolving door and that everyone went around and around and got out exactly where
they got in. For all the sophistication of the theory-saturated part of the profession,

---

and the Rules of the Academic Game," in *Religious Advocacy and American History*, ed.
Bruce Kuklcik and D. G. Hart (Grand Rapids: Eerdmans, 1997), 8; Kelly, *Truth Considered
and Applied*, 8n34, 112–15, 127, 198, 201, 206, 212, 216–18.

[227] McCullagh, *Truth of History*, 308 (emphasis added).

[228] Breisach, *Historiography*, 407–8; Nancy F. Partner, "Historicity in an Age of Reality-
Fictions," in *A New Philosophy of History*, ed. Frank Ankersmit and Hans Kellner (Chicago:
University of Chicago Press, 1995), 22; Evans, *In Defense of History*, 4; Mark T. Gilderhus,
History and Historians: A Historiographical Introduction, 7th ed. (Upper Saddle River, NJ:
Prentice Hall, 2010), 118; John Tosh, *The Pursuit of History: Aims, Methods, and New
Directions in the Study of Modern History* (London: Longman, 1984), 194–200.

[229] Jenkins, "On Being Open," 1, also 12.

scholars in all the relevant disciplines that contribute to or depend on historical information carry on in all essential ways as though nothing had changed since Ranke, or Gibbon for that matter."[230] Brian Fay draws a rather forceful conclusion as well: "Except for some interesting exceptions at the margins of the discipline, historical practice is pretty much the same in 1997 as it was in 1967: historians seek to describe accurately and to explain cogently how and why a certain event or situation occurred. . . . For all the talk of narrativism, presentism, postmodernism, and deconstruction, historians write pretty much the same way as they always have."[231] Once again, even accurate surveys prove nothing except the apparent lay of the scholarly landscape. But in the case of the scholarly environment, it does appear as if the postmodernist movement in all its aspects has failed to significantly change the course of historical research.

In sum, it seems that while the five historical a priori challenges dealt with in this section generally exhibited their own flavor in line with this particular discipline, there were also a fair number of similarities between the challenges in this category and some of the earlier philosophical objections. Nevertheless, over two dozen responses were also made, and none of the historical objections seemed to be very troublesome as far as successfully eliminating miracle claims or their investigation.

Hume suggested several times in his major essay that alternate, nonmiraculous scenarios would always be more likely than miracles.[232] Much of the discussion in this volume from this point forward addresses the plethora of naturalistic and other attempts to better explain miracle claims.

Conclusion

We have entertained a total of twenty-two mostly a priori objections to miracle claims drawn from four basic categories. A variety of these challenges concerned topics such as the amount of evidence available, issues regarding the laws of nature and whether they could be adjusted to accommodate miracle claims, how a potential miracle could be identified as an act of God even if it had occurred, and several doubts regarding historical concerns such as postmodern trends.

---

[230] Partner, "Historicity in an Age of Reality-Fictions," in Ankersmit and Kellner, *New Philosophy of History*, 22.

[231] Fay, "Nothing but History?," 83.

[232] Examples include Hume, "Of Miracles," 212, 214–16, 225–26.

Overall, just slightly under 100 total responses were directed toward the various challenges to miracle claims (an average of approximately four and a half responses per critique). The entire cartel of a priori objections appeared to have ended up fairly far from dismantling the potential case for miracles. Of course, the final evaluation at this point depends largely on one's overall worldview outlook. Multiple responses and refutations greeted each of the challenges.

It is apparent that several of the responses raised in answer to questions concerning the occurrence of miracle claims recurred frequently enough that they could be divided into groups. Among the premier retorts to the critical challenges were the following groupings:

(1) A priori *questions* (which are certainly acceptable) too often morph into a priori *rejections*, which are illegitimate responses. The inappropriateness of the latter is both because the challenges reject inductive matters even prior to their investigations and because these retorts often commit a number of informal logical fallacies.

(2) Regarding the *possibility* of miracles, what was referred to here as the frame argument asks: Is it even possible that there could be a God who is able and chooses to act in spite of the framework of nature's laws, or without interfering with any of those laws? The intent, at least at this point, is *not* to try in any way to actually argue that God exists, but simply to raise the awareness that *if* this is even possibly the case, then openness is needed to pursuing particular miracle-claim arguments to which some might not otherwise be open.

(3) Whether or not a miracle *claim* most likely occurred in the space-time world is determined by checking the data and ascertaining the likeliest occurrence. This mostly consists of applying historical research procedures. This was even the bottom line for this chapter, as just noted above. Volume 1 of this study already presented the majority of that data.

(4) However, whether or not an event is actually recognized and *identified* as a true miracle is determined by whether these occurrences can be traced as most likely coming from God's hand. Two such involved approaches that purport to link the resurrection to God, each consisting of many subpoints, was attempted in the first volume of this study. One path moves from the likelihood of a theistic universe to the resurrection as an event performed by God actually requiring his attributes. The second route combines some of Jesus Christ's rather unique actions, teachings, and assertions with his additional resurrection claim in order to ascertain the possibility that such an event just may have provided further validation of these earlier claims.

As stated when this chapter began with its plethora of challenges to the belief in miracles, most of the objections as well as most of the responses were a priori in nature. Hence, the purpose was to set up the nature of potential disputes and responses without stopping to ascertain whether each side actually had justifiable grounds for their assertions. This is the nature of a priori give-and-take. While moving further through this study, however, these a priori comments on both sides need to be pursued, hence requiring further investigation beyond the treatment in these considerations here.[233]

This chapter on Hume and many of his successors pursued many of the pros and cons regarding the existence and recognition of miracles. It might be concluded from the robust number of responses to the objections that this survey ended at the place often arrived at in earlier studies as well. As Flew notes, every case must be examined on its own merits or lack thereof, but there is nothing that prohibits or otherwise stands in the way of the possibility that miracles have occurred in the past, occur in the present, and could occur in the future. Therefore, our search moves forward.

---

[233] Strangely enough, even Antony Flew stated: "The scholarly and the businesslike procedure is to examine arguments one by one." See Flew, *God and Philosophy*, 141. Then later, Flew rather incredibly declared that "our only way of determining the capacities and the incapacities of Nature is to study what does in fact occur" (149; 153 in the 2005 edition). It should be noted carefully that the earlier 1966 text cited here was written when Flew was a thoroughgoing atheist—indeed, the best-known philosophical example of this position in the world. Thus, the oddness of Flew making these assertions is that both statements represent key moves that the Christian apologist also desires to make. This is fantastic common ground to share in order to best investigate these miracle claims.

4

Nineteenth-Century Liberalism and Alternative Resurrection Theories

From approximately 1800 to 1930, German liberalism was the dominant expression of critical theology.[1] While slightly different time frames are sometimes cited, the movement roughly began with the initially anonymous appearance of Friedrich Schleiermacher's volume *On Religion: Speeches to Its Cultured Despisers*.[2] This scholar became known as the "Father of German Liberalism" and is usually also recognized as the most influential thinker of the nineteenth century. As Richard R. Niebuhr declared in his opening sentence of a biographical essay on this theologian, "Religiously speaking, we must concede the nineteenth century to Schleiermacher. No

---

[1] The descriptive term "liberal" in this chapter is far from a derogatory label that one may use to call an opponent. Rather, it is a common name for this movement. For example, see the same title used to characterize this movement in Kirk R. MacGregor, *Contemporary Theology, An Introduction: Classical, Evangelical, Philosophical, and Global Perspectives* (Grand Rapids: Zondervan, 2019), 23–33; and James C. Livingston, *Modern Christian Thought*, 2nd ed., 2 vols. (Upper Saddle River, NJ: Prentice Hall, 1997); see chap. 11 in vol. 1, titled "The Enlightenment and the Nineteenth Century."

[2] Friedrich Schleiermacher, *On Religion: Speeches to Its Cultured Despisers*, trans. John Oman (New York: Harper & Brothers, 1958).

other judgment is possible."[3] Even Karl Barth noted that among recent theologians, "Schleiermacher . . . has no rival."[4]

The movement is generally demarcated as having ended either with World War I or at the 1930 death of Adolf von Harnack, a major voice at the close of this era. German liberalism was preceded by some earlier initial forays into the almost uncharted waters of both biblical as well as theological criticism at the hands of the French and German rationalists, but particularly by the English deists.[5] Few of these deistic participants were well-known or well-respected scholars, with the majority of them being neither philosophically nor theologically trained. They more frequently featured rather roughshod, rambling, and sometimes totally inept attempts and were often characterized as ranting authors who too frequently "shot from the hip" and were ill prepared for serious academic interaction. As a result, according to Peter Gay, the deists "produced a great debate, and a debate the deists were bound to lose: the opposing side engrossed most of the talent."[6] The rationalistic and deistic writers chiefly from the eighteenth century continued the even earlier trends in biblical criticism that were beginning to be developed by their predecessors.[7]

---

[3] Richard R. Niebuhr, "Friedrich Schleiermacher," in *A Handbook of Christian Theologians*, ed. Dean G. Peerman and Martin E. Marty (Cleveland: World, 1965), 17. In reporting this, Niebuhr cites the importance of both Schleiermacher's *On Religion* as well as his theological "magnum opus," *The Christian Faith*, ed. H. R. Mackintosh and J. S. Stewart, 2 vols. (New York: Harper & Row, 1963). In his essay, Niebuhr adds that "Friedrich Schleiermacher may justifiably be called the Kant of modern Protestantism" (ix). Editors Mackintosh and Stewart go as far as to attest in their preface that *The Christian Faith* is, after Calvin's *Institutes*, "the most important work" in the area of Protestant theology to appear up until this time (xxi)! These comments by noteworthy scholars are indeed high praise for the extent of Schleiermacher's influence.

[4] Karl Barth, "Schleiermacher," in *Protestant Thought: From Rousseau to Ritschl*, trans. H. H. Hartwell (New York: Simon & Schuster, 1959), 306.

[5] Representative examples of the latter authors include the primary sources found in Peter Gay, ed., *Deism: An Anthology* (Princeton, NJ: Van Nostrand, 1968), as well as secondary analyses of deistic scholars and ideas, such as John Orr's *English Deism: Its Roots and Fruits* (Grand Rapids: Eerdmans, 1934), an older but valuable source.

[6] Gay, *Deism*, 10.

[7] Examples of the earlier biblical critics who preceded the English deists included more respected philosophers such as Thomas Hobbes (1588–1679) in his important work *Leviathan* (London: Penguin, 2017), along with the major Dutch philosopher Benedict Spinoza (1632–1677) in his *Theological–Political Treatise*, ed. Jonathan Israel (Cambridge: Cambridge University Press, 2007). Spinoza deals with the subjects of prophecy in chaps. 1–2, miracles in chap. 6, and Scripture in chaps. 7–13 of this text. Better known as well as

But the German liberals were a new breed of critical scholars that differed in several respects from these earlier precursors. Though not always the case, the chief representatives during this period were usually credentialed German university professors of theology or philosophy who were best known for devoting much lengthier and more systematic efforts chiefly to studies of the historical Jesus. As a result, so many "Lives of Jesus" were published during this time by a plethora of different scholars that this movement as a whole was later named the "First Quest for the historical Jesus." It was the first such distinctive historical search for Jesus to occur during the next two centuries as well as the longest-lived of the three quests that have emerged thus far.[8] Also, unlike their predecessors, even when the liberal trends eventually died out or changed direction, their development of such major ideas left an indelible imprint on subsequent movements in critical New Testament scholarship.

These German efforts included both new and creative interpretations of Jesus's life as well as other huge developments, such as evolving theses regarding the literary and historical nature of the Gospels. Some of these theses stood the test of time, while others were quite unfounded and supplanted within a generation. Many of these scholars became the forerunners of crucial developments in critical theology long after their time, while others became infamous for particular research with which they have become associated.

More positively, some of the earliest major steps during this period were taken in the huge area of textual (lower) critical studies of the Greek New Testament text. While this is often taken for granted today, a critical Greek text of the New Testament was not really available during the first half of the liberal era. The twelve major developments in New Testament studies noted by Stephen Neill and Tom Wright from 1861 onward include such items as establishing substantially the original Greek text, with Mark increasingly thought to be the earliest Gospel written and with Paul

---

more nuanced and thoughtful were the slightly later critiques of biblical subjects by Scottish skeptical philosopher David Hume, such as his *Dialogues concerning Natural Religion*, ed. Norman Kemp Smith, 2nd ed. (New York: Social Science Publishers, 1948) or his *The Natural History of Religion*, in *Hume on Religion*, ed. Richard Wollheim (London: Collins, 1963), 31–98. An even earlier forerunner in biblical criticism was the Italian philosopher Pietro Pompanazzi (1462–1525).

[8] Further, between the First and Second Quests, a few decades were dominated by Karl Barth and Rudolf Bultmann plus other scholars and often termed the "No Quest" period since, although these scholars were far different from one another, they agreed in opposing historical quests for Jesus.

steadily being considered the most crucial Christian witness.[9] These advances, in turn, facilitated much more careful studies during the last few decades of liberalism.

There was a vast diversity of ideas during the reign of this movement, with scholars taking positions all the way along the philosophical and theological spectrum—from a few scholars who rejected the historical existence of Jesus to those who defended both his miracles as well as high Christology. Emerging during these years, then, was a rather steady stream of critical ideas pertaining to the historicity of the Gospel accounts and the establishment of the main groundwork for Jesus's life. Doubts continued to emerge regarding some of the more dogmatic theological doctrines held in the early church, along with a serious questioning of Jesus's miracles in particular. Foremost on this list were many responses to the resurrection appearances of Jesus.

Nineteenth-Century Liberals and Supernatural Events

Criticism of Jesus's miracles, especially early in the liberal movement, usually took the form of rationalistic attempts to dismiss the supernatural portion of the Gospel narratives. Most frequently (and differing as well from many contemporary critical treatments), liberal interpreters took a Gospel account largely at face value except when it came to the miraculous portions.[10] At that point, a natural alternative hypothesis was usually inserted instead, rendering the entire story as a quite normal episode.

Examples of such a rationalistic approach are supplied often in the famous overview of this liberal period by one of its own, Albert Schweitzer, the highly accomplished scholar with three earned doctor's degrees (including one in medicine). His best-known work by far was *The Quest of the Historical Jesus* (1906), which remains unsurpassed in its reputation for its intricate survey and evaluations of the liberals and has been treated ever since as a primary source for the period, especially its descriptions of more obscure works that have become quite difficult to obtain.[11]

---

[9] See the highly informative discussion by Stephen Neill and Tom Wright, *The Interpretation of the New Testament: 1861–1986*, 2nd ed. (Oxford: Oxford University Press, 1988), 121–23, 360–67.

[10] The other main target of the liberal aim was dogmatic theological pronouncements, where a roughly similar treatment was often applied in order to view more singular, original theological notions as actually being simply untrue for any of several reasons, such as being similar to teachings found in other religious systems.

[11] The first German edition was entitled *Von Reimarus zu Wrede*.

One of the best known of the early liberal rationalists was Kantian scholar Heinrich Paulus, whose own lengthy *Life of Jesus* (almost 1,200 pages) was published in 1828.[12] Its reputation notwithstanding, Schweitzer seems not to have held an overly high view of the work, stating that it was even "inferior to Venturini," who had previously been categorized as one of the writers of a fictitious life of Jesus! As if that comment were not enough, Schweitzer remarks further that Paulus's work was basically just a notated Gospel harmony based on the Fourth Gospel![13]

Schweitzer points out that, in the hands of a rationalist interpreter like Paulus, Jesus's healing miracles were of central concern and were explained creatively. Jesus made good use of his spiritual power and influence as well as various medicines, sometimes described merely as "oil" in the Gospels, and sedatives. Even diet and "devotional exercises" were encouraged! Sometimes the Gospel writers actually knew the secrets of Jesus's use of particular remedies, but their knowledge on these matters was not for public consumption.

Walking on the water during a storm could have been due to the tempest being so severe that the disciples in the boat simply failed to realize that Jesus was merely walking along the shoreline while the boat had blown too close to land. When Jesus was asleep in a boat during another storm, the disciples had perhaps been blown behind the cover of a hill, shielding them from the tempest. So, when Jesus awoke at approximately the same moment and made a comment regarding the storm, his disciples concluded that he had actually been responsible for calming the weather.[14]

On the other hand, the feeding of the 5,000 people was possible because Jesus encouraged everyone who brought food with them (especially the rich who were in attendance) to share, thereby providing plenty of nourishment for everyone. The transfiguration was due to Jesus talking to two men who the three disciples incorrectly assumed were Moses and Elijah, and in the early-morning rays of the sun coming up over the mountaintop, they appeared to be shining. Raising people from the dead had more to do with the sick emerging from comas, or with Jesus noticing signs of life in them.[15]

---

[12] Heinrich Eberhard Gottlob Paulus, *Das Leben Jesu als Grundlage einer reinen Geschichte des Urchristentums*, 3 vols. (Heidelberg: Winter, 1828). See below for more specific details from this volume.

[13] Schweitzer, *The Quest of the Historical Jesus*, trans. William Montgomery (New York: Macmillan, 1968), 50. On Venturini, see 44–47.

[14] Schweitzer, 52.

[15] Schweitzer, 52–53.

Less frequently employed and chiefly appearing a few decades after Schleier-macher, other liberal volumes touted much more radical methodologies that questioned large portions of the Gospel text altogether, including both miraculous and many nonmiraculous passages. In these latter cases, the Gospel accounts were often viewed largely as the later growth of mythical encrustation upon simpler stories that grew in the retelling, totally obscuring the original form.

Often missed is that this later developing mythical method questioned not only the more orthodox, supernatural approaches to the Christian faith regarding both its miracu-lous and dogmatic theological elements, but largely also eliminated cherished notions found in the earlier rational methodologies. In these cases, many of the nonmiraculous Gospel scenarios were typically viewed as lacking historical credentials, hence challeng-ing many of the older views. This did not please the more dominant, rationalistically inclined German liberals, who were not so drastic in their treatment of the Gospel texts.

The best-known nineteenth-century scholar who employed this mythical approach (as well as the most attacked!) was undoubtedly David F. Strauss. Schweitzer reports that Strauss's initial *Life of Jesus*, first published in two volumes in 1835–1836, created one of the greatest theological furors ever.[16] In fact, in July 1835, not very long after its publication, Strauss was relieved of his teaching position at Tübingen University and "exiled."[17]

After losing his teaching position, Strauss's example no doubt served to ensure that this mythological approach would remain the minority methodology during the dominance of the liberal period. Although of lesser reputation (and not to be confused with the earlier and much more influential New Testament scholar F. C. Baur, Strauss's former teacher), Bruno Bauer also engaged in this mythical meth-odology and arrived at more radical conclusions than did Strauss, such as his view that Jesus never even lived![18] Schweitzer was also very critical of Bauer's theses,

---

[16] David Friedrich Strauss, *The Life of Jesus Critically Examined*, trans. George Eliot, ed. Peter C. Hodgson (Mifflintown, PA: Sigler, 1972). Sorting out the early German editions of *Das Leben Jesu* can be a very tricky enterprise, especially given the differing titles and slightly different dates found in various publications. This volume was taken from the second English translation of the fourth German edition. Regarding Strauss, see chaps. 7–9 in Schweitzer, *Quest of the Historical Jesus*, esp. 72, 95–97.

[17] Peter C. Hodgson, "Editor's Introduction: Strauss's Theological Development from 1825–1840," in Strauss, *Life of Jesus*, xxiv.

[18] Bruno Bauer's last theological work was his *Christus und die Cäesaren: Der Ursprung des Christentums aus dem römischen Griechentum*, 2nd ed. (Berlin: Grosser, 1879), where he

viewing them as arbitrary, ungrounded, and self-refuting.[19] Perhaps not surprisingly, Bauer was also forced to stop lecturing after his own crisis of faith.[20] French scholar Ernest Renan is still another who followed this mythical methodology and was likewise removed from teaching in his own country of France as a reaction to his life of Jesus.[21]

Regarding Strauss's approach, Schweitzer remarked, "The distinction between Strauss and those who had preceded him upon this path consists only in this, that prior to him the conception of myth was neither truly grasped nor consistently applied."[22] So the ideas of Strauss, Bruno Bauer, Ernest Renan, and a few other scholars emerged on either side of the midpoint of the nineteenth century. Although they were too radical for the majority of their colleagues in their own day, their notions certainly served as forerunners for some highly influential concepts approximately a century later, championed particularly by Rudolf Bultmann along with certain others. Later, the Jesus Seminar also saluted Strauss's efforts.[23]

---

spends an inordinate amount of space (seven of the eight total sections, and well over 300 pages) on the history of the Roman Caesars. Roman statesman Seneca receives special treatment, beginning with section 1 on Seneca's "Religious Contributions." Incredibly, Bauer charged that Seneca's life and teachings were the basis for much of the Christian message, as Paul (whose epistles Bauer dates by fiat into the second century!) particularly drew out the more mystical components of Seneca's message and adapted them accordingly in order to become Christianity. These last ideas, including the application to Christianity, are developed through the eight chapters of sec. 8 of *Christus und die Cäesaren*. The bottom line is that Jesus's life was therefore invented and that he never actually lived at all.

[19] Schweitzer, *Quest of the Historical Jesus*, 157, 159.

[20] In his indignation after being relieved of his position, Bauer wrote a treatise against Christianity, though its publication was canceled. See Schweitzer, 137–38.

[21] Schweitzer, 180. Incidentally, a comparison of Ernest Renan's French volume *Vie de Jésus* (Paris: Calmann-Levy, 1864), particularly chap. 15 on "La légend de Jésus" (esp. 235–40) and chap. 16, "Miracles" (esp. 243–48, 251), indicates that his thinking is closer to that of Strauss and Bauer than to the rational gyrations of Paulus mentioned above, who tried to invent everyday substitutes for the supernatural portions of Jesus's miracles without disturbing much of the remainder of the Gospel accounts. (We will return below to Renan's treatment of the resurrection.)

[22] Schweitzer, *Quest of the Historical Jesus*, 78.

[23] Robert W. Funk, Roy W. Hoover, and the Jesus Seminar, *The Five Gospels: The Search for the Authentic Words of Jesus* (New York: Macmillan, 1993); the authors dedicate this volume to Galileo Galilei, Thomas Jefferson, and David Strauss, whom these scholars view as contributors and pacesetters before the twentieth century (3).

Naturalistic Theories regarding the Resurrection of Jesus

Still viewed as the central event in the Christian faith, Jesus's resurrection in particular received much attention during the dominance of the German liberal ideas. This
period of time served as the heyday for the development of many natural alternative
responses. With the many lives of Jesus being penned during these years, responding
to the cause of the resurrection experiences and the corresponding deep conviction
of the early disciples played a central role in these discussions. The purpose here is
to outline many of these naturalistic theses along with their supporters, with many
critiques and other responses coming later.

The Swoon or Apparent Death Hypotheses

One of the earliest attempts to question the historicity of the resurrection appearances
was to suppose that Jesus never really died by crucifixion in the first place. Up until
Strauss's multipronged critique against this view in his initial publication of *The Life
of Jesus*, it was the most popular of the naturalistic theories against the resurrection.
Somehow, Jesus avoided the intended outcome of his Roman death sentence. This
initial and popular approach was that Jesus escaped death, either purposefully (as
with an orchestrated setup) or accidentally (as in passing out and recovering later).
Differing "plot" scenarios may have involved others who worked variously to ensure
that Jesus would be rescued before the Romans' intended outcome. The perpetrators
in some of these volumes were often identified as the Essenes, involving narratives
that Schweitzer rather derisively termed the "fictitious lives" of Jesus.[24] The second
alternative generally involved Jesus being injured seriously and considered dead by
friends and enemies alike, though recovering sufficiently at a later time so that he
could appear to his followers and live a more or less normal life after that, perhaps like
Paul after being stoned and left for dead at Lystra. Some slightly different variations
existed here as well.

    One of the earliest to hold the second option of the swoon or apparent death
position was English deist Peter Annet. He wrote several brief treatises against the
Gospel accounts of Jesus's resurrection, most of them directed to critics who had published against his views and often repeating his salient points time and again.

---

[24] Schweitzer, *Quest of the Historical Jesus*, chap. 4.

Written in the mid-eighteenth century, Annet's works address many of the key areas that were most associated with skeptics who criticized Christianity. By today's critical standards, these books read as antiquated and outdated tracts that address questions very few are asking today, though some are still relevant. Examples of the latter would include the more general criticisms of belief in the notion of miracles, asserting that such events are an "absurdity" to common sense and even "contrary to the attributes of God."[25] The last statement is probably due to Annet's belief that God does not break his own created laws of nature.[26] Further, presupposing the infamous words repeated by a large chorus of skeptics today, he writes, "I ought to have *extraordinary evidence*, to induce me to believe *extraordinary things*, that are supernatural."[27]

More specifically regarding Jesus's resurrection, one of Annet's most frequent claims is that the Gospel accounts in general and the resurrection stories in particular are filled with discrepancies and contradictions of various sorts, lacking harmony throughout.[28] If we can judge from the amount of time he spent on two subjects in particular, a constant bother to Annet were apparently the Gospels' claims that Jesus repeatedly predicted the event of his resurrection ahead of time, and Matthew's lone account that guards were placed in front of his tomb after it had been sealed. In one volume, these two issues occupied approximately a quarter of his entire text.[29] One can only surmise, but perhaps the reason for the concerted efforts at these two points (with his arguments often being repeated) was that to allow these issues to go

---

[25] Peter Annet, *The Sequel of the Resurrection of Jesus Considered* (London: Rose, 1749), 4–5. Of Annet's little volumes on the resurrection, this one in particular spends more space talking around issues while rarely addressing the most significant aspects that he poses himself.

[26] Peter Annet, *Supernaturals Examined: In Four Dissertations on Three Treatises* (London: Page, n.d.), 20, 65, respectively. Other ideas against the belief in miracles are expressed in Annet's *The Resurrection Defenders Stript of All Defense* (London: Printed by the Author, 1745), 21–27, including some thoughts on telling the difference between the Devil's miracles and God's miracles (25–26). The work is signed as "Moral Philosopher" at the end of the volume, 95.

[27] Peter Annet, *The Resurrection of Jesus Considered: In Answer to the Tryal of the Witnesses* (London: Printed by the Author, 1744), 65. Here also the author is identified as a "Moral Philosopher."

[28] Annet's works mention this recurring theme rather regularly, such as in *Resurrection of Jesus Considered*, 35–37, 50–52, 59–60, 70; *Supernaturals Examined*, 8, 22–23; and *Resurrection Defenders*, 4, 42–45, 50–53, 59–67, 86.

[29] Annet, *Resurrection of Jesus Considered*, 20–49; cf. also Annet's *Resurrection Defenders*, 4–6, 10–14, 27–31; *Supernaturals Examined*, 23.

uncontested would make his postulated natural hypotheses more difficult to establish and maintain.

While Annet was probably one of the first modern critics to suppose the possibility that Jesus avoided death by crucifixion, he mentions this option quite infrequently in his works despite his many repetitions of his arguments elsewhere. It is also clear that this hypothesis was not the only natural suggestion he ventured as to what might have occurred. For example, asserting that reason is his only rule, he declared that "all Men die, and rise no more," and since the notion of a resurrection is contrary to nature, resurrections "never" occur.[30] As to potential natural causes in Jesus's case, Annet mentions the possibility of apparitions, faulty imagination, confusion, credulity, or even deception (though apparently without questioning the disciples' own sincerity).[31]

Amazingly, regarding the sources of information that Paul was citing in 1 Cor 15:3, Annet states that these reports were hearsay accounts. Mentioning a couple of reasons for this conclusion, Annet states that since Paul was "born out of due time" (15:8 KJV), this indicated that Paul had not even been born yet. Therefore, these testimonies were from before his own time and thus provide no eyewitness data at all. If that is not enough, he takes Paul's comment that some of the 500 witnesses to a resurrection appearance of Christ had fallen asleep (15:6) to mean that maybe they had been dreaming or just coming out of their sleep when Jesus appeared to them.[32] It seems from the immediate context that Annet means these statements seriously.

Then we arrive at what Annet is best known for questioning. He addresses the time when Jesus was in the tomb, asking whether Jesus was dead or alive. If the latter, perhaps he broke the seals from inside the sepulcher.[33] But if the Roman spear wound reported in the Gospel of John was doubted, then one could indeed also question Jesus's death by crucifixion altogether. After all, John adds that Jesus's legs were not broken (John 19:31–33) with all the complications that would entail. Further, Pilate

---

[30] Annet, *Resurrection of Jesus Considered*, 10, 91–92.

[31] Annet, 63, 66, 85–86; *Supernaturals Examined*, 66.

[32] Annet, *Resurrection of Jesus Considered*, 65–66.

[33] Annet, 46–51. While this may seem like a difficult question to reconcile with his longer treatment in the immediate context where he is contesting Matthew's account of the guards and seal being authentic in the first place (34–49), he is still raising a long string of questions. Beginning with the words "if sealed" (46) may indicate that he is simply making a hypothetical statement in the case that the tomb sealing did occur anyway.

himself wondered how Jesus had died by crucifixion so quickly, summoning the centurion to hear the report for himself (Mark 15:44–45). So perhaps Jesus was not dead when Joseph buried him.[34]

Annet spends more time on the apparent death hypothesis than on the other suppositions, which may indeed indicate he holds it as the most likely view of what really happened to Jesus. But it cannot be concluded that this was his only option, for as we have seen, he raises a few other possibilities along the way. Nonetheless, it still may have been the best known of his responses, perhaps because it appeared to be quite a novel position at that time, just a couple of hundred years after the Protestant Reformation itself.

Not long after Annet's series of small volumes on the resurrection of Jesus, Karl Friedrich Bahrdt and Karl Heinrich Venturini also supported the swoon or apparent death theory. Including their works in his chapter on the "fictitious lives of Jesus," Schweitzer introduced this chapter with the unflattering comment that these and other authors consisted of "a few imperfectly equipped free-lances" who nonetheless "first attempted to apply, with logical consistency, a non-supernatural interpretation to the miracle stories of the Gospel."[35]

However, as Schweitzer commented further, since they were unable to pinpoint any causes in the Gospels to make the necessary connections for their story, these authors had to resort to inventing this backdrop for themselves. To do so, both writers resorted to hypothesizing a secret society, which was "rather a sorry makeshift." Hence, this "colouring of fiction" is the reason for the moniker of the fictitious lives of Jesus.[36]

The first of the two writers, Bahrdt, composed his work *Ausführung des Plans und Zwecks Jesu: In Briefen an Wahrheit suchende Leser* in eleven volumes over an eight-year period (1784–1792).[37] He hypothesized that Nicodemus and Joseph of Arimathea were secret members of the Essene community. On the lookout for a good messianic figure, they adopted Jesus to fit their needs. These and other well-placed friends assisted Jesus, orchestrating many of the events during his life, among them his miracles.

---

[34] Annet, 61–64.

[35] Schweitzer, *Quest of the Historical Jesus*, 38.

[36] Schweitzer, 38–39.

[37] Karl Friedrich Bahrdt, *Ausführung des Plans und Zwecks Jesu: In Briefen an Wahrheit suchende Leser*, 11 vols. (Berlin: Mylius, 1784–1792).

For example, following the sort of rationalistic design agenda already described above, Luke the physician directed Jesus's healing efforts. The crucifixion was a staged event that worked out exactly as planned in spite of a few close calls. Luke made drugs available that were capable of helping Jesus cope with the horrible pain and also resist death. These men also made sure that Jesus was only on the cross for a minimal amount of time. The Roman centurion was bribed so that Jesus's ankles were not broken, and Joseph took Jesus down from the cross and placed him in the Essenes' cave so that he could be nursed back to health.

Since Jesus was healthy, he healed quickly, incredibly being able to walk by just the third day even though the nail wounds remained open and unhealed by that time! He was able to appear numerous times to his followers, retreating to his cave after each visit. After the last appearance, Jesus encouraged his followers and then walked up the Mount of Olives into a low cloud as they watched, causing them to think that he had ascended to heaven. Only rarely was he seen again, such as when he appeared to Paul on the Damascus road. Still, though unseen, he could quietly direct the members of his enclave until he died.[38]

Our second author, Karl Heinrich Venturini, developed another plot thesis in his text *Natürliche Geschichte des grossen Propheten von Nazareth*, published in four volumes from 1800–1802.[39] His chief idea was that Jesus's spiritual message had to be draped in material garb so as to appeal to the masses. So, Jesus's miracles were performed with an ethical intent in mind—to hasten the acceptance of his message. But these events were not actually miraculous. For example, Jesus employed medicines in healing people and always carried around his medicine bag! The dead were raised from comas.

On the other hand, the nature miracles were performed more by the knowledge of the natural order along with good timing rather than by any sort of supernatural control on Jesus's part. Changing the water to wine was "performed" with some jars of wine that Jesus had brought to the wedding as a gift.

The Essenes were also active in Venturini's story. They watched over and guided the child Jesus even while he still lived in Egypt and trained both him and John the Baptist. Also, in true rationalistic fashion, the supernatural elements in stories such as Jesus's baptism, the temptation, his paying taxes with the fish that

---

[38] Schweitzer, *Quest of the Historical Jesus*, 39–44.

[39] Karl Heinrich Venturini, *Natürliche Geschichte des grossen Propheten von Nazareth*, 4 vols. (Copenhagen: Bethlehem, 1800–1802).

Peter caught, and so on were all explained quite naturally in order to keep the basic story intact.

However, quite unlike Bahrdt and all the gyrations that he claimed occurred at the crucifixion, Jesus was really arrested and killed. Jesus expected to die and then meet his disciples later in eternity rather than being raised to life again. But Joseph of Arimathea acted quickly, procured permission from Pilate, bribed the centurion, and took down Jesus's body. He and Nicodemus washed the body, with blood from the spear wound still flowing freely from Jesus's side wound, and placed him in the tomb. The other "Essene Brethren" helped out as well, and those who were seen the next morning walking around the tomb area in their white garb were taken to be angels. But then Jesus actually revived and was nursed back to health. He came out of his hiding place on occasion to see his followers and got better with the assistance of the Essene brothers. After forty days, he left his disciples.[40]

Early in the nineteenth century, Friedrich Schleiermacher was on his way to becoming the lead liberal voice of the nineteenth century. This is the real beginning of German liberalism. The pens of Annet, Bahrdt, and Venturini began popularizing the swoon hypothesis before the liberal voices. But while the English deists and the authors of the fictitious lives of Jesus were read and no doubt affected views, they did not present the sort of gravitas of many of the leading liberal scholars. With these more scholarly pacesetters, a much more influential critique could be articulated.

To say that Schleiermacher's view of the death and resurrection of Jesus is not the easiest to discern is somewhat of an understatement, and for more than one reason. Different passages in Schleiermacher's writings appear to conflict with each other, and at any rate seem to use imprecise language. That is why seasoned interpreters among other scholars frequently disagree regarding the final stance of this German theologian.

At least one background matter is relevant here as well. Like many intellectuals of his time, especially after the publications of David Hume, Schleiermacher thought that the concept of miracle was very difficult given what we know concerning the laws of nature. When and where miracles are embraced, there seems to be little knowledge of these laws, whereas when the laws are fully appreciated in scientific terms, there tends to be much less talk of miracles. But why would God disrupt the "original immutable course" of nature by suspending its laws? Actually, "every absolute

---

[40] Schweitzer, *Quest of the Historical Jesus*, 44–47.

miracle would destroy the whole system of nature." Such events, if introduced, would "completely abrogate the conception of nature." Hence, "we should abandon the idea of the absolutely supernatural."[41]

Along with views such as these, Schleiermacher concluded that some miracle accounts in the New Testament should not be taken literally but symbolically, while the supernatural portions of others could best be explained naturalistically. Nature miracles, in particular, are the most questioned variety.[42]

From the outset, then, it might seem from these considerations that the likelihood does not favor Schleiermacher thinking that Jesus actually rose from the dead. But this is where the details tend to grow somewhat murky and are disputed by various commentators and are more difficult to unravel.[43] For starters, Schleiermacher asserts that, for him, it is "a matter of complete indifference" whether or not Jesus actually died due to crucifixion, which he then repeats. Actually, he thinks it may even be easier to presume that Jesus had not yet died, due to the brief time that he spent on the cross. Regardless, there are no grounds to prove the issue either way, so the answer is simply unknown.[44]

---

[41] All the quotations above were taken from Schleiermacher, *Christian Faith*, 1:178–84. Some similar matters are also discussed in 2:448–50.

[42] Friedrich Schleiermacher, *The Life of Jesus*, trans. S. Maclean Gilmour, ed. Jack C. Verheyden (Mifflintown, PA: Sigler, 1975), 193, 196–98, 206–10, 226, 420–22, 441. Schweitzer explains that Schleiermacher's response to the nature of miracles is why he should still be considered as a rationalist. See Schweitzer, *Quest of the Historical Jesus*, 58. A crucial matter should also be mentioned regarding Schleiermacher's specific volume here. The text was reconstructed chiefly from the notes of his 1832 lectures on the historical Jesus and combined with the notes from five of his students. Hence, such a format is not necessarily as "tight" as one might wish. It may also serve to explain some of the questions regarding the contents of this volume, such as the issue of whether Schleiermacher thought that Jesus was truly dead before the conclusion of the crucifixion. The original editor of the volume, K. A. Rütnik, presented Schleiermacher's notes first in the text, followed by the student's notes, indicated by lecture numbers along with a date. The volume was published in 1864, thirty years after Schleiermacher's death in 1834, which came two years after the original lectures were given. These editorial details are contained in Verheyden's introduction (xvi, xix).

[43] Though we will not in this context be able to sift through the pros and cons of the larger interpretation of Schleiermacher's views, we will remark briefly on the most salient aspects of the direct discussion regarding the death and resurrection of Jesus.

[44] Schleiermacher, *Life of Jesus*, 415–17. Without in any sense making a similar suggestion regarding Schleiermacher, one may be reminded here of the comment made by Søren Kierkegaard at about this same time, who charged that Gotthold Ephraim Lessing

However this remark may be taken, some major theological commentators have judged that Schleiermacher actually held that Jesus was only "apparently" dead, from which he recovered. This of course would seem to necessitate some species of the swoon or apparent death theory.[45] The operative terms in the conversation, used by both Schweitzer and Barth, seem to be "apparent death," while Strauss simply stated that Schleiermacher and Paulus agreed that "Jesus was not quite dead," which Strauss terms a "lame" position to hold (probably no pun intended).

However, Schleiermacher makes other statements on this topic that must be considered, however briefly, due to their relevance to our topic here. For example, following both Heinrich Paulus and Karl August von Hase, Schleiermacher asserts that the only sure way to know that someone is dead is by the presence of decomposition. But then Schleiermacher adds that the presence of the separated blood and water after the Roman spear entered his side may very well indicate that "chemical decomposition" had already begun, in that the act would seem to have been a test to indicate whether or not Jesus had already died. Even so, Schleiermacher adds, all we may be able to say is that the soldier "thought of Christ as really dead."[46] So even here, it appears that we cannot be sure, hence his stated doubts.

---

affirmed his belief in certain major Christian doctrines even while raising some critical issues, since he was only agreeing by way of concession. See Søren Kierkegaard, *Concluding Unscientific Postscript*, trans. David F. Swenson (Princeton: Princeton University Press, 1941), 88. But it must be asked, if Schleiermacher actually meant to defend Christianity (or at least to affirm it) at the absolute central point of the gospel message, how could it be simply "a matter of complete indifference" to him as to whether or not Jesus died by crucifixion? Even so, this question is not meant to make assertions regarding his position, but only to note that these may be some of the reasons why scholars have long missed or even questioned his comments.

[45] Some of the influential scholars who make this assertion concerning Schleiermacher include David Friedrich Strauss, *A New Life of Jesus*, 2nd ed., 2 vols. (London: Williams & Norgate, 1879), 24. This volume by Strauss (German: *Das Leben Jesu für das deutsche Volk bearbeitet*) should not be confused with his 1835–1836 *Life of Jesus* (*Das Leben Jesu*). Other prominent critical scholars who agree with Strauss's view of Schleiermacher on this point include German liberals Schweitzer, *Quest of the Historical Jesus*, 64; and Theodor Keim, *The History of Jesus of Nazara: Considered in Its Connection with the National Life of Israel, and Related in Detail*, trans. Arthur Ransom (London: Williams & Norgate, 1883), 6:328; as well as prominent twentieth-century scholar Karl Barth, *Church Dogmatics*, vol. 4.1, *The Doctrine of Reconciliation*, trans. G. W. Bromiley, ed. G. W. Bromiley and T. F. Torrance (Edinburgh: T&T Clark, 1956), 340.

[46] Schleiermacher, *Life of Jesus*, 415, 427–28. But strangely enough, Schleiermacher also makes the rather odd comment that "crucifixion was carried out by people who had no skill

One other item should be mentioned here. In a comment quite reminiscent of Strauss's famous critique of the swoon or apparent death thesis, Schleiermacher remarks:

> If we think of Christ as bearing the external marks of his crucifixion . . . the journeying hither and yon seems quite improbable, but this improbable action took place as early as the first day. Then he appears as one quite healthy, who walks without difficulty to Emmaus and back again. . . . We cannot represent him as those do who maintain the hypothesis of an apparent death. We cannot think of him as spending this time with his life force at a low ebb.[47]

This relevant comment would appear to end the question for many, but it really has not done so. Hence, editor Jack Verheyden chides Schweitzer and Strauss for not observing what he thinks are clear distinctions in the works of their fellow German theologian that Jesus had in fact truly died due to crucifixion.[48]

In his own day, even Karl August von Hase complained that his view along with that of Schleiermacher needed to be distinguished much more clearly from the position of Paulus. But frankly, Hase's own distinctions are quite confusing in themselves. It makes one wonder what the actual difference is between a more "obvious" *apparent* death where the body later revives (see below for Paulus's position) and an *actual* death that can still receive life back into it again (Hase, Schleiermacher, and Venturini).[49] Schleiermacher's distinctions are very difficult to discern as well.[50]

Candidly, of the two positions, it is the view held by Schleiermacher and Hase that requires the most explaining! But if Schleiermacher and Hase wanted to distinguish their understanding from a rather straightforward apparent death thesis, why would

---

in execution" (419). It is rather difficult to decipher what his particular comment here may or may not reveal regarding the direction of his view. Is he allowing or making way for less than a full and complete death on the cross? Or is he simply mistaken, even though in his day the prowess of the Roman soldiers was certainly known? On the positions of Hase and Paulus regarding bodily decomposition, see Schweitzer, *Quest of the Historical Jesus*, 60 (Hase) and 64 (Paulus).

[47] Schleiermacher, *Life of Jesus*, 455–56.

[48] Jack Verheyden, "Introduction," in Schleiermacher, *Life of Jesus*, 456n60.

[49] Karl August von Hase, *Geschichte Jesu: Nach akademischen Vorlesungen* (Leipzig: Breitkopf and Härtel, 1876), see section 112 on the resurrection, esp. 600–603. Hase's version of this thesis from almost fifty years earlier was published in his volume chiefly for the use of students: *Das Leben Jesu zunächst für akademische Studien* (Leipzig: Breitkopf and Härtel, 1829).

[50] Schleiermacher, *Life of Jesus*, 431–32, 444, 447.

they argue so confusingly and tortuously for Jesus's *actual* death on the cross that nonetheless left behind a body that could *still* receive life back into it?

Of course, the distinction just made from the statement of Hase's own view above—as well as Schleiermacher's—could also describe Jesus's resurrection itself. But that would require a little "unpacking" since that does not seem to be the only possible meaning of their wording. So in spite of Schleiermacher's strong comment above concerning Jesus's seeming healthy appearances, as well as Hase's attempted clarifications, these scholars could have helped themselves immensely in the understanding of their views. True, Hase helpfully states that Jesus was not rescued by any human means. But at the end of the day, why do both he and Schleiermacher insist that either an apparent death or a resurrection could be true, that neither position hurts Christianity, and that they basically seem not to care whether or not Jesus actually died by crucifixion?[51] Arguably, no one should have to work this hard to figure out someone's position and at such a crucial point as well.

Among the views of Annet, Bahrdt, Venturini, Hase, and Schleiermacher, then, Heinrich Paulus was probably the best-known proponent of the swoon or apparent death position during the heyday of liberal theology.[52] In his life of Jesus published in 1828, Paulus proposed that when Jesus was on the cross, he fell into a death-imitating trance. The soldier's lance thrust was simply a superficial wound, and Jesus revived after being placed in a cool tomb surrounded by pungent spices. The storm and the earthquake in particular caused the stone to roll away from the front of the tomb and Jesus was able to walk out. His severe crucifixion injuries explained why he was not always recognized, especially at first, but the nail wounds in his hands (though Paulus held that Jesus's feet were not nailed to the cross) served most to identify him to his followers.[53]

Thomas's doubts and Jesus's actual presence before his disciples served to indicate that he was not some sort of phantom but was genuinely present with them. Because

---

[51] Hase, *Geschichte Jesu*, 602–3; Schleiermacher, *Life of Jesus*, 414–15.

[52] Of course, the ambiguity in Schleiermacher's position may be what keeps him from holding this dubious distinction.

[53] Paulus, *Das Leben Jesu*, 1:265, 281–82. Heinrich Eberhard Gottlob Paulus's later work, *Exegetisches Handbuch über die drei ersten Evangelien*, 3 vols. (Heidelberg: Winter, 1830–1833), includes a very detailed discussion of the crucifixion and resurrection of Jesus in all four Gospels (in spite of the volume's title). In the 1842 edition of this text, this material occupies pages 660–928 of vol. 3. Key pages pertaining to the discussion are 3:669–750, 785–86, 793–94, 834–35, 866, 881–83, 893.

he was still recovering, however, he was unable to remain with them for long periods of time or to overexert himself. After concluding that he was actually dying, Jesus appeared to his followers one last time on the Mount of Olives, blessed them, and then walked off into a low cloud. Nobody knew when or where he died.[54]

Schweitzer lists three later "imaginative" or "fictitious" lives of Jesus that also embraced the swoon or apparent death hypothesis. These are the texts written by Charles Hennell, August Gfrörer, and Joseph Salvador—all appearing about the same time as Strauss's volume *Das Leben Jesu*. Hennell was a London businessman who patterned his work on Venturini's earlier "fictitious" text and similarly employed a plot thesis. For Hennell, Jesus was the son of an Essene and entered his ministry under their supervision. After his crucifixion, the Essenes removed him from the cross and resuscitated him.[55]

Gfrörer was a church curate and lecturer at Tübingen University who had jettisoned his Christian faith. He was at Tübingen while Strauss was still there. The second of his two volumes took a different methodological tact than the first, as he adapted Strauss's mythical approach to the Gospels. Gfrörer considered Luke to be the most historically reliable of the Gospels, with John still being treated fairly positively. Matthew was written later, utilized worse sources, and invented some material. Mark is even dated in the first quarter of the second century.[56]

When it came to the crucifixion and appearances of Jesus, Gfrörer's plot thesis is also apparent. Since there is no historical basis for the conjuring act that he conceives, his scenario earned him the "imaginative" moniker bestowed by Schweitzer. Like so many of these interpretations, Joseph of Arimathea was an Essene, whose group made use of Jesus for their own purposes. The Roman guards were bribed. Jesus was removed from the cross before dying and taken to Joseph's tomb nearby, where he

---

[54] In Paulus's German text, *Das Leben Jesu*, the discussion of the burial occurs in 2:256–66 (sections 204–6), while the resurrection appearances are discussed in 2:266–344 (sections 207–15). Schweitzer's earlier derogatory comment that Paulus's *Life of Jesus* was even inferior to Venturini's (one of the so-called "fictitious lives" authors) was because Paulus was said to have basically built a harmony of the Gospels with added notes. See Schweitzer, *Quest of the Historical Jesus*, 50, 54–55. Paulus's *Das Leben Jesu* indicates that Schweitzer's comment is quite accurate, where the Gospel texts are grouped by subject matter, juxtaposed and interspersed with Paulus's own discussion following.

[55] Schweitzer, *Quest of the Historical Jesus*, 161–62; Charles Christian Hennell, *Untersuchungen über den Ursprung des Christentums* (Stuttgart: Hallberger, 1840).

[56] Schweitzer, *Quest of the Historical Jesus*, 163–64; August Friedrich Gfrörer, *Kritische Geschichte des Urchristenthums*, 2 vols. (Stuttgart: Schweizerbart, 1831, 1838).

was successfully resuscitated. Understood in this manner, Jesus's appearances were historical events, even though they were definitely not postmortem miracles as in orthodox Christian teaching. Then the Essene community developed its own ideas into what became the church![57]

Joseph Salvador was a French Jew who postulated that Jesus stood in the long line of those who drew inspiration from the ancient tales of Middle Eastern gods and goddesses.[58] In terms of Jesus's "death" and later appearances, Salvador's version of the plot thesis hypothesized the involvement of Pilate's wife, the Roman centurion, and Joseph of Arimathea. The thrust of the Roman lance was simply a scratch that was not meant to kill Jesus. All of these items contributed to Pilate being surprised that Jesus had been pronounced dead so quickly. The result is that Jesus's death was only apparent, and he was alive when he was taken down and buried. Secret disciples placed him in a garden tomb. Later, Jesus actually appeared to his followers.[59]

This ends some of the major treatments of the well-known German liberal versions of the swoon or apparent death hypotheses.[60] This general notion seems clearly to be the most popular of the naturalistic hypotheses pertaining to Jesus's

---

[57] Schweitzer, *Quest of the Historical Jesus*, 165–66.

[58] Joseph Salvador, *Jésus-Christ et sa doctrine: Histoire de la naissance de l'église* (Paris: Guyot et Scribe, Libraires, 1838), esp. incl. his fairly lengthy list of mythological examples on 152n2. Other instances appear on 184–86, 563.

[59] Salvador, 144–206, esp. 193–98. Other areas of interest in this volume include Salvador's discussion of the importance of the resurrection message, especially in Paul (180–82), as well as his evaluating the issue of the Jewish leaders entreating Pilate for a guard for the tomb entrance (197). Like perhaps even the vast majority of critical scholars, Salvador also lists a lengthy number of proposed Gospel contradictions found in these same accounts (esp. 199–200n2).

[60] Another of the more outlandish treatments singled out by Schleiermacher in *Life of Jesus*, 451, was that by "the notorious" Jacob Andreas Brennecke, *Biblischer Beweis, dass Jesus nach seiner Auferstehung noch 27 Jahre leibhaftig auf Erden gelebt, und zum Wohle der Menschheit in der Stille fortgewirkt habe*, 2nd ed. (Lüneburg: Gerold and Wahlstab, 1819). As his title indicates, Brennecke proposed that Jesus lived on earth for twenty-seven more years after his "resurrection," appeared to Paul while he was still living in his earthly body, and also managed to direct other events in the early church. In Schleiermacher, *Life of Jesus*, 451–52n58, editor Verheyden mentions Brennecke's proposal that Nicodemus used ointments and spices to rouse Jesus from his stupor in a manner slightly reminiscent of some of the questions raised above concerning Schleiermacher's and Hase's own treatments. However, much more clearly than in the latter two German scholars, Brennecke's Jesus dies at sixty in either late AD 60 or early 61.

resurrection during the first third of the nineteenth century. These theses could come in the form of the ungrounded, plot-oriented, "fictitious" attempts of Bahrdt, Venturini, Hennell, Gfrörer, and Salvador, which usually feature Essenes affecting events from behind the scenes—facetiously, as if they were stationed even behind bushes and the like! Or they could concern the best-known, more serious example by Paulus. Or the disputed views of Schleiermacher and Hase could be the topic of discussion. But few liberal discussions are more intriguing than these versions. As we will observe in the next chapter, even these German liberal scholars themselves freely critiqued each other's positions, and these apparent death views surely received their share of the criticisms and then some. Although being quite popular at the time, the apparent death scenarios were not the only brand of natural "resurrection" flavors.

Fraud Type 1: Jesus's Disciples Stole Jesus's Dead Body and Lied about His Appearances

Probably owing to the highly problematic issues raised by this alternative approach, this hypothesis was arguably not employed by any of the better-known German liberal scholars. Yet it still needs to be documented here briefly due to the role that certain of these ideas played in critical thinking during both this period as well as later times. Just as the English deist Peter Annet held the swoon or apparent death theory just before the beginning of the liberal era, another English deist, Thomas Woolston, employed a fraud thesis decades earlier than Annet. Woolston is usually thought to have been mentally ill and was imprisoned in 1730 for blasphemy. Since he could not pay the fine, he remained in prison until his death in 1733.

Woolston maintained that he was indeed a Christian, but one who disbelieved literal interpretations (which he said nauseated him) in favor of allegorical notions. He enumerated three major religious ideas that he stood for: restoring the place of allegorical interpretations, striving for a "universal and unbounded Toleration of Religion," and abolishing a "hired and establish'd priesthood." Altogether, he wanted "a spiritual *Jesus*" without the miracles and other physical manifestations.[61]

In his sixth and last discourse on miracles, written particularly on Jesus's resurrection, Woolston proposed that a physical resurrection would "be the most

---

[61] Thomas Woolston, *A Defence of the Discourses on Miracles* (London: Printed for the Author, 1729), edited and reproduced in editor Gay's compilation, *Deism*, esp. 131–35, 138.

notorious and monstrous Imposture, that ever was put upon mankind."[62] Rather, Jesus's disciples stole his dead body out of the burial tomb: "The Body was to be removed and a Resurrection pretended to the Delusion."[63] Again, the body was taken away and "a Resurrection talk'd of."[64] Yet again, the disciples stole the body "in order to pretend a Resurrection" and then they later spoke about Jesus's appearances to them, including his giving them messages.[65]

Woolston plainly and repeatedly refers to his naturalistic thesis as "Fraud" or even the "Argument of Fraud" or the "Proof of Fraud," presumably because both stealing the body and the disciples' proclamations of Jesus's appearances (which were, of course, lies) were all perpetrated as duplicitous and deceitful actions.[66] Further, Woolston calls Jesus a "Deceiver," mentions the possibility of the disciples bribing the guards at the tomb, and points out conflicts in the texts. He even calls the entire ignominy "the most bare faced, and the most self evident Imposture that ever was put upon the World," all of which also points to various species of fraud.[67]

But why would the disciples be willing to die for a lie? Woolston declares that this is not an issue at all, because many "Cheats and Criminals . . . have asserted their Innocency" even to the point of death. Woolston thought this was the most successful farce in the universe, were it not for his taking the necessary steps to expose it.[68]

A few decades after Woolston wrote, but still before the birth of liberalism, German rationalist and professor of oriental languages at the University of Hamburg Hermann Samuel Reimarus (1694–1768) also championed the fraud or stolen body thesis. He wrote a 4,000-page manuscript entitled *An Apology for the Rational Worshippers of God*. It was not penned for publication, though it circulated anonymously among some individuals. Then, between 1774 and 1778, a librarian at Wolfenbüttel named Gotthold Ephraim Lessing published seven fragments from

---

[62] Thomas Woolston, *A Sixth Discourse on the Miracles of our Saviour, In View of the Present Controversy between Infidels and Apostates* (London: Printed for the Author, 1729), 5. Woolston begins this work on page 2 by pronouncing once again that he supports "the mystical Resurrection of *Jesus* . . . mystical Resurrection of our *spiritual Jesus*."

[63] Woolston, 16.

[64] Woolston, 17.

[65] Woolston, 29, also similarly, 20–21, 25.

[66] Woolston, 15, 18, 20, 21, 28, 30, 32, 33.

[67] Woolston, 5, 14, 19, 27, 47.

[68] Woolston, 27.

Reimarus's larger work. One of the fragments was entitled "Concerning the Story of the Resurrection."[69]

Reimarus conjectured that after Jesus's death, the disciples experienced a great amount of anxiety and fear, which lasted for a while. Still, they gathered their courage, reasoning that they could pretend to be brave and courageous even in the face of death. Further, they could preach the kingdom of God themselves, appearing to perform miracles, just as they had seen Jesus do repeatedly. So within a mere twenty-four hours, they stole Jesus's body out of the tomb. When the empty tomb was discovered by others, the disciples feigned their actual surprise and ran to the tomb, only to discover it to be empty. The disciples hid Jesus's body for fifty days so that it would be unrecognizable by that time, just in case anyone should challenge them. Then they could never be disproven.

Afterward, they began preaching and proclaimed boldly that they had actually seen Jesus alive again at several times and places, even in groups, as well as touched and walked with him and frequently even spoke with and ate with him. Later, he ascended to heaven, promising to return. To be sure, they accepted all the payments and gifts that they were offered. Of course, they had to agree unanimously in all of these aspects too, so as not to expose the plan.[70]

The element of the disciples' fraud, from which this hypothesis gets its name, is more than evident here, being observed many times over. Numerous of these "shady" items are quite apparent, such as the disciples stealing Jesus's body in the first place, feigning their surprise at seeing the empty tomb, hiding the dead body of their master, preaching a message they knew to be false (at least in its most central claim), faking their bravery and life changes when they were not really true, and lying about all the details of Jesus's appearances, including the ascension. Along the way, of course, they willingly accepted many gifts for their dishonest efforts. Of course, all of these false stories and actions had to be duplicated many times over and kept up consistently throughout their lives, with everyone in the group relating the same lies, even when it resulted in death for many of them.

---

[69] Many relevant details are provided by Schweitzer, *Quest of the Historical Jesus*, 14–26. Also helpful is the information in Daniel P. Fuller's account in *Easter Faith and History* (Grand Rapids: Eerdmans, 1965), 31–35; and in Gregory W. Dawes, ed., *The Historical Jesus Quest: Landmarks in the Search for the Jesus of History*, rev. ed. (Louisville: Westminster John Knox, 2000), esp. chap. 1, "The Gospels as Fraud."

[70] Some of the recent section demarcations in Reimarus's text are rather confusing and actually differ with each other. The text utilized here is Charles Voysey, ed., *Fragments from Reimarus* (London: Williams & Norgate, 1879), see chap. 5, sections 54–57.

What a wild scenario! It is hardly any wonder that the scholars of the nineteenth-century German liberal establishment strictly avoided the hypotheses of Woolston and Reimarus with their many required idiosyncrasies, including features that demanded exact timing, personalities that revolved back and forth while always remaining uniform with regard to their central message and actions, and the ability to live with an untold number of contradictions, not to mention a host of other foibles. Still, the view remains a historical fixture of the resurrection landscape.

Fraud Type 2: Non-disciples Stole Jesus's Dead Body and Other Tomb Theories

To proceed to another critical option, it is necessary to develop some background. It was evident to critical scholars from the start that the chief weaknesses with what we have termed the "Fraud Type 1" hypothesis was that the perpetrators, namely Jesus's own disciples, most likely could *not* have been the culprits. They were the exact same individuals who basically turned their world upside down with their preaching and teaching, and who sometimes went quite willingly to their deaths for their message, all the while proclaiming the truth of another world beyond this one. They were also the ones who followed Jesus by being away from their families for long periods of time. Viewed from another angle, the theology, morality, and lives of the ones who preached Jesus's resurrection so consistently, as well as their strict ethical actions toward others, contradicted these purported fraudulent actions.

Of course, we do have many examples of fraudulent teachings and deeds enacted by various persons throughout history, even diabolical examples by those who portray contradictory public personas. Some have even died for lies. But this charge cannot simply be stated in a vacuum, so we will return to this theme in much detail in another chapter. But as far as anyone knows in this present case, the apostles gave up their private careers and did so over a period of decades with ongoing consistency, without changing their message, and happily facing death rather than recanting. Further, their lifelong devotion to others cries out against such fraudulent actions.

A crucial indication sounding the death knell of "Fraud Type 1" is that the nineteenth-century liberal critical scholars themselves, who largely *already* disbelieved the resurrection anyway and just wished to pick the best alternative thesis to oppose this event, consistently ignored this hypothesis. Critical scholars followed suit in the twentieth century with virtually no exceptions. So how do we explain the more than two centuries of virtual rejection of the idea that the disciples stole Jesus's dead body, even by critics themselves? This utter lack of scholarly critical support is a stark testimony to its failure. And this conclusion is decidedly *not* due to the headcount of the authorities deciding against this option, but rather because the scholars making this move are *following the facts* of the situation. But as we will perceive in the next chapter, the critics did more than simply ignore this option.

Enter the next critical move, which is really an alternate *burial* view that could morph into a position of fraud: if the removal of Jesus's dead body plausibly explains the empty tomb teaching, yet it looks like the apostles are exceptionally poor candidates for this task, then another option is to have someone else do the dirty work. This might involve a more "innocent" explanation, such as someone simply changing the initial burial plans and placing the body somewhere other than Joseph of Arimathea's tomb from the beginning. Or perhaps Joseph or someone else simply reburied Jesus's dead body elsewhere soon after the initial interment.

The notion that the disciples were uninvolved in the stashing of Jesus's body removes several huge problems involved with the first scenario and potentially provides other benefits. Most of all, this approach leaves the disciples innocent of their "crimes against humanity" and allows them to preach their message in all sincerity, which clearly makes the most sense. It also has the potential of explaining a huge puzzle piece, namely the report of the empty tomb. If it were plausibly advanced that an *unknown person* was the one who actually performed the actions, it could also effectively remove the perpetrator from the watchful eyes of the critics who would like to interrogate the first-century perpetrators and issue countless countercharges right up through the present time.

It seems to be the case that the first culprits conjured by those advocating this approach may have been either the Roman soldiers or the Jewish leaders, perhaps due to the adversarial roles they played in the lives of Jesus and the early church. Further, we are told that representatives from both of these groups were present at the crucifixion, placing them in the immediate vicinity. One scholar who held some of the Jewish leaders responsible is French scholar Albert Réville, in whose estimation it was that the Jewish Sanhedrin in Jerusalem most likely planned for Jesus's body to be stolen. Then the body was hidden where it was unlikely ever to be discovered.[71]

---

[71] Albert Réville, *Jésus de Nazareth: Études critiques sur les antécédents de l'histoire évangélique et la vie de Jésus*, 2 vols. (Paris: Fischbacher, 1897), 2:250–52, 347, for the Sanhedrin's role in Jerusalem.

But actually, these options almost never show up from the pens of any critical scholars due to many factors, beginning with the lack of a strong motive. Why should either the Jews or the Romans want the grave to appear empty? Further, any involvement from either of these two enemies would very likely be rectified quickly, whether it had happened purposely or inadvertently, since presumably none of them would want the Christian message of Jesus's resurrection from the dead to gain momentum either, though for quite different reasons. So, it appears that the best option available here would be to implicate a unanimous person (or party) with innocent motives.

In spite of the wide range of possibilities included in the category we have termed "Fraud Type 2," there still seem to be fewer examples here than one might think among the German liberal scholars. The specific charges that others stole Jesus's body are surprisingly difficult to locate among this group of researchers.

Although his reasoning is a little dubious and his wording somewhat more difficult to grasp than usual at this particular juncture, David Strauss thinks it is most likely that Jesus was not buried in Joseph's tomb. At any rate, he still seemed to think that Jesus's body was buried in a nearby tomb and was probably not moved. Though referring to the matter as a contradiction, Strauss still seems to allow some room for the traditional option and states that there is no way to know for sure from the narratives that we possess.[72] Still, Strauss's questions do not really change much of anything in the total picture, especially since there is no firm conclusion here and no real data to support his view.

However Strauss is interpreted, other liberal scholars did conclude that Jesus was not buried in Joseph's tomb. Oskar Holtzmann in his *Das Leben Jesu* (1901) considers the possibility of Jesus's disciples taking his dead body with them back to Galilee but rejects the idea. Instead, he supposes that Joseph of Arimathea buried Jesus, but then moved his body after the Sabbath because he decided it was inappropriate to have a crucified man's body buried in the same tomb as his other family members.[73]

Arnold Meyer took a very similar position in that Joseph considered his tomb to be only a temporary burial place and always intended for Jesus's body to be moved. Joseph only volunteered it because of his respect for Jewish burial laws, not because

---

[72] Strauss, *Life of Jesus*, 704–5.

[73] Oskar Holtzmann, *The Life of Jesus*, trans. J. T. Bealby and Maurice A. Canney (London: Black, 1904), 499. However, Holtzmann does not use Joseph's name in this context, simply calling him "the distinguished member of the Synedrium" who had offered to bury Jesus in his own tomb.

Joseph was a disciple of Jesus, which Meyer rejected.[74] The distinguished Jewish critical scholar Joseph Klausner states the matter so similarly to Holtzmann that his statement may have been inspired by Holtzmann's earlier work.[75]

In some "out of the box" thinking for his time that certainly foreshadowed similar contemporary views several decades later, French liberal scholar Alfred Loisy held that Jesus died by crucifixion. However, the soldiers probably just tossed his dead body into a trench or common grave for those who did not deserve a decent burial, "perhaps after giving a finishing blow to the half-dead sufferer." Loisy thus held that the story of Joseph of Arimathea's burial was a "legend" and that the empty tomb teaching in the Gospels was similarly just "a fiction."[76] We will return below to Loisy's additional thoughts on Jesus's appearances.

Arguably the best known of the liberal hypotheses in this category is the celebrated "wrong tomb" thesis of Kirsopp Lake.[77] Strangely enough, in his 1907 book Lake only speaks of it briefly and more than once specifies that it is only a "possibility" or a "suggestion."[78] For Lake, after Jesus's arrest, his disciples either returned to their homes in Galilee or were in hiding in Jerusalem. The women in all likelihood watched the burial from a distance and were not in the proper position to have been good witnesses. So it is certainly plausible that when they returned on Sunday morning, they took the man they met near an open tomb to be an angel. When he simply tried to explain that Jesus's body was not there *because* the women had come to the wrong location, the women rushed to conclusions and thought the man really meant that the empty tomb was due to Jesus having been raised from the dead![79] But as we will see

---

[74] Arnold Meyer, *Die Auferstehung Christi: Die Berichte über Auferstehung, Himmelfahrt und Pfingsten* (Tübingen: Mohr Siebeck,1905), 118.

[75] Joseph Klausner, *Jesus of Nazareth*, trans. Herbert Danby (New York: Macmillan, 1926), 357.

[76] Alfred Loisy, *The Birth of the Christian Religion*, trans. L. P. Jacks (London: Allen & Unwin, 1948), 90. While being born just after the mid-nineteenth century, Loisy outlived many of his liberal colleagues, writing this volume in French in 1933 just a few years before his death.

[77] Later, it was also adopted by P. Gardner-Smith, *The Narratives of the Resurrection: A Critical Study* (London: Methuen, 1926), 134–39.

[78] Quotes taken from the reprinted edition of Kirsopp Lake, *The Historical Evidence of the Resurrection of Jesus Christ* (London: Williams & Norgate, 2012), 250, 252.

[79] Lake, 237–38, 248–53. Like the other critical scholars, Lake also finds contradictions and discrepancies in the Gospel accounts (183–89, 203, 206–7, 219).

later, this supposition does not mean that Lake doubts that Jesus actually appeared to his followers after his death. This suggested wrong tomb scenario actually plays another role for him.

For reasons that will become more obvious later, a disadvantage of the "Fraud Type 2" theses is that they attempted a less specific approach than the general direction favored by the "Fraud Type 1" perspective. However, "Fraud Type 2" does not implicate the disciples, thereby avoiding what the vast majority of scholars think is without much question the Achilles' heel of the latter position. As with all these hypotheses, much more will be remarked later concerning all the responses in this chapter.

The Hallucination or Subjective Vision Theory and Similar Subjective Views

Toward the middle of the nineteenth century, what would become the most popular German liberal hypothesis began to emerge.[80] Just as David Strauss's overall mythical approach largely trumped the earlier, rather piecemeal rationalistic surmisals, so Strauss's hallucination or subjective vision hypothesis convinced other

---

[80] Many liberal and conservative scholars during and just after the German liberal period produced lists of those critical researchers who were thought to have held each of the naturalistic views during these times. On the lists of subjective vision theorists, Schweitzer in *Quest of the Historical Jesus* lists David Strauss (83), Ernest Renan (187), and Friedrich Wilhelm Ghillany, who wrote under the name Richard von der Alm and favored the legend thesis (167). But Schweitzer also referred briefly to Ghillany's notion of subjective visions (70). Liberal German theologian Theodor Keim in *History of Jesus of Nazara* lists Strauss, Renan, Albert Réville, Jan Hendrik Scholten, and C. Holsten as holding to hallucination of one sort or another (6:334). Scottish theologian James Orr mentions Strauss, Renan, Karl Heinrich Weizsäcker, Adolf von Harnack, Arnold Meyer, Oskar Holtzmann, and Alfred Loisy as preferring the hallucination explanation in *The Resurrection of Jesus* (London: Hodder & Stoughton, 1908; repr., Grand Rapids: Zondervan, 1965), 219n1. Doremus A. Hayes lists Renan, Weizsäcker, Loisy, Harnack, Otto Schmiedel, and Otto Pfleiderer as proponents in *The Resurrection Fact* (Nashville: Cokesbury, 1932), 285. Former Pittsburgh-Xenia Theological Seminary professor John McNaugher lists Strauss, Renan, Harnack, Loisy, Pfleiderer, Schmiedel, and Oliver Lodge as taking this position in *Jesus Christ: The Same Yesterday, Today, and Forever* (New York: Revell, 1947), 150–51. Former Fuller Seminary professor Wilbur M. Smith adds Joseph Klausner to the lists in *The Supernaturalness of Christ: Can We Still Believe in It?* (Boston: Wilde, 1940), 216.

scholars that it was the most likely alternative approach to account for the resurrection experiences.[81]

Subjective Visions and the Disciples

One major reason that many of the German liberals accepted Strauss's assessments
is because the New Testament sources agree that the central component of the apostles' experiences was *visual* in nature. The texts claimed that the disciples really saw
something—appearances of the risen Jesus. Therefore, to explain how the witnesses
could actually have thought that they had visual perceptions of the risen Jesus, even
though they were still mistaken, gave Strauss's explanation an advantage over the
other theses.

Also, many of Strauss's liberal peers were well known for natural responses that
were sometimes only mere suggestions and were usually stated quite briefly. By comparison, rather remarkably, Strauss spent considerably more time explaining and
detailing his alternative views along with the relevant data surrounding these events,
spending approximately eighty pages on the subject in his earlier *Das Leben Jesu*.[82]
So what were the main points of Strauss's subjective vision critique here? We may
delineate a few layers.

According to Strauss, there is no doubt that the women were the first ones who
saw these visions of Jesus. The disciples left town to return to their old haunts in
Galilee somewhere around the time of the crucifixion. These men were definitely
depressed and forlorn after Jesus's seeming defeat. This required that more than
just a short duration of time would be necessary to change the disciples' powerfully
negative mindsets to an elevated enthusiasm in order for them to imagine that Jesus
was alive again.[83]

---

[81] Besides the long lists of scholars above, for straightforward comments on this thesis
being the most prominent one in nineteenth-century German thought (especially in the
latter half of this period), see Keim, *History of Jesus of Nazara*, 6:334, 358. Smith also names
the vision thesis as the most popular (*Supernaturalness of Christ*, 216).

[82] In his earlier *Life of Jesus*, Strauss discusses the mythical approach as it addresses the
details of Jesus's crucifixion (677–701), his burial (701–9), the resurrection (709–44), and
the ascension (745–56).

[83] Besides Strauss's *Das Leben Jesu*, his last work, *The Old Faith and the New: A Confession*,
trans. Mathilde Blind, 2 vols. (New York: Holt, 1874), likewise treats many of these same
subjects (see 1:79–83).

Hence, the New Testament proclamation that the resurrection occurred just the third day after the crucifixion is simply too brief a time frame for these changes in the disciples to occur. Even the fifty days until Peter's Pentecost sermon in Acts is not enough time for such occurrences. But in order for such a drastic change to occur in the disciples, an unspecified amount of time would have had to pass before these men would be revived in their outlook. Their conviction, courage, and enthusiasm had to be elevated significantly in order for them to begin proclaiming their message of hope with enthusiasm.

Only such a change could account "for the mental state of the disciples to become exalted in the degree necessary, before this or that individual amongst them could, purely as an operation of his own mind, make present to himself the risen Christ in a visionary manner." Once entire assemblies could also develop such a similarly "highly wrought enthusiasm," they "could believe that they heard him [Jesus] in every impressive sound, or saw him in every striking appearance."[84]

Obviously impressed with the performance of this German theologian, editor Peter Hodgson in his annotated notes in the 1972 edition of Strauss's *Life of Jesus* even makes the rather bold pronouncement, "Strauss demonstrates with devastating effectiveness that it is no longer possible to regard the empty tomb and appearance traditions as factual historical reports." However, even for the rationalists with whom Strauss was quite often sparring, Hodgson's reason for this conclusion is definitely underwhelming: Strauss defeated the historicity of the Christian claims by pointing out the contradictions in the various Gospel accounts. From these contradictions, we arrive at this bottom line: "The unavoidable conclusion is that the resurrection stories cannot be regarded as historical reports but as theological interpretations."[85]

We will return later to the overall evaluations of each natural hypothesis, but it will just be noted here briefly that several items seem exceptionally puzzling regarding Hodgson's comments above. How can he justify either this overall conclusion regarding Strauss or the chief details for thinking that this was the case?

Was Hodgson addressing Strauss's critique of the rationalistic liberals here? However, nearly all of the German liberals agreed with Strauss and had long taken

---

[84] See section 140 of Strauss, *Life of Jesus*, 739, 743–44 in particular.

[85] Hodgson's annotations in Strauss, 794–95n735. To provide a few details regarding these contradictions, Hodgson refers mostly to the three prior sections in Strauss (137–39), then notes that Strauss's chief, devastating conclusion arrives in section 140, the same one that we referenced above.

great relish in indicating and making assertions regarding Gospel contradictions, as we have pointed out quite regularly above. Since especially the more scholarly rationalists like Paulus agreed wholeheartedly, why would Strauss's moves be considered at all devastating? Further, wherever there were historical *agreements* between the liberals regarding the Gospel data, the evidence for these particulars took precedent over problem texts located elsewhere. Hence, it is unclear where or how Hodgson thinks that Strauss scored his victory at this specific juncture, except perhaps only in the general sense that his mythical approach superseded their rationalistic method.

Of course, Hodgson also could have been referring to the effects of Strauss's critiques on the conservative scholars at that time, though that does not seem as likely in the context.[86] Still, Schweitzer describes the firestorm that arose after the publication of Strauss's earlier *Life of Jesus*, noting that some forty or fifty responses appeared within just five years.[87] Strauss even responded by penning a volume defending himself against these opponents.[88] But if that was Hodgson's intent here, there is no apparent indication of it. Further, in this case, the point is still quite unclear and will have to await our detailed treatment of the major conservative scholarly responses below.

French scholar Ernest Renan is another who held the subjective visionary hypothesis and utilized very strong words for the atmosphere that he thinks developed gradually among the disciples after their retreat to Galilee to get away from the scene of the crucifixion. Renan describes the evolving occasions as "s'enivrant" (intoxicating) and a "fievre intense" (intense fever) where "les visions se multipliaient sans cesse" (visions multiplied incessantly).[89]

Moreover, on the matter mentioned earlier regarding having to stretch out the visions over a much lengthier time period to allow the disciples to have the necessary interval to upgrade their emotions from their discouragement, despondency, and forlornness after Jesus's death into this excited state of mind, Renan holds that the

---

[86] For example, in the same note (140), Hodgson refers to Strauss's criticisms of the resurrection views of both rationalist philosopher Benedict Spinoza as well as of fellow German liberal scholar and contemporary Christian Hermann Weisse, which makes it likely that he is responding chiefly to other liberals.

[87] Schweitzer, *Quest of the Historical Jesus*, 96–97.

[88] David Friedrich Strauss, *Streitschriften zur Verteidigung meiner Schrift über das Leben-Jesu und zur Charakteristik der gegenwärtigen Theologie* (Tübingen: Osiander, 1838).

[89] Hence Ernest Renan, *Les apôtres, histoire des origines du christianisme* (Paris: Calmann-Lévy, 1880), 2:25.

apostles did not return from Galilee to Jerusalem until much later in the same year Jesus died, or perhaps not even until the next year at Passover. So, beyond the forty-day period mentioned in Acts 1:3, this would stretch the time of respite up to one full year.[90]

Schweitzer reports that the success of Renan's volume gave rise to a French tradition of "life of Jesus" works, beginning immediately afterward in the 1860s. One of the most influential scholars was Alfred Loisy, who published works such as his almost 1,000-page study of the Gospel of John in 1903, a two-volume work on the Synoptic Gospels the next year, and another study on ecclesiology in 1908.[91]

Loisy's prominent text *The Birth of the Christian Religion* was written later.[92] He begins by mentioning the fourteen epistles of Paul in the New Testament, perhaps surprisingly counting Hebrews. However, he only decides positively in favor of the probable Pauline authorship of six of these texts: 1 Thessalonians, 1 and 2 Corinthians, Galatians, Romans, and Philippians, which is a larger number than either Baur or Strauss allowed and comes much closer to the late-twentieth and twenty-first-century list of "undisputed" Pauline Epistles. Loisy dates both 2 Thessalonians and Colossians to the second century, terms Ephesians as "spurious," and states the three Pastoral Epistles were written "much later than the apostolic age."[93]

Regarding his views on the last days of Jesus's life, we already noted earlier in this chapter that Loisy actually foreshadowed some similar contemporary views by holding that Jesus died by crucifixion, but his executioners afterward probably flung his body, "perhaps after giving a finishing blow to the half-dead sufferer," into a trench or common grave. The teaching of the honorable burial by Joseph of Arimathea along with the empty tomb are simply fictional developments.[94]

---

[90] Renan, 2:45–46. Strangely enough, Renan's earlier volume *Vie de Jésus* was his most popular and frequently cited writing and hence is almost always the one that gets discussed predominantly. However, on our present subject of the death and resurrection of Jesus, *Vie de Jésus* actually (and surprisingly) discusses very little about the early Christians' subjective visions. Renan develops his notion of hallucinations and their chiefly Galilean environment in much more detail in *Les apôtres*, esp. chaps 1–3 of vol. 2 (2:1–56).

[91] Schweitzer, *Quest of the Historical Jesus*, 296n2.

[92] The French volume, *La naissance du christianisme*, was published in 1933. The English translation by L. P. Jacks was published several years later as Alfred Loisy, *The Birth of the Christian Religion* (London: Allen & Unwin, 1948).

[93] See chapter 1 of Loisy, *Birth of the Christian Religion*.

[94] Loisy, 89–90.

Suffering a sense of overwhelming confusion, disillusionment, shock, and loss due to this absolutely jolting turn of events, Jesus's disciples fled back to Galilee. Their faith was "awakened" while they recovered over a period of time there, actually having their belief "created anew" by experiencing "apparitions" or "visions." These hallucinations were due to "an inward conviction" or "insight" that was created by faith and "objectified into outward occurrences." Still, these were clearly subjective experiences and not resurrection appearances but simply "fictions which faith produced." For the disciples, this served as the convincing indication that their faith had been justified. The resulting transformation propelled these followers into "a bolder affirmation" of Jesus's message.[95]

Before moving on to the visionary nature of Paul's conversion experience, a related (and perhaps even derivative) alternative view should be noted, one that sometimes constitutes a different angle on the subjective vision scenario and in other cases is a bit more of a distinct approach, especially in its late twentieth-century versions.[96] The first person to have "seen" the risen Jesus was sometimes supposed to have been either Mary Magdalene or Peter. They basically reported their own "appearance" to Jesus's other followers and the contagion spread, as the others either then had their own visions or were simply satisfied to report that Jesus had risen and appeared to them.

So, it was possible that either at that time or later, the other followers also supposed that they had seen similar visions of their risen Lord, with or without any direct visionary stimulus of their own. In fact, it is sometimes implied that Mary Magdalene or Peter may have been the lone recipient of a subjective vision at first before the others also joined in and reported their own experiences or simply their personal convictions.

It was sometimes concluded by these German liberal scholars that it was Mary Magdalene who served as the initial conduit for faith.[97] No one describes this hypothesis more ably than William Milligan of the University of Aberdeen, even though he does not take this position. Milligan nicely summarized the view like this: "That spark was applied by Mary Magdalene—a sensitive and nervous woman; and

---

[95] Loisy, esp. 92–99.

[96] Examples of what I have termed the "Illumination Theory" are found in twentieth-century critical scholars such as Willi Marxsen, Thomas Sheehan, Donald Cupitt, and John Shelby Spong and will be considered and critiqued in a later chapter.

[97] Plus, concluded by a French scholar in the case of Renan, and some other exceptions as well.

no sooner was it applied than the flame was kindled. Her story that she had seen the Lord was eagerly embraced; it spread with the rapidity and force of an epidemic." This process happened on numerous occasions: "what she believed that she had seen others immediately believed that they too must see . . . the conviction seized all the members of the early Church that their Lord had really risen from the grave."[98]

Another scholar who held a position like this was Renan, who postulated that, through her excitement, enthusiasm, and especially her imagination, Mary Magdalene's hallucination bequeathed a gift to the world: a resurrected God! The glory of Jesus's resurrection is due to her reports. The events were contagious, and others caught the infection from her and experienced their own visions.[99] Close to Renan's view here is that of the French theologian Réville, mentioned earlier. Hysteria initially on the part of Mary Magdalene, followed by similar experiences from many others, accounted for the belief in Jesus's resurrection.[100]

On the other hand, H. J. Holtzmann postulated that Peter's regret and penitence drove him to subjective visions of the risen Jesus. No doubt due to Peter being the apostolic leader, his experiences were central and served as a sufficient enough impetus to encourage Jesus's other followers to hallucinate similarly.[101]

---

[98] William Milligan, *The Resurrection of Our Lord*, 4th ed. (London: Macmillan, 1899), 83. Strangely enough, Milligan quotes here from Ferdinand Christian Baur, *The Church History of the First Three Centuries*, trans. Allan Menzies, 3rd ed., 2 vols. (London: Williams and Norgate, 1878–79), 1:42. It would seem, then, as if Baur's own original context included such a reference to Mary Magdalene, though she is not mentioned by name in Baur's section on Jesus's death and resurrection (1:41–43). Milligan's point was that this was a more general position among the liberal scholars of that day.

[99] Renan's examples can be found in *Les apôtres*, 2:11–17, with his especially pithy line above regarding the resurrected God from *Vie de Jésus*, 356, with related comments in the "Appendice" sections 40 (418) and 42 (419–20) as well as another similar description found in *Les apôtres*, 2:13.

[100] Réville, *Jésus de Nazareth*, esp. 2:152, 422.

[101] H. J. Holtzmann, *Lehrbuch der neutestamentlichen Theologie*, 2 vols. (Tübingen: Mohr Siebeck, 1897), with relevant details being found esp. in 1:356–62, 430–31. It may be noted that for Renan, Peter was also one of the leaders who quickly got on board here after Mary Magdalene's vision (*Les apôtres*, 2:12). Orr reports that such a view where Peter has the original subjective experience(s) and that the "contagion spreads" to the other disciples and even to the 500 at once was held by Harnack, Loisy, Weizsäcker, and A. Meyer. This unlikely scenario is especially what drew Orr's criticism on the same page that such visional theories require that virtually all the many details in the Gospel reports must be changed to accommodate it. See Orr, *Resurrection of Jesus*, 222.

As to how these visions spread, Renan is particularly graphic, not to mention exceptionally creative. Renan postulates that the atmosphere among Jesus's followers after his death had reached such a sufficient crescendo that virtually anything could have served to initiate one of these hallucinations. It need not have taken any more than a wisp of air, a squeaking window, or a fortuitous murmur in the room to produce a vision in those who already believed! Such stimulants would be sufficient intoxicants to prove that Jesus was actually standing there among them.[102]

Subjective Visions and Saul/Paul of Tarsus

But can the case of Saul—hereinafter called Paul—be approached as an extension of the subjective vision thesis? Or must he be treated differently? This will be addressed elsewhere in this study in much detail. Even a few hints above indicate enough issues involved with the disciples being the recipients of subjective visions of Jesus. But Paul's case seems to be an especially thorny situation for the hallucination alternative, for how could this radical, self-proclaimed church persecutor be a real candidate for such subjective experiences as the catalyst for his resurrection belief?

Enter Ferdinand Christian Baur, David Strauss's former professor and one of the most accomplished German liberal New Testament theologians. F. C. Baur's published scholarship amounted to some 16,000 pages of academic work. As Stephen Neill and N. T. Wright attest, "Baur was a heroic figure, a representative of German scholarship at its best."[103] Baur was probably best known for his monumental work on Paul, a major study that has even been described as "perhaps the most influential book of nineteenth-century New Testament scholarship," with ongoing influence even to this day.[104]

Baur was the dominant figure in the tremendously influential Tübingen University school of thought, in spite of holding several major views that definitely would be eschewed by today's scholars, such as dating much of the New Testament

---

[102] Renan, *Les apôtres*, 2:22.

[103] Neill and Wright, *Interpretation of the New Testament*, 21.

[104] Ferdinand Christian Baur, *Paul the Apostle of Jesus Christ: His Life and Works, His Epistles and Teachings; A Contribution to a Critical History of Primitive Christianity*, trans. A. Menzies, 2 vols. (London: Williams & Norgate, 1873, 1875; repr., Peabody, MA: Hendrickson, 2003). This comment was made by A. Andrew Das of Elmhurst College, on the back cover of the Hendrickson printing.

to later than AD 130, placing John in the latter half of the second century, and dating even Mark to about 150. Mark was further thought to be based upon the Gospels of Matthew and Luke, and of these last two texts, Matthew was the one to be preferred. Even so, Matthew contained much mythical material, though it also included some authentic traditions.[105]

For Baur, like recent scholarship, Paul was clearly the best source of information in the New Testament. But more skeptically than today's average New Testament scholar, Baur only accepted four of Paul's Epistles as undisputed: Romans, 1 and 2 Corinthians, and Galatians. With the highest praise, Baur held that "there has never been the slightest suspicion of unauthenticity cast on these four Epistles, on the contrary, they bear in themselves so incontestably the character of Pauline original-ity, that it is not possible for critical doubt to be exercised upon them with any show of reason."[106]

Baur does not totally dismiss the other nine epistles that bear Paul's name (which he terms "the shorter Pauline Epistles," excepting only the authentic Galatians) and states some considerations in their favor. However, in the end, though leaving open a few possibilities, he still concludes that there are too many signs in these nine epistles of non-Pauline tendencies.[107]

What happened during Paul's conversion, then, as mentioned by the apostle in his authentic statements such as 1 Cor 9:1 and 15:8, where he testified that he had seen the risen Jesus? Baur disallowed some of the popular rationalistic options in his day, like Paul somehow witnessing an external flash of lightning while he was on his way to Damascus, leading to a change of perspective.

Rather, Baur's approach was more refined—he preferred the internal route and advocated that Paul's conversion was the result of a private, subjective experience that the apostle nonetheless expressed objectively. This occurrence was a natural consequence of Paul's "downcast, introspective" personality arising from his growing conviction that he had sinned in the recent events in his life, presumably due to his persecuting the early Christians. A real experience resulted, one that Paul believed to be an appearance of the risen Jesus, just like what Jesus's other disciples had wit-nessed. The result was that Paul's life changed dramatically. Still, all of this happened

---

[105] See Neill and Wright, *Interpretation of the New Testament*, esp. 20–29 for a helpful summary of these thoughts on the four Gospels.

[106] See the second part of vol. 1 of Baur, *Paul*, esp. 1:255–59.

[107] Baur, 2:1, 44–64, 79–80, 84–85, 96–97, 105–11.

without his actually having seen Jesus at all, since nothing had actually occurred in reality. Rather, it was the result of "an inward process which becomes an outward one, a transition from the subjective to the objective."[108]

Baur's view, or one very close to it, became what was probably the predominant critical approach to Paul's transformation. A drastic conversion was obviously required, one that was sufficient to account for the apostle's 180-degree life change in spite of there seeming to be no apparent explanation for such an impetus. It was repeated widely that the foundation of Paul's transformation resulted from the tremendous stress that had built up inside him over his own culpability regarding Stephen's stoning and the Christian persecution that he had led. The result of this stress was Paul's private, inward experience that he was convinced was nothing short of a resurrection appearance of the risen Jesus himself. The outward expression of this new conviction was manifested in the strong conviction that the early Christians were somehow correct in their beliefs.

David Strauss also held similar views to Baur's. For example, at least later in his career, Strauss denied that any of the four traditional authors or anyone close to them actually wrote any of these Gospels. Like his former professor, Strauss also placed the writing of these books and Acts into the second century. Further, Strauss credits "Baur's epoch-making investigation" with indicating that the Gospel of John does not date until "the middle of the same century." He also agreed that the same four primary Pauline Epistles favored by his old professor Baur (Romans, 1 and 2 Corinthians, and Galatians) were foremost among the New Testament books and were "undisputed writings" by the apostle Paul.[109]

Paul's new convictions were actually quite similar to those of Jesus's disciples, though for different reasons and in spite of Paul's prior unbelief in the message and messiahship of Jesus. But like the majority of the older critical scholars, Strauss concluded that Paul experienced a spiritual crisis after witnessing Stephen's stoning to death. His emotions after this event were depressed, but eventually the situation issued forth into "a decisive spiritual crisis, concerning which it need not surprise us that in an oriental it took the form of a Christophany." When the feelings finally emerged, they rose "to a pitch of exaltation which issued in a Christophany, and a total change of sentiment." Just as with the other disciples, this change of outlook

---

[108] Baur, 1:67–81, also 264.
[109] Strauss, *Old Faith*, 1:45–46, plus 52 on John.

resulted in "the experience of similar visions."[110] But these heightened experiences were manifested "in a purely subjective manner."[111]

Whether or not it was due at least in part to the virulent criticism that he received throughout his life, Strauss reached some very negative conclusions in the end. In his last published text, *The Old Faith and the New*, he proclaimed that we could know very little about the historical Jesus. Moreover, he declared "the conclusion that we can no longer either hold to the idea of a personal God, or of life after death." Two pages later he stated that Ludwig Feurerbach was right and that religion was simply a wish. Last, we can no longer even call ourselves Christians![112] Two years after he published this last book in 1874, Schweitzer noted wistfully that "death set him free."[113]

Regarding Paul, Renan also makes some very similar moves to those of both Baur and Strauss. In his *Vie de Jésus* he mentions in sparse detail Paul's report that he saw the risen Jesus, adding that he does not reject "la véracité de saint Paul."[114] But again, it is in Renan's *Les apôtres* that the longer, more detailed discussion ensues.[115] His ideas here are somewhat similar to the report above regarding Renan's notion that Jesus's disciples experienced a range of high emotions when they thought that they had seen the risen Jesus, even describing these passions as "intoxicating" and an "intense fever."[116] Similarly, Paul was also wildly excited: "Paul était sous le coup de la plus vive excitation," a state described as some sort of "feverish delirium" or even a "sunstroke."[117]

We have provided some key examples of the many commentators who have ascribed to Paul a different mindset than the one found in Paul's own writings as well as the book of Acts. But other scholars agreed that it was very difficult to account for these alternative responses as coming from the early church persecutor. Seeming to straddle the fence in some sense, Otto Pfleiderer is one scholar who seems to be torn between the two views, speaking both about Paul's personal doubts and morbid

---

[110] Strauss, *Life of Jesus*, 741.

[111] Strauss, 742.

[112] Strauss, *Old Faith*, 1:87, 90, 107, 140–46 (esp. 141–44), 153, 155.

[113] Schweitzer, *Quest of the Historical Jesus*, 73–76.

[114] Renan, *Vie de Jésus*, 422.

[115] See chap. 10 in Renan, *Les apôtres*, esp. 2:174–81.

[116] Renan, 2:25.

[117] "Qu'un délire fiévreux amené par un coup de soleil ou une opthalmie." See Renan, 2:181–82.

introspection while sounding like what happened to Paul was a more independent work of God.[118]

As noted by former Princeton Theological Seminary professor J. Gresham Machen with regard to the older German liberal endeavors in his day, there were many other attempts to explain Paul's experience in less than supernatural terms. The apostle could have suffered from some variety of heat stroke. Or a violent thunderstorm with or without lightning could have played a crucial role in his conversion (to which Baur also responded critically, as we saw above). Likewise, nervous exhaustion, hallucinations, and even epilepsy were all posited at various times as potentially filling the need for a natural occurrence.[119]

One of the options mentioned by Machen was defended by prominent Jewish critical scholar Joseph Klausner of the Hebrew University, who researched and penned his classic volume on Paul between the years 1929 and 1939. He postulated that while Paul was traveling on the road to Damascus, this devout, passionate, and zealous Pharisee was considering the major role that he played in Stephen's martyrdom. Suddenly, Paul thought that Jesus was standing directly before him, although Jesus was not actually there in reality. This gripping experience was sufficient to cause Paul's conversion.

Klausner concluded that this experience was due "clearly" to Paul suffering from a case of epilepsy. Just before his epileptic episode here, Paul was probably contemplating the new and revolutionary idea that Jesus could have been the suffering Messiah. Perhaps the Christians were correct about this. Paul's disease could therefore account for the subjective experience of perceiving a "heavenly light" and would also align Paul with the "long list of epileptics" who have lived throughout history.[120]

These approaches to Paul's conversion tend to serve as instances of the rationalistic propensity among the older liberal scholars to work within the general New Testament framework while offering various sorts of natural explanations in place of the supernatural elements. While the contrast between the rational and mythical approaches described earlier is often more pronounced than this with regard to the disciples' resurrection appearances, the approaches to Paul's conversion seem not to

---

[118] As in Otto Pfleiderer, *Das Urchristentum, seine Schriften und Lehren in geschichtlichem Zusammenhang beschrieben*, 2nd ed., 2 vols. (Berlin: Reimer, 1902), esp. 1:43, 46.

[119] J. Gresham Machen, *The Origin of Paul's Religion* (Grand Rapids: Eerdmans, 1925), esp. 58–61, 65.

[120] Joseph Klausner, *From Jesus to Paul*, trans. William F. Stinespring (New York: Macmillan, 1944), chap. 11, esp. 322–30.

differ quite so much from one another. In order to explain Paul's conversion, even Baur and Strauss appear willing to work within this general rationalistic framework, even though they had strongly criticized the same context on other occasions.[121]

The Objective Vision Theory

While still affirming that Jesus's resurrection appearances were in some sense visionary events, a rival view to that of hallucinations and other subjective positions proposed the notion that although Jesus appeared in a nonbodily manner, there was an objective element as well. Jesus had *actually* been raised from the dead, was currently alive, and truly appeared to his disciples, though in a nonbodily manner. Hence, such a view acknowledges that the resurrection was an actual miracle.[122]

We have already mentioned that Strauss criticized an early forerunner of this view, that of another German scholar, Christian Hermann Weisse, who began teaching philosophy and theology at the University of Leipzig just before the time that Strauss published his initial version of *Das Leben Jesu*. While writing about what happened

---

[121] Such as when Baur, in the same context and immediate discussion, is repeatedly very critical of the traditions found in the book of Acts, treating them as subpar reports (*Paul*, 1:5–8, 13, 34, 63–65, 79–80). However, Baur utilizes freely the same three descriptions of Paul's trip to Damascus found in the same book he just criticized as not being accurate enough portrayals of the general historical circumstances that occurred. The compliments here seem to be due to their favoring the points that he is making (1:67–69, 73, 76–78)! True, all scholars need to be careful of this sort of inconsistency, but it is amazing how frequently critical scholars appear to make this sort of move when convenience is at stake. It seems that it simply takes less data when it is deemed helpful for one's case.

[122] Schweitzer in *Quest of the Historical Jesus* lists Christian Weisse as holding this position (130–31, cf. 136), though strangely enough he glosses over this aspect in his relevant discussions of the views of Theodor Keim (such as 211–14 and intermittently on 344–60) and Johannes Weiss (238–41, 267–69), possibly due to Schweitzer's near obsession at this point in his volume with more clearly eschatological matters. Although the various scholars held different perspectives on some of the relevant issues, W. J. Sparrow-Simpson, *The Resurrection and the Christian Faith* (Grand Rapids: Zondervan, 1968), 115, lists Theodor Keim, Hermann Fichte, Hermann Lotze, Fernand Ménégoz, and Eduard Riggenbach as holding this position. Orr mentions Keim, Weiss, and Kirsopp Lake as the chief proponents of this theory (*Resurrection of Jesus*, 227). McNaugher notes the views of Keim and Canon Streeter (*Jesus Christ*, 155) on this subject. Wilbur M. Smith also mentions Streeter in Smith's book *Therefore Stand: A Plea for a Vigorous Apologetic in the Present Crisis of Evangelical Christianity* (Boston: Wilde, 1945), 397. Another similar position is advocated by Gardner-Smith, *Narratives of the Resurrection*, 133–39.

to Jesus after his death and having rejected what he considered to be the myths of the empty tomb and Jesus's bodily appearances in the process, Weisse proposed that the risen, glorified Christ actually did appear to his disciples in visions. *How* such events occurred is another matter, but it remains that for Weisse, the resurrection was a historical fact and Jesus actually did appear to his followers.[123]

In spite of Weisse's appreciation of Strauss's work, he criticized Strauss for not offering solid ground between rational and supernatural approaches.[124] Strauss, for his part, noted some of Weisse's critical moves but did not appreciate Weisse retaining the position that Jesus's appearances were "objective magical facts." Interestingly, Strauss had already criticized the well-known Jewish philosopher Spinoza for holding a similar view—visions of the risen Jesus "produced by miraculous means" which, as with Weisse, Strauss referred to as "the magic circle of the supernatural"![125]

By far the best known liberal version of the objective vision theory was the lengthy *Die Geschichte Jesu von Nazara* by Theodor Keim, a study of the historical Jesus published in three volumes (1867–1872).[126] The English translation appeared eleven years later.[127] Schweitzer identified these texts by Keim as "the most important Life of Jesus which appeared in a long period."[128]

Like many of the German liberal scholars of his day, Keim rejected the early dates and traditional authorship of the four Gospels. Even Matthew and Mark, for him the earliest Gospels, depict numerous contradictions and other legendary problems, especially the account of the guards at the tomb in Matt 27:62–28:4, 11–14. Further, Luke and John have even more issues, and Keim dates the Gospel of John to about AD 130. Further, not only was Keim inclined to reject miracles, but he also disallowed the likelihood of the women's visit to Jesus's sepulcher as well as the empty tomb itself

---

[123] Christian Hermann Weisse, *Die evangelische Geschichte: Kritisch und philosophisch bearbeitet*, 2 vols. (Leipzig: Breitkopf and Hartel, 1838), 2:305–448.

[124] Schweitzer, *Quest of the Historical Jesus*, 121–31.

[125] Strauss, *Life of Jesus*, where his critique of Weisse is found on 744 and his criticism of Spinoza is on 740.

[126] Theodor Keim, *Die Geschichte Jesu von Nazara, in ihrer Verhaltung mit dem Gesamtleben seines Volkes frei untersucht und ausführlich erzählt*, 3 vols. (Zurich: Orell and Füssli, 1867–1872), esp. 3:506–621, on Jesus's burial and resurrection. Like Strauss, Keim spent much more time on the events at the end of Jesus's life than did many of the other German liberal scholars.

[127] Keim, *History of Jesus of Nazara*.

[128] Schweitzer, *Quest of the Historical Jesus*, 211.

as Gospel legends. Still, as with many of these other critical scholars, Keim is more than able to find a number of probable historical facts in these texts.[129]

Along with Strauss, Renan, and almost all other scholars who take visionary positions of one sort or another, Keim also held that the disciples fled to Galilee about the time of the crucifixion, and that this was the location where Jesus appeared to his followers. This was especially necessary so that they were able to relax somewhat and overcome their initial shock and fear. In fact, like the other "visionary scholars," being transformed from these adverse emotions was required as they waited until the transformations into moods of "religious enthusiasm and ecstasy" even reached a fevered pitch. Once they regrouped emotionally, they were able to be open to God's revelation.[130]

In order to ascertain if a strong case could be maintained *in favor of* the subjective vision theory, like the versions argued by Strauss, Renan, and others, Keim decided to build a case to actually argue in their favor. He agreed with many others that Peter was the first disciple to see Jesus after his crucifixion. He even went so far as to argue against bodily appearances and conceded the possibility of a contagious atmosphere giving rise to subjective visions.[131] Quite remarkably, Keim did such an exemplary job of arguing for hallucinations that Sparrow-Simpson even thought that his case was stronger than that of Strauss![132]

But just when it seemed that he might be convinced of the overall Strauss-type argument, Keim declared that he could no longer argue the case, due to the failings of the subjective vision thesis.[133] Having completed this process, Keim then turned around and critiqued the hallucination theory in a long treatment that involved a number of arguments, including some strong criticisms. In fact, Sparrow-Simpson argued of Keim's finished product that "no more penetrating discussion of the theory of self-generated visions has since been given us . . . his was certainly the most learned work on the Resurrection."[134]

---

[129] In the German edition, Keim, *Die Geschichte Jesu von Nazara*, 3:533–70. In the English edition, Keim, *History of Jesus of Nazara*, 6:281–323; cf. Schweitzer, *Quest of the Historical Jesus*, 211; Orr, *Resurrection of Jesus*, 113–14, 215–19.

[130] German: Keim, *Die Geschichte Jesu von Nazara*, 3:592–606; English: Keim, *History of Jesus of Nazara*, 6:345, 348–49, 364, quotation on 348.

[131] Keim, *History of Jesus of Nazara*, 6:333, 339–41, 344–50.

[132] Sparrow-Simpson, *Resurrection and the Christian Faith*, 112–13.

[133] Keim, *History of Jesus of Nazara*, 6:351.

[134] Sparrow-Simpson, *Resurrection and the Christian Faith*, 110. To gain the proper perspective here, Sparrow-Simpson's comment would extend from approximately the final

In place of the subjective vision hypothesis of Strauss and others, Keim argued for what came to be referred to more accurately as the objective vision theory, since the "originating source" of the early Christian experiences was none other than "God and the glorified Christ." Keim famously referred to these visions as "telegrams from heaven," from which they get their more popular name, since they were events inaugurated by God himself.[135]

In other words, these resurrection experiences were subjective in the sense that Jesus did not appear in a normal, physical body that could be touched.[136] However, these experiences were objective in the sense that they really did occur—by no means were they simply hallucinations or any other sort of self-generated occurrences that happened in someone's mind but not in the real world. Moreover, these appearances could be seen by more than one person at a time, each witness could perceive the same message sent to the others, and so on. They were supernatural occasions because they were generated by God himself from heaven.[137]

Most incredibly, Keim even concludes the matter by stating, "Though much has fallen away, the secure faith-fortress of the Resurrection remains."[138] Apparently Keim thinks that, though criticism has taken its toll on the Gospel texts, the fact of the resurrection still emerges from the critical research. Admittedly, this is not language heard very often from the nineteenth-century German liberal scholars!

---

form of Strauss's defense of the hallucination theory, perhaps in his *A New Life of Jesus*, which was published less than ten years before Keim's critique in 1872, until the time of the first printing of Sparrow-Simpson's volume some forty years later, in 1911, when this comment was made.

[135] Keim, *History of Jesus of Nazara*, esp. 6:361–65. Keim lists Hermann Fichte, Christian Weisse, and Rudolf Seydal as other liberal scholars who held his or a similar position (3:361). See also Keim, *Die Geschichte Jesu von Nazara*, 3:602–3.

[136] However, Keim even seems to state that he does not deny that Jesus's appearances could possibly have been corporeal in nature. See Keim, *History of Jesus of Nazara*, 6:362; Keim, *Die Geschichte Jesu von Nazara*, 3:603.

[137] It is rather intriguing and perhaps even strange that Keim thinks that in his day, "even conservative circles do not seem averse to the vision theory" as long as there is the "proviso" that Jesus's appearance be recognized as "not simply a human projection, but rather a divine objective manifestation in human form." See Keim, *History of Jesus of Nazara*, 6:334. It would be intriguing to be able to ascertain if he were actually right on this comment.

[138] Keim, *History of Jesus of Nazara*, 6:365; Keim, *Die Geschichte Jesu von Nazara*, 3:606. The German term "Glaubensburg" here could also intriguingly and graphically be translated as "faith-castle"!

Two additional scholars who held to objective resurrection visions also should be mentioned here, if only briefly. Influential German liberal scholar Johannes Weiss seems to follow Keim when he argues that after his death, the heavenly Jesus revealed himself: "It was in this state of heavenly glory that he manifested himself to his disciples." Then Weiss adds, "The bold proclamation of the message of the resurrection by the first disciples would be simply inexplicable had they felt the slightest doubt of the objective reality of the Lord's appearances."[139]

Though Kirsopp Lake is often considered to be a critic of Jesus's resurrection due to his well-known wrong tomb thesis, he actually defended the event as an objective vision that really occurred. Of course, agreeing with many of the vision theorists both subjective and objective alike, such positions need to explain the empty tomb somehow, since it is basically a superfluous claim when less than bodily appearances are in view. Nonetheless, after dismissing the subjective vision thesis (i.e., hallucinations) as inadequate, Lake concluded, "The objective hypothesis is that the appearance was independent of the belief or feelings of the disciples . . . because there really was a spiritual being that had an existence independent of them and produced the appearance."[140]

As the nineteenth century was drawing to a close, the objective vision thesis of major scholars such as Keim, Weiss, and Lake was gaining in popularity, even to the point of being thought of as more sophisticated than the subjective vision view of Strauss, Renan, and others.[141] The contrast between the two approaches is that, whereas the subjective version was probably beset by far more difficulties than any other naturalistic resurrection theory, the objective vision theory was growing in popularity partially because of the rise of psychical research especially in Britain but also in America, giving the latter view an aura of empirical support.[142]

---

[139] Johannes Weiss, *Earliest Christianity: A History of the Period A.D. 30–150*, trans. Frederick C. Grant, 2 vols. (New York: Harper & Row, 1959), 1:27, 28. The German publication was first entitled *Das Urchristentum* (Göttingen: Vandenhoeck & Ruprecht, 1917). This work was completed by Rudolf Knowles three years after Weiss's death.

[140] Lake, *Historical Evidence*, 267, esp. in the context of 266–79.

[141] One point to note here is that Eduard Riggenbach, *The Resurrection of Jesus* (New York: Eaton & Mains, 1907), is sometimes mentioned as an objective vision theorist (as Sparrow-Simpson does in *Resurrection and the Christian Faith*, 115). Yet, while saying some positive things about this position (49–62), Riggenbach eventually decides against it (65–67) in favor of bodily resurrection appearances, in that the latter best explains all of the data that we possess.

[142] As recognized by many scholars, including Lake, *Historical Evidence*, 272–73; Orr, *Resurrection of Jesus*, 226–27; Sparrow-Simpson, *Resurrection and the Christian Faith*, 436–42; and McNaugher, *Jesus Christ*, 181–82.

Legend or Myth Theories

In the late nineteenth and early twentieth centuries, a potpourri of other alternative hypotheses began to grow in popularity, largely due to new interests in other cultures, philosophies, and religions. Buoyed by the interdisciplinary and still-fledgling undeveloped areas of cross-cultural anthropological studies, other seemingly parallel religious accounts of virgin births, demon possession, miracles, humans who were in some sense taken to be deities, and even resurrections were noised around, challenging the Christian message and its sense of uniqueness in areas that rivaled the gospel message. It might have seemed that there was no end to the number of accounts that seemed to appear rather suddenly. For example, one prominent variety contrasted Jewish with Hellenistic ideas in attempts to ascertain where particular notions like the deity of Jesus may have originated.

These natural alternative approaches based on myths and legends of some sort were manifested in different flavors. A few varieties will be mentioned here.

(1) These teachings could reflect much simpler forms where the main emphases were just on stories that grew with the retelling, where critical scholars thought this pathway might be traced across the Gospels, for instance, from earlier to later volumes. Comparisons might be made to storytelling, where details were often obscured while others were added as the stories grew. This was especially the case when the reports being spread were extraordinary accounts of gods, goddesses, and miracles.

The majority of critical scholars accepted, recognized, or employed some notion of this creeping legendary distortion just described. Yet it should be noted here carefully that simply to assume or even to embrace such a common position of general textual change is by no means the same as employing the full-blown naturalistic legend thesis regarding, say, Jesus's resurrection.

The watershed question in these discussions is whether the necessary historical elements of whatever item is being discussed could still be maintained in spite of these legendary or mythical accretions. For example, many scholars readily accept literal resurrection appearances of Jesus in spite of also allowing some sorts of legendary textual issues. But as just mentioned, this is *not* the legend thesis as we are describing it here, because the essentials still remained. However, those who conclude that the resurrection appearances were actually nullified by the accumulation of such legendary considerations *would* be utilizing such a thesis as a naturalistic theory.

(2) Among the most common nineteenth-century mythical comparisons were those that presented more of a frontal challenge to the Gospel accounts. This version

of the legend thesis compared the Christian gospel proclamation to ancient stories in various fictional settings. The best-known versions of these accounts frequently involved the tale of a wife or queen who descended into the underworld to rescue her captured husband or king. If successful, she brought him back to the land of the living—hence he experienced a sort of return to life. Often referred to as "vegetation myths" or "vegetation gods," these stories arose in ancient agrarian societies and served to help commemorate the annually celebrated cyclical sequences of vegetation dying in the autumn, followed by its "rebirth" the next spring.

One immediately obvious issue here is that the majority of heroes in these accounts, such as Dumuzi, Inanna, Venus, Astarte, Isis, Osiris, Tammuz, Adonis, and Attis, were of course fictional characters, perhaps comparable in some respects to Snow White or Cinderella. Lacking historicity makes these cases much less comparable to Jesus's life, however the stories developed, which they did as they spread from one ancient culture to another.

(3) But another sort of legendary thesis concerned the "tall tales" and exploits of historical persons such as Alexander the Great, Apollonius of Tyana, or Sabbatai Zevi. Cases involving any similarities between real individuals of the past and Jesus's life would of course be a closer fit and more meaningfully compared than would the resemblances between Jesus and fictional personages. Unfortunately, the two very different kinds of stories were often mixed together, with readers not always knowing whether or not the characters were historical.[143]

---

[143] Regarding these second and third varieties of myth or legend in particular, Lake lists T. K. Cheyne, Hermann Gunkel, H. Winckler, P. Jensen, and Zimmern as "perhaps the best-known names." See Lake, *Historical Evidence*, 197. Orr lists Gunkel, Cheyne, Jensen, Winckler, A. Jeremias, and others as holding what the old liberal scholars sometimes considered to be parallel or comparative events or teachings. See Orr, *Resurrection of Jesus*, 21, 238. McNaugher also includes Gunkel, Jensen, Cheyne, along with Karl Weizsäcker and others; see McNaugher, *Jesus Christ*, 157. Influential thinkers Otto Pfleiderer and Wilhelm Bousset should be added to this list. The classic and influential collection of these sorts of stories, along with many other tales, is anthropologist James George Frazer's well-known study, *The Golden Bough: A Study in Comparative Religion* (New York: Macmillan, 1890). In a later edition, the subtitle was changed to *A Study of Magic and Religion*. The original research expanded from its initial two volumes in the first printing of 1890 to a dozen volumes by 1915. While Frazer was a scholar (he was a Fellow of Trinity College, Cambridge University) and included copious and detailed notes, his works still found a ready audience with readers of Thomas Bulfinch's popular *Mythology*, which was composed of three earlier volumes by Bulfinch: *The Age of Fable* (1855), *The Age of Chivalry* (1858), and the *Legends of Charlemagne* (1863), combined into a single volume only after Bulfinch's death.

(4) As mentioned, one of the most influential works to appear during the entire liberal period was *Kyrios Christos* written by the German New Testament theologian and Göttingen professor Wilhelm Bousset. He was perhaps the best-known proponent of the *religionsgeschichtliche Schule* of the late nineteenth and early twentieth centuries.[144] While roughly championing a more sophisticated version of some aspects of similar legendary ideas, Bousset argued that the worship of Jesus in the early church would not have begun in the monotheistic Jewish church but must have come from the early Hellenistic atmosphere where the Gospel message had spread, since there was much more openness to the notions of divinized humans and similar sorts of ideas. Thus, the teaching of the deity of Jesus Christ did not represent the earliest, Palestinian version of the Christian proclamation but developed later in more fertile, Hellenistic areas.[145]

Another influential scholar who was often associated with the history of religions movement was German theologian Ernst Troeltsch. Like Bousset, he also thought that the central question for scholarship was whether the ideas of Jesus's divinity and the Christian notion of salvation were original to the apostolic community or whether they developed in a non-Jewish or even non-Christian atmosphere, such as that of the mystery religions with their interest in a "savior-god." Yet, with the possibility of the latter origin, Troeltsch pointed out that no one has ever identified the non-Christian culprit, that the similarities raised were too superficial, and that there was no evidence that "such a grafting ever occurred."[146]

Sometimes it is difficult to draw hard and fast lines between these different sorts of myths and legends enumerated above. An influx of legend creeping into the text might look like the first category. But such could lead to utilizing examples of

---

[144] Note that the *religionsgeschichtliche Schule* is not synonymous with the legendary or mythical approach to Christianity. Rather, it is being treated here as one of the groups in this general category that approached some of these issues from an angle that exhibited certain relevant interests.

[145] Wilhelm Bousset, *Kyrios Christos: A History of the Belief in Christ from the Beginnings of Christianity to Irenaeus*, trans. John E. Steely (Nashville: Abingdon, 1970), esp. chap. 4. This idea was developed further by the highly influential German New Testament scholar Rudolf Bultmann, for example, in his *Theology of the New Testament*, trans. Kendrick Grobel, 2 vols. (New York: Scribner's Sons, 1951, 1955), such as 1:82–83, 125–33, 293–303.

[146] Ernst Troeltsch, *The Christian Faith*, ed. Gertrud von le Fort, trans. Garrett E. Paul (Minneapolis: Fortress, 1991), esp. 87–88. Troeltsch's original German volume was entitled *Glaubenslehre*, ed. Gertrud von le Fort (Berlin: Duncker and Humblot, 1925).

dying-and-rising gods or Hellenistic divine men to illustrate how Jesus's incarnation could have been conceived in gentile circles. This is similar to the "watershed question" above and, since it morphs into a different position, it might best be considered as a version of the second type.

On the other hand, another influential and well-published German theologian, Otto Pfleiderer, also took the second and third options mentioned above. Pfleiderer recounted dozens of potential parallels to the Christian ideas of heroes being sons of God, demonic exorcisms, miracles such as virgin births and resurrections, along with notions that Jesus was the King of kings and Lord of lords.[147]

For example, Pfleiderer states, "From the very beginning it was the belief of the Christian community that Jesus was the Son of God," but he argues that this idea could mean different things. However, the orthodox view that Jesus was the Son of God as indicated by being virgin born, as taught in Matthew 1 and Luke 1, are second-century views.[148] Further, the beliefs that Jesus was the Son of God and Son of Man could not have developed "in the circles of Judaism" but rather in pagan-influenced areas.[149] Here Pfleiderer actually predated Bousset's *Kyrios Christos* by several years. But exchanges of ideas had to take place. After all, the preaching of the gospel "was compelled to accommodate itself to the prevailing heathen ideas, in short to the myths."[150]

Unfortunately for Pfleiderer's thesis, he far too uncritically cited many of his sources, in that many of them both arose long after the origin of Christianity and were written literally centuries after the person whose life and exploits they describe. It could even be the case that these later tales were drawn from and borrowed their messages from Christianity rather than the other way around, as has actually been shown to be the case since the early twentieth century!

Earlier in this chapter we briefly viewed another skeptical development that some may be inclined to list as another trend within the mythical or legendary camp. We are speaking here of Bruno Bauer's notion that Jesus never actually lived. Though Bauer did widely employ some of these ideas discussed here, we will resist the idea that it was another specific *trend* within these legendary camps, strictly because it was

---

[147] These topics actually make up the various chapter headings for Otto Pfleiderer's consecutive topics in his volume, *The Early Christian Conception of Christ: Its Significance and Value in the History of Religion* (London: Williams & Norgate, 1905).

[148] Pfleiderer, 16–19.

[149] Pfleiderer, 24–25, cf. 154–55, 161.

[150] Pfleiderer, 166.

held by hardly anyone and hence cannot properly be thought of as a movement in itself. Yet, there were similarities.

Bauer was not the only German liberal during this century who held that Jesus never lived or walked the earth. Decades after Bauer, lesser-known scholar Peter Jensen of the University of Marburg agreed with this general assessment, though for different reasons. He could be included largely alongside scholars like Pfleiderer. After a very lengthy study of what he considered to be a host of Jewish legends, Jensen postulated that Jesus's life was an Israelite Gilgamesh legend. Like a patch-work quilt, the Gospel descriptions were taken and simply pieced together from Old Testament stories, as with its accounts of individuals being raised from the dead. Thus, the man described in the New Testament, Jesus, never lived.[151]

Of course, there are many other trends that could be pursued in this context, both similar as well as dissimilar. These German liberal paths truly include a labyrinth of movements. However, we will have to be satisfied to leave the various theses here for now, awaiting critiques in the chapters to come.

Conclusion

We have discussed at length some of the major naturalistic hypotheses that were proposed among the German liberal scholars throughout the nineteenth century and for a couple of decades afterward in the twentieth century to account for Jesus's death and resurrection. We have identified this movement that lasted more than a century as the heyday of these alternative theses. Whether using rationalistic explanations to replace primarily the miraculous portions of the Gospel accounts or treating the entire texts in a more wholesale manner as mythical compositions, the supernatural claims were systematically at least questioned if not totally rejected. But as will be seen in the next chapter, these liberal scholars were often merciless in their critiques of their colleagues' formulations as well.

Many reasons have been given to explain why the age of German liberalism drew to a close after leading critical theological trends for over a century. Among the most popular suppositions are that the romantic, "rose-colored glasses" notion of liberal anthropology was thoroughly dashed from its moorings by the realistic jolt of a world at war in 1914, which signaled that a human "sin nature" might truly be evident

---

[151] Peter Jensen, *Das Gilgamesch-Epos in der Weltliteratur* (Strasburg: Trübner, 1906), esp. 1026–28.

in civilization after all, despite the denials. Arguing in a similar though theological direction was Karl Barth's *Römerbrief,* which appeared in 1918 with its emphasis on the sovereignty of God and human sinfulness.[152]

For Albert Schweitzer, one of the chief failures of liberalism was the debacle that the search for the historical Jesus had become. At the end of his historical master-piece, Schweitzer states that liberalism "has not been destroyed from without, it has fallen to pieces, cleft and disintegrated by the concrete historical problems which came to the surface one after another."[153]

William Hordern adds a rather intriguing perspective. He states, "The Bible became a problem for liberals. . . . Why spend all the trouble in searching for the historical Jesus when he says nothing but love God and your neighbor, things which we can figure out for ourselves?" Then he adds, "Why do we spend more time dissecting the Bible than the *Analects* of Confucius if there is nothing unique about the Christian faith?"[154]

Whatever reasons are correct regarding the fall of German liberalism, new ideas arose rather quickly. The first great Quest for the historical Jesus ended somewhat abruptly but was followed directly by a group of scholars who had studied under the last of the German liberals. Unlike their professors, this new group generally eschewed historical Jesus studies altogether. These emerging and highly influential individuals, such as pacesetters Karl Barth, Rudolf Bultmann, and others, generally came to be called the "No Quest" scholars, although these two hugely influential German researchers often exhibited more differences than similarities between one another.

---

[152] Karl Barth, *The Epistle to the Romans,* trans. Edwyn C. Hoskyns (Oxford: Oxford University Press, 1933). A helpful overview regarding the fall of liberalism can be found in William Hordern's text, *A Layman's Guide to Protestant Theology* (New York: Macmillan, 1956), particularly chap. 5. Concerning the World War I scenario alone, Hordern states that "somewhere between 1914 and 1918 liberalism died in Europe" (101).

[153] Schweitzer, *Quest of the Historical Jesus,* esp. 398–403. The quotation is from 398.

[154] Hordern, *Layman's Guide to Protestant Theology,* 103–4.

5

Nineteenth-Century Liberals versus Liberals on Alternative Theories

T hroughout the more than a century of New Testament scholarship dominated by the reign of German liberalism, we have seen that various major naturalistic theories were proposed to account for at least the supernatural portion of the resurrection accounts. These theories came in a number of different subvarieties as well. But one of the most intriguing aspects of this back-and-forth dialogue is that while each of the liberal scholars of course supported their own personal alternative formulations, they quite frequently attacked the positions taken by their liberal colleagues. Neither did they shy away from leveling some of the strongest, most potent critiques against those who held positions other than their own, often pointing out some of the most serious issues with these natural responses, ones that are still employed today more than a century later. Several of the critiques even rather surprisingly went well beyond substance alone to comments that contained very caustic flavors.

Thus, some of the most memorable critiques of these natural hypotheses came from the pens of these German liberal scholars as they sparred with their colleagues. The best-known comment by far is David Strauss's unforgettable denunciation of the swoon or apparent death theory held by Heinrich Paulus and others. This criticism by Strauss remains the most common single rejoinder to the swoon thesis still voiced today.

Another example is that of Theodor Keim's detailed, multifaceted critique of Strauss's subjective vision theory, which arose after Keim's best initial efforts to unpack and understand the hallucination thesis. Keim's comments were also a major, well-evaluated effort, exhibiting criticisms that are still heard presently.

But even the briefer criticisms and one-liners were sometimes quite memorable, pertinent, and insightful. In this chapter we will view a number of these liberal German critiques of the resurrection hypotheses supported by contemporary liberal scholars. However, it ought to be noted that not the slightest effort is being made to construct a systematic, multifaceted, or detailed critique, let alone a complete one. The very nature of reporting these complaints from fellow liberals rather necessitates that the comments be far scantier and piecemeal, as well as more disorganized than might be hoped. Still, these efforts should be helpful in grasping the historical atmosphere of these debates as well as revealing the substance of key complaints and some of the very best retorts to these alternative ideas.

Schweitzer's Critiques of Historical Jesus Studies

In earlier chapters, we identified the two most popular paths that the German liberal scholars took in approaching the historical Jesus. The earlier, rationalistic tendency was inclined to accept most of the underlying, particular Gospel account as historical while substituting a natural hypothesis in place of the supernatural portion. On the other hand, the more radical mythical approach tended to reject large portions of the account or even the entire passage altogether, considering it to be the result of later, nonhistorical accretion in various ways. These two methods were in competition that sometimes sparked rivalries along with some agreed-upon similarities.

Albert Schweitzer very helpfully described this and other liberal rivalries throughout his major work on German liberalism. In the process, he definitely had a knack for getting to the heart of controversies and locating key flash points. For example, the setting for one of these memorable clashes was the intersection of ideas between two of the liberal giants: Schleiermacher and Strauss. When Schleiermacher lectured on the historical Jesus for the last time in 1832, Schweitzer graphically asserted with his frequent flair for words that Schleiermacher's work was already "rendered obsolete by the work of Strauss. For the questions raised by the latter's *Life of Jesus*, published in 1864, Schleiermacher had no answer, and for the wounds which it made, no healing."[1] Further, according to Schweitzer, the rational method "received its death-blow at the hands of Strauss" (56).[2]

Schweitzer frequently critiqued the nineteenth-century German scholars for making assumed, a priori decisions and rejections, and did so in some graphic language as well. For example, he remarked further concerning Schleiermacher, who he thought "comes to the facts with a ready-made dialectic apparatus and sets his puppets in lively action" (62). Likewise, Schweitzer thought that Otto Pfleiderer failed to ground his own Christology: "He laboriously brings together wood, straw, and stubble, but where he gets the fire from to kindle the whole into the ardent faith of primitive Christianity he is unable to make clear" (314–15).

Schweitzer also commented regarding the competing rational versus mythical approaches within German liberalism as well as internal group debates. For example, he discussed in great detail Bruno Bauer's theses, such as his critique of F. C. Baur's "four great Pauline Epistles, which the Tübingen school fondly imagined to be beyond the reach of criticism." But Schweitzer judged that Bauer's "transference of the Epistles to the second century is effected in so arbitrary a fashion that it refutes itself" (157). But as if that were not enough, Bauer also moved the Gospels to the second century as well.

Moreover, Bauer's last book on *Christ and the Caesars* "is even more unsatisfactory than that suggested in the preliminary work on the Pauline epistles." This is due to Bauer abandoning the historical method altogether and attempting to base his thesis about Christianity on "an imaginary picture of the life of Seneca." Here, Seneca's ideas are seen as some sort of mystical precursor for Paul's writings (157). In the process of evaluating these ideas, Schweitzer repeatedly uses terms for Bruno Bauer's research such as "subjective," "arbitrary," "unsatisfactory," and "eccentric" (148, 157, 159). That these negative terms were employed on separate pages where Bauer was addressed perhaps indicates that this caricature was essentially what Schweitzer thought of him.

---

[1] Albert Schweitzer, *The Quest of the Historical Jesus*, trans. William Montgomery (New York: Macmillan, 1968), 62. Throughout the rest of this section, page references to this work will appear in-text.

[2] Another example is David Strauss's criticism of Daniel Schenkel's work on the historical Jesus, *Das Charaktererbild Jesu*. After Schenkel criticized Strauss in this work, Strauss fired back his own critique of Schenkel's work, censuring it for being too unoriginal as well as taking a "both-and" perspective of the various views that he entertained. Strauss published his own text against Schenkel, entitled *Der Schenkel'sche Handel in Baden*. Schweitzer seemed to agree with Strauss's critique (210).

As a result of missteps such as these in his research, Bruno Bauer's views were largely disregarded by the German liberal scholars of his day. This includes his position that Jesus never existed, which was simply judged to be too far off the beaten scholarly path to have gained much influence, especially when, as Schweitzer argued, Bauer's theses were far too poorly reasoned. Placing even Paul's authentic epistles as well as the Gospels in the second century in order to support his thesis of Jesus's non-existence was also too uninformed and ungrounded. As a result, Schweitzer reported that Bauer "failed to exercise any influence. His work was simply ignored" (138). Further, "he had long been regarded by theologians as an extinct force; nay, more, had been forgotten" (158).

For Schweitzer, in discussing two of the more radical German liberal thinkers, another of Bauer's chief problems was his being overshadowed by Strauss. Born just one year apart (Strauss in 1808 and Bauer in 1809), Strauss's ideas commanded much more attention. One reason for this was due to the relative outlandishness of too many of Bauer's views, as just noted. The result was that, therefore, "Bauer passed practically unnoticed, because every one was preoccupied with Strauss." Yet, whereas Bauer's arguments themselves were misplaced, it might be concluded that his critical spirit alone made a mark (158–59).[3]

Needless to say, then, the view that Jesus never existed was a trial balloon tested among the German scholars, though it never went anywhere. With Bauer, the thesis barely made it a few feet off the ground before it was either shot down by Strauss, or, more likely, simply ignored by other researchers.

Some of the liberal critiques of other liberals were quite trenchant as well. After the appearance of Strauss's first *Life of Jesus*, forty or fifty essays on the subject appeared during the next five years alone. This is quite a number when the state of printing at that time is considered. Still, Schweitzer thinks that only four or five of them

---

[3] Adding to the interest here is that Strauss and Bauer critiqued each other's views both regarding the subject of the historical Jesus as well as their respective interpretations of Hegel. These works are David Friedrich Strauss, *In Defense of My "Life of Jesus" against the Hegelians*, trans. and ed. Marilyn Chapin Massey (Hamden, CT: Archon, 1984); Bruno Bauer, *Philo, Strauss, Renan, und das Urchristentum* (Berlin: Hempel, 1874); Bauer, "Rezension: *Das Leben Jesu, kritisch bearbeitet* von David Friedrich Strauss," *Jahrbücher für wissenschaftliche Kritik* 109 (1835): 879–80; 111 (1835): 891; 113 (1835): 905–12; 86 (1836): 681–88; 88 (1836): 697–704, the last source as listed by Douglas Moggach, "Bruno Bauer," *The Stanford Encyclopedia of Philosophy*, ed. Edward N. Zalta, December 18, 2013, http://plato.stanford.edu/entries/bauer/.

were valuable responses. To one of his interlocutors, Tübingen pastor Eschenmayer, Strauss replied with this ad hominem: "This offspring of the legitimate marriage between theological ignorance and religious intolerance, blessed by a sleep-walking philosophy, succeeds in making itself so completely ridiculous that it renders any serious reply unnecessary" (97).

In spite of this, Schweitzer asserts immediately after this last comment by Strauss that, "for all the sarcasm Strauss does not show himself an adroit debater in this controversy, any more than in later times. . . . It is indeed remarkable how unskilled in polemics is this man." However, "Strauss on his part seemed to be stricken with a kind of uncertainty, lost himself in a maze of detail, and failed to keep continually re-formulating the main problems which he had set up for discussion" (97). No doubt, at least some of Strauss's readers may have thought otherwise after studying and digesting his works.

On a different topic, Schweitzer also noted that French critical scholars from "the Strassburg school" [*sic*] of interpretation were disappointed with Ernest Renan's volume *Vie de Jésus*. Schweitzer explained that they did not appreciate Renan's reliance on the Gospel of John, judging that his work could not be termed the life of the Jesus of history, for it was more like the Christ of the Fourth Gospel (189)!

Even from these few hints, controversies over various interpretations and other aspects of the historical Jesus (always the major occupation during this era) were quite common. Just as these German liberal scholars would often challenge those with whom they disagreed, so it was with Jesus's resurrection in particular. Scholars who had developed their own naturalistic responses to this key event often seemed to think that it was necessary for them to detail and critique the other liberal responses before them that would take alternate paths to the same goal of sidestepping the resurrection! It often appeared as if it was not enough to be on the same side in denying the event of the resurrection; presumably, these authors seemed to think that they all needed to agree on the best natural alternative road to take, and it had better be the approach of the one doing the writing!

The Swoon or Apparent Death Hypotheses

We have already deliberated in some detail regarding the much-discussed topic of Schleiermacher's view of Jesus's death by crucifixion. We concluded that it was undetermined whether or not Schleiermacher truly thought that Jesus had died on the cross. Schweitzer was one of the many scholars who thought that, for Schleiermacher,

Jesus was less than fully dead. So Schweitzer offered at least two critiques of what he took to be Schleiermacher's stance here: "By what right does Schleiermacher currently speak of it as a 'resurrection,' as if resurrection and reanimation were synonymous terms?" Further, did Schleiermacher truly think, as he states, that it makes absolutely no difference whether or not Jesus was actually risen from the dead or merely reanimated?[4]

Strauss noted different varieties of swoon hypotheses, such as Jesus slumping into a coma, there being a plot to rescue him (complete with the administering of drugs or potions), or Jesus being taken off the cross before his death. He refers to Karl Venturini's "arbitrary suppositions" that tended in some similar directions as Bahrdt.[5] Although the rationalist Heinrich Paulus conveniently rejected nails having been placed in Jesus's feet, Strauss protested that the evidence favored their presence, asserting that if there were nails in Jesus's feet, then Paulus's swoon thesis had weighty and severe troubles. Strauss added that the Roman spear wound in the chest would also have killed Jesus in very short order anyway. Altogether, it would be exceptionally difficult to understand how Jesus could have survived crucifixion without medical assistance. Finally, the common cognate hypothesis that Jesus's ascension consisted of Jesus simply walking off in a cloud "falls to the ground of itself." Hence, all the probabilities are against the suppositions of apparent death.[6]

Though he did not aim his celebrated comment directly at Schleiermacher, Strauss's critique of the swoon or apparent death thesis remains the most famous of the German liberal criticisms aimed at other alternative resurrection views, as mentioned above: "It is impossible that a being who had stolen half-dead out of the sepulcher, who crept about weak and ill, wanting medical treatment, who required bandaging, strengthening and indulgence . . . could have given to the disciples the impression that he was a Conqueror over death and the grave, the Prince of Life."[7] Thus, Strauss held that the most damaging roadblock to postulating the notion that

---

[4] Schweitzer, *Quest of the Historical Jesus*, 65, as per Friedrich Schleiermacher, *The Life of Jesus*, ed. Jack Verheyden, trans. S. Maclean Gilmour (Mifflintown, PA: Sigler, 1997), 415–17, esp. 415.

[5] David Friedrich Strauss, *The Life of Jesus, Critically Examined*, ed. Peter C. Hodgson, trans. George Eliot (Mifflintown, PA: Sigler, 1997), 698, 718, 737–38.

[6] Strauss, 678–79, 737–38, 751, also 473, 485, quotation on 751.

[7] David Friedrich Strauss, *The New Life of Jesus*, 2nd ed., 2 vols. (London: Williams & Norgate, 1879), 1:408–12.

Jesus never died on the cross was not whether this or that life-ending blow had been administered to him during the crucifixion process. Rather, the chief point is the events that transpired after he emerged from the burial tomb and visited his followers. His disciples would observe for themselves that he was obviously alive, but they would know equally well that by no means had he been raised from the dead. A stooped, pale, badly limping, bleeding individual who clutched constantly at his side and tried to catch his breath would demand the immediate attention of a physician rather than passing for being the risen Son of God!

The major issue here is that from the very outset Jesus's appearances were preached exactly the opposite way: that after his death, Jesus was seen alive, vibrant, appearing and disappearing, teaching, and so forth. The two views were polar opposites, but how would the preaching of the earliest eyewitnesses embrace both images, alternating from the Jesus of the swoon thesis to the orthodox view? This was Strauss's chief concern, and the majority of scholars ever since him have agreed.[8]

Strangely enough, and adding to the mystery of his own position, Schleiermacher made a similar comment himself concerning the swoon thesis in a volume that was not published until about the same time as Strauss issued his famous quotation:

> If we think of Christ as bearing the external marks of his crucifixion and of his body as it had been before, that is to say, as a sick man with weakened life force, the journeying hither and yon seems quite improbable, but this improbable action took place as early as the first day. Then he appears as one quite healthy, who walks without difficulty to Emmaus and back again. All this clearly belongs to the picture of his state. We cannot represent him as those do who maintain the hypothesis of an apparent death. We cannot think of him as spending this time with his life force at a low ebb.[9]

---

[8] One could of course postulate that the disciples who were the original witnesses of the sickly Jesus could have been a different group than the ones who were proclaiming the joyous appearances of Jesus. Strauss did not need any help to think of this idea on his own, but evidently rejected it. This thesis would run aground of much of the data in the first volume of this study. For example, critical scholars agree that Paul interviewed the original eyewitnesses in Jerusalem just three years after his conversion, thus about AD 35–36. The original apostles knew nothing of the sickly Jesus, but only the risen Jesus who was healed immediately after the crucifixion. The continuity here is crucial.

[9] Schleiermacher, *Life of Jesus*, 455–56. A cautionary note is in order here, since it is at least possible that this quotation came from one of the students who put this volume together some thirty years after Schleiermacher's death.

Keim was familiar with Strauss's critique, which is evident both from the similarity of the wording below and, more precisely, because he cites Strauss at this point as well as mentions similar sentiments from Neander and Holtzmann: "Then there is the most impossible thing of all: the poor, weak, sick Jesus, with difficulty holding himself erect, in hiding, disguised, and finally dying—this Jesus, an object of faith, of exalted emotion, of the triumph of his adherents, a risen conqueror and Son of God! Here, in fact, the theory begins to grow paltry, absurd, worthy only of rejection."[10]

Schleiermacher also criticized the rational form of liberal theses that involved plots to rescue Jesus from the cross before his death (presumably regarding positions such as those of Karl Venturini and Karl Bahrdt), calling them "groundless."[11] Renan concluded that the Jewish leaders' hatred toward Jesus alone would be a sufficient guarantee that Jesus was indeed dead![12] Réville thought that the Gospel texts, which indicated that the disciples doubted and failed to recognize Jesus after his resurrection, plus the additional abilities that Jesus manifested, such as appearing and disappearing, were all further indications that this was not a case of Jesus simply avoiding death.[13]

These critiques by their fellow German liberals apparently had their effect on those who held or considered swoon theories during the early rationalistic phase of liberalism. This is especially the case with many scholars being quite aware of Strauss's devastating comments. Quite intriguingly, this alternate position was the

---

[10] Theodor Keim, *The History of Jesus of Nazara: Considered in Its Connection with the National Life of Israel, and Related in Detail*, trans. Arthur Ransom, 6 vols. (London: Williams & Norgate, 1883), 6:330–31.

[11] Schleiermacher, *Life of Jesus*, 443.

[12] W. J. Sparrow-Simpson is the scholar who reports this but lists the source only as Renan's *Life of Jesus*, without a page number. See Sparrow-Simpson's text, *The Resurrection and the Christian Faith* (Grand Rapids: Zondervan, 1968), 44.

[13] Albert Réville, *Jésus de Nazareth: Études critiques sur les antécédents de l'histoire évangélique et la vie de Jésus*, 2 vols. (Paris: Fischbacher, 1897), 2:455. Of course, it should be remembered here that Réville himself did not take the Gospels at face value but rather was just remarking how the texts point otherwise than to Jesus's apparent death. It still should be mentioned concerning his statement, however, that those few scholars who wished to defend the swoon thesis could respond to Réville that the doubting and the failure to recognize Jesus could simply be normal reactions when one thinks he has seen a dead person. The differences in Jesus's appearance could also have resulted from the scourging and the results of crucifixion. However, Réville certainly would be correct that such natural explanations could not account for Jesus's appearing and disappearing!

most popular option during the earlier portions of the nineteenth century, though Schweitzer lists no proponents of the thesis after about 1840.[14]

Fraud Types 1 and 2: Jesus's Disciples or Others Stole Jesus's Dead Body (and Other Tomb Theses)

We have seen earlier that only a few of the German liberal scholars preferred any of the more minor burial alternative considerations, such as Jesus's body not being buried in Joseph's tomb or the women going to the wrong tomb. The more major challenges proposing that the disciples (Fraud Type 1) or someone else (Fraud Type 2) stole Jesus's dead body were exceptionally rare. Apparently due to the general neglect of these tomb theses ever since the eighteenth-century writings of English deist Thomas Woolston and German rationalist Hermann Samuel Reimarus, there is even less mention in these nineteenth-century writings of any critiques of the various versions of fraud or stolen body views. The result is that one has to look carefully for critiques pertaining especially to the second fraud category that non-disciples stole Jesus's body from the tomb and other somewhat-related tomb theses. This entire category of approaches was neither popular, respected, nor well regarded.

For instance, Schweitzer refers to Reimarus's early work *Von dem Zwecke Jesu und seiner Jünger*, published by Gotthold Lessing in 1778, as an anonymous work and calls it "a polemic, not an objective historical study." Reimarus had "a wrong perspective" and that resulted in his arriving at "a mere makeshift hypothesis to derive the beginnings of Christianity from an imposture." The imposture or deception mentioned here is the disciples' actions in stealing Jesus's body, not to mention their ensuing lies about what happened.[15]

Regarding the idea that Jesus's own disciples could have stolen Jesus's body out of the tomb, even Strauss attests that such a motive "could not possibly have animated them . . . amid the greatest perils" or otherwise account for "the astonishing revolution from the deep depression and utter hopelessness of the disciples at the death of

---

[14] Schweitzer does mention Karl von Hase's *Geschichte Jesu: Nach akademischen Vorlesungen*, published in 1876, but this is a revised and edited version of Hase's earlier text, *Das Leben Jesu zunächst für akademische Studien*, first published in 1829, where his views are actually quite close to Schleiermacher's position. This means that the 1876 work is still basically before 1840. Moreover, in the end, it must be remembered that the works of these two scholars may not actually teach the swoon theory anyway!

[15] Schweitzer, *Quest of the Historical Jesus*, 22–23.

Jesus, to the strong faith and enthusiasm." But if they had acted in this manner, the exuberant change in Jesus's followers "would be inexplicable."[16]

Strauss also complained concerning the deists, specifically referring to Thomas Woolston by name, along with others from that era who held similar views involving fraud. Pointing to the comment above regarding the nineteenth-century scholarly lack of regard or interest in these fraud hypotheses, Strauss noted that the views of Lessing and the others were opposed by the "great majority of German theologians."[17]

In sum, the loose collection of tomb theories that we have termed the fraud theses, including that Jesus's disciples or someone else stole Jesus's body along with a variety of other odd suggestions concerning Jesus's burial, tend more or less to be blips on the nineteenth-century critical screen. Only the brief suggestion by Lake (who interestingly actually supported the view that Jesus was truly raised from the dead!) that the women could possibly have gone to the wrong tomb garnered much interest at all, perhaps because of its novelty. The idea also arrived toward the end of this era, meaning it could have received even more attention had it been produced earlier. As it was, the conservative scholars of this time noticed it more frequently. Otherwise, this group of theses were pretty well rejected *en toto* by other liberal scholars.

The Hallucination or Subjective Vision Theory and Similar Subjective Views

Due to Strauss's prominence in popularizing the subjective vision theory, many of the German liberal scholars aimed their comments at him pertaining to this hypothesis. This applies to Strauss's treatments of the disciples' experiences as well as the apostle Paul's, so we will treat each subject in turn.

Subjective Visions and the Disciples

Schleiermacher aimed many comments at this general idea. He argued that the appearances were "so substantiated that I cannot entertain the idea that they were either an invention of a later time or were due to self-deception on the part of the disciples."[18] Since the risen Jesus was both seen and heard, the likelihood of halluci-

---

[16] Strauss, *Life of Jesus*, 739.

[17] Strauss, 45–48, 707.

[18] Schleiermacher, *Life of Jesus*, 474.

nation plummets considerably. For Schleiermacher, the accounts are specific, realistic, and sufficient enough to conclude the certainty that Jesus appeared to his disciples and lived with them again after his death.[19]

In agreement with Schleiermacher, Paulus also held that the sorts of appearances recorded in the Gospels of the risen Jesus were not the sorts of manifestation that could be accounted for by hallucinations, for they were too real, including physical confirmation. This is especially the case in the last two canonical Gospels, and it must be remembered here that John was the preferred Gospel at this time.[20]

For Christian Weisse, writing about the same time that Strauss's initial edition of *Das Leben Jesu* first appeared, Strauss's concept of myth was ungrounded historically. As such, it would simply consist of a critical objection that was not linked to good theory. The result is that Weisse judged that Strauss had not found a way between the rationalistic and supernatural views of Jesus's resurrection.[21]

Schweitzer leveled several detailed critiques at Strauss. For instance, similar to Weisse's comments, Schweitzer also thought that Strauss "sometimes rules out statements by assuming their impossibility on purely dialectical grounds." But a priori dismissals are no place to begin building a thesis. Further, Strauss is often very arbitrary, such as in his spiritualizing of unwanted aspects of the Gospel depictions of Jesus or his attempts to take Jesus's resurrection teachings in a metaphorical manner (which actually foreshadows a few twentieth-century scholars). What many of these items have in common is Strauss's "awkward, arbitrary handling of the history." He spends much more effort as a critic tearing down texts instead of also creatively building the portions that are well grounded.[22]

More specifically, Schweitzer thinks that Strauss overestimates "the importance of the Old Testament motives in reference to the creative activity of the legend." But even if one knows the *form* taken by the legend, this does not explain its *origin*. Further, Schweitzer judged that the Gospels "must have as [their] basis some historical fact. . . . The substratum of historical fact in the life of Jesus is much more extensive

---

[19] Schleiermacher, 440, 442, 473–74. Some related thoughts also can be found in Friedrich Schleiermacher, *The Christian Faith*, ed. H. R. Mackintosh and J. S. Stewart, 2 vols. (New York: Harper & Row, 1963), 2:417–24, esp. 420. Schweitzer provides a few more details concerning this response by Schleiermacher; see *Quest of the Historical Jesus*, 64.

[20] Heinrich Eberhard Gottlob Paulus, *Das Leben Jesu als Grundlage einer reinen Geschichte des Urchristentums*, 3 vols. (Heidelberg: Winter, 1828), 1:265, 281–82.

[21] Schweitzer, *Quest of the Historical Jesus*, 130–31.

[22] Schweitzer, 84, 196–99.

than Strauss is prepared to admit."[23] But being critical of the Gospel content fails to disprove it. Any sort of report can be riddled with problems while still being substantially accurate in at least key portions of what is being described.

Subjective Visions and Paul of Tarsus

Kirsopp Lake adds another substantial angle on this matter, stating the problem rather succinctly. As he explains, the subjective vision hypothesis "seems to fall to pieces against the experience of St Paul. . . . Thus, to explain St Paul's experience in this way demands the reconstruction of an elaborate psychological process."[24]

Lake's prediction is, in fact, exactly what we find both before and since that time—that in order to apply the subjective vision (or almost any other natural theory) to Paul's conversion, an entire alternate scenario generally has to be contrived around Paul's own reports, usually without any data whatsoever. This seems to be what Lake is referring to here. Further, this approach is all done in spite of the critically ascertained "authentic" Epistles of Paul clearly teaching very different views!

As an example of precisely Lake's last point, German liberal scholar F. C. Baur criticized proposed natural scenarios such as Paul encountering thunder or lightning on his way to Damascus, noting "how unsatisfactory this is" since these options have "no foundation in the text."[25] The same should be said of probably the most popular natural view concerning Paul, which postulates that he had some species of subjective reaction due to an overwrought guilt complex from persecuting Christians, a state of mind which is absolutely contrary to everything we know about Paul. As incredible as it sounds, Baur's comment above was made in spite of the fact that he even crossed his own line. He is one of those scholars who concludes (and quite confidently too, it might be added) that Paul experienced some species of subjective experience contrary to the authentic information concerning Paul that Baur himself recognized and accepted![26]

---

[23] Schweitzer, 84.

[24] Kirsopp Lake, *The Historical Evidence of the Resurrection of Jesus Christ* (London: Williams & Norgate, 2012), 266–67.

[25] Ferdinand Christian Baur, *Paul the Apostle of Jesus Christ: His Life and Works, His Epistles and Teachings; A Contribution to a Critical History of Primitive Christianity*, trans. A. Menzies, 2 vols. (London: Williams & Norgate, 1873, 1875; repr., Peabody, MA: Hendrickson, 2003). The two quotations are taken from 63–64 and 70–71, respectively.

[26] Baur, 1:67–92, 255–59, 264; 2:251–53.

Arnold Meyer makes almost the same point as does F. C. Baur, although he was criticizing Baur and Carl Holsten regarding their attempts to formulate Paul's psychology on the way to Damascus. Meyer, an exegete, charges that Baur and Holsten depart from the New Testament texts at will, supposing in an a priori manner that Paul had developed "scruples of conscience as to his persecution proceedings" in spite of what Paul himself states. Meyer thinks that much of this reaction is due to Baur's school of thought embracing pantheistic rationalism with a prior disbelief in miracles.[27]

Pfleiderer also follows Baur in making this move. After referring to Paul's doubts, Pfleiderer remarks how these misgivings must have weighed heavily on Paul. Thus, his vision most likely originated from Paul's nervous and agitated disposition. One must wonder where these assertions about Paul were derived. Yet, Pfleiderer makes what appears to be a surprisingly enigmatic reference here, apparently asserting that whether Paul's conversion was due to natural or supernatural reasons, God was the ultimate cause of whatever occurred to the apostle.[28] Depending on Pfleiderer's meaning, this may potentially have other than a typically naturalistic meaning.

Hermann Fichte critiqued Strauss's view of Paul's conversion on some related grounds. First, for Paul to have had a vision of the risen Jesus would have contradicted psychology's laws, in that these subjective experiences should not have arisen from the previous and contrary unbelieving mental state that Paul himself describes for us. Second, no preexisting Christian faith could be found in Paul. Third, Strauss's imagining of Paul's mindset of supposed remorse and guilt at his persecuting of Christians is totally contrary to Paul's own accounts.[29]

Fichte's three responses as observed in this critique of Strauss and the many other scholars like Baur who so commonly adjusted Paul's mindset despite and even against the known data supplied by the apostle himself to meet their own theoretical needs actually can be quite a sophisticated analysis, even in twenty-first-century psychological terms. This is especially the case when considering the 1869 date of Fichte's original composition.

---

[27] Arnold Meyer, *Die Auferstehung Christi: Die Berichte über Auferstehung, Himmelfahrt und Pfingsten* (Tübingen: Mohr Siebeck,1905), xxii, xxvi.

[28] Otto Pfleiderer, *Das Urchristentum, seine Schriften und Lehren in geschichtlichem Zusammenhang beschrieben*, 2nd ed., 2 vols. (Berlin: Reimer, 1902), esp. 1:40–46.

[29] Immanuel Hermann Fichte, *Vermischte Schriften zur Philosophie, Theologie und Ethik*, 2 vols. (Leipzig: Brockhaus, 1869), 2:164–66.

The Most Detailed Critique of Strauss's Hallucination Theory

During the nineteenth century, the criticisms leveled by German liberal scholar Theodor Keim were the most comprehensive with regard to the popular subjective vision theories. Since Keim was often inclined to write by backtracking and repeating earlier points in his writings, it is difficult to produce an ordered list of his complaints regarding Strauss's thesis, at least in precise order. Still, an approximate enumeration of his major critiques is possible. Keim makes at least each of the following points:[30]

(1) According to the prevailing view among German liberal scholars (as favored by Strauss, Renan, and others), it was necessary for the disciples to switch from their previous negative mental states of depression, despair, and hopelessness caused by Jesus's sudden death by crucifixion and being ripped away from their ministry. But it was thought that a significant amount of time was needed for their mindsets to change, and up to a year had been suggested for this process to occur.[31] In place of the prior hopelessness, the apostles needed to exude self-generated excitement, enthusiasm, and optimism in order to produce the necessary visions.

But Keim pointed out some of the problems involved with demanding this new outlook, which were never observed or otherwise hinted at in the early New Testament texts. The sources agree that the appearances before Paul's began to take place almost immediately—within three days or so. Once again, as already remarked above, a number of these German critical scholars adjusted the narratives to fit their alternative thesis, like hallucinations. On the other hand, if the relevant writings are established, then alternative views such as Strauss's and Renan's have a major problem. According to the prevalent thinking at that time, the disciples would not have been in the proper frame of mind to produce subjective visions.[32]

---

[30] Keim, *History of Jesus of Nazara*, 6:338–64, esp. 338, 342–43, 353–61. See also Theodor Keim, *Die Geschichte Jesu von Nazara, in ihrer Verhaltung mit dem Gesamtleben seines Volkes frei untersucht und ausführlich erzählt*, 3 vols. (Zurich: Orell and Füssli, 1867–1872), esp. 3:506–621, on Jesus's burial and resurrection, with some specific pages from both the German and English versions listed in this and the previous chapter.

[31] Ernest Renan, *Les apôtres, histoire des origines du christianisme* (Paris: Calmann-Lévy, 1880), 2:45–46.

[32] The reason for this emphasis at the middle to end of the nineteenth century was that exuberance and excitement were necessary for the positive experiences that followed. However, this emphasis has shifted in some studies today. While this positive frame of mind is still thought to be necessary in some sorts of subjective experiences, it is not the case with postmortem visions, for example. The latter do indeed occur to persons who

(2) Throughout the New Testament, subsequent visions witnessed by the apostles, including Paul, were clearly distinguished from Jesus's resurrection appearances, signaling that the latter were a qualitatively different sort of phenomena. This distinction also argues against the disciples' resurrection appearances being subjective visions since the subsequent visions were of that sort.

(3) The cessation of the appearances after a few weeks (except for Paul's) makes sense if they were caused by God. But if they were self-generated, subjective visions, it would seem that these occurrences actually should have increased, even exponentially, as more converts entered the church and claimed to have seen the risen Jesus just as the apostles did. Hence it would seem that many more such visions would be a natural development, given the circumstances. So how is this sudden discontinuation to be explained?

It is also worth making a critical observation here. Some of the strongest and most common objections aimed at the subjective vision hypotheses over the past few decades were seldom raised during the late nineteenth century, presumably due to the content of these particular items simply not being known from the textual or psychological research at that time, or perhaps because certain New Testament reports were simply regarded as legendary and thus ignored. Several examples may be very briefly helpful here.

Initially, one of the most potent objections in current parlance, backed by the early appearance reports, testifies to groups of believers seeing the risen Jesus together. But rather incredibly, this was seldom mentioned in the nineteenth century. This was no doubt the case for more than one reason. The best data that favors these group appearances (1 Cor 15:3–7) were generally untreated in much of the research of that time. Further, the important considerations provided by the scientific developments in the field of psychology were quite unknown then. Moreover, even some conservative authors actually conceded the reality of group manifestations.[33] But the tide has

---

are still forlorn, downcast, and depressed after a loved one has died. Then again, not all scholars take this last category of experience to necessarily be hallucinatory anyway, but that is another discussion. On this subject, see for instance, see J. Steve Miller, *Deathbed Experiences as Evidence for an Afterlife* (Acworth, GA: Wisdom Creek, 2021). Another volume in this set by Miller is forthcoming. Thus, to make a similar or equivalent point today, much more nuance would be necessary here. But that's hardly surprising in our time after well over 100 years of further research have ensued.

[33] For example, see James Orr, *The Resurrection of Jesus* (London: Hodder & Stoughton, 1908; repr., Grand Rapids: Zondervan, 1965), 219; Sparrow-Simpson, *Resurrection and the*

certainly shifted today, for instance, with group appearances in the case of the earliest Christian witnesses generally being allowed by the majority of critical scholars who address the issue.

Another contemporary argument contrary to subjective visions is that of Jesus's tomb being unoccupied on the first Easter morning, which is also allowed by the majority of critical scholars today, whereas the empty tomb was probably more often than not considered by the German liberals simply to be a straightforward legend. Even Keim accepted this legendary view. Still other serious considerations at present are derived from facts such as the conversions of Paul and James the brother of Jesus, who were almost assuredly not in the proper frames of mind to hallucinate the risen Jesus.

But given the scholarly situation at the end of the reign of German liberalism, believers and others were largely left to critique the subjective vision thesis apart from what are now considered to be the best comebacks. This is all the more reason why strong critiques such as Keim's multifaceted case against hallucinations were so remarkable.

The Objective Vision Theory

The telegram, telegraph, or objective vision hypothesis popularized by Keim and a few others was of course not a naturalistic thesis (as recognized freely by critical scholars), for it postulated that Jesus was really raised from the dead and taken to heaven by God the Father, from which they cooperated to send nonbodily images to his disciples. These appearances were for the purpose of convincing Jesus's followers that he was indeed alive and that he was sending them out to tell others the good news of God's kingdom. Hence, these events were recognized as supernatural miracles from start to finish.

Nonetheless, it will just be mentioned briefly that the objective vision theory was not without its detractors. Schleiermacher may have had something like this

---

Christian Faith, 113; John McNaugher, *Jesus Christ: The Same Yesterday, Today and Forever* (New York: Revell, 1947), 151. However, this was sometimes denied by conservative scholars such as Wilbur M. Smith, *The Supernaturalness of Christ: Can We Still Believe in It?* (Boston: Wilde, 1954), 217. As noted in the material in this volume on hallucinations and related phenomena, this discussion requires that careful distinctions be made. While group phenomena such as more objective illusions (as with magical show performances) certainly do occur, subjective hallucinations in groups are quite a different matter altogether.

notion in mind, though as with his position on Jesus's death, he once again seems to be confused here.[34] Even though the chief work of Christian Weisse came slightly after Schleiermacher's death, this may be an indication that such concepts were involved in the conversation at that time, decades before Keim seemed to favor nonbodily appearances.

Schweitzer was critical of Weisse for only accepting the Galilean appearances of the risen Christ, a move that was judged for not helping his overall thesis very much. But it was thought further to be rather one-sided because it failed to solve the problem of the two traditions of appearances in both Galilee and Jerusalem.[35] But this was actually a rather odd thing for Schweitzer to blame on Weisse, given that most of the scholars who held either the subjective or objective vision theses at that particular time placed the appearances in Galilee.

Strauss made a few rather snide remarks about those who thought that a supernatural cause was behind Jesus's resurrection appearances. Responding to the well-known philosopher Spinoza, for example, Strauss referred to this scholar's view as "the magic circle of the supernatural."[36] With regard to Christian Weisse's conception of objective visions, Strauss similarly blamed him for holding on to "objective magical facts."[37] Common to both of these responses is Strauss's accusation that belief in miracles is akin to invoking magic.

The critiques directed at the objective vision theory were both milder and less common than those of the natural resurrection hypotheses. This could have been for more than one reason, such as the view having attracted several major German liberal scholars as well as Keim's major effort coming slightly past the time of some of the more critical and creative alternative liberal responses.

The Legend or Myth Theory

In the late nineteenth century, certain theological trends may have seemed quite unrelated to earlier aspects of German liberalism, even while still manifesting some similar core characteristics. One of the most influential was the *religionsgeschichtliche Schule* and its prominent quest to separate Hellenistic from Jewish influences on early

---

[34] Schleiermacher, *Christian Faith*, 2:420.
[35] Schweitzer, *Quest of the Historical Jesus*, 131.
[36] Strauss, *Life of Jesus*, 740.
[37] Strauss, 744, esp. n. 29.

Christianity. Another conspicuous, overlapping trend attempted to trace myriads of mythological stories through various cultures, implying or stating that Christianity may have been just another of these alternative accounts.

There is a sense that many of these scholars often had their readers at a disadvantage. For example, their attempts to parse out Hellenistic from Jewish influences drew some very fine lines, making it appear that only very specialized scholars could actually participate. However, decades later it turned out that a large portion of this research was largely guesswork.

While there was some specific knowledge at this time regarding the ancient mythical tales of god-men, miracles, and demons, there was not enough generally available, accurate data to make certain the most crucial distinctions. This resulted in the presence of many troublesome issues. For example, there were such wildly variant tales of the same pagan stories (such as Isis and Osiris) that it was even difficult to refer to them as the same accounts. Another simply huge issue was the date of these ancient tales. If some of the earliest forms of the most crucial stories were *post*-Christian, this would obviously be highly relevant to the question of whether Christians simply borrowed from these tales. But that's precisely the problem; because much of this more specific information was unavailable, many crucial distinctions could not be made at that time.

Particular scholars were aware of some of these issues but were still cautious of drawing tight conclusions. For Kirsopp Lake, "The difficulty is to decide how far this theory is based on fact, and how far it is merely guess work. . . . The evidence is not sufficient at present to prove that this is so."[38] Specifically pertaining to the resurrection, Lake goes on to say that "there is a solid basis of history" in the Markan empty tomb and Paul's appearance account "which cannot be explained as efforts of the imagination. . . . It is history, not theology or mythology."[39]

Actually, both of Lake's points are well supported. These general mythic or legendary hypotheses are indeed particularly well known for incorporating much conjecture. By stating or even just overemphasizing something in just a slightly different manner, or by arbitrarily choosing one version of a story over others, relevant comparisons can appear more similar than they are in reality. For instance, mentioning mystery religions where the heroes were said to have been raised after

---

[38] Lake, *Historical Evidence*, 262–63.
[39] Lake, 263–64, cf. 198–99.

three days of course makes a much closer comparison to Christianity. But what about the cases where the same hero is raised one, two, or perhaps even four days later?

Lake's second critique is even more penetrating. As many scholars have mentioned over the years, the Christian claim is not merely that Jesus must have been raised since he was a great hero like the others. Thus, the resurrection was not an event that was merely added to the end of Jesus's life as if it were the "thing to do." Rather, Jesus's followers claimed to actually have *seen* him again after his death. Moreover, they claimed to have found an empty tomb. The point is that they could have been mistaken, but hearing other tales would not account for empirical experiences.

Troeltsch thought that perhaps the most crucial issue for contemporary scholarship to solve was whether the ideas of Jesus's divinity and the Christian notion of salvation were originally based upon reports from the apostolic community. Or could these beliefs have progressed in a non-Christian or non-Jewish context like those of the mystery religions, featuring their interests in savior-gods? Though the pagan origin was a possibility, Troeltsch pointed out that no one had ever identified accurately the non-Christian culprit. Further, and like Lake's earlier question, Troeltsch thought that the similarities that were raised were too superficial and arbitrary. Last, we need to see the actual evidence that "such a grafting ever occurred."[40]

Then quite surprisingly, and also similar to Lake, Troeltsch went on to state that justice must be done to the indispensably historical nature and character of the Christian claims: "The development of the Christian belief in salvation and in the saving death of Christ must be traced back to the impact of the person of Jesus himself, i.e., to the resurrection faith." This includes the "resurrection appearances" along with other aspects of the "assured body of facts," among other aspects of Christianity that are "clearly historical."[41] In these aspects, Troeltsch even sounds rather conservative rather than like a distinguished member of the German liberal camp.

Therefore, even though similarities among the various stories were reported during the end of the liberal period, scholars called for careful substantiation. Claiming that a particular belief is of a similar or identical nature to another one and demonstrating it as such are often two different things. As a matter of fact, we will see later that as this specific research continued, the history of religions claims were not sustained.

---

[40] Ernst Troeltsch, *The Christian Faith*, ed. Gertrud von le Fort, trans. Garrett E. Paul (Minneapolis: Fortress, 1991), 87–88.

[41] Troeltsch, 88.

Conclusion

The reign of nineteenth-century German liberal thought marked the beginning of systematic studies of the historical Jesus. Schweitzer states that the very first lecture on this subject by a theologian was given by Schleiermacher in 1819.[42] Edited slightly from the title of Schweitzer's famous volume, this period has been termed the First Quest for the historical Jesus. Though it would be greatly exaggerated to say so, it does seem sometimes that almost every major liberal scholar who wrote during more than a century penned a volume with some variety of the words *Das Leben Jesu* in the title!

This German liberal period also marked the heyday of naturalistic theories directed at the resurrection of Jesus. The development of these suggested natural suppositions to replace Jesus's resurrection is an intriguing phase of critical thought. It might be expected that some major "pushback" would be forthcoming from the conservative scholars during this time to challenge firmly these alternative liberal ideas and critique them, and that is precisely what occurred. Holding honored positions in major universities such as Oxford, Cambridge, Aberdeen, Harvard, Yale, Princeton and elsewhere, these equally well-trained conservative scholars opened their own chapter of resurrection studies. When the smoke cleared, quite an impressive body of pro and con literature was available.

While the conservative onslaught was naturally to be expected, it was much more surprising to witness the German liberals critiquing each other's alternative theories. As we have seen, sometimes the critiques took on the appearance of quite nasty attacks! The usual result is that each of the hypotheses had considerations aimed in the direction of their often quite "creative" ideas. Occasionally the critical comebacks may have successfully convinced scholars to move in other directions![43]

---

[42] Schweitzer, *Quest of the Historical Jesus*, 62.

[43] This may have been the case with Schleiermacher, and it could possibly explain the apparent conflicts in his own testimony as described above, but that is difficult to determine for sure. Keim reports an example where Ludwig Noack, in his partially fictional account of Jesus's life, changed his earlier alternative response to the resurrection, but it is quite difficult to know if it was due to liberal critiques. While Noack still rejected the literal event later, it seems that he embraced Spinoza's view in his 1876 volume, *Die Geschichte Jesu auf Grund freier geschichtlicher Untersuchungen über das Evangelium und die Evangelien* (Mannheim: Schneider, 1876). See also Keim, *History of Jesus of Nazara*, 6:326n2, 332–33; cf. Schweitzer, *Quest of the Historical Jesus*, 174–79.

More striking, some of the liberal criticisms of their own colleagues were so damaging that the general consensus by even the German liberal community was that particular naturalistic hypotheses had been rendered passé and hence were no longer considered to be live options. Such instances were noted by many liberal scholars. Such was certainly the case, for example, with Strauss's leveling of the swoon or apparent death thesis in a devastatingly thorough yet brief critique. An incredible indication of this, mentioned already, is that Schweitzer basically does not mention a swoon theorist after 1840, even though it was the most popular thesis before that time.

We also saw that other major scholars, such as Schleiermacher and Keim, "piled on" against the swoon thesis, employing critiques that seem to be borrowed from Strauss's critique, especially in Keim's case.[44]

After producing more criticisms of the swoon thesis, Keim even reports in 1872, "On these grounds, the theory of apparent death has in recent times been rejected by critics almost without exception." Then he mentions several liberals who agree regarding this conclusion.[45] Toward the end of the German liberal reign, Eduard Riggenbach among others even added that the swoon theory was no longer a live option and was not to be found among the liberal scholarly ranks![46] Other examples of these conclusions from the contemporary conservative scholars will be mentioned in the next chapter.

Another example is Schweitzer's comment that the first version of the fraud theory, whereby Jesus's disciples stole his dead body and then lied about the appearances,

---

[44] Though Schleiermacher died two years before the release of Strauss's second volume of his *Das Leben Jesu*, and his own text *Das Leben Jesu* was not published until his students reassembled his lectures posthumously thirty years later, it is certainly possible, if not fairly likely, that Strauss's critique was already "in the air" both because Strauss and Schleiermacher spent time together personally and because Strauss had already been lecturing for two years before Schleiermacher's death. See Schweitzer, *Quest of the Historical Jesus*, 70. Even more importantly, when Schleiermacher's students published his notes from decades earlier, the notes contained their own strong criticism of the swoon theory; see Schleiermacher, *Life of Jesus*, 455–56. Perhaps Schleiermacher had been reconsidering these matters later in his life, especially if he and Strauss had discussed these specific matters. But at the least, these words were quite likely what his students considered to be Schleiermacher's view at that earlier time.

[45] Keim, *History of Jesus of Nazara*, 6:331, citing Strauss, Neander, Holtzmann, Noack, and Schleiermacher.

[46] Eduard Riggenbach, *The Resurrection of Jesus* (New York: Eaton & Mains, 1907), 48–49.

was long rejected by the liberal scholars as a whole.[47] Strauss likewise commented that the majority of German liberal scholars had rejected such an option.[48] We have already commented earlier in this chapter that Fraud Type 2—at least the option where someone else besides the disciples stole Jesus's body from the tomb as an act of deception—was never supported in the first place by the German liberal community but was only propounded by English deists such as Thomas Woolston and German rationalists like Herman Samuel Reimarus, who wrote before the beginning of the liberal era.

In fact, Keim attested the crucial observation that critical scholars had abandoned all "explanation from external facts." In other words, the German liberals had stopped seeking to reject the resurrection due to alternative influences from nature, human actions, or otherwise *outside* the mind of individuals. The latter was therefore the only realm worth looking at regarding the subject—that of "mental facts . . . thoughts . . . feelings which established itself in the inner life of men."[49]

Thus, it might be said that as nineteenth-century German liberalism was coming to an end, only the hallucination or subjective vision theory, and perhaps a version or two of the legend or mythical hypotheses, were still on the table, even though they had also been criticized in much detail. But the final dismantling of these last options remained for later twentieth-century scholarship to get involved with.

The objective vision option was not a naturalistic thesis, yet it definitely survived the First Quest for the historical Jesus. Not only did it endure, but during the middle third of the twentieth century, a modified version of Keim's creative formulation may well have been the most popular approach to the resurrection appearances of Jesus, and it has had its representatives on into the twenty-first century.

So ends for now the discussion here of the German liberal quest for a plausible naturalistic theory for the resurrection of Jesus. Though initially there were several categories of such nineteenth-century hypotheses, only a couple of species survived, along with the supernatural objective vision option. This is the state of the issue as scholars moved further into the twentieth century.

---

[47] Schweitzer, *Quest of the Historical Jesus*, 26, also 22–23.

[48] Strauss, *Life of Jesus*, 45–48, 707.

[49] Keim, *History of Jesus of Nazara*, 6:331.

6

Nineteenth-Century Conservatives versus Liberals on Alternative Theories

Shortly after the midpoint of the nineteenth century, several major, well-accomplished, and more conservative professors began publishing responses to the German liberal scholars and their theories regarding the New Testament. Many key responses were aimed at the liberal treatment of the resurrection of Jesus in particular.

The majority of these scholars were British or American, and many held positions at world-renowned universities, such as Oxford, Cambridge, Edinburgh, Aberdeen, Yale, Princeton, and Harvard. In terms of training and prestige, these respondents were roughly the equivalent from the English-speaking world of the German scholars they were challenging. In short, it was a colossal collision of ideas by accomplished scholars who were contemplating the greatest topics within Christianity.

This chapter will begin by following the same procedure as in the previous discussion. The five major naturalistic theories plus the supernatural objective vision thesis will be reviewed while offering several critiques of each. This time, the critiques will be presented by these conservative scholars. Responses will also be given to a few other prominent and related critical resurrection issues from the perspectives of these same researchers. Afterward, a list of conclusions that emerged from these debates will be addressed.

Like the previous chapter, this one does not purport to be either a systematic or an exhaustive treatment of naturalistic resurrection theories. Refutations will once again be tabled until future chapters in this volume.[1] Rather, the intent just mentioned is to catch a historical glimpse of what a number of prestigious conservative scholars wrote in response to the German liberal resurrection hypotheses and how they critiqued them.

The Swoon or Apparent Death Hypothesis

Actually, the conservative scholars of the nineteenth and early twentieth centuries wrote comparatively little regarding the swoon thesis, with one noteworthy exception. The most likely reason for this dearth stems from their personal comments explaining that they shared with German liberals the conviction that David Strauss's famous critique (along with similar thoughts from other liberal scholars) was not only the best refutation of the apparent death hypothesis, but that it had also accounted almost singlehandedly for the demise of this supposition.[2]

---

[1] Many other scholarly, conservative works from this time period were written in whole or in part on the resurrection but are cited in this chapter only sparsely or not at all. For some examples of such texts, see Cambridge scholar H. C. G. Moule, *The Resurrection of Christ: Expository Studies of St. John 20 and 21* (Minneapolis: Klock and Klock, 1898); Université de Neuchâtel (Switzerland) professor Frédéric Louis Godet, *Lectures in Defense of the Christian Faith*, 2nd ed. (Edinburgh: T&T Clark, 1883), featuring chapter 1 on the resurrection and chapter 2 on the visionary thesis; William Milligan, *The Ascension and Heavenly Priesthood of Our Lord* (London: Macmillan, 1892); Princeton Seminary's J. Gresham Machen, *Christianity and Liberalism* (Grand Rapids: Eerdmans, 1923), see chapter 5. From a few years after the close of the liberal period, other noteworthy scholars could be added here, such as Wilbur M. Smith, *The Supernaturalness of Christ: Can We Still Believe It?* (Boston: Wilde, 1940), with chapter 4 on Jesus's miracles and chapter 6 on Jesus's resurrection; Smith, *Therefore Stand: A Plea for a Vigorous Apologetic in the Present Crisis of Evangelical Christianity* (Boston: Wilde, 1945), with chapter 8 on Jesus's resurrection; John McNaugher, *Jesus Christ: The Same Yesterday, Today, and Forever* (New York: Revell, 1947), with chapter 4 on Jesus's miracles, chapter 6 on Jesus's resurrection, and chapter 7 on the ascension.

[2] Strauss's *Das Leben Jesu* was published in two volumes from 1835–1836. Even in the first few of numerous editions there were many references that hinted at the mature critique of the swoon or apparent death thesis that would emerge in Strauss's later editions almost three decades later. See David Friedrich Strauss, *The Life of Jesus, Critically Examined*, ed. Peter C. Hodgson, trans. George Eliot (Mifflintown, PA: Sigler, 1972). Strauss mentioned many of these hinted critiques on 678–79, 734, 737–39, 751. However, the most famous

Strauss made it evident that the thesis of Jesus's apparent death had failed as a mature factual supposition in itself when compared to the known factual data. But as Orr asserts further, Strauss also pointed out that it never answered the question in the first place as to how the disciples were persuaded that Jesus was not just simply alive, but that he had conquered death and the grave altogether.[3] Sparrow-Simpson asserted that earlier forms of the apparent death scenario such as that by Venturini belonged to "the school of rationalistic romance" featuring "no historical restraint" and based on imagination. But Strauss's refutation was the most complete.[4]

Reflecting on Jesus's supposed swoon and moving somewhat akin to Strauss's critique by looking at the scenario from the disciples' standpoint, University of Aberdeen professor William Milligan raised many questions. One question pertains to the lack of the disciples' despondency and why they did not venture to help such a severely wounded Jesus. Further, when, where, and how did Jesus actually die? Against these criticisms, Milligan noted that Jesus's appearances did not evoke pity and sympathy from his followers but rather engendered joy, boldness, and

---

version of Strauss's criticism of the swoon hypothesis was not contained in his 1836 text, as is often thought and repeated, but in his 1864 volume, *Das Leben Jesu für das deutsche Volk bearbeitet* (*The Life of Jesus for the German People, Revised*). The English translation is entitled *A New Life of Jesus*, 2nd ed., 2 vols. (London: Williams & Norgate, 1879), with Strauss's renowned comment appearing in 1:412 as the concluding paragraph to the discussion of this topic on 1:408–12.

In addition to the German liberal theologians who agreed readily, as enumerated in the previous chapter, the conservatives also credited Strauss (often by name) and referred to his now-famous paragraph originally published in 1864, concluding in general that his critique of the apparent death thesis was the very best of the refutations. For details, see James Orr, *The Resurrection of Jesus* (London: Hodder & Stoughton, 1908; repr., Grand Rapids: Zondervan, 1968), 11n2, 43; W. J. Sparrow-Simpson, *The Resurrection and the Christian Faith* (Grand Rapids: Zondervan, 1968), 44, 160; Doremus A. Hayes, *The Resurrection Fact* (Nashville: Cokesbury, 1932), 285; Frank Morison, *Who Moved the Stone?* (London: Faber & Faber, 1930), 64, 96; cf. George P. Fisher, *The Grounds of Theistic and Christian Belief*, rev. ed. (New York: Scribner's, 1883), 193; cf. also Alfred Edersheim, *The Life and Times of Jesus the Messiah*, 2 vols. (Grand Rapids: Eerdmans, 1883), 2:629; Smith, *Supernaturalness of Christ*, 208; Smith, *Therefore Stand*, 382; McNaugher, *Jesus Christ*, 148. This agreement across both the liberal and conservative sides of the critical aisle (as well as today, as will be indicated in subsequent chapters) on behalf of Strauss's critique is simply amazing.

[3] Orr, *Resurrection of Jesus*, 43.

[4] Sparrow-Simpson, *Resurrection and the Christian Faith*, 43–44.

enthusiasm. From these responses alone it can be ascertained that their conviction was that Jesus had indeed been raised from the dead in a triumphant manner rather than, say, merely limping around in his previous body with all of its torturous injuries. As Milligan notes, it was a critic like Strauss who "heaped contempt upon the old theory of a swoon."[5]

Yale University professor George Park Fisher raised four questions for the swoon hypothesis. He asked how Jesus would have made it throughout the crucifixion process without dying? Then, like Strauss's question, what physical condition would Jesus be in soon afterward, even if he cheated death on the cross? If not at this time, when did Jesus finally die? Finally, was there ever a time when Jesus and his disciples made plans for him to pretend that he had died on the cross?[6]

More or less minor considerations regarding the swoon theory would include other issues, including the fact that Jesus's severe pain and other deadly medical issues would cause him personally to realize that he had not been raised from the dead in a new body! As such, his actions would be better viewed by a healthy mind as a charade aimed at the ultimate goal of deception.[7] Like Fisher and Milligan inquire, what were the conditions under which Jesus finally did die? Are we to suppose that not a single one of those who were the closest to him—his family members, the women, disciples, or other followers—ever discovered anything amiss?[8]

Altogether, as will be argued at the end of this chapter, the prevailing critical testimony is that the swoon or apparent death theory attracted very little scholarly attention during the late nineteenth century and probably not much past the first half of the century, as already noted. Too many pieces of data were stacked against it. But in the view of many scholars (and perhaps even the majority), Strauss's critique alone buried it forever.

---

[5] William Milligan, *The Resurrection of Our Lord* (London: Macmillan, 1881), 75. The quotation above concerning Strauss is from the 1899 fourth edition, 77. The swoon theory is discussed there on 76–80. Milligan also wrote what he termed "a sequel to those [lectures] on the Resurrection of our Lord published by the same writer a few years ago." See Milligan, *Ascension and Heavenly Priesthood*, vii. This second volume was fairly lengthy (367 pages) for this particular subject. Chiefly a theological assessment, Milligan did not direct many of his comments in this text to alternative or critical theses but concentrated on a few other issues, such as how a tangible body could ascend to or even exist in heaven, whether heaven was located "up" in the clouds, and so on.

[6] Fisher, *Theistic and Christian Belief*, 193.

[7] Milligan, *Resurrection of Our Lord*, 76.

[8] Milligan, 78.

Fraud Type 1: Jesus's Disciples Stole Jesus's Dead Body and Lied about His Appearances

Before the birth of German liberalism in the works of Schleiermacher, Thomas Sherlock composed a volume that featured a court case centering largely on this first version of the fraud thesis. Arranged as a series of charges and countercharges with many responses, Sherlock's 1729 work was directed at the English deists, and Thomas Woolston in particular, who as pointed out earlier, had argued this view himself. These early critical discussions occurred precisely during the general time when this view was the most commonly aired, well before Schleiermacher.

Some of Sherlock's responses were as follows: There is no evidence in support of this mere contention. This thesis would truly be "the hardest plot in the world to be managed," apparently a reference to how such an elaborate heist could be kept secret and under the disciples' total control. What would be the disciples' motive for these actions? Whatever the answer, they seemed to gain little in exchange for their all-encompassing, potentially life-threatening effort. When the disciples stood before the Jewish leaders in the early chapters of Acts, they were commanded to stop preaching Jesus's message, but they were never accused of stealing Jesus's dead body. Perhaps most of all, how do we explain the disciples' life changes, especially their boldness in proclaiming this message?[9]

Many scholars have emphasized predominantly this last point. Milligan thought that the disciples were utterly changed in personal terms, with their lives being affixed on the message of God's kingdom, even to the point of dying for this message, and that these facts totally refuted this fraud thesis. Moreover, Milligan asserted rather strikingly that there was no reason to discuss this view any further.[10] Westcott, Fisher, and Edersheim are more commentators who, during the time of the German liberals, also emphasized the noteworthy transformation of the disciples as being quite inconsistent with their stealing the body and perpetrating such an obvious deception.[11]

Fisher raised quite succinctly a question for the first fraud thesis: "Why should men make up a story which was to bring them no benefit, but only contempt,

---

[9] Thomas Sherlock, *The Trial of the Witnesses of the Resurrection of Jesus* (London: Pemberton, 1733), with these ideas appearing on 9, 18–19, 38, respectively.

[10] Milligan, *Resurrection of Our Lord*, 79–80.

[11] Brooke Foss Westcott, *The Gospel of the Resurrection: Thoughts on Its Relation to Reason and History*, 4th ed. (London: Macmillan, 1879), 4, 121; Fisher, *Theistic and Christian Belief*, 197–98; Edersheim, *Jesus the Messiah*, 2:625.

persecution, and death?" There is still the question of what happened to Jesus's body as well.[12] Like Sherlock, Orr also asked, if the Jewish leaders thought that the disciples had stolen Jesus's body, why were they never blamed for their actions?[13]

Doremus Hayes of the Graduate School of Theology cites some of these same reasons concerning the disciples' lives of preaching, suffering persecution, and death, at least for many of them. These are not normally considered to be the preferred sorts of activities that we associate with willful lying. Besides, sooner or later, it certainly seems most likely that someone would have allowed the real fraudulent story to slip out, not to mention likewise revealed where Jesus's body was really buried. Therefore, he concludes, "The charge of fraud fell flat from the very beginning. . . . That faith did not rest upon invention or myth but upon the facts of their own experience."[14]

Sparrow-Simpson points out that some versions of the fraud theory can actually end up launching their own refutations. These theses best establish a single bottom line: not that the disciples' actions were fraudulent but that "both sides alike agreed upon the fact that the grave was empty."[15] Twentieth-century critical scholars have emphasized that such admissions by the first-century critics actually point to the concept of enemy attestation, that what one's opponents concede can be taken either as true or at least as admissible data for the ensuing discussion.

The version of the fraud theory that holds that the disciples were the culprits who removed Jesus's crucified body received much less attention among the German liberal scholars than did the swoon theory. This thesis faltered at many weak points, but none of these was more obvious than blaming the ones who were quite willing to die for their faith with being the very same ones who knowingly perpetrated all of the evil and unethical acts in the first place, as asserted by some of the earliest conservative scholars such as Sherlock and Milligan.

Fraud Type 2: Non-disciples Stole Jesus's Dead Body and Other Tomb Theories

The German liberals spent less time discussing the ideas contained in this rather catch-all category plus the previous Fraud Type 1 thesis than with any of the other

---

[12] Fisher, *Theistic and Christian Belief*, 193.
[13] Orr, *Resurrection of Jesus*, 213.
[14] Hayes, *Resurrection Fact*, 276–82.
[15] Sparrow-Simpson, *Resurrection and the Christian Faith*, 41.

major natural resurrection scenarios. To be fair, since these liberals rarely even proposed these two stolen body hypotheses themselves, the conservatives who responded to them could hardly be blamed for not spending much time on them either. Nevertheless, comments and critiques here and there can be located in the scholarly literature. For instance, we have already viewed French scholar Albert Réville's opinion that the Jewish Sanhedrin in Jerusalem arranged for Jesus's dead body to be stolen, afterward hiding it where it could not be discovered.[16]

Sparrow-Simpson opposed this specific suggestion and proposed a few critiques. Among them, he remarked that the Sanhedrin did not have to go to such an extreme, since they often cooperated with Pilate and could have worked out the situation in some other way than by stealing the corpse with all of the attendant complications. But more telling, if the Sanhedrin had actually taken Jesus's dead body, then by producing it again or at the very least making public their role in purposely emptying the tomb, they could presumably have dealt a decisive blow to the disciples' preaching at a very early stage in the process. This would have been a far more forceful alternative than the tame option of simply settling for commanding the disciples not to preach any longer in Jesus's name.[17]

Then there was Arnold Meyer's position noted earlier that Joseph of Arimathea only meant for his tomb to be used temporarily in order to fulfill the law with regard to having bodies buried before the Sabbath began at sundown. So he moved the dead body of Jesus later, for any of several potential reasons, which was Joseph's intention from the beginning, since he did not want Jesus's body in the same tomb as his own family members or because he was not a disciple of Jesus anyway, contrary to the Gospel reports.[18] We already observed that Strauss made similar moves.

Sparrow-Simpson also addressed this hypothesis, pointing out that there is no evidence at all for such a scenario. To the contrary, even the Gospels present better data than either Meyer or Strauss, for why should no specific data count against some early, definite data? Furthermore, Meyer cannot seem to keep his story straight, for he presents at least three scenarios that appear to conflict with one another: that

---

[16] Albert Réville, *Jésus de Nazareth: Études critiques sur les antécédents de l'histoire évangélique et la vie de Jésus*, 2 vols. (Paris: Fischbacher, 1897), 2:250–52, 347, for the Sanhedrin, their beliefs, and actions.

[17] Sparrow-Simpson, *Our Lord's Resurrection*, 2nd ed. (London: Longmans, Green, 1909), see particularly 100–101.

[18] Arnold Meyer, *Die Auferstehung Christi: Die Berichte über Auferstehung, Himmelfahrt und Pfingsten* (Tübingen: Mohr Siebeck,1905), 118.

Joseph moved Jesus's body, Meyer's denial that Joseph even had a grave in Jerusalem in the first place, and that Joseph's grave was not empty after all.[19]

Morison offered a few considerations against this Meyer-type fraud thesis, and additional suggestions may augment the possibilities. On the view that Joseph of Arimathea moved the body, there would have been a very short window of opportunity to do all that needed to be done, since he would have to be finished presumably within a maximum twenty-four hour or so span, basically during the Sabbath. Hence, his actions at a maximum would most likely have taken place between Friday after sundown or Saturday morning and very early Sunday morning. Moreover, if Joseph did not know that the women were coming to finish the burial process, this would also have been another potential snag in that he would not have been forced into an early decision by that knowledge, though the tomb would still have to be empty by the time they arrived.

Continuing, if Joseph was indeed a secret disciple of Jesus, then this probably would have given away his position to the other Jewish leaders, whether or not he did the actual removing himself. But on this scenario, why would Joseph have wanted to move Jesus's dead body in the first place? Plus, this alternative raises the possibility of tomb worship at the new site, should the word ever have gotten out from those who knew or found out later where Jesus had been reburied. Still worse, explaining why the original tomb was now empty or that Jesus's reburied body was nearby could have involved huge problems for friends and foes alike.[20]

The details here, whatever they were, could potentially have been worked out even after all these issues. But the worst problem for the German liberals was that changing the location of Jesus's original tomb would not have explained the more serious issue of all, namely, the disciples' unflinching belief that they had actually seen the risen Jesus.

Hayes adds that it would have taken several people to perform all the requirements of moving Jesus's body to another tomb, wherever the new one was located, so at a minimum these persons would have known the particulars. Yet, neither the Jews nor anyone else ever produced Jesus's body or disclosed any of the moving or secret plot scenarios, though any of them could have revealed truly dicey and unforgettable stories indeed![21]

---

[19] Sparrow-Simpson, *Our Lord's Resurrection*, 42.

[20] Morison, *Who Moved the Stone?*, 89–94.

[21] Hayes, *Resurrection Fact*, esp. 279–81.

The difficulties for Joseph of Arimathea moving Jesus's body before the women's Sunday morning trip to the tomb should not be underestimated. For example, if Joseph refused to move the body on the Sabbath, like the law-abiding Jewish leader that he was, this alone would have put everything in a brief Saturday night window— a very fast job. If he did not know that the women were returning so early the next morning, there would have been virtually no reason for him to finish the job so abruptly in the dark.

On the other hand, if either the Jewish leaders or any of the Romans had moved Jesus's body for any reasons whatsoever, one problem would be their motive for doing so. What sort of gain would have made such a move worth the potential religious or political risk, especially given the many touchy issues involved? This would be especially difficult for Jews with their cleanliness regarding dead bodies. After all, each group appeared to have been finished with the entire situation.

On the other hand, it may have been understandable if either the Jews or the Romans might have thought it wiser to act a little later, after it was obvious that the Christian teaching had begun spreading.[22] Presumably, nothing could be more important than crushing the Christian message during its infancy. It might be surmised that this could have been done up to a month or so later, while the body still could be identified as that of Jesus, especially given the nail and spear wounds.[23] Waiting much longer makes less sense, but even then the story of why the body had been moved would still have been helpful in thwarting the Christian cause, in that even the fact of an empty tomb would have taken on an entirely new meaning contrary to the apostolic preaching. However, on each of these options, what is to be done with the initial female testimony of the original tomb being found empty, along with all of the attendant indications that this was precisely the case?

Kirsopp Lake's suggestion was that the women possibly could have proceeded to the wrong tomb and when Jesus's body was not found there, they proclaimed an empty sepulcher.[24] The conservative scholars responded to this scenario. For instance, Orr states: "The theory, it need hardly be pointed out, is itself an invention, without

---

[22] Morison, *Who Moved the Stone?*, 94–96. A "wait and see" hint could have been taken here that may have been reminiscent of the advice given in Acts 5:38–39.

[23] In our discussion of Jesus's death in volume 1, information is provided on an approximate timetable for recognizing a crucified and now-dead body at this geographical location and time of the year.

[24] Kirsopp Lake, *The Historical Evidence of the Resurrection of Jesus Christ* (London: Williams & Norgate, 2012), 237–38, 248–53.

historical support or probability—a travesty of the narratives as we have them. There is no evidence of a mistake of the women, who knew too well where the Lord was laid."[25] But as pointed out often, even ungrounded details without evidence are often preferred by critical scholars and given precedent over straightforward statements in the Gospels, especially when the alternative option fits better with the direction of their worldviews.

Sparrow-Simpson charged that the liberal critics do not require solid historical reasons in order to reject items in the Gospels that they do not favor. Regarding the empty tomb in general and Lake's wrong tomb supposition in particular, these critics discarded this teaching simply because it did not fit with their preconceptions. Thus, these liberal scholars rewrote the Gospels at will in order to mold these writings to their own private notions, even from a distance of many centuries later.[26]

Morison raised a few questions of his own pertaining to Lake's thesis. If it was so dark when the women went to the tomb on that Sunday morning that they even got confused about where it was located, it is also highly unlikely that the young man who met them there, whether he was the gardener or merely a passerby, would even have been there in the first place! Who rakes the ground in the dark? Moreover, that the disciples were not available to correct the situation, as Lake seems to surmise, is quite another tenuous suggestion that Morison rates as being "of a very doubtful and precarious character."[27]

Then rather creatively, Morison asks for further clarification: Why would the male disciples either be in hiding or on their way to Galilee strictly out of fear for their lives, while leaving the women to finish Jesus's burial alone in Jerusalem? After all, the women were their own kin or fellow disciples! Did they not care a bit for the women's safety, when they "were in like peril"? Further, did the women then remain in Jerusalem for weeks or even up to a year longer after the burial itself until the disciples returned (as surmised by some critical scholars like Strauss and especially Renan)? Moreover, why would the Jewish leaders not seek out the young man at the tomb until they found him, since his side of the story would be yet another way to disprove the women's message?[28]

---

[25] Orr, *Resurrection of Jesus*, 131.

[26] Sparrow-Simpson, *Resurrection and the Christian Faith*, 44–45.

[27] See the discussion on this point below.

[28] Morison, *Who Moved the Stone?*, 237–38, 248–53.

Admittedly, the wrong tomb thesis seems to be quite confused at best, and at many places. It is no wonder that, after considering a related view, Orr again retorts: it would have been so easy—did not anyone else check out the women's claim to be sure? "It has only to be said of this flight of fancy that, when compared with the narrative of the Gospels, it has no substance or feature of reality to it. It contradicts the tradition at every point. There is no 'historical kernel,' for the ground of history is abandoned for imagination."[29]

Actually, this last conundrum seems to be the case with each of the fraud and tomb scenarios, whether involving the disciples or not. Even these less than coherent options no doubt were still strong factors given the critical rejection of the empty tomb teachings. Thus, some of the critics thought that certain ideas of this nature still remained helpful or even necessary in an attempt to deny the empty tomb. This was especially so in the case of those scholars who preferred one of the vision options (either subjective or objective) or to a lesser degree one of the legend scenarios, for whom the open sepulcher was a potent comeback to these skeptics.

Once again, these critics apparently thought that alternative circumstances sometimes had to be invented to support basically anything besides Jesus's resurrection or, to a lesser extent, the empty tomb. But at what price? These critical scholars occupied an exceptionally tough position between preferring either a far less than powerful explanatory thesis, perhaps even one that was filled with issues, or embracing the resurrection. However, the latter was clearly not an option for many of them, even though the historical options evidently favored the disciples' proclamation on these subjects.

The Hallucination or Subjective Vision Theory and Similar Subjective Views

As with the liberal scholars, so the conservatives also spent significant space on the hallucination and other similar subjective positions. Some acknowledged that they did so because it was the most popular natural alternative thesis at the end of the nineteenth century, therefore demanding more attention.

As a brief background for the liberal views at this time and the texts from which their natural positions were frequently drawn, most of the German liberals favored one Gospel over the others. In roughly the first half of the nineteenth century, that

---

[29] Orr, *Resurrection of Jesus*, 131–32, quotation on 132.

favorite was the Gospel of John. Sometimes the priority accorded to John was such that it was considered as largely reliable in historical terms and was treated occasionally as if the contents of this Gospel were simply true. Even the skeptic Renan,[30] among many others like Schleiermacher,[31] held a similar view. One major reason for this conclusion, especially among the rationalistic liberals, was that John recorded fewer miracles than the other Gospels, presumably indicating that it was more interested in historical matters. In this context, Strauss was the first to revoke the Gospel of John's favored status.[32] Thus it should be noticed that most liberal scholars would not judge all of the Gospels to be equally unreliable, whereas with Strauss the overall skepticism grew more apparent than with the earlier rationalistic liberals.

While the Gospels were commonly criticized, the question could be asked as to what criteria established the liberal's favorite naturalistic theories, be it swoon, hallucinations, legends, and so on? Was the favored alternative view the best option merely because the critics simply decreed it such? Or was it thought that each was actually defensible on its own grounds, due to being favored by worthwhile arguments? It has already been argued in this volume in detail that the liberals frequently criticized each other's views. Perhaps they did indeed mistrust one or more of the hypotheses due to their inherent weaknesses. But one key question pertains to whether each view was *established factually* over the other natural options?

Hallucination or Subjective Visions and the Disciples

James Orr

Also mentioned earlier was that the strongest and most detailed German liberal critique of the subjective vision hypothesis was probably that by Theodor Keim.[33] On

---

[30] Ernest Renan, *Vie de Jésus* (Paris: Calmann-Lévy, 1864), 423–24, especially Renan's pronouncement that the Fourth Gospel keeps or maintains its superiority over the other Gospels: "le quatrième Évangile garde sa supériorité" (423). But Renan is also clear that he values this Gospel's narratives rather than its discourses.

[31] Friedrich Schleiermacher, *The Life of Jesus*, ed. Jack C. Verheyden, trans. S. Maclean Gilmour (Mifflintown, PA: Sigler, 1997), 223, 417–18, 435, 441, 447–50, 454. In several places Schleiermacher refers to John's Gospel as the work of eyewitnesses, such as, "I know no rule to set up except this: The Gospel of John is an account by an eyewitness" (433).

[32] Schweitzer, *Quest of the Historical Jesus*, chiefly 85.

[33] This is widely acknowledged. Besides the German liberals who agreed in the previous chapter, a few of the conservative examples also should be mentioned here.

the conservative side of the ledger not long after Keim, that honor for the strongest treatment of the subjective vision theory probably goes to Scottish theologian James Orr, who devotes a fairly lengthy chapter to the many issues with visional theories of various types.[34] In fact, Orr's detailed arguments are probably the premier example of comebacks to Strauss and others during the liberal era. We will reproduce a few of Orr's criticisms here.

Orr argues over many pages that the historical case to be made for the disciples actually observing appearances of the risen Jesus is quite strong. Agreeing with Schleiermacher, Paulus, and others before him, Orr contends that these events were simply both too real and too persistent. Subjective events have their own laws too, and they are not free to operate just any old way.

Moreover, Orr thought that there were many critiques of the hallucination theses and concluded that these criticisms were often ignored by those who favored them. He defended his arguments from any of the Gospels of Matthew, Luke, or John alone. With the exception of Mark (because there were most likely no appearances recorded in the original text), the situation is that basically any liberal who championed one of these three Gospels would still have to come to grips with these critiques.

Orr was very helpful in pointing out an entire string of items taught in the Gospels that must be avoided or changed by the hallucination theorists, including: (1) The three Gospels that narrated the appearances (Matthew, Luke, and John) placed the initial experiences in or around Jerusalem rather than in Galilee, as do almost all visionary proponents.[35] (2) The disciples experienced bouts of grief, doubt, and despair after Jesus's death, again as expressed in all three of these Gospels. But because the subjectivist theorists acknowledged that the disciples' negative states of mind were entirely accurate, they felt compelled to delay the appearances by up to a year to accommodate these negative emotional experiences in order to change these

---

These would include scholars such as Orr (*Resurrection of Jesus*, 219), Fisher (*Theistic and Christian Belief*, 198), and Edersheim (*Jesus the Messiah*, 2:628n2). Sparrow-Simpson even asserted rather surprisingly that Keim did a better job of setting forth the case for the subjective vision position—which he did not hold—and that Keim even "expresses it more learnedly and forcibly than Strauss" (*Resurrection and the Christian Faith*, 112–13)!

[34] Orr, *Resurrection of Jesus*, 205–31.

[35] Notice that the emphasis here is on the initial appearances. Virtually no one denies that these experiences also took place in Galilee.

adverse mindsets to positive states of mind so that the visions could begin developing more readily and joyously.[36]

(3) Orr holds that "in no case is there the slightest trace of preparatory excitement" such as scholars like Strauss, Renan, and other critics portrayed as being necessary. (4) Rather than "momentary glimpses," the Gospels depict several of Jesus's appearances as "prolonged interviews" between the risen Christ and his followers. (5) That the disciples' unbelief, doubt, and fear continued even *after* they saw the risen Jesus is not the best background for hallucinations, where the disciples would have been observing precisely what they wanted to see, hence the lack of these negative emotions. (6) Jesus presented himself corporeally rather than ethereally. Obviously, if Jesus had also been touched, as all three of these Gospels either teach or imply, then the subjective vision thesis is badly mistaken.[37]

As with this and many other German liberal dialogues, contemporary critical scholars could comment on differences in how such a discussion on the Gospel accounts and some other matters might proceed today vis-à-vis the nineteenth century. Due to these contrasts, such a modern response would not be entirely inappropriate either. Yet for the very early twentieth century, Orr's response was an insightful reply to the natural theses of Strauss and a few other researchers from just a few decades earlier. More crucially, while it is the case that some of the issues discussed above would be considered outdated in the present, other matters here could have been entirely welcome today, depending on the nature of the specific dialogue. On still other subjects, the German liberals could take even more critical stances than what is done today.[38]

---

[36] This is especially located in Renan, *Les apôtres, histoire des origines du christianisme* (Paris: Calmann-Lévy, 1880), 2:45–46. Other helpful comments in this direction are found in Renan, *Vie de Jésus*, 355–56; David Friedrich Strauss, *The Life of Jesus, Critically Examined*, trans. George Eliot, ed. Peter C. Hodgson (Mifflintown, PA: Sigler, 1997), 739–40.

[37] For these and other comments, see Orr, *Resurrection of Jesus*, 222–25; the quotations utilized in points 3 and 4 above were each taken from 223.

[38] Such as how many of Paul's epistles were considered genuine. F. C. Baur, perhaps the most accomplished Pauline critical scholar among the German liberals, allowed only four authentic epistles: Romans, 1 and 2 Corinthians, and Galatians. He was followed by other liberals in this conviction. See Ferdinand Christian Baur, *Paul the Apostle of Jesus Christ: His Life and Works, His Epistles and Teachings; A Contribution to a Critical History of Primitive Christianity*, trans. A. Menzies, 2 vols. (London: Williams & Norgate, 1873, 1875; repr., Peabody, MA: Hendrickson, 2003), 1:256–58. The subject of this chapter on the very wide acceptance of naturalistic theories as supported by the German liberals would be another such difference.

Much of the interaction here is in the vein of the classic German liberal dialogue. Since some of the more skeptical German scholars are involved at this juncture at approximately the halfway point of the liberal "century"—among them F. C. Baur, Strauss, Bruno Bauer, along with the French scholar Renan—a couple concluding comments from Orr will be directed to this historic liberal context.

As noted, Orr provided lists of several criticisms of the subjective vision hypothesis, and his arguments against other natural hypotheses should not be ignored either. The force of Orr's overall critique is that hallucinations require many adjustments to the Gospel records to adopt its own critical parameters. Orr summarizes the matter: "It will be seen, to begin with, that to gain for this visional theory any semblance of plausibility, every fact in the Gospel history has to be changed—time, place, nature of the events, mood of the disciples, and so on—while scenes, conditions, and experiences are invented of which the Gospels know nothing. It is not the facts on record that are explained, but a different (imaginary) set of facts altogether."[39] This initial assessment by Orr led to his overall criticisms as parsed out in the comments above. Must all of the historical data in the Gospels be changed or ignored if hallucination theses are potentially to obtain? Conversely, if the Gospel data remain, especially in key places, would this be a formidable task or even a multifaceted roadblock that must be answered by those who prefer the hallucination views?

Another more specific critique of Strauss should perhaps be classified as Orr's strongest historical argument against hallucinations. In fact, this insight by both Strauss and Orr alike may actually rank as being ahead of both their times in accord with more contemporary views. Orr reasoned that Paul's list of appearances in 1 Corinthians 15 is very impressive "and well attested." Then Orr quotes Strauss, the major German skeptic and foremost hallucination proponent who actually conceded much crucial information regarding this text. Strauss acknowledges that Paul apparently received his material at this point precisely from Peter, James, and the other original eyewitnesses, as described in Gal 1:18–2:10.[40] Yet, he knew of these data much earlier.

Amazingly, Strauss admits a rather major scenario, almost as if constructing a positive case himself, by maintaining that Paul received the message of the appearances

---

[39] Orr, *Resurrection of Jesus*, 222–23.

[40] Orr, 26–27. It must not be overlooked that the Gal 2:1–10 text to which Strauss refers includes the apostle John as also being present as one of the "others" whom Strauss explicitly mentions by name elsewhere—see below.

in 1 Cor 15:3–7 three years after his conversion when he traveled to Jerusalem. Strauss affirms that "there is no occasion to doubt that the apostle Paul had heard this from Peter, James, and perhaps from others concerned" as per his own testimony in Gal 1:18–19 and 2:9. Then he specifies that Paul went "to Jerusalem, to get more accurate information about Jesus in general, and in particular about those appearances of him after his death which others also professed to have had." Further, Strauss thinks that Paul "had heard in many ways of these appearances even at an earlier period, while he was persecuting the confessors of the new Christ."[41]

So Strauss confirms his position that Paul received the testimony in 1 Cor 15:3–7 just three years after his conversion via his travel to Jerusalem to interview Peter and James (Gal 1:18–20).[42] For Strauss, Paul's precise purpose in making this trip was to gather reliable information regarding Jesus's resurrection appearances from the original witnesses themselves. Strauss also thinks that Paul had probably heard often of these appearance reports even *before* his conversion, precisely during his persecution of Christian believers.[43]

One reason to emphasize Strauss's approach and the information gained by its use is that it is enormously crucial in making a case precisely against his own hallucination thesis as well as in the overall evidence for Jesus's resurrection appearances that this approach generates. Paul naturally would have been utilizing the study skills that were built into his early training as a Pharisee when he heard these testimonies of these eyewitnesses. In fact, Paul even utilized the same terms for passing on tradition as explained by Josephus, who was himself a Pharisee.[44] This knowledge, combined

---

[41] Strauss's major acknowledgment here is found in his volume mentioned earlier, *A New Life of Jesus*, 2nd ed., 1:400. Fisher makes a similar point concerning the data in *Theistic and Christian Belief*, 192–93.

[42] Strauss includes John along with Peter and James as the Jerusalem "pillars" (see Gal 2:9) in his earlier, less detailed treatment of Paul's meeting them in Jerusalem. See *Life of Jesus*, 147.

[43] This is another critical example of what was termed in volume 1 of this study the pre-Pauline 1 creedal statements that predated Paul's own transformation. This would increase even further the historical weight of the early traditions contained chiefly in the New Testament Epistles.

[44] On the passing of tradition as practiced by the Pharisees, see Josephus, *Ant.* 13.297; *Ag. Ap.* 1.49–50; *Life* 361. Translation, including different demarcations of the references, from *The Works of Josephus*, trans. William Whiston (Philadelphia: McKay, 1820; repr., Grand Rapids: Kregel, 1963), see *Ant.* 13.10.6; *Ag. Ap.* 1.9; *Life* 65, cf. 75–76. On Paul employing these same skills, using precisely the same language, see also Richard Bauckham,

with Strauss freely admitting that Paul learned from the apostolic witnesses that the appearances occurred to *groups* of individuals, creates a roadblock to these appearances being hallucinations.[45]

Admitting this group of crucial events, as Strauss clearly does, places him in a bind that necessitates a response. Strauss thinks that Paul still downplayed the experiences of the other apostles due to his belief in the primacy of his own encounter, plus some jealousy on his part.[46] But this suggestion is unverified from the available data while being opposed by several considerations. For instance, Strauss's stance here is contrary to Paul's firm and quite positive assertion that all the apostles just mentioned reported the same appearances that he did (1 Cor 15:11).[47]

But beyond Strauss's clear teachings at this point, the overall introduction of these ideas in this chapter was that conservative scholar James Orr had singled out Strauss's admissions here as militating against Strauss's own views that Jesus's appearances after his death were due to natural hallucinations. Since Orr considered that Strauss's views were mistaken for these as well as other reasons, he asks

---

Jesus and the Eyewitnesses: The Gospels as Eyewitness Testimony, 2nd ed. (Grand Rapids: Eerdmans, 2017), 36–37, 264–71.

[45] For the importance of group appearances of the risen Jesus, see especially both volume 1 of this study on the evidence for these events plus the treatment of hallucinations and similar approaches in this volume.

[46] Strauss, *New Life of Jesus*, 1:401–2.

[47] Additional factors also militate against Paul's resistance to fully appreciating the valuable testimony regarding the other apostles' appearance testimonies. For example, why would Paul take the difficult and dangerous journey to Jerusalem in the first place (Gal 1:18–20) and then return again after fourteen years (2:1–10) in order to interview (Greek: *historēsai*; 1:18) these apostles regarding their own testimony if he hardly cared about it or was taking it less seriously than his own? Moreover, why was Paul pleased to include his own testimony along with that of the other apostles (1 Cor 15:14–15), downgrading himself in the process (15:9)? Strauss strangely chides Paul for taking three years to make his initial trip to Jerusalem, holding that he was quite satisfied with the veracity of his own appearance of Jesus (*New Life of Jesus*, 1:402)! That's an exceptionally odd stance when in other examples from ancient history, this is an *exceptionally brief time*— perhaps even without parallel. See Paul Barnett, *The Birth of Christianity: The First Twenty Years* (Grand Rapids: Eerdmans, 2005), 210, cf. 12. After all, it must be remembered that Paul had other things on his mind at this time, such as being in danger himself. Strauss's complaints sound like he is judging ancient times by more modern parameters. But then again, Strauss clearly did not believe in Jesus's resurrection, so it appears that since he had admitted this crucial data that Paul records in Galatians 1–2, this may well have been his best way to mitigate it somewhat.

whether Jesus may actually have appeared to his followers but in less than a real body.[48] The treatment of this latter option by conservative scholars is entertained later in this chapter.

Other Conservative Commentators

At the close of the German liberal era, prominent New Testament professor C. H. Dodd, of both Oxford and Cambridge Universities, also discussed this last theme of Paul's two trips to Jerusalem (Gal 1:18–20; 2:1–10) in specific detail. Dodd agreed with Strauss in holding that Paul probably received the traditional material regarding Jesus's appearances in 1 Corinthians 15 when he visited with Peter and James the brother of Jesus in Jerusalem. These events occurred no more than a maximum of seven years after Jesus's crucifixion, and they could have happened earlier.[49]

Edersheim adds that Paul's use of the verb *historeō* here in 1:18 "implies a careful and searching inquiry on his part."[50] One more major corollary here is that this text continues in Gal 2:1–10, where, in addition to other subjects as well, Paul indicates that he and Jesus's apostles were on the same page, agreeing on the nature of the gospel message, which of course included the resurrection event (Rom 1:3–4; 10:9; 1 Cor 15:3–4).[51]

In 1907, Lake noted another argument of equal importance: the material in 1 Cor 15:3–7 not only preserves eyewitness testimony, but it is also dated exceptionally early—in fact all the way back to Jesus's original disciples in the earliest church, probably at Jerusalem![52] These ideas are true forerunners of the most crucial, consensus conclusions from late twentieth- to twenty-first-century research![53]

---

[48] Orr, *Resurrection of Jesus*, 26–27. Orr treats later the notions of both the hallucination hypotheses (205–26) as well as real but less than bodily appearances (226–31).

[49] See C. H. Dodd's volume *The Apostolic Preaching and Its Developments* (London: Hodder & Stoughton, 1936; repr., Grand Rapids: Baker, 1980), particularly his conclusions on 16–20, 26.

[50] Edersheim, *Jesus the Messiah*, 2:625. As just mentioned above, that Paul chose a term that implies checking out testimony firsthand is certainly a strong comment as well as a notion of central importance. We will return to this topic in our presentation of the evidence for Jesus's resurrection.

[51] Lake, *Resurrection of Jesus Christ*, 223.

[52] Lake, esp. 37–43, 192–96, also 254, cf. 223.

[53] By Dodd's time, some thirty years after Orr and Lake wrote, this conclusion was just starting to be mentioned more frequently; see Dodd, *Apostolic Preaching*, 15–16, 21, 31.

The force of these last points is easy to miss. If Paul procured his information on the deity, death, and resurrection appearances of Jesus from the most influential of the apostolic eyewitnesses (Peter, James the brother of Jesus, and John), then the reports are indeed difficult to treat offhandedly. In fact, Paul and the other apostles taught the same gospel message (as stated in Gal 2:2, 6, 9, and as Paul confirms in 1 Cor 15:11). As such, this testimony indeed constituted a strong critique of hallucinations or any other naturalistic theory for that matter, since the message dated back to the direct experiences of the earliest eyewitnesses themselves, who saw the risen Jesus collectively.

Even without mentioning many other proposed weaknesses with suppositions that involve hallucinations, Orr sums up much of his case against these subjective notions in just one sentence: "Even on its own ground, however, it must be held that the vision theory breaks down in the most essential points."[54]

Listing hallucinations as the "only hypothesis which has any plausibility at the present day," Fisher also presents a multifaceted case against this approach. In no particular order, Fisher lists Schleiermacher's criticism regarding the disciples that this view "attributes to them a mental imbecility" that would invalidate their testimony. Further, it would question "our moral respect" for Jesus himself. Moreover, Paul distinguishes his appearance of the risen Jesus from his other subsequent revelations from God, indicating that the appearance was a more objective disclosure.[55]

Add to these reasons the disciples' mental condition after the crucifixion. They were sorrowful and dejected, as almost all critical scholars allow. But how would they recover from this state of mind? No ecstasy or excitement was found in their demeanors. Seeing Jesus "took them by surprise."[56] Westcott and Lake among many other scholars likewise emphasize the disciples' exceptionally negative psychological outlook.[57]

Hence we see the insightful research of Orr, Lake, and just a few others from a couple of decades earlier.

[54] Orr, *Resurrection of Jesus*, 223–24.

[55] Fisher, *Theistic and Christian Belief*, 194.

[56] Fisher, 196–97.

[57] Westcott, *Gospel of the Resurrection*, 120–21; Lake, *Resurrection of Jesus Christ*, 190, 193, 218. As Lake states forcefully, "None of the other disciples were present, for they had scattered after the arrest of Jesus (St Peter a little later than the rest), and had either already returned home, or were in hiding in Jerusalem until they could find an opportunity of escape" (237–38).

Continuing Fisher's critique, the resurrection appearances were quite reserved. One might expect that they would grow in numbers, but such was not the case. As Keim taught, the appearances were limited in time and "ceased in a short period." Also, the disciples were profoundly changed by their experience. This newly discovered enthusiasm must be explained adequately.[58]

After summarizing these eight arguments, Fisher issued a bit of a challenge. Everyone concedes and "nobody questions" that the disciples thought that the risen Jesus had actually appeared to them after his death by crucifixion. Therefore, those who refuse to accept this testimony should propose naturalistic theories that "explain in some satisfactory way the origin, strength, and persistence" of the disciples' faith![59]

Milligan also interjected his own list of critiques of the subjective vision thesis: Paul states in 1 Cor 15:8 that Christ appeared to him "last of all." That (along with Acts 1:3, it might be added) is a direct statement that Jesus's last appearance ended the series at a very specific time. There was definitely a demarcation in this matter. That was in spite of all of Paul's subsequent revelations and visions, which he thus had to think of as different phenomena and not as appearances. The expectancy and excitement required by several of the major German liberal theorists is not present; in fact it is quite the contrary. Moreover, if the appearances had been incorporeal, they would be more consistent with light surrounding Jesus, but such is nowhere to be found during the forty days of appearances preceding Paul's later experience.

Continuing, Milligan points out that Jesus's appearances ended abruptly without any fresh events even during the early days of persecution. There are good reasons to think that the appearances also occurred in Jerusalem rather than just in Galilee, as opposed to the majority of the vision theorists. The time that Jesus remained with his disciples during some of these appearances is inconsistent with the brief character of hallucinations. If the witnesses were seeing hallucinations as constructs from within their own minds, why did they disbelieve them after they saw them? Moreover, Milligan's strongest critique was probably that

---

[58] Fisher, *Theistic and Christian Belief*, 197–98. We have already mentioned other scholars who agree on their transformation, namely Westcott, *Gospel of the Resurrection*, 4, 121; Milligan, *Resurrection of Our Lord*, 79–80; Edersheim, *Jesus the Messiah*, 2:625; Lake, *Resurrection of Jesus Christ*, 2:193, 226.

[59] Fisher, *Theistic and Christian Belief*, 199.

Jesus manifested himself to many people and personalities in many different ways and circumstances.[60]

Hayes mentions several other problems with the hallucination approach. Some of these items are already mentioned above, such as the appearances ceasing and there being no state of ecstasy in the disciples and just despair. Further, subjective visions are brief but some of the appearances lasted quite long, and subjective visions later in the New Testament are distinguished from the resurrection appearances.[61]

Like Orr's exceptional critique above, Hayes was one of the earliest commentators, either liberal or conservative, to emphasize two other critiques of hallucination scenarios. He pointed out that *group* appearances where the same details were reported is a very powerful refutation.[62] This is quite a major insight, in that a few early conservative commentators wrongly conceded that such visions were contagious, a concept that was later disproven after the birth of psychology.[63] But this improper view may still have accounted for group appearances being mentioned seldom, perhaps because others had also incorrectly thought that this contagion was the case, hence making group sightings less consequential.

Further, Hayes also asserted that the witnesses to the appearances exhibited *quite different dispositions*, from Peter, to James, to Thomas and others (and we may certainly add here the women too), yet they all agreed that they had seen Jesus and that he was risen from the dead.[64] Fisher had also pointed out this huge observation even decades before Hayes, stating that Jesus appeared to a wide "number and variety" of people, comprising "all varieties of temperament."[65] But this was still not a common critique at that time.

Agreeing with Fisher that it was the only worthwhile theory to respond to, Edersheim also produced a list of reasons against the hallucination thesis. He charged that it was impossible to reconcile this notion with what we know from the New Testament, and it fails to explain Paul's appearance. Further, the motif of the disciples

---

[60] Milligan, *Resurrection of Our Lord*, 87–114.

[61] Hayes, *Resurrection Fact*, 287–90.

[62] Hayes, 289. Morison (*Who Moved the Stone?*, 114) is another who mentions this component, offering a strong version of this critique, declaring that if some of the appearances are not collective, then they are "of no use to us."

[63] Unfortunately, this even includes Orr (*Resurrection of Jesus*, 219) and Sparrow-Simpson (*Resurrection and the Christian Faith*, 113).

[64] Hayes, *Resurrection Fact*, 289–90.

[65] Fisher, *Theistic and Christian Belief*, 196–97.

returning immediately to Galilee and the meaninglessness of "third day" references are failed attempts. As per Keim, the appearances ceased, which is not the likely path for hallucinations.[66]

Unlike the German liberal scholars, the conservative scholars exhibited many more insights and made far more crucial critiques of the hallucination thesis in relation to the disciples. By comparison, the liberal response seemed almost half-hearted!

Amazingly, many of these conservative assessments were major and are still considered today to be among the very best criticisms of this hypothesis. These insights would include the concession from Strauss and others that Paul acquired the list of appearances in 1 Cor 15:4–7 from *apostolic testimony* (Orr) at a *very early* date (Lake), and that *groups* of people saw Jesus alive again (Hayes). The term *historeō* indicates the "searching inquiry" into these events by Paul (Edersheim). The wide variety of times and places (Milligan) and the personalities involved (Hayes) are also crucial factors, as is the other apostles agreeing with Paul regarding the nature of the gospel message (Hayes). Just a few years later, Dodd and others went into far more detail into many of these same features. So with Fisher, the challenge is for those who deny the resurrection appearances to compose a natural hypothesis that will incorporate these and other data. We will return to these points in particular when we construct the best case against hallucinations.

Hallucinations or Subjective Visions and Paul

Brook Foss Westcott was the Regius Professor of Divinity at Cambridge University and was without much of a doubt one of the most prominent scholars of his or any other era. As strange as it may sound, the German liberals during almost the entire nineteenth century, as the pacesetters of the world of contemporary theological trends, did not possess a critical text of the Greek New Testament! Since this absolutely crucial tool was unavailable to them, they did their studying and theorizing without one, unable to make objective comments regarding the original textual readings! Westcott was part of the famous trio of British scholars who largely made just such a New Testament text available in 1881 along with a critical text of the Apostolic Fathers (1889–1890). Working with F. Hort and J. B. Lightfoot, all three as Fellows

---

[66] Edersheim, *Jesus the Messiah*, 2:626–28.

of Trinity College, Cambridge University, they changed the world of Gospel and New Testament scholarship.[67]

In his volume on Jesus's resurrection, Westcott objected especially to the notions that the German liberals (such as Strauss, Weizsäcker, and Pfleiderer) frequently assumed regarding Paul's subjective "vision" on the road to Damascus.[68] Perhaps their chief reason for this conclusion was the idea that since Paul included his appearance (1 Cor 15:8) along with the other appearances in the list (15:3–7), he therefore considered them all to be of the same nature (i.e., closer to spiritual visions of some sort). But Westcott argued that Paul's point was not metaphysical sameness but that each of the appearances was "equally actual." For Paul, the appearances were "essentially objective and outward."[69]

Orr also argued against this prominent German liberal idea that the list of appearances in 1 Corinthians were all spiritual visions. Like Westcott, he also pointed out that Paul's emphasis was not that the experiences were therefore all visionary in nature, but that his was just as real as theirs.[70]

Fisher addressed a different aspect of the German liberal attempts to explain away Paul's conversion on the road to Damascus in natural terms due to some sort of subjective hallucination or other similar experience. Discussing alternative efforts that were often suggested, such as Paul undergoing a mental crisis due to secret doubts caused by his persecuting the church, or because he encountered a horrible thunderstorm or even suffered a sunstroke, Fisher describes each of these attempts as being "not only without historical warrant, but [it] is directly in the teeth of Paul's own assertions."[71]

---

[67] Stephen Neill and Tom Wright, *The Interpretation of the New Testament, 1861–1986*, 2nd ed. (Oxford: Oxford University Press, 1988), 35, 120–23. Speaking quite pointedly and addressing primarily the conclusions of prominent German scholar H. J. Holtzmann, Neill and Wright assert, "Scientific work on the Gospels was hardly possible in 1863" (120).

[68] On Pfleiderer in particular at this point, see the analysis by Sparrow-Simpson, *Resurrection and the Christian Faith*, 161–65.

[69] Brooke Foss Westcott, *The Gospel of the Resurrection: Thoughts on Its Relation to Reason and History*, 4th ed. (London: Macmillan, 1879), 110–12.

[70] Orr, *Resurrection of Jesus*, 38–39. Fisher comments very closely at this juncture as well (*Theistic and Christian Belief*, 195).

[71] Fisher, 194–95. Hayes adds along this same line that anyone who would blame Paul with having had a fit of epilepsy "can be accepted only by those who are capable of a boundless credulity, to say the least" (*Resurrection Fact*, 291).

Another key charge to make in this discussion is that once it is recognized that there are no grounds for claiming that Paul was reacting out of any kind of remorse, guilt, or doubt, as just mentioned, there are also no grounds for the claim that Paul could have hallucinated the risen Jesus. The way he describes himself in his unanimously accepted epistles is the exact opposite of the mindset required to be open to such subjective experiences. As Lake states, "an elaborate psychological process" for Paul must be construed. But showing this would be "extremely cumbrous and improbable" and thus be "a serious objective to the purely subjective hypothesis."[72] Paul clearly had no desire to see Jesus resurrected!

So these are other areas like those mentioned above where, in order to avoid the New Testament text's clear conclusions, critical scholars are often willing to invent new circumstances that are not grounded either in the Gospel reports or elsewhere. In this case, Paul's firsthand statements, especially in Gal 1:13–14 and Phil 3:4–6 (which are acknowledged as genuine by virtually every single critical scholar), clearly outweigh invented possibilities that suggest his state of mind *must* have been something totally different. This is one of the reasons why historians today generally eschew doing psychological analyses of persons who lived in the past, even more so for those of almost two thousand years ago, especially when these modern analyses contradict the sources that we possess.

Altogether, it is difficult to arrive at any good reasons for thinking that Paul was (or must have been) desirous to see the risen Jesus. All the ideas to the contrary are based on "happenstance" and "what if?" scenarios and oppose the evidence that we possess. Hence, there is simply a decisive lack of any confirmation that pushes us toward the notion that Paul hallucinated. On all accounts, he simply does not seem to be a very strong candidate to have manufactured these subjective visions.

The Objective Vision Theory

As mentioned often already, this is not a naturalistic hypothesis but an alternative view regarding the nature of Jesus's resurrection appearances. As such, in addition to its historical connections as a sort of opposite to Strauss's view, we will treat it in this chapter as well. According to this position, Jesus was raised from the dead, taken to heaven, and he and his Father cooperated to send nonphysical visions of

---

[72] Lake, *Resurrection of Jesus Christ*, 267; also, Milligan, *Resurrection of Our Lord*, 91; Hayes, *Resurrection Fact*, 291.

himself back to his followers to convince them that he was alive and to call them to ministry.

By far the chief benefit of, or problem for (depending on one's perspective!), this thesis is that it clearly involves the existence of God, his son Jesus, an afterlife, and the supernatural realm, as German liberal scholar Keim himself admitted.[73] It is even the case that virtually all the major Christian doctrines could still be true on this view except for the *bodily nature* of Jesus's resurrected form. In other words, Jesus was raised from the dead and appeared as a glorified spirit-being rather than bodily.

So if the objective vision thesis is true, naturalism is still mistaken at the very center and most crucial part of this worldview, since the natural world would *not* be all there is to reality. Not only was Jesus raised as a glorified spirit-being after his death, but his Father (God) exists. On the other hand, while orthodox Christianity would be incorrect in its belief that it was Jesus's *body* that was raised, it would still be correct that Jesus was raised from the dead. Moreover, it could potentially be correct about almost all other major doctrines. Naturalism clearly loses the most on this thesis. On this, there is widespread agreement.

However, the defeat of naturalism alone is clearly not the goal of Jesus's resurrection. As Orr also properly reminds us, "The survival of the soul is not resurrection."[74] So whether the underlying position is close to a view like Plato's idealistic notion of immortality or to another philosophical position, it clearly represents neither the New Testament teaching nor the predominant Jewish view of the resurrection of the body of Jesus's day, as we will argue later.

Edersheim mentions that although Keim's objective thesis has fewer unexplained facts than Strauss's subjective vision supposition, the empty tomb is an especially major problem for both of them. Plus, how did Jesus's dead body disappear from the tomb? Other questions for Keim include Jesus showing the disciples his wounds and his followers' inability to touch Jesus though the traditions speak of this.[75]

---

[73] Theodor Keim, *The History of Jesus of Nazara: Considered in Its Connection with the National Life of Israel, and Related in Detail*, trans. Arthur Ransom, 6 vols. (London: Williams & Norgate, 1883), esp. 6:361–65; Keim, *Die Geschichte Jesu von Nazara, in ihrer Verhaltung mit dem Gesamtleben seines Volkes frei untersucht und ausführlich erzählt*, 3 vols. (Zurich: Orell and Füssli, 1867–1872), 3:602–4.

[74] On these points of discussion, among others, see Orr, *Resurrection of Jesus*, 229; Milligan, *Resurrection of Our Lord*, 81–82; see even Lake, who holds this view in *Resurrection of Jesus Christ*, 267, 272.

[75] Edersheim, *Jesus the Messiah*, 2:627–28.

Similarly, Orr charges that ongoing, serious problems for the objective vision thesis exist chiefly when the view is compared to the New Testament reports themselves. The largest issues are the lack of *bodily* resurrection appearances (including Jesus actually being seen by and conversing with his followers) and the denial of the empty tomb, which are very well attested in the texts. But this is not all. Orr also cites A. B. Bruce, who asks, "Why send messages that were certain to produce an opposite impression?"[76] The implication here, of course, is that the Father and his son Jesus were guilty of sending misleading "telegrams," verging on deceit in that they clearly portrayed Jesus as standing right there in front of his disciples, not to mention the bodiless notion itself. Orr asks that, since "a theory of supernaturalism is not escaped" by the objective vision theory, why trade the Gospel accounts for Keim's thesis?[77]

It seems that we definitely need to proceed past the fact that the objective vision theory would be a supernatural thesis for several reasons. The most common version by Keim requires at least the notions of the existence of God, Jesus being raised from the dead (even if only as a spirit-being), what appears to be a miracle, and an afterlife for both Jesus and believers. So if this thesis is true, naturalism is false and some major Christian beliefs could still be true. So unlike the natural theories where believers are largely required to do the refuting, the naturalists are on the defensive for this supernatural alternative.

Still, there are serious problems with Keim's view, to be sure. For example, it fails in minimizing especially the Gospel accounts and descriptions of Jesus's resurrection appearances, and it denies the historicity of the empty tomb. Further, it adopts a nonbiblical anthropology that affects the future state in which Jesus and his followers exist.

The Legend or Myth Theory

When discussing the nineteenth-century German liberal hypotheses, we saw that a number of the later researchers were convinced that the Christian message had developed and grown due to the likely assimilation of various pagan myths. A variety of these ideas coalesced to form an entire category of potential responses rather than a single thesis. In this sense, differing types of overlapping legendary accretion were

---

[76] Here Orr quotes from A. B. Bruce, *Apologetics; or, Christianity Defensively Stated* (Edinburgh: T&T Clark, 1892), 393.

[77] Orr, *Resurrection of Jesus*, 229–30, with the quotation on 230.

thought to have merged. The Jewish or Christian narratives might have grown over time due to any number of factors, even from the simple retelling of fantastic stories and feats, especially as applied to miraculous accounts or claims of divinity.

According to one hypothesis, ancient, mythical "divine men" (Greek: *theios anēr*) or other semifictitious or fictitious "superheroes" could have been the original inspirations for the biblical accounts. Even the so-called vegetation gods or the tales surrounding them could have served as prototypes that developed into their grandiose "exploits," including the sense in which these ancient stories were thought to have served as archetypes for biblical persons or teachings.

It was thought that Christian and Jewish comparisons may have been made to historical individuals like Alexander the Great, Apollonius of Tyana, or Sabbatai Zevi. Efforts were made to trace various possible influences of Hellenistic ideas on these Jewish and Christian traditions. Best known for emphasizing some of these trends, the impact of the *religionsgeschichtliche Schule* was dominant. The apparent similarities and differences were tracked through the pagan accounts into their possible influences on Jewish and Christian teachings with regard to how these emphases could be parsed or teased out of various religious texts of this period, including the New Testament.

As mentioned with the other natural resurrection hypotheses as a whole, it is particularly true here that to provide anything close to a thorough critique of these notions is quite far from our purposes in this chapter. That will be pursued in a later chapter. Our intent at this point is just to delineate some of the various sorts of critiques that were leveled against these positions by the most influential conservative scholars at that time. These researchers made a number of thoughtful comments, as reflected in their writing during the last half of the German liberal reign and slightly afterward.

Lake raises an absolutely crucial complaint. While some of the critical charges are possible, "the difficulty is to decide how far this theory is based on fact, and how far it is merely guess work." Lake's chief emphasis, as he explains, is to begin with what conclusions we can ascertain directly from the harder data, such as historical reports. That material would go a long way toward providing some needed explanation apart from any mythological rumors. In short, "it is history, not theology or mythology." We move best, then, from the known to the unknown data.[78]

---

[78] Lake, *Resurrection of Jesus Christ*, 262–66, cf. 198–99. The two quotations are from 262 and 264, respectively.

To see what this might mean with regard to Jesus's resurrection, for example, critical scholars basically all agree that Jesus's disciples were utterly convinced that they had seen the risen Jesus after his death. As well established as this historical fact is, *their experiences* are the central core that needs to be explained, regardless of what sort of teachings may be scattered through other stories.

Westcott claims, "There was no popular belief at the time which could have inspired [the apostles] with a faith in an imaginary Resurrection. There was none among the Greeks whose mythology might appear at first sight to offer scope for its spontaneous growth." The key idea here is that "to the Greeks the Resurrection, whether as the type or as the spring of a new life, was a strange idea." Then Westcott adds, as pertaining to the Christian gospel, "Nor was it otherwise with the Jews."[79]

Hayes comments similarly regarding the empty tomb. He declares, "It cannot be accounted for by any suggestion in Jewish prophecy or in Oriental myths."[80] Then more like Lake, he adds regarding the early belief in Jesus's resurrection, "That faith did not rest upon invention or myth but upon the facts of their own experience."[81]

Finally, very few trained scholars followed Bruno Bauer or Peter Jensen in rejecting Jesus's very existence, yet this position should still be mentioned here, since it made extensive use of various concepts of myth and legend. As the better established of the two, Bauer's ideas were influential even though his entire position was not embraced. However, references to the view that Jesus never lived are relatively rare among the researchers of the German liberal period.

In the preceding two chapters, it was pointed out that Schweitzer dismissed Bauer's work as consisting of poor research, such as arbitrarily dating the Gospels and even Paul's critically accepted epistles into the second century, seemingly to give more credence to his own views. Schweitzer was exceptionally critical of Bauer's thesis and flatly blamed this German theologian for his arbitrariness, ungrounded arguments, and self-refuting ideas. As a result, Schweitzer reports that Bauer's conclusions were simply ignored by his peers, concluding among other things that "he had long been regarded by theologians as an extinct force; nay, more, had been forgotten. . . . For his contemporaries he was a mere eccentric."[82]

---

[79] Westcott, *Gospel of the Resurrection*, 115–19. The three quotations are from 115–16, 117–18, and 118, respectively.

[80] Hayes, *Resurrection Fact*, 37.

[81] Hayes, 282.

[82] Schweitzer, *Quest of the Historical Jesus*, 138, 157–59.

Hayes also critiques Bruno Bauer and several other mostly later popularizers who denied Jesus's existence. Citing Schweitzer's harsh words regarding these writers being out of their fields and using their imagination rather than strong research, Hayes states, "There seems to be general consensus of opinion today that these ultra-destructive critics have failed, and utterly failed, to establish their negative positions concerning this most important fact in the history of the race." He ends the matter with the words, "Practically all the authorities are agreed that there was a man Jesus and that he died and that he was buried."[83]

But it was also mentioned in an earlier chapter that Marburg University professor Peter Jensen likewise postulated that Jesus had never lived, though from a different angle. Jensen traced his notions to a collage of ideas and stories adopted from the Old Testament, which he termed a Jewish Gilgamesh myth. The Gospel writers recycled these mythical accounts in order to totally fabricate the details of Jesus's life. For instance, Old Testament resurrections and similar ideas found their way into the Gospel writings.[84]

But Orr argues, "Jensen is an extremist, and his book may be regarded as the *reductio ad absurdum* of a theory which, before him, had been getting cut more and more away from the ground of historical fact." Orr suggests treating historically the recognized, accredited evidence for Jesus's death, burial, and resurrection instead of simply showing "no concern with the facts" and trying to deny everything perceived to be in one's way. Orr continues, "You do not get rid of facts by simply proposing to give an artificial mythological explanation of them."[85]

Orr continues critiquing Jensen: "Where is the faintest trace of evidence of such a pre-Christian Jewish sketch of the Messiah embracing Virgin-born, Resurrection, and Ascension? It is nothing but an inferential conjecture from the Gospel narratives." Then, sounding quite similar to Lake's point above, Orr states, "The Resurrection of Jesus was no nature-myth, but an event which happened three days after His Crucifixion, in an historical time, and in the case of an historical Personage. Parallels to *such* an event utterly fail."[86]

---

[83] Hayes, *Resurrection Fact*, 35–38, with all of the quotations here from 36.

[84] Peter Jensen, *Das Gilgamesch-Epos in der Weltliteratur* (Strasburg: Trübner, 1906), especially 1026–28.

[85] Orr, *Resurrection of Jesus*, 241–47. The three quotations in this paragraph are taken from 244, 245, and 245–46, respectively.

[86] Orr, 249.

Regarding that mythological explanation, Orr makes two additional critiques. First is Jensen's *baselessness*. Jensen's starting point here is a wide-ranging theory concerning "the general astral Babylonian hypothesis" and "the assumed universal diffusion of this astral theory throughout the East." Orr notes that the remainder of the thesis is arranged such that it stands or falls on the success of this initial, far-reaching astral thesis. However, in a general Near Eastern ethos, *almost any* idea can be located somewhere!

The second critique is Jensen's *arbitrariness*. Supposed similarities between Babylonian, Jewish, and Christian ideas are reproduced as if there were one-to-one correspondences between them. However, the original, underlying liberal thesis had never been corroborated in the first place, and no apparent connections existed between these ideas. So Orr adds: "Where facts fail, imagination is invoked to fill the gaps." Then again, "this ingenious construction—[is] wholly in the air, as if there was no such thing as history in the matter."[87]

For example, Jensen and others who support the legendary thesis draw comparisons between the Gilgamesh tales and the Christian message, especially with regard to Jesus's resurrection. But there is no resurrection or anything like it in the Gilgamesh tale! In fact, the story ends with an almost opposite moral: human beings can never obtain immortality, for that is simply not in their power or nature. As per Orr's comments, the stretch needed to even compare these two accounts is mind-boggling!

Jensen's response is that the earliest version of Gilgamesh probably did include a translation to heaven and that this would be like a resurrection. This is, no doubt, what Orr means by his statements regarding Jensen's utilization of the imagination to fill the gaps in factual comparisons and his thesis being constructed in air apart from history.[88] We will simply add two brief comments: we cannot and must not assume what is missing in the text! Further, translation to heaven (or apotheosis) is definitely *not* an inference for the idea of a resurrection! But we will return to this subject in later chapters.

The conservative scholars from the second half of the German liberal period leveled at least two principal charges against the proponents of the legendary or mythical hypotheses. Most significantly, these legend theses predominantly sidestep or bypass the chief issue: *even if there were* such data consisting of ideas that have apparently grown more complex as time went on, or ancient, pre-Christian stories that typify crucial Christian messages in whole or in part, these overlook how the disciples' experiences are to be understood. The reason for the priority of the latter is

---

[87] Orr, 247–253. The quotations are from 247, 250, and 252, respectively.

[88] Jensen, *Das Gilgamesch-Epos*, 923–24; Orr, *Resurrection of Jesus*, 251.

clear: since critical scholars are quite unanimous that the historical evidence indicates that the disciples really thought they had seen the risen Jesus, then *that* is the center of what must be explained. Other stories may be relevant in some sense, but they do not account for the crux of these experiential convictions.

Further, the conservative scholars denied that parallel accounts of this nature existed before Jesus's time anyway, as the comments indicate above. If so, then there were no stories containing crucial elements like the gospel message to copy. So these legendary or mythical ideas fail on both ends of the suppositions.

Orr adds a few more general thoughts: the evidenced link or point of connection between the pagan and the Jewish or Christian ideas is sadly lacking. In other words, how do we demonstrate that the latter were derived from the former? Moreover, the extent to which these ideas are even found in earlier religious or other contexts to begin with is a serious issue too, such as with Persian or Zoroastrian sources on the subject of bodily resurrection. Further, many have questioned the degree to which these ideas are even found in the Old Testament, especially at an early date.[89]

We must not glide past this important point. As vital as explaining the confirmed historical data is, as we have seen, the causal connection linking two or more claimed similarities is just as critical. It is no stretch of the imagination to line up similar events, teachings, or holy books in order to make comparisons, while all the time thinking that such moves are sufficient to somehow "prove" a connection between them. Similarities are just that—similar! They may even be coherent to some extent.

But similarities simply do not translate to causal relations. Life is absolutely full of any number of ideas, events, or even ball games that seem to be related closely in some select sense, but which have absolutely no causal connection in any way what-soever. Regarding the causal assertions made by the German liberals that a certain pagan idea inspired a similar-sounding biblical idea, the burden is on them to show the causal connections between the one and the other. They must show how we know that the one led directly to the other and make that all-important causal link. Without it, the comparisons at their very best still remain unproven similarities.

Not only are causal connections between pagan ideas and Jewish or Christian ideas lacking, but Orr concludes that we cannot even produce a single example of resurrection belief regarding a historical person like Jesus. Further, "The Christian Resurrection is thus a fact without historical analogy."[90] If statements such as these

---

[89] Orr, *Resurrection of Jesus*, 256–58.
[90] Orr, 224.

obtain, it would seem that the Christian message may just be inching closer to some notion of uniqueness. But we do not wish to move too quickly here—that is a topic for ongoing discussion.

By the end of the German liberal reign, many criticisms had been aimed at the various legend or mythical theses. But very little was known or published at that time regarding such necessary information as the time frames of the mythical stories, which aspects were present in the earliest accounts, the question of the earliest sources for the historical persons being compared to Jesus and the resurrection accounts in particular, and so on. If the mythical stories dated before Christianity or were composed sufficiently close to the lives of the real persons they recount, there obviously would be more of a point to be made. But as this era ended, these huge topics remained largely unsearched and unsolved. As such, the crucial components for these discussions were simply missing and unknown.[91] So debates could only, by their very nature, beat the air. How could causal links be established without clear information on the sources thought to be precedents for the gospel message?

Still, this was not the chief point being made by the conservative scholars anyway. Their oft-repeated message was that *regardless* of when the pagan stories were dated, since virtually all scholars, whether liberal or conservative, agreed that Jesus's disciples were utterly convinced that they had seen the risen Jesus and that these events were central to their message, it is *these experiences* that must be explained adequately. So we are talking first and foremost about these experiences rather than the state of the non-Christian materials, about which not enough was known anyway.

Was Paul the Founder of the Christian Church?

A cognate issue that sometimes functions as an extension of the last subject above should be mentioned here quickly. For our present purposes, did Paul originate the gospel message involving the early high Christology along with the teachings of Jesus's death and resurrection appearances? Or was this early Christian gospel core in existence before Paul's teaching and preaching?[92]

---

[91] Another example in this vein, though more indirectly, is James G. Frazer, *The Golden Bough: A Study in Comparative Religion* (New York: Macmillan, 1890).

[92] This is a huge subject, with many of its considerations extending well beyond our subject of the death and resurrection of Jesus. It has been pursued in full treatises of its own.

It will be argued in much detail later in this volume that legendary and mythical theses of various species concerning either fictitious or living persons that seek to disprove the gospel message have not only been thoroughly refuted in each of their major claims, but they have even been basically abandoned by the critical scholars themselves. Similar refutations also apply to arguments that would suggest Paul's implementation of mythical ideas, which are likewise rejected by the vast majority of scholars.

Although the basic idea is not a naturalistic theory as normally understood, it was argued periodically in German liberalism and particularly by the *religionsgeschich-tliche Schule* that Paul was perhaps the mastermind behind Christianity or even its true founder, while Jesus was more simply a Jewish prophet and teacher loyal to the teachings of Judaism. Direct and indirect comments alike were aimed at how some of the Christian teachings of the first century were due either to Paul's ideas or to the larger influx of Hellenistic Christianity that he helped to introduce. For Bousset, for example, the primitive Jewish concept of the "Son of Man" was contrasted with the Hellenistic community's concept of "Lord."[93]

Some of these distinctions were only beginning toward the close of German liberalism. As with the other subjects in this chapter, the conservative scholars pushed back firmly against these ideas as well, even though the most developed aspects from both sides did not truly emerge until decades later in the mid-twentieth century.

At the very end of the German liberal era, Princeton Theological Seminary professor J. Gresham Machen published his own detailed discourses on the topic, discussing separate aspects of this thesis. Machen began by arguing specifically against Bousset that the early church's strong emphasis on the full deity of Jesus Christ began unequivocally with the original disciples in Jerusalem rather than with Paul and Hellenistic thought. After all, it was Paul who traveled to Jerusalem on at least two occasions to meet with his predecessors to make sure that they were all of one mind on this teaching, ascertaining that they stood in agreement (Gal 1:18–20; 2:1–10).

Nonetheless, a few particular aspects will still be addressed here where applicable. For a full treatment, see the excellent study by David Wenham, *Paul: Follower of Jesus or Founder of Christianity?* (Grand Rapids: Eerdmans, 1995).

[93] A major example from the most influential voice of this school of thought is that of Wilhelm Bousset, *Kyrios Christos: A History of the Belief in Christ from the Beginnings of Christianity to Irenaeus*, trans. John E. Steely (Nashville: Abingdon, 1970), with these ideas being contrasted on 151–52. A longer discussion of these contrasts appears on 200–210.

Paul traveled to them in order to gain the answer.[94] After a further discussion of the matter, Machen concluded, "Thus the Pauline Epistles contain not the slightest trace of any conflict with regard to the person of Christ. . . . Paul appears to have been in harmony with all Palestinian Christians."[95] Other nineteenth- and early twentieth-century conservative researchers also defended Jesus's deity as an early teaching that clearly predated Paul's efforts and said that these early claims and messages were verified by Jesus's resurrection from the dead.[96]

During the heyday of the *religionsgeschichtliche Schule*, various German critical scholars began to research and study the hymns, prayers, liturgical texts, and other similar traditions chiefly found in Paul's Epistles as well as in other New Testament works.[97] As the research progressed, it was concluded that these generally brief, formally oral texts reflected pre-Pauline beliefs and teachings in the very early church, a view that is commonplace in recent scholarly research, including among critical researchers. For the purposes of this chapter, many of these creedal or traditional passages not only predate Paul's writings, but they almost always address early statements about Jesus and frequently teach high Christology.[98] Clearly, these teachings were

---

[94] See chap. 5 in Machen, *Christianity and Liberalism*, esp. 80–85 on this last theme. See also chap. 2 in this volume by Machen.

[95] J. Gresham Machen, *The Origin of Paul's Religion* (Grand Rapids: Eerdmans, 1925), 130–37, with the quotation on 135. See also chap. 8 in Machen.

[96] Examples would include scholars like another very well-known Princeton Theological Seminary professor who predated Machen, Charles Hodge, *Systematic Theology*, 3 vols. (New York: Scribner's, 1873), see vol. 1, chap. 7; Fisher, *Theistic and Christian Belief*, chap. 7; Orr, *Resurrection of Jesus*, 269–71, 277–80.

[97] Among the most detailed and influential scholars here were Alfred Seeberg, *Der Katechismus der Urchristenheit* (Leipzig: Deichertschen, 1903); Eduard Norden, *Die antike Kunstprosa vom VI: Jahrhundert vor Christus bis in die Zeit der Renaissance*, 2 vols. (Leipzig: Teubner, 1898); Norden, *Agnos Theos: Untersuchungen zur Formengeschichte religiöser Rede* (Leipzig: Teubner, 1913); Johannes Weiss, "Beiträge zum paulinischer Rhetorik," in *Theologische Studien: Festschrift für Bernhard Weiss*, ed. C. R. Gregory (Göttingen: Vandenhoeck & Ruprecht, 1897); Eduard von der Goltz, *Das Gebet in der ältesten Christenheit* (Leipzig: Hinrichs, 1901); Ernst Lohmeyer, *Die Briefe an die Philipper, an die Kolosser, und an Philemon*, 2 vols. (Göttingen: Vandenhoeck & Ruprecht, 1928, 1930). For a lengthy list of critical works published on this subject after these early volumes, from 1921 onward, see Richard N. Longenecker, *New Wine into Fresh Wineskins: Contextualizing the Early Christian Confessions* (Peabody, MA: Hendrickson, 1999), 9–10.

[98] Some of these major Pauline examples include Rom 1:3–4; 4:24–25; 10:9; 1 Cor 8:6; 11:23–26; 15:3–7; Phil 2:6–11. Other nominees by scholars often mentioned include Rom 8:34; 1 Thess 1:9–10, among many other candidates.

present in the earliest church before Paul's Epistles. This argument alone consists of a major indication that Paul did not invent the early church's high Christology.

Shortly after the German liberal theological reign ended, C. H. Dodd wrote an influential volume on these early creedal traditions and the Acts sermon summaries, comparing the Pauline confessions to other New Testament texts. Reflecting on the similarities in light of Paul's first trip to Jerusalem to confer with Peter and James the brother of Jesus, Dodd penned a now-famous quip to describe these leaders' influential fifteen days together: "We may presume they did not spend all the time talking about the weather." Dodd argued, "Thus Paul's preaching represents a special stream of Christian tradition which was derived from the main stream at a point very near to its source."[99]

Moreover, the death of Jesus was not invented by Paul, as would hardly be charged by any specialist scholars. Bousset does not dispute this, attesting that even the notion of Jesus's sacrificial death was recognized and accepted in both the primitive Palestinian community as well as by gentile Christians.[100] Further, Bousset also thought that Jesus's earliest disciples in the "first Christian community" apparently had spiritual visions of some sort and believed that in spite of his death, Jesus was perceived as being alive and exalted in glory.[101] Otto Pfleiderer was another very influential member of the *religionsgeschichtliche Schule*, who, though he rejected the resurrection, still attested that the "most direct source" of these occurrences was "the historical fact of the death of Jesus, and the following visions seen by His disciples."[102] Hence, dating back to Jesus's disciples, their belief in Jesus's resurrection and his appearances were not due to Paul's invention.

So the earliest gospel teaching of the deity, death, and resurrection appearances of Jesus was birthed in Jerusalem with Jesus's apostles. The status of the ultimate facticity of their church-founding message makes all the difference. Once Jesus was raised from the dead, the gospel center was thereby established. There are, of course, far more of Paul's overall teachings. Yet Paul met and conversed with the major apostles who held these gospel doctrines before he did (Gal 1:18–20). After his conversion, he agreed with this proclamation and was commended by the apostolic

---

[99] See Dodd, *Apostolic Preaching*, 16–20, 26. Both of the quotations were taken from 16.

[100] Bousset, *Kyrios Christos*, 305.

[101] Bousset, chiefly 49–51.

[102] Otto Pfleiderer, *The Early Christian Conception of Christ: Its Significance and Value in the History of Religion* (London: Williams & Norgate, 1905), 157–58, also 78, 102.

leaders (Gal 2:6, 9), explaining later that they were all teaching the same central gospel message that he was regarding Jesus's resurrection appearances (1 Cor 15:11). On this core theme, then, as Dodd asserted, it should be concluded that "anyone who should maintain that the primitive Christian Gospel was fundamentally different from that which we have found in Paul must bear the burden of proof."[103] There was agreement in these essentials.

Naturalistic Theses at the Demise of German Liberalism

As in so many fields of study, conservatives are expected to criticize liberals and vice versa. One of the items that makes the material in this chapter so intriguing is that the majority of these conservatives held equally prestigious positions at major universities, making this a clash between colossal competitors.

Another fascinating item presaging interest in this battle is that it concerned the issue of naturalistic challenges to the resurrection of Jesus, which is generally taken as the most crucial, central, and important event in Christianity. Further, the German liberals themselves also offered many criticisms of each other's hypotheses as well, sometimes even agreeing on the same sorts of critiques as those made by the conservative scholars, as depicted in the previous chapter. This comparison of opposing scholars on the similarities and dissimilarities between those who critiqued the various German liberal views would make an incredible study in itself.

Why were these naturalistic options composed in the first place? Edersheim insightfully comments for many researchers that the chief reason is that the resurrection would presumably be a miracle, and some worldviews simply cannot allow supernatural events.[104]

So as we have seen several times already in this chapter, critics even preferred poor options over ones that offended their own worldview sensibilities. Such an example is the common effort to thoroughly rewrite Paul's state of mind as to what happened when he was converted on the way to Damascus, in spite of it being Paul's unanimously accepted epistles that were being freely adjusted without the necessary data to support these moves, while other liberals objected to these moves themselves. This caused Sparrow-Simpson, among others, to note that while the presence of worldviews is quite influential and personal, this still does not allow a scholar to

---

[103] See Dodd, *Apostolic Preaching*, 16–20, 26. The quotation was taken from 16.
[104] Edersheim, *Jesus the Messiah*, 2:626.

theorize just about anything except precisely what the facts indicate, as in the case of Paul's conversion.[105]

One of the fascinating results of this research was discovering that several testimonies from both the German liberal scholars as well as their contemporary conservative colleagues agreed that particular naturalistic theories had been decimated by their own challenges, causing some of them to be abandoned and no longer held by any scholars at the close of this theological epoch. Some of the scholarly language treated particular hypotheses like museum exhibits!

For example, after having remarked earlier that the swoon thesis "is now hopelessly discredited," Orr asserted confidently, "No one now holds that Jesus did *not* die!"[106] Morison reported of the apparent death hypothesis a couple decades later that "it is really little more than an historical curiosity."[107] Hayes stated strongly from the same time that, "it is not surprising, therefore, that the swoon theory has been rejected by all recent writers."[108] Sparrow-Simpson overstated the situation, but the thought expressed here is clear enough: "Probably no living person could be induced to credit it."[109]

It is likely that most of these scholars would attest that the very weakest of the alternative theses were the fraud hypotheses. Of the view we called Fraud Type 1, Orr explains, "The disciples, indeed, are now usually exonerated from participation in a deliberate fraud."[110] Then he adds, "The old theory of fraud on the part of the disciples has now no respectable advocates, and may be put out of account."[111] Hayes states strongly that "practically all authorities are willing to agree that conscious and continuous deception with such men as the apostles is an impossibility."[112] Fisher declares, "That some of the disciples stole his body, nobody will for a moment credit."[113] Milligan disregards the matter even quicker than the others: "It is not

---

[105] Sparrow-Simpson, *Resurrection and the Christian Faith*, 168–69.

[106] Orr, *Resurrection of Jesus*, quoted on 42, 92, respectively.

[107] Morison, *Who Moved the Stone?*, 96.

[108] Hayes, *Resurrection Fact*, 285. Also in agreement with this conclusion is Fisher, *Theistic and Christian Belief*, 193.

[109] Sparrow-Simpson, *Resurrection and the Christian Faith*, 43.

[110] Orr, *Resurrection of Jesus*, 212.

[111] Orr, 128.

[112] Hayes, *Resurrection Fact*, 278.

[113] Fisher, *Theistic and Christian Belief*, 193. While it is true that most of the scholars above are addressing what we have termed the "Fraud Type 1" views, this was not always the case. Besides, slight modifications of Fraud Type 1 critiques could also be at least imagined

necessary to discuss the theory. It has been abandoned by every inquirer to whom a moment's attention is due."[114]

Concerning what we called Fraud Type 2, few of these options were even defended by the German liberals anyway. After mentioning Pilate, Joseph of Arimathea, or the Sanhedrin as possibly removing Jesus's body, Orr made an astute comment, citing the critics Renan and Loisy as agreeing with him on his sentiment: "Others, more wisely, leave the matter in the vagueness of ignorance."[115] After all, if a critic takes one of these directions, it makes much more sense to cite some unnamed, unknown person as the perpetrator, thereby not leaving a trail that is so liable to be confronted by the inevitable barrage of critical responses that descend whenever some specific person or group is named! But even with an unnamed culprit, difficult questions are still forth-coming. This is simply another indication of the strength of the traditional evidence.

Besides the contrary testimony, another reason for the unpopularity of the Fraud Type 2 charges is that, even if true, they explain far too little of what the liberals need. Among other things, they fail to respond adequately to—let alone solve—the questions regarding the appearance claims. Without these puzzle pieces, they are far away from workable solutions anyway.

Indicting both the swoon and fraud theories, Edersheim pronounces toward the end of the nineteenth century that "we may here put aside two hypotheses, now universally discarded even in Germany," and follows by naming these two views. Then he asserts several times later, a little too strongly and confidently perhaps, that all versions of fraud as well as the vision alternatives are just "impossible."[116]

But not terribly far away from Edersheim's comment, Orr considered that the following resurrection alternative theses had already been refuted thoroughly: swoon, fraud by the disciples, subjective visions or hallucinations, and objective visions.[117]

---

for the other positions. It is actually even surprising to have so many more or less applicable negative comments here, given the negligible number of German liberal scholars who supposed these ideas. The German rationalist Reimarus did prefer Fraud Type 1, but it may be recalled that his work predated Schleiermacher's by a few decades, and he was not considered to be a member of the German liberals who we are addressing in this chapter.

[114] Milligan, *Resurrection of Our Lord*, 81.

[115] Orr, *Resurrection of Jesus*, 212–13. In his volume *Les évangiles synoptiques*, 2 vols. (Ceffonds: Loisy, 1907), Alfred Loisy remarks that it is "useless" to dialogue about the different ideas on who may have removed Jesus's body from the tomb (2:720).

[116] Edersheim, *Jesus the Messiah*, 2:626 and 629, respectively.

[117] Orr, *Resurrection of Jesus*, 12.

Summarizing the issues more generally but similarly, Hayes also reported, "All of these theories are practically discredited now."[118]

Thus, whichever scholarly train of views we follow, whether we are citing the German liberals themselves or their conservative scholarly counterparts, there was some initial agreement that, by the end of the nineteenth century or a little later, most of the once-prominent naturalistic theories had run their course and were now passé. At a minimum, most scholars appear to have thought that this extended at least to the swoon or apparent death theses, plus the varieties of the two fraud views. Even as a general conclusion, this is a valuable result of how scholarly interaction should take place by honing the various theses.

A Few Cognate Issues in the German Liberalism Debate

As these scholarly exchanges continued during the First Quest for the historical Jesus, several questions of a similar nature emerged from the discussions. A few of these matters are worth commenting on and summarizing, given the overall conversation, including providing some hints of some potential directions through the territory that developed during the ensuing decades.

Joseph's Burial and the Women's Visit to the Tomb

With few serious doubters, Jesus was believed by the majority of German liberal scholars to have died by crucifixion. Where does that leave the state of the Gospel accounts pertaining to Jesus's body being buried in Joseph of Arimathea's tomb, as well as the accounts of the women coming to Joseph's tomb on the morning of that first weekday to finish the burial process?

As will be observed below, at least for the German liberal scholars who favored one of the major visionary hypotheses, Jesus's appearances were generally held to have taken place at least initially in Galilee. For these and similar positions, this affected their views of the testimony regarding the Jerusalem tomb and what could be done with it. After telling his readers, "No one now holds that Jesus did *not* die!" Orr explains that most critical scholars of that time did allow that Joseph of Arimathea buried Jesus's body in his own tomb. However, Orr offered the caveat that this

---

[118] Hayes, *Resurrection Fact*, 294.

acceptance usually came "with qualifications and explanations which deprive the act of the character it has in the Gospels."[119]

One example of such a view that is not quite a straightforward affirmation of the Gospel data is Schleiermacher's, who thinks that while Joseph made sure that Jesus's body was placed in the tomb, there is still room for the possibility that others were sent by Joseph (to move the body?) before the arrival of the women on Sunday morning.[120] But not all scholars took this Joseph option at all. Orr even notes that some of those among the liberals, such as Strauss and Réville, even favored the position that Jesus's body was simply tossed in the garbage heap![121] This may come as a surprise to some modern readers who may think of this as a phenomenon that has arisen just during the past few decades.

Further, Orr thinks that most German liberal scholars even accepted the women's trip(s) to the tomb. He cites the negative votes of Weizsäcker, Keim, and Pfleiderer along with the positive affirmations of Renan, Réville, H. J. Holtzmann, O. Holtzmann, and Lake, concluding that "indeed most—accept the fact as historical."[122] Schleiermacher is another of those who could have been added to the positive side.[123] Lake is an intriguing case here. While writing about the same time as Orr, he has the women going to the wrong tomb, one in which Jesus was never buried. Yet, he explains these things amid caveats and with what appears to be hesitant ideas.[124]

The Empty Tomb

Generally speaking, the subject of the empty tomb did not command as much historical attention or thoughtfulness during the First Quest for the historical Jesus as it presently does in the Third Quest. But that does not eliminate some significant distinctions that were presented during the earlier movement. Several outspoken and influential German liberals such as Strauss, Keim, and A. Meyer are well known for their opposition to the empty tomb, holding that it was a nonhistorical report.[125] Lake, with his wrong tomb hypothesis, should be included among the deniers

---

[119] Orr, *Resurrection of Jesus*, 92, 94, respectively.

[120] Schleiermacher, *Life of Jesus*, 442.

[121] Orr, *Resurrection of Jesus*, 93–94.

[122] Orr, 112–13.

[123] Schleiermacher, *Life of Jesus*, 439–45.

[124] Lake, *Resurrection of Jesus Christ*, 248–53, cf. 237–38.

[125] For instance, Strauss, *Life of Jesus*, 704–5; Keim, *History of Jesus of Nazara*, 6:297–98.

too, as just cited. It must be recognized that many if not most of those who denied the empty tomb did so because they were committed to visionary views of one sort or another.

On the other hand, Renan and O. Holtzmann are among those skeptical scholars who perhaps surprisingly accepted the historicity of the empty tomb. In fact, even Keim, speaking from the "unhistorical" side of the question and continuing to hold that position, still acknowledged that "a hundred voices" were raised in protest against the naysayers. Rather incredibly, Keim himself noted that these positive votes were cast both by the liberals as well as by the conservatives among their ranks. Then he provided a list of over a dozen scholars who argued affirmatively for the empty tomb, such as Schleiermacher, Hase, Weizsäcker, Godet, and Riggenbach.[126] Writing several decades later, Adolf von Harnack added his considerable testimony to the discussion, at least concerning the likelihood of Paul's knowledge of the empty tomb.[127]

Having noted some of the positive support for the empty tomb, it clearly remains the New Testament teaching that the disciples' resurrection faith was *not* derived from this empty tomb data. Rather, it was Jesus's appearances that prompted their faith and proclamation. Scholars definitely recognize this aspect as well. As Harnack explains, "What [Paul] and the disciples regarded as all-important was not the state in which the grave was found, but Christ's appearances."[128]

The Location of Jesus's Appearances

One prominent issue during this time was the location of the appearances or visions, with two chief preferences being found in the literature: Galilee, and Jerusalem plus Galilee. In particular, the German liberals who championed *either* the subjective or objective vision theses were the chief proponents of the Galilean-only preference. The main reason for this was the predominant view at that time that the disciples would be incapable of working through all of their negative emotions in light of the unexpected crucifixion of Jesus and the dashing of their fondest hopes both for

---

[126] Keim, 6:296–301, esp. 297n2; Sparrow-Simpson names a half dozen advocates (*Resurrection and the Christian Faith*, 46–47), while Orr provides a slightly shorter list (*Resurrection of Jesus*, 113). Schleiermacher's view can be found in *Life of Jesus*, 441–42.

[127] Adolf von Harnack, *What Is Christianity?*, trans. Thomas Bailey Saunders, 3rd. ed. (London: Williams & Norgate, 1912), 164–65.

[128] Harnack, 164–65; see also Sparrow-Simpson, *Resurrection and the Christian Faith*, 47–48; Sparrow-Simpson, *Our Lord's Resurrection*, 105.

themselves and Israel. The disciples' resulting depression, despair, and unrest would take some time to work through before they were able to respond by rejoicing in the news that Jesus had been raised. As Orr summarizes the matter, "The third day also is set aside as affording too little time for the recovery of the disciples from despair."[129]

Accordingly, it was concluded that the disciples must necessarily be given some "space" to recover. On the Galilee view, the disciples' rest time was encouraged by Strauss's quite straightforward mention of the need for "some time for the mental state of the disciples to become exalted in the degree necessary, before this . . . highly wrought enthusiasm could believe."[130] Being more specific regarding the length of time that may have been required, Renan allowed for up to one year for the apostles to rest, rejuvenate, and heal.[131] Keim and others roughly followed a similar scenario, in spite of postulating actual appearances of Jesus, though of the objective visionary sort. So the reason for the Galilee location appears to be more than clear: in order to postulate either subjective or objective visions, it was thought that the time and location of these events must simply be changed from the details identified in the Gospel reports to accommodate these scholars' hypotheses.

The chief pushback came from scholars who thought that Jesus appeared to his disciples and others in Jerusalem first and then later in Galilee. This is reported by Matthew and John, while Luke only has appearances in Jerusalem.[132] But it must be noted carefully at this point that it is definitely not being argued here in a

---

[129] Orr, *Resurrection of Jesus*, 222. Orr lists such liberal scholars as "Strauss, Weizsäcker, Keim, Pfleiderer, A. Meyer, Professor Lake" as the leading proponents who held that "the disciples, immediately after the Crucifixion, fled to Galilee, there, and not at Jerusalem, receiving the visions which convinced them that the Lord had risen" (114). Later, Orr adds Harnack, O. Holtzmann, and Loisy to the supporters of the Galilee scenario (215, 222).

[130] Strauss, *Life of Jesus*, 743.

[131] Renan, *Les apôtres*, 2:45–46.

[132] It must be pointed out that even in the Gospel of Mark, which most scholars think purposely did not narrate any of Jesus's resurrection appearances while still favoring these events taking place at least in Galilee, it cannot be taught positively that there were no indications whatsoever of Jerusalem appearances. Some contemporary scholars in particular (as we will note below) hold that the message of the young man or angel at the tomb to "go, tell his disciples *and Peter*" (Mark 16:7, emphasis added) is actually a further indication if not a prediction of the appearance to Peter, as in the dual early traditions in 1 Cor 15:5 and Luke 24:34. Both Luke and John locate at least Peter and a few others in the city on Sunday morning (and John 20:19–20 places other disciples along with Peter and John there as well). Luke specifically places the appearance to Peter in Jerusalem (24:34). By the time Mark wrote, the appearance to Peter would be well known and could have preceded any

straightforward, one-to-one manner that all of the following material can be worked out simply by studying and attempting to harmonize these texts. If that were the case, there would be less need for much else besides parallel Gospel accounts or harmonies. Other options, such as Mark's addition of his "and Peter" comment, are possible nuances. There are certainly some potential questions among these passages.

It is only being pointed out for now that since reading through each of the earliest narratives does not automatically work out all the possibilities or decide between paths that differ from the ones chosen by this or that scholar, as just listed above, questions cannot simply be ignored. For starters, at least according to three of the Gospel reports, the disciples were still in Jerusalem on that first Easter Sunday morning. The angel at Jesus's burial tomb instructed the women to go tell the disciples that Jesus had been triumphantly raised from the dead and that Jesus would go ahead of them to Galilee as well as meet them there (Matt 28:7). Even in Mark 16:1–8 it certainly seems that when the women were instructed to go tell the apostles, they did not have to run to Galilee on a multiday trip! The women delivered their message to the disciples (Luke 24:5–9; Matt 28:8, 11; John 20:18), who left sometime later for Galilee (Matt 28:16).[133]

In the meantime, the texts relate that at least Peter and John ran to the burial tomb in order to check out the women's message (John 20:3–9; cf. Luke 24:12, 24). During that same Sunday, Luke and John (plus Matthew) indicate that Jesus appeared a few times in and around the city of Jerusalem. He appeared to one or more of the women who came to the tomb (Matt 28:9; John 20:14–18), and then to two of his followers just outside the city (Luke 24:13–31). Later he appeared to Peter (Luke 24:34), and then to *all eleven* of his disciples in Jerusalem (Luke 24:33–49; cf. John 20:19–22).[134]

---

appearance(s) in Galilee. The Gospel of Mark after 16:8 is still frequently listed, though as a later, secondary source.

[133] On the famous comment by Mark, who presumably ended his Gospel with the words that the women did not speak to anyone upon leaving the vicinity of the tomb (16:8), Allison begins his worthwhile discussion of scholarly rejoinders with the quip, "This claim wobbles." See Dale C. Allison Jr., *The Resurrection of Jesus: Apologetics, Polemics, History* (London: T&T Clark, 2021), 125–27.

[134] Rather extraordinarily and in spite of all these Gospel comments, Keim thinks that it is better to conclude that the women at the tomb were not charged to stay in Jerusalem to tell the disciples, but to go on a several-day journey to Galilee to tell them (traveling by themselves?), since that is where the men were. See Keim, *History of Jesus of Nazara*, 6:297. Even for Keim, presuppositions and prior decisions seem to get in the way more than need be the case.

According to John alone, the disciples were still in the city of Jerusalem one week later when Jesus appeared to them again (20:26–29). So all four Gospels want readers to know that the women and probably the male disciples had not yet left Jerusalem before Jesus's resurrection from the dead. Luke also relates that the ascension occurred later, just outside of Jerusalem (Luke 24:50–53; Acts 1:6–11).

It is also the case that two of the four Gospels do indeed teach clearly that Jesus appeared to the disciples in Galilee, while Mark reports this prediction by both Jesus himself (14:28) as well as by the young man (or angel) at the tomb (16:7). Since it can hardly be thought that such predictions would be mentioned if Mark intended to convey the idea that Jesus had been mistaken about a Galilee appearance, Mark's Gospel reports can safely be added to the Galilee list. Matthew actually reports such a Galilee appearance (28:16–20), as does the last chapter of John (21:1–23), whether or not it is taken to be an appendix or an addition. So Galilee clearly has its place in the majority of the Gospel appearance narratives.

At least a couple of other considerations also clearly favor the Jerusalem plus Galilee scenario for the appearances. Even if the majority of the disciples had fled for Galilee soon after Jesus's arrest in Gethsemane, they would very possibly (if not likely) still have failed to arrive there until Sunday night or possibly even later, especially if they were traveling carefully to avoid arrest, or if they had rested at all on the Sabbath.[135] This would actually have amounted to *four* or more days later by Jewish reckoning. If so, this would not have constituted Jesus being raised and appearing on the third day after his death (as with the early creedal material in 1 Cor 15:3–4 and frequently elsewhere). But the trip to Galilee could easily have fit into the longer period of Jesus's appearances *after* Jerusalem.

Further, it makes little sense for the men to go running away to Galilee anytime during the entire weekend while leaving the women behind—their friends, colleagues, and perhaps even their family members! Since the commonly stated reason for the disciples fleeing was out of fright, how could they possibly justify exposing these women to similar troubles? Moreover, in John 20:19, that fear drove the men inside behind locked doors in the city rather than out on the road to Galilee.

---

[135] Notice that Orr above cites the German liberals as holding that the disciples' flight from Jerusalem to Galilee occurred "immediately after the crucifixion" (*Resurrection of Jesus*, 114). This would delay further their trip and ensure that they would not have arrived in Galilee by Sunday.

For these reasons, then, a Jerusalem-followed-by-Galilee scenario for the appearances easily makes the most sense. The clear teaching of the Gospels, especially when multiply attested at this point, the lack of travel time to Galilee before the third day, and the disciples leaving the women behind in Jerusalem during what they *thought* was a very dangerous time are powerful considerations favoring both locations for the appearances. Perhaps for reasons such as these, this question has generally received much less attention after the German liberal era, and certainly without the deliberative force of the earlier liberal discussions. This could well have been due to the lessened emphasis on both major versions of the visionary hypotheses as well, which were the chief engines motivating the "Galilee first" agenda, plus the decided lack of more dogmatic evidence.

The "Galilee thesis" certainly seems to reject a stronger thesis in order to fit preferred critical presuppositions. Thus, it needs to be emphasized regarding the immediate move of the disciples to Galilee that this option was widely pursued by the liberal critics even though it was opposed to the best data and reasoning. This indicates yet another move that rather arbitrarily favored their notions over what the texts taught. This time, the motives that were even admittedly identified by the German liberals were to allow their visionary alternative hypotheses instead of bodily resurrection appearances and to undermine the women's message regarding the empty tomb (which would have created even worse problems for them, given the notion of visions).

Paul's Appearances of the Same Sort as the Others?

An exceptionally common assertion found among the German liberal scholars is that, since Paul added his name at the end of the early traditional lists of resurrection appearances in 1 Cor 15:3–7, he was thereby asserting that his appearance on the road to Damascus was of the same or similar species of those to the other apostles. As Lake states, there is no "reason to suppose that [Paul's] experience was essentially different from that of the other disciples."[136] Similarly, Johannes Weiss extrapolated from Paul's vision to all of the others as also being visionary.[137] F. C. Baur was another scholar who apparently tended to tie what he thought was the subjective vision of

---

[136] Lake, *Resurrection of Jesus Christ*, 265–66.

[137] Johannes Weiss, *Earliest Christianity: A History of the Period AD 30–150*, trans. F. C. Grant, 2 vols. (New York: Harper & Row, 1959), 1:27.

Paul to the other visions.[138] Orr explains the German liberal idea like this: "From St. Paul's 'vision' of Jesus on the way to Damascus, it is argued that the earlier appearances which he enumerates must have been visionary also."[139]

Another consideration must be borne in mind here before this view is evaluated. As just noted, there are overriding reasons for the frequent liberal tandem positions on the appearances of Jesus taking place in Galilee, largely in order to get past the apostles' grief and despair, plus the late report of the empty tomb. These are additional examples that most likely indicate some rather self-serving motives on the part of the German liberals who made this move. Like the earlier example, the chief reason here seems to be the popularity of both the subjective and objective vision theses. Therefore, if the comparison could be successfully established between Paul's appearance vis-à-vis the others as well as the late proclamation of the empty tomb, this dual support for the liberal thesis would help it along considerably, pointing in the direction of visionary events of some sort rather than bodily appearances for all the recipients. This was the preferred interpretation even if the visions were taken in the objective visionary sense, as both Lake and Weiss did.

However, there are several indications that this was not at all the point that Paul was attempting to establish in 1 Cor 15:3–8, though we will again only be able to mention these responses here very succinctly.[140] First, Paul argued at the outset that he was not a participant during the initial time frame with the other apostles. Rather, the Lord's appearance to him was "as to one untimely born" (15:8 ESV).[141] Since Paul at least acknowledged that he was out of the appearance time sequence proper, this temporal difference of two to three years could well indicate that he knew of other variations between the appearances as well.

Further, the Greek term *ōphthē* (from the verb *horaō*) used in this text indicates that the recipients "were appeared to," with Christ clearly being the initiator of the experience. Therefore, the emphasis is placed on the initiative of the one doing the appearing as opposed to internal, self-generated experiences of the recipients. The kind of sight spoken of here can refer to either bodily or spiritual sight. However,

---

[138] This is according to Milligan, *Resurrection of Our Lord*, 83–88.

[139] Orr, *Resurrection of Jesus*, 220, also 38.

[140] Gary R. Habermas, *Philosophy of History, Miracles, and the Resurrection of Jesus*, 3rd ed. (Sagamore Beach, MA: Academx, 2012) provides a list of reasons on 35.

[141] Beyond "untimely born," Paul's term here (*ektrōmati*) is sometimes translated either as "miscarriage" or even as "abortion."

the Greek terms refer most often to normal, physical sight.[142] For instance, in the Gospel of John (20:18, 25, 29), this same term is utilized to speak of Jesus's very physical resurrection appearances, including his being touched by Mary Magdalene. Thus, there is no exclusive, textual, or other dogmatic use to appeal to this term in order to indicate some inner, subjective form of perception.

While discussing the German liberal tendencies here, Orr raises another worthwhile consideration. He thinks that to hold the liberal contention of the sameness of the appearances "is to miss the very point of the Apostle's enumeration. St. Paul's object in his use of 'appeared' is not to suggest that the earlier appearances were visionary, but conversely to imply that the appearance vouchsafed to himself on the road to Damascus was as real as those granted to the others."[143] Westcott provides a similar argument.[144] Comments by Wilhelm Michaelis and N. T. Wright are reminiscent of one another.[145]

Moreover, a crucial point mentioned precisely in this text is that Paul was careful to proclaim his apostleship on a number of occasions (1 Cor 15:8–11; see also 9:1), and he asserted that he was granted this honor straight from Jesus Christ personally, when Jesus chose and called Paul, rather than by the recognition of men (Gal 1:11–17; 2:6–9). This call to Paul to join the ranks of apostleship, by itself, could certainly have been the sole reason why Paul added his appearance to those

---

[142] For a number of major thoughts here, especially on the specific definitions of the key words along with their textual usages, the following are very helpful: Allison, *Resurrection of Jesus*, 39, 46–93, 184, 198, 209–10; Michael R. Licona, *The Resurrection of Jesus: A New Historiographical Approach* (Downers Grove, IL: InterVarsity Academic, 2010), 330–33; N. T. Wright, *The Resurrection of the Son of God*, vol. 3 of *Christian Origins and the Question of God* (Minneapolis: Fortress, 2003), 317–29; Marion L. Soards, *1 Corinthians*, New International Biblical Commentary: New Testament (Peabody, MA: Hendrickson, 1999), 317–24; Craig S. Keener, *The Historical Jesus of the Gospels* (Grand Rapids: Eerdmans, 2009), 342–44; Murray J. Harris, *Raised Immortal: Resurrection and Immortality in the New Testament* (Grand Rapids: Eerdmans, 1993), 44–49.

[143] Orr, *Resurrection of Jesus*, 39.

[144] Westcott, *Gospel of the Resurrection*, 111.

[145] Wright, *Resurrection of the Son of God*, 477, 606–7, 609; Wilhelm Michaelis, *"horaō,"* in *Theological Dictionary of the New Testament*, ed. Gerhard Kittel and Gerhard Friedrich, trans. and ed. Geoffrey W. Bromiley, 10 vols. (Grand Rapids: Eerdmans, 1967), 5:359. Though it is difficult to make out his exact meaning in terms of his context, Michaelis comments that Paul in 1 Cor 15:8 "regards this appearance as similar in kind. In all the appearances the presence of the risen Lord is a presence in transfigured corporeality."

of the other apostles, even if he were aware of differences such as the timing aspect that he had just mentioned. Paul's intention here was at least that he had received the apostolic seal from the risen Christ, so that he and the others were all on the same ground, rather than there being no differences in the mode or manner of their experiences. After all, Paul had already acknowledged at least one variance between the appearances.

The last and probably the most important argument here would be rather anachronistic in our present context because it was not a very powerful or popular scholarly position during the First Quest for the historical Jesus. It will only be mentioned here that if the strongest case that could be made from the New Testament turned out to be that the resurrection appearances of Jesus were believed to be bodily in nature, even most especially if this applied to Paul's case as well, then this would have tremendous implications for this discussion. Since the predominant view of first-century Jewish interpreters was that of bodily resurrection, it could assist mightily in reaching a conclusion on the matter of bodily post-resurrection appearances too. Then if bodily resurrection appearances were shown to be the established and strongest textual position here, this most likely would be the sense of the appearance narrative mentioned in 1 Cor 15:3–8, having a tremendous bearing on Paul's meaning throughout.[146]

But this last point is not totally in vain even in the late nineteenth century. We have already seen in the previous chapter that Keim's critique of the subjective vision theories of Strauss and others involved the point that Paul had clearly differentiated between resurrection appearances and later visions. What were thought to be the chief characteristics involved in this contrast? Could it be that the original resurrection appearances were considered to be more realistic in some sense than the latter ones? Further, the Luke-Acts corpus records both the very physical appearances to Jesus's disciples (Luke 24; Acts 1:1–11) as well as Paul's conversion story on three separate occasions (Acts 9:1–9; 22:1–11; 26:12–18) without recognizing any inherent problems or inconsistencies in doing so. So perhaps the work of Keim and a few others foreshadowed some of the beginnings of what, in the hands of later New Testament researchers, became criticisms of both subjective and objective vision theses in favor of bodily appearances.

---

[146] It is argued later in this study that this view is probably in fact the majority position today in the twenty-first century, even for the apostle Paul. But this discussion later in this study will have to wait.

Strangely enough, it was Keim once again who even disagreed with the common argument among his fellow German liberals here as to why Paul had added his appearance to the list in the 1 Corinthians 15 creedal statement in the first place. Just as we mentioned the relevant point above, Keim asserted that it was the time span between Paul's appearance and those of the other apostles (which Paul himself acknowledges in 1 Cor 15:8) that made the difference. As Keim states: "Having made such a sharp and clean division, it is to be taken as proved that there lay between the first five or six appearances and the later oft-repeated visions such a great and broad gulf of time, and indeed of character, as rendered it impossible to reckon the latter appearances with the former." As a result, Keim termed his position the "imparity" of Paul's vision with the other appearances.[147] To drive a final point home, Keim was willing to concede that "even the corporeal appearance may be granted" to those who thought they needed the classical position to be true![148]

The Disciples' Belief That Jesus Had Been Raised from the Dead

The note on which to end this discussion of the German liberal treatment of Jesus's resurrection is the unanimous agreement of virtually all scholars—German liberals and conservatives alike—that whatever else may be the case, Jesus's disciples actually and fully believed that they had seen Jesus alive after his death. James Orr states the matter well: "It is granted on all sides that the Christian Church was founded on, or in connexion [sic] with, an energetic preaching of the Lord's resurrection from the dead. The *fact* may be questioned: the belief will be admitted."[149]

The German liberal scholars were hardly less convinced of this than were their conservative counterparts. Even Strauss declares, "*It is still certain* from the epistles of Paul and the Acts that the Apostles themselves had the conviction that they had seen the risen Jesus."[150] As Lake asserts, "There is convincing evidence that the disciples believed that the Lord had appeared to St Peter and to others. . . . It is quite plain that the disciples were all firmly convinced that the Lord had appeared to them, and no one more firmly than St Paul."[151] Lake then indicates later, "critical methods point

---

[147] Keim, *History of Jesus of Nazara*, 6:353, including n. 1.

[148] Keim, 6:362.

[149] Orr, *Resurrection of Jesus*, 33, afterward citing Strauss, Wellhausen, Gardner, Henson, Burkitt, and Lake (33–34, 115).

[150] Strauss, *Life of Jesus*, 739 (emphasis added), see also 727–28, 795.

[151] Lake, *Resurrection of Jesus Christ*, 265.

just as clearly to the existence of a conviction among the disciples that the Lord had appeared to them."[152]

Other liberal scholars freely admitted the disciples' belief in Jesus's resurrection and his appearances. To the positive comments above, many others could be appended, such as the thoughts of prominent German liberals like Schleiermacher, Baur, Renan, Troeltsch, Harnack, and Pfleiderer.[153] The conservatives, of course, were even more convinced of this truth. Fisher states the matter rather clearly: "The immovable faith of the apostles that Jesus 'showed himself alive to them' is a fact that nobody questions. Without that faith Christianity would have died at its birth."[154] Fisher is joined here by influential conservative scholars such as Westcott, Milligan, and Orr.[155]

That the early disciples were utterly convinced that they had witnessed appearances of the risen Jesus has always been (and still remains) at the center of the New Testament message, as well as a key component that is held in common by virtually all commentators, whatever their various theological commitments. Further, along with Jesus's death by crucifixion, which is held just as strongly by scholars, the disciple's beliefs regarding Jesus's afterlife appearances to them formed the crucial blocks on which to build the best case for historicity, at least according to those who have argued in favor of the gospel message. The acceptance of the disciples' belief in the resurrection and Jesus's appearances has continued through German liberalism and on through the Third Quest for the historical Jesus. As Allison states, going a bit further, "I am under the impression that, since David Friedrich Strauss, most skeptical scholars have also had no qualms about attributing visions to the first resurrection witnesses." In fact, "a significant number of critical scholars" have always recognized that this was the case.[156]

---

[152] Lake, 275, just as Lake expresses it elsewhere too (191, 193, 227, 266–67).

[153] Schleiermacher, *Life of Jesus*, 461; Baur, *Paul*, 1:67–69; Renan, *Vie de Jésus*, 422; Ernst Troeltsch, *The Christian Faith*, ed. Gertrud von le Fort, trans. Garrett E. Paul (Minneapolis: Fortress, 1991), 88, 96; Harnack, *What Is Christianity?*, 163–67; Otto Pfleiderer, *Early Christian Conception of Christ*, 157–58.

[154] Fisher, *Theistic and Christian Belief*, 199.

[155] Westcott, *Gospel of the Resurrection*, 113, 135; Milligan, *Resurrection of Our Lord*, 39–45; Milligan, *Ascension and Heavenly Priesthood*, 4, 8; Edersheim, *Jesus the Messiah*, 2:625; Orr, *Resurrection of Jesus*, 34–36, 115, 147, 231; Hayes, *Resurrection Fact*, 294 (citing esp. Lake); cf. Sparrow-Simpson, *Resurrection and the Christian Faith*, 161.

[156] Dale C. Allison Jr., "Explaining the Resurrection: Conflicting Convictions," *Journal for the Study of the Historical Jesus* 3 (2005): 125.

Conclusion

Albert Schweitzer concluded his epochal volume *The Quest of the Historical Jesus* on a rather downcast note. In the opening paragraph of his last chapter he states, "There is nothing more negative than the result of the critical study of the Life of Jesus."[157] Then he followed with this additional thought: "The historical foundation of Christianity as built up by rationalistic, by liberal, and by modern theology no longer exists; but that does not mean that Christianity has lost its historic foundation."[158]

Schweitzer criticized the entire nineteenth-century Quest as an imploding movement that devoured itself. Perhaps we could say that the German liberal apple never fell far enough from the tree. To Schweitzer's mind, the majority of commentators rejected the notion of the eschatological Jesus, leading to much of the confusion and wrongheadedness of their approaches. Actually, the liberal mindset consumed and demolished its own edifices, while all the time missing the main points in the discussion.[159] Another major problem is that those in the movement were more interested in the historical questions than those matters of spirituality, ethics, love, piety, and the spirit of Jesus.[160]

A little more in line with Schweitzer's first criticism, his major work revealed some of this personal bickering and infighting between the German liberals[161]—some of it being quite vicious at times. But the bottom line for our purposes is that the

---

[157] Schweitzer, *Quest of the Historical Jesus*, 398.

[158] Schweitzer, 399.

[159] Schweitzer, 331, 398–401. Many years later, Schweitzer recalled again his bitterness in realizing these conclusions; see Schweitzer, *Out of My Life and Thought: An Autobiography*, trans. C. T. Campion (New York: Holt, 1949), 47–48, 50, 58. Asking whether he considered himself to be a pessimist or an optimist, he chose the former but declared that he was still willing to hope (240).

[160] Schweitzer, *Quest of the Historical Jesus*, 399–403; Schweitzer, *Out of My Life*, esp. 50–51, 56, 59.

[161] As with the note made at the outset of our three chapters on nineteenth-century German liberalism and those scholars' efforts to establish what has come to be called the First Quest for the historical Jesus, neither of the words in the moniker "German liberals" is meant derogatively. It is being used the way it often is in the literature, speaking of a specific movement. This is in spite of the fact that certain French scholars like Renan, Réville, Salvador (along with how Schweitzer himself is often categorized), plus even an occasional British scholar such as Kirsopp Lake, were often numbered roughly as members of the movement. Still, German scholars made up the predominant number of members in this group.

weaknesses of the various naturalistic hypotheses pertaining to the resurrection were all exposed fairly efficiently. This was true of the liberal themselves, as they leveled some of the best-known critiques against the others here. Then just a little later, the mostly British and American conservative scholars from major universities finished off the lingering leftovers of the feast, often with more detailed and searching criticisms. At the end of the First Quest for the historical Jesus, then, not much remained of the liberal alternative attacks on the resurrection; little of the criticism was left standing. As will be seen, though, some of these views even appear to have gone into hiding, only to reappear later.[162]

A systematic treatment might have drawn together some of the loose ends of these critiques made piecemeal since they were drawn from many different perspectives, sources, and worldviews as well as being written in three different languages. Some of this will be attempted later in this study.

---

[162] Strangely enough, in a passage regarding the end of Jesus's life, Schweitzer discusses Jesus's own view of his atoning death, mentioning afterward that "the disciples find the grave empty, and in their enthusiastic expectation of the glory in which their Master is soon to appear, have visions of Him as risen from the grave, they are certain that He is with God in heaven, soon to appear as Messiah and bring in the Kingdom" (*Out of My Life*, 40–41). Especially since the portion about the disciples seeing visions of Jesus as risen and their relating these to Jesus being in heaven with God sounds possibly reminiscent of some of Keim's notions, it is unfortunate that this comes at the end of a chapter and is left unexplained by Schweitzer.

7

Twentieth Century:
Barth, Bultmann, and Beyond

Throughout most cycles of contemporary Western theology, there has been widespread agreement among critical scholars across a very wide conceptual spectrum that Jesus's preaching of the kingdom of God plus his death and resurrection appearances represent the central message of Christianity. Of course, such recognition requires none of these scholars to acknowledge the existence of a literal kingdom or an actual resurrection event. Rather, this agreement requires only the understanding that this teaching and proclamation occupied a central position in the early proclamation of the faith. Within these parameters, many nuances abound.

This position has long been asserted by orthodox believers based on New Testament passages such as the highly influential text in 1 Cor 15:12–20.[1] Uniqueness and significance is also admitted by many critical scholars surrounding these elements. Many examples may be drawn from scholarly works published in the mid-twentieth century.

---

[1] Many additional texts for consideration might include Matt 12:38–40; Luke 24:45–48; Acts 4:2, 33; 17:30–31; and 1 Pet 1:3–9. The early sermon summaries likely contained in Acts 1–5, 10, 13, and 17, as well as the early pre-Pauline creeds such as Rom 1:3–4; 4:24–25; and 10:9 all center on the proclamation of the resurrection and definitely could be brought into these discussions too.

One instance is New Testament scholar Willi Marxsen, who asserts that among the vast array of subjects in Christian theology, "the question of Jesus' resurrection plays a decisive part; one might even say *the* decisive part." Actually, if we are uncertain about the faith or if our hope is obscure, since these are "closely connected" to the resurrection message, then "there is a risk of jeopardizing more or less everything to which a Christian clings."[2]

Marxsen is not the only scholar who analyzes the subject in this manner. Günther Bornkamm likewise acknowledges the ultimate importance of the resurrection: "There would be no gospel, not one account, no letter in the New Testament, no faith, no church, no worship, no prayer in Christendom to this day without the message of the resurrection of Christ."[3] Jürgen Moltmann affirms strongly that "Christianity stands or falls with the reality of the raising of Jesus from the dead by God. In the New Testament there is no faith that does not start *a priori* with the resurrection of Jesus."[4]

If we are anywhere close to being accurate regarding these assessments, then the subject of Jesus's resurrection has always been of prime importance since the time of the earliest church. We will observe later how most scholars also agree that the historicity of this event is a major factor in knowing whether, or to what extent, the truthfulness of Christian theology and practice follows.[5] Repeated appraisals and

---

[2] Willi Marxsen, *The Resurrection of Jesus of Nazareth*, trans. Margaret Kohl (Philadelphia: Fortress, 1970), 12.

[3] Günther Bornkamm, *Jesus of Nazareth*, trans. Irene and Fraser McLuskey with James M. Robinson (New York: Harper & Row, 1960), 181.

[4] Jürgen Moltmann, *Theology of Hope*, trans. J. W. Leitch (New York: Harper & Row, 1967) 165.

[5] Marxsen denies typical Christian arguments, for instance, that because Jesus's resurrection happened, other theological beliefs such as the believer's resurrection will also follow directly (*Resurrection of Jesus of Nazareth*, 174, 184, 186), even though he recognizes that these sorts of teachings are certainly found in the New Testament (168–69 and elsewhere). This probably has much to do with his not holding to either Jesus's literal resurrection (147) or the bodily resurrection of others (187). Still, perhaps strangely enough for those who think that only conservative Christians make these sorts of moves, Marxsen still sees some crucial benefits to truths in the present that, without being somehow "proven" by Jesus's resurrection, are still related to it or follow from it. This includes beliefs that God somehow endorsed who Jesus was, the need for repentance, and the benefits of faith and hope for the future (esp. 125, 168–69, 187–88). We will address this subject in a later chapter, where it will be seen that, in a more recent work, Marxsen argues much more clearly that doctrine and practice do indeed follow in some sense from the resurrection.

various other considerations of the resurrection appear regularly in Christian stud-ies, but these are justified by both its centrality and the new varieties of contempo-rary criticism.

Our primary purpose in this chapter is to survey five approaches to the historic-ity of Jesus's resurrection that typified the critical scholarly scene from the wake of German liberalism's fall through just past the mid-twentieth century. This will lead into the next formative period of thought that occupies most of our attention in this study: from 1975 to the present.[6] Even the testimony just given regarding Marxsen's thoughts on how truths may follow from the resurrection is only one indication of how views can vary widely on this subject. Among other benefits, the survey in this chapter will indicate the contrast between how scholarly trends can change and how they may typically lead naturally into the next generation of study.

Before viewing these five models that survey and demarcate recent views regard-ing the relationship between the resurrection and history, we will overview briefly the resurrection positions of the two most prominent theologians in the twentieth century: Karl Barth and Rudolf Bultmann. This will be helpful in order to build the "historical resurrection bridge" all the way from the eighteenth-century deists through Friedrich Schleiermacher to present thinkers. Further, these two giants will also figure prominently in the remainder of the chapter, so the overview should serve as a much-needed introduction to these trends.

Karl Barth

Albert Schweitzer's critique of the perceived failure of the First Quest for the historical Jesus was a big blow to be sure. However, the appearance of Barth's volume *The Epistle to the Romans* was one of the chief reasons for the actual death of nineteenth-century German liberalism along with the outbreak of World War I. Having studied under some of the greatest minds of the early twentieth century, like Wilhelm Hermann and Adolf von Harnack, Barth reacted against the dominant message of unbiblical views regarding God; sin; and real, supernatural truth, among other issues. He called

---

[6] The emphasis here is not so much on specific dates, though these will often be in view, but rather on the sweeping trends and eddies of the last century before 1975. The point here is not so much the formulations of hard and fast time demarcations as much as noting key tendencies in thought that predate and lead up to the time period with which the majority of this overall study is concerned, from approximately the last quarter of the twentieth century to today.

for renewed emphasis on the sovereignty of God, the reality of human sinfulness, and the need for salvation. This volume sought to reassert that biblical message, and it shocked the theological establishment.[7]

Barth never hesitated to challenge what he took to be nonbiblical preaching and teaching, whether it was that of nineteenth-century liberalism or otherwise. For example, in another volume of eight very early messages, some of which even predate *The Epistle to the Romans*, Barth develops many key theses that follow a particular set of themes.[8] Chief among these are the inability of human effort to reach God, therefore eschewing all man-made efforts and religions;[9] human sinfulness;[10] the transcendence and sovereignty of God, who is "Wholly Other";[11] and the necessity of faith.[12] Throughout, there is a pervasive emphasis on Scripture and allowing God's Word to speak truth to us, replacing our own thoughts on this subject.[13]

Especially in his latter messages, Barth also takes on major German liberal scholars and themes, such as "the all-leveling and uncreative spirit of the nineteenth and twentieth centuries."[14] Schleiermacher particularly is named quite frequently. In one instance, he is not a good theological teacher because "he is disastrously dim-sighted in regard to the fact that man as man is not only in *need* but beyond all hope of saving himself."[15] Schleiermacher is also called out for his experience-centered theology.[16] Others named include Troeltsch, Ritschl, and Rothe, while Kierkegaard is praised and placed in a list with Luther, Calvin, Paul, and Jeremiah![17]

In the process of challenging liberal theology, the immense combined influence of Karl Barth along with Rudolf Bultmann (though for quite different reasons)

---

[7] Karl Barth, *The Epistle to the Romans*, trans. Edwyn C. Hoskyns, 6th ed. (Oxford: Oxford University Press, 1933).

[8] Karl Barth, *The Word of God and the Word of Man*, trans. Douglas Horton (New York: Harper & Brothers, 1956).

[9] Barth, *Word of God*, mainly when he speaks of building the tower of Babel in chap. 1 (15, 20–24, 27) and also chap. 8 (282–83, 285, 323–24).

[10] Barth, 11, 17, 167.

[11] Barth, 24, 41, 45, 74–75, 168, 288.

[12] Barth, 25, 27.

[13] This is the theme of entire messages in Barth, *Word of God*, such as chaps. 2–4 as well as chap. 6 (199, 200, 214, 216) and chap. 7 (229–30, 235, 240–42, 247, 249, 266).

[14] Barth, 226.

[15] Barth, 195–96.

[16] Barth, 285–86.

[17] Such as the additional comments like those in Barth, 148–49, 197.

had an inhibiting effect on the Jesus of history landscape—neither of these scholars appreciated historical Jesus studies very much. Through their influence on a couple generations of students, this interlude came to be known as the "No Quest" period. Neither of these thinkers appreciated the First Quest for the historical Jesus, and they maintained those objections throughout their careers.[18] Both also reacted strongly to the theology of German liberalism as a whole.

Particularly for Barth, who was easily the more conservative of the two scholars, it is often missed that he hardly denied either the truth or the historical facts of the New Testament gospel message. Rather, it was the exercise of discovering or requiring historical *evidence* that Barth considered to be outside the pale of faith. As he asserts in one of his most authoritative venues speaking of Jesus's resurrection: "There is no proof, and there obviously cannot and ought not to be any proof, for the fact that this history did take place (proof, that is, according to the terminology of modern historical scholarship)."[19]

Unfortunately, especially earlier in his career, Barth juxtaposed a number of comments that often appeared to confuse the *fact* and even *truth* of the resurrection with its *evidential* moorings. Examples from his earlier works indicated his overly dialectical emphasis and included thoughts such as: "In the Resurrection the new world of the Holy Spirit touches the old world of the flesh, but touches it as a tangent touches a circle, that is, without touching it." This was followed directly by the straightforward comment, "The Resurrection is therefore an occurrence in history, which took place outside the gates of Jerusalem in the year A.D. 30." Immediately after that: "The Resurrection is not an event in history at all."[20] Still another rather strange-sounding comment in the same volume reads: "We have already seen that the raising of Jesus from the dead is not an event in history elongated so as still to remain an event in the midst of other events. The Resurrection is the non-historical."[21]

---

[18] Barth complained, though rather mildly, concerning the New Testament scholars "who to my amazement have armed themselves with swords and staves and once again undertaken the search for the 'historical Jesus'—a search in which I now as before prefer not to participate." Karl Barth, *How I Changed My Mind*, trans. John D. Godsey (Richmond, VA: Knox, 1966), 69.

[19] Karl Barth, *Church Dogmatics*, vol. 4.1, *The Doctrine of Reconciliation*, ed. G. W. Bromiley and T. F. Torrance, trans. G. W. Bromiley (Edinburgh: T&T Clark, 1956), 335.

[20] These three comments are all found just a few lines apart and are each included in the very same paragraph; see Barth, *Epistle to the Romans*, 30.

[21] Barth, 195, cf. 203.

Further, in *The Word of God and the Word of Man*, the resurrection is "not in time. It is not one temporal thing among others." Again, "the resurrection of Christ . . . is not a historical event." But immediately afterward, Barth states, "though it is the only real happening *in* is not a real happening *of* history."[22] So we should apparently not pursue with arguments whether or not the resurrection was a historical event. Barth frequently answers such historical questions as "the see-saw of 'Yes' and 'No.'"[23]

About a decade after these early sermons and messages, Barth's language seemed to change very subtly. He still plainly emphasized the unprovability of the empty tomb and the resurrection—Paul didn't mean to evidence these events, and neither should we. These occurrences are "not to be counted, weighed, and measured." They can "only be proved by revelation itself."[24] On the negative side, if we wish to rely on historical investigation alone, how do we know that negative natural results might not emerge toward which, strangely enough, Barth seemed rather nonchalant?[25] But on the positive side, there was little talk of the "Yes, it's historical . . . No, it's not" sort of dialectic, regardless of the caveats that follow.

Still, the biggest change occurred another two decades later when the first part of the fourth volume of his *Church Dogmatics* was written. Clearly the dialectic could still be seen: "The death of Jesus Christ can certainly be thought of as history in the modern sense, but not the resurrection." Yet Barth went on to affirm that the resurrection did indeed happen, commenting just a little later that "the New Testament is speaking of an event in time and space."[26]

As Barth worked his way to the conclusion of the matter, he stated in surprisingly strong terms: "If Jesus Christ is not risen—bodily, visibly, audibly, perceptively, in the same concrete sense in which He died, as the texts themselves have it—if He is not also risen, then our preaching and our faith are vain and futile; we are still in our sins." Thus, the apostles, as true observers of the resurrection "were witnesses of an event which was like that of the cross in its concrete objectivity." So when the disciples saw Jesus alive, "He encountered them formally (eating and drinking with them) in the

---

[22] Barth, *Word of God*, 89–90.

[23] Barth, *Epistle to the Romans*, 204. For other examples, see Barth, *Word of God*, 207, 216, 256.

[24] Karl Barth, *The Resurrection of the Dead*, trans. H. J. Stenning (New York: Revell, 1933), 131–43. The two quotations are taken from 137 and 140.

[25] Barth, 135–36.

[26] Barth, *Church Dogmatics*, 4.1:336.

same way as He had encountered them before . . . (eating and drinking with them)."[27] In these last words, then, Barth states the matter rather straightforwardly.

We will address later the subject of what Barth was attempting to accomplish by making these seemingly confusing statements. However, in spite of the dialectical language that has no doubt frustrated many readers, Barth affirmed the historicity of Jesus's resurrection from the dead.

Approaching Jesus's resurrection in what has been described as a fideistic manner, we will include Barth in that "faith only" camp in the survey of the five resurrection models below. Overall, Barth's influence was immense. Godsey states that Barth "more than any other, has shaped the theology of the church for almost half a century."[28] Later, Godsey remarks, "In him a Church Father has walked among us, a theologian of such creative genius, prodigious productivity, and persuasive influence that his name is already being associated with the elite group of Christian thinkers that includes Athanasius, Augustine, Anselm, Aquinas, Luther, and Calvin."[29] There is no shortage of scholars who identify Barth as the most influential theologian of the twentieth century or repeat similar accolades.[30]

A Critique of Barth's Notion of Prehistory

For Barth, Jesus was definitely raised from the dead in a bodily manner that was observable to the witnesses' physical senses.[31] But his repeated shying away from the actual specifics of historical research or other evidence for this event that might indicate this to be a fact of the past was criticized on many occasions. A few vulnerable points will be mentioned briefly. Strictly for our purposes in these volumes, the initial conundrum appears to be the most serious one for Barth. In a sense, the additional criticisms and concerns here could be viewed more as extensions of the initial aspect rather than separate items, though with projections that reach out into other areas.

---

[27] Barth, 4.1:351–52.

[28] Godsey, "Preface," in Barth, *How I Changed My Mind*, 3.

[29] Godsey, "Portrait of Barth," in Barth, *How I Changed My Mind*, 9.

[30] Such as Daniel Jenkins, "Karl Barth," in *A Handbook of Christian Theologians*, ed. Dean G. Peerman and Martin E. Marty (Cleveland: World, 1965), 396, 398, 409; Gregory W. Dawes, ed., "Karl Barth (1886–1968)," in *The Historical Jesus Quest: Landmarks in the Search for the Jesus of History*, rev. ed. (Louisville: Westminster John Knox, 2000), 268–70.

[31] Barth, *Church Dogmatics*, 4.1:336, and esp. 351–52.

The primary as well as the most comprehensive critique involves the belief that Jesus's resurrection occupies a sort of "prehistory" or "saga" that definitely includes some aspects of objective history, while other facets such as providing strong evidence in favor of the event must be abandoned. This may be the chief problem of Barth's interpretation, for he asserts that the resurrection is not history in the modern sense of this term. Rather, this event really occurs in some species of redemptive or religious history.[32] However, how do we define, categorize, or indicate the essence or truth of events that history simply cannot ascertain? Such an in-between ground, whether it is termed prehistory, saga, legend, or referred to, as Barth does, as the "boundary" or "frontier" of history, keeps it from the watchful eye of careful research and the ability to ascertain factuality.[33]

As former Oxford University historian William Wand perceptively points out, "History is concerned only with such events as happen within the space-time continuum. Events, real or imagined, which occur in an eternal or spiritual sphere are not the proper subject of history. The reason is that history has no tools by which it can deal with such events."[34] Thus, historiography can only be occupied with claimed events that are thought to have occurred in time and can be investigated by the tools of historical research. Since there are no means whereby events that occur in a religious or other in-between sphere can be so investigated, they do not actually fall within the scope of history. As Wand contends, events thought to have happened only in such an elusive realm cannot be properly regarded as history, even if they were real events. Historical facts must therefore be open to verification and research.

Admittedly, a resurrection would have a different origin from other events if it entered the realm of the past as a direct act of God.[35] If Jesus's resurrection had occurred by strictly natural means, such as historical causation, such a response might be shown by examining other alternatives.[36] Barth is correct in asserting that it is

---

[32] Barth, 4.1:300–301, 334, 336.

[33] Barth, 4.1:336, and cf. his earlier *Resurrection of the Dead*, 134, 139.

[34] J. W. C. Wand, *Christianity: A Historical Religion?* (Valley Forge, PA: Judson, 1972), 23.

[35] This is what C.S. Lewis referred to as the backward direction of a miracle being linked to God, while its forward direction "is interlocked with all Nature just like any other event." See Lewis, *Miracles: A Preliminary Study* (New York: Macmillan, 1947), 82–84, quotation on 82.

[36] Barth refers to other options for explaining the resurrection and clearly rejects them. After listing many of them, he states: "To-day we rightly turn up our nose at this" not only

possible for an event to be caused by divine action and still be a part of history, which could indeed make it unique. But such a divine origination may not be investigated, evidenced, or known to be the case. This would hardly bother Barth, however. If research into the resurrection is exempted from the process of historiography, can faith alone simply plug that gap?

There is an immense difference between simply proclaiming that this occurrence was unique due to its being a direct result of God's revelation and holding that it ought not be investigated or known to have occurred. If such an occurrence did happen in history, even though its entry would definitely be unique, becoming part of the natural process would make it open to historical investigation.

Yet, for Barth this is not why this process will not work. It is simply not a matter of whether or not the proper tools are available to proceed with such a historical study. Rather, the underlying rejection is caused by his presuppositions regarding the split between historical research and faith in God's revelation. Back to the days of leaping over Lessing's ugly ditch,[37] there is an absolute and unsolvable separation between historical investigation on the one side and faith in God's revelation on the other. God has spoken and requires faith in his person and message. Biblical belief does not come from doing good research but from stepping out in commitment to God. Hence, Barth removes revelatory events from the scope of historical study, thereby isolating them from these procedures, because such an act is required. In the process, he removes them from any historical inspection.

It will convince very few scholars to assert the truth of the resurrection, announcing that certain events actually occurred, while adding that a historical examination is just not allowed. In such instances the response from both believers and unbelievers very well may be that the dialectic is nauseating. Either the resurrection really happened in verifiable history or it did not occur in normal history at all. But employing fancy theological verbiage to affirm its occurrence in an unverifiable, unobservable realm of thought presents all the marks of a contradiction. It appears to desire all the benefits of historicity but without taking any of the risks!

Barth's own backdrop of being a victim to his predetermined theological views might be why he struggled so much in explaining his position and frustrated many

---

because of "the many inconsistencies in detail" but because they fail in various other ways to be the best explanations of the existing reports. Barth, *Church Dogmatics*, 4.1:340–41.

[37] Gotthold Ephraim Lessing, *Lessing's Theological Writings*, ed. Henry Chadwick (London: Black, 1956), 53–55, esp. 55.

readers in the process! His sentences weave back and forth continually until the reader wonders if they can ever be reconciled. However, Barth had no choice but to reject historical evidence and to embrace a faith commitment, yet he was absolutely required to believe that Jesus's resurrection and appearances occurred in real history. The double requirement did not fit together well.

German theologian Wolfhart Pannenberg agreed with this initial criticism of those who took positions such as this one. He asserts:

> If we would forgo the concept of a historical event here, then it is no longer possible at all to affirm that the resurrection of Jesus or that the appearances of the resurrected Jesus really happened at a definite time in our world. There is no justification for affirming Jesus's resurrection as an event that really happened, if it is not to be affirmed as a historical event as such. Whether or not a particular event happened two thousand years ago is not made certain by faith but only by historical research, to the extent that certainty can be attained at all about questions of this kind. . . . The only method of achieving at least approximate certainty with regard to the events of a past time is historical research.[38]

As pointed out, it is another mere confusion for a theologian like Barth to say that an event actually occurred in history, but not in the same realm of history as other events do. As Pannenberg adeptly points out, it is improper to make comments concerning Jesus's resurrection being a historical event if, as such, it can only be known by faith and not by historical research. If one asserts that an occurrence is not even able to be investigated, it cannot be proclaimed with any certainty that the event ever happened at a certain time and place in this world. Such an event is not really known historically because, on this view, no measurable concept of history exists in this particular realm. Therefore, without sufficient grounds, it cannot be known for sure that this event still happened just like other incidents in the past. Simple claims do not determine the historicity of events.

Another historian, John Warwick Montgomery, also objects to Barth's use of prehistory. The following statement points out the folly of such a concept: "To claim objectivity, but to remove any possibility of determining it, is by definition to

---

[38] Wolfhart Pannenberg, *Jesus: God and Man*, trans. Lewis L. Wilkins and Duane A. Priebe, 2nd ed. (Philadelphia: Westminster, 1977), 99.

destroy objectivity."[39] If a historical event is not open to investigation in some sense, in what sense can it be knowable other than perhaps as a faith statement? The historical "middle ground" of prehistory, removed from such processes of verification, is next to meaningless.[40] Montgomery thus agrees with others that this particular area of Barth's idea of history is foreign both to the discipline itself as well as to the biblical records.[41]

Many other scholars have also noted Barth's tendency to rely on the concept of prehistory and similar ideas and the subsequent weaknesses in his approach to Jesus's resurrection that have resulted. They realize both that historians recognize no such realm of history and that the very assertion that such a realm exists with both historical and nonhistorical characteristics is itself contradictory.[42]

The next concern extends from this critique of Barth regarding his stance on Jesus's resurrection to a greater tension. Unless there is a way out of the earlier dilemma, there would appear to be little hope of ascertaining if other portions or even the whole of the Christian faith can be shown to be true. If Barth's notion of faith cannot stand alone as its own justification, serving as its own standard, then where may a believer turn? Of course, this is assuredly not to say that Christianity is false or anything of the sort. In fact, many believers would probably take a stance fairly close to Barth's while never doubting their faith.

The potential upshot of this approach is that it might otherwise be difficult to show that Christianity as a whole is actually true by other means. The subjective, personal stances above provide no reason why someone else should believe this particular system or accept Christianity over alternative views. Faith simply is not a panacea for

---

[39] John Warwick Montgomery, *History and Christianity* (Downers Grove, IL: InterVarsity, 1971), 87–88.

[40] Montgomery, 106–7.

[41] John Warwick Montgomery, *Where Is History Going?* (Grand Rapids: Zondervan, 1969), 111–12, cf. 115.

[42] In addition to Carl F. H. Henry, ed., *Jesus of Nazareth: Saviour and Lord* (Grand Rapids: Eerdmans, 1966), 11–12, compare Henry's comments in the dialogue on the resurrection in the appendix to Montgomery's *History and Christianity*, 85, 96, 105; Daniel P. Fuller, *Easter Faith and History* (Grand Rapids: Eerdmans, 1965), 69, 71, 82–84; Bernard Ramm, *A Handbook of Contemporary Theology* (Grand Rapids: Eerdmans, 1966), 90. Barth's position in contrast to Bultmann's here is summarized by Charles C. Anderson, *Critical Quests of Jesus* (Grand Rapids: Eerdmans, 1969), 128–39. Clark Pinnock also agreed with what he considered to be contradictory aspects of Barth's concepts in personal correspondence with the author, dated July 19, 1971.

320 REFUTATIONS

all theological problems because there are no grounds upon which its claims may be based. In spite of Barth's defense of faith in revelation as the only way (as opposed to either historical research or rational approaches), it still remains that this faith cannot verify itself or demonstrate its own validity. This can only mean that one cannot know if the grounds for belief are solid or not. Barth was not interested in verifying the grounds of Christianity, and neither are many other Christians, but for those who wish to build on solid, knowledge-producing doctrines, how are we to know if faith is true and secure? Perhaps worse yet, how is Christianity to be distinguished from other views or able to answer evidential questions from other faith systems?

These initial two criticisms of Barth are internal critiques. The next concern applies to Barth's understanding of God's revelation in human events. Barth contends that God reveals himself in certain revelatory acts, like Jesus's resurrection, which occur in man's prehistory and not as an actual part of verifiable history.[43] But if revelation is not given via evidence in historical facts, which are open to historical research, or based on natural revelation or theology, then how is Jesus's death revelatory? Barth definitely holds that the crucifixion is part of God's revelation, since Jesus died a substitutionary death to pay for the sins of those who surrender their lives to God in faith.[44]

Yet, Barth is also quite clear that the crucifixion is fully historical: "The death of Jesus Christ can certainly be thought of as history in the modern sense, but not the resurrection."[45] Here it seems that there is an internal inconsistency in a major area of theology. If one holds that the death of Jesus is an indispensable part of God's revelation (as Barth is correct in doing), then it would seem that one must abandon the previously held idea that God never acts meaningfully in this "secular" kind of history. But since the cross is a regular historical fact in every sense of the term, as Barth also acknowledges, then this means that the resurrection could likewise be objective, verifiable history and still be a revelatory event as well.[46] This should particularly be the case when in both the New Testament and Barth these two events are inseparable, being the flip sides of each other.[47]

---

[43] Ramm, *Handbook of Contemporary Theology*, 90.

[44] Barth, *Church Dogmatics*, 4.1:248–54, for instance; cf. Ramm, *Handbook of Contemporary Theology*, 16, 108.

[45] Barth, 4.1:336, cf. 334–38, 353.

[46] See Henry, *Jesus of Nazareth*, 10, where a similar criticism is developed.

[47] However, the Barth who wrote *The Resurrection of the Dead* was closer to his former liberal days and made some strange comments. About the empty tomb, he states that

The next critique of Barth's treatment of the resurrection is that he holds that the New Testament does not make any attempt to demonstrate that the resurrection of Jesus did occur. He holds, rather, that the earliest Christians were only interested in accepting this event by faith and preaching it. Thus, Paul was not even trying to present evidence for this occurrence by citing the famous list of witnesses in 1 Corinthians 15.[48] As already noted for Barth, this text makes it quite plain that although Paul is speaking of the faith of the first-century Christians, he is also explaining how this faith has its basis in historical fact. However, he thinks that the text clearly shows that Paul does not at all intend to cite any kind of "proof" or objective basis here. As always for Barth, the twin issues are God's revelation and faith, not evidence.

Even Bultmann disagrees with Barth here, noting that Paul *does* mean to use the list of the appearances of Jesus as evidence for the resurrection.[49] Bultmann notes that there were two current "proofs" for this event in the early church, both of which are found in 1 Corinthians 15. There was the appeal to eyewitness testimony, as just mentioned (especially 15:5–8) and the appeal to the fulfillment of Old Testament prophecy (15:3–4).[50] This testimony is valuable at this point mainly because it is apparent that Barth desires to utilize Scripture to reinforce his own polemic,[51] whereas Bultmann actually objects to Paul using such evidence in spite of believing that he does just this.[52] Barth's desire of course does not in itself mean that he is necessarily mistaken here. But it does appear that Bultmann is more accurate in ascertaining Paul's obvious motives here, even though Bultmann does not agree with Paul.

---

whether it was truly empty or not "is really a matter of indifference" (135). Later (136–38), he makes the cryptic comment that perhaps some issues might drive us to the liberal side regarding the idea of visions. (Incidentally, Barth mentions both objective and subjective visions in this context, though without evaluating either.) There are aspects of this early Barth in *The Resurrection of the Dead* that one does not witness in *Church Dogmatics*, where he criticizes the subjective vision thesis (4.1:340).

[48] This tendency to believe that the New Testament never intends to *demonstrate* that the resurrection happened is evident in both the early and the late Barth. Compare his *Resurrection of the Dead*, 131–38, with his later *Church Dogmatics*, 4.1:335, where many of the comments could even be switched with very little if any loss of meaning!

[49] Rudolf Bultmann, "New Testament and Mythology," in Bultmann et al., *Kerygma and Myth: A Theological Debate*, ed. Hans Werner Bartsch, trans. Reginald H. Fuller (New York: Harper & Row, 1961), 39.

[50] Rudolf Bultmann, *Theology of the New Testament*, trans. Kendrick Grobel, 2 vols. (New York: Scribner's Sons, 1951, 1955), 1:82.

[51] See Barth, *Church Dogmatics*, 4.1:334–36.

[52] Bultmann, "New Testament and Mythology," 39.

Reginald Fuller's own position is somewhat close to Barth in his view on this question. He holds that Paul's primary intention was to identify his preaching of the resurrection with that of the earliest eyewitnesses. But he also believes that Paul intended to include the eyewitness accounts in order to indicate that Jesus actually appeared to his followers. He likewise agrees that 1 Cor 15:6 is the chief pointer to the fact that Paul was establishing evidence to be used on behalf of these appearances.[53]

It must be kept in mind during this entire discussion that the overall point being discussed is whether Barth or Bultmann thought that Paul and the Gospel authors were attempting to provide evidence for Jesus's appearances, *not* whether any of these texts are critically acclaimed. The general point was that Barth did not want to indicate that evidence was being given, whereas Bultmann and Fuller thought it was clear that Paul was doing so.

There are additional passages in the New Testament besides Paul's writings that also endeavor both to provide evidence for Jesus's resurrection appearances and to use this event as the basis for establishing other beliefs, contrary to Barth's view. It has been argued quite frequently that the Gospels in particular sought to demonstrate the reality of Jesus's resurrection by emphasizing that he appeared to his disciples in bodily form. Although Jesus's new body had undergone changes, it is reported that Jesus allowed his followers to examine this new body. We are even told that Jesus was touched and "held," thus demonstrating that he was alive. This emphasis is especially evident in passages like Luke 24:36–43, which undeniably indicates that Jesus had risen.[54]

It is even taught plainly in Acts 1:3 that Jesus "presented himself alive after his passion by many proofs" (RSV). In fact, the Greek word used here for "proof" (*tekmēriois*) literally means a positive or certain proof. Hence it *was* the intention of several New Testament authors to show that Jesus had risen.

In addition, it should be mentioned that the resurrection is also used in the New Testament to support other Christian doctrines. For instance, Acts 17:30–31 shows that the earliest church believed that God verified Jesus's earthly teachings by raising

---

[53] Reginald H. Fuller, *The Formation of the Resurrection Narratives* (New York: Macmillan, 1971), 29.

[54] Besides this portion and 1 Cor 15:3–8, see such passages as Matt 28:8–9; John 20:17 (in the Greek), 19–31; Acts 10:39–41. Bultmann also believes that the Gospels and Paul endeavor to provide evidence that Jesus had appeared to the apostles. Besides his recognition that 1 Cor 15:3–8 clearly does so, Bultmann likewise recognizes that Luke 24:39–43 is another good example of this tendency ("New Testament and Mythology," 39).

him from the dead.[55] Further, Acts 2:22–24, 36, and Rom 1:4 are other examples that point to Jesus being accepted as the Lord, Messiah, and the Son of God based upon the resurrection.[56]

Barth was unsuccessful in teaching his untenable notion of history, including that an event could have occurred literally without being able to investigate it. One huge problem was leaving believers without grounds for their faith, both here and in other major areas of theology. Barth's emphasis on early Christian preaching instead of the need to also provide evidence shows that his interpretations of Scripture at these points were mistaken, being rather clearly governed by his overpowering presuppositions. His discussions with Bultmann pointed clearly to these issues. Finally, the claim that the New Testament does not attempt to establish the historicity of Jesus's resurrection appearances is simply not supported by the facts.

For the reasons given above, it becomes evident that Barth's thesis fails. These critiques point out some of the key weaknesses to which this view is most vulnerable as well as the inadequacies involved. In short, Barth declares clearly that there "cannot and ought not to be any proof" in these matters.[57] But since there *is* very strong historical evidence for Jesus's resurrection appearances, then his view of prehistory's characteristics is seriously mistaken.

Rudolf Bultmann

In spite of Barth's incredible influence, by the mid-twentieth century, Rudolf Bultmann may have surpassed him in that respect. Barth and Emil Brunner, another highly acknowledged theologian in his own regard, both recognized in an interview that "Bultmann is king."[58] However, Brunner thought that Bultmann and Barth remained "the strongest contenders for this leadership." Another theologian, Edmund Schlink, parsed their influence this way: "In the field of systematic theology

---

[55] This is admitted by both Bultmann, "New Testament and Mythology," 39, and by Marxsen, *Resurrection of Jesus of Nazareth*, 169. Marxsen notes that the preaching of repentance and belief in the lordship of Jesus are both based on the evidence that Jesus rose from the dead, according to these verses.

[56] Bultmann, *Theology of the New Testament*, 1:27.

[57] Barth, *Church Dogmatics*, 1.4:335, see also 334–36.

[58] Carl F. H. Henry, "Has Winter Come Again? Theological Transition in Europe," *Christianity Today*, November 21, 1960, 3.

Barth still has more control, while in the New Testament field, it is Bultmann who holds more influence."[59]

Just before turning to a survey of five models of resurrection research in the mid-twentieth century, we would do well to survey Bultmann's early position on the resurrection of Jesus since it exacted so much influence on this mid-century research. From the beginning of his theological career, Bultmann treated the resurrection as a mythical occurrence. In one of his earlier writings, he stated that the resurrection teaching was due to "devout imagination."[60]

In his famous 1941 essay "New Testament and Mythology," which furthered the demythologization agenda, Bultmann responded in more detail. In one sentence, he mentioned "the historical event of the crucifixion," while then commenting on the "definitely non-historical event of the resurrection."[61] Then in his opening words in the section on "The Resurrection" he stated rather boldly, "But what of the resurrection? Is it not a mythical event pure and simple? Obviously it is not an event of past history."[62] Shortly afterward, he judged that "a historical fact which involves a resurrection from the dead is utterly inconceivable!"[63] Related components of the resurrection message, such as the empty tomb and the ascension, are likewise mythical.[64]

So how should the early church's central message be treated today? For Bultmann, as with other supernatural claims, the meaning of the resurrection proclamation must be demythologized. Unlike his qualms with the nineteenth-century German liberal approach to myth, which often simply excised the mythical language from the text,

---

[59] Henry was the editor of *Christianity Today* (and was himself an eminently qualified scholar in the fields of both philosophy and theology). He toured western Europe in the early 1960s to interview a large number of the leading, best-known theologians to assess areas such as current research trends along with matters of influence. The result was a very informative series of absolutely fascinating articles that appeared in this influential magazine. The articles were later included, along with some new material, in Henry's volume *Frontiers in Modern Theology: A Critique of Current Theological Trends* (Chicago: Moody, 1965), see 13 for the citations from Brunner and Schlink. (The Barth and Brunner quotation above is on 11.)

[60] Originally published in 1934, Rudolf Bultmann, "The Study of the Synoptic Gospels," in *Form Criticism: Two Essays on New Testament Research*, trans. Frederick C. Grant (New York: Harper & Brothers, 1962), 64.

[61] Bultmann, "New Testament and Mythology," 34.

[62] Bultmann, 38.

[63] Bultmann, 39.

[64] Bultmann, 34–35, 39.

Bultmann held that it has to be inquired as to what the ancient authors intended the mythical language to signify. He combined Christ's death and resurrection into "an inseparable unity . . . a single, indivisible cosmic event." In spite of the resurrection not being literally true, the result brings "the possibility of authentic life."[65]

This emphasis continued far past this influential 1941 essay. In the Shafer Lectures at Yale University Divinity School and the Cole Lectures at Vanderbilt University, both in the fall of 1951, Bultmann explained his view that this demythologization process had already begun in the pages of the New Testament in the writings of Paul and even more earnestly in John's writings.[66]

Providing a crucial distinction, Bultmann provided further instruction on the demythologized meaning of the resurrection: "Belief in the resurrection and the faith that Christ himself, yes God Himself, speaks in the proclaimed word (II Cor. 5:20) are identical. . . . If he heeds it as the word spoken to him, adjudicating to him death and thereby life, then he believes in the risen Christ." In other words, Bultmann explains that belief in the resurrection is one and the same with believing that Christ is being proclaimed as the Word of God. So heeding Jesus's words means believing in the resurrection, taken not as a literal historical event but as one's living authentically.[67]

In sum, for Bultmann the resurrection of Jesus Christ is not a historical event,[68] but a myth.[69] But rather than simply expunging myth from the text as ancient

---

[65] Bultmann, 38–39.

[66] Rudolf Bultmann, *Jesus Christ and Mythology* (New York: Scribner's Sons, 1959), esp. 32–34, also 60–62, 80.

[67] Bultmann, *Theology of the New Testament*, esp. 1:305–6.

[68] As per our earlier discussions in volume 1 on the philosophy of history, Bultmann demarcated some of the influences on him from the writings of Benedetto Croce and especially R. G. Collingwood, pertaining to the historian's "participation in history." This concerns topics such as the subjectivity of the historian's conclusions and even some rather startling comments such as: "Therefore, historical research includes the readiness to hear the claim which meets one in the historical phenomena." These requirements include "the demand for freedom from presuppositions, for an unprejudiced approach, which is valid for all science, is also valid for historical research. The historian is certainly not allowed to presuppose the results of his research, and he is obliged to keep back, to reduce to silence, his personal desires with regard to these results." Rudolf Bultmann, *History and Eschatology: The Presence of Eternity* (New York: Harper & Row, 1957), 118–22, also chaps. 8 and 9, both on "The Nature of History."

[69] After our earlier treatment of Barth, we presented a critique primarily of his prehistorical interpretation of history with regard to Jesus's resurrection. No separate

trappings, it must be demythologized and retained, as with other myths, in order to unpack and apply its existential significance and meaning. Christ did not die an ordinary death, for this event signifies salvation and judgment for the world (though again, not literally or in any orthodox understanding of these doctrines). In him, we are confronted with the message of God's risen messenger, requiring a decision with authentic life consequences.[70]

Contemporary Approaches

By the early 1960s, Carl Henry had completed his interviews with many of Europe's most influential theological and New Testament scholars. But in spite of the testimonies of both Karl Barth and Emil Brunner above that Bultmann was the theological leader at that time, this New Testament scholar's influence was definitely waning. Strikingly, the first sentence of Henry's lead chapter read as follows: "After ruling German theology for more than a decade, Rudolf Bultmann is no longer its king." Or as Georg Werner Kümmel, Bultmann's successor at the University of Marburg, attested, the Bultmannian school of thought had "broken to pieces."[71]

It would be impossible to deny, however, that Bultmann still undoubtedly cast a very long shadow over critical theology in the mid-twentieth century.[72] It would take a couple more decades before this German scholar had lost virtually all of his influence. But when the time finally came, the change was definitely thoroughgoing.

Rather than a unified movement arriving on the scene and pushing out previous scholarly strongholds, as largely had been the case with German liberalism in the nineteenth century as well as with Barth's and Bultmann's movements earlier in the

---

critique was given for Bultmann since, unlike Barth, Bultmann rejected the historicity of Jesus's resurrection and his appearances. Thus, as with other naturalists and those of similar positions, the response to Bultmann appears in the resurrection evidence presented in volume 1, plus the additional critiques throughout this present volume, since Bultmann made comments from time to time addressed by some of the chapters here.

[70] Bultmann, "New Testament and Mythology," 38–39; Bultmann, *Theology of the New Testament*, 1:305–6.

[71] Henry, *Frontiers in Modern Theology*, 13.

[72] As per the comment of John Macquarrie in his essay "Rudolf Bultmann," in Peerman and Marty, *Handbook of Christian Theologians*, 462.

century, the field was now exhibiting a wide degree of fracturing. Kümmel divided the "competition" into at least four different camps.[73]

Risking the possibility of oversimplification, we will list five theological models that may be demarcated during the middle of the twentieth century, specifically with regard to the state of resurrection research. Each model is a critical attempt to describe a specific position regarding the nature of Jesus's resurrection appearances. Occasionally, the differences between each type will be based on only slight, carefully nuanced distinctions. Our list will begin with those scholars who deny or doubt seriously the historical reality of Jesus's resurrection appearances, usually because they question the existence of the supernatural realm itself. Then we will move to other views that culminate, finally, in the position that the risen Jesus actually appeared bodily, mostly to his followers, and that these events are well supported by historical and other data.

Granted, there are numerous potential angles from which to study Jesus's appearances, so it ought not be pretended by any means that the only important perspective or angle is one of historicity.[74] However, agreeing with Paul (1 Cor 15:12–20) and against Marxsen at this point, many scholars still hold that any theological meaning for this event depends on the prior question of historicity.

It should also be acknowledged fully that it is always risky to attempt to identify the positions of a broad cross-section of scholars on almost any issue, let alone an absolutely crucial one. This is particularly true with regard to the resurrection appearances, due to the numerous subtle shades of meaning that may be apparent (or not so apparent!) even to the trained eye. In fact, it is rather frustrating to

---

[73] Kümmel listed these mostly German scholarly groups as the conservatives, the *Heilsgeschichte* scholars, the post-Bultmannians, and the so-called Wolfhart Pannenberg school of thought. Then he listed some independent scholars who presumably did not fit very easily into any of these four categories. Some of these theological scholars were apparently listed in more than one of these groupings. See Henry, *Frontiers in Modern Theology*, 13–14.

[74] Gerald O'Collins notes six contemporary interpretive models of Jesus's resurrection, only one of which emphasizes the historical aspect. These categories emphasize the resurrection as history, redemption, revelation, the ground of faith, the ground of hope, and the ground of kerygma. See O'Collins, *What Are They Saying about the Resurrection?* (New York: Paulist, 1978), 7–34. On the other hand, we are basically dividing the historical question regarding the appearances into five distinct perspectives. However, in later sections of these volumes, especially volume 4, we will also turn to other angles that emphasize the relationship between the resurrection and theology, ministry, and even personal practice.

read certain well-known scholars on this topic and to come away still attempting to understand their positions, as if they were purposely being obscurantist. Intriguingly, this latter practice was more common in the decades we are discussing here than is the case today.

Although our procedure here is potentially somewhat hazardous for more than one reason, it should be helpful to sort out the plethora of resurrection views plus the accompanying philosophical outlooks involved. There will necessarily be some overlap since some scholars exhibit tendencies toward more than one model. Other scholars can be identified only in fairly approximate terms due to their incomplete descriptions of their own positions. Still, even these broader categorizations will hopefully still serve our purpose here, while at the same time reveal some "strange bedfellows."

The first model comprises those mid-twentieth-century scholars who manifest the tendency either to dismiss or at least to question seriously the reality of both the resurrection and Jesus's appearances, often due to the influence of eighteenth-century Scottish philosopher David Hume's essay "Of Miracles." The empty tomb is usually rejected as well, though some of these researchers do recognize its historicity. While being more radical in their criticisms, these academics still accept a number of the basic surrounding facts as being historical. Quite surprisingly, they also tend to either reject or at least disregard the naturalistic explanations for the appearances. A widespread preference here is just to assert that an undefined "something" occurred to Jesus's followers—some real and actual though private experience—while concluding that a more exact description of these experiences cannot be ascertained.

Bultmann and his followers claimed that the real cause of the disciples' transformation is obscured by the New Testament texts and is of little interest anyway. So, it is not crucial to inquire into the exact nature or cause of these experiences: "The resurrection itself is not an event of past history. All that historical criticism can establish is the fact that the first disciples came to believe in the resurrection. The historian can perhaps to some extent . . . reduce the resurrection appearances to a series of subjective visions. But the historical problem is not of interest to Christian belief in the resurrection."[75] Similarly, Marxsen also believes that reconstructing the

---

[75] Bultmann, "New Testament and Mythology," 42. It should be noticed that Bultmann does not personally endorse these subjective visions here. He could well be open to them, but that he does not really endorse particular naturalistic hypotheses elsewhere in any detailed way is a further indication that such is not his intent.

nature of these encounters cannot and should not be attempted, including whether the disciples actually experienced appearances of the risen Jesus. It simply makes very little difference since the chief point is that, regardless of what happened, faith is still warranted.[76]

Some scholars in this first model could be better characterized by what they *do not* (or feel they *cannot*) say than by what is stated explicitly. So it is with the later view of Helmut Koester, who asserted that it was not his concern to inquire into the nature of Jesus's appearances, but that they may nevertheless best be characterized as the "catalyst" that started the early Christian missionary activity and church-planting activities in the first place. Whatever else may be said, the resurrection revealed nothing new, but it did change life for the first believers.[77]

For another German theologian, Hans Küng, the resurrection should not be considered "a supernatural intervention which can be located and dated in space and time." Once again, it is "not an event in human space and human time." It can be known that Jesus died, and that this event was followed by the disciples' rise of faith and their proclamation of the Easter message. But nothing objective can be apprehended, observed, or checked out concerning either the resurrection event itself or Jesus's appearances.[78]

---

[76] Marxsen, *Resurrection of Jesus of Nazareth*, chaps. 3–4, esp. 77, 96, 111, 119, 147, 152.

[77] Helmut Koester, *Introduction to the New Testament*, 2 vols. (Philadelphia: Fortress, 1982), 1:84, 86. Another tendency to notice here is that while those influenced by Bultmann, such as his pupil Koester, usually acknowledged that the resurrection event, however it is taken, is the center of Christian belief (as Marxsen, Bornkamm, and Koester all indicated above), they often comment very little regarding it. Koester's two large volumes and Bultmann's own two-volume New Testament theology say exceptionally little about the resurrection. But how is this the case in a multivolume New Testament introduction or theology when it is the central focus point in the development of the historical Christian faith? Or how can Koester assert above that "the resurrection revealed nothing new"? How can this be the case when it opened a new door for the Christian church and propelled it in a new direction? It seems that we see here the influence of how worldviews often trump the data. When historical events, and supernatural ones in particular, impinge on our thinking in such a central way that we cannot speak of the development of entire movements without them, which we largely ignore in practice, it would seem that these are quite revealing scenarios. In fact, these tendencies seem to shout the disparity between the founding event and one's theory. Needless to say, something is deficient here.

[78] Hans Küng, *On Being a Christian*, trans. E. Quinn (New York: Doubleday, 1976), 348–53.

As part of the so-called Death of God movement, theologian Paul Van Buren likewise held "something happened" that changed the disciples' outlook from one of initial discouragement to faith. While these experiences were more than subjective and were articulated in terms of actual appearances of the risen Jesus, their nature remains a mystery and still cannot be ascertained.[79]

Another researcher who probably best fits this model, despite some differences, is former Oxford and London professor C. F. Evans. Placing much more emphasis on textual and theological considerations, Evans spent much less time on historical concerns. Yet, he judged that both strong and weak positions regarding the historicity of the empty tomb and resurrection appearances were unwarranted. Instead, he preferred rather agnostic conclusions, including some inconclusive moves.[80] Another influential New Testament exegete who was also strongly influenced by Bultmann's work and preferred some similar positions was German scholar Hans Conzelmann.[81]

Certain recent trends still reflect views that resemble the scholarly positions constituting this first model, though the position as a whole appears to be much less popular today. Possibly the waning of Bultmann's widespread influence has caused this position to suffer a similar fate with thinkers supporting these options.[82]

There are a few other indications that this last point is accurate. For example, Norman Perrin, formerly of the University of Chicago, was often viewed during these decades as a major American representative of at least some of Bultmann's positions, frequently exhibiting similarities to the latter's New Testament interpretations. But strangely enough, in a volume on this subject written very shortly before his death, Perrin concluded that the tradition behind Jesus's appearances was firmly based. In

---

[79] Paul Van Buren, *The Secular Meaning of the Gospel* (New York: Macmillan, 1963), 126–34.

[80] C. F. Evans, *Resurrection and the New Testament* (London: SCM, 1970), esp. 130, including the critical view that exaltation preceded resurrection as the earliest Christian position (136–43). O'Collins (*What Are They Saying*, 12) concurs in this interpretation of Evans's view.

[81] Some of Hans Conzelmann's thoughts on the resurrection appearances are found in his *1 Corinthians: A Commentary on the First Epistle to the Corinthians*, trans. J. Leitch (Philadelphia: Fortress, 1975), 251.

[82] Of course, some scholars still hold similar views, including dismissals of supernatural events, frequent denials of the empty tomb, and resistance to the actual resurrection appearances. Yet, embracing specific naturalistic theories and taking a stand there still remains the minority option at present. This should all become more obvious when we look at views of scholars such as Thomas Sheehan, John Dominic Crossan, Marcus Borg, and Bart Ehrman.

fact, his synopsis of what actually happened appears at least to allow for some sort of objective visions whereby Jesus actually commissioned the apostles for a new mission.[83] Beyond this, Perrin did not think that anything further could be said.[84] Here it seems clear that Perrin may have moved quite far beyond Bultmann.

Another example comes from Helmut Koester, Bultmann's former pupil mentioned above. When writing a brief section on the cross and resurrection, Koester asserted, "We are on much firmer ground with respect to the appearances of the risen Jesus and their effect." He then concludes the matter: besides Paul, from whom we have "immediate testimony," the fact that "Jesus also appeared to others (Peter, Mary Magdalene, James) cannot very well be questioned."[85] Like Perrin, this testimony clearly exceeds anything Bultmann would have concluded.

So this first model expresses a disbelief or at least agnosticism concerning both Jesus's resurrection as well as his postmortem appearances. Instead, some sort of actual, private experiences are postulated without any further description. The empty tomb is sometimes accepted but usually dismissed. Even though the natural alternative hypotheses are usually either simply ignored or sometimes even rejected, the events regarding the miracle claims are still assumed never to have happened, often with a salute to Hume and his famous essay that argued against the existence of miracles. A number of the best-attested events adjoining these occurrences are still thought to be historical, however.

The mid-twentieth-century scholars constituting the second model are distinguished from the first group by their increased interest in the nature of the disciples' experiences and their more frequent acceptance of a literal resurrection event.[86] Further, although the naturalistic theories opposed to this event are generally rejected and the empty tomb is sometimes affirmed, the *chief earmark* of the scholars in this second model is that they insist that these original experiences still cannot be verified historically, even probabilistically, or otherwise evidenced. They can only be apprehended, recognized, and accepted by an act of faith.

---

[83] This opens the possibility that Perrin had actually moved from the most skeptical position to being a proponent of the third model below.

[84] Norman Perrin, *The Resurrection according to Matthew, Mark and Luke* (Philadelphia: Fortress, 1977), 78–84.

[85] Koester, *Introduction to the New Testament*, 2:84.

[86] It is difficult in all examples below to ascertain precisely which scholars espouse faith in *literal* resurrection appearances of Jesus to his followers because some of these authors do not answer the question directly. But it is sufficiently clear in most cases here.

Thus, while the resurrection is quite often considered a historical event, it is known in a distinctly different way than the crucifixion or other regular historical events. The resurrection is sometimes even proclaimed as having occurred in a different type or species of history, which is *very seldom defined or described* in any detail in these scholars' works. These thinkers insist that while the cross is a normal historical event (described in German as *historisch*), the resurrection is a type of revelatory history or story (described as *geschichtlich*) that can only be understood, grasped, or believed through the eyes of a faith commitment. Or it might be concluded that a particular event even encompasses both aspects of history and revelation. For instance, the crucifixion is an event of regular history (*historisch*), while the *interpretation* that this event manifests the possibility of redemption or the atonement is therefore a revelatory occasion (*geschichtlich*).

The theologians and exegetes placed in this second model have usually been influenced heavily by Søren Kierkegaard and by Barth, who held that the resurrection should be accepted by faith as a literal event, but that it cannot be ascertained by any historical investigation or other "proofs."[87] Barth could scarcely have rejected the naturalistic alternative theories any more emphatically than he did. Further,

---

[87] See especially Søren Kierkegaard's works *Philosophical Fragments,* trans. David F. Swenson (Princeton: Princeton University Press, 1962), chaps. 3–4; and *Concluding Unscientific Postscript,* trans. David F. Swenson (Princeton: Princeton University Press, 1941), chap. 1, and 86, 188–90. In a number of usually philosophical sources, the twentieth-century witnessed a huge shift as to whether, or to what extent, Kierkegaard really deserved to be treated as a forerunner to scholarly views such as those of Barth and Bultmann in their fideist (or fideist-like) positions on the epistemic value or even the usefulness of history as an evidential ally for Christian truth. On the newer position, see Stephen F. Evans, "Apologetic Arguments in Philosophical Fragments," in *Philosophical Fragments and Johannes Climacus* (Macon: Mercer University Press, 1994), chap. 4, esp. 82–83; Evans, *Passionate Reason: Making Sense of Kierkegaard's Philosophical Fragments* (Bloomington: Indiana University Press, 1992). While doubting but not contesting such a position on Kierkegaard, a more practical solution may be twofold: (1) Even if Kierkegaard is ultimately not guilty of teaching this anti-evidential view of history, and if the proper angle depends on his frequent use of pseudonyms and other rather obscure notions that only philosophers could basically decipher and figure out, and with perhaps a few exceptions only in the twentieth century, then Kierkegaard himself is apparently in for a good deal of the blame for the misinterpretations and misunderstandings of his views. After all, some of Kierkegaard's publications, such as those listed above, certainly display much of the "old" language. (2) Perhaps more importantly for our purposes, even if the new view of Kierkegaard is completely correct, at least much of the interpretation by Barth, Bultmann, and their colleagues took the old interpretation of Kierkegaard, thinking that these were

he asserted that Jesus appeared empirically to his disciples, yet these occurrences happened in a different domain of history and cannot be verified historically. As he states rather enigmatically, "We cannot read the Gospels without getting the strong impression that as we pass from the story of the passion to the story of Easter we are led into a historical sphere of a different kind." Barth continues, referring to "the peculiar character of this history."[88]

Similar views closely aligned with Barth's position were held by other major "neoorthodox" theologians, such as Emil Brunner,[89] Dietrich Bonhoeffer,[90] and Reinhold Niebuhr,[91] including related comments by others regarding this nonverifiable species of "history." These frankly odd statements often concerned comparisons between the different modes of the past in which the event of Jesus's crucifixion occurred in normal history and the resurrection "occurrence" in this revelatory realm.[92]

---

plainly Kierkegaard's own positions. So *at the very least*, according to their interpretations, Kierkegaard was interpreted as inspiring many of their notions at this point.

[88] The progress in Barth's ideas on this subject is both very intriguing and informative. Barth's most authoritative statement of these views is found in *Church Dogmatics*, esp. 1.4:334–36, 351–52. The quotations above are from 334 and 335, respectively.

[89] See, for instance, Emil Brunner, *The Christian Doctrine of Creation and Redemption*, vol. 2 of *Dogmatics*, trans. Olive Wyon (Philadelphia: Westminster, 1952), 366–72.

[90] Dietrich Bonhoeffer, *Christ the Center*, trans. John Bowden (New York: Harper & Row, 1966), 71–77.

[91] Reinhold Niebuhr, *Faith and History: A Comparison of Christian and Modern Views of History* (New York: Scribner's Sons, 1949), 145–50.

[92] The contrast exhibited in Niebuhr's *Faith and History* plus various comments by Barth are examples of some of the difficulties involved in ascertaining the precise differences regarding how these researchers defined the respective realms in which they surmised that Jesus's crucifixion and his resurrection are thought to have occurred. This lack of clarification was a common feature with members of this school of thought and was presumably due to the seemingly steadfast refusal by these scholars to define or quantify these or various other notions. Specifications are virtually never provided in the relevant resurrection literature, perhaps being due to factors such as the dialectic nature of their message, the lack of clarity among these researchers themselves, the resistance concerning measuring and specifying such ideas, or even the realization that making such distinctions would be very difficult to parcel out, clarify, and defend. A fair guess as to the meaning from some of these writings might be that whereas the crucifixion was virtually always taken as a straightforward historical event, the resurrection was viewed as a revelatory occurrence, and God's revelation is not open to investigation. If this demarcation is anywhere close to the mark, it should be added that this distinction would be true whether the particular scholar held that the resurrection actually occurred, as with Barth, or if it were either doubted

These contrasts grew somewhat less common in the decades after these scholars discontinued their formative writing, but aspects remained popular in some later circles. For instance, Bornkamm noted the failure of naturalistic hypotheses pertaining to Jesus's resurrection, but still, in a style quite reminiscent of Barth, asserted that the resurrection appearances could only be accepted by faith apart from any historical examination.[93] Reinhold Niebuhr remarked in a more puzzling manner for some that "the story of this triumph over death is thus shrouded in a mystery which places it in a different order of history than the story of the crucifixion."[94]

Likewise, influential Roman Catholic theologian Karl Rahner pointed out that just because the resurrection cannot be incorporated "into the normal world of space and time" does not mean that this event should be denied.[95] For Marcus Barth, Jesus's resurrection was actually a real occurrence in history but, in words quite reminiscent of his famous father, it "is an event which occurs at the boundary of empirical scientific knowledge . . . beyond the realm of experience and sensation which is accessible to rationality and empirical investigation."[96]

An exceptionally informed view (that also reaches beyond this second model) is the position of Thomas Torrance. A well-known Scottish translator and interpreter of Karl Barth's theology, not to mention a major theologian in his own right, Torrance carefully and repeatedly explained his acceptance of the literal resurrection of Jesus. He placed more "objective" emphasis on the historicity of this event than did Barth, such as his identification of the resurrection as "an event that happens within history . . . a happening within the same order of physical existence to which we belong . . . an event in space and time."[97] He even drew a distinction between his position and that of the early Barth, whom Torrance surprisingly identifies as holding that the resurrection was "not . . . really historical." A footnote there implies

or denied, as with Niebuhr. In all cases, the resurrection was revelatory, should not be evidenced and, in the end, was basically almost inscrutable.

[93] Bornkamm, *Jesus of Nazareth*, 180–86.

[94] Niebuhr, *Faith and History*, 147.

[95] See chap. 3 of Karl Rahner, *Belief Today*, vol. 3 of *Theological Meditations* (New York: Sheed & Ward, 1967), 127.

[96] Marcus Barth and Verne H. Fletcher, *Acquittal by Resurrection* (New York: Holt, Rinehart, and Winston, 1964), vi–vii. Compare 14–15, 29 with 25, 31 for this contrast. An intriguing parallel is found in Karl Barth, *Resurrection of the Dead*, esp. 134, cf. 131–42.

[97] T. F. Torrance, *Space, Time, and Resurrection* (Grand Rapids: Eerdmans, 1976), 86–88, cf. also 21, 89–91, 94–95, 171–75.

that Barth only held such a view in his earlier stages (1910–1931).[98] But it should be objected that Barth continued to speak of the resurrection having occurred in a different sphere of history long after this.[99] At any rate, Torrance still agrees with Barth that the resurrection cannot be proven, but is "apprehended only by faith."[100]

Like Torrance in the sense of being a bit removed from this second model in some of his responses, Neville Clark also proceeded beyond the scholars in this group. But then, he failed to go as far as they do in other places. For examples, Clark pointed out the nature of the early creedal evidence for the resurrection appearances and emphasized the "indisputable facts" in their favor, including "the belief of the early church that he has risen." This "reality . . . seems to defy definition but demand explanation."[101] This last assertion was because, like others taking this approach, he disliked naturalistic hypotheses. Yet Clark also seemed to differ in being a little more equivocal about the empty tomb and in questioning the bodily nature of Jesus's appearances.[102] Moreover, very much like the other scholars here, Clark held that the resurrection cannot be proven but can only be known to believers by faith.[103]

Other scholars, like Helmut Thielicke, held similar views. For Thielicke, the resurrection is the center of the Christian faith and grounds Christian theology as a whole. Stated more strongly than some earlier scholars might have liked, this occurrence is definitely "established as a factual event, taking place within time and space," even though inexplicably so. In spite of the presence of contradictions in the various texts (which Thielicke termed "quite edifying"), naturalistic theses cannot explain away the event itself. However, there is no objective proof to be had and, "the believer alone can apprehend this event. . . . Apart from this situation of faith, Easter is indeed unverifiable." Still, for believers, it is exceptionally well attested.[104]

---

[98] Torrance, 95n8.

[99] Karl Barth, *The Faith of the Church*, trans. Gabriel Vahanian, ed. J. L. Leuba (New York: Meridian, 1958), 105–8.

[100] Torrance, *Space, Time, and Resurrection*, 18–19, also 220.

[101] Neville Clark, *Interpreting the Resurrection* (Philadelphia: Westminster, 1967), 96.

[102] Clark, 89–91, 97–98, 100, 104.

[103] Clark, 93–95, 98–99, 104.

[104] For instance, see Helmut Thielicke, "The Resurrection Kerygma," in Leonhard Goppelt, Helmut Thielicke, and Hans-Rudolf Müller-Schwefe, *The Easter Message Today: Three Essays*, trans. Salvator Attanasio and Darrell Likens Guder (New York: Nelson, 1964), esp. 59, 61, 70–73, 77. On the inability of critical hypotheses to disprove the resurrection, which is one of Thielicke's chief emphases, see 72, 77–78, 81–91, 103–4. For another of his themes of the resurrection grounding Christian theology, see 59–61, 76, 80, 91.

These are the earmarks of this second model. Scholars within this model usually affirm the resurrection appearances and hold a more positive view toward them and often the empty tomb as well. Naturalistic hypotheses are also viewed as failed explanations. But neither the resurrection nor the appearances can be "proven" in any sense. These scholars eschew evidential verification, including photographs (even if cameras had been present in the first century) or any other sort of objectification. Rather, these events represent private occurrences that can only be apprehended, truly understood, or believed by the eye of faith. Especially for those closer to Barth's position (who was apparently the pacesetter here), while these more miraculous events really happened, they did so in this undefined and undeveloped notion of history, seemingly a type of revelatory space where normal historical investigation cannot occur.

The third model consists of scholars who generally exhibit more significant interest in the actual aspects of the resurrection appearances themselves, although from a different angle. Like the researchers from the second model and even some of those from the first category, naturalistic theories are also rejected. Similar to those in the second model as well, these scholars quite often hold that the resurrection event can chiefly be known or appropriated by faith apart from evidential methods. But there are at least two significant dissimilarities between those who championed this third view and those who gravitated to the previous position. Scholars in this third group usually proceeded a step further, developing a more or less abstract reconstruction of the historical appearances of the risen Jesus. Additionally, they tended to produce a few arguments for the empty tomb being the best explanation for the data as opposed to the more straightforward faith approach.

The chief difference between these last two models, then, is the attempt by those in the third group to go beyond undifferentiated, generalized statements of resurrection faith without descriptions of the phenomena behind the New Testament texts in an effort to ascertain at least a minimal understanding of what really happened, including providing some details for the acceptance of Jesus's appearances and the empty tomb.[105] However, those constituting this third model still agreed that the resurrection was an eschatological event that was not demonstrable by

---

[105] This is not to imply that these third model scholars approved or engaged in the practice of apologetic argumentation, for this was not the case. Whatever their intent at this point, there was nonetheless a tendency among some of these researchers to provide reasons, including what might be considered defenses of their position, in contrast to the absence of this activity in the second model.

historical methodology per se, although some held that this event will be verifiable in the future. The chief difference here is the willingness to identify some outward characteristics of the appearances while still holding that faith was not to be placed in these reconstructions per se.

The popularity of this third position derived most significantly from the 1956 publication of a volume on the resurrection by a German theologian at the University of Marburg, Hans Grass. Arguing that the Gospel depictions of Jesus's corporeal resurrection appearances were legendary, Grass contended that the application of critical procedures to the New Testament texts nonetheless revealed that Jesus actually did appear to his disciples. Yet the appearances were of a more spiritual body that could not have been photographed.[106] Unlike most of the scholars in this model, Grass also rejected the empty tomb accounts as legendary.[107] Other researchers followed Grass's lead in interpreting Jesus's resurrection appearances as veridical visionary manifestations that truly occurred, rather than as physical phenomena.[108]

Influential Tübingen University theologian Jürgen Moltmann likewise held that the disciples witnessed visionary appearances of the risen Jesus involving spoken messages that charged his followers with a mission of service in the world. These events were not verifiable but occurred in eschatological history that would be subject to future verification.[109] Ulrich Wilkens likewise concluded that the historical process cannot determine exactly what happened. While naturalistic theories can be refuted and the historical facticity of the empty tomb upheld, Jesus's appearances were private revelations, being indications of a future, eschatological existence.[110]

---

[106] Hans Grass, *Ostergeschehen und Osterberichte*, 2nd ed. (Göttingen: Vandenhoeck & Ruprecht, 1962), 93, 226–49, also 232.

[107] Grass, 93.

[108] The term "visions" is perhaps more often than not employed without sufficient care. We are *not* utilizing the word here as a synonym for hallucinations or some entirely subjective phenomena. The scholarly discussions differentiate between subjective and objective visions, with the initial experiences being closer to the subjective, internal variety, while the latter type are like Grass's view and were thought to be actual appearances of a less than physical body, perhaps accompanied by light. This more visionary notion of Jesus's appearances explains, for instance, why the literal empty tomb was considered to be superfluous.

[109] Jürgen Moltmann, *Theology of Hope*, trans. J. W. Leitch (New York: Harper & Row, 1967), 172, 181, 188, 190, 197–98, 202; Moltmann, *Religion, Revolution and the Future*, trans. M. D. Meeks (New York: Scribner's, 1969), 49–55.

[110] Ulrich Wilckens, *Resurrection: Biblical Testimony to the Resurrection. An Historical Examination and Explanation*, trans. A. M. Stewart (Atlanta: Knox, 1978), particularly 116–25.

Reginald Fuller's chief work on this subject was a major, detailed effort that roughly did for English-speaking audiences what Grass's volume did for Germans. Fuller insisted that the disciples' thorough transformations necessitated an adequate explanatory cause. This cause was Jesus's appearances, which are defined historically as visionary experiences of light accompanied by auditory messages communicated to the earliest witnesses. The messages both proclaimed that Jesus had been raised to a new eschatological existence and imparted a mission to his followers, such as Paul's commission to preach to the gentiles. Such phenomena were not subjective visions but were actual experiences occasioned by an external source. But even though these appearances of Jesus provided the source of the Easter faith and message, these occurrences were removed from historical demonstration.[111]

For Cambridge University's Michael Perry, while there was no clear match between Jesus's resurrection appearances and the phenomena studied in psychical research, these latter cases were still helpful in making certain comparisons.[112] Intriguingly, Perry opts for the historicity of the empty tomb because the "historical evidence for it is powerful."[113] Yet he also appreciates the similarities with "spontaneous apparitions of the dead." At the end of the day, however, Perry judged that the resurrection appearances were actual events that point to the believer's resurrection.[114]

In an exceptionally brief description, eminent German New Testament scholar Joachim Jeremias similarly stated his view that the resurrection appearances of Jesus occurred as spiritual visions of shining light. Through these experiences, Jesus's disciples experienced their teacher as the risen Lord.[115]

---

[111] Fuller, *Formation of the Resurrection Narratives*, 46–49, 169–72, 181.

[112] In fact, Perry finds much disparity between psychical theses and the resurrection appearances. See Michael C. Perry, *The Easter Enigma* (London: Faber & Faber, 1959), 125, 157, 175–88, 190, 239–40.

[113] Perry, 228, also 101–2, 218–28.

[114] Perry, 157, 171, 240–41. More than once, Perry mentions Jesus's being raised bodily (194–95, 240–41) but seems to settle, all things considered, for less than real bodily events (157, 171, 196, 240–41). Even the striking possibility of more than one type of bodily appearance is at least alluded to as a possible position in the early church (238). How this fits with the empty tomb, which Perry clearly appears to hold, is difficult to tell. Admittedly, there is much skipping back and forth in this volume, and if some potential areas of confusion have been noticed in this brief discussion, it is most likely because such confusion exists! In fact, Perry seems to state or at least infer that he has not always landed on unchanging conclusions either (241–43)!

[115] Joachim Jeremias, "Easter: The Earliest Tradition and the Earliest Interpretation," in *New Testament Theology*, trans. John Bowden (New York: Scribner's, 1971), esp. 308–9.

Preferring to study the resurrection as a historical question, Roman Catholic theologian Gerald O'Collins postulated that Jesus's appearances ought to be termed "Christophanies" since they involved manifestations of Jesus as "glorified and divinized as fully as that is possible." Though he often produced reasons for his conclusions, similar to the others here, O'Collins held that these appearances cannot be known except by the exercise of faith.[116] Throughout at least his earlier publications on Jesus's resurrection appearances, O'Collins surprisingly stated little else about the actual nature of the appearances. They involved sight, although it is unclear if they were experiences of light, and they differed from other visions or revelatory encounters in the New Testament.[117] While realizing that these comments were not very detailed, he held that "we have to follow the austere Pauline lead (1 Cor 15:5–8; Gal 1:12, 16)."[118] Still, very helpfully, Collins emphasized the "language of sight," which is a dominant feature in the major New Testament texts.[119] Other scholars likewise concurred on these and other similar points.[120]

---

[116] O'Collins, *What Are They Saying*, 14, 55, 62.

[117] These clarifications are made in O'Collins's responses to the emphases of Reginald Fuller, Pheme Perkins, and Hans Kessler. See Gerald O'Collins, *Interpreting the Resurrection: Examining the Major Problems in the Stories of Jesus' Resurrection* (Mahweh, NJ: Paulist, 1988), 5–21.

[118] O'Collins, 20.

[119] Though chiefly in books subsequent to the period that we are considering here, see the examples in O'Collins's volumes *Interpreting Jesus* (London: Chapman, 1983), 112–14, 116–17, 122–23; *Jesus Risen: The Resurrection—What Actually Happened and What Does It Mean?* (London: Darton, Longman & Todd, 1987), 118–19; and *Interpreting the Resurrection*, 12–19.

[120] It also seems likely that Cambridge University professor G. W. H. Lampe could probably best be construed as taking a similar position to others in this third model. Like Grass, Lampe holds that the Christian teaching of the empty tomb is a myth (17, 40, 53, 58–59). Although very few details are provided, Jesus's appearances were nonbodily in nature (15, 39, 59), and these appearances cannot be proven in any way but only accepted by faith (32–33, 36–37, 58). Yet, these occurrences were probably not hallucinations (19–20, 37–38), and they are the best reason for holding that believers will also rise from the dead (58–60, 98). Page citations from G. W. H. Lampe and D. M. MacKinnon, *The Resurrection: A Dialogue*, ed. William Purcell (Philadelphia: Westminster, 1966). Rather incredibly, in a slightly later publication where the specifics of his precise position are difficult to identify at a few specific points, Jewish New Testament scholar Pinchas Lapide firmly accepts the facticity of Jesus's resurrection and his subsequent appearances, even though they are recognized by faith. Further, he also provides good reasons to accept these conclusions. See Lapide, *The Resurrection of Jesus: A Jewish Perspective* (Minneapolis: Augsburg, 1983), esp. 92, 95–99, 118, 125, 127–28.

In sum, the researchers included in the third model were among the first critical scholars to begin breaking away from the rather nonevidential molds of both Barth and Bultmann. Going even further back to the heart of nineteenth-century German liberalism (against which these two renowned German scholars also revolted), the few small steps taken by those within this third emerging model to unpack some of the historical details of the resurrection appearances were still quite crucial. Further, providing details regarding the nature of these objective visions was something that groups of scholars had hardly done in well over a century. Even though these researchers maintained the central importance of faith and some of them rejected the empty tomb, they presaged some changing times on the horizon.

The fourth model comprises scholars who held that the available textual and historical data were actually sufficient to demonstrate the probability both that Jesus's burial tomb was discovered to be empty soon after his burial and that Jesus was raised from the dead and appeared literally to his followers. The naturalistic alternative theories fail to explain these events as well. But unlike any of the forgoing models (with the possible exception of a few individual scholars here and there), the scholars within this fourth model maintained that strong historical evidence could be assembled for these occurrences. History is an ally, and faith alone is not the best way to adjudicate these events.

The best-known theologian to detail these conclusions during this period was Wolfhart Pannenberg, who argued strongly against any naturalistic theories and who championed the hypothesis that God's use of historical facts was his chief revelatory mode, hence promoting what came to be recognized as a strong reaction to the previous dominance of Barth and Bultmann on these subjects.[121] Yet, Pannenberg tended to dismiss a corporeal resurrection body, instead favoring appearances that were described in terms of a spiritual body that appeared from heaven and was recognized as Jesus. He imparted to his followers an auditory message that, at least in Paul's situation, was accompanied by a light phenomenon.[122]

Somewhat similar to Pannenberg's position in a few places while still holding a view that was not as carefully developed and stopped short of Pannenberg's overall

---

[121] Most notably, Wolfhart Pannenberg et al., *Offenbarung als Geschichte*, ed. Wolfhart Pannenberg (Göttingen, Germany: Vandenhoeck & Ruprecht, 1961), as pointed out on 132 in particular. The English version is *Revelation as History*, trans. David Granskou (New York: Macmillan, 1968), esp. Pannenberg's "Introduction," 1–21.

[122] See particularly Pannenberg, *Jesus: God and Man*, 88–106, esp. 92–93 for details.

thesis, Richard R. Niebuhr took a few steps in this general direction. But the moves taken by Niebuhr remain significant given both the publication of his views before Pannenberg's chief theses were generated and the initial emergence of a number of these elements, particularly as viewed against his background in the well-known Niebuhr family.[123] Richard R. Niebuhr preferred a position on the resurrection appearances that at least drew somewhat upon historical investigation. The appearances are affirmed often as real historical events, and they were probably bodily in nature. Yet, hard evidence is available, hence indicating that there is a limited historical ability to probe the details of these events.[124]

New Testament scholar A. M. Hunter employed textual considerations and applied some initial forms of historical investigation to conclude that Jesus's tomb was empty and that his resurrection appearances were clearly indicated by the facts.[125] New Testament theologian John A. T. Robinson pointed out that while historical studies cannot ascertain the exact details, they may be sufficient to formulate a probable case for this event.[126] A premier American New Testament scholar, Raymond Brown, after conducting an extensive study of the textual data, likewise supported the facticity of the empty tomb as well as Jesus's bodily resurrection appearances.[127]

---

[123] His father was the well-known professor H. Richard Niebuhr of Yale University Divinity School, while his uncle was the even more influential Reinhold Niebuhr, professor at New York's Union Theological Seminary—both of whom were also close to previous conversations on a few of these matters.

[124] Richard R. Niebuhr, *Resurrection and Historical Reason: A Study in Theological Method* (New York: Scribner's Sons, 1957), 23, 95, 171, 175–78. Both Evans (*Resurrection and the New Testament*, 177) and Daniel Fuller (*Easter Faith and History*, 172–77) were among the researchers who discussed aspects of Niebuhr's position on the historicity of the resurrection appearances while offering critiques.

[125] For example, see A. M. Hunter, *Jesus: Lord and Savior* (Grand Rapids: Eerdmans, 1976), 98–107; Hunter, *Bible and Gospel* (Philadelphia: Westminster, 1969), chap. 10.

[126] John A. T. Robinson, *Can We Trust the New Testament?* (Grand Rapids: Eerdmans, 1977), 120–29. For an earlier, positive comment on the evidence for the empty tomb, see Robinson, *Exploration into God* (Stanford: Stanford University Press, 1967), 113. This comment was made during the Raymond Fred West Memorial Lectures at Stanford University in 1966.

[127] Raymond E. Brown, *The Virginal Conception and Bodily Resurrection of Jesus* (New York: Paulist, 1973), 125–29. For a brief article that makes many strong and helpful comments, see Brown, "The Resurrection and Biblical Criticism," *Commonweal*, November 24, 1967, 232–36.

In a similar though less systematic manner, Leonhard Goppelt found that the available data favored both the empty tomb as well as the resurrection appearances of Jesus. He critiqued Hans Grass's thesis in that it did not go far enough in its conclusions.[128] A professor at both Cambridge and Durham who employed a more positive perspective on the Gospel traditions than some of his colleagues, A. M. Ramsey was even clearer in his defense of the empty tomb and Jesus's appearances.[129]

Though written a few years later, it would be worthwhile to mention one other view here. After a close look at the research, influential British theologian James D. G. Dunn examined the pros and cons for both the empty tomb and the resurrection appearances of Jesus. He concluded that it is almost impossible to reject the assertion that the disciples' experienced visionary phenomena that cannot be explained by alternative natural hypotheses. Further, the empty tomb is "almost as difficult to deny."[130] In much more recent publications, Dunn continued to express similar conclusions.[131]

The scholars constituting the fourth resurrection model broke even more demonstrably from the former theological movements than did the ideas expressed in the last group. On a greater scale, some influential scholars found that views such as Pannenberg's Christology were the most creative and original in some forty years.[132] This newly championed emphasis on the role of history is perhaps typified by Brown's complaint that just because Jesus's resurrection and exaltation alongside the giving of the Holy Spirit all have strong eschatological dimensions, this does not necessitate the removal of Jesus's appearances from historical research.[133] For sure, even though some of these scholars hedged on the bodily nature of Jesus's appearances, it is more than obvious that several new ideas had now been placed on the table for further research and discussion.

---

[128] Leonhard Goppelt, "The Easter Kerygma in the New Testament," in Goppelt, Thielicke, and Müller-Schwefe, *Easter Message Today*, 44–52.

[129] A. M. Ramsey, *The Resurrection of Christ* (London: Collins, 1961), 35–74.

[130] James D. G. Dunn, *The Evidence for Jesus* (Philadelphia: Westminster, 1985), 66–78.

[131] James D. G. Dunn, *Jesus Remembered*, vol. 1 of *Christianity in the Making* (Grand Rapids: Eerdmans, 2003), 828–41, 855, 864–65, 873–79, 882; Dunn, *Why Believe in Jesus' Resurrection?* (London: SPCK, 2016), 31–34, 39–40.

[132] Such as the comments by theologians Carl E. Braaten and even John B. Cobb Jr. on the dust jacket of the first English edition of Pannenberg's volume, *Jesus: God and Man*.

[133] Brown, *Virginal Conception*, 125–26.

The fifth and last model to be discussed here comprises scholars who agreed with the previous group that the historical and other evidence refutes naturalistic theories, that Jesus's burial tomb was discovered to be empty very soon after his death, and that Jesus actually rose and then appeared alive to his followers. But the primary difference between this model and the prior two is that, additionally, the scholars in this fifth group held firmly to the position that Jesus rose and appeared bodily. Granted, there are many different conceptions of the term "body" as well as shades of meaning, frequently making this a difficult issue to decipher precisely.[134]

For our purposes here, it will be specified that the chief notion utilized by those in this last group is the sense more or less described in the Gospels, though with occasional caveats. But it ought to be noted carefully that this view is generally not necessarily held because the Gospels state such a position but because it is often held increasingly by scholars at present that Paul also held a comparable view. On the one hand, these reports do describe several indications that Jesus's body had been transformed in some sense. The stone walls did not impede Jesus leaving the burial tomb. He appeared and disappeared elsewhere as well. Additionally, he was not always recognized by those who saw him. Yet, he still rose and appeared in a physical body, with the wounds of Roman crucifixion still present.[135]

It must be admitted that it is still sometimes difficult to ascertain who holds this general concept of Jesus's resurrection body and who does not for more than one reason. Some of the scholars already discussed above also espouse the position that Jesus was raised bodily. This appears to be quite clear, for example, in the works of Karl Barth and Thomas Torrance.[136] Although Marcus Barth, Goppelt, and Ramsey likewise make this point, at least the last two regard the view taken by Luke and John as being too drastic.[137] In the case of Richard R. Niebuhr, though

---

[134] This important topic is discussed in more detail in volume 4 of this study.

[135] As noted above, these five positions incorporate a number of close nuances. Some interpreters may well even conclude that there is too narrow a focus precisely at this point and collapse the fifth model back into the fourth. Or as a sort of halfway position, this fifth view could be categorized as a development of the previous view and treated as a subcategory.

[136] See Karl Barth, *Church Dogmatics*, 4.1:351–42; Torrance, *Space, Time, and Resurrection*, 26, 164, 171.

[137] Goppelt, "Easter Kerygma in the New Testament," 43, 47–49; Ramsey, *Resurrection of Christ*, 108–9; cf. M. Barth and Fletcher, *Acquittal by Resurrection*, vi, 9, 11.

he affirms the historicity of the resurrection appearances, the bodily element is not quite as clear.[138]

Many (though not necessarily all) of the scholars who constitute this fifth model were generally more conservative.[139] One example of distinctive contributions by some of these scholars can be observed in the volumes they published on these subjects. Fuller Seminary professor George Eldon Ladd situated a defense of the resurrection within the context of a brief apologetic for both the Gospel passages as well as Paul's testimony, one that faced squarely the contemporary critical challenges.[140] Another Fuller Seminary professor, Daniel Fuller, presented a masterful survey of contemporary twentieth-century trends on the resurrection followed by championing the Luke-Acts corpus as an excellent means of answering critical objections.[141] Both of these texts supported treatments of the empty tomb and the bodily nature of Jesus's post-resurrection appearances.

At least one crucial observation describes some scholars whose views extend across all five of these models and thus should be mentioned here as well. Namely, a stream of sophisticated research has provided very intricate evaluations of the New Testament data concerning the sort of body in which Jesus's early followers *believed* that he appeared after his resurrection. These observations and others like them have even grown in influence to the extent that these researchers across all five models have tended to move in the direction of embracing what has been identified as bodily appearances in the biblical accounts, even if the commentator making the point did not personally endorse that position. In other words, it has progressively been recognized that the New Testament witnesses regarded Jesus's appearances as being bodily in nature, with different nuances among these commentators.

Robert Gundry's influential work on New Testament anthropology included a chapter devoted to the crucial subject of Paul's agreement with the Gospel authors regarding the nature of Jesus's resurrection body. Gundry concluded,

---

[138] Niebuhr, *Resurrection and Historical Reason*, 175.

[139] It could likewise be remarked here that this is in contrast to the first model above, which consisted of positions that were generally held almost entirely by nonconservative scholars, while the other three models may be viewed as various stages between these two positions.

[140] George Eldon Ladd, *I Believe in the Resurrection of Jesus* (Grand Rapids: Eerdmans, 1975), see chaps. 7–8 in particular.

[141] Daniel P. Fuller, *Easter Faith and History* (Grand Rapids: Eerdmans, 1965), esp. chaps. 7–8.

"Paul uses *sōma* precisely because the physicality of the resurrection is central to his soteriology."[142]

Later volumes devoted to this same theme have continued to emerge, arriving at quite similar conclusions on the New Testament teaching. These include massive works on the intricate meanings of the relevant terms, such as N. T. Wright's *The Resurrection of the Son of God* and John Cook's *Empty Tomb, Resurrection, Apotheosis*.[143] Wright asserts that the key terms for resurrection (such as *anastasis* and *egeirō*) had a constant bodily meaning "until we come to a new coinage in the second century."[144] The initial theme of Cook's volume is that "there is no fundamental difference between Paul's conception of the resurrection body and that of the Gospels."[145] These sources agree in concluding that even Paul viewed Jesus's appearances as being bodily in nature. Likewise, Michael Licona's *The Resurrection of Jesus* contains a detailed treatment of these matters.[146] Licona's conclusion, which is similar to Wright's, is that no "known author from the eighth century B.C. through the third century A.D. employed these terms to contrast *physical* and *immaterial* bodies."[147] Thus, bodily events are often thought to be in view with regard to Jesus's appearances. Other major works have added to these conclusions.[148]

---

[142] Robert Gundry, *Sōma in Biblical Theology: With Emphasis on Pauline Anthropology* (Cambridge: Cambridge University Press, 1976; repr., Grand Rapids: Zondervan, 1987), esp. chap. 13, entitled "The Sōma in Death and Resurrection."

[143] N. T. Wright, *The Resurrection of the Son of God*, vol. 3 of *Christian Origins and the Question of God* (Minneapolis: Fortress, 2003), 3:85–398, featuring crucial ideas here on xvii, xix, 31, 71, 82–83, 201–6, 273, 314, 321, 350–74, 414, 476–79; John Cook, *Empty Tomb, Resurrection, Apotheosis* (Tübingen: Mohr Siebeck, 2018), 1, 54–55, 591, 618, 623, and elsewhere throughout this text.

[144] Wright, *Resurrection of the Son of God*, 31 and elsewhere.

[145] Cook, *Empty Tomb*, 1.

[146] Michael R. Licona, *The Resurrection of Jesus: A New Historiographical Approach* (Downers Grove, IL: InterVarsity Academic, 2010), with his linguistic study on 400–437.

[147] Licona, 416.

[148] For just a few more of these sources that at least lean in this general direction, see Brown, *Virginal Conception*, 85–92; Torrance, *Space, Time, and Resurrection*, xi, 87, 164, 171; William Lane Craig, *Assessing the New Testament Evidence for the Historicity of the Resurrection of Jesus* (Lewiston, NY: Mellen, 1989), 158, 393–95, cf. 345–46; cf. also Andrew Loke's conclusions in his *Investigating the Resurrection of Jesus Christ: A New Transdisciplinary Approach* (Oxford: Routledge, 2020), 201–6; and in Loke, "The Resurrection of Jesus: An Engagement with Dale Allison: A Review Essay," in *Philosophia Christi* 24 (2022): 121–38, particularly 125–26. Michael R. Licona even thinks that the bodily aspect of Jesus's postresurrection appearances is strong enough according to recent scholars to consider the

It must be noted carefully here once again that the issue being discussed is *not* whether or in what form Jesus may actually have appeared, but rather what the canonical authors are thought to have held on the subject of Jesus's resurrection body. This conclusion alone is very important because the situation has essentially changed since the mid-twentieth-century ideas that have largely been discussed in this chapter.

At present, the overall current view has perhaps even reached the tipping point in this matter, with many scholars agreeing with the thesis that, at least for the earliest Christians, the primary view in the New Testament writings was that Jesus appeared bodily to his followers. At present, this view is shared by many recent scholars, including representatives from each of the five models introduced in this chapter, that is, across the entire liberal-conservative spectrum. This includes atheist, agnostic, and self-identified non-Christian researchers.[149] Of course, such scholarly agreement does not make this view true, but it must be recognized that some major changes of opinion have emerged on this issue due not to any sort of headcount but to the textual data thought to account for these trends.

In sum, the fifth model holds many of the characteristics of the fourth, though exhibiting a firmer commitment to the historicity of the empty tomb, including

---

inclusion of this notion as a minimal fact; see Licona, "In Reply to Habermas, McGrew, and McCullagh," *Southeastern Theological Review* 3 (2012): 55–56. In the volume *Resurrection: Theological and Scientific Assessments*, ed. Ted Peters, Robert John Russell, and Michael Welker (Grand Rapids: Eerdmans, 2002), several of the authors favor these more bodily elements in the resurrection appearances of Jesus, with this aspect also being extended to Jesus's followers. See in this volume Robert John Russell, "Bodily Resurrection, Eschatology, and Scientific Cosmology: The Mutual Interaction of Christian Theology and Science," 25; Michael Welker, "Theological Realism and Eschatological Symbol Systems," 38; John Polkinghorne, "Eschatological Credibility: Emergent and Teleological Processes," 49; Jeffrey P. Schloss, "From Evolution to Eschatology," 69–71; Peter Lampe, "Paul's Concept of a Spiritual Body," 105–10; and Hans-Joachim Eckstein, "Bodily Resurrection in Luke," 116–23.

[149] Some of the very critical scholars who basically agree on this view, as categorized above, include Dale C. Allison Jr., *The Resurrection of Jesus: Apologetics, Polemics, History* (London: T&T Clark, 2021), 131–36, 224–25; Allison, *Resurrecting Jesus: The Earliest Christian Tradition and Its Interpreters* (London: T&T Clark, 2005), 317, 324–25; John Dominic Crossan and Jonathan L. Reed, *In Search of Paul: How Jesus's Apostle Opposed Rome's Empire with God's Kingdom. A New Vision of Paul's Words and World* (New York: HarperCollins, 2004), 6–10, 173, 296, 341–45; Gerd Lüdemann, *The Resurrection of Jesus: History, Experience, Theology* (Minneapolis: Fortress, 1994), 35, 177, 200–201n145; Bart D. Ehrman, *How Jesus Became God: The Exaltation of a Jewish Preacher from Galilee* (New York: HarperCollins, 2014), 132–33, 168–69, 176–78; cf. Geza Vermes, *The Resurrection* (London: Penguin, 2008), 6–7, 75–78, 134.

developing further arguments for this event. The major distinctive here is the firm position regarding the bodily nature of Jesus's resurrection appearances. Intriguingly, it was hardly realized by critical scholars at the time that this fifth emerging view would become a major critical position just a few decades later. This was not the overall position in the mid-twentieth century.

Conclusion

In retrospect, several significant observations may be drawn from across this overview of mid-twentieth-century resurrection models. One major conclusion derived from both this chapter as well as from discussions elsewhere in these volumes is that amid the opposition to the resurrection event characteristic of scholars categorized in the first model, the utilization of naturalistic theses that oppose this occurrence seems to have diminished significantly among them, and even more so moving into the twenty-first century.[150] Scholars in the first model objected to the historicity of this event, but often did so without espousing specific alternative theses. This is particularly the case where a scholar was willing to embrace just a single hypothesis, including the possibility of having that view disproven.

A second aspect is found too commonly among both very influential scholars and less prominent writers during this period. Even while addressing the specific historical subjects that have most concerned us here, these authors tended to either utilize tendencies such as dialectical "back-and-forth" language or employ imprecise terms like "vision," making it difficult to identify precisely their historical responses to the central questions being addressed. As a result, even a very experienced resurrection scholar who is used to such moves can still feel unsure publishing their description of another scholar's views, despite having read over their work several times.

This can be a frustrating characteristic of some authors, perhaps as holdovers from the dialectical methods of the Barth and Bultmann eras when these tendencies were far more common.[151] Now it is certainly possible that the reader is the one who

---

[150] It is noteworthy that two of the best-known critical scholars who embraced single naturalistic resurrection theses, Gerd Lüdemann and John Shelby Spong, both passed away in 2021, leaving even fewer of those who made these choices.

[151] For example, as already noted, in his early work Barth had the habit of answering questions regarding the historicity of the resurrection with both yes and no responses. An instance could be taken from Barth's famous 1918 commentary, *The Epistle to the Romans*, where he entertains the historical question pertaining to Jesus's resurrection and refers to

missed something. However, it seems likely that on other occasions some authors may have been somewhat unsure of their *own* positions on the current state of the research or perhaps changed their view at some later time. Such propensities likewise could have occurred chiefly among those who do not wish to be labeled or pinned down on these difficult issues. Or perhaps the effort was to protect a position from the watchful eye of modern science. It is even likely that for some researchers, especially at the beginning of the breakaway from their former major German liberal professors, it was simply easier in human terms not to upset the status quo so completely. Others may simply have adjusted their positions later.[152]

"the see-saw of 'Yes' and 'No'. . . which is characteristic of all that happens on the historical plane" (204). In his 1920 address, "Biblical Questions, Insights, and Vistas," Barth stated his early views on this subject: "The resurrection of Christ . . . is not a historical event . . . though it is the only real happening *in* is not a real happening *of* history" (*Word of God*, 90). Many readers, it is feared, would respond after reading these last words with "Huh?" accompanied at the very least by a shrug of the shoulders. Then in his 1922 address, "The Word of God and the Task of the Ministry," we have still other instances where Barth also applies his yes and no response to issues (*Word of God*, 207, 216).

    While not as commonly as with Barth, Bultmann's ambiguity was often manifest in his constant interchanging of the German terms *geschichtlich* and *historisch*, the translations of which need constantly to be kept in mind at the risk of severely misunderstanding a discussion on the historicity of the event in question. In Bultmann's essay "New Testament and Mythology," where the gospel message is the focus esp. on page 37, the translator supplies the German terms in an attempt to keep confusion to a minimum. This also might be contrasted with Hans Küng's yes and no response while addressing the question of bodily resurrection in his *Eternal Life? Life after Death as a Medical, Philosophical, and Theological Problem*, trans. Edward Quinn (Garden City, NY: Doubleday, 1984; repr., Eugene, OR: Wipf & Stock, 2002), 111.

    [152] Another scholar who was at least a candidate for these difficult expressions in his resurrection view is John Hick in his volume *Death and Eternal Life* (New York: Harper & Row, 1976), esp. 171–77. (A new edition of this book was published by Westminster John Knox in 1994, including the same pagination in both editions.) This situation was at least doubly puzzling in Hick's case because, in another of his books published at about the same time as the earlier edition here, he appeared to report his view quite differently; see Hick, *The Center of Christianity* (New York: Harper & Row, 1978), 25–26. Then, in a dialogue that we had on the historicity of the resurrection appearances (along with a few other scholars) just a few years later at Louisiana State University, Hick concluded by espousing an entirely different position from his response in *The Center of Christianity*, favoring a view that is probably closest to our third model in this chapter!

    Still another candidate for such a difficulty of expression was Hans Küng, especially in his views on the resurrection found in two of his volumes (*On Being a Christian*, 348–53;

A third fascinating feature that emerges from the study of these resurrection models is that it could matter significantly when the individual works were written. For example, those scholars who were publishing in the 1950s and the early 1960s were far more likely to be quite reticent both in what stance they took as well as how they expressed it. The overall earlier tendency was not to express much exuberance or bombast when mentioning pro-historical comments or positive considerations in favor of Jesus's resurrection appearances, but rather to discuss them only briefly, often with hints, and perhaps even downplay these angles just a bit. It seems that this hesitance might have disappeared entirely if the same author were writing on this subject just a couple of decades later.[153] There were several times in reviewing these

---

Eternal Life?, 91–112) where his positions are contrasted. A lesser-known example is that of James McLeman, *Resurrection Then and Now* (Philadelphia: Lippincott, 1967), esp. chaps. 12–18, where many of our key historical issues of interest are discussed.

[153] Most of these moves appear to have migrated in the direction toward greater acceptance of the resurrection's historicity, as will be noted below, because these were the overall predominant trends in both theology as a whole as well as with the specific resurrection questions. Of course, these views could have moved in the other direction as well, from more to less historical views. An example of the latter was theologian William Hamilton, whose early, popularly written little commentaries on the Gospels still mildly registered some critical points here and there but plainly affirmed the resurrection and appearances of Jesus in historical terms. See Hamilton's *The Modern Reader's Guide to Mark* (New York: Association, 1959), 121–25; or his *The Modern Reader's Guide to John* (New York: Association, 1959), 119–24. Of the two, his historical comments on Mark are slightly more positive. In a more scholarly volume, Hamilton still affirmed the following strongly worded comments in 1961: "I find myself in fairly strenuous opposition to that tradition in contemporary theology which denies the resurrection as an ordinary event on the one hand, while giving it a profound existential meaning on the other." Continuing, he stated rather clearly, "I believe that the resurrection of Jesus can be affirmed as an ordinary event; the empty tomb tradition, at least, seems to me to contain historical material of a high degree of probability." Then he drew these comments together: "But there can be no meaning for faith, I am sure, without this historical texture." See William Hamilton, *The New Essence of Christianity: Laying Claim to Those Few Things That Are Certain* (New York: Association, 1961), 115–16n34. But Hamilton grew more and more "radical" in later years, even being one of the better-known proponents of the Death of God movement during the 1960s. One of his works that is quite far removed from the ones just mentioned was coauthored with Thomas J. J. Altizer, *Radical Theology and the Death of God* (Indianapolis, IN: Bobbs-Merrill, 1966). Another is William Hamilton's *On Taking God out of the Dictionary* (New York: McGraw-Hill, 1974).

An example of a slight move in the opposite direction from more to less skepticism is that of influential New Testament scholar Willi Marxsen, listed in our first model in this

publications when taking a guess at the copyright date based on *how* the author expressed their views sometimes hit the vicinity quite closely.

A fourth observation is that some intriguing connections *between* these five models appear to have emerged, although it is difficult to be dogmatic here. The third group seems to be a more recent development growing out of the second, where it was seemingly concluded that Karl Barth and the others upon whom he had such a powerful influence placed too much emphasis on the disjunction between history and faith. In that sense it could be seen as a parallel move made by the Second Quest for the historical Jesus scholars as they similarly developed out from the so-called No Quest period led by Barth and Bultmann, due to the stated failure of these two luminaries to employ much historical investigation.

Model four is a more recent defense of the resurrection among critical scholars who might be viewed partially as reacting against the naturalistic assumptions held by those in the first model. Like the third model, the fourth also contains scholars who objected strenuously to the emphasis of those we located in the second model who opposed historical reasons for faith. But it did not proceed as far as the more traditional, often orthodox view represented by those constituting the fifth model, perhaps due to the latter placing more emphasis on the Gospel data.[154] On the last point, it is rather intriguing that a few of N. T. Wright's and Stephen Neill's dozen

---

chapter and whose volume *The Resurrection of Jesus of Nazareth* has been mentioned above. Later in his career, he wrote another text on the same subject entitled *Jesus and Easter: Did God Raise the Historical Jesus from the Dead?*, trans. Victor Paul Furnish (Nashville: Abingdon, 1990), one that is more measured and a little more positive in its conclusions, tending away from some of his earlier, more radical comments that were somewhat in the direction of agnosticism.

[154] This is not to say that there is antipathy between the scholars of the fourth and fifth models over the historical nature of the four canonical Gospels. Actually, many scholarly volumes that are not easily labeled as to their theological stripe have made major advances in recent years by defending the historicity of the Gospels, either as a whole or in part. Just a very small group of such instances would include Richard Bauckham, *Jesus and the Eyewitnesses: The Gospels as Eyewitness Evidence* (Grand Rapids: Eerdmans, 2006); Richard A. Burridge, *What Are the Gospels? A Comparison with Graeco-Roman Biography* (Cambridge: Cambridge University Press, 1992); James D. G. Dunn, *Jesus Remembered*; Dunn, *Beginning from Jerusalem*, vol. 2 of *Christianity in the Making* (Grand Rapids: Eerdmans, 2009); Dunn, *The Oral Gospel Tradition* (Grand Rapids: Eerdmans, 2013). Some older critical texts also exhibited some of these positive characteristics as well, such as A. T. Hunter, *Bible and Gospel*, and John A. T. Robinson's *Can We Trust the Gospels?*, both mentioned above, plus Robinson's magnum opus, *The Priority of John*, ed. J. F. Coakley (London: SCM, 1985).

developments they identified in New Testament studies since 1861 concern positive developments related to the state of Gospel study.[155]

Conversely, models one and five may be viewed as direct antitheses with almost totally divergent views on the nature of the New Testament as a reliable historical document. Models two and four are also rivals on the issue of historicity, especially, as alluded to earlier, where the so-called Christology from below of the Pannenberg school was widely seen as a reaction to Barth's and Emil Brunner's Christology from above.[156]

It is also very important to note that of these five models, only the first is specifically characterized by a rejection of (or an agnostic attitude toward) the resurrection and appearances of the risen Jesus. Each of the other four groups accepts the historicity of these events,[157] in spite of downplaying the role of historical research by the second model,[158] plus perhaps a few other caveats here and there.

Just as significant in terms of the last consideration is the observation that the first model is largely represented by those scholars who have lost the vast majority of their influence in recent decades. As indicated in the very first line of Carl F. H. Henry's published interviews with many of the major early 1960s European theologians, "After ruling German theology for more than a decade, Rudolf Bultmann is no longer its king."[159]

True, other advocates of the nonhistoricity of the resurrection have taken up much of the slack. However, those engaged in the most recent research almost uniformly

---

[155] Stephen Neill and Tom Wright, *The Interpretation of the New Testament, 1861–1986*, 2nd ed. (Oxford: Oxford University Press, 1988), 360–64.

[156] Henry states, "Pannenberg represents the farthest contemporary break from Barth and Bultmann and the dialectical theology." See Henry, *Frontiers in Modern Theology*, 40.

[157] Once again, as mentioned at the outset, the overview in this chapter was broad, hence necessitating generalities rather than detailed expositions of these five positions. Concerning the second group in particular, it has already been noted specifically that it is difficult to ascertain in all instances whether or not the resurrection is actually being affirmed as a literal event due to the language employed. However, since many in this group do indeed accept a literal resurrection, rejecting this event is therefore not some sort of internal characteristic of the second group as a whole, as it is with the first.

[158] It needs to be emphasized that even the Barthian school (and most certainly Barth himself) did not necessarily reject the resurrection as a historical event. Though sometimes placing this event's factual status in another, undefined historical realm, as we have seen, this model's chief issue was the concern over the search for historical data, evidence, and what it thought was the downplaying of the importance of faith and revelation.

[159] Henry, *Frontiers in Modern Theology*, 9.

utilize different methods than those who held these views in the middle of the twentieth century. In other words, the more recent critical scholars have moved on to new territory. Still, the new skeptical researchers neither possess the magnetism nor the influence that Rudolf Bultmann's views did during the mid-twentieth century.[160] Moreover, varying positions that support the facticity of the resurrection appearances are presently much more popular than the highly skeptical positions.

Fifth and last, we alluded during this chapter to what some may view as quite a strange but largely uniform phenomenon in resurrection studies. Across all five models, there is a strong tendency throughout the twentieth and into the twenty-first century to find enormous amounts of meaning in the resurrection event, especially for practical application to Christian lives today. This quite intriguingly includes even some very skeptical thinkers for whom Jesus never rose in the first place! This trend extends to the majority of the researchers across all five models.

For example, Bultmann's famous pronouncement is that even though Jesus's resurrection is mythical, Jesus is somehow still risen in the church's preaching. As he asserts: "Christ meets us in the preaching as one crucified and risen. He meets us in the word of preaching and nowhere else. The faith of Easter is just this—faith in the word of preaching."[161]

Another instance is Marxsen's somewhat similar proclamation that "one cannot believe in the resurrection *as an event which happened in the past*."[162] So Marxsen ends his book *Jesus and Easter* with the proclamation that, as such, the resurrection "cannot

---

[160] Only Karl Barth surpassed Bultmann in influence during the twentieth century. Interestingly, Barth's views also appear to be much more popular and influential today than are Bultmann's. This is especially true in places such as graduate schools and seminaries where many of Barth's ideas are still in vogue.

[161] Bultmann, "New Testament and Mythology," 41. Comments like this can be found throughout Bultmann's writings. Thomas Oden pointed out that, for Bultmann, the Christ event is the key to Christian ethics as well, *not* in the sense of God breaking into the natural or historical world with a miracle, which cannot be taken seriously. Nor can such acts be demonstrated in any way as historical fact. Rather, these realities are known only to "the eye of faith" since only faith apprehends their meaning. But Oden stated that he was not going to inquire in detail as to the specific nature of the Christ event. Thomas C. Oden, *Radical Obedience: The Ethics of Rudolf Bultmann* (Philadelphia: Westminster, 1964), esp. 82–88. Rudolf Bultmann wrote a response in the same volume, expressing his appreciation for the clear and accurate portrayal of his views, though with some caveats (141–47, particularly 144, 147).

[162] Marxsen, *Jesus and Easter*, 42.

provide any security for faith." However, the key to "all of this is on the basis of Jesus's invitation to faith. It is the living Lord who" can lead to the apprehension of truths such as our being able to "bring reconciliation," forgiveness, brotherhood, peace, faith, and so on. Further, we can still claim, "*To me* he is still present. *He*, the Jesus whom God has raised from the dead, has led me into this faith."[163]

This rather incredible juxtaposition maintained by those who do not accept the historicity of this event but still make these and other moves from Jesus's resurrection to theology, ethics, action, and involvement with others is simply amazing. But it is definitely a prominent feature of the contemporary theological landscape. The resurrection of Jesus has always "preached"![164]

---

[163] Marxsen, 91–92.

[164] Two more nonskeptical scholars from this time period who also developed detailed theses especially on the theological significance of the resurrection include G. Ernest Thomas, *The Meaning of the Resurrection in Christian Experience* (Nashville: Tidings, 1964); and Laurence W. Miller, *Jesus Christ Is Alive!* (Boston: Wilde, 1949).

8

Discrepancies and the Resurrection

Without much question, in terms of the frequency of the statements, the most common objection to the historical reliability of the Gospels in general, and to the resurrection accounts in particular, is that these texts contain numerous discrepancies and contradictions in the details. These comments are probably far more widespread among nonacademic critics than with the scholars. The implied (or often blatant) claim particularly among the more popular commentators is that such errors disqualify these sources from commenting on the message of Jesus's resurrection. More specifically, this position may include the notion that such erroneous claims indicate that the biblical authors could have gotten a lot more reports incorrect as well, especially since they were writing about supernatural occurrences.

The intent in this chapter is to comment on these claims in general by first surveying the scholarly horizon to illustrate this prevalent tendency while commenting more specifically on applications to resurrection studies. While making no effort whatsoever to harmonize the resurrection accounts here, a few representative examples will hopefully clearly indicate that sometimes it is a matter of simply allowing the text to speak for itself.[1] Many, though not all, of our examples of discrepancies and

---

[1] It is not so much that attempting to harmonize the crucifixion, burial, resurrection, and appearance accounts in the Gospels is an unscholarly pursuit, or that it does not work, or that it has been disproven, or that it is just plain silly, or so on. Discussions surrounding a single case or a small number of incidents are more commonly addressed

the critical sources are drawn from the resurrection and appearance accounts in the New Testament.

To set the stage here, critical scholar Reginald Fuller begins his influential book on the resurrection by framing the chief issue the way it is often thought of:

> The best way to discredit a witness in court is for the cross-examiner to tie him up in knots and make his evidence appear to be such a tissue of in- consistencies that the jury becomes convinced he is entirely untrustworthy. One does not need to be a scientific New Testament scholar to do that with the resurrection narratives.[2]

Fuller then adds: "It is no wonder that many have found these discrepancies a major obstacle to belief in the resurrection." Then he provides a few examples of those who

---

in the relevant literature than larger endeavors, where the overall goal seems to be to explain everything. Quite a surprising number of strong points have been made in the historical studies of the past, including even by liberal scholars themselves. A number of newer and more recent approaches have also indicated even ingenious paths to solving sometimes difficult scenarios. In the latter portion of this chapter, viable approaches in answering a few of these well-known cases will be attempted by way of example. But the *chief* reason for the hesitation on harmonizing is that when the minimal facts method is employed, seeming discrepancies are definitely secondary—not because they are unimportant or given up for lost causes, but because if the very center of the gospel message (at a minimum) of the deity, death, and resurrection appearances of Jesus obtains, the case itself is established. Thus, if additional time needs to be spent on the tough questions for any reason, so be it. But the straightforward point here is that this is not an absolute necessity. Virtually nothing turns on cases that are decided to the satisfaction of most. Having stated this, however, it is important to indicate that the Gospel texts can still be shown to be reliable, especially where they stand strongly in the face of strong accusations.

[2] Reginald H. Fuller, *The Formation of the Resurrection Narratives* (New York: Macmillan), 2. Then Fuller lists some of these inconsistencies (2–5, also 125), yet he calls them "minor" (5). James D. G. Dunn also makes the comparison between conflicts in testimony and court cases in *The Evidence for Jesus* (Louisville: Westminster, 1985), 64. Howard Clark Kee begins one of his volumes similarly, except that Kee employs the court case scenario very positively due to the fact that the Christian message would actually make the grade in the courtroom! This seems to be high praise, especially from a scholar who is listed as a member of the Jesus Seminar on the Westar Institute website as of July 23, 2018 (https:// www.westarinstitute.org/membership/westar-fellows/fellows-directory/)! See Kee, *What Can We Know about Jesus? Understanding Jesus Today* (Cambridge: Cambridge University Press, 1990), esp. 1–2.

have struggled with these issues.[3] And yet, Fuller holds that Jesus did indeed appear to his disciples![4] It is intriguing to observe how critical scholars pose the problem, sometimes thinking of modern courtroom situations, and then observe the responses. Actually, many other scholars make similar moves as Fuller.

A Historical Survey on the Near Unanimity of Citing Contradictions

The purpose of this initial section is to present a historical review of critical responses to these issues. Beginning with nineteenth-century German liberalism and a few of its forerunners, the goal is to work toward the present in a fairly detailed overview. For well over 200 years, the charge of New Testament (especially Gospel) discrepancies and contradictions is easily the most commonly raised objection to the belief that these texts present reliable information, especially concerning Jesus being raised from the dead. Conversely, addressing and answering this overall problem successfully would be a very helpful means of opening the way for the many additional chapters later in this volume that treat and address the more specific naturalistic hypotheses aimed at these Christian claims.

The scholars treated below are organized according to their time periods and schools of thought. While the bottom line may be close to the same, each set of similar views emerges from particular backgrounds and sets of presuppositions. Strangely enough, the wide variety of criticisms could move across a spectrum from the charge of errors and contradictions in Scripture, as addressed in this chapter, to a variety of similar critical allegations. Later chapters focus on the problems with biblical miracles and supernatural claims, the assimilation of mythology, and so forth. A large variety of these examples could be found across differing groups and views.

Old German Liberalism

The precursors and forerunners to the German liberalism of the nineteenth and early twentieth centuries were much clumsier, to be sure. But the assumption that the Gospels were errant in some sense was common in English deism as well as with

---

[3] Fuller, *Formation of the Resurrection Narratives*, this additional quotation is on 5, with a short list of those who stumbled over these problems on 5–6.

[4] Fuller, 46–49, 180–83.

the various strands of continental rationalism, such as those of Benedict Spinoza or Hermann Samuel Reimarus.[5]

Old German liberalism hit the ground running. Early to mid-nineteenth-century liberals who often held a mixture of these critical positions included Friedrich Schleiermacher,[6] F. C. Baur,[7] David Strauss,[8] and Ernest Renan.[9] More than a few of their positions were aimed at the resurrection of Jesus.[10]

Mid-nineteenth to early twentieth-century liberals often went in new directions. Perhaps taking their leads from a few of the more radical thinkers who emphasized mythology, such as Strauss, Bruno Bauer, and Renan, these later writers often followed the paths of searching for rival mythologies in the ancient world. While not being the case for Johannes Weiss,[11] the movement known as the *religionsgeschichtliche Schule* (history of religions school) was contributed to by the works of scholars

[5] For English deism, note Thomas Woolston, *A Sixth Discourse on the Miracles of our Saviour, In View of the Present Controversy between Infidels and Apostates* (London: Printed by the Author, 1729), 5, 14, 16, 19, 27, 47; Benedict Spinoza, *Theological–Political Treatise*, ed. Jonathan Israel (Cambridge: Cambridge University Press, 2007), in his chapters that comment on prophecy (1–2) and Scripture (7–13) in particular. Note also Reimarus's text as edited by Charles Voysey, *Fragments from Reimarus* (London: Williams & Norgate, 1879), chap. 5, sections 54–57.

[6] Friedrich Schleiermacher, *The Life of Jesus*, ed. Jack C. Verheyden, trans. S. Maclean Gilmour (Mifflintown, PA: Sigler, 1997), 205–9, 476, and esp. the pages listed in note 10.

[7] Ferdinand Christian Baur, *Paul the Apostle of Jesus Christ: His Life and Works, His Epistles and Teachings; A Contribution to a Critical History of Primitive Christianity*, trans. A. Menzies, 2 vols. (London: Williams & Norgate, 1873, 1875; repr., Peabody, MA: Hendrickson, 2003), 1:5–8, 13, 34, 65, 112, 119–27, 255.

[8] David Friedrich Strauss, *The Life of Jesus, Critically Examined*, ed. Peter C. Hodgson, trans. George Eliot (Mifflintown, PA: Sigler, 1972), 86–92, 441, 461–62, 495, 518, 534.

[9] Ernest Renan, *Vie de Jésus* (Paris: Calmann-Levy, 1864), particularly chap. 15, "Commencement de la légende de Jésus. Idée qu'il a lui-même de son rôle surnaturel" (esp. 235–40) and chap. 16, "Miracles," plus esp. 243–48, 251.

[10] Schleiermacher, *Life of Jesus*, 415–17, 428–36, 440–44, 455–58, 463–65; Baur, *Paul*, 1:63–81, 109–11, 264; 2:251–53; Strauss, *Life of Jesus*, 563–74, 702–23, 741–44, 753, 755; Renan, *Vie de Jésus*, 310, 418–22.

[11] Johannes Weiss, *Jesus' Proclamation of the Kingdom of God*, trans. and ed. Richard Hyde Hiers and David Larrimore Holland (Philadelphia: Fortress, 1971; repr., Mifflintown, PA: Sigler, 1999), 65–66, 73–74, 129–30. The original edition of the German of this work was published in 1892.

like Otto Pfleiderer,[12] Wilhelm Bousset,[13] and perhaps, to a somewhat lesser extent, Ernst Troeltsch.[14] As earlier in German liberalism, the resurrection was still often the main target.[15] For believers, Jesus's resurrection was the center of the Christian faith, so for many unbelievers it was the chief target!

Albert Schweitzer's monumental study *The Quest of the Historical Jesus* cast its very long shadow over much of German liberalism.[16] This work is absolutely replete with dozens of references to different authors, some from more than a century in the past, and their unanimous persuasion of the contradictions, errors, and other problems in the New Testament along with many different and rather wild scenarios, including naturalistic comments against the resurrection.[17] (Schweitzer includes very few positive comments on the subject.)[18]

---

[12] Otto Pfleiderer, *The Early Christian Conception of Christ: Its Significance and Value in the History of Religion* (London: Williams & Norgate, 1905), 7–9, 14. This entire volume consists of a comparison between Christianity and many claimed parallel beliefs in ancient religious views on the subjects of "Christ as the Son of God" (chapter 1), "Christ as Conqueror of Satan" (chapter 2), "Christ as a Wonder-Worker" (chapter 3), "Christ as the Conqueror of Death and the Life-Giver" (chapter 4), and "Christ as the King of Kings and Lord of Lords" (chapter 5).

[13] Wilhelm Bousset, *Kyrios Christos: A History of the Belief in Christ from the Beginnings of Christianity to Irenaeus*, trans. John E. Steely (Nashville: Abingdon, 1970), 47–48, 188–94. The original German edition was first published in 1913.

[14] Ernst Troeltsch, *Writings on Theology and Religion*, ed. and trans. Robert Morgan and Michael Pye (Louisville: Westminster John Knox, 1990), 189, 192; Troeltsch, *The Christian Faith*, ed. Gertrud von le Fort, trans. Garrett E. Paul (Minneapolis: Fortress, 1991), 88.

[15] Johannes Weiss, *Jesus' Proclamation*, 83–84, cf. 130; Pfleiderer, *Early Christian Conception of Christ*, chapter 4; Bousset, *Kyrios Christos*, 57–59, 191–94, though positive notes on the resurrection are also present (58, 120); Troeltsch, *Christian Faith*, 88–89, 96.

[16] Albert Schweitzer, *The Quest of the Historical Jesus: A Critical Study of Its Progress from Reimarus to Wrede*, trans. W. Montgomery (New York: Macmillan, 1968).

[17] Schweitzer, *Quest of the Historical Jesus*, includes brief comparisons to Buddha (291), Jesus being mistaken about the time of his return (353, 358–60), and many naturalistic resurrection hypotheses, a few of which include the fictional swoon theories of Karl Friedrich Bahrdt (42–43) and Karl Heinrich Venturini (44–47), and Heinrich Paulus's more serious swoon theory (53–54), all from 1782 to 1828; the emphasis on myths and subjective visions by Strauss, Renan, and some of the attendant problems as well (83–84, 187).

[18] But see Albert Schweitzer's provocative though unexplained comments in his volume, *Out of My Life and Thought: An Autobiography*, trans. C. T. Campion (New York: Holt, 1949), 40–41.

But Schweitzer also notes the downfall of German liberalism: "There is nothing more negative than the result of the critical study of the Life of Jesus. . . . He is a figure designed by rationalism, endowed with life by liberalism, and clothed by modern theology in an historical garb."[19] For Schweitzer, liberalism's Jesus "has fallen to pieces" from within because they made Jesus in their own image. The liberal Jesus is "too small," and these scholarly liberal studies "cannot call spiritual life into existence."[20]

So even though Schweitzer thought that several liberal scholars were correct in pointing out that Jesus was quite mistaken about the "delay" and "non-occurrence" of the Parousia, his teachings were still meaningful in the present because of his "mighty spiritual force" that flowed through him into our present world.[21] He is in some sense "spiritually arisen within men . . . not the historical Jesus, but the spirit which goes forth from Him . . . is that which overcomes the world." Emphasizing the last thought is the comment: "The abiding and eternal in Jesus is absolutely independent of historical knowledge and can only be understood by contact with His spirit which is still at work in the world."[22] Then Schweitzer closes his study by affirming the "world-accepting ethic" and "the world-affirming spirit" of the Jesus who called to us, "Follow thou me."[23]

The First Half of the Twentieth Century

If Schweitzer's shadow loomed large over the lengthy rise as well as the demise of nineteenth-century German liberalism, the shadows cast by Karl Barth and Rudolf Bultmann were even larger in the twentieth century. Barth (in particular) as well as Bultmann began by lending very willing and helping hands to the fall of German liberalism, under whose last leaders these two scholars had studied. Having treated at some length earlier the passing of the torch from this form of liberalism to the

---

[19] Schweitzer, *Quest of the Historical Jesus*, 398.

[20] Schweitzer, 398–400.

[21] Schweitzer, 353, 358–60, with the words quoted above from 360.

[22] These citations are from Schweitzer's forceful close to this study on 399 and 401.

[23] Schweitzer, 402–3. Many years later in his autobiography, still repeating that Jesus's future expectations were incorrect (*Out of My Life*, 39, 57), Schweitzer still issued these same words with which he ended his *Quest* volume many years earlier: "Follow thou Me!" (56, similarly, 54).

decades-long hiatus of studies on the historical Jesus, this changeover will not be belabored here.

Yet, even with Barth's more conservative tendencies, he too located "obscurities and irreconcilable contradictions" in New Testament texts, even finding fault with Paul's treatment of the resurrection in 1 Corinthians 15. Barth especially objected to notions that favored claims that Paul was attempting to give "proof" of the resurrection appearances. Barth preferred terms such as "pre-historical" even though the resurrection is definitely "an event in space and time."[24]

Elsewhere, Barth stated clearly enough: "Unquestionably, the resurrection narratives are contradictory. A coherent history cannot be evolved from them." He then specified that appearances in both Galilee and Jerusalem "cannot be harmonized. It is a chaos." He also made his normal comment opposed to trying to prove the resurrection. He even added that harmonizing the accounts should not be attempted.[25]

In comparison to Barth's views on textual contradictions and the nature of history, Rudolf Bultmann was much more direct as well as radical. From the beginning, Bultmann was quite clear that the New Testament writings and the historical events they describe, in particular, were quite muddled. As such, Bultmann had no doubt that there were errors of various sorts and species. For example, prophetic preaching in the Old Testament was apparently translated into events in the New Testament.[26] The

---

[24] Karl Barth, *The Doctrine of Reconciliation*, vol. 4.1 of *Church Dogmatics*, ed. G. W. Bromiley and T. F. Torrance, trans. G. W. Bromiley (Edinburgh: T&T Clark, 1956), 334–37, 340, with the quoted phrases on 335 and 336. Barth's repeated opposition to "proof" is found especially on 335–36, 341, though Barth gives his unquestioned support for the historicity of Jesus's resurrection and appearances (esp. 351–53). More opposition to this notion of proof without sacrificing the truth of the resurrection is found especially in Barth's earlier works, such as *The Epistle to the Romans*, trans. Edwyn C. Hoskyns, 6th ed. (Oxford: Oxford University Press, 1933), 30, 195, 203–5, 381–82; Barth, "Biblical Questions, Insights, and Vistas," in *The Word of God and the Word of Man*, trans. Douglas Horton (New York: Harper & Brothers, 1956), 89–92; and perhaps most of all, Barth, *The Resurrection of the Dead*, trans. H. J. Stenning (New York: Revell, 1933), 130–43. Locating some of these ideas in Barth, though, can be *very difficult*, as these ideas are often not well stated and changed somewhat over the years. Even seasoned commentators often differ in discussions of Barth's ideas here.

[25] Karl Barth, *The Faith of the Church: A Commentary on the Apostle's Creed according to Calvin's Catechism*, ed. Jean-Louis Leuba, trans, by Gabriel Vahanian (London: Collins, 1960), particularly 92.

[26] It is difficult to read this distinction and not think of John Dominic Crossan's catchy notion of "History Remembered and Prophecy Historicized" as stated in the first chapter

result was our lack of assurance regarding the "considerable uncertainty" pertaining to the sorting out of Jesus's sayings. While Jesus definitely lived in history, many details were unknown.[27]

In Bultmann's famous 1941 essay "New Testament and Mythology," he began his section titled "The Resurrection" with the opening line: "But what of the resurrection? Is it not a mythical event pure and simple? Obviously it is not an event of past history."[28] These and similar themes show up throughout Bultmann's work, whether it was carrying on the German liberal theme of Jesus being mistaken about the time of his coming;[29] there being no proof or historical evidence for miracles;[30] reported events that never occurred, such as Jesus's predicting his resurrection;[31] or the subjectivity of history and its events.[32] While he agreed with Barth that there was no historical evidence for the resurrection, Bultmann disagreed with Barth in that he thought that Paul really intended the list of Jesus's appearances to serve as evidence, while Barth disagreed.[33]

Bultmann took such a strong stand against history as evidence for Christianity that some of his own disciples and former students reacted in an effort to bring back what would today be considered quite a nominal amount of historical

(and elsewhere) of his volume *Who Killed Jesus? Exposing the Roots of Anti-Semitism in the Gospel Story of the Death of Jesus* (New York: HarperCollins, 1995), 1–4.

[27] Rudolf Bultmann, "The Study of the Synoptic Gospels," in *Form Criticism: Two Essays on New Testament Research*, trans. Frederick C. Grant (New York: Harper & Brothers, 1962), 57–61.

[28] Rudolf Bultmann, "New Testament and Mythology," in Bultmann et al., *Kerygma and Myth: A Theological Debate*, ed. Hans Werner Bartsch, trans. Reginald H. Fuller (New York: Harper & Row, 1961), 38. Other relevant texts include 4–5, 10–11, 34–44 (including here and elsewhere the constant theme that we viewed in Barth regarding there being no historical proof for revelatory truths).

[29] Rudolf Bultmann, *Theology of the New Testament*, trans. Kendrick Grobel, 2 vols. (New York: Scribner's Sons, 1951, 1958), 1:22, 92–93; Bultmann, *Jesus Christ and Mythology* (New York: Scribner's Sons, 1958), 12–13.

[30] Bultmann, *Jesus Christ and Mythology*, 61–62, 71–72, 80, 84.

[31] Bultmann, *Theology of the New Testament*, 1:29, 83.

[32] Rudolf Bultmann, *History and Eschatology: The Presence of Eternity* (New York: Harper & Row, 1957), 118–22.

[33] Bultmann, "New Testament and Mythology," 39; Bultmann, *Theology of the New Testament*, 1:295.

information about Jesus backed by a relatively small amount of historical data. It was held that such information was necessary and indispensable to ground Jesus and his teachings as a real historical individual, not to be confused with mythology. Bultmann disagreed.[34] But that did not dissuade scholars like Ernst Käsemann, Günther Bornkamm, and James M. Robinson from a rather short-lived undertaking that came to be called, in the title of Robinson's book, *A New Quest of the Historical Jesus*.[35]

Having discussed this development in an earlier chapter, do we find anything changed regarding the reduction of interest on discrepancies or other critical stances in this new quest? While surely not as negative as Bultmann's research, similar critical emphases reoccurred. Most commonly seen was a similar resistance to "proof" or strong evidence for key kerygmatic historical truths along with emphasis still being placed on existential factors.[36] Also a similar emphasis on discrepancies and the growth of legend is found among these scholars, or the lack of assurance regarding

---

[34] Such as Bultmann, "New Testament and Mythology," 34–43; Bultmann, *Theology of the New Testament*, 2:250–51; Bultmann, *History and Eschatology*, 70, and chap. 8, esp. 115–22. Barth likewise disagreed on this matter when, late in his life, he also noticed this trend back toward history. See Barth, *How I Changed My Mind*, trans. John D. Godsey (Richmond, VA: Knox, 1966), 68–69.

[35] James M. Robinson, *A New Quest of the Historical Jesus* (London: SCM, 1959). Stephen Neill and N. T. Wright make a comment that may be summarized in terms of this movement not drifting overly far from Bultmann; see their volume, Stephen Neill and Tom Wright, *The Interpretation of the New Testament, 1861–1986*, 2nd ed. (Oxford: Oxford University Press, 1988), 288n1. This interlude in historical Jesus studies is now more commonly referred to as the Second Quest for the historical Jesus. For example, see Ben Witherington III, *The Jesus Quest: The Third Search for the Jew of Nazareth* (Downers Grove, IL: InterVarsity, 1995), 11–12. Witherington notes that the movement was "dead in the water by the early 1970s" (11) but some of the ideas also morphed into the period that is usually termed the Third Quest for the historical Jesus.

[36] Ernst Käsemann, "The Problem of the Historical Jesus," in *Essays on New Testament Themes* (London: SCM, 1962), also included in the anthology by Gregory W. Dawes, ed., *The Historical Jesus Quest: Landmarks in the Search for the Jesus of History*, rev. ed. (Louisville: Westminster John Knox, 2000), 281–84, 288–89, 299; Günther Bornkamm, *Jesus of Nazareth*, trans. Irene and Fraser McLuskey with James M. Robinson (New York: Harper & Row, 1960), 131–32, 180, 184; Robinson, *New Quest*, 90–92.

accurate reports in the Gospels.[37] But a fairly large number of more positive trends developed too.[38]

The End of the Twentieth Century to the First Quarter of the Twenty-First Century

Moving from those who may be considered earlier forerunners, such as Wolfhart Pannenberg,[39] into the Third Quest for the historical Jesus scholars,[40] we continue to

---

[37] Käsemann, "Problem of the Historical Jesus," 297, 300, 304; Bornkamm, *Jesus of Nazareth*, 66–67, 131, 175–78, 182–83. Though decades removed from this time, Robinson's later work on the mostly gnostic works from the Nag Hammadi find seemed to open up areas that may be thought to revert back to some of Bultmann's *religionsgeschichtliche* roots of alternate, even rival, movements to Christianity. See James M. Robinson, ed., *The Nag Hammadi Library in English* (New York: Harper & Row, 1977).

[38] This takes us beyond the focus here. But some examples are not difficult to locate, such as critical assessments and even critiques of these scholars' German liberal and Bultmannian forerunners, being more open to research options such as the value of the Gospels, sources for Jesus's existence, the new emphasis on historical aspects in Jesus's life including Jesus's healings and exorcisms, the centrality of the kingdom of God, the importance of personal decision-making and ethical actions, total commitment to Jesus, and last but most importantly in terms of this study, more positive evaluations of the empty tomb and the resurrection of Jesus. Details are found in Käsemann, "Problem of the Historical Jesus," 284, 288–89, 299–303, 306–7, 312; Bornkamm, *Jesus of Nazareth*, 27–29, 54–63, 67–69, 96–108, 130–31, 169–75, 180–86; Robinson, *New Quest*, 37, 64, 111–12, 121–22.

[39] Wolfhart Pannenberg, "Die Auferstehung Jesu—Historie und Theologie," in *Zeitschrift für Theologie und Kirche*, 91 (1994): 318–28; Pannenberg, *Die Auferstehung Jesu und die Zukunft des Menschen* (Munich: Minerva, 1978), 12–18; Pannenberg "Response to the Debate," in Gary R. Habermas and Antony G. N. Flew, *Did Jesus Rise from the Dead?*, ed. Terry Miethe (New York: Harper & Row, 1987), 125–35, esp. 132. Of course, one of Pannenberg's original efforts was his monumental break from Barthian and Bultmannian christological trends in his volume *Jesus: God and Man*, trans. Lewis L. Wilkins and Duane A. Priebe (Philadelphia: Westminster, 1968), 53–106, esp. 65–73, 89–106; Pannenberg, Rolf Rendtorff, Trutz Rendtorff, and Ulrich Wilckens, *Revelation as History*, ed. Wolfhart Pannenberg, trans. David Granskou (New York: Macmillan, 1969), see Pannenberg's introduction plus chap. 4, particularly 11–12, 125, 130, 140, 143; cf. G. E. Michalson Jr., "Pannenberg on the Resurrection and Historical Method," *Scottish Journal of Theology* 33 (1980): 345–59.

[40] It is worth being reminded again of the periodic discussions that emerged as to whether the scholars of the "New" or "Second Quest for the historical Jesus" were early forerunners of the "Third Quest for the historical Jesus" at all, or more accurately belonged

find that the majority of critical scholars place themselves somewhere along a lengthy continuum that holds that there are some very difficult texts in the Gospels that are best considered as inconsistencies if not actual discrepancies and even contradictions. Though fewer in number, some researchers still opted for the presence of legends and myths in these texts. The scholars entertained here are specialists in at least one of the relevant fields that impinge on the areas discussed.[41]

It will not always be easy to categorize recent scholars due admittedly to subjective categorizations as well as factors like when they hold positions in more than one group. This goal here will to be include researchers into three very general categories: (1) skeptics (including atheists, agnostics, and adherents of other religions who self-identify as non-Christians); (2) moderates (who at times may share similar views with the groups on either side of them); and (3) conservatives (who usually side with the New Testament texts in most situations, while still potentially agreeing that there clearly may be issues of one sort or another).[42]

---

either to the previous Bultmannian camp or even to Schleiermacher's German liberal movement before that. The views seem to favor the latter Bultmannian view. Again, see Neill and Wright, *Interpretation of the New Testament*, 288n1, cf. also 379, 397–99.

[41] When Bart D. Ehrman discusses examples of the relevant subjects that are pertinent as a background for studying the historical Jesus, he includes those trained in New Testament or early Christian studies (2), classics (19, 167), and ancient history and theology (20), though he also cites relevant contributions from other scholars as well. Other areas might include archaeology, Jewish studies, church history, religion, or philosophy (especially religious philosophy or philosophy of religion). The page numbers above are from Ehrman's text, *Did Jesus Exist? The Historical Argument for Jesus of Nazareth* (New York: HarperCollins, 2012).

[42] Other lists by scholars may be reminiscent here in one way or another. For example, John A. T. Robinson noted four categories of researchers in his book *Can We Trust the New Testament?* (Grand Rapids: Eerdmans, 1977). He included one radical view each on the far left and on the far right, which he termed "The Cynicism of the Foolish" and "The Fundamentalism of the Fearful." In between were two, more moderate positions: "The Skepticism of the Wise" and "The Conservatism of the Committed" (13–29). Robinson thinks that the last group of conservative scholars is quite well entrenched, and he even seems to identify it most with his own position (28–29). These are interesting comments, since Robinson had often been categorized with the radicals, as in his revolutionary text, *Honest to God* (Philadelphia: Westminster, 1963). Another study of this general sort was that by New Testament scholar Raymond E. Brown. Surveying four views as well, the radical views on the right and the left were, respectively, "Nonscholarly Conservatism" and "Nonscholarly Liberalism." The two more respected positions in between were "Scholarly Liberalism" and "Scholarly (Moderate) Conservatism" (4–15). Like Robinson, Brown

Only the third group here contains researchers who refer to themselves as inerrantists with regard to the New Testament. Though there are different definitional stances along with nuances even among these researchers, to be sure these scholars reject at least the presence of clear factual errors, particularly in the Gospel texts. Nonetheless, there are still scholars in this group who possess terminal degrees (quite often from nonconservative schools), specialize in relevant areas of research, usually have publications (sometimes major ones), and generally hold teaching positions in accredited colleges, universities, or seminaries. Among the reasons for including these scholars and their views in this chapter is that different definitions, nuances, and other issues preclude the knowledge of exact cookie-cutter responses as well as how strictly this is done. When explanations are given, even in critical settings, the response is often one of understanding and even agreement.[43]

Perhaps most importantly of all, it will be argued here that the greater scholarly community probably includes comparable numbers of researchers who also hold crucial worldview commitments with every bit as much equal intensity and in areas that are similarly just as relevant as they are to the inerrantists. After all, it may well be the case that liberals frequently appear to be just as unlikely to change their own positions as the conservatives! In other words, all sides may have an analogous amount

---

concludes that "moderate conservatism" was "perhaps the most agreed upon scholarly approach to christology" (102), the topic of his volume. Brown's own conclusions seem to be firmly in this moderate conservative camp as well (85–89, 92–102, 112–15, 189–92, 203n304). See Raymond E. Brown, *An Introduction to New Testament Christology* (Mahwah, NJ: Paulist, 1994).

[43] It may be objected that conservatives frequently sign doctrinal statements that identify them as holding certain specific theological positions to which they are bound. While that is often the case, increasing numbers of conservatives either teach in secular institutions or denominational schools where these positions are not spelled out. Further, many professors who sign these statements do so after nuancing their own views and making those known, since there is a range of possible clarifications, as noted in the sources below. Last, it is strange to overlook liberal expectations and commitments to their own schools and especially to their own colleagues who may well be quite bothered if they disagreed with the guild. Each side has its own enforcement measures, and the liberals' unspoken rules may possibly be even more stringent, as often manifested and observed in present political and social conversations. On several of these nuanced options, see especially R. Albert Mohler Jr., Peter Enns, Michael F. Bird, Kevin J. Vanhoozer, and John R. Franke, *Five Views on Biblical Inerrancy*, ed. J. Merrick, Stephen M. Garrett, and Stanley N. Gundry (Grand Rapids: Zondervan, 2013); Benjamin C. F. Shaw, "What's Good for the Goose Is Good for the Gander: Historiography and the Historical Jesus," *Journal for the Study of the Historical Jesus* 15 (2017): 291–309.

of nuancing of prior intellectual commitments that tend to level out the playing field when it comes to being open to differing scholarly positions and areas of belief. But this remains to be seen.

Skeptical Scholars

Many recent skeptical scholars may be thought of as being situated across the aisle from those who take conservative stands on New Testament issues.[44] But this is frequently not the case, as friendships have often developed even after debates. The group of scholars known as the Jesus Seminar probably provides a representative example here, representing a large number of usually skeptical scholars.[45] According to their own tabulations, as a whole the members of the Jesus Seminar rejected some 82 percent of the so-called red-letter words of Jesus in the Gospels.[46] Further, of all the purported events concerning Jesus or his close followers, less than 6 percent of these were considered by this group to garner "a relatively high level of confidence that the event actually took place."[47] That would seem to qualify for a strong definition of skeptic.[48]

---

[44] The scholars listed in all three areas in this chapter are not listed in any particular order. Nor was any attempt made to be anywhere near exhaustive or to purposely exempt anyone. These lists are hopefully to present some of the representative examples of these many researchers.

[45] The group has grown considerably over the years. The roster published in their second group volume in 1998 listed over seventy-five fellows. See Robert W. Funk and the Jesus Seminar, *The Acts of Jesus: The Search for the Authentic Deeds of Jesus* (New York: HarperCollins, 1998), with the roster being found on 537–42. Later, the website of the Westar Institute, "the home of the Jesus Seminar," listed more than 200 scholars, including charter and deceased members (https://www.westarinstitute.org/membership/westar-fellows/fellows-directory/). Without attempting to identify several members in particular, some of the Jesus Seminar fellows appear from their own publications to hold more conservative views than the group as a whole. *The Acts of Jesus* also addresses this question in a few places (1, 37–38, 549).

[46] Robert W. Funk, Roy W. Hoover, and the Jesus Seminar, *The Five Gospels, The Search for the Authentic Words of Jesus* (New York: Macmillan, 1993), 5; Funk and the Jesus Seminar, *Acts of Jesus*, 1.

[47] Funk and the Jesus Seminar, *Acts of Jesus*, 1.

[48] The comment above that the Jesus Seminar may be representative of skeptical scholars refers to their numbers and the fact that several members have been well published rather than their speaking on behalf of other skeptics. But this is not to say that they are overly

Some of the better-known members of the Jesus Seminar, each of whom has questioned the veracity of a large number of major New Testament texts (from the Gospels in particular), would include John Dominic Crossan,[49] Marcus Borg,[50] Robert Funk,[51] and Gerd Lüdemann.[52] Another major list of Jesus Seminar scholars

---

respected as a group even by their fellow critical scholars. In fact, the sorts of criticisms that have sometimes been aimed at them are often harsh enough to be surprising—not at all the kinds of comments that are often heard by one scholar toward another. For example, in a no-holds-barred critique, Luke Timothy Johnson aimed numerous harsh volleys their way. Johnson referred to the Seminar as "a ten-year exercise in academic self-promotion . . . a far better example of media manipulation than of serious scholarship." See Johnson, *The Real Jesus: The Misguided Quest for the Historical Jesus and the Truth of the Traditional Gospels* (New York: HarperCollins, 1996), 1. Of the Seminar's scholarship expressed in their first volume, *The Five Gospels*, Johnson added, "It is not of an impressive quality. The most notable lack in the publication is any discernible *demonstration* or even *argument*. Much is asserted here without either evidence or even substantial logic" (25). Elsewhere, in a written dialogue, Johnson remarks concerning John Dominic Crossan, the Seminar's best-known scholar: "What is perhaps most disappointing . . . is the way [Crossan's] essay plays fast and loose with the sources, with logic," which Johnson considered to be "a product of Crossan's imagination." See Johnson, "Response to John Dominic Crossan," in *The Historical Jesus: Five Views*, ed. James K. Beilby and Paul Rhodes Eddy (Downers Grove, IL: InterVarsity Academic, 2009), 140–41. In the same work, James D. G. Dunn asserted, "I have no doubt that Birger Gerhardsson and David Aune are better guides on these features than the most prominent members of the Jesus Seminar" (221). Dunn also referred to Crossan's work: "The selective acceptance of one sequence of texts, and effective dismissal or denigration of others . . . is poor scholarship" (145). Dunn's first statement is located in his chapter, "Remembering Jesus: How the Quest for the Historical Jesus Lost Its Way," and Dunn's second comment comes from his essay, "Response to John Dominic Crossan" in *Historical Jesus: Five Views.*

[49] John Dominic Crossan, *The Birth of Christianity: Discovering What Happened in the Years Immediately after the Execution of Jesus* (New York: HarperCollins, 1998), 558, 561–62; John Dominic Crossan and William Lane Craig, "Dialogue," in *Will the Real Jesus Please Stand Up? A Debate between William Lane Craig and John Dominic Crossan*, ed. Paul Copen (Grand Rapids: Baker, 1998), 53, 55.

[50] Marcus J. Borg, "Thinking about Easter," *Bible Review* 10 (1994): 15; Borg, "The Truth of Easter," in Marcus J. Borg and N. T. Wright, *The Meaning of Jesus: Two Visions* (New York: HarperCollins, 1999), 132–33.

[51] Robert W. Funk, *Honest to Jesus: Jesus for a New Millennium* (New York: HarperCollins, 1996), 267.

[52] Gerd Lüdemann, "Opening Statement," in *Jesus' Resurrection: Fact or Figment? A Debate between William Lane Craig and Gerd Lüdemann*, ed. Paul Copan and Ronald K. Tacelli (Downers Grove, IL: InterVarsity, 2000), 43, and "Closing Response," 154–56.

with views on a number of widely dispersed subjects includes James M. Robinson,[53] John Kloppenborg,[54] Howard Clark Kee,[55] Richard Carrier,[56] Robert Price,[57] Burton Mack,[58] Barbara Thiering,[59] and John Shelby Spong.[60] Still more Jesus Seminar members include Robert J. Miller,[61] Roy W. Hoover,[62] and Thomas Sheehan,[63] some of whom have produced other detailed treatments of New Testament issues.

Numerous other scholars across a wide but relevant interdisciplinary swath, counting atheists and many other skeptical varieties along with some non-Christian authors

[53] James M. Robinson's earlier-mentioned works above include his *New Quest of the Historical Jesus* and his influential *Nag Hammadi Library in English*.

[54] Especially relevant for this present study is John Kloppenborg's important essay "An Analysis of the Pre-Pauline Formula 1 Cor 15:3b–5 in Light of Some Recent Literature," *Catholic Biblical Quarterly* 40 (1978): 351–67.

[55] Howard Clark Kee, *Medicine, Miracle and Magic in New Testament Times* (Cambridge: Cambridge University Press, 1988); Kee, *Miracle in the Early Christian World: A Study in Sociohistoric Method* (New Haven: Yale University Press, 1986); Kee, *What Can We Know*, 1–2, 86, 111–13.

[56] Richard Carrier, *On the Historicity of Jesus: Why We Might Have Reason for Doubt* (Sheffield: Sheffield Phoenix, 2014). On the burial of Jesus and afterward, see Carrier, "The Spiritual Body of Christ and the Legend of the Empty Tomb," 105–231; Carrier, "The Plausibility of Theft," 349–68; and Carrier, "The Burial of Jesus in Light of Jewish Law," 369–92; all three essays being found in *The Empty Tomb: Jesus beyond the Grave*, ed. Robert M. Price and Jeffery Jay Lowder (Amherst, NY: Prometheus, 2005).

[57] Robert M. Price, "Is There a Place for Historical Criticism?," *Religious Studies* 27 (1991): 380–81; Price, *Deconstructing Jesus* (Amherst, NY: Prometheus, 2000), chaps. 1 and 7; Price, "Apocryphal Apparitions: 1 Corinthians 15:3–11," 69–104; and Price, "By This Time He Stinketh: The Attempts of William Lane Craig to Exhume Jesus," 411–31, in Price and Lowder, *Empty Tomb*.

[58] Burton L. Mack, *The Lost Gospel: The Book of Q and Christian Origins* (New York: HarperCollins, 1993), 5–11, 245–61.

[59] Barbara Thiering, *Jesus the Man: Decoding the Real Story of Jesus and Mary Magdalene* (New York: Atria, 2006), esp. chaps. 24–27.

[60] John Shelby Spong, *The Easter Moment* (New York: Harper & Row, 1987), chaps. 15, 17–18; Spong, *Resurrection, Myth or Reality? A Bishop's Search for the Origins of Christianity* (New York: HarperCollins, 1994), chapters 15, 19–20.

[61] Robert J. Miller, "What Do Stories about Resurrection(s) Prove?," in Copan, *Real Jesus*, 82–85.

[62] Roy W. Hoover, "A Contest between Orthodoxy and Veracity," in Copan and Tacelli, *Jesus' Resurrection*, 131–36.

[63] Thomas Sheehan, *The First Coming: How the Kingdom of God Became Christianity* (New York: Random, 1986); Sheehan, "Two Easter Legends," *Philosophy and Theology* 1 (1989): 36–47.

who mention a number of negative problems with the New Testament accounts, include Willi Marxsen,[64] Maurice Casey,[65] Ingo Broer,[66] Norman Perrin,[67] Bart D. Ehrman,[68] Michael Martin,[69] Michael Goulder,[70] Evan Fales,[71] Larry Shapiro,[72] A. J. M. Wedderburn,[73] Gregory J. Riley,[74] J. K. Elliott,[75] Schubert M. Ogden,[76]

---

[64] Willi Marxsen, *The Resurrection of Jesus of Nazareth*, trans. Margaret Kohl (Philadelphia: Fortress, 1970), 27, 55, 68, 75–76, 146–48; Marxsen, *Jesus and Easter: Did God Raise the Historical Jesus from the Dead?*, trans. Victor Paul Furnish (Nashville: Abingdon, 1990), 42, 91.

[65] Such as Maurice Casey's text *Jesus: Evidence and Argument or Mythicist Myths* (London: Bloomsbury, 2014), 4–8, 134, 207, 243, 245.

[66] Ingo Broer, "'Seid stets bereit, jedem Rede und Antwort zu stehen, der nach der Hoffnung fragt, die euch erfüllt' (1 Peter 3,15): Das leere Grab und die Erscheinungen Jesu im Lichte der historischen Kritik," in *"Der Herr ist wahrhaft auferstanden" (Lk 24,34): Biblische und systematische Beiträge zur Entstehung des Osterglaubens*, ed. Ingo Broer and Jürgen Werbick (Stuttgart: Katholisches Bibelwerk, 1988), 60–61.

[67] Raymond Brown treats Norman Perrin as within the critically conservative fold in *Introduction to New Testament Christology*, 15, and in some respects that may be deserved. Perrin also followed Bultmann in other aspects as well, such as his comments on 38, 58, 77 in Perrin, *The Resurrection according to Matthew, Mark, and Luke* (Philadelphia: Fortress, 1977), esp. 78–84; Perrin, *Rediscovering the Teachings of Jesus* (New York: Harper & Row, 1967), with more thoughts at least somewhat reminiscent of Bultmann particularly on 11–12, 37–47.

[68] Ehrman, *Did Jesus Exist?*, chaps. 2–5; Bart D. Ehrman, *How Jesus Became God: The Exaltation of a Jewish Preacher from Galilee* (New York: HarperCollins, 2014), chaps. 4–5.

[69] Michael Martin, *The Case against Christianity* (Philadelphia: Temple University Press, 1991), 83–84, 89–90; Martin, "Reply to Davis," in *Philo* 2 (1999): 62–76, esp. 71–73.

[70] Michael Goulder, "The Empty Tomb," *Theology* 79 (1976): 206–14, particularly 210.

[71] Evan Fales, "Taming the Tehom: The Sign of Jonah in Matthew," in Price and Lowder, *Empty Tomb*, 307–48.

[72] Larry Shapiro, *The Miracle Myth: Why Belief in the Resurrection and the Supernatural Is Unjustified* (New York: Columbia University Press, 2016), xiv–xv, 57, 77, 93–95.

[73] A. J. M. Wedderburn, *Beyond Resurrection* (Peabody, MA: Hendrickson, 1999), 8, 24–37, 124.

[74] Gregory J. Riley, *Resurrection Reconsidered: Thomas and John in Controversy* (Minneapolis: Fortress, 1995), 65, 90, 155.

[75] J. K. Elliott, "The First Easter," *History Today* 29 (1979): 211–18.

[76] Schubert M. Ogden, *Christ without Myth: A Study Based on the Theology of Rudolf Bultmann* (New York: Harper & Row, 1961), 177–81.

G. A. Wells,[77] Morton Smith,[78] Jack Kent,[79] Geza Vermes,[80] Daniel Cohn-Sherbok,[81] Hans Küng,[82] Duncan M. Derrett,[83] John E. Alsup,[84] Adela Yarbro Collins,[85] James Keller,[86] Robert Greg Cavin,[87] John A. T. Robinson,[88] Keith Parsons,[89] Rudolf

---

[77] G. A. Wells, *A Resurrection Debate* (London: Rationalist, 1988), 24–27.

[78] Morton Smith, *Jesus the Magician: A Renowned Historian Reveals How Jesus Was Viewed by People of His Time* (New York: Harper & Row, 1978; repr., Newburyport, MA: Hampton Roads, 2014), 48.

[79] Jack A. Kent, *The Psychological Origins of the Resurrection Myth* (London: Open Gate, 1999), 17, 20, 67, 86–87.

[80] Geza Vermes, *The Resurrection* (London: Penguin, 2008), 86, 109–11; Vermes, *Jesus and the World of Judaism* (Philadelphia: Fortress, 1983), 23–24.

[81] Daniel Cohn-Sherbok, "The Resurrection of Jesus: A Jewish View," in *Resurrection Reconsidered*, ed. Gavin D'Costa (Oxford: Oneworld, 1996), 197, 199.

[82] Hans Küng, *On Being a Christian* (Garden City, NY: Doubleday, 1976), 346–48; Küng, *Eternal Life? Life after Death as a Medical, Philosophical, and Theological Problem*, trans. Edward Quinn (Garden City, NY: Doubleday, 1984), 100–103, 107.

[83] Duncan M. Derrett, *The Anastasis: The Resurrection of Jesus as an Historical Event* (Shipston-on-Stour: Drinkwater, 1982), 59; Derrett, "Financial Aspects of the Resurrection," in Price and Lowder, *Empty Tomb*, 393–409.

[84] John E. Alsup, *The Post-Resurrection Appearance Stories of the Gospel Tradition: A History-of-Tradition Analysis with Text-Synopsis* (Stuttgart: Calwer, 1975), 117.

[85] Adela Yarbro Collins, "The Empty Tomb and Resurrection according to Mark," in *The Beginning of Gospels: Problems of Mark in Context*, ed. Adela Yarbro Collins (Minneapolis: Fortress, 1992), 119–48, esp. 133.

[86] James Keller, "Contemporary Christian Doubts about the Resurrection," *Faith and Philosophy* 5 (1988): 113–14; Keller, "Response to Davis," *Faith and Philosophy* 7 (1990): 112–16.

[87] Robert Greg Cavin, "Is There Sufficient Historical Evidence to Establish the Resurrection of Jesus?," in Price and Lowder, *Empty Tomb*, 19–41; Robert Greg Cavin and Carlos A. Colombetti, "Swinburne on the Resurrection: Negative versus Christian Ramified Natural Theology," *Philosophia Christi* 15 (2013): 253–63.

[88] John A. T. Robinson, *Can We Trust the New Testament?* (Grand Rapids: Eerdmans, 1977), 125–26.

[89] Keith Parsons, "Peter Kreeft and Ronald Tacelli on the Hallucination Theory," in Price and Lowder, *Empty Tomb*, 433–51.

Pesch,[90] Hansjürgen Verweyen,[91] Frank Miosi,[92] Theodore M. Drange,[93] and Randel
Helms.[94] Still more authors are skeptical at points but are not necessarily skeptics in
the same sense as the others above (not all of whom are specialists). These authors,
who nevertheless doubt various aspects of the New Testament text, could also be
listed here.[95]

---

[90] This especially applies to the writings of the early Rudolf Pesch: "Zur Entstehung
des Glaubens an die Auferstehung Jesu," *Theologische Quartalschrift* 153 (1973): 201–28, esp.
212–18; Pesch, "Materialien und Bemerkungen zu Entstehung und Sinn des Osterglaubens,"
in Anton Vogtle and Rudolf Pesch, *Wie kam es zum Osterglauben?* (Dusseldorf: Patmos,
1975).

[91] Hansjürgen Verweyen, "Die Sache mit den Ostererscheinungen," in Broer and
Werbick, *Der Herr ist wahrhaft auferstanden*, 77–78; cf. John P. Galvin, "The Origin of
Faith in the Resurrection of Jesus: Two Recent Perspectives," *Theological Studies* 49 (1988):
35–40, 43–44, particularly 36.

[92] Frank T. Miosi, "The Resurrection Debate." *Free Inquiry* 8, no. 2 (1988): 55–57.

[93] Theodore M. Drange, "Why Resurrect Jesus?," in Price and Lowder, *Empty Tomb*,
55–67.

[94] Randel Helms, *Gospel Fictions* (Amherst, NY: Prometheus, 1988), 121, 130–32.

[95] Not all of the sources here are opposed to the resurrection per se, nor are these authors
always skeptical of this event. Not all fit our stricter mold of critical scholars who specialize
in relevant areas. Such a list might include Peter F. Carnley, *The Structure of Resurrection
Belief* (Oxford: Clarendon, 1987), 64, 69–72, 79, 82, 244–45; Carnley, "Response," in
Resurrection: An Interdisciplinary Symposium on the Resurrection of Jesus, ed. Stephen T. Davis,
Daniel Kendall, and Gerald O'Collins (Oxford: Oxford University Press, 1998), 35–40;
C. F. Evans, *Resurrection and the New Testament* (London: SCM, 1970), esp. 130–31; Brooke
Hopkins, "Jesus and Object-Use: A Winnicottian Account of the Resurrection Myth,"
The International Review of Psychoanalysis 16 (1989): 93–100, 93 in particular; Kenneth
Grayston, "The Empty Tomb," *Expository Times* 9 (1981): 263–67; Charles W. Hedrick,
"Paul's Conversion/Call: A Comparative Analysis of the Three Reports in Acts," *Journal of
Biblical Literature* 100 (1981): 415–32, esp. 422, 427, 428, 432; Rolland E. Wolfe, *How the
Easter Story Grew from Gospel to Gospel* (Lewiston, NY: Mellen, 1989), 91, 101, 124, 128;
B. C. Johnson, *The Atheist Debater's Handbook* (Buffalo, NY: Prometheus, 1983), 119–22;
Lloyd M. Graham, *Deceptions and Myths in the Bible* (New York: Bell, 1975), 356–62. Frank
J. Tipler initially rejected the resurrection before changing his position and embracing this
event; see Tipler, *The Physics of Immortality: Modern Cosmology, God and the Resurrection
of the Dead* (New York: Doubleday, 1994), 308–9. Dale Allison is a special case here. This
influential New Testament scholar and friend is often thought of as a skeptic, though he
denies it in his recent volume, Dale C. Allison Jr., *The Resurrection of Jesus: Apologetics,
Polemics, History* (London: T&T Clark, 2021), 338, but then cf. 4. See also Allison, *The
End of the Ages Has Come: An Early Interpretation of the Passion and Resurrection of Jesus*
(Philadelphia: Fortress, 1985), chaps. 11–12, and excursus; Allison, *Resurrecting Jesus: The*

Moderates

Just as skeptical scholars cover a wide swath of theoretical territory and feature much variety, so do the moderate scholars. Similarly too, there is always a risk that some researchers will be misidentified, or that a single facet of their thought may be overemphasized. Though it is difficult to ascertain, the moderates across the board may be more influential than the skeptics, at least among the Third Quest for the historical Jesus researchers. This comparison would also seem to parallel Raymond Brown's survey of contemporary christological trends as well as John A. T. Robinson's investigation of recent scholarship regarding the reliability of the New Testament accounts. These two studies were mentioned earlier and in these two crucial areas of Christian thought, both Brown and Robinson concluded that the moderate to conservative positions were the most influential. While skeptics raise more critiques and tend to question far more passages, moderates are just as likely to locate problems, including many of the same issues, though they frequently think that a solution is actually close at hand.

Among the more influential moderate scholars are Jürgen Moltmann,[96] Wolfhart Pannenberg,[97] Karl Rahner,[98] E. P. Sanders,[99] Raymond E. Brown,[100] Joseph A.

Earliest Christian Tradition and Its Interpreters (London: T&T Clark, 2005), particularly 199–219, 228–69, 299–337, 340, 346–50.

[96] Jürgen Moltmann, *Theology of Hope: On the Ground and the Implications of a Christian Eschatology*, trans. James W. Leitch (New York: Harper & Row, 1967), 165–66, 172, 197–202; Moltmann, "The Resurrection of Christ: Hope for the World," in D'Costa, *Resurrection Reconsidered*, 76.

[97] Wolfhart Pannenberg, "Die Auferstehung Jesu," 318–28; Pannenberg, *Die Auferstehung Jesu*, 12–18; Pannenberg *Jesus: God and Man*, 53–106.

[98] Karl Rahner, *Foundations of Christian Faith: An Introduction to the Idea of Christianity*, trans. William V. Dych (New York: Seabury, 1978), 276.

[99] E. P. Sanders, *The Historical Figure of Jesus* (London: Penguin, 1993), 276–77, 279; Sanders, "But Did It Happen?," *The Spectator* 276 (1996): 12–13, incl. the three accounts of Paul's conversion according to Acts. Intriguingly, Sanders identifies himself as a liberal in his book *Jesus and Judaism* (Philadelphia: Fortress, 1985), 334.

[100] Raymond E. Brown, *Virginal Conception*, 116–19nn197 and 198, incl. the chart on 118; Brown, *Introduction to New Testament Christology*, 166–70 (incl. a detailed list of issues); Brown, *A Risen Christ in Eastertime: Essays on the Gospel Narratives of the Resurrection* (Collegeville, MN: Liturgical, 1991), 25–28; Brown, "The Resurrection of Jesus," in *Jerome Biblical Commentary* (Englewood Cliffs, NJ: Prentice-Hall, 1968), 1373–77, esp. 1375 incl. a detailed chart on 1376; Brown, *The Death of the Messiah: From Gethsemane to the Grave*, 2 vols. (New York: Doubleday, 1994).

Fitzmyer,[101] James D. G. Dunn,[102] John Meier,[103] Gerald O'Collins,[104] and Reginald H. Fuller.[105] Other significant moderates might include Luke Timothy Johnson,[106] Walter Künneth,[107] Jacob Kremer,[108] Ben F. Meyer,[109] Ulrich Wilckens,[110] Jerome

---

[101] Joseph A. Fitzmyer, "The Resurrection of Jesus Christ according to the New Testament," *The Month* 20 (1987): 402–10, 409 in particular, 418–20; Fitzmyer, "The Ascension of Christ and Pentecost," *Theological Studies* 45 (1984): 409–40.

[102] James D. G. Dunn, *Jesus Remembered*, 329, 335, 490, 670, 836, 864, 879; Dunn, *Beginning from Jerusalem*, 105–8, 333, 348–50, 368–69; Dunn, *Evidence for Jesus*, 74–76.

[103] John P. Meier, *A Marginal Jew: Rethinking the Historical Jesus*, vol. 3, *Companions and Competitors* (New York: Doubleday, 2001), 9–12, 251–52, 433–44, 625, 641–42, 646.

[104] Gerald O'Collins, *The Easter Jesus*, 2nd ed. (London: Darton, Longman & Todd, 1980), 18–19; O'Collins, *What Are They Saying about the Resurrection?* (New York: Paulist, 1978), 51, 55, 61, 78; O'Collins, *Interpreting the Resurrection: Examining the Major Problems in the Stories of Jesus' Resurrection* (Mahweh, NJ: Paulist, 1988), 11, 20–21; O'Collins, *Interpreting Jesus, Introducing Catholic Theology* (Mahwah, NJ: Paulist, 1983), 125; Daniel Kendall and Gerald O'Collins, "The Uniqueness of the Easter Appearances," *Catholic Biblical Quarterly* 54 (1992): esp. 306–7.

[105] Fuller, *Formation of the Resurrection Narratives*, 2–6, 46, 130, 136; also Reginald H. Fuller, Eugene LaVerdiere, John C. Lodge, and Donald Senior, *The Passion, Death and Resurrection of the Lord: A Commentary on the Four Gospels* (Mundelein, IL: Chicago Studies, 1985), 54.

[106] Luke Timothy Johnson, "Luke 24:1–11: The Not-So-Empty-Tomb," *Interpretation* 46 (1992): 57–61, esp. 59–60; Johnson, *Real Jesus*, 24–25, 119–26, 151–52, 172, 175–77; Johnson, *Living Jesus: Learning the Heart of the Gospel* (New York: HarperCollins, 1999), 10, 130–32.

[107] Walter Künneth, *Theologie der Auferstehung* (Munich: Claudius, 1951), 82–99.

[108] Jacob Kremer, *Die Osterevangelien: Geschichten um Geschichte*, 2nd ed. (Stuttgart: Katholisches Bibelwerk, 1988), concerned with the appearance accounts in all four Gospels (30–229) and the conclusions that can be drawn regarding the "Stories about History" (the subtitle; see 231).

[109] Ben F. Meyer, *The Aims of Jesus* (London: SCM, 1979), chap. 4 on "Jesus and Critical History," including the known data, the nature of history, and verification (81–92); Meyer, *Critical Realism and the New Testament* (Allison Park, PA: Pickwick, 1989).

[110] Ulrich Wilckens, *Resurrection: Biblical Testimony to the Resurrection. An Historical Examination and Explanation*, trans. A. M. Stewart (Atlanta: Knox, 1978), 1, 83–88, 112, 117, 119, 121, 124–25, 132.

Murphy-O'Connor,[111] Pheme Perkins,[112] Walter Kasper,[113] Xavier Léon-Dufour,[114] Brian Hebblethwaite,[115] Barnabas Lindars,[116] Jean-Marie Guillaume,[117] Frans Neirynck,[118] as well as Jewish New Testament scholar Pinchas Lapide.[119] Still others should also be numbered among these scholars, though some might be uneasy matches in one way or another.[120]

---

[111] Especially Jerome Murphy-O'Connor, "Tradition and Redaction in 1 Cor 15:3–7," *Catholic Biblical Quarterly* 43 (1981): 582–89, with his summary on the last page.

[112] Pheme Perkins, *Resurrection: New Testament Witness and Contemporary Reflection* (Garden City, NY: Doubleday, 1984), 91, 198; Perkins, "Reconciling the Resurrection: The Central Act of the Christian Faith," *Commonweal* 112 (1985): 202–5.

[113] Walter Kasper, *Jesus the Christ*, trans. V. Green, rev. ed. (Mahwah, NJ: Paulist, 1977), 125, 127–29.

[114] Xavier Léon-Dufour, *Résurrection de Jésus et message pascal* (Paris: Seuil, 1971).

[115] Brian Hebblethwaite, "The Resurrection and the Incarnation," in *The Resurrection of Jesus Christ*, ed. Paul Avis (London: Darton, Longman & Todd, 1993), 158.

[116] Barnabas Lindars "The Resurrection and the Empty Tomb," in Avis, *Resurrection of Jesus Christ*, 32; Lindars, "Jesus Risen: Bodily Resurrection but No Empty Tomb," *Theology* 59 (1986): 90–96.

[117] Jean-Marie Guillaume, *Luc interprète des anciennes traditions sur la résurrection de Jésus* (Paris: Gabalda et Cie, 1979), particularly 50–52, 65, 201, 265–74.

[118] Frans Neirynck, "John and the Synoptics: The Empty Tomb Stories," *New Testament Studies* 30 (1984): 161–87, esp. 172–75, 179.

[119] Pinchas Lapide, *The Resurrection of Jesus: A Jewish Perspective* (Minneapolis: Augsburg, 1983), 34–35, 112–15.

[120] A few scholars who may fit here uneasily according to the assessment of some, for whatever reasons, might include Richard R. Niebuhr, *Resurrection and Historical Reason: A Study in Theological Method* (New York: Scribner's Sons, 1957); Joseph Doré, "Croire en la résurrection de Jésus-Christ," *Études* 356 (1982): 525–42, particularly 531–32, 537–38, 541–42; A. M. Ramsey, *The Resurrection of Christ: A Study of the Event and Its Meaning for the Christian Faith*, rev. ed. (London: Fontana, 1961); the spiritualist interpreter Michael C. Perry, *The Easter Enigma: As Essay on the Resurrection with Special Reference to the Data of Psychical Research* (London: Faber & Faber, 1959), chaps. 13 and 17. Others include Thorwald Lorenzen, *Resurrection and Discipleship* (Maryknoll, NY: Orbis, 1995), 169, 183; Carolyn Osiek, "The Women at the Tomb: What Are They Doing There?," *Ex Auditu* 9 (1993): 97–107; John Frederick Jansen, *The Resurrection of Jesus Christ in New Testament Theology* (Philadelphia: Westminster, 1980); Neville Clark, *Interpreting the Resurrection* (Philadelphia: Westminster, 1967); Hugo Staudinger, "The Resurrection of Jesus Christ as Saving Event and as 'Object' of Historical Research," *Scottish Journal of Theology* 36 (1983): 309–26, particularly 318, 320, 324; Donald Viney, "Grave Doubts about the Resurrection," *Encounter* 50 (1989): 132; Charles Austin Perry, *An Interpretation of the Easter Narratives* (Grand Rapids: Eerdmans, 1986); Alan E. Lewis, *Between Cross and Resurrection: A*

One last, intriguing volume, edited by Ted Peters, Robert John Russell, and Michael Welker, contains eighteen essays, argued by scholars trained in either (or both) theological or scientific fields, that favor "embodied" existence after death based on the model of Jesus's resurrection. Many of these essays argue for a non-reductive materialism or some other species of discontinuity at death, after which "God will draw into the divine memory the pattern of information that constitutes the human soul; and in the eschaton God will reinstate human personhood within the transformed material creation." The information is "extracted from our present earthly bodies and reinstated in a future resurrected body."[121] Several of the essays in this text are of the moderate variety discussed here.[122]

Conservatives

Although it may surprise some, as with skeptics and moderates there is much variety among conservative Christian authors on the questions being addressed in this chapter. Conservatives generally believe in the occurrence of miracles in the past and often in the present. While many of these scholars think that various levels of data may be produced on behalf of these events, even generating verification of one species or another, others—especially those who tend toward fideistic positions—do not think that such events can or even should be evidenced at all. Likewise, the latter

---

Theology of Holy Saturday (Grand Rapids: Eerdmans, 2001), 35–36, 57–58, 70–74; Violaine Monsarrat, "Le récit de la passion: Un enseignement pour le disciple fidèle," in *Foi et Vie* 81 (1982): 40–47, esp. 44, 46–47.

[121] As Ted Peters explains in his introduction, the description just given is drawn chiefly from the well-known physicist John Polkinghorne, whose essay "Eschatological Credibility: Emergent and Teleological Processes," 43–55, is included in this volume. The volume is entitled *Resurrection: Theological and Scientific Assessments*, ed. Ted Peters, Robert John Russell, and Michael Welker (Grand Rapids: Eerdmans, 2002).

[122] Besides Polkinghorne's and Peters's later essay "Resurrection: The Conceptual Challenge," 297–321, examples of other moderate essays would probably include at least those by Michael Welker, "Theological Realism and Eschatological Symbol Systems," 31–42, and Nancey Murphy, "The Resurrection Body and Personal Identity: Possibilities and Limits of Eschatological Knowledge," 202–18.

often believe that while these events truly occurred, they are not exactly historical events in the same "objective" sense as are other nonmiraculous events.

Further, it is well known that a plethora of conservative views are held on various theological doctrines as well as other issues, as indicated clearly by the successful publication of dozens of so-called three-, four-, and five-views books. For example, while holding that Jesus Christ is the only path to salvation, some may think (taking more than one view on the way to this conclusion) that it is possible that some who do not even know specifically who Jesus was can still be "saved" through him, in spite of this lack of explicit knowledge. Divergent stances are taken on the importance and mode of baptism, the time of creation, whether God used evolution as the method of creation, and many aspects concerning the time of the end, the future mode of existence, and many other topics.

More directly on our topic in this chapter, many conservative scholars also hold that the New Testament contains various amalgams of discrepancies or even contradictions, legends, or other issues. Skimming the list below would probably show this to be the case here as well.[123] These researchers usually hold that scholars should interact with those who disagree in a congenial and helpful manner, even when one's dialogue partners are also conservatives!

Not to forget some of the conservative voices from before the Third Quest for the historical Jesus, Karl Barth,[124] Dietrich Bonhoeffer (at least on Jesus's death and resurrection),[125] and C. S. Lewis were among the most influential.[126] Very prominent

---

[123] In the sources beginning in the next note and listed further below, the page numbers reference the divergences just noted as related further to the overall topics of these volumes, namely regarding the scholar's stance on whether or not miraculous events have occurred, whether they can potentially be verified in whole or in part, specifics on the resurrection appearances of Jesus, as well as regarding the issue of discrepancies in the New Testament.

[124] Barth, *Church Dogmatics*, 4.1:334–53.

[125] Dietrich Bonhoeffer, *Christ the Center*, trans. John Bowden (New York: Harper & Row, 1966), see the discussion on 63–66, and especially 71–77.

[126] On the topics that we have been discussing, C. S. Lewis's most influential book has easily been *Miracles: A Preliminary Study*, rev. ed. (New York: Macmillan, 1960), chaps. 3, 8, 13.

since that time are Alvin Plantinga,[127] Martin Hengel,[128] Thomas F. Torrance,[129]

---

[127] Plantinga's influence with regard to our discussions here is not directly on the subjects of the death and resurrection of Jesus so much as his groundbreaking theorizing on topics such as belief in God apart from evidence and his notion of proper warrant for religious belief. Even on the latter topic, where he has been critical of historical arguments from the past, his further clarifications still have been very helpful. On believing in God without evidence, see Alvin Plantinga, "Reason and Belief in God," in *Faith and Rationality: Reason and Belief in God*, ed. Alvin Plantinga and Nicholas Wolterstorff (Notre Dame, IN: University of Notre Dame Press, 1983), 16–93. (Incidentally, this volume does contain an essay on Jesus's resurrection by D. Holwerda, "Faith, Reason, and the Resurrection," 265–316.) On the issue of warrant specifically with reference to historical arguments of the past, a rigorous, enlightening dialogue ensued between Plantinga and Timothy McGrew: see Timothy McGrew, "Has Plantinga Refuted the Historical Argument?," *Philosophia Christi* 6 (2004): 7–26; and Alvin Plantinga, "Historical Arguments and Dwindling Probabilities: A Response to Timothy McGrew," *Philosophia Christi* 8 (2006): 7–22. Crucially, Plantinga clarified that his volume *Warranted Christian Belief* (Oxford: Oxford University Press, 2000) was not primarily attempting to disallow historical arguments per se as much as to postulate that they were not strictly necessary moves for a religious argument to succeed. Plantinga concluded that if there were also strong historical arguments, then he was "delighted to discover that" and "I admire his [i.e., McGrew's] way of making the point" (20–21). Plantinga ended his essay by noting that this dialogue had been "a real step forward and contributes substantially to our understanding of historical arguments" (22).

[128] Martin Hengel, "Ist der Osterglaube noch zu retten?," *Theologische Quartalschrift* 153 (1973): 252–69; Hengel, "Das Begrabnis Jesu bei Paulus und die leibliche Auferstehung aus dem Grabe," in *Auferstehung-Resurrection*, ed. Friedrich Avemarie and Hermann Lichtenberger (Tubingen: Mohr Siebeck, 2001); Hengel, "Maria und die Frauen als Zeugen," in *Abraham unser Vater: Juden und Christian im Gespräch über die Bibel. Festschrift für Otto Michel zum 60. Geburtstag*, ed. Otto Betz, Martin Hengel, and Peter Schmidt (Leiden: Brill, 1963), 243–56; Hengel, *Crucifixion in the Ancient World and the Folly of the Message of the Cross*, trans. John Bowden (Philadelphia: Fortress, 1977), esp. 25, 28, 31–32, 83, 87, cf. 73; on the theological ramifications of Jesus's death, see Hengel, *The Atonement: The Origins of the Doctrine in the New Testament*, trans. John Bowden (Philadelphia: Fortress, 1981), 31–39, 57–60, 65–75; Hengel, *The Son of God: The Origin of Christology and the History of Jewish-Hellenistic Religion*, trans. John Bowden (Philadelphia: Fortress, 1976), 89–93.

[129] Thomas F. Torrance, *Space, Time, and Resurrection* (Grand Rapids: Eerdmans, 1976), 3–4, for the recognition of "difficulties and contradictions" in the resurrection accounts.

N. T. Wright,[130] Richard Bauckham,[131] Larry W. Hurtado,[132] Richard Swinburne,[133] C. F. D. Moule,[134] Carl F. H. Henry,[135] William Lane Craig,[136] John Warwick Montgomery,[137] Ben Witherington III,[138] Craig A. Evans,[139] Peter Stuhlmacher,[140]

[130] Such as N. T. Wright's four-volume magnum opus, *Christian Origins and the Question of God*, including (especially for our purposes) vol. 3, *The Resurrection of the Son of God* (Minneapolis: Fortress, 2003).

[131] Richard Bauckham, *Jesus and the Eyewitnesses: The Gospels as Eyewitness Testimony* (Grand Rapids: Eerdmans, 2006), esp. 25, 264–287, 304–8. See also the update on the earliest resurrection data in the second edition of this work (8); Bauckham, *Jesus and the God of Israel: God Crucified and Other Studies on the New Testament's Christology of Divine Identity* (Grand Rapids: Eerdmans, 2008), ix–xii, 182–232.

[132] Larry W. Hurtado, *Lord Jesus Christ: Devotion to Jesus in Earliest Christianity* (Grand Rapids: Eerdmans, 2003), 11–26; Hurtado, *One God, One Lord: Early Christian Devotion and Ancient Jewish Monotheism* (Philadelphia: Fortress, 1988), 68, 94, 116–19, 124.

[133] Richard Swinburne, *The Resurrection of God Incarnate* (Oxford: Clarendon, 2003), esp. chaps. 9–13; Swinburne, *The Concept of Miracles* (London: Macmillan, 1970); Swinburne, ed., *Miracles* (New York: Macmillan, 1989).

[134] C. F. D. Moule, *The Origin of Christology* (Cambridge: Cambridge University Press, 1977), chaps. 1, 4.

[135] Carl F. H. Henry, *God, Revelation and Authority*, 2nd ed., 6 vols. (Wheaton, IL: Crossway, 1999).

[136] William Lane Craig, "On Doubts about the Resurrection," *Modern Theology* 6 (1989): 53–75. Craig comments, "Discrepancies in secondary details could exist" (62); also, Craig, *Assessing the New Testament Evidence for the Historicity of the Resurrection of Jesus* (Lewiston, NY: Mellen, 1989), particularly chaps. 9–10.

[137] John Warwick Montgomery, *Where Is History Going? Essays in Support of the Historical Truth of the Christian Revelation* (Grand Rapids: Zondervan, 1969), chaps. 1–3; Montgomery, *The Shape of the Past: A Christian Response to Secular Philosophies of History* (Minneapolis: Bethany, 1975), 138–45, 288–93, 296–98; Montgomery, *History and Christianity* (Downers Grove, IL: InterVarsity, 1971); Montgomery, *Faith Founded on Fact: Essays in Evidential Apologetics* (Nashville: Nelson, 1978), chaps. 2–3; Montgomery, *Tractatus Logico-Theologicus*, 5th ed. (Eugene, OR: Wipf & Stock, 2013).

[138] Ben Witherington III, *The Christology of Jesus* (Minneapolis: Fortress, 1990), 22–31 on the critical textual criteria, also 157–60, 164–67; for a more popular presentation and critique of critical claims, see Witherington, *The Gospel Code: Novel Claims about Jesus, Mary Magdalene and Da Vinci* (Downers Grove, IL: InterVarsity, 2004), 36–37, 80–109 on Gnosticism.

[139] A serious volume that still exposes popular renditions of Jesus is Craig A. Evans's *Fabricating Jesus: How Modern Scholars Distort the Gospels* (Downers Grove, IL: InterVarsity, 2006), esp. chaps. 3–5 on the gnostic and other newer approaches to Jesus.

[140] Peter Stuhlmacher, *Was geschah auf Golgatha? Zur Heilsbedeutung von Kreuz, Tod und Auferweckung Jesu* (Stuttgart: Calwer, 1998), particularly 43–64; Stuhlmacher, "The

I. Howard Marshall,[141] Darrell L. Bock,[142] Craig L. Blomberg,[143] Paul Barnett,[144] Ronald H. Nash,[145] and Donald Guthrie.[146]

Resurrection of Jesus and the Resurrection of the Dead," trans. Jonathan M. Whitlock, *Ex Auditu* 9 (1993): 45–56, esp. 46–49; Stuhlmacher, *Jesus of Nazareth–Christ of Faith*, trans. Siegfried Schatzmann (Peabody, MA: Hendrickson, 1993), 8, 22–28; Stuhlmacher, *Schriftauslegung auf dem Wege zur biblischen Theologie* (Gottingen: Vandenhoeck & Ruprecht, 1975).

[141] I. Howard Marshall, *I Believe in the Historical Jesus* (Grand Rapids: Eerdmans, 1977). Marshall concludes in chaps. 10–11 by dealing specifically with what can be known of Jesus from history, beginning with a bare minimum of Jesus's factual teachings according to Norman Perrin. Marshall terms this list "extremely meagre" even for "the most skeptical of scholars" (217) and works up to more material. Then in chap. 11 he sets out parameters for what the historian may conclude if supernatural-looking data should appear in his or her research; see also Marshall, *The Origins of New Testament Christology*, rev. ed. (Downers Grove, IL: InterVarsity, 1990).

[142] Darrell L. Bock, *Studying the Historical Jesus: A Guide to Sources and Methods* (Grand Rapids, Baker, 2002); also Bock, *Blasphemy and Exaltation in Judaism and the Final Examination of Jesus* (Tübingen: Mohr Siebeck, 1998); reprinted by Baker in 2000 with the title *Blasphemy and Exaltation in Judaism: The Charge against Jesus in Mark 14:53–65*.

[143] Most of Craig L. Blomberg's work is on the Gospel texts and related questions, such as *The Historical Reliability of the Gospels*, 2nd ed. (Downers Grove, IL: InterVarsity, 2007), chap. 4 is devoted to the question of Gospel contradictions. Also Blomberg, *The Historical Reliability of John's Gospel: Issues & Commentary* (Downers Grove, IL: InterVarsity, 2011); David Wenham and Craig Blomberg, eds., *The Miracles of Jesus*, vol. 6 of *Gospel Perspectives* (Sheffield: JSOT Press, 1986).

[144] Historian Paul Barnett's works include: *Is the New Testament Reliable? A Look at the Historical Evidence* (Downers Grove, IL: InterVarsity, 1986); *Jesus and the Logic of History* (Grand Rapids: Eerdmans, 1997); *The Birth of Christianity: The First Twenty Years* (Grand Rapids: Eerdmans, 2005); *Finding the Historical Christ* (Grand Rapids: Eerdmans, 2009). On the question of ancient accuracy and discrepancies, Barnett notes some discrepancies in the New Testament (*Birth of Christianity*, 18, 65 for example) and asserts that in this earliest time frame, "nothing hangs on absolute precision" (9). But Barnett also points out, "In terms of the historical reference to noted persons in antiquity, this would represent a brevity without parallel" (210, cf. 11–12).

[145] Ronald H. Nash, *Christian Faith and Historical Understanding* (Grand Rapids: Zondervan, 1984), chaps. 3, 5–7; Nash, *Christianity and the Hellenistic World* (Grand Rapids: Zondervan, 1984), chaps. 7–13, 16.

[146] Donald Guthrie, *New Testament Theology* (Downers Grove, IL: InterVarsity, 1981), 365–407.

Other major conservative scholars writing specifically on the issues discussed in this chapter and this study as a whole include Markus Barth,[147] Stephen T. Davis,[148] Paul L. Maier,[149] Paul Rhodes Eddy and Gregory A. Boyd,[150] Craig S. Keener,[151] Robert Gundry,[152] C. E. B. Cranfield,[153] Robert H. Stein,[154] Graham H. Twelftree,[155] Norman

---

[147] Markus Barth and Verne H. Fletcher, *Acquittal by Resurrection: Freedom, Law, and Justice in the Light of the Resurrection of Jesus Christ* (New York: Holt, Rinehart, and Winston, 1964), with Barth's material on v–96; Markus Barth, "Introduction," in Leonhard Goppelt, Helmut Thielicke, and Hans-Rudolf Müller-Schwefe, *The Easter Message Today: Three Essays*, trans. Salvator Attanasio and Darrell Likens Guder (New York: Nelson and Sons, 1964), 9–25.

[148] Stephen T. Davis, *Risen Indeed: Making Sense of the Resurrection* (Grand Rapids: Eerdmans, 1993), 180–85 on the rationality of the resurrection, 169–70 on discrepancies in the accounts.

[149] Paul L. Maier, *First Easter: The True and Unfamiliar Story in Words and Pictures* (New York: Harper & Row, 1973), chap. 9 on the historical facts favoring the resurrection, chap. 11 on the empty tomb, and chap. 10 plus pages 94, 96 on "Doubts and Criticism." See also Maier, "The Empty Tomb as History," *Christianity Today* 19, no. 13 (1975): 4–6.

[150] Paul Rhodes Eddy and Gregory A. Boyd, *The Jesus Legend: A Case for the Historical Reliability of the Synoptic Jesus Tradition* (Grand Rapids: Baker Academic, 2007); Eddy and Boyd, *Lord or Legend: Wrestling with the Jesus Dilemma* (Grand Rapids: Baker, 2007); Boyd, *Cynic Sage or Son of God? Recovering the Real Jesus in an Age of Revisionist Replies* (Wheaton, IL: BridgePoint, 1995).

[151] Craig S. Keener, *The Historical Jesus of the Gospels* (Grand Rapids: Eerdmans, 2009), 330–48. For those interested, Keener's two-volume work *Miracles: The Credibility of the New Testament Accounts* (Grand Rapids: Baker Academic, 2011) has already become a classic.

[152] Robert H. Gundry, *Sōma in Biblical Theology: With Emphasis on Pauline Anthropology* (Cambridge: Cambridge University Press, 1976), see esp. the exceptional chapter, "The Sōma in Death and Resurrection," 159–83.

[153] C. E. B. Cranfield, "The Resurrection of Jesus Christ," *Expository Times* 101 (1990): 167–72, esp. Cranfield briefly addressing several of the main issues (167–68).

[154] Robert H. Stein, *Jesus the Messiah: A Survey of the Life of Christ* (Downers Grove, IL: InterVarsity, 1996), 260–62 on the difficulty of working out harmonizing details, including Stein listing many of the issues; also Stein, *Gospels and Tradition: Studies on Redaction Criticism of the Synoptic Gospels* (Grand Rapids, Baker, 1991), chaps. 1, 4, 5, 8–9 on critical methodology, incl. a note on the resurrection in Mark (chap. 7).

[155] Graham H. Twelftree, *Jesus the Miracle Worker: A Historical and Theological Study* (Downers Grove, IL: InterVarsity, 1999), 304–10, 314–28, esp. Twelftree's conclusions on 328–30, 345.

L. Geisler,[156] Colin Brown,[157] Frank J. Beckwith,[158] Robert A. Larmer,[159] Daniel P. Fuller,[160] and William Alston.[161] Additional conservative scholars have likewise contributed to the overall discussion on the subjects that we are considering here.[162]

In the context of the earlier conversation in this chapter, an interesting phenomenon may be observed among the conservative researchers listed here. Although it is impossible to be objective, a quick estimate seems to indicate that the

---

[156] Norman L. Geisler, *Miracles and the Modern Mind: A Defense of Biblical Miracles* (Grand Rapids: Baker, 1992); Geisler, *The Battle for the Resurrection* (Nashville: Nelson, 1989).

[157] Colin Brown, *Miracles and the Critical Mind* (Grand Rapids: Eerdmans, 1984), 281–92, 370–71.

[158] Francis J. Beckwith, *David Hume's Argument against Miracles: A Critical Analysis* (Lanham, MD: University Press of America, 1989).

[159] Robert A. Larmer, *The Legitimacy of Miracle* (Lanham, MD: Lexington, 2014), chaps. 3, 6, and 7 in particular; Larmer, *Dialogues on Miracle* (Eugene: Wipf & Stock, 2015).

[160] Daniel P. Fuller, *Easter Faith and History* (Grand Rapids: Eerdmans, 1965), 145–261.

[161] William P. Alston, "Biblical Criticism and the Resurrection," in Davis, Kendall, and O'Collins, *Resurrection*, 148–83, particularly Alston's own critical comments (160–61, 179).

[162] F. X. Durrwell, *La résurrection de Jésus, mystère de salut*, 10th ed. (Paris: Cerf, 1976), esp. chap. 1:3, 1:5.i–ii; David Wenham, *Paul: Follower of Jesus or Founder of Christianity?* (Grand Rapids: Eerdmans, 1995), esp. 380–92, where Wenham differentiates the items about the historical Jesus known to Paul as "Highly Probable," "Probable," and "Plausible," plus states a cumulative case argument regarding these data, see also 3–7; Laurence W. Miller, *Jesus Christ Is Alive* (Boston: Wilde, 1949), particularly chap. 1:1–12 and 45–52; Floyd V. Filson, *Jesus Christ, The Risen Lord: A Biblical Study Based on the Resurrection* (Nashville: Abingdon, 1941), 31–57, 270–72 in particular; Leonhard Goppelt, "The Easter Kerygma in the New Testament," in Goppelt, Thielicke, and Müller-Schwefe, *Easter Message Today*, 27–58; Helmut Thielicke, "The Resurrection Kerygma," in Goppelt, Thielicke, and Müller-Schwefe, *Easter Message Today*, 59–116; Grant R. Osborne, *The Resurrection Narratives: A Redactional Study* (Grand Rapids: Baker, 1984); Murray J. Harris, *Raised Immortal: Resurrection and Immortality in the New Testament* (Grand Rapids: Eerdmans, 1983), 52, 68–71; Bernard L. Ramm, *An Evangelical Christology: Ecumenic and Historic* (Nashville: Nelson, 1985), 87–99; Norman Anderson, *Christianity and World Religions: The Challenge of Pluralism* (Downers Grove, IL: InterVarsity, 1984), chaps. 2–4 on comparing the early Christian historical record to that of other ancient religious claims; Norman Anderson, *Jesus Christ: The Witness of History*, 2nd ed. (Downers Grove, IL: InterVarsity, 1985); Stephen Neill, *Christian Faith and Other Faiths* (Downers Grove, IL: InterVarsity, 1984), 280–87 in particular, listing unique features of the early Christian message; John Drane, *Introducing the New Testament* (New York: Harper & Row, 1986), 101–3; David Basinger and Randall Basinger, *Philosophy and Miracle: The Contemporary Debate* (Lewiston, NY: Mellen, 1986); Richard B. Gaffin Jr., *Resurrection and Redemption: A Study in Paul's Soteriology*, 2nd ed. (Philadelphia: Presbyterian and Reformed, 1987).

majority of the people listed are quite likely not inerrantists. One reason is seen in the frequent report that inerrantist evangelical scholars outside the United States are in the minority. This is a major response to those who tend to raise the question of prior doctrinal commitments by conservatives.[163]

So far in this chapter, the attempt has been made to document some of the various types of textual issues that scholars often think can be located within the topics with which this study is most interested. After our foray into the scholarly trends from nineteenth-century German liberalism through the twentieth century and up to the present, it seems clear that the vast majority of researchers thinks that the New Testament writings contain various sorts of problems that have been treated as inaccuracies of several sorts, including outright errors and contradictions.

Frankly, the historical territory that has concerned us the most in this study regarding the crucifixion, burial, and resurrection appearances of Jesus has received more than its share of the scholarly concern. In fact, among the hundreds of separate sources mentioned in this chapter, it is probably safe to state that no objection to the Christian message has been mentioned more frequently over the past two centuries than the sheer presence of these textual issues.

Does this general objection have merit? Does such a move leave us with serious, intractable problems in other major areas of the texts? As the old question is asked, if the New Testament texts cannot be trusted or ascertained for sure in certain areas, how may it be known if the texts in other areas are reliable? We will begin here by surveying a few of the historical areas most frequently questioned. Then we will turn to some potential treatment options. Finally, it will be pointed out why none of these questions or objections is sufficient to nullify the force of the historical case presented in this study, consisting of data that are accepted *even by the very skeptical scholars who raised these questions in the first place.*

Specific Textual Questions

Among the best known and most common instances of discrepancy-type problems raised from the Gospel texts as a whole are those that zero in on aspects regarding the burial and resurrection appearance accounts. It may even be accurate to say that the post-crucifixion examples comprise the most popularly mentioned examples in the

---

[163] See Michael F. Bird, "Inerrancy Is Not Necessary for Evangelicalism outside the USA," in *Five Views on Biblical Inerrancy*, 145–73.

entire New Testament. There are several conundrums from which to choose here. These questions are expressed by commentators in a variety of ways too, from detailed charges and concise listings in the form of charts and diagrams to a large number of accusations enumerated in rapid-fire succession or even just tossed together in just a few words each.

Another couple of intriguing facets may be stated here as well. Even conservative scholars, including some who identify themselves as inerrantists, frequently acknowledge some of the difficult issues involved. So it simply will not do for the inerrantists to blame the examples that are raised below on the attacks of more critical scholars alone, as if they were due, perhaps, to liberal tendencies.

Moreover, the most important overall observations for our purposes will be indicated later in this chapter, and a number of these issues are addressed in more detail in other volumes in this study and will not be repeated here, as noted below. Except in a few cases, the potential concerns are more or less just identified in this context. Still, the popular, most commonly mentioned problems raised are sometimes also precisely the ones that appear to be the most readily solved.

The following list notes several of the most popular instances of discrepancy claims found in the literature, which are stated as questions. Many critical scholars only note the issues in passing, so being included among the listed researchers does not mean that they either necessarily agree or disagree with a particular position. A few crucial points will be addressed afterward in detail.

Was Jesus's body buried by Joseph? The negative answer to this question is held only by a minority of commentators and is occasionally alleged to be anachronistic by some scholars.[164] However, it has received more attention in recent years due to the press and influence of those who champion one or more related positions. It is variously suggested or held that the dead body of Jesus simply could have been unceremoniously dumped into a common pit for unclaimed bodies or for criminals, or perhaps buried in a rectangular plot dug in the ground, since this was the most common form of burial. As Crossan popularized, the body would have become food for ravaging dogs in the latter case. Similar to our interests, it is also claimed that Acts 13:29 may contradict the Gospel burial accounts by claiming that the Jewish leaders took Jesus's body off the cross and buried it themselves.[165]

---

[164] Craig, "Opening Address," 25–26, and Craig, "Resurrection and the Real Jesus," 160–61, both in Copan, *Real Jesus*.

[165] For examples, John Dominic Crossan, *The Historical Jesus: The Life of a Mediterranean Peasant* (New York: HarperCollins, 1991), 391–94; Crossan, *Jesus: A Revolutionary Biography*

Though it is not our purpose to critique each of the options here, a simple and multifaceted rejoinder to the last point is easily made. Initially, this would allow virtually the entire point regarding the Jewish leaders doing the burial to turn on the meaning of a Greek antecedent referring to the two prior verses. While antecedents are often worthwhile considerations, they are seldom capable of turning away by themselves a number of opposing rejoinders that argue otherwise. Further, Luke apparently saw no contradiction whatsoever between Acts 13:29 and his far more detailed Gospel report in Luke 23:50–56, where Joseph indeed was clearly indicated as the one who buried Jesus's body.[166] So Luke most likely did not consider it to be a straightforward clash. Could it be that Luke never understood the Acts account that way at all?

Even stronger, in contrast to the many sources that favor the traditional burial in a private tomb by Joseph of Arimathea (see the chapter in volume 1 of this study on the burial of Jesus's body), this interpretation of Acts 13:29 has no first-century support. Where are its additional sources to place up against the traditional texts that argue otherwise? Finally and most pointedly, the Jewish leaders mentioned in Acts 13:27 could simply have been a reference to Joseph (a member of the Jewish council himself, after all) and those other members who probably knew of his planned action and simply concurred since they too would be concerned that the Jewish law not be broken by removing and burying the body during the Sabbath.[167]

Is Matthew's account of the guards stationed in front of Jesus's tomb (27:62–66; 28:11–15) some variety of legend? It has already been mentioned that, without much

---

(New York: HarperCollins, 1994), 152–58, 160; Ehrman, *How Jesus Became God*, 7, 141–42, 151–64, 173–74, esp. 155; Spong, *Resurrection*, 239–42; Dale Allison mentions this as a popular view, though it is one with which he disagrees, in *Resurrecting Jesus*, 202–3, 352–63.

[166] It is true that Acts 13:29 is usually identified as one of the Acts sermon summaries that predates the Gospels and may even go back to the early 30s, as in Ehrman, *How Jesus Became God*, 154–55, 225–26. But that should not have a bearing on why Luke included this description if he considered it to constitute a contradiction with his Gospel report.

[167] Ehrman makes a point of arguing that Acts 13:29 states that the Sanhedrin "council as a whole" buried Jesus's body whereas Joseph is only a single individual; see Ehrman, *How Jesus Became God*, 154. But there is no reason that one of their own members could not have been taken as operating on their behalf as well, especially if, as just mentioned, others in the Sanhedrin also knew of Joseph's actions and agreed in order to uphold the law. After all, the reader is told that Joseph was a prominent or respected member of the council (Mark 15:43). So multiple assent is a serious possibility. But regardless, in normal parlance, one member of a group could stand for the whole. It is just too narrow of a way to push the meaning here. One scholar who agrees is Raymond Brown, *Virginal Conception*, 114–15.

question, the majority of critical researchers view these events as never having occurred. But especially since these are not supernatural occurrences, the fact that this detail is only recorded by Matthew deserves some attention. As with the previous question on the Gospel accounts of Jesus's honorable burial in Joseph of Arimathea's tomb, both of these subjects are handled in much more detail in the lengthy chapter on Jesus's burial in volume 1 of this study.[168]

Which women (and how many) are named on their return trip to Jesus's burial tomb? Three women are mentioned in the Gospel of Mark—Mary Magdalene, Mary the mother of James, and Salome (16:1). Two women are mentioned by Matthew—Mary Magdalene and another Mary (28:1). Three women are named in Luke—Mary Magdalene, Joanna, and Mary the mother of James, though Luke does not list them until a little later in the story after they had gone back to tell the disciples (24:10). John mentions only Mary Magdalene by name as coming to the tomb (20:1), though the plural pronoun "we" is used when explaining to the disciples that they do not know the whereabouts of Jesus's body (20:2).[169] Beyond mentioning this single comment here, we will return to this situation later in the chapter.[170]

---

[168] These questions are chiefly discussed in the previous volume, as just noted, though a list of a very few critical scholars may be pertinent: Perrin, *Resurrection*, 45–46; G. W. H. Lampe, "Easter: A Statement," in G. W. H. Lampe and D. M. MacKinnon, *The Resurrection: A Dialogue*, ed. William Purcell (Philadelphia: Westminster, 1966), 38; Miller, "What Do Stories about Resurrection(s) Prove?," in Copan, *Real Jesus*, 83.

[169] Bornkamm views the entire episode as a legend, thus concluding that a response "need not be assessed in detail here" (*Jesus of Nazareth*, 183). Some of the scholars here who mostly just note the overall situation while sometimes making just a few additional comments include Wright in Borg and Wright, *Meaning of Jesus*, 121; Miller, "Stories about Resurrection(s)," 83; Ehrman, *How Jesus Became God*, 134; Vermes, *Resurrection*, 109; Helms, *Gospel Fictions*, 132; George Eldon Ladd, *I Believe in the Resurrection of Jesus* (Grand Rapids: Eerdmans, 1975), 80, 84–86; John M. G. Barclay, "The Resurrection in Contemporary New Testament Scholarship," in D'Costa, *Resurrection Reconsidered*, 24; James McLeman, *Resurrection Then and Now* (Philadelphia: Lippincott, 1967), 138–39; Osborne, *Resurrection Narratives*, 199–200, 216–17, cf. 233–35; Allison, *Resurrecting Jesus*, 247–53; Dunn, *Jesus Remembered*, 828–34, noting differences though without mentioning problems here; Brown, *Virginal Conception*, 117–18, where little comment is provided, except that two separate traditions may be present in Mark; Kaspar, *Jesus the Christ*, 127, 129; Perkins, *Resurrection*, 91, 126, 156, 172, including a chart of differences on 91–93; cf. Robinson, *Can We Trust the New Testament?*, 125–26.

[170] One suggestion may be helpful regarding what the canonical Gospels actually state concerning which women visited the tomb on that first Easter morning. As several specific examples indicate during that weekend from the crucifixion until the burial and

How many angels or "young men" do the women find at the empty tomb? Mark mentions that the women encountered a young man dressed in white inside Jesus's empty tomb (16:5), while a single angel is mentioned outside the tomb in Matt 28:2.[171] Luke reports two men in dazzling clothing apparently inside the tomb

---

empty tomb stories, it is quite clear that the Gospel authors never intended to exhaustively name each of the individual women. Regarding the crucifixion, Mark relates that some women had been watching "from a distance," naming Mary Magdalene, another Mary, and Salome. Then Mark specifies that these were among the "many other women" who had accompanied them up to Jerusalem, but the others remain unnamed (15:40–41). Matthew records that "many women" were present in the vicinity of the crucifixion scene, naming in particular Mary Magdalene and another Mary (27:55–56). However, it would seem that "many women" at the crucifixion in Matthew would number more than just these two named individuals, hence Matthew presumably chose not to name the others. Luke similarly records that women were present at the crucifixion, without naming a single one of them in this context 23:49). At Jesus's burial, Luke again mentions that the women watched and saw how Jesus's body was buried, though still not naming any (23:55–56). Each of the Synoptic Gospel authors narrates that the women went to the tomb that first Sunday, though Luke does not name them until they report to the men, adding clearly that there were "other women with them who told these things to the apostles" (24:10 ESV). This statement that Luke did not name all the women going to the tomb shows that, like the early pericopes, this was simply not the intent of the narration.

Last of all, John mentions only Mary Magdalene (by name) going to the tomb. However, when she ran to the apostles and told them what she saw, the plural "we" was used (20:2). The use of "we" in 20:2 is intriguingly contrasted with the reversion to the singular just a few verses later in John 20:13. On the strength and potential meaning of the plural in the last point here, see Raymond E. Brown, *The Gospel according to John XIII–XXI*, Anchor Bible 29A (Garden City, NY: Doubleday, 1970), 984.

The chief point here is that when the four authors address the crucifixion, the burial, or the empty tomb, the presence of the women observers is mentioned frequently in each Gospel. However, all four accounts state that women were present at least once without mentioning the specific names of the women involved in that particular story. So why should the Gospel authors be held to some random modern standard that attempts to pin them down on naming *each* of the specific women on *each* occasion, with discrepancies being freely acclaimed when the writers do not measure up to what appears to be a modern counting preference? Incredibly, these modern charges are made even when the writers have already indicated over and over that an exhaustive naming of all the women was *not* their intention. Yet, this regular critical practice is done so commonly, even blatantly so. It is the modern error that is egregious here. This ought not even have to be pointed out, especially when it runs counter to perhaps the best-known rule of contemporary literary criticism, namely, never judge an author for something that they clearly indicated was beyond their intentions.

[171] Another issue that may garner the attention of some scholars is why or if the young men in Mark and Luke should be identified as angels. Of course, the issue here is not

(24:4). In John, no angels are mentioned until Mary Magdalene's second trip to the tomb (which was the third trip overall, counting Peter and John running to the tomb in between Mary's trips). When Mary Magdalene returned, bent down, and peered inside the tomb, she saw the two angels there (20:11–12).[172] It should be noticed that each of the Gospels counts the number of angels as either one or two, even if they are located a little differently. This is a slight variance here, well within the constraints of common usage that is employed in everyday descriptions of the same event by different witnesses.[173]

---

whether contemporary scholars think that these men were *actually* angels or even whether they themselves believe in such beings. The question being answered here is who do Mark and Luke think they are? Actually, scholars generally do identify the "young man" dressed in white clothing in Mark 16:5 and the "two men . . . in dazzling clothes" in Luke 24:4 as angels due to several considerations. To start with, the white, festive or special occasion clothing worn by the men, even when viewed inside a dark tomb, along with Luke's use of the adjective "dazzling" for the appearance of their garments (*en esthēti astraptousē*) is quite striking and out of place inside the burial chamber. After all, it should be kept in mind that Luke describes the return of the Son of Man with this term too (17:24), a word often translated as "lightning," having the same root (*astrapē*). Further, in his account, Luke specifically identifies these two "men" as "angels" just a little later (24:23). Moreover, the response of the women to these messengers was one of bewilderment or fright (*emphobōn genomenōn autōn*, Mark 16:5). Thus, referring to these men as angels in these two Gospel texts is hardly a stretch, but is entirely appropriate in each case, fitting well with the contexts. (Reginald Fuller is among the many critical scholars who agrees that the young men at the tomb in both Mark and Luke are most likely angels; see *Formation of the Resurrection Narratives*, 2–3).

[172] As with the names and numbers of the reported women who went to Jesus's tomb, so here as well many scholars simply mention that there were slightly different numbers of angels or young men at the tomb, without much by way of critical interaction; see Karl Barth, *Resurrection of the Dead*, 137; Wright in Borg and Wright, *Meaning of Jesus*, 121; Miller, "Stories about Resurrection(s)," 83; Ehrman, *How Jesus Became God*, 134; Vermes, *Resurrection*, 109–10; Ladd, *Resurrection of Jesus*, 80; Osborne, *Resurrection Narratives*, 210–11; Allison, *Resurrecting Jesus*, 252–53; Dunn, *Jesus Remembered*, 829n12, in reference to the differences though without mentioning any issues or concerns; Brown, *Virginal Conception*, 118–19, who simply notes the situation but with seemingly little else to say; Kaspar, *Jesus the Christ*, 127, 129; Perkins, *Resurrection*, 92, including the chart already mentioned above; cf. Robinson, *Can We Trust the New Testament?*, 125–26.

[173] As John Wenham states concerning the angelic headcounts, this "does not constitute a contradiction or discrepancy. If there were two, there was one." See John Wenham, *The Easter Enigma: Are the Resurrection Accounts in Conflict?* (Grand Rapids: Zondervan, 1984), 87.

Is there a contradiction between the Gospel writers and Paul, who does not explicitly mention the empty tomb? This question is also discussed elsewhere in this study, though it is listed here due to its being a frequently addressed topic in the literature.[174] Initially, no contradiction whatsoever is involved because Paul simply does not comment directly. There is no opposition to a Gospel statement here, and hence no juxtaposition of assertions in the same time, place, or manner. Additionally, a highly significant argument in this context that several major researchers have developed carefully and at much length is that *Paul did not even actually have to mention the empty tomb at all in order to affirm it!* Specifically in Jewish parlance, to be raised from the dead (*anastasis*, meaning to stand or rise up) involved a bodily event, thereby *requiring* that the burial tomb be vacated.[175]

Did Jesus's resurrection appearances occur in Jerusalem or Galilee, as presented in the Gospels? Back to the somewhat outdated discussions in the days of German liberalism, this was one of the most mentioned issues of all. But as the research moved closer to the present, particularly within the past two to four decades, the importance of this subject has fallen off considerably. Today the subject is mentioned by fewer critics and with much less concern than in the past.[176] Those who do make remarks regarding this issue tend to do so more in passing, perhaps due to its former importance, and almost always without urgency.[177]

---

[174] Lindars, "Jesus Risen," 90–91, 94–95; Vermes, *Resurrection*, 111–12; Helms, *Gospel Fictions*, 130; Ehrman, *How Jesus Became God*, 7, 142, 151, 157, 164–69, 173–74, 184–86; Lampe, "Easter," 17, 40, 53, 58–59; Clark, *Interpreting the Resurrection*, 90–91; Allison, *Resurrecting Jesus*, 299–337; Pannenberg, *Jesus: God and Man*, 91, 100; and Alan Lewis, *Between Cross and Resurrection*, 57, who speaks for many scholars when he points out simply that an empty tomb is not explicitly mentioned in Paul's Epistles, hence he may simply have chosen to remain silent on this subject.

[175] Detailed linguistic studies that make this argument include John Granger Cook, *Empty Tomb, Resurrection, Apotheosis* (Tübingen: Mohr Siebeck, 2018), which Cook considers to be one of the chief conclusions in this entire lengthy study (591–93, 618, 623); Gundry, *Sōma in Biblical Theology*, 164, cf. 176; Wright, *Resurrection of the Son of God*, see some of these many comments in xix, 31, and elsewhere, driving the point home quite clearly in 321, 691, 694.

[176] Dunn, *Why Believe in Jesus' Resurrection?* (London: SPCK, 2016), who states, "The answer is hardly very clear, but the question itself may not be very important in the event" (20–21). In this context, Dunn raises other related questions as well (16–25).

[177] A. M. Ramsey terms the Galilee-Jerusalem question the biggest discrepancy of them all in *Resurrection of Christ*, 68–69. Even a little more recently than Ramsay, Ladd refers to the Galilee or Jerusalem subject as "the most foreboding problem" (*Resurrection*

Of the four Gospels, only Mark does not explicitly narrate any appearance stories, though there are several reasons why scholars very rarely question whether Mark knew about Jesus's appearances. For example, Jesus clearly predicts several times that he would rise from the dead after his impending death (Mark 8:31; 9:31; 10:33–34). He further tells his disciples that he would appear to them again after his death in Galilee (Mark 14:28). Plus, the young man at the tomb announces clearly that Jesus already had been raised from the dead, was no longer present in the tomb, and would appear to the disciples in Galilee "just as he told you" (Mark 16:7). Some scholars also think that Mark meant to foreshadow Jesus's private appearance to Peter (as reported in 1 Cor 15:8 and Luke 24:34) by singling him out by name during the narrative at the empty tomb (16:7). So, Jesus's earlier predictions plus the angel's report foreshadow an appearance in Galilee and perhaps another one to Peter.

Matthew describes two appearances of the risen Jesus: the first appearance is to the women in Jerusalem on their way away from the tomb, after also hearing the message of the angel that the disciples were to meet him in Galilee (28:5–10). Then Jesus appears to the disciples later in that location (28:16–20). Interestingly in this last case, Matthew added that the latter location was "to the mountain to which Jesus had directed them" (28:16 NRSV).

Luke is the only canonical Gospel author who narrates only resurrection appearances in Jerusalem and its environs. These involve Jesus walking with two disciples on the road to Emmaus (24:13–33, 35), the report that Jesus had also appeared to Peter (24:34), then his appearance to all his disciples (24:36–49) followed by the ascension (24:50–53).

John narrates an appearance to Mary Magdalene during her second trip to the tomb (20:14–17), then another to the disciples without Thomas in Jerusalem (20:19b–25), plus another appearance in Jerusalem a week later to the disciples

---

of Jesus, 81–82, 86–90). In 1967, McLeman called the subject one of the biggest disputes (*Resurrection Then and Now*, 140, 145, but see 152). Reginald Fuller referred to it as "major" (*Formation of the Resurrection Narratives*, 5). Other scholars who either express doubts or sometimes simply note the issue include Bornkamm, *Jesus of Nazareth*, 182; Miller, "Stories about Resurrection(s)," 84; Hoover, "Orthodoxy and Veracity," 135; Ehrman, *How Jesus Became God*, 134–35; Vermes, *Resurrection*, 110–11; Robinson, *Can We Trust the New Testament?*, 125; Barclay, "Resurrection in Contemporary New Testament Scholarship," 25; Lampe, "Easter," 40; Clark, *Interpreting the Resurrection*, 90; Osborne, *Resurrection Narratives*, 212–14, 272, 281–82; Lorenzen, *Resurrection and Discipleship*, 122, 127–28, cf. 184; Pannenberg, *Jesus: God and Man*, 104–5; Sanders, *Historical Figure of Jesus*, 278.

while Thomas was present (20:26–29). In the so-called Gospel appendix in the final chapter, Jesus appears to seven of his disciples on the shore of the Sea of Tiberias (Galilee) while they are fishing, followed by an early morning meal plus a chat with Peter and John (21:1–23).

One of the chief reasons why the Galilee-Jerusalem question has tended to calm down considerably in recent years is the way that the research is both viewed and carried out today, including how the relevant textual issues are presently framed. The different varieties of source, redaction, tradition, and narrative criticism have yielded an increased sense not only that the New Testament authors were relatively autonomous and freely investigated their preferred interests, but also that they sometimes focused on their chosen geographical areas and the themes that were most crucial there. Therefore, concentrating on a geographical region by no means rules out other venues. A particular theme that may have seemed absolutely necessary to one writer or area may not have had the same import elsewhere. As a result, perhaps even most critical scholars tend more frequently to view the overall subject as being of less vital impact and most frequently recognize appearances in both locations.[178]

Are there contradictions between Paul, the Gospels, and Acts regarding the nature of Jesus's resurrection appearances? This has long been a key issue where skeptics, moderates, and conservatives do not always "line up" where one might think. Often lurking behind the scenes in this question is whether, by adding his appearance (1 Cor 15:8) to the early creedal list in 1 Cor 15:3–7, Paul was stating or assuming that all the earlier resurrection appearances were of the same nature as his? Varying crucial responses are given here.[179] This involved issue has been treated in volume 1 of this study and comes up again later.

---

[178] One indication of this growing change is that even Rudolf Bultmann stated many years ago that "after Jesus's arrest, the disciples fled to Galilee" (a common critical view) and the first appearances occurred there. However, "the appearances of the risen Lord probably were not confined to Galilee but also occurred at Jerusalem after the disciples had return[ed] there (Luke reports only such)." See Bultmann, *Theology of the New Testament*, 1:45. Of course, it should be noted that Bultmann by no means recognized literal resurrection appearances of Jesus at all; see Bultmann, "New Testament and Mythology," 34–44.

[179] Karl Barth, *Church Dogmatics*, 4.1:335; Borg in Borg and Wright, *Meaning of Jesus*, 132–33; Hoover, "Orthodoxy and Veracity," 131; Robinson, *Can We Trust the New Testament?*, 125; Reginald Fuller calls this one of the two "major" questions (*Formation of the Resurrection Narratives*, 5); Barclay "Resurrection in Contemporary New Testament Scholarship," 17, 24; Lampe, "Easter," 18, 40, cf. 58; Allison, *Resurrecting Jesus*, 265–68, 317; Sanders, *Historical Figure of Jesus*, 276–78; Pannenberg thinks that the Gospel appearance

Does the very early creedal list of resurrection appearances in 1 Cor 15:3–7 differ markedly from the combined list of appearances as reported in the Gospels and Acts? This is a very puzzling charge for more reasons than one. For starters, at least there appears to be a fairly strong similarity between these separate accounts. Only the appearance to James plus the one to the 500 persons at one time do not potentially correspond to narratives in the Gospels and Acts. But on second thought, why would these appearances have to line up precisely with each other anyway—as if there is some exhaustive list of appearances that must somehow be coordinated in virtually the same way?[180]

Are statements that Jesus's resurrection occurred on the "third day" or on the "first day of the week" meant to be taken literally or are these more general or even figurative comments?[181] Like some other issues that have been mentioned, this discussion was also more common decades ago. But this question is addressed in more than one context, such as in the initial volume of this study.

Were the resurrection appearances meant to be legitimatization formulas for purposes of signifying those who were the leaders in the early church? In other words, was there less concern regarding the nature (or even the reality?) of the resurrection appearances themselves in favor of a means in the early church to position leaders? Given the early pre-Pauline creedal statement in 1 Cor 15:3–7 plus Paul's addition in 15:8, the most frequently suggested names for appearances that indicated leadership roles are those of Peter, James the brother of Jesus, and Paul.

---

narratives are much too physical and of "such a strongly legendary character that one can scarcely find a historical kernel"! See Pannenberg, *Jesus: God and Man*, 89, also 92. For Ehrman along with many other researchers of late, Paul at least believed that Jesus was raised bodily. See Ehrman, *How Jesus Became God*, 133, 137.

[180] Barth, *Church Dogmatics*, 4.1:335; Bornkamm, *Jesus of Nazareth*, 182; Lüdemann, "First Rebuttal," 54–55, and "Second Rebuttal," 60–61, in Copan and Tacelli, *Jesus' Resurrection*; Barclay "Resurrection in Contemporary New Testament Scholarship," 17, 24; Osborne, *Resurrection Narratives*, 281; Lorenzen, *Resurrection and Discipleship*, 178–80; Helms, *Gospel Fictions*, 130.

[181] Ehrman, for example, argues that these times are "not necessarily a historical recollection of when the resurrection happened, but a theological claim" (140). Further, "But as I argued . . . the idea that Jesus rose on the 'third day' was originally a theological construct, not a historical piece of information" (175). See Ehrman, *How Jesus Became God*. This is a popular position, as in Lorenzen, *Resurrection and Discipleship*, 267–68, among other commentators.

But the general conception here seems to be firm that, while these ideas may figure somewhere into the equation, as noted frequently by commentators, it is not the primary purpose or focus of the appearances. Nor does the notion of positioning override in any way the events themselves.[182] For example, Crossan is perhaps the foremost defender of this position concerning the legitimatizing of apostolic leadership, without attempting to explain away appearances/real experiences of some sort. Whatever the latter were, they were real experiences, though not supernatural, according to Crossan.[183]

Related to the previous question, did the resurrection appearances also serve as an apostolic (as well as a general) call to believers to engage in Christian ministry? Beyond issues related to historical and theological matters, by far the majority response from critical scholars on this idea is in the affirmative. The risen Jesus exhorted his followers to participate in various ministry endeavors such as preaching, teaching, and

---

[182] As recognized, for example, in Rudolf Pesch's major position change, as observed in his 1973 publication, "Zur Entstehung," 96–97, 201–28, esp. 212–18. After many critical responses to his ideas and the ensuing interaction, he moved to a more robust view that involved the necessity of the postresurrection visions and appearances of Jesus, as expressed in Pesch, "Zur Entstehung des Glaubens an die Auferstehung Jesu: Ein neuer Versuch," *Freiburger Zeitschrift für Philosophie und Theologie* 30 (1983): 73–98. The key words here are in the addendum to the title: "Ein neuer Versuch," or "A New Attempt." Other pertinent works by Pesch include "Materialien und Bemerkungen." See also Crossan, *Historical Jesus*, 397–404. Additional relevant works by other critical scholars include Crossan, *Jesus: A Revolutionary Biography*, 169–92; Wilckens, *Resurrection*, 13, 16, 48–50, 65, 114; Fuller, *Formation of the Resurrection Narratives*, 49; Lorenzen, *Resurrection and Discipleship*, 130–31, 136–37, 143–44, 185; Perkins, *Resurrection*, 131–32; Allison, at least in part, rejects this view of positioning within the early Christian leadership (*Resurrecting Jesus*, 237–38, 245, 268); Pannenberg agrees with many in thinking that this understanding may be possible, though without negating the actual resurrection appearances of Jesus themselves (*Jesus: God and Man*, 90–91, 97); cf. Williams, *Resurrection*, 116–17.

[183] John Dominic Crossan and N. T. Wright, *The Resurrection of Jesus: John Dominic Crossan and N. T. Wright in Dialogue*, ed. Robert B. Stewart (Minneapolis: Fortress, 2006), see esp. the "Dialogue," 33–34, 38, and Crossan, "Opening Statement," 24–25; also, Crossan, *Historical Jesus*, 397–98; Crossan, *Jesus: A Revolutionary Biography*, 190.

baptizing.[184] For many scholars, radical discipleship is the reasonable result.[185] These last themes are pursued in depth in the last volume of this study.

---

[184] For instance, Reginald Fuller thinks that Jesus's tomb was empty and Jesus actually appeared to his followers (though in a less than fully bodily manner), while speaking of how Jesus's message to his disciples "involved a communication of meaning: God revealed his Son." Further, for Fuller, this message was often an auditory communication from Jesus that set up the apostolic leadership and inaugurated the mission to the Aramaic-speaking Jews in Jerusalem, Judea, and beyond, to the Hellenistic Jews, and finally to the Gentiles (*Formation of the Resurrection Narratives*, particularly 46–49, also 169, 172, 181). Jürgen Moltmann divides the structure of the resurrection appearances into "three different dimensions." First, the "*prospective* visions of hope" due to "God's coming glory." Second, the *retrospective* remembrance of the past: "The One who will come is the One crucified on Golgotha." The third aspect is comprised of Jesus's "*personal call*"—an invitation to men and women to heed his call and follow him in ministry and mission. See Moltmann, "The Resurrection of Christ," in D'Costa, *Resurrection Reconsidered*, 76; also, Moltmann, *Theology of Hope*, 202. Another instance is Thorwald Lorenzen's extensive emphasis that projects outwardly from Jesus's resurrection appearances to every area of the Christian worldview and the ensuing Christian life, including faith and praxis (part 3) as well as the new relation to the God who raised Jesus from the dead, salvation, and the mission of the church (269–74, plus all of part 4). See Lorenzen, *Resurrection and Discipleship*, 191–320. A few more of the many examples here include Pannenberg, *Jesus: God and Man*, 93–95; Perkins, *Resurrection*, 72, 136, 167; Allison, *Resurrecting Jesus*, 145.

[185] As a brief but relevant excursus, a major theological line of interpretation proceeds through Barth's view of radical discipleship, such as in Barth's *Church Dogmatics*, 4.1:102–22 (and also *Church Dogmatics* 4.2 on Bonhoeffer's contributions), and to those theologians whom Barth influenced. Barth's view similarly reflects earlier influences from key aspects of Søren Kierkegaard's thought too, as in *Kierkegaard's Attack upon "Christendom,"* trans. Walter Lowrie (Princeton, NJ: Princeton University Press, 1944), esp. "What Christ's Judgment Is about Official Christianity," 115–24, and "The Instant, Nos. III–VII," 125–52; also, Kierkegaard, *Purity of Heart Is to Will One Thing: Spiritual Preparation for the Office of Confession*, trans. Douglas V. Steere (New York: Harper & Brothers, 1956), esp. essays 7 and 8. Dietrich Bonhoeffer is best known for this theme of radical discipleship, including how this subject is tied to the death and resurrection of Jesus Christ. See Bonhoeffer, *The Cost of Discipleship*, rev. ed., trans. Reginald H. Fuller (New York: Macmillan, 1963), 340–44. This also includes Bonhoeffer's thoughts on the basis for human government as emanating from the cross, atonement, resurrection, and exaltation of Christ. See Bonhoeffer, *Ethics*, ed. Eberhard Bethge, trans. Neville Horton Smith (New York: Macmillan, 1986), particularly 336–39. For ideas on the Anabaptist tradition of thinkers that he terms "Radical Protestantism," including both Bonhoeffer and Kierkegaard, see Donald F. Durnbaugh, *The Believer's Church: The History and Character of Radical Protestantism* (New York: Macmillan, 1968), particularly chap. 8, "Discipleship and Apostolicity," 209–25. Durnbaugh states, "Nothing has called attention recently to the demands of Christian obedience as has Dietrich Bonhoeffer's book *The Cost of Discipleship*, sealed as it was by his martyrdom

These are some of the most commonly raised questions from perhaps a majority of critical scholars regarding the items in the Gospel texts and elsewhere that they think may range from apparent discrepancies all the way to outright legends and myths. Some of the scholars produced easily accessible charts or lists of various sorts.[186] It should be acknowledged as well that, depending on how selective one wishes to get, there are other potential issues to inquire about, though they tend to be usually of a more minor nature.[187]

Going back further into the critical literature of the past two centuries, the question of whether Jesus's appearances occurred or at least began in Galilee or Jerusalem would still have to rank very highly in terms of the topics that have evoked the most scholarly responses and interest. It is perhaps even the most commonly raised subject.[188] But sticking to the original overview and proposed study that

---

in 1945 at the hands of the SS troopers" (209). Later in the same chapter, Durnbaugh places Kierkegaard in the same radical tradition (211). Though separated somewhat in theological terms, this theme also emerges in Bultmann's writings, such as in *Theology of the New Testament*, 1:11–22; 2:203–31, esp. 229–30 on Christian views on personal property. Bultmann's position is also mapped out well in Thomas C. Oden's volume, *Radical Obedience: The Ethics of Rudolf Bultmann* (Philadelphia: Westminster, 1964), including a response from Bultmann that notes some of his concerns about Oden's interpretation on 141–47. Cf. also James D. G. Dunn, *Jesus' Call to Discipleship* (Cambridge: Cambridge University Press, 1992), and N. T. Wright, *Following Jesus: Biblical Reflections on Discipleship* (Grand Rapids: Eerdmans, 1994), along with many other scholars.

[186] Such as those by Perkins on the narratives of the empty tomb and the women's trips to the tomb (*Resurrection*, 91–93) and the three charts by Miller with regard to the empty tomb accounts (83), the resurrection appearance stories (84), and the post-Easter appearance accounts (85). See Miller, "Stories about Resurrection(s)."

[187] For examples, Perkins along with others mention additional items, like the time of day that the women visited the tomb, their purpose in going there, the state of the tombstone, what they discovered upon reaching or entering the tomb, their reactions to the situation, the angelic message to the women, their physical and emotional responses, plus the type of report that they imparted to the others (Perkins, *Resurrection*, 91–93). Miller includes many of the same additional questions, plus whether or not there was a guard posted at the tomb, who else was involved, and a conclusion. As far as post-Easter appearance accounts, Miller also inquires concerning the times, persons involved, places, messages, reactions, any confirmation plus another conclusion. See Miller, "Stories about Resurrection(s)," 83–85.

[188] It is rather intriguing that this issue seems to be framed fairly often as two opponents being pitted against each other, as in Galilee "versus" Jerusalem options, when they are very far from being directly opposed. Even Bultmann was clear about the "both/and approach"

began as a survey of scholarship from 1975 to the present, it appears that the names and numbers of the women who visited Jesus's tomb might be the most popular questions, followed closely by the cognate issue of the number of angels that the women encountered at the tomb. Also, ever since the age of German liberalism began well over two centuries ago, the contrast between the nature of the appearance to Paul "versus" those to the disciples has been a popular question.[189]

Additional suggestions regarding the cases of the women and the angels will be offered in this chapter. Elsewhere in this study the nature of Paul's appearance as compared to those of the others who claimed to have seen the risen Jesus is examined in the context of discussing the nature of Jesus's resurrection body. Our earlier comments regarding Galilee and Jerusalem will have to suffice for now.

To Harmonize or Not to Harmonize?

Most critical scholars today, including even the conservative ones, generally eschew harmonizing scenarios. For example, after mentioning a list of textual issues and making a limited number of potential suggestions as to how a few inquiries might be explained, E. P. Sanders states, "We are still left with an intractable problem."[190] After mentioning various examples of discrepancies, Raymond Brown notes that "we must reject the thesis that the Gospels can be harmonized."[191] Yet, Brown describes these issues as "minor" and still affirms Jesus's appearances in spite of them, as do many scholars.[192] G. B. Caird and L. D. Hurst think that it is "unlikely" that a harmony could ever be produced.[193] In agreement with the other scholars, Walter Kaspar holds that "no harmonization is possible."[194] "At almost every point, the accounts go in separate directions. It is impossible to harmonize them in such a way as to produce a

---

in his citation quoted in this chapter above, and that probably remains the most frequent response.

[189] It must be noted here carefully that given all the other more careful tallies throughout this entire study, the question about which apparent discrepancies are mentioned most commonly by scholars is definitely not meant to be an exact count.

[190] Sanders, *Historical Figure of Jesus*, 276–79, quotation on 279.

[191] Brown lists some of these problems in *Virginal Conception*, 101–29. The quotation above is from 106.

[192] Brown, 106, 125–29. The one-word quotation is from 106.

[193] G. B. Caird and L. D. Hurst, *New Testament Theology* (Oxford: Clarendon, 1994), 239.

[194] Kaspar, *Jesus the Christ*, 128.

single, simpler tradition," states Perkins.[195] C. F. Evans asserts more strongly that it is "quite impossible" to harmonize the accounts.[196] Neville Clark agrees that these sorts of efforts are "doomed to failure."[197]

General responses even from conservative academics, most of whom are not inerrantists anyway, are not all that different. N. T. Wright remarks that it is "notoriously difficult" to explain all the problem areas, and we shall never know "some of the details."[198] Grant Osborne concurs: "No true harmonization of the appearances is possible since they originally appeared as isolated units in kerygmatic situations; the actual chronology of them is unknown."[199] Speaking of the problem areas in question, Paul Rhodes Eddy remarks, "though we may agree that they are not fatal, nevertheless some are not small," and they "cannot be harmonized."[200]

After providing a list of some of the problematic details that are tough to reconcile completely, Robert Stein comments on the difficulty of working out a harmonization.[201] William Lane Craig observes briefly: "Discrepancies in secondary details could exist."[202] On another occasion, like Brown above, Craig also observes that "the sort of disparities in the secondary details . . . do not suffice to undermine the historical core" of the resurrection appearance details. Then Craig correctly adds, "No professional historian jettisons his sources because disparities exist at points," using the example cited by Murray Harris of the "two irreconcilable accounts" by Livy and Polybius of Hannibal crossing the Alps in his wars against Rome. Yet, "no historian doubts that Hannibal did carry out such a campaign."[203]

A few conservative scholars have nonetheless tried to assemble a harmony of the reported events that took place after the crucifixion, though usually only pertaining to a limited number of occurrences at a time rather than attempting to reconcile an entire, long-range scenario. Often preferable to actual harmonized lists are the attempts to treat individual problem areas by explaining enough details in order to

---

[195] Perkins, *Resurrection*, 93.

[196] Evans, *Resurrection and the New Testament*, 128.

[197] Clark, *Interpreting the Resurrection*, 84.

[198] Wright, in Borg and Wright, *Meaning of Jesus*, 121–22.

[199] Osborne, *Resurrection Narratives*, 282.

[200] Eddy, "A Response to William Lane Craig," in Davis, Kendall, and O'Collins, *Resurrection*, 328.

[201] Stein, *Jesus the Messiah*, 260–62.

[202] Craig, "On Doubts about the Resurrection," *Modern Theology* 6 (1989): 53–75.

[203] Craig, "Resurrection and the Real Jesus," 164.

shed some light on particular recalcitrant issues. But even inerrantists do not make these attempts very often.[204]

Well-respected theologian George Eldon Ladd did attempt to construct a basic route to account for the details concerning the women's trip to the empty tomb as well as the resurrection appearance accounts.[205] New Testament scholar Murray Harris comments, "A harmonisation of the resurrection narratives is not impossible, at least in principle. There is at present a strong antipathy among New Testament scholars to the procedure of harmonisation, although it is one of the historian's tools of trade."[206] Then he directs some initial comments to the individual issues of the Galilee and Jerusalem appearance scenarios plus, like Ladd, attempting a potential listing of events from the women's trip to the tomb through the appearance accounts.[207] Philosopher Richard Swinburne provides a chart to align the resurrection appearances along with an accompanying discussion.[208] But none of this should be construed as harmonizing attempts per se, especially in light of Swinburne's straightforward comments that such cannot be done.

Moderate scholars have also done similarly, as we have already seen above in a few instances. More typically, these efforts are briefer suggestions directed to fewer events, seemingly those where it appears that a few well-placed comments could be really helpful. Thus, without being a traditional harmonization, Brown still produced helpful tables that line up the crucifixion and burial accounts in the Synoptic Gospels as well as produce another comparison of the events in all four Gospels from before Jesus's death on Friday to the empty tomb occurrences of Easter.[209] Elsewhere, Brown makes precisely the point just mentioned here, actually arguing against a harmonization in the context while making a number of pertinent and helpful comments regarding how the resurrection appearances of Jesus might fit into the Gospel scenario.[210]

---

[204] No effort is made here to single out those scholars who are inerrantists and those who are not, chiefly because of the often extreme efforts of some writers to attempt to force upon others their own definitions and interpretations of what inerrancy *must* indicate.

[205] Ladd, *Resurrection of Jesus*, 90–94.

[206] Harris, *Raised Immortal*, 68–69.

[207] Harris, 52, 68–71.

[208] Swinburne, *Resurrection of God Incarnate*, 147–59, with the chart on 157.

[209] Brown, *Death of the Messiah*, with the charts on 2:902–3 and 1016, respectively.

[210] Brown, *Virginal Conception*, 99–111, with a chart on 100 that shows variations that also indicate similarities.

Then there are what might be called the "un-harmonies" of some moderate scholars who, while shunning or perhaps even disdaining harmonizations, nonetheless make some excellent efforts themselves to work out some of the tangled details. This includes James D. G. Dunn's scholarly work that unpacks a number of the key questions that we have discussed in this chapter.[211] Another example could occur where a single issue is addressed and dissected, such as Gerald O'Collins devoting a chapter to a question in Luke 24, weighing and suggesting various options as to whether the risen Jesus ate fish.[212] Then there are William Alston's thoughts on Reginald Fuller's attempts to "make a coherent harmonization impossible," after which Alston develops his own efforts at making some progress in this regard.[213]

Without much question, one of the most ambitious efforts at harmonizing the death, burial, empty tomb, and resurrection appearance accounts regarding Jesus in recent decades was produced by British New Testament scholar and theologian John Wenham. Not going into the project with his head in the sand, so to speak, Wenham acknowledges from the outset that the five major and relevant New Testament authors present accounts that "differ from each other to an astonishing degree" and cites much scholarly testimony to that fact.[214] Going beyond the call of duty,

---

[211] Dunn, *Jesus Remembered*, chap. 18, particularly 828–32, 840–57, 861–62, including the chart of Jesus's resurrection appearances in all four Gospels on 841–42. Cf. also Dunn's earlier volume *The Evidence for Jesus*, when, treating the empty tomb and appearance traditions, he includes in each section a discussion of "Conflicting evidence" followed by more detailed "Considerations in favour" (63–72). See also Dunn, *Why Believe in Jesus' Resurrection?*, which states, "The answer is hardly very clear, but the question itself may not be very important in the event" (20–21). In this context, Dunn raises other related questions as well (16–25).

[212] O'Collins, *Interpreting the Resurrection*, 39–52.

[213] Alston, "Biblical Criticism," 170–73. Alston was listed above as more likely being closer to the conservative camp, though he makes numerous concessions to moderate scholars like Reginald Fuller.

[214] John Wenham, *Easter Enigma: Are the Resurrection Accounts in Conflict?* (Grand Rapids: Zondervan, 1984), 9, with a lengthy list of scholars who agree on tough issues being apparent in the text (9–12). A dozen tables and diagrams throughout the volume are also very helpful. Wenham acknowledges freely that harmonizing efforts are "generally frowned on in modern study of the gospels" (126). In recommending this book on its cover, another British New Testament scholar R. T. France states that Wenham's text is "clearly and deliberately refusing to play the critical game according to the accepted rules, and is for that reason to my mind refreshing and deserving of notice. . . . Some of the major reconstructions which are offered on the basis of odd hints and bits of New Testament information carefully drawn together I find extraordinarily suggestive."

Wenham includes a few chapters of background information, followed by incorporating details regarding the crucifixion and the burial of Jesus, the women's trips to the tomb, and each of the appearances. Wenham also designates some appendices that include more brief thoughts on harmonizing efforts as well as an attempt to work out details pertaining to "theories of relationship" in Jesus's family as well as the identities of the "Marys" who are quite apparent throughout, such as in their heading to the empty tomb. In the process, Wenham claims that his own harmonized account could be construed differently and thus makes no claims to "any infallibility of detail" on his part.[215]

True Contradictions and Easy Explanations

Here we will direct some comments to the more general philosophical issue of what constitutes a "contradiction" and then will make some suggestions regarding two of the most common and frequently raised Gospel questions of all, both having been listed above. Namely, what were the names and numbers of women who visited the empty tomb on the first Easter Sunday morning? Also, how many angels did the women encounter when they arrived at the tomb? As already mentioned, these two subjects are perhaps the most frequently raised inquiries in the most recent studies of these specifics.

In an article that received much acclaim, prominent philosopher Eleonore Stump questioned the methodology taken by well-known New Testament theologian Raymond Brown. Stump complained of methodologies where "any tension in a narrative will constitute an apparent inconsistency."[216] Her chief point was that scholars sometimes reveal their personal biases, interpretations, or other attitudes

---

[215] Wenham, *Easter Enigma*, 54. It must be confessed that for years my copy of Wenham's book was kept on a library shelf off by itself due to its lack of consultation and use. But of late, several factors have shown it to be very useful. Besides some very creative suggestions in keeping with R. T. France's comment directly above, some of which seem quite likely (such as those on 49, 57, 66–67, 81–85, 87–89, 93–99, 114), there are a few considerations that leave one wondering why this or that solution had not been proposed more frequently in the past. On the other hand, additional comments indicated Wenham's humility and recognition of the tentative nature of certain other of his comments (9, 32–33, 42, 46, 54, 64, 78–79, 84, 147n8).

[216] Eleonore Stump, "Visits to the Sepulcher and Biblical Exegesis," *Faith and Philosophy* 6 (1989): esp. 369.

when scenarios that could be explained without much effort are simply passed off as problems, conflicts, discrepancies, or even contradictions when they are not necessarily anything of the sort. Stump thinks that these overly easy generalizations often reveal more of the author's own attitude *about* the documents in question. Instead of an apparent solution being offered, which would not have been difficult in many circumstances, the real problem is thought by the exegete to be a lack of ancient historical acumen or even the writers' fabrication of the stories in question or other issues. Stump comments, "I find this claim very difficult to believe."[217]

Stump objects throughout this essay to subjective judgments that are justified neither historically nor philosophically but are too commonly based on the exegete's presuppositions and expectations. For instance, Stump chooses the examples of the differences in the Gospel accounts concerning the women coming to Jesus's tomb on Sunday morning, noting Brown's many areas where he thinks there are issues, no matter how small. Brown often attempts to account for these differences by suggesting various sources and editors of the material. The different issues are summarized in a chart.[218]

Stump remarks that, for all the "good judgment" that Brown shows, his surmisals do not constitute historical demonstration—in fact, they are often quite subjective in nature: "It is important to see that Brown's suppositions are not themselves demonstrated by historical evidence."[219] Rather, they "remain more a matter of speculative inference than of historical data."[220] In short, Brown's approach is problematic because of tendencies such as too easily concluding that discrepancies are present, that editors freely invented new material, and that very little effort is made to ascertain how these accounts may actually be compatible when he needs instead to back up his suppositions with data and sound reasoning. Perhaps the implied weak areas could be propped up with relatively simple explanations.[221] But as is, Brown is overly subjective without appropriate support for too many of his conclusions.

Another prominent philosopher, William Alston, likewise critiqued influential New Testament scholar Reginald Fuller along similar lines, though Alston makes many concessions to Fuller's critical stance.[222] Fuller accepts the actual though nonbodily

---

[217] Stump, 368–69.

[218] Brown, *Gospel according to John XIII–XXI*, 974.

[219] Stump, "Visits to the Sepulcher," 366.

[220] Stump, 367.

[221] Stump, 355–59, 366–72.

[222] William P. Alston, "Biblical Criticism," 161, 163, 169–70, 177, 79, 182.

resurrection appearances of the risen Jesus, and Alston concentrates on Fuller's denial of bodily appearances. He announces that Fuller's argument "is extremely weak" and, later, identifies it as "much too weak."[223] Alston is quite critical of New Testament scholars who too frequently champion the slogan "*It is possible that it happened this way, therefore it did.*" Or if something could have happened because the Gospel writers enjoyed telling stories, "then we will assume that they did." If sayings of Jesus could have originated elsewhere, "then we will suppose that they did."[224]

Briefly, Alston's chief complaints pertain to Fuller's "*extremely speculative suggestions that are allowed to play a major role in an argument.*" Further, "recent Gospel critics seem driven to achieve definite results at any cost, despite the thinness of the data at their disposal." The critics rely too much on the argument from silence, having "produced much chaff along with this wheat." Is there a hidden agenda somewhere?[225]

Often when scholars "cross lines" and critique researchers in other fields, they are criticized themselves. This may be the case with some of the items in these two examples here and the New Testament scholars could no doubt defend themselves at several critical junctures. But two comments can be made very briefly. First, the definition of a "contradiction" as well as the structure of argumentation are within the areas of logic and critical thinking.[226] Second, it is not necessarily a matter of two different disciplines here. New Testament scholar John Wenham likewise critiqued the tendency of critical scholars who tend to overuse terms such as "discrepancy" and "contradiction" when these are not always present.[227]

Again, to repeat, many other important issues like those raised in this chapter are also treated elsewhere throughout this study. For example, two such instances are the similarities between the exceptionally early pre-Pauline creedal list of resurrection appearances in 1 Corinthians 15 and those appearance accounts narrated in the Gospels, and a comparison of Paul's teaching concerning his own appearance of Jesus to the other appearances as to whether or not they were bodily in nature.

---

[223] Alston, 160,

[224] Alston, 181.

[225] Alston, 181–82.

[226] Cf. Stump's somewhat similar comments here ("Visits to the Sepulcher," 365, 367). Stump remarks, "It is important to recognize the difference between historical evidence, on the one hand, and philosophical presuppositions and methodological commitments, on the other," whereas Brown relies too heavily on the latter (371).

[227] Wenham, *Easter Enigma*, 85, 87.

Evangelicals and Inerrantists in These Discussions

Evangelicals

Evangelical *scholars* should not shy away in the least from historical Jesus studies and conversations. For several reasons, they should be involved, participating in this research. Conservatives should be willing to acknowledge their presuppositions as well, but so should liberals and skeptics. This is an absolutely crucial issue because there is a need for everyone to acknowledge, initially, that *all scholars* have presuppositions. None are exempt here. *Everyone* views the world through their own variously colored glasses. Some of the lenses on these glasses are rose colored and others are opaque, but is one better than the other? Or does one guarantee truth while the other does not? No one owns the market on presuppositions.

Of course, there are large differences between liberals and conservatives. However, some disputes are between liberals and their fellow liberals, or between conservatives and their fellow conservatives. All of these can be equally as strident. So why are radical or liberal presuppositions often somehow viewed as seemingly privileged, more intelligent, or more scholarly? It could have much to do with liberals more frequently composing the leadership in the best universities, or the "left" often being thought of as the "freethinkers." But is that a well-celebrated perception or the actual state of affairs in the world? Regardless, good arguments do not follow one group or another.

As asked earlier in this chapter, are conservatives too tied to their creeds, as liberals often assert, daring not to venture too far away from these standards for fear that they will be viewed as liberal or moving over to the opposition's side? Is it not also the case that skeptics are perhaps just as unlikely to wish to appear narrow-minded by crossing into conservative territory and trying to avoid the raised eyebrows of *their* colleagues? Frankly, there are places where *neither* side can venture—the fear of movement is definitely not all on one side or the other. The retort may be that liberals are freer to roam. But again, is that simply the perception? It often seems that both sides are roughly as unlikely to cross over the invisible lines of separation. Conservatives, on the other hand, often claim that liberals prefer window dressing to strong arguments, whether or not the latter are popular.

However, whatever the angle taken, a more basic ground of measurement remains. While the arena of ideas is where these dialogues and discussions should be aired, heard, and decided, this ultimately concerns the discourse of ideas. More crucial than the issues of whether or where lines can or should be drawn and crossed is the subject of where the data lie. If there is truth to be gained and it may be ascertained, according to the canons of probability, how is it determined?

More specifically for our present purposes regarding the study of the historical Jesus or New Testament studies as a whole, there are many issues that conservatives discuss and ought to be interested in dialoguing through and prepared to exchange ideas or even change views. If this is not the case, as has already remarked more than once, why are the multiple-views volumes currently so popular? This seems to be a clear enough indication.

For examples, who wrote each of the four Gospels? What were their most likely dates of composition? Especially in the Epistles, what is the nature of the early creedal traditions, such as Rom 1:3–4; 10:9; 1 Cor 11:23–26; 15:3–7, or the sermon summaries in Acts? How early are such statements and confessions held by scholars of all persuasions to precede the writings of the canonical New Testament books?[228] How accurate are these reports likely to be?[229] How do we evaluate the uses of coauthors, amanuenses, or other writers in addition to the critically assigned authors of the epistles?[230] Conservatives and liberals both, in fact, dialogue regularly through each of these subjects.

Further, what about questions concerning which both conservatives and liberals have frequently or even generally changed their minds, chiefly in the last few decades. These might include whether or not the Gospels fit most closely the genre of the Greco-Roman *bios*?[231] Was Jesus a healer and an exorcist?[232] What role might

---

[228] As per Bauckham, *Jesus and the Eyewitnesses*, 264–71, 578; James P. Ware, "The Resurrection of Jesus in the Pre-Pauline Formula of 1 Cor 15.3–5," *New Testament Studies* 60 (2014): 475–98; Ehrman, *Did Jesus Exist?*, 92–93, 97, 109–13, 140–41, 251, 254; Ehrman, *How Jesus Became God*, 139, 225–30.

[229] The answers to some of these latter questions pertaining to the early pre–New Testament creeds play a central and crucial role in this present study and were addressed in much detail in the initial volume of this study.

[230] Examples might include the words, "I Tertius, who wrote this letter, greet you in the Lord" (Rom 16:22); or the opening, "Paul, Silvanus, and Timothy" to the church in 2 Thess 1:1; or the role played by "Silvanus" in 1 Pet 5:12.

[231] One of the very best discussions of some of these topics, including a few of the many ramifications here, written by a conservative author is the excellent volume by Michael R. Licona, *Why Are There Differences in the Gospels? What We Can Learn from Ancient Biography* (Oxford: Oxford University Press, 2017), particularly chaps. 3–5; John H. Walton and D. Brent Sandy, *The Lost World of Scripture: Ancient Literary Culture and Biblical Authority* (Downers Grove, IL: InterVarsity, 2013), 279–80, ask about the issues involved with "applying modern genre criteria to ancient literature."

[232] Intriguingly, arguably the two best investigations of this subject were written by a moderate researcher and a conservative scholar. See Meier, *Marginal Jew*, 2:507–1038,

be played by writings that are sufficiently close to New Testament times to be helpful, but which are admittedly noncanonical? Is there a particular time of demarcation within which noncanonical writings may be most helpful?[233]

There are also relevant philosophical and religious issues where all sides converse freely. These include questions concerning God's existence, the problem of evil, the question of miracles, and the afterlife, among other topics.[234] Occasionally, conservatives have engaged in debates or dialogues with other conservatives, moderates, and especially skeptics, either as live or written events. This has furthered the exchange of ideas on many of the important issues that have been raised in this study.[235]

---

for the treatment of miracles, and conservative scholar Twelftree, *Jesus the Miracle Worker*, 328–59, for the conclusions. Here in particular, it is the skeptical views that have changed somewhat, at least in terms of the frequency of the exceptionally widespread amount of recent assent. For instance, after a lengthy discussion, Marcus Borg writes, "Despite the difficulty which miracles pose for the modern mind, on historical grounds it is virtually indisputable that Jesus was a healer and exorcist." Then Borg follows this comment by providing three reasons for backup. See Marcus J. Borg, *Jesus, A New Vision: Spirit, Culture, and the Life of Discipleship* (New York: HarperCollins, 1987), 61 for the quotation in the context of pages 47, 59–61, 65–67, 71. Jarl Fossum is in basic agreement with Borg's assessment in "Understanding Jesus' Miracles," *Bible Review* 10 (1994): 16–23, 50.

[233] Bock, *Studying the Historical Jesus*, which surveys historical criticism (chap. 6), source criticism (chap. 7), form criticism (chap. 8), redaction criticism (chap. 9), tradition criticism (chap. 10), narrative criticism, plus some thoughts on Greco-Roman biographies in relation to the Gospels (chap. 11), including treatments of places where evangelical scholars can and have made many contributions (40–41, 148–52, 161–62, 171–79, 187, 196–97, 203, 213–16); also Darrell L. Bock, *The Missing Gospels: Unearthing the Truth behind Alternative Christianities* (Nashville: Nelson, 2006), see especially the earlier-than-might-be-expected composition dates for books, like the possible dating of the *Gospel of Thomas* to the late first century by an evangelical scholar (218–19). Conservative New Testament scholar Robert Stein also covers many of these same critical categories in his volume on redaction criticism as well as the use of the criteria for authenticity; see Stein, *Gospels and Tradition*, chaps. 1–4, 8–9 in particular.

[234] J. P. Moreland, Chad Meister, and Khaldoun A. Sweis, eds., *Debating Christian Theism* (Oxford: Oxford University Press, 2013), featuring a who's-who lineup of scholars debating twenty key philosophical, religious, and theological themes over more than 500 pages. See also R. Douglas Geivett and Gary R. Habermas, eds., *In Defense of Miracles: A Comprehensive Case for God's Action in History* (Downers Grove, IL: InterVarsity Academic, 1997).

[235] Mark Allan Powell, "Editorial Foreword," *Journal for the Study of the Historical Jesus* 9 (2011): 1–2; Darrell L. Bock, "A Brief Reply to Robert Miller and Amy-Jill Levine," *Journal for the Study of the Historical Jesus* 9 (2011): 107–11; Bock, "Faith and the Historical

Inerrantists

Granted, when the subject of evangelicalism arises, a huge question concerns the subject of inerrancy. Yet, very few religious subjects today are more misunderstood by nonevangelicals and evangelicals alike. Probably the major, detailed statement pertaining to this movement, in a doctrinal sense, was from the International Council on Biblical Inerrancy (ICBI), which produced "The Chicago Statement on Biblical Inerrancy."[236]

Each of the nineteen articles contains an affirmation and a denial. The latter statement for article 13 reads:

> *WE DENY* that it is proper to evaluate Scripture according to standards of truth and error that are alien to its usage or purpose. We further deny that inerrancy is negated by Biblical phenomena such as a lack of modern technical precision, irregularities of grammar or spelling, observational descriptions of nature, the reporting of falsehoods, the use of hyperbole and round numbers,

---

Jesus: Does A Confessional Position and Respect for the Jesus Tradition Preclude Serious Historical Engagement?," *Journal for the Study of the Historical Jesus* 9 (2011): 3–25; Craig S. Keener, "Assumptions in Historical-Jesus Research: Using Ancient Biographies and Disciples' Traditioning as a Control," *Journal for the Study of the Historical Jesus* 9 (2011): 26–58; Robert L. Webb, "The Rules of the Game: History and Historical Method in the Context of Faith: The Via Media of Methodological Naturalism," *Journal for the Study of the Historical Jesus* 9 (2011): 59–84; Robert J. Miller, "When It's Futile to Argue about the Historical Jesus: A Response to Bock, Keener, and Webb," *Journal for the Study of the Historical Jesus* 9 (2011): 85–95; Amy-Jill Levine, "Christian Faith and the Study of the Historical Jesus: A Response to Bock, Keener, and Webb," *Journal for the Study of the Historical Jesus* 9 (2011): 96–106; Keener, "A Brief Reply to Robert Miller and Amy-Jill Levine," *Journal for the Study of the Historical Jesus* 9 (2011): 112–17; Robert L. Webb, "Methodological Naturalism: Engaging the Responses of Robert J. Miller and Amy-Jill Levine," *Journal for the Study of the Historical Jesus* 9 (2011): 118–23; Mark Allan Powell, "Evangelical Christians and Historical-Jesus Studies: Final Reflections," *Journal for the Study of the Historical Jesus* 9 (2011): 124–36; James G. Crossley, "Everybody's Happy Nowadays? A Critical Engagement with Key Events and Contemporary Quests for the Historical Jesus," *Journal for the Study of the Historical Jesus* 11 (2013): 224–41; Michael R. Licona, "Historians and Miracle Claims," *Journal for the Study of the Historical Jesus* 12 (2014): 106–29; Shaw, "What's Good for the Goose," 291–309. Also, Beilby and Eddy, *Historical Jesus: Five Views.*

[236] See http://library.dts.edu/Pages/TL/Special/ICBI_1.pdf for what is sometimes called the short statement or summary statement.

the topical arrangement of material, variant selections of material in parallel accounts, or the use of free citations.[237]

For all of the "woodenness" with which the Chicago Statement is sometimes blamed, it would seem that the majority of biblical scholars would want to affirm that the actual phenomena of the New Testament writings may well contain "a lack of modern technical precision" as spelled out in each of the subject areas above, such as grammar; spelling; a lack of scientific descriptions of the world; topical arrangements of material rather than, say, a strict chronological or other means of citation; and the use of hyperbole, round numbers, and free citations in parallels or other formats.

Many scholars would no doubt appreciate even more details being spelled out here, but it would seem that there was widespread agreement on these particular matters across the conservative spectrum. After all, it cannot be denied that these phenomena exist in the biblical texts, so these elements were exempted from a

---

[237] "The Chicago Statement" article 13, denial statement, page 5. A small book by well-known New Testament theologian Clark H. Pinnock, written even earlier, also employed a list of items regarding "What infallibility does not mean." See Pinnock, *A Defense of Biblical Infallibility* (Philadelphia: Presbyterian and Reformed, 1967), 19. In addition to the excellent information itself, the purpose of the list (18–31) was to show that these characteristics "mark the Bible off to be an ancient book, but which in no way lessen or impair its claim to infallibility or inerrancy" (20). Pinnock quoted Princeton theologian B. B. Warfield, who asserted that "so long as the proper evidence by which a proposition is established remains unrefuted, all so-called objections brought against it pass out of the category of objections to its truth into the category of difficulties to be adjusted to it" (18–19n37). Pinnock cited Warfield's volume, *The Inspiration and Authority of the Bible* (Philadelphia: Presbyterian and Reformed, 1948), 174. On such a position, having a firm foundation for one's view of Scripture allows the individual not to have to "rush to judgment" and define a conundrum that they were unable to explain as an error. Rather, they could hold the problematic issue in tension with the rest of their views, since they have good reasons for their foundation, thus, waiting for the opportunity to do further research. In a slightly later text, Pinnock expanded his treatment of items that do not invalidate the belief in inerrancy; see Clark H. Pinnock, *Biblical Revelation: The Foundation of Christian Theology* (Chicago: Moody, 1971), 185–207. In the place of the above statement by Warfield, this time Pinnock quoted John Warwick Montgomery, who remarked that, when there is no potential answer to an apparent discrepancy, "the exegete must leave the problem open" (179–180), here citing Montgomery's *The Validity and Relevance of Historic Lutheranism versus Its Contemporary Rivals*, vol. 1 of *Crisis in Lutheran Theology* (Grand Rapids: Baker, 1967), 103. Later, Pinnock stated that "minor imperfections in the text do not obscure the message of the Scripture," so we should attempt to "show that these discrepancies are not original errors" (196).

definition of the inerrancy, reliability, or even a description of the text, since these traits were already simply part of the text that was the starting point of the study.

Further, in the "Exposition" section following shortly after article 13, these additional comments appear:

> So history must be treated as history, poetry as poetry, hyperbole and metaphor as hyperbole and metaphor, generalization and approximation as what they are, and so forth. Differences between literary conventions in Bible times and in ours must also be observed: since, for instance, non-chronological narration and imprecise citation were conventional and acceptable and violated no expectations in those days, we must not regard these things as faults when we find them in Bible writers.[238]

It should be acknowledged as well that words like "generalization and approximation" are presumably quite surprising to many who thought otherwise regarding a statement on the nature of inerrancy, especially when found in the most widely accepted document signed by nearly 300 conservative scholars.

The last portion of the "Exposition" paragraph, just cited, ends as follows:

> When total precision of a particular kind was not expected nor aimed at, it is no error not to have achieved it. Scripture is inerrant, not in the sense of being absolutely precise by modern standards, but in the sense of making good its claims and achieving that measure of focused truth at which its authors aimed.[239]

The next paragraph spells out and repeats the items just mentioned in the earlier "denial" statement, but adding the comment, "The truthfulness of Scripture is not negated by . . . seeming discrepancies between one passage and another." Further, Scripture is not "culture-bound" but "it is sometimes culturally conditioned."[240]

Of course these comments from the Chicago Statement are still considered too narrow for many scholars today. Others no doubt would like to work through it and hammer out some of the details expressed here in even more detail. But once again, what this text does state explicitly may surprise many readers, especially given that this is probably the most widely accepted statement of inerrancy among inerrantists.

---

[238] "The Chicago Statement," 9.
[239] "The Chicago Statement," 9.
[240] "The Chicago Statement," 9.

A couple of observations might follow, even on statements of this nature, without much further explanation here. First, there is perhaps a surprising amount of potential room here, especially for not judging the biblical texts by standards that were foreign to them and beyond the aims, intentions, and purview of the writers. This may even be called the first rule of literary criticism—that authors are not to be judged for what was specifically excluded from the discussion. Especially for those who may have expected that there was no room for them in the "inerrancy inn"—or rather at the discussion table—this understanding may have come as a pleasant surprise. Even taken at its apparent face value, these words may surprise many. Second, these words may have a bearing on some or even many of the "contortions" within evangelicalism in recent years or even decades.

Of all the scholars who might weigh in on these issues, Jesus Seminar member Robert Price addressed the subject of the Chicago Statement a few years ago.[241] Sporting provocative titles, as he is known to do, Bob included chapter titles such as "Prodigal Fundamentalists: The Neo-Evangelical Ferment," "Inerrancy, Ltd.: The Inerrancy of (Some) Assertations," and, "It Ain't Necessarily So: Do Evangelicals Demythologize?" His Conclusion was titled: "Onward to Post-Evangelicalism"! Recommendations on the back of Price's book were written by a variety of commentators (including the present writer). Another Jesus Seminar member, J. Ramsay Michaels, wrote provocatively, "To the many voices reminding us that 'evangelicalism' is a highly unstable coalition comes another, from outside the camp. The charm of Bob Price's work is that everyone gets skewered for their inconsistencies and evasions, the non-inerrantists as much (or more) than the inerrantists. Price demonstrates convincingly that there is about as much diversity within so-called evangelicalism as within Christianity as a whole."[242]

Perhaps the hardest-hitting conclusion Price draws about the inerrantist Chicago Statement is his comment that article 13 "sounds remarkably like the non-inerrantist (or limited inerrantist) position it purports to challenge."[243] He then cites an essay by Clark Pinnock, asserting in Price's words that "inerrantist polemicists often wind up condemning non-inerrantists who hold virtually their own position minus the slogan." For Price, one anomaly of the document is that

---

[241] Robert M. Price, *Inerrant the Wind: The Evangelical Crisis of Biblical Authority* (Amherst, NY: Prometheus, 2009).

[242] Michaels's comment appears on the back cover of the book's dust jacket.

[243] Price, *Inerrant the Wind*, 22.

it could include Francis Schaeffer, who held strictly to the literal, nonallegorical existence of Adam and Eve, while allowing that J. I. Packer need not endorse Schaeffer's position.[244]

The upshot of Price's comments here seems to be that article 13 of the Chicago Statement is fairly lenient and open to some important interpretation, enough so that it at least fails to separate strictly between inerrantists and noninerrantists who could potentially hold close but different views. Price illustrates this by the juxtaposed positions of Schaeffer and Packer. As such, Price apparently thinks that noninerrantist critics of the Chicago Statement could even conclude that the document contradicts itself.[245] This last comment possibly means or implies that article 13 actually nullifies, or at the very least strains against, the remainder of the document.

Price then follows up these important and insightful comments by repeating the observations and fears of those inerrantists who pointed out that, without a rudder or other stopping point, there was very little to keep scholars or others from sliding further away toward higher critical approaches to Scripture. As Price noted, the "fundamentalists sought to push the Trojan horse back outside of the gates."[246]

Bob Price's criticism here is certainly challenging. If he is correct, then article 13 of the "Chicago Statement on Biblical Inerrancy" might be said to be quite open to questions such as how exactly could researchers know the "focused truth at which its authors aimed"? Stating that texts can be inerrant as long as they have "violated no expectations in those days, [then] we must not regard these things as faults when we find them in Bible writers" could open the field to the genre of New Testament times. If the Gospels follow the genre of Greco-Roman *bioi*, then will inerrantists be open to the sorts of compositional devices employed by these classical authors, since they were fine in that genre but would not be favored today? This would be to allow methods such as transferral, displacement, conflation, compression, spotlighting, or even expanding and inventing details.[247]

It would seem that if the Chicago Statement comments were taken in a straightforward manner, Price could be correct that it would sometimes be difficult

---

[244] Price's words summarizing Pinnock's essay "The Inerrancy Debate among the Evangelicals," apparently came from *Theology, News and Notes* (1976), though Price notes that he referred to page 9 of Pinnock's essay and that Price's own copy was mimeographed without a publisher or a date; see Price, *Inerrant the Wind*, 22.

[245] Price, 21.

[246] Price, 36 in the context of 34–42.

[247] As in Licona, *Differences in the Gospels*, 19–21 and elsewhere.

to tell inerrantists from noninerrantists. One indication of this is precisely the case that Price raised—namely, how to determine and decide between the positions of Francis Schaeffer and J. I. Packer on the matter of Genesis and creation. After all, there is potentially a long range of views between a literal Adam and an allegorical one. Interactions such as these above have been defended or denied for years since the publication of this document.

Final Thoughts on Conservative Research and the Historical Jesus

At any rate, several lessons may hopefully be drawn from this overview regarding whether or not conservative scholars should be involved in the recent studies of the historical Jesus. In a chapter on potential discrepancies in the canonical Gospels following Jesus's crucifixion, these are important overall considerations to be discussed. And all views are welcome to the ensuing discussions. A few last thoughts are worth noting.

First, it could easily be argued from more than one direction as to whether skeptics and liberals are better equipped than moderates and conservatives in their abilities to express their views on this subject more freely, fairly, and accurately. As pointed out, there are many factors to consider here. Undeniably, researchers on all sides think that their views are correct, while at the same time wearing glasses that are colored variously, and anyone could be guilty of prejudice, drawing faulty conclusions, and so on. Liberals and conservatives *both* can be just as likely to begin with preconceived ideas. Further, it is often the case that *neither* group wants to give in or concede to the opposite positions. Like political discussions, these exchanges can grow very heated. As an antidote here, all anyone can do is to investigate the data in the best way possible and decide where the strong and weak points are laid out in a case-by-case basis. Dialoguing through the issues step by step is the best way to proceed, preferably with both sides operating on friendly grounds.

Second, there are *many* relevant topics in the study of the historical Jesus that interest scholars from all sides of the aisle where the major options are not necessarily either liberal or conservative. One's personal perspective may have a bearing on some of these discussions, but the outlooks do not seem to be quite as overbearing here. Questions regarding the Gospel genre provide some good examples. But pro and con angles potentially could be pursued with perhaps even significantly more freedom.

Third, while personal beliefs in the inerrancy of the New Testament might be relevant in some of these discussions, relevant questions concerning how these terms are being used could also be important. Robert Price has shown that it should not be taken for granted that everyone is clear on what is being discussed. There is plenty of room for dialogue, even between researchers who hold very similar theological positions. As Price's examples indicate, it is not impossible that roles might even be reversed on occasion.

Fourth, it is often thought to be the case that conservatives are more likely inclined to prejudge the issues based on a prescribed regimen of beliefs, rules, or doctrinal statements. But it should also be recalled that the members of the Jesus Seminar began both of their major treatises by listing some three dozen parameters that circumscribe what should and should not be concluded concerning the historical Jesus, at least from *their* perspectives. Their color-coded *rejection* of at least 82 percent of all the so-called red-letter words of Jesus (depending on which colors are counted) lead to their comments like these, which are common:[248] "Jesus was a social deviant"; he apparently did not perform any nature miracles; he did not as a rule "initiate dialogue or debate"; he rarely "speaks about himself in the first person"; he made "no claim" to being the Messiah; and of course he never uttered comments after the crucifixion simply because dead men neither rise nor talk.[249]

These may be good examples of how skeptics can likewise enforce their agendas due to their own presuppositions, but from the "left" this time, perhaps rivaling the conservatives in that regard. Strangely enough, this last list of restrictions is located in volume 2 of the Jesus Seminar under the heading "Additional Tests for Historicity," when they are actually nothing of the sort but rather serve as what might be called prejudicial guidelines—not unlike those of some conservatives, although emanating from opposite directions.

Add to these issues the charges from respected scholars like Eleonore Stump and William Alston that the critics themselves almost always impose other, highly subjective standards when there are contradictions in the Gospels. For example, why cannot two seemingly different things both be uttered during a normal conversation

---

[248] Funk, Hoover, and the Jesus Seminar, *Five Gospels*, 5; Funk and the Jesus Seminar, *Acts of Jesus*, 1.

[249] The quotations above are taken from Funk and the Jesus Seminar, 32–35, where some of the long list of "rules" from volume 1 are discussed further. For the original, longer list of just more than three dozen presuppositions that are included in their first major study, see Funk, Hoover, and the Jesus Seminar, 19–36.

even in today's world? Regarding the women who visited the empty tomb, why should phrases such as "plus others" not normally mean that additional women were also present *besides* the few whose names were specifically mentioned? Such simple, straightforward language seems quite difficult to twist and appears to solve a number of questions. This side of the agenda is rarely mentioned when skeptics address the problems introduced by conservatives.[250]

A Last Crucial Issue: The Place of the Minimal Facts Argument

Throughout this present study we have favored an overall probable case for the historicity of Jesus's resurrection that is based primarily on what has been termed the "minimal facts argument" for this event. Namely, this method is based on two features: most crucially by far, each individual historical fact employed in this process is itself established by a large number of other probable, well-evidenced historical facts, such that, as a result, the vast majority of critical scholars across the entire skeptical-to-conservative spectrum of theological views recognizes the historical status of these events. Few scholars would reject these events themselves.[251]

Where does this approach fit here? Employing this argument at this juncture applies a final perspective to this charge of Gospel discrepancies, since the minimal facts argument builds on what we might call the lowest common denominator of the most basic historical facts. Obviously, none of these facts is thought by scholars to be contradictory. In other words, the case for Jesus's death by crucifixion followed by his resurrection appearances can be established in probable terms on these foundational, hardly objectionable data alone. As such, if these individual puzzle pieces are true, established by secure research, then that is the case whatever else may be known. So even if the exact number or the specific names of the women who visited the empty tomb on the first Easter morning are not finally known, or even if the number of

---

[250] It should be noted carefully that these thoughts at the close of this chapter are not at all to accuse the skeptics of being the real culprits here or anything like that. Rather, it is an effort to indicate that *all sides* have their own presuppositions and perspectives and need to be sensitive to each other in these conversations. But since it is often the views of the conservatives that are thought to be more problematic in this context (as in the series of articles cited above from the *Journal for the Study of the Historical Jesus*), it is simply being pointed out that there is more than one angle to this discussion.

[251] Of course, interpretations of these facts do vary. That is precisely why this present volume is devoted to these alternative suggestions.

angels that were present remains a question, the tomb was empty. Or again, even if it is unknown as to whether Jesus appeared first in Galilee or Jerusalem, the point is that the best data confirm his death and subsequent appearances, so these events are all well established.

To view this matter from another angle, this chapter introduced Reginald Fuller's comparison of the burial and empty tomb Gospel scenarios to a situation in a court of law, implying that the overall Gospel accounts would not fare well if they had been on trial. But the intriguing situation here was that even while Fuller wrote these words, he actually embraced both the empty tomb as well as Jesus's appearances.[252] How could this be the case? Fuller's conclusion actually follows from an argument that is not all that far removed from the one used here. Rather than regarding the more objectionable details as being the more crucial facts, Fuller viewed the best-established data as the key to this discussion.

So it is in our present case as well. It is precisely these latter, more crucial data that serve as the ones that are capable by themselves of establishing the empty tomb and resurrection appearances. That is a normal move in historical research—to establish the more central foundation that *is then capable of providing the needed answers* for the most important research at hand. In other words, while there are situations where scholars think that only the best guess is available, the more vital, probable arguments can indeed be established in historical terms. This is the normal historical approach, since conflicts are noted by the majority of scholars. What follows from this, especially in terms of this chapter, is that nonessential issues do not stand in the way of viewing and verifying the essential, established ones.

Conclusion

It is fair to say that the majority of critical scholars across the theological schools of thought, all the way from atheists and skeptics to conservatives, think that various sorts and levels of problems, such as apparent discrepancies, clear discrepancies, or contradictions, are found within the Gospel texts. However, few of these scholars think that any of these issues annul the Gospel message any more than similar differences in the classical texts nullify the existence or exploits of Alexander the Great, Julius Caesar, or other ancient heroes. As ancient historian Paul Meier attests, "The earliest sources telling of the great fire of Rome, for example, offer far more serious conflicts

---

[252] Fuller, *Formation of the Resurrection Narratives*, 46–49, 180–83.

on who or what started the blaze and how far it spread, some claiming that the whole city was scorched while others insist that only three sectors were reduced to ash. Yet the fire itself is historical: it actually happened."[253]

Similarly, with historians and other scholars, our method must include weighing the strength of the most probable historical sources and facts available over against the likelihood that there are serious problems at hand, all the time searching for potential explanations. Then how do the troublesome questions along with the possible interpretations stack up against the most likely, favorable data? Which are the strongest overall conclusions? As Meier pointed out, historians can be unsure of a good many details, but still quite certain about the chief underlying event.

Again, Bart Ehrman lists some fifteen early, independent sources for the crucifixion of Jesus, all dating within the first 100 years after the crucifixion of Jesus, with at least four of these texts being found outside of the New Testament.[254] Ehrman also argues that the Gospels as a whole are not very reliable texts.[255] Yet he nonetheless recognizes that the sources for Jesus's crucifixion are among the very strongest arguments for the historicity of Jesus, as are several other items in Jesus's life.[256] This is yet another angle from which to view the comments that have been made throughout this chapter. Textual problems in areas that do not seriously affect the central items under consideration do not annul the overall essential conclusions.

[253] Paul L. Meier, *In the Fullness of Time: A Historian Looks at Christmas, Easter, and the Early Church* (New York: HarperCollins, 1991), 180.

[254] Ehrman, *Did Jesus Exist?*, 140–41, 163, 290–91, cf. 92–93, 156–58, 171–72, 251.

[255] Ehrman, 70–71, 268–69.

[256] Ehrman, with chap. 2 (35–68) listing some important arguments for the historicity of Jesus's life, some of which derived from pagan sources.

9

Fraud Type 1: The Disciples Stole the Body

As already addressed in the initial volume and elsewhere in this study, several angles have been suggested over a century of scholarly studies regarding potential burial locations and circumstances pertaining to Jesus's deceased body. Though hardly the only possible suggestion, most scholars still tend to think along more traditional lines regarding the burial cave owned by Joseph of Arimathea. As such, this chapter will treat primarily this alternate hypothesis regarding scenarios involving Jesus's followers, and his immediate disciples in particular, rather than a theft from a common grave or from a second burial in another tomb. Yet it should be noted carefully that the location from which the disciples may have stolen Jesus's body is far from the principal issue here. The major question concerns the likelihood that they perpetrated this act from whatever location it could have taken place. On the chief version of this view, then, Jesus's disciples stole his dead body out of Joseph of Arimathea's personal tomb. Afterward, the disciples freely invented stories of his resurrection appearances.

Actually, this is a very ancient hypothesis—perhaps even the oldest alternative appearance theory of all. A few hints of the details have already been mentioned. The charge of the Jewish elders in Matt 27:63 that Jesus was a "deceiver" or an "impostor" (*ekeinos ho planos*) employs a somewhat technical term similar to other accusations that had been brought against Jesus, suggesting that this theme was perhaps a common one.[1] Incidentally, the more simple assertion that Jesus's body was stolen from the tomb is not necessarily connected at all to Matthew's more complicated report that guards were placed at the tomb to stop any shenanigans.[2]

What is called here the Stolen Body Hypothesis 1 (or simply Fraud Type 1) is also probably the most maligned of the better-known naturalistic resurrection theories due to what are considered to be the more obvious refutations.[3] Yet, for whatever reason, it often seems to be one of the initial retorts for some critics, at least on the popular, nonscholarly front. Due to the highly problematic issues raised by this alternative scenario, it was ignored almost completely by the major German liberal scholars of the nineteenth century, when naturalistic resurrection theses were rampant. However, it still needs to be treated here, at least briefly, due to the role it played at particular junctions in both earlier and later discussions.

Two Early Proponents of Fraud Type 1

A few decades before the writings of Friedrich Schleiermacher and the birth of German liberalism, English deist Thomas Woolston employed the stolen body thesis. Often thought to have been mentally ill, Woolston was imprisoned for blasphemy in 1730. Unable to pay his fine, he remained imprisoned until his death in 1733.

While insisting often that he was a Christian, Woolston conceded his dislike for literal biblical interpretations, which he said nauseated him, and favored allegorical

---

[1] The revised doctoral dissertation by Matti Kankaanniemi is quite helpful here: *The Guards of the Tomb (Matt 27:62–66 and 28:11–15): Matthew's Apologetic Legend Revisited* (Åbo: Åbo Akademi University Press, 2010). Kankaanniemi argued that Matthew had an earlier source (95–106) and especially that the words *ekeinos ho planos* (i.e., "the deceiver") indicate that the term came from the Jewish leaders rather than from the author. N. T. Wright argues similarly in *The Resurrection of the Son of God*, vol. 3 of *Christian Origins and the Question of God* (Minneapolis: Fortress, 2003), 403–4, 637, also, 633–40.

[2] Matthew's story of the guards at the tomb is evaluated in detail in the initial volume of this study.

[3] The two names for this challenge to the resurrection indicate the difference in the angles being viewed or presented. The "Stolen Body" naturally depicts what the disciples (or others) did with Jesus's dead body, while the "Fraud" appellation depicts the lies or false reports that were spread afterward, proclaiming that Jesus appeared to them after his death when he had obviously not done so, which supposedly launched the teaching that Jesus had risen from the dead. The number 1 differentiates this species of stolen body or lie theory perpetrated by Jesus's disciples as contrasted with the next view, where one or more persons *other than* the disciples did the dirty work.

notions. He singled out three major religious ideas that he preferred: allegorical interpretations, a "universal and unbounded Toleration of Religion," and the eradication of the "hired and establish'd priesthood." Woolston desired a "spiritual *Jesus*" minus the miracle reports and other physical expressions.[4]

Woolston's sixth and last treatise on miracles, concentrating particularly on Jesus's resurrection, proposed that a physical resurrection from the dead would "be the most notorious and monstrous Imposture, that ever was put upon mankind."[5] Rather, Jesus's disciples stole his dead body from the tomb: "The Body was to be removed and a Resurrection pretended to the Delusion."[6] After Jesus's body was stolen, the "Resurrection [was?] talk'd of."[7] So Jesus's disciples performed the theft "in order to pretend a Resurrection" and later preached regarding Jesus's appearances to them, concocting the messages.[8]

The various stolen body theories, whether the culprits were Jesus's disciples or others, were also referred to as Fraud Theses. Interestingly, Woolston repeatedly used this same term himself: "Fraud," the "Argument of Fraud," or the "Proof of Fraud." These ideas were presumably drawn from the two-part idea that stealing Jesus's body was followed by the false proclamation of appearance messages from him, with both being clearly fraudulent and duplicitous.[9] Woolston even criticized Jesus as a "Deceiver," while maintaining the possibility that the disciples bribed the guards at the tomb, as well as asserting like almost all critics that the Gospel texts contained discrepancies and so forth. Overall, in Woolston's opinion, the entire ignominy was "the most bare faced, and the most self evident Imposture that ever was put upon the World," pointing out several varieties of fraud.[10]

Since at least some of Jesus's disciples were willing to die for their belief that they had actually seen the risen Jesus alive again (with some having actually suffered

---

[4] Thomas Woolston, "A Defence of the Discourses on Miracles," in *Deism: An Anthology*, ed. Peter Gay (Princeton, NJ: Van Nostrand, 1968), esp. 131–35, 138.

[5] Thomas Woolston, *A Sixth Discourse on the Miracles of our Saviour, In View of the Present Controversy between Infidels and Apostates* (London: Printed by the Author, 1729), 5. As mentioned, Woolston begins this treatise by affirming his support for "the mystical Resurrection of *Jesus* . . . mystical Resurrection of our *spiritual Jesus.*"

[6] Woolston, 16.

[7] Woolston, 17.

[8] Woolston, 29; similarly on 20–21, 25.

[9] Woolston, 15, 18, 20, 21, 28, 30, 32, 33.

[10] Woolston, 5, 14, 19, 27, 47.

martyrdom), this generally stopped most liberals in their tracks from employing this thesis. After all, martyrdom is usually a good antidote with which to face liars. But such was not the case with Woolston. He proclaimed that many "Cheats and Criminals . . . have asserted their Innocency" even to the point of death, totally missing the crucial distinction that the disciples died willingly for their message. Woolston thought that this would have been the most successful religious farce of all time, had it not been for his taking the necessary steps to unmask the entire travesty for the rest of the world![11]

A few decades after Thomas Woolston was writing in England, German rationalist Hermann Samuel Reimarus (1694–1768) likewise advocated the first version of the stolen body or fraud thesis, where Jesus's disciples were the perpetrators. While spending most of his life teaching oriental languages at the gymnasium (an academic high school) in his native city of Hamburg, Germany, Reimarus penned a 4,000-page manuscript that he did not intend for publication, named *An Apology for the Rational Worshippers of God.* The document circulated anonymously. However, between the years 1774 and 1778, a librarian in Wolfenbüttal, Germany, Gotthold Ephraim Lessing, published seven fragments from Reimarus's work, one of which was entitled "Concerning the Story of the Resurrection." Lessing published this account in 1777.[12]

Reimarus postulated that after Jesus's death, his disciples underwent a time of much fear and anxiety, which dominated their thinking for some time. Gathering their courage, they pretended to be fearless even in the face of death. Jesus had preached an uncomplicated message that opposed the legalism of the Jewish leaders of his day. At the center of Jesus's proclamation was that the kingdom of God was coming on earth as a temporal kingdom and the initiation into it was through the act of repentance. This was accompanied by kingdom morality, about which Jesus taught much. Jesus thought that a popular Jewish movement would place him as the head of this kingdom, and on at least a couple of occasions he came close to seeing it happen. But Jesus had miscalculated. Instead, he was crucified, which dashed the disciples'

---

[11] Woolston, 27.

[12] Many of the pertinent background specifics here are found in Albert Schweitzer, *The Quest of the Historical Jesus: A Critical Study of Its Progress from Reimarus to Wrede*, trans. W. Montgomery (New York: Macmillan, 1968), 14–26; Gregory W. Dawes, ed., *The Historical Jesus Quest: Landmarks in the Search for the Jesus of History*, rev. ed. (Louisville: Westminster John Knox, 2000), 54–56. Daniel P. Fuller also adds further relevant material in *Easter Faith and History* (Grand Rapids: Eerdmans, 1965), 31–35.

dreams of being a part of this grand kingdom scenario. They did not get over this shock for some time.[13]

After Jesus's apparent and unexpected failure caused by his untimely death, the disciples recast Jesus's earthly kingdom message as a spiritual one, to that of Jesus being the suffering Savior who died for the world's sins and was then raised from the dead by his Father. To further this message, they stole Jesus's dead body out of the tomb before any serious decomposition took place. When the empty tomb was discovered by others, the disciples feigned their surprise and ran to the tomb, only to discover that it was empty. The disciples hid Jesus's body for fifty days so that it would be unrecognizable by that time. Just in case anyone should challenge them, they could never be disproven and hence have their plot exposed. Then they disposed of the body and spread the stories that the risen Jesus had appeared to them, spoken with them, eaten with them, and later ascended to heaven, promising to return again. The conspiracy worked well and having taken the proper steps, they could never be branded with the fraud.[14]

So, the disciples began preaching, proclaiming boldly that Jesus had risen, was alive again, and had appeared to them. Like Jesus had taught them, the disciples also performed events that seemed to the people to be miracles, which of course increased their appeal. Just as when Jesus was alive, the disciples found that their audiences were very generous. Here too as before, the disciples never lacked for food or money. Some people sold their property and gave the proceeds to the apostles, having been promised eternal rewards as a result. To be sure, Jesus's followers accepted all the payments and gifts that they were offered, amassing wealth and power. Of course, these men agreed unanimously that none of them would expose their scheme. While

---

[13] Charles H. Talbert, ed., *Reimarus: Fragments* (Philadelphia: Fortress, 1970). Selections from Talbert's work here are also reproduced in Dawes, *Historical Jesus Quest*, 56–86, such as Reimarus, *Fragments*, part 1, fragment 7:6, 8, 29; part 2, fragment 6:54. Some of the section demarcations in Reimarus's text are rather confusing and actually differ with each other. Besides Talbert, another example is found in Charles Voysey, ed., *Fragments from Reimarus* (London: Williams & Norgate, 1879). For example, Fuller places Reimarus's denial of the resurrection in the fifth fragment (32), while Talbert has the main resurrection denial in the sixth fragment (81–83). Also relevant here are Schweitzer, *Quest of the Historical Jesus*, 19–21, 24, and Dawes, *Historical Jesus Quest*, 55–56.

[14] Following Reimarus here, *Fragments*, part 2, fragment 6:54, 56–57. See the comments by Dawes, *Historical Jesus Quest*, 56; Schweitzer, *Quest of the Historical Jesus*, 21; Fuller, *Easter Faith and History*, 33.

Reimarus thought that the Gospels got many things wrong and were hopelessly contradictory, this much of the story could be ascertained![15]

The element of the disciples' fraud in Reimarus, from which this hypothesis gets one of its names, certainly presents an easy target. As Daniel Fuller remarks: "Reimarus' reconstruction of New Testament history never gained general acceptance because it failed to explain how, if the disciples were perpetuating what they knew to be a fraud, they were yet willing to suffer and die for Jesus."[16] Other scholars have also been critical of Reimarus, given his ineptitudes.[17]

Numerous problematic puzzle pieces are apparent here and reinforce Fuller's observation, such as the disciples stealing Jesus's body in the first place, thereby occasioning the empty tomb; their counterfeited surprise at the discovery from others; their hiding Jesus's deceased body, then preaching a resurrection message that they knew was false; feigning their bravery and true life changes when that was really not the case; and lying about the many details of Jesus's appearances to them, including his ascension. Subsequently, they grew rich while accepting countless gifts by way of dishonest gain.[18]

Of course, all the retelling of these false stories as well as the disciples' accompanying deceitful actions had to be duplicated many times through the remainder of their lives. The lies had to be reinforced in a consistent manner too, with everyone in the group relating the same falsehoods, even when it resulted in uncertainty, continual discomfort, physical mistreatment of the worst sorts, and even premature deaths for a number of them. Further, none of Jesus's disciples ever recanted, as far as is known, or confessed the fraudulent details of the story during moments of weakness.

Such an extraordinary scenario obviously required so many elements to occur precisely on cue without any slipups! It is hardly any wonder that the nineteenth-century

---

[15] Reimarus, *Fragments*, part 2, fragment 6:1, 54–55, 57. Also, Schweitzer, *Quest of the Historical Jesus*, 21; Fuller, *Easter Faith and History*, 33.

[16] Fuller, *Easter Faith and History*, 33n4.

[17] Especially David Friedrich Strauss, *The Life of Jesus, Critically Examined*, trans. George Eliot, ed. Peter C. Hodgson (Mifflintown, PA: Sigler, 1972), 738–40; Schweitzer, *Quest of the Historical Jesus*, 22–23; Dawes, *Historical Jesus Quest*, 56.

[18] Atheistic philosopher Michael Martin made a point worth thinking about here: there are many forms of wishful thinking and self-deception and not all of them involve "deliberately perpetrating a fraud." See Michael Martin, "Reply to Davis," *Philo* 2 (1999): 68. But it needs to be recognized that there is still a vast difference between explaining the known data well and not really explaining it at all.

German liberal establishment quite strictly eschewed the hypotheses of Woolston and Reimarus with their plethora of idiosyncrasies, including features that demanded exact timing, the fact that many different personalities could easily have ruined everything by not remaining true to their false message with all of the contradictions that might be imagined, or even a drunken confession.[19] Each of the actors certainly knew the basic falsity of the tale too. Their lives at times must have been balanced on a razor's edge. It is not easy to live in the midst of all of these potential foibles with all of these moving parts. Still, the view remains a historical fixture of the resurrection landscape, with a similar accusation being recorded ever so briefly in Matt 28:11–15.

Neither Woolston nor Reimarus were very sophisticated compared to the standards of many nineteenth-century German liberal critics who emerged and redirected theological trends just a few decades later. Nonetheless, while these later liberal scholars definitely did not follow Reimarus's notion that the disciples stole Jesus's dead body, certain other elements of Reimarus's eschatological ideas did exercise some influence among the later liberals.[20]

For example, Schweitzer concluded that Reimarus was the first researcher in eighteen centuries to veer in the direction of a particular angle on eschatology being a central emphasis in his work. Various aspects in eschatological thinking might be mapped from the early centuries of the church. But Schweitzer seemed to think that these views encapsulated an interlude of misinterpretations until Reimarus, whose thesis was *also* mistaken according to Schweitzer.[21] But the latter at least brought

---

[19] Actually, Reimarus even rather incredibly mentions just such a possibility on the part of the disciples; see *Fragments*, part 2, fragment 6:54!

[20] In his volume *Das Leben Jesu* (1901), Oskar Holtzmann briefly entertained the hypothesis that the disciples may have carried Jesus's deceased body back to Galilee, followed later by this German scholar abandoning the idea. See Holtzmann, *The Life of Jesus*, trans. J. T. Bealby and Maurice A. Canney (London: Black, 1904), 499.

[21] For instance, Schweitzer judged that Reimarus was mistaken in holding to an earthly hope—that "the Messianic ideal which dominated the preaching of Jesus was that of the political ruler, the son of David" (Schweitzer, *Quest of the Historical Jesus*, 23). The emphases of Johannes Weiss and Schweitzer were chiefly on the futuristic concepts of Jesus's eschatology, termed consistent eschatology. In fact, for Schweitzer, Weiss's concept of Jesus's kingdom teaching was "wholly future." Only Jesus's casting out of demons is an exception (239–41). Schweitzer moved further in this futuristic eschatological emphasis (239–41 and chapter 19). In Weiss's own repeated words, Jesus and the early church thought that the kingdom was quite near, but it was still "not yet here" (74 and stated similarly on 66); Johannes Weiss, *Jesus' Proclamation of the Kingdom of God*, trans. and ed. Richard Hyde Hiers and David Larrimore Holland (Philadelphia: Fortress, 1971), esp. 65–74.

further attention to the subject from a more promising angle. Some of the critical reemphases were reborn more than a century later in the writings of those researchers such as Weiss and Schweitzer.[22] But to repeat, on his theme of Jesus's disciples stealing his dead body and lying about the appearances, Reimarus was basically ignored except for the criticisms of his view.

It will remain difficult for many to compare the early church perspectives on eschatology to those of the eighteenth- and nineteenth-century liberal scholars. More specifically, there is a huge conceptual gap between those very early Christian scholars who actually accepted and believed the truth of Jesus's proclamations concerning the future as contrasted with those like Reimarus, Weiss, and Schweitzer. While the latter may have emphasized the role of eschatology in Jesus's teachings, they rejected the time-space realities of these categories, such as Jesus's virgin birth, the resurrection, Jesus's return, a literal kingdom of God, and so on. Hence, there is a huge conceptual gap between the views of the earliest church thinkers, however diverse, and those particularly of late nineteenth- and twentieth-century scholarship, which were both diverse as well as dismissive of the literal positions held by Jesus and the early church writers.

Dawes makes the additional point that in spite of Reimarus's historical shortcomings, he recognized that the early church interpreted Jesus's teachings "in the light of later Christian beliefs."[23] This insight can lead in different directions. Though Reimarus rejected the historicity of the resurrection as well as much of the remaining literal message of Jesus, he realized that Jesus's chief emphasis for both the early church and contemporary theologians had to do with answering the questions pertaining to his identity as well as his other teachings. If in fact Jesus had actually been raised from the dead, this would have shed a different light on his teachings.

Such insights potentially left these liberal scholars in a tough spot. According to the New Testament, the reality of Jesus's resurrection potentially changed the import and truth of his preaching and teaching. Which portions of Jesus's teaching might thereby have been shown to be true by virtue of this event, if it occurred? If Jesus was not the Son of God, for example, then why did God raise him from the dead? And what would the truth of the resurrection potentially dictate about other aspects of Jesus's message?

---

[22] Schweitzer, *Quest of the Historical Jesus*, 22–24, 241, 313, 321, 346, 367.
[23] Dawes, *Historical Jesus Quest*, 56.

Multiple Problems with the Fraud Type 1 Hypothesis

The tenor of scholarly acceptance or rejection of various ideas is not always an accurate gauge of either truth itself or whether a particular idea served as a strong or weak thesis. Sometimes a general vote follows the evidence and other times it does not—popularity can be fickle. But perhaps this time, the virtual ignoring of Reimarus's stolen body option throughout the more than a century-long heyday of naturalistic resurrection options during the reign of German liberalism is an indication that the Fraud Type 1 thesis may simply have fallen short in its ability to explain away this event. Add to this the virtual continued absence of any supporters to speak of during the twentieth century, and that makes about two centuries with nary a taker! So what were some of the serious problems with this idea?

(1) Naturalistic resurrection hypotheses may not generally be thought of as being overwhelmed by what might be referred to as one-punch knockouts. But this does seem to be the case with Fraud Type 1 hypotheses. Martin's cautions above notwithstanding, it would be virtually impossible for Jesus's disciples to go through all the motions involved in suffering the totally unexpected shock of Jesus's crucifixion and their loss of hope for eternity, hiding in fear for their own lives, then in quite short order removing his dead body from one tomb to another location while acknowledging that this deceased individual had actually been raised from the dead, as he had predicted several times. To top off the entire story, the disciples would have lied repeatedly, claiming to have been with the risen Jesus often. They arguably would have made the jump from the very lowest time ever in their lives to hatching a plot that would affect the entire world from that time onward! This hardly seems workable.

Rather than questioning the promise of the coming kingdom and Jesus's presumed reign, together with them, the disciples would have moved in the very opposite direction by preaching a series of falsehoods. They would have realized that their own presumed futures had still vanished, gone for naught, but the crowd was encouraged to believe that all was well. What a comedy of errors amid hatching several new problems in the process!

As for some of the additional problems posed by this "solution," why would the disciples even be inclined to carry on their "ministry" after those dark moments? Worse yet, how would they respond later whenever their lives may have been on the line once again? Would at least some of them continue to be willing to go to their deaths, knowing full well that Jesus did not conquer death himself? Such decisions would have to be revisited regularly during many new situations. Having decided to lie and otherwise contort the truth about Jesus having appeared to them, what could there possibly be in the future given this obviously false message, especially seen from the perspective of years later when still nothing had changed?

True, other religious and political movements discovered new ways to carry on in the face of defeat.[24] But in how many of these cases had such an involved scenario ensued, with falsehoods perpetrated at every turn in just this way? The very center of their message had been destroyed—this time regarding the present and future kingdom and all that it signified in the future—followed by a string of falsehoods. That very message involved the disciples' outright fabrications many, many times over. Now the original center of the message that Jesus had proclaimed had been disproven, negated, and defeated. The very heart of their hopes, dreams, and messages had been dashed. It is virtually impossible to understand this situation in any way other than as total defeat.

Sometimes it is remarked that the disciples may have gotten rich in the process. But rather than simply pull suggestions out of thin air, critics need to produce the compelling first-century data for this claim—where is this support? And how useful are riches in such circumstances, both conceptually as well as physically, when the disciples apparently did not even enjoy such wealth? Critical scholars must have agreed with these critiques as well, for as we have seen, virtually no one supported this position in some 250 years.

Again, the ultimate one-punch knockout refutation of the Fraud Type 1 view is that liars do not make willing martyrs. At the very least, liars do not yield persons who put themselves in danger constantly and remain at least willing to become martyrs. Sure, the story might be recast otherwise in new plot theses, but apparently not persuasively enough to convince the critical scholars. The hallmark of being willing to die for one's faith begins with individuals who truly believe what they teach, especially when the teachings concern the very center of their theology. On this development alone, this natural hypothesis fails. The disciples would more likely have denied their belief or simply have slipped away and said nothing further, since they already knew that Jesus was truly dead, since they stole his dead body, followed

---

[24] See, for example, Michael L. Brown's discussion of a modern Jewish movement in Brown, *Resurrection: Investigating a Rabbi from Brooklyn, a Preacher from Galilee, and an Event that Changed the World* (Lake Mary, FL: Charisma, 2020), 61–72.

by concocting misrepresentations and fakeries regarding his "appearances." How does this scenario breed real-life transformations?

(2) If the disciples stole their teachers' dead body and Jesus therefore never rose from the dead or appeared to them, how do we then explain the known extent of the radical and complete transformations of the apostles? This is a huge problem in itself because the disciples could have stolen Jesus's dead body, misrepresented the situation a few times in their preaching, and then called it quits and gone back to their families and jobs. But what led to the subsequent, lifelong changes in the apostolic cases where the details are largely known?

Again, other movements present changed lives too, but no message in the history of religions can claim this revolutionary of a change that was based squarely on real experiences that were thought to be resurrection appearances. We are told repeatedly that Jesus's apostles were transformed by the truth of their central message—that of their resurrection faith and its further application for eternity.[25] But on this alternate thesis, there was no truth in the disciples' message whatsoever, and they knew it. It would be absolutely remarkable if the apostles both chose and preached the resurrection of Jesus and his appearances as their central, transforming message even when they knew without question that their centermost, weight-bearing column could hold no weight whatsoever, since there was no reality to it. So how can their utter transformations, as even admitted by the strongest critics, be explained adequately?

(3) Another unlikelihood followed soon after the disciples' initial "changes." What could account for the conversion of James the brother of Jesus? James's previous unbelief during Jesus's public ministry, plus his conversion that most likely occurred due to an appearance of Jesus, have been both supported by the historical facts and recognized by critical scholars. How should especially the latter be accounted for if Jesus neither rose from the dead nor appeared to anyone?

(4) A few years after the crucifixion the infamous church persecutor Saul (i.e., Paul) became totally convinced that he had also seen the risen Jesus. If Jesus's appearances never occurred and the resurrection was untrue, Paul would most likely have never come to faith. So what was the impetus in each of these additional cases for these pious men to become believers in Jesus Christ from their previously unbelieving states?

---

[25] For just a few of these texts, see Acts 4:2, 33; 1 Cor 15:32; Phil 1:21–23; 3:10–11, 18–21; Col 3:1–4; 1 Pet 1:3–5.

(5) As far as is known, none of Jesus's disciples recanted or otherwise turned away from the faith that they preached after having reported witnessing his resurrection appearances. As Sean McDowell stated after completing his doctoral dissertation on this subject, "And yet not a single account exists that *any* of the Twelve, including Paul and James, recanted their belief that Jesus had appeared to them alive after his death."[26] It is incredibly amazing on more than one level that if the disciples knew that Jesus had not really appeared to them, this staunchness in their faith would have remained their trademark, without anyone having recanted! Under these circumstances, as far as is known, why would they all have remained steadfast in their faith until the end?

(6) There is no serious evidence in favor of the Fraud Type 1 hypothesis. The view simply hangs out there in space on mere assertions without support.[27] Stephen T. Davis notes the "radical change that came over the disciples" and then emphasizes that there is "not one bit of evidence to support [the stolen body thesis]." Further, "no such secret ever 'leaked out,'" nor are there any data to support turmoil among the disciples or that some did not truly believe the resurrection. All of the evidence makes it clear that they "believed wholeheartedly in the resurrection of Jesus."[28]

(7) This last reason still remains just a possibility at present. But if the Shroud of Turin turns out finally to be Jesus's burial garment, as now appears to be quite possible to many careful scientific and other researchers, then this would be an additional, huge reason against the Fraud 1 Type hypothesis. But the indications so far are that due to the intact condition of the bloodstains on this cloth, the body in the shroud, in all probability, was not unwrapped by the disciples or by anyone else. Rather, there are indications that the body left the cloth in some other way than by being unwrapped.

The multiple factual problems for the Fraud Type 1 alternative hypothesis to the resurrection appearances of Jesus are significant.[29] But major critical scholars only

---

[26] See Sean McDowell, *The Fate of the Apostles: Examining the Martyrdom Accounts of the Closest Followers of Jesus* (Surrey: Ashgate, 2015), 263, cf. also 6, 8, 243, 259–65.

[27] Some seemingly offhanded statements may appear occasionally as if the view were actually being asserted by critical *scholars*. But as has been mentioned repeatedly, though a few researchers here and there have made some positive comments along the way during the past 250 years, as if to mention a consideration, virtually no scholars have actually preferred or taken this position. This must be kept in mind.

[28] Stephen T. Davis, *Risen Indeed: Making Sense of the Resurrection* (Grand Rapids: Eerdmans, 1993), 181–82.

[29] Gerd Lüdemann makes a strange comment that sounds like he is also arguing against the disciples stealing the body, and that may have been indeed what he was doing. He states that fraud by the disciples is disproven. Though Lüdemann's language here seems to be a

rarely get past citing the initial critique alone, since it is so devastating; time and again this is their chief concern. It seems quite straightforward: the evidence works strongly against the thesis. Agnostic New Testament scholar A. J. M. Wedderburn asserts, "We have no reason to suggest that these early Christians deliberately lied."[30] Self-styled liberal scholar E. P. Sanders adds, "I do not regard deliberate fraud as a worthwhile explanation" since Jesus's followers spent their lives preaching that he was risen and several of them died for their message.[31] Wolfhart Pannenberg points out that "it is hard to understand how [the disciples] could risk their lives for such a conspiracy."[32] Hugo Staudinger adds the point, "Even less can we reckon with some kind of conspiracy . . . for this conspiracy would run directly counter to their own personal interest."[33]

G. T. Eddy summarizes the issue here: "We may agree at once that conscious, deliberate, concerted and sustained fraud is unthinkable as the origin of the Easter

---

little convoluted (possibly due to the translation?), the strangeness is due to Lüdemann's comment that the disciples did not even know where Jesus was buried. The reason for this lack of knowledge is apparently linked somehow to *"their utter disappointment"* which also seemed to keep them from being *"in a position to perpetrate such a fraud."* See Gerd Lüdemann with Alf Özen, *What Really Happened to Jesus: A Historical Approach to the Resurrection* (Louisville: Westminster John Knox, 1995), 52. This seems incredibly strange from start to finish, and for a large number of reasons. So *why* did the disciples not know where Jesus was buried? Was it because of *"their utter disappointment"*? If so, does this mean that no one can ever be severely disappointed about life and still carry out their responsibilities? Further, is it to be thought that not a single one among the disciples, due to differences of temperament or whatever, was less affected emotionally and could then have been the one to go and check where Jesus was being buried? Are we also to believe that after they were utterly devoted to Jesus for perhaps three years, not a single one of them would care one iota where Jesus's final resting place would have been? Was not even one of the disciples able to inquire *later* as to who ended up burying the body by checking with Joseph of Arimathea? Perhaps most of all, did the women never go to the tomb on Sunday morning, as per the testimony of all four Gospels, because they were also so disappointed? Last, even if it could be imagined that neither the disciples nor the women had anything to do with Jesus's burial, would neither Joseph nor Nicodemus have sought them out and initiated the conversation regarding the burial that they had performed? This is all very strange indeed.

[30] A. J. M. Wedderburn, *Beyond Resurrection* (Peabody, MA: Hendrickson, 1999), 123.

[31] E. P. Sanders, *The Historical Figure of Jesus* (London: Penguin, 1993), 279–80.

[32] Wolfhart Pannenberg, "The Historicity of the Resurrection and the Identity of Christ," in *The Intellectuals Speak Out about God*, ed. Roy Abraham Varghese (Chicago: Regnery Gateway, 1984), 257–64, with the quotation on 262.

[33] Hugo Staudinger, "The Resurrection of Jesus Christ as Saving Event and as 'Object' of Historical Research," *Scottish Journal of Theology* 36 (1983): 309–26, quotation on 321.

faith."[34] Historian Paul Maier provides the chief reason for this conclusion: "Would [the disciples] have gone on to give their very lives for this fraud? Clearly . . . myths do not make martyrs."[35] Many other scholars share similar views and critiques such as these.[36]

Conclusion

All told, Fraud Type 1 and its implication of Jesus's disciples stealing their master's dead body frankly does not come anywhere close to making the grade necessary to explain adequately all of the known data regarding Jesus's appearances. It is most likely the very weakest of the major naturalistic theses, as indicated by one knockout

[34] G. T. Eddy, "The Resurrection of Jesus Christ: A Consideration of Professor Cranfield's Argument," *Expository Times* 101 (1990): 327–29, quotation on 328.

[35] Paul L. Maier, *In the Fullness of Time: A Historian Looks at Christmas, Easter, and the Early Church* (New York: HarperCollins, 1991), 5.

[36] Karl Barth, *Church Dogmatics*, vol. 4.1, *The Doctrine of Reconciliation*, trans. G. W. Bromiley, ed. G. W. Bromiley and T. F. Torrance (Edinburgh: T&T Clark, 1961), 340; James D. G. Dunn, *Jesus Remembered*, vol. 1 of *Christianity in the Making* (Grand Rapids: Eerdmans, 2003), 838; N. T. Wright, *Resurrection of the Son of God*, 3:637–39; Raymond E. Brown, "The Resurrection and Biblical Criticism," *Commonweal* 87 (1967): 233; Thomas C. Oden, *The Word of Life*, vol. 2 of *Systematic Theology* (Peabody, MA: Hendrickson, 1989), 484–86; Richard Swinburne, *The Resurrection of God Incarnate* (Oxford: Clarendon, 2003), 183–84; Ulrich Wilckens, *Resurrection: Biblical Testimony to the Resurrection. An Historical Examination and Explanation*, trans. A. M. Stewart (Atlanta: Knox, 1978), 117; Michael Grant, *Jesus: An Historian's Review of the Gospels* (New York: Macmillan, 1992), 176–77; Walter Kasper, *Jesus the Christ*, trans. V. Green (New York: Paulist, 1976), 130; William Lane Craig, "The Guard at the Tomb," *New Testament Studies* 30 (1984): 52, 279; Michael R. Licona with Gary R. Habermas, *The Case for the Resurrection of Jesus* (Grand Rapids: Kregel, 2004), 93–95; Paul W. Barnett, *Jesus and the Logic of History* (Grand Rapids: Eerdmans, 1997), 130–31; Craig S. Keener, *The Historical Jesus of the Gospels* (Grand Rapids: Eerdmans, 2009), 340–42; Murray J. Harris, *Raised Immortal: Resurrection and Immortality in the New Testament* (Grand Rapids: Eerdmans, 1983), 34–39; George Eldon Ladd, *I Believe in the Resurrection of Jesus* (Grand Rapids: Eerdmans, 1975), 133–34; C. E. B. Cranfield, "The Resurrection of Jesus Christ," *Expository Times* 101 (1990): 171; Robert Stein, *Jesus the Messiah: A Survey of the Life of Christ* (Downers Grove, IL: InterVarsity, 1996), 269; Robert Geis, *Life of Christ* (Lanham, MD: University Press of America, 2013), 318–19; Charles C. Anderson, *The Historical Jesus: A Continuing Quest* (Grand Rapids: Eerdmans, 1972), 168–69; Grant R. Osborne, *The Resurrection Narratives: A Redactional Study* (Grand Rapids: Baker, 1984), 276.

critique along with several other solid refutations. These are a substantial number of considerations against the position, especially given its major weaknesses.

While it is the facts that demonstrate the falseness of this hypothesis rather than the critical evaluations per se, it is still significant that virtually all scholars seem to agree with assessments such as this, including many of the most skeptical researchers as well. This failure to explain the data best explains why this thesis basically has not been a popular alternative view taken by critical scholars for some 250 years, even during the nineteenth century, when these alternate options were so popular. The multiple refutations indicate these problems quite clearly. Yet this natural response frequently seems to come quickly to the minds of nonscholars who question the resurrection appearances. But the thesis is even rejected by a rather diverse collection of skeptical as well as non-Christian scholars of many stripes, among whom are John Dominic Crossan,[37] Bart Ehrman,[38] Dale Allison,[39] and John A. T. Robinson,[40] along with major Jewish scholars,[41] including Joseph Klausner,[42] Geza Vermes,[43] and Pinchas Lapide.[44]

Another way to view this matter is to unpack the second critique already mentioned above: virtually every scholar researching these questions recognizes that at

---

[37] N. T. Wright and John Dominic Crossan, "Dialogue," in *The Resurrection of Jesus: John Dominic Crossan and N.T. Wright in Dialogue*, ed. Robert B. Stewart (Minneapolis: Fortress, 2006), Crossan's comments are found on 38, see also 33.

[38] Bart D. Ehrman, *How Jesus Became God: The Exaltation of a Jewish Preacher from Galilee* (New York: HarperCollins, 2014), 164–65.

[39] Dale C. Allison Jr., *The Resurrection of Jesus: Polemics, Criticism, History* (London: T&T Clark, 2021), 339; Allison, *Resurrecting Jesus: The Earliest Christian Tradition and Its Interpreters* (London: T&T Clark, 2005), 207–8.

[40] John A. T. Robinson, *Can We Trust the New Testament?* (Grand Rapids: Eerdmans, 1977), 123–25, who well before it was a popular option, referred seemingly disparagingly to the common grave scenario as the view where "his corpse as that of a convict was simply dissolved in a lime-pit," adding that "the *burial* of Jesus is one of the best attested facts about him" and listing a handful of sources in its favor.

[41] For an excellent summary of where non-Christian Jewish scholarship is on the relevant issues discussed here, see David Mishkin, *Jewish Scholarship on the Resurrection of Jesus* (Eugene, OR: Pickwick, 2017), esp. 76–89, 201–11.

[42] Joseph Klausner, *Jesus of Nazareth: His Life, Times, and Teaching*, trans. Herbert Danby (New York: Macmillan, 1929), 357; Klausner, *From Jesus to Paul*, trans. William F. Stinespring (New York: Macmillan, 1944), 323–24.

[43] Geza Vermes, *The Resurrection* (London: Penguin, 2008), 144–45, 149.

[44] Pinchas Lapide, *The Resurrection of Jesus: A Jewish Perspective* (Minneapolis: Augsburg, 1983), 126.

the center of the lives of Jesus's disciples were the experiences that they believed absolutely to be appearances of the risen Jesus. These events changed their lives completely. As Ehrman attests: "Their conviction on this matter eventually turned the world on its ear. Things have never been the same since."[45] These disciples believed that they had seen Jesus alive after his resurrection from the dead and, as a result, Jesus was presently alive too. For them, this belief carried with it the ultimate meaning of life, both here and eternally, shaping how they lived in the present. They embraced this message wholeheartedly with both their beliefs and their actions. It revolutionized everything they thought, taught, and believed. It is this basic conviction that also so radically cuts against the Fraud Type 1 thesis.[46]

That Jesus's disciples had these experiences and beliefs is basically not disputed in the current theological literature. As Ehrman states again, "When speaking as historians . . . we can say with complete certainty" that Jesus's disciples believed these things. Therefore, Ehrman "has no difficulty whatsoever" embracing the apostles' beliefs at this point. Why not? After all, the disciples' conviction here is "a matter of public record . . . it is a historical fact."[47] This is what birthed the church.

Since this is as well-known and accepted as anything we know about the disciples, how could they (apart from mental illness) have held so tenaciously to their belief in Jesus's resurrection as the very dearest of all their views and, at the same time, know that they were the ones who had stolen Jesus's dead, lifeless body? But if they had stolen Jesus's body, then the resurrection could not have occurred. And if the resurrection had not happened, they were indeed liars, and none of their key theological beliefs were true. As Paul stated, if their claims were untrue, then they had never been forgiven of their sins, their loved ones had died without Christian hope, and their own Christian vision of eternity, likewise, was nonexistent. Paul recognized this and encapsulated it all so clearly that, apart from the resurrection, they would have been "of all people most to be pitied" (1 Cor 15:19 NRSV; cf. vv. 12–19).

Perhaps the chief point here is that, in addition to all the other severe problems with the Fraud Type 1 hypothesis noted above, what scholars know most assuredly about Jesus's disciples—their all-encompassing belief that Jesus had risen from the

---

[45] Bart D. Ehrman, *Jesus: Apocalyptic Prophet of the New Millennium* (Oxford: Oxford University Press, 1999), 230.

[46] Marcus J. Borg is another scholar who also accepts the fact of the disciples' transformations; see Borg, *Jesus, A New Vision: Spirit, Culture, and the Life of Discipleship* (New York: HarperCollins, 1987), esp. 184–85.

[47] Ehrman, *Jesus: Apocalyptic Prophet*, 230–31.

dead and had appeared to them—was *most directly* at odds with them having been the ones who had stolen Jesus's body. As mentioned, liars do not make good martyrs. This was the initial knockout punch against the Fraud Type 1 view. But the second major critique above regarding this approach is also an exceptionally powerful blow. The disciples' incredible transformations were not short-lived, as they well might have been. Rather, at least several of their cases are known to have been extended, lifelong commitments that lasted for decades after the initial resurrection events. How do such enormous, honorable changes result from the combination of losing both one's best friend and mentor along with one's most deeply cherished beliefs, perpetrating perhaps the greatest heist in human history with repeated lies followed by lives of service and more, all without a foundation? No wonder this hypothesis has been almost entirely ignored.[48]

---

[48] The first two critiques of this naturalistic thesis that we termed Fraud Type 1 are alone devastating. First, that the disciples stole Jesus's dead body and then were still willing to die for the truth of their resurrection message, especially when some of them actually did die gruesome deaths, is what we called a knockout punch. Second, the disciples' ultimate transformations that are sometimes known to have lasted a lifetime are also another strong indication of the falsehood of this Fraud Type 1 scenario. If Fraud Type 1 were true, these huge initial changes could alternately have stopped altogether just a short time later after a few very brief forays followed by the disciples' retirements due to the defeat of their message. The two critiques just noted are both strong arguments that favor the resurrection argument and refute the Fraud Type 1 scenario. Together, these two considerations are powerful roadblocks to this alternate thesis even by themselves. It is no surprise that these two counterresponses are the most-often-cited reasons not to opt for the Fraud Type 1 approach.

10

Fraud Type 2: Someone Else Stole the Body

To be sure, more critical scholars are attracted to this second, more general version of the stolen body hypothesis. In this case, one or more persons *other than* Jesus's disciples supposedly performed the feat of moving, reburying, or even stealing Jesus's dead body. Since it explains so little of the known and recognized scholarly data, it is virtually always intended to serve as an auxiliary hypothesis, not as a position that stands on its own, as will be pointed out directly below. Many options have been suggested here.

Though still unpopular, this second fraud variety has been more common than implicating Jesus's own disciples by postulating that they stole Jesus's dead body and then lied by claiming to have seen him alive while experiencing major transformations in the process. But all the while (according to Fraud Type 1), the disciples would have behaved as if they were truly convicted in their beliefs (Acts 4:33), plus being quite willing to suffer (5:40–41). But after Stephen in Acts 7:54–60 (an early leader though not an apostle) and James the son of Zebedee in Acts 12:1–2 were martyred for their beliefs, it might have seemed as if the fakery would not be able to be maintained much longer. Nonetheless, the evangelism and rejoicing simply continued unabated.

According to this second stolen body view, the chief idea was that someone else—almost anyone could potentially be cited to perform the job—must have stolen, reburied, or perhaps simply moved Jesus's dead body to a different location.

The involved person or persons could even have been unknown perpetrators. This hypothesis was not as far-reaching as the Fraud Type 1 proposal, and that probably helped it gain more momentum than its counterpart that blamed Jesus's disciples; hence, it was held more commonly. Further, a couple of the major natural responses needed an additional hypothesis in order to explain the empty tomb.

If Jesus's disciples were the perpetrators as in Fraud Type 1, one advantage is that a built-in explanation for Jesus's appearances would be included as well—they simply lied. But in making that move, the view went way too far overboard. The more direct way to characterize the situation would be to respond that the disciples lied about having seen the resurrected Jesus. True, certain subexplanations might enter the conversation and soften this report somewhat, making it look like some sort of mistake. But the obvious difficulty in believing such a hypothesis would have been that it essentially implicated the very persons who would never have been involved in the first place. These are most likely the chief reasons behind the virtual abandonment of this position over the past 250 years of critical interaction.

So why employ this second, weaker thesis at all? Several reasons account for the quite irregular though occasional appearance of this second option that identifies a culprit(s) *other than* one of Jesus's disciples, definitely making it more popular than the Fraud Type 1 since at least the time of English deism. The short answer is that it was sometimes thought that this secondary scenario was able to plug some apparent holes in the overall critical approach to the resurrection.

Most crucially, this view at least does not implicate the very preachers and teachers whose lives had almost undeniably changed most radically after Jesus's death, such that they were at least willing to die for the proclamation of the resurrection message. Such famous transformations, especially when they involve as many individuals as this thesis does, hardly seem possible if the proclaimers themselves were the same ones who were radically changed—all based on falsehoods or even lies. As William Lane Craig states, "To my knowledge, the only naturalistic explanation of the empty tomb that deserves any consideration is the suggestion that some third party stole the body."[1]

The chief weaknesses with implicating Jesus's disciples as the perpetrators were not the only reasons why this view attracted somewhat more attention. There are

---

[1] William Lane Craig, "The Empty Tomb of Jesus," in *In Defense of Miracles: A Comprehensive Case for God's Action in History*, ed. R. Douglas Geivett and Gary R. Habermas (Downers Grove, IL: InterVarsity Academic, 1997), 259.

a few other advantages with this Fraud Type 2 hypothesis. For starters, there are more options for the potential identification of the offenders, including the "crafty" selection of an unknown person(s). Further, there are also more motives available that may have driven them to their decision and actions. Moreover, not all these possibilities were equally drastic, as in cases where Jesus's body may simply have been moved, perhaps even rather innocently.[2]

But the chief reason for those researchers who chose a version of this Fraud Type 2 thesis is probably some species of visionary view being selected as the individual scholar's major option regarding Jesus's appearances. Speaking generally, this could either have been a natural subjective hypothesis such as hallucinations, illusions, or another species of postmortem scenarios. Conversely though, it could even have involved a supernatural option such as Jesus *actually* having appeared to his followers, though in more glorified, nonbodily appearances. Strangely enough, a number of scholars especially since the days of German liberalism chose the latter option, still arguing that Jesus actually rose from the dead, though rejecting what they considered to be the overly physical testimony of the Gospels and other New Testament texts.

When more visionary theses (either subjective or objective versions) were chosen, a reason to empty the tomb was often thought to be necessary, for these visionary conceptions by themselves would fail to do the job on their own. Of course, that immediately complicated the alternative thesis as well. But there obviously must have been an explanation for what happened to Jesus's deceased body.

Varieties of the Fraud Type 2 Position

Several different angles on alternative tomb hypotheses will be presented in this chapter. Basically, the category potentially includes any person or group who stole, reburied, or moved Jesus's body after his burial other than Jesus's disciples. In fact, the hypothesis that might meet the overall group requirements may qualify for a tongue-in-cheek moniker termed something like the "Potpourri Jesus Tomb Collection"!

Different categories of perpetrators are extant. One option is that *friends* could have stolen, taken, or moved Jesus's dead body for reasons outside the burial process (such as Joseph of Arimathea, Nicodemus, or possibly even the women

---

[2] As with the quite unintentional secondary burial thesis by Joseph of Arimathea that was evaluated in the burial chapter in volume 1.

in the case of those few scholars who do not consider any of these persons to be disciples).[3] Another option is that *enemies* might have done the same (like the Romans or the Jewish leaders).[4] Though neither (necessarily) friends nor enemies,

---

[3] Strangely enough, James Tabor postulated that Jesus's mother, Mary, and the other women moved Jesus's body after the initial burial, and while this is a *burial* thesis instead of a stolen body view like those we are considering here, there is a parallel in that the action was performed by the women, which is rarely proposed. See James D. Tabor, *The Jesus Dynasty: The Hidden History of Jesus, His Royal Family, and the Birth of Christianity* (New York: Simon & Schuster, 2006), 235. Perhaps Tabor agreed as well, because in a later blog he changed or reframed the scenario from the women to Joseph of Arimathea doing the reburial; see Tabor, "Two Burials of Jesus of Nazareth and the Talpiot Yeshua Tomb," *Society of Biblical Literature Forum*, 2007; reprint, 2; also found in *Bible History Daily* (blog), March 14, 2007, https://www.biblicalarchaeology.org/daily/archaeology-today/biblical -archaeology-topics/two-burials-of-jesus-of-nazareth-and-the-talpiot-yeshua-tomb/.

[4] In the earlier burial chapter in volume 1, an interesting angle was that the hypotheses discussed there postulated the possibility that the Roman soldiers may have tossed Jesus's body into an unknown, common pit (such as the view of John Dominic Crossan). This may actually exhibit some secondary similarities for this chapter too. While those burial accounts belong strictly in that chapter, and although the Roman soldiers did not "steal" the body per se, they were the ones who performed the nontraditional burial on this option. Albert Réville was a nineteenth-century French scholar who thought that the Jewish leaders were responsible for what happened to Jesus's dead body. More specifically, the Jerusalem Sanhedrin probably made arrangements for Jesus's dead body to be stolen. Then the body was placed where it most likely would never be discovered. See Réville, *Jésus de Nazareth: Études critiques sur les antécédents de l'histoire évangélique et la vie de Jésus*, 2 vols. (Paris: Fischbacher, 1897), 2:250–52, 347, for the Sanhedrin's crucial role in Jerusalem. Dale Allison refers to the (seeming) sheer possibility that "the Jewish authorities filched [the body] to prevent veneration of Jesus' remains" then "dumped" it when things got out of hand, but by then were either "unable or unmotivated to recover it later" (334). Allison also alludes to the text in Acts 13:29 as potentially hinting that the Jewish leaders themselves may have buried Jesus in the first place (362–63). But pertaining to this general scenario among others, Allison asserts, "We have no reason to endorse any of these speculations, for which there is not a shred of evidence. They must all be deemed unlikely. Yet they are not impossible" (334). His comments in the last half of this note are taken from Dale C. Allison Jr., *Resurrecting Jesus: The Earliest Christian Tradition and Its Interpreters* (London: T&T Clark, 2005). Robert Stein mentions the claim that the Jewish leaders were the perpetrators but scoffs at it, including mentioning the guard at the tomb; see Robert H. Stein, *Jesus the Messiah: A Survey of the Life of Christ* (Downers Grove, IL: InterVarsity, 1996), 267–68, 270.

Jack A. Kent makes what seems to be one of the most general, idle suggestions that either friends or enemies simply removed the body. See Kent, *The Psychological Origins of the Resurrection Myth* (London: Open Gate, 1999), 88.

a third option is the enigmatic proposal that necromancers might have taken the body in order to salvage the organs and other body parts of a powerful man.[5] Also, we will mention a few catchall ideas, such as what is probably the most popular idea in this category—that the women went to the wrong tomb on the first Sunday morning—as well as the thesis that the dirty work was done by an "unknown" thief or perpetrator.[6]

---

[5] The best-known contemporary proponent of the possibility of necromancers having stolen Jesus's deceased body is Dale Allison, who makes some suggestions involving this idea but never finally adopts it in his text *Resurrecting Jesus*, 202–3, 334. Richard Carrier also mentions this option in his essay "The Plausibility of Theft," in *The Empty Tomb: Jesus beyond the Grave*, ed. Robert M. Price and Jeffery Jay Lowder (Amherst, NY: Prometheus, 2005), 350, 365.

[6] These details can often be mixed and matched as well. For instance, John A. T. Robinson thinks that about the only empty grave hypothesis that "cannot be so easily dismissed" is the idea of "foul play," where some (presumably unknown) "extremist fanatics" moved or took Jesus's body; see Robinson, *Can We Trust the New Testament?* (Grand Rapids: Eerdmans, 1977), 123–24. French scholar Réville named the Sadducees as the perpetrators, but the place where they finally placed Jesus's body was apparently unknown according to his volume *Jésus de Nazareth*. Kent is one of those who suggests briefly that Jesus may have been buried in an unknown grave; see Kent, *Psychological Origins of the Resurrection Myth*, 88. A very different idea mentioned by Duncan Derrett, who also held the swoon or apparent death theory—see the material on Jesus's death in both volumes 1 and 2 of this study for many specific details there—who adds that Jesus's body was later cremated! See Derrett, *The Anastasis: The Resurrection of Jesus as an Historical Event* (Shipston-on-Stour: Drinkwater, 1982), 128. Cf. Wolfhart Pannenberg's critique at the end of this essay as well. Allison includes many different twists and turns among the sorts of options within this Fraud Type 2 alternative category (*Resurrecting Jesus*, 302–3, 307–10, 320, 324–26, 331–34). Yet, in spite of listing these possibilities, Allison seems to be mentioning what he thinks are not serious alternatives at all. As a case in point, he pronounces that many of these suggested scenarios invoke poor reasoning (302, 303, 305, 308, 313, 317, 325, 328, 329, 331–32). Further, Allison points out that these theses often have little or no evidence in their favor (312, 317, 334, 340). As just mentioned above, he also asserts that these options cannot be endorsed because "there is not a shred of evidence" on their behalf (334). He also rejects outright several of these options (303, 308, 311, 314). Quite intriguingly, when all the dust settles, although somewhat tentatively, Allison still decides in favor of the historicity of the empty tomb (331–34, 344, 346), as well as strongly endorses Jesus's appearances to his followers (346, cf. also 343). In a more recent work, Allison begins the volume by affirming his personal recognition of the resurrection appearances: "I believe that the disciples saw Jesus and that he saw them." See Dale C. Allison Jr., *The Resurrection of Jesus: Apologetics, Polemics, History* (London: T&T Clark, 2021), 3.

The Wrong Tomb Theory

Even in the heyday of nineteenth-century German liberalism with its penchant for a variety of naturalistic resurrection theses, only relatively few scholars would even venture in the direction of choosing the challenges presented by one of the Fraud Type 2 hypotheses. One of the ones who did so was Oxford University–trained Harvard Divinity School professor Kirsopp Lake (1872–1946). Lake is one of the few scholars who ever proposed the wrong tomb theory, and it is not usually acknowledged that this was only a brief suggestion on his part. He explained the possibility like this: Joseph of Arimathea indeed buried Jesus's body, but the women probably only witnessed the procedure from a distance. No male disciples were present due to their fear and despair caused by Jesus's death. On Sunday morning the women headed back to what they thought was the correct tomb to finish the burial process, but they found it open and unoccupied. Then the women were told by a young man standing there that Jesus was not in the tomb.

The women were obviously "overwrought" when they came to the tomb. But given the "already firm belief" in the resurrection that these women had, they apparently took the young man's words to mean that the closest tomb nearby had been that of Jesus, but that his body was now gone.[7] But the fellow was probably saying no more than that neither Jesus nor anyone else had been buried in that particular tomb. So of course, this tomb was obviously empty! Since the women were not physically close when Joseph was doing the burying, they could not be sure that this particular tomb was the same one. The young man even "tried to tell them that they had made a mistake . . . and probably pointed to the next tomb."[8]

Perhaps due to their excitement, the women were in no position to understand the young man completely. Further, Lake commented that the women and virtually

---

[7] These words along with a few other phrases by Kirsopp Lake show how critical views have changed in the intervening almost 125 years since Lake wrote this treatise. The comment that the women going to the tomb already believed in the resurrection, made in more than one place in Lake's work, would be made by very few critical scholars today. But there is also a practical warning here for us today that we should not think that staunch views held solidly today by liberals, moderates, or conservatives alike will necessarily still be in force decades from now.

[8] Lake, *The Historical Evidence for the Resurrection of Jesus Christ*, 2nd ed. (London: Williams & Norgate, 1912; repr., Eugene, OR: Wipf & Stock, 2004), 237–38, 248–53.

all believers in their day believed that if Jesus had been raised, then the tomb would have been empty. Hence, they were naturally interpreting these events in light of their own background beliefs. Nonetheless, the women had, in fact, gone to the "wrong tomb," which constituted Lake's "natural explanation."[9]

Intriguingly, Lake was clear that he was not offering this idea as some sort of irrefutable view about which he was positive. He took great care to state a few times that the various portions of his scenario were only "possible" or at most "probable." He even concluded the discussion with these words: "These remarks are not to be taken as anything more than a suggestion of what might possibly have happened."[10] But this caution has rarely been repeated regarding his thesis since that time.[11]

Even stranger is that Lake actually *affirmed* the resurrection along with Jesus's appearances, though as nonbodily occurrences. Hence, he had no need to affirm the empty tomb and may have preferred to explain it away.[12] His book title even states as much—he thought that he was providing "Historical Evidence" for the resurrection. However, he thought that the empty tomb was defenseless anyway, in that it "is for us doctrinally indefensible and is historically insufficiently accredited."[13] Lake thought that he was following Paul and the other apostles in this matter by holding to real appearances of Jesus as "a spiritual being" rather than as a material body without the

---

[9] Lake, 238, 241, 249–50.

[10] Lake, 252, cf. 248, 250.

[11] Thrall states that while Lake's wrong tomb theory is a "very unlikely" option, it is the "most plausible" of the natural theses pertaining to the empty tomb; see Margaret E. Thrall, "Resurrection Traditions and Christian Apologetic," *The Thomist* 43 (1979): 199. Barry W. Henaut simply mentions the "wrong tomb" thesis in passing; see Henaut, "Empty Tomb or Empty Argument: A Failure of Nerve in Recent Studies of Mark 16?," *Studies in Religion* 15 (1986): 180.

[12] This is the scholarly move mentioned above where even those who actually affirmed Jesus's resurrection appearances but as less than bodily events still thought that they had to do something with the empty tomb accounts in the Gospels.

[13] The quotation is from Lake, *Historical Evidence*, 253. Here again, as mentioned above, Lake's expression of over a century ago certainly runs contrary to where the scholarly meter on the empty tomb is today, with Lake making it sound almost as an embarrassment to scholars. Today, easily a majority of critical researchers accept the historicity of the empty tomb. In fact, there are more *critical* arguments in its favor than there are on behalf of almost any of the remaining resurrection evidences.

empty tomb.[14] Further, Lake also opposed strenuously the naturalistic theories that were leveled against Jesus's resurrection appearances.[15]

Such views have still not been very common in the past few decades. Michael Martin asks why we can rule out the thesis that someone other than the disciples stole the body of Jesus from the tomb.[16] A. N. Wilson suggests the possibility that the young man at the tomb stole the body and took it elsewhere, but admits that we will never know for certain.[17] But these sorts of theories are few and far between.

An Overview of Responses to Stolen Body by Non-disciples Theory

Before offering several very specific responses to what we have called the stolen body by non-disciples hypotheses (i.e., Fraud Type 2), Craig's earlier comment noted

---

[14] Lake, 252–54, 265–79. Here is at least the third area in only a short space where scholarly views have shifted significantly in recent times. Probably the predominant view today holds that the New Testament teaching, *including* Paul's view, is that the nature of Jesus's appearances was bodily in nature. The words "resurrection of the flesh," prominent in many classical Christian creeds down through the centuries, is still eschewed in many contemporary circles today. But Jesus appearing in an actual body is probably the most popular scholarly position at present concerning the New Testament view, *even among those who reject this position personally*. It should be noted once again that this view is definitely not to be decided by scholars according to their colleagues' headcount, but due to the way the New Testament data are now construed. Thus, it was a change based on the strength of the arguments themselves. The published treatment that is often cited as favoring the bodily view of Jesus's appearances most strongly is the nearly exhaustive treatise specifically on this subject by N. T. Wright, *The Resurrection of the Son of God*, vol. 3 of Christian Origins and the Question of God (Minneapolis: Fortress, 2003), particularly 32–552. See also the shorter but weighty argument in Michael R. Licona, *The Resurrection of Jesus: A New Historiographical Approach* (Downers Grove, IL: InterVarsity Academic, 2010), 400–436. For an assessment of where scholarship lines up on this issue today, see Gary R. Habermas, "Mapping the Recent Trend toward the Bodily Resurrection Appearances of Jesus in Light of Other Prominent Critical Positions," in *The Resurrection of Jesus: John Dominic Crossan and N. T. Wright in Dialogue*, ed. Robert B. Stewart (Minneapolis: Fortress, 2006), 78–92.

[15] Some examples of Lake's critiques of major alternatives to the resurrection appearances include his dismissals by the *religionsgeschichtliche Schule* (history of religions school) movement of his time, with its parallel mythological conjectures (198–99, 262–66), plus hallucinations and other subjective views (266–67, 271, cf. 212).

[16] Michael Martin, *The Case against Christianity* (Philadelphia: Temple University Press, 1991), 95.

[17] A. N. Wilson, *Jesus* (London: Sinclair-Stevenson, 1992), 242. This work was written before Wilson's conversion to Christianity.

that a third party removing Jesus's deceased body is the only natural tomb thesis "that deserves any consideration." After all, as Craig notes, an inscription written on a fifteen by twenty-four-inch marble slab, called the Nazareth Decree, "seems to imply that tomb robbery was a widespread problem in first-century Palestine" as well as possibly elsewhere in the Roman Empire. Then Craig adds that no positive evidence regarding such hypotheses of this nature occurred, making it merely an ungrounded assertion.[18]

Having made these comments, Craig then provides six brief reasons that militate against someone other than the disciples removing Jesus's body from the tomb, especially if these considerations are used in tandem. While these reasons of course do not guarantee that such a removal could not have taken place, they raise the bar and hence make it more difficult for such a thesis to succeed.

Craig begins, first, by saying that we have no knowledge of a third party where a motive was harbored to steal Jesus's dead body, especially when nothing of value was apparently buried along with it. Even if the tomb was simply desecrated for whatever reason, taking the body does not make very much sense, especially given the factor of the body weight.

---

[18] Craig, "Empty Tomb of Jesus," 259. It might be added regarding the Nazareth Decree that this stone was reportedly found in the city where Jesus was raised, perhaps not long after his death. That may possibly reflect one or more of these grave-robbing scenarios in Palestine, or even that the stories of Jesus's resurrection appearances were being told around the Mediterranean area and may have created quite a stir. But no clear decision can be made on these options based on this stone message alone. This archaeological discovery is also mentioned and commented on in volume 1. For a more technical treatment of the matter, including both a photograph of the stone and the Greek text of the inscription that also mentions sealing gravestones, see F. Cumont, "Un rescrit impérial sur la violation de sèpulture," *Revue Historique* 163 (1930): 242, for the photo appearing on the unnumbered page that follows this page, with the translation on 243. For a more popular treatment that begins with the words "Ordinance of Caesar," see Paul L. Maier, *In the Fullness of Time: A Historian Looks at Christmas, Easter, and the Early Church* (New York: HarperCollins, 1991), 202–3. However, as explained in volume 1 of this study, an alternate thesis has appeared recently that the incident in question may have referred to the grave of Nikias, a famous dictator from Kos (Greece) during the time of Caesar Augustus. More research will hopefully be done on these options. See Kyle Harper, Michael McCormick, Matthew Hamilton, Chantal Peiffert, Raymond Michels, and Michael Engel, "Establishing the Provenance of the Nazareth Inscription: Using Stable Isotopes to Resolve a Historic Controversy and Trace Ancient Marble Production," *Journal of Archaeological Science: Reports* 30 (2020): 1–7.

Second, according to the available sources, only a few men plus several women appear to even have known where the tomb was located. This might complicate things for a third party stealing Jesus's body unless the news had spread further.

Third, since the data favor the women discovering the empty tomb just some thirty-six hours after the crucifixion, this provides very little time for a conspiracy to be arranged, develop, and launched. Working within this narrow window to perform such a task and steal the body would involve a tight, seemingly well-planned operation, especially with the available working time being between the evening of the Sabbath until very early on Sunday morning.

Fourth, leaving graveclothes in the tomb also does not make a lot of sense during a hurried operation. Even if the clothes were left behind because the spices made them heavy, they would hardly have been folded neatly, as appears to be the case (John 20:5–7). Two independent traditions vouch for this second trip to the tomb by the men (with Luke 24:12, 24 being the second one).

Fifth, plots often get exposed later whether by rumor, discovery, or secret-telling. The disciples' preaching in the same city could well be what exposed a potential conspiracy. A payoff could well be a motivating factor too.

Sixth, perhaps the most compelling response to the hypothesis that someone other than Jesus's disciples stole Jesus's deceased body is left untouched by this hypothesis. This stolen body scenario fails to address the data favoring the tradition that Jesus appeared alive again mostly to his followers after his death. Hence, another alternative response is needed in order to address the most troublesome portion of the picture for the one denying this scenario, and this fails the criterion of explanatory scope to make the two scenarios work.

For Craig, the conclusion to this matter is that no plausible natural responses are "yet available" to explain the empty tomb. However, the resurrection of Jesus fits the data very well and is just what we would expect on this supposition. The rejoinder that *any* hypothesis is more likely than a resurrection draws us back precisely to the overall question of miracles itself, which as Craig points out, runs aground against the other responses such as those in the volume in which his response here appears.[19] Of course, this assumes that the other components of the overall positive case must also obtain.[20]

---

[19] Craig, "Empty Tomb of Jesus," 259–60. The brief quotation above is found on 260.

[20] Richard Carrier responded specifically to Craig's six points above, judging affirmatively that these positive points "encompass all the objections anyone might raise

Turning Matthew's Stolen Body Account on Its Head

Concerning just Craig's fifth comeback to stolen body accounts alone, he mentioned that conspiracies and plots "tend to come to light eventually, either through discovery or disclosure or at least rumor."[21] But Carrier provocatively conjectures further on this matter. Carrier asks, "What if the theft was indeed brought to light? Imagine, for example, that what the guards said (28:13–15) was not a lie after all, but the truth."

In Carrier's alternate, imagined scenario, Matthew would still have been defending the empty tomb account. But rather than simply buttressing the main story by providing the account regarding the guards, which is almost always thought by critical scholars to be the motivation for this explanation, "certain fanatical Christians" (probably not the ones who stole the body, Carrier notes) were actually *answering* the quite real rumor that had gotten started *because* of the historical attempt by some to steal Jesus's dead body.[22] In such a case, the author could have been responding to the objection (either real or imagined) that Jesus's body had been stolen. Following the

---

that are worthy of attention." Of course, a bit of personal interest could well be present here as Carrier circumscribes the territory in such a way that there are no other plausible views to which he must respond. Then Carrier could claim that he had handled all of the major or worthwhile responses. Carrier objects to Craig's first response regarding the need for a motive to rob the tomb, by asserting that body parts and crucifixion nails were valuable at that time, especially for necromancers. Other potential motives are also suggested, even pertaining to the possibility of robbery being recognized in Matt 27:63–64, whether or not the story was an invention. (See Carrier, "Plausibility of Theft," 350–52). To Craig's second comment that only very few men and women would know where the body had been interred, Carrier responded that the thief could have been someone in Joseph's own party, or one who either followed behind and viewed the procedure or perhaps simply inquired later concerning the group and then bribed one of those who were present (352). Third, regarding Craig's thought that there was only a very brief time frame in which to facilitate all the requirements of such a heist, Carrier answered chiefly that there were two nights during which the activity could have been accomplished (352–53). Fourth, addressing Craig's comment on the graveclothes being left behind in Jesus's tomb, Carrier retorted that "bodysnatchers want the body parts," so they would have discarded the remainder (353). Fifth, regarding Craig's charge that conspiracies are usually discovered, Carrier responded that criminals do not usually announce their crimes, plus there were no press corps, forensic scientists, or other such modern means of discovery available at that time (353–54). Sixth, Carrier of course holds that the resurrection appearances can be explained quite naturally (354–55).

[21] Craig, "Empty Tomb of Jesus," 260.
[22] Carrier, "Plausibility of Theft," 355.

speculated scenario, Matthew's account would more or less *accurately* be witnessing the additional development that this particular explanation had spread in answer to the Christian proclamation (Matt 28:15).

While being a strange and fanciful twist to Matthew's account, to be sure, this is not to retort that it could never have been the case.[23] Still, a few problems count against Carrier's comeback here. These must be mentioned.

(1) Carrier no doubt intends his rejoinder to serve as conjecture rather than as a potent volley drawn from the reported data. For in the same context, he freely postulates other countermoves as well, while pointing out somewhat properly in his conclusion that "of course, we cannot know whether the body of Jesus was stolen, since all direct evidence has been erased by secrecy and time."[24] Thus, though the rumor *could* have been true, with Matthew hinting at its actual existence, this is not really being asserted by Carrier as a historical occurrence. Carrier's attempt seems simply to take the Gospel account in one, two, or many directions at once, so that it is maneuverable in whatever form is necessary in order to avoid a direct answer to Matthew's resurrection claim. This seems to be indicated best by Carrier's word choices of "perhaps," "what if," and "imagine."[25]

This lessens the ultimate value of Carrier's response, in that while it does not count in any *direct* way as a blow against Matthew's report, it serves rather as a reply that, in effect, says, "Maybe so . . . We cannot tell for sure." So the critical comeback could even flip back and forth as needed between responses of "What if . . . ?" and "Remember, I suggested that . . ." and "Well, what do you want? It was only a suggestion." This certainly at least seems to be the case here. But playing both ends against the middle while thinking of many *just barely possible* scenarios obviously does not qualify as refuting the Gospel accounts.

(2) If Carrier is right that Matthew may have been referring to or addressing an early rumor, one where he reported "the truth" of the matter, then we have a serious

---

[23] Carrier mentions some half dozen well-known cases of fraud or cover-ups in both secular as well as religious settings, such as UFO reports, a "face" being visible on Mars, plus the results of the movements and followers of David Koresh, Heaven's Gate, Jim Jones, and Rastafari groups, where additional details emerged later (356–57). Carrier tries hard too, in his attempt to compare the influence of some of these movements to the influence of Christianity! Yet, he goes overboard in this last aspect (357).

[24] Carrier, 354, quote on 364.

[25] Carrier, 355.

issue regarding who was being implicated by that rumor.[26] In terms of being guilty of snatching Jesus's body, who were the ones to whom the fingers pointed in Matthew's account? While Carrier could always respond that Matthew changed the storyline or just plain missed the point, it was clearly Jesus's own disciples who were the ones implicated with the theft according to the potential rumor (28:11–15). The way Carrier presents the story, the truthful report by the guards at the tomb was twisted into a plot by the disciples and spread that way by unknown, non-apostolic perpetrators "probably not involved in the theft themselves."[27] But the point here is that, in Matthew, the apostles were clearly the culprits rather than any others.

Around AD 150 Justin Martyr spread an account drawn from or otherwise similar to Matthew's story. Justin told his Jewish interlocutor Trypho that the Jews had sent emissaries "throughout all the world to proclaim that . . . his disciples stole him by night from the tomb . . . and now deceive men by asserting that he has risen from the dead and ascended to heaven."[28] Again, as in Matthew, the perpetrators of the theft here were Jesus's disciples.

Similarly, Tertullian wrote approximately fifty years after Justin and sarcastically asserted that the same Jesus who was beat up, dead, and buried "is He whom His disciples secretly stole away, that it might be said He had risen again, or the gardener abstracted, that his lettuces might come to no harm from the crowds of visitants!"[29] Here we see what appears to be the same or similar accounts woven together from both the story in Matthew, coupled with another, later account in the Gospel of John, where Mary Magdalene supposes that the gardener moved (rather than stole) Jesus's dead body (John 20:11–16). However, Tertullian added the odd twist that the gardener seemed to be most concerned lest his lettuces get trampled by the presumed numbers of people that were sure to come in order to visit Jesus's empty sepulcher.

Then in the despised fifth-century anti-Christian Jewish text *Toledot Yeshu* (which is sometimes dated earlier and also reflects earlier traditions), the gardener

---

[26] Carrier, 355.

[27] Carrier, 355.

[28] Justin, *Dial.* 108, cf. also 17. For this translation, see the *Ante-Nicene Fathers*, ed. Alexander Roberts and James Donaldson (1886–1889; repr., Grand Rapids: Eerdmans, 1971), 1:253.

[29] Tertullian, *Spect.* 30, with the quotation also taken from Roberts and Donaldson, *Ante-Nicene Fathers*, 3:91.

reappears.[30] Seemingly surprised that everyone was so perplexed, he leads the priests to the place where he had reburied Jesus's body and sells it to the leaders, receiving thirty pieces of silver in return. Then the Jewish leaders drag Jesus's body down the streets of Jerusalem.[31]

So clearly, the accounts in Matthew, Justin, Tertullian—along with another late document, the *Acts of Pilate* (10:16–17)[32]—portray Jesus's disciples as the chief culprits in the prolonged deceit. John, Tertullian, and the later *Toledot Yeshu* mention the gardener (named Juda?) as simply moving Jesus's dead body, and the reason for that mistake is quickly uncovered. Tertullian mentions both traditions—the disciples and the gardener.

In at least the earliest couple of texts plus the majority of sources here, Jesus's disciples are still the ones who were said to have stolen Jesus's dead body, opening the door to the preaching of the resurrection message. The alternate accounts of the gardener in Tertullian and the *Toledot Yeshu* are not only much later, but the gardener's mistake was quickly discovered and corrected—it was not a permanent solution to the issue.

The overall chief point not to be missed here is that even on Carrier's clever rearranging of numerous possibilities, the sources are clearly against him. Carrier even admits that, "We have no texts attacking Christianity from the first century, not even fabrications or slanders."[33] Carrier's explanation is that Christianity was too small of a sect to rate on anyone's "literary radar."[34] Nonetheless, the earliest texts that we have concerning this matter—Matthew's echoed rumor and Justin Martyr's similar account from halfway through the second century—both implicate the disciples. Without much specificity on the matter, it appears that Carrier would

---

[30] David Mishkin has pointed out that while the earliest extant copy of an Aramaic version of the *Toledot Yeshu* dates only to the tenth century, "some have argued that it originates as early as the third century." See Mishkin, *Jewish Scholarship on the Resurrection of Jesus* (Eugene, OR: Pickwick, 2017), 3.

[31] See the account and explanations by Maier, *In the Fullness of Time*, 200, 202, 348 (incl. chap. 24n4) on the story in the *Toledot Yeshu* along with the extant manuscript copies and dates that detail this tale. Cf. also Gary R. Habermas, *The Historical Jesus: Ancient Evidence for the Life of Christ* (Joplin, MO: College Press, 1996), 205–6.

[32] Carrier seems to list this reference in the *Acts of Pilate* (also known as the *Gospel of Nicodemus*) as 1:13; see "Plausibility of Theft," 351. Cf. Raymond E. Brown, *The Death of the Messiah: From Gethsemane to the Grave*, 2 vols. (New York: Doubleday, 1994), 2:1232–34.

[33] Carrier, "Plausibility of Theft," 357.

[34] Carrier, 357.

rather have the body snatchers be other, perhaps even unknown persons. Yet the earliest texts that we have do not favor his position.

But further and much more seriously, Carrier now faces a rather devastating logic tree. If one is inclined to prefer the earliest and majority view that Jesus's own disciples did the dirty work stealing Jesus's body, then as we have already shown in the previous chapter, this view is faced with many insuperable problems, most of all from the scholarly, specialist perspective. As a note of advice, Carrier should resort instead to one of his other options rather than this one concerning Jesus's closest followers.[35]

But if Carrier prefers the possibility of his original suggestion here regarding a (mere) rumor of theft, then he needs most likely to settle for another person or group against the earliest data and facing a number of tough questions. For example, who else might be the candidate(s)? Would he also argue against the earliest view that soldiers fell asleep on the job but that they could still accurately identify the bandits? Or perhaps they were just afraid to act? But if Carrier also abandons the account of the soldiers altogether, then he must be careful here, for it will soon look as if he is now picking and choosing whatever and whenever simply in order to weave *any* view except the New Testament position![36]

Of course, Carrier might take none of the above options and never choose who might be the perpetrator. He could simply say, for example, that he was merely exploring the possibility that Matthew knew of a rumor critical of the Christian report of the empty tomb and that such a possibility was worth pointing out. But such a response would seem to settle for a very unsubstantial possibility. While Carrier might protest this characterization, it would probably look to most observers as if, once being forced into a tough situation, he had settled for a lesser road that now seemed to be the only way open.

---

[35] Carrier, 354.

[36] Carrier would no doubt resort at this or other points to his frequent comments that *any* view is preferable to a miracle or other supernatural event, so therefore he is simply open to alternative natural explanations of any or all sorts. As he states in the conclusion of this essay on 364 when mentioning Jesus's resurrection, "We have no good evidence that any form of supernaturalism is true." But it must be remembered that we are discussing here a cause for the empty tomb report, and it has not been concluded on these data alone that a miracle or supernatural occurrence has taken place. Furthermore, his naturalistic-type worldview outlook is most likely unprovable in itself, eliminating any exalted perch from which he may judge all other events.

But Carrier needs to head in a more specific direction beyond commenting on *potential* motives and some undiscovered "what if" plots that lack evidence, and toward the *possible* rumor specifically *hinted* at in Matt 28:11–15. Then he should indicate clearly that he has moved from the original notion in Matthew that implicates Jesus's disciples in the process. Carrier comments, "There is simply nothing improbable in an empty tomb being the result of theft."[37] Improbable or not, we need more than just his say-so speculations throughout this entire process. Namely, we need a comprehensive, likely hypothesis—one that explains the detailed circumstances in this specific case while avoiding the hard problems and pitfalls in the process. Beyond these "what ifs" alone, we need some *actual and strong historical evidence* for Carrier's favored option, so that it can be checked against the known, agreed-upon data.[38] After all, Craig responded with historical data.

(3) Further, even if Carrier or another critical scholar decided to take the route that we have termed the Fraud Type 2 or stolen body thesis, opting for someone other than one of Jesus's disciples, he or she would now need to develop at least one other alternative hypothesis to complete the naturalistic response to this event. This is necessary because the most crucial data to be explained are not those items pertaining to the empty tomb, as important as they are, but rather how, specifically, should Jesus's resurrection appearances be explained.[39]

To expand further on the last point, unless Jesus's appearances are accounted for naturally, dismissing the empty tomb by any approach(es) whatsoever will not disprove the resurrection. Theoretically at least, Jesus's body could hypothetically have been stolen from the tomb by anyone, only to have Jesus rise from the dead in a secret hiding place such as another burial tomb or even from a private home, still appearing

---

[37] Carrier, 354.

[38] On another subject, Carrier mentions that, in his opinion, his thesis on that occasion addresses my list of critically recognized historical facts with the exception of the empty tomb, which, as we have seen, he rejects (197). Whether he has done that adequately in the first case is open to question. But the point here is that he needs that sort of specificity in explaining his hypothesis on behalf of the empty tomb, instead of the generalities that allow him to skip anywhere he desires.

[39] Regarding the appearances, Carrier provides a hint concerning one of the places that he might head while responding to Craig: "The physicality of appearances in the Gospels can be a doctrinal and legendary development" given that these appearances are not found in Mark and because the epistles do not teach "physical appearances" (354). But if Carrier took this option, his claims in this statement alone would already be both outdated as well as incorrect.

to his followers later! These other locations, wherever they were, would then serve only as temporary lodgings from which Jesus would have resurrected—to "stand up again" (Greek *anastasis* and *egeirō*).

As already mentioned, and without developing either the details here or a critique, some researchers over the years have proposed literal appearances of Jesus that did not depend on his physical, crucified body or the empty tomb.[40] Of course, this would differ from the New Testament teachings.[41] But the point being made here is that explaining the identities and methods employed by those who robbed the tomb and stole Jesus's deceased body certainly does not necessarily prevent his resurrection or

---

[40] One effort along these lines is hinted at by New Testament scholar Dale C. Allison Jr., in his two volumes *Resurrecting Jesus* and *The Resurrection of Jesus*. Allison clearly explains, "I am sure that the disciples saw Jesus after his death" (*Resurrecting Jesus*, 346) and "I believe that the disciples saw Jesus and that he saw them" (*Resurrection of Jesus*, 3). He leans somewhat more so than not in favor of the empty tomb, though he is still not positive of this last event, remaining rather agnostic about it (269, 331–34, 343–44). Further, Allison finds no need for an empty tomb or a physical body for there to be a meaningful afterlife (*Resurrecting Jesus*, 225, 344), though he thinks that the Jewish plus the New Testament views were that of raised bodies (*Resurrecting Jesus*, 317, 324–25; *Resurrection of Jesus*, 131–36, cf. 224–25). On the other hand, Murray J. Harris takes quite a different angle on the subject in *Raised Immortal: Resurrection and Immortality in the New Testament* (Grand Rapids: Eerdmans, 1983) and his follow-up work, *From Grave to Glory: Resurrection in the New Testament: Including a Response to Norman L. Geisler* (Grand Rapids: Zondervan, 1990). Although Harris clearly accepts the historicity of the empty tomb (*Raised Immortal*, 37–44), he holds concerning the risen Jesus that, "after his resurrection *his essential state was one of invisibility and therefore immateriality*" (53, similarly, 54–58). Yet in his postmortem appearances, Jesus could be touched (55) due to his assuming materiality (54, 57). A very different thesis with a similarity or two is that held by Barnabas Lindars, who thought that Jesus's resurrection appearances were supported by strong evidence, whereas the empty tomb was a late legend argued backwards from the appearances. See Lindars, "Jesus Risen: Bodily Resurrection but No Empty Tomb," *Theology* 59 (1986): 90–96. A slightly later version of Lindars's ideas appeared in his essay "The Resurrection and the Empty Tomb," in *The Resurrection of Jesus Christ*, ed. Paul Avis (London: Darton, Longman, & Todd, 1993), 128–34. We will respond to similar theses below and elsewhere in this study.

[41] For detailed responses to Allison's overall views, see Licona, *Resurrection of Jesus*, 623–41; Gary R. Habermas, "Dale Allison's Resurrection Skepticism: A Critique," *Philosophia Christi* 10, no. 2 (2008): 303–13. Norman L. Geisler objects strongly to Harris's position in Geisler, *The Battle for the Resurrection* (Nashville: Nelson, 1989), esp. chap. 8; as does Francis J. Beckwith, "Identity and Resurrection: A Review Article," *Journal of the Evangelical Theological Society* 33 (1990): 369–73. Many of the items in these sources also apply to Lindars's argument.

the subsequent appearances. Thus, another thesis is necessary. Carrier should carry on with both projects in detail. Carrier has mostly bantered around the edges of the issues regarding some theory that somewhere *may* explain what happened to Jesus's body, freely offering caveats here and there. But he has plainly not done the hard work of naming the person(s) and describing the methods used. Even so, he may still say that he offered a hypothesis.[42]

A More Detailed Critique of the Fraud Type 2 Hypotheses

The preceding chapter emphasized the most obvious problems noted by most scholars who readily recognize that the double knockout blow to the Fraud Type 1 hypothesis

---

[42] Carrier also ends his main chapter above with further details regarding the guards at the tomb, raising additional points that have been discussed in much detail in the chapter on Jesus's burial in volume 1 as well as elsewhere in this study, so his items will simply be listed here briefly. He joins almost all critical commentators in rejecting Matthew's account of the guards at the tomb (Matt 27:62–66; 28:11–15), noting "several positive reasons to disbelieve it." See Carrier, "Plausibility of Theft," 358. These include the supposition that stealing Jesus's body was a possibility in the first place or the guards presumably would not have been introduced into Matthew's text at all. Further, Jesus predicted his resurrection in the context (Matt 27:63), thereby "priming his disciples to expect" the resurrection. Then "more importantly," the guard is not placed at the tomb until Saturday, hours after a potential theft. In conclusion, "even if the story of the guards is true it does little to argue against the possibility of theft." Several other considerations also cause Carrier to doubt the presence of the guards. For starters, they appear in the Gospel of Matthew alone. Next, when the women arrive, the tomb is already open, and they are unimpeded by the presence of the guards. Carrier dismisses Craig's supposition that the women did not arrive until *after* the guards left due to the presence of the angel, because this version takes too many liberties with the text. However, it is difficult to understand very specifically why Carrier would be able to make much of this point. After all, frankly, reading Carrier's complaints that Craig or anyone else takes too many liberties with the Gospel text is almost comical, given what has already been noted in the discussion concerning Carrier! More than perhaps any other commentators, Carrier is prone to take positions that are not supported by the text in question, seemingly in an effort to try and explain some convoluted idea—using exegesis "as a torture chamber" according to Licona. On this last tendency, see Licona, *Resurrection of Jesus*, 411n453, cf. also 57n104. Additionally, Carrier thinks Matthew's story reads more like fiction and that there is an overt apologetic function to the entire account (358–59). As an aside, Carrier repeats the term "entail" or "entails" several times in this discussion (such as 358), apparently without realizing that logical entailment is a property of deductive arguments rather than the inductive points that he is making here. In this strict sense, at least, no strict entailment follows from his arguments at all.

was that the same disciples who stole Jesus's dead body were necessarily the very ones who were both so exuberant in their resurrection faith, even being willing to die for their faith, which some of them did. While no single, equally lethal bomb sinks the Fraud Type 2 scenarios, the initial refutation is nearly as fatal.[43]

(1) Even asserting the strongest considerations, the collection of Fraud Type 2 responses basically only speaks to the matter of the empty tomb while failing altogether to touch the central data on behalf of the resurrection appearances of Jesus. Of course, it cannot be denied that the empty tomb is certainly a valuable part of the resurrection picture. But as a result, though this thesis might pick around some of the other edges, it basically ignores what is both the strongest as well as the most important indications that the risen Jesus was seen by others.

Pertaining to the minimal facts method, the empty tomb is not even included among these data, though it is definitely part of the second half dozen or so accepted historical facts listed in volume 1 of this study. But as stated several times now, Jesus's body could theoretically have been stolen from wherever it was buried and placed in some hidden, unknown grave or other spot, only to have Jesus rise from that alternate location and still appear. While a number of New Testament comments would be mistaken if such a series of occurrences had obtained, the point being made here is that Jesus would still have been risen and appeared to his disciples, and Christian truth would follow.[44]

(2) Additionally, besides not addressing the appearances, the Fraud Type 2 naturalistic views need to be demonstrated and not simply stated as possible what-if scenarios, like those critical scholars who prefer this angle so often choose to do. But this may be a nigh impossible task, as both Dale Allison and Richard Carrier have noted that these hypotheses lack any data, especially from the first century.[45]

In spite of the comment stated immediately above, Dale Allison in his later book on the resurrection provides several considerations against those scholars who make critiques such as this one. At the very end of that discussion in the book, Allison still remarks, "This means that any skeptical scenario will, in the nature of the case, lack positive, cast-iron evidence. Every alternative history will, in other words, necessarily be speculative and indeed oppose the texts at important points. Given how little we

---

[43] As Craig also noted in his critique above. Other scholars have noted similarly.

[44] Though we have taken great pains to argue against this entire cartel of burial and stolen body hypotheses.

[45] Allison, *Resurrecting Jesus*, 334, with a related comment appearing on 340; Carrier, "Plausibility of Theft," 357.

know, this is not the fatal flaw some imagine it to be."[46] And a page later, Allison adds that the overall evidential case for Jesus's resurrection is extraordinary and that he is unaware of a parallel case elsewhere.[47]

The comment regarding an absence of any "cast-iron evidence" for these natural Fraud Type 2 scenarios is of course not being requested and is an overstatement. Likewise, many theses *could* be true as well. However, these are not the specific points in view at this juncture. What *is* being discussed and remains the issue is that substantially more than happenstance is required by the supporters of these ideas, but the actual, specific data are seldom provided. Allison's favorite suggested option on the negative side appears to be the work of necromancers, though as cited above, even he comments on the same page that it is one of the views of which he maintains, "We have no reason to endorse any of these speculations, for which there is not a shred of evidence. They must all be deemed unlikely. Yet they are not impossible."[48] Thus, in spite of Allison's several caveats, even he considers what we have termed the Fraud Type 2 hypotheses to be improbable solutions.

(3) As pointed out in much detail throughout various places in this study, many of the events in the canonical Gospels, including several particulars of Jesus's burial in Joseph's tomb, are supported by good data. In the case of Jesus's entombment, a number of important features have an advantage—they are *multiply attested*.[49] As Bart Ehrman notes on this subject, independent sources that relate the same details or aspects were most likely not invented on their own. Rather, this means that the underlying traditions, sources, or actual facts that gave rise to the accounts and upon which they are based must predate them and be even earlier still. Ehrman explains the bottom line here: the presence of these factors in independent sources increases the probability that the material is credible.[50]

---

[46] Allison, *Resurrecting Jesus*, 345.

[47] Allison, 346.

[48] Again, Allison, 334, similarly 340. To be clear in this context, though Allison cites sources for grave robbers such as necromancers, he apparently means by this evaluative statement that there are no specific data that connect them to Jesus's burial tomb, so in this case the idea is deemed to be "unlikely."

[49] There is a distinction between the overall number of different sources that record a saying or event and how many of these resources are actually independent. *Multiple attestation* concerns the number of independent sources that are present and confirm the items in question.

[50] Bart D. Ehrman, *Did Jesus Exist? The Historical Argument for Jesus of Nazareth* (New York: HarperCollins, 2012), 290. Ehrman's comment is cited below.

These interment texts may also include briefer, multiply attested snippets of information that together assist in encapsulating an overview of Jesus's entire burial process. Different texts also report individual aspects of the burial process. For some examples, each of the following particulars is arguably also multiply attested by at least two independent sources: Joseph of Arimathea's role in requesting Jesus's body from Pilate; Pilate's permission; Joseph retrieving Jesus's deceased body from the cross, preparing it, and burying it in a new tomb; and even that a guard was posted in front of the tomb.

Altogether, there are approximately seven independent texts for Jesus's traditional burial, depending on how a couple of them are counted.[51] They are Mark 15:42–47 (and the Synoptic parallel passages); John 19:38–42; the fairly well-supported pre-Markan burial source; the exceptionally early and authoritative, pre-Pauline creedal statement recorded in 1 Cor 15:4; the highly accredited sermon summaries in Acts, such as those attributed to Petrine preaching in Acts 2:24, 27, 31 (especially taken in tandem); the Pauline argument in Acts 13:34–37; and the *Gospel of Peter* (2:3–5; 5:15; 6:21–24).[52] More than a half dozen independent sources is an amazingly strong number. But do they help confirm the same incidents? If so, alternate critical theories would have to oppose this combined collection of data, with much less actual evidence on their behalf, which is a highly questionable scheme.

Even skeptical scholars like John Dominic Crossan and the Jesus Seminar members voting as an entire group agree to the multiple attestation of various burial events

---

[51] Some might consider adding sources such as the additional portions of traditions that many scholars think lie behind the burial accounts in Mark, Matthew, Luke, and John. It was argued in the chapter on Jesus's burial in volume 1 that there may well have been a tradition behind the guard that was posted at Jesus's tomb, as found in Matthew and the *Gospel of Peter*, though it may well be later than the other pre-Gospel traditions. Some might question counting separately the two Acts traditions above, but the point here is that they are separate, earlier reports, even though they are contained in a single book. For those who object, one of them can always be subtracted to make a half dozen.

[52] While the *Gospel of Peter* is by far the weakest of these texts in historical terms, Ehrman also counts this writing as one of those dated within 100 years of the crucifixion. See Ehrman, *Did Jesus Exist?*, 163, 171; Bart D. Ehrman, *The New Testament: A Historical Introduction to the Early Christian Writings*, 2nd ed. (Oxford: Oxford University Press, 2000), 44. Even Darrell Bock dates the *Gospel of Peter* to the mid-second century, or just some twenty to forty years after Ehrman, so there has been some movement on the date of this text. See Darrell L. Bock, *The Missing Gospels: Unearthing the Truth behind Alternative Christianities* (Nashville: Nelson, 2006), 218–19.

here.[53] Going a little further, the Jesus Seminar members also agreed as a group that the empty tomb accounts are likewise multiply attested.[54] While this last subject is not the topic for this chapter, it still serves the purpose here of pointing to and augmenting the traditional burial scenario depicted in the Gospels.[55]

---

[53] Crossan puzzlingly lists Jesus's burial as having "Double Independent Attestation," which should be noted is still very good in itself. But his list of corroborating texts includes 1 Cor 15:4; *Gos. Pet.* 2:3–5a; 5:15b; 6:21, 23–24; Mark 15:42–47 (plus the Synoptic parallels) along with John 19:38–42, which most critical scholars would probably count as *four* independent sources, which would be incredibly strong. Yet it seems that Crossan *apparently* counts all these texts except 1 Corinthians 15 as aspects of a single source, which yields his two-source total instead of the usual critical count of perhaps four here. See Crossan, *The Historical Jesus: The Life of a Mediterranean Jewish Peasant* (New York: HarperCollins, 1991), 438.

The Jesus Seminar lists three Gospel sources for Jesus's burial: Mark 15:42–47 plus the Synoptic parallels; John 19:38–42; and the *Gos. Pet.* 2:1–5; 6:1–4 (562). It additionally lists the obvious reference to Jesus's burial in 1 Cor 15:4 (453), which may be the most highly acclaimed text of all. Yet, in spite of these *four* total sources attesting to Jesus's burial, the Seminar still judges that the traditional burial did not occur (562). Most incredibly, the Jesus Seminar declares at the beginning of its study of Jesus's actions that they had no preconceptions in coming to this topic, for their views were "not predetermined by theological considerations" (1). See Robert W. Funk and the Jesus Seminar, *The Acts of Jesus: The Search for the Authentic Deeds of Jesus* (New York: HarperCollins, 1998).

[54] The Jesus Seminar lists three sources for the empty tomb: Mark 16:1–8 and the Synoptic parallels; John 20:3–10; and *Gos. Pet.* 12:1–13:3. But like the burial of Jesus, it still concludes that this event did not occur; see Funk and the Jesus Seminar, 563. (The Jesus Seminar references to the *Gospel of Peter* are not necessarily listed the same way that other researchers number these same references.)

[55] The number of independent sources listed for Jesus's burial by Crossan and the Jesus Seminar is less than the above list of seven. A few comments are in order here: (1) Crossan's list of two sources often equals four by most scholarly counts (he does list four total references, though). But even by critical standards, it would seem highly problematic for Crossan to legitimately count comments from Mark, John, and the *Gospel of Peter* all as the same source, as if they were interconnected puzzle pieces. It would at least seem that very few other scholars would make the move that these three texts in Mark, John, and the *Gospel of Peter* all report variations of the same passage in speaking of Jesus's burial. (2) Four is also the number of sources provided by the Jesus Seminar, of which Crossan is a member anyway. (3) In spite of studying the views of scholars that are far from conservative, four sources are quite substantial anyway and provide plenty of material with which to make the case here, as indicated by other scholars who comment concerning source counts. See historian Maier, *In the Fullness of Time*, 197; cf. also another historian, E. P. Sanders, *The Historical Figure of Jesus* (London: Penguin, 1993), particularly 2–11. Additionally, see the comments on source attestation by Ehrman in the next couple of notes.

While multiple attestation of independent texts does not guarantee historicity, it is one of the most important tests for the historical status of events, for it can provide substantiation and confirmation from multiple angles, including the early dates of the tradition.[56] Hence, the seven sources mentioned above as favoring both the burial as a whole as well as noting the individual aspects from the Gospels regarding Joseph of Arimathea specifically approaching Pilate, gaining permission, taking down Jesus's body, and preparing and placing it in his own grave all point powerfully in the same direction and favor the traditional scenario.[57]

The overall point of this third critique regarding the multiply attested sources for the traditional burial of Jesus is not only to defend this event per se. The additional purpose here is to indicate that critical scholars who wish to move in a different direction by holding that someone stole or otherwise moved Jesus's body have to show initially some very strong evidences for their own alternate position and indicate the superiority of the opposed view in addressing the numerous angles of this traditional burial material above. As already mentioned, critics too often like to just list several possible moves here without buttressing their data.

Next, the further question needs to be addressed regarding how Jesus's appearances are to be understood by Fraud Type 2 theses, which we have asserted is by far the major issue in the initial critique above. But even without knowing which of the Fraud Type 2 options the critical scholar might choose to take, this would be a very difficult hill to climb, due to the fairly strong source data that support the traditional burial.[58]

---

[56] As Bart Ehrman states strongly in his text mentioned above: "But if a word or action is found in several sources and they did not collaborate with one another, then none of them made it up; the tradition must predate them. If it is found independently in a number of sources, the probability of its being reliable is increased, assuming, of course, that it is contextually credible." See Ehrman, *Did Jesus Exist?*, 290; also 111, 130–31, 251, 261.

[57] Plus the sources that were noted earlier for the guard at the tomb. On the same page as the quotation in the prior note, Ehrman contrasts the difference between "a saying or deed" that is present in only one source and one that is corroborated in several sources, with the latter being far more evidential (290). Interestingly enough, when he argues similarly regarding one versus several sources earlier in the book, Ehrman uses as his example a case that is corroborated by seven sources (92)—the same number that we argued for here regarding the traditional view of Jesus's burial.

[58] Ehrman changed his view on the traditional burial and empty tomb accounts in the Gospels, which he now accepts. For an explication of his new argument against the traditional views and a critique of it, see the earlier chapter on Jesus's burial plus the chapter

With regard to any of the Fraud Type 2 paths, then, what are the facts and sources that are comparable to those that support the traditional view? How much first-century data supports the alternate view? Of course, the critic has many options and much freedom in weaving their chosen hypothesis. But the view cannot simply be asserted as true. Nor can a number of negative assertions alone be piled up against the traditional case without being accompanied by many positive reasons that support an alternative thesis. The traditional position has some evidence backing it, such as the multiple sources from this third critique alone. What sources back the other options?

(4) The next problem for the alternate Fraud Type 2 positions is this: how would any of these suggested views totally captivate the apostle Paul? Could any of these proposals feature a message that would completely change the remainder of Paul's life? Would they be capable of causing his swift and immediate about-face, even when he constantly and repeatedly faced death, always being willing to die at every turn, as he mentions frequently?

The story began with Saul of Tarsus, the Pharisee and expert in the Old Testament and its history and theology plus all its legalities, additional rules, and traditions as well as their applications. On top of that, he had advanced beyond his peers, as indicated by his being singled out to carry on the message of Judaism even to the point of imprisoning believers and hounding them to their deaths and doing so with great relish.[59] According to Acts, Saul was trained in these areas and disciplines under the well-known scholar Gamaliel (22:3), and he was "a Pharisee, a son of Pharisees" (23:6; 26:5).

Totally steeped in Jewish tradition, Saul (now referred to as Paul) would later testify that at that point he was chosen and called, becoming an eyewitness to the majesty of the risen Jesus Christ, whom he saw on the road to Damascus (1 Cor 9:1; 15:8; cf. 10:32–33). The apostle Paul marched faithfully to the beat of Christ's message through to the end of his life (Phil 3:10–11), which almost surely ended in martyrdom.

The purpose of this chapter is not to defend and argue for Paul's appearance per se, but to lay out in abbreviated form how his message opposed each of the Fraud Type 2 options. It does not seem like any of the stolen or moved body views enacted

---

on the empty tomb in volume 1. Bart D. Ehrman's more recent view is expressed in his volume *How Jesus Became God: The Exaltation of a Jewish Preacher from Galilee* (New York: HarperCollins, 2014), 151–64.

[59] Gal 1:11–17; Phil 3:4–9; cf. Acts 7:58–8:1; 9:1–2; 22:3–5; 26:4–11.

by a person or persons other than Jesus's disciples serves as an option here with even a chance of enticing Paul and his cause, not to mention doing so in a way that would change him radically for the remainder of his life, thus fulfilling what we know about him, particularly from his own writings plus Acts.

One other item might be mentioned here. We have indicated that critical hypotheses are often stated without evidence, as if simply mentioning potential "what if" options is sufficient. In very few places is this latter practice more obvious than it is with alternate views pertaining to the cause of Paul's conversion on the road to Damascus. Some of the best-known scholars have made their own diagnoses, supposing the possibility or perhaps even being almost certain that Paul had a stroke, experienced a bout of epilepsy or a hallucination, was a victim of the heat, or had a breakdown of some sort.[60] Several of these may even be piled up in the space of a sentence, taking no longer than the few words necessary to simply state them.[61] Thus, "what if" type suggestions occur in more than just the stolen body chapters.

More careful scholars have attempted to calm the situation by pointing out that we simply do not have the data to determine the matter one way or the other.[62] Princeton Theological Seminary New Testament professor J. Gresham Machen charged repeatedly many years ago concerning these theories regarding Paul at the end of German liberalism's theological reign: "There is not the slightest evidence . . . totally insufficient data . . . no real basis" for many of these suppositions.[63]

So how is Paul's conversion to be explained alternately? The total assurance he manifested repeatedly was that he had actually seen the risen Jesus, and he never deviated from that. Nor was he ever forced to deviate from it! The remainder of his

---

[60] Such as historian Michael Grant, *Saint Paul: The Man* (London: Weidenfeld and Nicholson, 1976), 107–9, who mentions several options. So also major Jewish historian Joseph Klausner, *From Jesus to Paul*, trans. William F. Stinespring (New York: Macmillan, 1944), 325, 329–30, who was convinced (along with other scholars) that Paul suffered from epilepsy.

[61] Such charges and ones like them regarding their application to the apostle Paul are treated and critiqued in both the chapter on Paul in volume 1 of this study, plus in the appropriate chapters on these particular versions of naturalistic theories. The positive historical and other backup for Paul's appearance was also treated in the minimal facts chapters of volume 1, which include Paul's conversion.

[62] Grant, *Saint Paul*, 109. In spite of his own comment above, Grant states: "Our evidence is too fragmentary and enigmatic, to allow us to do more than guess at an answer."

[63] J. Gresham Machen, *The Origin of Paul's Religion* (Grand Rapids: Eerdmans, 1925), 47, 59, 61, 65, with the quotations appearing on 47 and 59 as well as in many similar phrases.

life argues against the options above, almost all of which involve a sickness of some sort. But the cause awaits another discussion. We only wish to point out here that any natural hypothesis needs to be detailed to the point of doing at least an equally good job of accounting for all of the information that we possess. The Fraud Type 2 hypotheses fail to do so.

(5) Further, how are we to account similarly for the conversion of Jesus's skeptical brother James? Along with his family members, James's earlier stance was apparently to reject Jesus and his message, along with joining the public sentiment (*hoi par' autou*) that Jesus was out of his mind (*exestē*; Mark 3:21, 31–35; John 7:3–5).[64] Yet later, after he met the risen Jesus, James appears to have been converted from his early position to his subsequent leadership of the Jerusalem church.[65]

Admittedly, this was a rather abrupt about-face for James—a change from thinking that his brother was mentally ill to following him even to the point of being willing to be stoned to death for his belief in him (Josephus, *Ant.* 20.9.1). The majority opinion among critical scholars is that the apparent and awe-inspiring change in

---

[64] The Greek text in Mark 3:21, 31–35 is difficult in its own right, such as regarding the question of the identity of those who attempted to restrain Jesus. The Greek literally indicates that these were people nearby (*hoi par' autou*), but both the way the terms are used plus Jesus seemingly ignoring his family, at least temporarily (3:31–35), favors the notion that Jesus's family agreed with this public sentiment. It no doubt looked quite embarrassing for both Jesus and his family, hence raising its likelihood of authenticity. R. T. France notes the traditional interpretation that Jesus's family attempted to get Jesus out of the public view, having concluded themselves that Jesus was "out of his mind" (165). After entertaining some alternate interpretations, France concludes that the traditional view "seems the least unsatisfactory solution" (166) and "seems to make the best sense" of the language here. The family, then, was concerned for both theirs as well as Jesus's reputation, since he apparently was not sane (167). See France, *The Gospel of Mark: A Commentary on the Greek Text* (Grand Rapids: Eerdmans, 2002). Larry W. Hurtado basically agrees with this interpretation, as well; see Hurtado, *Mark*, New International Biblical Commentary (Peabody, MA: Hendrickson, 1989), 65.

[65] James the brother of Jesus is even initially present in the upper room among a crowd of about 120 persons (Acts 1:13, 15), along with the other brothers of Jesus, the disciples, Mary the mother of Jesus, and others, immediately after Jesus's ascension (Acts 1:13–14). So James was numbered from the beginning as being present among those who would begin the church just a few days later. Then, at the epochal Jerusalem council of Acts 15:1–35, James gives what turns out to be the decisive word on the soteriological fate of the gentiles (15:13–21), even sounding as if he were handing down the final decision himself (15:19). Whether or not Gal 2:1–10 depicts the same meeting as the one in Acts 15, James's presence is also unmistakable there (cf. Gal 1:18–19).

James was due to an appearance of the risen Jesus.[66] This event was recorded in both the very early creedal tradition in 1 Cor 15:7 as well as narrated briefly in chapter 7 of the later, noncanonical *Gospel of the Hebrews*.[67]

James's move away from his previous unbelief has to be accounted for adequately both in his conversion and in his leadership position in the early church. Scarcely has anyone stated this more succinctly than critical scholar Reginald H. Fuller, who went as far as to retort, "It might be said that if there were no record of an appearance to James the Lord's brother in the New Testament we should have to invent one in order to account for his post-resurrection conversion and rapid advance."[68] Quite similarly, N. T. Wright also asserts regarding Jesus's brother James, "it is difficult to account for his centrality and unrivalled leadership unless he was himself known to have seen the risen Jesus."[69]

Taking a different angle altogether concerning James, Ehrman argues other specifics in a chapter entitled "Two Key Data for the Historicity of Jesus."[70] Of perhaps the two strongest arguments for the historicity of Jesus, Ehrman's first is that of Paul's personal acquaintances, beginning with a very crucial meeting that occurred when Paul visited Jerusalem and spent fifteen days with Peter and James the brother of Jesus just a few years after the crucifixion.[71] During this discussion, Ehrman unpacks a number of historical items indicated by Paul's visit, such as listing four independent

---

[66] Two of the very few protests here are those from John Painter, "Who Was James? Footprints as a Means of Identification," 25–29, 57–62, and, quite surprisingly to many, Richard Bauckham, "James and Jesus," 106, with both essays being found in Bruce Chilton and Jacob Neusner, eds., *The Brother of Jesus: James the Just and His Mission* (Louisville: Westminster John Knox, 2001). Both of these authors also produced earlier writings that voiced these views: see Painter, *Just James: The Brother of Jesus in History and Tradition* (Columbia: University of South Carolina Press, 1997); Bauckham, *Jude and the Relatives of Jesus in the Early Church* (Edinburgh: T&T Clark, 1990), 46–57. Bauckham does acknowledge that the predominant view among scholars is that James's resurrection appearance was the occasion of his conversion in "James and Jesus," 106.

[67] Crossan dates the *Gospel of the Hebrews* quite early (*Historical Jesus*, 434–36), while Bock apparently dates it to the second century (*Missing Gospels*, 218). Licona comments on these subjects in *Resurrection of Jesus*, 450, 458.

[68] Reginald H. Fuller, *The Formation of the Resurrection Narratives*, 2nd ed. (New York: Macmillan, 1980), 37, after citing Gal 2:1–10, 12; Acts 15:13; 21:18.

[69] Wright, *Resurrection of the Son of God*, 325. Wright likewise follows the majority view that James probably came to believe in Jesus due to a resurrection appearance (560).

[70] Ehrman, *Did Jesus Exist?*, 142–74.

[71] Ehrman, 146–56.

sources for the existence of Jesus's brothers, and even rather incredibly notes that this trip by Paul and his new acquaintances could just possibly constitute the closest occasion we have for gaining eyewitness testimony about Jesus![72] Referring to Paul's comment in Gal 1:19–20, Ehrman even states a little earlier, "When Paul swears he is not lying, I generally believe him."[73]

In fact, Ehrman thinks that this just-mentioned meeting in Jerusalem is probably where and when Paul first heard the details concerning James's vision of the risen Jesus. Further, bringing together the larger picture, Ehrman thinks that James, Peter, Paul, Mary Magdalene, and the other women all had some sort of visions or, at the very least, believed that and interpreted their experiences that way. But they all believed that Jesus had indeed been raised.[74]

Michael Licona takes a different approach to James, drawing from the minimal facts approach. He discusses in depth James's skepticism, Jesus's appearance to him, and the results afterward, including why James was converted. Licona's summary of what we know about James is very instructive.[75] Licona definitely recognizes that Jesus appeared to James and that, as a result, James became a Christian leader in Jerusalem. Further, James's conversion was most likely due to a resurrection appearance.[76]

---

[72] Ehrman, 145, 151, and to a lesser degree 148.

[73] Ehrman, 120.

[74] Ehrman, *How Jesus Became God*, 203–4, 192. Ehrman has held this view for a long time; see Ehrman, *Jesus: Apocalyptic Prophet*, 201, 229–30, cf. 231–32.

[75] Licona, *Resurrection of Jesus*, 440–51 on James's skepticism, 455–58, 499 with regard to Jesus's appearance to James and afterward, and 458–60 concerning the reason for James's conversion. The very helpful summary of what we know about James is found on 460.

[76] Licona, 460–61, 618 for succinct comments to this effect. Licona considers the evidence for this appearance to James to be quite strong, but he no longer counts this event as one of the minimal facts. This has nothing to do with any lack of historical evidence whatsoever. But the definition we gave of the minimal facts also requires a very significant amount of scholarly support—a high percentage of critical scholars. Licona tightened up the initial historical criteria for the scholarly consensus that favors historical events (esp. 64–66), and as a result he does not count James's appearance as a minimal fact, strictly because of this tighter second criterion for these facts. True, the critical scholars who comment on the matter virtually always think that James was converted from skepticism either by the risen Jesus himself appearing to him, or at the very least by what James *thought* or *believed* was the risen Jesus's appearance. Licona's new application is that the overall scholarly sample size of the commentators on the matter is simply too small. In the research, those who comment on these details regarding James almost always conclude the same thing, as just stated, but Licona prefers a broader cross-section of views on the subject. Given the strength of the evidence itself, even without a larger number of scholars,

Against the cross-section of these views that range all the way from scholars like Licona, Wright, Reginald Fuller, and Ehrman above, along with many others, which optional view of the stolen, moved, or reburied body of Jesus by a person or persons besides Jesus's disciples can account for James's conversion better than his having experienced an appearance of the resurrected Jesus? In short, what view most accords with the best evidence? It must be remembered at this juncture too, that what is being requested is *not* a response to each of the individual critiques of the Fraud Type 2 hypotheses. Rather, a *single* thesis needs to be chosen that accounts for *all* this data, and equally well or better than the resurrection appearances. What other thesis, then, makes a response that equally well explains the fact that this Fraud Type 2 thesis basically only explains the empty tomb, making it necessary to come up with another account for the appearances, the strong number of ancient, multiple sources that favor the traditional burial of Jesus as opposed to virtually no data on the other side, plus answers to the lifelong transformations of Paul and James, when their answer was that they had seen the risen Jesus?

(6) Then there are the twin problems of motives and any indications that these intentions were actually the case. In other words, even beyond much of the actual data themselves, which have been posited throughout this chapter, which views are accompanied by the best inside track on the clearest, strongest motivations *behind* their actions?

We have already discussed in the preceding chapter as well as this one, in a fair amount of detail, the better-known or more common alternate scenarios. These include options such as dumping Jesus's body in a common pit, burying it in a trench, Joseph quite innocently reburying the body in another tomb or location for whatever reasons, or even the actions of necromancers. But if these options are the closest that we can get to more possible rival circumstances, then potential Fraud Type 2 positions seem to be clearly in trouble. These latter suggestions do not appear to "size up" in likely ways by comparison with the traditional scene in the Gospels. The traditional burial in Joseph's tomb is stronger in almost every comparison and evaluation, including the

---

Licona considers James's conversion due to Jesus's resurrection appearance to be a second-order fact (461, cf. 618), along with three other second-order facts: namely, the empty tomb, Jesus's predictions of his death and resurrection, and the bodily nature of the appearances (468–69). Regarding the historical evidence per se, Licona's view still reflects closely the position that he and I took in chap. 4 of our volume *The Case for the Resurrection of Jesus* (Grand Rapids: Kregel, 2004), which includes James's appearance as one of the minimal facts (67–69, 224).

most probable motives, the presence of multiple independent sources, pre-Gospel
sources with very early dates for the material, the sometimes-determinative meaning
of the Greek terms, and so on. Thus the traditional burial is easily the best of the two
categories in terms of the considerations in its favor.

On the other hand, where are the similar sorts of multiple evidences that would
signify that another of the candidates for stealing or otherwise disturbing Jesus's dead
body would replace or dismantle the traditional thesis with its own data? It seems
that the remaining "contenders" have few established motives, no legal standing for
its option alone, and especially no serious testimony in its favor. For instance, what
Romans or Jews would desire to encourage the growth and development of a new,
large body of enthusiastic followers, rumors of other possible rival religious leaders
in Jerusalem or elsewhere, or yet another new religious movement to concern them?

Or in the case of the potentially intriguing suppositions that necromancers might
have taken the body, perhaps hoping for something to gain from robbing Jesus's
tomb, where is the specific evidence here with regard to *this particular case involving Jesus's body?*[77] As even Allison allows, these views are "speculations, for which
there is not a shred of evidence."[78] Moreover, Carrier himself points out, "We cannot
expect any other evidence of a discovered theft to survive. We have no texts attacking
Christianity from the first century, not even fabrications or slanders."[79] The honest
concessions by these skeptical researchers indicate some of the lack of hypothetical
toeholds that oppose the historicity of Jesus.

Hence, these alternate charges are only bare possibilities—the often proposed
"what ifs"—as is even acknowledged by some of the most critical scholars. Options
like these face huge uphill struggles largely in competition against a great deal of
early evidence. This regular lack of evidenced, competing situations is certainly damaging to these views. Earlier in this chapter we mentioned another possibility: that
of an *unknown* performer or location. But as Wolfhart Pannenberg wisely remarked
along similar lines:

---

[77] Allison, *Resurrecting Jesus*, 202–3, 334; Carrier, "Plausibility of Theft," 350, 365n1,
365n5. See also Carrier's earlier article, "The Guarded Tomb of Jesus and Daniel in the
Lion's Den: An Argument for the Plausibility of Theft," *Journal of Higher Criticism* 8
(2001): 304–18.

[78] Allison, *Resurrecting Jesus*, 334; a similar statement by Allison appears on 340. See
the further treatment of necromancers in the chapter on the empty tomb in volume 1.

[79] Carrier, "Plausibility of Theft," 357. Ehrman makes a strictly unrelated but still
helpful concession here as well (*Did Jesus Exist?*, 290).

It has been suggested that the burial place of Jesus might have been unknown. But this is a pure invention of modern scholarship without the slightest evidence. Moreover, it does not seem very likely that nobody would have been interested in where Jesus's body had gone when his followers proclaimed his resurrection in that city, and friends and foes of that proclamation would take for granted that there is a connection between resurrection and the dead body.[80]

Perhaps needless to say, positing unknown persons and locations hardly helps with questions of understanding or knowing the motivations of those involved!

In sum, it is already problematic that very little or no actual data support the *motivations* behind these alternate actions, which is the specific angle being examined at this point. But further, what proper conclusions should be drawn when the persons or locations are proclaimed to be unknown and therefore can hardly be evaluated (as just mentioned), or when the suggestions make essentially no real sense (like the Jews or Romans having been the culprits, again without historical data or divulged motives and so on) or are illogical (such as happenstance proposals)? This lack of data and reasons seems to contribute to the comparative absence of many takers regarding the Fraud Type 2 option.

(7) The wrong tomb thesis, barely even suggested by Kirsopp Lake, is an intriguing option by itself. The women watched the burial, supposedly from a distance, though this point both opposes the available texts and possesses no support, besides obviously being postulated in order for the women to fail to recognize the correct tomb on Sunday morning. Then, when the young man near the tomb saw their confusion at mistaking his verbal correction as well as his pointing in the proper direction, it would make sense for him to correct their misconception as well, but he fails to do the latter. Additionally, Robert Stein makes the point that it is simply amazing that everyone promptly forgot the location of the tomb after such a brief time![81]

So, in their enthusiasm and armed with their assurance that Jesus had indeed been raised from the dead (a conviction that would have existed before the appearances, though such a view on their part is denied by virtually all scholars today), the women

---

[80] Wolfhart Pannenberg, "History and the Reality of the Resurrection," in *Resurrection Reconsidered*, ed. Gavin D'Costa (Oxford: Oneworld, 1996), 69.

[81] Stein, *Jesus the Messiah*, 267–68. As mentioned above, Stein cites the presence of the guard at Jesus's tomb.

never cared to locate the correct tomb. Rather, they were pleased to run off without further inquiry. Likewise, the later trip to the tomb by the male disciples, attested by multiple sources, also apparently ended up at the exact same mistaken tomb, even though the young man tried to correct that. However, what about the account, which is also attested by multiple sources, of the men discovering the graveclothes inside the wrong tomb? Perhaps the women or the men (or both) had indeed gone to the correct tomb (Luke 24:12; John 20:5–7) after all? Or were the graveclothes found in a tomb where Jesus was never buried at all? All the time, as Margaret Thrall reminds us, "then the right grave would still contain the body of Jesus."[82] On this view, then, Jesus's dead body was apparently never discovered even as it lay right there in the correct burial chamber.

Then, as has been noted above, this actually fascinating hypothesis stops there and explains nothing else because Lake himself thought that the best evidence actually *established* the fact of the objective resurrection appearances of Jesus, though in nonbodily form. So, Lake's story is refuted at a number of places, yet still allows that Jesus both rose from the dead and appeared to his followers in the process!

(8) As already mentioned elsewhere, the Jewish leaders plus the early believers as well as the Romans themselves all had a stake in keeping track of Jesus's dead body, though for clearly different reasons. Too many adverse outcomes from various perspectives could have occurred otherwise. Hence the chief point here is that none of these persons or groups would have wanted Jesus's body to simply disappear by whatever means. Too many potential negative outcomes were at stake for everyone. This is illustrated well by the point that the Gospel of John records Mary Magdalene talking to the person she mistakenly thought was the gardener who had removed Jesus's body. Understandably, she wanted to retrieve it (20:15).

Such issues indicate that there were reasons to think that Jesus's burial place would most likely have been watched carefully or at least checked periodically. C. E. B. Cranfield agrees, noting, "The Jewish and Roman authorities had, in fact, a very strong interest in Jesus's being securely dead." Thus, going to the wrong tomb or other such developments would have been "quickly corrected."[83] While not necessar-

---

[82] Thrall, "Resurrection Traditions," 199. Thomas C. Oden is another of the many scholars critical of the wrong tomb thesis (484) as well as other Fraud Type 2 options; see Oden, *The Word of Life*, vol. 2 of *Systematic Theology* (Peabody, MA: Hendrickson, 1989), 485–86.

[83] C. E. B. Cranfield, "The Resurrection of Jesus Christ," *Expository Times* 101 (1990): 171.

ily being fail-safe, these other problems add to the conditions that make stealing or removing the body more unlikely.

Conclusion

This chapter has presented an overview of the troubled fate of the hypotheses that we have labeled Fraud Type 2, where Jesus's crucified and dead body was supposedly stolen or moved by someone other than Jesus's disciples. These actions could have occurred either purposely or innocently, but each option is beset by several problems. Many hypotheses have been gathered under this rubric, often mentioned only once by a couple of scholars or nonscholars. Then when the alternate refutations are mentioned, the original challenge is often simply dropped or else reduced to a mere notation or suggestion without any further explanation.

Altogether, comparatively few critical scholars have ever chosen any of these Fraud Type 2 options. There are at least three good overall reasons for this dearth, accompanied by a variety of subpoints under each one. First, the hypotheses all fall short for a variety of reasons, with none of them getting even close to solving a large number of key puzzles to which they need to respond. Very critical researchers have even acknowledged this.[84] Second, there would seem to generally be too small a prize for these critical efforts—such as the "right" to attempt to explain the empty tomb to enemies, not to mention a healthy payment no doubt being offered and paid for

---

[84] Other additional or secondary considerations may also arise while addressing challenges in extended discussions regarding the plethora of Fraud Type 2 suppositions. For instance, as with other critical questions, such as those surrounding the empty tomb, much is properly made of the location of Jesus's burial being found precisely in the city of Jerusalem, where the initial preaching also began—since that message could have been checked out within the local vicinity. But if both friends and foes alike were keeping a general or specific eye on the whereabouts of Jesus's body, which seems to make sense, as mentioned in the previous section above (along with Pannenberg's very helpful quotation on page 465), then we are again confronted with the juxtaposition of the dead body within the proximity of the city where the preaching occurred. Thus, especially in light of the absence of any alternate archaeology or supported accusations having occurred (as helpfully also pointed out in the concessions above by Allison, Carrier, and the last comment by Ehrman), the city of Jerusalem remains a very strategic place of advantage for early Christian preaching, thereby providing the opportunity for disproof of the alternative Fraud Type 2 hypotheses, especially without any actual evidence against the preaching from these charges. Once again, while this is not a failproof situation, these are strong cognate considerations just the same.

the correct information. Third and perhaps most crucially, besides failing to claim any potential benefits, it was pointed out in this chapter that the "holy grail" of this entire discussion would still fail to have been accomplished—namely, solving the far more difficult task of explaining the resurrection appearances, since these events are not really addressed by the Fraud Type 2 alternate theses. So who wants to spend all this exceptional time and effort without solving by far the major, most central issue?

11

The Swoon or Apparent Death Theory

One of the most popular rejoinders to the Christian belief in the resurrection particularly during the reign of older nineteenth-century German liberalism was that Jesus was never dead in the first place when he was removed from the cross. Conversely, this hypothesis has been proposed quite rarely by scholars during recent decades. Yet, it still appears periodically. The oft-mentioned cognate point is that such an oversight would be particularly more common in light of these events occurring almost 2,000 years ago when medical knowledge was far less developed than today. The less-magnanimous way to pose the same question would be to inquire where the centurion received his medical degree, or whether there was a power outlet located on the Galilean hilltop for the EEG and EKG machines.

While several of the best-known natural alternative hypotheses actually show up in the Gospels, having occurred to both believers and unbelievers alike, this was not really one of them. However, it is recorded that Pilate was surprised at the report that Jesus died so quickly, so he summoned the centurion to inquire if this were indeed the case. Only when he was persuaded of the truth of Jesus's death did he give the body to Joseph of Arimathea for burial (Mark 15:42–45). So the basic idea behind this supposition may actually have occurred to Pilate.

After a brief survey of some scholars who have held this view, chiefly during the periods of English deism, European rationalism, and German liberalism in the eighteenth and nineteenth centuries, this chapter will briefly review the major data included in the initial volume of this study on the cause of Jesus's death by crucifixion. That earlier treatment should be consulted for far more details, given that this second volume is devoted to alternative resurrection theses.

Scholarly Suppositions

The German liberalism movement in the nineteenth century provided the major birthplace for the development of the naturalistic theories concerning Jesus's resurrection. The liberal scholars involved in the movement fostered the heyday where one thesis after another was brought to the floor for consideration, but often only after naturalistic hypotheses favored by others were first critiqued. It was the heyday of alternative critiques not only directed at Jesus's resurrection but also toward a few other theological and historical topics that were likewise deemed unacceptable. The latter subjects included other miracle claims like the virgin birth or nature miracles such as Jesus calming a storm, or what were considered dogmatic theological beliefs like the deity of Jesus Christ, the Trinity, or the atonement.

During their lengthy time of more than a century of theological dominance, a number of liberal scholars championed the swoon or apparent death thesis, though almost always during the first third of this historical period. Not unlike some of the more popular, less scholarly treatments today, a number of the early efforts beginning just before nineteenth-century liberalism (such as eighteenth-century English deism and German rationalism) consisted of different fictional "plot" scenarios where the perpetrators were often the Essenes. Albert Schweitzer rather derisively termed these latter accounts the "fictitious lives" of Jesus.

One of the early English deists to hold the swoon or apparent death position was Peter Annet. He wrote several brief treatises against the Gospel accounts of Jesus's resurrection, often repeating the same points time and again, such as criticizing the notion of miracles.[1] Annet probably spent more time on the apparent death hypothesis than almost any other skeptic.

---

[1] Peter Annet, *The Resurrection of Jesus Considered: In Answer to the Tryal of the Witnesses* (London: Printed by the Author, 1744); Annet, *The Sequel of the Resurrection of Jesus Considered* (London: Rose, 1749); Annet, *The Supernatural Examined: In Four Dissertations on Three Treatises* (London: Page, 1750); Annet, *The Resurrection Defenders Stript of All Defense* (London: Printed by the Author, 1745).

A few decades after Annet's series of small volumes on the resurrection were published, a couple of examples from Schweitzer's list of "fictitious lives" also supported the swoon or apparent death theory. Schweitzer introduced his chapter on these authors with the unflattering comment that they consisted of "a few imperfectly equipped free-lances" who nonetheless "first attempted to apply, with logical consistency, a non-supernatural interpretation to the miracle stories of the Gospel."[2]

The first of these two writers, Karl Friedrich Bahrdt, composed his work *Ausführung des Plans und Zwecks Jesu: In Briefen an Wahrheit suchende Leser* in eight volumes over an eight-year period (1784–1792).[3] Bahrdt hypothesized that Nicodemus and Joseph of Arimathea were secret members of the Essene community who worked with Luke the physician to keep Jesus from dying during the crucifixion and then nursed him back to health so he could appear to his disciples.[4]

The second author, Karl Heinrich Venturini, developed another plot thesis in his text *Natürliche Geschichte des grossen Propheten von Nazareth*, published in four volumes from 1800–1802.[5] Similarly, Jesus was crucified and later nursed back to health by the Essene brethren while he was in hiding, from which he appeared to his followers.[6]

Early in the nineteenth century, Friedrich Schleiermacher was becoming the lead voice marking the beginning of German liberalism. Annet, Bahrdt, and Venturini had popularized the swoon hypothesis before this time. But while the English deists and the fictitious lives authors were influential, they did not represent the sort of gravitas that many of the leading liberal scholars did. With these more scholarly pacesetters, a much more influential stance could be articulated.

However, Schleiermacher's view of the death and resurrection of Jesus, especially whether or not he accepted some version of the apparent death thesis, is very difficult to discern for more than one reason, as discussed in far more depth in volume 1 in the chapters on German liberalism. The short answer is that there are insufficient grounds to prove either way whether Schleiermacher held this thesis, hence the

---

[2] Albert Schweitzer, *The Quest of the Historical Jesus: A Critical Study of Its Progress from Reimarus to Wrede*, trans. W. Montgomery (New York: Macmillan, 1961), 38–39.

[3] Karl Friedrich Bahrdt, *Ausführung des Plans und Zwecks Jesu*, 8 vols. (Berlin: Mylius, 1784–1792).

[4] Schweitzer, *Quest of the Historical Jesus*, 39–44.

[5] Karl Heinrich Venturini, *Natürliche Geschichte des grossen Propheten von Nazareth*, 4 vols. (Copenhagen: Bethlehem, 1800–1802).

[6] Schweitzer, *Quest of the Historical Jesus*, 44–47.

bottom line is that it is simply unknown and debated in various directions.[7] Karl August von Hase is another German liberal scholar who is also quite confusing on this topic of whether Jesus really died by crucifixion.[8]

Annet, Bahrdt, Venturini, Hase, and Schleiermacher aside, Heinrich Paulus was probably the best-known proponent of the swoon or apparent death position during the heyday of liberal theology.[9] In his *Life of Jesus* published in 1828, Paulus proposed that when Jesus was on the cross, he entered a death-like trance, though he revived later in the tomb. His severe crucifixion injuries kept him from always being recognized clearly, though the nail wounds in Jesus's hands were the most helpful indicators. Paulus held that Jesus's feet were not nailed to the cross.[10] Nobody knew when or where Jesus died.[11]

Schweitzer also listed three later "imaginative" or "fictitious" lives of Jesus that also embraced the swoon or apparent death hypothesis. These texts were written by Charles Hennell, August Gfrörer, and Joseph Salvador, all appearing about the same time as Strauss's earlier volume *Das Leben Jesu*. Hennell patterned his work on

---

[7] For example, Friedrich Schleiermacher, *The Life of Jesus*, trans. S. Maclean Gilmour, ed. Jack C. Verheyden (Mifflintown, PA: Sigler, 1975), 415–17, where Schleiermacher states that the question "*cannot be resolved*" (416), and he expresses indifference on the subject.

[8] Karl August von Hase, *Geschichte Jesu: Nach akademischen Vorlesungen* (Leipzig: Breitkopf and Härtel, 1876), section 112 on the resurrection, esp. 600–603. Hase's version of this thesis from almost fifty years earlier was published in his volume chiefly for the use of students: *Das Leben Jesu zunächst für akademische Studien* (1829).

[9] The ambiguity in Schleiermacher's position could well be the factor that keeps him from holding this dubious distinction.

[10] Heinrich Eberhard Gottlob Paulus, *Das Leben Jesu als Grundlage einer reinen Geschichte des Urchristentums*, 3 vols. (Heidelberg: Winter, 1828), 1:265, 281–82. Paulus's later work, *Exegetisches Handbuch über die drei ersten Evangelien*, 3 vols. (Heidelberg: Winter, 1830–1833), includes a very detailed discussion of the crucifixion and resurrection of Jesus in all four Gospels. In the 1842 edition of this text, this material occupies 660–928 of volume 3. Key pages pertaining to the discussion in the text above are 669–750, 785–86, 793–94, 834–35, 866, 881–83, 893.

[11] In volume 2 of Paulus, *Das Leben Jesu*, the discussion of the burial occurs in sections 204–6 (pages 256–66), while the resurrection appearances are discussed in sections 207–15 (pages 266–344). Schweitzer made the derogatory comment that Paulus's *Life of Jesus* was actually inferior to Venturini's "fictitious life" in that Paulus's had basically just offered a harmony of the Gospels with added notes (Schweitzer, *Quest of the Historical Jesus*, 50, 54–55). Paulus's *Das Leben Jesu* indicates the accuracy of Schweitzer's comment, where the Gospel texts were grouped by subject matter, juxtaposed, and interspersed with Paulus's discussion.

Venturini's earlier "fictitious" text, similarly employing a plot thesis. After his crucifixion, the Essenes removed Jesus from the cross and resuscitated him.[12]

Gfrörer had jettisoned his Christian faith and was a lecturer at Tübingen
University while Strauss was still there. In the second of his two volumes he took a
different methodological tact, applying Strauss's mythical approach to the Gospels.[13]
Gfrörer's plot thesis is also apparent regarding the crucifixion and appearances of
Jesus. The conjuring of his story without a historical basis led to the "imaginative"
moniker bestowed by Schweitzer. Jesus was removed from the cross before death,
taken to Joseph's tomb nearby, and was successfully resuscitated. Jesus's appearances
were thus historical events, though he had never died.[14]

Joseph Salvador was a French Jew who postulated that Jesus stood in the long
line of those who were inspired by the ancient tales of gods and goddesses.[15] In
terms of Jesus's "death" and later appearances, Salvador's version of the plot thesis
hypothesized the involvement of Pilate's wife, the Roman centurion, and Joseph of
Arimathea. Jesus only apparently died, was taken down, and buried, appearing alive
later to his followers.[16]

Thus ends some of the major treatments of the well-known German liberal versions of the swoon or apparent death hypotheses.[17] This notion seems clearly to be

---

[12] Schweitzer, *Quest of the Historical Jesus*, 161–62. Charles Christian Hennell,
Untersuchungen über den Ursprung des Christentums: Vorrede von David Friedrich Strauss
(Stuttgart: Hallberger, 1840). Hennell's work *An Inquiry concerning the Origin of Christianity*
was published previously in English in London in 1838.

[13] Schweitzer, *Quest of the Historical Jesus*, 163–64. August Friedrich Gfrörer, *Kritische
Geschichte des Urchristenthums*, 2 vols. (Stuttgart: Schweizerbart, 1831, 1838).

[14] Schweitzer, *Quest of the Historical Jesus*, 165–66.

[15] Joseph Salvador, *Jésus-Christ et sa doctrine: Histoire de la naissance de l'église* (Paris:
Guyot, 1838), as indicated by his fairly lengthy list of mythological examples on 152n2.
Other related instances appear on 184–86, 563.

[16] Salvador, *Jésus-Christ*, 144–206, esp. 193–98. Other areas of interest in this volume
include Salvador's discussion of the importance of the resurrection message, esp. in Paul
(180–82), and his evaluation of the Jewish leaders entreating Pilate for a guard for the
tomb entrance (197). In common with perhaps even the vast majority of critical scholars,
Salvador thinks there are many Gospel contradictions, a number of which he lists in the
long note 2 on 199–200.

[17] Another of the more outlandish treatments singled out by Schleiermacher himself
in *Life of Jesus*, 451, was that by "the notorious" Jacob Andreas Brennecke in *Biblischer
Beweis, dass Jesus nach seiner Auferstehung noch 27 Jahre leibhaftig auf Erden gelebt, und
zum Wohle der Menschheit in der Stille fortgewirkt habe*, 2nd ed. (n.p., 1819). As his title

the most popular of the naturalistic hypotheses pertaining to Jesus's resurrection during the first third of the nineteenth century. These theses were regularly developed in
the form of the ungrounded, plot-oriented, "fictitious" attempts of Bahrdt, Venturini,
Hennell, Gfrörer, and Salvador, often with the Essenes posing as the coconspirators.
The more respectable and serious example of the swoon theory was that developed
by the scholar Heinrich Paulus. Besides Paulus, the disputed views of Schleiermacher
and Hase also would have proceeded from scholars, if in fact these two authors
favored these notions. But as has been noted more than once, that is a very difficult
issue to determine.[18] Even these German liberal scholars freely critiqued each other's
positions. Although being quite popular at the time, the apparent death scenarios
were not the only brand of natural "resurrection" flavors.[19]

After a lengthy hiatus of several decades brought about largely by the relative
conservatism of Karl Barth and the chiefly fideistic views of Rudolf Bultmann, the
swoon theory began to reappear in a few places. However, seldom were the authors of
these efforts specialist scholars in a qualifying field.

One of the only exceptions to this trend of nonspecialist theorizing is the brief
article by theologian Margaret Lloyd Davies and physician Trevor A. Lloyd Davies,
which develops the hypothesis that Jesus lost consciousness, which caused the

---

indicates, Brennecke proposed that Jesus lived on earth for twenty-seven more years after
his "resurrection," appeared to Paul while he was still living in his earthly body, and also
managed to direct other events in the early church!

[18] As Schweitzer himself even noted in *Quest of the Historical Jesus*, 58. One huge consideration that could at least help solve this situation here in the case of Schleiermacher's
view, is that his *Life of Jesus*, from which the strong anti-swoon comment was reproduced
below, was not only a posthumous work, but was "reconstructed from students' note-books"
(62). Other questions would remain to be solved in this matter of Schleiermacher's views
on the death of Jesus, but the nature of his volume of notes could still be a helpful factor
for consideration.

[19] Many prominent German liberal scholars disputed or totally rejected the apparent
death hypothesis. Among these liberals were David Strauss, Albert Schweitzer, Theodor
Keim, and a couple of French authors, Ernest Renan and Albert Réville. These views and
sources are listed below in this chapter. Even Schleiermacher himself criticized the view
in Strauss-like fashion: "As a sick man with weakened life force, the journeying hither and
yon seems quite improbable, but this improbable action took place as early as the first day.
Then he appears as one quite healthy, who walks without difficulty to Emmaus and back
again. . . . We cannot represent him as those do who maintain the hypothesis of an apparent
death" (*Life of Jesus*, 455–56). (The other sources here are also found in our earlier chapter in
volume 1 on German liberalism that favors these scholars critiquing each other.)

bystanders to think that he was truly dead. The spear wound was only the prick of a blister! After he was taken down from the cross, Jesus revived and was treated. Rather surprisingly, instead of Jesus simply appearing to his disciples after his recovery, some unspecified sort of "perceptions but not visualizations" occurred, raising the possibility of internal perceptions such as hallucinations or even a species of diatribe illumination view here.[20]

The medical outcry against the Davies' stance was quite instructive, with multiple reasons being provided from many letters to the editor, mostly written by British medical professors, to indicate that Jesus really died by crucifixion. Dominating these letters were comments regarding the Davies' assertion that the spear wound was probably merely the prick of a blister, the reality of Jesus's death by asphyxiation, the Roman spear having pierced the heart, and the assumptions that the Davies favored something such as hallucinations, which were judged to be untenable in medical terms.[21]

Barbara Thiering has published some rather nontraditional ideas regarding Jesus. Among those is her view that Jesus married Mary Magdalene, had children, got divorced, and also married Lydia of Philippi. Jesus was crucified at Qumran along with Judas Iscariot and Simon Magnus. But none of the three men died, in spite of Judas and Simon having had their ankles broken. Jesus was drugged, given an antidote later, and traveled all around the Mediterranean with his followers, dying sometime after AD 64.[22] Not surprisingly, scholars have not taken her hypotheses very seriously.[23]

---

[20] Margaret Lloyd Davies and Trevor A. Lloyd Davies, "Resurrection or Resuscitation?," *Journal of the Royal College of Physicians of London* 25 (1991): 167–70. It is difficult to know the precise specifics concerning the very briefly mentioned "appearance." In fact, the entire article is less than two pages long, plus the endnotes.

[21] "Letters to the Editor," *Journal of the Royal College of Physicians of London* 25 (1991): 268–72.

[22] Among her books that develop these ideas are Barbara Thiering, *Jesus and the Riddle of the Dead Sea Scrolls: Unlocking the Secrets of His Life Story* (New York: Harper & Row, 1992).

[23] N. T. Wright remarks regarding ideas such as these: "Once again, it is safe to say that no serious scholar has given this elaborate and fantastic theory any credence whatsoever. . . . The only scholar who takes Thiering's theory with any seriousness is Thiering herself." See Wright, *Who Was Jesus?* (Grand Rapids: Eerdmans, 1992), 22–23. Edwin M. Yamauchi labels her ideas "an Alice-in-Wonderland scenario." See Yamauchi, "Jesus outside the New Testament: What Is the Evidence?," in *Jesus Under Fire: Modern Scholarship Reinvents the Historical Jesus*, ed. Michael J. Wilkins and J. P. Moreland (Grand Rapids: Zondervan, 1995), 210.

The swoon theory has appeared from time to time over the years, almost always in popular writings and often along with a number of other strange and off-the-beaten-path notions about Jesus.[24] But among scholars, even self-identified non-Christian researchers, the apparent death scenario has not really been overly popular since Strauss's devastating critique, stated most forcefully in 1864.[25] By the beginning of the twentieth century, it was declared to be only a curiosity of the past.[26]

---

[24] Some of these popular examples include Hugh J. Schonfield, *The Passover Plot: New Light on the History of Jesus* (New York: Bantam, 1965); Donovan Joyce, *The Jesus Scroll* (New York: Signet, 1972); Gaalah Cornfeld, *The Historical Jesus: A Scholarly View of the Man and His World* (London: Macmillan, 1982); Duncan M. Derrett, *The Anastasis: The Resurrection of Jesus as an Historical Event* (Shipston-on-Stour: Drinkwater, 1982); Michael Baigent, Richard Leigh, and Henry Lincoln, *Holy Blood, Holy Grail* (New York: Delacorte, 1982); David Mirsch, *The Open Tomb: Why and How Jesus Faked His Death and Resurrection* (Bangor, ME: Footlocker, 2011); Rolland E. Wolfe, *How the Easter Story Grew from Gospel to Gospel* (Lewiston, NY: Mellen, 1989), 92–103; Robert M. Price, *Deconstructing Jesus* (Amherst, NY: Prometheus, 2000), 222–24. Derrett's text employs other naturalistic theories as well, further supposing both that the disciples cremated Jesus's body after his later death and that the disciples experienced visions of the departed Jesus. Two other exceptionally brief mentions of the swoon thesis are B. C. Johnson, *The Atheist Debater's Handbook* (Buffalo: Prometheus, 1983), 121–22; and Rupert Gethin, "The Resurrection and Buddhism," in *Resurrection Reconsidered*, ed. Gavin D'Costa (Oxford: Oneworld, 1996), 206. Another example of a popular treatment is Richard Andrews and Paul Schellenberger, *The Tomb of God: The Body of Jesus and the Solution to a 2,000-Year-Old Mystery* (Boston: Little, Brown, 1996). A special case is that of the Quran, which states that Jesus did not die by crucifixion (QS 4:156–158), thus making this the Muslim's regular response on this subject. However, since the Quran has not spelled out the exact way that Jesus's death was avoided, Muslims are free to employ more than one supposition as to how the mistake or oversight came about. Popular responses include Jesus being placed on the cross with Allah removing him before his death or another person (perhaps a look-alike individual) being crucified in place of Jesus. However, the Quran was written more than 600 years after Jesus's death, far too long afterward and far too removed from the events themselves to be considered a historical treatment of Jesus, as agreed even by Muslim author Ahmed Deedat, *Crucifixion or Cruci-fiction?* (Jeddah: Abul-Qasim, 1984), 5–6.

[25] David Friedrich Strauss, *Das Leben Jesu für das deutsche Volk bearbeitet*, 8th ed. (Leipzig: Brockhaus, 1864), 299. Schweitzer comments on the influence of Strauss's devastating attack on rationalism (*Quest of the Historical Jesus*, 56–57) and does not list any nineteenth or early twentieth-century proponents of the swoon theory after 1838.

[26] See Eduard Riggenbach, *The Resurrection of Jesus* (New York: Eaton and Mains, 1907), 48–49; James Orr, *The Resurrection of Jesus* (London: Hodder & Stoughton, 1908; repr., Grand Rapids: Zondervan, 1965), 92, cf. 42. Orr also remarks on the influence of Strauss's crushing critique of the swoon thesis (11n2, 43).

Thus, with few exceptions, even the vast majority of very critical scholars willingly concede Jesus's death by crucifixion as a given, as some examples indicate. Atheist New Testament scholar Bart Ehrman summarizes the matter this way: "The most certain element of the tradition about Jesus is that he was crucified on the orders of the Roman prefect of Judea, Pontius Pilate. The crucifixion is independently attested in a wide array of sources and is not the sort of thing that believers would want to make up about the person proclaimed to be the powerful Son of God."[27]

Other skeptical researchers who write similarly include John Dominic Crossan, who makes a comment similar to Ehrman's: "That he was crucified is as sure as anything historical can ever be."[28] Elsewhere, Crossan likewise asserts, "I take it absolutely for granted that Jesus was crucified under Pontius Pilate."[29] Marcus Borg agrees with Ehrman and Crossan about the crucifixion: "The most certain fact about the historical Jesus is his execution as a political rebel."[30] Today it is safe to state that the vast majority of these critical scholars dispute or reject entirely the swoon or apparent death thesis.[31]

---

[27] Bart D. Ehrman, *The New Testament: A Historical Introduction to the Early Christian Writings*, 2nd ed. (Oxford: Oxford University Press, 2000), 233. Concerning his own personal viewpoint, Ehrman specifies: "I am not a Christian, and I have no interest in promoting a Christian cause or a Christian agenda. I am an agnostic with atheist leanings." See Ehrman, *Did Jesus Exist? The Historical Argument for Jesus of Nazareth* (New York: HarperCollins, 2012), 5. In his blog Ehrman states, "So I'm an agnostic atheist. Or an atheistic agnostic. Take your pick!" See Ehrman, "On Being an Agnostic Atheist," *The Bart Ehrman Blog*, May 23, 2021, https://ehrmanblog.org/on-being-an-agnostic-or-atheist/.

[28] John Dominic Crossan, *Jesus: A Revolutionary Biography* (New York: HarperCollins, 1994), 145, cf. 154, 196, 201 as well.

[29] John Dominic Crossan, *The Historical Jesus: The Life of a Mediterranean Jewish Peasant* (New York: HarperCollins, 1991), 372, cf. 372–75.

[30] Marcus J. Borg, *Jesus, A New Vision: Spirit, Culture, and the Life of Discipleship* (New York: HarperCollins, 1987), 179, cf. the context of this comment here in 178–84.

[31] Besides the influential authors just listed, additional skeptical thinkers who could be listed in this category against the swoon thesis include Gerd Lüdemann, Robert Funk, James Tabor, Thomas Sheehan, Geza Vermes, Elaine Pagels, Helmut Koester, A. J. M. Wedderburn, and John Shelby Spong. A long list of other influential scholars who oppose the apparent death idea for Jesus would include Dale Allison, N. T. Wright, Peter Stuhlmacher, Hans Küng, James D. G. Dunn, Jürgen Moltmann, Wolfhart Pannenberg, E. P. Sanders, Raymond Brown, Reginald Fuller, John Meier, John A. T. Robinson, Luke Timothy Johnson, Victor Paul Furnish, Gerard Sloyan, Walter Kasper, Gerald O'Collins, Thomas Torrance, Traugott Holtz, Pinchas Lapide, Pheme Perkins, Ulrich Wilckens, Craig Evans, Stephen Davis, George Eldon Ladd, William Lane Craig, Richard Swinburne,

Problems for the Swoon Hypothesis

In the response to the swoon or apparent death theory in this section, a large number of serious problems with this view will only be summarized. While the categories will progress while working through each (medical, historical, and David Strauss's critique), the count of numbered criticisms will follow in succession for the sake of gaining an overall impression of the strength of the contrary argument.[32] Many additional details not presented in this chapter may be gleaned from the two earlier chapters devoted to Jesus's crucifixion in the initial volume of this study.

Medical Problems for the Swoon or the Apparent Death Hypothesis[33]

(1) For most medical researchers, by far the most common cause postulated for the death of Jesus by crucifixion is asphyxiation or suffocation.[34] In fact, as remarked in the earlier treatment in this study on Jesus's death by crucifixion, it is likely that this option garners more total adherents than all the other medical options combined.[35]

The asphyxiation explanation is often presented similarly. When an adult male is hung so that the weight of the body pulls downward, the intercostal, pectoral, and deltoid muscles surrounding the lungs tend to constrict them. When this occurs, the victim can still inhale with difficulty, though it is increasingly difficult to exhale. Of course, the inability to either inhale or exhale causes asphyxiation quite quickly.

Michael Licona, Charles Perry, John Carroll, and Joel Green. The more than three dozen total researchers cited here are only examples of a much larger number of recent major researchers who reject the swoon or apparent death theory and embrace the historical fact of Jesus's death by crucifixion.

[32] The categories will be treated in reverse order from the original chapter in volume 1.

[33] The five medical problems to be mentioned here should be thought of more as categorical responses than as individual issues, since each critique generally contains several problems each.

[34] These two terms can be easily confused, depending on different emphases within the definitions, though with the first term often being preferred.

[35] Confirming this tally, see Gary Habermas, Jonathan Kopel, and Benjamin C. F. Shaw, "Medical Views on the Death by Crucifixion of Jesus Christ," *Baylor University Medical Center Proceedings* 34 (2021): 748–52. This article was more about the medical and historical *fact* of Jesus's death, along with a tally of medical researchers, rather than a dogmatic view on the exact cause of Jesus's death per se (as mentioned at 751).

Unless the process is halted, death will occur. Moreover, being nailed to a wooden cross, which is by far the more common description in the ancient world, would cause far more stress on the body.[36]

On this explanation, the centurion at the crucifixion site did not need a medical degree or modern technologies such as those supplied by EKGs or EEGs to determine if the offenders were dead. If the victim had been hanging in the "low" position on the cross for any significant amount of time, death would result, whether the individual was in a coma, faking death, or just plain worn out. The position of the person's body would provide much of the necessary information, since further up-and-down movements would obviously signal that more time was needed before death would ensue.

Death could be prolonged for perhaps even a considerable time if the victim could continually push down on their severely injured feet, pull up with their likewise brutally wounded arms and wrists, and contort their pain-wracked bodies into new positions to relieve the stress on their lungs in order to breathe. Even this drawn-out, incredibly painful process, recurring repeatedly, probably only resulted in just a few brief, halting and wheezing gasps before the person sank back down again. This obviously would be an incredibly painful process, especially given that nails were most often used. Further, such constant action would quickly tire out a victim. Not being able to continue these movements meant certain death in the low position, so there was a constant and repeated choice between staying alive or giving up and dying.

But if the legs of the crucified persons were smashed or severed, as with an instrument like a heavy mallet or an axe, the ability to push up to breathe certainly would be, at the very least, severely restricted if not thereby made impossible. This

---

[36] In a detailed footnote, Michael Licona provides a list of ancient sources that identify how the feet, arms, or wrists of crucifixion victims were affixed to the wood. He found that nails were mentioned much more frequently in these ancient works than were ropes. Virtually nothing pertaining to the time of death is determined by which fastening methods were employed. See Michael R. Licona, *The Resurrection of Jesus: A New Historiographical Approach* (Downers Grove, IL: InterVarsity Academic, 2010), 304n98. Cf. also John Granger Cook, *Crucifixion in the Mediterranean World*, 2nd ed. (Tübingen: Mohr Siebeck, 2019), esp. 425–26n45, also 190, 451; Ruben van Wingerden, "Crucifixion Practices: How to Attach a Patibulum to a Stipes," *Novum Testamentum* 64 (2022): 269–76.

would be in addition to the effect of the blow itself on the substantially weakened human body and perhaps the impending shock as well.[37]

For many reasons, then, asphyxiation has easily been the most popular choice among medical researchers to explain the chief factor in what was probably a multi-faceted cause of Jesus's death due to the process of crucifixion, perhaps even more than the other medical options combined. Of course, as mentioned often in this study, the most popular views are not always correct.[38] But whatever combination of factors may have been involved in the actual, physical process of Jesus's death by crucifixion, several additional considerations indicate clearly that Jesus was certainly dead when his body was placed in the tomb. This last fact is easily the most crucial consideration here, as agreed by the vast majority of critical scholars such as those listed above.

(2) According to the Gospel of John, the two crucified men on each side of Jesus had their legs broken to hasten their deaths before the start of the Sabbath, as per Jewish custom. But when they came to Jesus the soldiers saw that he was already dead, probably due to his hanging in the low position on the cross for a significant amount of time, plus there could have been other factors as well. So, a soldier pierced his side (*pleura*), and blood and water came from the wound (19:31–34).

Many of these details have already been discussed in volume 1 and will not be repeated here. It will only be remarked in this context that many sources in the ancient world evidence both the practice of breaking the legs of crucifixion

---

[37] For some of the fairly large number of descriptions available in the medical literature, see particularly the many details in our earlier chapter in volume 1, "Jesus's Death." Cf. here William D. Edwards, Wesley J. Gabel, and Floyd E. Hosmer, "On the Physical Death of Jesus Christ," *Journal of the American Medical Association* 255 (1986): 1455, 1461; Robert Bucklin, "The Shroud of Turin: Viewpoint of a Forensic Pathologist," *Shroud Spectrum International* 1, no. 5 (1982): esp. 9. Thomas A. Miller's explanation of a different perspective on asphyxiation is also a major consideration here. Miller explains that results from "inadequate oxygen availability to body tissues because of disturbed lung function" can impact the major organs and result in unconsciousness. See Miller, *Did Jesus Really Rise from the Dead? A Surgeon-Scientist Examines the Evidence* (Wheaton, IL: Crossway, 2013), esp. 78–85. Joseph W. Bergeron describes clearly the process of asphyxiation, even though this is not his own position. See Bergeron, *The Crucifixion of Jesus: A Medical Doctor Examines the Death and Resurrection of Christ* (Suwanee, GA: St. Polycarp, 2018), 144–53.

[38] Cf. Thomas W. McGovern, David A. Kaminskas, and Eustace S. Fernandes, "Did Jesus Die by Suffocation? An Appraisal of the Evidence," *The Linacre Quarterly*, August 22, 2022, https://doi.org/10.1177/00243639221116217; plus Bergeron, *Crucifixion of Jesus*.

victims (*crurifragium*) as well as administering other forms of death blows for the purpose of ending a crucified person's life more quickly, not to mention breaking legs in noncrucifixion cases to cause death.[39] Several sources also record examples of piercing chests and hearts in both crucifixion and other scenarios to ensure the death of someone who has apparently already died.[40]

---

[39] Ancient sources recording examples of the three scenarios mentioned above are as follows: cases of crurifragium during crucifixion include John 19:31–35; the independent *Gos. Pet.* 4:14; *Acts Andr.* 51:1, 54:4; two more archaeological examples of crucifixion victims that appear to have received crurifragium in the ancient world as explained by archaeologist Kristina Killgrove in her discussion "Line on the Left, One Cross Each: Bioarchaeology of Crucifixion," *Powered by Osteons* (blog), November 4, 2011, http://www.poweredbyosteons .org/2011/11/line-on-left-one-cross-each.html. The source to which Killgrove refers is A. C. Aufderheide and C. Rodriguez-Martin, *The Cambridge Encyclopedia of Human Paleopathology* (Cambridge: Cambridge University Press, 1998). There are also at least three more mentions of crurifragium in Cicero (*Fat.* 5, *Phil.* 11.14; 13.27), plus additionally the possible or likely Jewish archaeological scenario of crurifragium in the case of Jehohanan mentioned often elsewhere in this study, such as the volume 1 discussions of crucifixion. Martin Hengel describes ancient cases of non-crurifragium death blows of crucifixion victims, such as a ruler who ordered that ten crucified men have their skulls crushed with cudgels in order to finish the process. Also, in an ancient fictional account in Aristophanes, retold by Hengel, while a man nailed to a plank was writhing in pain, a bowman taunted him and threatened to finish him off with an arrow; see Martin Hengel, *Crucifixion in the Ancient World and the Folly of the Cross*, trans. John Bowden (Philadelphia: Fortress, 1977), 70. Other medical or archaeological authorities also report the general use of crurifragium plus other death blows during crucifixion; among these, F. P. Retief and L. Cilliers, "The History and Pathology of Crucifixion," *South African Medical Journal* 93 (2003): 938; a separate archaeological case noted more recently in Emanuela Gualdi-Russo, Ursula Thun Hohenstein, Nicoletta Onista, Elena Pilli, and David Caramelli, "A Multidisciplinary Study of Calcaneal Trauma in Roman Italy: A Possible Case of Crucifixion?," *Archaeological and Anthropological Sciences* 11 (2019): 1783–91. Last, the Roman historian Suetonius mentions cases in noncrucifixion scenarios where Augustus had a man's legs broken in order to kill him (*Aug.* 67), along with another situation where two men had their legs broken without mentioning whether or not they died as a result (*Tib.* 44).

[40] The prime example of piercing the chest to ensure death is that by Roman author Quintilian, as discussed in detail in the main crucifixion chapter in volume 1, where this writer states in Latin that executioners allow that the dead bodies of crucifixion victims who have been taken down from the crosses to be pierced (presumably as a last step in assuring their deaths) and then given over to those who would bury the bodies (*Decl.* 6.9). Much later (sixteenth-century) anecdotal cases are reported by Oxford University professor and religious historian John Foxe, who cited scenarios where Christian martyrs were tied or nailed to posts and, after much pain, "their sufferings were ended by lances being thrust

In both instances, reports of breaking legs and piercing chests are found in various Greco-Roman accounts as well as other religious and archaeological sources. Moreover, a number of major critical scholars have also concluded that John's accounts of the death blows for crucified victims in general and Jesus's specific postmortem chest wound are well attested as being historical.[41]

It is true that Jesus's legs were not broken. Yet the upshot of these two conclusions is the importance of establishing the Roman practices of issuing death blows to hasten an individual's death (either breaking ankles or some other death-ensuring method) and delivering a final death blow to ensure an apparently deceased person had really died, which appears to be how the Roman soldiers addressed the situation with Jesus. In both cases, the existence of these practices in the time of Jesus is well established.

Crucially and not to be missed here, the lack of a final death blow such as crurifragium in Jesus's case *only serves to make the spear wound even more likely*. Since the soldiers were basically killing the other two men on each side of Jesus at the same time as they passed by him, doing something to his body too makes absolute sense because these actions were for the purpose of *ensuring the deaths of all three men*. The soldiers' lives may possibly even have depended on all three crucifixion victims being dead, especially given the potentially explosive political situation with Jesus at Passover season.[42] So the well-documented truth of crurifragium is directly

---

through their bodies." See John Foxe and others, *Foxe's Christian Martyrs of the World*, rev. ed. (Chicago: Moody, 1960), 96. Although without describing crucifixion, other ancient texts describe cases where prodding or piercing dead bodies was a method of insuring that the persons were really deceased (as in Plutarch, *Cleom.* 37). In another instance, Roman soldiers were in the habit of piercing with lances the dead bodies of Jews to ensure their deaths. The same Jewish incident is related in both *Lam. Rab.* 1.5.31 and in b. Gittin 56a. Last, other recent scholars report that piercing the heart (plus other methods) was a regular example of ensuring death by crucifixion. See Retief and Cilliers, "History and Pathology of Crucifixion," 938; also Gualdi-Russo et al., "Calcaneal Trauma in Roman Italy," 1783–84.

[41] Among the scholars cited in the earlier chapter on Jesus's death as affirming John's crucifixion scenarios especially at these two points are Raymond Brown, James D. G. Dunn, C. H. Dodd, and John Wilkinson.

[42] Although not totally analogous, the story of Peter's imprisonment and release by an angel in Acts 12 is instructive at this point. Herod (Agrippa I) had lived in Rome where he was educated, so he was quite familiar with Roman law. According to Acts 12:18–19, when Herod heard the news about Peter's escape, he interviewed the guards, who had done nothing wrong, and then he had them killed.

connected to the coup de grâce in the specific case of Jesus. Finally, his pierced chest came after he had already died and served as the final indication of that reality, as in Quintilian's report.[43]

(3) Another vital medical observation must also be added here. Assuming the likelihood that Jesus's chest wound from the Roman spear pierced at least Jesus's lung, in the unlikelihood that Jesus was still alive at that time a pneumothorax (lung collapse) would have resulted. This condition would have developed since the pressure outside his chest would have exceeded the inside pressure, resulting in the incidence of a very audible sucking sound proceeding from the blood and other bodily fluids in the chest cavity that "would have been obvious to the centurion and to the individuals who took Jesus down from the cross." Pathologist Frederick Zugibe even witnessed such a sound that he could hear distinctly all the way across a room from a wounded and unconscious man.[44]

Beyond the centurion, others who were present at the crucifixion site also would have heard the sound and naturally would have concluded that Jesus was breathing and hence still alive. That would no doubt have resulted in still more radical steps being taken by the Roman soldiers to ensure his death.

(4) Michael Licona mentions another thoughtful argument favoring Jesus's death due to crucifixion. There "is a very low probability of surviving crucifixion." Of all the specific details and many references to crucifixion in the ancient world, "only one account exists in antiquity of a person surviving crucifixion."[45] Jewish historian Josephus narrates the case where, during a Roman siege, he discovered that three of his friends had been crucified. Josephus beseeched another friend, the Roman general Titus, who "immediately commanded them to be taken down, and to have the

---

[43] Quintilian, *Decl.* 6.9. This is not simply the verdict of modern medical testimony, but John's account relates that the soldiers had come to the same conclusion regarding Jesus's previous death. On the medical data, see Edwards, Gabel, and Hosmer, "Physical Death of Jesus Christ," 1463; John Wilkinson, "The Incident of the Blood and Water in John 19.34," *Scottish Journal of Theology* 28 (1975): 155; Bucklin, "Shroud of Turin," 8–9. Once again, the evidence for these comments is supplied in the myriads of details provided in volume 1.

[44] Frederick T. Zugibe, *The Cross and the Shroud: A Medical Examiner Investigates the Crucifixion* (Cresskill, NJ: McDonagh, 1981), 165.

[45] Licona, *Resurrection of Jesus*, 311–12. Josephus himself attests that "I saw many captives crucified" (*Life* 75). The translation used here is William Whiston's *Josephus: Complete Works* (Grand Rapids: Kregel, 1960).

greatest care taken of them." In spite of being given Rome's very best medical care available, only one of Josephus's friends survived even their shortened crucifixion. The other two "died under the physicians' hands."[46]

The point here is that besides this single case of a *rescued* crucifixion victim, we know of no other survivors of crucifixion in antiquity. There are *no known cases of unrescued survival* in the ancient documents of those who were crucified and mistakenly thought to be dead. Further, as Licona asserts, "Thus, even if Jesus had been removed from his cross prematurely and medically assisted, his chances of survival were quite bleak. In addition, no evidence exists that Jesus was removed while alive or that he was provided any medical care whatsoever, much less Rome's best."[47]

We need to add a major consideration here: recognizing the highly likely reality of death by crucifixion indicates that *even without* the crucifixion death blows and the postmortem wounds, Jesus would most likely have died anyway from any of several medical causes. Josephus witnessed many crucifixions with zero unassisted swoon events, either purposeful or otherwise. Therefore, all told, those who suppose that Jesus did not die by crucifixion are banking on slight possibilities rather than historical probabilities. All the best historical and medical data that we possess on death by crucifixion oppose this naturalistic alternative view. This is precisely why so few of even the most skeptical scholars support the swoon or apparent death hypotheses.

(5) Amid all of these detailed considerations that favor so strongly Jesus's death by crucifixion, another one has historically been the most influential critique in scholarly terms among both believing and unbelieving researchers. Developed and popularized by David Strauss, the most famous (or infamous) of the skeptical German liberals, this astute refutation of the swoon or apparent death hypothesis is not medical but rather logical or historical in nature.

When Strauss began his teaching career, the apparent death thesis was the most popular alternative view regarding Jesus's resurrection. However, Strauss did not value it very highly. In fact, judging from his remarks, he thought it was ridiculous.[48] After stating the essence of the swoon theory, Strauss then struck his tar-

---

[46] Josephus, *Life* 75. Translation again from Whiston.

[47] Licona, *Resurrection of Jesus*, 311.

[48] As with other criticisms aimed at Jesus's death by crucifixion that were dealt with in more detail in the initial volume in the major chapters on Jesus's death, Strauss's critique will simply be summarized briefly here in far less detail, so as not to be overly repetitious.

get in its very weakest place, brandishing his now-infamous and stylishly worded critique:

> It is impossible that a being who had stolen half-dead out of the sepulcher, who crept about weak and ill, wanting medical treatment, who required bandaging, strengthening and indulgence, and who still at last yielded to his sufferings, could have given to the disciples the impression that he was a Conqueror over death and the grave, the Prince of Life. . . . Such a resuscitation could only have weakened the impression which he had made upon them in life and in death . . . but could by no possibility have changed their sorrow into enthusiasm, have elevated their reverence into worship.[49]

Strauss's criticism works like this: *even if* Jesus had escaped this Roman death, which was highly unlikely in itself, this would not account for his disciples' *belief* in his resurrection, a belief that virtually every single scholar today concedes without question to be historical. To be sure, the Jesus of the swoon theory would have convinced his disciples that he was undeniably alive. But "just alive" was hardly good enough. Since the resurrection is the center of the Christian faith in all its fullness, the disciples needed to see Jesus's resurrection body appearing to them gloriously, grounding their newfound faith from that point onward.

However, on the opposite view, the severely wounded Jesus standing before them would have been very far from risen. The truth would have been rather straightforward: standing before them would have been a recently beaten and crucified and barely living Jesus, who would have appeared in absolutely horrible physical shape. True, it would have been clear that he had survived crucifixion, at least for a brief time, but this was not their risen Savior. Scourged horribly, with gaping wounds that were now dripping blood anew, pale and sickly looking, hunched over and limping badly, holding his side with his breath sounding in gasps, disheveled with unwashed hair caked with blood, Jesus would have been very much in obvious need of immediate medical assistance!

Then Strauss asks a few exceptionally pointed questions. Could this Jesus really have convinced his followers that he was the "Prince of Life"? Could this Jesus have

---

[49] Strauss, *Das Leben Jesu für das deutsche Volk*, 295–99, which is the section aimed at the apparent death thesis, with the now-famous quotation on 299. Strauss uses the term "swoon" on 297. English translation from David Friedrich Strauss, *A New Life of Jesus*, 2nd ed., 2 vols. (London: Williams & Norgate, 1879), 1:408–12, quotation on 412.

changed their grief and sadness into fervor and passion? Most of all, would this Jesus's disciples have worshiped him?[50]

Strauss's questions were precisely on the mark, striking precisely at the key problems. At least two other related issues follow. Jesus's condition obviously would have contradicted his disciples' initial belief that he had appeared in a glorious, new resurrected body. Similarly, could Jesus's highly disappointing appearance have led to their excitement that they would someday have a "resurrected" body just like this Jesus who now stood before them?

Strauss's overall critique of the older liberal version of religious rationalism in general, and more specifically the swoon or apparent death theory featuring particularly this critique, were so devastatingly hard-hitting and influential that he has regularly been cited by liberals, moderates, and conservatives alike since the nineteenth century. This trend of citing Strauss's criticism as a one-punch knockout of the idea that Jesus survived crucifixion was popular during and after liberalism, surely contributing to the demise of this natural thesis.[51] As was noted earlier, several scholars

---

[50] Strauss, *Das Leben Jesu für das deutsche Volk*, 299. English translation from Strauss, *New Life of Jesus*, 1:412. Some commentators over the years thought that David Friedrich Strauss's famous quotation above against the swoon theory was located in the initial publication of his earlier two-volume *Life of Jesus* (1835–1836). Though that is not the case, the initial four editions of the earlier work, published from 1835 to 1840, do contain a number of strong and sometimes pithy denunciations of this theory (such as 678–89, 734, 737–39, 751 in the English translation of the fourth German edition of 1840, entitled *The Life of Jesus, Critically Examined*, trans. George Eliot, ed. Peter C. Hodgson [Mifflintown, PA: Sigler, 1972]). Still, none of Strauss's other stated criticisms of this hypothesis come close to the 1864 nugget in terms of its succinctness, elegance, and power. As intriguing as it is remarkable, it is worthwhile to be reminded that after Strauss's devastating attack on rationalism and its methodology as a whole, Schweitzer once again does not list any new proponents of the swoon theory after 1838, perhaps because this natural response to the resurrection came chiefly from commentators in the rational camp of liberal critics themselves. There is a precipitous drop in German liberal interest in the swoon thesis, which was the most popular approach among the critics before this year; see Schweitzer, *Quest of the Historical Jesus*, 56–57.

[51] Critical scholars writing during the nineteenth century and slightly after this liberal onslaught, among the German liberals and the conservatives alike, recognized that Strauss's criticisms basically destroyed the rationalistic critique in general and the swoon thesis in particular. On the German (and French) liberal side, several of these responses included the writings of Schleiermacher (*Life of Jesus*, 455); Ernest Renan, *Vie de Jésus* (Paris: Calmann-Lévy, 1864), 314–15, 347–51, 358–60 regarding Jesus's enemies; Theodor Keim, *The History of Jesus of Nazara: Considered in Its Connection with the National*

went as far as to observe at the beginning of the twentieth century that the apparent death thesis had become basically nonexistent.[52]

Further, comparatively few scholars in relevant fields of study well over a century after Strauss hold the swoon theory today.[53] As a result of examining the data as well as hearing such denunciations of this thesis, more scholars have since agreed that Strauss indeed authored the strongest refutation of this naturalistic thesis. Gerald O'Collins also employs the term "knockdown," similar to the verbiage above.[54] Some perhaps do not even mention the point any longer due to the conviction that the view is both outdated as well as false. Nonetheless, Strauss's criticism has remained the nemesis of swoon theories even in more recent decades, appearing regularly when the view is discussed.[55]

Life of Israel, and Related in Detail, trans. Arthur Ransom, 6 vols. (London: Williams & Norgate, 1883), 6:330–31; Albert Réville, *Jésus de Nazareth: Études critiques sur les antécédents de l'histoire évangélique et la vie de Jésus*, 2 vols. (Paris: Fischbacher, 1897), 2:455; and Schweitzer, *Quest of the Historical Jesus*, 56–57, 62. For the conservatives, comments concerning the force of Strauss's views were made by William Milligan, *The Resurrection of our Lord* (London: Macmillan, 1881), 75; George P. Fisher, *The Grounds of Theistic and Christian Belief*, rev. ed. (New York: Scribner's, 1883), 193; Orr, *Resurrection of Jesus*, 11n2, 42–43; W. J. Sparrow-Simpson, *The Resurrection and the Christian Faith* (Grand Rapids: Zondervan, 1968), 44, 160; Frank Morison, *Who Moved the Stone?* (London: Faber & Faber, 1930), 64, 96; Doremus A. Hayes, *The Resurrection Fact* (Nashville: Cokesbury, 1932), 284–85; cf. also Alfred Edersheim, *The Life and Times of Jesus the Messiah*, 2 vols. (Grand Rapids: Eerdmans, 1883), 2:629. That both major liberal and conservative scholars alike agreed on the force of Strauss's thoughts here as the final word on the swoon theses is a tribute to the lasting influence of Strauss's critique.

[52] As noted above, Riggenbach, *Resurrection of Jesus*, 48–49; and Orr, *Resurrection of Jesus*, 42, 92, are two such examples. In addition, others who noted quite similar thoughts were Morison, *Who Moved the Stone?*, 96; and Hayes, *Resurrection Fact*, 285. Hayes creatively concluded the matter like this: "It is not surprising, therefore, that the swoon theory has been rejected by all recent writers. Strauss was largely responsible for its death and burial, and he has left it without any hope of a resurrection."

[53] With apologies to any possibly mischaracterized authors here, many recent writers were noted above in this chapter who still favor the swoon thesis but are better described as popular writers who are rarely cited positively by the scholars. A few of the authors are scholars but in unrelated fields rather than specialists in these subjects, hence they would be out of their research areas to draw these conclusions.

[54] Gerald O'Collins, *Jesus Risen: The Resurrection—What Actually Happened and What Does It Mean?* (London: Darton, Longman, & Todd, 1987), 100–101.

[55] Allison comments similarly on the denunciation by Strauss, whom he footnotes after this comment: "How a flagellated, half-dead victim of the hideous torture of crucifixion

Just to summarize briefly these five medical categories, the medical cause of death by crucifixion was probably multifactorial, with asphyxiation mentioned most frequently by far.[56] But it also should be noted very carefully that if other major causes of death actually predominated instead of asphyxiation, they were likewise fully capable of ensuring Jesus's death. Therefore, the other arguments for Jesus's death presented in this chapter would also assure this same result.

Second, very strong textual and archaeological evidences confirm the practices of administering death blows to living crucifixion victims as well as providing additional support for a final coup de grâce being administered in the case of deceased victims like Jesus. The postmortem chest piercing was connected to the treatment of the other two victims in the same context, which lends further historical likelihood to the chest wound. The latter would certainly have assured Jesus's death, which had already occurred.

Third, assuming that Jesus had been stabbed in the chest, a pneumothorax would have occurred. Such an event would have ensured Jesus's death from another angle, since the ensuing sucking and gurgling sounds originating from that wound would have sounded to bystanders, Romans and others alike, as if Jesus were still alive. In such an instance, Jesus would necessarily have been struck again, probably even more severely.

---

could impress others as triumphant over death is hard to envisage." See Dale C. Allison Jr., *Resurrecting Jesus: The Earliest Christian Tradition and Its Interpreters* (London: T&T Clark, 2005), 203–4. Among the many contemporary critical scholars who have argued that Strauss's main critique and related evaluations were decisive and ended any thoughts of swoon, see N. T. Wright, "Christian Origins and the Resurrection of Jesus: The Resurrection of Jesus as a Historical Problem," *Sewanee Theological Review* 42 (1998): 119; A. E. Harvey, "A Short Life after Death," review of *The Anastasis: The Resurrection of Jesus as a Historical Event*, by J. Duncan M. Derrett, in *The Times Literary Supplement*, No. 4153 (1982); Pheme Perkins, review of *The Anastasis: The Resurrection of Jesus as a Historical Event*, by J. Duncan M. Derrett in *Catholic Biblical Quarterly* 45 (1983): 684–85; T. S. M. Williams, review of *The Anastasis: The Resurrection of Jesus as a Historical Event*, by J. Duncan M. Derrett in *Journal of Theological Studies* 36 (1985): 445–47; Norman Anderson, *Jesus Christ: The Witness of History* (Leicester: InterVarsity, 1985), 87, 158–64, esp. 163, where Anderson remarks that "Derrett's 'reconstruction' runs up against Strauss' trenchant criticism." Cf. Otto Merk, review of *The Anastasis: The Resurrection of Jesus as a Historical Event*, by J. Duncan M. Derrett in *Gnomon: Kritische Zeitschrift fur die gesamte klassische Altertumswissenschaft* 59 (1987): 761–63.

[56] Repeating the earlier point once again, the five medical issues listed above are more like categories that usually involve several critiques each.

Fourth, though there are many crucifixions described or discussed in antiquity, there are no known cases among them where the full crucifixion process failed to result in the death of the victim. Thus, given his completed crucifixion scenario, Jesus's chances of survival were very bleak, *even without additional wounds or death blows*. This is highly significant.

Fifth, David Strauss's absolutely devastating critique by itself has traditionally convinced most scholars, liberals and conservatives alike, that swoon or apparent death scenarios are badly mistaken. After a botched crucifixion, Jesus would only have succeeded in convincing his followers that he was *barely alive* and incredibly wounded, but definitely not *raised* from the dead! This actually would have shown that Jesus had not been raised—the exact opposite of a resurrection.

In sum, though the swoon or apparent death hypothesis was popular primarily in English deism and continental rationalism just before and then for a few decades after the beginning of German liberalism, the supposition fell out of popularity immediately thereafter, and very quickly at that. The failure of rationalistic trends within liberalism at the hands of Strauss's mythical methodology, plus Strauss's famous critique, combined to signal the death knell of this naturalistic option.[57]

Historical Problems for Swoon or Jesus's Apparent Death

There are many exceptionally serious medical problems regarding the multiple failures of the swoon thesis, as just indicated. These issues have no doubt contributed to the serious shortage of scholars in relevant fields who have proposed this option. Additionally, there are also many positive historical indications that the New Testament texts attesting to Jesus's death are accurate. Here we will chiefly be drawing on the so-called historical criteria that biblical scholars have borrowed from

---

[57] Schweitzer makes this first claim more than once; see *Quest of the Historical Jesus*, 10, 56–57, 62. Occasionally, other arguments against swoon are also raised. For instance, New Testament professor John McNaugher argues that the best argument against the apparent death thesis is the resulting moral charge against Jesus's character. If he had escaped death on the cross by whatever means, "then Jesus allowed Himself to be palmed off as one risen from the dead when He knew He was nothing of the sort." He would then be guilty of willfully allowing His followers even to worship him when he was actually "an archimposter" because he would have known the truth that He was neither moral nor divine. See John McNaugher, *Jesus Christ: The Same Yesterday, Today and Forever* (New York: Revell, 1947), 148–49.

historians. Rather incredibly, even very skeptical scholars generally agree with the majority of these applications, as will be indicated below. But we will have to be brief here, leaving out many additional points.

Multiple Attestation

The idea that Jesus died by crucifixion is well supported both in the New Testament and in additional ancient texts and archaeology, as well as recognized virtually unanimously by critical scholarship. For example, Bart Ehrman states, "That Jesus died by crucifixion is almost universally attested in our sources, early and late."[58] Then he lists a minimum of fifteen independent sources composed within 100 years of Jesus's death that mention the crucifixion.[59] For the ancient world, in particular, this is simply a plethora of sources. Scholars would largely look in vain for very many other personages in antiquity that have close to this number of independent testimonies. As Ehrman asserts, "For a historian these provide a wealth of materials to work with, *quite unusual for accounts of anyone, literally anyone, from the ancient world.*"[60]

Other radical and strongly critical scholars agree with Ehrman as well. The Jesus Seminar corporately lists three independent Gospel sources (Mark, John, and Peter) for Jesus's crucifixion.[61] Crossan mentions the same three Gospels as the Seminar, plus four additional texts (1 Corinthians, 1 Clement, Ignatius, and Barnabas), for a total of seven sources that record the crucifixion of Jesus.[62] Crossan summarizes: "I take it absolutely for granted that Jesus was crucified under Pontius Pilate."[63] That skeptical researchers also agree so readily on these data and details of Jesus's death should be sufficient to settle the matter.

---

[58] Ehrman, *Did Jesus Exist?*, 163.

[59] Ehrman lists at least the following New Testament and nonbiblical sources that teach or imply (usually the former) the crucifixion of Jesus: Mark, Matthew's source (M), Luke's source (L), John, "the speeches in Acts," "everywhere in Paul," 1 Timothy (because it is not one of the seven undisputed Pauline Epistles allowed by Ehrman), Hebrews, 1 Peter, Revelation, plus 1 Clement, Ignatius, the *Gospel of Peter*, Josephus, and Tacitus. See Ehrman, 156–58, 163–64, 290–91, cf. also 140–41, 173, 327–31.

[60] Ehrman, 78 (emphasis added).

[61] Robert W. Funk and the Jesus Seminar, *The Acts of Jesus: The Search for the Authentic Deeds of Jesus* (New York: HarperCollins, 1998), 562. Other affirmations on the fact of Jesus's death are found on 8, 259, 567–68.

[62] Crossan, *Historical Jesus*, 435.

[63] Crossan, 372.

Early Attestation

Continuing with Ehrman's research, this scholar admits freely and very frequently (well over a dozen times) that many of the early pre-Pauline creedal statements at least mention Jesus's crucifixion or death—such as those in Rom 1:3–4; 10:9; 1 Cor 15:3–7; Phil 2:6–11—along with a number of the key Acts sermon summaries, especially those in Acts 2:36 and 13:32–33, plus other passages.[64] He thinks that such comments clearly go back to the 30s.[65] Several times, Ehrman states further that some of these creeds and Acts summaries extend back to within one to three years after the crucifixion.[66] Truly, this is the very definition of *early* dates for these texts that report Jesus's death and other areas.

Ehrman is by no means the only critical author to make such comments about the exceptional earliness of similar creedal statements. However, that he is an atheist New Testament specialist does make this research highly significant.

As part of a discussion of several relevant New Testament passages that center on the ministry and personal claims of Jesus, G. B. Caird claimed, "The further back we go, the more we discover the intense conviction of Jesus that God is his Father and he is His son."[67] Richard Bauckham wrote that the earliest Easter-oriented message revolved around the death and resurrection of Jesus, indicating that "the earliest

---

[64] Of the Acts sermon summaries, Ehrman especially seems to gravitate to Acts 2:36 and 13:32–33 because he thinks they teach an adoptionist Christology, which is his view. Ehrman concludes that a few other texts like Rom 1:3–4 (at least before Paul probably added the words "with power" in 1:4) were also adoptionist in nature. See Ehrman, *Did Jesus Exist?*, 110–13, 130, 172; Bart D. Ehrman, *How Jesus Became God: The Exaltation of a Jewish Preacher from Galilee* (New York: HarperCollins, 2014), 154–55, 218, 220–30. Ehrman also discusses adoptionism in *How Jesus Became God*, 5, 44, 49, 209, 218, 231–35, 249–52. Issued at the same time as the second of Ehrman's books mentioned here, a division of HarperCollins also co-released a rejoinder by a number of other scholars that is an excellent critique of Ehrman's ideas. See the highly detailed chapters and discussions in Michael Bird, ed., *How God Became Jesus: The Real Origins of Belief in Jesus' Divine Nature. A Response to Bart Ehrman* (Grand Rapids: Zondervan, 2014).

[65] Ehrman, *Did Jesus Exist?*, 27, 92–93, 97, 132, 141, 144–45, 155–56, 171–74, 260–63; also, though not mentioned as often, this also appears in Ehrman, *How Jesus Became God*, 216–18.

[66] Ehrman, *Did Jesus Exist?*, 130–31, 141, 163–64, 170, 251, 254.

[67] G. B. Caird and L. D. Hurst, *New Testament Theology* (Oxford: Clarendon, 1994), 398–404, with the above quotation on 400.

Christology was already the highest Christology."[68] This is one of the most radical things a scholar could report in terms of recent research. This would have been quite a significant insight for the early church after Jesus had been slain recently by the authorities as some sort of false prophet or criminal, but later was reportedly raised from the dead.[69]

Closer to Bauckham (though agreeing with some of Ehrman's conclusions too), Larry Hurtado specialized for some forty years on the question of the earliest Christian worship of Jesus. Hurtado held that the "earliest devotion to Jesus" dates from very soon after Jesus's death and manifests an exceptionally high Christology. For Hurtado, this devotion occurred "very early at or near the outset of the early Christian movement."[70] It may even have been manifested just *months* after Jesus died![71] Therefore, this development is "so early that practically any evolutionary approach is rendered invalid as historical explanation."[72] After the disciples' post-crucifixion experiences, "honorific titles" were given to Jesus incorporating pre-existence and issuing forth into hymns, prayers, and worship.[73]

---

[68] Richard Bauckham, *Jesus and the God of Israel: God Crucified and Other Studies on the New Testament's Christology of Divine Identity* (Grand Rapids: Eerdmans, 2008), quote on x, see also 268, cf. ix, 30, 128, 259. In this same work Bauckham moves on to the early worship of Jesus Christ and follows up on this provocative statement with a number of related statements pertaining to the exceptional earliness of these events: "The practice of worshipping Jesus goes far back into early Jewish Christianity" (25). Pointing "to the earliest Palestinian Jewish Christianity . . . Jesus was already understood to be risen and exalted to God's right hand in heaven" (128). Last, "the worship of Jesus was central . . . beginning in the early Palestinian Christian movement" (151).

[69] Bauckham, *Jesus and the God of Israel*, 268.

[70] Larry W. Hurtado, *How on Earth Did Jesus Become a God? Historical Questions about Earliest Devotion to Jesus* (Grand Rapids: Eerdmans, 2005), 23, also 42. Earlier in this text, Hurtado states, "Jesus' exalted status 'at God's right hand' had been affirmed by the one God," who willed that Jesus be given "heavenly glory with the intention of all creation acclaiming Jesus as Lord" (6).

[71] Hurtado, 36.

[72] Hurtado, 25, also 37. Hurtado adds here rather graphically that far from this process taking any significant amount of time, it was "a more explosively quick phenomenon . . . more like a volcano" (25).

[73] Hurtado, 27–30. Strangely enough, Hurtado seems to include surprisingly little time on the nature or other details of Jesus's resurrection appearances themselves beyond what we have mentioned here. On these further matters, see Hurtado, 6, 93, 192–94; Hurtado, *Lord Jesus Christ: Devotion to Jesus in Earliest Christianity* (Grand Rapids: Eerdmans, 2003), 72, 78, 170; Hurtado, *One God, One Lord: Early Christian Devotion and*

Providing an estimated date reminiscent of Ehrman, James D. G. Dunn points out that the early Christian tradition, including the famous creed on the death, resurrection, and appearances of Christ in 1 Corinthians 15, preceded Paul's conversion about one to two years after the crucifixion.[74] Of the early text in 1 Corinthians 15, Dunn asserts: "This tradition, we can be entirely confident, was *formulated as tradition within months of Jesus's death*."[75] For Dunn, this leaves room for this very early tradition to potentially be dated to the very same year in which Jesus died.

Even the Jesus Seminar concluded similarly on this issue! Likewise speaking of the early creed in 1 Corinthians 15, which included the report of Jesus's death, they attested: "Most fellows think the components of the list reported there were formed prior to Paul's conversion, which is usually dated around 33 C.E."[76] It is difficult to overestimate the force of this conclusion from a group of scholars who only voted in favor of 18 percent of Jesus's oral statements and only 16 percent of the Gospel events![77]

Many other scholars could be cited here as well for the exceptionally early date at which the Christian proclamation of Jesus's death by crucifixion and some of the surrounding beliefs is thought to have emerged in antiquity. Due to the data that favor the extraordinarily close proximity that these proclamations enjoyed in relation to the events themselves, the teaching of these beliefs is acknowledged and endorsed to one degree or another by most critical scholars who deal specifically with this material. This last comment applies to atheist, other self-identified non-Christian, agnostic, moderate, and conservative researchers alike. But especially given the immense reputations of many of the researchers presented here, these affirmations will suffice to indicate the force of this conclusion.

Eyewitness Testimony

Continuing an aspect of the previous argument regarding the amazing closeness of the earliest proclamation of Jesus's death by crucifixion, at least some of those who

---

Ancient Jewish Monotheism (Philadelphia: Fortress, 1988), esp. 118–19, also 68, 94–95, 116–17, 124.

[74] James D. G. Dunn, *Jesus Remembered*, vol. 1 of *Christianity in the Making* (Grand Rapids: Eerdmans, 2003), 864.

[75] Dunn, 854.

[76] Funk and the Jesus Seminar, *Acts of Jesus*, 454.

[77] Funk and the Jesus Seminar, 1.

spread the accounts presumably had access to eyewitness information pertaining to the crucifixion events. Many scholars also agree and add to the veracity of these conclusions in that either the Gospel authors or their sources could have included eyewitness material, which could potentially yield substantial amounts of testimony behind the crucifixion occurrences and these early beliefs, increasing the amount of advantageous material here.

The Jesus Seminar members overall voted and decided that Jesus's execution and death deserved a red rating as an assured "core event." The red indicates, "The historical reliability of this information is virtually certain."[78]

Did any eyewitness comments inform the crucifixion and death reports that we possess? Who might have observed the actual details of the crucifixion and then provided their witness regarding these details? The multiply attested accounts of several women witnesses could qualify here.[79] The likewise multiply attested testimony concerning Joseph of Arimathea (and possibly Nicodemus in John 19:39–40) would probably count as well.[80] The likelihood of Joseph actually being present at the cross seems assured, since he went to Pilate immediately and asked for Jesus's body, surprising Pilate with the early information that Jesus had already died on the cross. The best explanation here is that Joseph came straight from the crucifixion site itself, where he witnessed the details up close, since he knew immediately when Jesus had breathed his last (Mark 15:43–45).

We have already seen that major scholars such as C. H. Dodd, Raymond Brown, and James D. G. Dunn, along with researchers like John Wilkinson and still others, are inclined to accept John's testimony even though it is not multiply attested, largely due to his general crucifixion descriptions being supported in other ancient reports.[81] If so, this could add John's testimony to the list of crucifixion witnesses. Though it would be less assured, it is additionally possible that one or more other witnesses at

---

[78] Funk and the Jesus Seminar, 453, 567, 568. The quotation on the red rating is found on 36.

[79] Cf. Mark 15:40–41; Matt 27:55–56; Luke 23:27–28, 49; John 19:25–27. See also, along with many other scholars, Craig S. Keener, *The Gospel of John: A Commentary*, 2 vols. (Peabody, MA: Hendrickson, 2003), 2:1141–45.

[80] Cf. Mark 15:42–43; Matt 27:57–58; Luke 23:50–52; John 19:38; *Gos. Pet.* 2:3. Cf. Keener, 2:1158–62; Merrill C. Tenney, *John: The Gospel of Belief. An Analytic Study of the Text* (Grand Rapids: Eerdmans, 1976), 270–71.

[81] Wilkinson is also listed above. Others include Keener, *Gospel of John*, 2:1151–57, and Tenney, *John*, 266–67.

the cross stepped forward, especially if they had later become believers, contributing their own observations. At any rate, perhaps a half dozen or more eyewitnesses are possibly in view here.

One probable and exciting development is the seeming majority critical view, based on strong evidence from even quite skeptical researchers, that Mark used a number of earlier sources in the composition of his Gospel. In Marion Soards's influential study on this subject, several key findings emerged.[82] For example, concerning Mark 15:24–37, which demarcates the details in the Gospel from the initiation of Jesus's crucifixion until his ensuing death, the critical scholars surveyed by Soards concluded firmly that twelve of these verses derived from Mark's earlier sources, with the only exception (15:31) garnering equal pro and con numbers in his survey.[83]

Even Rudolf Bultmann concluded that Mark's passion narrative included elements that extended from Jesus's arrest to his death by crucifixion.[84] Rudolf Pesch concluded, "Mark used extensive sources" involving "at least seven blocks of preMarkan [*sic*] tradition."[85] Soards's overall conclusion was, "We may safely conclude that Mark used a source in writing his [passion narrative]."[86]

In treating this question, Kirk MacGregor followed Pesch in arguing further, "Accordingly, the *terminus ante quem* of the pre-Markan passion narrative is 37 CE."[87] Further, MacGregor drew the important conclusion that the narrative extends to the empty tomb account in Mark 16:1–4, including parts of vv. 5–6 and parts of v. 8, though with far fewer details than are present in the Gospel of Mark. Moreover, of further importance is that the tradition here "originated quite independently of the pre-Pauline resurrection tradition" in 1 Corinthians 15.[88]

---

[82] This study was originally published by Soards in the journal *Bible Bhashyam* in 1985, and it was included later as appendix 9 in Raymond E. Brown's major study, *The Death of the Messiah: From Gethsemane to the Grave*, 2 vols. (New York: Doubleday, 1994), 2:1492–24.

[83] Due to a variant reading, Mark 15:28 was not included in Soards's list or in a number of translations such as the NRSV. See Brown, *Death of the Messiah*, 2:1512–14.

[84] Brown, 2:1494, where Bultmann's view is included in Brown's chart.

[85] Brown, 2:1498–1499, with Brown summarizing Pesch.

[86] Brown, 2:1523. Soards concluded that the main issue here is that "we cannot be absolutely certain about where Mark's source would have ended" (2:1523).

[87] Kirk Robert MacGregor, "The Ending of the Pre-Markan Passion Narrative," *Scriptura*, vol. 117 (2018, repr.), 1–2.

[88] MacGregor, "Ending of the Pre-Markan Passion Narrative," 8.

The two possibilities mentioned above concerning Peter or a Petrine source plus a pre-Markan passion text used extensively by Mark involves an upside and a downside pertaining to the crucifixion question sources in this chapter. These developments are definitely pluses in terms of Mark having very early and potentially reliable sources at his disposal. However, in one or even both cases, exploring the possibility of there being eyewitnesses for Jesus's crucifixion is conceivable but not necessarily a given.

Throughout his massive work *Jesus Remembered*, Dunn attempts to unite a number of these ideas to explain how the earliest church brought together its message. As Dunn states, his overall theme is that how the historical Jesus was remembered by his followers is the necessary key to understanding the earliest movement. Information regarding Jesus was chiefly gathered, organized, and disseminated through oral testimony. This "original and immediate impact made by Jesus" was accomplished by eyewitnesses who had observed Jesus. This was how it began.[89]

Key ideas and actions among early believers involved bearing witness as well as formulating and passing along traditions as observed chiefly in the New Testament Epistles. But the most striking idea, at least at the outset, was remembering what was taught and modeled initially by Jesus, which was passed on orally. In this process, Jesus's apostles were the custodians. Chief among these leaders were Peter, John, and James the brother of Jesus—those referred to as the "pillars" (Gal 2:9). In spite of any differences, Paul contributed much during the early years. Different contemporary commentators have emphasized particular elements. But for Dunn, those who fail to see the significance of Jesus's original message being remembered and passed along, chiefly orally, to those who would assimilate the teachings for themselves and pass them on to others have misunderstood the process. This is the key to early Christian growth after Jesus: the eyewitnesses were the leaders, playing an indispensable role.[90]

According to Paul (and other New Testament writers) the gospel message certainly included at least the teaching of Jesus's deity, death, and resurrection, as in other very early and major creedal passages that we have discussed elsewhere (Rom 1:3–4; 4:24–25; 10:9; cf. 10:10–13; Gal 2:6–11; and several other texts including the many Acts sermon summaries). Even these passages that simply mention or detail

---

[89] Dunn, *Jesus Remembered*, 335–36, 882, cf. 223–24 for further details on the storytelling component.

[90] Dunn, 176–81, 242–43, 882.

Jesus's resurrection or appearances at the very least imply Jesus's death. Hence, the early appearance creeds would entail a very early mention of Jesus's death.

That the other most influential apostles agreed with Paul concerning the nature of this gospel message (as in Gal 2:2, 6b, 9; 1 Cor 15:11) adds a highly crucial component here. Besides his conversion, Paul's most important contribution to the early church, then, may have been his discussing with or interviewing of Peter and James the brother of Jesus in Jerusalem (Gal 1:18–20) and his subsequent meeting with Peter, James, and John in his trip back to the city fourteen years later (Gal 2:1–10). In so doing, he ascertained and passed on their eyewitness agreement on the gospel message and thereby confirmed the topic of this present chapter.[91] Even Ehrman rates Paul making these two trips to Jerusalem and obtaining these apostles' testimonies as one of the two most important historical developments in the early church, including being the closest we may have gotten to eyewitness testimony regarding these events.[92]

Dissimilarity

This historical criterion is usually taken to be the toughest one to fulfill. But according to Ehrman, the crucifixion "clearly passes the criterion of dissimilarity." This is because "no Jews would have expected a crucified Messiah" and "the story that Jesus was crucified created enormous headaches for the Christian mission." This event was the ultimate stumbling block for Christian preaching. In short, neither Jews nor Christians would have invented the crucifixion if it had not actually occurred. Therefore, especially along with the exceptionally strong case from multiple independent attestation, Ehrman states, "It appears highly probable that in fact Jesus was crucified."[93]

---

[91] There may be a parallel here in that the Jesus Seminar colored the risen Jesus's appearance to Peter as pink instead of red (like Paul's) because the comment about Peter came indirectly through Paul; see Funk and the Jesus Seminar, *Acts of Jesus*, 453–54, 533, 568. Accordingly, besides the creedal text in 1 Cor 15:3–5, it was also Paul's testimony that communicated the agreement on the gospel in Gal 2:1–10, indicating the pink rating for Peter, since it was also derived indirectly from Paul. Nonetheless, pink for the Jesus Seminar still means, "This information is probably reliable. It fits well with other evidence that is verifiable" (36).

[92] Ehrman, *Did Jesus Exist?*, esp. 144–46.

[93] Ehrman, 292.

Embarrassment

Many incidents before, during, and after the crucifixion were especially embarrassing, hence these awkward and uncomfortable occurrences favor these incidents being reliable. At the very heart of the gospel message, why would any first-century Christian want to preach that although their Savior had been accused of being cursed by God for hanging on a tree (as per the Old Testament law in Deut 21:22–23), that event was actually the very key to salvation?

What about the male disciples abandoning Jesus when he was captured and taken prisoner, eventually to die? Further, the chief disciple and later church leader, Peter, denied his Lord repeatedly. Most of the disciples went into hiding for the next few days. This left the women to attend to Jesus's burial and the return trip on Sunday morning to finish the job. Earlier, Jesus's own brother James, later the leader of the largest church in the ancient world at Jerusalem, did not even believe his own brother when he came to town during his public ministry and basically thought that Jesus was mentally disturbed and ought to be ushered out of sight. Sometime afterward, Saul—later the great theologian and missionary—persecuted, imprisoned, and even sent believers to death. It can hardly be questioned that this series of embarrassments was quite stunning.

Christians overlook these enormous glitches and complications, presumably because they are comfortable having heard them repeatedly and knowing how the story plays out. However, it would seem that many major events would not have survived this series of massive setbacks and immense roadblocks, especially when they happened to such influential persons in the young movement. Humanly speaking, if only a few occurrences would have transpired in a slightly different direction, perhaps the church would not have survived. And yet, the church was born and even flourished beyond all expectations.

Enemy Attestation

There are also a number of examples where it is at least claimed that enemies corroborated or confirmed aspects of the Christian message. The best known is Matthew's account of the guards being placed at Jesus's tomb (also found in the *Gos. Pet.* 8:28–33 plus in some manuscripts of the *Gospel of the Nazareans*). By far the majority critical view is that this event never occurred, though in our treatment earlier in this study we pointed out that on the basis of the available data alone, the account fared pretty well. This is especially the case when there is no supernatural claim involved.

Regardless whether Jesus's tomb was guarded, the Jewish leaders did not produce any data contrary to the claims of either the empty tomb or the appearances of Jesus. While this is a bit of an argument from silence, it is not entirely so. The Jewish leaders no doubt heard these claimed events announced all over Jerusalem. Plus, Acts asserts specifically that the Jewish leaders both heard and confronted the apostles about these resurrection teachings on more than one occasion (4:1–2, 5–12; 5:27–33) without making any accusations regarding the details. Further, we are even told provocatively, soon after these challenges, that "a great many of the priests became obedient to the faith" (6:7 ESV), though without any comment concerning the specific details. Thus, it appears at least from the information available that the disciples made unrefuted claims concerning the resurrection.

An additional insight is provided by Marcus Borg, one that is made frequently by other skeptical and critical scholars. Borg points out that various Jewish leaders in Jesus's day had often witnessed his supernatural actions and freely admitted their occurrence. However, they attributed these quite real healings and exorcisms to "the lord of the evil spirits." Hence Jesus was "seen as a holy man with healing powers."[94] So virtually everyone in Jesus's own day recognized that he was doing miracles.[95] These responses to Jesus's actions by the Jewish leaders alone would seem to constitute a more straightforward example of enemy attestation.

In this portion of this chapter, we have emphasized several historical indications that Jesus was crucified without yielding any major questions concerning the reality of Jesus's death. In particular, we concentrated on several historical criteria that point firmly to Jesus's crucifixion and death having taken place. For starters, these reports are multiply and independently attested, which is a prime signal that they are

---

[94] Borg, *Jesus, A New Vision*, 61. Borg states on the same page, "Despite the difficulty which miracles pose for the modern mind, on historical grounds it is virtually indisputable that Jesus was a healer and exorcist."

[95] Ehrman also agrees with Borg here (*Did Jesus Exist?*, 261–62). Depending on how Josephus is read, many scholars think this Jewish historian who was born just a very few years after Jesus's death most likely admitted at least that Jesus performed "wonderful works" (*Ant.* 18.3.3). As Licona attests, the predominant scholarly position pertaining to this text, known as the *Testimonium Flavianum*, is that, save for a few Christian interpolations, Josephus wrote this passage (Licona, *Resurrection of Jesus*, 238).

reliable. To repeat the above significant report acknowledged by prominent atheist New Testament scholar Bart Ehrman, there are at least fifteen different sources in the relevant ancient literature that record this event.[96] Additionally, there are very strong signs that there are both exceptionally early and also eyewitness reports concerning the reality of Jesus's death as well. These three indicators alone are powerful witnesses. Other helpful pointers include both embarrassing details and enemy reports. That there were plenty of examples of each criterion here strengthens further these considerations.

The earliest sources for the crucifixion (and for the resurrection appearances) of Jesus consist of a large number of very brief creedal testimonies and sermon summaries that were originally oral in nature. The strong majority of these oral traditions date from the first twenty years after the crucifixion. This means that though the main examples in this group were included chiefly in the Acts sermons and in Paul's earliest works, these initial creeds among them actually predated the first New Testament writings. The canonical New Testament books are often dated from about AD 50 onward, from the time of Paul's earliest epistles.[97]

Therefore, most of these creedal traditions were actually pre-Pauline in origin. Even far beyond this, a select number of these creeds are often thought by critical scholars across the board (including the Jesus Seminar) to have existed before Paul's conversion, which is usually thought to have occurred two or three years after the crucifixion. Predating Paul becoming a believer, the earliest of these pre-Pauline traditions thus would most likely have extended within one to two years after Jesus's death. Needless to say, this is about as early as these reports could possibly get.

Besides multiple, independent sources along with the earliest testimony available, some of these creeds appear strongly to have eyewitness roots, either from within the eyewitness apostolic community itself or else at the very least being

---

[96] Ehrman, *Did Jesus Exist?*, 156–58, 163–64, 290–91, cf. also 140–41, 173, 327–31. Some of the explanations and details pertaining to these texts are found earlier in this chapter.

[97] The material on these subjects has been summarized from our earlier chapters and arguments detailed in volume 1 of this study. Particularly for our purposes here, see the earlier chapters on Jesus's death as well as those on the creeds themselves. On the date of Paul's Epistles, beginning in about AD 50, see esp. Helmut Koester, *Introduction to the New Testament*, 2 vols. (Philadelphia: Fortress, 1982), 2:1–3, 101–4; and Ehrman, *New Testament*, 44 (chart), cf. 262, 290.

based on these apostolic reports.[98] This qualifies these data even more positively still. That these early reports likewise also pass assessments that may be made from the historical criteria such as those viewed above just deepens the richness of the foundation here.

Many scholars would conclude that the key markers for authenticity are multiple attestation, early and eyewitness testimony, and discontinuity, which are well represented in these sources. These historical markers indicate that the chances of Jesus being taken down off the cross alive were virtually nil.

Conclusion

According to the comments of New Testament critical scholars extending over a century, the swoon or apparent death theory has fallen on tough times and has remained

---

[98] For some of the early and best of the classical scholarly texts on the nature of these creeds, including some of the conclusions above such as their very early and apostolic nature, see the following sources: Oscar Cullmann, *The Earliest Christian Confessions*, trans. J. K. S. Reid, ed. Gary R. Habermas and Benjamin Charles Shaw (London: Lutterworth, 1949; repr., Eugene, OR: Wipf & Stock, 2018), particularly 13, 16, 49–50; C. H. Dodd, *The New Testament Preaching and Its Developments with an Appendix on Eschatology and History* (London: Hodder & Stoughton, 1936; repr., Grand Rapids: Baker, 1980), 17–31; Vernon H. Neufeld, *The Earliest Christian Confessions* (Grand Rapids: Eerdmans, 1963), esp. Neufeld's conclusions on 140–46. Also very helpful in this regard are Max Wilcox's summaries in his volume *The Semitisms of Acts* (Oxford: Clarendon, 1965), particularly 79–80, 165–69, 171, 177. For more recent studies, see Dunn, *Jesus Remembered*, where some of the creedal texts are both dated before Paul's conversion (855, 864) and drawn from eyewitness sources (856, 864, 882); Dunn, *Beginning from Jerusalem*, vol. 2 of *Christianity in the Making* (Grand Rapids: Eerdmans, 2009), where "very old," "primitive," and possibly "Semitic" tradition was utilized in the creeds and sermon summaries (87–98), with key teachings in the creedal texts reflecting Christian teaching before Paul's conversion (105–8, cf. 190–91). In James D. G. Dunn's more popular text, *Why Believe in Jesus' Resurrection?* (London: SPCK, 2016), 4, 10–11, he also opts for Paul having received material that dated from before his conversion. See also Hurtado, *How on Earth*, on the exceptionally early date of the material (2–9, 23–30, 36–42), which most likely originates before Paul's teachings (36); Hurtado, *Lord Jesus Christ: Devotion to Jesus in Earliest Christianity* (Grand Rapids: Eerdmans, 2003), on the very early date of the teachings (110, 144–49, 169). Richard Bauckham emphasizes the role of the eyewitnesses in this early material in *Jesus and the Eyewitnesses: The Gospels as Eyewitness Testimony*, 2nd ed. (Grand Rapids: Eerdmans, 2017), esp. 264–71, but see also 6, 25, 30, 307–8, 389, cf. 330–35, 341–46.

that way for many decades. Though it still appears periodically, it is always plagued by numerous issues, chiefly those of a medical or historical nature.[99]

The medical arguments are more decisive in the sense of indicating reasons for knowing not just that Jesus was crucified, but that the situation actually resulted in his death. Five such arguments were presented in this chapter. The predominant medical response is that death by crucifixion is most likely multifactorial, with the chief cause of death being asphyxiation. But any other medical causes could of course kill too. The further likelihood was that Jesus was stabbed in the chest, probably piercing the heart, and that the wound would have resulted in his death had he not already been deceased when it occurred. A collapsed lung would have been the likely result from the spear wound, with the subsequent sucking sound making it appear that Jesus was alive. Such a situation would definitely have occasioned a second serious death blow from a Roman soldier. Moreover, the fact that none of the recorded descriptions of unrescued crucifixion victims in the ancient world ever depict an individual escaping death makes it highly unlikely that Jesus would have survived, *even without any death blows being administered.*

The last medical response was popularized by David Strauss, who was probably the best-known skeptical scholar of nineteenth-century German liberalism and an ardent critic of Jesus's resurrection. To hold that a crucified Jesus who somehow survived this process would be half dead and sickly looking would be a vast understatement. How would Jesus even walk the distance to where the disciples were hiding in the city? Jesus would be limping severely, pale, bleeding once again (especially from his side wound), his body covered from barely scabbed beating and thorn wounds, with his breath coming in gasps due to untold injuries to his internal organs. He probably would have died anyway just a brief time later. Even if he arrived at the disciples' hideout, would anyone have believed him if he held up his arms and announced that he had been crucified, but now he was the *risen* and *glorified* Lord of life? There would have been no doubt that he had been crucified, but raised from

---

[99] In addition to the examples listed earlier in this chapter, a more detailed listing of critical scholars appears in Gary R. Habermas, "The Late Twentieth-Century Resurgence of Naturalistic Responses to Jesus' Resurrection," *Trinity Journal* 22 (2001): 179–96. However, during the ensuing two decades-plus since this article appeared, it at least seems that the researchers who prefer natural responses have again slowed down considerably, as already discussed in some detail in this study.

the dead? Where was the glorious body that believers would someday possess? Was this a joke?

Sure, Jesus's disciples would be thankful that he was alive, but they would not have been tempted to declare him risen. Just seeing him in that sickly, wounded state would probably divest them of ever thinking of him as raised and glorified. Strauss's critique was powerful and has had an enormous and lasting influence on scholarship. One and a half centuries later, it has remained the main reason cited by critical scholars as to why the swoon theory is untenable. Perhaps the disciples would have thought that God had spared Jesus from death (probably only temporarily), but his appearance would never cause them to conclude that he had been raised from the dead or especially that he had been glorified. Is this how believers would live in heaven (as in 1 John 3:2)? Strauss's critique also includes a strong logical component, precisely because the experience would have convinced the disciples of the *exact opposite* of what it was supposed to accomplish. Jesus definitely had not been raised from the dead; he was alive, yes, but raised and glorified, never. The visual impression would simply be too strong to overcome.

Just to mention again, even briefly, the historical evidence for the crucifixion and death of Jesus will reveal that the amount of data available is simply astounding. More than a dozen independent sources within 100 years attest to these events. The majority of these sources date before the end of the first century AD, placing them within the first seventy years after the cross, or roughly from that time until the writing of the Gospel of John. This is an amazingly, almost unbelievably rich situation, even more so considering its ancient context. How many people or events from antiquity possess this many religious or other sources and traditions that date so close to the historical situations that they describe? The sources during this time period encompass Christian, Jewish, gnostic, and pagan texts, both canonical as well as noncanonical. It should be no wonder that the vast majority of critical researchers never question the crucifixion of Jesus.

In short, since Jesus died, then he obviously must have lived as well.[100] As mentioned elsewhere in this study, ancient historian Paul Barnett also has noted the brief

---

[100] For further details on this evidence, see Gary R. Habermas, *The Historical Jesus: Ancient Evidence for the Life of Christ* (Joplin, MO: College Press, 1996), particularly chaps. 7–11. Ehrman's earlier comment is appropriate here as well, that the excellent number of historical sources for Jesus is perhaps unparalleled in the ancient world (*Did Jesus Exist?*, 78).

gap at the beginning of this time period from Jesus's death until the earliest oral and written sources: "In terms of the historical reference to noted persons in antiquity, this would represent a brevity without parallel."[101]

All these historical data include a plethora of multiple, independent sources. Further, many examples of these texts begin from a time *exceptionally* close to the crucifixion itself. They are even traceable to eyewitnesses or those who were quite close to them. These early and evidenced reports likewise pass the dissimilarity test since they were neither inspired nor derived from earlier Jewish or later Christian ideas. Since a number of the comments are highly embarrassing to early Christian believers, one wonders why they would be shared at all. Finally, some nonpartisan confirmation (or enemy attestation) is present in this information.

We will not spell out here in any more detail this historical material summarized above. But to say that the available evidence is incredibly early, multiply and independently attested, or potentially drawn from eyewitnesses might even be considered as huge understatements. Moreover, Jesus's death by crucifixion is probably the most firmly established event in his entire life. That even *very critical scholars* in relevant fields of study so seldom challenge this evidence is entirely astonishing in itself.

For example, well-known skeptical scholar John Dominic Crossan has declared of Jesus: "That he was crucified is as sure as anything historical can ever be."[102] He again inserts above, "I take it absolutely for granted that Jesus was crucified under Pontius Pilate." Crossan also states how non-Christian writings by the Jewish historian Josephus and the Roman historian Tacitus provide final security for these events, plus the fact that Christians definitely would not have invented this story.[103]

Other skeptical scholars agree readily. Marcus Borg concludes that Jesus's execution was "the most certain fact about the historical Jesus."[104] Bart Ehrman observed,

---

[101] Paul Barnett, *The Birth of Christianity: The First Twenty Years* (Grand Rapids: Eerdmans, 2005), quotation on 210. For specifics on some of these data, see also 7–13, 45–59, 67–70, 111–17, 185–86, 198–200.

[102] Crossan, *Jesus*, 145, cf. 154, 196, 201.

[103] Crossan, *Historical Jesus*, 373. Crossan provides further details on 372–76. More relevant to Jesus's crucifixion, Crossan adds that "leg breaking was considered a merciful act" because it "removed any support from the legs and rendered breathing impossible," prompting asphyxiation or shock. See Crossan, *Who Killed Jesus?*, 135.

[104] Borg, *Jesus, A New Vision*, 179, cf. 178–84.

"The most certain element of the tradition about Jesus is that he was crucified on the orders of the Roman prefect of Judea, Pontius Pilate."[105]

E. P. Sanders observes that one of the historical facts that is "almost beyond dispute" is that Jesus "was executed on the orders of the Roman prefect, Pontius Pilate."[106] Helmut Koester remarks firmly that "Jesus's death on the cross" was certain.[107] Atheist New Testament professor Gerd Lüdemann states firmly, "The fact of the death of Jesus as a consequence of crucifixion is indisputable, despite hypotheses of a pseudo-death or a deception which are sometimes put forward."[108] This is quite an impressive array of endorsements regarding Jesus's death by crucifixion from skeptical scholars who are not obliged to arrive at such conclusions unless they are previously warranted by the facts.

---

[105] Ehrman, *New Testament*, 233.

[106] E. P. Sanders, *The Historical Figure of Jesus* (London: Penguin, 1993), 10–11.

[107] Koester, *Introduction to the New Testament*, 2:84.

[108] Gerd Lüdemann with Alf Özen, *What Really Happened to Jesus: A Historical Approach to the Resurrection*, trans. John Bowden (Louisville: Westminster John Knox, 1995), 17.

12

Legend 1: Dying-and-Rising Gods

Like certain other natural hypotheses, mythical or legendary theses also come in several varieties with multiple subcategories. That is hardly surprising, since embellishment of more than one sort is often expressed in different ways with varieties of tales concerning the same person, mythical or otherwise, often found in various geographical areas. On other occasions, the gods may morph together, taking on characteristics of each other. The purpose in this chapter and the next is to discuss a few prominent alternative views, including some of these additional cognate ideas.

A convenient demarcation is to concentrate on three broad categories. (1) The initial set of fantastic tales from ancient mythology usually consist of individuals who never lived. Many or even most of these cases concern the so-called dying-and-rising gods of the Greco-Roman, Egyptian, and Mesopotamian areas all the way over to the Tigris and Euphrates Rivers and even beyond. Though the majority of characters in this group were nonhistorical, some examples might be debatable, as in situations where a person may have lived but where their mythical personae and actions usually dominate the stories. Even when the person(s) in these tales did not exist or were largely unknown, their make-believe portions nonetheless were capable of exerting much influence in the ancient world. This category will be the subject of this chapter on the dying-and-rising god figures. (2) The following chapter treats historical persons who are usually intermixed with myth, where supernatural items such as miracles were often reported. (3) Additionally, chapter 13 also treats the New Testament Gospel cases where it is sometimes alleged that particular accounts grew significantly in subsequent retellings.

Other categories could be mentioned, but these are among the most prominent as well as representative types. As such, these will also serve to indicate potential directions in which treatments of such extra theses may arise in still other situations. The examples from the first category will treat the mythical accounts of the so-called mystery religions and their prominent dying-and-rising god figures, such as Osiris, Adonis, or Attis, some of which were called "vegetation gods" and others "storm gods." The second group treated in the next chapter is concerned with largely historical persons about whom a good amount of material is available, like Apollonius of Tyana and Sabbatai Zevi. The third species includes examples of what are sometimes challenged as resurrection stories in the canonical New Testament texts that appear to grow in length or detail from earlier to later accounts, as in the Gospels.

Some stories, especially in ancient times, were told in mythical terms. Lofty and seemingly inexpressible ideas were frequently articulated in other than factual terms. Pertaining to the initial group above, Rudolf Bultmann famously defined "myth" as "the use of imagery to express the other worldly in terms of this side," such as articulating the concept of transcendence in spatial terms.[1] Regarding the second group engaged in the next chapter, a "legend" might be defined as a "narrative, often tied in with a particular place or locality, which tells an apparently historical story which has little basis in actual fact."[2] In spite of some confusion or overlap here among these notions, more emphasis in group two will be placed primarily on the actual historical nature of the persons, their claims, or influential ideas being treated by or about them.[3]

---

[1] Rudolf Bultmann, "New Testament and Mythology," in Bultmann et al., *Kerygma and Myth: A Theological Debate*, ed. Hans Werner Bartsch, trans. Reginald H. Fuller (New York: Harper & Row, 1961), 10n2. Irving Hexham defines "myth" similarly, as "to express in imaginative form a belief" of theological or other importance. Hexham, *Concise Dictionary of Religion* (Downers Grove, IL: InterVarsity, 1993), 153.

[2] Hexham, *Concise Dictionary of Religion*, 135.

[3] Paul Rhodes Eddy and Gregory A. Boyd, *The Jesus Legend: A Case for the Historical Reliability of the Synoptic Jesus Tradition* (Grand Rapids: Baker, 2007), see 133–46, with another breakdown demarcation set out on 136–38.

Mythical Stories

In terms of being the most relevant and popular examples in our initial study category, arguably the best-known pattern of these ancient stories is "the myth of the dying and rising god, seen in its earliest form in the Tammuz myth" but which moved elsewhere beyond the Near East across the Greco-Roman world.[4] In spite of there being very few specialists (atheist, liberal, moderate, or conservative) who hold that this approach provides a viable alternative thesis capable of explaining Jesus's resurrection, this area of study has still attracted some of the top researchers in the world.

Arguably one of the most respected specialists in the field of comparative religion, the late Jonathan Z. Smith, defined the dying-and-rising gods as "a generic appellation for a group of male deities found in agrarian Mediterranean societies who serve as the focus of myths and rituals that allegedly narrate and annually represent their death and resurrection."[5] Before attempting to address the chief issues here, a few crucial questions need to be identified. There is an exceptionally wide range of statements in print pertaining to the identification of the dying-and-rising gods along with related tales. Emanating from the nonscholarly crowd that tends often to question or deny Jesus's existence, a large number of comments about dying-and-raising gods contain false information regarding these ancient tales.

Even among the experts, however, there is more than one way to view the specifics; hence, the dialogue in this chapter. The chief issue being discussed here concerns whether any of the pre-Christian myths involved stories about ancient gods who were truly said to have been dead and then resurrected. But it always must be kept in mind throughout these discussions that when a specialist argues that this or that myth really did concern a story of a dying-and-rising god, no judgment is being made

---

[4] S. H. Hooke, *Middle Eastern Mythology* (London: Penguin, 1963), 173. In addressing potential New Testament parallels, Hooke appears to make comments that hint that these mythical considerations may have influenced New Testament writings somehow (148, 173–74) while apparently asserting that this did not occur (16, 174, 176, cf. 166). At any rate, in a subsequent volume on Jesus's resurrection, Hooke speaks positively of this event as having actually taken place (119–127) while de-emphasizing the need to demonstrate it in historical terms (130). See Hooke, *The Resurrection of Christ as History and Experience* (London: Darton, Longman & Todd, 1967). The latter angle is consistent with a similar comment he made in *Middle Eastern Mythology*, 16.

[5] Jonathan Z. Smith, "Dying and Rising Gods," in *Encyclopedia of Religion*, ed. Mircea Eliade, 2nd ed., 16 vols. (New York: Macmillan, 2005), 4:2535. Henceforth, this author's name will be shortened to J. Z. Smith.

as to whether these events *actually occurred* in space-time history. Thus, deciding that "the story in this tale was truly one that concerned a dying-and-rising god" refers to *how the mythical story itself taught the matter* that is being recounted.

Someone *could* of course charge that the heroes in these tales truly were historical characters who really rose from the dead, or that even a nonhistorical story still influenced the Christian accounts to teach that Jesus was dead and raised at a somewhat later time. But these are not the scenarios in the discussions here precisely because such alternate scenarios are not considered scholarly theses. Nonetheless, the critiques presented later in this chapter will still apply to these additional claims. But again, it is rare for specialists on any side of the discussions to think that these ancient myths either describe actual resurrected heroes or inspired and served as the basis in some "copycat" fashion for the New Testament teaching of Jesus's death and resurrection.

Who are the main mythical characters and what is known about their tales? What species of story are they—seasonal vegetation accounts, cloud-riding deities, and so on? Do the approximate time and location of the stories help or hinder these demarcations? More specifically, do the accounts predate the time of Jesus? Is the hero *clearly* said to have died and, if so, in what manner? Is there anything specifically in these tales that *clearly* could be called in any sense a resurrection? These last two questions are critical, since many endings of these ancient accounts are missing and, in other cases, particular items must be assumed or interpolated since they are not mentioned directly. How about any similar or related ideas, such as apotheosis or being immortalized in the afterlife in some sense?

One particularly crucial subject needs to be clarified at the outset. The bottom line as to whether there were dying-and-rising gods that predate Christianity has much to do with how the relevant concepts are defined and dated. Another of the recognized experts here is Mark S. Smith, who employs four indicators to identify the presence of this concept. We need "the divine status of the figures"; "their death and their return to life"; the "correspondence" of these themes to "the seasonal cycle"; and "a series of rituals which provides a cultic context for the recitation" of these myths. Smith explains that this sequence is drawn heavily from the famous nineteenth-century work of J. G. Frazer titled *The Golden Bough*.[6]

---

[6] Mark S. Smith, "The Death of 'Dying and Rising Gods' in the Biblical World: An Update, with Special Reference to Baal in the Baal Cycle," *Scandinavian Journal of the Old Testament* 12 (1998): 257–313, as summarized nicely on 262. Smith explains that

It is easy to miss the crucial nature of the "ritual" and "cultic" elements of Smith's fourfold indicators, especially when other researchers leave them out. But for Smith, the lack of ritual and cultic beliefs and celebrations may hint that any possible accounts of rebirth or rising heroes in these mythological stories would indicate that these portions probably do not occupy the central perspective in these belief systems. In other words, without these two aspects, it would be very difficult to distinguish between a nice story and an essential belief to ground a particular culture's deepest beliefs.

In response, another specialist, John Granger Cook, implies that following Frazer in these matters may not be the best way to handle this subject, in that Frazer "has not fared well among historians of religion." Cook thinks that Smith's first two categories can be fulfilled "in an attenuated sense."[7] But then, what qualifies as such a weakened or diminished sense? How much of the story can be missing from the ancient accounts and have them still considered virtually the same concept? For example, Walter Burkert qualifies the matter this way: "The evidence for resurrection is late and tenuous in the case of Adonis, and practically nonexistent in the case of Attis; and not even Osiris returns to real life, but instead attains transcendent life beyond death."[8]

Cook responds that his primary interest is whether there is a death and resurrection element in the ancient accounts comparable to the New Testament concepts, meaning that he "will dispense with the third and fourth markers" preferred by Smith. Thus, Cook maintains that even this "more minimalistic category" still "remains quite useful" for comparison to the New Testament—is there a clear dying-and-rising in these ancient tales?[9] It must be remembered that this is not to say that the mythical accounts actually inspired the Christian teachings.[10] But as will be seen, definitions can and do make a difference in the final outcomes here, including how they are stated.

---

he draws these characteristics from James George Frazer, *The Golden Bough: A Study in Comparative Religion*, 2 vols. (London: Macmillan, 1890). Henceforth, this author's name will be shortened to M. S. Smith.

[7] John Granger Cook, *Empty Tomb, Resurrection, Apotheosis* (Tübingen, Germany: Mohr Siebeck, 2018), 57.

[8] Walter Burkert, *Structure and History in Greek Mythology and Ritual*, rev. ed. (Berkeley: University of California Press, 1982), 100–101. Cook also quotes Burkert, though from the first edition, with the same page numbers.

[9] Cook, *Empty Tomb*, 58, cf. 62.

[10] Cook, esp. 56n1, also 69.

Some of the Main Characters in the Ancient Literature

The distinctions provided above should assist in providing a path for introducing some of the chief characters in our discussion, including how scholars interpret the distinctions and contradictions between the various religious paths just mentioned. A few of the definitional distinctions here should be kept in view as well.

Dumuzi/Tammuz: Jonathan Z. Smith states, "The assessment of the figure of Tammuz (Sumerian: Dumuzi) as a dying-and-rising deity in the scholarly literature has varied more than any other deity placed in this class."[11] The ends of both the Sumerian and Akkadian texts are missing and in their current state contain only the death and disappearance of Dumuzi/Tammuz without anything that might be treated as a return to life. But changing perspectives came as the result of later published material indicating more than one potential ending. In one, Dumuzi's lover Inanna (Akkadian: Ishtar) consigned him to the underworld on her behalf. In an Akkadian version, Ishtar is allowed to get a substitute so that she could go free, but when she finds Tammuz rejoicing over her problems, she has him killed by demons and taken into the underworld!

That there was no celebration of Dumuzi's return may indicate that such an event was not a central or significant part of the tale. Smith states that any ritual evidence is "unambiguously negative . . . a relentlessly funeral cult. The young Tammuz is dead and he is mourned."[12] Smith adds, "In the Akkadian version, Tammuz is dead and remains so."[13] In sum, there is virtually no strong reason to consider Dumuzi/Tammuz and Inanna/Ishtar to be examples of dying-and-rising gods.[14]

---

[11] J. Z. Smith, "Dying and Rising Gods," 4:2535–40, with the quotation on 2538.

[12] J. Z. Smith, 4:2538.

[13] J. Z. Smith, 4:2539.

[14] On these conclusions, cf. J. Z. Smith, 4:2538–39; M. S. Smith, "Death of 'Dying and Rising Gods,'" 310–12; Edwin M. Yamauchi, "Tammuz and the Bible," *Journal of Biblical Literature* 84 (1965): 283–90; Yamauchi, "Descent of Ishtar," in *The Biblical World: A Dictionary of Biblical Archaeology*, ed. Charles Pfeiffer (Grand Rapids: Baker, 1966), 196–200; Yamauchi, "Did Christianity Copy Earlier Pagan Resurrection Stories?," in *The Harvest Handbook of Apologetics*, ed. Joseph M. Holden (Eugene, OR: Harvest House, 2018), 149–55, 471–74; Bendt Alster, "Tammuz," in *Dictionary of Deities and Demons in the Bible*, ed. Karel van der Toorn, Bob Becking, and Pieter W. van der Horst (Leiden: Brill, 1999), 833; Günter Wagner, *Das religionsgeschichtliche Problem von Römer 6, 1–11* (Zurich: Zwingli, 1962), 142, 146–79, 268–69; Cook, *Empty Tomb*, 57–58, 69–73, esp. 72–73.

Baal: Often considered to be a storm god rather than a vegetation god, particularly in the Ugaritic accounts, there is emphasis in some texts that Baal died and descended to the underworld. But it is very difficult to be specific in the crucial details here because all agree that the relevant accounts are riddled with gaps in the most vital places.

This is one of those instances mentioned above where definitions can make a difference. In a detailed treatment of new manuscript evidence for the Baal Cycle, Mark Smith argues that whatever the known copies of the Baal Cycle may include, the most recent discoveries confirm that the text possesses a heavy ceremonial emphasis having to do with Baal's "royal funerary rites."[15] In fact, Smith argues that "the rich indigenous corpus of Ugaritic ritual texts does not contain a single reference to the death and rising of Baal"; hence, "the burden of demonstration for Baal as a dying-and-rising god, with its attendant ritual background, falls on those who argue for it."[16]

Jonathan Z. Smith seems close to Mark Smith here, at least pertaining to Aliyan Baal (lit. "the lord") who descends to the underworld "as if he is dead" and then returns later. Smith concludes that "this is a disappearing-reappearing narrative. There is no suggestion of death and resurrection."[17] Yamauchi leaves the matter open regarding the specifics of the Baal account.[18]

However, while Scandinavian scholar Tryggve Mettinger of Lund University follows Mark Smith in his ordering of the "major lacunae and unreadable passages," he still disagrees with both Mark Smith and Jonathan Z. Smith in thinking it is clear that Ugaritic Baal dies and his corpse is located.[19] It is also clear that Baal lives afterward, with Mettinger producing and translating a text that seems to state this. Yet, Mettinger speaks straightforwardly concerning the state of the data: "I am painfully aware of the hypothetical nature of the following interpretation, but it is the one I have arrived at" and acknowledges after citing the text that "the passage in

---

[15] M. S. Smith, "Death of 'Dying and Rising Gods,'" 310–11.

[16] M. S. Smith, 290.

[17] J. Z. Smith, "Dying and Rising Gods," 4:2536.

[18] Yamauchi, "Pagan Resurrection Stories," 151. This conclusion specifically concerning Baal does not extend to this or any other pre-Christian account influencing the Christian concepts of the death and resurrection of Jesus (153–55).

[19] Tryvvge Mettinger, *The Riddle of Resurrection: 'Dying and Rising Gods' in the Ancient Near East* (Winona Lake, IN: Eisenbrauns, 2013), 57.

question contains a number of interpretive problems, but even so some main points seem to be possible to ascertain."[20]

Interestingly enough, Mettinger finds two other alternatives to Baal being a dying-and-rising god: either "there was a ruse" and Baal "never actually went down to the Netherworld" or Baal was "rather a god of the vanishing gods type." Yet, Mettinger concludes against these views that these two alternatives are mistaken, and in spite of the "disturbing gaps in the material," Baal's "return is a return to full and active life" connected to seasonal changes, with the autumn rains after the summer drought being "the proof of his return." Admittedly, cultic ritual motifs are "more difficult to ascertain."[21] In the end, Mettinger lists Baal as a dying-and-rising god.[22]

In his conclusion, Cook follows Mettinger against Mark Smith. Cook also concedes, "The opposition in the texts between Baal's death and life may not have a ritual background, but they do indicate that in the myth Baal finally overcomes death."[23] This includes that the epic "associates rain with Baal's return to life."[24] There two elements of the absence of cultic ritual in Baal and the importance of rain as a sign of his being alive will be entertained further below.

Osiris and Isis: Perhaps the best-known names from the dying-and-rising gods genre, especially in an Egyptian context, are Osiris and Isis. There is simply an amazing array of twists and turns to these particular mythical stories, often coming from well before the Christian era. Yamauchi states, "The most complete and coherent account of the myth is narrated by a Greek writer from the Roman period, Plutarch (AD 50–129)."[25] According to an abbreviated summary of this myth, Osiris's brother Seth tricked him into getting inside a chest, which Seth then deposited into the Nile River. The chest traveled around the eastern end of the Mediterranean Sea and ended up in Phoenicia.

Isis, Osiris's sister and wife, found the chest and brought it back to Egypt. With the assistance of magic, Isis revived Osiris. But not to be outdone, Seth killed his brother, cut his body into fourteen pieces, and dispersed the fragments around

---

[20] Mettinger, *Riddle of Resurrection*, 68 and 69.

[21] Mettinger, 80–81.

[22] Mettinger, 218.

[23] Cook, *Empty Tomb*, 74.

[24] Cook, 73. This is reminiscent of Cook's earlier disagreement with Mark Smith on the notion of including the context of cultic rituals as a crucial factor in the definitional notion of dying-and-rising gods (57–58).

[25] Yamauchi, "Did Christianity Copy Earlier Pagan Resurrection Stories?," 152.

Egypt. Isis collected thirteen of the fourteen pieces but had to fashion a new reproductive organ for Osiris, with which Isis got pregnant and bore a son named Horus, who eventually avenged his father's death by killing Seth. Horus became the god of the living, while Osiris descended into Hades and became the god of the dead in the underworld.[26]

The story of Isis and Osiris had such longevity that it is hardly a wonder that the tale is full of various twists and turns, many of them quite out of the ordinary. Some of the changes include an earlier version of the story where Osiris drowned accidentally or was rescued from the Nile before ending up in Phoenicia. Another popular version involved Isis flapping her wings over her husband's body, thereby breathing the breath of life back into his nostrils. Ideas involving magic, sorcery, incantations, and the like are often mentioned. Sometimes Isis herself is the hero and sometimes it is her son Horus. Osiris is better known for being the god of the underworld, but he is referred to as a "solarized deity" in some versions, which seems to conflict with his home in what is presumed to be the darkness of the underworld.[27]

According to Mark Smith, Osiris has generally been considered "as a funerary deity" rather than a rising god.[28] Jonathan Z. Smith similarly points out, "Osiris was considered to be the mythical prototype for the distinctive Egyptian process of mummification" and is almost always depicted as a mummy. Then he adds, "In no sense can Osiris be said to have 'risen' in the sense required by the dying and rising pattern."[29]

Rudolf Bultmann was, to some extent, one of the last major supporters of the famous *religionsgeschichtliche Schule* (at least to a certain extent) of the late nineteenth and early twentieth centuries. Frazer's work *The Golden Bough* was highly influential in the earlier phases of this movement, such as in teaching that dying-and-rising gods were very common in the ancient world.[30] Yet Helmut Koester, a critical New Testament scholar

---

[26] Yamauchi, "Pagan Resurrection Stories," 152–53.

[27] Many of these different angles are recounted in R. E. Witt, *Isis in the Graeco-Roman World* (Ithaca: Cornell University Press, 1971), esp. 36–40, 45, 197, cf. 189. The differences between Osiris being described as the solar eye of the sun or the ruler of the netherworld is discussed on 17, 38, 51, 54.

[28] M. S. Smith, "Death of 'Dying and Rising Gods,'" 271.

[29] J. Z. Smith, "Dying and Rising Gods," 4:2538.

[30] For example, the best-known New Testament representative on this position was Wilhelm Bousset, *Kyrios Christos: A History of the Belief in Christ from the Beginnings of Christianity to Irenaeus*, trans. John E. Steely (Nashville: Abingdon, 1970), 57–59, 191–94 on the common notions of dying-and-rising gods in the first century. Bultmann himself wrote the "Introductory Word" to the 1964 fifth edition (7–9) and seems already to be

and former student of Bultmann's, commented, "To be sure, Osiris died and became the lord of the realm of the dead, but it is never said that he rose." Besides, Osiris is not the hero of the story anyway.[31] Like Koester, another skeptical New Testament professor, atheist scholar Bart Ehrman, agrees: "Osiris does not—decidedly does not—return to life. . . . And so for Osiris there is no rising from the dead."[32]

The majority scholarly view at present appears to follow the line of thought from Mark Smith, Jonathan Z. Smith, Koester, and Ehrman that whatever happened in the various stories, Osiris was not resurrected in any normal, meaningful way.[33] Mettinger and Cook are worthy representatives among the dissenters.[34]

Heracles/Melqart: These two figures have been combined at least since Frazer's work at the end of the nineteenth century. For Mettinger and Cook, this is one of the

---

acknowledging cracks in the general direction of key *religionsgeschichtliche Schule* theses. Bultmann states, "Still it must be said that the correctness of Bousset's total view and of his representation of the cultic Kyrios worship in Hellenistic Christianity is in no way dependent upon the correctness of this thesis." One issue Bultmann goes on to mention is that "it can be regretted above all that in his presentation, essential motifs of the New Testament, especially of Pauline theology, have not been brought into operation adequately" (8–9). This seems to be an odd comment on Bultmann's part. Of course, it is possible that Bousset could have been mistaken at any of several crucial points while other important features still remain intact. But it almost sounds more like an attempt by Bultmann to save the overall thesis in spite of some major misses, while still offering a preemptive strike against Bousset's detractors. Of course, as many have remarked, the Frazer/Bousset thesis has indeed gone on to suffer so many central blows that most scholars at present would probably attest to the overall theory being rendered rather incapable of doing what it was intended to do in the first place. This issue will also be discussed further.

[31] Helmut Koester, *Introduction to the New Testament*, 2 vols. (Philadelphia: Fortress, 1982), 1:190.

[32] Bart D. Ehrman, *Did Jesus Exist? The Historical Argument for Jesus of Nazareth* (New York: HarperCollins, 2012), 228.

[33] Besides these four scholars, see also Günter Wagner, *Das religionsgeschichtliche Problem*, 1–11, esp. the strong statement on 273: "Osiris erlebte keine Auferstehung, sondern wurde zum Herrscher der Unterwelt wiederbelebt" (Habermas translation: "Osiris did not undergo a resurrection but was revived as the lord of the underworld [or Hades]"). See also Yamauchi, "Pagan Resurrection Stories," 152–53. Bruce M. Metzger's comments seem very close to those of Mark Smith and Jonathan Z. Smith above. See Metzger's excellent essay, "Methodology in the Study of the Mystery Religions and Early Christianity," in *Historical and Literary Studies: Pagan, Jewish, and Christian* (Grand Rapids: Eerdmans, 1968), 1–24, particularly the critiques and detailed scholarly sources on 20–21.

[34] Mettinger, *Riddle of Resurrection*, 182, while still admitting questions on 218; Cook, *Empty Tomb*, 76, 78, but see 80.

potential cases of a dying-and-rising god where a variety of positive arguments are posed, especially regarding both literary texts and Greek inscriptions. For instance, Josephus (*Ant.* 8.5.3) uses the Greek noun *egersis* (a rising up, awakening) in a phrase that has been translated "the awakening of Heracles."

Many discussions have ensued concerning the best interpretation of the Jewish historian at this point. In a section discussing the achievements of King Hiram of Tyre (e.g., 2 Sam 5:11; 1 Kgs 5), Josephus also mentions that Hiram was the first Tyrian ruler to "celebrate the awakening of Heracles in the month of Peritus." Mettinger and Cook both acknowledge the serious issues here, since Josephus in his *Against Apion* (1.119) "gives similar information" yet Josephus is not at all speaking about the awakening of Heracles but is discussing the building of a couple of temples. Admittedly, however, the text in *Against Apion* is plagued by the reading of just a single imperfect text. At any rate, both Mettinger and Cook conclude that the best solution is still to regard Josephus as addressing "a cultic celebration of the resurrection of Heracles."[35]

A Greek inscription from Amman-Philadelphia also bears on the situation here. After another difficult discussion, Mettinger concludes that it makes the most sense to refer to a person described in the inscription as the "resuscitator" of Heracles. An inscription from Ramleh is similar. Additionally, iconography from the Melquat Stele and a vase from Sidon are interpreted similarly in spite of raising crucial questions, and are also supported by other considerations. This all leads Mettinger and Cook to conclude that Melquat is a dying-and-rising god.[36]

These interpretations are difficult indeed, as admitted on all sides. Are the references to the "raising" of temples or to Heracles's dying and rising? Mettinger refers to the Josephus issue as the "vexed problem" that had been called "a hopeless case." He and Cook both acknowledge additional issues that keep this from being as solid as they would like, since the texts can be interpreted differently.[37]

Mark S. Smith similarly recognizes the difficulties here, but he raises a number of problems for the more positive views like those of Mettinger and Cook. These include the exact identity of the god or the person being addressed in more than one place. More serious questions concern the strength of the data that Melquat/Heracles was

---

[35] Mettinger, *Riddle of Resurrection*, 88–90, containing the quotations above; also, Cook, *Empty Tomb*, 127–29.

[36] Mettinger, *Riddle of Resurrection*, 90–111; Cook argues similarly (*Empty Tomb*, 129–32).

[37] Mettinger, *Riddle of Resurrection*, 89, cf. also 109–11; Cook makes similar concessions (*Empty Tomb*, 130–31).

actually dead in the first place, especially given the contradictory methods by which this supposedly came about (death and burial versus a body burned on a funeral pyre), though Smith seems inclined to think that the interpretation of death still makes sense. Yet, Smith rejects that there is a clear death account at all, denying that the sources actually affirm this event.[38]

Moreover, Smith also wonders about the material in Josephus, in that it is secondhand, and it is difficult to know its dependability for the material on Heracles. Moreover, the various accounts are diverse enough between the different geographical regions to produce still other questions. Beyond all this, Smith also balks concerning questions as to whether some sort of resurrection is part of the overall accounts. Even on some of these assumptions, there is virtually no information or description on this rising from death. A large problem for Smith is the lack of ritual or cultic connections as well.[39]

As Smith sums up the matter, "There is simply insufficient evidence to prove the case or to dismiss it entirely." Hence, he thinks that the attempted solution is very difficult and that it is better to conclude that the reconstruction "remains hypothetical."[40] Thus, if even a few of Smith's questions obtain, it remains very difficult to prove that a single, major interpretation stands head and shoulders above any other views, particularly when a wrong turn in any of several places could cause much or even most of the entire knot to unravel.

Adonis: Wagner provides the details of one of the two best-known versions of the Adonis myth. Adonis is usually considered to be a vegetation god who, according to the most prominent narrative, was killed by a wild boar while on a hunt. Two goddesses, Aphrodite and Persephone, were both enthralled with Adonis's beauty and quarreled over whether or not he would be claimed by the underworld or remain in the world of the living. The goddesses settled their dispute by allowing Adonis to spend half of his time with each of them in each of their respective realms. Wagner asks if that qualifies as a resurrection.[41] In the second version, Jonathan Z. Smith relates how, after being killed by the boar, Adonis is commemorated as a flower.[42]

---

[38] M. S. Smith, "Death of 'Dying and Rising Gods,'" esp. 279, 282.

[39] M. S. Smith, particularly 279–80, 282, cf. 310.

[40] M. S. Smith, esp. 277–82, with the quotations above on 279.

[41] Wagner, *Das religionsgeschichtliche Problem*, 187, 190.

[42] J. Z. Smith, "Dying and Rising Gods," 4:2535–36; cf. Cook similarly here (*Empty Tomb*, 87–88).

Wagner maintains that none of the forms of the Adonis story contains a resuscitation. Nor are there any explanations that Adonis ate magical food or drank living water or something like that. In fact, in the earliest form of the story from the fifth century BC, Adonis is not even said to have died.[43] In short, there is not even a minor hint of his resurrection in these myths.[44] Jonathan Z. Smith agrees: there is "no suggestion of death and rebirth." In fact, strangely enough, Adonis's "alternation between the upper and lower worlds precedes his death."[45]

Not until the middle of the second century do we find a classical text that mentions a festival commemoration for any resurrection of Adonis. Jonathan Z. Smith notes that these late mentions, which continue into the fourth century and beyond, were "largely influenced by or written by Christians." It is quite intriguing that with several of these mythological gods in the ancient world, there is a recurrent pattern of an indigenous mythology that contained at most the death of the hero but then that was changed later by Christians inserting or influencing an element of resurrection that is "nowhere found in the earlier native sources."[46]

Jonathan Z. Smith notes that the reason for Christians seemingly introducing those resurrections into the pagan accounts is difficult to determine. It might be that the believers' interpretation was to take the non-Christian stories to be precursors to the New Testament accounts, hence representing a sort of general human longing or hope that actually expressed itself in mythical stories but which became historical events in Jesus Christ.[47] Perhaps this sort of fulfillment motif was used as a preaching tool. References to the third day appear periodically but not universally so, and this

---

[43] Wagner, *Das religionsgeschichtliche Problem*, 191: "Sie weiss überhaupt nichts von einem Tode des Adonis."

[44] Wagner, 190–93. Wagner states, "Der Mythus weiss nichts von einer Auferstehung im Sinne Aktes" (Habermas translation: "The myth knows nothing of a resurrection in the sense of action").

[45] J. Z. Smith, "Dying and Rising Gods," 4:2536. For Smith's much-quoted comments on Adonis and other claims of dying-and-rising gods, see "On Comparing Stories," in *Drudgery Divine: On the Comparison of Early Christianities and the Religions of Late Antiquity* (Chicago: University of Chicago Press, 1990). On 101 we read that the account of Adonis contains "no hint of rebirth."

[46] J. Z. Smith, "Dying and Rising Gods," 4:2536.

[47] Besides Jonathan Z. Smith below, Mettinger also mentions this possible theme of Christians who may have wanted to showcase the death and resurrection of Jesus as unique. Mettinger, *Riddle of Resurrection*, 221.

also could have been introduced by Christians since it was *their* message.[48] On the other hand, the cultists themselves could have originated the use of the time factor in the form of mimicry of the Christian belief, as was done in other aspects. But commentators remark that the third day element cannot be established for sure from the data alone.[49]

At any rate, the strong consensus is that the ancient accounts of Adonis emphasize his death but do not contain a resurrection or anything like it either in texts or pictorially until very late, post-Christian times.[50] Even Bart Ehrman states, "There is nothing here to suggest either death or resurrection for Adonis."[51]

Attis: In this case, there is widespread agreement. Jonathan Z. Smith begins his hard-hitting lead paragraph like this: "The complex mythology of Attis is largely irrelevant to the question of dying and rising deities." In two of the old versions of the Attis myth, Attis is killed either by being castrated or by a boar. In neither case does he return to life. In later accounts he does not even die from his wounds, so there is neither a death nor a rebirth. Then Smith summarizes: "Attis is not, in his mythology, a dying-and-rising deity; indeed, he is not a deity at all."[52]

Metzger, Yamauchi, Mark S. Smith, Craig Keener, and Günter Wagner are all examples of scholars who join Jonathan Z. Smith in agreeing on the chief point here.[53] There seems to be very little to report by way of a reference to a resurrection

---

[48] Metzger addresses this in "Methodology," particularly 19, along with J. Z. Smith.

[49] J. Z. Smith, "Dying and Rising Gods," 4:2536; Mettinger, *Riddle of Resurrection*, 221.

[50] J. Z. Smith, "Dying and Rising Gods," 4:2536; Wagner, *Das religionsgeschichtliche Problem*, 205–11; Metzger, "Methodology," esp. 21; Cook, *Empty Tomb*, 95–96 (esp. on Frazer's error at this point), 97n239, 98–110, and the summary statement on 143 all concerning the second century AD and later accounts; Yamauchi, "Pagan Resurrection Stories," 151; M. S. Smith, "Death of 'Dying and Rising Gods,'" 282–86. Even Mettinger lists the Adonis resurrection as second century but states that, before that, "Adonis' resurrection is possible but not proved" (*Riddle of Resurrection*, 218; but cf. 153–54).

[51] Ehrman, *Did Jesus Exist?*, 227.

[52] J. Z. Smith, "Dying and Rising Gods," 4:2536; see also J. Z. Smith, *Drudgery Divine*, 101–4 on Attis.

[53] Yamauchi also confirmed to Habermas that he did not consider there to be any actual resurrections reported in the pre-Christian material (personal email to Habermas, dated May 18, 2019). Keener's more general point needs some explication. Craig S. Keener does list many examples of pre-Christian dying-and-rising gods in Keener, *The Historical Jesus of the Gospels* (Grand Rapids: Eerdmans, 2009), 336, along with 582n57. Yet, he is also careful to point out a few times that none of these cases qualify either as resurrections or as parallels to Jesus. As he states, "These are not *resurrection* appearances" (333), and they

for Attis before at least the latter portion of the second century and even much later. A number of scholars note that even Christian writers may have gotten involved in support of the idea of a resurrection here, perhaps as a harbinger to their own claims of resurrection.[54] Keener claims that "there is no possible evidence for [Attis's] resurrection before the third century CE."[55] Wagner finds nothing in support of Attis's resurrection in the classical works up into the post-New Testament times and even into the fourth century. He concludes that Attis is definitely not a "Heilgott"— not a healing god.[56]

Cook and Mettinger, quite often two of the major dissenters on some of these matters, even agree on this topic. Cook states clearly: "The narratives of a resurrection of Attis are late, at best. There is no shred of evidence in classical sources that he returned to life." Quoting Jan Bremmer, Cook adds, "Attis' 'resurrection' is not mentioned before the third century and seems closely connected with the rise of Christianity, just like the 'resurrection' of Adonis is not mentioned before the third century."[57] Mettinger states, "While the mythological material is broadly silent on a resurrection of Attis, the situation is slightly different when we turn to ritual." But even the references to the Hilaria or the Day of Joy are "perhaps as late as the third and fourth centuries."[58] So far, Attis clearly seems to be the least likely candidate for a dying-and-rising god, with this time factor serving to nullify direct questions with regard to Christian beliefs.

Other candidates for rising and dying gods: Among other possible suggestions that have been raised in the past, a few have fallen by the wayside more quickly than

---

are not "parallels" to resurrection appearances because such a definition here "stretches the category of parallel too far to be useful" (334, also 336). Keener's negative verdict here was further verified in personal emails to Habermas (dated May 18 and 20, 2019).

[54] Metzger, "Methodology," 20; Yamauchi, "Pagan Resurrection Stories," 152; Mark S. Smith does not discuss Attis in his lengthy study that we have been discussing, but he cites approvingly the work of Jonathan Z. Smith and P. Lambrechts, concluding that "Attis is said to be dead, but not resurrected; nor is he a divinity." See M. S. Smith, "Death of 'Dying and Rising Gods,'" 269n46; J. Z. Smith, "Dying and Rising Gods," 4:2536–37.

[55] Keener, *Historical Jesus*, 336.

[56] Wagner, *Das religionsgeschichtliche Problem*, 224–25, 229–31. Short and sweet, Wagner quotes M. P. Nilsson on 229: "Attis starb und tot blieb" (Habermas translation: "Attis died and remained dead"). The "Heilgott" quotation is on 233. Among Günter Wagner's other direct and hardest hitting comments are those on 230–31, 241.

[57] Cook, *Empty Tomb*, 110–24, with the two quotations on 110 and 121, respectively.

[58] Mettinger, *Riddle of Resurrection*, 157–59, quotation on 158.

Adonis and Attis. Ronald Nash states that at one time, Mithraism "eventually became Christianity's most serious rival." It was championed by one of the Roman emperors, Julian the Apostate, who ruled from AD 360–363. But any momentum on behalf of Mithraism lost ground to Christianity, particularly when Emperor Constantine embraced the latter. Very little is known of Mithraism's doctrine, with no detailed accounts of the cult's beliefs except that it was apparently dualistic like Zoroastrianism, "promoted an ethical life," and celebrated a sacred meal as well as a baptism-like ritual. Mithra's birth came about when he reportedly emerged out from under a rock![59]

Besides being far too late to have influenced Christianity's central beliefs and teachings, Mithraism differs in many key areas. Jonathan Z. Smith argues that "there has never been a claim for the 'rising' of Mithras in any late Antique document."[60] Yamauchi points out, "The scholarly consensus today is that Mithraism arose as a Roman phenomenon late in the first century AD at the earliest." Then he continues: "Given the relatively late formation of Mithraism, there is no possibility that this mystery religion could have influenced nascent Christianity, nor is there any evidence that it did so later."[61]

In another case, according to Jonathan Z. Smith, Marduk was the "king-god of Babylon," the "canonical instance of the Myth and Ritual pattern." However, "there is no hint of Marduk's death" in the ancient account in the *Enuma elish*. Rather, Marduk was apparently imprisoned, with this confinement being taken by "an older generation of scholars" to be the "equivalent to his death, and his presumed ultimate release represented his resurrection"! However, "there is no evidence that the Babylonian Marduk was ever understood to be a dying-and-rising deity, that such a myth was reenacted during the New Year festival, or that the king was believed to undergo a similar fate."[62] In fact, the case for Marduk being a dying-and-rising god "is based on a misreading of the ancient Near Eastern sources."[63]

Living at the end of the nineteenth century during the heyday of the German *religionsgeschichtliche Schule* movement, where reports such as these were common,

---

[59] Ronald H. Nash, *Christianity and the Hellenistic World* (Grand Rapids: Zondervan, 1984), 143–48; also, Yamauchi, "Pagan Resurrection Stories," 153.

[60] J. Z. Smith, *Drudgery Divine*, 101; J. Z. Smith, "Dying and Rising Gods," 4:2537–38; Nash, *Christianity and the Hellenistic World*, 147.

[61] Yamauchi, "Pagan Resurrection Stories," 154; Nash agrees completely (*Christianity and the Hellenistic World*, 143, 147–48).

[62] J. Z. Smith, "Dying and Rising Gods," 4:2537–38.

[63] J. Z. Smith, *Drudgery Divine*, 101.

Scottish theologian James Orr even cited A. Jeremias's comment that there was still no definite evidence for a festival that commemorates the death and resurrection of Marduk-Tammuz.[64] Wagner agrees totally on this general question. Nothing in the text points to any sort of victorious resurrection for Marduk. Hence, such an event should not be spoken of at all.[65]

On the specific question of Marduk, even Mettinger agrees with Jonathan Z. Smith. It was determined that the important text in question "was a propaganda work composed in Assyria and had nothing to do either with the death and resurrection of Marduk or with the New Year festival."[66] Later Mettinger explained further: "Already by the 1950's a drastic reduction in the claims for Dumuzi/Tammuz (and Marduk) had thus taken place." Hence the milieu for dying-and-rising deities had been reduced.[67] But still other candidates besides Mithras and Marduk have been suggested from time to time.

As Mettinger and others have pointed out, these mythical gods were of quite different types, such as Adonis often being identified as one of the famous vegetation gods that "die" like the foliage in the fall or winter, only to reappear or "rise" in the spring. This can be compared to a fertility god, as Dumuzi is sometimes called, or a storm or weather god like Baal, or a sun god like Marduk. There is also a shepherd god like Dumuzi or Eshmun, who "is a god of healing." Some gods seem to die and rise, but not all who expire live again afterward. For example, "it seems that storm gods are not generically gods who die and rise. Baal of Ugarit was here an exceptional case." On the other hand, "Adon(is) of Byblos . . . is an independent god"! Mourning and celebration also take place at different times of the year. Hence, the gods definitely should not be cast into a single category.[68]

---

[64] James Orr, *The Resurrection of Jesus* (London: Hodder & Stoughton, 1908; repr., Grand Rapids: Zondervan, 1965), 250, citing the work of A. Jeremias, *Babylonishes im New Testament.*

[65] Wagner, *Das religionsgeschichtliche Problem*, esp. 173, also 175. Wagner states clearly on 173, "Nichts im Text . . . deutet auf einen 'Triumph' oder eine 'Auferstehung' Marduks hin" (Habermas translation: "Nothing in the text signifies [or points to] a 'victory' or a 'resurrection' of Marduk").

[66] Mettinger, *Riddle of Resurrection*, 23. Cf. Jonathan Z. Smith, who also makes a similar comment elsewhere regarding the misunderstanding of the texts ("Dying and Rising Gods," 2537).

[67] Mettinger, *Riddle of Resurrection*, 40.

[68] The quotations above are from Mettinger, 218–20; cf. also M. S. Smith, "Death of 'Dying and Rising Gods,'" 310; Wagner, *Das religionsgeschichtliche Problem*, 169. Though

A Critique of the Various Dying-and-Rising Gods Theses

How should the pros and cons regarding our discussion in this chapter be evaluated? The dialogue was quite detailed at particular points, so we will begin here by providing a brief summary regarding the scholarly consensus, including the reasons for these positions. This will serve the purpose of viewing the current lay of the land. Of course, scholarly views do not "prove" one view or another; they may be mistaken, and new evidence may emerge, especially in the form of ancient manuscripts. Further, entire landscapes are sometimes reversed, as indicated on a smaller scale above when academic positions changed a few decades ago regarding the views concerning both Marduk and Mithraism. Still, the specialists can help direct nonspecialists to carefully access the predominant avenues and implications of the many issues involved. Afterward, some of the major reasons for these positions will also be presented as support for the various positions that are held so that the most likely cases may be established more easily vis-à-vis the data.

Scholarly Views

For our purposes here, at least two primary questions are paramount. First, were there *any* examples of dying-and-rising gods before the first century AD and the time of Jesus? The minimal required characteristics for these stories of the gods have been developed and debated throughout this chapter. But the candidate must at least, in the same tradition, clearly be reported to have died and then have been seen alive *afterward*.[69] Second, could any or all of these ancient accounts of dying-and-rising gods, or even the general Mediterranean ethos itself, have influenced in any

---

older, S. H. Hooke discusses many of the differences among the ancient myths both concerning the ones discussed here as well as beyond the range of our more specific focus (*Middle Eastern Mythology*, particularly 19–23, 67–70).

[69] The reason that the death as well as the life *afterward* must be contained "in the same tradition" is due to a number of ancient stories that, for whatever reason, do in fact include one without the other, or where the latter seems to precede the former, whether or not it was discussed that way. Of course, people can die and people can also walk around and communicate with each other. But unless the latter occurs *after* the first, and in the same account, we do not know if the intent is to teach a dying-and-rising god. As Jonathan Z. Smith and others have reminded their readers, these sorts of accounts simply cannot be combined automatically on the assumption that they are both teaching the very same ideas. J. Z. Smith, *Drudgery Divine*, 100–101.

significant way(s) the many New Testament accounts that report that Jesus did in fact die, clearly followed later by his own resurrection appearances, suggesting that Jesus was some sort of a copycat account?

The popular *religionsgeschichtliche Schule* of interpretation in the late nineteenth and early twentieth centuries at least thought that the first question could be answered affirmatively: these dying-and-rising cases were indeed thought to exist.[70] On the other hand, today it is probably the case that the majority of scholars who specialize in these subjects have decided negatively on the first question, favoring the notion that there were few, if any, clear cases of dying-and-rising gods before Jesus. Most prominent researchers presently appear to doubt that specific cases may be located and identified with assurance, at least when careful definitions are allowed.

There are numerous possible candidates for ancient dying-and-rising gods, but the chief view appears to be that in every or virtually every case, the clear factual and dating constraints are missing, plus the causal data to bridge the strands between the various arguments are often lacking or just collapse under scrutiny. This results in the breakdown of the hypothesis, making the stories quite susceptible to other cogent explanations.

Many problems here no doubt have emerged due to the presence of several key factors. Many of these stories were told hundreds or even thousands of years before Jesus lived! The scarcity of the available data aside, many of the sources are also mutilated in various places, exhibit missing endings, or contain wording that is indeterminately garbled. After all, literally thousands of years obviously can make a difference.

The second, follow-up question regarding whether these pagan beliefs in the ancient pre-Christian world provided any serious inspiration for the Christian notions of the deity, death, and resurrection of Jesus is solved much more assuredly, and the scholarly majority seems overwhelmingly to line up on the same side. Very few, if any, specialist scholars at present, regardless of their own religious convictions, respond positively that any ancient dying-and-rising ethos inspired the Christian notions of Jesus's deity, death, and resurrection appearances. This would essentially serve as a naturalistic hypothesis, though scholars almost always agree that such a notion fails to answer many key and known factors.

---

[70] An example from a prominent member of the *religionsgeschichtliche Schule* is Otto Pfleiderer's volume *The Early Christian Conception of Christ: Its Significance and Value in the History of Religion* (London: Williams & Norgate, 1905), 84–133. Chapter 3 treats the related subject of Jesus as a miracle worker.

Hence, the majority of researchers who reject the overall category of ancient dying-and-rising gods itself surely also reject its influence on Christianity, given that then there would be no clear cases with which to make the additional charge. The percentage of scholars who object to the second question, holding that the dying-and-rising god accounts definitely did not inspire the Christian reports of Jesus's deity, death, and resurrection, is much higher than with the views regarding the initial question. Both general and specific comments will address the reasons for these affirmations and the rejections, hence providing some of the details for these stances.

Major Question One

Were there any ancient pre-Christian accounts of dying-and-rising gods?

With the outlined "battle lines" drawn in this chapter, which arguments enjoy the most support? Why do so many major scholars take such a variety of positions? Most crucially, which notions are supported by the best arguments? To begin, it must be remembered, as mentioned often in this discussion, that the textual artifacts with which these researchers are dealing are quite far from optimum. In fact, they are admittedly quite poor. Often the scholar must render an intelligent guess in order to speculate on where the ancient writer was heading before this or that lapse in the source. This always leaves room for disagreements followed by the guarding of one's research territory.

Further, another very important consideration that has been kept in view throughout this evaluation was also mentioned from the outset. Namely, these scholars are largely arguing according to their own definitions, as mentioned above, and this is an important source of misunderstanding, according to which they do not always agree.

One example discussed was Mark Smith favoring four indications as best defining an account of a dying-and-rising god.[71] However, Cook disputes these four markers, which he states were drawn from the outdated position taken more than a century ago by Frazer in his volume *The Golden Bough*. Accordingly, Cook especially disputes Smith's third and fourth criteria, namely, that the stories in question need to correspond to the seasonal cycles and that the context of these ancient myths should include cultic rituals.[72]

---

[71] M. S. Smith, "Death of 'Dying and Rising Gods,'" esp. 262.
[72] Cook, *Empty Tomb*, 57–58.

While also being quite critical of Frazer, the last measure regarding the presence of rituals is particularly crucial in that Jonathan Z. Smith and Mark S. Smith use this marker regularly as one of the chief indications that disallows particular stories as being considered as tales of dying-and-rising gods. The lack of ensuing rituals may indicate that these stories were essentially dying funeral and burial tales. However, as noted often, Cook and Mettinger do not require these two criteria.

It is difficult to reach hard-and-fast decisions on this difference. Cook seems to be more correct regarding the third point in Mark Smith's definition, in that these ancient stories can be quite different from one another with regard to particular aspects, and therefore corresponding to seasonal cycles would seem to limit the consideration of particular accounts. As will be delineated below, these dying-and-rising gods are plainly not exactly of the same vintage; a storm god may be distinct from a seasonal vegetation god. So, it appears too radical to force them all into a single mold typified by the seasonal mystery religions.

On the other hand, it appears that Mark Smith and Jonathan Z. Smith have included a crucial additional consideration regarding the import of ritual celebrations. Our most cherished beliefs often emerge and play crucial roles in our festivals and rituals, especially when these items are religious in nature. It would therefore seem that the presence of rituals that build up around particular beliefs may well serve as important windows into the nature and centrality of these notions in the particular ancient belief systems. Further, the additional point here is that the lack of ritual and celebration may in fact indicate cases of dying alone rather than being followed by an afterlife.

Cook states that he is most interested in comparing the exceptionally ancient dying-and-rising accounts "with resurrection in the New Testament" but to do so *analogically* by comparing "the NT images of resurrection and similar images in paganism and Judaism" rather than *genealogically*, which would attempt "to demonstrate pagan influence . . . on Paul and early Christianity or vice versa."[73] To be clear then, Cook's

---

[73] Cook, *Empty Tomb*, compare 58 and 56, also 7, 69. Intriguingly, John Granger Cook refers initially to his two-part definition as a more "attenuated" description than what might emerge when Smith's four markers are required. Cook's point is apparently that the first two insignia alone are by far the major ones and are sufficient in themselves to identify an ancient dying-and-rising god, at least on a less-detailed scale, even without Mark Smith's two remaining considerations (57). Cook follows this up by identifying his chief emphasis as being to compare the ancient dying-and-rising accounts to the notion of resurrection found in the New Testament, referring to this as a "more minimalistic category" (58). Cook's comments

aim is a comparison of the similarity between the ideas, *not* to argue whether the earlier pagan notions gave rise to or otherwise influenced the Jewish and Christian beliefs.

Could it not follow similarly that, in this case, the centrality of the dying-and-rising myths might well be manifest in the ritual patterns of the people? On the other hand, if these stories do not show up in the ancient rituals and celebrations, this may be a means of indicating that those accounts were perhaps more extraneous and superficial within those cultures, or that they predominantly demarcated the processes of dying and burial.

Overall, then, which factors might help to address our first question regarding the viability of recognizing any pre-Christian dying-and-rising accounts? Mark S. Smith begins his best-known essay with the provocative title, "The Death of 'Dying and Rising Gods' in the Biblical World."[74] At the outset, Smith acknowledges the death knell with regard to our initial question above: "For historians of religion the death of 'the dying and rising god' may have passed."[75] But was this actually the case?

Next, in his article, Mark Smith cites Jonathan Z. Smith's doctoral dissertation "The Glory, Jest and Riddle: James George Frazer and *The Golden Bough*."[76]

---

together could actually be taken as descriptions that might be understood as the way to contrast his scaled-down definition with the more robust delineation taken by Jonathan Z. Smith and Mark Smith's longer list of conditions. Of course, some researchers will prefer Cook's more minimalistic definition as the stronger one, and more concentrated arguments are sometimes harder hitting. Others will support the more detailed approach of the Smiths as being built on a greater amount of data. On the larger playing field, this sort of back-and-forth set of comparisons is a microcosm of choosing the best options in this entire discussion and may at least partially explain why there are so many differences of opinion among the specialists. Whether one uses an "attenuated" definition or a more detailed one could quite easily account for many of the differences between the interpreters in this chapter. Here's the chief point to be noticed at this juncture: it would appear to be obvious that a two-tiered bar may produce a longer list of dying-and-rising gods than a four-tiered test with its greater number of hurdles to clear! In the end, the Smiths along with other scholars think that the more detailed qualifications are necessary in order to demarcate the nature of these ancient beliefs, but they may also in fact leave us with no such dying-and-rising gods at all.

[74] Mark Smith's essay is subtitled "An Update, with Special Reference to Baal in the Baal Cycle," *Journal of the Old Testament* 12, no. 2 (1998): 257–313, https://doi.org/10.1080/09018329808585140.

[75] Mark S. Smith, *The Origins of Biblical Monotheism: Israel's Polytheistic Background and the Ugaritic Texts* (New York: Oxford University Press, 2001), 104.

[76] Jonathan Zittell Smith, "The Glory, Jest and Riddle: James George Frazer and *The Golden Bough*" (PhD diss., Yale University, 1969), 366–75. See M. S. Smith, "Death of 'Dying and Rising Gods,'" 257–58.

Frazer's famous work stood out as the crown jewel of the *religionsgeschichtliche Schule* onslaught over a century ago. Then Mark Smith continues by stating his aims in his lengthy essay, which include critiquing Frazer's late nineteenth-century work on comparative religion, which too often seemed to study chiefly the similarities in these ancient tales. On the other hand, Smith determines to look at the contrasts in these ancient tales. This comment was no doubt meant to counteract the prevalent tendency of the *religionsgeschichtliche Schule* to overly emphasize these resemblances between ancient accounts when prominent divergences were also present.[77] Smith also wishes "to suggest an alternative interpretation" to the conclusions drawn in the history of religions tradition.[78]

Mark Smith charges that Frazer wove his own textual tapestry in a highly selective way, piecing together various ancient stories and conclusions that were not always what the ancient authors and texts taught. Thus, Frazer erred especially in matters of method and data, since these accounts were often taken unsystematically from across centuries and cultures alike, then mixed and matched along the way with dissimilar and late reports. In the process, "Frazer's work came at a major cost to the ancient texts." Frazer invented "his own new mythology of 'dying and rising gods,'" essentially by manipulating the sources in unnatural ways.[79]

Smith concludes that "Frazer's driving motivation to 'explain' Jesus's death and resurrection against the backdrop of the category of 'dying and rising gods' entirely misses the background of Jewish resurrection. . . . Jesus's resurrection had little or nothing to do with rituals for a 'dying and rising god.'" The ancient mystery stories were likely more related to "mortuary traditions" and a possible human afterlife.[80] When these allowances are made, Smith concludes that it is uncertain that *any* of the

---

[77] A prominent example might consist of carefully noting the instances in the ancient world where a mystery god was said to have been raised on or after the third day while largely ignoring those cases where this was celebrated on earlier or later days, especially when the third day references began to appear in sources that were dated later than the emergence of Christianity, as with Adonis and Attis. In those cases, many scholars concluded that the copycat process moved in the reverse direction of what the *religionsgeschichtliche Schule* scholars tended to argue—namely, that Christian views were sometimes mimicked in these sources.

[78] M. S. Smith, "Death of 'Dying and Rising Gods,'" 259.

[79] M. S. Smith, 310. Other scholars besides Smith have made similar critiques of Frazer's work.

[80] M. S. Smith, 312–13.

dying-and-rising accounts actually taught what Frazer and those who agreed with him thought.[81]

Jonathan Z. Smith similarly reviews the various ancient accounts that purportedly exhibited dying-and-rising scenarios. Some texts are obscure with unknown or even missing "major lacunae at the most crucial points."[82] Scholars have presented possible reconstructions of these lost portions, but it is impossible to tell if the missing portions have been rendered properly. Later discoveries indicate that some proposed restorations were not only wide of the mark, but that the early accounts actually moved in an opposite direction! Some texts lack the clearly stated death of the hero or heroine, while still others are devoid of anything that could be understood fairly as a resurrection.

Jonathan Z. Smith concludes that some stories, like those about Aliyan Baal, describe "disappearing-reappearing" gods rather than dying-and-rising gods. Others, such as the Adonis and Attis narratives, contain no rebirth until well after the origins of Christianity and are thus "largely irrelevant to the question of dying and rising deities." Osiris exemplifies the Egyptian process of mummification and the life among the dead, but not of the living. Many of these purported dying-and-rising tales are not the celebration of a new life at all but rather its very opposite—the domination of death and the underworld. As Smith concludes regarding the several options of half-years in Hades followed by half-years on the earth, this "is not what is usually meant in the literature when speaking of a deity's 'rising.'"[83]

But all the considerations in this dialogue are far from being just one-sided. Cook and Mettinger are two well-qualified, representative scholars who hold that several of the mystery gods actually do meet the criteria and thereby qualify as dying-and-rising gods. Cook thinks that "Osiris is the closest analogy to the resurrection of Jesus" but also lists Osiris's son Horus as "a clear analogy." Dionysus is deemed to be "a fairly close analogy," as are Heracles and Melqart. The accounts of Dumuzi, Baal, and Adonis "are less useful as comparisons." The accounts of Adonis and Attis are simply too late, but there are still benefits to be gathered from among the more

---

[81] M. S. Smith, 288. Some of the more specific details and charges against Frazer are outlined here.

[82] J. Z. Smith, "Dying and Rising Gods," 4:2536.

[83] J. Z. Smith, 4:2536 and 2539; see also J. Z. Smith, *Drudgery Divine*, 99–105.

questionable examples here and there, even from those that do not otherwise provide very strong cases overall.[84]

For Mettinger, the list of possibilities does not seem quite so lengthy as for Cook, but Dumuzi, Baal, and Melqart are singled out for special mention, as well as Osiris to some extent. However, Eshmun, Adonis, and Attis raise other, sometimes serious issues and questions and thus must be considered too.[85] Even so, the parameters of these discussions are not always easy to navigate, and dissenting scholars from multiple and often opposing directions have offered similar and sometimes even original objections, some of which are quite weighty, as we will outline briefly.[86] How are

---

[84] Cook, *Empty Tomb*, esp. 143 for these quotations.

[85] Mettinger, *Riddle of Resurrection*, 217–18.

[86] For example, Mark T. Finney has switched the usual theoretical tables in a recent volume, arguing that it was the Greek writers who held to an afterlife view that "insisted on the importance of the physical body whereas a wealth of Jewish texts from the Hebrew Bible, Second Temple Judaism and early (Pauline) Christianity understood post-mortem existence to be that of the soul alone." Only later, when influenced by Greco-Roman writers, did canonical New Testament authors move toward a bodily afterlife position! See Finney, *Resurrection, Hell and the Afterlife: Body and Soul in Antiquity, Judaism and Early Christianity* (New York: Routledge, 2016), with the quotation here from the opening abstract in the book. Finney explains that he originally took the more usual position that the Greco-Roman view was disembodied while the predominant Jewish and Christian positions in the Second Temple period were bodily positions. But his more recent study changed the direction of his conclusions, even to the point of holding that Paul embraced the view that the afterlife was about souls but not about bodies (1–5). Especially relevant for our chief questions in this present chapter, and illustrative of his thesis, Finney counts more than ten mortals (Asclepius, Hercules, Memnon, Alcmeme, Melicertes, Castor, Menelaus, Dionysus, Rhesus, Hector, among others) who died and were "resurrected to immortal *bodily* life" (14, emphasis added).

In support, Finney cites on 13–14 another recent study by Dag Øistein Endsjø, *Greek Resurrection Beliefs and the Success of Christianity* (New York: Palgrave MacMillan, 2009), who somewhat similarly holds that immortality was essentially a bodily state (see esp. chap. 4 and page 120 for a summary; and chap. 6 and pages 157–58 for a key summation). But see Cook's review of Finney's work *Resurrection, Hell, and the Afterlife*, which covers much ground and offers several insightful objections in *The Enoch Seminar Online*, February 2, 2017, http://enochseminar.org/review/12675. To these studies, an intriguing essay by Stanley E. Porter also should be added, particularly Porter's related thesis arguing that bodily afterlife views moved from Greek to Greco-Roman, to Jewish ideas, and then into New Testament thought; see Porter, "Resurrection, the Greeks and the New Testament," in *Resurrection*, ed. Stanley E. Porter, Michael A. Hayes, and David Tombs (Sheffield: Sheffield Academic Press, 1999), 68–70, 80. Still another thesis arguing along related lines

these sometimes direct disagreements to be resolved in the major discussions in this chapter, chiefly those between Jonathan Z. Smith and Mark Smith on the one side, and Cook and Mettinger on the other?

(1) To begin, the negative position argues that there are no clear cases that exhibit all the required aspects which indicate that a positively dead god then also clearly reappeared. As Jonathan Z. Smith asserts, there are "major lacunae" in some of the writings; others exhibiting portions that cannot be deciphered, let alone interpreted. Some clearly lack deaths, whereas others *apparently* do so as well, and what might be

---

is the chapter by M. David Litwa, "We Worship One Who Rose from His Tomb," in *Iesus Deus: The Early Christian Depiction of Jesus as a Mediterranean God* (Minneapolis: Fortress, 2014), 141–79.

In contrast, skeptical New Testament scholar Gregory J. Riley takes what is by far the majority, more traditional view on many of these matters, with Greek disembodied afterlife notions being contrasted with the generally more bodily notions of much Second Temple Judaic thought and New Testament Christian views. Seemingly contrary to Finney's view above and sandwiched into Riley's treatment is the comment that mythical heroes like Sisyphus, Odysseus, Heracles, Orpheus, Dionysus, Theseus, and Pirithous, among others, descended to Hades and returned. However, in what appears to be a dramatic shift, Riley points out that rather than occurring *after* death, these trips to the underworld happened while the hero of the story was "still alive"! See Riley, *Resurrection Reconsidered: Thomas and John in Controversy* (Minneapolis: Fortress, 1995), 23n46. This introduces yet another potential angle on the views that have been discussed throughout this chapter. Riley's thoughts from Homer to Plato (*Resurrection Reconsidered*, 23–34) would present an interesting contrast to Porter's treatment of Homer and the Greek views ("Resurrection," 68–71) as well.

Likewise, N. T. Wright argues very strongly over several hundred pages against many of the various aspects of what might be thought of as the reversed-order theses propagated by Finney, Endsjø, Porter, and Litwa above. See Wright, *The Resurrection of the Son of God*, vol. 3 of *Christian Origins and the Question of God* (Minneapolis: Fortress, 2003), particularly chaps. 2–5. Other strong critiques of several items found in these newer theses above can be found in Michael R. Licona, *The Resurrection of Jesus: A New Historiographical Approach* (Downers Grove, IL: InterVarsity Academic, 2010), esp. 400–37; Robert H. Gundry, *Sōma in Biblical Theology: With Emphasis on Pauline Anthropology* (Cambridge: Cambridge University Press, 1976), 159–83; and Cook, *Empty Tomb*, particularly the detailed introduction and chaps. 1–2, plus Cook's review of Finney's volume, as mentioned above. Even Bousset, the best-known representative of the nineteenth-century *religionsgeschichtliche Schule*, also favored the traditional position in the comparison between the Hellenistic versus the majority Hebrew and nearly unanimous Christian positions in the early church (*Kyrios Christos*, 256, for one of the examples among many that could be chosen).

termed "resurrections" are frequently missing too, while other heroes disappear and appear again with neither a death nor a resurrection.

Examples that illustrate these many difficulties are easily located. Though being closer to the Cook-Mettinger side of the dialogue while surveying three prime candidates as significant examples of dying-and-rising figures (Asclepius, Heracles, and Romulus), M. David Litwa admits that there are doubts regarding whether the last two actually died at all. He notes further that whatever the bottom line is here, the deaths of these figures at least are not emphasized.[87] Riley lists more than a half dozen of these figures who descended to Hades "while still alive." Riley's observation would clearly disallow resurrections in these cases.[88] In a very crucial summary comment, Jonathan Z. Smith even reports that "*it is now held that the majority of the gods* so denoted appear to have died but not returned; there is death but no rebirth or resurrection."[89]

Continuing, atheist New Testament scholar Bart Ehrman goes even further. After commenting that Osiris never "returned to life on earth by being raised" Ehrman states, "In fact, no ancient source says any such thing about Osiris (or about the other gods)."[90] As was noted above, another New Testament skeptic, Helmut Koester, agrees concerning Osiris in particular: "To be sure, Osiris died and became lord of the realm of the dead, but it is never said that he rose."[91] Summarizing the matter and concluding that Jonathan Z. Smith is correct on the question of the dying-and-rising gods, Ehrman states, "Some die but don't return; some disappear without dying and do return; but *none of them die and return*."[92]

Some may assert that only a few clear cases are needed to hypothesize a general ethos here, with even more examples making the situation all the merrier. But that's the chief question: Are these perhaps uncommon or even rare examples actually available? Mark Smith's point should be remembered too that Frazer pieced together a *composite* picture, creating a makeshift case that brought together elements from many different cases.[93]

---

[87] Litwa, "We Worship," 171.

[88] Riley, *Resurrection Reconsidered*, 23n46.

[89] J. Z. Smith, *Drudgery Divine*, 100–101 (emphasis added). After noting this, Smith provides several examples as illustrations.

[90] Ehrman, *Did Jesus Exist?*, 26, also 222.

[91] Koester, *Introduction to the New Testament*, 1:190.

[92] Ehrman, *Did Jesus Exist?*, 228–29 (emphasis added).

[93] M. S. Smith, "Death of 'Dying and Rising Gods,'" 310.

(2) An amazing feature in this dialogue appears to be the surprising lack of substantial overlap or major agreement that might be expected between Cook, Mettinger, and others in their general camp when it comes to which cases of dying-and-rising gods each considers to be the strongest instances. This is especially so since they seemingly hold quite similar philosophical positions on these matters, issuing into the position that there are *indeed* dying-and-rising gods. Cook apparently prefers Osiris, Horus, Dionysus, and Melqart/Heracles. Mettinger favors Dumuzi, Baal, Melqart, and possibly Osiris. Osiris and Melqart/Heracles are the only two major mythical figures shared in common here. But further, Cook states his apparent lack of high regard for Dumuzi, Baal, and Adonis, whereas Dumuzi and Baal are Mettinger's favorites! Then, Cook elevates Horus and Dionysus, while the other commentators in this chapter, including Mettinger, barely even discuss and evaluate them.[94] Even worse, of a combinational preferred list between Cook and Mettinger, *most* of their purported dying-and-rising gods are debased or largely ignored by the other scholars here!

The different emphases between these two excellent scholars in regard to their favorite cases is quite noticeable. To be sure, Cook and Mettinger are both straightforward concerning a number of weaknesses in their positions, too. But here is the huge consideration at this juncture: given that Cook and Mettinger are two of the very best researchers on this subject, and assuming that they are tightly matched on their knowledge of the specifics as well as being close in their overall perspectives, why is there the seeming distance between their best-case scenarios?[95] Further, why do the additional differences exist on the examples that Cook almost dismisses while Mettinger readily appreciates? It is of course true that two close scholars can disagree in their positions. Yet this example is a little more direct: the specific cases preferred by one seem frequently not valued as highly in evidential terms by the other, yet they are both so seemingly and firmly convinced of the data regarding their own arguments. This causes one to wonder if Cook or Mettinger actually agrees with the criticisms that have been made by those on the opposite side of the fence?

---

[94] As already mentioned above, Cook, *Empty Tomb*, esp. 143; Mettinger, *Riddle of Resurrection*, 217–18.

[95] See, for example, Cook's praise of Mettinger's major work here: "It is the most comprehensive investigation of the problem since the original study by Frazer. . . . My debt to Mettinger's analysis will be readily apparent in the references below." Cook, *Empty Tomb*, 61, cf. also 57.

To restate the matter, if the best cases between these two close positions are presumably the ones that are accompanied by the strongest empirical evidence, then why does a comparison not yield far more common ground between them? Sure, there are always the customary allowances to be made between differing views and interpretations, and that could certainly be the key here as well. But when the overall perspectives are so close, one is inclined to question in a case of this nature if it is primarily the specific data that are chiefly being evaluated somewhat differently. Could the divergent views be due primarily to the force of the criticisms from the two Smiths, Metzger, Wagner, Yamauchi, or others on the "other" side? Of course, this is what we are endeavoring to determine.

(3) It may be helpful to zero in on a specific case of a prominent dying-and-rising god in order to compare the two major sets of interpretations. Melqart/Heracles is one of two major dying-and-rising gods (the other being Osiris) for which both Cook and Mettinger express strong support.[96] In Cook's defense, simply a plethora of data are presented in favor of this god's death and resurrection. The many pieces of evidence include writings, inscriptions, and an especially helpful stone vase that Cook describes in great detail. In these multiple sources in the ancient Near Eastern world, Melqart is variously declared, praised, or pictured as being resuscitated or as a "resuscitator."[97]

As mentioned above, one of Cook's particularly intriguing arguments in this context is taken from Josephus, who makes more than one relevant comment on this subject. In one instance while speaking about the region of Tyre (where Melqart was thought of as the lord), Josephus refers to the celebration of "the awakening of Heracles." The language here (especially the use of the Greek verb *egeirō*) is employed in other contexts by Josephus to indicate "resuscitation" or even "resurrection."[98] The verb is also one of the major New Testament words used to describe Jesus's own resurrection. Witnessing this verb being used by the Jewish historian Josephus is particularly helpful too, given the often-stricter language used predominantly in Jewish circles during the time of Second Temple Judaism.

Mettinger reviews much of the evidence as well, using very technical scholarly analysis and ancient language study. His overview includes providing a very helpful

---

[96] It may be recalled above that Litwa also considers Heracles to be one of the better-established dying-and-rising gods in "We Worship," 171.

[97] Cook, *Empty Tomb*, 124–27, 131–32.

[98] Cook, 127–29.

depiction of the four-sided vase described by Cook, along with helpful summaries of the arguments and subconclusions along the way.[99] Mettinger also expresses frustrations on a few occasions with various problems regarding either the state of some data itself or with the way critics argue against the case for Melqart/Heracles.[100]

How would the likes of Jonathan Z. Smith and Mark Smith, among other scholars who oppose these arguments, respond to this amassed data? A few of the details mentioned earlier in this chapter should provide the gist of their replies. It is admitted on all sides, including by Cook and Mettinger, that the data are not as clear as the straightforward way the arguments are often presented. Much nuance is absolutely required.

Mark Smith raises an abundance of problems with a positive case here. Sometimes the exact identity of the god or another person being addressed in the particular text must be guessed or assumed, for the subject of the story is too often missing, unclear, or simply unidentified.[101] Mettinger concedes this point of identity, acknowledging that "we must be open to the possibility that an other [sic] deity than Melqart may be envisioned."[102]

Further, the alternative translation of a number of these references need not be "resurrected" at all, but simply "awakened." Obviously, then, the latter may refer to sleeping, as when Elijah taunted the prophets of Baal by charging that their god may be asleep (1 Kgs 18:27).[103] Both Cook and Mettinger acknowledge this issue as well.[104]

Concerning Josephus's seemingly helpful comments regarding the worship of Heracles in Tyre, Mark Smith points out, "The evidence came secondhand to Josephus, and it is hard to know what to make of these texts' reliability as a source for understanding the cult of Herakles." Thus, in procuring the information from another source, key ideas could have been confused as well. Besides, when Josephus employs the same Greek root (*egeirō*) in another work, *Against Apion*, while discussing Tyre and the cult of Heracles, it is apparently used in reference to the erection of

---

[99] Mettinger, *Riddle of Resurrection*, 83–103, with the representation and description of the vase on 100, with the argument summaries and conclusions on 90–95 and 102–3.

[100] Mettinger, 89, 93. At one point he makes a somewhat humorous swipe at Mark Smith: "He grants the evidence the benefit of maximal doubt" (84).

[101] M. S. Smith, "Death of 'Dying and Rising Gods,'" 279, 282.

[102] Mettinger, *Riddle of Resurrection*, 109.

[103] M. S. Smith, "Death of 'Dying and Rising Gods,'" esp. 277–79.

[104] Cook, *Empty Tomb*, particularly 127, also 129; Mettinger, *Riddle of Resurrection*, 88.

temples.[105] Both Cook and Mettinger admit these issues in Josephus. It was mentioned that Mettinger refers to the Josephus citations as an aggravating puzzle and has even deemed them hopeless.[106]

Still another problem according to Mark Smith is the mixing and matching of various accounts from the ancient Near East and elsewhere: "It is still unknown that the traditions at the opposite ends of the Mediterranean basin were uniform."[107] But as already mentioned, we cannot assume that the different portions of perhaps diverse accounts can be combined and reconciled in this manner, as if they addressed the same content.

While Cook and Mettinger acknowledge a number of Mark Smith's critiques, there are a few issues over which there is genuine disagreement. Two major examples concern the death and resurrection of Melqart/Heracles. Smith questions both aspects. Regarding Melqart, Smith claims firmly that "no text provides information about the putative death of the god."[108] Smith asserts the same concerning Heracles.[109] One problem here is the contradictory reports on how this event supposedly occurred, whether by the more normal process of death and burial or due to the god's body being consumed on a funeral pyre. While still noting the problems at this juncture, Smith appears to have fewer problems here, since he seems to conclude that the interpretation of death still makes sense.

However, even if a death may be inferred, Smith especially draws the line at the notion of resurrection. He states, "It should not be assumed that any resurrection was involved." Even on some of the assumptions and suggested reconstructions, there is virtually no information or description on this aspect.[110]

Finally, Smith questions the presence of ritual or cultic connection with Melqart/Heracles.[111] We have seen that at least Cook rejects the ritual aspect of Smith's definition, while Mettinger disputes it in the case of Melqart/Heracles.[112]

In conclusion regarding this third discussion point, should Melqart/Heracles be considered as a dying-and-rising god? Those who argue affirmatively sometimes

---

[105] M. S. Smith, "Death of 'Dying and Rising Gods,'" 281–82 in particular.

[106] Cook, *Empty Tomb*, 127–28; Mettinger, *Riddle of Resurrection*, 89.

[107] M. S. Smith, "Death of 'Dying and Rising Gods,'" 282.

[108] M. S. Smith, 279.

[109] M. S. Smith, 282.

[110] M. S. Smith, 282.

[111] M. S. Smith, 282.

[112] Cook, *Empty Tomb*, 57–58; Mettinger, *Riddle of Resurrection*, 110.

point to utilizing a shortened definition that requires fewer information checkpoints. Then, the question turns on whether it can be argued successfully that Melqart/ Heracles was considered a god, that he died, and that he then was observed afterward. Scholars like Cook, Mettinger, Litwa, and others have marshaled various sorts of data in support of each of these three criteria of deity, death, and resurrection.

Those who argue negatively, such as Mark Smith, make use of a more detailed definition for a dying-and-rising god, afterward offering numerous critiques of the affirmative proposals in each of the three areas listed above. Scholars like Cook and Mettinger more or less agree with about half of Smith's critiques while offering rejoinders to the others.

It appears that when the smoke has settled, the result is a fairly even argument, with scholars and other readers then making their own judgments. As Mark Smith states seeming fairly, "There is simply insufficient evidence to prove the case or to dismiss it entirely." He concludes that the solution is very difficult to ascertain and that it is better to conclude that the reconstruction "remains hypothetical."[113] According to this route, it is a very difficult task to prove that one argument or interpretation should rank head and shoulders above the other. This is particularly the case when a wrong turn in one or more of several key places for discussion could cause much or even most of the entire knot to unravel.

But it must also be borne in mind that Melqart/Heracles may present the strongest case in the ancient world in terms of the actual evidence on behalf of a particular dying-and-rising god, as mentioned earlier. This was the reason for showcasing this example. *If* in fact this is the best scenario for the affirmative position, where do the other less-demonstrated examples stand? At the very least, since Melqart/Heracles is certainly *one* of the very best examples, that may indicate some difficulties for those who wish to make a strong case on behalf either of the dying-and-rising gods in general, or especially so for those who may care to argue that *many* strong cases obtain. We will continue to push forward for an answer here.[114]

Regarding the overall question of whether there are any cases of pre-Christian dying-and-rising gods, it would seem that the Melqart/Heracles case may serve to determine the path here, at least in the sense of verified examples of these accounts.

---

[113] M. S. Smith, "Death of 'Dying and Rising Gods,'" esp. 277–82, quotations on 279.

[114] No doubt some will appreciate and perhaps agree with this conclusion to this third consideration, while others may not. Of course, many will press onward to their own conclusions. That has always been the case with arguments.

As mentioned in the very first consideration above, it is difficult to analyze ancient texts, inscriptions, pottery, and so on that are dated several hundred years or even longer before the New Testament period. There are so many lacunae, missing pieces, undecipherable passages, and words that can have multiple meanings that often occur in the very worst places for this research, not to mention modern interpretations of this lost or jumbled material that have been proven false when new data are discovered.

Several of these issues were present in some of the Melqart/Heracles material dealt with earlier, including missing names of the gods, a lack of explicit deaths, contradictory versions of key events, the two apparent meanings of *egeirō/egersis* used by Josephus, the mixing of geographically and philosophically different texts to obtain a sense of what is being taught, the lack of distinctions in the meanings of terms for "awakened" or "raised," and so on. These can be exceptionally crucial issues that are not necessarily solvable dilemmas.

Perhaps in large part due to the plethora of individual problems, either these questions or similar scenarios could account for our second perspective above as to why Cook, Mettinger, and other scholars *within the same interpretive camp that favors the existence of resurrected gods* still disagree about the best and worst examples of dying-and-rising gods. But further, by undercutting the arguments of their colleagues, these scholars can actually showcase the fact that the best cases preferred by others are not necessarily so exemplary!

The bottom line here is quite difficult, to say the least. Whether or not it can be determined on all these various notions of awakenings, rebirths, returns (especially from the underworld), and possibly even resurrections following actual deaths as well as comprising genuine raisings to new lives seems almost impossible to conclude with any assurance. Further, in case there are genuine examples of raisings, do these beings die again like Lazarus or do they become immortal?

All told, it would appear that the best conclusion to our first question is to extend the specific judgment regarding Melqart/Heracles to serve as the overall response to whether or not there are any such examples of dying-and-rising gods. The issue appears to have ended in a stalemate, one that is potentially even unanswerable, largely due at least to the current, often unfortunate state of the ancient data. Moreover, from a different epistemic angle, even if there were some cases of dying-and-rising gods, it seems extraordinarily difficult to *demonstrate* factually that this was the case. After a highly detailed study, Wagner asserts a potentially helpful observation here: "The mystery religion *par excellence* has never existed, and quite certainly did not in the first century A.D."[115] Of course, one may disagree with Wagner at this point, but the alternative argument that avoids all the pitfalls mentioned above would have to be demonstrated clearly. The overall response, then, may lean just slightly to the denial that dying-and-rising gods predated Jesus, but again, this is difficult to ascertain.

Major Question Two

Did any pre-Christian tales of dying-and-rising gods influence seriously the New Testament resurrection and appearance accounts, as per some proponents of the older German *religionsgeschichtliche Schule*? Are these former views still held by many critical scholars today?

What about this second key inquiry? Could any potential accounts of ancient dying-and-rising gods, or even that general ethos or attitude that surrounded these tales, have influenced the New Testament teaching of Jesus's resurrection and appearances in whole or in part? Asked from another angle, could any such pre-Christian stories serve as a viable naturalistic hypothesis against the resurrection, as held at the end of the old German liberal heyday under the influence of the history of religions scholars.

It will simply be mentioned at the outset that by far the stance even of critical scholars across the board is to reject the thesis that the apostolic teachings of Jesus's resurrection were in any way invented or influenced seriously by any dying-and-rising mythical accounts of the past. For instance, it has already been noted that Bart Ehrman has criticized these scenarios in no uncertain terms in a lengthy response.[116] Numerous other critical scholars have also repudiated these mythical positions, as will be illustrated in more detail below. This general rejection was occasioned by at least ten objections.

First, the historical life, death, and reported resurrection appearances of Jesus stand in marked contrast to the totally, or at least chiefly, mythical characters involved in the dying-and-rising scenarios. Writing less than a century after Jesus's crucifixion, Plutarch reminded his readers of this very point when composing his story of Isis and Osiris, mainly, that the contrast should be apparent between the lives of truly

---

[115] Günter Wagner, *Pauline Baptism and the Pagan Mysteries: The Problem of the Pauline Doctrine of Baptism in Romans VI.1–11 in the Light of Its Religio-Historical 'Parallels'* (Edinburgh: Oliver & Boyd, 1967), 268.

[116] Ehrman, *Did Jesus Exist?*, 207–30.

historical persons and those heroes of the tall tales. As Plutarch states concerning Isis and Osiris, "You must remember what has been already said, and you must not think that any of these tales actually happened in the manner in which they are related."[117] Later in the same story, Plutarch adds, "We must not treat legend as if it were history at all, but we should adopt that which is appropriate."[118]

This initial criticism arises time and again throughout these discussions. For instance, former Princeton Seminary Greek scholar Bruce Metzger also leveled this critique rather forcefully: "A most profound difference between Christianity and the Mysteries was involved in the historical basis of the former and the mythological character of the latter." After all, Jesus was "a real Person on earth only a short time before the earliest documents of the New Testament were written."[119] Even Cook acknowledges this criticism clearly in what he terms his "major point" concerning the dying-and-rising gods: "None of the figures from the history of ancient Mediterranean religions are 'live options' for faith any longer. . . . Dionysus, Osiris, Heracles, and Attis are mythical beings who never existed."[120]

Second, an additional point follows from this initial objection. There is plenty of evidence for various aspects in the life of the historical Jesus in areas such as his central preaching message of the kingdom of God, his self-reference as both the Son of God and the Son of Man, and his healings and exorcisms. The empty tomb is also supported by many independent pieces of historical data. Moreover, the data that we have identified as the minimal historical facts, which support the reports of Jesus's resurrection appearances, are also highly significant and are supported by virtually all critical scholars. Many more historical events and nuances can be verified as well.[121]

Third, that no historical evidence to speak of exists in favor of any dying-and-rising god scenarios goes without mentioning. Even those ancient figures who may just possibly have some partial historical roots are not accompanied by sources

---

[117] See *Isis and Osiris* 11 (*Moralia* 355b). Translation from Plutarch, *Moralia. Isis and Osiris*, trans. Frank Cole Babbitt (Cambridge: Harvard University Press, 1911).

[118] Plutarch, *Isis and Osiris* 58 (*Moralia* 374e).

[119] Metzger, "Methodology," 13.

[120] John Granger Cook, "Resurrection in Paganism and the Resurrection of Jesus Christ," *The City* (Houston Baptist University), September 9, 2016, https://hc.edu/news-and-events/2016/09/09/resurrection-paganism-resurrection-jesus-christ/.

[121] See volume 1 of this resurrection series for dozens of considerations in further support of these comments above.

temporally close to the events in question to provide adequate evidence whatsoever.[122] Further, the documents are often in terrible enough shape that many of the relevant questions cannot even be answered. What about the mythological stories of living six months of the year in the underworld? Particularly when the claims in question concern the possibility of resurrections and the like, this lack of evidence presents massive differences with the New Testament accounts. There is simply an enormous contrast in the historical disparity between the two positions.

Fourth, phenomenologically, New Testament statements regarding Jesus's resurrection appearances by their very nature employ the language of sight. In other words, statements or descriptions pertaining to Jesus being present with his followers again after his crucifixion are always explained in terms of those who saw him. Never is the sense given that this doctrine was simply a thought drawn from copying religious teachings garnered from other foreign (especially pagan) ideas or systems. Nor did the conviction arise as merely being due to some inner conviction or insight, to a lie or misunderstanding, or to hearing about some faith healer somewhere.

To the contrary, since this is the unanimous nature of the earliest appearance statements, justice must be done to what was at least claimed. Whether natural or supernatural hypotheses are proposed as explanations for these occurrences, they must account for the statements that human sight was involved, or commentators will be guilty of responding to teachings other than the combined message of the very earliest claims. This is recognized by the majority of both critical and believing scholars alike across a very diverse theoretical landscape.[123]

---

[122] For details and specific responses, see Gary R. Habermas, "Resurrection Claims in Non-Christian Religions," *Religious Studies* 25 (1989): 167–77.

[123] A comparative sample of the wide range of scholars across theological positions and resurrection views who nonetheless acknowledge this point regarding the language of sight include the following: Gerd Lüdemann, *The Resurrection of Jesus: History, Experience, Theology*, trans. John Bowden (Minneapolis: Fortress, 1994), 30–31, 177; Ehrman, *Did Jesus Exist?*, 249, 252, 257–58; Geza Vermes, *The Resurrection* (London: Penguin, 2008), 121–22, 141–42, 147–49; Dale C. Allison Jr., *Resurrecting Jesus: The Earliest Christian Tradition and Its Interpreters* (London: T&T Clark, 2005), 249, 343–44, 346; James D. G. Dunn, *Jesus Remembered*, vol. 1 of *Christianity in the Making* (Grand Rapids: Eerdmans, 2003), 854–57, 861–62; Luke Timothy Johnson, *The Real Jesus: The Misguided Quest for the Historical Jesus and the Truth of the Traditional Gospels* (New York: HarperCollins, 1996), esp. 119–20; Larry W. Hurtado, *How on Earth Did Jesus Become a God? Historical Questions about Earliest Devotion to Jesus* (Grand Rapids: Eerdmans, 2005), 30, 36, 48, 192; E. P. Sanders, *The Historical Figure of Jesus* (London: Penguin, 1993), 11, 13, 278, 280; Pinchas Lapide, *The*

The significance of this fourth theme cannot be overestimated in terms of this chapter. The more it is known that the sight of Jesus's disciples and others was involved, the more it is known that the far away stories of dying-and-rising gods fail to fit the conditions here, at least not as any sort of primary causal thesis. It would seem that this critique alone weighs exceptionally heavily in dismissing the naturalistic dying-and-rising gods thesis here. As Wolfhart Pannenberg noted years ago after noting the nature of the historical evidence for Jesus's resurrection: "Under such circumstances, it is an idle venture to make parallels in the history of religions responsible for the *emergence* of the primitive Christian message about Jesus's resurrection."[124] The point here is that whatever is thought of the dying-and-rising gods theses, since we are dealing with the disciples' *sight* as the chief mechanism, ancient stories do not possess the requirements to explain at least the very earliest beginnings of Christianity.

Fifth, an absolutely crucial logical point must also be raised here. Even if some of the comparisons discussed above were tighter than they in fact were, similarities simply do not prove causal connections. In other words, even if the comparisons between the ancient mysteries and Jesus's life were closer, this is still not the same as demonstrating that some of these similar ideas actually *caused* the later ones. Too many other possibilities could also explain these related concepts. This requires a far

---

Resurrection of Jesus: A Jewish Perspective (Minneapolis: Augsburg, 1983), 15–16, 92, 95–99, 125, 127–28; John Dominic Crossan, *The Historical Jesus: The Life of a Mediterranean Jewish Peasant* (New York: HarperCollins, 1991), 435–36, cf. 407; Crossan, "Dialogue," in John Dominic Crossan and N. T. Wright, *The Resurrection of Jesus: John Dominic Crossan and N. T. Wright in Dialogue*, ed. Robert S. Stewart (Minneapolis: Fortress, 2006), 31, 33, 177; Marcus J. Borg, *Jesus, A New Vision: Spirit, Culture, and the Life of Discipleship* (New York: HarperCollins, 1987), esp. 184–85; Borg, "Thinking about Easter," *Bible Review* 10 (1994): 15, 49; Reginald H. Fuller, *The Formation of the Resurrection Narratives*, 2nd ed. (Minneapolis: Fortress, 1980), 47–49, 182; Raymond E. Brown, *The Virginal Conception and Bodily Resurrection of Jesus* (New York: Paulist, 1973), 78–96; Gerald O'Collins, *Jesus Risen: The Resurrection—What Actually Happened and What Does It Mean?* (London: Darton, Longman, & Todd, 1987), particularly 118–19, also 100–109; Wright, *Resurrection of the Son of God*, 317–29, 476–79; Richard Bauckham, *Jesus and the Eyewitnesses: The Gospels as Eyewitness Testimony* (Grand Rapids: Eerdmans, 2006), 264–71, 307–8; Licona, *Resurrection of Jesus*, 329–33, 468–69; Paul Barnett, Peter Jensen, and David Peterson, *Resurrection: Truth and Reality* (Sydney: Aquila, 1994), 23; Keener, *Historical Jesus of the Gospels*, 342–44.

[124] Wolfhart Pannenberg, *Jesus: God and Man*, trans. Lewis L. Wilkins and Duane A. Priebe, 2nd ed. (Philadelphia: Westminster, 1977), 91.

tighter argument than any that has been shown here.[125] This is one of the key reasons why some of the researchers above distinguish between analogy and genealogy. There are various sorts of the former that do *not* at all indicate the latter. As Jonathan Z. Smith asserts succinctly, "Analogies do not yield genealogies."[126] In fact, genealogy is specifically stated *not* to be in view in some of these studies.[127]

Plus, the *differences* between systems must also be considered, as well—how distinct are the contrasts between them? As Metzger asserts wisely, when specifically comparing the mystery religions and Christianity: "The formal resemblance between the two, however, must not be allowed to obscure the great difference in content."[128] More recent commentators have remarked that Frazer spun too many of his ancient stories so that the similarities stood out as being more substantial than the differences, causing this oversight to be one of the reasons for the demise of the entire thesis of the *religionsgeschichtliche Schule*.[129]

These initial five critiques are highly significant in that they probably represent the most crucial and demarcating contrasts between the mystery beliefs and those of the New Testament, arguing that these belief systems are not just different, but actually quite opposed to each other and in the most vital and essential areas as well. Even so, there are still additional considerations that increase the degree of separation here.

Sixth, while researchers almost always single out the initial element above regarding Jesus's historicity as contrasted with the more or less mythical dying-and-rising heroes, an additional development is that several of Jesus's individual actions and teachings were quite original. Equally important though, Jesus's theological and ethical themes were grounded in particular ideas that could be traced to the Old Testament and other ancient Semitic contexts and ideas. At the same time, Jesus's teachings were often also quite unique in nature, moving far beyond these points. In other words, Jesus's milieu both originated in the context of his time, as well as being

---

[125] Similar points are made by Eddy and Boyd, *Jesus Legend*, 145; Keener, *Historical Jesus of the Gospels*, 334; O'Collins, *Jesus Risen*, 103; Thorwald Lorenzen, *Resurrection and Discipleship: Interpretive Models, Biblical Reflections, Theological Consequences* (Maryknoll, NY: Orbis, 1995), 117–19.

[126] J. Z. Smith, *Divine Drudgery*, 104.

[127] J. Z. Smith, 47–51, 112–14, 118; Cook, *Empty Tomb*, 57–58, also 7, 69; Metzger, "Methodology," 12, 14, 17–18, 24.

[128] Metzger, 18.

[129] M. S. Smith, "Death of 'Dying and Rising Gods,'" particularly 310–13.

uniquely different from the Greco-Roman and ancient Near Eastern cultures. This could well explain some of his incomparable influence.

The principal thrust of this sixth point is that there is virtually no reason to trace Jesus's actions or teachings to origins in the mystery religions or as reflecting elements from among the dying-and-rising mythical themes. Discovering the roots of Jesus's world-changing ideas flows from a far more direct and meaningful source.

Moving in this same direction, Wagner published a study that illustrated these and additional trends. He produced twenty-two *theological* considerations against the thesis that the mystery religions gave rise to (or affected severely) the New Testament teachings regarding the early Christian practice of baptism, including the death and resurrection of Jesus. The following seven reflections are among the stronger contentions that Wagner concluded separated Christianity from the mystery systems drawn from both Jesus's life as well as Paul's teachings: (1) Paul never even utilizes many of the same terms that he is often blamed with adopting from the mystery belief systems.[130] (2) The only key words that do overlap between Paul and the mystery sources are also present in Judaism. Further, when this common language is used, Paul utilizes totally different meanings than those employed in the mysteries, favoring the Jewish sources and their meanings.[131] (3) The New Testament teaching that Jesus's death paid for sin is never taught of the dying-and-rising gods.[132] (4) The death and resurrection of Jesus were *onetime events* rather than a "mythisches Drama" (mythical drama).[133] For example, this is a key theme to the arguments in the book of Hebrews, which emphasizes the unique, never-to-be-repeated death of Jesus.[134] (5) The death and resurrection of Jesus are "salvation-events"—nothing like the mystery gods who often died by unrelated incidents, such as being killed on a hunt or by personal emasculation or by the evil gods from the underworld, and so on.[135] (6) Contrary to the initiations in the mystery religions, Christian baptism signified and typified a connection based on real historical events derived strictly from Jesus's life and the gospel message.[136] (7) The mystery conception of a magical imparting of

---

[130] Wagner, *Das religionsgeschichtliche Problem*, 283–84.

[131] Wagner, 287–88.

[132] Wagner, 297.

[133] Wagner, 297.

[134] For instances, see Heb 5:8–9; 7:24; 9:12, 25–28; 10:12.

[135] Wagner, *Das religionsgeschichtliche Problem*, 297.

[136] Wagner, 298. Wagner adds, "Ist noch kein einziger Text aus den Schriften der apostolischen und der Kirchen-Väter vorgelegt worden, in dem Röm 6 unter Hinweis

benefits to those who were baptized is in full contrast to the radical faith-surrender required of Christian believers as they grew utterly committed to God and others while in this world.[137]

Other key distinctions of various sorts could be listed between Jesus and Paul on the one side and the dying-and-rising gods on the other, but these above should be sufficient to make the general point. There are both serious and major contrasts that argue clearly that the very center of the Christian faith, especially at the specific point of the gospel message, is significantly independent and unrelated to the teachings associated with the ancient gods and goddesses.

Seventh, besides Wagner's theological areas of critique, a ceremonial aspect also needs to be considered. We saw earlier that Cook offered what he termed "an attenuated sense" of the required characteristics of dying-and-rising gods that disagreed with Mark Smith's definition, in that Cook expunged the last two of Smith's four markers.[138] The last definitional indicator that is supported by the likes of Mark Smith and Jonathan Z. Smith but rejected by Cook and others concerns the presence of rituals that provide a basis for a cultic recitation of the mystery myths. Although there are various disagreements among the commentators as to the extent to which the dying-and-rising god accounts incorporated these elements, as noted above, the two Smiths charge that rituals were quite often absent from these pre-Christian tales. But a lack of cultic celebrations here may hint that any possible rebirth or rising portions of these mythologies do not occupy the central perspective in these belief systems.[139]

If this is indeed the case, then such a lack of ritual and potentially also the notion of centrality for the dying-and-rising portions of the mystery accounts would of course be a major contrast that is very much unlike the place given to the death and resurrection of Jesus within Christianity, where this message is at the very epicenter

---

auf oder im Gegensatz zu 'analogen' Riten oder Erfahrungen (symbolisches Sterben und Auferstehen) der Attis-, Adonis-, oder Osirismysten gedeutet worden ist" (Habermas's basic translation/paraphrase: "Not a single text from the writings of the apostolic community and the church fathers has been produced where Romans 6 was interpreted in terms of analogous rites or experiences from the dying-and-rising cases of Attis, Adonis, or Osiris"). Metzger agrees that the differences on the subject of baptism are the most obvious of all between these belief systems in "Methodology," 15–17.

[137] Wagner, *Das religionsgeschichtliche Problem*, 298.

[138] Cook, *Empty Tomb*, 57–58.

[139] M. S. Smith, "Death of 'Dying and Rising Gods,'" esp. 313, cf. also 279, 310.

of New Testament teaching. This would then serve as another potential indication that these ancient pre-Christian Mediterranean tales were neither the basis for nor a major influence upon the Christian accounts.

Eighth, comparing the roots of major worldview concerns offers a direct challenge to the thesis that ancient Mediterranean and Near Eastern myths influenced Christianity in a major way. Important studies by scholars like N. T. Wright and Mark Smith, among many others, charge that the most crucial background for understanding the Christian ideas about bodily resurrection come from Judaism rather than any pagan belief systems.[140]

Ninth, Jonathan Z. Smith (as well as others) has added a last powerful insight. Probably the predominant scene in the dying-and-rising god's tales is that of a hero or heroine descending to the underworld and returning again after some prescribed amount of time (often for six months) as long as another person had agreed to take their place. As Smith points out, there is no way that these events can be termed resurrections at all. This is because in all of these specific scenarios, hell, Hades, or the underworld is paramount. The rules and requirements are those of hell, not those of heaven. But a hell-dominated return to earth is not to be confused with a heavenly resurrection. And while the persons reside in hell, it is anything but a trip to eternal life, the celestial heights, or even to the Emerald City! If that were not true, why would they care to return repeatedly to the world above in the first place rather than simply staying and seeking to enjoy themselves in the nether realm?

Jonathan Smith describes the problem powerfully in these words: "The myth emphasizes the inalterable power of the realm of the dead, not triumph over it." Then Smith continues: "Such alternation is not what is usually meant in the literature when speaking of a deity's 'rising.'"[141] That this view is neither a resurrection nor an example to inspire Christian teachings to emulate needs to be acknowledged!

Tenth, Metzger reminds his readers that the mystery religions differ from New Testament teachings in the very heart of their notions regarding the philosophy of history. The former were typically concerned with "the cyclical recurrence of the seasons . . . leading nowhere." Conversely, for Christians, "the time-process comprises

---

[140] Wright, *Resurrection of the Son of God*, particularly chaps. 2–4; M. S. Smith, "Death of 'Dying and Rising Gods,'" 312.

[141] J. Z. Smith, "Dying and Rising Gods," 4:2539. Cf. Metzger, who points to this problem as well in "Methodology," 21.

a unique series of events, and the most significant of these events was the death and resurrection of Jesus Christ."[142]

Eleventh, we may return to a lesson from history. Even going back to the *religionsgeschichtliche Schule* of the late nineteenth and early twentieth centuries, though some lines of influence were certainly thought to exist, the scholars usually stopped short of thinking that these ancient tales actually gave rise to the key New Testament accounts. For example, the most influential scholar in this school, Wilhelm Bousset, argued that the foundations of the early Christian resurrection beliefs were built, first and foremost, on the unique and incomparable personality and teachings of the historical Jesus. For Bousset, the second basis for resurrection belief was the visions of the risen Jesus that the early disciples thought that they had experienced.[143] Thus, though he was convinced that the pre-Christian tales of dying-and-rising gods clearly existed, Bousset did not conclude that these stories directly caused the disciples' beliefs and the teachings regarding Jesus's resurrection appearances, which originated from Jesus's influence and the postmortem visions.[144]

Likewise, another major *religionsgeschichtliche Schule* proponent, Otto Pfleiderer, took a position similar to Bousset's response above. In addressing this subject, Pfleiderer agreed that there were many cases of dying-and-rising gods and delineated a large number of them.[145] However, one very serious research problem with the scholars in this era, and for Pfleiderer in particular, is that they too seldom, if ever, differentiate the origin of these myths in terms of the dates or other key markers for each. Hence, post-Christian resurrection stories might be grouped along with earlier accounts. This frequently resulted in a jumbled assortment of heterogeneous stories being indiscriminately lumped together side by side without distinctions of date, culture, geographical location, and so on.[146]

---

[142] Metzger, "Methodology," 23.

[143] Bousset, *Kyrios Christos*, 49–52. Coming close to some of the same differences mentioned above, beyond the foundations that were supplied by Jesus Christ himself and then by the disciples' postmortem visions of Jesus, the overall background was also gathered from the Old Testament teachings (49). Presumably the Mediterranean dying-and-rising ideas provided some added background impetus here as well.

[144] Bousset, 56–59, 191–194.

[145] See Pfleiderer, *Early Christian Conception of Christ*, chap. 4.

[146] See Pfleiderer, where Romulus (108), Mithras (121, 133, 155), Adonis (94, 99), and Attis (94–95, 99) are among those who are cited, in spite of serious historical issues like those that have been pointed out above. True, very little of this may have been known

Specifically regarding Jesus's resurrection, Pfleiderer acknowledged that though there were many such dying-and-rising myths, neither their existence nor this wide-ranging ethos around the Mediterranean world and beyond could explain the resurrection. Like Bousset, the chief overall reason here is because the example of Jesus was situated in history rather than in mythology. Further, the rise of the resurrection belief was occasioned more specifically by Jesus's postmortem visions, as reported by his disciples, and not by their recitation of copycat scenarios. Pfleiderer summarized very directly: "But the Christian myth is not to be derived from this nature-myth, because it has its most direct source in the historical fact of the death of Jesus, and the following visions seen by his disciples."[147]

Though the dying-and-rising myths cannot explain Jesus's life, death, and resurrection visions, Pfleiderer still thought that "those parallels are surely of significance." Pfleiderer seems to think that the similarities in different religious beliefs indicate that they stem from similar human longings, as foreshadowed in many religions. Likewise, Pfleiderer also acknowledged that the many differences in belief systems need to be studied.[148] The responses of Bousset and Pfleiderer contain

---

in Pfleiderer's day. However, this lack of knowledge does not apply to the citations of a comet that was deemed to indicate that Julius Caesar had been apotheosized and made immortal, plus another reference to a Roman Senator thinking he may have seen Augustus's soul soaring through the flames of the funeral pyre (109–10), in spite of souls presumably being invisible and no one else present having mentioned the same, makes Pfleiderer's judgment seem a little questionable in matters where he did know better. The same might be said of citing Buddhist legends and using them side by side with the Christian accounts such as the Gospel of Luke (43–45). Still another example used by Pfleiderer is the miracle stories concerning Buddha, which are termed "parallels" (65–68, 71), as if Buddha's miracles were on a level playing field, such as Buddha's birth and Jesus's birth (154–55). Perhaps even the worst of the religious cases in terms of the historical data available, Krishna also gets compared to Matthew on the subjects of births (155)! To be sure, Pfleiderer thinks the Buddhist stories are legends (43, 51, 65, 71, etc.), but the closeness of the Christian sources to the events in question as compared to a cited Buddhist text, which apparently dates from close to a millennia after Buddha's birth, is just one major issue that makes Pfleiderer's comparisons rather troublesome! For details on these "parallels" from a historical viewpoint, see Edward Conze, *Buddhist Scriptures* (London: Penguin, 1959), 11–12, 34; Paul Gwynne, *Buddha, Jesus and Muhammad: A Comparative Study* (Oxford: Wiley-Blackwell, 2014), esp. 2, 5–6, 18–19.

[147] Pfleiderer, *Early Christian Conception of Christ*, 157–58, cf. 78, 102.

[148] Pfleiderer, 158–59.

a number of similarities here. To this we may also add the testimony of another very prominent German scholar, Ernst Troeltsch.[149]

It should be noted that the views of these *religionsgeschichtliche Schule* scholars are *not* being counted here as a critique of this natural thesis, since critical views one way or another do not demonstrate the truth or falsity of a view. Yet, these scholars who support this natural thesis still acknowledge freely that their thesis does not account for the resurrection teachings in the New Testament, especially when some of their reasons are the same or similar to the critiques given above. This is at least a pointer to the evaluation in this chapter.

Hence, even these German liberal scholars realized that the overall foundation of Christianity was built upon history rather than the assimilation of foreign mythologies untethered to history. These mythological tales did not occasion the founding of the church. More specifically and succinctly, these German liberal scholars correctly recognized, as do commentators today, that the New Testament resurrection teaching involved the *language of sight*—real persons thought that they had actually observed the risen Jesus visiting them in space and time. This has been mentioned many times throughout this chapter. The central point here is that while the naturalistic charge that the disciples were possibly mistaken in their claimed perceptions may still have to be answered, that charge nonetheless involved the early believer's *sight* and their *observations*, but *not* their having catered to the retelling of pagan mythical myths, legends, and stories.

Of course, it might theoretically be questioned whether some borrowing could still have taken place in spite of all these distinctions along with the critical scholarly opposition to these ideas. But a variety of the conditions just mentioned above make it far less likely than is judged by these previous scholars to be the case. As already pointed out, there is no genealogical evidence that such borrowing took place and much data indicating that it did not. Apparent similarities turn out upon closer

---

[149] Toward the close of the period of German liberalism, Ernst Troeltsch was sometimes referred to as one of the originators of the *religionsgeschichtliche Schule* and was certainly another major thinker at the end of this era (as commented by Garrett E. Paul in his introduction to the English edition below, see xv). In what could perhaps be a harbinger or even a forerunner of the later Barthian position just a few years later, Troeltsch commented that history cannot make a judgment on the resurrection: "But no insuperable difficulties stand before those who wish to hold that there was a real spiritual vision" (96). See Ernst Troeltsch, *The Christian Faith*, Fortress Texts in Modern Theology, ed. Gertrud von le Fort, trans. Garrett E. Paul, Fortress Texts in Modern Theology (Minneapolis: Fortress, 1991), also 88.

inspection not to be so with many differences besides. The Jewish origins for many or even most of these ideas further taught that pagan ideas were an abomination to God, so why look elsewhere when the roots of these ideas were near at hand, *such as Old Testament raisings from the dead*? Perhaps most of all, the New Testament language is that of *sight* and *real experiences*. Even critics allow that these encounters were truly believed to have occurred rather than representing mythic tales. Something happened to Jesus's followers, and this has to be accounted for rather than being glossed over in favor of stories from far-off lands. As Ehrman asserts, the disciples' conviction that they had seen Jesus "eventually turned the world on its ear."[150]

Conclusion

Returning to our initial comment in the treatment of the second question above, it is clearly the case that very few specialist critical scholars today think that the dying-and-rising god scenarios birthed Jesus's resurrection appearance accounts in the New Testament. Neither these ancient tales nor the general ethos emanating from them greatly or significantly influenced the Christian accounts in the sense of inspiring or formulating their central gospel message. Whether atheist, agnostic, skeptical, liberal, moderate, or conservative, there are very few, if any, scholars who charge that the ancient mystery tales can actually account completely for the New Testament resurrection data and message. Even critical scholar Robert Price, who at least *doubts* that Jesus ever existed, rejects the ancient dying-and-rising gods thesis, referring to it as "untenable."[151]

Obviously, the scholars who were surveyed earlier in this chapter who doubt or even deny that there are dying-and-rising god tales in the first place would not likely think that there is any influence here on the Christian notion of Jesus's resurrection appearances! Likewise, even the vast number of those critical scholars who think that there *were* such pre-Christian tales almost always deny such a causal thesis regarding the resurrection of Jesus.

Decades after the fall of German liberalism, specialists across the entire scholarly spectrum generally agree that the dying-and-rising gods, whether or not

---

[150] In agreement here is Bart D. Ehrman, *Jesus: Apocalyptic Prophet of the New Millennium* (Oxford: Oxford University Press, 1999), 229–31.

[151] Robert M. Price, "Is There a Place for Historical Criticism?," *Religious Studies* 27 (1991): 383 (unless of course his position has changed since that time).

they predated Jesus, neither created nor otherwise gave rise to the origins of the message that Jesus had risen from the dead and appeared to his followers.[152] This well-researched conviction is the case wherever these scholars are on the personal belief spectrum.

For example, it has been pointed out above that very influential scholars Jonathan Z. Smith, Mark S. Smith, Bruce Metzger, Günter Wagner, Bart Ehrman, Helmut Koester, Edwin Yamauchi, and Ronald Nash are all examples of those researchers who doubt or deny that there were any such pre-Christian dying-and-rising gods in the first place.[153] Add to this other scholars such as New Testament specialist Craig Keener and the former quite influential University of Chicago history of religions professor Mircea Eliade, who agree that while there *were* pre-Christian mythical dying-and-rising figures, they provide *no* real parallels to the historical Jesus.[154] Nor

---

[152] One reason for constantly specifying these terms and categories is to make it clear that only those with sufficient training are being referred to here. They of course may hold any positions they choose on these matters, but they must be specialist scholars in relevant areas. The Jesus mythers who do not possess scholarly qualifications often consider themselves to be scholars. This author has been told more than once that his scholarly counts on various historical issues are incorrect because they do not include these generally self-published, untrained mythicists. The note here is not to demean anyone, only to answer this common charge from the mythicists and other nonscholars that they need to be included in these and other counts. For further, relevant details, see Gary R. Habermas and Benjamin C. F. Shaw, "Agnostic Historical Jesus Scholars Decimate the Mythical Jesus Popularists: A Review Essay on *Jesus: Evidence and Argument or Mythicist Myths?*," *Philosophia Christi* 18 (2016): 485–95.

[153] This must be considered to be rather amazing in the cases of atheist New Testament scholar Ehrman and his skeptical counterpart Koester, or Jewish New Testament scholar Pinchas Lapide, *Resurrection of Jesus*, 124.

[154] To repeat some earlier comments, Keener lists many instances of pre-Christian dying-and-rising mythical figures (*Historical Jesus of the Gospels*, 336, esp. 582n57). Yet he is adamant enough to make a few comments in a relatively brief space that none of these accounts may be termed resurrections. These stories cannot be understood as either parallels or rivals to Jesus. Keener states rather firmly that "these are not *resurrection* appearances" (333). Nor do they serve as "parallels" to Jesus's resurrection appearances because such a definition "stretches the category of parallel too far to be useful" (334, also 336; personal emails from Keener to Habermas, May 18 and May 20, 2019).

For Eliade, like Keener, there were pre-Christian dying-and-rising gods, such as Dionysus and Osiris; see Mircea Eliade, *Patterns in Comparative Religion* (Cleveland: Meridian, 1963), 98–99. However, Eliade refers to these sorts of raisings as "periodic resurrection" (99), clearly differentiating them from Jesus's resurrection, which had no sense of "periodic" about it! Further, Eliade speaks about some of these ancient mythical

did these ancient myths influence the New Testament texts that mention Jesus's death, resurrection, and appearances. According to this long list of researchers just mentioned, we must look elsewhere for the origins of the Christian resurrection beliefs, specifically to the early creedal and other traditions and teachings in the New Testament.

On the other hand, Tryggve Mettinger and John Cook are two of the best and ablest defenders of the existence of pre-Christian dying-and-rising gods tales. Yet, neither scholar opts for the view that one, many, or all of these stories can account naturally for the origin of the early Christian resurrection message. Nor does a more general Mediterranean ethos fulfill the task. In other words, there is no antecedent naturalistic causal thesis here.

As Mettinger states, "The figures we have studied are deities. In the case of Jesus, we are confronted with a human (for whom divinity was claimed by himself and by his followers). For the disciples and for Paul, the resurrection of Jesus was a one-time, historical event that took place at one specific point in the earth's topography. The empty tomb was seen as a historical datum." Then Mettinger continues, responding more directly to our second question: "There is, as far as I am aware, no *prima facie* evidence that the death and resurrection of Jesus is a mythological construct, drawing on the myths and rites of the dying-and-rising gods of the surrounding world . . . the death and resurrection of Jesus retains its unique character in the history of religions."[155]

No matter how many pagan analogies there may have been, similarly to so many other scholars, Cook likewise finds that the Jewish background was the central forerunner to the Christian view. When coupled with the historicity of Jesus's resurrection appearances, whatever one might think of the non-Christian

---

personages where each person can "become a 'sun'" where, like the sun, they rise again every single morning (135–36). Similarly, other ancient notions involve the moon, as it rises anew daily (174–75). Certain views have sometimes been viewed as a variety of pantheism, though Eliade prefers the term "panontism" (459), including some disjunction from reality and even history, while other views embrace at least aspects of history (460–65). It would seem to be a fairly straightforward comment that, from these expressions, the senses of rising from the dead in these ancient mythic contexts where there are "periodic" resurrections and being made alive in the rising sun or in the moon are not in any sense related to the New Testament teachings. In short, there are "raisings" in these myths that seem quite unrelated to anything biblical or literal.

[155] Mettinger, *Riddle of Resurrection*, 221.

analogies, the resurrection occurred in space and time. This sets off this occurrence as a singular event.[156]

Thus, none of the recent, major scholars who participated in the dialogue throughout this chapter would answer our second question positively. None would conclude that the resurrection of Jesus can be explained naturalistically by responding that this central teaching of Christianity was a tale that was totally or mostly inspired by the dying-and-rising myths from the Mediterranean world or the Near East. Beyond that, at least three of the most influential German liberal *religionsgeschichtliche Schule* scholars of the late nineteenth and early twentieth centuries, even in the heyday of this movement, also agreed specifically that such a response would be insufficient to disprove the early church's resurrection teachings, based as they were on historical lives and events, including most of all the appearances of the risen Jesus.

But we can also move beyond these individual responses from the narrowest specialists on these questions to the evaluations of additional influential scholars in the next most specialized circle. This group of researchers not only concluded similarly that the dying-and-rising gods failed to account for the teachings of Jesus's resurrection, but additionally that the influence of at least the liberal arm of the *religionsgeschichtliche Schule* and other similar hypotheses have lost most or all of their influence today.

For example, in speaking about the past attempts to show that "the world of pagan philosophy and mystery-religions" may have influenced Paul (probably the major point of attack for these views), N. T. Wright concluded, "All have failed, as virtually all Pauline scholars now recognize."[157] In fact, Wright finds the arguments against these views of pagan influence to be "overwhelming."[158]

One massive study on an aspect of this research is A. J. M. Wedderburn's specialized tome, *Baptism and Resurrection: Studies in Pauline Theology against Its Graeco-Roman Background*. Wedderburn charges that the *religionsgeschichtliche Schule*, as developed further by Rudolf Bultmann and other scholars, failed in its attempt to prove its chief theses. In fact, while being an agnostic on the historical question of Jesus's resurrection, Wedderburn still asserts that his "purpose" in this volume

---

[156] Cook, *Empty Tomb*, specifically chap. 7 and the conclusion; Cook, "Resurrection in Paganism."

[157] N. T. Wright, *What Saint Paul Really Said: Was Paul of Tarsus the Real Founder of Christianity?* (Grand Rapids: Eerdmans, 1997), 172, cf. similarly 20, 70, 173.

[158] Wright, 77.

was to "call into question" the entire enterprise of this movement, in that further advances "in our understanding of the mystery-cults of the Graeco-Roman world" have "fatally undermined" the theological foundations of the *religionsgeschichtliche Schule* and its conclusions.[159]

Another academic pursuit of these matters, in this case over a lifetime of research, is Larry Hurtado's exploration of the very early date at which a high Christology burst onto the scene in the earliest church. Pertaining to our vital question here, Hurtado concludes that the combination of this exceptionally early proclamation of Jesus as deity along with this teaching having occurred in Judea, indicates that pagan myths such as the influential ideas of Bousset could not have been what gave rise to these Christian beliefs.[160] Rather, these latter beliefs were based on historical occurrences from locally in the Jerusalem area, rather than Jesus's disciples and others reflecting on far-away pagan ideas.[161] Therefore, the time frame according to Bousset's thesis began way too late. But recognizing the earlier date at which these events really did occur would have disproved his hypothesis.[162]

James D. G. Dunn's emphasis on the epicenter of the Christian message being based on the message of Jesus's disciples having *seen* their teacher in some sense after his crucifixion has already been mentioned above. Dunn goes further in order to ground the disciples' sight in first-century history, namely, in the life of Jesus himself. The center revolved around him, not the disciples, and most of all not distant tales. These early followers reveled in "preserving, promoting, and defending the memory of [Jesus's] mission."[163] There is no room or historical place here for emulating pagan myths from far-away lands. The antecedents were much closer at hand, as these views plus similar ideas were grounded in Jewish thought that "should have killed stone dead" the heart of Bousset's polemic![164]

---

[159] A. J. M. Wedderburn, *Baptism and Resurrection: Studies in Pauline Theology against Its Graeco-Roman Background* (Tübingen: Mohr Siebeck, 1987; repr., Eugene, OR: Wipf & Stock, 2011), 5–6.

[160] Hurtado, *How on Earth*, esp. 42.

[161] Hurtado, particularly 30, but also 29–38. Hurtado charges that Bousset "worked with a seriously inaccurate and somewhat simplistic view of earliest Christian history and also of Roman-era Jewish tradition" (17).

[162] Larry W. Hurtado, *Lord Jesus Christ: Devotion to Jesus in Earliest Christianity* (Grand Rapids: Eerdmans, 2003), specifically 18, cf. 5–18, 24.

[163] Dunn, *Jesus Remembered*, 185–86, 876.

[164] Dunn, 709n15.

Continuing, Luke Timothy Johnson likewise argues, "The best work in Paul in recent years has demonstrated that Paul was not the inventor of the 'Christ cult' but was, rather, the inheritor of liturgical and creedal traditions already in place before his conversion."[165] Craig A. Evans has judged that the Hellenistic approach to Jesus's historicity, along with its trends, have "been largely abandoned."[166] Reginald Fuller also mentions a critique similar to the one supported by Wedderburn and other scholars, namely, that the nineteenth-century *religionsgeschichtliche* movement built its chief theses on "dubious evidence" where the parallels were inexact and the material was insufficiently related to the New Testament.[167] Thorwald Lorenzen is among the many scholars who have been critical of the history of religions school's repeated reliance on claimed similarities with virtually no concentration on the larger numbers of differences.[168]

Metzger similarly reminds his readers of the extreme differences between the Jewish and Christian notions of philosophy of history that involve linear history as contrasted with the mystery religions' ideas favoring the cyclical repetition of events.[169] Another intriguing comeback from recent critical scholars like Leon McKenzie and others pertains to those who think that the less than impressive accounts of the dying-and-rising gods may have been precursors to the one truly historical resurrection in history—that of Jesus Christ.[170]

---

[165] Johnson, *Real Jesus*, 119.

[166] Craig A. Evans, "Life-of-Jesus Research and the Eclipse of Mythology," *Theological Studies* 54 (1993): 18–19.

[167] Fuller, *Formation of the Resurrection Narratives*, 25.

[168] Lorenzen, *Resurrection and Discipleship*, 117–19, who notes for example that a key group of words in the Hellenistic tales, such as *epiphaneia* and *epiphainesthai*, does not even appear at all in the New Testament. A few of the many authors who mention this critique include John P. Meier, *A Marginal Jew: Rethinking the Historical Jesus* (New York: Doubleday, 2001), 3:493; Metzger, "Methodology," 12, 14, 17; O'Collins, *Jesus Risen*, 103, where O'Collins mentions that this mystery thesis "ignores the radical differences"; cf. Dale C. Allison Jr., *The End of the Ages Has Come: An Early Interpretation of the Passion and Resurrection of Jesus* (Philadelphia: Fortress, 1985), 165–66.

[169] Metzger, "Methodology," 22–23.

[170] Leon McKenzie, *Pagan Resurrection Myths and the Resurrection of Jesus* (Charlottesville, VA: Bookwright's, 1997), 58–61; Grant R. Osborne, *The Resurrection Narratives: A Redactional Study* (Grand Rapids: Baker, 1984), 277. Even Justin Martyr and other early second- and third-century Christian thinkers might be mentioned briefly for some similar ideas (for instance, Justin, *1 Apol.* 23.1). Cook appears to take this position too, at least in

According to recent scholars, still other concerns impede the liberal *religion-sgeschichtliche Schule* tradition from returning to the front page of critical scholarship. Included in these oft-mentioned criticisms are the general lack of mystery-religion influence in Israel during the first century, that Jesus's case fits the Jewish and Old Testament pattern rather than a Hellenistic one, the predominant view among scholars today regarding the huge anthropological differences that exist between the Hellenistic and Jewish views of persons, ancient understandings of exactly what sort of body was thought to be raised from the dead, and other similar issues, some of which have been mentioned in the critique above.[171]

Last, it should be mentioned once again that the New Testament texts and early Christian convictions were that Jesus's resurrection appearances were established by claims involving the recipients' *sight*. This alone is a huge hurdle for any view claiming that foreign ideas were actually the primary cause. The two concepts stand quite opposed to one another, constituting a contradiction.[172]

So we close this chapter with a qualified agnostic position on whether there were actual dying-and-rising gods before Jesus, with perhaps a slight edge in the direction of the negative position. But this is admittedly quite a problematic issue to solve definitively. Still, it is clear for a large number of reasons that these ancient tales did not create or even significantly influence the New Testament teachings of Jesus's death and resurrection. For this conclusion there are many favorable reasons and almost unanimous scholarly agreement.[173] Finally, a large number of recent and often quite influential researchers also agree that the liberal *religionsgeschichtliche* tradition retains exceptionally little weight today.

---

part; see Cook, "Resurrection in Paganism"; cf. also Cook's potential hints in this direction in *Empty Tomb*, 1–2, 143.

[171] See Michael Grant, *Jesus: An Historian's Review of the Gospels* (New York: Macmillan, 1992), 199–200; Metzger, "Methodology," 7; Paul Barnett, *The Birth of Christianity: The First Twenty Years* (Grand Rapids: Eerdmans, 2005), 70; O'Collins, *Jesus Risen*, 102–3.

[172] As mentioned earlier in Pannenberg's pointed comment (*Jesus: God and Man*, 91).

[173] It should be noticed that the heaviest emphasis here or elsewhere in this study is not weighted in the direction of a scholarly headcount serving as the prime indication of the bottom line. As done elsewhere, the chief emphasis is clearly on the reasons and evidences that determine these overall issues and views. While it is helpful to recognize where the scholarly lay of the land is located, due to these scholars knowing the issues better than nonscholars, this aspect was clearly kept subservient to the available data itself.

13

Legend 2: Historical Persons Resurrected?

The previous chapter concentrated chiefly on the ancient mystery religions, frequently retelling the stories of dying-and-rising gods, including an array of subtopics and issues. Geographically, a variety of these pre-Christian accounts were found chiefly throughout the vicinities of Rome and Greece, down into Egypt, and then around and past the eastern end of the Mediterranean world over to the Tigris and Euphrates Rivers and beyond. We directed special reference throughout to two major questions: Were there any clear examples of pre-Christian dying-and-rising gods? If so, did these tales exhibit any significant amount of influence on the New Testament formulations of the death and resurrection of Jesus?

Regarding the initial question, it was concluded for several reasons that it is very difficult to determine whether there were any clear pre-Christian cases of dying-and-rising gods. Specialist scholars line up on different sides of the issues, often due to the thousands of years separating some sources and the present plus the many relevant pieces of mutilated data. Further, the researchers frequently began from dissimilar starting points by utilizing different definitions. We concluded that the data indicated a slight preference for there being no such clear resurrection tales in pre-Christian times.

The answer to the second question is much more settled. Only rarely do recent specialists, whatever their personal outlook from atheist to conservative, hold that pre-Christian tales of dying-and-rising gods gave rise to the Christian teaching of

the death and resurrection of Jesus. Nor did these ancient stories provide any significant influence on these Christian positions.

These original arguments were popularized chiefly by the late nineteenth-century
religionsgeschichtliche Schule, with holdover views in the early twentieth century, often
in brief statements or hints from the highly influential writings of Rudolf Bultmann
and others. But even Bultmann began to shift away from these positions.[1] Yet it often
escapes notice that even Bousset and Pfleiderer did not think that the resurrection
parallels could explain the disciples' visions.

Eventually the cracks in the claims of the history of religions supporters became
apparent. A huge problem was that the original theses proclaimed by Frazer, Bousset,
and Pfleiderer among others were cobbled together from disparate sources, sometimes without regard for which myths were being combined (especially in terms of
time, geography, and independent provenance of the myths). New critiques emerged
decades later, especially from members of the Third Quest for the historical Jesus,
such as emphasizing the Jewish rather than the Hellenistic origin of the earliest Christian teachings along with the recognition of the exceptionally early New
Testament creeds and their role.[2] Under this large amount of pressure, the original

---

[1] Much of the negative response to Wilhelm Bousset's work in recent decades, noted in
the preceding chapter, was in reaction to his views on the ancient dying-and-rising gods in
relation to the historicity of Jesus's life. Of the many places where Bousset's strong influence
on Rudolf Bultmann can be seen, one the clearest is reported by Bultmann himself in
his "Introductory Word to the Fifth Edition" of Bousset's work *Kyrios Christos: A History
of the Belief in Christ from the Beginnings of Christianity to Irenaeus*, trans. John E. Steely
(Nashville: Abingdon, 1970). Here, Bultmann praises Bousset's volume by recounting that
when he used to recommend works to his students, the primary place "above all belonged
to Wilhelm Bousset's *Kyrios Christos*" (7). Later, Bultmann realized that Bousset's volume
exhibited some shortcomings, especially regarding the explication of Paul's theology (9).
But just reading a variety of Bultmann's writings, chiefly his early, formative texts, will
indicate some major inclinations toward Bousset's conclusions. Intriguingly and somewhat
coincidentally, the more recent scholarly reaction contrary to Bultmann's own thought had
to do with *both* his work on Paul as well as his own views on the historicity of Jesus.
Especially on the latter topic, see E. P. Sanders, *Jesus and Judaism* (Philadelphia: Fortress,
1985), 26–36 for example.

[2] One intriguing comparison is that Bultmann repeatedly acknowledged fully the
existence of early creedal teachings in the New Testament, including their probably being
pre-Pauline and present in the very earliest church, with at least some of these traditions
perhaps even originating in Jerusalem, and yet claimed that they were somehow derived
from Hellenistic sources. See Rudolf Bultmann, *Theology of the New Testament*, 2 vols.,
trans. Kendrick Grobel (New York: Scribner's, 1955), 1:46, 82–83, 86, 125–26, 293–96.

positions occupied by the *religionsgeschichtliche Schule* scholars have largely evaporated as they were addressed and refuted.[3]

Another Angle

This chapter chiefly moves beyond the material from the dying-and-rising gods to another species of legendary accretion. The principal interest here is largely with historical figures (or those who were largely historical) in order to examine the potentially legendary miraculous sorts of occurrences that were sometimes attributed to them. World religions scholar Irving Hexham defines a "legend" as a "narrative, often tied in with a particular place or locality, which tells an apparently historical story which has little basis in actual fact."[4] Among the many accounts in this genre, the amounts of history and legend that appear in each example understandably often differ.

We will begin by discussing some Jewish rabbinic figures who were considered to be miracle workers and exorcists, moving to ancient magicians and the notion of the Hellenistic "divine men," of which the best-known example is that of Apollonius of Tyana, and back to the key Jewish messianic figure of Sabbatai Zevi (or Sevi). A few other historical figures will be viewed as well regarding certain related ideas. Throughout, from New Testament times to much closer to the present, it will be our intent to evaluate particular claims that certain individuals had or utilized special powers. Two of the specific areas of concentration in this chapter are examples of apotheosis (being taken to heaven and divinized either before or after death) and some empty tomb or resurrection appearance accounts.[5]

Today it would no doubt be asked by many scholars how these ideas could have replaced Jewish thought in their own backyard almost immediately after the birth of the church, not to mention several other concerns.

[3] One example of such negative responses to both of the two major questions considered here plus the recognition that the *religionsgeschichtliche Schule* has failed is argued strongly by atheist New Testament scholar Bart D. Ehrman in his work *Did Jesus Exist? The Historical Argument for Jesus of Nazareth* (New York: HarperCollins, 2012), 207–18, 221–30.

[4] See "Legend," in Irving Hexham, *Concise Dictionary of Religion* (Downers Grove, IL: InterVarsity, 1993), 135.

[5] Part of the discussion at various points in this and the prior chapter also involves another species of both myth or legend, namely stories that more simply grow over time in the process of retelling. In more than one location in this study, such as the individual

Ancient Parallels?

One reason the question of early, non-Christian miracle claims is intriguing is that these descriptions are plentiful in the ancient world.[6] In this regard, comparisons to Jesus would be natural if not actually expected. Moreover, some of the Jewish or pagan incidents told concerning Jewish holy men, magicians, and the group known as the Hellenistic "divine men" seem similar in places to those events that were reported regarding Jesus in the canonical Gospels. As a result, some critical scholars in the past couple of centuries have even charged that a number of these ancient parallels may have provided different sorts of inspiration either for the Gospel portrayals of Jesus's miracles (perhaps even contributing ideas for entire Gospel episodes) or in otherwise encouraging Jesus's own ideas or actions in a copycat fashion.[7]

What should be concluded regarding these Jewish and pagan parallels? These are some of the major issues at hand in this chapter, with particular examples revealing some of the variety of these ancient miracle claims. It should also be remembered throughout this chapter that to challenge the *origin* or *source* of an idea instead of addressing the truth or falsehood of the actual concept or position itself is to commit the informal logical falsehood known as the genetic fallacy.[8] Even if some relationship or similarity could be shown between Hellenistic or other ideas and any Gospel stories, this still does not at all prove that the reports of Jesus's miracles are either false or derived from earlier examples.

Gospel treatments, this matter is also evaluated in relation to the possible growth in the resurrection narratives from the earliest to the latest of the canonical Gospels.

[6] Portions of this present section are a much enlarged and updated treatment taken from Gary R. Habermas, "Did Jesus Perform Miracles?," in *Jesus Under Fire*, ed. Michael J. Wilkins and J. P. Moreland (Grand Rapids: Zondervan, 1995), 119–21.

[7] This chapter does not consider the fantastic feats often attributed to Jesus in the apocryphal Gospels, especially because the sources are not contemporary with the canonical texts, besides often not consisting of true parallels to Jesus's miracles. Rather, these writings are usually of a different genre and quality than that of the canonical Gospels, have an extremely low likelihood of having utilized early testimony and sources, and teach philosophical ideas that are opposed to the overall Gospel ethos. Taken as a whole, the apocryphal Gospels exhibit a decided lack of historical attestation for the claims they recount, even while appearing to speak in a historical manner. These texts will also be treated elsewhere in this study.

[8] Irving M. Copi, *Introduction to Logic*, 7th ed. (New York: Macmillan, 1986), 92.

Jewish Holy Men

Jewish historian Josephus describes "a righteous man . . . beloved of God" named Onias (or Honi, as he is usually called) who lived in the first century BC. He prayed to God to send rain in order to end a drought, and God answered his prayer by granting the request.[9] The Mishnah reports additional specifics, explaining that God did not answer the prayer initially. So Onias the Circle-Maker drew a ring and stood within it, telling the Lord that he would not leave until it rained—and it did.[10]

On another occasion, Josephus relates, "I have seen a certain man of my own country whose name was Eleazar" who cast demons out of tormented individuals by holding a root up to the person's nose and drawing the demon out through the nostrils! Then Eleazar commanded the demon never to return again, citing the authority of King Solomon and "reciting the incantations which he had composed." As a final step, Eleazar would command the demon to overturn a nearby "cup or basin full of water" to indicate for those present that the demon had, indeed, left the possessed individual. The purpose throughout this narrative was to indicate Solomon's greatness and abilities (*Ant.* 8.2.5).

It was a common Jewish belief about the time of Jesus that certain rabbis were able to perform miracles. Hanina ben Dosa, for example, was reputed to be able to heal the sick, even when the latter were located a distance away. On one occasion he prayed in order to cure a boy who had a high fever, afterward pronouncing that the child had been healed. This was later confirmed to be the case by the lad's father.[11]

Could the Gospel authors who related the accounts of Jesus's miracles have known such Jewish stories and incorporated portions of them into their own writings due to the influence of such Jewish holy men?[12] Or further, could particular

---

[9] Josephus, *Ant.* 14.2.1; quotations from *Josephus: Complete Works*, trans. William Whiston (Grand Rapids: Kregel, 1960).

[10] Mishnah Ta'anit 3:8. This text is also found in C. K. Barrett, ed., *The New Testament Background: Selected Documents* (New York: Harper & Brothers, 1956), 150–51. Barrett explained that this action may have been connected to magic.

[11] Babylonian Talmud, *Berakot* 34b. See Israel W. Slotki, ed., *The Babylonian Talmud*, trans. S. Daiches (London: Soncino, 1936); cf. Jarl Fossum, "Understanding Jesus' Miracles," *Bible Review* 10 (1994): 18 for this plus another example as well.

[12] Jewish historian Geza Vermes is a major example of the many scholars for whom a chief theme is to describe Jesus as a popular Jewish rabbi, holy man, and magnetic personality from Galilee who was particularly well-known for his miracles and exorcisms. For example, Vermes, *Jesus and the World of Judaism* (Philadelphia: Fortress, 1983), 1–2, 27–28, 57.

Gospel accounts even have been "borrowed" or invented on behalf of Jesus in order to increase his acclaim? It is difficult not to notice how Hanina ben Dosa's account of healing at a distance is reminiscent of Jesus's own curing of the centurion's servant (Matt 8:5–13; Luke 7:1–10).

By way of evaluating and responding to such questions or charges, several items may be noted. (1) To start, it is perhaps needless to remark that the Gospels do indeed exhibit much influence from the Old Testament and also reflect Jewish tradition in many places. For example, the Gospel of John reports that Jesus himself was referred to as a rabbi as was John the Baptist.[13] The point to observe here is that from the beginning of Jesus's teachings, the Jewish background to his message was not denied, covered up, or even downplayed. Jesus openly based many of his examples, lessons, and good theology on sound Old Testament principles, referring directly to many key figures in the process. In light of this dependence on Jewish Scripture, principles, and teachings, the presence of additional similarities between these sources should actually be *expected*.

(2) While many Jewish similarities are thus present and expected, *dissimilarities* and certain odd-sounding aspects are also present too, like Eleazar's employing a root and pulling a demon through the nostrils of the possessed individual. And why utter a Solomonic incantation as one's authority to exercise the demon? Or what about Honi's circle-drawing as an act in itself, especially if it had been done by magical powers?

Moreover, on the surface at least, these differences even exhibit the *superiority* of Jesus's person and authority over that of the Jewish rabbis and other teachers. Why cite Solomon for one's authority in casting out demons? As Jesus remarked, someone greater than Solomon was now present (Matt 12:42; Luke 11:31). Further, often in the New Testament, Jesus places his own authority above that of the sacred Old Testament text and commands (as is remarkably the case in Matt 5:21–48). Or other writers teach that Jesus was far superior to the angels (Heb 1:5–14), Moses (3:1–6; 8:5–6), or the Jewish priests (4:14–16; 8:1–6). Last, magical and occultic powers were regularly condemned throughout both the Old and New Testaments, so miracles or exorcisms done by such powers were not only considered inferior but were condemned.[14]

---

[13] Regarding Jesus, see John 1:38, 49; 3:2; 6:25; for John the Baptist see John 3:26.
[14] Such as Lev 19:31; 20:6, 27; Deut 18:10–12; Acts 16:16–18; 19:18–19; Rev 21:8.

Another huge difference is noted by many critical scholars today, both liberal and conservative. As Marcus Borg asserts, "Typically, Jesus exorcised evil spirits by verbal command alone" apart from using instruments of any kind, incantations, and so on. The people who witnessed this knew the difference—they were absolutely amazed by Jesus's new teaching and authority (Mark 1:23–28) in that he did not heal or do exorcisms the same way that other Jewish authorities did them.[15]

(3) But the other potential challenges from these Jewish accounts still remain. Could any of these similarities just mentioned in the writings of Josephus and the Mishnah actually explain the Gospel records of Jesus's miracles and exorcisms, including individual portions of these accounts? In particular, the Talmud's account of Hanina ben Dosa appears to be especially close to the Gospel accounts in the Q passages in Matthew and Luke.

To begin, we have no solid bridges that indicate any such mythical mimicry of these Jewish traditions in the Gospel portions regarding stories being passed on as Jesus's healings or exorcisms. Further, the written forms of these Jewish writings date at a minimum after the Synoptic Gospels. The earliest of these works is Josephus's *Antiquities*, probably dating from late in the reign of Roman emperor Domitian, perhaps AD 93–94.[16] This places it at about the same time as John's Gospel, *after* the Synoptic Gospels, and almost certainly several *decades* after the possible dating of any Q source material containing either Jesus's healings or exorcisms. Thus, it would be quite difficult to argue that Josephus's material affected any of these possible accounts in the Synoptic sources, whereas earlier oral sources for this material could still be cited.

The initial portions of the Mishnah date from no earlier than about AD 200, when it was completed by Rabbi Judah and later became part of the Talmud.[17] Though there are certainly earlier roots to these Jewish documents, the Babylonian Talmud, from which the account of Hanina ben Dosa was drawn, dates from about AD 500.[18] Thus this completed material dates some 450 years after the Q material accounts of the centurion's son in Matthew and Luke, presumably dating from the

[15] Marcus J. Borg, *Jesus, a New Vision: Spirit, Culture, and the Life of Discipleship* (New York: HarperCollins, 1987), esp. 61–65, with the quotation on 63.

[16] Paul L. Maier, ed. and trans., *Josephus: The Essential Works* (Grand Rapids: Kregel, 1994), 12; also, Barrett, *New Testament Background*, 190.

[17] For details, see Barrett, 141, 143, 145, 190.

[18] Barrett, 145.

mid-first century AD. Therefore, it can be safely concluded that while there still could have been some earlier origins of the Jewish stories, neither the Mishnah nor the Talmud inspired or affected in any way these healing and exorcism stories noted above. Finally, the possible existence of earlier Jewish stories would still have to be demonstrated in their own right, with historical lines being drawn to the Gospel accounts.

(4) Furthermore, it must also be remembered that the Jewish leaders in the Gospels actually acknowledged the reality of Jesus's miracles and exorcisms in spite of their best interests.[19] This is understandable on more than one front in light of both the early attestation of Jesus's wonders plus Jesus's own apparent recognition that the Jews also performed actual exorcisms.[20] But if Jesus also seemed to acknowledge the reality of the Jewish exorcisms, this likewise serves to disarm a good deal of the initial objection above as to whether or not Jewish prophets, holy men, and the like were performing supernatural works. In light of Jesus's seeming comment, this could involve an overall response that questions whether there is even a further point to be made here. Does a further critique even matter at this point?

The major issue at hand in this chapter concerns alternative challenges to the historicity of Jesus's miracles. Jesus was a Jew, and there can be no doubt that long-standing Jewish concepts exerted influence on the Gospel writers. But unless it can be shown that Jesus's miracles were either invented wholesale or that the supernatural element was significantly colored by such bias, this Jewish element is not a problem. This is especially the case when Jesus himself seemed to acknowledge that Jewish exorcists were doing their own work too. Hence, there are no immediate issues here. The historicity of the Gospel miracles is treated elsewhere in this study as well.

---

[19] See Mark 2:1–12; 3:22; Luke 13:10–17; John 11:47. Borg agrees with this specific point here, in addition to acknowledging three strong reasons to admit that Jesus was both a healer as well as an exorcist (*Jesus, a New Vision*, 61).

[20] Besides the above accounts by Josephus and the Talmud, see the both early and powerful Q passage in Matt 12:27–28; Luke 11:19–20. Homer Kent remarks regarding Jesus's own comment to the Jewish leaders, "If, however, Jesus implies that at least some of the Pharisaic exorcisms were genuine, then it must be assumed that the power came from God (otherwise Christ's argument is greatly weakened)." See Homer A. Kent Jr., "The Gospel according to Matthew" in *The Wycliffe Bible Commentary*, ed. Charles F. Pfeiffer and Everett F. Harrison (Nashville: Southwestern, 1962), 950.

Magicians

The two preceding examples from Josephus indicate some overlapping territory between the category of Jewish holy men and that of magicians. The holy men appear to have employed some techniques that were often connected with magic to accomplish their ends (e.g., the use of special roots and Solomonic incantations). In the case of Honi, Josephus continues by reporting that Simeon ben Shetah made a complaint against him, charging him with unorthodoxy in his use of magical circle-drawing, among other implications, and Honi was stoned.[21]

Other magical accounts beyond Judaism also abound in the ancient world. Edwin Yamauchi reports the existence of a thousand cuneiform texts in ancient Mesopotamia that depict the healing of diseases by means of magic. Since many diseases were attributed to demons, those cures often resulted in casting out the demons by specific formulas.[22] Is there perhaps credible evidence that such ancient pagan cases either inspired or even led to the creation of particular Gospel miracles? Or can Jesus's miracles and exorcisms as they are reported in the Gospels be taken as the work of a magician?

Yamauchi's detailed analysis sufficiently addresses the major concerns of these questions. A crucial roadblock to understanding Jesus as a magician is the ancient concept of magic itself, which was exceptionally negative. Both Christians and non-Christians characterized magic as including elements such as demons, sorcery, incantations, the casting of evil spells, and even trickery. It definitely involved persons of dubious or doubtful moral character.[23] Perhaps worse, Morton Smith, arguing that Jesus was a magician, asserts that "cannibalism, incest, and sexual promiscuity were reported of magicians."[24] He links Jesus and early Christianity to magic primarily because Jesus was considered to be a miracle worker as well as his claims to be divine. Smith also includes the early Christian belief in mutual love, the use of "brother" and "sister," the practice of having all personal possessions in common, and the custom of

---

[21] Josephus, *Ant.* 14.2.1. See Barrett, *New Testament Background*, 150–51 for both the original text and for further comments.

[22] See Edwin M. Yamauchi's impressive and well-documented chapter "Magic or Miracle? Diseases, Demons and Exorcisms," in *The Miracles of Jesus*, ed. David Wenham and Craig Blomberg, vol. 6 of *Gospel Perspectives* (Sheffield; JSOT, 1986), 89–183. Barrett, 31–35, includes an instance of an ancient incantation from the Paris Magical Papyrus.

[23] Yamauchi, "Magic or Miracle?," 89–91, 97.

[24] Morton Smith, *Jesus the Magician* (New York: Harper & Row, 1978), 66.

the Lord's Supper (which some critics of Christians in the ancient world considered a form of cannibalism).[25]

It is difficult to understand how the presence of almost any of these items absolutely proves or requires someone to be a magician. If all miracle workers—people who claim to love one another as brothers and sisters, along with those who share their material possessions—qualify as designating devotees of magic, then such generalization has robbed the word of any crucial meaning. And though it is true that some unbelievers charged that the Lord's Supper was actually a belief in cannibalism, this hardly amounts to evidence for Christian cannibalism or that Jesus was a magician.

Smith's tangential arguments are even more outrageous and highly questionable. He postulates that Jesus travelled to Egypt purposely to study magic, that the marks on Paul's body (Gal 6:17) were actually magical tattoos, and that the Roman historian Tacitus's comments that Christians were charged with "hatred for the human race" probably referred to their practicing magic. So the list goes on![26]

Such arguments hardly even require a response. Each one stretches credulity beyond any normal meaning, lacks crucial historical or other evidence, and is opposed to the clear and early data that are available. For example, there is no early testimony that Jesus studied magic in Egypt or anywhere else, for that matter.[27] According to Paul's own self-identification, the scars on his body were plainly due to the extraordinary and repeated physical suffering that he explicitly enumerates more than once (such as 2 Cor 11:23–28). Further, though Tacitus does not explain his comments in detail, exhibiting hatred for others has no necessary connection with magic or cannibalism. It seems that for Smith, simply stating something in a particular way may provide enough warrant, by itself, to establish these claims, even when direct statements exist to the contrary, as with Paul's wounds.

In short, if one defines magic the way that it was described in ancient times (or even today), then Jesus is certainly not a magician, for none of the unique concepts connected with the subject can be applied to him. If, on the other hand, the notion of magic is defined so broadly that Jesus is included, as with Smith, then the concept

---

[25] Smith, 46, 64–67.

[26] Smith, 47–48, 50–53.

[27] For a detailed examination of some versions of what I refer to as the "Jesus as international traveler" hypothesis, see Gary R. Habermas, *The Historical Jesus: Ancient Evidence for the Life of Christ* (Joplin, MO: College Press, 1996), 89–98.

loses any distinctive meaning, as it can be applied to just about anyone and anywhere.[28] Still, we need to ask whether ancient accounts of magic somehow inspired Jesus's miracles or their reports. A few relevant issues regarding the historicity of some related claims will also be treated below.

Hellenistic "Divine Men"

Besides Jewish holy men and magicians, one of the best-known parallels to the Gospel miracles was once claimed to be that of the Hellenistic "divine men." A very popular notion decades ago, it has proved exceptionally difficult if not impossible to actually discover consistent data that can provide criteria to establish these ancient "superheroes."[29] To the extent to which this once-popular idea can even be defined, it was often said to have been concerned mostly with two types of phenomena: divination and miracles.[30]

However, Holladay summarizes powerfully the conclusion that this hypothesis lost credibility as it was "repeatedly based upon the same few bits of data" that became recognized both for "their paucity but also for their ambiguity."[31] Problematically, "a half-century of scientific research has shattered this oversimplified picture of the ancient world" into which the concept of the *theios anēr* supposedly fit.[32] As the most accredited research was nearing its conclusions, the evidence for *both* the two chief ingredients of divination plus the appeals to miracle-working abilities as authentication was found wanting and failed to obtain, especially in a Jewish context. The

---

[28] For other germane issues, see the lengthy and well-reasoned treatment in the remainder of Yamauchi's well-documented essay above.

[29] In the excellent chapter by Barry L. Blackburn, "Miracle Working ΘΕΙΟΙ ΑΝΔΡΕΣ in Hellenism (and Hellenistic Judaism)," in Wenham and Blomberg, *Miracles of Jesus*, the author begins by citing major defenders of the divine man thesis, but the three sources listed date from 1934, 1935–1936, and 1964 (see 206). In a major work resulting from his doctoral research at Cambridge University, Carl R. Holladay explains both the scholarly popularity as well as the opposition of other major critical scholars in the 1970s. See Holladay, *Theios Aner in Hellenistic Judaism: A Critique of the Use of this Category in New Testament Christology* (Missoula, MT: Scholar's Press, 1977), 1–5, 44.

[30] Blackburn, "Miracle Working," 185–218. Blackburn includes a very helpful chart that lists pre- and post-Christian representatives, with the former being subdivided into seers, healers, and other miracle workers (187).

[31] Holladay, *Theios Aner*, 44.

[32] Holladay, 12–13.

result is that the usefulness of this *theios anēr* concept "is extremely questionable, for using it in Christological discussions merely introduces into an already confused field of study yet another ill-defined, if not undefinable category." Thus, the notions of "Jesus's divine sonship and his miracles" must be sought "along lines other than Hellenistic Sitz im Leben or in terms of a process of Hellenization."[33]

The best-known of the Hellenistic divine men was Apollonius of Tyana, a first-century traveling Neopythagorean bard of whom it was claimed that he had exhibited special powers, including miracles.[34] For example, on one occasion Apollonius ordered a demon to leave a young man and to prove he had done so by exhibiting a visible sign. The demon responded that he would knock down a nearby statue, which promptly fell to the ground. The young man rubbed his eyes as if he had just awakened from sleep, being totally healed.[35]

While the conclusion to this exorcism might remind some of the Gospel account of Jesus exorcising a demon from the Gadarene man (Mark 5:1–20), Graham Twelftree argues that the latter case of the demons' entering the pigs should not be understood as confirming their exit, but simply as Jesus granting the demons' request to inhabit other bodies. In other words, entering the pigs was not meant as a sign that the demons had exited.[36]

On another occasion, while visiting Alexandria, Apollonius watched while twelve men were being led away to their executions. He identified one as being innocent, which was confirmed by a messenger who reported new evidence that Apollonius was correct (*Vit. Apoll.* 5.24). The special cognizance of an innocent man facing execution may remind some of the many times that Jesus exhibited supernatural knowledge.[37]

However, few if any of these Hellenistic sources provide the careful grounds necessary in order to establish the veracity of the miracles and other supernatural items that they record. Philostratus's work on Apollonius is one of the best-known examples of such miracle stories. Yet, this text is problematic on many accounts:

---

[33] Holladay, 235–38, with the latter quotations above being located on 238.

[34] His life is detailed in a major biography, written in the first half of the third century AD by Flavius Philostratus, *The Life of Apollonius of Tyana*, trans. F. C. Conybeare, 2 vols. (Cambridge: Harvard University Press, 1912).

[35] Philostratus, *Vit. Apoll.* 4.20. Actually, demonic exorcisms were quite rare among the Hellenistic divine men. This case is one of the only such reports.

[36] See Graham H. Twelftree, "EI ΔΕ . . . ΕΓΩ . . . ΕΚΒΑΛΛΩ ΤΑ ΔΑΙΜΟΝΙΑ! . . . [Luke 11:19]," in Wenham and Blomberg, *Miracles of Jesus*, 381–84.

[37] See Luke 5:4–10; John 1:47–49; 2:24–25; 4:17–19; 6:64; 11:11–15; 18:4.

- Philostratus wrote in the third century AD, more than 100 years after the end of Apollonius's life. This is not an absolutely horrible gap for ancient history, though it is a long enough time lapse to require a cautious examination of the author's reports. How does he fare? Atheist New Testament scholar Bart Ehrman summarizes the matter of Philostratus's biography this way: "Our one source dates from long after the fact and is thoroughly biased."[38]

- Very serious historical inaccuracies mar significant portions of Philostratus's work, such as Apollonius's lengthy journeys to cities like Nineveh and Babylon. Not only were these wonders of the ancient world lying in ruins during the first century, but at least Nineveh had been destroyed even hundreds of years earlier. To say that these lacunae also raise serious questions about Apollonius's dialogues with the kings in each of these locations, if not invalidating the information entirely, is admittedly a vast understatement. Then what is the status of the other materials in this entire work?

- Philostratus identifies his major source of information concerning Apollonius as having come from one of his disciples, named Damis. But Damis could well be a fictitious individual, especially since he is identified as being from the nonexistent city of Nineveh, thus raising these doubts. This in turn increases the number of additional questions about the sources for this work by Philostratus.[39]

- Many scholars think that Philostratus's work is primarily an example of romantic fiction, a popular literary form existing in the second century AD. There are a number of indications that Philostratus's primary intent was not to present an accurate picture of Apollonius's life.[40] This does not mean that there is an absence of history altogether in this text. It just appears that Philostratus may have been attempting to do otherwise than writing

---

[38] Ehrman, *Did Jesus Exist?*, 288. Even though Robert M. Price also considers the Gospels to be quite problematic, he considers Philostratus's work on Apollonius of Tyana to be fictional; see Price, *Deconstructing Jesus* (Amherst, NY: Prometheus, 2000), 38, 221.

[39] Howard Clark Kee, *Miracle in the Early Christian World* (New Haven: Yale University Press, 1983), 256; John Ferguson, *The Religions of the Roman Empire* (Ithaca: Cornell University Press, 1970), 182; Charles Bigg, *The Origins of Christianity* (Oxford: Clarendon, 1910), 306.

[40] Details are found in Kee, 253; J. Bidez, "Literature and Philosophy in the Eastern Half of the Empire," in *The Cambridge Ancient History*, ed. S. A. Cook et al. (Cambridge: Cambridge University Press, 1965), 12:611.

straightforward history. Besides, huge issues in historical epistemology are present here; even granting at least the possibility of some history being present, how could the reader ascertain where and when it obtains, or even if some reports are accurate but attributed to wrong persons, occasions, or dates?

- The similarities between Apollonius and Jesus may well be more than just coincidental. Philostratus was commissioned to write these accounts by Julia Domna, the wife of Roman emperor Septimius Severus, and it is regularly held that she did so in order to specifically orchestrate "a counterblast to Jesus."[41]

- Perhaps even more difficult with regard to this present study, Philostratus specifically admits that his chief source by Damis actually ended before Apollonius's death, and thus neither his death nor any further information was even found in the only extant source available. Philostratus then indicates that he therefore must be satisfied to record a variety of conflicting "stories" that have been repeated about the death of Apollonius up until Philostratus's own time over a century later (*Vit. Apoll.* 8.29). This claimed loss of his chief source of material, whatever that may have been, only makes his account all the more questionable.

- One of the later stories told by Philostratus apart from his source relates that Apollonius was observed entering a temple and that he was not seen again, from which it was thought that he must have ascended to heaven (*Vit. Apoll.* 8.30). Entering a temple rather obviously indicates nothing supernatural, let alone being a case of apotheosis. Later, a young skeptic who denied immortality dreamt that he saw Apollonius who told him that, indeed, the soul is immortal. This too falls far short of any evidence for an afterlife, a resurrection included, especially when we are told explicitly that the others who were present saw nothing (8.31).

- Philostratus is known to have embellished Apollonius's life, particularly in regard to the supernatural claims presented in his work, with the miracles among the fictitious items that he added. In this sense, Philostratus's text is "not altogether . . . credible."[42] Even far more crucial, no other historical data validate or otherwise confirm the miracle claims in Apollonius's life. But as has been mentioned on more than one occasion in this study, the

---

[41] Ferguson, *Religions of the Roman Empire*, 51; cf. Bidez, "Literature and Philosophy," 613.

[42] For these problems, see F. C. Conybeare's introduction to Philostratus, *Life of Apollonius of Tyana*, 1:7–10.

potential acceptance of supernatural reports does require some careful source work. Not only is that missing here, but the available data that is present unfortunately militates strongly against good history on these occasions.

To be sure, problems with Philostratus's example of Apollonius of Tyana do not invalidate miracle stories in other ancient sources. But just as critical scholars regularly question the very nature of the New Testament text, the same questions need to be addressed regarding the non-Christian sources as well. It is insufficient simply to *claim* that a miracle actually occurred in any tradition, Christian or otherwise. All such data must be scrutinized, including aspects like the dates and circumstances of the writing in relation to the original situation, the vantage point and sources of the author if any purported evidence is presented, and whether alternative proposals better explain the data.

The Hellenistic divine men are in some ways an odd group exhibiting many differences. Among these differences, however, is a last crucial aspect to note. The Gospels do not even hint that Jesus's abilities were connected with divination or the use of occult powers. But since divination was "the most prevalent power" displayed by the Hellenistic divine men, Blackburn notes another stark contrast here with the Gospel accounts.[43]

Could the Gospel picture of Jesus's miracles have been inspired by the Hellenistic divine men?[44] As with the dying-and-rising gods theses, these comparisons are also generally thought to be specious, for several reasons: (1) One issue is that these Hellenistic wonderworkers were not a group that can be easily defined; there was no

---

[43] Blackburn, "Miracle Working," 190.

[44] As discussed and evaluated in the previous chapter with regard to our former subject of the dying-and-rising god scenarios in the ancient Mediterranean world, the classic expression of a positive connection between the divine men and Jesus is Wilhelm Bousset's *Kyrios Christos*. A slightly earlier forerunner, also from the history of religions school of thought (*religionsgeschichtliche Schule*) is Otto Pfleiderer's *The Early Christian Conception of Christ* (London: Williams & Norgate, 1905), which also addresses parallels to Jesus's miracles in chap. 3. One of the best-known twentieth-century supporters of this school of interpretation is Rudolf Bultmann, in *Theology of the New Testament*, 1:128–33. For an evaluation and critique of some of these and related positions, see Reginald H. Fuller, *The Foundations of New Testament Christology* (New York: Scribner's, 1965), 68–72, 86–101; and especially Oscar Cullmann, *The Christology of the New Testament*, trans. Shirley C. Guthrie and Charles A. M. Hall, rev. ed. (Philadelphia: Westminster, 1963), 195–99, 239–45, 270–72.

fixed type or list of common characteristics.[45] It has been stated that some of these ancient mighty men sometimes claimed to heal and to otherwise utilize the power of divination, but of course that is claimed on behalf of several ancient persons who are not thought of as Hellenistic divine men. So, it has been concluded more recently that it is difficult to support the contention that Jesus's miracles were patterned after such an ill-defined class. The point here is that while individual cases of claimed miracles being similar to those of Jesus would still need to be investigated, the category itself cannot be applied to Jesus because of the confusion on the classification.

(2) Even if the pre-Christian Hellenistic concept is honed significantly, the examples in the Gospel accounts are still distinguished in several ways from those of the divine men. As even Bultmann notes, two of these differences are that the examples in the Gospels exhibit much more reserve and restraint in their descriptions of miracles, and, even more crucially, they lack the magical traits that generally characterize the Hellenistic accounts.[46]

(3) Additionally, while there may be some similarities between the Gospel accounts and the Hellenistic stories, almost all the Gospel motifs are also paralleled in the Old Testament, Palestinian Jewish, or rabbinic literature. This observation alone makes it difficult to prove that any particular Gospel miracles must have been drawn from the Hellenistic genre.[47]

(4) Furthermore, an absolutely huge issue for the alleged Hellenistic parallels is that most of these stories actually *postdate* the New Testament. As Reginald Fuller crucially affirms: "Now it cannot be denied that most of the evidence adduced for the Hellenistic concept of the divine man by the History of Religions school is later

---

[45] Blackburn, "Miracle Working," 187–92, 205; cf. Fuller, *Foundations of New Testament Christology*, 97.

[46] Agreeing on both aspects, Bultmann similarly points out that "the New Testament miracle stories are extremely reserved" in not attributing magical aspects to the miracle accounts, as do many of the Hellenistic stories. Intriguingly, one of Bultmann's two cases in our earlier examples is where Eleazar used a root to cast out a demon, though this was seemingly treated as a "Hellenistic" instance. Bultmann's second Hellenistic case is that of a healer who employed a chip from a virgin's gravestone to heal a person of a snake bite. See Rudolf Bultmann, "The Study of the Synoptic Gospels," in *Form Criticism: Two Essays on New Testament Research*, trans. Frederick C. Grant (New York: Harper & Brothers, 1962), 38.

[47] Blackburn, "Miracle Working," 169–99; Fuller, *Foundations of New Testament Christology*, 70–72, 97–98; Cullmann, *Christology of the New Testament*, 199–217, 241–45, 272–75. This distinction was also observed in the previous chapter concerning the tales of the dying-and-rising gods.

than the NT."[48] Even more pointedly, Fuller declares further of the pre-Christian redeemer myth, "It is no more than a scholarly reconstruction. . . . But there is no evidence for a pre-existent redeemer who becomes incarnate."[49] Perhaps no other problem with the Hellenistic redeemer myths and *theios anēr* concepts has been more devastating than this one, which almost single-handedly brought down the huge influence of Bousset, Bultmann, and other critics.[50]

(5) Another blow against this Hellenistic view was leveled by Blackburn regarding the miraculous activity of these ancient heroes. After an extensive study of the Hellenistic miracle accounts, he concluded: "In fact, among the undoubtedly pre-Christian traditions I can adduce only three stories formally reminiscent of the Gospel accounts."[51] As already mentioned in various ways, it is impossible to build what purports to be a powerful case in favor of Hellenism on such a small number of examples.[52]

(6) Moreover, at the very center of Christianity are the utterly unique historical events of the crucifixion and resurrection of Jesus Christ, which cannot be accounted for by references to Hellenistic mythical motifs. After noting the vastly different nature of the death and resurrection of Jesus, Fuller states, "The idea of resurrection in the biblical sense appears to be foreign to antiquity."[53] Mark Smith agrees that the New Testament notions of death and resurrection are clearly drawn from Old Testament backgrounds rather than Hellenistic ideas.[54] Similarly,

---

[48] Fuller, *Foundations of New Testament Christology*, 98. On a related topic, Fuller judges that the gnostic redeemer myth "is not directly attested in pre-Christian sources" (93). Later he adds, "Only in second-century 'Christian' Gnosticism does the incarnate redeemer figure finally penetrate the gnostic tradition" (97). These are devastating comments directed at the inability of the divine man scenario to make its case.

[49] Fuller, 93 and 97, respectively, cf. also 98.

[50] Fuller, 68–72.

[51] Blackburn, "Miracle Working," 199–202, quotation on 199.

[52] Holladay, *Theios Aner*, 237.

[53] Fuller, *Foundations of New Testament Christology*, 90, cf. also 142–43. On the atonement as the very early theological side of Jesus's death by crucifixion, see Martin Hengel, *The Atonement: The Origins of the Doctrine in the New Testament*, trans. John Bowden (Philadelphia: Fortress, 1981), 31–32, 65–75. For more on the uniqueness of Jesus's resurrection, see 34–39; see also Norman Anderson, *Christianity and World Religions: The Challenge of Pluralism* (Downers Grove, IL: InterVarsity, 1984), 48–81.

[54] Mark S. Smith, "The Death of 'Dying and Rising Gods' in the Biblical World: An Update, with Special Reference to Baal in the Baal Cycle," *Scandinavian Journal of the Old Testament* 12 (1998): 312–13.

I. Howard Marshall concludes concerning the deity of Christ, "the influence of pagan ideas is minimal."[55]

(7) The last issue here is more of a further indication of systematic failure than it is a specific refutation per se. It has been shown that the data on behalf of the *theios anēr* concept not only turned out to be quite different from what certain skeptical scholars expected, but what was discovered was that the information often tended in opposite directions away from their central theses. Any of several derivations of copycat scenarios originally touted by particular scholars who may have entertained these ideas at some time in the past largely have been abandoned decades ago. This was especially the case when the notion of a gnostic redeemer myth crumbled, as mentioned above. It is difficult to find specialist scholars who remain entranced by many of these ideas, especially in the centermost aspects of their interpretation.[56]

It must be concluded, therefore, that the evidence points very far away from the hypotheses that the Gospel records of Jesus's divinity, miracles, or other specific aspects of Jesus's life were invented, duplicated, or otherwise initiated and explained due to the influence of the Hellenistic hero stories. The slow and steady rise of this stream of thought followed by a swifter collapse can alone explain a plethora of other related (mis)understandings in New Testament exegesis that garnered so much influence during the late nineteenth through the middle of the twentieth centuries centered in the writings of scholars such as Bousset, Bultmann, and others.

There are many indications of a failed hypothesis here. For starters, the very lack of a robust definition, including clarity in the central concept of divine men, the significant areas of divergence between these pagan ideas and the Gospels, and that Old Testament and Jewish parallels do indeed lie behind and ground the Gospel

---

[55] I. Howard Marshall, *The Origins of New Testament Christology*, rev. ed. (Downers Grove, IL: InterVarsity, 1990), 128, see also 112–23, 126–29. On the deity of Jesus Christ vis-à-vis the Hellenistic options, see Cullmann, *Christology of the New Testament*, 203–37, 270, 275–90, cf. 150–64; Martin Hengel, *The Son of God* (Philadelphia: Fortress, 1976); Blackburn, "Miracle Working," 189, for the comment that the author knows of no example where a pagan miracle worker was called the Son of God, or where his divinity was argued from his miracles. Fuller, *Foundations of New Testament Christology*, 69–72, adds that the title "Son of God" is never used in Hellenistic Judaism for the divine man concept but has its chief roots in the Old Testament.

[56] As noted above, the overall failure of this general thesis contributed mightily to the downfall of Bousset's influential ideas at the close of the German liberal theological era as well as the crumbling of Bultmann's vast influence, including similar ideas that were carried on by Bultmann's school of interpretation; see Fuller, particularly 69, 93–98.

accounts, are all key problems. Even more critically, the absence of clear, pre-Christian Hellenistic accounts from which the Gospels were supposed to have borrowed, the inability to establish that these mighty men were even supposed to be miracle workers, as well as the absence of the most crucial components of the historical Christian Gospel message of the death and resurrection of Jesus Christ all militate even more seriously against the Hellenistic divine man thesis. As Blackburn concludes forcefully, belief in the "pervasive assimilation" of Hellenistic sources into the Gospel accounts, as is often claimed, is "without justification." That such pagan influence can be proven even in particular cases is "questionable" and ought not be concluded with any confidence.[57]

If "the proof is in the pudding," so to speak, then the fact that this message disappeared even among the critical scholars who, along with their disciples, popularized it appears to be the final death knell on this once-popular thesis. Whatever was left amid the dust was crushed further during the Third Quest for the historical Jesus, which has centered most of all in linking Jesus and his ministry to the roots of his Jewish background.

Apotheosis

Moving somewhat beyond the consideration of parallels such as those in the earlier examples, we are getting closer to our central interest in this entire study, namely that of the question of Jesus's resurrection from the dead. Certain historical individuals especially in the ancient world were not resurrected but were said to have been taken upward before or after their deaths, where they were subsequently divinized. Since this chapter concerns historical individuals, comparatively little will be mentioned in this section regarding nonhistorical (or primarily mythical) persons who were reportedly either apotheosized or raised from the dead.[58] In each of these

---

[57] Blackburn, "Miracle Working," 198–99, 205–6. The quoted words are from 205.

[58] An instance that was explained variously in the sources as either a resurrection, apotheosis, or murder is the case of Romulus, who was said to have been taken to heaven and glorified, later appearing to Julius Proculus (Ovid, *Metam.* 14.805–851; *Fast.* 2.481–509). However, other conflicting accounts concerning Romulus were related by Livy, who reported that Romulus either disappeared in a storm and was later declared to be a god, or that he was actually killed by senators. See Livy, *The Early History of Rome, Books 1–5*, trans. Aubrey de Sélincourt (Harmondsworth: Penguin, 1960), 1.16. As with the problems pointed out below regarding more clearly historical persons, both Ovid and Livy wrote

cases (either fictitious or largely fictitious), numerous problems plague the accounts. Most notably, where these issues concern stories about largely mythical persons who never lived, there is obviously a decided lack of historical data. Even where there is a possibility that someone may actually have lived, the reports are far too late to be helpful in historical terms, such that these accounts would thereby constitute claims without evidence.

Attention will be placed here on the comparatively fewer number of claims that historical persons were either apotheosized or raised from the dead. Examples of apotheosis in regard to historical individuals include Julius Caesar, Augustus Caesar, Apollonius of Tyana, and Antinous.

In ancient times, apotheosis may have been the most common expression of the afterlife experience in the Greco-Roman world. Historical persons were frequently reported to have been snatched up to heaven or to the gods and divinized.

---

approximately 700 years after Romulus was supposed to have lived. This exceptionally large time gap exempts these treatments as historical records, in addition to other questions pertaining to the likelihood that Romulus even existed at all, or that he did exist but where the reports were accompanied by much nonhistorical or mythical storytelling. Hercules (also spelled Heracles), a mythological hero, is said to have burned to death on a funeral pyre, afterward being taken to heaven and glorified by Jupiter. See Thomas Bulfinch, *Bulfinch's Mythology* (New York: Dell, 1959), 122–23. But W. H. D. Rouse reports the conflicting tale that Heracles was performing a sacrifice for personal safety, and he put on an enchanted robe that began to burn him. He was then laid on a couch but died a short time later, after which his soul went to heaven; see Rouse, *Gods, Heroes and Men of Ancient Greece* (New York: New American Library, 1957), 70. The story is told of Aristaeus, who reportedly entered a fuller's shop where he died. When his relatives arrived, he could not be found anywhere, so it was assumed that he had been taken to heaven. It was also said that Aristaeus reappeared seven years later, disappeared, and reappeared yet again, a full 340 years later (Origen, *Cels.* 3.26). Origen critiques this account of Aristaeus by providing numerous criticisms (3.27–29). Last, Asclepios was a physician who was able to heal people through administering medicines and ointments. He was killed by a thunderbolt sent by Jupiter/Zeus after using a herb to raise a man from the dead. But Jupiter/Zeus revived Asclepios and placed him either among the stars, so that "we may think that the kind, good Asclepios is not quite dead and finished" (Rouse, 87–88). Or Aesclepios may have been "received" among the gods (Bulfinch, 106). For evaluations of the so-called mythical dying-and-rising gods, see the detailed discussion provided in the previous chapter. The sections on apotheosis and non-Christian resurrection claims in this chapter is a much larger, more detailed, and updated treatment taken from Gary R. Habermas, "Resurrection Claims in Non-Christian Religions," *Religious Studies* 25 (1989): 168–70.

Several mythical expressions of this have already been mentioned above. In the Roman era, this process was frequently portrayed by the sighting of a comet or a star in the sky, which was believed to be the departed soul of the hero. For instance, Suetonius explains that after the death of Julius Caesar, "a comet appeared about an hour before sunset and shone for seven days running. This was held to be Caesar's soul, elevated to heaven; hence the star, now placed above the forehead of his divine image" (*Jul.* 88).[59]

During the cremation of Augustus Caesar, Suetonius similarly relates, "An ex-praetor actually swore that he had seen Augustus' spirit soaring up to Heaven through the flames" (*Aug.* 100). Another example concerns Antinous, Emperor Hadrian's favorite slave. When Antinous died, Hadrian approved of the teaching that a particular star was created from the soul of his slave. Hadrian built a city at the site of Antinous's death and erected several statues at various locations around the Roman Empire in Antinous's honor.[60] One statue of Antinous announced that he was now glorified in heaven and that he was actually Osiris.[61]

Rather intriguingly, Suetonius explains that comets likewise reportedly signaled the deaths of Emperors Claudius and Vespasian (*Claud.* 46; *Vesp.* 23). These sorts of accounts were most likely related to the Roman belief that their emperors were frequently elevated after death, with Suetonius noting that five of the twelve Caesars concerning whose lives he wrote were later deified.[62]

A last, major example of apotheosis was mentioned earlier concerning first-century Neopythagorean philosopher Apollonius of Tyana. Apollonius's lengthy story was told in much detail by his major biographer, Philostratus, who concludes his work by claiming that Apollonius was not seen after he entered a temple, apparently indicating that he was probably transported to heaven and divinized. Many years later Philostratus mentioned that a man saw Apollonius in a dream, convincing the young skeptic of the truth of immortality (*Vit. Apoll.* 8.30–31).

Are such accounts of apotheosis in any way evidentially credible? It is virtually impossible to ascertain how this in any way could be the case. Several insurmountable

---

[59] Quotations in this chapter taken from Suetonius, *The Twelve Caesars*, trans. Robert Graves (London: Penguin, 1957).

[60] Cassius Dio, *Hist. Rom.* 69.11.2. This account is also reproduced in David R. Cartlidge and David L. Dungan, *Documents for the Study of the Gospels* (Cleveland: Collins, 1980), 199.

[61] Cartlidge and Dungan, *Documents for the Study of the Gospels*, 198.

[62] These five emperors were Julius Caesar, Augustus, Claudius, Vespasian, and Titus.

problems immediately surface. First, each of the sources that report these details
above are relatively late and otherwise highly questionable. While Suetonius was a
good ancient historian and did have access to some official Roman records, he still
wrote about 150 years after Julius Caesar and about 100 years after Augustus. While
this certainly does not invalidate his work by itself, it should make modern readers
very cautious. For instance, both sources were written a far greater temporal gap from
the events they describe than the oft-criticized distance between the Gospel of John
and the end of Jesus's life, with the gap back to the life of Julius Caesar being over
twice the length of time between John and Jesus. Cassius Dio also wrote his history
approximately 100 years after Hadrian, which is about the same distance of time
separating Philostratus and Apollonius of Tyana, as pointed out earlier.

Further, habitual inclusions of paranormal phenomena, often of an incredible
nature, are a known feature of Greco-Roman history, including Suetonius's historical
writing.[63] Examples from both Livy and Suetonius are located easily.[64] Moreover, the
Roman acceptance of emperor worship helps explain references to apotheosis too, as
almost half of Suetonius's twelve emperors were later reportedly deified.[65]

---

[63] As will be mentioned directly below, it is not so much the astonishing nature of
these claims as it is the questions as to whether there is any sort of confirmation for the
assertions. See Robert Graves's foreword to Suetonius, *Twelve Caesars*, 7.

[64] For Livy in his *History of Rome*, many examples are found throughout. Even in just
the first third of the first book alone, we find emphases on subjects like stories of the gods
(1.3–4; 6–7, 9–10, 12, 16), the occurrence of miracles (1.16), the role of fate (1.3), portents,
prophecies, and signs (1.6–7), a possible case of apotheosis (1.16), immortality (1.7, 16),
and other incredible stories, like the temporary nursing of baby twins by a wolf (1.4). This is
not to say that Livy was as gullible as others around him, for he does recognize, for example,
the presence of fable (1.4, 6) and no doubt questioned many of these tales himself. But
that it was the general ethos of his times can hardly be questioned. Likewise, Suetonius in
The Twelve Caesars similarly reports stories of the gods or the supernatural (*Jul.* 47; *Nero*
56–57), the potential virginal conception of Augustus (*Aug.* 94), Augustus seeing Julius
Caesar's ghost (*Aug.* 96), the importance of omens (*Aug.* 81, 92; *Vesp.* 5), portents and
prophecies (*Jul.* 88; *Aug.* 96; *Vesp.* 5, 7, 23–25; *Cal.* 57–58; *Claud.* 46; *Nero* 56; *Dom.* 23),
and apotheosis (*Jul.* 88).

[65] As at other places in this study, the imagined catcalls here from skeptics are quite
loud. "What hypocrisy! How in the world can someone complain about blatant, stupid, and
even weird paranormal phenomena from other ancient authors when the Bible includes
worse things? But most of all, you question paranormal items elsewhere and all the time
evaluating whether Jesus is the Son of God who returned bodily from the dead? And it all
must be taken by faith! Just what is the problem here?" Initially and very briefly, a few items
ought to be mentioned. We have discussed in several places in this study how the New

Second, and more damaging to the presence of the miraculous statements being made, are the reports claiming that a spirit ascended to heaven or that stars and comets indicate the presence of a deceased person's glorified soul. Needless to say, these do not qualify as historical or as any other sort of evidence. Usually even worse are the plethora of statements both from chiefly mythological figures (like Romulus or Aristaeus) as well as historical persons (such as Apollonius of Tyana) of whom it was reported that their disappearance from a particular location was taken as a sign that the individual was taken to heaven and divinized. Since when do doubts about a person's whereabouts automatically mean that he or she was whisked away to heaven?

The nature of these inferences is frankly ludicrous, whether taken poetically, mythologically, or otherwise, especially if they are meant to influence others. They almost make one want to facetiously respond, "Sure, that is the very first thing that occurs to me, too, when someone is not where they are supposed to be. It just seemed that they must have risen straight up to heaven!" Hence, Apollonius's disappearance from a temple provides no indication, signal, or even a mere suggestion that anything supernatural has happened there, and especially not apotheosis and the resulting divinization. Nor does a skeptic's dream decades after the historical individual's

---

Testament is incredibly reserved when addressing the presence of the supernatural, unlike the cases of Livy and Suetonius directly above, particularly when it is remembered that all of the examples from Livy were drawn from just the early pages of the first book alone of the dozens of his books that have survived. This point is often conceded, even by rather radical skeptical scholars, as we have seen. For one example from earlier in this chapter, no less a skeptic than Rudolf Bultmann asserted that "the New Testament miracle stories are extremely reserved" in not attributing magical or other similar aspects to the miracle accounts, unlike those observed in many of the Hellenistic stories. See Bultmann, "Study of the Synoptic Gospels," 38. Further, no serious evidence exists for the large number of Greco-Roman tales, certainly nothing that is enough to substantiate them. On the other hand, the entire initial volume in this study is devoted to the excellent evidence on behalf of Jesus's resurrection, which it is fair to say is head and shoulders above any other miraculous claim at the center of a religion, especially from ancient times. Former eminent atheist philosopher and later deist Antony Flew is an example of an unbeliever who has conceded much of this material. Flew readily admitted that "the evidence for the resurrection is better than for claimed miracles in any other religion. It's outstandingly different in quality and quantity." See Flew in Gary R. Habermas, "My Pilgrimage from Atheism to Theism: A Discussion between Antony Flew and Gary R. Habermas," *Philosophia Christi* 6 (2004): 197–211, esp. 209–11. Readers are of course able to make up their own minds regarding the historicity of this event, but we have seen enough even to this point to indicate that the New Testament is clearly not just a matter of stories for gullible persons generated by silly and poor thinking.

life ended provide any sign pointing to the truth of immortality, especially when the author states that the others present saw nothing (Philostratus, *Vit. Apoll.* 8.31). At best, these are subjective testimonies without supporting data that are hardly even open to any verification whatsoever.[66]

Third, it is difficult to conceive how apotheosis reports, whether true (though without any evidence whatsoever) or false, can necessarily either help or hinder conclusions concerning resurrection anyway. In other words, it has been argued that the belief in an afterlife is nearly "universal" but this by itself is vastly different than the claim that a historical person was actually raised from the dead and appeared to his followers in space and time, which is the subject of this study.

Resurrection Claims in Non-Christian Belief Systems

Concerning historical persons for whom a resurrection is claimed, several cases will be mentioned briefly followed by a critique. Rabbi Judah I was a major Jewish wise man, teacher, and scholar who was instrumental in completing the compilation of the Mishnah about AD 200. The Gemara texts report concerning Rabbi Judah is that after his death in 220, "he used to come home again at twilight every Sabbath Eve." On one particular occasion, a neighbor came to the rabbi's door but was denied entrance by his maid. When the incident was made known to Rabbi Judah, he refrained from coming back to his home so as not to upstage other righteous persons who did not return to their houses after death.[67]

Kabir, a forerunner to the Sikh religious movement, was a religious teacher of the fifteenth and sixteenth centuries who endeavored to combine specific facets of both the Hindu and Muslim religions. After his death, usually placed at 1518, many sources indicated that Kabir's followers argued over the question of whether his body should be cremated in accordance with Hindu customs or buried as preferred by Muslims. A later text reports that, in order to end the controversy, Kabir himself is

---

[66] Granted, the point will be made by some that these sorts of comments concerning comets, stars, disappearances, and the like should be responded to more gracefully, in the spirit of the times in which they were made. To a certain extent this is certainly true, but sometimes they are made by scholars who do believe them, like Pliny, Suetonius, Josephus, Tacitus, and Plutarch, among others. So the reports may be offered as true either by the authors themselves or on behalf of others of their day. Regardless, it must be noted that this is not evidence.

[67] See b. Ketubbot 103a in Slotki, *Babylonian Talmud.*

said to have appeared to his followers and directed them to peel back the cloth that had been placed over his body. When this request was performed, living flowers were found underneath the material instead of Kabir's body, which was gone. The Hindus burned half of these flowers while the Muslims buried the other half.[68] Virtually the same story was also told of another Sikh teacher and arguably the religion's founder, Nanak, who died in 1539.[69]

Seventeenth-century Jewish teacher Sabbatai Zevi was one of the most prominent individuals who proclaimed that he was the Messiah, a teaching that was further agreed to by Nathan, a contemporary Jewish prophetic figure who served as Sabbatai's key follower. After Sabbatai's death in 1676, it was reported that his brother Elijah went to his tomb and discovered that a dragon was guarding the entrance. Being allowed to enter, Elijah did not discover Sabbatai's body but saw that the cave was full of light. Strangely enough though, it was also reported that Sabbatai did not actually die but only appeared to do so, which became a prominent teaching that gained wide acceptance among his followers. In fact, Nathan also agreed that Sabbatai had not died and stated that he would soon reveal that this was the case.[70]

Nineteenth-century Hindu guru Lahiri Mahasaya died in 1895 and was cremated. After reportedly stating to his followers that he would rise again, it was claimed that he had appeared to three of them individually. These meetings were reportedly rather brief and happened in three different cities at approximately the same time, during which it was also commented that Mahasaya's body appeared to be transfigured.[71]

Last, another Hindu guru, Sri Yukteswar, died and was buried in 1936. A chief disciple, Paramhansa Yogananda, explains that one week after seeing a vision of the Hindu avatar Krishna and more than three months after his master's death, he received a flesh-and-blood appearance of the dead Yukteswar while he was meditating. He said that he touched his teacher's body and also enjoyed a two-hour conversation with

---

[68] Cf. James Hastings, ed., *Encyclopedia of Religion and Ethics* (New York: Scribner's Sons, 1955), s.v. "Kabir, Kabirpanthis" (7:632–34).

[69] W. Owen Cole and Piara Singh Sambhi, *The Sikhs: Their Religion, Beliefs, and Practices* (London: Routledge & Kegan Paul, 1978), 16. Both cases are documented in detail below.

[70] Especially authoritative is Gershom Scholem's massive work, *Sabbatai Sevi: The Mystical Messiah* (Princeton: Princeton University Press, 1973), 917–29.

[71] Paramhansa Yogananda, *Autobiography of a Yogi* (Los Angeles: Self-Realization Fellowship, 1956), 348–50.

him, chiefly concerning the nature of the afterlife. Yogananda also commented that on another occasion that happened approximately three months earlier, an elderly woman also reported seeing Yukteswar after his death.[72]

When examples of apotheosis and resurrection such as these are reported in a straightforward manner apart from any critical investigation (as is often done today), some might presume that claims of postmortem phenomena are common, and some might even conclude that such occurrences happen quite regularly. Some researchers, like Robert Price, encourage skepticism in regard to all such claims in light of the various parallels between them.[73] Others, such as Yogananda, conclude that there have been numerous spiritual masters throughout the world religions who have been raised from the dead. Intriguingly, Yogananda illustrates this comment by referring to the resurrection of Jesus![74] Are any of these positions warranted by the data that we possess?

Concerning the non-Christian resurrection claims, critical investigation reveals numerous problems, with the most significant issue by far being the state of the historical evidence in each of these examples. Regarding the date of Rabbi Judah's postresurrection appearance testimony, while the rabbi died in AD 220, the gemara in which the incident is actually recorded is dated from about the fifth century.[75] This is a major time gap of a couple of hundred years in the testimony. Additionally, the text lists the maid as the only witness to the phenomena, and there is no attempt to provide any evidence. This late date of the material plus the lack of evidence does not completely disprove the story, but it shows that it would be virtually impossible even to begin to demonstrate it as historical.

In the case of Kabir, scholars have noted often that the overwhelming problem is the absence of any early or historical documentation, as the late stories that do exist indicate a proliferation of unevidenced data. In fact, only a few facts about Kabir's life are known with assurance. No primary, evidentially relevant records are available for examination, and none of these document a postmortem appearance.[76] Some of

---

[72] Yogananda, 413–33.

[73] Robert M. Price, "Is There a Place for Historical Criticism?," *Religious Studies* 27 (1991): esp. 373–88.

[74] Yogananda, *Autobiography of a Yogi*, 313, cf. 349.

[75] Personal conversation with Asher Finkel, Seton Hall University, May 24, 1988; cf. Hexham, "Talmud," in *Concise Dictionary of Religion*, 93.

[76] For instance, see David Lorenzen, *Kabir Legends and Ananta-Das's Kabir Parachai* (Albany, NY: SUNY Press, 1991), 3–8, 18. Lorenzen explains, "Two texts compete for the

Kabir's likely preserved writings consisted of hymns and poetry, comparable to the Old Testament book of Psalms. Kabir "taught through his poems."[77]

Several important studies indicate that legend crept up in the aftermath of Kabir's life, especially at each of the points involving supernatural claims like a miraculous birth, miracles performed during his life, and the account of his appearing to his disciples after death. In fact, the earliest source regarding Kabir's death does not relate the postmortem appearance mentioned above at all. Rather this key source along with others explains the incident of Kabir's deceased body being covered with flowers, but a later check did not reveal the body—much like some of the apotheosis stories of disappearance related above. Intriguingly, given the story that Kabir's body had disappeared, more than one place of death is listed in the literature, plus two different tombs are also reported.[78] Mohan Singh argues that "in the Indian setting" this was a "very normal process by which a creature of legend is made."[79]

Additionally, virtually the exact same story as the earliest source told about Kabir and the flowers was also related as occurring to Nanak, the founder of what later would be Sikhism. Like the earliest Kabir material, while Nanak was apparently close

---

honor of being the oldest to contain a coherent set of legends about Kabir," but research indicates that one, almost assuredly, dates about 100 to more likely 200 years after Kabir in the eighteenth century (9). Another quite negative appraisal of the data is found in Hastings, *Encyclopedia of Religion and Ethics*, s.v. "Nānak," 9:181–84, particularly 181–82.

[77] While some of Kabir's words were apparently written down decades after his death, these were devotional in nature, consisting chiefly of hymns and poetry. Further, scholars are uncertain exactly which of these writings are actually his and which are from others, especially since the poems and verses were frequently mixed with those of other authors. See Hilda Wierum Boulter, "Sikhism," in *Religion in the Twentieth Century*, ed. Vergilius Ferm (New York: Philosophical Library, 1948), 195. Much more crucially for our purposes, these earlier writings *do not* include historical data regarding anything happening after Kabir's death, as related above. Similar details often can be found, for example, in W. H. McCleod, *Guru Nanak and the Sikh Religion* (Oxford: Oxford University Press, 1968), 50–51; John Clark Archer, *The Sikhs* (Princeton: Princeton University Press, 1946), 50, 52–55; S. A. Nigosian, *World Religions: A Historical Approach*, 3rd ed. (Boston: St. Martin's, 2000), 46, 345–50.

[78] Lorenzen, *Kabir Legends*, 42.

[79] Mohan Singh, *Kabir and the Bhakti Movement*, 3 vols. (Lahore: Ram and Sons, 1934), with the points arranged by Archer, who summarizes Singh's demarcation of the steps by which legend may have appeared in the life and teachings concerning Kabir, as Archer poses the question of Singh's success (*Sikhs*, 63–65).

to death and was still speaking to his followers, he was not yet deceased.[80] Nor was Kabir. The followers of both of these teachers thought that these men were taken to heaven.[81] Therefore, attempting to reconstruct the events surrounding both Kabir and Nanak's deaths beyond some of the very earliest details is seemingly impossible given the dearth of historical materials. But to repeat, no postmortem appearances are mentioned for either individual in the earliest sources.[82]

Moreover, beyond the obvious historical concerns here, several other criticisms chiefly in the form of alternative formulations of the data could be leveled at the cases of either Kabir or Nanak, as will be indicated below with another such account. For just one example, what other options are available regarding the disappearances of the bodies? Unfortunately, these questions need not even be asked and cannot be investigated due to the same problems with the available data. But the demonstrated presence of legend, especially in the crucial portions of the reports, along with the absence of any early, verifiable historical documentation are decisive enough in this investigation since they effectively block research into these later resurrection claims.

The critiques here of Rabbi Judah, Kabir, and Nanak indicate that miracles, postmortem appearances, apotheosis, and other legendary events are claimed but are hardly comparable to Jesus.[83] Rather, the central concern is that there are no reliable

---

[80] Lorenzen, *Kabir Legends*, 125–28 for the text of the earliest Kabir account; regarding the same story being found in Nanak, cf. Nigosian, *World Religions*, 346; Boulter, "Sikhism," 201; Max Arthur MacAuliffe, *The Sikh Religion*, 2 vols. (Oxford: Clarendon, 1901), 1:189–91; Dorothy Field, *The Religion of the Sikhs* (London: Murray, 1914), 16; Charles Potter, "Nanak," in *The Great Religious Leaders* (New York: Simon & Schuster, 1958), 313.

[81] Cole and Sambhi, *Sikhs*, 16; John Clark Archer, *Faiths Men Live By* (New York: Ronald, 1958), 339; Robert Hume, *The World's Living Religions* (New York: Scribner's Sons, 1959), 94–95.

[82] Harbans Singh, *Guru Nanek and the Origins of the Sikh Faith* (Mumbai Asia Publishing House, 1969), 193–98; Lorenzen, *Kabir Legends*, 9, 125–28. Personal correspondence with Jasvir Basi, whose book of interaction, *Sikhism: Cross-Examined*, is forthcoming.

[83] Some scholars may no doubt be critical that the entire point of this critique has been missed in these cases by being too intent on looking for historical data in what are no doubt simple texts that are plainly not of that more rigorous nature. In other words, this criticism would be that these texts cannot be studied by the application of more demanding standards of historicity to texts that are meant to be taken as stories and poetry to inspire, not to be investigated historically. However, while this is probably indeed the case here, this just seems to be a very similar way to make the original points in the evaluation. If these sources are not to be taken as historical, then that seems precisely another way to say that the incidents in question cannot be confirmed by normal research procedures.

historical data from early, eyewitness sources against which later claims can be critically weighed, compared, and ascertained. So the crucial point is not that resurrection appearances may be claimed, which is hardly an anomaly. What is important is the lack of verification for these claims. Thus, in the absence of this crucial documentation, such negative conclusions are necessary.

A major character in such discussions is that of Sabbatai Zevi. However, like that of Apollonius of Tyana, numerous very serious historical problems exist for anyone who would argue for a resurrection or even for other supernatural elements in his life. Here are some of the more damaging issues:

- Miracle stories purporting to have been performed by Sabbatai spread almost immediately after his trips to various cities, with letters from Palestine being sent to various communities even in northern Europe. These communications, which were sent far and wide, contained many rumors and unsubstantiated reports. As Stephen Sharot states: "There were often wide gaps between the teachings of Nathan, the events around Zvi in the Middle East, and the content of the news. . . . The letters and rumors told of miracles and mythological and apocalyptic events occurring in the present."[84] Some of these tales concerned rather incredible and certainly mistaken claims, such as the lost ten tribes of Israel reappearing in Arabia, that the city of Mecca had been destroyed, and that particular Christian churches had sunk into the earth.[85]

- Additionally, some Christian reports did not help matters at all. Dependent upon the Jewish rumors, these tales "added distortions, exaggerations, and embellishments of their own."[86]

- Nathan, Sabbatai's prophetic "forerunner," even argued against the truth of such miraculous tales himself, on the grounds that faith alone should suffice for the faithful![87]

- Concerning Sabbatai's claims to be the Jewish Messiah, additional problems surfaced. Some of Sabbatai's activities and statements can presumably be

---

[84] Stephen Sharot, *Messianism, Mysticism and Magic: A Sociological Analysis of Jewish Religious Movements* (Chapel Hill, NC: University of North Carolina Press, 1982), 87–88, 90.

[85] Sharot, 88.

[86] Sharot, 88.

[87] Sharot, 87–88.

explained in that it is known that he was manic-depressive, which could have
been a strong factor in these grandiose thoughts and pronouncements.[88]

- An enormous and even more devastating blow to his efforts was that Sabbatai
  was imprisoned by the Turkish Muslims and given the choice of either dying
  or converting to Islam. Not only did Sabbatai deny that he had made any
  messianic claims, but he also converted to the Islamic faith! Further, he then
  encouraged some of his disciples to also become Muslims too! At this point,
  most of his followers admitted that they had been mistaken in their beliefs,
  with some even turning to Christianity.[89]

- What about Sabbatai's death and afterward? Several even more serious problems can be detected here. Although Sabbatai died in 1676, the major teaching of Nathan and the Sabbatians was that he only *appeared* to die, perhaps
  involving a swoon thesis of sorts. In principle, portions of this view may actually be comparable to the apotheosis cases described earlier, chiefly regarding
  those of the Roman emperors.[90]

- Pertaining to the report that Sabbatai's brother Elijah discovered his tomb
  to be empty and guarded by a dragon, Scholem notes the specific stages
  through which this legend grew, evidenced by the internal documents of
  Sabbatai's followers.[91]

- While one of the group's letters notes Nathan's teaching that Sabbatai was
  still alive and that Nathan would soon meet with him again, Scholem points
  out that when this letter was written, Nathan himself had been dead for a
  month, without having rendezvoused with Sabbatai.[92]

- Lastly, actual claims with specific details that Sabbatai appeared after his
  death are lacking anyway, especially when the official group stance taught
  by Nathan denied Sabbatai's death in the first place, hence removing a
  resurrection from the picture. At any rate, there is no historical evidence
  for any resurrection or subsequent appearances of Sabbatai and thus, no
  rivals to Jesus.

---

[88] Sharot, 91; Gershom G. Scholem, *Major Trends in Jewish Mysticism* (New York:
Schocken, 1974), 90.

[89] For Sharot's report of these events, see *Messianism, Mysticism and Magic*, 115–17.

[90] Scholem, *Sabbatai Sevi*, 920, 922–24; Sharot, *Messianism, Mysticism and Magic*, 122.

[91] Scholem, *Sabbati Sevi*, 919–20.

[92] Sharot, *Messianism, Mysticism and Magic*, 925.

All told, the story of Sabbatai Zevi is lengthy and quite detailed, involving many strange and almost unparalleled twists and turns. Few well-known religious figures probably had as many strange and even contradictory items reported of them.

Regarding the claims that Hindu leaders Lahiri Mahasaya and Sri Yukteswar appeared to their followers after their deaths, similar types of critical questioning such as those already proposed must still be applied. Even though it was said that Mahasaya appeared to three individual people, and it is claimed that Yukteswar appeared to two people, one of whom touched him, numerous queries must still be made.

For example, all five reported appearances were to single individuals while they were alone. Especially in light of this fact, along with the possibility that most of these persons were grieving, hallucination is certainly very possible (if not likely). Or what about other subjective hypotheses such as autosuggestion, especially with persons who so readily accepted belief in such phenomena?[93] Or could parapsychological phenomena such as occultic activity be factored in here, which is certainly a possibility if not actually hinted at by those involved in some of these cases?[94]

Embellished accounts that grow over time are a known reality in religious literature, as pointed out earlier in this essay, and the above accounts certainly do not erase that possibility. The practice of Eastern meditation also needs to be mentioned as a possible contributory factor, at least in the example here where Yogananda claims to have seen and touched his former guru Yukteswar while meditating. Making this experience even more likely is Yogananda's comment that he saw Yukteswar "one week after the vision of Krishna," whom he saw poised above the roof of a nearby building as Krishna "waved to me, smiling and nodding in greeting."[95] This last element alone seems to affect the credibility of the testimony given in the ensuing appearance comment.[96] And we must not rule out even the possibility of plain

---

[93] Yogananda, *Autobiography of a Yogi*, 313, 349.

[94] For instance, one former Indian guru attests, "My world was filled with spirits and gods and occult powers, and my obligation from childhood was to give each its due." See Rabindranath R. Maharaj with Dave Hunt, *Escape into the Light* (Eugene, OR: Harvest House, 1984), 24. This volume was formerly published under the title *Death of a Guru* (Philadelphia: Holman, 1977).

[95] Yogananda, *Autobiography of a Yogi*, 413.

[96] It would seem that the simply incredible nature of the claim to have seen Krishna apparently suspended above a nearby building would bother many researchers. But beyond even this statement, and in an effort to remain open to various possibilities without rejecting religious claims in an a priori manner, how could Yogananda recognize and identify Krishna in the first place, *even if* he had seen him? A problem here would definitely also have a

misreporting of various types in some such accounts. Price cites a report of blatant examples in the Muslim tradition.[97] It must be remembered that no single alternative hypothesis need necessarily account for all reported appearances. Different (or even combined) natural theories potentially could be the answer.[98]

Here again, as we have done throughout, we must also note that it is not enough simply to report a miracle. Such a case must be substantiated in detail, especially if it is to serve as a basis for one's personal beliefs. The burden of proof would seem to be on the shoulders of those who claim that a resurrection has occurred. A miracle claim would appear to require strong attestation since such events are not the normal fare.[99] But the necessary evidence has not been provided in any of the non-Christian cases before us. Simply to claim or even to report a resurrection is obviously not the same as substantiating it.

Conclusion

It is exceptionally intriguing to note how often some skeptical scholars who are otherwise very critical in their approach to Christian claims are not at all critical, or at least much less so, when they address non-Christian claims of apotheosis and resurrection. For example, while discussing Jesus's resurrection, the well-known skeptical New Testament scholar John A. T. Robinson tells the story of a possible case of Buddhist apotheosis. In 1953 a saintly man died and was wrapped in a blanket and kept briefly in a locked room inside a home. When the locals went to retrieve the

---

bearing on the next instance with Yukteswar. In other words, if Yogananda presumably cannot positively identify Krishna for sure from perhaps millennia beforehand before any photos, what can be said about the next appearance claim, which was also quite subjective? In fact, many researchers might retort that Yogananda has hereby seriously compromised his testimony as a reporter, at least in any evidential sense.

[97] Price, "Historical Criticism," 378–379.

[98] Of course, we have already raised and addressed in much detail the same sorts of issues in this study with regard to the resurrection of Jesus.

[99] Generally speaking, it is usually the case that persons require more evidence to believe an extraordinary event than to accept a regular occurrence. But it is not the case, whether or not this is taken to be David Hume's position in his famous essay on miracles, that virtually no evidence (or none at all, as in certain recent statements and debates) can ever establish a miracle. Strong evidence is needed, but it must remain a condition that can at least potentially be met. Hume's position is found in his essay "Of Miracles," in his volume *An Enquiry concerning Human Understanding*.

body, it was not there. The local villagers concluded that the man was "absorbed and transmuted" and thus taken into the afterlife. As far as the matter is explained, no one investigated or raised any countertheories such as swoon, a stolen body, legend, and so on. Nor did Robinson respond in such a critical manner in his own presentation of the story. The incident was simply reported in a straightforward manner.[100]

In another instance, prominent process philosopher Charles Hartshorne discussed the resurrection of Jesus in response to a debate between Antony Flew and me. He mentions that "all the religions tell of miracles." Then after mentioning a couple of such occurrences attributed to Buddha, Hartshorne remarks, "I do not feel that I can choose among such accounts."[101] He adds, "I can neither explain away the evidences to which Habermas appeals, nor can I simply agree with Flew's or Hume's positions."[102] But just for starters, according to critical scholars, Buddha's miracles were described hundreds of years after his death, while Jesus's resurrection was reported immediately, as seen throughout this study! How are they to be compared in terms of the research?[103] But as noted, here is another example where the Christian claims are subjected to the strictest critique while the Buddhist teachings are left alone!

But just because miracle reports may very well abound in the various religions, there is no reason to think that they therefore must remain on the same epistemic footing. Again, one issue raised repeatedly in this study concerns that of critical interaction with miracle reports. Are all miracle claims in the world's religions to be accepted, rejected, or placed on hold en masse simply because even a wide variety of these reports may exist, as Hartshorne seems to favor? Once again, where is the critical study of these matters?

As already asserted in this chapter, one must be critical of both Price's skepticism concerning all potentially supernatural accounts as well as Yogananda's seeming ready

---

[100] John A. T. Robinson, *The Human Face of God* (Philadelphia: Westminster, 1973), 138–39.

[101] Charles Hartshorne, response to the debate between Gary R. Habermas and Antony G. N. Flew, in *Did Jesus Rise from the Dead? The Resurrection Debate*, ed. Terry L. Miethe (San Francisco: Harper & Row, 1987), 137.

[102] Hartshorne response to Habermas and Flew, 142.

[103] For some initial comparisons by a Buddhist scholar between the sources for Buddha and those for Jesus and his followers, admitting that the later are far stronger, see Edward Conze, ed. and trans., *Buddhist Scriptures* (London: Penguin, 1959), 11–12, 34, cf. 62–64. See also Paul Gwynne, *Buddha, Jesus, Muhammad: A Comparative Study* (Oxford: Wiley-Blackwell, 2014), 1–19, 127–31, 242–44.

acceptance of many or perhaps even most of them. The chief problem with both of these and similar approaches is precisely that the conclusions are too frequently held far too easily apart from critical, mostly historical, analyses of the data. More specifically, Price, Yogananda, Robinson, and Hartshorne have all declined to apply rigorous critiques to non-Christian claims, perhaps for more than one reason. Further, all but Yogananda seem more than willing to apply much skepticism in the other direction toward Christianity, including very specific criticisms. Dare we raise the question here that perhaps there is a very strong desire to keep all religions on basically the same footing regardless of their potential evidential considerations? Further, is there a strong bias that has perhaps only grown stronger in the years since these four scholars wrote that, whatever Christianity has to offer, it cannot be allowed to be placed above other religious systems, even if the evidential considerations outweigh the other traditions?[104]

Whatever the reasons for this general one-way view among many skeptical researchers, it must be recognized that such non-Christian claims have not fared well in terms of historical investigation. This lack of evidence among the non-Christian beliefs does not necessarily disprove these beliefs. But it certainly seems to suggest at least that they have not been established (or known) by historical methodology.[105]

What if more evidence is discovered or produced on behalf of some of these non-Christian claims in the future, or if entirely new cases are utilized? What if early evidence for one or more non-Christian reports appears? Initially, such suppositions are somewhat arbitrary in that one could almost always postulate the possibility of future evidence for just about any proposition. Further, while such new data might help to eliminate major naturalistic alternative views here and there, they could fail to rule out other elements or strengthen possible hypotheses or even create new criticisms. The cases from long periods of time in the past potentially could be more difficult as far as gathering data. But to be sure, all viable naturalistic theories need to be addressed, whether Christian or not, even if simply a host of data would be

---

[104] Again, see Anderson's treatment in comparing several major religious claims from both the past and present across a number of key features in *Christianity and World Religions*, 48–81.

[105] Perhaps strangely enough, one potential exception must be mentioned on behalf of Price's research. Even though he is very critical of Christian claims, he still concludes his earlier discussion of the resurrection of Jesus with the exceptionally intriguing but largely unexplained comment: "One need not assume that there was no resurrection. Indeed it was precisely because of experiences of some kind (such as those intriguingly listed but not described by Paul in I Corinthians 15) that anyone cared to glorify Jesus." See Price, "Historical Criticism," 383.

required to change some of these evaluations. Still, having commented along these lines, all grounded challenges need to be considered.

As a final, brief word on these two chapters regarding both mythical and historical persons as well as apotheosis and resurrection claims in non-Christian religions that involve living persons of the past, such events have not been demonstrated by the evidence. Frankly, it is not even close. By far the largest challenge in these other examples is the lack of early plus well-evidenced, authoritative data. Each case misses by a large margin the strength of the data that favors the resurrection of Jesus.

Any of several naturalistic hypotheses may certainly be applicable to some of the examples that were investigated in the previous two chapters, and seemingly none were without serious rejoinders. Again, this is largely because there is insufficient data with which to counteract these alternative suppositions, unlike the excellent evidence for Jesus's resurrection. In some cases, one or more alternative counterhypotheses may specifically be postulated as a probable cause. In short, simply to report a miracle claim is not sufficient to establish it. This is especially the case if that miracle claim has to bear the additional burden afterward as the key support for a religious system of belief.

To answer a question posed at the outset of this chapter in light of the ensuing research here, claims such as the ones examined in the previous two chapters are quite insufficient in showing that the evidence favors any specific accounts of apotheosis, resurrection, or other similar phenomena in non-Christian stories. Further, this lack of data concerning these non-Christian claims themselves leaves any ensuing theological beliefs that depend on the supernatural cases in particular as likewise being unsubstantiated teachings.

In a day of "live and let live," especially in religious matters, this may appear to some as a harsh epitaph regarding other belief systems. But without being pejorative, the data either make the case or they do not. In court cases or certain other adjudications, sometimes preciseness in the preponderance of evidence is absolutely crucial, even if some cases just do not succeed. In the examples viewed here, if the same amount of intense scrutiny is applied to the non-Christian accounts as have been applied in this study to Jesus's resurrection, it is simply the case that needs to be recognized: the comparisons do not exonerate even one or two of the other stories. But if Jesus's message to follow him is also true, even eternal life may stand in the balances this time.[106]

---

[106] Further thoughts on these concluding matters can be found in Habermas, "Resurrection Claims," 176–77.

14

Illumination and Illusion Hypotheses

This chapter considers two naturalistic theses that are enigmas. Both have been seldom considered and have virtually never been identified by name while still finding support by some major researchers. Their ideas are somewhat related, as both potentially involve sight and can be confused with hallucination or other subjective theses. This often accounts for the multiple confusions and the often strange ways they are grouped. Few researchers actually champion either one as their primary suggestion, and most of those who mention them do so almost as side issues or illustrations.[1] Even then, these writers sometimes only attempt to mix and match dissimilar ideas rather than buttress these theses as primary theories. It would be a mistake to consider these naturalistic theories as hallucinations, as should be clear after this treatment, but the inaccuracies are hardly even noticed by those who make the connections, hence some of the reasons for the misunderstandings.

The Illumination Hypothesis

Perhaps taking hints from Luke 24:36–40, both natural as well as supernatural varieties of visionary hypotheses have been a popular means of explaining the nature of

---

[1] A few exceptions would include the primary scholars listed below who take the illumination view as their naturalistic theory of choice, but they are usually alone in doing so.

Jesus's resurrection appearances since the birth of the Christian faith. In the second century AD, the Greek philosopher and severe critic of Christianity, Celsus, commented that a hysterical and deluded woman hallucinated Jesus as being alive after his crucifixion.[2]

Among the subjective visionary theories, the charge of hallucinations has been the most popular. Though far from a widespread view, what I have dubbed as the illumination thesis argues that, through an almost completely nondescript internal process, the disciples became convinced that Jesus had been raised from the dead.[3] Rarely are many details provided. Almost always, the apostle Peter is the key. His insights provided the initial impetus, and his enthusiastic encouragement was the engine that empowered and persuaded his friends. As a result, the nearly contagious-sounding conviction that Jesus was alive spread to the others. Some idea of autosuggestion or other form of transmittable faith is thereby suggested.

Championed largely by German New Testament scholar Willi Marxsen in a day when his treatment was a rare but perennial example of a naturalistic attempt to dismiss the historical nature of the resurrection, his prototypical position espoused an inner, organized enlightenment on Peter's part, which led to the belief of the other disciples that Jesus was alive.[4] In a later volume, Marxsen continued to hold that

---

[2] The lost but reconstructed argument is taken from Origen's systematic critique *Against Celsus*; see Celsus, *On the True Doctrine: A Discourse against the Christians*, trans. R. Joseph Hoffmann (Oxford: Oxford University Press, 1987), 67–68.

[3] In Gary R. Habermas, "The Late Twentieth-Century Resurgence of Naturalistic Responses to Jesus' Resurrection," *Trinity Journal* 22 (2001): 188–89, 196. The next page and a half of this chapter has been edited and adapted from this article by permission of *Trinity Journal*.

[4] Willi Marxsen, *The Resurrection of Jesus of Nazareth*, trans. Margaret Kohl (Philadelphia: Fortress, 1970), esp. 88–97. The overall tone is critical in nature and tends to devalue the results of historical research. In that sense it is more reminiscent of Bultmann's conclusions on the resurrection, as expressed in the latter's exceptionally influential essay, "New Testament and Mythology," in *Kerygma and Myth: A Theological Debate*, ed. Hans Werner Bartsch, trans. Reginald H. Fuller (New York: Harper & Row, 1961), esp. 34–39, 42. This approach by Marxsen, emphasizing faith over history, presents an intriguing contrast with an earlier essay on the same subject by Marxsen that was argued in a different vein: "The Resurrection of Jesus as a Historical and Theological Problem," in *The Significance of the Message of the Resurrection for Faith in Jesus Christ*, ed. C. F. D. Moule (London: SCM, 1968), 5–50. This earlier writing by Marxsen tends to be more positive and presents more emphasis on recent historical research, such as that in the early pre-Pauline creed in 1 Cor 15:3–7.

Peter's faith was the primary motivation for the faith that was generated in the other disciples, although Marxsen concluded that he did not know whether this vision(s) of Jesus to Peter was subjective or objective.[5] There is a marked sense here in which the fading influence of Rudolf Bultmann may be seen, though it had grown less over the years.[6] Edward Schillebeeckx expressed some quite similar thoughts to Marxsen's, though without necessarily denying the resurrection appearances.[7]

Philosopher Thomas Sheehan perhaps supplied the most details concerning the new understanding of Jesus arrived at by Peter and the other disciples. In a flash of revelatory "insight," they understood that Jesus had been exalted and glorified by God. So, in some "ecstatic" occurrence that could have been as "ordinary as reflecting," they "saw" Jesus and "believed." Peter and the others began proclaiming that Jesus had been raised from the dead. Like Marxsen (and Cupitt below), we do not really know what happened in the first century, although Sheehan is quite clear that no resurrection event took place. Rather, all we have is the interpretation of what Peter and the other disciples experienced.[8]

---

[5] Willi Marxsen, *Jesus and Easter: Did God Raise the Historical Jesus from the Dead?*, trans. Victor Paul Furnish (Nashville: Abingdon, 1990), 70–74. The "signs of the times" perhaps were detected in this writing by Marxsen, in the sense that we all are generally influenced in some ways by the contemporary trends around us. Marxsen's 1970 *Resurrection of Jesus of Nazareth* reflects a time when Bultmann's influence was waning but was still strong. A larger number of naturalistic comments were made freely during that era. But in 1990, the major influence of the growing Third Quest for the historical Jesus was underway, and even critical scholars were often much more open to historical research, revealing for instance that Jesus was a healer and often viewing even the resurrection appearances more positively, as pointed out often in this study. One may wonder if that new historical outlook and greater openness to the Gospels exercised an influence on Marxsen's backing off the more avowed and open naturalistic stance of his 1970 text. At least the slight appearance of openness is noticeable toward the possibility that the risen Jesus may have appeared to his followers.

[6] Karl Lehmann is rather reminiscent of Bultmann's emphasis on the centrality of the disciples' faith rather than being grounded in any event, as explained in Lehmann, "Zugang zum Ostergeschehen Heute: Am Beispiel der Emmauserzählung," *Internationale Katholische Zeitschrift* 11 (1982): esp. 45–49; also Robert F. Scuka, "Resurrection: Critical Reflections on a Doctrine in Search of a Meaning," *Modern Theology* 6 (1989): esp. 79, 85, 90.

[7] Edward Schillebeeckx, *Jesus: An Experiment in Christology*, trans. Hubert Hoskins (New York: Crossroad, 1987), 369, 385–90.

[8] Thomas Sheehan, *First Coming: How the Kingdom of God Became Christianity* (New York: Random House, 1986), 103–9, 112–14, 118; Sheehan, "How Did Easter Originally

Some of Sheehan's comments were absolutely stunning, such as these gathered from a single article: "Perhaps the point is not to salvage Catholicism or Christianity but to let go of them." "Christianity begins with Simon, not with Jesus," so anyone who holds this tradition regarding Simon "can also rightly claim the title 'Christian,' even if he or she believes that Jesus is as dead as a doornail. For ultimately Jesus is not essential to Christianity. But Peter is."[9] Sheehan also ends his volume *The First Coming* with the words, "That means learning to live at the uncertain point that is the present-future, without any appeal to the 'beyond.' . . . It is the same message that Jesus preached."[10]

Theologian Don Cupitt is another who expresses some reluctance to precisely outline the nature of these experiences. But like Marxsen, he is also much more interested in the disciples' faith than in any event, for contrary to the vast majority of recent commentators, Cupitt thinks that the former precedes the latter. Through "a shocking flash of recognition everything fell into place and they saw the meaning of this man."[11]

Exhibiting several similarities sufficiently close to the ideas of Marxsen, Sheehan, Cupitt, and Spong, theologian Edward Schillebeeckx also holds that after Peter was converted, he was then instrumental in bringing the other disciples to convert. It is difficult to decipher the precise intent and direction of the (purposely?) vague language, but it seems that Schillebeeckx proposes that the disciples' experiences were not really visual appearances, at least not as reported by Paul and the Gospel writers.[12] Schillebeeckx later explains further that religious parallel legends can account for the empty tomb and appearance reports.[13]

Happen? An Hypothesis," in *The Resurrection of Jesus: A Sourcebook*, ed. Bernard Brandon Scott (Santa Rosa, CA: Polebridge, 2008), 110–15.

[9] Thomas Sheehan, "On Satan and Catholic Liberals: A Response to David Tracy," *Commonweal*, September 21, 1984, 498 and 500.

[10] Sheehan, *First Coming*, 227.

[11] Don Cupitt, *Christ and the Hiddenness of God* (Philadelphia: Westminster, 1971), 143, cf. esp. 164–67. Cf. also C. F. D. Moule and Don Cupitt, "The Resurrection: A Disagreement," in Cupitt, *Explorations in Theology* 6 (London: SCM, 1979). Peter Carnley, in *The Structure of Resurrection Belief* (Oxford: Clarendon, 1987), 154–82 provides an in-depth critique of both Marxsen and Cupitt, as do others (including directing additional comments at Sheehan and Spong).

[12] Edward Schillebeeckx, *Jesus: An Experiment in Christology*, trans. Hubert Hoskins (New York: Crossroad, 1987), 369, 385–90 for some of these comments.

[13] Schillebeeckx, 336, 441–515.

Yet, theologian Gerald O'Collins cautions that Schillebeeckx still allows the possibility that the disciples' experiences with the risen Jesus could have been real events and that he never denies that possibility.[14] This caution aside, N. T. Wright (writing at a later date) is clear in his own evaluation that Schillebeeckx did indeed hold that the disciples reported only subjective experiences rather than appearances of a living Jesus.[15]

John Shelby Spong's writings on the subject created quite an uproar when published, perhaps because he was an Episcopal bishop. Once again, for Spong, Peter was the key individual, for it was Peter rather than Jesus himself who "was resurrected to new life, a new being." Standing "as if in a trance," Peter was "suddenly aglow with life." But there were no visions, hallucinations, or anything to do with the real world. No one else in the room (including Peter) really saw Jesus. Peter then helped to open the eyes of the other followers of Jesus.[16] In a later work, Spong provides the disclaimer that, after all, we really cannot know what happened to Peter and the others. Reminiscent of the views of the influential nineteenth-century German liberal scholar David Friedrich Strauss, Spong also removes Peter's transformative experience to about six months after Jesus's death.[17]

A last, similar thesis to be mentioned here is Milan Machoveč's ideas that Peter "was the first to assimilate the tragedy and absurdity of a Calvary without a parousia . . . and to realise that Jesus's crucifixion was his victory." Hence, Peter led the other

---

[14] O'Collins, *Jesus Risen: The Resurrection—What Actually Happened and What Does It Mean?* (London: Darton, Longman, & Todd, 1987), 115, referring especially to the Schillebeeckx volume, *Interim Report on the Books 'Jesus' and 'Christ,'* trans. John Bowden (New York: Crossroad, 1982), 147n43, 148n46. This volume was reissued as *The Collected Works of Edward Schillebeeckx*, vol. 8, *Interim Report on the Books* Jesus *and* Christ (London: Bloomsbury, 2014).

[15] N. T. Wright, *The Resurrection of the Son of God*, vol. 3 of *Christian Origins and the Question of God* (Minneapolis: Fortress, 2003), 559, 692, 701–2, 704–5.

[16] John Shelby Spong, *The Easter Moment* (New York: Harper & Row, 1987), 196–98.

[17] John Shelby Spong, *Resurrection: Myth or Reality?* (New York: HarperCollins, 1994), 239–41, 255–57. Strauss also separates the beginning of the disciples' experiences from the time of the crucifixion in order to make the situation more conducive for his theory! The point, as Strauss states specifically, is so that the disciples have a sufficient time to get over the shock of the sudden, unexpected crucifixion and allow for their mental states to clear sufficiently for their "highly wrought enthusiasm" to grow. See David Friedrich Strauss, *The Life of Jesus Critically Examined*, ed. Peter C. Hodgson, trans. George Eliot (Mifflintown, PA: Sigler, 1994), 743–44. One wonders why Spong feels as if he too must adjust the time element?

disciples to grasp Jesus's death in this new light, in order "to regard Calvary not as the end but as the transition to victory and exaltation."[18] In this sense, Peter is thought to have had an insight that snatched victory from the apparent embarrassment and ignominy of crucifixion by somehow interpreting Jesus's death event as the true victory! By dying especially in that manner and remaining dead, Jesus's defeat somehow still turned into his means of exaltation. Further, Peter successfully convinced the other disciples of the same message and thereby inspired the Christian ideas that changed the world.

One other more sophisticated view will be cited here, although it was different in several respects from the ramifications of the illumination thesis as just outlined. Prominent German scholar Rudolf Pesch's early research is probably the most notable example of a few scholars who thought that Jesus's pre-crucifixion authority and message were in themselves so incredibly influential, riveting, and magnetic that they were largely sufficient in themselves to cause his followers to survive the horrors of the crucifixion with their faith intact. Even in the absence of the "flash of insight" views in the illumination theses outlined earlier, Pesch's position still utilized the utterly transforming power of Jesus's teachings to inspire his disciples to the same level of transformation in the absence of either an empty tomb or actual resurrection appearances, which he rejected as not being sufficiently established on historical grounds.[19]

A major firestorm against Pesch's views developed with a cadre of prominent German scholars largely arguing against several angles of Pesch's research. There was a strong sense among these German critics that the level of transformation in the apostles after the crucifixion was far greater than anything that possibly could be accounted for by Pesch's pre-crucifixion transformation ideas alone. This is especially the case when their convictions would have had to survive the tremendous psychological jolt of Jesus's unexpected and heinous crucifixion, which realistically

---

[18] Milan Machoveč, *A Marxist Looks at Jesus* (Philadelphia: Fortress, 1976), with the citations above from 163, 161, 164, 171, as cited by Gerald O'Collins, "Peter as Easter Witness," *Heythrop Journal* 22 (1981): 5, although the edition being cited here is different from that used by O'Collins.

[19] Rudolf Pesch, "Zur Entstehung des Glaubens an die Auferstehung Jesu," *Theologische Quartalschrift* 153 (1973): 219–26; Pesch, "Materialien und Bemerkungen zu Entstehung und Sinn des Osterglaubens," in Anton Vogtle and Rudolf Pesch, *Wie kam es zum Osterglauben?* (Dusseldorf: Patmos, 1975), 157–68.

would have tended to crush their hopes and may even have caused them to view Jesus as a failed messiah figure. John Galvin presents a masterful overview of this controversy, headlined by a remarkable reaction among many very prominent and influential German scholars such as Martin Hengel, Peter Stuhlmacher, Hans Küng, Jacob Kremer, Walter Kasper, Anton Vögtle, Hans Werner Bartsch, and several others.[20]

Under the scholarly onslaught, Pesch actually changed his position, still not granting the historicity of the empty tomb narratives but embracing the idea that Jesus's resurrection appearances could be established by careful historical research, and that these events took the form of visions of Jesus in his heavenly glory as the Son of Man exalted to the right hand of God.[21] Galvin notes that these moves were sufficient for Pesch to have "joined a widespread consensus among contemporary exegetes and systematic theologians" though there was still some question about how he fit the Son of Man visions into his scenario.[22]

Intriguingly however, largely due to the influence exerted by Pesch's earlier position, another German scholar, Hansjürgen Verweyen, continued to emphasize the role that the pre-Easter message of Jesus played in preparing his disciples. Like Pesch, Verweyen also was not very positive toward the historicity of the empty tomb but realized, also like Pesch, that the disciples' turnaround and their ability to get past the severe psychological roadblock of Jesus's crucifixion would only have been possible due to the appearances of the risen Jesus.[23]

---

[20] John P. Galvin, "Resurrection as *Theologia Crucis Jesu*: The Foundational Christology of Rudolf Pesch," *Theological Studies* 38 (1977): particularly 517–20.

[21] Rudolf Pesch, "Zur Entstehung des Glaubens an die Auferstehung Jesu: Ein neuer Versuch," *Freiburger Zeitschrift für Philosophie und Theologie* 30 (1983): esp. 87; John P. Galvin, "The Origin of Faith in the Resurrection of Jesus: Two Recent Perspectives," *Theological Studies* 49 (1988): with 27–35 containing an excellent summation of the shift in Pesch's thought.

[22] Galvin, "Origin of Faith," 31. The Son of Man role is outlined by Galvin on 31–33.

[23] Hansjürgen Verweyen, "Die Ostererscheinungen in fundamentaltheologischer Sicht," *Zeitschrift für Katholische Theologie* 103 (1981): 429. See Galvin's excellent contrast of Pesch and Verweyen ("The Origin of Faith in the Resurrection of Jesus," 35–40). A later contribution to the subject is Verweyen's "Die Sache mit den Ostererscheinungen," in *"Der Herr ist wahrhaft Auferstanden" (Lk 24,34): Biblische und systematische Beiträge zur Entstehung des Osterglaubens*, ed. Ingo Broer and Jürgen Werbick (Stuttgart: Katholisches Bibelwerk, 1988), esp. 77–78.

The illumination theses definitely share a common core.[24] The single key element throughout is undoubtedly the priority of Peter's experience(s), which could have consisted of a range of just about anything from a simple idea bursting in upon his personal radar to some sort of full-blown mystical experience. As the leader of the apostles, Peter would have had tremendous influence on the others. Somehow, Peter relating his thoughts and conclusions plus any potential mystical experiences on his part must have impressed the group enough that, after some unspecified amount of time, the others either had similar insights or experienced something that made them likewise comfortable in agreeing that they too had somehow "experienced" the risen, exalted Jesus. Machoveč's main idea adds a bit of an enhanced twist here—that Peter's insight involved the idea that even the crucifixion, in spite of all its embarrassment and other horrid aspects, did not truly mark the end, but was actually the means by which Jesus was exalted.

These scholars agree that this hypothesis is naturalistic in nature.[25] Whatever the nature of the disciples' thoughts, intuitions, or experiences, they were all strictly internal and subjective in nature rather than based on any sort of actual events. But the result was very similar: they all responded by exercising faith and came to believe that Jesus Christ had been raised from the dead, or at least that he had been exalted to heaven after his death, perhaps in some sort of apotheosis. The key emphasis, then, is strictly on the disciples' internal faith rather than on any sort of external resurrection appearances by Jesus. The potential delay in these experiences, such as that mentioned by Spong, further highlights these ideas.

Critiquing the Illumination Hypothesis

An enormous scholarly outcry has ensued regarding both the general positions taken above as well as the various ideas among the individual thinkers. Several of these numerous critiques appeared in print quite early, even before the majority of the publications that argue in favor of the illumination views were published. These critiques were delivered over a wide range of related issues as well. Perhaps

---

[24] Though similar in a few regards, we are not counting here the view just described, formulated by the early Pesch and later by Verweyen, given the aspects that are significantly different, such as these two German scholars not even denying the resurrection appearances.

[25] Depending for example on one's evaluation of O'Collins's caution regarding being open to Schillebeeckx allowing real appearances of Jesus.

surprisingly, these critical responses were chiefly delivered mostly from a large number of very influential researchers, in spite of the frequent tendency among many researchers of this caliber not to engage overly often in these sorts of exercises, which is sometimes eschewed.[26]

---

[26] Raymond E. Brown, "The Resurrection of Jesus," in *Jerome Biblical Commentary*, ed. Raymond Brown, Joseph A. Fitzmyer, and Roland E. Murphy (Englewood Cliffs, NJ: Prentice-Hall, 1968), 81:1375; C. F. D. Moule, "The Resurrection: A Disagreement," in Cupitt, *Explorations in Theology*, 27–41; Gerald O'Collins contributed to the critique in spite of his caution on behalf of Schillebeeckx, as mentioned above in *Jesus Risen*, 63–66, 103–7, 115–17; O'Collins, "Peter as Easter Witness," 5; O'Collins, *What Are They Saying about the Resurrection?* (New York: Paulist, 1978), 91–92, 106–15. For Francis Schüssler Fiorenza's critique of especially the thesis by Schillebeeckx, see "The Resurrection of Jesus and Roman Catholic Fundamental Theology," in *The Resurrection: An Interdisciplinary Symposium on the Resurrection of Jesus*, ed. Stephen T. Davis, Daniel Kendall, and Gerald O'Collins (Oxford: Oxford University Press, 1997), 221, cf. 243–44; G. B. Caird with L. D. Hurst, *New Testament Theology* (Oxford: Clarendon, 1994), 241; Hans Küng, *Eternal Life: Life after Death as a Medical, Philosophical, and Theological Problem*, trans. Edward Quinn (Garden City, NY: Doubleday, 1984), 106; Peter Carnley, *The Structure of Resurrection Belief* (Oxford: Clarendon, 1987), 156–82, 199–222; Wolfhart Pannenberg, *Systematic Theology*, trans. Geoffrey W. Bromiley, 3 vols. (Grand Rapids: Eerdmans, 1991), 2:355–56; Pannenberg, "History and the Reality of the Resurrection," in *Resurrection Reconsidered*, ed. Gavin D'Costa (Oxford: Oneworld, 1996), particularly 70. Without referring to specific thinkers, Peter Stuhlmacher critiques similar ideas in his essay, "The Resurrection of Jesus and the Resurrection of the Dead," *Ex Auditu* 9 (1993): 47–50; Luke Timothy Johnson, *The Real Jesus: The Misguided Quest for the Historical Jesus and the Truth of the Traditional Gospels* (New York: HarperCollins, 1996), 138–39; Reginald H. Fuller, "John 20:19–23," *Interpretation* 32 (1978): 94–96; Pheme Perkins, *Resurrection: New Testament Witness and Contemporary Reflection* (Garden City, NY: Doubleday, 1984), 55, 108n53; Perkins, "The Resurrection of Jesus of Nazareth," in *Studying the Historical Jesus: Evaluations of the State of Current Research*, ed. Bruce Chilton and Craig A. Evans (Leiden: Brill, 1974), 424; N. T. Wright, *Resurrection of the Son of God*, particularly 692, 698, 701–12, cf. 558–59; Wright, "Christian Origins and the Resurrection of Jesus: The Resurrection of Jesus as a Historical Problem," *Sewanee Theological Review* 41 (1998): 115–16, 119–21; Wright, *Who Was Jesus?* (Grand Rapids: Eerdmans, 1992), 62–63; Wright, *The Challenge of Jesus: Discovering Who Jesus Was and Is* (Downers Grove, IL: InterVarsity, 1999), 147–48; Robert C. Ware, "The Resurrection of Jesus, I: Theological Orientations," *Heythrop Journal* 16 (1975): 25, 27, 29; Ware, "The Resurrection of Jesus, II: Historical-Critical Studies," *Heythrop Journal* 17 (1975): 190; John Muddiman, "'I Believe in the Resurrection of the Body,'" in *Resurrection: Essays in Honour of Leslie Houlden*, ed. Stephen Barton and Graham Stanton (London: SPCK, 1994), 129–37; Stephen T. Davis, *Risen Indeed: Making Sense of the Resurrection* (Grand Rapids: Eerdmans, 1993), 16.

Thus the illumination theorizers had definitely struck a few scholarly nerves, some of which seemed a little "raw," judging from the tone of the remarks! Those scholars who were the most frequently critiqued for holding the illumination views were Marxsen, Schillebeeckx, and Sheehan. In fact, Sheehan's comments sparked such a huge outburst from major scholars (mostly in the Roman Catholic tradition) that questions were asked in terms of whether his onslaught may mark the end of traditional theological Catholicism. For instance, an entire series of articles was published by Sheehan and others responding to him over a few months in *Commonweal*.[27]

Besides the exceptionally long list of critiques and remarks cited in various studies, a mostly different array of major problems will be enumerated below. A few of the many comments raised by other scholars will be mentioned along the way, often to illustrate the evaluations below.

First, regarding the available details, it is almost impossible to imagine how the lasting, utterly transformed lives of Jesus's disciples would have resulted from the suppositions of the illumination thesis. The claimed details seem to be based on such a thin gruel for lifelong makeovers, including the willingness to die for the truth of the message! These are the same apostles who were for years constantly on the move away from their homes, sacrificing the bulk of their personal time away from their

---

[27] Some of the major scholarly interaction with Sheehan's views, largely within the Roman Catholic community, include Alvin Plantinga, "Sheehan's Shenanigans: How Theology Becomes Tomfoolery," *Reformed Journal* (1987): 19–25; Raymond E. Brown, *Biblical Exegesis and Church Doctrine* (Mahweh, NJ: Paulist, 1985), see chap. 3, "Liberal Misunderstanding of the Interaction between Biblical Criticism and Dogma," with 58–65 devoted specifically to Sheehan. The three *Commonweal* magazine issues on these topics related to Thomas Sheehan were published on August 10, September 21 (chiefly consisting of short articles and letters to the editor, often by major Catholic scholars), and October 5, 1984. Some of the representative *Commonweal* articles included: Editors, "The End of Catholicism?," *Commonweal* (1984): 425–26; David Tracy, "Levels of Liberal Consensus: Exegesis, Tradition, and Authority," *Commonweal* (1984): 426–31; Andrew M. Greeley, "The Ways of Knowing: Neither Fundamentalism nor Agnosticism," *Commonweal* (1984): 431–33; Greeley, "The Provisional Path to Mystery: The End of Catholicism, Part 3," *Commonweal* (1984): 530–32; Greeley, "The Ways of Knowing: Neither Fundamentalism nor Agnosticism," *Commonweal* (1984): 530–32; David Tracy, "To Trust or Suspect: The End of Catholicism, Part 3," *Commonweal* (1984): 532–34. A number of key book reviews of Thomas Sheehan's volume *The First Coming* also appeared from the pens of scholars; see those by Paul L. Maier in *The Christian Century*, January 7–14, 1987, 28–30; J. M. Cameron in *The New York Review*, December 4, 1986, 23–27; William M. Thompson, *Commonweal* (1986): 377–79.

family and livelihoods, not requesting personal wealth and eschewing fame, while all the time exposing themselves to constant and serious pressures and threats of danger. How could their motivation be simply due to their having heard someone's testimony, however stirring that may have been, even if Peter had given his own assurance of his supposed mystical experience? He may have been their leader, but he had also denied his Lord. The accessible specifics of the traditional view are conceded by virtually all critical researchers.

Granting that hearing a leader like Peter testifying in inspiring terms could carry some weight, would even that be enough in itself to result in an enduring, lifelong commitment of this nature? Would the public ministry that the apostles exercised have continued to last even after some of them began suffering martyrdom? Moreover, could we reasonably expect that all of these results would be the unquestioned result of unevidenced, subjective experiences? Could this basis account for no apostles quitting their ministries or recanting their faith, as far as is known, in spite of such a flimsy foundation?[28] It might more likely engender a few incredulous responses of "Really? Just because you say so?"

Then further, even concerning Peter himself, how could he continue to be so sure and settled through all the intervening years since his initial insight or mystical communication? Without any sort of external evidence to which he could point, could he know that his experience was really from the Lord? Was this subjective conviction alone enough to assuage any of Peter's ongoing questions and break forth into his sweeping, encompassing, all-conquering triumph of faith followed by probable martyrdom? Even the nature of doubt in general is such that virtually no one escapes without questions, especially in the most crucial beliefs in one's life.

Would Peter's intensely personal, subjective experience have caused him to forget his deep knowledge of Jesus's gruesome death as well as his own previous denials and resulting utter despair? This anguish and hopelessness is acknowledged by the vast majority of even skeptical scholars today (including Sheehan, as pointed out elsewhere in this study) since it is a normal psychological consequence of losing one's closest friend in a sudden, horrendous, and unplanned manner. Then there is the constant turmoil and physical grief during Peter's ongoing ministry, including

---

[28] On the lack of any evidence regarding Jesus's apostles recanting their faith, see Sean McDowell, *The Fate of the Apostles: Examining the Martyrdom Accounts of the Closest Followers of Jesus* (Surrey: Ashgate, 2015), 6, 8, 243, 259–65.

ignoring the endangerment to his life that resulted from being convinced by some insights, however profound. Did Peter meet others throughout these years of ministry who likewise claimed subjective religious experiences that were *opposed* to his own experiences? Were his own subjective experiences many years earlier still sufficient enough to keep his personal reservoirs full, unaccompanied as they were by any real event, his own physical sight, or anything else of a tangible nature?[29]

Sheehan admits Peter's tortured mental state here, but he moves too easily in the space of just five lines from admitting Peter's "despair" as a "drowning man" to Peter being the recipient of an inward, subjective "ecstatic vision."[30] Worse, the claim is made without any external evidence whatsoever.[31] Is the latter capable of overpowering forever the extreme emotional weight of the former issues? If the inward emotional experience of Peter could fire up the other disciples to this extent, then other opposing, inward emotional experiences could potentially plague any of the recipients with overwhelming doubts. The foregoing problem is a precarious situation indeed, and this alone points to the tenuousness of the illumination thesis. It plainly does not have the substance to secure a long-term commitment from its experiencers, chiefly when the original occurrence extended from one person to many others who frankly were not witnesses themselves, which is what the evidence indicates.

Second, those who favor this hypothesis may prefer to emphasize subjective religious experience and the value of faith apart from evidence.[32] Or they may simply want

---

[29] One could imagine a more cynical critic asking how we know that the disciples' commitment went on until the end of their lives anyway rather than occupying some shorter time commitment? One response is that there are far more data favoring the disciples' continuing ministries after the crucifixion (as pointed out in the Sean McDowell volume just mentioned in the prior note; see esp. chaps. 2–4) than there are that favors only a brief experiment in faith. Then these more cynical critics are still confronted with the severe problem of how a rather simple insight or other subjective experience rather magically inspired a number of total life transformations and not a few martyrdoms. In at least the cases of Peter, Paul, and James the brother of Jesus, the approximately two plus decades of total sacrifice and service before their likely martyrdoms is sufficient testimony to the force of their convictions.

[30] Realizing of course that five lines does not describe the time element involved, but it still sounds from the description that a fast turnaround is envisioned.

[31] Sheehan, *First Coming*, 105.

[32] While neither holding this position nor speaking about this specific issue, Bart D. Ehrman intriguingly makes several quite positive comments about the value of faith; see

to arrive at a viable naturalistic thesis for the Gospel accounts. But one of the chief issues in this discussion is whether this or any alternate position squares with what the New Testament teaches. It must be noted immediately that the point here is definitely *not* that what the New Testament teaches is automatically the case. Rather, the critique is that in order to postulate what happened to Jesus's disciples, we must at least attempt to come to grips with the data we possess, even if it is rejected. But the illumination hypothesis does not do so; on a comparison of hypothesis to data, it misses widely.

But what is to be done with the actual, exceptionally early evidence that Jesus *really did* appear to his followers after his death by crucifixion? This or any hypothesis needs to begin there. The influential list(s) of resurrection appearances in 1 Cor 15:3–7, not to mention other data, such as that garnered from the Acts sermon summaries, the Gospel appearances, and elsewhere, indicates that those present at the outset actually *claimed* to have seen Jesus in bodily form. The majority of scholars today, including skeptical ones, actually acknowledge that the data itself indicate that this represents the view in the early church, whether or not contemporary scholars themselves believe these accounts.[33] To state it another way, Jesus's appearances were described in the New Testament with the language of sight.[34] Group appearances add to the force of this theme. To begin with a notion that fails to take this language seriously is not the way to do justice to the texts.

Again, the chief point of this second critique is *not* to announce simply that the resurrection is a fact because Jesus's disciples may have proclaimed that to be the case.

Ehrman, *How Jesus Became God: The Exaltation of a Jewish Preacher from Galilee* (New York: HarperCollins, 2014), 132, 143, 150.

[33] Gerd Lüdemann, *The Resurrection of Jesus: History, Experience, Theology*, trans. John Bowden (Minneapolis: Fortress, 1994), 35; Lüdemann, "Closing Response," in *Jesus' Resurrection: Fact or Figment? A Debate between William Lane Craig and Gerd Lüdemann*, ed. Paul Copan and Ronald K. Tacelli (Downers Grove, IL: InterVarsity, 2000), 151; Carnley, *Structure of Resurrection Belief*, 64, 82, 170, 246.

[34] For more on this topic, see the treatments in this study of the various visionary hypotheses. Few commentators on the issue are as clear as Gerald O'Collins, as in his *Saint Augustine on the Resurrection of Christ: Teaching, Rhetoric, and Reception* (Oxford: Oxford University Press, 2017), 11, 16, 43–44, 75–76, 79; O'Collins, *Interpreting the Resurrection: Examining the Major Problems in the Stories of Jesus' Resurrection* (Mahwah, NJ: Paulist, 1988), 12–17, 19. Moule makes this point against Cupitt's illumination view too in C. F. D. Moule and Don Cupitt, "The Resurrection," 34; note as well as some similar points by Cupitt, "Ghosts, Visions and Miracles" in *Christ and the Hiddenness of God*, 143–44, 157. Cf. also Richard Bauckham, "The Eyewitnesses and the Gospel Traditions," *Journal for the Study of the Historical Jesus* 1 (2003): 51–52.

Rather, the point here is that to characterize what caused the incredible change in Jesus's disciples as other than being due to visible appearances of the risen Jesus, as done in this naturalistic manner, does justice neither to the New Testament accounts nor to the historical evidence that clearly favors these accounts.

In fact, the illumination hypothesis turns the entire scenario around almost totally backwards by making the inner workings of the individual apostles themselves the central object lesson instead of placing the attention exactly and squarely where all the data place it: firmly resting on the risen Jesus and his appearances. In short, we must account for what the earliest and most authoritative texts claim rather than totally sidestepping them and heading in another direction altogether. It is not about the disciples' inner psychology or experiences in their minds but about their outward perceptions, whatever they were.[35]

The predominant scholarly view at present appears to be that Jesus's earliest followers held not just that Jesus had appeared to them, but that he did so in bodily form.[36] Of course, this does not require that the contemporary scholars themselves accept the historicity of the resurrection, let alone believe that the appearances were actually bodily in nature. But these researchers do acknowledge generally that this was at least the major position held by the initial witnesses in the early church. Buoying this majority view is that a sizeable number of skeptical and even radical researchers hold this position, among them, John Dominic Crossan, Gerd Lüdemann, Bart Ehrman, James Crossley, Dale Allison, and Jonathan Reed.[37]

---

[35] N. T. Wright, "Early Traditions and the Origin of Christianity," *Sewanee Theological Review* 41 (1998): 125, 128–40.

[36] Gary R. Habermas, "Mapping the Recent Trend toward the Bodily Resurrection Appearances of Jesus in Light of Other Prominent Critical Positions," in *The Resurrection of Jesus: John Dominic Crossan and N. T. Wright in Dialogue*, ed. Robert B. Stewart (Minneapolis: Fortress, 2006), 199–204.

[37] John Dominic Crossan, "The Resurrection of Jesus in its Jewish Context," *Neotestamentica* 37 (2003): 29, 42–43, 48–52, 55–56; Crossan and Jonathan L. Reed, *In Search of Paul: How Jesus's Apostle Opposed Rome's Empire with God's Kingdom. A New Vision of Paul's Words and World* (New York: HarperCollins, 2004), 6–10, 173–74, 296, 341–45, cf. 133–35; Lüdemann, *Resurrection of Jesus*, 35; Lüdemann, "Closing Response," 151; Ehrman, *How Jesus Became God*, 132–33, 137, 168–69, 176–78; Ehrman, *Did Jesus Exist? The Historical Argument for Jesus of Nazareth* (New York: HarperCollins, 2012), 256–58; James Crossley, "Against the Historical Plausibility of the Empty Tomb Story and the Bodily Resurrection of Jesus: A Response to N. T. Wright," *Journal for the Study of the Historical Jesus* 3 (2005): 178; Michael F. Bird and Crossley, *How Did Christianity Begin? A Believer and Nonbeliever Examine the Evidence* (London: SPCK, 2008), 52; Dale C. Allison Jr., *Resurrecting Jesus: The*

Most of these critical scholars would add that this was Jesus's own notion of the afterlife as well.[38]

The significance of these areas for our present discussion concerns both Jesus's own beliefs in this matter as well as those of his disciples. The illumination hypothesis once again inverts this early distinction and teaches the opposite: it is a view held by some contemporary critical scholars in recent times but is clearly *not* the view that Jesus or his followers held in the earliest times.

It may be asserted that this distinction by itself does not make illumination theorists wrong. But this comment also misses the chief point, in that it clearly does not address or represent the earliest teachings of those closest to the resurrection experiences that were thought to be appearances of the risen Jesus. As such, the hypothesis fails to resolve the question of what really occurred at the outset of Christianity. The disjunction here between the original New Testament teachings and a modern reductionist rendition are the chief issue here. In the words of Wright, "Schillebeeckx first sweeps all the evidence under the carpet, and then exclaims, 'Look! No evidence!'"[39] Ancient historian Paul Maier states that, on historical grounds, Sheehan's thesis is "pure conjecture."[40]

Third, the illumination hypothesis by itself neither requires nor explains the empty tomb. Yet, the empty tomb accounts are strongly evidenced and, as a result, a strong majority of recent critical scholars favor the historicity of this event. True, the scholars who hold this thesis generally reject the idea that Jesus's burial tomb was discovered to be empty just a short time later. Some may even favor an alternate burial in another location. But on what grounds? These theorists seldom actually argue the details involved in this line of thought. Yet most recognize that the data favoring a vacated tomb are strong enough to overcome both theses involving alternate burials as

---

Earliest Christian Tradition and Its Interpreters (London: T&T Clark. 2005), 317, 324–25, cf. 226 among others.

[38] A major critical study on this subject is William Strawson, *Jesus and the Future Life*, rev. ed. (London: Epworth, 1970), particularly 177–83, 196–97, 209–10, 225–30. An oft-cited classic is Oscar Cullmann's volume, *Immortality of the Soul or Resurrection of the Dead? The Witness of the New Testament* (London: Epworth, 1964; repr., Eugene, OR: Wipf & Stock, 210), esp. chap. 4 and conclusion; cf. also Cullmann's text *Christ and Time: The Primitive Christian Conception of Time and History*, trans. Floyd V. Filson, 3rd ed. (London: SCM, 1962; repr., Eugene, OR: Wipf & Stock, 2018).

[39] Wright, *Resurrection of the Son of God*, 705.

[40] Maier, review of *The First Coming* (by Sheehan), 30.

well as naturalistic accounts for the actual tomb being open. If not, then the majority of scholars most likely would not embrace its historicity.

But it remains the case (as enumerated elsewhere in this study) that the empty tomb accounts in the Gospels possibly comprise the single report after Jesus's crucifixion accompanied by more strong reasons than any of the other data points! Though not a point to be developed here, it often appears that objections to the empty tomb, especially the seeming majority that are mentioned without early or specific backup evidence, are proposed simply because another thesis is needed to explain this fact, in addition to whatever is suggested to account for the appearances.

Should the empty tomb be a historical fact, as we have argued in this study, this would be a powerful reason alone for disfavoring the illumination thesis. It would seem that a separate alternative account would need to be devised to explain each of the almost two dozen pieces of data that have been provided on behalf of this event. Further, as many have pointed out, an empty tomb would best indicate that something happened to Jesus's physical body.

Do natural hypotheses work better for the empty tomb? If so, which ones? Critics generally tend to be slow about coming up with powerful alternative views here, perhaps because none of these alternate positions is accompanied by much evidence—certainly nothing approaching the empty tomb accounts presented in the Gospels. As skeptical New Testament scholar Dale Allison reminds us after mentioning several of the possible empty tomb options, "We have no reason to endorse any of these speculations, for which there is not a shred of evidence. They must all be deemed unlikely."[41] But if something still happened to the body, and if natural hypotheses are rather problematic, then a view that totally ignores Jesus's body or any other external physical explanation seems not to make the grade. Thus, the probable emptiness of Jesus's tomb needs to be explained, but quite clearly the illumination theory does not do so.

Fourth, among those who argue for less than physical appearances of Jesus, including those embracing the illumination thesis, a common tendency is to assert that the Greek verb *horaō* often (or even usually) indicates less than physical sight.[42]

---

[41] Of course, as Allison adds, the naturalistic tomb theories "are not impossible" (*Resurrecting Jesus*, 334).

[42] Noteworthy examples here come from Thomas Sheehan, *First Coming*, 114–18; Sheehan, "Resurrection," 96–97, 101; and Sheehan, "How Did Easter Originally Happen," 111–13, both of the latter essays in Scott, *Resurrection of Jesus*. Many of the works that make statements like this are of older vintage, and Sheehan is not the only scholar who argues like

Sometimes this pronouncement is followed by the assertion that the resurrection appearances of Jesus as described in the New Testament, even in Paul, therefore teach, indicate, or at least allow the meaning that Jesus never really *appeared* to anyone. Rather the phenomena, whatever they were, are then referred to as some sort of internal, subjective experiences or even just simply due to unique insights or the drawing of personal conclusions. Once again, seldom is there specific argumentation given that would confirm or support these points.[43]

It needs to be acknowledged from the outset that determining word meanings here will not solve this question, for there are too many other components involved in the discussion. For just one example, a definition may be interpreted or even manipulated, "held hostage" as it were and virtually overpowered by the way it is construed from within one worldview or another. Thus, the "spinning" of a meaning can easily make it appear that an entirely different thesis is true. Of course, this problem cuts both ways; all sides in a debate can make use of this tactic.

In our case, rather than attempting to make an argument stand on a definition, the point here is to answer those who charge that particular terms, such as the Greek verb *horaō* and its aorist passive form *ōphthē*, actually support a nonliteral sense of Jesus's appearances. It seems safe to say that this issue is more often suggested from the critical side against those who would argue for the historicity of the resurrection. It can be a fairly common plank in a platform, so the claim must be answered.

The chief question regarding this particular argument concerns whether the illumination theorists and other similar subjective thinkers are correct that the key New Testament terms do indeed point to the experiences of the original witnesses being subjective and revelatory in nature.[44] It is noteworthy that by far the majority

---

this. Another example is Paul Badham, "The Meaning of the Resurrection of Jesus," in *The Resurrection of Jesus Christ*, ed. Paul Avis (London: Darton, Longman & Todd, 1993), 31.

[43] For example, Sheehan jumps from how *horaō* could possibly be translated in a nonphysical way, even when referring to Paul's view in 1 Cor 15:5–8, to comments in the same context that "the text makes no claim that Jesus appeared in a body . . . those stories would come thirty years later" ("Resurrection," 97). He repeats elsewhere comments such as these, declaring that the appearances need not be actual events at all. In Sheehan's sequence, "might" seems too easily to become "was," and "was" morphs into the basis for proclaiming a natural thesis involving no actual appearances (as in Sheehan, *First Coming*, 104–9, 112–18). Sheehan calls this idea his "hypothesis" (108–9). The sleight-of-hand moves are simply amazing!

[44] Tracing where this claim may have started can be tricky. Some (like Sheehan, *First Coming*, 115) mention Wilhelm Michaelis's lengthy article on *horaō* in the highly influential

view in contemporary scholarly circles is that the textual basis to support the more subjective interpretation fails, and quite badly. Of the times where *horaō* and its related variants occur in the New Testament, many of the usages refer to neither physical nor nonphysical sight (involving other meanings such as "understand," "discern," "perceive" and so on) and thus have very little if any bearing on this discussion. For our purposes, these meanings are subtracted from the overall word count since they do not indicate a particular sort of sight at all, thereby favoring neither category.

Theological Dictionary of the New Testament, by Geoffrey W. Bromiley, ed. Gerhard Kittel and Gerhard Friedrich, trans. Geoffrey W. Bromiley, 10 vols. (Grand Rapids: Eerdmans, 1967), 5:315–82, and it may have provided some push in this direction. Michaelis makes it clear that *horaō* has a variety of meanings, including spiritual and physical sight (325, 341). Still, he cautions against overemphasizing the eyewitness aspects of *horaō* (347–50). Regarding its import for the resurrection passages, some of the comments that Michaelis makes shows his hand on what theological positions he prefers, sometimes by making statements that would be questioned at least by many scholars today (355–61). He thinks that the resurrection appearance accounts emphasize chiefly the subjective, revelatory aspects (356, 358), downplaying the more physical aspects of sight (358–59). Rather strangely, Michaelis even employs the less clear usage of *horaō* in 1 Cor 15:3–8 to interpret the clearer reference to Paul's seeing the risen Lord in 1 Cor 9:1, where Paul uses a straightforward Greek term (*heoraka*) that indicates regular sight to refer to his viewing the resurrected Jesus. Yet Michaelis turns the situation around backwards in order to interpret even *heoraka* in terms of the less-clear *horaō*, arguing that all these experiences were probably revelatory and internal in nature rather than being more indicative of normal sight (358)! (Compare Wright's thoughts on 1 Cor 9:1 in the next point immediately below.) Michaelis does note, however, that Barth "resolutely opposed" this emphasis, and Michaelis still comments that Paul thought of Jesus's appearances as "transfigured corporeality" (359). But as remarked above, the theological aspects in Michaelis's article appear to trump the grammatical responses. In line with this, in another article from the same set of volumes, Gerhard Kittel argues regarding the terms *akouō*, *blepō*, and *horaō* in almost direct contrast to Michaelis's article that sight is usually emphasized over hearing, especially with the specific cases of the appearances of the risen Lord (Kittel, *Theological Dictionary of the New Testament*, 1:216–25, particularly 220). Responding to some of Michaelis's thoughts, James D.G. Dunn noted "the famous attempt by W. Michaelis, '*horaō*', TDNT 5:355–361, to argue that *ōphthē* indicated 'revelation', a 'perception' of non-visionary reality.'" In response, Dunn noted from similar texts that the aspect viewed here is one of "a visual seeing, not a mental perception" alone. Then Dunn objected to views like Michaelis's by citing Jesus Seminar scholar Gerd Lüdemann's comments on 1 Cor 15:3–8, where the latter emphasized the "inescapable conclusion" that Paul clearly "had in mind an experience of 'seeing'" Jesus. See James D. G. Dunn, *Jesus Remembered*, vol. 1 of *Christianity in the Making* (Grand Rapids: Eerdmans, 2003), 872n211.

Of the seventeen remaining times *horaō* and its forms appear in Paul in reference to either objective or subjective sight, sixteen of them clearly refer to physical sight, with only one reference indicating a heavenly vision. Of the 118 relevant usages of these terms in Luke-Acts, 107 clearly refer to physical sight, while only 11 refer to a personal vision![45]

These definitional counts far from solve the overall issues here. But whatever is made of this usage tally, it should be clear that it is incorrect for critics to make ungrounded comments about *horaō* and its cognates, claiming that they usually refer more often to nonphysical sight or attempting to make these terms more conducive to inner, subjective states of mind. This is especially the case when the context from critical scholars makes it more than obvious that these comments are made chiefly to embarrass or belittle those who disagree, especially when the bombast is clearly incorrect in itself![46]

More helpful in terms of the overall meaning of these terms is how the verbal forms of *horaō* are actually employed specifically in narrative passages to describe Jesus's resurrection appearances. These terms even refer to the very physical resurrection appearances of Jesus as depicted in the Gospels of both Luke and John. In the most physical references to Jesus's resurrection body in the entire New Testament, Jesus offered himself to be touched and held, eating in the presence of his disciples, and is observed by many people at once.[47] By no means, then, does *horaō* veer away from highly physical meetings with the risen Jesus. It needs to be remembered at this point that the immediate issue here is *not* what actually happened on these occasions, but the nature of the original language that was employed to *describe* these events.

Even further, Michael Licona attests that both the Greek terms and the context in these texts and elsewhere make it clear that, for both Luke and Paul, it was Jesus's physical body that was actually raised from the dead! For Luke, the tomb was empty while Jesus's graveclothes remained behind, though Jesus himself was not present.

---

[45] Ten times in Acts the references are to resurrection appearances, but these were not included in the above count so as not to beg the question by favoring either type of sight. The word counts here for the usages of *horaō* were taken from Michael R. Licona, *The Resurrection of Jesus: A New Historiographical Approach* (Downers Grove, IL: InterVarsity Academic, 2010), 330–33.

[46] As seems more than evident in Sheehan, "Resurrection," 100–104. These sorts of comments and additional innuendos are definitely out of place in scholarly discussions.

[47] For examples, Luke 24:34, 39; John 20:18, 20, 25, 29.

Jesus appeared to his disciples as "flesh and bones" and later ascended in a fully bodily manner. For Paul as well, Licona concludes that resurrection is "an event that happens to a corpse," as depicted in Rom 8:10–11, 23.[48] Of course, saying that Jesus's corpse was raised by no means rules out that, in the process, his body was transformed and, as some would add, glorified, in keeping with Paul's teachings in 1 Cor 15:35–55. After all, the New Testament hardly teaches that Jesus rose as some sort of zombie corpse to die once again.

From a perspective slightly different from that of word studies alone, the usage of *horaō* in these original contexts from Luke and Paul above, especially in reference to Jesus's resurrection appearances, increases the likelihood tremendously that these authors are referring to normal, physical sight when they speak of how Jesus appeared when the original witnesses saw him postmortem. So even these brief word studies and other comparisons seem to make it obvious by a large margin that there is far more support for *horaō* and related terms being references that indicate external rather than subjective sight or revelation.[49] It would appear, then, that the critical refrain that tries to argue that it means something subjective is far less likely.[50] It is

---

[48] Licona's strong reference to a resurrected corpse will no doubt startle and even alarm many readers because this is one of the items that contemporary scholars often avoid stating whenever possible. For instance, the Jesus Seminar is fond of repeating, "The resurrection of Jesus did not involve the resuscitation of a corpse." See Robert W. Funk and the Jesus Seminar, *The Acts of Jesus: The Search for the Authentic Deeds of Jesus* (New York: HarperCollins, 1998), 461. Without embracing what we have termed the illumination thesis, great pains are taken by the Seminar members to separate what the New Testament states about Jesus's resurrection appearances from any inkling of bodily vestiges (454, 458–62). See Licona, *Resurrection of Jesus*, where 332–33 are especially hard hitting. See also the argument by Robert H. Gundry, a specialist in these matters who concurs with at least the general tenor of Licona's remarks in "The Sōma in Death and Resurrection," in Gundry, *Sōma in Biblical Theology: With Emphasis on Pauline Anthropology* (Cambridge: Cambridge University Press, 1976), 176–77, 182; compare also Gundry's comments in "Trimming the Debate," in *Jesus' Resurrection: Fact or Figment? A Debate between William Lane Craig and Gerd Lüdemann*, ed. Paul Copan and Ronald K. Tacelli (Downers Grove, IL: InterVarsity, 2000), esp. 116. See also William Hendriksen, *Exposition of Paul's Epistle to the Romans* (Grand Rapids: Baker, 1981), 251–53, 269–71.

[49] Again, while a word count may not totally solve the issue of the word meanings here, it still remains instructive that in the examples above from the writings of Paul and Luke-Acts, 121 of 133 relevant New Testament references favor physical, objective meanings for the term *horaō* and its cognates.

[50] As when the Jesus Seminar comments, "It is difficult to distinguish Stephen's vision of Jesus from other resurrection appearances." Funk and the Jesus Seminar, *Acts of Jesus*, 460.

difficult not to notice that more radical critical arguments such as these appear to be rather self-serving, in that they are not confirmed by the actual data.

Fifth, N. T. Wright provides strong additional force to the notion that Paul clearly referred to his own appearance of Jesus being physical in nature. Without concentrating on the verb *horaō* and its aorist passive form *ōphthē*, Wright develops a completely separate argument that also centers on New Testament language. More generally, Wright argues that whether the relevant terms were used by Christians, Jews, or pagans in the ancient world from the third century BC up until the (late) second century AD, the key Greek terms *anastasis* (noun: resurrection, a standing up) and *egeirō* (verb: to raise up, arise) virtually always and only were used to described *bodily* events, which is the basic root meaning of the words. While it is true that ancient peoples also spoke of ghosts and other sorts of disembodied wraiths, the point is that they never utilized terms like *anastasis* for these latter beliefs, since this term signified bodily events alone.[51]

The insight to be gained from this argument is that if Wright is correct about the virtually "universal" usage of the terms *anastasis* and *egeirō*, then these are horrible word choices by the New Testament authors if they are trying to describe illumination-like, subjective, or personal insights. Rather, other words were readily available to them other than the ones chosen by Paul. For example, when Luke explains that the disciples thought that the risen Jesus standing in front of them was really a disembodied spirit, the term *pneuma* is used (Luke 24:37). Or earlier when the disciples saw Jesus walking across the sea and thought that he was a ghost, the Greek term *phantasma* (apparition, ghost, specter) is utilized (Mark 6:49). But it must be kept in mind that the illumination thesis usually concerns subjective experiences rather than visionary occasions, creating an even larger gap between these descriptions immediately above and resurrection appearances.

---

[51] Wright states, "'Resurrection' (*anastasis* and its cognates) was not in use elsewhere in the ancient world as a description of non-bodily life after death. It did not denote the passage of the soul into the life beyond or below, or even the migration of the soul into a different body." *Resurrection of the Son of God*, 83–84. See also Wright, xix, 31, 71, 82–84, 127, 201–6, 273, 314, 321, 350–74, 477–79, 551–52. Also important are: Licona, *Resurrection of Jesus*, 400–440, 468–69; John A. T. Robinson, *The Body: A Study in Pauline Theology* (Philadelphia: Westminster, 1952), esp. chap. 1; see also Ronald J. Sider, "The Pauline Conception of the Resurrection Body," *New Testament Studies* 21 (1975): 428–39; Sider, "St. Paul's Understanding of the Nature and Significance of the Resurrection in 1 Corinthians 15:1–19," *Novum Testamentum* 19 (1977): 124–41.

Some critics may charge that, in their opinion, since the Gospels are not written by eyewitnesses, these volumes might simply be reflecting the bodily ethos a few decades after the crucifixion. But bracketing the question of the Gospels' authorship, this would definitely not apply to Paul, who was a scholar and knew better. Yet, after claiming to have seen the resurrected Jesus (1 Cor 9:1; 15:8), he repeatedly made quite powerful comments strongly favoring the bodily resurrection of both Jesus as well as believers.[52]

Next, Wright moves on to a specific application of his general argument. Paul states clearly in 1 Cor 9:1 that he was an apostle who had seen the risen Lord (possibly referring to the early tradition that being a witness to Jesus's resurrection was a condition for apostleship in Acts 1:21–22). Wright notes that the perfect verb *heoraka* in 9:1 "is a normal word for ordinary sight. It does not imply that this was a subjective 'vision' or a private revelation . . . it was a real seeing, not a 'vision.'"

Then Wright moves from 1 Cor 9:1 to 15:8 and argues that "four factors tell strongly in favour of Paul's intention to refer to a real 'seeing' with his ordinary eyes, rather than a non-physical 'seeing' in the sense of a private or internal 'experience.'" These factors, drawn from 15:8, are (1) the textual proximity of 9:1 argues that the seeing of the resurrected Jesus in 15:8 refers to the same sense of sight as previously mentioned—meaning that neither episode was a private experience. (2) There is a sequence of appearances in 15:3–7 followed by the phrase "last of all" in 15:8, most likely indicating that the series of real events came to an end at that point. In particular, Paul is hardly referring to a lineup of those who had spiritual experiences or insights! Nor would such a lineup of testimonies have stopped. (3) First Corinthians 15:6 clearly indicates that Paul considers the appearances to be public events with witnesses who were capable of providing real evidence. No one is going to travel back to Judea to check out witnesses regarding their internal intuitions. (4) The remainder of 1 Corinthians 15 indicates that Paul really thinks that believers will be raised from the dead, which correlates well with the idea that Jesus's resurrection body was literal as well.[53]

Stephen Davis adds a few more reasons of a similar nature for Jesus's bodily appearances being perceived by normal sight. Davis considers a half dozen arguments

---

[52] Such as Rom 8:11, 23; 1 Cor 15:12; Phil 3:11, 21; cf. the incident Acts 23:6–9, which may be helpful in this context, as well. Cf. Gundry, *Sōma in Biblical Theology*, 164, 169, 176, 180, 182; Gundry, "Trimming the Debate," particularly 116.

[53] Wright, *Resurrection of the Son of God*, 381–84, cf. also 321–22.

in favor of objective visions of a resurrected Jesus who was really present, though involving actual, "enhanced perception." Then Davis considers reasons in favor of the resurrected Jesus being seen via normal sight.[54] He considers the strongest counterpoint to be "the massive physical detail of the appearance stories" even though these come primarily from Jesus being held by the feet in Matthew plus the accounts in Luke and John. One supporting reason is that the earliest postapostolic church also interpreted the resurrection appearances as normal sightings perceived by physical eyes.[55]

Sixth, how does the illumination hypothesis square up with the resurrection appearance to Paul, leading to his revolutionary, lifelong conversion followed by his martyrdom? That Paul was a previous enemy and scholar with an opposing mindset further heightens the force of this argument. As unlikely as it would be in itself, even an internal conviction or insight for Peter—a believer, insider, and the leader of the apostles—would not command the force of an actual appearance of the risen Jesus to Paul the persecutor. What best accounts for Paul's complete transformation—the beauty of an internal understanding and insight, or actually having met the resurrected Jesus, as Paul proclaimed himself? Which experience would best account for his radical, lifelong reversal?

Seventh, as with the previous question concerning Paul, how does the illumination hypothesis explain the appearance to James, the longtime family skeptic, who had apparently concluded that his brother had lost his mind (Mark 3:20–21; cf. John 7:5)?[56] James's experience, like Paul's, had to be far greater than Peter's personal

---

[54] These six common arguments listed by Davis often cited on behalf of objective visions of the risen Jesus are (1) Jesus appearing only to believers (causing Davis to retort, "If this claim were true, it might constitute a powerful argument"); (2) the resurrection not being a resuscitation; (3) the meaning of the Greek term *ōphthē*; (4) some of those to whom Jesus appeared experienced doubts, plus some did not always recognize him; (5) the three accounts in the book of Acts that describe Paul's conversion, which sometimes seems to be less than physical; and (6) Paul's emphasis on the spiritual body of raised believers. See Stephen T. Davis, "'Seeing' the Risen Jesus," in Davis, Kendall, and O'Collins, *Resurrection*, 130–40.

[55] Davis, 140–44.

[56] John A.T. Robertson, the acclaimed Greek scholar of a couple of generations ago, explained that the idiom in Mark 3:31 implies strongly that it was Jesus's family who had concluded these negative things about him. Then Robertson remarked that in modern parlance, "We say that one is out of his head." See A. T. Robertson, *Word Pictures in the New Testament*, vol. 1, *The Gospel according to Matthew and the Gospel according to Mark* (Nashville: Broadman, 1930), 281.

intuition and internal cognition from an insider in order to explain his conversion from unbelief to his absolute transformation and leadership in the early church, as well as following his brother in martyrdom.

Eighth, how does this hypothesis explain Jesus's probable death and resurrection predictions, which many critical scholars recognize as historical?[57] On the surface, it might be thought that such comments from Jesus might precisely "prime the disciples' internal pumps" for personal experiences like those proclaimed by the illumination theorists.

But it must also be remembered that on these occasions, we are told that the disciples misunderstood Jesus and even went as far as to object strenuously to Jesus making these comments.[58] In fact, we are told that Jesus even rebuked Peter in the strongest of terms for denying that he would be killed (Mark 8:33), qualifying as a highly embarrassing statement. The Gospel writers also reported that the disciples had to be reminded later of Jesus's predictions (Mark 16:6–7; Matt 28:7), since they still did not expect Jesus to rise from the dead even on resurrection morning (John 20:9).

But if Jesus's predictions are historical, as the best textual and historical evidence indicates, this points favorably to Jesus having special knowledge of these events ahead of time, thereby comprising a worldview consisting of items beyond the resurrection itself. By increasing the explanatory range of the resurrection message, this leans further in the direction of a literal resurrection explanation than toward a naturalistic hypothesis that attempts to account for these occurrences as normal internal convictions.[59]

---

[57] For perhaps the best summation of individual arguments for and against Jesus's resurrection predictions, including the conclusion that the positive evidence is much weightier, see Licona, *Resurrection of Jesus*, 284–302, with 299–302, 468–69 addressing the positive conclusion that Jesus did make these predictions. Hans F. Bayer has written a major treatment of the relevant issues here; see Bayer, *Jesus' Predictions of Vindication and Resurrection: The Provenance, Meaning and Correlation of the Synoptic Predictions* (Tübingen: Mohr, 1986); also Allison, *Resurrecting Jesus*, 230; Dale C. Allison Jr., *The Resurrection of Jesus: Apologetics, Polemics, History* (London: T&T Clark, 2021), 184–88, 198.

[58] As in Mark 8:31–33; 9:31–32; 14:27–31.

[59] It might be objected here that the illumination thesis could be broadened to favor the real though still nonobjective appearances of Jesus. But it must be remembered that a naturalistic hypothesis is being evaluated here, which is its major weakness. Further, if an objective visionary thesis is being suggested instead, that is the subject of the later chapter in this volume.

A little background is necessary before continuing with our next critique of the illumination hypothesis. Like many ideas, this option (along with a few other negative responses) thrived at particular times due to the more fertile ground of the prominent ideas available. The close of the Bultmannian era was quite compatible with the more positivistic presuppositions that still remained in the 1970s and early 1980s as a hangover from the more anti-supernatural hypotheses still in vogue during the time in which the illumination stance had gained a little attention. Some scholars have pointed out that highly reductionist responses such as this thesis stood in fairly stark contrast to the emerging times, methods, and historical approaches that were gaining more prominence. The new trends were changing significantly, producing important rejoinders to older ideas due to being more open and less naturalistic.

This does not deny that the illumination hypothesis could still have sprung up in more recent times, for more severe critics may always feel constrained to defend their positions that oppose the chief New Testament event of Jesus's resurrection. However, today's research often emerged from far different perspectives where some of the old doorways no longer appeared to have been left as wildly open. The critical responses in recent decades, frankly, has been far more balanced, less one-sided, and much more desirous of producing reasons (usually historical) for the views that were taken. Good arguments are far more often conceded by virtually all sides, even when they do not necessarily mesh with every other view. Of course, the interpretations of those ideas vary.

The best example here is that of the most influential area of study in the New Testament at present, that of the Third Quest for the historical Jesus. Far different from the more sterile and hard-line divisions of a few decades ago, conservatives, moderates, and liberal scholars alike, even those who count themselves as non-Christian, agnostic, or even atheist thinkers, are much more conversant in spite of their sometimes quite wide differences.

This new approach to the historicity of Jesus, based on different research methods and often featuring new historical insights, has definitely emerged in recent decades, even drawing together scholars of differing theological outlooks.[60] While the spirit of

---

[60] In all fairness, an important example here is Ehrman's works, such as his volume *Did Jesus Exist?* Because Ehrman refers to himself as an atheist New Testament scholar, one must of course allow for his anticipated conclusions that the New Testament is not generally a reliable text (70–71, 268–69), that there are no direct eyewitness reports of

the times might simply account for some of these more open attitudes, it may also be the case that mutual respect for the results of historical and other empirical research has grown.[61] Since we have pursued each of these subjects elsewhere in this study, we will simply mention here briefly a few of these new historical emphases.

Jesus in the New Testament (46, 49, 101, cf. 145), that Jesus did not refer to himself as deity (22–23, 159, 167, 170, cf. 172, 305–7), that Jesus's miracles cannot be confirmed historically (315–16), and that Jesus was incorrect about the time of his return (1, 313–14, 316, 336). But Ehrman also seems to acknowledge the historical likelihood of many quite positive areas pertaining to Jesus's historicity, including that mythicist attacks on the existence of Jesus are fully unwarranted (2, 17, 20–34, 167, 194–96, 268), that there are more than sufficient independent sources and historical attestation for Jesus's existence (56, 77, 92, 97, 140–41, 163, 171, 251, 262, 290–91, cf. 140–41), and that there are more than a dozen independent sources for the historicity of Jesus's crucifixion within 100 years (71, 156–58, 163–64, 173, 290–91, 327–31). Ehrman challenges thoroughly any notions that Christian origins were based on the mystery religions and related positions, which are totally wrongheaded (26, 207–18, 221–30, 256–58); he defends the notion that the earliest Christian preaching of the Gospel message dated from as early as one to two years after the crucifixion and certainly to no later than the 30s (22, 27, 92–93, 97, 109–13, 130–32, 141, 144–45, 155–58, 163–64, 170–73, 232, 249–51, 254, 260–63), that the historical sources for Jesus are the best among similar religious founders in the ancient world (78, 291), that there are good data for Paul's early conversion (131, 144, 157, 246, 261), Paul's holding to bodily resurrection appearances of the risen Jesus (257–58), the legitimate use of historical criteria as applied specifically to the Gospels (151, 163, 193, 262, 271, 288–93), and that the gnostic beliefs postdated the birth of the Christian message (290). In this overall process, Ehrman comes across as a fair-minded dialogue partner who concedes ground when the evidence determines it, while still holding to skeptical views when he thinks that they are warranted. Further, Ehrman is not the only critical scholar who exemplifies these attitudes. Other similar examples among major critical scholars include James Crossley, Dale Allison, James D. G. Dunn, E. P. Sanders, Luke Timothy Johnson, Paula Fredriksen, John P. Meier, Larry Hurtado, and, in different areas, Antony Flew. But in my opinion, that sort of fair attitude and willing give-and-take is also exhibited among some more or less conservative authors, such as N. T. Wright, Scot McKnight, Nancey Murphy, Craig A. Evans, Ben Witherington, William Lane Craig, David Wenham, Michael Licona, Richard Bauckham, and Greg Boyd. I believe this general ethos is far more common today but would not have characterized the more positivistic and dogmatic generation of Bultmann and others.

[61] When longtime atheist Antony Flew shocked the intellectual world by changing his mind and becoming a deist/theist (with those words being used interchangeably by Flew), he famously declared repeatedly that he had to follow the argument and its evidence, wherever it might lead him. See Antony Flew with Roy Abraham Varghese, *There Is a God: How the World's Most Notorious Atheist Changed His Mind* (New York: HarperCollins, 2007), 22–23, 42, 48, 52, 56, 75, 89, 147, 155.

Heading the list of the underlying historical developments was the predominant, unifying theme of the Third Quest regarding the Jewishness of Jesus, including the Jewish backgrounds found in New Testament thought. Complementing this refrain is the apparently majority view and growing conviction that the Gospels are actually a species of Greco-Roman biography (*bioi*).[62] To be sure, there are differences in how this emphasis has played among the various ancient historians themselves, such as the second-century authors Plutarch (in his *Lives of the Noble Greeks and Romans*) and Suetonius (in his *The Twelve Caesars*), though some trends were similar.

For instance, some of the chief ideas in these texts involved factual accuracy, including the notion that other ancient sources had been employed as data. In the New Testament accounts, these additional sources included the potential use of the Q text (from the German *Quelle*, "source"), a sayings text, or Luke's sources mentioned in 1:1–4, a passage often recognized for its research element, along with the majority scholarly view that Mark employed a pre-Markan passion and empty tomb narrative, or John making use of an earlier miracle document.

Another highly influential recognition among the Third Quest researchers is the presence of early oral sayings that were embedded as creedal texts particularly in the New Testament Epistles as well as in the sermon summaries in Acts. The early dates of these traditions, chiefly centering on the Gospel message of the centrality of the deity, death, and resurrection of Jesus, reflect the content of the earliest historical reports and go back to the time of the apostles. Even very critical scholars have particularly recognized the value of these confessions as records of the very earliest Christian proclamation.[63] But only in the last generation have the incredible benefits of these early confessions been recognized more fully.

---

[62] The most influential study that accounted for the shift was Richard A. Burridge, *What Are the Gospels? A Comparison with Graeco-Roman Biography* (Cambridge: Cambridge University Press, 1992).

[63] The beginning of this creedal recognition even extended back into the days of the German liberalism of the nineteenth and early twentieth centuries, particularly toward the latter portions of this theological movement. David Strauss does not show much recognition of the creedal element when he treats the resurrection appearances in 1 Cor 15:3–7 (*Life of Jesus, Critically Examined*, 727–28, 738–44). However, several decades later Wilhelm Bousset conceded the traditional nature of the pre-Pauline creeds but did not trace them to the Jerusalem church, preferring a Hellenistic origin, which reflected the popular ideas of the time, as just mentioned. See Bousset, *Kyrios Christos: A History of the Belief in Christ from the Beginning of Christianity to Irenaeus*, trans. John E. Steely (Nashville: Abingdon, 1970), 58, cf. 120. A few more decades after Bousset, Bultmann began to recognize the value of

Last, the employing of historical criteria, applied primarily to the Gospels, has produced insights that have helped determine when a report probably recorded reliable data. Examples would be the presence of early or eyewitness material and embarrassing or enemy reports that point to backhanded indications of what really occurred in the first century. Multiple independent attestation of sources has become another major indication that an account is probably trustworthy. The overall impact of these criteria have pushed further in the direction of locating dependable reports in antiquity.

Ninth, back to the effect of worldviews and changing perspectives on the illumination thesis, some of the Third Quest critical scholars who responded to this view were fairly strong in their denunciations, even being sarcastic at times. Regarding Schillebeeckx, along with a few similar subjective views, N. T. Wright concluded, "It requires enormous credulity to suppose that, even allowing Peter and Paul to have had such fantasies or hallucinations, they would have generated more than a passing comment of sympathy among their colleagues or contemporaries."[64] Elsewhere, Wright commented that undergoing such a postmortem vision of someone in this manner would convince them of precisely the opposite view—reminding them rather forcefully that their loved one was indeed dead.[65] Hence, the thesis is actually counterproductive in producing the disciples' conviction that Jesus has been raised from the dead. Theses like these tend along reductionist lines of thinking, similar to those of Bultmann and Marxsen.[66]

Plantinga scolds Sheehan repeatedly. For example, in an age where liberal theologians manifest "a kind of desperate quest for novelty" and "vie with each other to

---

these creedal texts along with brief snippets in the Acts sermon summaries, listing several of them and referring to their pre-Pauline character; see Rudolf Bultmann, *Theology of the New Testament*, trans. Kendrick Grobel, 2 vols. (New York: Scribner's Sons, 1951), 1:81–83, 86, 125–26. Unlike Bousset though, Bultmann traced the resurrection tradition in 1 Cor 15:3–7 to the earliest Jerusalem church (1:295–96). Though the creedal scholarship was not yet honed in a way that recognized the full, incredible value of these traditions, early volumes were already pointing out their importance. Among these were the influential studies by C. H. Dodd, *The Apostolic Preaching and Its Developments: With an Appendix on Eschatology and History* (London: Hodder & Stoughton, 1936); and Oscar Cullmann, *The Earliest Christian Confessions*, trans. J. K. S. Reid, ed. Gary Habermas and Benjamin Charles Shaw (London: Lutterworth, 1949; repr., Eugene, OR: Wipf & Stock, 2018).

[64] Wright, "Christian Origins," 121.

[65] Wright, "Dialogue," in Crossan and Wright, *Resurrection of Jesus*, 35.

[66] Wright, *Resurrection of the Son of God*, 701.

see who can make the most outrageous pronouncements," we should give "credit where credit is due: Sheehan, it seems, has topped it." While some theologians (like Thomas J. J. Altizer) have in the past encouraged atheism, "now Sheehan adds, in a spectacular burst of insight, that this is the gospel Jesus Christ himself brought! Colossal!" Now the only remaining move to make is "to hold that God himself . . . was an atheist even before Jesus. . . . But even this suggestion, logically impossible though it is, doesn't have quite the sheer bite and panache of Sheehan's preposterous claim."[67]

Raymond Brown states that Sheehan sometimes has a tendency "to set up straw men easily knocked down."[68] Sociologist and Roman Catholic priest Andrew Greeley stated that Sheehan was guilty of "dismissing myths in a fashion which suggests he is not paying attention to anything written on the subject since Bultmann."[69] In a later article, Greeley accused Sheehan of being "serenely innocent of understanding," "blithely unaware," guilty of "oversimplifications," and of displaying "his own sad and rather shabby ignorance" across several fields of research, indicating "that he does not know what he is talking about."[70]

Moule also compares Don Cupitt's version of the illumination thesis to a Bultmann-type move.[71] Wright states similarly regarding Schillebeeckx's "variations on the Bultmannian scheme."[72] Carnley critiques Marxsen's view in the context of

---

[67] Plantinga, "Sheehan's Shenanigans," 21, with numerous other similar critiques throughout the essay.

[68] Brown, *Biblical Exegesis and Church Doctrine*, 61.

[69] Greeley, "Ways of Knowing," 432. Greeley seems to be insinuating here that Sheehan was overly dependent on Bultmann's ideas while neglecting key ideas since that time. Though the idea could have come from more than one place, of course, including from his own study, Sheehan emphasizes that the earliest resurrection teaching was about Jesus's exaltation rather than about any resurrection "event" (*First Coming*, 106–7, 117–18), which was also a key teaching of Bultmann's (*Theology of the New Testament*, 1:45, 82). Whether or not the idea came from Bultmann's writings, Sheehan's bold assertion that the idea of exaltation first is "the virtually unanimous opinion of mainstream scholars of the New Testament" is assuredly false. Sheehan, "Resurrection," 94.

[70] Greeley, "Provisional Path to Mystery," 530–32. Frederick J. Crossan makes a similar point to the previous one, that Sheehan "dogmatically leaps beyond his data" in Crossan, "A Challenge, Not a Threat," *Commonweal* (1984): 491.

[71] C. F. D. Moule and Don Cupitt, "The Resurrection: A Disagreement," in Cupitt, *Explorations in Theology*, 27, 33–34, cf. 29.

[72] Wright, "Christian Origins," 120–21.

the reductionism of David Strauss and especially Bultmann.[73] Ancient historian Paul Maier refers to Sheehan's thesis as "St. Peter's happy hunch."[74]

Of course, strong comments do *not* demonstrate that other views are false. But behind these criticisms is the general ethos of the Third Quest researchers and especially the *research* that fuels their comments, such as those observed in the details mentioned by Wright and Carnley.

Tenth, a very crucial point in its own right is that those who hold the illumination hypothesis rarely provide historical or any other reasons that indicate the nature of their interpretation of Peter's actual experience, or anyone else's for that matter. In this regard, their thesis suffers mightily from not having any significant historical data that evidences these testimonies. Not only do many arguments stand against this thesis, such as those above, but like Bultmann himself, this approach exhibits a rather fideistic approach, perhaps not far from Bultmann's own angle, in that it is simply proclaimed to be the case. Scholars have referred to such an approach as groundless.

Wright argues that naturalistic treatments like that of Schillebeeckx are built on taking solely internal insights in place of external appearances and "are at best unprovable and at worst wildly fantastic."[75] Moule responded to Cupitt that there is nothing in either Scripture or experience that would trigger Cupitt's internal view giving rise to the resurrection faith.[76] O'Collins faults Machoveč for reducing and altering the New Testament claims in a way that allows him to state whatever he wants without answering the central questions.[77] Greeley refers to Sheehan's "shallow agnostic arguments" where he is constantly guilty of asserting "once again as proven that which remains to be proven."[78] J. M. Cameron asserts confidently that there is "no text, no primitive record, no known fragment, to which we can appeal to justify this view . . . Sheehan's interpretation is implausible."[79] Paul Meier judges that Sheehan's proposal is "pure conjecture."[80]

However, these skeptical scholars do not hesitate to challenge other positions by asking for their evidence while not producing many positive reasons in return.

---

[73] Carnley, *Structure of Resurrection Belief*, 156–58.

[74] Maier, review of *The First Coming* (by Sheehan), 30.

[75] Wright, "Christian Origins," 121.

[76] Moule and Cupitt, "Resurrection," 33.

[77] O'Collins, "Peter as Easter Witness," 5.

[78] Greeley, "Ways of Knowing," 432.

[79] J. M. Cameron, review of *The First Coming* (by Sheehan), 27.

[80] Maier, review of *The First Coming* (by Sheehan), 30.

Thus, those who embrace the illumination hypothesis need to do more than simply assert their own positions, especially when requested to produce their reasons. Some historical backup should be forthcoming.

Altogether, the illumination thesis quite simply comes up very far short of the mark at every turn. The ten critiques above began with there simply not being enough transformative power to last for many years, including potential martyrdoms, all because of a personal insight or reflection, as most scholars have agreed. Another problem includes this view not coming to grips with the strong data favoring the New Testament descriptions of the disciples' experiences. The strong evidence for the historicity of the empty tomb is likewise a large issue, remaining unrefuted but necessarily having to be denied nonetheless. Moreover, the Greek verb *horaō* and its aorist passive form *ōphthē* speak far more of ordinary sight than of mental or spiritual events alone, contrary to several illumination claims. Wright's arguments for the terms *anastasis* and *egeirō* always being bodily terms also weigh heavily against illumination. The argument from 1 Cor 9:1 on Paul's resurrection appearance is also impressive.

Further, illumination is not the best way to explain the conversions of Paul or James the brother of Jesus. Jesus's resurrection predictions of literal occurrences also militate against the subjective understandings of these occurrences. Being formulated during the influence of the Bultmannian era without facing the challenges of the Third Quest, plus the lack of purported evidence for the position, plagues this view as well. The overall weight against the illumination hypothesis is impressive.

The Illusion Hypothesis

This often-unrecognized natural supposition occurs when one physical object or condition is mistaken for another actual object. Illusion may thus be defined as the "misperception or misinterpretation of real external sensory stimuli."[81] Though very much unlike hallucinations (which are subjective sense stimulations, usually sight, in the absence of any actual physical presence), illusions can quite often be confused or categorized with hallucinations. The illusion thesis, involving genuine objects or

---

[81] See Jerrold S. Maxmen and Nicholas G. Ward, *Essential Psychopathology and Its Treatment*, 2nd ed. (New York: Norton, 1995), 483–85; Harold I. Kaplan, Benjamin J. Sadock, and Jack A. Grebb, *Synopsis of Psychiatry*, 7th ed. (Baltimore: Williams & Wilkins, 1994), 306–7.

events, concerns situations where people mistake actual phenomena for something other than what they are actually experiencing. These occasions can occur singly or in groups.

Examples of Illusion

With regard to the resurrection question, examples of illusion would be a "twin brother" thesis, such as those by A. N. Wilson or Robert Greg Cavin, where a look-alike was taken to be Jesus himself.[82] For Wilson, the second individual was most likely James, Jesus's brother, though we cannot say for sure. More creatively, Frank Miosi suggests what we might call the "John the Baptist Theory." In this case, just as some thought that Jesus was actually John the Baptist having returned from the dead (Mark 6:14–16), Miosi thinks that early Christians may have considered later that Jesus was raised when they saw someone else who reminded them of Jesus.[83]

Atheist philosopher Michael Martin also mentions the possibly of a look-alike individual seen by the followers of Jesus. Other potential illusions have been mentioned as possible parallels, including UFO cases![84] Michael Goulder cites some odd illusional incidents that he considers analogous to certain aspects of the resurrection accounts—such as statues of the Virgin Mary that reportedly move, concentrating especially on stories of Bigfoot appearances![85]

---

[82] A. N. Wilson, *Jesus* (London: Sinclair-Stevenson, 1992), 242–44; Robert Greg Cavin, "Miracles, Probability, and the Resurrection of Jesus: A Philosophical, Mathematical, and Historical Study" (Ph.D. diss., University of California at Irvine, 1993), 314–58. Some related thoughts are found in Cavin, "Is There Sufficient Historical Evidence to Establish the Resurrection of Jesus?," *Faith and Philosophy* 12 (1995): 361–79.

[83] Frank T. Miosi, "The Resurrection Debate," review of *Did Jesus Rise from the Dead? The Resurrection Debate*, by Gary R. Habermas and Antony G. N. Flew, ed. Terry L. Miethe, *Free Inquiry* 8, no. 2 (1988): 56–57.

[84] Michael Martin, *The Case against Christianity* (Philadelphia: Temple University Press, 1991), 83, 92–95.

[85] Michael Goulder, "The Baseless Fabric of a Vision," in D'Costa, *Resurrection Reconsidered*, 48–61. A briefer version of these thoughts is found in "Did Jesus Rise from the Dead?," in Barton and Stanton, *Resurrection*, esp. 58–62. Some parallels are also mentioned by Frank J. Tipler, *The Physics of Immortality: Modern Cosmology, God and the Resurrection of the Dead* (New York: Doubleday, 1994), 310–12. Tipler denied the resurrection in this work (309–13) but later changed his naturalistic views and embraced the historicity of Jesus's resurrection and his appearances; see Tipler, *The Physics of Christianity* (New York: Doubleday, 2007), chaps. 1, 8 in particular!

What illusion theorists hold in common is that *something real* was mistakenly thought to be *something else* that was also real. For our purposes, something or more likely someone was wrongly thought to be the risen Jesus. As Martin suggests, "A person who looked like Jesus could have triggered a collective delusion."[86] Then

---

[86] Martin, *Case against Christianity*, 93. The word "delusion" in Martin's quotation most likely should be "illusion," especially so as to remove the notion of mental or psychotic problems; see Kaplan, Sadock, and Grebb, *Synopsis of Psychiatry*, 488–89. In many places throughout this volume, Martin employs simply exasperating comments and unsubstantiated claims to make his points, as if he needs no backup data in many key places. For just a very few examples, it seems that anytime Martin dates a New Testament writing or an early Christian author like Ignatius or Polycarp, he can be counted on to add one or two decades to the date of the writing. After all, what's a decade or two extra among friends! *And it must be noted very carefully* that these are not cases where Martin's personal dates simply differ from those of the specialists, because it still would be his right to disagree. But in almost all the cases cited here, Martin purports to be telling his readers where the critical scholars themselves line up on these subjects today, and he is usually quite far from being accurate. We will list several examples, drawn from just his two chapters on the historicity of Jesus and his resurrection, where he is seriously in error. While most critical scholars date Mark at about AD 70–75 (see Ehrman below), Martin thinks that scholars place the date for Mark at AD 70–135, stating that the Gospel of Mark may actually have originated in the second century AD (44)! While most critical scholars date Luke at about 80–85, Martin adds fifteen years to make it AD 100. Polycarp magically moves from about 110 to 120–135 (43). Martin pronounces that virtually all scholars "are almost in uniform agreement" that the famous *Testimonium Flavianum* passage in Josephus's *Antiquities* is spurious, even though almost the exact opposite is the case and, in fact, a number of the very scholars he lists in his endnote (including Habermas!) specifically disagree with his statement here, stating otherwise (48). He basically repeats this again on 85 and 91. He is badly mistaken on where critical scholars are with regard to the unanimously accepted Pauline Letters, numbering seven (see Ehrman at the end of this note), whereas Martin lists only four of Paul's Epistles being allowed by scholars for sure (52–53). It must be remembered, once again, that Martin is telling his readers where he thinks critical scholars line up, but he frequently misses the mark by miles. Against the vast majority of scholars today, Martin downgrades the value of 1 Cor 15:5–8 (83). More cases of his exceptionally weak claims can be found on 45, 55–56, 75, 85, 88, 89, 90, 92, 94, 95. Often throughout, Martin seems frequently to set a very low threshold for his own comments and what he thinks is worth reporting, noting in one place that even if a particular thesis of his cannot be shown to be probable, "Surely, it is not beyond the realm of psychological possibility" (95). Really? This is not the only place where he reasons in this manner either (with another major example on 55–56). So is he trying to present probable arguments, or only ones that are psychologically *possible*? For substantiation of my own arguments against Martin on the subject of where the majority of contemporary critical scholars are today, note that atheist New Testament scholar Bart Ehrman dates Mark from the 60s to the early 70s rather than possibly into the

presumably, other early Christians probably would have approved enthusiastically of the idea that they had seen their Lord raised from the dead.

A Critique of the Illusion Hypotheses

These ideas are difficult to evaluate because they span a very wide array of phenomena and often involve quite odd, even outlandish, ideas. Perhaps the best way to appraise them is to treat separately cases where Jesus was witnessed from a distance from those encounters that occurred at a closer range.

Examples from a distance obviously lend themselves to easier responses for more than one reason. At any rate, there are fewer instances of such encounters with regard to the New Testament reports of Jesus's resurrection. John 21:1–10 relates that while seven of Jesus's disciples were fishing in the Sea of Tiberias (the Sea of Galilee), the risen Jesus stood on the shore and called out to them. But the text states that Jesus was about 100 yards away from them, far enough away that they did not recognize him (21:4, 8). But as might be expected, when the disciples arrived back on land, they were close enough to ascertain that it was indeed Jesus who had been on the shore and had called out to them. Once being in his presence, no one needed to ask Jesus who he was (21:10, 12). In another possible instance, we are not told how far away Jesus was while he was teaching on a mountain (Matt 28:16–17), but it would have been counterproductive to stand very far from his audience without voice-projection devices.

First, as the passage in John 21 states, once the distance gap was closed and the men were all together, Jesus was close enough to be properly identified. The distance factor was clearly the problem, and no further questions were necessary. This would certainly seem like the chief answer in such cases.

Second, on a few occasions the Gospel texts state that Jesus was not readily recognized even when he was close by, such as in the garden with Mary Magdalene (John 20:14), or on the walk to Emmaus with the two companions (Luke 24:16; cf.

second century as per Martin, while Ehrman dates both Matthew and Luke from 80 to 85 (Martin says AD 100 for Luke). On other places where we have reported on Martin, notice Ehrman's views: Polycarp wrote shortly after 110 (415), not 120–135 like Martin, and Paul wrote seven "undisputed" epistles (262, 290), not the four epistles allowed by Martin when he claims to be speaking for critical scholarship as a whole. Page citations from Bart D. Ehrman, *The New Testament: A Historical Introduction to the Early Christian Writings*, 2nd ed. (Oxford: Oxford University Press, 2000).

Mark 16:12 in pseudo-Mark). Regarding the two men walking, one issue concerns the interpretation of the Greek words in question, that they were *ekratounto tou mē epignōnai auton* (unable to recognize him) in Luke 24:16 and then their eyes were *diēnoichthēsan* (opened, or no longer restrained) in Luke 24:31, plus *en heterāi morphēi* (in another guise) in the longer ending of Mark 16:12.

There are a few possible explanations that may be applicable in these texts. The implications in Luke 24:16, 31 (as well as the long ending of Mark 16:12) seem to be that the witnesses were supernaturally kept from recognizing Jesus until that was no longer the case. In the case of Mary Magdalene, paintings often picture her with her back turned to Jesus or with her face covered at the graveside, or looking through tear-blurred eyes. Of course, we do not know for sure. Others might surmise that the emotional shock of seeing someone who was so brutally executed and buried just a brief time before might militate against allowing themselves to admit recognizing Jesus.

But it seems that the major and probably best rejoinder overall is simply that people's appearances certainly change over the years. When people think they have just spotted an old friend whom they have not seen in some time, they often do a double take, especially if the experience is unexpected. The verbal response is almost always the same: "Is that really you?" And they might be mistaken in their guess as often as they are correct. The same thing may have been the case with the risen Jesus, even though the time difference was not a factor. Crucially, Paul states that the believer's resurrection body will change after death too (1 Cor 15:35–55; Phil 3:21). We are also told that this change will be patterned after Jesus's own resurrection body (cf. 1 John 3:2). The point here is that it would make perfect sense if Jesus's body and outward appearance had actually changed just enough to make his followers do a double take as well.

Of course, no one knows how closely the risen Jesus may have appeared if compared to his pre-crucifixion body, but when combined with the emotional shock given that the resurrection was so unexpected (see John 20:9), this could very plausibly explain the couple of situations where certain persons did not recognize Jesus. But most crucially, whatever the reasons, each of the texts agrees that the situation was rectified very quickly.

Third, concerning the suggestions of look-alike persons being mistaken for Jesus, such as his own brother James or any other cases that might be mentioned, these scenarios come crashing down pretty quickly when a variety of angles and circumstances are considered. The Gospel narratives teach that one or more of

Jesus's disciples were usually present during the appearances,[87] as were his mother or the other women,[88] his brother James,[89] and others who knew Jesus exceptionally well.[90] Virtually everyone mentioned in these groupings could probably tell the difference between Jesus and his brother James or other look-alikes, but certainly Jesus's mother Mary knew the difference between her two sons. Plus, would James or any others allow the confusion to go uncorrected had a misunderstanding of this sort occurred?

Additionally, Jesus's crucifixion wounds (Luke 24:39; John 20:25–28) were also crucial for the purposes of identification, and neither James nor anyone else but Jesus possessed them. Virtually no matter how someone construes these Gospel texts, there were enough people who knew Jesus well who could answer these suppositions.

On the other hand, the John the Baptist scenario was suggested as a potential rumor that was conceivably noised about, circulating at that time concerning Jesus, not at all in the sense of folks making that claim after seeing the two men side by side. In the cases regarding Marian statues, these are obviously not living people and these reported phenomena could have been cleared up quickly enough by empirical

---

[87] Such as Matt 28:16–20; Luke 24:34, 36–53; John 20:19–25, 26–29; 21:1–22; cf. Acts 2:32; 3:15; 5:30–32; 10:39–41; 13:30–31; 1 Cor 15:5–8; *1 Clem.* 42; Ignatius, *Smyrn.* 3.

[88] Depending on whether Jesus's mother, Mary, is identified in Matt 28:1, 9; Mark 16:1; Luke 24:10; cf. Acts 1:14. Even without specific texts, how could it be questioned that Jesus's own mother Mary would have seen her resurrected son at least a few times?

[89] See 1 Cor 15:7 (cf. the *Gospel of the Hebrews* 7), as applied to Jesus being together with his brother James as well.

[90] Critics occasionally suggest some rather wild and chaotic scenarios, perhaps like an impersonator attempting *deliberately* to play the role of Jesus for some unknown reason. Perhaps naturally looking just a little like Jesus, or keeping his distance whenever possible, conceivably faking the scars somehow and so on, he could get away with this charade. Yet the number of contrary responses would mount rapidly, such as the fake scars being discovered very quickly, family members and close friends like the male or female disciples not discovering anything amiss, the Jewish leaders who were present at his crucifixion to ensure his death not discovering the ruse either, the exceptionally brief time limitations involved in a two-day window before the caper beginning, even imagining a worthwhile alibi that would "inspire" someone to take such chances in the first place, and more. Then what about the empty tomb? Another thesis of some sort would be needed here. And then perhaps last of all, where is the evidence that anything of such a nature ever occurred anyway? It probably would not take much thought to realize that such a situation would not exactly be at the very top of the naturalist's options to expose Jesus's resurrection!

testing or other data-gathering. With the Bigfoot suggestions mentioned by more than one critic, we are presumably back to distant-sight situations that would have been corrected at close range.[91]

Again, it could hardly be maintained seriously in any of these situations, whatever scenario was devised, that the one(s) drawing the false conclusions would continue to maintain their thesis once they were surrounded by all the witnesses among Jesus's family members and best friends. When confronted by those who knew Jesus and the facts well, or even by the risen Jesus himself, it would certainly seem that the doubting individual(s) could not plausibly keep holding their look-alike, distant-sight, or rumor-based alternative claims. After all, in John's narrative (20:24–28), the apostle Thomas played precisely the sort of role that is represented by the cynics here, having concluded that his colleagues had misapprehended the situation at hand. As mentioned, these are precisely the sorts of matters that are straightened out by those who best know the situations, this time by the Lord Jesus himself, and we are told that Thomas went away believing!

Illusions do indeed occur often in normal, everyday life, perhaps even on a daily basis. One reality is quite often thought to be something, and sometimes it turns out to be something quite different altogether. This is especially the case when the perception happens at night or at a distance, and the further away it is, generally the less likely is the report. When these situations occur, we are normally aware of ways to sort out our observations by checking our perceptions against the data that we can find at our disposal or by inquiring of living eyewitnesses. So it was in the first century AD as well. The testimony favoring Jesus's resurrection appearances could be

---

[91] Examples such as Bigfoot, UFOs, and statues of Mary as used by Goulder ("Baseless Fabric," 52–55), as well as UFOs, cattle mutilations in the western United States, witchcraft, satanic cults, and the very odd species of psychosis (*folie à deux*) referred to by Martin (*Case against Christianity*, esp. 93–95), seem designed to explain how people in sometimes large numbers can be tricked, deceived, or otherwise duped, which can hardly be denied, rather than being the sorts of visual illusions that we are considering in the present context. Note here that *folie à deux* is a psychosis. Regarding what skeptics sometimes refer to as mass or collective delusions (such as Martin, *Case against Christianity*, 93; Goulder, "Baseless Fabric," 52–55; Tipler, *Physics of Immortality*, 310–13), these are different phenomena and are treated in the chapter on hallucinations. As per the explanation above, note also that the use of "delusions" here should probably be understood as collective *illusions*, so as both to be much more accurate and to not imply psychotic situations that are not necessarily warranted. Further, recall that the illusory objects in question are real, not hallucinatory.

checked against any of the alternative hypotheses, as we have done in this chapter. The process continues unabated.

Conclusion

In this chapter, we have addressed two scenarios that in literature are quite often confused with hallucinations but are, strictly speaking, not the same. The first option was termed here the illumination hypothesis and refers to the supposition that Peter, followed by the other disciples, experienced an internal conviction, insight, or understanding that persuaded them that after Jesus's crucifixion and death, Jesus was actually alive and had been exalted to God's right hand. This view was formulated as a reflection of the time in which it was birthed, during the Bultmannian era, when fideistic expressions of faith were frequently postulated as the way the earliest Christian preaching began. But its ideas were short-lived in light of the Third Quest for the historical Jesus and its historically based search for data that accounted for the foundations of the church.

Specifically, most scholars were much dissatisfied with the illumination hypothesis, as indicated by the huge backlash and outcry aimed at these ideas. That these repercussions even emerged from major researchers, which is very seldom the case, is an indication of how far this view was judged to have differed from the early records. In particular, it was determined chiefly that the suppositions were far too inconsequential, exaggerated, and ungrounded to have supported grand notions of transformation, all based on foundations that were far too inadequate. In short, the views were much too top-heavy and unsupported. We also noted nine additional problems, some of which were also quite severe. These included the lack of correspondence to the New Testament claims, the empty tomb, the Greek terms in the very early accounts, plus the conversions of Paul and James. Not surprisingly, this natural thesis has basically come and gone without standing the test of time.

The second scenario of illusions is derived from false conclusions due to incorrectly thinking that a particular visual object is in fact something else. It comes in many different forms, some of which are quite wild (UFOs, cattle mutilation, *folie à deux*, and witchcraft, for examples). Accordingly, these mistaken perceptions were suggested as the grounds on which Jesus was falsely thought to have appeared to his followers though on this view, he had not in fact done so at all. Rather, something or someone quite different was seen and mistakenly identified by the witnesses.

However, this second, often strange concoction of false examples fails rather miserably as well. It almost appears as if this set of responses represents a catchall for any remaining odd ideas that might just possibly be invented. In a sense, the cases would have been confronted by the light of day, so to speak. The risen Jesus was either there or he was not, and the evidence that was gained "close up" should sort out the matters, curing any ongoing instances of misapprehension and confusion.

15

Hallucination

In the heyday of nineteenth-century German liberalism, the majority of influential skeptical scholars chose a single naturalistic hypothesis aimed at Jesus's resurrection and defended it, usually throughout their careers. Heinrich Paulus chose the swoon or apparent death view, David Strauss championed the subjective vision thesis, and Wilhelm Bousset opted for what might be termed the legend or mythical approach. Theodor Keim embraced the nonnaturalistic objective vision alternative.

Several decades later, until past the halfway point of the twentieth century, the influence of Barth, Bultmann, and others led to what was later termed the "No Quest" for the historical Jesus that eschewed history coming to the aid of faith. One could even get the idea that those scholars who believed firmly in Jesus's resurrection appeared to be somewhat reticent about stating this, especially in detail, perhaps due to the length of Barth's and Bultmann's shadows! Comparatively few major defenses of the resurrection appeared.[1] Conversely, historical rejections of Jesus's resurrection had likewise fallen on hard times. Very few skeptical specialists in relevant areas of study had clearly chosen just a single natural thesis rejecting the resurrection and

---

[1] One exception was Wolfhart Pannenberg. Though he had only written comparatively short treatments of the resurrection as part of his other volumes, such as in his celebrated text *Jesus: God and Man*, trans. Lewis L. Wilkins and Duane A. Priebe (Philadelphia: Westminster, 1968), he was still acclaimed the new champion of resurrection studies, especially among conservative scholars.

championed that idea alone, as had been the case with so many of the nineteenth-century German liberals. In short, historical arguments either for or against the faith were not gaining much traction.

At the end of the century and the beginning of the next, there was a measurable upturn of interest in alternative approaches.[2] And probably due to the quickly growing popularity of the Third Quest for the historical Jesus, studies of the past again have been on the move. But while strong defenses of Jesus's resurrection have reappeared, many critics have tended to eschew alternative theses all together.[3] Even fewer skeptics have been willing to choose just a single natural proposal and move forward with it, perhaps implying an unwillingness to chance having that view dismantled.

While many scholars reject miraculous events as a whole, these more general viewpoints are still not the same as defending specific alternative positions. Ehrman has emphasized, "I don't subscribe to any of these alternative views." But he notes that, though it was an "unlikely" option, even the notion that Jesus's disciples stole Jesus's deceased body and then lied about it was still superior to a miraculous event.[4] Critical scholars are usually open to a host of potential responses in principle, often without choosing a particular option, almost as if to keep a "back door" ajar just in case it goes badly for their favorite options![5] Far fewer major

---

[2] Gary R. Habermas, "The Late Twentieth-Century Resurgence of Naturalistic Responses to Jesus' Resurrection," *Trinity Journal* 22 (2001): 179–96.

[3] These volumes included Pinchas Lapide, *The Resurrection of Jesus: A Jewish Perspective* (Minneapolis: Augsburg, 1983); Gerald O'Collins, *Jesus Risen* (London: Darton, Longman & Todd, 1988); William Lane Craig, *Assessing the New Testament Evidence for the Historicity of the Resurrection of Jesus* (Lewiston, NY: Mellen, 1989); Stephen T. Davis, *Risen Indeed: Making Sense of the Resurrection* (Grand Rapids: Eerdmans, 1993); Gary R. Habermas and Michael R. Licona, *The Case for the Resurrection of Jesus* (Grand Rapids: Kregel, 2003). Most noteworthy among these publications were especially N. T. Wright, *The Resurrection of the Son of God*, vol. 3 of *Christian Origins and the Question of God* (Minneapolis: Fortress, 2003); and Michael R. Licona, *The Resurrection of Jesus: A New Historiographical Approach* (Downers Grove, IL: InterVarsity Academic, 2010).

[4] Bart D. Ehrman, *How Jesus Became God: The Exaltation of a Jewish Preacher from Galilee* (New York: HarperCollins, 2014), 165.

[5] Rather humorously, Ehrman points out how apologists (perhaps himself in his Christian days?) "have a field day" in their responses when critics pick particular natural theories, such as retorting that Jesus "would have looked like death warmed over" when the swoon thesis was proposed (164)! Only he knows if these memories lie behind his not willing to choose a specific naturalistic comeback.

researchers, comparatively speaking (and often the older ones), will stick with a single natural position.[6]

What reasons may account for this seeming shift in recent critical scholarly approaches? Probably the chief reason for discarding these naturalistic theses is that each alternative is rather decisively answered by the data, with this becoming even more the case in the latest research. This has become increasingly evident in recent years. After viewing some of these challenges, New Testament theologian James D. G. Dunn concludes, "Alternative interpretations of the data fail to provide a more satisfactory explanation."[7] Philosopher Stephen Davis agrees that critics "are unable to come up with a coherent and plausible story that accounts for the evidence at hand. All of the alternative hypotheses with which I am familiar are historically weak; some are so weak that they collapse of their own weight once spelled out . . . the alternative theories that have been proposed are not only weaker but far weaker at explaining the available historical evidence."[8] Is this the case with all naturalistic theses, including hallucinations?

The Recent Limited Popularity of the Hallucination Hypothesis

In spite of this adjusted attitude regarding naturalistic theories on the part of critical scholars, including the overall shrinkage among influential researchers, hallucinations still appear to be the most popular natural option, at least speaking generally (in the sense of not always making this an assertion). Still, the numbers holding this view have decreased since the nineteenth century. Further, of those who now prefer hallucination explanations, only a few scholars have pursued this approach in much detail.[9] A few of the attempts will be unpacked, while several other scholars who

---

[6] More recently, as this study was being written, Gerd Lüdemann (subjective vision theory) and John Shelby Spong (what has been termed in this volume the illumination thesis) both passed away, leaving two fewer examples of those embracing single alternatives.

[7] James D. G. Dunn, *The Evidence for Jesus* (Louisville: Westminster, 1985), 76.

[8] Stephen T. Davis, "Is Belief in the Resurrection Rational? A Response to Michael Martin," *Philo* 2 (1999): 57–58.

[9] One of the more prominent examples where hallucinations have been developed in more detail than normal would include Richard Carrier's research in "The Spiritual Body of Christ and the Legend of the Empty Tomb," in *The Empty Tomb: Jesus beyond the Grave*, ed. Robert M. Price and Jeffery Jay Lowder (Amherst, NY: Prometheus, 2005), 184–88, 193–95. After his exposition, Carrier freely introduces specific evidenced claims of contemporary Jesus sightings that he hardly even attempts to refute (187–88). Later, Carrier

turns a discussion of possible group appearances of Jesus into a melting-pot concoction of concepts that virtually encourages playing a shell game among the possibilities (194–95, 387), only to end up even admitting that these experiences are *still* individual hallucinations rather than group sightings (195, 387), thereby conceding the chief point! Also, Carrier thinks that hallucinations are the best possibility of the naturalistic theses (184), only to give that award later to the legend theory (370), seeming to have forgotten his earlier preference in the same book, nicely illustrating the principle raised above of recent scholars not wishing to stick with a single alternative thesis! And if that is not enough, Carrier also challenges the empty tomb scenario in terms of Jesus's body being moved or stolen by others, even by his own disciples, though he does not think that these possibilities are as strong as the other options (see his chapter 9, "The Plausibility of Theft," 349–68, esp. 349, 364 and chap. 10, "The Burial of Jesus in Light of Jewish Law," 369–92, particularly 369, 385, 387). Carrier also supposes that there were multiple modalities in the sightings of Jesus, which he thinks were hallucinations (190), which is also troublesome in light of the scientific hallucination data, as we will see below.

Ehrman discusses more details in *How Jesus Became God*, such as hallucinations in general (186–204), mentioning the possibility of group appearances (138–40, 202), Marian apparitions (191, 198–99), and bereavement hallucinations (195–97, 203–4). In each category, one may get the opinion that the topics are being glossed over without hard looks and specific data. Examples would include the claims that "the Blessed Virgin Mary has appeared to hundreds or thousands of people at once, even though we have modern, verified eyewitness testimony that she has" (202). Having done some specific study on this thesis myself, I will leave the matter at Ehrman's comments being highly questionable. One very crucial inquiry concerns who was claiming to see Mary in the best known of these situations: the thousands of people who may have been present, or just the few children? Further, did the children all report seeing the exact same phenomena? Many, I'm sure, would love to see the sources that reveal either these "verified eyewitnesses" or the refutations so that the data may really be examined carefully! Another instance is Ehrman's dismissing the group appearances in 1 Cor 15:3–7, especially in verses 3–5 (137–43), which will also be discussed below. His ideas about grief hallucinations will also be critiqued in detail below. And it is truly interesting, in fact quite odd, when Ehrman states, "I am not going to take a stand on this issue of whether Jesus really appeared to people" or whether it was really "visions" or "hallucinations" of some sort (186–87, cf. 149, 203–4). Further, Ehrman will not "subscribe to any of these alternative views" because any one is possible (165), just like our statement above that this is a very common trend today, almost like scholars need a fallback plan as assurance. Another potential question is that, for Ehrman, history can neither prove nor disprove that Jesus was raised from the dead (132). These are honest admissions on his part but are very revealing nonetheless, and no doubt will raise some eyebrows! For example, if he thinks there is hard testimony that Mary appeared to many, then why is he not a Christian (perhaps a Roman Catholic)? After all, it is a belief held by Christians.

Keith Parsons, in his chapter, "Peter Kreeft and Ronald Tacelli on the Hallucination Theory" (433–52), in Robert M. Price and Jeffery Jay Lowder, *The Empty Tomb: Jesus beyond*

simply mention their preference or the mere possibility of the hallucination thesis will be mentioned briefly.[10]

---

the Grave (Amherst, NY: Prometheus, 2005), challenges many of the thirteen apologetic arguments against hallucinations that are presented by Peter Kreeft and Ronald Tacelli in their *Handbook of Christian Apologetics* (Downers Grove, IL: InterVarsity, 1994), 186–88. Parsons summarizes Kreeft and Tacelli's negative argument against hallucinations (435), with most of his comments being quite straightforward, sometimes addressing apologetic oversteps. Most of his challenges will be dealt with in due course throughout this chapter.

But for now, Parsons states quite boldly that "mass hallucinations . . . are extremely well-documented phenomena" (436). Really? If so, then how does this statement correspond to the apparent lack of even a *single such reference* to mass hallucinations being discovered in the medical and psychological literature over the past few decades (see below)? To make matters worse, Parsons follows this statement by presenting a number of empirical claims taken from recent news phenomena, but too frequently failing to supply sources for the key claims made (436–37). He responds by citing cases of Marian apparitions under the category of "*mass delusions*" (436), accompanied by references to the "spinning and dancing" of the sun, and still more examples of "collective delusions" of "weeping icons and moving statues" (436–37).

In terms of a quick response to some items that are likewise discussed later in detail, one wonders why UFO reports (434) and especially "collective delusions" are inserted several times here by Parsons, instead of the collective *hallucination* cases that he just promised? Moreover, the items that he freely calls *delusions* seem more probably to be *illusions*. It is crucial that accurate distinctions be made between group illusions, delusions, and hallucinations, which are distinguished below. It is difficult to tell for sure here, but the notions seem to be confused. Parsons claims the mass hallucinations are "extremely well-documented phenomena" without presenting any documented cases cited from the research literature. Then he interjects delusions into his discussion precisely at this point, instead of the claimed "well-documented phenomena" that he thinks favor mass hallucinations (436–37). Or perhaps Parsons realizes that the claim he just made of there being major evidence that favors mass hallucinations is simply not available, necessitating some irrelevant "packing" with different species of occurrences—UFO reports and especially delusions—the latter of which often emanate from diseased minds. Further, is the forty days and nights of Noah's flood *really* a sort of Old Testament motif for Jesus's forty days of appearances on earth (441)? Was this a serious comment? See Parsons, "Peter Kreeft and Ronald Tacelli," esp. 435–49. I will comment on most of the other areas on the coming pages.

[10] Some of these rather brief mentions are made by Michael Martin, "Swinburne on the Resurrection," in Price and Lowder, *Empty Tomb*, 464–66; Dan Cohn-Sherbok, "The Resurrection of Jesus: A Jewish View," in *Resurrection Reconsidered*, ed. Gavin D'Costa (Oxford: Oneworld, 1996), 197; John Barclay, "The Resurrection in Contemporary New Testament Scholarship," in D'Costa, *Resurrection Reconsidered*, 25–26; Michael Grant, *Saint Paul: The Man* (London: Weidenfeld and Nicholson, 1976), 108; M. Lloyd Davies and T. A. Lloyd Davies, "Resurrection or Resuscitation?," *Journal of the Royal College of*

In a few recent volumes, Gerd Lüdemann has outlined a more detailed case quite reminiscent of nineteenth-century liberal attempts, holding that subjective visions can be applied to all the chief participants in the earliest church: the disciples, Paul, the 500 witnesses (1 Cor 15:6), and James the brother of Jesus.[11] Lüdemann perhaps surprisingly concludes that it is clear from Paul's language that the Greek verb ōphthē in 1 Cor 15:8 means that he was speaking of actual sight, of "his own active sensual perception" as well as that of the other apostles. So, Paul "must have expected the Corinthians to understand the term historically."[12] Lüdemann concludes that hallucinatory visions are required along with "auditory features" that produced a "stimulus," "enthusiasm," "religious intoxication," and "ecstasy" for Peter. This spread to the other disciples by "an incomparable chain reaction." Paul, the other apostles, the 500 witnesses, and James all similarly experienced these subjective visions. The appearances were collective, amounting to a "mass ecstasy."[13]

Although his approach is quite different at various points, Jack Kent also thinks that hallucinations explain the claims of the disciples, Paul, and James.[14] Kent combines two naturalistic theories to explain the resurrection appearances of Jesus. The disciples and women experienced "normal, grief-related hallucinations." Paul, on the other hand, experienced inward conflict and turbulence over participating in the death of Stephen and his persecution of Christians. As a result, he underwent a "conversion disorder," a psychiatric malady that Kent thinks accounts for his con-

---

Physicians of London 25, no. 2 (1991): 168; Antony Flew, in Gary R. Habermas and Antony G. N. Flew, *Did Jesus Rise from the Dead? The Resurrection Debate*, ed. Terry Miethe (New York: Harper & Row, 1987), 50–59; John Hick, *The Center of Christianity* (San Francisco: Harper & Row, 1978), 25. Although Peter Carnley thinks that Jesus's resurrection actually occurred, he states that the subjective vision supposition is very difficult to disprove; see Carnley, *The Structure of Resurrection Belief* (Oxford: Clarendon, 1987), 64, 244–45, cf. 69–72, 79, 82.

[11] Gerd Lüdemann's best-known works that develop these ideas are *The Resurrection of Jesus: History, Experience, Theology*, trans. John Bowden (Minneapolis: Fortress, 1994); a more popular rendition was written in collaboration with Alf Özen, *What Really Happened to Jesus: A Historical Approach to the Resurrection*, trans. John Bowden (Louisville: Westminster John Knox, 1995). A more recent volume is Lüdemann's *The Resurrection of Christ: A Historical Inquiry* (Amherst, NY: Prometheus, 2004).

[12] Lüdemann, *Resurrection of Jesus*, 50, 37; Lüdemann with Özen, *What Really Happened to Jesus*, 103.

[13] Lüdemann, *Resurrection of Jesus*, 106–7, 174–75.

[14] Jack A. Kent, *The Psychological Origins of the Resurrection Myth* (London: Open Gate, 1999).

version on the road to Damascus, including his stumbling and blindness.[15] Unlike Lüdemann, however, Kent wishes to avoid the notion of collective hallucinations.[16]

Closer to Kent, Michael Goulder applies a related explanation to the experiences of Peter, Paul, and some of the other apostles.[17] Nonetheless, mixing hallucinations and conversion disorder, Goulder thinks that Peter and Paul experienced what he calls "conversion visions," hallucinations of various sorts that are produced during times of great stress, guilt, and self-doubt. The result for these apostles, one of whom had denied his Lord and another who had persecuted Christians, was a new orientation to life—a transformation leading to "subsequent heroism and martyrdom."[18]

Another notion that has gotten some attention in the past few decades is that Jesus's resurrection was somehow akin to, or perhaps just another species of, other sorts of widespread experiences where deceased individuals interacted with living persons, usually during dreams or otherwise soon after the individual's death.[19] The most commonly reported occurrences of this sort consist of interactions between spouses or visions of deceased loved ones that usually occur fairly soon after death.[20]

Strangely enough, this option comes in several versions and is not even necessarily a naturalistic theory. Of the phenomena in this group, a wide-angle lens on these visions of deceased loved ones would indicate much variation. Some supporters argue that at least a fair number of these usually spousal experiences are probably real sightings, indicative of an afterlife. Others take the polar opposite position, denying that anything supernatural is going on at all and that all of these sightings are common hallucinations. Beginning our three examples below is another take from a medical

---

[15] Kent, 6–11, 21, 33, 41, 47–61, 85–90. Few details will be mentioned here on the idea of conversion disorder, since it is treated in detail in our chapter on this subject.

[16] Kent, 89–90.

[17] Michael Goulder, "Baseless Fabric of a Vision," in D'Costa, *Resurrection Reconsidered*, 48–61. A briefer version of Goulder's thesis was published as part of a debate with James D. G. Dunn in *Resurrection*, ed. G. N. Stanton and S. Barton (London: SPCK, 1994), 58–68.

[18] Goulder, 48–52. Incidentally, Goulder argues that the disciples, especially regarding group appearances, experienced "collective delusions." These are significantly different from subjective hallucinations in that they pertain to the misapprehension of actual, physical objects (52–55).

[19] These experiences especially as discussed here have nothing to do with seances or other attempts to communicate with the dead but are experiences in the everyday world.

[20] For a detailed discussion of the similarity to the resurrection appearances of Jesus, see the chapter in this volume on objective visions.

researcher who did a hallmark study of these cases, apparently deciding that either of the first two views could potentially be correct, without trying to emphasize one view over the others.

Dewi Rees's influential 1971 study of bereavement in widowed persons reported many crucial details pertaining to these personal experiences, including visionary experiences of their deceased spouses.[21] In a later book, Rees unpacked the implications of his study, including the possible emotional and religious significance of these bereavement experiences. Some visions may provide spiritual benefit, namely consolation and assurance of Christian faith.[22] For Rees, these postmortem visions can affirm the reality of an afterlife in general and, for some, even belief in Jesus's resurrection.[23]

Rees acknowledges differences between bereavement visions and the disciples' resurrection encounters with Jesus but does not conclude that the latter are distinctly separate. Instead, he proposes that the disciples' encounters with the resurrected Jesus are comparable and should not be excluded from the bereavement experience genre. Further, for Rees, beliefs in Jesus's resurrection are undiminished as to whether or not Jesus appeared bodily.[24] However, Rees does admit that bereavement experiences cannot account for the disciples' simultaneous group encounters with the risen Jesus.[25]

After the death of a loved one it is fairly common for family members (particularly spouses) and close friends to sense in some way the presence of the deceased. Not infrequently it is even claimed that the deceased individual was seen in some sense. Surprisingly, even folks who were not connected very closely

---

[21] W. Dewi Rees, "The Hallucinations of Widowhood," *British Medical Journal* 4 (1971): 37–41.

[22] Dewi Rees, *Pointers to Eternity* (Talybont: Y Lolfa, 2010), 198.

[23] Rees, 205.

[24] Rees, 193–95.

[25] Rees, 205. After a lengthy analysis, including parallels between apparitions of the dead and the resurrection appearances of Jesus, such as both phenomena being real after-death occurrences (269, 278–82, 299, 343), New Testament scholar Dale Allison still argues that there are also major differences too. Hence, these apparitions are not some natural hypothesis or phenomena that explains Jesus's appearances; see Dale C. Allison Jr., *Resurrecting Jesus: The Earliest Christian Tradition and Its Interpreters* (London: T&T Clark, 2005), esp. 283–85. His more recent study also reviews these subjects in Allison, *The Resurrection of Jesus: Apologetics, Polemics, History* (London: T&T Clark, 2021), 221–22, 346, 356.

to the deceased have claimed to have experienced these occurrences as well. The percentages can differ widely. Aleman and Larøi report that 36 percent of Swedish widows in one study "had experienced at least one type of hallucination," while in another, almost 90 percent of Japanese widows experienced hallucinations of their deceased husbands.[26] Results in two other studies tallied nearly half and nearly two-thirds of those surveyed.[27]

Goulder and Kent both would be examples of scholars who entertained the idea of grief-induced visions as less than actual events. Their views above have already been mentioned, and it is clear that neither one thinks that any such experiences should be explained by the actual presence of the deceased individual.[28]

John Dominic Crossan seems to have lined up in more than one place on these questions. In an earlier journal article, he states quite directly, "*Resurrection is not post-mortem apparition.*"[29] Then in a later dialogue on the subject with N. T. Wright, Crossan either affirms this option or at least seems open to the idea.[30] But if Crossan does indeed entertain this view, it is still clear that, like Goulder and Kent, his position does not affirm either Jesus's actual resurrection

---

[26] André Aleman and Frank Larøi, *Hallucinations: The Science of Idiosyncratic Perception* (Washington, DC: American Psychological Association, 2008), 31.

[27] Aleman and Larøi, 67, with the first one here being Rees's study.

[28] Goulder, "Baseless Fabric," 48–52; Kent, *Psychological Origins*, 21. Maurice Casey's thesis also seems to fit best into this category of trying to utilize subjective notions of bereavement apparitions or hallucinations in order to deny the veracity of any actual resurrection appearances of Jesus, at least with regard to the disciples. However, also like both Goulder and Kent, Casey seems to confuse some important aspects of the relevant ideas here, seemingly causing a would-be interpreter to feel yanked back and forth in an effort to follow his comments in Casey, *Jesus of Nazareth: An Independent Historian's Account of His Life and Teaching* (London: T&T Clark, 2010), esp. 490–96.

[29] John Dominic Crossan, "The Resurrection of Jesus in Its Jewish Context," *Neotestamentica* 37 (2003): 46. Yet this comment can be taken in more than one way.

[30] John Dominic Crossan and N. T. Wright, "Dialogue: N. T. Wright and John Dominic Crossan," in *The Resurrection of Jesus: John Dominic Crossan and N. T. Wright in Dialogue*, ed. Robert B. Stewart (Minneapolis: Fortress, 2006), 35–38. As far as Crossan possibly taking more than one view on the issue of grief hallucinations, of course one's views sometimes do change. But it is also the case that in live dialogues such as this one, commentators are often pressed into places where they would prefer not to go in more normal circumstances or that can more easily be misunderstood. Thus, the idea of Crossan taking different or perhaps conflicting views is not being pressed here.

appearances or a general afterlife. Yet neither does Crossan think that these experiences were hallucinations.[31]

Stephen H. Smith also seems to support the idea of nonveridical grief events as the original experiences of Jesus's disciples, though some key distinctions seem to be lacking.[32] Other scholars mention grief visions or hallucinations without necessarily specifying whether or not they consider the possibility that they were actual occurrences.[33]

We will examine psychologist Ken Vincent's defense of a particular afterlife thesis in our discussion of objective vision theories. Vincent holds that Jesus is divine and remains alive today, having concluded that Jesus actually rose from the dead though in nonbodily fashion. Paul is the only eyewitness to a resurrection appearance whose testimony we have, though Paul also reports "verified second-hand reports of the resurrection" from his interviews with the other apostolic witnesses Peter and James the brother of Jesus.[34]

For Vincent, Paul's view should be favored—Jesus was resurrected and appeared in a spiritual body rather than a more substantial one, and this appearance to Paul

---

[31] Crossan, "Dialogue," 33, also 38.

[32] Stephen H. Smith, "'Seeing Things': 'Best Explanations' and the Resurrection of Jesus," *Heythrop Journal* 61 (2020): 689–700. For his other articles see: "Assessing the Mode of Jesus's Post-Resurrection Appearances: Does Parapsychology Help?," *Religion and Theology* 26 (2019): 255–81; "He Appeared to Peter: Reconsidering the Hallucination Hypothesis," *Neotestamentica* 53 (2019): 53–78; "The Post-Resurrection Appearances of Jesus as Bereavement Experiences: An Engagement with Gerald O'Collins," *Irish Theological Quarterly* 85 (2020): 109–26; "Christic Visions and the Resurrection Appearances of Jesus: Comparisons, Contrasts and Conclusions," *Religion and Theology* 28 (2021): 41–63.

[33] Gerald O'Collins unpacks and then critiques John Hick's view of bereavement visions as a potential explanation for Jesus's resurrection in his essay "The Resurrection: The State of the Questions," 10–13; and Peter F. Carnley retorts that perhaps O'Collins does not take Hick's suggestions seriously enough in his "Response" essay to O'Collins (32, 37, 39–40), with both essays being included in *The Resurrection: An Interdisciplinary Symposium on the Resurrection of Jesus*, ed. Stephen T. Davis, Daniel Kendall, and Gerald O'Collins (Oxford: Oxford University Press, 1997). Hick elsewhere takes a more naturalistic view of the resurrection appearances in terms of hallucinations; hence, his view is being considered in this category; see his *Center of Christianity*, particularly 24–26.

[34] Ken R. Vincent, "Resurrection Appearances of Jesus as After-Death Communication," *Journal of Near-Death Studies* 30 (2012): 137–39, 142, 147.

should be considered an instance of "After Death Communication" (ADC), which is a form of postmortem communication common throughout world religions. Moreover, for Vincent "the most impressive aftereffect" of any mystical or religious encounter concerns "how they have changed people's lives for the better."[35]

Another approach that was treated in an earlier chapter and dubbed the illumination theory should also be mentioned briefly. Several contemporary scholars prefer this strategy that, while it has a few similarities to the hallucination thesis, is not closely related. In general, the idea is that Peter was the first to have some sort of subjective experience or conviction that Jesus was alive. It may even have been a private hallucination or no more than a personal insight. This conviction was later communicated to Jesus's other followers, who concluded that Jesus was risen, perhaps even being willing to adopt Peter's experience and language as their own. Conveniently, these researchers hold that we cannot now speak about the historical nature of this incident, as it has been lost in the retelling. It is the *faith* of the early believers that is really of chief importance here, not the nature of the experiences.[36] It is often remarked that these experiences were not hallucinations, but many of our critiques below will still apply to this thesis that has already been critiqued in depth in the earlier treatment.[37]

---

[35] Vincent, 145–47. Other prominent researchers besides Vincent have also held that there are some strong similarities between Jesus's resurrection appearances and postmortem experiences, such as at least some examples of both having actually occurred, but without necessarily being the same type of phenomena. Two distinguished examples are current Princeton Seminary New Testament theologian Dale Allison in his volume *Resurrecting Jesus* (particularly 278–83) as well as former Cambridge University professor Michael C. Perry, *The Easter Enigma: An Essay on the Resurrection with Special Reference to the Data of Psychical Research* (London: Faber & Faber, 1959), 31, 125, 157, 171, 175–89, 190–91, 218–28.

[36] Similar views were held by Willi Marxsen, *Jesus and Easter: Did God Raise the Historical Jesus from the Dead?* (Nashville: Abingdon, 1990), 65–74; Marxsen, *The Resurrection of Jesus of Nazareth*, trans. Margaret Kohl (Philadelphia: Fortress, 1968), esp. chaps. 3–5; Don Cupitt, *Christ and the Hiddenness of God* (Philadelphia: Westminster, 1971), 143, 165–67; Thomas Sheehan, *The First Coming: How the Kingdom of God Became Christianity* (New York: Random House, 1986), 95–118; John Shelby Spong, *Resurrection: Myth or Reality?* (New York: HarperCollins, 1994), 255–260; Spong, *The Easter Moment* (New York: Harper & Row, 1987), esp. 39–68.

[37] Spong, *Easter Moment*, 196; Sheehan, *First Coming*, 262–63n38; cf. Marxsen, *Jesus and Easter*, 71–74.

A Critique of Hallucination and Similar Hypotheses

Before beginning this assessment, it must be remarked (if it were not already obvious) that there is an incredible amount of confusion on this topic, as stated in the critical remarks above. Much of this muddle is due to how the various aspects of these positions have been expressed by commentators, including inaccuracies, blurred lines, and mistaken concepts regarding various theses. Sometimes, the way a critical scholar's views are stated appears contradictory. On more than one occasion similarities between illusions, delusions, and hallucinations are made apparent, but at other times not so much. There is much confusion regarding whether these claimed similarities with hallucinations really have much overlap. One huge problem has been that theological scholars explaining the details of their ideas often do so in ways that do not accord with psychological or psychiatric parameters. For example, conversion disorder has nothing to do with religious conversions and how they occur. Unfortunately, however, many scholars expressing their views have controlled how they thought the concepts worked without recourse to psychological or psychiatric research. We must thus address this confusion here; otherwise the angle of the critique might be missed, and engaging this critique of the resurrection might be a lost cause.

In this critique, many critical conceptions will have to be changed in order to be understood. Others may have to be ignored. But the central point concerns whether or not the critique hits its mark. If not, it will hopefully be obvious afterward why this was the case. It will probably be most helpful to differentiate between three sorts of psychological phenomena. These distinctions must be kept clearly in view, or it may be very difficult to make exact judgments.

Key Definitions

Hallucinations

Hallucinations are false perceptions of sights, sounds, touches, and smells for which there are *no external referents*—perhaps like observing something where there is essentially only "thin air." One of the major works on the subject by André Aleman and Frank Larøi follows the definition by Anthony S. David, defining hallucination as "a sensory experience which occurs in the absence of corresponding external stimulation of the relevant sensory organ."[38] Al-Issa defines it as "sensory experience such as seeing persons or objects, hearing voices, and smelling odors in the absence of environmental stimuli."[39] If otherwise healthy, the hallucinating person often gives up the story when they more clearly perceive the lack of reality or evidence. An actual case here was a person who was taking prescription medicines who thought that there were rabbits inside their house, but these creatures were not present, and no one else observed them. But when the person was told the very first time that there were no rabbits there, they actually agreed and responded that they just must have been seeing things. It is often not so simple, but the point is that reality is the best antidote to misapprehension.

Illusions

Illusions are distorted perceptions of *something that really is there* but is misidentified. Aleman and Larøi define an illusion as "a misperception that is based on an existing stimulus."[40] Mark Cosgrove defines this illusory element as a "distorted perception that misrepresents external stimuli."[41] An example might be the presence of a winter coat perched on the back of a bedroom chair that is taken during the night to be an intruder in the room. While a coat and a chair are really present, these objects are obviously not a human person. Moreover, a big bear may actually be present nearby, but hopefully it will not be misrepresented through the trees as Bigfoot!

Delusions

Delusions can be a more serious matter because they may imply some species of sickness, including mental illness. These are untrue beliefs often held with great fervor in spite of factors that prove that the beliefs are definitely mistaken. A technical

---

[38] Aleman and Larøi, *Hallucinations*, 15; other relevant definitions and restatements are found on 3, 18, 20, 23, cf. 118.

[39] Ishan Al-Issa, "Hallucinations," in *Baker Encyclopedia of Psychology and Counseling*, ed. David G. Benner and Peter C. Hill, 2nd ed. (Grand Rapids: Baker, 1999).

[40] Aleman and Larøi, *Hallucinations*, 18.

[41] Mark Cosgrove, "Illusion," in Benner and Hill, *Baker Encyclopedia of Psychology and Counseling*.

definition is a "false belief based on incorrect inference about reality that is firmly
sustained despite what almost everyone else believes and incontrovertible evidence
to the contrary."[42] Such an instance might be an individual who has undergone every
possible medical test that turned out negatively, while the person remains adamant
that they have a serious cancer, where only they know the exact location. This situation
might be exacerbated if the individual insists that they absolutely know this to be the
case because a malicious voice keeps whispering inside their head that this is true.
This subcategory might be termed "somatic."[43]

Our topic in this chapter is chiefly hallucinations, though unfortunately the lines
on the above phenomena are often blurred by critics and others. For some instances,
some may use examples like group sightings of UFOs, several hunters seeing a
large furry bear and misnaming it Bigfoot, or any of several Medjugorje (Bosnia
and Herzegovina) Marian sightings where observers reported that they saw the sun
spinning in the sky as being examples of group hallucinations. Yet, none of these is
even a hallucination at all, let alone a group hallucination.[44] Each is quite clearly an
illusion, since what was actually seen in every instance were actual objects that were
really present, such as various objects in the sky, a big furry creature, or a real sun.

---

[42] C. D. Campbell, "Delusion," in Benner and Hill, *Baker Encyclopedia of Psychology and Counseling*; cf. Aleman and Larøi, *Hallucinations*, 55.

[43] Philip C. Kendall and Constance Hammen, *Abnormal Psychology* (Boston: Houghton Mifflin, 1995), 296, where several other examples are also given. For further prominent distinctions here, see Benjamin J. Sadock and Virginia A. Sadock, *Kaplan and Sadock's Synopsis of Psychiatry: Behavioral Sciences, Clinical Psychiatry* (Philadelphia: Lipincott, 2003).

[44] Michael Goulder mentions phenomena such as people observing statues of Mary that reportedly move, UFOs, and the resurrection appearances of Jesus all under the category of "Collective Delusions" in "Baseless Fabric," 53. According to our definitions above, Goulder's examples here are better termed "illusions" without implicating many of these participants as having mental illness. Here are some of the examples of confusion between these terms. But more seriously, though treating these phenomena as other than hallucinations, Goulder insists in this section on comparing these experiences to the 1 Cor 15:3–8 major creedal listing of appearances to the apostles, the 500 brethren, and Paul himself (52–53) while frequently employing terms such as "visionary experience" or "visions" (esp. 54). This clearly blurs the categories, no doubt causing readers to think that he is using these underlying concepts correctly to deal with hallucinations as well. These confusions are as misleading as they are unnecessary. This is also reminiscent of Parsons's comments above where he switches back and forth between delusions and hallucinations, especially when illusions seem to be in view; see Parsons, "Hallucination Theory," 436–37.

Distinctions such as these must be kept in mind constantly because they make huge differences in evaluation.[45]

Summarized briefly, hallucinations are false perceptions about what is not present at all in the real world, and which are often not maintained vociferously when the evidence is pointed out.[46] The mistake is often acknowledged fairly quickly. Illusions are distorted interpretations of something that is really present, but not in that manner. Delusions are false beliefs that are held virtually no matter what is shown to the person, who may even get highly agitated when others attempt to talk them out of their convictions.[47]

While hallucination theses can vary among critics, sometimes revealing several key differences, there tend to be more similarities among these positions.[48] We will

---

[45] It is difficult to know for sure but are these sorts of category mix-ups the reason why Parsons reported, "Mass hallucinations . . . are extremely well-documented phenomena" (436)? Parsons is a friend and I have no desire to belittle or embarrass him, but if some of this is the root of the problem here, there are problems indeed.

[46] As pointed out in Joseph W. Bergeron and Gary R. Habermas, "The Resurrection of Jesus: A Clinical Review of Psychiatric Hypotheses for the Biblical Story of Easter," *Irish Theological Quarterly* 80, no. 2 (2015): 161. There can be many psychophysiologic or other causes of hallucinations, such as "structural injury to the brain, such as tumors, midbrain strokes, or localized dysfunction of brain structures" including lesions, progressive neurologic disease processes like dementia, biochemical derangement, or delirium of many differing species. "Hallucinations in delirium are often unpleasant: for example, seeing snakes crawling in the bed. Hallucinogenic drugs, as signified by their drug category name, are also associated with hallucinations. Mental illnesses, such as psychotic conditions like schizophrenia, can be associated with visual hallucinations. At times, symptoms of psychosis may even include thoughts and hallucinations with religious content. While auditory hallucinations are more common, visual hallucinations can occur and have a greater association with more severely affected patients."

[47] See also the brief discussion in Habermas and Licona, *Case for the Resurrection*, 104–5.

[48] Some of the most helpful, authoritative, and recent studies on the subject of hallucinations are as follows: American Psychiatric Association, *Diagnostic and Statistical Manual of Mental Disorders*, 5th ed. (Washington, DC: American Psychiatric Publishing, 2022); Aleman and Larøi, *Hallucinations*; Frank Larøi, Tanya Marie Luhrmann, Vaughan Bell, William A. Christian Jr., Smita Deshpande, Charles Fernyhough, Janis Jenkins, and Angela Woods, "Culture and Hallucinations: Overview and Future Directions," *Schizophrenia Bulletin* 40, no. 4 (2014): S213–S220; Harold G. Koenig, "Religion, Spirituality and Psychotic Disorders," *Revista de Psiquiatria Clínica* 34 (2007): 40–48; R. P. Bentall, "The Illusion of Reality: A Review and Integration of Psychological Research on Hallucinations," *Psychological Bulletin* 107 (1990): 82–95; Frank J. Prerost, Donald Sefcik, and Brian D. Smith, "Differential Diagnosis of Patients Presenting with Hallucinations," *Osteopathic Family Physician* 6 (2014): 19–24; B. S. Kasper, E. M. Kasper, E. Pauli, and H. Stefan,

begin by evaluating a crucially important side issue: the possibility of group hallucinations, followed by a few other specific idiosyncrasies of this view.[49] Then the central
hypothesis will be weighed as a whole.

Collective Hallucinations

One of the central issues in this entire discussion of Jesus's resurrection appearances
concerns whether a group of people can witness the same hallucination together.
Virtually all psychologists and psychiatrists question or dispute the reality of such
occurrences, as pointed out below. A very rare attempt suggesting that collective hallucinations are at least potentially possible, without any application whatsoever to Jesus's
resurrection, is made by Leonard Zusne and Warren Jones. They point to phenomena
such as claimed sightings of the Virgin Mary and other accompanying reports from
groups of people. In cases like these, "expectation" and "emotional excitement" are
"a prerequisite for collective hallucinations." In such groups we see the "emotional
contagion that so often takes place in crowds moved by strong emotions."[50]

But favoring the possibility of collective hallucinations is highly problematic on
any scenario and on several grounds. (1) To begin, the chief examples of "collective

---

"Phenomenology of Hallucinations, Illusions, and Delusions as Part of Seizure Semiology,"
Epilepsy and Behavior 18 (2010): 13–23; W. Leslie Mackenzie, review of *Review of
Hallucinations and Illusions: A Study of the Fallacies of Perception*, by Edmund Parish, *Mind* 7
(1898): 541–47; M. Manford and F. Andermann, "Complex Visual Hallucinations: Clinical
and Neurobiological Insights," *Brain* 121 (1998): 1819–40; Ryan C. Teeple, Jason P. Caplan,
and Theodore A. Stern, "Visual Hallucinations: Differential Diagnosis and Treatment,"
Primary Care Companion to the Journal of Clinical Psychiatry 11 (2009): 26–32; Diogo
Telles-Correia, Ana Lúcia Moreira, and João S. Gonçalves, "Hallucinations and Related
Concepts—Their Conceptual Background," *Frontiers in Psychology* 6 (2015): 1–9; A. Y.
Tien, "Distribution of Hallucinations in the Population," *Social Psychiatry and Psychiatric
Epidemiology* 26 (1991): 287–92; T. X. Barber and D. S. Calverley, "An Experimental
Study of 'Hypnotic' (Auditory and Visual) Hallucinations," *Journal of Abnormal and Social
Psychology* 63 (1964): 13–20; Gilles Fénelon, Soulas Thierry, Franck Zenasni, and Laurent
Cleret de Langavant, "The Changing Face of Parkinson's Disease-Associated Psychosis: A
Cross-Sectional Study Based on the New NINDS-NIMH Criteria," *Movement Disorders*
25 (2010): 763–66.

[49] Again, the conversion disorder thesis as proposed by Kent and Goulder, among
others, will be critiqued in part in this chapter, plus in further details elsewhere.

[50] Leonard Zusne and Warren H. Jones, *Anomalistic Psychology: A Study of Extraordinary
Phenomena of Behavior and Experience* (Hillsdale, MI: Erlbaum, 1982), 135–36.

hallucinations" provided by Zusne and Jones (plus many critics) were group religious experiences such as Marian apparitions. However, since these occasions are purportedly theological, *by their very nature* they simply beg the question regarding whether such experiences could ever actually have occurred *under natural conditions* in the real world. If these events happened as described, and if they were even possibly miraculous in some sense, then almost assuredly they could not have been hallucinations as normally understood. In other words, what Zusne and Jones *assume* to be normal, naturalistic, subjective explanations in the first place could be miraculous![51] By so doing, *they ruled out even the possibility of real religious occurrences in an a priori manner*, before alternative possibilities were considered. Perhaps these events did occur naturalistically, but that does not follow without *evidence. Assuming* them to be natural occurrences as a starting point without showing that to be the case is unwarranted.[52]

(2) A further clarification and critique needs to be made regarding the Marian apparitions in general and the comparison to illusions in particular. There is sometimes much confusion regarding the large crowds of spectators that come to Medjugorje, Bosnia-Herzegovina. For example, it is fairly common to hear comments that many people in the large groups actually "saw" Mary.[53] But such claims on these occasions are made incorrectly. The people in attendance have often claimed to see signs in the heavens, such as the sun "dancing" in the sky. But there is a real sun located up in the sky and members of the crowd could view that object, so these are clearly illusions, not hallucinations. Moreover, a dancing sun is also a misperception because, for example, normal pedestrians in the town or elsewhere without interest in the situation apparently do not observe the sun behaving in such

---

[51] For a number of critical observations and responses to such phenomena, see Elliot Miller and Kenneth R. Samples, *The Cult of the Virgin Mary: Catholic Mariology and the Apparitions of Mary* (Grand Rapids: Baker, 1992), especially chapters 11–14 and appendix A.

[52] This entire species of maneuver has been regular naturalistic fare since before Hume and is virtually always taken for granted without argument. See the two detailed critique chapters on Hume and more recent kindred moves above, as well as a critique of another such effort: Gary R. Habermas, "A Recent Attempt to Disprove the Resurrection of Jesus and Supernatural Beliefs," *Journal of Theological Studies* 69 (2018): 191–97.

[53] Recall Ehrman's comment that Mary was seen by "hundreds or thousands of people at once" in Ehrman, *How Jesus Became God*, 202. But which cases are being described here—where did these occur? And what is the empirical data for or against these sightings? We are not told in this context.

a manner![54] It is often remarked that such observations are due to the unhealthy practice of staring at a bright sun without appropriate eye protection, but that is not necessary, as Parsons remarks. Moreover, members of the crowd may watch the children who attest that Mary appeared to them but without viewing Mary for themselves, as mentioned below.

On other occasions elsewhere in the world, what is taken for an image of Mary has literally turned out to be a shadow on glass windows that does not look like a human being at all, let alone someone identifiable. Other instances could be "faces" in cloud photographs or even faces on oil leakages on cement (!) that remind a few folks of a person but are thought by virtually everyone who sees them to be unequivocally nothing of the sort.[55] But whatever is thought about such examples, these are clearly instances of illusions. We know this because real objects were involved; actual, physical views of the sun, window glass, clouds, or even oil drippings on cement were incorrectly identified as something else. These are very far from mass hallucinations and are not technically in the same category, as pointed out above with the initial definitions.[56]

---

[54] Parsons mentions rather incredibly that a personal friend "set up a telescope with a solar filter" in the vicinity in order to show "to anyone that cared to look—that the sun was not spinning or dancing." But "hundreds" in the vicinity still kept up their claims anyway. See Parsons, "Hallucination Theory," esp. 435–49, quotation on 436–37.

[55] Over the years, literally dozens of photographed examples like these situations have been sent to me. One location was reportedly visited by droves of observers. These pictures were then shown to many others who often remark that the photograph did not even appear to be a person at all! Thus, seldom was it agreed that they might be viewing Mary the mother of Jesus. The original photographers then actually agreed with these negative assessments. Of course, it might be true that some people could simply have agreed for other reasons, such as not to doubted or even teased. But those present did not tease them, and the matter was simply dropped and not brought up again as far as is known.

[56] To summarize very briefly and generally some potential responses to the Marian phenomena in Medjugorje: (1) A barely concealed a priori rejection of supernatural possibilities is easily noticed. Why assume from the outset that it is all a natural mistake of some sort and without *evidence* to the contrary? (2) The heavenly sightings reported by the majority of observers are illusions, not hallucinations. There is a real sun in the sky that has been observed by eyewitnesses, but it has been shown *not* to be spinning and dancing during that time! (3) The adults basically watched the children rather than seeing Mary for themselves. (4) Reports mention the children even years later with different levels of mistaken or contradictory comments that have been checked out. (5) Reportedly, not even all of the children saw Mary every time, and the descriptions of her clothing and so on differ between them. (6) Questions have been raised about there being errors of one sort or another in what the children report Mary teaching. (7) Many have pointed out that these stories are

As commented by Frank Larøi, the coauthor of one of the most highly accredited research volume on hallucinations, "in general, 'true' collective (mis)perceptions are more commonly illusions."[57] In this sense, these occasions could be collective without being hallucinations.

(3) It may be asked what difference it would make if particular data indicate *group illusions* rather than group hallucinations? The distinction is this: illusions are disproven by falsifying the reports.[58] Thus, it is known that the sun is not spinning and dancing in the sky because both uninvolved people and telescopes prove this to be the case. Likewise, hunters know the grizzly bear is not Sasquatch as they get closer to it or examine the photographs.

(4) Further, claims regarding the collective hallucination thesis are somewhat or even largely unfalsifiable, at least in the specific sense of solving the overall issue, chiefly because even if the occasions turn out actually to be some other sort of illusory phenomena, hallucinations may still be maintained even after the criteria are properly identified, as with the telescope example above.[59] On the one hand, an identification of a group hallucination could be applied to real, objective events with religious overtones, as we just saw with a real sun or children. On the other hand, purely natural group events also could simply be called group hallucinations too—like many persons reporting UFOs or other odd sightings. In both sets of circumstances, such identifications also could be very much mistaken. This sort of misapplication could potentially happen in both directions. Thus, either religious or secular sightings could be misidentified as group hallucinations, as Larøi mentions above, making this thesis quite haphazardly applied almost whenever and wherever. But crucial epistemic criteria seem to be missing in both.

---

all within the broader Christian camp, whatever one might think of Roman Catholicism or Orthodoxy; cf. Allison, *Resurrection of Jesus*, 299–300. Sample questions such as these do not disprove the reports one way or the other, but conflicting data need to be researched.

[57] This comes from Larøi's personal correspondence with Habermas (July 29, 2019) and is used by permission. In Larøi's and Aleman's volume *Hallucinations*, other relevant and potentially helpful information can be found on 3, 14–15, 18, 20, 23, 31, 46–47, 55, 77, 83–84, 102, 118, 120. See 118 for their comment on hallucinations as private events.

[58] Incidentally, this can be done, often quite simply, in hallucination cases as well, if there is someone present who recognizes the details of the situation and points out what is actually happening. I have been present and done this myself on more than one occasion.

[59] Presumably in such circumstances, believers may still maintain that these events are miracles, while more skeptical persons could still resort to mass hallucinations, claiming that the believers are still imagining what they report. Strangely enough in these cases, both groups would be categorizing true illusions in their own ways.

(5) Even if it could be established that people in groups witnessed hallucinations, it is absolutely critical to note that it does not at all follow that these experiences were therefore collective, as in every person witnessing the exact same things. If, as most psychologists and psychiatrists assert, at least the vast majority of hallucinations are private, individual events, then how could groups share exactly the same subjective visual perception? Rather, it is much more likely that the phenomena in question are either illusions—perceptual misinterpretations of actual realities such as the spinning sun example above—or a collection of *individual* hallucinations. Many specialists have agreed on this as well.[60]

(6) Moreover, perhaps the largest number of serious problems for utilizing the group hallucination explanation to account for Jesus's group appearances results from comparing the requirements for these occurrences to the critically recognized portions of the New Testament accounts of Jesus's postmortem sightings.[61] It may be precisely at this interval that the explanatory power of this natural hypothesis is most severely challenged, since much of the accredited New Testament data not only differs from the psychological requirements but actually contradicts the necessary conditions for "collective hallucinations." In other words, the necessary conditions are precisely what are *not* reported.

For instance, Zusne and Jones argue that "expectation" and "emotional excitement" are "prerequisites" before these group experiences will even occur. In fact, expectation "plays the coordinating role."[62] As observed above, even Lüdemann remarkably agrees with this sentiment, employing quite similar terms to describe Jesus's appear-

---

[60] Zusne and Jones repeatedly refer to collective hallucinations. Yet surprisingly, they conclude their treatment, conversely, by admitting that these persons may still be seeing actual phenomena. So the "final answer to these questions has not been obtained yet" (*Anomalistic Psychology*, 135–36)!

[61] As has been pointed out at key intervals, the distinction must always be kept in mind that critical scholars often concede certain beliefs *on behalf of New Testament authors*, even if these contemporary researchers personally do not accept these positions.

[62] Zusne and Jones, *Anomalistic Psychology*, 135. Jake O'Connell develops a thesis similar to Zusne and Jones in a few major ways, especially in terms of the required emotional and excited reactions of the recipients. But O'Connell at least asks if these concepts are similar to Jesus's resurrection appearances, and he decides negatively—they do not explain these appearances. Very oddly, in spite of this positive application, O'Connell defines group hallucinations as two or more individuals together who are experiencing private hallucinations! See Jake O'Connell, "Jesus' Resurrection and Collective Hallucinations," *Tyndale Bulletin* 60 (2009): 69–105. For a critique of this notion, see Licona, *Resurrection of Jesus*, 485n64.

ances, brought about "unexpectedly" and described as "enthusiastic experience," "mass ecstasy," and "enthusiasm." These emotions lead to "an incomparable chain reaction" that spawned what is described as "religious intoxication" and was "infectious," and these emotional scenes were "passed on to others."[63]

But how many scholars would agree that these highly emotionally charged terms and descriptions truly applied to Jesus's post-crucifixion disciples, thereby accounting for their experiences? Rather, this scenario contradicts the emotional state of the early witnesses of Jesus's resurrection appearances, as recognized regularly even by critical scholars.[64] Psychologically, the early believers were confronted face-to-face with the utter reality of the very recent and unexpected death of their best friend, who they had hoped would both rescue Israel as well as reward them. They had sacrificed much in the process as well. Then the horrific events unfolded in a whirlwind: the disciples' own bewilderment at the fast-moving chaos; Jesus's physical beatings, crucifixion, and seeming abandonment by his Father, along with their guilt in the situations. The normal human response would have been severe fear and anxiety, disillusionment, and depression, and that is precisely what we observe in the accounts, whether it be Peter's denials (Mark 14:66–72), the absence of the disciples at the cross, or the disciples hiding in fear (John 20:19).

To suppose that these believers would exhibit "expectation," "emotional excitement," "enthusiasm," and' "intoxication" is simply far over the top of a normal psychological response especially in the face of these stark circumstances beginning just a day or so later. This would require of them responses that would scarcely be exhibited even at a normal funeral, let alone a death of this magnitude! That Zusne and Jones postulate that expectation "plays the coordinating role" in all this is most likely the least applicable to Jesus's disciples, in that it would need to be present in order to get the entire process moving. Yet it was the characteristic that was probably lacking most in them. All indications are that Jesus's disciples exhibited the very *opposite* emotions from these that Zusne and Jones assert are the *necessary prerequisites* for their thesis (though they were not at all considering Jesus's situation).

Because of this powerful objection, Lüdemann and many other critical scholars going back to David Strauss in the mid-nineteenth century and before have suggested separating the disciples' experiences from the crucifixion by several days, months,

---

[63] Lüdemann, *Resurrection of Jesus*, 106–7, 174–75, at least for Peter.

[64] As discussed at length in volume 1 under the category of the disciples' despair, depression, and severe disappointment after Jesus's crucifixion.

or perhaps even years. But what data support such moves? Even just a few days later would be too soon for such monumental emotional changes in Jesus's followers. There are several other issues with such scenarios as well.

By comparison, the disciples' experiences were totally unlike those in the Marian cases above where pilgrims frequently traveled long distances, hoping dearly and even expecting to witness wonderful events, gathering exuberantly with anticipation. These would seem to be very meager grounds of comparison with any of the emotions belonging to Jesus's disciples after his death.[65]

(7) Separate studies of both the relevant psychological and medical literature going back even decades have revealed no clear data indicating that group hallucinations have ever actually occurred or at least been observed. Individual hallucinations of course happen, as do illusions and delusions—the latter even in more than one person. But Aleman and Larøi note "the general supposition" made by a number of theorists that "hallucinations are private events."[66] Group hallucinations have not been observed or confirmed in the relevant literature. This by itself does not make them impossible events, but given the huge collections of

---

[65] The rejoinder might be suggested that perhaps a few individual disciples hallucinated individually, thereby inducing excitement in the others, preparing them for even more hallucinations. In the first place, the initial hallucinations would more likely have been negative in character given the recent past events. From our critique, it is *far more likely* from the statistics alone that these secondary hallucinations would be individual in nature rather than collective. An additional multifaceted response could be fashioned. To begin, human nature being what it is given a variety of different personalities, a few disciples experiencing hallucinations would hardly get everyone in the entire group excited, given that it would have to overpower the reality of the horrible things that they had seen and heard firsthand, especially including changing all the other friends who had gathered around them at this time as well. In fact, such hallucinations, even if positive, may not even have significantly changed the forlornness of the very ones who experienced them. And again, a few may have required some empirical means such as touching (as suggested in John 20:24–29). Last, critiques 4–5 especially in the next section regarding the two cases of Paul and James still would be highly problematic for this view because of the former skepticism and later conversions of these two apostles, as would (to varying extents) the remainder of the critiques in the "Additional Problems" section below. This last group of problems alone would be quite troublesome for this rejoinder. On the existential depth of Friday and Saturday's effects on the disciples' suffering, see the personal, moving, and highly acclaimed account by Alan E. Lewis, *Between Cross and Resurrection: A Theology of Holy Saturday* (Grand Rapids: Eerdmans, 2001).

[66] Aleman and Larøi, *Hallucinations*, 118.

relevant scientific literature in these areas, this is almost an overwhelming critique by itself.[67]

(8) Possibly the two best critiques of group hallucinations are the previous point that such occurrences have highly questionable empirical status either medically or psychologically along with this present assessment. The absence or rarity of these group events is noticeably an exceptionally difficult issue for critics, judging from the ways they attempt to respond and often even back off the issue when challenged. However, easily the majority of all the claimed New Testament appearances of Jesus were to groups. Of these, the best attested were the ones arguably to the twelve disciples, "all the apostles" (1 Cor 15:7), the 500 individuals at once, the group of women, the appearance on the Galilean mountain, and Paul's sighting along with his companions. Amazingly, even Crossan and the Jesus Seminar note two instances where separate lists of multiple, independent sources record these occurrences, as noted just below.

So here is the additional knockout criticism: *Even if there had been* some exceptionally rare realities like mass hallucinations in the world, several group events of that nature were proclaimed in the earliest and strongest Christian sources. Therefore, the chief issue according to the data is that to deal a blow to these appearances, it would *not* be enough to mount arguments against a single group sighting of the risen Jesus. Even though group hallucinations have arguably never happened in the past, these group events *reportedly reoccurred* frequently after Jesus's death.[68]

Under such circumstances, what could the critic report? They could hardly report this: "The only time that *multiple* mass hallucinations have likely ever happened in history in the presence of just one individual over a brief time span, they were witnessed by the followers of Jesus, perhaps the most unique person who ever lived, including critically accepted healings, likely predictions of the events, and probably the most acclaimed ethical teachings ever. And in his case, the events happened repeatedly!" In

---

[67] Bergeron and Habermas, "Resurrection of Jesus," 157–72. See 161 for the details of two such research reports, one medical and the other psychological in nature. Licona cites a personal contact (an email dated 2009) from Aleman and Larøi that makes a helpful and relevant conversational comment to him, though of course without the experimental force of the comments above (*Resurrection of Jesus*, 484–85n64).

[68] Even John Dominic Crossan, *The Historical Jesus: The Life of a Mediterranean Jewish Peasant* (New York: HarperCollins, 1991), 435–36; and Robert W. Funk and the Jesus Seminar, *The Acts of Jesus: The Search for the Authentic Deeds of Jesus* (New York: HarperCollins, 1998), 454, 533, both list several independent sources that record group appearances of the risen Jesus.

other words, if the true nature of the naturalistic claim here regarding these proposed group hallucinations were emphasized, this situation might more accurately be named something like this: "This hypothesis might be termed the natural group hallucination, natural group hallucination, natural group hallucination, and so on view."[69] The chief point here is that if group hallucinations are at least very rare events, then several examples in the life of Jesus alone might appear to be miraculous in themselves!

Many other crucial problems also plague the application of hallucinations to Jesus's resurrection appearances, including a few more considerations with a bearing on group hallucinations. Several more of these issues are pursued directly below. Zusne and Jones never apply their approach to Jesus's resurrection. Moreover, they even rather astonishingly end their examination of this subject with the admission that group hallucinations have a "dubious status" because it is not possible to ascertain whether these individuals were actually even hallucinating in the first place![70] This is truly an amazing concession for a treatment that largely places the proverbial icing on the hallucination cake, almost causing one to wonder why they conducted this discussion in the first place!

Having critiqued group hallucinations in some detail, we will now move on to additional critiques of hallucinations in general.[71] Then we will turn to a couple of specific conditions that are often linked with hallucinations but are not directly related.

---

[69] These words are reworked and adapted from Gary R. Habermas, *Philosophy of History, Miracles, and the Resurrection of Jesus*, 3rd ed. (Sagamore Beach, MA: Academx, 2012), 21.

[70] Zusne and Jones, *Anomalistic Psychology*, 136, cf. 134–35. For more regular assessments against group hallucinations, see Aleman and Larøi, *Hallucinations*, 118; Phillip H. Wiebe, *Visions of Jesus: Direct Encounters from the New Testament to Today* (Oxford: Oxford University Press, 1997), 210; J. P. Brady, "The Veridicality of Hypnotic, Visual Hallucinations," in *Origins and Mechanisms of Hallucinations*, ed. Wolfram Keup (New York: Plenum, 1970), 181; Weston La Barre, "Anthropological Perspectives on Hallucinations and Hallucinogens," in *Hallucinations: Behavior, Experience and Theory*, ed. R. K. Siegel and L. J. West (New York: Wiley & Sons, 1975), 9–10.

[71] In his recent volume *The Resurrection of Jesus*, Dale Allison provides many examples of what might qualify as group hallucinations. He raises some worthwhile questions about cases of visions, appearances, and similar issues, asking how we can ascertain the differences between group and individual occasions (63, 230–35, 244, 340)? For example, in general cases some persons who were present clearly did not perceive what others saw, perhaps being talked into the experience later (76, 235, 340n27). Allison recognizes the existence of collective *illusions* (233, 340n27) and mass *hysteria* (14, 340) and seems to think that there is decent evidence for group hallucinations. However, he far too indiscriminately mixes Marian apparitions (14, 74n200, 76, 294–300), near-death experiences (86n280,

Additional Problems for Hallucinations

Many other issues remain regarding the various types of hallucination hypotheses. (1) Even multiple individual hallucinations are questionable because they are generally far more rare than is commonly thought to be the case.[72] Unless they are somehow induced, including by abnormal methods, they do not just occur anytime at all without cause, not to mention that some personalities are much less prone to experiencing them.[73] So the sheer rarity of "hallucinations" among those individuals involved in each of the New Testament reports might be expected to yield a far smaller number of individual hallucinations than is often assumed or stated to be the case, where it is sometimes acted as if anyone can have one on the spot.

(2) Further, hallucinations of the extended sort as required by the New Testament and other reports (i.e., ones that involved multiple senses such as sight, hearing, and touch) are even rarer phenomena.[74] Of course, as with other aspects being raised in this section, certain aspects in these accounts could be denied by critics if there are good reasons for doing so, but the overall point is that these considerations make the appearance narratives more difficult to explain. That these multisensory cases

---

252), ghosts (356), and spectral armies in the clouds (340) without the sort of adequate differentiation that could make a significant difference in such discussions.

So, are group hallucinations and the like Allison's natural thesis to explain Jesus's resurrection and appearances? Certainly not (99, 101–2, 107, 222), for after all of this is said and done, Allison still clearly believes in Jesus's resurrection appearances (3, 61–62, 146, 209–10), especially the appearance to the twelve disciples (61, 66), and he further acknowledges that no other religious case is as strong in terms of the data (esp. 346, also 344, 356). In fact, Allison opens this volume with this statement: "I believe that the disciples saw Jesus and that he saw them, and next Easter will find me in church" (3). Another affirmation from his earlier volume on this topic states similarly: "I think that the tomb was probably empty, although I am sure that the disciples saw Jesus after his death" (*Resurrecting Jesus*, 346). See also Licona's exceptionally careful study of Allison's work plus his interview with him on Jesus's resurrection, concluding that Allison thinks that Jesus rose from the dead and appeared to his followers in Licona, *Resurrection of Jesus*, 623–41. So whatever Allison thinks about the possibility of group hallucinations, he does not consider it to be incompatible with the arguments for Jesus's appearances and still favors the overall strength of the resurrection argument.

[72] A. Y. Tien places the "underlying vulnerability to hallucinations in the population" at only a 1 to 3 percent general incidence depending on multiple factors such as gender and especially age; see "Distributions of Hallucinations," 292.

[73] Aleman and Larøi, *Hallucinations*, 84.

[74] Aleman and Larøi, 46.

were reported on several occasions as occurring regularly during Jesus's appearances militates further against Jesus's disciples being the recipients.[75]

(3) According to the early texts, the wide variety of times and places when Jesus appeared, along with the differing mindsets and underlying personalities of the witnesses, are all simply huge obstacles. This retort is thought by some to be the best response to hallucinations. Men and women, hard-headed and soft-hearted alike, of different ages, all believing that they truly had seen Jesus, as far as is known from the data, both indoors and outdoors, in light and in darkness, by itself provides a virtually insurmountable barrier.[76] These various details significantly complicate the cases of private hallucinations, let alone the much tougher cases of group appearances. Further, it must be kept in mind here that group appearances are much more commonly reported in the accredited historical literature.[77] Thus, the odds that every person, each with his or her quite different characteristics and idiosyncrasies, would be in precisely the proper frame of mind to experience a hallucination, even individually, decreases exponentially.[78] Many commentators take these aspects for granted, as if hallucinations can just "pop up" virtually anywhere, in almost any circumstance, with almost anyone.

(4) Generally, hallucinations do not transform lives, even less so over a period of many years. Studies have argued that even with persons who hallucinate, it is quite frequently (or even usually) the case that they abandon or disavow such experiences once they realize that they "saw" things that did not happen or when others present

---

[75] For many details, see Wiebe, *Visions of Jesus*, 199–200, 207–11. To repeat an earlier point, many of the objections throughout this section also apply to what we have termed the illumination theory, treated earlier.

[76] Aleman and Larøi do not address the question of Jesus's resurrection but do mention this aspect of variance of factors; see *Hallucinations*, 84.

[77] To repeat, in spite of rejecting Jesus's resurrection appearances, Crossan (*Historical Jesus*, 435–36) and Funk and the Jesus Seminar (*Acts of Jesus* 454, 533) both list several independent sources that record group appearances of the risen Jesus. And Crossan rejects hallucinations and other natural theses regarding these occurrences as well. See Crossan, "Dialogue," in Crossan and Wright, *Resurrection of Jesus*, 33–34, 38, and the appendix, "Bodily-Resurrection Faith" (177); Crossan, "Resurrection of Jesus," esp. 47.

[78] See the list of hallucination characteristics above, including S. J. Segal, "Imagery and Reality: Can They Be Distinguished?," in Keup, *Origins and Mechanisms of Hallucinations*, 103–13. Zusne and Jones remark that even if hallucinations in groups have occurred somewhere, not everyone would have experienced these subjective experiences (*Anomalistic Psychology*, 135). This comment is somewhat similar to the interviews by Miller and Samples in *Cult of the Virgin Mary*, 157, 178.

around them state that they did not see the same thing.[79] Jewish New Testament scholar Pinchas Lapide, though a non-Christian, still asserts, "In none of the cases where rabbinic literature speaks of such visions did it result in an essential change in the life of the resuscitated or of those who had experienced the visions." Lapide adds, "Only the vision remains . . . but it did not have any noticeable consequences." Not so with Jesus's disciples—they were thoroughly changed.[80]

Critics acknowledge freely that Jesus's disciples were transformed even to the point of being quite willing to die for their faith.[81] Additionally, no early texts report that any of them ever recanted.[82] As far as we know, the disciples were faithful to the end of their lives, however each one ended. To suppose that this quality of conviction came about through false sensory perceptions without anyone rejecting it later seems highly problematic, as Lapide's insights detail.

(5) Of course, if the appearances were hallucinations, then Jesus's body should have been located safely and securely in its grave just outside the city of Jerusalem. But the hallucination theory is what we might label a "full tomb view" rather than an empty tomb position. Producing Jesus's dead body from wherever it was buried would undoubtedly be a rather large disclaimer to the disciples' efforts to preach that Jesus was raised. But hallucinations fail to even address this situation, so it is necessary that another naturalistic thesis be developed to explain the empty sepulcher. However, it is not in the critics' best interests to have to come up with yet another unlikely thesis and then try to turn it into a likely one. It is no wonder that there are several scholars in recent years who seem to talk themselves out of the empty tomb belief, or who try to list comebacks that cancel the more than twenty major and minor arguments to which critics have agreed.

Still other issues impede the hallucination hypothesis. While these following reasons are perhaps not as weighty in this context, they must still be addressed. (6) Unquestionably, the experiences that were believed strongly to be resurrection appearances were reported by Jesus's disciples at an exceptionally early date. Even critical researchers usually agree in placing them from just days after the crucifixion

---

[79] Segal, "Imagery and Reality," 103. I was also benefited greatly by an unpublished MA study of hallucinations by former Navy SEAL Shea Lambert, titled "Hallucinations and the Post Death Appearances of Jesus," September 20, 2000. Unfortunately, to date, this study does not appear online.

[80] Lapide, *Resurrection of Jesus*, 125.

[81] See volume 1 of this study with a chapter plus other comments on this subject.

[82] McDowell, *Fate of the Apostles*, 259, 261–65, cf. 243.

to at most five or six years afterward.[83] Individual hallucinations could occur immediately, though they would have to overcome all the potential objections here. But this critique does answer the critical charge that the proclamation of the gospel message came too long afterward. This is especially the case when the time frame is compared to the religious documentation in other faiths. Perhaps the analogy helps here that, as in a chess match, moves are sometimes made to forestall another later move!

(7) Jesus's resurrection was the disciples' central teaching, and people usually take extra care with matters that are the closest to their hearts and that mean the most to them. This is what drove Paul to travel more than 100 miles to Jerusalem in order to investigate (*historēsai*) the nature of the gospel data with other key disciples on at least two occasions to make sure he was preaching the truth on this subject (Gal 1:18–19; 2:1–10). He found that the other apostles were also teaching the same message that he was about Jesus's appearances to them (1 Cor 15:11). Are we to assume that, given all of Paul's vigilant care, no one discovered that any of these experiences were subjective and ungrounded?

(8) What about the natural human tendency among at least some people to touch in order to confirm what they are witnessing? Assuming that at least a few disciples would have attempted to touch their best friend, who was supposedly standing just a few feet away, why wouldn't someone have discovered, even once, that he was not physically there at all? This very human scenario is described in Luke 24:36–43 and other places

---

[83] Even many of the more critical commentators stand in agreement on this point, which is very widely conceded. Interested readers may also consult the two detailed chapters on the early Gospel date in volume 1 as well as the other discussions on this topic throughout this study. Francis X. Durrwell states a common position today: "La formulation est, sans doubte, antérieure à la conversion de Paul" (Habermas translation: Speaking of 1 Cor 15:3–5: "The expression [or formulation] is, without doubt, prior to the conversion of Paul"). See Durrwell, *La résurrection de Jésus: Mystère de salut* (Paris: Cerf, 1976), 22. Additional critical scholars who date these apostolic experiences and their proclamations from the initial days to just a very few years after the crucifixion include the following: Funk and the Jesus Seminar, *Acts of Jesus*, 454, 533; Hans Grass, *Ostergeschehen und Osterberichte*, 2nd ed. (Göttingen: Vandenhoeck & Ruprecht, 1962), 96; Bart D. Ehrman, *Did Jesus Exist? The Historical Argument for Jesus of Nazareth* (New York: HarperCollins, 2012), 92–93, 131–32, 141, 144–45, 155–58, 170, 251, 254, 260–63; James D. G. Dunn, *Jesus Remembered*, vol. 1 of *Christianity in the Making* (Grand Rapids: Eerdmans, 2009), 854–57, 864–85; Dunn, *Why Believe in Jesus' Resurrection?* (London: SPCK, 2016), 4. On the New Testament consensus regarding this exceptionally early date, see James Ware, "The Resurrection of Jesus in the Pre-Pauline Formula of 1 Cor 15.3–5," *New Testament Studies* 60 (2014): 475–98; Richard Bauckham, *Jesus and the Eyewitnesses: The Gospels as Eyewitness Testimony*, 2nd ed. (Grand Rapids: Eerdmans, 2006), 264–71, 308.

in the Gospels (Matt 28:9; John 20:17, 24–29). Discovering that Jesus was a phantom would seemingly have ended the speculation in favor of hallucinations or worse!

(9) Why did the hallucinations stop after just forty days?[84] Why didn't these inward experiences continue to spread to other believers, just as other Christian experiences and expressions expanded, and just like other non-Christian phenomena at that time, as an initiation or badge of entry into the cultic beliefs?[85]

(10) The resurrection of an individual contradicted general Jewish theology, which held to a corporate event at the end of time. That is why Paul wrote of the resurrection of the dead in the plural—the righteous dead are raised together (such as Rom 1:3–4). So Jesus's individual resurrection did not fit normal Jewish expectations. Of course, new views certainly do emerge, but this is at least an additional roadblock.

(11) Of all the prophet, messiah, and "superhero" figures or stories of the past, why are Jesus's resurrection appearance accounts so unique? Where are the additional historical examples? And where is the comparable evidence for these other reports?[86]

There is no shortage of reasons that oppose the range of hallucination theses, some even strongly so. Further, some additional, equally weighty critiques of several look-alike hypotheses have also been treated in this study, such as what we have called the illumination and illusion options.[87] Altogether, it is rather amazing that hallucination remains the most commonly chosen option, although these alternative ideas are generally supported in smaller numbers today.

Conversion Disorder

Perhaps misled by the term "conversion," this illness is often thought to be related to religious changes of heart to different belief systems. But this phenomena is quite

---

[84] In the nineteenth-century German liberal heyday of the hallucination theorizing, Theodor Keim also made this point against David Strauss and the other subjective vision supporters. See Keim, *Die Geschichte Jesu von Nazara, in ihrer Verhaltung mit dem Gesamtleben seines Volkes frei untersucht und ausführlich erzählt*, 3 vols. (Zurich: Orell and Füssli, 1867–1872), 3:355–57.

[85] Dunn, *Evidence for Jesus*, 71–72.

[86] Two lengthy chapters on a variety of both nonhistorical and historical characters that arise in ancient mythological, legendary, and even historical accounts are evaluated in earlier chapters of this present volume. Cf. also Gary R. Habermas, "Resurrection Claims in Non-Christian Religions," *Religious Studies* 25 (1989): 168–70.

[87] These examples were distinct enough to treat in an earlier chapter in this volume.

distinct from experiencing changes in one's religious beliefs. "The term 'conversion' in psychiatric parlance is conceptually unrelated to religious 'conversion.'"[88] Rather, it refers to "disturbances of bodily function" due to distress, perhaps like an individual who suffers real paralysis when made to do something that they object to strenuously.[89]

Of the different angles on hallucination in this chapter, this particular option is the outlier, because hallucinations are not normally connected with conversion disorder.[90] As some critics suggest, Paul experienced a conversion disorder, a psychological condition characterized by physical symptoms like blindness or paralysis in the absence of specific neurological or medical causes. Such was brought about by his inner turbulence, conflict, doubt, and guilt. Goulder agrees with this claim about Paul, but adds that Peter and others, including perhaps James, were also suffering from the same problem. Hallucinations and illusions were mixed in here too.[91]

Once again, we must align our hypotheses with the facts, and multiple problems oppose this interpretation of conversion disorder. (1) Initially, only Paul is known to have manifested any of these symptoms, so while Goulder's and Kent's inclusion of the other apostles is very convenient for their thesis, it fails to be grounded either factually or medically. Regardless, the likelihood that each of the other disciples would all just "happen" to have this malady is ridiculous.[92]

Further, showing that Goulder does not understand this subject, he even defines conversion disorder as a personal transformation due to adopting a different religious mindset![93] But again, this malady is unrelated to religious conversion. There are just way too many examples here among these critics where almost magically accumulating apostles, additional symptoms, and utilizing faulty definitions all add to the overall

---

[88] Bergeron and Habermas, "Resurrection of Jesus," 165.

[89] Bergeron and Habermas, 164. Additional symptoms and characteristics will be unpacked in the critique.

[90] It is nonetheless being considered in this context because a few critics seem rather unfamiliar with this juxtaposition and have combined conversion disorder with other hallucination issues, thereby almost forcing the specific issues to be treated here as opposed to potentially being "called out" with not responding to them, as if admitting that the confused view is hereby correct!

[91] Goulder, "Baseless Fabric," 48–55, 58–59.

[92] Another very serious instance of Goulders's overreach is when he brings hallucinations into his discussion of conversion disorder, and rather prominently so ("Baseless Fabric," 49), as pointed out below.

[93] Goulder, 54.

mix that allows them to improperly extend this mixture and attempt to custom-fit the hypothesis to the biblical descriptions. These are clearly instances of abusing the data and committing a large case of overreach in the process.

(2) A huge problem for Goulder's position is that, from what we know personally about Paul and James in particular, there were no mitigating grounds to suppose any conversion disorder. We have no evidence or indication that there was the slightest inner conflict, doubt, or guilt concerning their previous rejection of Jesus's teachings, nor any present questionable states of mind in general. Critics generally agree that James was an unbeliever during Jesus's earthly ministry (John 7:5; cf. Mark 3:21). Paul's skepticism is even better known, since he admittedly persecuted early Christians (1 Cor 15:9; Gal 1:13, 23). But we do not know of any guilt on Paul's part, for he considered his actions to have been both zealous and faultless (Phil 3:4–6).[94] In short, there is no indication of any inner turmoil for either of these apostles. Nor are there any other factors that might contribute to conversion disorder. To suppose otherwise is groundless. In short, these men are exceptionally poor candidates for this problem.

But not to miss the chief point at hand, these responses are to answer critics who are heading down the wrong path. These improperly mentioned religious characteristics above are not the domain of conversion disorder cases.

(3) Further, in addition to Paul and James's internal states of mind not showing similarities to patterns of conversion disorder, the psychological profile for this ailment strongly opposes its application to either of these apostles. Conversion disorder most frequently occurs to women (up to five times more often), adolescents, and young adults, as well as less-educated persons, those with low IQs, individuals of low socioeconomic status, or combat personnel.[95]

(4) Conversion disorder does not generally take overly long to heal; Bergeron attests that "complete spontaneous resolution would be expected within a few days and nearly all cases resolve within 30 days."[96] This usual outcome hardly seems

---

[94] Again, while conversion disorder has nothing to do with religious conversion, we will see below that the states of mind just described for Paul and James definitely do not foreshadow any apparent desire for a religious conversion.

[95] Harold Kaplan, Benjamin Sadock, and Jack Grebb, *Synopsis of Psychiatry*, 7th ed. (Baltimore: Williams & Wilkins, 1994), 621.

[96] The quotation is from Bergeron and Habermas, "Resurrection of Jesus," 166. For further confirmation, see especially Kaplan, Sadock, and Grebb, *Synopsis of Psychiatry*, 649–50.

applicable to Paul or James in particular, both of whom experienced critically ascertained, lifelong conversions, both dying as martyrs for these convictions.[97]

(5) Regarding other facets pertaining to the question of conversion disorder, these critical scholars often hold that these sufferers were strong candidates for both visual and auditory hallucinations. But this is exaggerating the case again, and by quite a bit since hallucinations are uncommon characteristics of this disorder.[98] Not only have we commented that Paul and James were poor candidates for this illness in the first place, but even apart from this sickness, they were additionally not predisposed to experiencing hallucinations. These were two separate men here, in very different life circumstances, and hence we have two separate critiques of their likelihood for this condition. To extend our earlier critique, there is no indication that either James or Paul longed to see Jesus. In fact, when they had their chances, they refused the opportunities. Their previous unbelief was a poor basis for producing hallucinations due to any imagined desires to see the risen Jesus! Nor did their outlooks on life and faith contain indications that they wanted to believe in Jesus. As before, to say otherwise is mere conjecture apart from any historical data whatsoever.

(6) Concerning his conversion, James agreed with his family in concluding that Jesus had "gone out of his mind" (Mark 3:21 NRSV). Jesus's mother and family members wanted to remove him from a ministry situation, but Jesus apparently did not go with them (3:31–35). Jesus's own townspeople were offended at him as well (6:2–3). John remarks that Jesus's family wanted him out of the area, adding that "not even his brothers believed in him" (John 7:5 NRSV). James does not seem at this point in his life to have had a pious reputation or any leadership position in Judaism. Responses to Jesus such as these account for why the majority of scholars hold that James the brother of Jesus was an unbeliever before Jesus's resurrection.[99]

---

[97] Sean McDowell, *The Fate of the Apostles: Examining the Martyrdom Accounts of the Closest Followers of Jesus* (Surrey: Ashgate, 2015), chaps. 5–6, 19.

[98] Cf. Kaplan, Sadock, and Grebb, *Synopsis of Psychiatry*, 621–22. I am also indebted to clinical psychologist Gary Sibcy, PhD, for this last response.

[99] As argued by John Painter, "Who Was James? Footprints as a Means of Identification," 27–29, 57–62; and Richard Bauckham, "James and Jesus," 106, with both essays in *The Brother of Jesus: James the Just and His Mission*, ed. Bruce Chilton and Jacob Neusner (Louisville: Westminster John Knox, 2001). Painter and Bauckham are among the few scholars who disagree with the majority conclusion that these men were unbelievers before their resurrection appearance.

(7) As Luke explains, Saul (Paul) seemed to be minding the coats of those who stoned Stephen to death (Acts 7:57–59), and he clearly approved of Stephen's martyrdom (8:1). Then we are told that, "Saul was ravaging the church by entering house after house; dragging off both men and women, he committed them to prison" (8:3 NRSV). In Paul's own words: "I was violently persecuting the church of God and was trying to destroy it. I advanced in Judaism beyond many among my people of the same age, for I was far more zealous for the traditions of my ancestors" (Gal 1:13–14 NRSV). Paul also states that he was "a Hebrew born of Hebrews; as to the law, a Pharisee; as to zeal, a persecutor of the church; as to righteousness under the law, blameless" (Phil 3:5b–6 NRSV).

In the cases of James and Paul, some have claimed that these two men were forlorn, repentant, depressed, or no doubt many other things. To be sure, they were living in very different positions, probably sporting dissimilar states of mind. But the chief problem here is that all the actual evidence under consideration supports conclusions that head in different directions, including that their conversions to Christianity were most likely due to Jesus's resurrection appearances to them that are mentioned in the pre-Pauline creedal statement of 1 Cor 15:7–8 (cf. 9:1 for Paul's appearance too). Saul (Paul) apparently held a more respected position in Judaism, but most conclude that either man exhibited good reasons to consider them as longing for conversion—just the opposite. Further, once again, conversion disorder is not concerned with religious changes of mind.

(8) Nor does the conversion disorder hypothesis account for what might otherwise be considered as these two apostles' delusions of grandeur—namely, their beliefs that God himself had imparted special revelation to them for the sake of enlightening the entire world and that others must embrace their message. But there appear to be no other apparent delusions involved here, occurring at precisely the same time, so the original conversion disorder case is further weakened. But are we to suppose that each of these two apostles had *both* of these psychological conditions?

In sum, charging that these apostles were victims of conversion disorder and accompanying hallucinations simply does not fit the facts on many key counts, neither historical nor medical. It is clearly an overreliance on a hypothesis apart from the data, hence their initial theses fail to be anchored in reality. From the outset, conversion disorder has nothing to do with religious changes of mind, in spite of some popular descriptions. Then to charge that each of the claimed contributing factors converged simultaneously and multiplied for several disciples at once, occurring to Paul and James the brother of Jesus along with many other apostles at roughly the same time, is over the top. There is no evidence for this misapplied category. Moreover, attaching the charge of any species of hallucinations to this concept at all is still very much out of place, since they basically are not symptoms of this malady, let alone the far more difficult charge of establishing mass hallucinations. As will be seen now, there remain still many other serious difficulties for hallucination theses.

Bereavement Hallucinations or Visions and Post-death Visions/ After-Death Communications

Initially, there are some similarities between the resurrection appearances of Jesus and the post-death visions (PDVs) and spontaneous after-death communications (ADCs) mentioned various places in this volume.[100] These reports concern claims of after-death data. The grief of the recipients may definitely play a role in these scenarios as well.

From the outset, it needs to be clear throughout this entire section that the object of critique here is *not* any opposition to the study or even the potential reality of evidenced PDVs.[101] Thus, the critical remarks here are *not* aimed at reports of these sightings per se or the potential reality that those experiences may be backed with evidence.[102] Some of these ADC claims may very well be hallucinations or other

---

[100] See especially the following chapter on objective visions for a detailed analysis.

[101] As commented in the next chapter too, neither spontaneous PDVs nor ADCs as described here have anything to do with seances or the purposeful communication with dead individuals. The unplanned PDVs/ADCs generally concern the death of a loved one or friend, most often that of a widowed spouse, and are often quite unexpected. The PDV/ADC contrast above is due in that not all these occurrences are visual (PDVs). Some may involve familiar sights, sounds (as with nostalgic music), and so on that are reminiscent in some other ways of a deceased loved one.

[102] To drive home this point more forcefully, several years ago I debated science scholar and atheist Michael Shermer, PhD, the founding publisher of *Skeptic* magazine, at the April 13–14, 2012 Greer-Heard Point-Counterpoint Forum at the New Orleans Baptist Theological Seminary. (The dialogue is available at www.greer-heard.com.) The topic for debate was "Is There Life after Death?" I argued for the reality of the afterlife, and three of my chief arguments were the resurrection of Jesus, very well-evidenced NDEs (see the first appendix in volume 1), and a few highly evidenced PDVs. The same year, I began my published debate with Ken Vincent (listed immediately below) by affirming the reality of the best-evidenced PDVs. So obviously in my view, certain examples of these visions, at least, are not to be taken lightly and neither are they the objects of any personal critique on my part. See Gary R. Habermas, "Resurrection Appearances of Jesus as After-Death

subjective experiences too. However, a good many appear to be genuine and well evidenced.[103] This judgment is not generally opposed even by proponents. But examining this evidence is not the issue in this discussion.[104]

The critique in this section, then, is predominantly on two specific and related points. Any evidenced resurrection appearances of Jesus would obviously qualify as postmortem phenomena, and Jesus's appearances do present some similarities in common with PDVs. Yet there are many reasons to deny that these appearances were the same or a very similar species of events as PDVs, as argued by Ken Vincent in his essay "The Resurrection of Jesus as an After-Death Communication." Rather, the argument in both the next chapter on this subject and in this section is that Jesus's resurrection appearances were unique historical events.[105] Further, any possible hallucinatory elements in some PDVs or ADCs do not at all relate to the reality of the evidenced cases or to the corroborated postmortem appearances of Jesus.

So what are some of these differences? Two items should be noted here. First, this subject overlaps somewhat and will also be treated in the following chapter on objective vision hypotheses as well. Thus, some of the information will be repeated as necessary in both places, though often with different angles of emphasis and sources. Some of the details will be different and more apropos to one place or the other. Also, the order of the responses to contrary arguments differs from the next treatment on objective visions.

Communication: Response to Ken Vincent," *Journal of Near-Death Studies* 30 (2012): 151, 157. Glenn B. Siniscalchi also summarizes some impressive evidence for what we have been calling PDVs (192–94). Siniscalchi cautions that there is lack of both strong evidence here, as well as a clear track for the interpretive value of PDVs, though many published cases have appeared since his publication. See Siniscalchi, "On Comparing the Resurrection Appearances with Apparitions," *Pacifica* 27 (2014): 184–205.

[103] For a number of evidenced cases, see J. Steve Miller, *Deathbed Experiences as Evidence for the Afterlife* (Acworth, GA: Wisdom Creek, 2021); see also J. Steve Miller, *Is Christianity Compatible with Deathbed and Near-Death Experiences?: The Surprising Presence of Jesus, Scarcity of Anti-Christian Elements, and Compatibility with Historic Christian Teachings*, vol. 3 (Acworth, GA: Wisdom Creek, 2023).

[104] Cf. Siniscalchi on the directions where some of these various data might indicate; "Comparing the Resurrection Appearances," 194.

[105] As argued in my response to Vincent (Habermas, "Resurrection Appearances," 149–58). In a nuanced treatment that makes a few strong thoughts, but after arguing primarily against Dale Allison's defense of postmortem apparitions, Siniscalchi concludes similarly on the strength of the case for Jesus's resurrection appearances ("Comparing the Resurrection Appearances," 205).

A second note concerns the relation of this section to hallucinations, as per this chapter. On the positive side, there is now a fair amount of agreement between Jesus's evidenced resurrection appearances and at least the corroborated PDVs in that they *both* point *away from* the subjective hallucination category due to this factual verification. But at the onset of the bereavement research, these experiences were commonly cast in terms of hallucinations.[106] Moreover, some later commentators still took these "visions" in the original, subjective sense.[107]

In this chapter more attention will be paid to the claim that at least some of these occurrences were evidenced in some way, since this argues against the charge that these phenomena are all hallucinations. Yet, it will be asserted on several grounds that they are still not exactly the same species of occurrences as Jesus's appearances but may still produce other evidence for an afterlife.

(1) Typically, the argument for sameness or strong similarity between Jesus's appearances and PDVs often progresses by comparing the similarities. But this move potentially commits more than one informal logical fallacy, depending on how the argument is construed.[108] In short, similarities or compatibilities do not prove that two or more items must be the same, or even that they are quite closely related. This is particularly the case when major differences exist to offset at least some of these similarities, as is certainly the case here.

(2) If Jesus's post-crucifixion appearances and the PDVs both have probable evidence in their favor, then this double situation of good data for each view is helpful in the sense that they both are able to share corroborated views, including the conviction that the afterlife is a reality. On this combined supernatural (while not necessarily miraculous) perspective, each of the positions could further share some similar worldview perspectives. From the angle of Christian theology, for example, there could be many similarities regarding Jesus. But there are some major differences

---

[106] Rees, noting the title of his 1971 medical journal article above: "Hallucinations of Widowhood."

[107] This is likewise why Joseph Bergeron and I include the interpretations of these bereavement events as hallucinations in our journal article "Resurrection of Jesus," 157, 167–71. Two of the scholars treated there who take the bereavement visions as hallucinations are Lüdemann and Kent, plus Goulder.

[108] Depending how the argument details, candidates for such informal fallacies might include hasty generalization (as in jumping to conclusions in situations where there is an insufficient amount of data to determine a particular outcome), or false cause (declaring something to be the cause, such as in situations where there are other options).

too, such as that PDVs are generally disembodied. Still, both could presumably agree on the demise of naturalism.

(3) An enormous issue in opposition to the argument that Jesus's appearances were the same (or a closely similar) phenomena to PDVs of a bereavement nature is the presence of almost two dozen strong primary and secondary critical arguments that favor Jesus's burial tomb being empty after Jesus's death. While other rival suggestions are of course possible, it has already been argued at length in volume 1 and elsewhere that these alternative hypotheses do not line up well with the established data available, as indicated by the majority of critical scholars who reject the viability of these alternatives.[109] This would be a vast difference from the disembodied theses. For example, recipients who report PDVs do not think that their loved one's graves have been vacated, which argues for different, unique qualities in Jesus's case when assessing the comparative data.

(4) N. T. Wright among others has raised another intriguing critique of the differences on these positions. When a loved one witnesses what they think is a brief

---

[109] In one objection that is not heard often, even Ehrman dates the sermon summary in Acts 13:29–30 as being very early, referring to it as "pre-Lukan," "pre-literary," and very old (*How Jesus Became God*, 154–55, 226). Ehrman takes the minority view here that the Sanhedrin *as a whole* did the burying here (154–55). But why cannot Joseph of Arimathea be the exact member of the Sanhedrin who is in view here, as per Mark 15:43 and Luke 23:50? The chief point in this immediate context is still that Jesus was buried in a tomb (*mnēmeion*, Acts 13:29). It was from that location that Jesus emerged (v. 30), necessitating an empty tomb. Further, the majority view among critical scholars, as pointed out above, is that Mark relied on a passion narrative that probably both contained the empty tomb and may well have been dated in the 30s. Additionally, even many critical scholars think that the very early creedal statement in 1 Cor 15:4 either teaches or at least implies the empty tomb. Two of the keys to this consideration include the creedal text being taught in a very Jewish context that drew the ire of the Greeks, namely, as Paul explains, that of Jesus being raised literally "out from among the dead ones" (*ek nekrōn*, as in the similar Pauline ideas in both 1 Cor 15:12 and Phil 3:11, 21). This is quite a literal, bodily view, even crassly so, as Jesus emerges out from among those who were dead. Further, since Jesus's burial is part of the creedal sequence of "died . . . buried . . . was raised . . . appeared" in 1 Cor 15:3–5, the strong implication here is that the body that went into the grave is also the body that came out and reappeared. Thus, these notions from this Acts 13:29–30 creed and Paul's accompanying thought, from a very early date, seem also to teach an empty tomb.

The emphasis above on most scholars rejecting the alternative empty tomb hypotheses is also addressed in detail in the treatment in volume 1. For one relevant example here, even Perry, who takes a very positive angle on the question of PDVs, agrees that the historicity of the empty tomb is a major difference (*Easter Enigma*, 101–2).

PDV of a loved one or friend, often a spouse, such an occurrence is certainly capable of producing comfort and often does so. In spite of that, what the vision does *not* do is cause the recipient to conclude that their loved one or friend is still alive somewhere in this world. As Wright asserts, even witnessing an after-death vision "doesn't mean they're alive again—it means they're dead. That's the point. . . . Uncle Joe ain't coming back again. That's how those things function."[110] The major distinction is that while both persons may presently be alive, the PDV individual is elsewhere. This contrasts the New Testament, which states that Jesus remained bodily with his followers, even for a relatively brief time. This is a massively distinct difference from typical reports of PDVs.

So, while the living individuals may certainly be consoled in some respects, such as in realizing that their loved one apparently is still alive in heaven or elsewhere, the body of the deceased remains dead and the realization is firm that the individual will not return to this world. Therefore, whatever these visions may mean, they are neither harbingers that inspired Jesus's resurrection nor grist for those who take this position and hypothesize that the resurrection appearances are simply the same as PDVs. Wright concludes pointedly, "That's precisely what [a grief vision] isn't."[111]

(5) Moreover, according to at least a half dozen critical arguments, Jesus quite often predicted both his death and his resurrection (see Mark 8:31; 9:31; 10:33–34; 14:27–28; Matt 12:38–40; cf. 16:1–4). These forecasts are found throughout the early literature; are established by multiple independent sources; fulfill several of the recognized critical historical tests of embarrassment, dissimilarity, and contextual plausibility; and lack Old Testament parallels or theological elaboration, all of which are well-recognized research methods in the scholarly community. Such positive indications appear to overwhelm the few opposing considerations.[112]

Such predictions by Jesus would indicate more than his mere ability to make good guesses or to read the tea leaves regarding current politics and ascertain that he had a good chance to be martyred for his beliefs. If that were it, what intelligent individual in their right mind would forecast a unique event like a resurrection, which had never before been witnessed? Such bold and repeated pronouncements would more likely indicate

---

[110] Wright has made this point in more than one context. He makes it in the dialogue with Crossan mentioned above ("Dialogue," chiefly 35–37, quotation on 35). See also Wright, *Resurrection of the Son of God*, 689–92.

[111] Wright, "Dialogue," 36.

[112] Licona, *Resurrection of Jesus*, 284–302. Cf. also Michael R. Licona, "Did Jesus Predict His Death and Vindication/Resurrection?," *Journal for the Study of the Historical Jesus* 8 (2010): 47–66.

that Jesus was well aware of his imminent death plus his resurrection and exaltation along with the role that he would play in God's kingdom and planned salvation.

Then what might it mean if these wild prognostications really happened just as they were forecast? This knowledge would further differentiate Jesus's foresight from those who experienced the PDVs or ADVs due to Jesus's knowledge of what awaited him in his fate, including his appearances. These teachings indicated Jesus's knowledge of and participation in a specific plan. Persons who experienced PDVs do not project such previous knowledge, let alone that God would raise them from the dead.[113]

(6) Critical theologian Theodor Keim argued influentially during the reign of German liberalism in the late nineteenth century that the New Testament is careful to differentiate Jesus's resurrection appearances from disembodied visions.[114] But these visions were well known in the ancient world too, and if all these afterlife occurrences were considered roughly the same or similar, then there is all the more reason not to distinguish or differentiate the resurrection appearances from other visions. But the appearances were nonetheless viewed separately and uniquely. Oddly enough, even though he made this distinction, Keim still held to disembodied appearances! As Allison points out, something other than postmortem visions must be going on here, especially when these visions were not expressed in terms of resurrections.[115]

(7) The majority of critical scholars today appear to hold that, at least according to the earliest New Testament witnesses themselves, including Paul, Jesus's resurrection appearances were believed to be bodily events.[116] Those who take this recent view include a number of skeptical thinkers.[117] Thus, in spite of rejecting personally all supernatural

---

[113] As in the case with Perry (see footnote 109), Dale Allison is another critical scholar who has studied extensively and is positive about the specifics of the PDV thesis, but also seems to accept Jesus's predeath predictions as well (*Resurrecting Jesus*, 230; *Resurrection of Jesus*, 184–88, 198).

[114] Keim, *Die Geschichte Jesu von Nazara*, 3:595. In the twentieth century, Raymond E. Brown among other scholars carried on this distinction as well; see Brown, *The Gospel according to John, XIII–XXI* (Garden City, NY: Doubleday, 1970), 966.

[115] Allison, *Resurrecting Jesus*, 261, 321–26.

[116] For an overview of this subject, see Gary R. Habermas, "Mapping the Recent Trend toward the Bodily Resurrection Appearances of Jesus in Light of Other Prominent Critical Positions," in Stewart, *Resurrection of Jesus*, 78–92.

[117] For examples of these see Habermas, "Mapping the Recent Trend," 88–90. Examples of these researchers include John Dominic Crossan and Jonathan L. Reed, *In Search of Paul: How Jesus' Apostle Opposed Rome's Empire with God's Empire. A New Vision of Paul's Words and World* (New York: HarperCollins, 2004), 6–10, 296, 341–45; Crossan,

events like miracles, and both Jesus's resurrection appearances and PDVs alike, a number of researchers still agree that the view taught by the New Testament authors, including the apostle Paul, was Jesus's bodily resurrection appearances. Other scholars have provided among the very best defenses of bodily resurrection views.[118] Wright is well known for hundreds of pages defending this concept, including describing the resurrection body as "immortal physicality,"[119] "transphysical," and "transphysicality."[120] This once again is a direct difference from the majority of PDVs, which are disembodied.

(8) An absolutely major contrast between Jesus's resurrection appearances and the PDVs is the extraordinary diversity of Jesus's many accredited resurrection appearance accounts. To my knowledge, no comparable combination of ADCs or PDVs regarding a single historical person who died, followed by various disembodied postmortem reports over a comparable length of time, even approaches the diversity of these appearance accounts of Jesus. No matter what category these postmortem events are placed in, these details make these Jesus sightings look rather unique as well.

In order to arrive at anything even remotely close to this early list of resurrection appearances that is so respected by contemporary critical scholars, one would have to string together a lengthy series of similar ADCs involving a single person over a relatively brief time. The resurrection reports of Jesus encompass highly attested appearances to both individuals and groups (including over 500 persons at one time), to believers and also to at least a couple of major skeptics, to both males and females, to people who were standing, walking, and talking, both indoors and outdoors in both

---

"Dialogue," 24–25; Crossan, "Resurrection of Jesus," 46–56; Lüdemann, *The Resurrection of Jesus*, 35, 177; Bart D. Ehrman, *The New Testament: An Historical Introduction to the Early Christian Writings* (Oxford: Oxford University Press, 2000), 296; Allison, *Resurrecting Jesus*, 317; Allison, *Resurrection of Jesus*, 131–36, 224–25.

[118] Wright, *Resurrection of the Son of God*, 32–552 (esp. xvii, 83, 321), plus the conclusion in 477–79; John Granger Cook, *Empty Tomb, Resurrection, Apotheosis* (Tübingen: Mohr Siebeck, 2018), esp. 1, 54, 591, 618; Licona, *Resurrection of Jesus*, 400–440 in particular; Robert H. Gundry, *Sōma in Biblical Theology: With Emphasis on Pauline Anthropology* (Cambridge: Cambridge University Press, 1976; repr., Grand Rapids: Zondervan, 1987), esp. 159–83; Gundry, "The Essential Physicality of Jesus' Resurrection according to the New Testament," in Gundry, *The Old Is Better: New Testament Essays in Support of Traditional Interpretations* (Tübingen: Mohr Siebeck, 2005), 171–87; also published in Joel B. Green and Max Turner, eds., *Jesus of Nazareth, Lord and Christ: Essays on the Historical Jesus and New Testament Christology* (Grand Rapids: Eerdmans, 1994).

[119] Wright, "Dialogue," 19.

[120] Wright, *Resurrection of the Son of God*, 477, 606, 609.

the daytime as well as the evening. The emphasis on group sightings, especially of more than a couple persons at a time, is particularly noteworthy.

Though holding views closer to those of Vincent, Perry made the similar point to the one immediately above that in terms of the sheer number of witnesses, appearances, and various other details, not even the best PDV cases approach the inclusive list of Jesus's resurrection appearances. Perry added in a detailed discussion that, if the Gospel data are also included, both the length of time involved in the appearances as well as the extent of the conversations serve as supplementary indicators of the distinctiveness of Jesus's appearances. As he affirmed, "It remains true that the overall scale of the Resurrection appearances is far greater than that of modern cases."[121]

Though Allison was likewise very impressed with the PDV cases while conducting a very lengthy evaluation of ADCs, he agreed with Perry regarding the strength and diversity of the resurrection appearance traditions.[122] His comparisons in his later resurrection study were remarkable, attesting that "if there is a good, substantial parallel to the entire series, I have yet to run across it."[123]

As mentioned earlier, the additional pointers to the unique resurrection events need to be kept in mind for supplementary assessment.[124] As O'Collins and Siniscalchi among others have noted, there are *far more differences* than similarities between Jesus's resurrection appearances and bereavement visions.[125] These distinctions between these

---

[121] Perry, *Easter Enigma*, 181–89, quotation on 188.

[122] Allison, *Resurrecting Jesus*, 228–69, 285.

[123] Allison, 346, also 344, 356.

[124] Gerald O'Collins produced his own list of some of the differences between the resurrection appearances of Jesus and regular bereavement apparitions. The latter usually concern widows, where those who died had virtually nothing in common with Jesus's violent death, the bereavement apparitions sometimes continued for years afterward, and many of those who had these experiences kept them to themselves, while Jesus's disciples were joyous with the opportunities to express their testimonies from the very beginning, and the bereavement cases usually occurred to individuals rather than to groups. Details can be found in Gerald O'Collins, "The Resurrection and Bereavement Experiences," *Irish Theological Quarterly* 76 (2011): 224–37. This article was also reprinted later as an appendix entitled "Easter Appearances and Bereavement Experiences," in O'Collins's volume, *Believing in the Resurrection: The Meaning and Promise of the Risen Jesus* (Mahwah, NJ: Paulist, 2012), 175–91; also Glenn B. Siniscalchi, "Maurice Casey on the Resurrection and Bereavement Experiences," *Irish Theological Quarterly* 80 (2015): 24–25; additionally, personal correspondence between Habermas and Gerald O'Collins, January 31, 2014 and February 3, 2014.

[125] O'Collins, "Resurrection and Bereavement Experiences," 229; Siniscalchi, "Maurice Casey," 24.

general accounts are absolutely crucial because they produce other areas of opposition that further drive a wedge between the concepts and against the idea that Jesus's resurrection appearances and PDVs are either the same or quite similar sorts of events.

(9) Besides Paul's personal statements pertaining to his own resurrection appearance of Jesus in 1 Cor 9:1 and 15:8, many recent scholars have also regarded seriously at least some of the various core elements that Luke includes in his three accounts of Paul's conversion in Acts 9:1–9; 22:6–11; and 26:12–18, in spite of the textual questions that might also be researched.[126] However Luke's descriptions are taken, then, they include a few essentials that seem foreign to at least most of the PDVs, like an extremely bright light from heaven seen by all those persons who were present in Paul's group on their trip to Damascus and caused everyone to fall to the ground. It is noteworthy too, that none of these observers were Christians. This occurrence seems unlike at least the general species of PDV.

Siniscalchi makes another important observation here. The appearance to Paul is postascension, and the same author (Luke) records both the quite bodily appearances of Jesus to his disciples (Luke 24:36–43; Acts 1:1–11) as well as the three episodes involving Paul. Thus, Luke is unaware of any problems between the earlier bodily sightings and the appearance to Paul and his companions that involved the blinding light. Nor does Luke have a problem with the emptiness of Jesus's tomb with regard to Paul's appearance.[127] In fact, Luke also includes the early sermon summary in Acts 13:29–31 and attributes it to Paul. So, it ought not be argued that the appearance to Paul is less than bodily. Further, it may be added that Paul's large number of teachings on the subject (such as Rom 8:11; 1 Cor 15:12; Phil 3:11, 21 among other texts) hold strictly to the bodily views as well, providing added backup that Paul's appearance was hardly less than bodily, as many scholars also recognize.[128]

---

[126] For just a few examples: James D. G. Dunn, *Beginning from Jerusalem*, vol. 2 of *Christianity in the Making* (Grand Rapids: Eerdmans, 2009), 346–53; Crossan and Reed, *In Search of Paul*, 4–10; Allison, *Resurrecting Jesus*, 236, 263–66; Marion L. Soards, *The Speeches in Acts: Their Content, Context, and Concerns* (Louisville: Westminster John Knox, 1994), 111–14, 124–25; Gerd Lüdemann, *Early Christianity according to the Traditions in Acts: A Commentary*, trans. John Bowden (Minneapolis: Fortress, 1989), particularly 106–16; Vincent, "Resurrection Appearances," 138–39.

[127] Siniscalchi, "Maurice Casey," 26–27. Siniscalchi criticizes Casey for not addressing this aspect too (25).

[128] Siniscalchi, 27–28; Wright, *Resurrection of the Son of God*, particularly chaps. 5–8 (esp. 370–74, 398, 477–79); Licona, *Resurrection of Jesus*, esp. 400–437; Habermas and Licona, *Case for the Resurrection*, 155–57, 161–64; Gundry, *Sōma in Biblical Theology*, esp.

Crossan and Reed note in addressing this same subject that Paul's primary sources need to be preferred over Luke's secondary ones. When this is done, the bottom line is this: "To take seriously Paul's claim to have *seen* the risen Jesus, we suggest that his inaugural vision was of Jesus's body simultaneously wounded *and* glorified." In this process, they bracketed Luke's "blinded-by-light sequence" in favor of Paul's vision in which he "both *sees* and hears Jesus as the resurrected Christ, the risen Lord."[129]

Taken as a whole, the various elements of the critically accredited sightings of Jesus after his crucifixion are time and again quite different in many major respects from the details of regular PDVs. As mentioned, it also must be considered that a number of events in Jesus's life before the resurrection were quite remarkably unique as well, which is amazing considering that we are dealing with a far briefer time range in terms of the years involved and an exceptionally miniscule number of cases when compared to ADCs. These more exceptional factors in Jesus's life include his very distinctive theological and ethical teachings, predictions of his death and resurrection, and critically recognized texts that record his healings and exorcisms alongside a multiply evidenced empty tomb and corroborated bodily appearances (including the amount, rarity, and the variety of the sightings themselves). The combination of factors particularly with the empty tomb and appearances is unique. Plus it is often overlooked that each underlying historical fact on which the appearances are based has been recognized and attested by the vast majority of critical researchers today, a number of whom personally disbelieve the resurrection of Jesus.

Scholarly Views Regarding Hallucinations

In spite of the critical scholarly attestation, the very frequent and quite shrill verbiage that often comes from *nonscholarly* critics still abounds, too often filling the comments on conservative blogs and book reviews, questioning Jesus's very existence, and brandishing a rule: always reject any evidence presented, no matter what it is, and *demand* even more evidence, no matter how much has already been given. The additional rule is often to ask more questions than anyone will take time to answer. The most prominent impression seems to indicate that these inquiries emanate

---

163–75; Allison, *Resurrecting Jesus*, 236, 263–66; and even Crossan and Reed, *In Search of Paul*, 4–10; Ehrman, *New Testament*, 296; Lüdemann, *Resurrection of Jesus*, 35, 177; cf. Brown's comment in his *Gospel according to John*, 966.

[129] Crossan and Reed, *In Search of Paul*, 6, 8–10.

largely from those who are simply willing to hear only what they prefer and do not have the sort of scholarly ammunition that they require to counteract the early New Testament data. The anger and vehemence that often flows so freely from this crowd in many of these sessions can sometimes sound alarming. Surprisingly, even critical scholars have admitted that this anger exists![130]

If this is largely how *nonscholarly* critics react, how do *scholarly* critics like Ehrman respond to the data that they know and almost always recognize? For starters, the ensuing conversations are usually much more civil. Across the scholarly spectrum, many of the reasons given in this chapter help to explain *why* hallucination theses are generally rejected by scholarly researchers. This last point is crucial too: while academics are humans with their own views, their comments no doubt can carry weight, usually because of the reasons and arguments that stand behind these stances.[131]

---

[130] During a very kind and civil written debate on the resurrection of Jesus between New Testament professor Craig Blomberg and atheist professor emeritus Carl Stecher, the latter remarked that "unlike most 'new atheists' I am not generally hostile to religious beliefs, Christian or other." The comment was definitely appreciated, but why did Stecher think that he needed to begin the dialogue with this initial comment about atheist hostility or anger? See Stecher and Blomberg, *Resurrection: Faith or Fact? A Scholars' Debate between a Skeptic and a Christian* (Durham, NC: Pitchstone, 2019), 51. On the other point above concerning nonscholarly critics who often tend to be out of their fields, Ehrman is to be credited with a hard-hitting volume aimed largely at these Jesus mythicist popularizers who "are not taken seriously . . . to their chagrin" (*Did Jesus Exist?*, 20). Continuing, Ehrman notes, "Mythicists of this ilk should not be surprised that their views are not taken seriously by real scholars, that their books are not reviewed in scholarly journals" (21). He states concerning one of these authors: "I list a few of the howlers" (23). Then Ehrman states, "The mythicist view does not have a foothold, or even a toehold, among critical scholars of the Bible" (268 along with 146, 149–56, 194–96). True, Ehrman often makes statements that oppose the typical views of evangelicals and conservative Catholics (such as 46, 49, 70–71, 268–69, 313–16, 336), but he also adds concessions here often enough, frequently treating fairly his conservative opponents (like 74, 98, 101, 140–41, 145, 248–50, 290, among many more such examples).

[131] Just a very few of the mostly skeptical researchers who have commented against hallucination hypotheses of various species include Grass, *Ostergeschehen und Osterberichte*, 96; E. P. Sanders, *The Historical Figure of Jesus* (London: Penguin, 1993), 278–80; Raymond E. Brown, *The Virginal Conception and Bodily Resurrection of Jesus* (New York: Paulist, 1973), 90–92; Lapide, *Resurrection of Jesus*, 125–26; Ingo Broer, "'Seid stets bereit, jedem Rede und Antwort zu stehen, der nach der Hoffnung fragt, die euch erfüllt' (1 Petr 3,15): Das leere Grab und die Erscheinungen Jesu im Licte der historichen Kritik," in *"Der Herr ist wahrhaft auferstanden" (Lk 24,34): Biblische und systematische Beiträge zur Entstehung des Osterglaubens*, ed. I. Broer and J. Werbick (Stuttgart: Katholisches Bibelwerk, 1988), particularly 55–56; John Dominic Crossan, "Dialogue," in *Will the Real Jesus Please Stand Up?*

Regarding the topic in this chapter, Jesus Seminar cofounder John Dominic Crossan stated regarding one of Jesus's appearances, "Now it's not a vision; it's not a hallucination . . . not in a hallucination."[132] Fellow Jesus Seminar cofounder Marcus Borg attested of the experience of Paul and his companions on the way to Damascus: "I do not put them in the category of hallucinations."[133] Speaking again of the appearance to Paul in another discussion, Borg commented: "I think visions can be true. . . . I never put them in the same category as hallucinations."[134] John A. T. Robinson likewise holds that it "seems certain" that hallucinations cannot account for all of the appearance data, especially that of Paul.[135]

In a written dialogue, skeptical Cambridge University philosophical theologian Don Cupitt commented on the issue in this chapter.[136] Cupitt asserted, "Of course religious experiences can be shared, but then there are plenty of hallucinations." For Cupitt, "collective visions of Mary" occurred in the present century.[137] His Cambridge University New Testament colleague C. F. D. Moule then responded: "As for collective hallucinations, the ones you cite seem to me negligible, in extent, persistence, and consequences, as compared with the Easter belief, and scarcely serious parallels to the genesis of the Christian church."[138]

An amazing aspect of resurrection and other Christian studies is the number of non-Christian Jewish scholars who are at least open to, or who even compliment,

---

A Debate between William Lane Craig and John Dominic Crossan, ed. Paul Copan (Grand Rapids: Baker, 1998), 63; Marcus Borg, "The Truth of Easter," in Marcus J. Borg and N. T. Wright, *The Meaning of Jesus: Two Visions* (New York: HarperCollins, 1999), 132–33; A. J. M. Wedderburn, *Beyond Resurrection* (Peabody, MA: Hendrickson, 1999), 96; Geza Vermes, *The Resurrection* (London: Penguin, 2008), 143–49; John Shelby Spong, *The Easter Moment* (New York: Harper & Row, 1987), 96; Samuel Vollenweider, "Ostern—der denkwürdige Ausgang einer Krisenerfahrung," *Theologische Zeitschrift* 49 (1993): 41–43.

[132] Crossan, "Dialogue," in Copan, *Real Jesus*, 66.

[133] Borg in Borg and Wright, *Meaning of Jesus*, 132–33.

[134] Borg, "The Irrelevancy of the Empty Tomb," in Copan, *Real Jesus*, 123.

[135] John A. T. Robinson, *Can We Trust the New Testament?* (Grand Rapids: Eerdmans, 1977), 125, esp. in the context of 123–25.

[136] Cupitt's view on Jesus's resurrection, treated here as the "Illumination Theory," is addressed in detail in this study in the chapter titled "Illumination and Illusion Hypotheses."

[137] C. F. D. Moule, "The Resurrection: A Disagreement," in Cupitt, *Explorations in Theology* (London: SCM, 1979), 6:40. Moule is a respondent to Cupitt in his book.

[138] Moule, "Resurrection: A Disagreement," 41. The point here is not the actual dialogue itself, but Moule being another prominent scholar who rejected hallucinations, especially collective ones, though Cupitt of course takes the opposite view.

the New Testament text in sundry ways, such as with various historical aspects (Jesus's healing miracles, claims to divinity, and so on).[139] New Testament Jewish scholar Pinchas Lapide famously wrote a book arguing that Jesus actually was raised from the dead.[140] Mishkin lists at least three other well-known Jewish thinkers (the agnostic Oxford University historian Geza Vermes, Claude Montefiore, and the early Joseph Klausner, though he appeared to change his view later in life) who at least allowed the resurrection visions as actual though private occurrences.[141] Jewish historian Alan Segal is very difficult to decipher on this matter due to his back and forth comments that seem to conflict at times and the difficulty of deciphering the difference between Paul's views and those of Segal himself. But Segal seems to fit comfortably in this category of Paul having had a real, spiritual, mystical experience.[142]

Like these three positions mentioned by Mishkin, Lapide even argues, "Most Jewish scholars consider this . . . possibility as the most likely one," and amazingly seems to think that the most popular Jewish scholarly position is similar to the "true" bereavement options that we discussed above, where the deceased individuals really do appear especially to their loved ones! Yet Lapide does not take this last position for Jesus's appearances personally, since he thinks that what Jesus's disciples saw was different from the bereavement cases. In terms of our topic in this chapter, Lapide affirms, "No vision or hallucination is sufficient to explain such a revolutionary transformation."[143]

---

[139] David Mishkin notes these aspects throughout his volume, *Jewish Scholarship on the Resurrection of Jesus* (Eugene, OR: Pickwick, 2017). His last chapter, "Conclusions" (201–14) serves as a very helpful overview.

[140] Lapide, *Resurrection of Jesus*, 92, 95–99, 125–29; cf. also the affirmative comments in theologian Carl Braaten's "Introduction" to Lapide's text, 15–16.

[141] Mishkin, *Jewish Scholarship*, 138, 142, 168.

[142] Alan F. Segal, *Life after Death: A History of the Afterlife in the Religions of the West* (New York: Doubleday, 2004), chaps. 10–11, esp. 389, 441–42, 446–56, 459–63. Perhaps the most puzzling comment is that Segal states that he agrees with Lüdemann that "the original experiences of the risen Christ must have been visionary appearances" (448), but in the context Segal seems to relate this agreement with Lüdemann to the experiences beginning on the initial Easter Sunday. How much further this agreement may extend is very difficult to say, especially when Segal closes his treatment by saying: "What actually happened at Easter is still an historical mystery as well as a mystery of faith" (477). Mishkin has some similarities to this interpretation of Segal's position as well (*Jewish Scholarship*, esp. 68, 83–87, 202–9).

[143] Lapide, *Resurrection of Jesus*, 124–25.

Another New Testament scholar, Ben Witherington, states the following: "The pattern of appearances to various people at various times in differing places—sometimes to individuals, sometimes to groups, and at least once to someone who had never been a believer (Paul)—makes clear that these events cannot be categorized as mass hallucinations or the dreams of the deluded or even mere subjective visions."[144]

Philosopher Stephen Davis affirms why the majority scholarly view rejects hallucinations: "The very idea of a group hallucination or vision is at best deeply problematical." Davis considers Jesus's appearances to have been bodily.[145] One of "several obvious reasons" why the hallucination is highly dubious is that the texts relate that, "on at least three occasions, the resurrected Jesus was not immediately recognized" and some expressed doubts. Davis's point seems to be that, among other characteristics, these are not likely when any hallucinations already would have been conjured up inside their own minds, so why would there be a lack of recognition and doubt afterward? Further, "many different people saw the risen Jesus, in different places and in different circumstances."[146]

In addressing David Strauss's famous hallucination thesis along with the history of other such subjective efforts, eminent German theologian Wolfhart Pannenberg concluded: "These explanations have failed to date." Pannenberg explains that this verdict follows due to two chief lines of argument: "positive points of contact for the application of the psychiatric concept of vision are lacking," plus the additional fact that "serious difficulties that argue against this are present in the tradition."[147]

---

[144] Ben Witherington III, L. William Countryman, Gail Ramshaw, and Mark I. Wegener, *New Proclamation: Year B, 2003, Easter through Pentecost*, ed. Harold W. Rast (Minneapolis: Fortress, 2003), 5–6.

[145] Stephen T. Davis, *Risen Indeed: Making Sense of the Resurrection* (Grand Rapids: Eerdmans, 1993), 179–80, quotation on 179. Davis's view on the bodily nature of Jesus's resurrection is made in a truly distinctive way in his chapter "'Seeing' the Risen Jesus," in Davis, Kendall, and O'Collins, *Resurrection*, 126–47.

[146] Davis, *Risen Indeed*, 183–84. The three Gospel passages that Davis cites for this nonrecognition and doubt are Matt 28:17; Luke 24:36ff.; and John 20:24–25.

[147] Pannenberg, *Jesus: God and Man*, 96–97; additional critiques on 94. Pannenberg comments similarly in his *Systematic Theology*, trans. Geoffrey W. Bromiley (Grand Rapids: Eerdmans, 1991), 2:354. Pannenberg thinks that the empty tomb is likewise a huge problem for hallucination theses; see *Jesus: God and Man*, 100; *Systematic Theology*, 2:359; Pannenberg, "The Historicity of the Resurrection and the Identity of Christ," in *The Intellectuals Speak Out about God*, ed. Roy Abraham Varghese (Chicago: Regnery Gateway, 1984), 257–64, particularly 260–62. See also Pannenberg, "Die Auferstehung Jesu: Historie

Of course, scholars can be found occupying all sides of the issues here, and head-counts, impressive quotations, or other statements will not resolve this question once and for all. However, it is at least worthwhile to note that among the views of such distinguished scholars on all sides, a sizeable number of the majority who reject hallucinations are skeptics or even unbelievers who likewise reject the resurrection of Jesus itself and sometimes even jettison belief in the supernatural world as a whole. In other words, this critical group may embrace hallucinations if they thought it was a superior view, but they fail to take this path. At the same time, while some pro-resurrection scholars have pondered seriously the hallucination thesis, it is certainly questionable how many pro-hallucination scholars include resurrection believers among those whose views they also study.

A Brief Encapsulation of the Hallucinations Critique

We have viewed three dozen considerations in this chapter that critique several types of hallucination theses from a variety of angles. In a nutshell, arguably the hardest-hitting combination from these blends integrates five features. Group hallucinations may well be nonexistent, particularly with regard to the absence of medical and psychological recognition. But even if they do exist rarely, the majority of Jesus's resurrection appearances were described as group events, sometimes accompanied by exceptional corroboration. That such rare occasions could occur fairly often after Jesus's crucifixion creates an amazing combination that leads to the conclusion that this repetition alone confirms the reality of Jesus's actual appearances instead of subjective visions.

Adding to these features are the medical views above that only 2 to 3 percent of individuals are affected by hallucinations and that multimodal cases involving sight, touch, and hearing together may be even more rare. These data severely complicate the issues as well, militating against all of these aspects coming together at once. Even individual hallucinations are fairly rare. Combined with the wide varieties of personalities, men and women, headstrong and sensitive, of different ages, indoors and outdoors, in the daytime and nighttime, it all adds another layer of attestation. Together, these five considerations provide virtually an insurmountable hurdle against the multiple occurrences of hallucinations having caused Jesus's resurrection appearances.

---

und Theologie," in *Zeitschrift fur Theologie und Kirche* 91 (1994): 318–28; Pannenberg, *Die Auferstehung Jesu und die Zukunft des Menschen* (Munich: Minerva-Publikation, 1978).

Conclusion

While the second half of the nineteenth and early twentieth centuries witnessed great numbers of hallucination theorists, there are far fewer specialist scholars holding such naturalistic hypotheses today. Hallucination and related subjective hypotheses may again be the most popular options but in smaller numbers overall. In other words, both the alternative theses as a whole and the hallucination views in particular are supported by dwindling numbers of researchers.

Further, very few specialist critical scholars today, especially among the younger researchers, seem to be willing to choose just a single natural theory and champion that view alone, as has been the more common approach since the early nineteenth-century explosion of alternative positions. It seems clear especially in terms of the newer data emerging in recent decades that to place all of one's eggs in a single basket in that manner can be a very risky business for skeptical researchers. The main path today seems to be for critics to champion any or all of these theses without choosing a favorite, because they are supposedly each better than the resurrection. But there is apparently an underlying reason for this maneuver: it seems that scholars seldom trust a single thesis to the exclusion of all the others. It is one of the wary critic's secrets to which many others may even be unaware.

Ehrman even warns about this: "Historians who do not believe that Jesus was raised from the dead should not feel compelled to come up with an alternative explanation for why the tomb was empty. Apologists typically have a field day with such explanations." Ehrman then goes on to explain, "I don't subscribe to any of these alternative views." He then points out that "any of these views is more plausible" than a resurrection.[148] This certainly seems like a loss of confidence in any particular view covering the necessary territory.

But we have argued in this chapter that these strategies regarding hallucinations have still failed to explain the known, critically ascertained data on several fronts. Three dozen total reasons were applied to these alternative theses.[149] We have concluded here that subjective visions in their various forms fall short in their attempts to provide an adequate alternative to the New Testament proclamation. Clinical psychologist Gary Collins summarizes a few of the problematic issues: "Hallucinations

---

[148] Ehrman, *How Jesus Became God*, 164–65.

[149] Some of these refutations may apply to more than one occasion as well, because they can provide excellent responses to more than a single variety of hallucination challenge.

are individual occurrences. By their very nature only one person can see a given hallucination at a time. They certainly are not something which can be seen by a group of people. . . . Since an hallucination exists only in this subjective, personal sense, it is obvious that others cannot witness it." In fact, the problems with this thesis are so serious that, in order to hold this view, Collins even thinks that these critical scholars "would have to go against much of the current psychiatric and psychological data about the nature of hallucinations."[150] Many commentators, both believers and unbelievers alike, seem to think that the notion of group hallucinations does not fare well versus our best psychological understanding on this point. This is a simply huge problem for the critics.

But Collins is stating more than that here by pointing out that these naturalistic options are at odds with most of our current scientific knowledge on this entire subject. In other words, he thinks that it should be concluded that applying hallucinations and similar subjective theses to Jesus's resurrection appearances is severely mistaken across both the disciplines of psychiatry and psychology, and at more than one point. These approaches oppose our entire spectrum of scientific knowledge on these subjects. This is an enormous issue for these views.

Yet, in spite of the comparatively rare percentages of even individual hallucination experiencers, and its nonexistence in group settings as far as is known from research studies, hallucination supporters have written and lectured for almost two centuries as if these occurrences are frequent occasions for individuals. Entire groups of observers are included in the incidents without effort. Further, hallucinations are quite frequently misidentified when illusions and delusions are actually in view, only to be touted and claimed afterward as group occurrences as well with regard to the resurrection appearances.

Recent New Testament studies have trended toward ascertaining greater amounts of historical information, especially regarding the life of Jesus. The evidence comes chiefly from very early creedal traditions that are often dated to the 30s plus the application of historical criteria to the texts. In these and other ways, numerous amounts of positive information have been used in support of particular events and teachings during these times, even by critical scholars themselves. Hallucinations are still suggested, but developed positions here are not as common as in the past.

Along with the relative rarity of even detailed individual hallucinations, other realities also need to be factored in here. The differing amounts of likelihood for

---

[150] Gary Collins, PhD, letter to the author, February 21, 1977.

various personalities, gender, age, and other fluctuations need to be considered as well as multiple hallucinatory modalities. These data are absolutely necessary in order to explain the accredited source data that instead support the occurrence of Jesus's resurrection appearances, which must all be considered carefully and explained adequately.

But the experimental information on hallucinations was nearly unknown during the nineteenth and early twentieth centuries. For example, as mentioned earlier, when hallucinations occur the situation has often been corrected by those present by various careful and accurate interventions, by pointing out the incongruities involved from better vantage points, and so on. Even so, critical scholars including David Strauss, Gerd Lüdemann, Ernest Renan, John Shelby Spong, Michael Goulder, and other subjective theorists often seem to have relied on various incorrect definitions, such as the differences between hallucinations, illusions, delusions, and other similarly subjective theses to explain the data. Individual traits unrelated to the psychological profiles could cause problems. But neither the conditions nor the applications always worked in these manners. These experiences could be proclaimed to be a fit even when the science was heading in other directions.

But we are addressing the possibility of hallucinations to both individuals and groups. The former class has a number of difficulties of its own and the latter is apparently impossible or nearly so. Radical transformations are generally also outside the normal scope of hallucinations. As far as is known, no disciples ever recanted, and it is generally admitted even by critical scholars that these same disciples were at least *willing* to give their lives for this gospel message, often standing in the line of fire on multiple occasions throughout their lives. These are difficult matches for any of these subjective theses. In short, the overall evidence that we possess simply points in all the wrong directions for hallucinations to obtain, as Gary Collins mentioned above, especially given the many different circumstances for which we have data. This is why the scholars have largely rejected the class of subjective theses. This is the conclusion here as well. The refutations of the hallucination theses are just overpowering.

16

Objective Visions

Throughout the past two centuries, many alternative notions have been proposed as rivals to the orthodox view of Jesus's resurrection from the dead and his bodily appearances. One such family of options actually comprised a different species altogether in that it held that the resurrection actually did occur, though not in the traditional, orthodox sense. While favoring Jesus's resurrection over the naturalistic suggestions, it was sort of a midpoint between the better-known stances.

Especially from the last third of the nineteenth century until the present, this less-influential rival to the conservative view of Jesus's bodily resurrection appearances has often been referred to as the telegram or telegraph thesis. A more accurate designation for this option would be the objective vision thesis. The early forms tended to hold that Jesus rose from the dead, went to heaven, and relayed objective visions back to his disciples. These bodiless but quite real appearances informed his followers that he was truly alive and with his Father, and that he would be with them as they spread his message. Later forms skipped the notion of *relayed* visions from heaven and held the simpler thesis that Jesus actually appeared to his disciples in this new form and visited with them, though in a nonbodily, usually nonevidential manner.[1]

---

[1] Hence the term "objective" here was not a reference to Jesus appearing in a regular body where he could be touched or eat food with his disciples, as in Luke 24 and John 20–21. The scholars who espoused this view, such as Theodor Keim, still generally

The Objective Vision Theory and Its Supporters

The notion of "telegrams" to describe earlier aspects of this outlook was derived from the older idea that after Jesus was truly raised from the dead, this event was followed by his spiritual ascension to heaven. From that location, Jesus and his Father relayed images of himself back to his followers in order to indicate that he was indeed alive and doing well in his exalted heavenly abode. By far the most influential nineteenth-century scholar to hold this view was German liberal theologian Theodor Keim, who referred to these notions as "telegrams from heaven."[2] After an influential set of criticisms of the subjective vision thesis of David Strauss and others, Keim defended his own position.[3] But these roundabout gyrations between earth and heaven involving some sort of telegraphed images turned out to be a far too convoluted set of unnecessary and difficult concepts, particularly if the living Jesus had sent the images without actually being present with the disciples, since this was clearly thought to be the case.

Others in the nineteenth and twentieth centuries likewise favored a similar view of Jesus's resurrection appearances. Another major scholar who did so shortly after Keim was Kirsopp Lake of Harvard University. Like Keim, Lake first criticized the subjective vision thesis as inadequately postulating that Jesus never actually rose or appeared in the first place. Then he defended the position that Jesus really did rise from the dead and showed himself to his disciples in what Lake described as "a real though supernormal psychological event" that nonetheless did not suspend

---

rejected the possibility of these more physical Gospel accounts, including the empty tomb. However, Jesus still at least could have appeared to groups of people in this manner, such as the appearances to "the Twelve," the large gathering of 500 persons, plus to the additional group called "all the apostles" as in the famous early creedal statement that Paul cited in 1 Cor 15:3–7. Rather, the word "objective" indicated that Jesus nonetheless *truly did appear* to people and was clearly seen by them, in contrast to the subjective vision theories of David Strauss and other scholars, where the disciples only *thought* (and probably hallucinated) that Jesus had appeared to them.

[2] Theodor Keim, *Die Geschichte Jesu von Nazara, in ihrer Verhaltung mit dem Gesamtleben seines Volkes frei untersucht und ausführlich erzählt*, 3 vols. (Zurich: Orell and Füssli, 1867–1872), 3:506–621 treating the burial and resurrection of Jesus. These specific comparisons above were made in 3:602–3. The English translation is Keim, *The History of Jesus of Nazara, Freely Investigated in Its Connection with the National Life of Israel, and Related Detail*, trans. Arthur Ransom, 6 vols. (London: Williams & Norgate, 1883).

[3] Keim, *Die Geschichte Jesu von Nazara*, 3:596, 602–3; Keim, *History of Jesus of Nazara*, 6:323–24, 353–58, 361–64.

nature's laws.[4] Already Lake seems to have dropped the notions of telegrams to simply describe these occurrences of Jesus showing himself to his disciples in his own "objective presence." But these events were not the sort of bodily occasions where Jesus could have been touched.[5]

Slightly less than a century after Keim published his major three-volume treatise (in German) a similar hypothesis was championed by another German theologian, Hans Grass. For Grass, like Keim and Lake, the empty tomb and bodily appearances of Jesus were due to legendary embellishment.[6] Yet it remains the case that Jesus really did appear to his disciples after his death by crucifixion, according to the early testimony in 1 Cor 15:3–5.[7] In fact, that Jesus's family members (such as James) were converted due to the appearances is one of the surest indications that Jesus appeared and could be observed as such.[8]

Finally, New Testament scholar Reginald Fuller was also a prominent supporter of this thesis. Perhaps surprisingly, unlike Keim, Lake, and Grass, Fuller accepted the historicity of the empty tomb.[9] Fuller also provided more details than most of the other commentators, defining Jesus's appearances as being revelatory in nature and meant for the disciples alone, as "visionary experiences of light, combined with a communication of meaning." Through these events, Jesus commissioned the disciples to a missional ministry. Like the others who held this view, Fuller considered these appearances to be real but unable to have been photographed or otherwise objectified.[10]

A number of other academics over the years have held the objective vision thesis in one form or another. A hallmark of this position is that the vast majority of these scholars generally describe their conceptions of the actual nature of these appearances

---

[4] Kirsopp Lake, *The Historical Evidence of the Resurrection of Jesus Christ* (London: Williams & Norgate, 2012), 269. Further details are found on 267–77.

[5] Lake, 272.

[6] Hans Grass, *Ostergeschehen und Osterberichte*, 2nd edition (Göttingen: Vandenhoeck & Ruprecht, 1962), 93. It is difficult not to wonder concerning those who take the objective vision theory if denying the historicity of the Gospel accounts of Jesus's bodily appearances and the empty tomb are somehow necessary moves that are simply required in order to allow for their preference for nonbodily appearances.

[7] Grass, 96.

[8] Grass, 102.

[9] Reginald H. Fuller, *The Formation of the Resurrection Narratives*, 2nd ed. (New York: Macmillan, 1980), 49, 69–70, 170–72.

[10] Fuller, 46–49, 170–72, 181.

in only the briefest of terms, with very few details. There is general agreement that the outward manifestations were in the form of visions of light, perhaps surrounding a human image that was not photographable or otherwise measurable, where Jesus imparted messages (possibly telepathically) to the recipients that chiefly commissioned them to missional endeavors and service to others.[11]

There is a marked contrast between the subjective vision thesis and the objective vision theory. The subjective version of David Strauss, Ernest Renan, and many others almost always relies on some species of hallucinations or other internal states of mind without any corresponding external reality whatsoever being present while seeming to the recipients to be real. On the other hand, the objective version presented in this chapter postulates quite real though revelatory experiences, sometimes with external indications. For instance, these occurrences were actually viewed by single persons or by groups of people at the same time. The latter included appearances to the twelve disciples, to the more than 500 "brothers" (*adelphois*) at once, as well as

---

[11] Besides the scholars listed above, others who employ this language include Jürgen Moltmann, *Theology of Hope: On the Ground and the Implications of a Christian Eschatology*, trans. J. W. Leitch (New York: Harper & Row, 1967), 172, 181, 188, 190, 197–98, 202; Moltmann, *Religion, Revolution and the Future*, trans. M. D. Meeks (New York: Scribner's Sons, 1969), 49–55; Wolfhart Pannenberg, *Jesus: God and Man*, trans. Lewis L. Wilkins and Duane A. Priebe (Philadelphia: Westminster, 1968), 92–93; Ulrich Wilckens, *Resurrection, Biblical Testimony to the Resurrection: An Historical Examination and Explanation*, trans. A. M. Stewart (Edinburgh: Saint Andrew, 1977), esp. 116–25; Joachim Jeremias, "Easter: The Earliest Tradition and the Earliest Interpretation," in *New Testament Theology*, trans. John Bowden (New York: Scribner's Sons, 1971), 308–9; Pinchas Lapide, *The Resurrection of Jesus: A Jewish Perspective* (Minneapolis: Augsburg, 1983), 92, 95–99, 118, 125, 127–28; Gerald O'Collins, *What Are They Saying about the Resurrection?* (New York: Paulist, 1978), 54–55, 76–81; Larry W. Hurtado, *How on Earth Did Jesus Become a God? Historical Questions about Earliest Devotion to Jesus* (Grand Rapids: Eerdmans, 2005), 30, 48. James M. Robinson argues that this is probably the earliest view of the resurrection appearances followed later by the more physical, bodily elements. Still, unlike many of the commentators above, Robinson asserts that the position should not be espoused literally today. However, in this critique Robinson follows the holdover Bultmannian scholars and later exegetes who rejected objective resurrection appearances altogether. These views are set forth in Robinson, "Jesus from Easter to Valentinus (or to the Apostles' Creed)," *Journal of Biblical Literature* 101 (1982): 37. For a thorough and detailed critique of Robinson's position, see William Lane Craig, "From Easter to Valentinus and the Apostles' Creed Once More: A Critical Examination of James Robinson's Proposed Resurrection Appearance Trajectories," *Journal for the Study of the New Testament* 52 (1993): 19–39.

to a group called "all the apostles," in 1 Cor 15:7, a group that was apparently larger than the Twelve noted in the pre-Pauline creed in 1 Cor 15:5.[12]

The objective vision thesis was most popular between the late period of German liberalism and the close of the "No Quest" period in the first half of the twentieth century, which was dominated at its close by Bultmann's strongly anti-supernatural views, to the time just before the initial publications later dubbed the "Third Quest for the historical Jesus."[13] Viewed over against these times, the popularity of the objective vision hypothesis seemed in some ways to have been a sort of middle ground for those mid-twentieth century scholars who thought that Jesus was raised from the dead in some sense. Most of the examples from Hans Grass onward were published in the 1960s and 1970s.[14] It may be wondered if some of the scholars just mentioned may have preferred stronger bodily appearance views (in some sense) had the theological climate been more conducive to it, as it became soon afterward.

Though it is difficult to know for sure, when stronger historical positions began to appear as part of the Third Quest's efforts or simply as part of the growing ethos of the day, the objective vision view seemed to lose a little of the urgency to make a case for Jesus's resurrection appearances. Many scholars in the late twentieth century and beyond have offered arguments that the predominant Jewish view in Jesus's day was that of the resurrection of the body, including that this was the primary New Testament position as well.[15] Even skeptical scholars who reject Jesus's resurrection

---

[12] The word *adelphois* raises the possibility that the count consists of men only (as with the feeding of the 5,000 men in Mark 6:44) and easily could have involved a much larger group of onlookers who witnessed this appearance of the risen Jesus.

[13] For example, Bultmann's famous 1941 essay asks the question without any further deliberation, "But what about the resurrection? Is it not a mythical event pure and simple? Obviously it is not an event of past history." See Rudolf Bultmann, "New Testament and Mythology," in *Kerygma and Myth: A Theological Debate*, ed. Hans Werner Bartsch, trans. Reginald H. Fuller (New York: Harper & Row, 1961), 38.

[14] Interestingly, against this comparison, the Hurtado volume above almost looks like an outlier among the other publications, though there are some other more recent works like it as well.

[15] In one intriguing collection of essays, though endorsing more than one subposition, all eighteen authors agreed on the notion of Jesus's bodily resurrection as well as on that of Christian believers. See Ted Peters, Robert John Russell, and Michael Welker, eds., *Resurrection: Theological and Scientific Assessments* (Grand Rapids: Eerdmans, 2002). Another evaluation of non-Christian Jewish authors also notes many who agreed that the predominant Jewish position was that of the resurrection of the dead. See David Mishkin, *Jewish Scholarship on the Resurrection of Jesus* (Eugene, OR: Wipf & Stock, 2017). On the

frequently agree that a bodily position was the major Jewish and New Testament view here.[16] Many other researchers have argued straightforwardly for the bodily nature of Jesus's resurrection appearances and usually for the empty tomb tradition as well.[17] While many arguments for the historicity of the empty tomb were constructed, as argued at length in volume 1 of this study, this approach usually went beyond what

---

Jewish view, see also Dale C. Allison Jr., *The Resurrection of Jesus: Apologetics, Polemics, History* (London: T&T Clark, 2021), 131–36; on Paul's view, note 224–25; John P. Meier includes some worthwhile discussions on this point in his volume *A Marginal Jew: Rethinking the Historical Jesus* (New York: Doubleday, 2001), 3:322–23, 432–44, 642. For the contrasting positions in Judaism, few studies are more valuable than Alan F. Segal's *Life after Death: A History of the Afterlife in Western Tradition* (New York: Doubleday, 2004), 368, 379–83, 404–77, 757n27. Without much question, two of the most authoritative studies on the various meanings of the relevant terms in both Judaism and the New Testament are N. T. Wright, *The Resurrection of the Son of God*, vol. 3 of *Christian Origins and the Question of God* (Minneapolis: Fortress, 2003), chiefly 32–552; and John Granger Cook, *Empty Tomb, Resurrection, Apotheosis* (Tübingen: Mohr Siebeck, 2018), esp. the introduction along with chaps. 6–7. Two other major studies endorsing this position are Michael R. Licona, *The Resurrection of Jesus: A New Historiographical Approach* (Downers Grove, IL: InterVarsity Academic, 2010), 400–440; and Robert H. Gundry, "The Sōma in Death and Resurrection," in *Sōma in Biblical Theology: With Emphasis on Pauline Anthropology* (Cambridge: Cambridge University Press, 1976; repr., Grand Rapids: Zondervan, 1987), 159–83.

[16] Such skeptical testimony includes John Dominic Crossan and Jonathan L. Reed, *In Search of Paul: How Jesus's Apostle Opposed Rome's Empire with God's Kingdom. A New Vision of Paul's Words and World* (New York: HarperCollins, 2004), 6–10, 133–35, 173–74, 296, 341–45; Gerd Lüdemann, *The Resurrection of Jesus: History, Experience, Theology*, trans. John Bowden (Minneapolis: Fortress, 1994), 34–35, 177; Geza Vermes, *The Resurrection* (London: Penguin, 2008), 6; Dale C. Allison Jr., *Resurrecting Jesus: The Earliest Christian Tradition and Its Interpreters* (London: T&T Clark, 2005), 317, 324–25; Bart D. Ehrman, *Did Jesus Exist? The Historical Argument for Jesus of Nazareth* (New York: HarperCollins, 2012), 257–58; Ehrman, *How Jesus Became God: The Exaltation of a Jewish Preacher from Galilee* (New York: HarperCollins, 2014), 132–33, 137, 176–78, 181.

[17] Licona, *Resurrection of Jesus*, 399–437, 461–63; Wright, *Resurrection of the Son of God*, particularly 375–98, 683–718; James D. G. Dunn, *Jesus Remembered*, vol. 1 of *Christianity in the Making* (Grand Rapids, Eerdmans, 2003), 825–79; Dunn, *The Evidence for Jesus* (Louisville: Westminster, 1985), 53–78; E. P. Sanders, *The Historical Figure of Jesus* (London: Penguin, 1993), 11, 13, 278–80; Raymond E. Brown, *The Virginal Conception and Bodily Resurrection of Jesus* (New York: Paulist, 1973), 69–113; Allison, *Resurrecting Jesus*, esp. 346, also 317, 343; Gerald O'Collins, *Jesus Risen* (London: Darton, Longman & Todd, 1988), 99–127.

most of the objective vision theorists were willing to argue, as we saw.[18] By the end of the twentieth century, then, the supporters of the objective vision position were no longer on an island by themselves. Yet they were outnumbered by the scholars who held to the bodily appearances of Jesus.[19]

Why does the objective vision thesis appear to have a less prominent role to play at present? After all, it acknowledges that Jesus was truly raised from the dead and really appeared to his followers, even if these were less than fully bodily events. Further, it might be viewed as a position that is somewhat less offensive to the modern mind. Additionally, if the evaluation above is correct, the approach should be given some credit for the valuable service it performed by opposing a large portion of the most influential theological trends at the mid-century mark. Still, we turn to some of the other issues involved.

Critiquing the Objective Vision Thesis

A number of shortcomings are also apparent in the objective vision position, as argued by those who opposed the view. Some of the critiques are major, cutting to the heart of this stance.

(1) Arguably the initial issue is that the objective vision theory is still a supernatural thesis that postulates and even basically requires the existence of God, a living Jesus, another world beyond this one, and the resurrection and immortality of believers. Actually, except for the crucial aspect of a nonbodily resurrection appearance, virtually everything else that is normally believed by orthodox Christians could potentially still be held in this thesis. It is at least possible on this scenario that Jesus was embraced as the divine Son of God who died for human sin, was buried, and rose from the dead. Most or even all of Christianity's other major doctrines could all be

---

[18] On the historicity of the empty tomb, see Dunn, *Jesus Remembered*, 828–41; Brown, *Virginal Conception*, 113–29; Sanders, *Historical Figure of Jesus*, 13, 276; Allison, *Resurrecting Jesus*, 311–34, 346; O'Collins, *Jesus Risen*, 121–27; Michael Grant, *Jesus: An Historian's Review of the Gospels* (New York: Macmillan, 1992), 175–76; cf. also Luke Timothy Johnson, *The Real Jesus: The Misguided Quest for the Historical Jesus and the Truth of the Traditional Gospels* (New York: HarperCollins, 1996), 135.

[19] Gary R. Habermas, "Mapping the Recent Trend toward the Bodily Resurrection Appearances of Jesus in Light of Other Prominent Critical Positions," in *The Resurrection of Jesus: John Dominic Crossan and N. T. Wright in Dialogue*, ed. Robert B. Stewart (Minneapolis: Fortress, 2006), 78–92.

true as well. For example, Keim even recognized that his thesis was supernatural in nature, and he held that Jesus and his Father cooperated to send the telegrams to the disciples in the first place, along with grounding human immortality in the process.[20] In fact, rather surprisingly for some, he even allowed that Jesus's appearances may actually have been corporeal in nature.[21]

So, the chief question here is how much actual difference is there between Keim's thesis and the orthodox view, especially given Keim's concession that Jesus's appearances still could have been bodily in nature? The advantage to be gained in the late nineteenth century may possibly have been thought to appeal more to the other German liberal scholars of that era. But the point here is that where the strong supernatural stances of orthodoxy are still maintained just the same, this reconfiguration does not appear to gain overly much by this middle ground. This is especially the case in circles where the stronger bodily appearance tradition followed more easily as per Keim's comment, with arguably fuller results, and a few decades later became the dominant appearance position anyway. Of course, in keeping with this consideration, if Jesus did not appear in a resurrected body, that would be a serious problem for later configurations.

(2) Further, a huge problem for the objective vision thesis is the strong historical data in favor of the empty tomb. Most of the older researchers who took this position dismissed the empty tomb basically out of hand without detailed arguments, most likely at least partially in order to solve their issue of Jesus's physical body.[22] It was an easier position to take because the historicity of the empty tomb was more unpopular throughout the nineteenth and early twentieth centuries. But the relevant historical research has changed much in the ensuing century since these earlier positions were adapted and the robust evidences that favor the historicity of the empty tomb are today held by the majority of critical scholars, as already detailed thoroughly in volume 1.

Fuller clearly recognized the state of the data here and argued for the empty tomb. This development would seem to place these older theorists in a bind. If the tomb had been found empty, though other options are possible, this would more likely seem to indicate a direct correlation between what happened to the body and

---

[20] Keim, *Die Geschichte Jesu von Nazara*, 3:602–3.

[21] Keim, 3:603.

[22] It may be recalled that Reginald Fuller was one of the exceptions here.

the subsequent appearances—it would seem that the one who vacated the tomb also would have been the same one who appeared. As Wolfhart Pannenberg asserted years after his earlier comments that leaned more to objective visions, this configuration favored more bodily appearances.[23]

(3) Although there were definitely differences in the overall Jewish outlook throughout the Second Temple period through the New Testament period and beyond, the predominant Jewish view remained that of bodily resurrection. This was especially the case regarding the Pharisees' view.[24] As such, this would provide some background milieu that would be helpful in arguing for the most likely background behind the New Testament teachings.

(4) The Third Quest for the historical Jesus arose during the last quarter of the twentieth century and remains a very influential movement today, centering most of all on the Jewish background of Jesus. Due in large part to these developments and building particularly on this Jewish soil with regard to the dominant resurrection background at that time, there has been an apparent shift in scholarship of late. As mentioned above, the newer emphasis has migrated toward understanding the entire New Testament ethos of Jesus's resurrection appearances in a more bodily manner, even if the modern researcher did not hold that position personally.

It is hardly disputed that Jesus's bodily resurrection appearances is the overall view that is taught in the Gospels. This position was increasingly held even for

---

[23] Pannenberg, *Jesus: God and Man*, 100–101, 105. See especially the later concession in Wolfhart Pannenberg, "The Historicity of the Resurrection and the Identity of Christ," in *The Intellectuals Speak Out about God: A Handbook for the Christian Student in a Secular Society*, ed. Roy Abraham Varghese (Chicago: Regnery Gateway, 1984), 260–62.

[24] See the relevant notes directly above, and compare Josephus, *Ant.* 18.1.3; *J.W.* 9.14; John Dominic Crossan, "The Resurrection of Jesus in Its Jewish Context," *Neotestamentica* 37 (2003): 29, 34–56; Crossan, "The Resurrection, Historical Event or Theological Explanation? A Dialogue," in Stewart, *Resurrection of Jesus*, 24–25; Crossan, "Bodily-Resurrection Faith," in Stewart, *Resurrection of Jesus*, 175–76; Wright, *Resurrection of the Son of God*, particularly 85–128; Larry W. Hurtado, *Lord Jesus Christ: Devotion to Jesus in Earliest Christianity* (Grand Rapids: Eerdmans, 2003), 547–48; Licona, *Resurrection of Jesus*, 335–36; Segal, *Life after Death*, 411–12, 415, 417, 429–31, 433, 441–42, 447, 456–57, 459; Vermes, *Resurrection*, 6; Lapide, *Resurrection of Jesus*, 44–65; Gundry, *Sōma in Biblical Theology*, 169, 175–77, 182. Interestingly, since he favored the bodily resurrection of both Jesus as well as believers, Paul is depicted in Acts 23:6–9 as pitting the Pharisees against the Sadducees, thereby earning the favor of the Pharisees. Lapide takes this passage very favorably (*Resurrection of Jesus*, 62).

Paul's views.[25] In fact, this even may be the majority view at present based on the

---

[25] Of course, there are still differences between the resurrection appearance details as described in the Gospel narratives and the brief statements in Paul's Epistles. Hence, while Paul likewise accepts the notion of bodily resurrection appearances, the descriptive approaches vary. Many of the differences may be due to the Gospel authors narrating their stories, while the epistolary genre is entirely different, given brief statements of the reported earliest beliefs instead of detailed accounts. For example, Paul never describes (or even mentions directly) an empty tomb. Nor does Paul state that Jesus's female followers held him by the ankles after his resurrection (Matt 28:9; John 20:17), that Jesus otherwise offered to be touched (cf. Luke 24:39–40; John 20:17, 27), or that he ate food in the presence of his followers (Luke 24:41–43; Acts 10:41, or as implied in John 21:9, 12). Consider this, though: these situations may have been described much differently if Paul had written a Gospel. But whereas the Gospel narratives in Matthew, Luke, and John make it clear throughout in their descriptions that Jesus's appearances were bodily in nature, Paul also develops his views in other more theoretical ways in his teaching that he also thought that Jesus appeared bodily. Paul communicated his ideas in a variety of ways, such as by elaborating on his Pharisaic background views of both corporate and bodily resurrection, plus his teachings that the righteous would inherit a refurbished earthly creation (which would seem rather irrelevant or even just plain metaphysical nonsense for Platonic disembodied spirits!). Most of all, Paul's notion of the resurrection body is further indicated by his usage and interaction between crucial terms such as *sōma*, *anastasis*, *egeirō*, and especially *exanastasin* in Phil 3:11, or similar phrases where the concept of *anastasis* was combined with *ek nekron* (as in Phil 3:11b; 1 Cor 15:12; or Rom. 8:11). In these instances, especially for the Pharisees and in the majority Jewish parlance, this would most likely indicate that for Paul, the *sōma* that went down into the ground in burial was essentially the same *sōma* that emerged in the resurrection appearances (as in the creedal statement in 1 Cor 15:3–5). Of course, there were significant changes in resurrection bodies too, as Paul argues rather pointedly, especially in 1 Cor 15:35–45. It is even obvious in the Gospels that there were differences in Jesus's resurrection body, such as when Jesus appeared and disappeared, or when he was already gone when the tomb was opened. Moreover, Jesus's wounds were already healed, and he no longer suffered any pain, and so on. But Jesus's physical body had died, was buried, was raised, and appeared afterward—that is, what "went down" in death and burial returned in the resurrection and appearances. Though there were marked differences, Jesus had not ceased having (or being) a body—his own body. This is why many scholars have added that an empty tomb is implied in the pre-Pauline creedal statement in 1 Cor 15:4 as well as in Paul's other teachings on these matters. (See the crucial works listed above by Wright, Cook, Licona, and Gundry.) As Cook declares succinctly on the opening page of his treatise, his primary hypothesis is that "there is no fundamental difference between Paul's conception of the resurrection body and that of the Gospels" (*Empty Tomb*, 1). To be sure, the notions were expressed differently in the Gospels and in Paul, but the shared concept is that of the same raised body instead of a raised and glorified spirit.

available data.[26] This shift is even acknowledged by many skeptical scholars, as has likewise been mentioned above. Thus, even among those researchers who personally doubt or deny the historicity of the resurrection, or hold to the objective vision thesis, many still acknowledge that the bodily resurrection concept was the New Testament position for Jesus's appearances, including for Paul.[27] This information would of course directly oppose much of the objective visionary suppositions along with the other critiques that argue that less than bodily notions of the resurrection appearances are out of step with the predominant Jewish views at that time. This argues for different philosophical understandings lying behind these interpretations.

(5) Even as asserted forcefully by Keim and many other scholars against *subjective* visionary views like hallucinations, commentators have pointed out that the New Testament authors regularly differentiated between the resurrection appearances of Jesus and other sorts of heavenly visions.[28] Examples of nonresurrection visions could include visionary phenomena such as Jesus's transfiguration (Mark 9:2–8; Matt 17:1–8; Luke 9:28–36), Stephen's premartyrdom vision of the exalted Jesus (Acts 7:55–56), Peter's vision of the large sheet of animals coming down from heaven (Acts 10:9–16), or other visions reported by Paul (Acts 16:9; perhaps 2 Cor 12:1–4).[29]

---

[26] The authors and sources above are also relevant here. Carefully researched works such as those by Wright, Cook, Licona, and Gundry, among others, have been especially worthwhile studies that have done much to "move the needle" in this direction.

[27] Again, see note 16 above and, once again, compare Habermas, "Mapping the Recent Trend," 78–92.

[28] Keim, *Die Geschichte Jesu von Nazara*, 3:596.

[29] Regarding the question of whether Jesus's transfiguration could have been a misplaced resurrection appearance, this effort has largely failed in the context, not to mention has possibly been suggested in the first place to provide some support to those who favor either the objective vision approach itself or a suggestion like James Robinson's that this was the earliest conception of the resurrection appearances, as mentioned above. But as R. T. France points out concerning the transfiguration passage in Mark, "The frequently repeated assertion of Bultmann that, 'It has long since been recognized that this legend was originally a resurrection story' (*History*, 259) is now widely discounted. At almost every point it differs in form from the resurrection appearances." See France, *The Gospel of Mark: A Commentary on the Greek Text* (Grand Rapids: Eerdmans, 2002), 349. Even Fuller, who supports an objective visionary scenario as we have seen above, rejects this suggestion as a weak argument (*Formation of the Resurrection Narratives*, 165–66). However, this view of the transfiguration as a resurrection appearance might appear to constitute a strange twist to those who ask the question of whether Mark actually reported one of Jesus's resurrection appearances, whether or not he knew that he did so! In such a case, in addition to Mark's several repetitions of Jesus's predictions to his disciples that he would both rise from the

But there is another application to be made here concerning this distinction between the resurrection appearances and other heavenly visions. While Keim applied this dissimilarity to subjective visions or hallucinations, if the resurrection appearances are also to be viewed as revelatory, disembodied visions as distinct from these others (as some of the objective vision theorists might want to do), then on what grounds would these later, clearly nonresurrection visions be differentiated from the position of Keim and those who took similar positions? In other words, might not their own objective visionary view be seen as lacking just such a differentiation here?

It is quite clear that Paul, for instance, made just such a separation between Jesus's resurrection appearances and these nonresurrection visionary experiences. For example, Paul held that the resurrection appearances were unique. Why else would he have included a creedal list of Jesus's resurrection appearances in his epistle with the original list apparently ending before his own appearance (1 Cor 15:3–7, 8)? Moreover, Paul thought that his appearance on the road to Damascus was the "last" one (15:8). Further, how would Luke have been able to state that Jesus's resurrection appearances ended after just forty days (Acts 1:3)? Of course, since Luke also reported Stephen, Peter, and Paul's visions, he clearly did not consider these to be appearances of the risen Jesus either!

But that is exactly the issue at hand here: on what grounds could these early New Testament authors differentiate so clearly between the two species of phenomena *if* they were both disembodied revelatory types? If the objective vision thesis is favored, the distinctions may seem to break down a bit.[30] This distinction favors a different

---

dead and appear to them (Mark 8:31; 9:31; 10:33–34; and esp. 14:27–28), a conclusion such as Bultmann's above might actually backfire to a certain extent! The descriptions in the cases of Stephen (Acts 7:55–56) and Paul (2 Cor 12:1–4) appear to be much closer to near-death or similarly reported phenomena.

[30] Holding that Jesus's tomb was empty, as did Fuller (*Formation of the Resurrection Narratives*, 49, 69–70, 170–72) or Pannenberg (*Jesus: God and Man*, 100–101, 105), gave them at least a bit of an advantage here over the likes of Keim, Lake, and Grass, who argued that the empty tomb was simply a later legend. For instance, Fuller and Pannenberg could always argue that an empty tomb provided at least one line of demarcation that contributed to the uniqueness of the resurrection appearances. For Pannenberg's views here, see also "Historicity of the Resurrection," 260–62. See especially Wolfhart Pannenberg's insightful comments in "Response to the Debate," in Gary R. Habermas and Antony G. N. Flew, *Did Jesus Rise from the Dead? The Resurrection Debate*, ed. Terry L. Miethe (New York: Harper & Row, 1987), 125–35, esp. 129–31. Pannenberg even quite intriguingly commented: "If one accepts the empty-tomb tradition, one is pushed

quality for the resurrection appearances. What was it, then? The bodily view of the resurrection appearances provides such a differentiation, and a major one at that. Of course, this does not by itself demonstrate the truth of bodily appearances but is at least a pointer in the right direction. There are of course other considerations besides this one, but here at least bodily appearances would have to be recognized as holding the upper hand.

(6) A further point also needs to be added here. Some evaluators throughout church history may have been content with glorified and disembodied appearances alone—such events may even have been impressive. But simply in terms of normal human psychology that differs from person to person, it also seems fair to say that many everyday people, both centuries ago as well as in the present, would *not* have been satisfied with such appearances—especially those who held the majority Jewish views of bodily resurrection. The disembodied proposals would assuredly seem to cause many more occasions for doubt and second-guessing afterward, possibly for the remainder of the witnesses' lives. Did Jesus truly appear to them after his death or was it merely imagined?

For those who believed in a bodily resurrection who also had the psychological make-up that generally favors more empirical data, something more substantial than a vision would seem to have been necessary. For this substantial portion of the witnesses, a desire to touch the risen Jesus would be necessary in order to be sure. Glorified appearances of Jesus that were perhaps located above or even beyond the witnesses, as some commentators have suggested, would seem not to satisfy a fair percentage of these witnesses. As such, visionary appearances would not seem to be objective enough to convince these kinds of followers that Jesus was really there in their presence, particularly upon later reflection.

Strangely enough, whatever is concluded regarding the Gospel writers, several passages argue precisely this way. The women are said to have held Jesus's feet (Matt 28:9), and Mary Magdalene desired to touch the risen Jesus and apparently did so on her second trip to the empty tomb (John 20:17). Granted, these occasions may have been more out of love for Jesus rather than to gain evidence. But in other texts, such as Luke 24:36–43 and John 20:24–29, Jesus offered to be touched, most likely because he sensed that some there, as with the depiction of Thomas, wanted or even

---

to a literal conception of Resurrection, so in liberal theology that particular tradition was not very popular" (131). This is surely a thoughtful insight, illustrating the influence of our presuppositions.

demanded it. At least one of the very earliest postcanonical texts stated that, after Jesus offered, the disciples did exactly that and touched him (Ignatius, *Smyrn.* 3).

The chief point here is easy to miss. This contrast is definitely *not* a question regarding the strength of this Gospel testimony or the reliability of these texts. The nature of the Gospel witness itself is not at all the point in view. Rather, the idea not to miss is that the Gospel writers seem to have precisely recognized these psychological needs for different people. In other words, particularly for the women as well as possibly some of the male disciples too, a fairly decent percentage probably would have been satisfied with less evidence and simply *believed* that they had seen Jesus. But this would clearly *not* have been the case for many others—namely, for the evidentially minded doubters (as in Matt 28:17). Jesus knew this too, and hence offered to be touched.

Thus, unless there had been a more solid experience than disembodied visions, as impressive as they might have been in their own way, what else could better explain a large number of these witnesses apparently going out and turning the world upside down without ever looking back (as far as is known)?[31] Once again, the Gospel writers capture just that need for such human differences in assurance—it is a built-in human response for many persons. Bodily appearances are obviously strong here and would fulfill this desire.

True, it is not a question here of which option leaves us with the stronger evidence, but the issue is which scenario actually obtained. Yet this component also must be considered and evaluated carefully: Could the disembodied scenario of the scholars who hold the objective vision thesis even have produced the resulting exuberance, strongest convictions, and the all-out missionary zeal that were clearly manifest in most or all of the disciples alone, as we have already investigated in volume 1 of this study? Most crucially, were there a few "doubting Thomas" personalities among them? Could the personal transformations have lasted as long as they apparently did for some of them, such as Peter, Paul, or James—probably during the entire lifetimes of these witnesses—unless there had been at least some attending evidence?

In summary, several items might be mentioned regarding the objective vision theory or particular aspects of it. Keim's view probably exhibited the most problems among these like-minded theorists—as in leaving unexplained why Jesus did not

---

[31] On the point of Jesus's disciples recanting, see Sean McDowell, *The Fate of the Apostles: Examining the Martyrdom Accounts of the Closest Followers of Jesus* (Surrey: Ashgate, 2015), esp. 259–65, see also 6, 8, 243.

simply appear to his disciples instead of sending the visions. Again, perhaps Keim did not want to press too far the German liberal psyche of his day, but it leaves a yawning question there. Others have remarked that Keim's thesis would have tended to make both Jesus and his Father appear to be deceivers by convincing the disciples that he was actually present with them when this was not the case. But Keim should at least be given credit for going as far as he did in postulating supernatural events that exposed some quite definite liberal shortcomings.

None of these objective visionary configurations account for the robust New Testament textual evidence that, even for Paul, Jesus's appearances were bodily in nature. Further, the predominant Jewish view of that time regarding bodily resurrection remains unexplained while the reigning nineteenth-century German idealistic philosophy was preferred. As we have also argued, objective visions would not have provided objective enough data to convince at least a fair number of Jesus's followers, though commentators like Fuller and Pannenberg had an advantage here in espousing the empty tomb, based on the strong evidence for that event, as well as moving in the direction of more carefully defined manifestations of Jesus's presence.

But some progress was definitely made here nonetheless by introducing solid considerations against the theological presuppositions of the times in which they appeared, perhaps somewhat like the way Karl Barth struck at the heart of nineteenth-century German liberal theology a few decades later, even though he failed to push forward in more evidential directions himself. Sometimes these huge endeavors needed to be taken in smaller steps. But especially given that objective visions affirmed the resurrection appearances against the naturalistic hypotheses, this particular step was a bit more substantial.

Responding to a Related Thesis

The objective vision thesis just considered generally holds that the risen Jesus really appeared to his followers in actual though nonbodily appearances. In both formal research as well as in quite popular, unevidenced testimonies, myriads of very common occurrences have often been reported in recent times where many individuals have described witnessing spontaneous visions of their deceased loved ones or friends very soon after those individuals' deaths. These sightings usually last just brief seconds or so. Many claimed occurrences include a variety of closely related phenomena of slightly different sorts, often termed after-death communications (ADCs). The visionary examples among these experiences might be termed post-death visions

(PDVs).[32] These experiences are usually perceived privately, but a number of these reports have also included multiple witnesses simultaneously or additional claims that could be checked.[33]

---

[32] The term "spontaneous" here generally indicates that these occasions just "happened," seemingly out of nowhere, usually after the individual's recent death, when the surviving and grieving loved one was simply going about their daily life routines, such as being at home, work, or wherever they were at the time. These accounts do not pertain to, and should not be confused with, seances or other efforts on the part of living individuals who purposely seek out contact with the dead.

[33] A number of these evidential examples are found in the researched literature. Some of the best research here are the volumes from J. Steve Miller, including *Deathbed Experiences as Evidence for the Afterlife* (Acworth, GA: Wisdom Creek, 2021), particularly 113–18, 139–42; and *Is Christianity Compatible with Deathbed and Near-Death Experiences?* (Acworth, GA: Wisdom Creek, 2023), esp. chaps. 2–3, 6–10. A third volume in this set is forthcoming. Former Cambridge University Fellow Michael C. Perry includes several discussions of the relevant data, including evidential accounts, agreeing with others in this volume that Jesus's resurrection both answers successfully the naturalistic hypotheses (17, 102, 157, 162–171, 192, 218) as well as presenting better evidence than that on behalf of modern cases (31–32, 181–83, 194–95, 218, 228, 239–43). See Perry, *The Easter Enigma: An Essay on the Resurrection with Special Reference to the Data of Psychical Research* (London: Faber & Faber, 1959). Another popular collection of PDVs and ADCs presented numerous testimonies of "firsthand accounts" involving a wide variety of stories, perhaps even dozens of which included reports of corroboration, though apparently without much careful backup research on these accounts. Readers are invited to make their own decisions. These examples were collected and reported by Bill and Judy Guggenheim, *Hello from Heaven!* (New York: Bantam, 1995). Evidential reports, often including numerous examples in each of these categories, included PDVs that occurred before or at the same time as the information was received of the individual's death, including the exact time of the occurrences (243–58). In some cases the deceased person in the PDV spoke (231, 233, 246, 260–61). Multiple witnesses have sometimes been present (205, 207–8). One PDVer appeared along with a long-deceased individual (257–58). Objects have sometimes moved (206–8) and hellish, scary, or negative situations have been reported (229–35, 239–42). Other odd circumstances have also been involved (202–4, 206, 208–9, 248). These phenomena also included seemingly quite out of the ordinary or spontaneous music, lights, sounds, or other surprising incidents (201–4, 206, 209, 260), or impressions of impending disaster or death before anything occurred involving the precise times of later deaths (243–58). Often, comforting words have been spoken with the deceased person (231, 233, 235). Many popular Christian works also include very similar testimonies, such as John Myers, ed., *Voices from the Edge of Eternity* (Old Tappan, NJ: Spire, 1968). Myers includes complicated, intertwining testimony with some confirmation (39–42, 55–56, 97–99), including a person who did not die but who witnessed the NDE of one who did die even though the family of the individual who died had not yet learned of their death (56), knowing the

A number of these studies pursue more rigorous compilations of a wide array of experiences. Probably the most common scenario is that of a recently widowed spouse or a bereaved parent who seemingly witnesses what appears to be the actual presence of their loved one who had recently died and was buried (though some of these experiences also happened years after the original events). These occasions quite often take the form where the deceased individual appears seemingly out of nowhere, usually for just seconds, as a spirit-like presence in the place occupied by their living loved one(s). A sparse number of spoken words, or even simply an under-standing expression without words, provides the expressly stated or other sense that the departed person is doing just fine. Hence, the living persons were not to be wor-ried about them. This scenario and responses are often essentially the same from case to case, with the brief, spoken messages being frequently very similar in this regard.[34] These reports have essentially developed into a genre of their own.[35]

---

correct time of one's death (63–66), hell visions (59, 239–241), and a shared case resulting in religious conversion (231–32). Similar Christian collections of these sorts of stories have also appeared, often from professionals trained in the relevant areas. These include Pete Deison, *Visits from Heaven* (Nashville: Nelson, 2016), particularly 51–56, 66–70, 78–81, 105–8; Trudy Harris, *Glimpses of Heaven: True Stories of Hope and Peace at the End of Life's Journey* (Grand Rapids: Baker, 2008), esp. 19, 24, 36–39, 51, 69, 112, 116–17, 152–53, 182–83, 186–87; Robert L. Wise, *Crossing the Threshold of Eternity: What the Dying Can Teach the Living* (Ventura, CA: Gospel Light, 2007), see 17–19, 22–23, 49–53, 75–77, 100–103, 158–59, 213–16; John Burke, *Imagine Heaven* (Grand Rapids: Baker, 2016), chiefly on the subject of NDEs. Some of these latter testimonies were gathered from hospice workers, nurses, chaplains, and pastors. Two important points need to be repeated: many of the above accounts consist of uncorroborated testimonies and, as far as is known, the stories were unconnected with seances or occultic practices. Throughout, there is a need for per-sonal evaluation and conclusions.

[34] We are not including here the various quite common existential senses in which the deceased individual is thought or felt by their loved one to be present nearby, though apart from any claimed manifestations. These sorts of convictions often take the form of living persons being convinced that the deceased individual is invisibly present in the room, or watching them from somewhere close by, and so on.

[35] A major and well-publicized pioneering report was provided by physician W. Dewi Rees in his essay "The Hallucinations of Widowhood," *British Medical Journal* 4 (1971): 37–41. In a much more recent study, Rees concluded that these bereavement experiences can produce both emotional and religious significance, such as comfort and assurance of faith, including affirming the reality of an afterlife in general and, for some, even increasing belief in Jesus's resurrection. See Dewi Rees, *Pointers to Eternity* (Talybont: Y Lolfa, 2010), 193–95, 198, 205. Crossan has also provided some updated statistics on the prevalence of

The occurrences such as these just mentioned most frequently resulted in a great amount of subjective assurance and peace for the loved ones. Even when the event was private and without any attending corroboration, the typical result for the living was still the assurance that their loved one was doing well. Seldom can the recipients be dissuaded from their assured conviction either. Evidential cases often provided still greater amounts of calmness and degrees of acceptance, though the typical results generally included a positive impact on grief resolution.

While it might be thought or simply assumed that there is a somewhat similar relationship between ADCs (and PDVs in particular) and Jesus's resurrection appearances, it is seldom made clear in the studies whether particular researchers considered these phenomena to be somewhat or essentially the *same species or family* of events, or whether it was just being pointed out that the cases exhibited *similarities but not sameness*, probably in the sense of being various afterlife indications.[36]

---

these experiences among recently bereaved individuals ("Resurrection of Jesus," 46–47). For an evaluation of the reports by Rees and others, including both the subjective and other potential manifestations, see Joseph W. Bergeron and Gary R. Habermas, "The Resurrection of Jesus: A Clinical Review of Psychiatric Hypotheses for the Biblical Story of Easter," *Irish Theological Quarterly* 80 (2015): 157–72, esp. 167–71, cf. 158–62.

[36] The former as argued by Ken R. Vincent, "Resurrection Appearances of Jesus as After-Death Communication," *Journal of Near-Death Studies* 30 (2012): 137–48, especially as indicated in the title of the article and the abstract (137, plus 146–47). Vincent and I dialogued in this same journal issue as to the form and uniqueness of Jesus's resurrection appearances, where Vincent again reiterated his position "that Jesus was raised from the dead" and that the available data from this event plus ADCs indicate the essential relatedness of these events and the reality of the afterlife. See Vincent, "Resurrection Appearances of Jesus as After-Death Communications: Rejoinder to Gary Habermas," *Journal of Near-Death Studies* 30 (2012): particularly 159, 165. Crossan appears to hold a view somewhat similar to that of Vincent, though his wording in this regard is a bit unclear at points ("Resurrection of Jesus," particularly 46–47).

The majority position appears to be that the various phenomena are *related or similar* while not being the same. To a large extent the difference between these positions could represent a matter of where the accent is placed in these discussions. Very notably on the more carefully nuanced side of the ledger is Dale Allison's 2005 work, *Resurrecting Jesus*. Allison notes quite carefully a list of highly evidenced characteristics of these apparition cases (294–95, also 279), and that many of these occurrences are "reminiscent" of New Testament appearances of Jesus (278–82, 285). Yet, Allison is also very careful to delineate the different characteristics between these two categories (283), holding that while the similarities between the modern apparitions and Jesus's appearances are very important, the former appear not to be the "Rosetta Stone" that links or interprets all of these experiences (285). Actually, it

These distinctions may be supported by various researchers or more likely left un-answered altogether.

Regarding the varieties of emphasis, these lesser-known PDV experiences and phenomena (to the extent that they occur at all) seem generally to be bodiless occur-rences rather than more bodily encounters.[37] A popular interpretation of PDVs is that deceased loved ones have sometimes appeared to their loved ones and friends in a disembodied state. As such, whether or not this was the intention of the reporter, some have asserted that this is similar to the form in which Jesus's real but nonbodily appearances may have occurred, similarly to objective vision theses. If this is the case, could these PDVs, ADCs, and resurrection appearances feasibly be viewed as the same species of phenomena? Of course, there could also be ramifications here not only concerning the literalness of Jesus's appearances, but especially pertaining to the *uniqueness* of these events too, if they in fact are also experienced by many others.

So, options that consider PDVs or other ADCs to be hallucinations or some similar variety of subjective, internal phenomena *without* external referents are not examined in this chapter. Such options are treated in detail along with other similar claims in the chapter in this volume on Jesus's appearances being interpreted as hallu-cinations or other subjective experiences.[38] These latter subjective cases are not at all

---

might be argued that "very little" follows from all the parallels and similarities that could be adduced (283). As the bottom line, Allison seems to say that Jesus's appearances are not the same as the apparitions, ADCs, or otherwise (283–85). In his later volume on the subject (*Resurrection of Jesus*, 210–26), Allison concludes similarly (esp. 222). What makes Allison's testimony more important, even strikingly so, is that he (along with several family members) has actually experienced several clear phenomena such as these described here (including specific PDVs), which he describes (*Resurrecting Jesus*, 275–77; *Resurrection of Jesus*, 215–16). Perry's view seems to fit well alongside the theses of Vincent and Allison in that Jesus's resurrection is quite closely related to "spontaneous apparitions of the dead" (*Easter Enigma*, 157, 171). However, Perry very carefully notes the many major, disanalogous distinctions between Jesus's appearances and the recent phenomena, ultimately seeming to arrive at a thesis that is very close to Keim's view or to the other objective vision theses pursued above regarding Jesus's unique appearances (125, 187–96), further illustrating the earlier point regarding the role of careful nuance.

[37] In spite of Allison's number of citations regarding the bodily element of these appari-tions (such as *Resurrecting Jesus*, 281nn327, 347), this is not the testimony of most research-ers into this phenomenon.

[38] Further evaluations of both hallucination scenarios with regard to Jesus's resur-rection appearances as well as an examination of Dewi Rees's studies on grief visions, including the relevant medical factors, can also be found in Bergeron and Habermas,

what is in view in this chapter, where the emphasis throughout has been on outward sightings, whether objective visions or more bodily appearances of Jesus. Nor will any potential evidential data in favor of PDVs or ADCs be investigated here, which is beyond the scope of this study.[39] The chief interest in this chapter has been placed more on the subjects of whether these more recent experiences are the same (or quite similar to) Jesus's resurrection appearances, the potential uniqueness of Jesus's sightings, and whether disembodied appearances like those that we have viewed are adequate to the task at hand.

Evaluating PDVs and Jesus's Appearances as the Same or Similar Phenomena

It is argued various ways in this study that Jesus's resurrection appearances are certainly examples of the afterlife in general. Further, throughout the New Testament the explicit Christian hope is that believers will be raised like Jesus, who became the "firstfruits" of the believer's resurrection.[40] It is undeniable from a Christian perspective that Jesus's resurrection and that of believers are rather intricately connected, manifesting various aspects of the afterlife as a whole. There is thus no effort to place a wedge between Jesus's resurrection and the afterlife: this comparison and relationship has strong connections on many levels.[41] In terms of our study, "Jesus's resurrection appearances would in some sense comprise after-death messages."[42]

At the same time, careful commentators who address this issue also note that Jesus's afterlife teachings and especially his resurrection appearances themselves reach far beyond other afterlife teachings and manifestations, such as the usually brief, far more general and generic reports already mentioned above. There are

---

"Resurrection of Jesus," esp. 158–64, 167–71. See also Gary R. Habermas, "Explaining Away Jesus' Resurrection: The Recent Revival of Hallucination Theories," *The Christian Research Journal* 23 (2001): 26–31, 47–49.

[39] Some similarities as well as critiques in these matters may also be found the appendix in volume 1 on NDE evidence.

[40] A few of the relevant New Testament texts include John 14:19; Acts 4:2; 1 Cor 6:14; 15:20–55; 2 Cor 4:14–18; 1 Pet 1:3–5; 1 John 3:2.

[41] William Strawson's remarkable volume *Jesus and the Future Life* (London: Epworth, 1970) pursues many of these inquiries throughout, such as chaps. 4–7.

[42] This is the initial sentence in the abstract of my response to Vincent in Gary R. Habermas, "Resurrection Appearances of Jesus as After-Death Communication: Response to Ken Vincent," *Journal of Near-Death Studies* 30 (2012): 149, see also 157.

certainly similarities to some PDVs and more general ADCs in both details as well as the overall sense of afterlife stories. Yet on these topics, Jesus's appearances indicate markedly unique characteristics when compared across the entire, broad subject. Several of these more exclusive aspects involved with Jesus's postmortem presence make rather difficult the identification that they comprise the same species of PDV phenomena.[43]

Earlier in this chapter, a half dozen major problems plus a few further issues were pointed out regarding the objective vision theory. These critiques, especially taken as a whole, point clearly in the direction of the bodily nature of Jesus's appearances being the best explanation of the New Testament teachings plus the additional developments in current research. We will summarize these concerns again briefly before emphasizing a couple of additional areas of difficulty with the intent of adapting these six considerations more narrowly to this second, somewhat-related hypothesis concerning PDVs and ADCs.

The initial critique of objective vision theories above was that both this as well as the traditional, bodily views of Jesus's appearances require the occurrence of supernatural events in ways that place them beyond the reach of the natural universe. Moreover, those who hold to objective visions, such as Keim, sometimes even acknowledge that such events would involve the miraculous actions of God. But incredibly, minus chiefly the embodied aspects, the heart of Christian theology could actually follow from disembodied appearances of Jesus, even though this thesis fails to account for the available data.

(1) Aspects of this initial observation could likewise still apply to differences with ADVs as well, such as Jesus's appearances being actual, *supernatural* events caused by God, and accompanied by incredible amounts of evidence. In other words, though not the New Testament teaching, those who hold the position that Jesus could have appeared as some type of ADV (or a series of these occasions) could also hold that Jesus Christ was nonetheless still the exclusive Son of God who offered himself as the exclusive path of salvation and similar doctrinal positions. This is a crucial point to make, in that the disembodied views can potentially still embrace much or even most of the unique New Testament theology, including Jesus Christ's deity and the

---

[43] See some of the additional ideas, such as the applicable background of Jesus's appearances, in Stephen Neill, *Christian Faith and Other Faiths* (Downers Grove, IL: InterVarsity, 1984), 27–29; Strawson, *Jesus and the Future Life*, 177–78, 196–97, 209–10, 225–30; Wright, *Resurrection of the Son of God*, 476–79.

miraculous nature of this event.[44] After all, as expressed earlier, disembodied appearances of the risen Jesus are still appearances.

(2) In volume 1 we collected almost two dozen primary and secondary historical arguments in favor of the empty tomb, with each one being drawn only from critical sources and arguments, as done with the minimal facts.[45] What happened to Jesus's body in the tomb is a strong consideration in terms of the nature of Jesus's appearances, for it would appear that the dead body that was buried was connected materially to the risen body that emerged from the tomb. Of course, other possibilities exist to explain this disappearance, and these options have been explored exhaustively by critical scholars during the past two centuries. But as seen chiefly in two chapters and elsewhere in this volume, the overwhelming testimony of recent researchers is that these suppositions have proved quite inadequate and increasingly unpopular over the years. As Allison emphasized after identifying several of these challenges to the empty tomb, "We have no reason to endorse any of these speculations, for which there is not a shred of evidence."[46] The inability of alternate theses against the empty tomb strengthens the likelihood that Jesus's resurrection was bodily in nature, driving a wedge between it and PDVs.

Given the general scholarly rejection of natural explanations for the empty tomb along with there being no decent evidence in their favor, the empty tomb is a remarkably well-evidenced factual challenge to Jesus's appearances being disembodied PDVs, since these are the majority of PDVs.[47] After all, would anyone think that even the strongest recent PDV cases would be accompanied by empty caskets in the ground?

This argument is weighty. In our 2012 dialogue on this topic, I argued that the empty tomb was one of the strong responses against Vincent's ADC thesis.

---

[44] Of course, on the view that Jesus's appearances were PDVs of some sort, the widespread similarity of PDVs could still diminish some of this uniqueness.

[45] While the number and quality of positive arguments favoring the historicity of the empty tomb were high enough to reach the most crucial standard for the minimal facts argument, this event was never placed in that list due to the much less important but still required secondary rule that a very high percentage of critical scholars needed to agree. Though that positive percentage of critical scholars who accept the historicity of this event has increased in recent years to 80 percent, as mentioned in volume 1, this was not deemed to be quite high enough.

[46] Allison, *Resurrecting Jesus*, 334.

[47] Allison expressed elsewhere there is "not a sliver of evidence" for other theses like these either (*Resurrecting Jesus*, 340).

He responded, "I prefer to leave the question of the empty tomb a mystery, as an empty tomb is simply unnecessary for Jesus's *spiritual* resurrection."[48] Of course he preferred not to respond—this argument *opposed* his position in a crucial place, leaving him without a comeback! Such a critique provides a powerful argument for the uniqueness of Jesus's resurrection appearances, which are not synonymous with PDV occurrences.

(3) The data indicate that the predominant Jewish view in the first century was that of bodily resurrection. While not overpowering by itself, this stance continues to add to the reasons why Jesus's appearances more likely point in the direction of bodily events rather than disembodied ones.

(4) Similarly, even if it is not the primary position of modern critical scholars themselves, the predominant notion among these specialists appears to be the recognition that the New Testament authors generally held that Jesus rose bodily. Thus, Jewish and canonical Christian views in the first century, including both anthropological and social factors in the New Testament, favor the notion of bodies being raised, both Jesus's and believers' alike. Such positions continue to favor Jesus's bodily appearances over against them having been the same as modern PDV notions.[49]

(5) Other supernatural visions in the New Testament (such as Acts 7:55–56; 10:9–16; 16:6–10; possibly 2 Cor 12:1–4; Rev 1:9–16) are clearly distinguished from the resurrection appearances. Each of these occasions, except for Stephen's martyrdom, occurred after Paul's conversion, but Paul stated clearly that his resurrection appearance was the last (1 Cor 15:8) and Luke seems to end the appearances with the ascension (Acts 1:1–3).

On the other hand, that the later, apparently bodiless appearances were of a different character is quite problematic for the view that Jesus's appearances were the same as PDVs according to the New Testament writers. In fact, on the PDV view, it should be quite difficult to distinguish the PDVs from these other spiritual visions at all. Why do the appearances end after forty days and why is Paul's appearance the very last one, thereby separating these events from the later disembodied occurrences?

---

[48] Vincent, "Rejoinder to Gary Habermas," 162.

[49] It has already been mentioned that bodily appearances are sometimes reported in the regular PDV literature as well; see Allison, *Resurrecting Jesus*, 281; Vincent, "Resurrection Appearances," 143; Perry, *Easter Enigma*, 182; though across the board, bodily PDVs appear to be much more uncommon. This will be addressed further in the critique below.

In short, the New Testament definitely considers these two phenomena to be quite different. What determines the difference here, if not that between bodily and non-bodily events? This distinction clearly seems to be the most likely difference. Once again, Jesus's appearances and PDVs are distinct.

(6) Moreover, the differing personalities regularly observed in normal human psychology would suggest that a number of the witnesses to Jesus's appearances most likely would have been less than satisfied had they been unable to touch or otherwise ascertain that Jesus was actually present with them. As mentioned, this normal human tendency is observed several times in the Gospels (Matt 28:9; Luke 24:36–43; John 20:17, 24–29). Without stronger confirmation than is usually gained from typical PDVs, it is difficult to understand the seeming group explosion out of the gate immediately after the resurrection appearances. If these experiences emanated from insubstantial manifestations alone, this simply seems to fall quite short of the immediate and especially the ongoing convictions that willingly placed at least many of these witnesses repeatedly in the line of fire and accounted for some deaths. Just like today, dispositions that tend in more empirical directions would appear to have much less assurance.[50]

Especially taken together, these six considerations favor bodily manifestations of the risen Jesus, making it far more likely than not that this comprised the original nature of the sightings. Given especially considerations such as the empty tomb without evidence to the contrary, the New Testament teaching of bodily appearances, the clear distinctions between visions and appearances, and personality differences, these appear to be a difficult case to overcome by the supposition of PDVs. Overall, it seems strong that Jesus's appearances and the ADCs above are not the same phenomena, though the best cases of the latter also evidence the afterlife.

A few additional considerations are likewise applicable to the differences between Jesus's appearances and PDVs that are not so crucial with objective visions. These will signify further distance between these experiences.

(7) Another indication that points away from comparisons between Jesus's resurrection and PDVs or ADCs being the same phenomena are the multiply attested data that Jesus regularly predicted a number of important details regarding

---

[50] Whatever is made of the gospel testimony, the sort of Jewish views and personalities involved in these circumstances would favor strong desires in at least some to touch Jesus, as actually observed in Matt 28:9; Luke 24:37–43; John 20:17, 24–28.

both his death and resurrection appearances on several occasions before his demise.[51] An initial glance might make it appear as if this simply specifies yet another odd characteristic of these events concerning Jesus. But it is actually far more momentous than this alone.

Jesus's predictions combine a number of important historical criteria that indicate the likelihood that these comments were indeed made by Jesus himself. For just a few examples of such details, these remarks are present in at least one early pre-Pauline creedal source and are multiply attested in a total of up to six independent sources. These predictions appear in multiple literary forms, which include the presence of Semitic elements and more than one example of embarrassing or surprise elements. Some of these predictions are also embedded in Son of Man passages, which are themselves multiply attested.[52]

These evidential elements help specify Jesus as occupying quite a different place among the claimed ADC cases where a comparison is being made. If Jesus indeed knew beforehand both the facts along with some details of these events at the end of his life, including the unlikely additional comment that he would rise from the dead afterward, this would be highly significant.[53] Such knowledge would indicate that Jesus was privy to wisdom and insight that others who may have seen their loved ones in a post-death manner presumably would not have understood in their own cases. But to know ahead of time such realities that actually did obtain later would seem to contribute additional reasons to think that Jesus was also a rather unique person,

---

[51] Examples include Mark 8:31–32; 9:31–32; 10:33–34; Matt 12:38–40; 16:1–4; John 2:18–22; cf. Mark 12:1–12; Luke 22:14–23; 1 Cor 11:23–26.

[52] For an impressive list of six affirmative reasons for Jesus's predictions, including a discussion of the attesting criteria, see Michael Licona, "Did Jesus Predict His Death and Vindication/Resurrection?," *Journal for the Study of the Historical Jesus* 8 (2010): 47–66. Cf. also the even more detailed accounts in Licona, *Resurrection of Jesus*, 284–302, 468–69. Licona also produces three arguments against Jesus having made these predictions (295–99), though he judges that the former half dozen positive reasons are much stronger as a cumulative case (300–302). These historical criteria are also discussed at length in volume 1 of this study.

[53] For example, many scholars have commented that Jesus could well have surmised that, like so many of the Old Testament prophets before him, he would probably sooner or later push the leaders too far, likely resulting in his own death. But to claim repeatedly and with such assurance that he alone would rise from the dead and be vindicated by God places him in an utterly unique category that had not been experienced by any of the former prophets, nor by anyone else for that matter.

in keeping with other singular claims regarding his person and nature. These factors taken together would once again signal a combination of indications that these rare events surrounding Jesus's life, death, and especially his appearances exceeded the cases in the PDV category. The results point further to Jesus's uniqueness. Indeed, no known individual has walked these paths previously, challenging even further the comparisons of sameness in these cases.[54]

(8) Even when compared to the vast amount of PDV and ADC literature, there do not appear to be any rivals to these combined resurrection reports of the risen Jesus. Consulting the myriads of modern PDV accounts does not seem to produce a parallel set of separate reports that is at all similar to these examples from Jesus. Further, modern similarities must be produced from among thousands of many diverse, cross-cultural accounts. While a distinct minority of PDV cases are both well documented and evidenced to certain extents, the vast majority are not only unevidenced but are very popularly obtained. Even with such a large body of PDV material, nothing is available that rivals even the known data that are critically derived concerning Jesus.

In fact, surprisingly, the ever-skeptical Dale Allison attests straightforwardly, "Nonetheless, I know of no close phenomenological parallel to the series of likely events as a whole. . . . Taken as a whole, this is, on any account, a remarkable, even extraordinary confluence of events and claims. If there is a good, substantial parallel to the entire series, I have yet to run across it."[55] Michael Perry, the former Cambridge University professor who both knew the nature of good research and strongly accepted the ADC thesis in cases beyond Jesus's resurrection appearances, still stated the matter similarly to Allison. In spite of "some striking similarities" to Jesus's appearances in the ADC literature, he still acknowledged, "All the same, it remains true that the overall scale of the Resurrection appearances is far greater than that of modern cases. . . . To find parallels for all the aspects of the Resurrection appearances, we have to *ransack* the literature of parapsychology and build up a composite picture from the most striking aspects of a number of cases."[56] Having stated this, Perry went on to assert, "There is no one modern case" like this, after which he listed elements concerning the appearances of Jesus that are very similar to those that we have mentioned above, including that Jesus "on several occasions" was "seen by a

---

[54] The hypotheses of those who have challenged these ideas are considered throughout this volume.

[55] Allison, *Resurrection of Jesus*, 346, cf. 344 for some similar thoughts.

[56] Perry, *Easter Enigma*, 188 (emphasis added).

group of his friends," talked, ate, stayed for a length of time, and disappeared. Even the "amount of conversation recorded . . . cannot be paralleled in a modern case."[57] This is an amazing concession that virtually spells the term "uniqueness" at every turn with regard to Jesus's appearances.[58]

As mentioned often, this is far from questioning the reality of PDVs. It is clear that these data deal with afterlife issues and sometimes do present some good evidence. Rather, the point evaluated here was to critically analyze the hypothesis that Jesus's postresurrection appearances and PDVs are the same phenomena or very nearly so. The assessment drawn from this comparison certainly moves more and more strongly away from any such scenario.

(9) One last line of reasoning moves totally away from historical and other empirical data to the field of logic and critical thinking. Central to the argument here is that there could be any number of exceedingly close similarities between Jesus's resurrection appearances and PDVs or other ADCs. But does such a list of similarities require that these occurrences be members of the exact same (or a very similar) class of events? Or may they more simply be related data—as in being varieties or indicators of an afterlife without sharing sameness?

Militating heavily against Jesus's appearances and PDVs being the same experiences is that even very close similarities do not prove sameness. The latter may be shown to be the case by normal comparisons that identify members of the same family, ethnic group, football team, student body, and so on. There are ways to indicate sameness, but mounting a number of close similarities can be quite superficial when not being done by more recognized means such as DNA and other chemical analyses, scientific testing, or legal records. Claiming sameness via tendencies, actions, or lining up events in a very similar manner does not necessarily indicate that these events, persons, or ideas are precisely the same.

For example, falling short of more minute means of testing or other types of inspection is one sort of comparison. However, an absolutely crucial question pertains to how many differences are also involved between these same reports, and how significant are these factors. Many differences can militate against the sameness thesis, and we have already noted a number of these vital distinctions between Jesus and the large body of ADC and PDV cases.

---

[57] Perry, 188–89.

[58] Cf. Neill's stunning comment regarding Jesus's uniqueness as compared to the other major world religious founders (*Christian Faith and Other Faiths*, 286, see also 23, 125, 284).

There are many examples in this last category. The American and French Revolutions may share some startling similarities without being the same events, let alone even from the same continent. Two historical tyrants that are amazingly alike in different parts of the world or even in different centuries are not the same and are scarcely related, though they may be quite similar. Two animals, insects, stars, or events may manifest amazingly similar traits without ranking anywhere near the same family lines. Doctoral dissertations may reveal ideas where collusion or plagiarism may be suspected, while still being proven later that nothing of the sort occurred.

So it is with our thesis. As has been maintained from the beginning, the resurrection appearances, PDVs, ADCs, and other afterlife categories, such as NDEs, can be quite amazingly similar at points without bearing the same DNA. The overall logical point is that a lineup of similarities does not prove that they are the same phenomena. Similarities, even close ones, are easy to show; sameness is not shown to be the case without more specific tests and rules. And again, how many differences are there and how significant are they?[59]

Along with the many similarities, it has also been argued that there are many significant differences between Jesus's resurrection appearances and PDVs/ADCs. Further, a number of these distinctions involve various categories that indicate substantial areas that fail to line up, as mentioned in this chapter. Neither are the similarities as close as often imagined.

These nine critiques plus a few possible secondary applications involve unique aspects that are also relevant to the questions here. Numerous strong indications were also mentioned that while Jesus's appearances to some extent would comprise PDVs to his disciples, they must be categorized differently than the other ADC accounts. Again, neither PDVs nor ADCs need be denied, and some are strongly confirmed. None of these categories or other similar possibilities should be denied in this discussion. Rather, the question concerns whether Jesus's appearances indicate a difference *in kind*, and this appears strongly to be the case, and from several angles.

What follows from a brief summary of these previous arguments? The initial consideration asserted that if bodily resurrection appearances of Jesus occurred, especially when accompanied by other relevant data, the objective vision theory most obviously would be mistaken. Six arguments were presented to evidence these claims.

---

[59] Examples of relevant or similar informal logical fallacies can include hasty generalization and its subcategory of biased statistics or false cause. See Charles W. Kegley and Jacquelyn Ann Kegley, *Introduction to Logic* (Columbus, OH: Merrill, 1978), 156–58.

The embodied scenario would also go a long way toward arguing that Jesus's appearances were not just different, but they were part of a unique pattern of an overall exceptional life of ideas and events confirmed by a significant amount of data. The sources claim that Jesus's life contained a number of exceptional wonders—forgiving sin, healing the sick, exorcisms, natural miracles, some of the greatest ethical and theological teachings ever, proclamations of his own deity, and many other phenomena of various sorts often agreed to by critical scholars.[60] These were capped off by arguably the greatest event of all time: Jesus's resurrection, which Jesus himself had predicted in detail and later confirmed with his many bodily post-resurrection appearances.

Attention was then directed to the ADCs, with nine arguments pointing out the significant distance between Jesus's resurrection appearances and especially the PDVs in particular. Other aspects of Jesus's uniqueness and worldview could also be pursued, as just mentioned, further separating Jesus from the recipients of PDVs and ADCs, but that remains for the final volume in this study.[61]

In addressing the uniqueness of Jesus's life including his appearances, comparisons have been made here between Jesus's appearances and various examples of the PDV and ADC material. However, the New Testament scenario presents stronger evidential aspects than the PDV material as well.[62] Other critical researchers argue

---

[60] Both Richard Swinburne in *The Resurrection of God Incarnate* (Oxford: Clarendon, 2003), esp. part 2; and Timothy McGrew and Lydia McGrew, "The Argument from Miracles: A Cumulative Case for the Resurrection of Jesus," in *The Blackwell Companion to Natural Theology*, ed. William Lane Craig and J. P. Moreland (West Sussex: Wiley-Blackwell, 2012), particularly 620–42, argue carefully how the technical importance of factors such as those listed above, along with still others, indicate how Jesus's life was unique in terms of other cases.

[61] For a few examples, see Gary R. Habermas, *The Risen Jesus and Future Hope* (Lanham, MD: Rowman & Littlefield, 2003), chaps. 2–10; Norman Anderson, *Christianity and World Religions: The Challenge of Pluralism* (Downers Grove, IL: InterVarsity, 1984), chaps. 2–4; Kenneth Richard Samples, *7 Truths that Changed the World: Discovering Christianity's Most Dangerous Ideas* (Grand Rapids: Baker, 2012), chaps. 1–10, 13–14; Stephen Neill, *The Supremacy of Jesus* (Downers Grove, IL: InterVarsity, 1984), chaps. 3–4, 6.

[62] Some will object that the Gospels are overly physical in their representations and portrayals of Jesus's resurrection appearances, perhaps in order to combat less than physical views. However, first, we have argued in volume 1 of this study as well as elsewhere that there are strong grounds for rejecting these concerns and for accepting the general Gospel depictions, citing many reasons that are opposed to such a doubtful stance. Many very influential scholarly commentators, including among them the likes of Martin Hengel, James D. G. Dunn, N. T. Wright, Richard Bauckham, Larry Hurtado, Robert Gundry, Michael

that the appearance to Paul was not bodily like the appearances that occurred to the disciples, the women, or others during what Acts states was a period of forty days.[63]

However one takes Paul's appearance, many unique aspects vis-à-vis the combined PDV and ADC reports still emerge.[64] The three secondary accounts of Paul's conversion in Acts 9:1–9; 22:6–16; and 26:12–18 present some out of the ordinary details that are rather uncommon in the PDV material. For examples, the extreme brightness of the sun (9:3; 22:6; 26:13), Paul's being blinded by the light for three days (9:8–9; 22:11), along with Paul and the other men with him falling to the ground (26:14a). Though not entirely unique, that Paul's companions witnessed many but not all of the items is rare in the literature (9:7; 22:9; 26:13).[65]

Licona, Darrell Bock, Ben Witherington, Craig Keener, Craig Blomberg, and many others, have noted one or more of the reasons for accepting the New Testament teachings here. Many details and sources are also cited throughout this study and elsewhere regarding these scholars and others who have argued, often in much detail, in favor of various portions of this argument. Second, a number of major arguments of a comparative nature put forth in this chapter do not even rely on the Gospel appearance narratives. Third, much of the ADC and PDV literature is very popular in nature, often citing personal testimonies and other stories as straightforward reports without any attending evidence, clear citation of data, or confirming testimony. Given that much of this recent material has been stated rather than having been argued carefully, it is hardly appropriate to reject evidenced Gospel testimony while not requiring appropriate backup arguments from those other sources to which the Gospels are being compared.

[63] See the various discussions in this study regarding the nature of Paul's resurrection appearance, especially the detailed defense of his appearance in volume 1.

[64] See especially note 24 and the surrounding material above. Compare the thoughts mentioned above by Crossan and Reed, among other critical scholars, on the primary New Testament evidence favoring bodily appearances, including that to Paul himself (*In Search of Paul*, 6–10, 133–35, 173–74, 296, 341–45). These researchers argue that the three narratives of Paul's appearance in Acts are secondary, while the firsthand accounts in Paul's writings do not give this impression. Moreover, the likelihood that Paul's writings also hold to bodily notions of Jesus's appearances changes the entire picture. As noted above, Crossan has even pointed out that his position on these matters is not much different from N. T. Wright's arguments (Crossan, "Resurrection of Jesus in Its Jewish Context," 29, 34–56; Crossan, "Historical Event or Theological Explanation," 24–25; Crossan, "Bodily-Resurrection Faith," in Stewart, *Resurrection of Jesus*, 175–76).

[65] In doing a synoptic comparison of these three accounts, atheist New Testament professor Gerd Lüdemann finds several historical and accurate reminiscences in these three reports. These include that the event occurred near the city of Damascus, which he describes as being "historically accurate," that it involved Paul the church persecutor, that the appearance of the bright light is described as being brighter than the sun, and that Paul was

So even for those who might question this or that aspect of the Gospel appearance narratives, the various New Testament texts present more than one example of each of the following scenarios: group appearances reported to both smaller and larger groups, instances of touching Jesus including his own offer to do so, eating together, Jesus communicating in spoken words, being seen by men and women alike both at different times of the day and the evening, appearing to unbelievers who converted to the faith when they saw the risen Jesus, and so on. The consensus even among critical scholars is that the exceptionally early creedal accounts of these details were proclaimed within the brief time span of a few months to a year or so after Jesus's crucifixion, and then were written down beginning just a couple of decades later in Paul's Epistles, with likely earlier sources behind each of the Gospels.[66]

Conclusion

This chapter considered two alternative views to what might be called the classical, orthodox understanding of Jesus's resurrection appearances. Both theses generally hold that Jesus actually did rise from the dead, though in less than a full bodily sense. Hence, when considered in this manner, neither of these options is a naturalistic hypothesis.

---

blinded. Moreover, Paul's traveling companions also observed some of the relevant details, with the supposition that Paul is the one who saw the glorified Jesus, along with the existence and role of the prophet Ananias. The accounts agree closely enough with Paul's own statements in his epistles and are multiply attested by the relevant texts, with the result being Paul's call by God to missionary service as the apostle to the gentiles. Lüdemann does not think that differences in the texts are due to Luke's carelessness or to any invention, though he thinks there is a legendary backstory that those who despise God are punished. See Gerd Lüdemann, *Early Christianity according to the Traditions in Acts: A Commentary*, trans. John Bowden (Minneapolis: Fortress, 1987), 106–10, 239–40, 255–56. Lüdemann also comments that studies that "defend the historical reliability of Acts" have increased. As such, "Acts remains an important source for the history of early Christianity" because "many of the traditions which it uses are historically reliable and enrich our knowledge of the earliest Christianity in addition to the letters of Paul." All the issues have not been solved, by any means; there remain issues to be worked out, especially in places where there are no backup data (17). For further comparison here, see especially Craig S. Keener's excellent four-volume commentary, *Acts: An Exegetical Commentary* (Grand Rapids: Baker, 2012, 2013, 2014, 2015), esp. the portions on Paul's conversion in 9:1–9; 22:6–11; and 26:12–18.

[66] See the multiple chapters in volume 1 especially on this subject plus some recent trends in the study of the Gospels.

The two positions support notions that can be fairly close in some of their ideas. The initial stance, that Jesus actually appeared as a more or less disembodied presence of some sort to reassure and commission his followers in ministry has a long prior history and is often termed the objective vision theory. These concepts can be found especially in the writings of a number of the nineteenth-century German liberal scholars, the best known of whom was Theodor Keim. The view has even postulated or at least allowed the possibility of what might be termed partially embodied appearances. As a rival to theses involving hallucinations, Keim and others offered some of the best rejoinders to this naturalistic option while acknowledging that their position required supernatural action.

Responding to this initial approach involves evaluating which thesis best fits the known circumstances. Approaching the question from more than one angle, six critiques were aimed at this initial scenario, beginning with the thesis that the objective vision theory was also supernatural in nature and could potentially involve the truth of the entire Christian worldview. The historical case favoring Jesus's empty tomb is a powerful corrective. The first-century Jewish majority view of bodily resurrection of the dead plus the New Testament Christian teachings of Jesus's bodily appearances also argued against the stance of objective visions. The New Testament distinction between Jesus's resurrection appearances and religious visions from God argues for something more substantial than Jesus making himself known as a disembodied presence alone. Moreover, the strong human desire in many personalities to determine these sorts of questions in empirical terms, as the Gospel narratives indicate, points in the same direction of at least some of the disciples confirming Jesus's actual presence. Such outlooks often require more palpable signs than are available in order to account for the radical changes in Jesus's followers. For these several reasons, then, a disembodied presence as presented in the objective vision thesis does not come close to being the best fit here.

The second hypothesis considered in this chapter concerns reports sometimes known as post-death visions or after-death communications. Here persons claim to have seen their recently deceased loved ones in what are most often very brief visits. Occasionally, it is thought that these scenarios best explain the nature of Jesus's resurrection appearances, either more rarely as the same events or as similar ones in the afterlife category. Scientific studies have argued that these experiences seem to occur more often than may be thought and are occasionally even reported as having been veridical in nature, such as by being seen by multiple persons at a time. Whereas the emphasis in the previous discussion was on the empirical fit of the views, the heart of this second discussion may be chiefly concerned with whether Jesus's appearances were a unique set of events or a specific species within the ADC and PDV family.

Refining the six critiques just raised above regarding the objective vision view allowed further honing of this response with regard to the ADC and PDV scenarios. These more recent theses still require an afterlife, though usually bodiless. The empty tomb is especially difficult for these scenarios, since it points more strongly to bodily appearances, given that natural alternatives are rarely thought to apply. This makes bodily appearances of Jesus far more likely to have occurred than spiritual visions of either of these varieties, given that there would be no necessary connection between an empty gravesite and more ethereal appearances. But since the bodies of loved ones are still buried when their disembodied PDVs were reported, this points out the serious point of separation between Jesus's appearances and PDVs or ADCs. Further, that the New Testament clearly separates Jesus's appearances from later visions (which sound much like PDVs!) plus the frequent human desire to affirm these things empirically for longer-lasting conviction is also quite difficult to explain in the ADC scenarios.

Additionally, the PDV and ADC suppositions are beset by still additional and serious issues beyond these initial six. Three more weaknesses were mentioned here for a total of nine critiques. Especially given the evidential considerations mentioned earlier—that Jesus predicted his death, resurrection, and exaltation ahead of time—is another unique indicator, this time in terms of his having exceptional prior knowledge concerning his worldview, which placed him in a singular position unoccupied by any other potential PDV "visitor."

Moreover, the New Testament accounts of Jesus's appearances, including the evidentially supported ones in particular, involved far more episodes with Jesus characterized by longer visits with far lengthier discussions than the entire field of PDVs can assemble together. As Perry (supporting a PDV thesis) was cited above, "The overall scale of the Resurrection appearances is far greater than that of modern cases."[67] This amazing concession states powerfully the uniqueness of Jesus's appearances. Allison offers a very similar comment to Perry's with regard to the uniqueness of the entire field of resurrection data.

Moreover, in spite of the similarities between Jesus's resurrection appearances and the ADC and PDV literature, parallels and resemblances certainly cannot determine

---

[67] Perry, *Easter Enigma*, 188.

that these events are the same, or even that they are necessarily of the same general family, though they would involve the category of the afterlife. A myriad of living creatures, circumstances, and events in the world can be quite incredibly similar on a number of levels while having been literally centuries or continents apart! Besides, the many incredible differences between Jesus's appearances and the PDVs and ADCs indicate that they are distinct occurrences.

One further matter should be mentioned at this point. It has been mentioned several times that both objective vision theories and PDV and ADC hypotheses would involve actual afterlife cases. However, if either view considered in this chapter (or Jesus's resurrection appearances as well) were proposed as a natural hypothesis apart from an afterlife, it would simply push that thesis into the category of hallucinations or similar subjective views. Hallucinations and their kin are treated at length in this volume, so they are not treated in this chapter. Leaving this natural matter aside, then, and as strange as this may seem, even if the objective vision thesis or PDVs and ADCs were true, virtually all of the chief Christian message could potentially follow, except of course for the bodily nature of Jesus's appearances. For example, the gospel message of Jesus's deity, death, resurrection, the truth of eternity, and so on could all be just as true, emanating from a less than physical body. Thus, while the effort here has been a defense of Jesus's unique bodily appearances, this last conclusion ought not be missed in the exchange of ideas.

In sum, numerous predominant features favor the New Testament proclamation that Jesus's appearances were both bodily events as well as being unique manifestations on a much larger scale as well. This is the case even though other phenomena could also indicate the truth of an afterlife.

17

Resurrection Agnosticism

Anoteworthy trend has appeared to become a more prominent option in recent years, though it has been evaluated and addressed very rarely. In this chapter we will be concentrating on agnostic positions in current scholarship, building a series of a half dozen steps that will, in subsequent chapters, lead to questions of what, if anything, may have occurred to Jesus in his death and afterward.[1] Is it possible to keep moving to a final view on these matters, or are scholars justified in more or less stopping along the route at a particular critical position that declares that no further moves can (or will) be made? At first glance, this latter position might appear to be an eminently defensible position without very many pitfalls. But appearances are not always what they seem to be!

Agnostic Default Positions

As we have discussed, the vast majority of recent critical scholars at least allow for and usually even accept what some might consider a surprisingly strong amount of known historical data surrounding the end of Jesus's life and the very earliest

---

[1] In several places along the way, it will be very helpful to mention or note atheistic notions, for various reasons, but these will be kept to a minimum. This inclusion will hopefully also augment some particular points being made here.

preaching of the gospel message. For example, virtually all scholars, whatever their personal beliefs, espouse or at least concede that Jesus died by Roman crucifixion, which was followed by his disciples experiencing grief and disillusionment at his death. Although the scholarly acceptance rates drop somewhat on the next two here, it is still accepted by a majority of commentators that Jesus was buried in a tomb and that it was later found empty.

Then, essentially all scholars think that the disciples experienced what they believed to be appearances of the risen Jesus. As a result, these believers were transformed, even being willing to die for their faith. Very soon afterward, they began to proclaim the death and resurrection of Jesus Christ, and the church was founded on this gospel message. Even a few former skeptics, such as James the brother of Jesus and then Paul, became believers after they believed that they had seen the risen Jesus.

In earlier chapters we divided these historical data into two slightly differentiated lists. A few of these particulars were singled out and termed the minimal facts due to the presence of two factors: each one was determined as being heavily evidenced, and each was also recognized as historical by virtually all critical scholars who work in the relevant fields.[2] These particular minimal facts will be employed later to argue for the historicity of Jesus's post-crucifixion appearances. The remainder of the facts referenced above are part of our slightly longer list made up of events that are almost always recognized by scholars due to their historical support, though not always with the same degree of recognition.

These agreements among recent critical commentators are intriguing. On the surface, these parameters appear to support, at least in outline, the New Testament teaching that Jesus appeared again after he was raised from the dead. At a minimum, they point to exceptionally important occurrences that can be neither dismissed nor

---

[2] There are a considerable number and variety of recent critical scholars who provide their own lists of historical facts that parallel (often quite closely) this list, with some frequently exceeding the number of events on our list. Some examples include Jesus Seminar founder Robert W. Funk, *Honest to Jesus* (New York: HarperCollins, 1996), 32–34, 40, 237, 239; highly skeptical scholar James D. Tabor, *The Jesus Dynasty: The Hidden History of Jesus, His Royal Family, and the Birth of Christianity* (New York: Simon & Schuster, 2006), 228, 310–11; self-styled liberal E. P. Sanders, *The Historical Figure of Jesus* (London: Penguin, 1993), 10–14, 278–80; and New Testament scholar Luke Timothy Johnson, *The Real Jesus: The Misguided Quest for the Historical Jesus and the Truth of the Traditional Gospels* (New York: HarperCollins, 1996), 119–36.

ignored easily. One such indication of this tendency is that only a minority of scholars actually hold that naturalistic hypotheses can account comfortably for the data.[3]

So, to repeat, it is virtually unanimous that critical scholars hold that Jesus's disciples *thought* they had witnessed appearances of the risen Jesus. But how many think that the disciples *really* saw Jesus in at least some form? From my recent and ongoing survey of the majority of critical scholars in relevant fields who have addressed these questions, a strong number do accept that Jesus's disciples actually saw him in some sense after his death by crucifixion, but this will be addressed in detail in a later chapter. But further, the majority scholarly view is that Jesus probably appeared in a bodily manner![4] While it is absolutely true that surveys do not indicate that any particular position is correct, an accurate assessment regarding the contemporary theological outlook may well provide at least some clues as to where recent scholars think the *data* point.

During the past 200 or more years of critical theological trends, this is perhaps the closest that the predominant view has come to embracing at least the general New Testament teaching on the nature of Jesus's resurrection body.[5] One obvious question is why more scholars do not willingly and openly acknowledge their recognition or belief that Jesus was raised from the dead and actually was seen afterward. Why are so many caveats sometimes added to the discussion that one wonders if the scholar meant what they seemed to say in their works? Moreover, when pressed, why do some scholars at least appear to take steps backward, ending their comments by asserting something like, "Well, when all is said and done, we cannot really be sure what happened. Sure, the disciples had real experiences of

---

[3] Of course, this also requires that these critical researchers provide clear indications that they hold these positions! A couple of decades ago, there was a bit of an upturn of interest in these alternative theses; see Gary R. Habermas, "The Late Twentieth-Century Resurgence of Naturalistic Responses to Jesus' Resurrection," *Trinity Journal* 22 (2001): esp. 179–96. However, the outlook and interest at present seem to have noticeably slowed.

[4] Gary R. Habermas, "Mapping the Recent Trend toward the Bodily Resurrection Appearances of Jesus in Light of Other Prominent Critical Positions," in *The Resurrection of Jesus: John Dominic Crossan and N. T. Wright in Dialogue*, ed. Robert B. Stewart (Minneapolis: Fortress, 2006), esp. 78–92.

[5] One may, of course, disagree with my survey of recent scholars or otherwise dispute these trends. But if my count is anywhere close to being accurate, the percentages are high enough that they would have to be mistaken by quite a large margin for these general observations to be overturned.

some sort, but we should perhaps just leave the issue there and not attempt to say what actually occurred."

My suggestion brings us to the heart of this chapter. This latter move sometimes appears to be made for a variety of reasons, many of which seem to be closely related. Some scholars simply do not want to be "pinned down" to a particular view. Others perhaps do not want to sound overly conservative, especially when they are in the presence of their colleagues. On the other hand, maybe still others do not wish to be known as "liberals" either! Peer pressure of various kinds is always a strong motivator. Still other scholars do not want faith or theology to be linked too closely to historical findings, even if they actually believe in Jesus's resurrection. And perhaps some simply think that the evidence cannot be pressed beyond the initial recognition that the disciples' had real experiences.

One last puzzle piece needs to be added. Rather intriguingly, in spite of these caveats that are often heard in public dialogue or in private conversation, comparatively few scholars appear to publish their position if it is agnostic, or at least overtly so.[6] On the other hand, other scholars who may even be positive toward either the resurrection appearances or their bodily form sometimes seem to lack enthusiasm in airing that view, even if their research provides support for these views.

Here is a potential suggestion worth considering. It is certainly arguable that although agnosticism may not be the first option for a scholar to set forth, it still may serve well as a "fallback" statement for those who perhaps feel that they have gone as far as they can in the direction of historicity, for reasons such as those just given. In other words, when scholars are pushed for specific details that indicate where they stand, some more clearly defend the historicity of the resurrection appearances, while others migrate to a different response. For the latter, then, the agnostic position often functions as a sort of default setting.[7] In this chapter we will present an overview of the agnostic position, followed by a general critique.

---

[6] Habermas, "Mapping the Recent Trend," 81–82, 91.

[7] This was also my conclusion in "Mapping the Recent Trend," 204n60. As a rather incredible and insightful aside, it is always amazing when this sort of specific clarification is requested, such that those who move to the conservative side, or who opt to present arguments for their position, are often termed "apologists" or perhaps even viewed as nonscholars, while those who take the agnostic stance are thought of as being "careful" or "scholarly" thinkers!

The Agnostic Position on Jesus's Resurrection

In keeping with these comments, it may not be surprising that there are relatively few *developed* agnostic positions on the resurrection appearances that have appeared during the past few decades. More frequently, we find a brief comment here or there that may indicate more questions.[8]

Willi Marxsen

One exception is Willi Marxsen's nuanced resurrection research, including his mostly slight changes of emphasis over the years. In older treatments that manifested Rudolf Bultmann's strong and ongoing influence, Marxsen favored the importance of faith and interpretation while downplaying history as a means to faith. In the process, Marxsen favored a natural understanding of Jesus's resurrection, such that the actual occurrence was not at all necessary for faith. If it were, he stated, then *all* Christians would have to see Jesus even today in order to make faith possible![9]

---

[8] For instance, G. T. Eddy pleads, "Let us allow more room . . . for a reverent agnosticism about bodies and tombs." See Eddy, "The Resurrection of Jesus Christ: A Consideration of Professor Cranfield's Argument," *Expository Times* 101 (1990): 329. Sometimes it is even difficult to know if agnosticism is what the scholar(s) is implying. One example of this possibility is the comment by Richard A. Burridge and Graham Gould that they are not sure of the sense in which Jesus was raised; see their volume, *Jesus Then and Now* (Grand Rapids: Eerdmans, 2004), 208. But they may simply be saying that Jesus *was* raised in some sense, but that they are not prepared to give specific empirical details. However, Dale Allison spends more creative time than most in musing on the sense in which it might be said that Jesus rose from the dead. See Dale C. Allison Jr., *Resurrecting Jesus: The Earliest Christian Tradition and Its Interpreters* (London: T&T Clark, 2005), 364–75.

[9] Willi Marxsen, *The Resurrection of Jesus of Nazareth*, trans. Margaret Kohl (Philadelphia: Fortress, 1970), esp. 88–97. An earlier essay by Marxsen was a forerunner while featuring its own phase of development: "The Resurrection of Jesus as a Historical and Theological Problem," in *The Significance of the Message of the Resurrection for Faith in Jesus Christ*, ed. C. F. D. Moule (Naperville, IL: Allenson, 1968), 15–50. There were a few themes in this earlier essay that were emphasized less frequently in later works by Marxsen, such as intriguing references to the empty tomb as history but without thereby getting from it to the resurrection (24–25), or to the early "pre-Pauline" creedal material regarding the resurrection witness, as found in specific New Testament texts such as 1 Cor 15:3–8; Luke 24:34; and even the Acts passages in 9:17 and 13:31 (26). Further, Marxsen emphasizes the sense in which history establishes the truth of Jesus's disciples believing

Still, there was much room for an agnostic stance here. For example, we can only get back to Peter's faith, not somehow "behind it" to the nature of any actual events themselves. Regarding those events, we can never really know what occurred—that information is "impossible" to obtain.[10] In a much later volume on the same subject, perhaps reflecting the changed scholarly climate more in favor of the resurrection, Marxsen rather strikingly concluded that he did not know whether Jesus appeared in a subjective or an objective manner.[11]

Peter Carnley

Peter Carnley's version of agnosticism is of a different sort. Like virtually all contemporary scholars, including Marxsen, he is sure that the disciples at least thought that they had seen the risen Jesus, who was alive after his death: "It seems clear enough that, on the basis of these alleged experiences, the disciples were convinced that they had seen the raised Christ."[12] Later he reaffirms this: "Meanwhile, there is no doubt that the first disciples interpreted the Easter visions or appearances as signs of the heavenly presence of Christ."[13]

---

that they saw the risen Jesus (17, 21–22, 36, and esp. 31), along with Paul's faith being based on him seeing the risen Jesus (22–23, 27, cf. 33). Marxsen's last emphasis on the importance of sight almost seems to suggest as if it were different for Paul and the disciples (in Lessing's terms) because they were contemporary with the occurrences themselves! But more fideistic themes that reverberate throughout his later thoughts on the resurrection can also be found here, like history being unable to establish either the resurrection or Jesus's appearances (18–19, 21, 25, 28, 31, 38, 48, cf. 36). Last, while subjective visions "cannot be excluded," we must not get back into the type of thinking that involves studying history to validate faith (28). Hans Grass's view of objective visions must also be rejected, again because it mixes history and "faith alone prevails" (29). Incidentally but not surprisingly, Marxsen's comment about subjective visions being possible rather parallels Rudolf Bultmann's similar thoughts in "New Testament and Mythology," in *Kerygma and Myth: A Theological Debate*, ed. Hans Werner Bartsch, trans. Reginald H. Fuller (New York: Harper & Row, 1961), 42.

[10] Marxsen, *Resurrection of Jesus of Nazareth*, 96–97, 119, 126, 152.

[11] Willi Marxsen, *Jesus and Easter: Did God Raise the Historical Jesus from the Dead?*, trans. Victor Paul Furnish (Nashville: Abingdon, 1990), 70–74.

[12] Peter Carnley, *The Structure of Resurrection Belief* (Oxford: Clarendon, 1987), 64.

[13] Carnley, 246.

However, while historical investigation does have some value, it is ultimately inconclusive regarding the resurrection.[14] The major theme of the volume, emphasized throughout his text, is Carnley's thesis that Christians have internal confirmation of the resurrected Jesus. Such assurance is due not to the rigors of historical research but to the witness of the Holy Spirit.[15] So Carnley's agnosticism is with regard to the unsure results of historical investigation rather than the truth of the resurrection itself.

A. J. M. Wedderburn

While Marxsen and Carnley are examples of scholars who hardly employ historical investigation at all, the most developed historical treatments of resurrection agnosticism are the theses of A. J. M. Wedderburn and Bart Ehrman. With a more clearly stated, robust appreciation of historical matters than most of the others in this category, Wedderburn begins his treatment of the question by clearly stating that many of the key resurrection questions *are* historical in nature. Examples of such historical questions include what happened to Jesus's body, whether or not various naturalistic theories apply to the empty tomb or appearance accounts, and whether particular events are necessary to explain what happened.[16]

After all, we need to do something with the claims "that human eyes have seen something and human ears have heard something."[17] Accordingly, Wedderburn at least lists, and sometimes affirms, data similar to that which we mentioned at the outset of this chapter, beginning with the central dictum of most scholars, whatever their ultimate views on the historical nature of the resurrection: "It is an indubitable historical datum that sometime, somehow the disciples came to believe that they had seen the risen Jesus."[18]

However, after looking at a host of subjects, Wedderburn concludes his study by supporting the verdict of a "reverent agnosticism." While there are good data that

---

[14] Carnley, 72, 95, 225–26, 264.

[15] Carnley, 248–65, esp. 248–49, 256, 259–65.

[16] A. J. M. Wedderburn, *Beyond Resurrection* (Peabody, MA: Hendrickson, 1999), 12–19, 21–22, 38.

[17] Wedderburn, 15.

[18] Wedderburn, 13.

favor the resurrection appearances, and the naturalistic alternatives are problematic (perhaps even clearly so), a supernatural event like a resurrection or the resulting afterlife are difficult barriers to overcome. The result is that skeptics will probably not be convinced by historical arguments. So the verdict is "Not proven."[19]

In a touching discussion of emotional matters following this verdict, Wedderburn admits that this leaves some very difficult pastoral problems with those who need assistance in areas of guilt, suffering, bereavement, and fear of the unknown, given a faith that is agnostic and "vulnerable at all points." One might be tempted to tell such hurting persons that they will be reunited with their loved ones after death, which would presumably be very comforting and otherwise helpful, but can this be affirmed in good conscience?[20]

Bart Ehrman

Bart Ehrman has described himself along the atheistic-agnostic continuum.[21] On the central datum of contemporary critical scholars, for example, "we can say with complete certainty that some of his disciples at some later time insisted that . . . he soon appeared to them, convincing them that he had been raised from the dead." Explaining further, "Historians, of course, have no difficulty whatsoever speaking about the belief in Jesus's resurrection, since this is a matter of public record. For it is a historical fact that some of Jesus's followers came to believe that he had been raised from the dead soon after his execution."[22]

Still, Ehrman thinks that as we work beyond these crucial questions, we also get into areas that we *cannot* know about the resurrection appearances. For instance, "we cannot be completely certain, historically, that Jesus's tomb was actually empty." Further, as historians, "we cannot say that Jesus was actually raised from the dead." Yet, each of these beliefs can be "affirmed" by faith.[23]

So here we find ourselves in a bit of a quandary between what we can know and what we cannot know. In fact, in one of his later books, Ehrman uses these subtitles

[19] Wedderburn, esp. 95–98, but also 134, 153, 218–19, 221, 225.

[20] Wedderburn, esp. 221–26.

[21] Bart D. Ehrman, *Did Jesus Exist? The Historical Argument for Jesus of Nazareth* (New York: HarperCollins, 2012), particularly 98–132, 140–41, and chap. 5.

[22] Bart D. Ehrman, *Jesus: Apocalyptic Prophet of the New Millennium* (Oxford: Oxford University Press, 1999), 230–31.

[23] Ehrman, 229. The sources below contain other references here.

for two chapters that deal with the resurrection. For examples, on the "cannot know" side, Ehrman has serious doubts regarding the historicity of Jesus's burial in Joseph of Arimathea's private tomb, and he also notes that he has changed his mind regarding the empty tomb.[24] As expected, however, we obviously cannot know historically that Jesus was actually raised from the dead.[25]

But quite surprisingly, Ehrman does not claim to be saying "that historians can use the historical disciplines in order to demonstrate that Jesus was *not* raised from the dead."[26] Stated simply, historians just cannot demonstrate the case "one way or the other."[27] As a result, and even more incredibly, Ehrman no longer subscribes to "any" particular naturalistic theory of the resurrection appearances, especially since all of these alternative theories are more likely than a miracle.[28] Yet, believers can always believe in the resurrection and appearances by faith.[29]

However, having said this about not choosing a particular naturalistic theory, the next chapter in Ehrman's book *How Jesus Became God*, entitled "What We

---

[24] Bart D. Ehrman, *How Jesus Became God: The Exaltation of a Jewish Preacher from Galilee* (New York: HarperCollins, 2014), examples on 7, 141–43, 151–69, 173–74, 184–86. Ehrman used to accept the empty tomb but now does not. The change of mind on this issue is noted on 164. For a number of relevant, detailed responses to Ehrman in a book released simultaneously by Zondervan (a sister publishing company to HarperCollins), written by a number of highly trained New Testament scholars (with additional endorsements by Richard Bauckham and Larry Hurtado), see Michael F. Bird, ed., *How Jesus Became God: The Real Origins of Belief in Jesus' Divine Nature. A Response to Bart Ehrman* (Grand Rapids: Zondervan, 2014). For a response specifically to the issue mentioned here of Ehrman's change on Joseph's burial tomb by a specialist in this area, that also includes a brief treatment of the empty tomb, see the chapter by Craig A. Evans, "Getting the Burial Traditions and Evidences Right," 71–93.

[25] Ehrman, *How Jesus Became God*, 132, 143–44, 148–49.

[26] Ehrman, 132.

[27] Ehrman, 146–48

[28] Ehrman, 164–65, 173, 186; also, Ehrman, *Did Jesus Exist?*, 315–16.

[29] Ehrman, *How Jesus Became God*, 132, 143, 150. However, just as Ehrman points out from time to time that too many people pontificate on subjects in which they are not trained (e.g., *Did Jesus Exist?*, 2–3, 14–30, 167, 194–96, 268), he should *never* have offered the comment that "religious faith and historical knowledge are two different ways of 'knowing'" (*How Jesus Became God*, 132). Taken at face value, this is nothing short of shocking! But if he meant this *seriously*, as any sort of epistemic comparison of these two avenues as differentiated ways of knowing something to be *true*, as we sometimes might hear chiefly in some preaching services (almost always seeming to invoke "amens"), then Ehrman is simply mistaken. This is a matter primarily for philosophers, not New Testament scholars!

Can Know," exhibits an extraordinary amount of interest in various *visionary* hypotheses.[30] This is strange for a couple of reasons. Initially, if *any* natural theory will do the job over against resurrection claims, as we just saw, then why spend half a chapter on a single thesis from several different angles? Further, why does Ehrman *raise questions* throughout this entire chapter rather than follow his own title as well as the previous chapter on what we *cannot* know and tell us what he thinks *we can know* about the resurrection? Hence, why is there comparatively little on what we can know, and why the preoccupation with visions here? This latter question in particular is a discussion to finish up what has been dealt with in the specific chapters on hallucinations and other notions of visions.

The agnostic positions mentioned here share several features. Historical study is deemed to be at least partially applicable and may even be able to establish a number of relevant data. For example, for each researcher it is clearly the case that the data indicate that Jesus's disciples were totally convinced that they had seen the risen Jesus after his death. Yet for at least Marxsen and Carnley, ultimately history is judged to be deficient as a basis for exercising faith as applicable to life and ministry, or perhaps even as grounds for supporting the facticity of the resurrection. One common element here, at least for Marxsen, Wedderburn, and especially for Ehrman, seems to be that Jesus's resurrection appears to require an acknowledgment of supernatural activity in the world, and this remains problematic, especially in that it involves the intrusion of an "alien" realm that we can know almost nothing about. Nonetheless, the resurrection can still be believed, though only as a tenet of faith.

Problems with the Agnostic Position on the Resurrection

However, the agnostic position on the resurrection of Jesus is problematic on multiple grounds. Here we will discuss a series of six problems with this approach, working from general to specific and progressing to the most crucial issues.

Overstated Positions

First, as often happens with responses to rival positions in presumably every sort of situation, occasionally the case against one's opponent is slanted unfairly. Expressed

---

[30] Ehrman, *How Jesus Became God*, 183–204, or exactly half of the entire chapter!

popularly, the cards are frequently stacked in such a manner that the task of establishing the contrary position from the outset is more difficult than it need be. This is a less serious offense and can certainly be corrected.

Wedderburn provides a couple of examples in his treatment. He states that the historical defense of the resurrection would not convince a skeptic.[31] Furthermore, the verdict against the supernatural positions of either Jesus's resurrection or life after death is "Not proven."[32] But since when is convincing a person of the opposite persuasion a prerequisite for arguing that anyone's view is fairly indicated by the data? So should it be concluded that the data are faulty when a person of another faith (or none at all) fails to "convert" after hearing the argument? Is it not the case that the opposite could also be said with assurance? How likely is it that the argument constructed by a skeptic or agnostic would convince a believer against his or her Christian theistic position? Doubtless, neither side wants this to be a prerequisite for their rationality or the truth of their own beliefs! After all, so many other things contribute to one's faith than arguments alone, such as family backgrounds, emotions, pain and suffering, and so on, that even a suggestion of this nature should rightly be considered naive.

Still, conversions do indeed move in every direction. Former evangelicals have become atheists, agnostics, or skeptics of one sort or another.[33] But without any question it can be attested from both public publications as well as private testimonies,

---

[31] Wedderburn, *Beyond Resurrection*, 95.

[32] Wedderburn, 225.

[33] Examples include perhaps the best-known former evangelical-turned-atheist, Robert M. Price, whose background figures heavily in works like *Inerrant the Wind: The Evangelical Crisis of Biblical Authority* (Amherst, NY: Prometheus, 2009) and *Beyond Born Again: Toward Evangelical Maturity* (Eugene, OR: Apocryphal Books, 1993). Already discussed is former evangelical-turned-agnostic Bart D. Ehrman, as in *Did Jesus Exist?*, with autobiographical reflections on 5, 35–37, 70–71, 94–95. Also in this category is John W. Loftus, *Why I Became an Atheist: A Former Preacher Rejects Christianity* (Amherst, NY: Prometheus, 2008). Geza Vermes, born into a Jewish-Hungarian family, later became a Roman Catholic priest and then later returned to Judaism. He is known as one of the early pioneers in the Third Quest for the historical Jesus; see Vermes, *Jesus the Jew: A Historian's Reading of the Gospels* (Minneapolis: Fortress, 1981); Vermes, *Jesus in His Jewish Context* (Minneapolis: Fortress, 2003), with autobiographical reflections in the preface and chap. 12. Vermes was also a professor of Jewish studies at Oxford University.

many (probably thousands) of persons have converted in recent decades *on evidential grounds* of some sort and become Christians.[34]

Moreover, regarding the second comment above, virtually no scholar on any portion of the theoretical spectrum requires that one's position be "proven." Stated succinctly, "proof" is simply not the measure in any inductive discipline, including history or even the experimental sciences. For an entire host of reasons, such as those discussed in our methodology chapters in volume 1, probability is the guide for research. Thus, to label the position taken by an opponent as "not proven" is, similarly, to assume or imply a standard that *no* historian can live by and is rather vacuous in nature. Nor can the atheist or agnostic positions be "proven," so this ought not be required by conservatives either. Speaking evidentially, then, we need to be satisfied with a probable argument. That is all that is required, though some are of far better quality, and hence much stronger arguments, than others. In our case, we therefore want to know if the resurrection is the most likely event given the data that we possess.

As already mentioned, this is not necessarily an egregious error; it is committed regularly and can be corrected, so we can move forward. However, it is a decent place to begin. The chief point here is that in evidential discussions of this nature, falsely

---

[34] The best-known example in the twentieth century is no doubt C. S. Lewis, *Surprised by Joy: The Shape of My Early Life* (New York: Harcourt Brace Jovanovich, 1955). Others include Sheldon Vanauken, *A Severe Mercy* (New York: Bantam, 1977); Josh McDowell with Christóbal Krusen, *Undaunted: One Man's Real-Life Journey from Unspeakable Memories to Unbelievable Grace* (Carol Stream, IL: Tyndale House, 2012), chaps. 7–10, on the resurrection of Jesus, see 78–81; Viggo Olsen, *The Agnostic Who Dared to Search* (Chicago: Moody, 1974). Olsen was a medical doctor before his conversion to Christianity (see chap. 1). Also Alister McGrath, *Why God Won't Go Away: Is the New Atheism Running on Empty?* (Nashville: Nelson, 2010); James S. Spiegel, *The Making of an Atheist* (Chicago: Moody, 2010), complete with surveys, reports, and other important information in chaps. 3–5 in particular; Dinesh D'Souza, *What's So Great about Christianity* (Washington, DC: Regnery, 2007); Nabeel Qureshi, *Seeking Allah, Finding Jesus: A Devout Muslim Encounters Christianity* (Grand Rapids: Zondervan, 2016). Qureshi is an adult convert from Islam and also a medical doctor, see esp. chap. 47 plus chaps. 48–53, including Qureshi's visions that paved the final steps for him to the gospel of Jesus Christ. For a treatment in the same book of the reported 100,000 or even far more visions of Jesus that have led to so many contemporary Muslims coming to Jesus, see appendix E: "Dreams and Visions" by Josh McDowell, including some statistics along with many testimonies (331–35). Abdu H. Murray, *Apocalypse Later: Why the Gospel of Peace Must Trump the Politics of Prophecy in the Middle East* (Grand Rapids: Kregel, 2009), esp. chaps. 6–7; note that Murray is also an adult convert from Islam and a practicing trial lawyer.

inflating even the inferred levels of evidence that seemingly must be reached by either side to be "successful" runs the risk of providing unfair emotional standards that may tend to stick especially in the minds of those who are unfamiliar with the canons of good research, leading to misconstrued evaluations of the data.

It must also be remembered that converting others to one's own opinion is not the gold standard of an effective argument. After all, people convert for all sorts of very poor reasons as well. Further, reaching "proof" in inductive arguments is not even strictly possible. So, bandying the word about is bad practice—that is no one's goal in this species of research.

The Burden of Proof

A second issue is that the agnostic position usually entails its own burden of proof. If a scholar is satisfied to assert what may be called the "weaker" or even the "private" agnostic stance and just respond that something is simply her private view without any encumbrance on any other position, then that may well be, of course, her opinion alone. But a "stronger" agnostic position may also be chosen, one that maintains that neither we nor others are able to ascertain the truth of particular religious positions.[35]

In our case, however, if the harder, more assertive line is taken that no one is justified in believing religious views, that position, in effect, crosses the line into another individual's "space." As such, this sort of assertion then assumes its own burden of proof, for it seeks to make decisions on behalf of another, thereby settling the issues for them. That would clearly seem to raise the relevant question as to why no one else is justified in moving further in belief on a particular subject—such as the origin of the disciples' faith regarding their thinking that they saw the risen Jesus. A critic can say that this and nothing further occurred, but now an assertion is being made. When challenged in these situations, certainly stronger reasons are needed in order to solve the issue at hand.

Now, is the Christian also justified in asking for the grounds on which this stronger agnostic position should be held? In this case, *both* the more forceful agnostic position

---

[35] A simple distinction between these two, using the terms "modest" and "aggressive" agnosticism, is given by C. Stephen Evans: "It is helpful to distinguish the 'modest agnostic,' who merely claims to be unable to decide the question of God's reality, from the 'aggressive agnostic,' who claims that no one can decide the question and that suspension of judgment is the only reasonable stance." See Evans, *Pocket Dictionary of Apologetics and Philosophy of Religion* (Downers Grove, IL: InterVarsity, 2002), 8–9.

as well as the more assertive theistic assertions about the disciples' resurrection beliefs should be prepared to evidence their positions. The agnostic position is not established simply by the *claim* that we can go no further. Nor is the believer's *view* now set in cement because it has been stated. How or why should the conclusion to the discussion remain at precisely this point, and on someone's say-so alone? *Why* is it the case that we cannot get behind the data and know what happened to the disciples?

But now, agnostic scholars may have reached a dilemma—perhaps one that they were unaware was their responsibility. They presumably may be satisfied with the very personal, more passive stance above and the resulting private view that it involves, devoid of any evidential force. In this sense, the weaker (nonargumentative) agnostic position might be comparable to those who hold to the weaker (nonevidential) Christian position that it is enough to believe firmly in the bodily resurrection of Jesus, but without any evidence or other data being produced in its favor. It is enough that Christianity is true "in our hearts." Christians often make such assertions. Both are personal positions without evidential confirmation.

On the other hand, both agnostics and Christians ought to accept their own burdens of proof, providing *reasons* for their beliefs.[36] But too often in dialogues of this nature, it is thought to be evidentially insufficient for Christians to "simply believe," while agnostics have the evidential right to "simply assert" their view. The reasoning is sometimes repeated even more frequently by atheists than by agnostics, but it is often said that the prefix "a" before either "theist" or "gnostic" only means that they do not subscribe to whatever word comes next, and hence they have absolutely nothing to prove—strictly speaking, they do not even hold a position on the matter![37]

---

[36] Or either could, of course, try to dispute who has the burden of proof.

[37] The more philosophical discussion here is represented by Antony Flew as he applies these terms to the term "atheism" in *The Presumption of Atheism and Other (Philosophical) Essays on God, Freedom, and Immortality* (London: Pemberton, 1976). Flew's earlier essay by the same title was published in the *Canadian Journal of Philosophy* 2 (1972): 29–46. Here, Flew makes the distinction between the "positive" use of the term "atheism," where God's nonexistence is being asserted, and the "negative" use of the term, where the individual simply means "someone who is simply not a theist." But note also that Flew is not so interested in applying this reasoning to agnosticism (30). Cf. the rejoinder by R. Douglas Geivett, "A Pascalian Rejoinder to the Presumption of Atheism," and Antony Flew's response: "Response to R. Douglas Geivett's 'A Pascalian Rejoinder to the Presumption of Atheism,'" with both of these latter essays appearing in Raymond Martin and Christopher Bernard, eds., *God Matters: Readings in the Philosophy of Religion* (New York: Pearson, 2003), chaps. 21 and 22.

Not being so careful philosophically, Sam Harris falls exactly into this trap, showing that he definitely does not understand the worldview implications of philosophical issues. He presents just such a straightforward comment featuring the mindset with which atheism is often plagued—that it is not a worldview or real position at all. Really? Harris asserts quite naively, "Atheism is not a philosophy; it is not even a view of the world; it is simply an admission of the obvious," like saying that atheists are simply not-somethings. Atheists are just persons who tell religionists to produce evidence for *their* views![38]

It may be true that neither agnosticism nor atheism are, in and of themselves, full-blown worldviews. But two things are important and should be mentioned here. Initially, the essence of these two views holds much in common with the very heart of naturalism, as can be seen in this definition: "Naturalism—very roughly—may be defined as the philosophy that *everything that exists is a part of nature and there is no reality beyond or outside of nature* . . . nature is all that exists and nature itself is whatever will be disclosed by the ideal natural sciences, especially physics."[39] So atheism, agnosticism, and naturalism appear to share quite closely the core beliefs regarding the nonexistence of the supernatural realm.

Further, Harris plainly does not stop with what we have identified as the weak or softer unbelieving position that may not need any defense—that of being satisfied to simply affirm one's own personal, private "faith." Rather, he goes on the offensive on many occasions, especially for such a short book. Harris piles up what he considers to be one critique of Christianity after another,[40] charging Christians numerous times with having insufficient evidence,[41] as well as offering what he considers to be positive arguments that favor his naturalism.[42] So this is plainly over the line that he set for himself and his colleagues. Harris goes far beyond his own limit of simply registering that he is not religious![43]

So, Harris thinks that atheism is neither a philosophy nor even a view of the world? Here's the atheist angle: there is no God, and the universe exists by accident,

---

[38] Sam Harris, *Letter to a Christian Nation* (New York: Random House, 2006), 51–52.

[39] Stewart Goetz and Charles Taliaferro, *Naturalism* (Grand Rapids: Eerdmans, 2008), 6–7, cf. 14.

[40] Harris, *Letter to a Christian Nation*, 23–32, 47, 50–61, 64–67.

[41] Harris, 6, 25, 33, 43, 49, 51–52, 64–65, 67, 87–91.

[42] Harris, x, 46, 68–87.

[43] Harris, 51.

perhaps eternally, perhaps emerging out of nothing. Is this "not a philosophy . . . not a view of the world"? Does this sound like a simple belief that needs no backup?

So as we just stated, it may be the case that neither agnosticism nor atheism is, in and of itself, a full-orbed worldview. We are certainly not saying that they are identical ideas. Nonetheless, the naturalistic worldview involves as a major tenet the belief that God does not exist (or perhaps that God may never be known to exist). With naturalism serving as one of the philosophical parents here, atheism and agnosticism certainly play large roles in the natural scenery that there is at least no traditional God. Many would identify naturalism as the dominant worldview in the Western world. Further, a dominant message here is that religious believers of all sorts are quite gullible and guilty of employing faith without good reasons.[44] However, if these theists and agnostics would have looked more closely, they might have found a plethora of recent Christian scholars who even agree with them that "faith only" positions (including secular ones!) are insufficient.[45]

---

[44] Many instances of these combinational comments can be located in the recent unbelieving literature. For example, Richard Dawkins blames Christians with throwing faith into discussions thinking that any reasons they have given (if any) have now been given a boost! See Dawkins, *The God Delusion* (Boston: Houghton Mifflin, 2006), 134. Christopher Hitchens as well as others have railed regularly on the absence of reason or evidence in religious arguments. See Hitchens, *God Is Not Great: How Religion Poisons Everything* (New York: Hachette, 2007), 150, 202, 204. Sam Harris has complained, "In fact, every religion preaches the truth of propositions for which no evidence is even *conceivable*. This put the 'leap' in Kierkegaard's leap of faith." See Harris, *The End of Faith: Religion, Terror, and the Future of Religion* (New York: Norton, 2004), 23, cf. 40. Broadly, there is insufficient evidence for religion, as noted above.

[45] Besides the dozens upon dozens of Christian scholars who hold this and similar positions, here are still more volumes that defend reason and science, directing the comments to the unbelievers such as those in the previous footnote: John C. Lennox, *God's Undertaker: Has Science Buried God?* (Oxford: Lion Hudson, 2007), esp. chaps. 1–3; David Marshall, *The Truth Behind the New Atheism: Responding to the Emerging Challenge to God and Christianity* (Eugene, OR: Harvest House, 2007), chaps. 1–2 in particular; Paul Chamberlain, *Why People Don't Believe: Confronting Seven Challenges to Christian Faith* (Grand Rapids: Baker, 2011), chaps. 4–5; Peter S. Williams, *A Sceptic's Guide to Atheism* (Milton Keynes: Paternoster, 2009), chaps. 3, 5–7; Spiegel, *Making of an Atheist*, chaps. 2–4, plus page 123 on the helpfulness of doubt; D'Souza, *What's So Great about Christianity*, chaps. 8–10; McGrath, *Why God Won't Go Away*, chaps. 4–5, 7; Alister McGrath and Joanna Collicutt McGrath, *The Dawkins Delusion: Atheist Fundamentalism and the Denial of the Divine* (Downers Grove, IL: IVP, 2007), chap. 2, where the absolutely stunning endorsement on the front of this book by well-known atheistic philosopher of science

Thus, some forms of agnosticism are plainly one-sided, quaint positions that stack up all the cards in their own corner, all in the absence of any real evidential data on their own behalf. It is a mere assertion—and an incorrect one at that. But it is incredibly convenient to tell someone else that *they* bear the entire burden of proof, while all "your side" has to do is to say, "No, not this," or "No, we're not that," without any further responsibility. This frequent disparity in roles and perceptions of occupied positions must change.

So, in the name of getting his foot in the front door, Harris then declares outright war! Since he freely both initiates and engages in the debate, it then becomes "put up or shut up time" for him rather than resting on his earlier "innocent routine"! He has made the charges against others as well as offered defenses of his own system (hence, offering a worldview!). So we are back to the original point: the duel has been offered and now it has been taken.

Harris and other atheists or agnostics who wish to argue against other philosophies or to suggest evidence in favor of their own views have every bit as much of a burden of proof as anyone else, for they have decided not to remain with a stated, undefended "faith" system. They may choose to run into a corner and hope to be overlooked, but when a position is argued in favor of or against others, a system is being favored. It should not even be pretended that such a critic can shoot darts left, right, and all around but never have any burden to indicate that the critic's underlying system is true!

This ploy may have been very useful while the ruse lasted, or whenever it goes unopposed. Perhaps a mere sneer and guffaw are enough to keep religious believers at bay. But as we will see next, perhaps naturalism and related views that reject the supernatural simply cannot be shown to be true! If so, perhaps agnostics and atheists are better off using ploys in order to distance themselves from producing evidence. Otherwise, it may be more widely known that the emperor is not wearing any clothes!

Michael Ruse reads, "*The God Delusion* makes me embarrassed to be an atheist, and the McGraths show why." Two other major research volumes by a major scholar are among the many that argue two of the themes that are among those that these atheists absolutely detest: namely, how Christianity led to both modern science as well as the voice of reason in the Western world; see Rodney Stark, *For the Glory of God: How Monotheism Led to Reformations, Science, Witch-Hunts, and the End of Slavery* (Princeton: Princeton University Press, 2003), esp. chap. 2; Stark, *The Victory of Reason: How Christianity Led to Freedom, Capitalism, and Western Success* (New York: Random House, 2005), chap. 1.

Naturalism and Related Views as Truth?

Third, before going further, an issue that ranks as crucially as any other in this discussion must be solved. What actual arguments determine that naturalism or materialism in general, along with atheism, agnosticism, or similar views in particular, are even true in the first place? It is easy to pretend to sit on a lofty height and throw stones down at someone else, all the while proclaiming loudly to be immune from having to establish one's *own* case, as in the second point just mentioned. But until a sufficient number of positive evidences and other good arguments arise that are capable of indicating the *actual truth* of the philosophical position from which the criticism is coming, the agnostic begs the question by assuming the truth of that position.

Thus, what are the *grounds* for denying the supernatural realm? How would these grounds be established in the first place? True, the existence of the supernatural is probably denigrated as much as any idea in these discussions, but is there more to these naturalistic attacks here than mere verbiage and bombast?

Sometimes the suggestion is made that the one–two punches of these philosophical positions are the problem of pain and evil along with the process of evolution. While these two areas can indeed be pithy issues that raise good questions, *neither one* disproves either the existence of God or the existence of a supernatural realm. Though nothing on these fronts can be solved here, a few brief observations that indicate this conclusion may be helpful.

Regarding the classic problem of evil, the best-known statements of the problem are the *logical* and the *evidential* versions. In perhaps the best-known example of the potentially stronger, logical version, J. L. Mackie states, "There seems to be some contradiction" between the theist's propositions. "However, the contradiction does not arise immediately . . . we need some additional premises."[46]

Years later, Alvin Plantinga challenged Mackie to produce the actual contradiction by indicating which additional premises would complete his argument and prove that theism was false. The result, as Plantinga notes, is that "no atheologian has produced even a plausible candidate for this role, and it certainly is not easy to see what such a proposition might be."[47]

---

[46] J. L. Mackie, "Evil and Omnipotence," *Mind* 64 (1955): 200–212; reprinted in Louis P. Pojman, ed., *Philosophy of Religion: An Anthology*, 2nd ed. (Belmont, CA: Wadsworth, 1994), 185–92, quotation on 185 of the Pojman edition.

[47] Alvin Plantinga, *God, Freedom, and Evil* (Grand Rapids: Eerdmans, 1974), 24.

In a surrejoinder by Mackie after he and Plantinga had "slugged it out," Mackie concluded the matter by conceding in the final two paragraphs of his treatment: "We cannot, indeed, take the problem of evil as a conclusive disproof of traditional theism, because, as we have seen, there is some flexibility in its doctrines, and in particular in the additional premises needed to make the problem explicit." The matter "leaves open several possibilities for revised religious views."[48]

So, while Mackie no doubt wanted to retain in some form his original thesis of a few decades before, he had to admit that it did not work. In short, theists simply have too many theological options to avoid getting pinned down on the logical problem of evil. As Mackie concludes the matter, theism has enough "flexibility in its doctrines" leading to "several possibilities" of avoiding any serious issues.

In fact, prominent atheist philosopher and specialist on the problem of evil, William Rowe, dismissed the discussion rather unceremoniously, concluding regarding the logically inconsistent form of the problem (like Mackie's) that "no one, I think, has succeeded in establishing such an extravagant claim . . . there is a fairly compelling argument for the view that the existence of evil is logically consistent with the existence of the theistic God."[49]

Thus, the stronger, contradictory form of the argument from evil suffered an inglorious death.[50] However, Rowe is best known for developing the evidential problem of evil. Could there actually exist such intense examples of human or animal suffering where God could have done something about it without losing either a greater good or by permitting an equal or worse evil in the process?[51]

But after pursuing this option for years, Rowe also had to concede that this chief question could not be demonstrated so as to discount God's existence: "The

[48] J. L. Mackie, *The Miracle of Theism: Arguments for and against the Existence of God* (Oxford: Clarendon, 1982), 176.

[49] William L. Rowe, "The Problem of Evil and Some Varieties of Atheism," *American Philosophical Quarterly* 16 (1979): 335–41, reprinted in William L. Rowe and William J. Wainwright, eds., *Philosophy of Religion: Selected Readings*, 3rd ed. (Fort Worth, TX: Harcourt Brace, 1998), 242–51. The quotation is from 243n1.

[50] Other examples of this wide recognition are common. Another similar evaluation by Rowe is his *Philosophy of Religion: An Introduction* (Belmont, CA: Wadsworth, 1978), 94; cf. also Ronald H. Nash, *Faith and Reason: Searching for a Rational Faith* (Grand Rapids: Zondervan, 1988), 212–15; C. Stephen Evans, *Philosophy of Religion: Thinking about Faith* (Downers Grove, IL: InterVarsity, 1982), 137.

[51] This question is paraphrased from Rowe, "Problem of Evil," 243 in the Rowe and Wainwright edition.

truth is that we are not in a position to prove" that evil refutes God's existence.[52] But Rowe does think that there are still some rational grounds for supporting atheism here, presumably in that there is just too much evil in the world. Even so, rather incredibly, Rowe also suggests that there are ways that theism can counteract these moves by atheists. Theists could defend one or more of the traditional arguments for God's existence, appeal to aspects of religious experience, or provide an "account for a variety of phenomena" in the world. Rowe thinks that an atheist like himself can even concede that the theist can be *justified* in believing in God on grounds like these![53]

So, neither the harder-line argument from *logical contradictions* in the theistic response to evil in the world nor the more popular *evidential* argument from even heinous cases of human and animal suffering have disproven theism, even as conceded by the strongest atheist defenders. As Mackie states, the theist just has too many options that do not allow the atheist to close all the doors.[54]

What about evolution? Critics should acknowledge that this subject has nothing like the force of the argument from evil. A huge indication of this is simply straightforward: many Christian scholars actually *affirm* some notion of evolution while also confessing their orthodox views of many of the central tenets of Christianity, including the inspiration of Scripture, the nature of sin, the atoning work of Christ via his crucifixion, and so forth, whereas evolution is seen as a peripheral issue involving the question of method.[55]

Of course, this is a hotly disputed issue and there is certainly enough disagreement to go around, with any number of items to debate.[56] So the presence of this evolutionary perspective hardly indicates that everyone is pleased with this or that reasoning. But this is not the matter we are discussing here. The point is that if even theologically sophisticated conservatives like J. I. Packer and many others can

---

[52] Rowe, 245.

[53] These last few comments are drawn from Rowe, 245, 250–51.

[54] Mackie, *Miracle of Theism*, 176.

[55] For example, Denis R. Alexander, *Creation or Evolution: Do We Have to Choose?* (Oxford: Lion Hudson, 2014), 11–12.

[56] Such as the response volume edited by prominent British geneticist Norman C. Nevin, *Should Christians Embrace Evolution? Biblical and Scientific Responses* (Downers Grove, IL: InterVarsity, 2009). Another example of the debate is Kenneth Keathley, J. B. Stump, and Joe Aguirre, *Discussing Origins with Reasons to Believe and Biologos: Old-Earth or Evolutionary Creation?* (Downers Grove, IL: InterVarsity, 2017).

be open to the subject, then it is hardly an issue that contradicts central Christian theology or requires that this theology be jettisoned.[57]

An additional issue beyond whether evolution is compatible with Christian doctrine is the cosmological angle. Apparently following the lead of the well-known twentieth-century philosopher Edgar Sheffield Brightman, Warren C. Young stated that Darwin's thesis indicates "the survival of the fittest without explaining the arrival of the fittest."[58] The idea here is that evolution describes the process of how already existing, living organisms flourish, but not how they came about in the first place. Since this is the case, some think that God's existence is even required before Darwin's descriptions of life in order to create the entire living system in the first place.

The upshot here is that without being grounded or otherwise known to be true, naturalism and similar positions cannot act as if they are able to judge other systems for lacking sufficient evidence. Yet, these philosophical positions seem not to hesitate to do just this. For example, it is often argued that we are justified in doubting or denying the existence of supernatural events, perhaps even on a priori grounds. Many have commented that the occurrence of a miracle is highly unlikely, if not impossible, since it involves a supernatural occurrence.[59]

But philosopher Stephen Parrish makes the point in forceful terms: "Why are miracles widely accepted as extremely improbable?" If one *knew* that a particular philosophical position that basically disallowed miracles was true, "then one would be completely justified in assigning miracles a very low order of antecedent probability."

---

[57] Among other endorsers, Packer, as perhaps the "dean" of evangelical theologians, states on the cover of Alexander's book that it is "surely the best informed, clearest and most judicious treatment of the question in its title that you can find anywhere today." That's hardly the move of someone who fears that this method will potentially replace treasured theological beliefs.

[58] Warren C. Young, *A Christian Approach to Philosophy* (Grand Rapids: Baker, 1954), 91. The statement by Brightman is found in his text *Philosophy of Religion* (New York: Prentice-Hall, 1940), 317.

[59] Ehrman asserts that miracles "by definition, are infinitesimally remote." See *Jesus*, 196, cf. 228. He makes similar comments in *Did Jesus Exist?*, 315–17; *How Jesus Became God*, 132–33, 143–51, 165, 172–73. Here he confuses the unlikelihood that a miracle will happen *at any given moment* with the overall near impossibility of miracles anytime and anywhere. But to hold that the latter is true by definition, as Ehrman clearly states, is more than a confusion. It also provides a good example of the error mentioned above, for he must *assume* a particular philosophical stance in order to "know" this about miracles, for he has certainly not proven that miracles virtually never occur. And by assuming such a perspective, he ignores and begs the very question that he is trying to address.

But this is the very position that must be demonstrated, not assumed. Apart from such a heavily evidenced positive case, the question has been begged against the possibility of miracles.[60] Thus, no matter how strongly such an agnostic or atheistic stance is asserted, it still fails, having committed an informal logical fallacy.

Miracle Claims and History

Fourth, the agnostic scholars above argue or imply that a major problem with affirming that God raised Jesus is that such an event involves supernatural activity. But many researchers, including even some of those who affirm the resurrection, note that it is problematic to argue *historically* that a particular event was a miracle. On this latter view, it is at least arguable that history as a discipline is unable to show that *God* is the one who acted in a particular event. History may only be able to decide on the status of the event itself, since, as historians, we may only be able to judge the evidence for what happens in the space-time world and decide on that, but there are no photographs or footprints when God works a miracle.[61]

---

[60] Stephen E. Parrish, *God and Necessity: A Defense of Classical Theism* (Lanham, MD: University Press of America, 1997), 156–57, cf. 172. Similarly on the importance of taking a strong stand when naturalistic and other similar options had failed in the previous century, former prominent Oxford University philosophical theologian Basil Mitchell read an essay at the C. S. Lewis Memorial Lecture in Belfast, Ireland, in 1986, which was published as "Contemporary Challenges to Christian Apologetics," *Journal of the Irish Christian Study Center* 4 (1989): 1–18. This essay was later included in Mitchell's volume, *How to Play Theological Ping-Pong and Other Essays on Faith and Reason*, ed. William J. Abraham and Robert W. Prevost (Grand Rapids: Eerdmans, 1990), 25–41. Mitchell argued that several philosophical movements had come and gone in recent years. These included positivism and Marxism as well as scientific versions of naturalism, humanism, and materialism. Each had fallen to a host of refutations, such as positivism's failure both to "give a convincing account of science" as well as also having failed to justify its rejection of metaphysics (27–33). Though these secular movements, including forms of naturalism, failed, Mitchell encouraged Christians to step into the gap and reassert their leadership in the philosophical, theological, and ethical spheres without keeping to themselves and settling for private goals. Mitchell encouraged conservatives to take the lead among current options just as C. S. Lewis had done in his day, to join the debate, and to hold up the gospel message as the truth rather than adding to the contemporary malady by treating the gospel as just one option among others (36, 40–41).

[61] Psalm 77 includes an intriguing metaphorical description of God taking the children of Israel through the Red Sea while escaping the Egyptians, and at the end we are told that though God's paths were through the sea, he left no footprints (v. 19)!

On such a distinction, then, we may study the historical ramifications of "normal" events, such as whether Jesus really died. All of the agnostic scholars surveyed above judge that this event occurred in space-time history. Did Jesus's followers see him after that point, without inquiring about any supernatural implications? A real death for a historical figure and seeing a person walk around and talk in space and time are both matters that historical and other inductive research techniques (such as documents, interviews, medical data, photographs, and so on) can determine.

In other words, it would hardly be disputed that historical methodology *can* study the side of the issue that occurred within its own domain. But whether this event was a *miracle* or whether *God raised Jesus from the dead*—these are distinct philosophical questions, and some would say that they must be treated differently. Or at least, different or additional "tools" or methods for getting at these issues need to be employed.[62]

On this specific point, though it is possible that we can be too strict at times, my tendency is actually to *agree* with the agnostic scholars! We can view the historical portion of the miracle *claim*, as Wedderburn states, by examining its this-worldly components. Therefore, in this chapter, we should concentrate on these same two questions: According to the canons of historical probability, can it be determined whether Jesus died? Then, can it be determined that human witnesses saw him afterward? We can agree not to cloud the issue with other questions.[63] So, for now, we will therefore suspend judgment on any potential supernatural portion of the issue with regard to the possible *cause* of Jesus walking around after his death.

---

[62] Granted, sometimes we may rely *too strictly* (or even too artificially) on graduate school or other research specializations in the sense of whether or not scholars had specialized training in particular study areas. For example, what if a person is not formally trained in philosophy but has a theological or historical background and happens to think very well in the philosophical mode? Sometimes decent treatises are written by scholars who are removed from the field in question. To Ehrman's credit, he makes some complimentary remarks regarding mythicists who either have no specialized training at all, or for those whose field is in other areas of study (such as *Did Jesus Exist?*, 17–21, 347n1, 348n11, 349n20). We will discuss the philosophical side of this question in later chapters as to whether God raised Jesus and how specifically and definitely these issues can be answered. For many details here, see Gary R. Habermas, *The Risen Jesus and Future Hope* (Lanham, MD: Rowman & Littlefield, 2003), esp. chaps. 2–3.

[63] For discussions of this distinction between the historical and philosophical sides of an issue, see Habermas, *Risen Jesus*, esp. 4–5; Habermas, *The Historical Jesus: Ancient Evidence for the Life of Christ* (Joplin, MO: College Press, 1996), 60–61.

Wedderburn correctly recognizes this crucial distinction between historical investigation and one's philosophical and theological positions, conclusions, and arguments.[64] Moreover, he also makes the same distinction between the historical portion of a claim and the philosophical portion. Answering those who argue that history and revelation are sometimes so intertwined that we cannot investigate the claims at all, Wedderburn states that even such events "have a side, a dimension, which *is* open to history and the historian . . . the fact that it is supposed to be a revelation *in history* means that human eyes have seen something and human ears have heard something. . . . This side of the revelatory act that is open to history . . . must be scrutinized to ascertain its trustworthiness and credibility."[65]

Ehrman is helpful here too, making some of the same sorts of distinctions as Wedderburn between initial historical observations and their meanings, interpretations, and so on. Similarly helpful is the dual discussion of the crucifixion and Paul's first visit to Jerusalem to see Peter and James. Other discussions are full of nuance as well as key distinctions throughout, whether or not one agrees with Ehrman. Given his background views, the data that Ehrman allows, in particular, and his rationale for allowing each piece of evidence are the most instructive items.[66]

How would this translate to a study of the resurrection? Here Wedderburn applies well his previous point: "The resurrection-event itself may be beyond the reach of historians, but they can still pass judgment on whether that event is needed at all to explain what *is* within their reach, namely the early Christians' claim that Jesus had been raised." So Wedderburn thinks that history cannot tell whether God was actually involved in the resurrection event, but it is still necessary to determine whether "some such event occurred and impinged upon and occasioned the more obviously human events of which we do know? This *is* a historical question to which the historian can attempt to give some sort of answer."[67]

However, distressingly, Wedderburn seems to forget his own distinction later when he decides in favor of agnosticism. When discussing naturalistic alternatives to the resurrection, he judges that, "however unconvincing they may seem," these

---

[64] Wedderburn, *Beyond Resurrection*, 97, cf. 12–19, 21–22, 38.

[65] Wedderburn, 15.

[66] Examples of these discussions are found, consecutively, in Ehrman, *Jesus*, 229–31; Ehrman, *Did Jesus Exist?*, 145–74; Ehrman, *How Jesus Became God*, 143–51.

[67] Wedderburn, *Beyond Resurrection*, 14–15.

options have an advantage over supernatural origins for this event.[68] So even though natural hypotheses do not seem to explain the data that we have, they may be better than looking to God for an explanation. But we have agreed that the discipline of history cannot answer the supernatural portion of the question! So why bring it up again and prejudice the decision?

Thus, rather than keeping the clear distinction that he called for earlier between human observations in space and time and any possible supernatural cause of this event, Wedderburn leaves the realm of historical investigation. He even decides rather "unconvincing" natural options are probably better than supernatural explanations. So, he crosses his own line of historical research and then opts for what he takes to be a less likely cause. But we should note that he does this *because* the miraculous possibility does not fit well with his own preconceptions—exactly what we have been discussing in this fourth point!

After many strong comments on the historicity of these events, Ehrman agrees with Wedderburn and makes very similar moves. In fact, even experienced readers may not be able to distinguish from one another the comments made by these two scholars. Once again, *any thesis at all, no matter how improbable, is more likely than a resurrection.*[69] This conclusion, it must be remembered, comes from a scholar who has stated that history can neither prove nor disprove the resurrection.[70] But as we have seen here, something always gets in the way when it comes to the final verdict!

We close this fourth critique by asking how, specifically, can agnostic forms of naturalism be shown to be true as the chief backdrop for this position? If evidencing this view strongly is not strictly an option in any rigorous way, then upon what foundation can this widespread and, in some places, fairly unanimous agreement against the supernatural realm and those sorts of events be grounded? Why should this skeptical view simply be assumed?

Incidentally, it will simply not do to respond that we just do not actually witness these supernatural events today, because dozens, if not hundreds, of these occurrences of various species have been documented carefully in medical and other researched literature—so many so that shrugging shoulders just does not work anymore. If the

---

[68] Wedderburn, 96–97.

[69] Ehrman, *Jesus*, 196, 227–28; Ehrman, *Did Jesus Exist?*, 315–16; Ehrman, *How Jesus Became God*, 165, 173.

[70] Ehrman, *How Jesus Became God*, 132, cf. 204.

naturalistic emperor is not wearing any clothes, as it appears that he is not, how can the *absence* of a grounding position eliminate potentially evidenced positions, especially with a guffaw and quick wave of the hand?[71]

Thus, Wedderburn, Ehrman, and other scholars first need to evidence strongly their agnosticism, followed by reaffirming their own methodologies. Even if it is decided that we cannot determine with historical tools whether *God* by his power raised Jesus from the dead, our attention here in the remainder of this chapter is still on a smaller, more focused goal: Did Jesus die? Then, was Jesus seen later at least one time, no matter what the cause?

The Role of the Minimally Known Facts

So far in this chapter, after surveying representative agnostic scholars, we have outlined four consecutive steps that build on one another. We began with a minor admonition not to use language in ways that build expectations to levels that will always be unachievable from any perspective, even according to the actual standards being employed. This led to discussing the burden of proof that all sides, agnostics included, must bear when discussing the relative strengths of their own positions.

Next, how do we know that naturalism in general, including agnostic, atheistic, and other similar components, are themselves true? If they are going to serve as the backdrop for truth, including whisking away other positions with which they disagree, then they must also pass muster. Finally, the question of actual interventions by God is addressed in volume 4 of this study.

Our fifth move, in working toward the case for Jesus's resurrection that we have forecast in this overall study, is our contention that by using only the recognized historical data that are conceded by virtually all critical scholars, including agnostics, we have the advantage of a powerful factual cartel from which we might draw for our discussion. The nature of agnostic questioning sometimes makes it appear that a particular scholar does not want to follow the evidence to its conclusion, thereby functioning as a way to stop the proceedings before they ever begin pointing in the direction of the resurrection.

---

[71] While we have definitely not yet surveyed this evidence, or decided that the resurrection probably occurred, or that it is more likely than not, we leave it here for now as only a potential option. The point we are making is that there seems to be very little if any evidence on the other, natural side of the ledger.

However, it is certainly possible that these shared data could be just what is needed to remove the agnostic question mark. Especially if naturalistic theories have failed to explain Jesus's resurrection appearances, or are even less likely options, then perhaps we have plenty of evidence already to decide the case. The crucial point, then, is that critical scholars ought not reject or arbitrarily pull up short of the results that proceed from their own research. That is, unless such is precisely their goal. It is of course possible that agnostics and others *want* to stop there in order not to arrive at a conclusion that they may not appreciate!

Instead of looking at less likely data, as scholars often do, such as concentrating on textual conflicts that cannot even hinder let alone halt these recognized historical findings, perhaps it can be determined that more than an undefined "something" occurred to Jesus's disciples. The key here is to highlight not what we think we *cannot* know, but what our own methodology indicates that we *can* know. Do we *already* have an adequate foundation from which we might answer our most vital questions? Scholars need to viably address the results of their own research. Of course, they can *deny* the conclusion of the resurrection, but this is different from providing an adequate explanation.

So, we may already possess precisely what we need—plenty of data to know what occurred. Since scholars readily concede that Jesus's disciples had experiences that they *thought* were appearances of Jesus after his death, these need to be explained. If naturalistic hypotheses do not do so viably, then we must look elsewhere for what *convinced them* of this.

In other words, did the disciples *really* see Jesus after his death, no matter the cause, or not? Anything less is an inadequate response. By using only those data to which virtually all scholars agree, we may already have adequate grounds to argue that Jesus's followers actually saw him alive after his death. So, we need to stay focused precisely on this particular issue. If the resurrection appearances follow, then we have successfully made a historical case for them. We must account for our commonly held data.[72]

By pulling up short with an agnostic response of "I do not know; let's stop right here" sort of reply, we may actually be curtailing the historiographical process, bypassing the very information that might be enough to establish Jesus's appearances as the most likely explanation of the sightings. Reginald Fuller is correct in asserting that the factual situation "therefore requires that the historian postulate some other event"

---

[72] This is the portion of the argument that has been the central focus of the minimal facts argument over the years, and precisely where the case is at its very strongest.

as an adequate reason for the disciples' conviction. We must have a real "cause of the Easter faith . . . outside of their belief."[73]

Near-Death Experiences and Supernatural Reality

Our sixth move takes aim at the frequent objection that any conclusions, like the one to which we have been pointing, would still involve a supernatural realm, hence invoking its automatic dismissal or, at the very least, a concession that it is just barely possible, since we know of no such realm.[74] This response seems about as common as a jerk of the knee when stimulated with a little medical hammer! When faced with the possibility of a supernatural event, the automatic retort is quite often that we must draw back to the agnostic stance, strictly to avoid the miraculous claim.

What makes this reaction so incredible is that its utter confidence follows from its position that frequently denies its own burden of proof while demanding of others that such a burden is theirs alone. This is sometimes followed up by begging the question by seldom, if ever, attempting to indicate the truth of its own worldview (without which they have no right to hold prisoner any supernatural views) as well as failing to distinguish what can be known on the historical (nonmiraculous) side, even when they already acknowledge the historicity of these data.

Although these last two steps of our half dozen definitely cannot be argued in this chapter, perhaps the central claim of this entire study is that the minimal facts argument is strong enough to indicate the historicity of Jesus's resurrection. Further, it has already been argued at length elsewhere that an exceptionally strong evidential case can be made for at least an initial afterlife based on individual, highly evidenced near-death experiences (NDEs). The latter could potentially supply an empirical case for a nonmiraculous but still supernatural reality, in the same realm (the afterlife) as the resurrection.

Cases cited elsewhere include many highly evidential reports where the individual is later able to recount minute details from their surroundings as well as other events while in a near-death state. For example, in dozens of documented cases of

---

[73] Reginald H. Fuller, *The Formation of the Resurrection Narratives* (Philadelphia: Fortress, 1980), 169, 181.

[74] As is the chief response in Larry Shapiro, *The Miracle Myth: Why Belief in the Resurrection and the Supernatural Is Unjustified* (New York: Columbia University Press, 2016), 29, 55–58.

NDEs where the individual was *without brain or heart activity of any measurable sort*, these individuals reported accounts that were later corroborated. Sometimes the subsequently confirmed events occurred *miles* away from their locations, while others provided evidence from minute descriptions in their *immediate environment*, such as an operating room.

In a few other reported cases, *healthy persons* have reported witnessing the NDEs of others! In another few accounts, the NDE patients had been blind all of their lives except during the experience. Once in a while, those experiencing an NDE seemingly brought back testimonies from deceased individuals whom they reported seeing again. These individuals, who had died years before, imparted information that apparently was unknown to anyone alive but was confirmed later, sometimes quite dramatically.[75]

The most likely conclusion to be drawn from this plethora of more than 300 interdisciplinary, exceptionally well-evidenced NDE cases is that at least the best of these strongly evidence what we have termed "minimalistic life after death," in that they indicate consciousness beyond the initial stages of death. Though NDEs are not miraculous events requiring God's intervention, they would evidence a supernatural realm, which is also anathema to naturalism and its relatives.

The relevance of NDEs for the resurrection is twofold, as these truths would be interconnected. Not only would a supernatural realm exist, but this confirmation concerns the specific area of life after death.[76] The claim of agnostic doubt is that we

---

[75] For many accounts of well-evidenced cases, relevant sources, data drawn from medical journals, plus detailed arguments for an afterlife, see Gary R. Habermas and J. P. Moreland, *Beyond Death: Exploring the Evidence for Immortality* (Wheaton: Crossway, 1998), chaps. 7–9; cf. also Habermas, *Risen Jesus*, 60–62; Habermas, "Near-Death Experiences and the Evidence—A Review Essay," *Christian Scholar's Review* 26 (1996): 78–85; Habermas, "Paradigm Shift: A Challenge to Naturalism," *Bibliotheca Sacra* 146 (1984): 437–50, esp. 444–49. For the work of others, see esp. J. Steve Miller, *Near-Death Experiences as Evidence for the Existence of God and Heaven: A Brief Introduction in Plain Language* (Acworth, GA: Wisdom Creek, 2012); Michael Sabom, *Light and Death: One Doctor's Fascinating Account of Near-Death Experiences* (Grand Rapids: Zondervan, 1998); Mario Beauregard and Denyse O'Leary, *The Spiritual Brain: A Neuroscientist's Case for the Existence of the Soul* (New York: HarperCollins, 2007), esp. chap. 6.

[76] It may be remembered that Wedderburn also links together these two topics (*Beyond Resurrection*, 129–34), citing John Hick in the process. An afterlife could help with Wedderburn's "most problematic" pastoral issues too (221–26), although we are bereft of a strictly Christian response if we leave out Jesus Christ's resurrection role in all of this discussion. Hick, on the other hand, *did* bring Jesus's resurrection into the discussion, including much more detail than Wedderburn. For our purposes here, an important

cannot decide on either such *events* or such a *realm*. But if an afterlife is a reality, the popular naturalistic objection against the resurrection that supernatural events are practically impossible loses a great deal of its force. Further, the resurrection could be investigated strictly on its own grounds in order to ascertain if it is a unique instance of this reality, since the path has already been opened. The evidence for the disciples seeing an appearance of Jesus after his death is strong, and this would be a final blow to the agnostic option. Hence, afterlife and resurrection play off one another.

Would Jesus's resurrection appearances still be unique events?[77] Even the straightforward historical events would indicate that this is the case. According to the fourth critique of agnosticism above, we are pursuing here this-worldly, historical aspects of this event. Did Jesus die? Was he seen afterward? The way is now totally clear to answer these two questions.

Is there is a path by which we may move from the most secure historical facts to the historical appearances of Jesus? That Jesus died and that afterward his early followers thought they saw him again are both held by virtually all critical scholars

---

example is Hick's argument that Jesus's resurrection provided additional support and confirmation for the disciples' belief in life after death, though they already believed in an afterlife both "before and independently of his resurrection." But now the ideas could work together. See John Hick, *Death and Eternal Life* (San Francisco: Harper & Row, 1976), particularly chap. 9 and page 179. Incidentally, in April 1987 I, John Hick, and a few others participated in a dialogue on the afterlife at Louisiana State University. On the second day of the dialogue, Hick opened his remarks by arguing that Jesus's resurrection experiences and NDEs were two of the very best indicators we have of the truth of the afterlife.

[77] After all, the resurrection appearances were not NDEs for several key reasons. The relevant texts indicate that Jesus (1) was really dead, (2) was raised in his own (although now-changed) body, and (3) would never die again. The apostle Paul taught that Jesus was the very first to be raised in this manner (1 Cor 15:20). Moreover, (4) what are we to make of the Acts descriptions (9:1–9; 22:6–11; 26:12–18) of brilliant light associated with Jesus's appearance to Paul, unlike NDEs? (5) If Jesus predicted his resurrection ahead of time, which we will also argue later on critical grounds, this indicates his not only being aware of the event beforehand, but his having had an actual part in worldview planning terms, surely unlike anything in NDEs. (6) The empty tomb by itself would be a simply huge point of differentiation from NDEs, where the body remains behind in some shape. (7) The amazing array of resurrection appearance details, including the reported number of appearances, to both groups and individuals, indoors and outdoors, and so on, are unique as well. For a dialogue that highlights a number of these points, see Gary R. Habermas, "Resurrection Appearances of Jesus as After-Death Communication: Response to Ken Vincent," *Journal of Near-Death Studies* 30 (2012): 149–58.

today, including the agnostics whose views we studied above. Most critical scholars also concede that natural alternative hypotheses are unable to explain these data. This scenario in tandem indicates that, at least for those who reject the alternative hypotheses, the best explanation for what occurred is that Jesus was indeed seen by his disciples after his death.

To repeat, then, that the early disciples really thought that they had seen Jesus after death, coupled with failing to disprove this naturally, indicates that they did see Jesus again. The more thoroughly these natural options are disproven, the more probably Jesus's appearances are indicated. This is the inference to the best historical explanation. No wonder the distinguished, self-described liberal scholar E. P. Sanders thought that Jesus's postmortem appearances were "secure facts" that we could know about Jesus.[78]

Conclusion: To Pull Back or Move Ahead?

So where does this discussion leave us? We began this essay with a brief list of facts that is accepted as historical by the vast majority of scholars who comment on the issues, regardless of their personal beliefs or theological outlook. Other pertinent data could be added to the list too. The relevant question for us here, then, is whether we ought to pull back and conclude that, in spite of all these data, almost anything is preferable to Jesus's appearances after death, as Wedderburn and Ehrman do? Or ought we to move ahead and affirm that an examination of the historical portion of Jesus's postmortem appearance claim pushes us to the conclusion that it is indeed the best explanation of our data?

Some scholars think that agnosticism has the advantage of always taking the natural path, hence its question marks have to do with the supernatural. But I have argued that the agnostic alternative is seriously troubled by an ascending series of six problems, many of which are quite troublesome. Besides some *overstatements* that need some adjusting, taking the agnostic stance on the resurrection may be simply a private notion, devoid of providing its own reasons. But if the agnostic position is asserted or thought to be held for good reasons, then the mere claim is insufficient; *a burden of proof* follows. *Why*, precisely, can we not get behind the data and know what happened to Jesus's disciples? Why are the data insufficient? Why should we stop exactly here?

---

[78] E. P. Sanders, *The Historical Figure of Jesus* (London: Penguin, 1993), 11, 13, 278–80.

Additionally, unless a deeper philosophical position that questions the supernatural realm is itself established, the agnostic begs the question against that conclusion. *On what grounds* are we justified in doubting the occurrence of the supernatural realm or of miracles? What determines that this agnostic outlook on the world is correct? After all, if it is to rule out all of nonnatural existence, we need some grounds for this move.

Moreover, it seems that the agnostic contention that historians are only able to investigate the historical side of a miracle claim makes a good deal of sense, though we must be careful not to overemphasize specializations. Yet, historical research *still* indicates both that Jesus died and that he was seen afterward by his followers. We tabled for now the supernatural portion of the question regarding the *cause* of the resurrection when speaking specifically of the historians' craft. But now the balance would be shifting well away from agnosticism anyway, because its skepticism of the supernatural would be a moot point at this juncture.[79]

Further, if the historical facts on which virtually all critical scholars agree strongly favor the resurrection appearances, then the central claim that Jesus was seen after his death would still obtain. For those agnostics who agree, they would be moving toward taking this stronger position!

Finally, if the many well-evidenced NDEs establish at least a minimal afterlife, it would appear that the nature of this reality drives a final nail in the agnostic position. For if life after death actually exists, we *now know* about the reality of a central, relevant tenet that agnostics have long questioned. So, even if we are pursuing only the historical side of the issue for now, Jesus could have lived after his death.

As just summarized above, the fact that the early disciples really thought that they had seen Jesus after his death, when juxtaposed with the failure of natural alternative hypotheses, indicates the strong likelihood that the early disciples did see Jesus again. The more these natural alternative options fail, the more Jesus's appearances emerge as the probable inference to the best historical explanation.

Therefore, the view that Jesus was indeed raised from the dead makes the best sense of the historical and other data. For those who already think that God exists or that there are other reasons to hold to a supernatural realm (see some examples in

---

[79] As William Lane Craig noted many years ago, if Jesus indeed rose from the dead, then "only a sterile, academic skepticism resists this inevitable inference," namely, that God was the one who had raised him. See Craig, *The Son Rises: The Historical Evidence for the Resurrection of Jesus* (Chicago: Moody, 1981), 137.

the other chapters in this volume), these would provide still additional "clinchers" to the argument here.

The agnostic position on the resurrection exhibits the modern charm engendered by a scholarly shoulder shrug and accompanied by a verdict of "We cannot always be sure." But it opts for the question mark without realizing that this maneuver exposes a position devoid of solid reasons that would establish its position. Exactly why can't we know the nature of the disciples' experiences? Further, how is the agnostic position itself established? And since we are only investigating the historical side of these claims for now, what about the strong evidence that Jesus was seen after his death, especially when NDEs indicate independently that agnostics are already mistaken regarding the cognate realm of an afterlife?

By championing the question mark, agnosticism works itself too quickly into a corner, opening itself up to the precise contrary data that can disprove it. Here it comes up very short on a number of crucial questions in areas where we already have plenty of data to draw positive conclusions.[80]

---

[80] An earlier, much briefer essay on this topic appeared as Gary R. Habermas, "The Resurrection of Jesus and Recent Agnosticism," in *Reasons for Faith, Making a Case for the Christian Faith: Essays in Honor of Bob Passantino and Gretchen Passantino Coburn*, ed. Norman L. Geisler and Chad V. Meister (Wheaton, IL: Crossway, 2007), 281–94.

18

Five Reasons for the Failure of
Naturalistic Theories

I n this volume, a wide range of naturalistic hypotheses have been treated in great detail, hypotheses aimed both at miracle claims in general and the resurrection of Jesus more specifically. Many refutations were given to each alternative, and different types of responses were sometimes arranged by category. Many responses to miracle claim objections were chiefly foreshadowed by David Hume, although some earlier skeptics were also discussed, such as Benedict Spinoza and the English deists. Critical responses to miracles that appeared later in the twentieth and twenty-first centuries were likewise entertained. A great many of these newer efforts support what were often recast as anti-miraculous arguments as well as new developments of other theses. We also encountered a great variety of critiques from the skeptics as well. There is much to digest from this long and challenging group of thinkers, with many readers being drawn to their favorite candidates.[1]

---

[1] Many scholarly writings have addressed these trends, some written before Hume's day, which was before the American Revolutionary War era. Most of those works before that time were supportive of miracles, as are an amazing number of writings in certain recent scholarly works today. The Western intellectual spectrum could include the following scholarly works. Living a little more than a century before Hume was the mathematician and philosopher Blaise Pascal, *Penseés: Thoughts on Religion and Other Subjects* (New York: Washington Square, 1965), particularly thoughts 801 and 802 plus section 13,

In many ways and in general, Hume is seemingly viewed and interpreted by many thinkers as being colored by some broad brushstrokes. On the one hand, Hume is the watershed philosopher who was interpreted as being chiefly responsible as the most influential scholar who turned critiques of miracles in the proper, modern direction. On the other hand, Hume was also seen as the lightning rod, as the philosopher who got much attention that he did not deserve, due to the publishing of an exceptionally faulty article that managed to get most of the central issues twisted.

We have taken a great deal of time in this text to understand Hume's argument against miracles. Initially, we set forth the major, most influential understandings of Hume and decided on what seemed to be the best interpretation, making use of today's premier scholarly insights. Next, we outlined the philosophical attempts chiefly in analytic philosophical circles to follow in Hume's footsteps by introducing some dozen and a half additional arguments against miracles. These twin efforts were followed by a third, closer look at a specific argument of Hume's that we numbered challenge 3:3, where Hume argued that miracles from rival religions, along with their competing teachings, would only serve to cancel out each other, leaving no viable candidates standing as for miraculous events.

"The Miracles," 803–56. Rick Kennedy presents an amazing study in *A History of Reasonableness: Testimony and Authority in the Art of Thinking* (Rochester: University of Rochester Press, 2004), esp. chaps. 2–5, tracking Augustine and the eleventh through the eighteenth centuries, with frequent thoughts on discussions of miracles (43–44, 105, 115, 137, 150–53, 158, 164–66, 172–73, 184–85, 196–213). Stanley Tweyman, ed., *Hume on Miracles* (Bristol: Thoemmes, 1996) is a collection of essays with half being written before Hume's death, and the other half from after Hume's time. From this same period is Richard Whately, *Historic Doubts Relative to the Existence of Napoleon Bonaparte* (London: Hatchard, Piccadilly, 1819); Robert Bruce Mullin, *Miracles and the Modern Religious Imagination* (New Haven: Yale University Press, 1996); philosopher of science Stanley L. Jaki, *Miracles and Physics* (Front Royal, VA: Christendom, 1989), esp. chaps. 1–2 for a couple of centuries of overview on this issue. Containing more on the current state of modern physics with regard to the question of miracles, see Werner Schaaffs, *Theology, Physics, and Miracles*, trans. Richard L. Renfield (Washington, DC: Canon, 1974); Colin Brown, *Miracles and the Critical Mind* (Grand Rapids: Eerdmans, 1984); Norman L. Geisler, *Miracles and the Modern Mind: A Defense of Biblical Miracles* (Grand Rapids: Baker, 1992), defending biblical miracles, as the title indicates, while covering critiques from Spinoza to the present; Richard Swinburne, ed., *Miracles* (New York: Macmillan, 1989), featuring a cross-section of both negative and positive responses.

This chapter briefly summarizes several *categories* of critiques against those scholars who oppose the existence of miracles. These classifications emerged from the lengthy discussions in this text and from the even more prolonged, drawn-out critique that still continues today. These group refutations draw together many of the subpoints that have been catalogued together.

The most recent research seems to agree largely and has trended chiefly in the direction of Hume being in error at a number of key points, as we pointed out in the specific details in our other treatments. This does not mean necessarily that a particular bottom line on the miracles question follows automatically, but only that Hume's approach has frequently been viewed as a less than helpful way of handling the issues. This has been emerging of late as the majority view. Additional arguments in this study on whether miracles have and do actually occur today are forthcoming as we move forward.

For many researchers, Hume appears to have presented a faulty case and, therefore, failed to reach his goal of disproving miracles. His essay was more general in nature but, far more specifically, subsequent naturalistic attempts that sought to explain away miracles, including the resurrection of Jesus in particular, arose later by taking alternate paths that Hume probably hinted were the best routes to take.[2] By dividing the refutations into families, the hope here is to pursue a helpful path through a maze of ideas. Further, more time will be spent on taking the next step by also including the failures of natural alternative efforts to explain miracle claims in nonmiraculous ways, another move that Hume similarly mentioned. This critique begins with overall failures of these tactics.

Reason 1

The skeptical backdrop against miracles provided by David Hume fails to provide good "cover" for the prospect of rejecting miracles.

After the appearance of Hume's essay "Of Miracles," there was a great deal of agreement among religious liberals that this work had put to rest the issue of miracles: they simply never occurred. For example, almost a century later, the equally famous skeptic, the nineteenth-century German liberal scholar David Strauss, concluded that

---

[2] David Hume, "Of Miracles," esp. as Hume sets forth in the last two paragraphs of part 1 in section 10 of his famous work *An Enquiry Concerning Human Understanding*.

Hume's treatise had settled forever the issue. Supernatural events that ran contrary to the course of nature just did not happen.[3]

In the first half of the twentieth century, prominent Columbia University philosopher John Herman Randall Jr. also maintained this line of reasoning, arguing, "Since Hume's critique of miracles in the eighteenth century, religious liberals have refused to believe in any such interferences with the order of natural law." So-called miracles were "the product of the natural causes of human credulity, imagination, and legend." Then Randall summarized the matter: "In the eighteenth century, miracles were the chief support of faith; in the next, they became the chief problem to be explained."[4]

To be sure, liberal critics did not need much reason or encouragement to take the stance that miracles were at best longshots. But as documented in our initial chapter on Hume, his case has received much less support in the past few decades, with many questions being raised about his assumptions, his science, and especially his use of induction in his arguments. While some scholars still support him,[5] more have opposed his ideas on miracles.[6]

---

[3] David Friedrich Strauss, *A New Life of Jesus*, 2nd ed., 2 vols. (London: Williams & Norgate, 1864), 1:199–201.

[4] John Herman Randall Jr., *The Making of the Modern Mind: A Survey of the Intellectual Background of the Present Age*, rev. ed. (Boston: Houghton Mifflin, 1940), 553–54.

[5] Rejoinders on behalf of Hume's basic ideas include Antony Flew, *Hume's Philosophy of Belief: A Study of His First Inquiry* (London: Routledge & Kegan Paul, 1961), esp. chap. 8, "Miracles and Methodology"; Robert J. Fogelin, "What Hume Actually Said about Miracles," *Hume Studies* 16 (1990): 81–87; Fogelin, *A Defense of Hume on Miracles* (Princeton: Princeton University Press, 2003); Fred Wilson, *Hume's Defense of Causal Inference* (Toronto: University of Toronto Press, 1997); Wilson, "The Logic of Probabilities in Hume's Argument against Miracles," *Hume Studies* 15 (1989): 255–75; Richard Otte, "Schlesinger and Miracles," *Faith and Philosophy* 10 (1993): esp. 93, 97; William L. Vanderburgh, *David Hume on Miracles, Evidence, and Probability* (Lanham, MD: Lexington, 2019).

[6] Contrary expositions include George I. Mavrodes, "David Hume and the Probability of Miracles," *International Journal for Philosophy of Religion* 43 (1998): 176–77; John Earman, *Hume's Abject Failure: The Argument against Miracles* (Oxford: Oxford University Press, 2000), esp. the entire host of critiques found in part 1; John Earman, "Bayes, Hume, and Miracles," *Faith and Philosophy* 10 (1993): 293, 305–6; Robert A. Larmer, *The Legitimacy of Miracle* (Lanham, MD: Lexington, 2014), esp. chaps. 2–4, specifically 60–61; Rodney D. Holder, "Hume on Miracles: Bayesian Interpretation, Multiple Testimony, and the Existence of God," *British Journal for the Philosophy of Science* 49 (1998): 60–62; George N. Schlesinger, "Miracles and Probabilities," *Nous* 21

Some of Hume's chief problems that were argued and documented earlier included the following: (1) The presence of a number of informal logical fallacies, including some major and rather obvious examples of circular argumentation and question-begging. Of course, these problems can be corrected, but in Hume's case they are woven so deeply within his argument that much of the seeming force of the charges would be removed too. (2) Pontificating on what can or cannot occur in nature, while failing to address the role that might be played by a greater power that chooses to act, is not the best way to ascertain if these events can occur. Even stranger here, the present sentiment seems to be that Hume was some species of deist or theist.[7] (3) Hume's four subarguments against miracles in part 2 of his essay sometimes raise thoughtful issues, but they tend to pick around the edges, while none comes close to indicating that miracles cannot occur. (4) If Hume was referring to the fellows at the pub or a few other places, then his sample size was obviously way too small with regard to his claim that "uniform experience" opposed all miracles. In such a case, his observations would have been almost valueless. But if Hume were to have extended his approach by asking enough people to make a decent sampling size, then the problem was that he almost certainly would have heard some miracle testimonies, just like present-day polling numbers. But either way, his major contention is inductively mistaken from the outset.[8] (5) If miracles do not break the laws of nature, as a number of philosophers claim, Hume's program probably could not even get started. (6) Elsewhere in his writings, Hume speaks out against some of the same principles that he employs in his argument, such as the very notion of our inability to demonstrate that uniformity and causality are true. Why the seeming discrepancy? (7) Finally, there are hundreds of documented miracle claims today, some even observed under stringent conditions. They have been published in medical

---

(1987): 219, 230–32; Schlesinger, "The Credibility of Extraordinary Events," *Analysis* 51 (1991): 125; Benjamin F. Armstrong Jr., "Hume on Miracles: Begging-the-Question against Believers," *History of Philosophy Quarterly* 9 (1992): 319, 327; Roy A. Sorensen, "Hume's Scepticism concerning Reports of Miracles," *Analysis* 43 (1983): 60; Stanley L. Jaki, *Physics and Miracles* (Front Royal, VA: Christendom, 1989), esp. 19–25, 32–33, 78–79, 92–93.

[7] See W. David Beck, *Does God Exist? A History of Answers to the Question* (Downers Grove, IL: InterVarsity, 2021), 130–32; cf. Jordan Howard Sobel, *Logic and Theism* (Cambridge: Cambridge University Press, 2004), section 7.5–6; also, William Lad Sessions, *Reading Hume's Dialogues* (Bloomington: Indiana University Press, 2002).

[8] For an excellent discussion here, see Mavrodes, "Probability of Miracles," 176–77.

journals, medical volumes, and elsewhere. This point alone could very well bring the downfall of Hume's thesis.[9]

Almost two dozen a priori objections to miracles were listed previously, some of which were inspired by Hume's approach along with a number of updates by analytic philosophers.[10] These charges were divided into five categories and over 100 responses were addressed to them, as follows: (1) A priori *objections* are usually fair game, but the problem is that they generally tend to either represent or become a priori *rejections*, where data are often ignored. The latter is *not* a fair approach for getting rid of ideas that we reject or even wish were not there. (2) Like the first set of critiques regarding Hume above, we still have not determined if there is a greater power in existence that can overcome any potential odds against miracles. For example, what good are the laws of nature if they are far from the ultimate force in the universe? (3) When miraculous-*sounding* claims are made, usually it is still possible to investigate the surrounding nonmiraculous "checkable" assertions, such as historical details or the structure of the arguments. Perhaps the measurable, weighable, observable aspects are enough to decide on the entire question. (4) Nature cannot be broadened in order to account adequately for events like Jesus's well-evidenced resurrection from the dead. (5) There are ways to trace an event back to a likely supernatural identification. In volume 4 of this study, we will present many details on two such detailed approaches—one moving from a theistic universe to Jesus's resurrection, and the other built on clear means of demarcation that already surround Jesus's resurrection.

Some of these critiques are quite forceful even by themselves. Unless Hume can answer or disprove at least each of the major ones plus a few others, his hypothesis is doomed. It is for these and other reasons that most scholars do indeed think that he has overextended himself. Additionally, those who depended upon Hume for their belief that miracles do not happen are likely to have built their interpretation of Jesus's resurrection on questionable foundations.

---

[9] For healing experiments confirmed by testing, see Candy Gunther Brown, *Testing Prayer: Science and Healing* (Cambridge: Harvard University Press, 2012). Reports containing multiple cases from physicians include H. Richard Casdorph, *The Miracles* (Plainfield, NJ: Logos, 1976), with photographs; Rex Gardner, *Healing Miracles: A Doctor Investigates* (London: Darton, Longman, & Todd, 1986).

[10] Gary R. Habermas, *Philosophy of History, Miracles, and the Resurrection of Jesus*, 3rd ed. (Sagamore Beach, MA: Academx, 2012), 10–24, 29–33.

Reason 2

Each natural hypothesis especially aimed at Jesus's resurrection is refuted by multiple reasons taken from the list of minimal historical facts and the data that confirm them.

Hume argued that whenever he heard of a claimed miracle, he always considered whether it was more likely that a supernatural event really did occur on such an occasion, or that the one reporting the event "should either deceive or be deceived." His rule was to "always reject the greater miracle."[11]

As an aside for right now, we have commented several times in this study that naturalism, including materialism or other possible forms of atheism and agnosticism whenever they may be assumed or employed, carry their own burdens of proof, depending on what is being asserted. It is helpful to recall once again that if Hume's rule of thumb in this matter is to always reject the greater miracle, then some forceful argument, evidence, or something else substantial must serve as a support as to why his view ought to be given preference above the others.

Hume might retort that those reporting miracles are frequently in error of some sort or another, and that miracles, by definition, are much rarer than normal events. No one is disputing that claim. But how many instantaneous healings or other events, or perhaps even very well-evidenced NDEs, would have to obtain before Hume's thesis would crumble, especially since he seems to admit *no* supernatural events, since the evidence is declared to be "uniform" against miracles?[12] So then, would one clear and very well-evidenced miracle or supernatural testimony do the job? Ten? A couple dozen? Given the available data, it seems like the theists would have the clear advantage on these comparative arguments.

The further matter is Hume's proposal to basically take *any* natural response over any supernatural one, and we have seen that this is a very common move among critics even today. But there is still the matter of why this is so. This sounds like prejudice unless there is sufficient data on the opposite side.

But here there is an additional kicker against the specific point that we are addressing. Every one of the naturalistic alternative suppositions that is lined up against Jesus's resurrection is itself opposed by an entire cartel of factual refutations of various sorts, as recognized by many critics themselves (and as will be pointed

---

[11] Hume, "Of Miracles," part 1, in *Essential Works of David Hume*, ed. Ralph Cohen (New York: Bantam, 1965), 128–29.

[12] Hume, 128.

out below). These reasons to reject the original naturalistic counter proposal, in turn, are themselves strengthened further. Since the refutations here are almost always drawn from and based on the minimal facts, this means that each refutation is backed by the very reasons affirmed by these very critical scholars who may be attempting to dismiss the resurrection! Thus, virtually all critical scholars, even the most skeptical ones, agree to the historicity of the minimal data that oppose these natural hypotheses. The combination is a strong listing of refutations—each multiply evidenced with additional full scholarly support regarding its historicity. That is probably why only a minority of critical scholars prefer these critical alternative theories anyway.

Reason 3

None of the major natural alternative theses covers all the minimal data, so more than one theory is probably necessary.

One of the chief means of choosing a natural path to explain the resurrection of Jesus is to cover as many historical aspects of the New Testament case as well as possible. Of course, these efforts will differ between individuals in that they are person relative to a large extent. Decisions are often based on particular *perceptions* of the known data, or even sound rather emotional in nature. So personal evaluations of which responses do the best job of explaining this or that aspect may differ. However, speaking broadly here, no single thesis does the job of covering well even all of the crucial information alone.[13] It seems inevitable that major components are neglected somewhere.

For example, various forms of hallucination theories may well remain the most popular views today.[14] But at a minimum, two huge hurdles and a host of smaller ones

---

[13] By twisting and turning this way and that, often in rather strange ways, some efforts may settle for saying *something* about most of the major aspects of the historical reports surrounding the resurrection. But the comments in this paragraph make the point that no single alternative thesis covers all the bases without exceptionally ad hoc requirements.

[14] Although, in the overall scheme of naturalists who respond on the subject of the historicity of the resurrection, relatively few scholars take one of the forms of this option. See Gary R. Habermas, "The Late Twentieth-Century Resurgence of Naturalistic Responses to Jesus' Resurrection," *Trinity Journal* 22 (2001): esp. 186–90, 194–96, including two generally unnamed theses that were named in this article: the "illumination" and "illusion" alternatives.

stand in their way.[15] The empty tomb with its incredible list of critically ascertained, positive reasons is really problematic here and clearly requires another explanation, for hallucinations would leave a body in the tomb untouched. The report that *groups* of witnesses saw the risen Jesus is even more troublesome, especially since these same reports are known to be multiply attested and exceptionally early.

That Jesus's disciples stole his dead body leaves a gaping hole when, as far as we know, these witnesses were clearly willing to die for their proclamation that Jesus had risen from the dead. Surely they would remember that they had stolen the body themselves! Virtually no critics get past this point. But what about *anyone else* stealing the body for *whatever* reasons—even unknown persons? That seems a little craftier, though, and is not plagued by the same reasons just mentioned. But to the extent that someone might argue this view successfully, they will have addressed only the empty tomb but basically almost nothing else. So, what about the toughest data to explain—namely, the appearances, plus everything else in the research that is well accredited?

The swoon (or apparent death) theory was popular mostly in the early nineteenth century but hardly at all today. Like the stolen body theses, there are knockout punches awaiting here—how could an undeniably hurting, exceptionally wounded, and sickly Jesus convince anyone that he was the risen Lord of life? And what about the Roman spear wound confirmed in a Roman source? Further, given the state of the medical findings today in dozens of studies, even the most critical scholars shy away and avoid this theory.

Other attempts to explain away the resurrection appearances of Jesus could be mentioned as examples, and many of these have been treated in great detail in this volume. But the chief problem we are raising at this point is that one natural alternative thesis does not cover very well all of the known facts that are considered to be solid by large numbers of critical scholars. Some of the evidence in favor of these facts seems altogether unanswerable in any coherent sense, particularly when there are remaining aspects of the data that have not been adequately addressed. Additional naturalistic riders may have to be added in order to address further uncovered aspects of the evidence that remain outstanding.

---

[15] Incredibly, perhaps the most popular natural thesis is actually beset by the most refutations. For example, see Gary R. Habermas, "Explaining Away Jesus' Resurrection: The Recent Revival of Hallucination Theories," *Christian Research Journal* 23 (2001): 26–31, 47–49.

Still, the argument against naturalistic theories being considered here is that a single alternative seems not to cover the knowable aspects, hence failing to do the job well. This alone is another difficult hill to climb. Lurking in the background, however, is the larger question of whether *any* of the natural hypotheses or adjustments are capable of doing the job.

Reason 4

Nineteenth-century German liberal scholars indicated many of the weaknesses in each of the natural theses by refuting individually each hypothesis on a piecemeal basis.

The last two reasons for the failure of naturalistic theories are not separate, stand-alone critiques but are additional indications that the previous three points were accurate. In other words, Hume was badly mistaken in his theorizing for a variety of reasons, and hence his thesis cannot serve as the backdrop for rejecting miracles. It is even more crucial that each natural hypothesis has been refuted for multiple reasons. This is shown further by the need for more than one of these alternate views to be correct at the same time in order to cover the factual landscape. These final two points provide additional corroboration of the first three by showing additional angles regarding the collapse of these alternative ideas.

The nineteenth century was the heyday of German liberalism, and German universities were the hotbed in developing naturalistic approaches to the resurrection of Jesus. Liberal theology dominated the leading schools and more than one of these professors even rejected the existence of Jesus.[16] To say the least, some of the critical approaches were very creative.[17]

Throughout the century, there was definitely a motive to expose this central Christian event of Jesus's resurrection as a myth, and in a glut of volumes with titles such as "The Historical Jesus," these scholars quite often indicated their willingness to engage the historical data. This was simply an intriguing trend in this century.

---

[16] Both Bruno Bauer and Peter Jensen took this position. As a contrast on the last point here, agnostic New Testament scholar Bart D. Ehrman notes that he knows of no scholar in a cognate field today who teaches in an accredited university, college, seminary, or divinity school who "has any doubts that Jesus existed." See Ehrman, *Did Jesus Exist? The Historical Argument for Jesus of Nazareth* (New York: HarperCollins, 2012), 2–3.

[17] Schweitzer devotes two chapters to the fictitious lives of Jesus in Schweitzer, *The Quest of the Historical Jesus: A Critical Study of Its Progress from Reimarus to Wrede*, trans. W. Montgomery (New York: Macmillan, 1968), chaps. 4, 12.

However, in the process of treating relevant subject areas in Jesus's life and giving their own nonsupernatural "remedies," several of these major researchers leveled hearty criticisms at their fellow German liberals. Several of the major refutations emerged during this historical period, including some of the truly crushing comments aimed squarely at rival hypotheses.[18]

For example, David Strauss's devastating critique of the swoon theory has stood the test of time, remaining the chief critique still being proposed today against various suppositions of Jesus's apparent death. Strauss popularized the hallucination thesis in its place. However, scholars like Friedrich Schleiermacher, Heinrich Paulus, and especially Theodor Keim eliminated the hallucination (subjective vision) theory that David Strauss had popularized, providing a number of key critiques in the process.

Form-critical scholars along with other researchers of various stripes in the late nineteenth and early twentieth centuries facilitated the spread of ancient mythical or legendary accounts promoted by the German history of religions school (*religionsgeschichtliche Schule*). However, at the end of German liberalism, these critical scholars who concentrated on ancient mythology and legendary interests could not provide adequate accounts of the early proclamation of the resurrection appearances, as they recognized themselves. These and other theses were negated by the German liberals themselves, the very scholars who, according to their own theological agendas, should have embraced them. But rather than supporting their colleagues, they chewed up the other liberal views and spat them out.[19]

So throughout nineteenth-century Germany during this liberal period, scholars quite frequently supported their own approaches while tearing through each other's naturalistic resurrection theses in a point-by-point fashion as they elevated their own critical visions. Their language toward one another was possibly more pointed than anything in the history of theology. For example, Strauss once commented about a pastor who had been attacking his views: "This offspring of the legitimate marriage between theological ignorance and religious intolerance, blessed by a sleep-walking

---

[18] See chaps. 4–6 of volume 4 of this study for specific details regarding the nineteenth-century liberal attacks on Jesus's resurrection, the key sources, and the fates of these efforts to disprove other liberal theses.

[19] Examples of such criticism as applied to the German *religionsgeschichtliche Schule* are the detailed critiques by Ehrman (*Did Jesus Exist?*, 26, 207–18, 221–30, 256–58). Again, these along with other related trends from the days of the German liberals' theological scholarship, including their naturalistic theories and the subsequent refutations by others of this group, are cited and discussed in the three chapters above on this school of thought.

philosophy, succeeds in making itself so completely ridiculous that it renders any serious reply unnecessary."[20] Normally far more reserved, Schweitzer himself remarked regarding Neander's *Life of Jesus* that "it is a patchwork of unsatisfactory compromises. It is the child of despair, and has perplexity for godfather. One cannot read it without pain."[21]

Given such an acidic atmosphere even when addressing often like-minded colleagues, perhaps it will not be a great surprise to find former distinguished New Testament professor J. Gresham Machen of Princeton Theological Seminary testifying that, at the end of the German liberal era with the scholarly attacks on the views of fellow liberals, "the advocates of one theory are often the severest critics of another."[22] Without such nastiness, Machen time and again added many comments on the views of some of liberalism's most influential scholars that, in his estimation, presented natural approaches to the resurrection appearances that were nothing more than suppositions with virtually no effort at producing any historical or other data in their own defense.[23] That Machen was one of the well-trained scholarly critics at the close of the German liberal era increases the value of his insights.

One other note is needed before moving forward. Even while criticizing each other's resurrection alternatives, the German liberals often devoted considerably longer treatments to these naturalistic options than did later scholars, as we will see next. Just a few of the more striking examples will be mentioned here. Schleiermacher took several jabs at other liberal natural theories,[24] while devoting several chapters and dozens of pages to discussing whether or not Jesus actually died (though his own view on this topic is often debated).[25] Influential New Testament scholar F. C. Baur took over thirty pages to explain that Paul was the recipient of subjective, nonmiraculous experiences at

---

[20] Schweitzer, *Quest of the Historical Jesus*, 97.

[21] Schweitzer, 101.

[22] J. Gresham Machen, *The Origin of Paul's Religion* (Grand Rapids: Eerdmans, 1925), 65.

[23] For examples, Machen (*The Origin of Paul's Religion*) remarked that the liberal "diagnosis rests upon totally insufficient data" and has "no real basis," "no evidence," and "prejudges" the case (59), "not the slightest evidence," "no evidence," and no "certain information" (65). An alternate thesis concerning Paul's appearance is judged to be "very romantic, but very un-Pauline" (66). On several other occasions, Machen asks for the critical evidence to be produced instead of being assumed (61, 64, 67).

[24] Friedrich Schleiermacher, *The Life of Jesus* ed. Jack C. Verheyden, trans. S. Maclean Gilmour (Mifflintown, PA: Sigler, 1975), 440, 442–43, 455 esp., 474.

[25] Schleiermacher, 415–17, 439, 441, 445, 447, 450–52, 455–58, 463–65, 469–71, 477–81.

his conversion, but that he mistook these inner events for outer, objective realities and concluded that Jesus had actually appeared to him. In the process, Baur still employed a few criticisms along the way for others who disagreed with his approach.[26] Strauss took far more swipes at the resurrection theses of others,[27] while spending less time on his favorite option—the subjective vision hypothesis.[28]

French scholar Ernest Renan devoted some sixty pages in two brief chapters to the death and burial of Jesus plus a lengthy appendix at the end of his book *Vie de Jésus*. He made some notable comments regarding Jesus's memorable character along with Mary Magdalene's enthusiasm and imagination, which gave way to the doctrine of the resurrection including the "apparitions" of Jesus to Peter and the others.[29] Yet, Renan was criticized heavily and actually relieved of his teaching position for almost ten years as well as roundly criticized by the "French school of critical theology."[30]

Occasionally there were surprising concessions by these authors themselves. Otto Pfleiderer, a member of the *religionsgeschichtliche Schule*, devoted two long chapters of about seventy pages in length to ancient pagan parallels that rivaled Jesus as a miracle worker and then turned to parallels to Jesus's resurrection in the ancient world.[31] But then Pfleiderer remarkably conceded that Jesus's predictions of his resurrection beforehand, plus some eyewitness testimony in the New Testament along with the "historical fact" of Jesus's death and the "visions" afterward to his disciples, were all unique vis-à-vis the pagan accounts.[32]

---

[26] Ferdinand Christian Baur, *Paul the Apostle of Jesus Christ: His Life and Works, His Epistles and Teachings; A Contribution to a Critical History of Primitive Christianity*, trans. A. Menzies, 2 vols. (London: Williams & Norgate, 1873; repr., Peabody, MA: Hendrickson, 2003), 1:63–92, particularly 67–81, see also 1:264; 2:251–53.

[27] David Friedrich Strauss, *The Life of Jesus Critically Examined*, ed. Peter C. Hodgson, trans. George Eliot (Mifflintown, PA: Sigler, 1994), 45–46, 678–79, 707, 718, 734, 737–41, 744, 751, besides criticizing the German liberal "rationalists" (423, 479–81, 485).

[28] Strauss, 742–44, plus the excellent editor's annotations on 794–95.

[29] Ernest Renan, *Vie de Jésus* (Paris: Calmann-Lévy, 1864), 343–56, esp. 351, 355–56; plus 418, 420–27, incl. the "apparitions" to Peter and the twelve disciples along with Paul later. Renan also affirms his preference for the Gospel of John (423), a typical liberal move, at least earlier in the movement.

[30] Schweitzer, *Quest of the Historical Jesus*, 180, 189–90.

[31] Otto Pfleiderer, *The Early Christian Conception of Christ: Its Significance and Value in the History of Religion* (London: Williams & Norgate, 1905), 63–133.

[32] Pfleiderer, 102, 157–58. This did not indicate, however, that Pfleiderer accepted the historicity of Jesus's resurrection.

It is rather amazing that the nineteenth-century German liberals labored over such details in order to exalt their theses, often while decimating their colleagues' alternate resurrection accounts. Similarly, it has already been argued that the conservative scholars who lived during this German heyday also critiqued the liberal scholars, assessing their naturalistic theses with the same zeal and detail. These conservatives quite often taught at some of the major British and American universities such as Oxford, Cambridge, Aberdeen, Harvard, Yale, and Princeton Theological Seminary. A few examples here should suffice.[33]

These comments have concerned the various hard-hitting criticisms between the treatments that these nineteenth-century liberal German scholars devoted to their own natural theories concerning what caused the disciples' resurrection beliefs, as contrasted with critiquing other liberal scholars with whom they disagreed. The conservative scholars from this same period followed suit, manifesting perhaps even more critical detail regarding the liberal attacks on the resurrection, while the latter's

---

[33] Perhaps the best example here of conservatives treating these liberal naturistic theories is Scottish theologian James Orr, where approximately half of his almost 300-page book on Jesus's resurrection was devoted to addressing these alternate theses plus other critical questions. See Orr, *The Resurrection of Jesus* (London: Hodder & Stoughton, 1908; repr., Grand Rapids: Zondervan, 1965), 205–61 for just hallucination, objective vision, and legendary theses alone. Earlier than Orr, both Brooke Foss Westcott's *The Gospel of the Resurrection: Thoughts on its Relation to Reason and History* (London: Macmillan, 1865), 7–14, 30–54, 108–20, and William Milligan's *The Resurrection of Our Lord* (London: Macmillan, 1881), 76–119 included almost fifty pages each of refutations. Also appearing very early, though with fewer pages of rebuttal against the liberals, is Alfred Edersheim's huge study, *The Life and Times of Jesus the Messiah*, 2 vols. (Grand Rapids: Eerdmans, 1883), 2:621–29, and George P. Fisher's text *The Grounds of Theistic and Christian Belief* (New York: Scribner's Sons, 1883), 193–99, 202. Frederic Louis Godet included a treatment of the hallucination hypothesis in *Lectures in Defense of the Christian Faith*, 2nd ed. (Edinburgh: T&T Clark, 1883); see also H. C. G. Moule, *The Resurrection of Christ* (Minneapolis: Klock & Klock, 1898). Kirsopp Lake included more than thirty pages of critical responses in *The Historical Evidence of the Resurrection of Jesus Christ* (London: Williams & Norgate, 2012), 187–99, 209–13, 218–19, 225–26, 237–38, 245, 262–67, 271–76. W. J. Sparrow-Simpson included some forty pages devoted to the liberal hypotheses in *The Resurrection and the Christian Faith* (Grand Rapids: Zondervan, 1968), 40, 44, 100–122, 159–65, 436–42. Some of the most penetrating refutations of liberal ideas were included in Doremus A. Hayes's volume, *The Resurrection Fact* (Nashville: Cokesbury, 1932), 35–38, 275–99. Often cited by critical scholars and available in many reprints is Frank Morison's *Who Moved the Stone?* (London: Faber & Faber, 1930), 64, 88–102, 114, which also treated alternative theories in a fair amount of detail.

sometimes-large page counts reflected their seriousness. It is noteworthy that both the nineteenth- to early twentieth-century liberal and conservative retorts often seemed far more meticulous when compared to the volume of similar efforts throughout the majority of the twentieth century, as will be discussed next.

Reason 5

In contrast, most twentieth-century critical scholars rejected wholesale the naturalistic theories.

Whereas nineteenth-century critical scholars generally attacked the alternative resurrection hypotheses piece by piece until none remained, twentieth-century researchers took a different approach altogether. In their treatment of naturalistic resurrection views, the majority of scholars during the past several decades, both liberal writers as well as other more moderate scholars, tended to eschew detailed line-by-line critiques.[34] Instead, after making references to these natural alternative approaches, today's skeptics and other scholars generally either cite just a few of these theses and then reject them briefly with a couple of details or comments, mention just the most influential comeback, or simply issue a blanket statement declaring that the alternative positions, overall, are rather misguided or even hopeless. Few of these examples, listed in note 35, below, exceed twelve pages in length while others are only a few lines long—far behind the average during the reign of nineteenth-century German trends for either the liberals or the conservatives, as we have seen.[35] Conservative critiques are usually much lengthier, including many more details.

---

[34] Elsewhere, the term "liberal" is a reference to scholars who take any of several views that are basically defined by Bernard Ramm as those holding "specifically to a spirit of inquiry to which nothing is sacrosanct." Citing Kenneth Cauthen, Ramm defines liberal views as rallying around the three themes of erasing supernatural-natural distinctions, elevating human autonomy above theology, and celebrating the world as an open system that is in process. See the very helpful volume of definitions by Bernard Ramm, *A Handbook of Contemporary Theology* (Grand Rapids: Eerdmans, 1966), 80–82.

[35] The many examples exemplify a very wide swath of scholars from different perspectives. They may include self-identified non-Christians, skeptics, or moderate researchers who still reject natural theses for the resurrection. These approaches encompass the views of Geza Vermes, *The Resurrection* (London: Penguin, 2008), 143–49; Pinchas Lapide, *The Resurrection of Jesus: A Jewish Perspective* (Minneapolis: Augsburg, 1983), 120–28; James D. G. Dunn, *Jesus Remembered*, vol. 1 of *Christianity in the Making* (Grand Rapids: Eerdmans, 2003), 1:831–32, 838, 873–79; Dunn, *The Evidence for Jesus* (Louisville:

Several additional works similarly express their critiques in few words, only making remarks concerning one or two of the best-known alternative views. Chief among the areas of defense here are the empty tomb and various problems with hallucinations.[36] Especially in these last examples, the overall appearance of

Westminster, 1985), 72, 76; E. P. Sanders, *The Historical Figure of Jesus* (London: Penguin, 1993), 277–81; Wolfhart Pannenberg, *Jesus: God and Man*, trans. Lewis L. Wilkins and Duane A. Priebe, 2nd ed. (Philadelphia: Westminster, 1977), 88–106; Jürgen Moltmann, *Theology of Hope: On the Ground and the Implications of a Christian Eschatology*, trans. James W. Leitch (New York: Harper & Row, 1967), 172–82, 186, 197–202; Karl Barth, *The Doctrine of Reconciliation*, vol. 4.1 of *Church Dogmatics*, trans. G. W. Bromiley, ed. G. W. Bromiley and T. F. Torrance (Edinburgh: T&T Clark, 1956), 303, 334–37, 340–41, 351–52; Raymond E. Brown, *An Introduction to New Testament Christology* (New York: Paulist, 1994), 162–70; John A. T. Robinson, *Can We Trust the New Testament?* (Grand Rapids: Eerdmans, 1977), 120–29; N. T. Wright, *The Resurrection of the Son of God*, vol. 3 of *Christian Origins and the Question of God* (Minneapolis: Fortress, 2003), 27–28, 77, 80–81n265, 318, 550, 638–39, 686, 689, 697–706, 709–10; Luke Timothy Johnson, *The Writings of the New Testament: An Interpretation* (Philadelphia: Fortress, 1986), 101–5; Johnson, *The Real Jesus: The Misguided Quest for the Historical Jesus and the Truth of the Traditional Gospels* (New York: HarperCollins, 1996), 133–140; Ulrich Wilckens, *Resurrection: Biblical Testimony to the Resurrection. An Historical Examination and Explanation*, trans. A. M. Stewart (Atlanta: Knox, 1978), 117–19; Markus Barth, introduction, in Markus Barth and Verne H. Fletcher, *Acquittal by Resurrection: Freedom, Law, and Justice in the Light of the Resurrection of Jesus Christ* (New York: Holt, Rinehart, and Winston, 1964), 23–31; Gerald O'Collins, *Jesus Risen: The Resurrection—What Actually Happened and What Does It Mean?* (London: Darton, Longman, & Todd, 1987), 99–109, 118–27; Richard Swinburne, *The Resurrection of God Incarnate* (Oxford: Clarendon, 2003), 174–86; Stephen T. Davis, *Risen Indeed: Making Sense of the Resurrection* (Grand Rapids: Eerdmans, 1993), 16, 179–84; George Eldon Ladd, *I Believe in the Resurrection of Jesus* (Grand Rapids: Eerdmans, 1975), 132–42; Charles C. Anderson, *The Historical Jesus: A Continuing Quest* (Grand Rapids: Eerdmans, 1972), 166–73; Thorwald Lorenzen, *Resurrection and Discipleship: Interpretive Models, Biblical Reflections, Theological Consequences* (Maryknoll, NY: Orbis, 1995), 117–24; Murray J. Harris, *Raised Immortal: Resurrection and Immortality in the New Testament* (Grand Rapids: Eerdmans, 1983), 57–62; Robert Geis, *Life of Christ* (Lanham, MD: University Press of America, 2013), 313–22; John Drane, *Introducing the New Testament* (New York: Harper & Row, 1986), 103–6; Paul L. Maier, *In the Fullness of Time: A Historian Looks at Christmas, Easter, and the Early Church* (New York: HarperCollins, 1991), 189–96; Laurence W. Miller, *Jesus Christ Is Alive* (Boston: Wilde, 1949), 35–45; Grant R. Osborne, *The Resurrection Narratives: A Redactional Study* (Grand Rapids: Baker, 1984), 275–78.

[36] For just a few of these briefer examples that often exemplify the hit-and-miss pattern just mentioned, see C. Stephen Evans, *The Historical Christ and the Jesus of Faith: The Incarnational Narrative as History* (Oxford: Clarendon, 1996), 352–55; Raymond E. Brown, *The Virginal Conception and Bodily Resurrection of Jesus* (New York: Paulist, 1973),

the criticism almost seems to be a half-hearted critique due to the author being convinced that the enterprise itself is unnecessary to spell out, hence the perception of a wholesale dismissal. The overall result and appearance is that, even for liberal scholars at this present time, the naturalistic theories have had their day in court and we need to move on elsewhere.[37]

122, 126–29; Neville Clark, *Interpreting the Resurrection* (Philadelphia: Westminster, 1967), 100, 104; A. M. Ramsey, *The Resurrection of Christ: A Study of the Event and Its Meaning for the Christian Faith*, rev. ed. (London: Fontana, 1961), 41, 49–50; Helmut Thielicke, "The Resurrection Kerygma," in Leonhard Goppelt, Helmut Thielicke, and Hans-Rudolf Müller-Schwefe, *The Easter Message Today: Three Essays*, trans. Salvator Attanasio and Darrell Likens Guder (New York: Nelson, 1964), 85–91, 103.

[37] Confessional evangelical scholars and other conservatives have sometimes been left out of the surveys on the last two points above, not necessarily because of their training or their views. Quite often, in fact, the conservatives' graduate training is stronger than other researchers as well as having been done with professors, mentors, and other colleagues who generally oppose their views, thereby making them even better equipped in the process. This last thought, in particular, is vastly neglected and underappreciated in terms of evangelical competence. On the subject of conservative voices in these resurrection discussions, see Benjamin C. F. Shaw, "What's Good for the Goose Is Good for the Gander: Historiography and the Historical Jesus," *Journal for the Study of the Historical Jesus* 15 (2017): 291–309. One important reason to note the diversity of the scholars in these lists was so that it may be seen even more forcefully that the points being made in this context are present across the scholarly landscape and do not at all depend on "loading up" with conservative voices. An excellent and highly acclaimed example is the work of Michael R. Licona, *The Resurrection of Jesus: A New Historiographical Approach* (Downers Grove, IL: InterVarsity Academic, 2010). Licona's careful examination of the oft-neglected role of historiography in these studies (31–198), the more than 250 pages on the historical, clearly ascertained bedrock events surrounding Jesus's resurrection (199–464) as well as the central task of entertaining rival resurrection hypotheses (465–582) is done so carefully that the final conclusion (582–610) is very difficult to resist, even from researchers who differ with Licona's conclusions. This final point is emphasized by more than one of the recent scholars who wrote recommendations and complimented these or other aspects of Licona's work, even though they clearly disagreed with his overall stance. Since the chief topic of this chapter is a wrap-up of the naturalistic countertheses that oppose the historicity of Jesus's resurrection, we will just note additionally that the coauthored volume by Gary R. Habermas and Michael R. Licona, *The Case for the Resurrection of Jesus* (Grand Rapids: Kregel, 2004), includes more than 100 pages (including the endnotes) of evaluation regarding these natural alternative suppositions. Another conservative work that clearly belongs in the heart of this discussion is Wright's text, *The Resurrection of the Son of God*, which includes lengthy treatments of the ancient pre-New Testament sources (1–206), about 375 pages devoted to the key New Testament texts and extending afterward (207–583), as well

A last aspect of this issue should also be mentioned. One indication of these trends is that there seems at present to be a shortage of influential specialist scholars who are satisfied to champion just a single naturalistic theory, stick with it, and live or die with that choice. Clearly, that was not true of the English deists, the continental rationalists, or the entire movement of German liberals from Schleiermacher through Strauss and Bousset into the early twentieth century along with a number of other scholars since those days. In the past few years, at least two of the major critical scholars who held only one naturalist position have passed away.[38] That there appears to be a dearth of those researchers presently who advocate for only one alternative is certainly significant.

One aspect of the current debate that could help account for this trend was expressed by philosopher Angus Menuge. He stated that "Habermas' 'minimal facts' approach . . . does explain why, over time, one skeptical alternative after another to the historical fact of the resurrection has been abandoned, leaving critics with shrinking cover to hide from Christ's claim on their life."[39]

Conclusion

Such is the summarized critical work of at least the more than a century of the German liberal dominance of theology, including the scholarly employment of naturalistic theories to Jesus's resurrection. Actually, the efforts that have been viewed here in the current four chapters on these hypotheses actually get fairly close to extending into a second century in duration if the thinkers mentioned earlier are counted, such as the (mostly) English deists and some continental rationalists like Spinoza and

---

as treating major historical matters (585–738). In fact, the texts by Licona and Wright are probably the two most celebrated of these studies in print.

[38] Reference is made here to Gerd Lüdemann's subjective vision thesis in *The Resurrection of Jesus: History, Experience, and Theology*, trans. John Bowden (Minneapolis: Fortress, 1994) and his other works, plus John Shelby Spong's view that the primacy of Peter's conviction and influence was responsible for bringing the other disciples to faith in the living Lord as well in Spong, *Resurrection: Myth or Reality? A Bishop's Search for the Origins of Christianity* (New York: HarperCollins, 1994) and his other writings.

[39] Angus Menuge, review of *Debating Christian Theism*, ed. J. P. Moreland, Chad Meister, and Khaldoun A. Sweis, *Philosophia Christi* 16 (2014): 456. Intriguingly, one evangelical critic of the minimal facts approach notes this method's "near-exclusive use in Christian apologetic circles." See Lydia McGrew, *Hidden in Plain View: Undesigned Coincidences in the Gospels and Acts* (Chillicothe, OH: DeWard, 2017), 220–21.

Reimarus with regard to their opposition to supernatural events, written in works before the writings of Schleiermacher and the birth of German liberalism.

Yet, we are taking nothing for granted here. Just because scholarly adherence to naturalistic alternative theories may be at an all-time "low" at present, it is not "dead in the water" just because of the present lull.[40] According to one recent estimate with regard to the period of the Third Quest for the historical Jesus, "less than one-quarter of critical scholars who addressed the historicity question offered naturalistic theories."[41] Still, the state of each major alternative hypotheses will be pursued in this volume.

---

[40] As noted in Habermas, "Late Twentieth-Century Resurgence," there was a resurgence of these theses that has more recently seemed to have evaporated, at least somewhat.

[41] Gary R. Habermas, "Mapping the Recent Trend toward the Bodily Resurrection Appearances of Jesus in Light of Other Prominent Critical Positions," in *The Resurrection of Jesus: John Dominic Crossan and N. T. Wright in Dialogue*, ed. Robert B. Stewart (Minneapolis: Fortress, 2006), 78–92, particularly 82–86, 91–92.

19

Conclusion

Reviewing the initial two overall arguments here, volume 1 argued the details of the mostly historical evidence in favor of Jesus's resurrection appearances. Volume 2 sought to address and answer the naturalistic and other alternative responses that dispute these resurrection facts and interpretations.[1] In a nutshell, it was the position here that none of these objections come very close to dismantling the best evidences.

---

[1] In spite of the length of this volume, it is not being claimed that the treatment here was exhaustive. Various other alternate approaches have been attempted by critical scholars. For example, postmodern historical approaches among others were also presented and evaluated in volume 1. Michael R. Licona, in his text *The Resurrection of Jesus: A New Historiographical Approach* (Downers Grove, IL: InterVarsity Academic, 2010), treated a specific postmodern scholar who has applied some of these postmodern ideas to Jesus's resurrection plus various other religious considerations. Licona argued that postmodernists might insert their views into the systems of others in the name of openness and acceptance, though often doing so somewhat forcefully. According to Licona, Pieter Craffert is a representative scholar who failed in almost every step of Licona's very detailed evaluation by importing outside views into his New Testament studies, while all the time attempting to be postmodern, magnanimous, and accepting of all beliefs and cultures. Yet, at virtually every step, Craffert obstructed the beliefs of others and attempted to inform them that they are not viewing their own data from the proper perspectives. For example, Craffert employed a postmodern historiography against the "overwhelming majority of historians identifying themselves as realists" (566). Further, ad hoc components such as psychohistory produced some of these results (581-582). Craffert holds that multiple views and realities

The general response that tends to reject miracles or supernatural events because they are deemed to be outdated, unscientific, or unevidenced does not refute the arguments made in these two volumes. While this sort of response is widely held, it fails to deal with the crux of the empirical matters developed in more than one area here.[2]

(1) In the first two volumes, it has *not been argued* that the resurrection was a miracle, only that Jesus's appearances after his death were historical events that were believed to be resurrection appearances; that is, after his death, Jesus was actually seen again (without arguing for God's action).[3] (2) In the initial appendix to volume 1, it was argued that near-death experiences (NDEs) provide more than enough evidence to indicate the nonmiraculous likelihood of some form of an afterlife. (3) Further, if there is an afterlife, this at least opens the door to an integral component of the resurrection argument. In other words, if there is an afterlife of some sort, then Jesus's resurrection becomes even more likely as a specific case that involves

---

are true (564), but in the end, he is an example of pushing his naturalistic worldview onto others who do not hold these positions (566-67, 574). In the process, he "proposes interpretations that clearly run contrary to the main sense of the texts" in question (580), thereby doing violence to these other positions (581). The bottom line is that Craffert "failed to fulfill every one of the most important criteria" of Licona's comparative study (582).

[2] Please note that what follows is definitely *not* to be taken as a detailed or step-by-step demarcation of the argument in these first two volumes. Rather, we are just accenting a few of the most important comments.

[3] This is far from a quaint avoidance of the miracles issue. The historicity of Jesus's resurrection appearances is exactly what was being pursued in these two volumes at this point. A case for the cause of the resurrection is to be treated in volume 4 of this work, though it has not been attempted yet. That this historical case alone may be a possible move even from an atheist view, Bart D. Ehrman even argues that historians can study the question of "whether the disciples really had visions of Jesus after his death." But historians cannot adjudicate whether God was the one who actually raised Jesus from the dead. Thus, historians may even say "that Jesus was crucified, and buried, and then he was seen alive, bodily, afterward." But again, the key is that the historian could do so as long as the discussion was done "without appealing to divine causality" by saying that God was the one who performed the event of raising Jesus. This is the potentially miraculous portion of this question, and for Ehrman, this conclusion cannot be argued by historians from within their own discipline. Ehrman, *How Jesus Became God: The Exaltation of a Jewish Preacher from Galilee* (New York: HarperCollins, 2014), 148–49. In this matter, as far as it goes here, these are the questions that also have been addressed in these initial two volumes since the miraculous possibilities were not argued. As Ehrman states, whether Jesus was crucified, buried, and then seen afterward walking around and talking are historical issues apart from the cause.

and took place in this realm.[4] (4) As per the direction of volume 2, it should be even clearer to understand why naturalistic and other alternative theses do not work and are improbable. (5) Finally, the resurrection evidence presented in volume 1 can now speak for itself.[5]

These considerations are far from questions concerning why more observers do not accept various arguments and change their views either one way or the other when they hear the data. Sometimes this does occur. Of course, this question could be asked the opposite way as well! Most of those who hold different positions read or hear the material, and *neither* side will be convinced. It is widely known that worldviews usually dominate evaluations of the data, but this is a separate issue, which once again is to be taken up in volume 4.

This brings us to the end of volume 2, so we will leave these matters here with a couple more works still on the way. But for now, this broad summary should remind us where we left several of the chief issues.

---

[4] Allison agrees on this point as well in Dale C. Allison Jr., *The Resurrection of Jesus: Apologetics, Polemics, History* (London: T&T Clark, 2021), 235, 350.

[5] Again, the term *resurrection* in these volumes refers to that belief in the earliest church, as explained in this minimal fact as it was described in volume 1.

APPENDICES

APPENDIX 1

THE TALPIOT TOMB

The contents of this appendix appeared in a longer form, including photographs, in Gary R. Habermas, *The Secret of the Talpiot Tomb: Unraveling the Mystery of the Jesus Family Tomb* (Nashville: Holman Reference, 2007). All citations in this appendix match the informal style of that earlier work.

The bodily resurrection of Jesus is and has been a core belief of Christians. This belief has been challenged almost from the beginning and will continue to be challenged. One of the boldest approaches to showing that Jesus's bodily resurrection is a myth or a theological embellishment and not fact is the claim that came in early 2007 that the odds strongly favored that Jesus's bones had been found in a tomb in a southeast suburb of Jerusalem. Comments such as these were strongly challenged by scholars as well (see chapter 4 for this specific discussion).

Many have criticized the sensationalism of the documentary and book that made this claim. One of the problems with the so-called Talpiot hypothesis is its clarity and boldness. It can be a faith shaker, as witnessed by the emails and telephone calls that Christian apologists started receiving after this hypothesis went public.

Much of the help these believers were seeking was already available on the internet, including my own website, which received a sharp increase in traffic in the days following the announcement. The press soon moved on to other stories as Easter came and went. But many whose faith was shaken by the discovery of the Jesus family tomb may not have come to a resolution concerning the claim that Jesus's bones had been found.

In this short appendix, I shall expose the claim that there is a high probability that Jesus's bones have been found and assess the evidence offered for it. Understanding how well this claim stands up to scrutiny can be important not just for evaluating this claim but for knowing the solid evidential ground on which Jesus's bodily resurrection rests. Every believer owes it to themselves to understand the case for the resurrection of Jesus.

The Talpiot Tomb and Jewish Burial Practices

Israeli archaeologist Amos Kloner notes that on March 28, 1980, the entrance to a Jewish burial tomb was discovered in the East Talpiot region of Jerusalem.[1] At the time, there was no hint of the controversy that would arise. Actually, little was published on the subject during the next fifteen years. Then, during the Easter season of 1996, the BBC broadcasted a documentary that was titled "The Body in Question."[2] Even then, there was not much of a splash.

In the Talpiot Tomb, ten ossuaries (stone bone boxes) were found, six of which had names inscribed on them. According to Simcha Jacobovici and Charles Pellegrino, professional archaeologist Eliot Braun was the first to be dispatched to the site. Yosef Gat, an antiquities inspector, went as well. Kloner, then a PhD student, also joined this team of investigators.[3]

Jewish Burial Practices and Jesus's Burial

The Jews required that bodies be buried within twenty-four hours after death. Typically, two sorts of Jewish burial practices were utilized in the first-century AD. The less common but better-known technique would involve a burial cave

---

[1] Amos Kloner, "A Tomb with Inscribed Ossuaries in East Talpiyot, Jerusalem," *Atiquot* 29 (1996): 15.

[2] James D. Tabor, *The Jesus Dynasty: The Hidden History of Jesus, His Royal Family, and the Birth of Christianity* (New York: Simon & Schuster, 2006), 23.

[3] Simcha Jacobovici and Charles Pellegrino, *The Jesus Family Tomb: The Discovery, the Investigation, and the Evidence That Could Change History* (New York: HarperCollins, 2007), 3–8.

or tomb cut out of the rock in the area that generally surrounded the city of Jerusalem. Each burial cave would include one or more chambers surrounded by rows of *loculi*, which were burial compartments about the length of a body cut into the rock.

Each tomb belonged to an extended family and the dead were buried there over several generations. After death, the body of the family member would be prepared and then placed in a *loculus*, with the opening being sealed with a stone slab. Another stone would then be placed over the outside entrance to the tomb.[4]

Before burial, the dead body would be washed, anointed with oil, and then wrapped in a burial shroud. The body would lie in the tomb for a year or so, during which time the flesh would decay. Then, when only the person's bones remained in the tomb, they would be gathered and placed in a stone ossuary and reburied. In a minority of circumstances—about one quarter of the time—names would then be carved on the side of the box. Complicating the issue is that more than one person was often buried in these bone boxes. These ossuaries were only used for 100 years or so.[5]

Because cut stone tombs were very expensive, the more common method, used chiefly by poorer members of Jewish society, was to bury the dead in the ground. In this case, loved ones would be buried in "simple, individual trench graves dug into the ground, similar to the way we bury our dead today." The dirt would then be moved back into the trench and a "crude headstone" would usually be placed at one end of the burial site to mark the spot. This was not considered dishonorable. In these cases, nothing would remain to rebury after a year.[6]

Of these two sorts of Jewish burial, the use of the rock tomb is more widely known today, probably due to the case of Jesus's death and burial. Jodi Magness notes that while the Gospels are not only our earliest sources, they do accurately describe the burial of Jesus by Joseph of Arimathea in a *loculus* of his family's own tomb. The body had to be buried before the Sabbath began that same day at sundown. Otherwise, the burial would have had to wait until Saturday night after the Sabbath

---

[4] Jodi Magness, "Has the Tomb of Jesus Been Discovered?," *SBL Forum*, February 2007, http://www.sbl-site.org/Article.aspx?ArticleId=640.

[5] Tabor provides details in *Jesus Dynasty*, 8; Christopher A. Rollston, "Prosopography and the Talpiyot Yeshua Family Tomb: Pensées of a Paleographer," *SBL Forum*, March 13, 2007, http://www.sbl-site.org/Article.aspx?ArticleId=649.

[6] Magness, "Tomb of Jesus."

ended. However, that would exceed the twenty-four-hour maximum for burying a dead body. Thus, Joseph had to act very quickly.

So, Joseph procured Jesus's dead body, wrapped it in linen, included spices, and made sure that it was buried hastily late Friday afternoon in his own family tomb. In this, the Gospels show familiarity with Jewish law.[7] The Gospels explain that the women returned to see the tomb on Sunday morning. Mark (16:1) and Luke (24:1) specify that they brought spices that they had prepared, apparently to finish Friday afternoon's hasty burial. But all four Gospels teach that when the women arrived, they found that the tomb was empty. Afterward, the women and others saw the risen Jesus.

But at least the traditional understanding of these events has been challenged by the ossuaries from the Talpiot Tomb. The news dominated the religious world for weeks, beginning days before the extended New York press conference on February 27, 2007, followed by the airing of the Discovery Channel documentary on March 4, 2007. The latter was followed by a scholarly discussion. In this appendix we will investigate many challenges, both pro and con, as to whether the claims of the Talpiot hypothesis can be upheld over against the New Testament view.

A Word about the Sources

To the chagrin of scholars, the Talpiot story has been widely aired in the popular press, from television and radio discussions to various news media and internet publications. To be sure, many of these stories and articles involve scholarly input, sometimes even doing an excellent job of finding the right specialists. Still, many other sources derive from popular news outlets as well as personal and group websites. Therefore, it is not surprising that from the beginning this has been a prevalent story, especially since the original television and book versions were largely associated with the claims of two film producers.

Therefore, as a mainstream story much of the information about the Talpiot Tomb as well as many of the best quotations and critiques have appeared in popular venues. Accordingly, the sources that are employed in this appendix will be derived from both popular and scholarly areas. We will strive to cite recognized scholars whenever we can, even if the citations are found in popular sources.

---

[7] Magness, 2–4.

The Talpiot Tomb: Setting up the Debate

The 2007 New York news conference, the Discovery Channel documentary, and the publication of the book *The Jesus Family Tomb* made it very plain that James Cameron, Simcha Jacobovici, and Charles Pellegrino thought that it was very likely that the Talpiot Tomb was indeed the final burial place for the family of Jesus of Nazareth.[8] In this section we will outline the grounds for their argument.

Incidence of Ossuary Names and DNA Testing

From the very beginning, one of the most confusing aspects of the Talpiot Tomb story was that the names on the six ossuaries looked very different. The chief reason is that the names appeared in three different languages: Aramaic, Hebrew, and Greek. As listed by Kloner, the names are as follows:

- Mariamene (written in Greek)—a rare variation of Miriam, Maryam, or Marya
- Yehuda son of Yeshua (written in Hebrew)—Judah son of Jesus
- Matya (written in Hebrew)—Matthew
- Yeshua son of Yehoset (written in Aramaic)—Jesus son of Joseph
- Yose (written in Aramaic)—a contraction of Yehosef (Joseph)
- Marya (written in Hebrew)—Mary[9]

Since the Talpiot Tomb, like other rock tombs in Jerusalem, is that of an extended family, DNA analysis would seem to be a natural test. But ossuaries are usually cleaned after discovery with the contents being reburied. So, most of the stone boxes did not have enough material in them to do any DNA testing. As Tabor reported, "The other four [inscribed ossuaries] had been cleaned out, even vacuumed, with nothing left that could be easily tested."[10] This finding was repeated during the Discovery Channel scholarly discussion, hosted by Ted Koppel, with

---

[8] Jacobovici and Pellegrino, *Jesus Family Tomb*, chap. 4.

[9] Kloner, "Tomb with Inscribed Ossuaries," 17–19. Cf. also Rollston, "Prosopography"; Tabor, *Jesus Dynasty*, 23.

[10] James Tabor, "The Top Twenty Fictions Related to the Talpiot 'Jesus Family' Tomb," *TaborBlog*, February 17, 2018, https://jamestabor.com/the-top-twenty-fictions-related-to-the-talpiot-jesus-family-tomb/.

Jacobovici and Tabor both reiterating that only two ossuaries contained enough material to test.[11]

The two ossuaries that still contained material in them were those of Jesus son of Joseph and Mariamene. These contents were tested in a laboratory at Lakehead University in Ontario, Canada, where researchers were looking for a mitochondrial DNA match that would potentially have linked these individuals through a common mother. However, the DNA test came back with negative results.

Arguing that the absence of a DNA match was significant, Jacobovici and Pellegrino concluded that "Jesus of Nazareth and Mary Magdalene, if their DNA could be read, would be two individuals who had no family ties. But what are the alternatives? People buried in the same tomb were related by either blood or marriage." Thus, since they were not related by blood, they concluded that, most likely, they would have been married.[12]

Mary Magdalene and Other Family Connections?

But Jacobovici and Pellegrino go much further than this. Postulating that Jesus and Mariamene were married, they also argue that the latter was really Mary Magdalene, reminiscent of Dan Brown's hypothesis in *The Da Vinci Code*.[13]

Here's how the argument progresses:

- "Mary" was known in Greek as "Mariamne."
- Her name was actually written as "Mariamn-u," that is "of Mariamne."
- The second portion of the inscription "Mara" is a Greek rendering of an Aramaic word meaning "Lord" or "Master."
- So, the full inscription "of Mariamne" means "also called Lord/Master."
- The title on the ossuary is "perfectly consistent with the Mariamne described in the Acts of Philip as the sister of Philip. There she is also explicitly equated with the woman the Gospels call Mary Magdalene."

---

[11] Jacobovici and Tabor in *The Lost Tomb of Jesus: A Critical Look*, interview by Ted Koppel, Discovery Channel, aired March 4, 2007.

[12] Jacobovici and Pellegrino, *Jesus Family Tomb*, 168. Cf. also Stuart Laidlaw, "Christ's Tomb Found? Canadian Filmmaker Claims Burial Boxes Belonged to Christ's Family," *Toronto Star*, February 25, 2007, https://www.thestar.com/news/christs-tomb-found/article _dd08a8fa-4d50-5ae0-977b-6dd0f7e1e215.html.

[13] Dan Brown, *The Da Vinci Code: A Novel* (New York: Doubleday, 2003), chaps. 56, 58.

- "The *Acts of Philip* was widely quoted by early Christina writers but was eventually lost save for a few fragments."
- In June 2000, Bovon and Bouvier published the complete French translation of the Mount Athos version of the *Acts of Philip*, with its identification of Mary Magdalene as "Mariamne," the sister of the apostle Philip.[14]

Therefore, since "Jesus the son of Joseph" was not related by blood to "Mariamene," then they must have been married. And since Mariamene is probably Mary Magdalene, as just indicated by the argument above, then the "Judah son of Jesus" who is also buried in another ossuary in the same tomb must be their son.[15]

Other probable connections to the holy family were also made by Jacobovici and Pellegrino. The other Mary was probably Jesus's mother, and the Joseph on Jesus's tomb was his father. "Yose" (Jose) was probably the name of Jesus's brother, which is spelled similarly in Mark 6:3, rather than a nickname for Joseph. The name Matthew is similar to some of the names of Jesus's ancestors (Luke 3:23–25).

A last probability, according to the Talpiot hypothesis researchers, pertains to the "missing ossuary" that came out of the tomb. Although there were originally ten ossuaries in the tomb, later inventories showed that one of them was missing. So, it has been asserted that this missing box might actually be the famous "James son of Joseph brother of Jesus" ossuary. This, of course, would argue for even tighter family connections.

As Tabor remarked quite recently, "I noticed that the dimensions of the missing tenth ossuary are precisely the same, to the centimeter, to those of the James Ossuary." Perhaps Oded Golan, the owner of the James Ossuary who went to trial on the supposition that he received the ossuary illegally, actually found the James Ossuary not in the 1970s, as he claims, but sometime around 1980, "when the Talpiot tomb was discovered."[16] Perhaps a little less sure than Tabor, Jacobovici and Pellegrino argue that, while not precisely the same, the James Ossuary is of similar size to the missing tenth ossuary. "So, the missing ossuary and the James ossuary may be one and the same after all."[17]

To examine further this possibility that the James Ossuary is the missing Talpiot bone box, in July 31, 2006, a series of tests were conducted on random ossuary samples that had been collected in Israel. These tests analyzed whether terra rosa—a rare red soil with high iron content found in the hills around Jerusalem—was present in the

---

[14] Jacobovici and Pellegrino, *Jesus Family Tomb*, esp. 76, 95.

[15] Brown provides another similarity here in *Da Vinci Code*, 249.

[16] Tabor, *Jesus Dynasty*, 33.

[17] Jacobovici and Pellegrino, *Jesus Family Tomb*, 210.

patinas of the ossuraries. According to the tests, "This was all consistent with the patinas on the James and Talpiot tomb ossuaries." While most of the ossuaries tested differently, "compared to other patina samples from ossuaries found in the Jerusalem environment, the Talpiot tomb ossuaries exhibited a patina fingerprint or profile that matched the James ossuary and no other."[18]

Another possibility exists too. Tabor credits Shimon Gibson as first suggesting that the James Ossuary might not have been the tenth ossuary at all, but merely another one that may have been stolen from the Talpiot Tomb the first weekend when the tomb was left open.[19]

So, the Talpiot hypothesis holds that the Talpiot Tomb is the burial site of Jesus of Nazareth's family. Marya is Jesus's mother and Joseph is his father. Mariamene is Mary Magdalene, Jesus's wife, and Judah is their son. Jose is Jesus's brother, not his father. And his brother James was probably also buried in this same tomb.

Statistical Analysis: Jesus's Tomb?

On the surface at least, and with a couple of potential exceptions, the family names in the Talpiot Tomb seem to fit nicely with the known family members in Jesus of Nazareth's household. Is there any way to be more specific about whether or not we could have a potential match here?

To check out their hunch, Jacobovici and Pellegrino sought the services of Andre Feuerverger, a statistician from the University of Toronto. While most of the Talpiot names are very common, what was the likelihood that this particular cluster of names would all be together?

Tabor explains that the initial statistics for the Talpiot grouping have nothing to do with whether or not they fit the family of Jesus of Nazareth. Rather, they were arrived at in a two-part process. First, the study tested the likelihood that such a cluster of names would be found in one place or in a single family. Second, these findings were then compared to Jesus's family according to the names presented in the Gospels.[20]

Based on the available information and the family connections mentioned above, Feuerverger arrived at the following figures for this cluster of names: there is a 1 in 190 chance of having a Jesus son of Joseph; a 1 in 160 chance for Mariamne; a 1 in 40

---

[18] Jacobovici and Pellegrino, 182, 188.

[19] James Tabor, email to select colleagues and friends, February 28, 2007.

[20] Tabor email.

chance for Matia; a 1 in 20 chance for Jose (Yose); and a 1 in 4 chance for Maria. Multiplying these odds yields a likelihood of a 1 in 97,280,000 chance of getting this specific list of persons together.

Then, the second set of computations was done, comparing the family buried in the Talpiot Tomb to the Gospel listings of Jesus of Nazareth's family members. The name Matthew was eliminated during this step, because he is not explicatively mentioned in the Gospels as a direct family member of Jesus's family. Then other adjustments were made for unintentional biases in the historical sources as well as to allow for all possible first-century Jerusalem tombs, arriving at a final probability factor of a 1 in 600 chance that the Talpiot Tomb was not the family tomb of Jesus of Nazareth. So, the conclusion was that the two families were the same to a very high degree of likelihood, and thus Jesus was probably buried in this tomb. But this argument was rejected by other researchers.[21]

Tabor's Summary of the Argument

James Tabor recently provided a very helpful summary of the arguments in favor of what we have called the Talpiot hypothesis. I have attempted to categorize the arguments under his twofold division, as stated above, by looking first at the Talpiot data and then comparing it to the family of Jesus of Nazareth.

First are the findings from the Talpiot Tomb:

- "Nothing like this [statistical grouping of names] occurs anywhere else." This is especially so when we consider that the names were discovered as belonging "in one family."

- To illustrate the statistical likelihood of these names being together in a single family, Tabor uses a range of population figures for Second Temple Jerusalem, estimating that between 25,000 and 75,000 people lived in the city. Consulting with several statisticians, he then compares Jerusalem to a football stadium filled with 50,000 people, including men women, and children. In that group, an estimated 2,796 men would be named Jesus. Of these, 351 would have a Joseph for a father and 173 of them would also

---

[21] Joe D'Mello, "The Correct Interpretation of Dr. Andrey Feuerverger's 1:600 Odds Calculation," *NT Blog*, March 2, 2007, https://ntweblog.blogspot.com/2007/03/correct -interpretation-of-dr-andrey.html.

have a mother named Mary. Only 23 of these men named Jesus would also have a brother named Joseph. If we also added having a brother named James, we would be left with only one person named Jesus. This presumes a "modest pre-70 CE family burial cave" with a "tighter time span" than three generations.

Then we compare these figures to the family of Jesus of Nazareth:

- Jesus's father Joseph probably died earlier and so he would have been buried in Galilee.
- Jesus's four brothers also seem to fit the Talpiot Tomb scenario too. Simon and Jude probably lived past AD 70, but Jesus and James died before then. The simple interpretation is that "Yose" is Jesus's brother rather than his father and is also the one buried in the Talpiot Tomb ossuary.
- Of the two Marys buried in the tomb, we have "the likelihood that *Maria* could well be the mother" of Jesus.
- There is also the "logical possibility" that Mariamene is Mary Magdalene, as indicated by "several early Christian texts" like the *Gospel of Mary*, Hippolytus, and the *Acts of Philip*, and based on research regarding Mary Magdalene's "place in earliest history of the Jesus movement."
- If Judah is Jesus's son, then Mariamene is "a likely candidate" for being Judah's mother, although we really "have no way of knowing" for sure.
- Matthew could be a family member.

Tabor's conclusion regarding the evidence is that it is "possible-to-likely" that the Talpiot Tomb is that of the Jesus of Nazareth family. But if the supposition is correct that the James Ossuary was also in the Talpiot Tomb, then Tabor thinks that this would make the identification "close to certain."[22]

Conclusion: Jesus's Spiritual Resurrection and Ascension?

Those who hold the Talpiot hypothesis favor the conclusion that it is highly likely that this tomb is the same one that contains the bones of Jesus of Nazareth and his family. Of the group, Tabor is the most cautious, claiming that this scenario is "possible-to-likely."

---

[22] James Tabor, "The Talpiot Jesus Tomb: An Overview," *The Jesus Dynasty Blog*, March 24, 2007. No longer accessible.

But since Tabor also thinks that it is likely that the James Ossuary came from the Talpiot Tomb, it would seem that he, too, believes that the entire hypothesis is "close to certain."[23]

An intriguing issue is that Jacobovici is reported many times as stating that these conclusions should not bother or offend Christians! He maintains this stance because he does not deny Jesus's resurrection or ascension to heaven, for these events could have happened spiritually. However, he does note that Christians who believe that Jesus rose bodily from the dead, or later ascended bodily to heaven would have issues with his conclusions.[24]

For example, the report on the Discovery Channel, in bold print, said, "Even if Jesus's body was moved from one tomb to another, however, that does not mean that he could not have been resurrected from the second tomb. Belief in the resurrection is based not on which tomb he was buried in, but on alleged sightings of Jesus that occurred after his burial and documented in the Gospels."[25] The report continues with regard to Jesus's ascension: "Some Christians believe that this was a *spiritual* ascension, i.e., his mortal remains were left behind. Other Christians believe that he ascended *with* his body to heaven. If Jesus' mortal remains have been found, this would contradict the idea of a physical ascension but not the idea of a spiritual ascension. The latter is consistent with Christian theology."[26] Tabor also stated his belief that the resurrection was not a material, bodily event, but a "spiritual resurrection."[27] Tabor develops this thesis, arguing chiefly that Paul held to less than bodily resurrection appearances, like the one he experienced. "God then raised Christ from the dead and transformed him back into his glorious heavenly body." Further, Christians will also experience such a resurrection, with their bodies being "instantaneously changed from flesh to spirit." It is only later that the Gospels portrayed Jesus's appearances as bodily in nature.[28]

Many scholars have reacted strongly against these ideas. The arguments on behalf of the Talpiot hypothesis will be addressed in much detail in the next two sections.

---

[23] Tabor, "Talpiot Jesus Tomb."

[24] Laidlaw, "Christ's Tomb Found?"

[25] "Theological Considerations," Discovery Channel "Tomb of Jesus" web page (2007?). Article no longer available.

[26] "Theological Considerations." The italics were original, and the last two sentences were written in bold type.

[27] Jacobovici and Tabor, *Lost Tomb of Jesus.*

[28] Tabor, *Jesus Dynasty*, 230–33, 262–66; both quotations are from 264.

A Talpiot Tomb Critique Part 1: Family Names, Mary Magdalene, the James Ossuary, and DNA

The Talpiot hypothesis began to circulate and gain attention after being popularized by the initial news conference, the Discovery Channel documentary, the book by Jacobovici and Pellegrino, and the seemingly countless interviews, articles, and news items that followed. Most of the major news television networks and periodicals reported the pro and con arguments. Almost as quickly, the scholarly response entered the discussion at a torrid pace. Interestingly, much of the response came from *non*-evangelical scholars who reacted strongly to the claims of the Talpiot hypothesis.[29]

Here we will address several of the major portions of the Talpiot hypothesis, concentrating on the issues regarding the family names, the possibility of a Mariamene or Mary Magdalene identification, and the DNA testing. Our format will be to isolate the key questions, and then provide lists of the scholarly counterarguments. Footnotes provide a wide variety of sources for these responses. The reader will hopefully then be in a position to judge the strength of each claim and response.

Incidence of Names: How Common Are the Names Found in the Talpiot Tomb?

Virtually all commentators, including those who agree with the Talpiot thesis, concur that most of the names in the tomb were very common in first-century Jerusalem.

- Tal Ilan, compiler of the *Lexicon of Jewish Names*, "disagreed vehemently" with the view that the Talpiot Tomb was Jesus's burial place and said that these names "are in every tomb in Jerusalem . . . you could expect to find them everywhere."[30]
- Citing L. Y. Rahmani's *A Catalog of Jewish Ossuaries*, Stephen Pfann highlighted that every one of the names for Jesus's family members were among the most popular sixteen male and female names found on ancient ossuaries.

---

[29] This was one of the real surprises after the story aired.

[30] Tal Ilan, quoted in Christopher Mims, "Special Report: Has James Cameron Found Jesus's Tomb or Is It Just a Statistical Error?," *Scientific American*, March 2, 2007, https://www.scientificamerican.com/article/jesus-talpiot-tomb-or-statistical-error/.

Four of those names (Simon, Mary, Joseph, and Judas) were among the top five male and female names in frequency and represent 38 percent of the entire list! Jesus was the eighth most common male name.[31]

- Richard Bauckham noted that the name Joseph is found on forty-five ossuaries, while the name Jesus is found on twenty-two ossuaries. "Mary" is found on forty-two ossuaries.[32]

- Even the particular congruence of names in the Talpiot Tomb is not absolutely unique. Near the Mount of Olives another burial tomb reportedly lists a number of ossuaries also inscribed in Hebrew, Aramaic, and Greek. The names include Jesus, Joseph, Mary, Martha, and Matthew.[33]

Moveover, can we even be sure of the name "Jesus" on the Talpiot Tomb ossuary?

- James Charlesworth, cited in the Talpiot presentation, states that the name "Jesus" before that of "Joseph" on that particular ossuary "is the most difficult name to read among all the names in the tomb." He adds, "The scribbling is not an inscription, it is sloppy graffiti."[34]

- Pfann is not sure that the name is Jesus. He thinks that "it's more likely the name 'Hanun.'"[35]

---

[31] Stephen Pfann, "The Improper Application of Statistics in 'The Lost Tomb of Jesus,'" *University of the Holy Land*, 1–2. This publication was previously found on the University of the Holy Land website but is no longer available.

[32] Richard Bauckham, "The Alleged 'Jesus Family Tomb,'" *Chrisendom* (blog), March 1, 2007, http://blog.christilling.de/2007/03/; Bauckham's ossuary statistics are also listed in Ben Witherington, "The Jesus Tomb? 'Titanic' Talpiot Tomb Theory Sunk from the Start," *Ben Witherington* (blog), February 26, 2007, http://benwitherington.blogspot.com/. See also Joe Zias, "Deconstructing the Second and Hopefully Last Coming of Simcha and the BAR Crowd," http://www.joezias.com/tomb.html. Unfortunately, the URL for Zias's article is no longer active.

[33] "Dominus Flevit," 2 (downloaded on March 22, 2007); email from Michael S. Heiser, March 13, 2007.

[34] James H. Charlesworth, "Reflections on the So-Called 'Lost Tomb of Jesus,'" February 7, 2007, 1.

[35] Stephen Pfann, quoted in Karen Matthews, "Documentary Shows Possible Jesus Tomb," Associated Press, February 26, 2007, 2. Article no longer available. See NBC11.com, "Director Claims Discovery of Jesus' Tomb," February 26, 2007, archived at https://web.archive.org/web/20070303084823/http://www.nbc11.com/entertainment/11116378/detail.html.

- Steve Caruso argues that "I cannot be *even 10% conclusive* about anything else in this inscription other than the name 'Joseph.'"[36]
- Tabor even acknowledges that the name "Jesus" is "nearly illegible."[37]

Mariamene and Mary Magdalene

Was Mariamene another name for Mary Magdalene? There are no good historical reasons to trace the name "Mariamene" to Mary Magdalene.

- Sources dating from the middle to late third to fifth centuries like Hippolytus, the *Gospel of Mary*, and the *Acts of Philip* are far too late to be helpful with historical questions pertaining to the life, death, and resurrection of Jesus.[38] It is amazing that Tabor refers to these sources as "several early Christian texts" and the "earliest history of the Jesus movement" while holding that the Gospels are often too late to be helpful![39]
- Further, even in Hippolytus's *Refutation of All Heresies* and the *Acts of Phillip* (dated by Bauckham to the late fourth to the early fifth century), the person "Mariamene" is never specifically identified as Mary Magdalene. Although Mariamene is mentioned several times in the *Acts of Philip*, Joseph Fitzmyer states that "there is not one instance that suggests she is Mary of Magdala."[40] Witherington adds that in Hippolytus the name is not even spelled the same as on the Talpiot ossuary.[41]

[36] Steve Caruso, "The Aramaic Blog," February 29, 2007, 3; also listed on "NT Gateway" site of Mark Goodacre of Duke University.

[37] Tabor, *Jesus Dynasty*, 23.

[38] Bauckham, "Jesus Family Tomb"; Pfann, "Improper Application of Statistics"; Ben Witherington, "Problems Multiply for Jesus Tomb Theory," *Ben Witherington* (blog), February 28, 2007, http://benwitherington.blogspot.com/2007/02/problems-multiple-for-jesus-tomb-theory.html.

[39] Tabor, "Talpiot Jesus Tomb."

[40] Joseph A. Fitzmyer, "Together at Last?" (a review of Simcha Jacobovici and Charles Pellegrino's *The Jesus Family Tomb*), *America: The Jesuit Review*, April 9, 2007, https://www.americamagazine.org/arts-culture/2007/04/09/together-last; Witherington, "Problems Multiply," 2.

[41] Ben Witherington, "The Jesus Tomb Show—Biblical Archaeologists Reject Discovery Channel Show's Claims," *Ben Witherington* (blog), March 5, 2007, http://benwitherington.blogspot.com/2007/03/jesus-tomb-show-biblical-archaeologists.html.

- Fitzmyer thinks that this lack of identification is the "biggest problem" for the claims by Jacobovici and Pellegrino. For example, the *-ou* ending of the Greek name *Mariamenou* is actually masculine or neuter, so how could it even be a woman's name? For these and other reasons, "the whole account about 'the Jesus family tomb' loses its most crucial piece of 'evidence.'"[42]
- Further, "Mara" does not mean "master" or "teacher," but is short for Martha. Joseph Fitzmyer calls the Talpiot thesis translation a gratuitous assumption.[43]
- Witherington says that Mary was known as being from Magdal or Magdala. Without that geographical designation, the name is far too common to tie to Mary Magdalene.[44]

What could the ossuary name "Mariamene" indicate?

- Bauckham thinks that the woman buried in the ossuary probably had two names: "Mariamenon" (Greek) and "Mara" (Semitic). Since the former is "a term of endearment" it probably indicates a bilingual family that spoke Greek at home, another problem for identifying this as Jesus's family.[45]
- Witherington also concluded that the ossuary probably contained the remains of two women, a woman and a child, or one woman with two names. Perhaps favoring the two-persons view is that there appears to be a "slash line" between the names. Still, none of these names is that of Mary Magdalene.[46]
- Pfann concluded that the "Mariamene" ossuary is really that of two persons: "Mariame" and ("*kai*") "Mara," the latter being added to the ossuary later.[47] Tabor responded to Pfann that a specialist, archaeologist Dr. Leah Di Segni, thinks Pfann is mistaken and still holds to the view that Mariamene is a double name for a single woman buried in the ossuary.[48]
- The bottom line is that scholars have uniformly rejected the suggestion that Mariamene is Mary Magdalene. Harvard scholar Francois Bovon, whose work

---

[42] Fitzmyer, "Together at Last?"

[43] Fitzmyer, "Together at Last?"; Witherington, "Problems Multiply."

[44] Witherington, "Jesus Tomb?"

[45] Bauckham, "Jesus Family Tomb."

[46] Witherington, "Jesus Tomb?"; Witherington, "Problems Multiply."

[47] Stephen Pfann, "Mary Magdalene Is Now Missing: A Corrected Reading of Rahmani Ossuary 701," *SBL Forum*, March 2007, 7, https://www.sbl-site.org/assets/pdfs/Pfann.pdf.

[48] James Tabor, "Tabor Responds to Phann," *SBL Forum*, March 2007, https://www.sbl-site.org/publications/article.aspx?ArticleId=654.

on Mary Magdalene is cited by Tabor and others holding the Talpiot hypothesis, still concludes, "I must say that the reconstructions of Jesus's marriage with Mary Magdalene and the birth of a child belong for me to science fiction."[49] Bauckham also concludes: "There is no reason at all to connect the woman in this ossuary with Mary Magdalene, and in fact the name usage is decisively against such a connexion."[50] Mark Goodacre of Duke University adds that "no reputable historian of Christian origins seriously thinks that Jesus was married to Mary Magdalene (or anyone else, as far as we know)."[51]

Was Jesus Married? Did He Have Children?

- It would seem that, in theological terms, nothing negative would follow either from Jesus being married or fathering children. It could be true even if the New Testament never recorded it. After all, it was normal for first-century Jews to marry and, if this were the case, Jesus would be the model for husband-wife relations as well as fatherhood! So, there is no need to disregard these hypotheses for such reasons. However, the chief problem is not the theoretical concept itself but the revisionist history that is the main ally of these ideas, as it attempts to invent this thesis without any evidence.

- Not one ancient historical source claims that Jesus was married, either to Mary Magdalene or to anyone else. Nor are there any ancient historical sources that teach that Jesus had children.

- There are several considerations in the New Testament that appear to argue against the claim that Jesus was married, although it probably should be acknowledged that none of these proves the case either. As just indicated, Jesus's wife is never mentioned, even though it would be normal. Arguments from silence are notoriously weak, so we cannot place too much emphasis on this point, but it is worth mentioning. Jesus's teaching about being single for the kingdom of heaven (Matt 19:12) is also a pointer. If Jesus had been married, this would have been a wonderful clincher to Paul's argument that

---

[49] Francois Bovon, "The Tomb of Jesus," *SBL Forum*, March, 2007, https://www.sbl-site.org/publications/article.aspx?ArticleId=656.

[50] Bauckham, "Jesus Family Tomb."

[51] Mark Goodacre, "The Statistical Case for the Identity of the 'Jesus Family Tomb,'" *NT Blog*, March 1, 2007, https://ntweblog.blogspot.com/2007/02/.

apostles have the right to bring their wives with them in ministry, although the best Paul could do was to refer to Peter and Jesus's brothers (1 Cor 9:5). That would have clinched Paul's argument by itself![52]

- Acts 8:30–34 implies that Jesus had no descendants. At the cross, Jesus committed his mother to John, not to his son (John 19:26). Jesus's brother James is the leader of the early church in Jerusalem (see Acts 15, for example), not Jesus's son. But since there is no evidence at all that Jesus was married, it should not be necessary to mention his lack of offspring!

- Goodacre states that the available evidence argues that Jesus did not have a son. It will not do to postulate otherwise without historical data by saying that "our evidence is incomplete," or that we should be open to it, or simply that we cannot rule out the possibility.[53] Positive evidence is needed.

The Missing Tenth Ossuary

Is the missing ossuary from Talpiot the same as the James Ossuary?

- This entire discussion assumes and depends on the assertion that the James Ossuary is itself authentic, which is highly disputed.[54] If it is a fake, this issue is a moot point. Or even if the ossuary is authentic, but the words "brother of Jesus" have been added, as some have charged, then the Talpiot hypothesis is weakened considerably.

- The James Ossuary appeared in a 1976 photo produced by its owner, Oded Golan, at his trial.[55] Reportedly, former FBI agent Gerald Richard testified in Israeli court proceedings that the photo comes from Golan's home and does indeed date to the 1970s, as indicated by tests performed in the FBI photo lab.[56] Jacobovici has even admitted that if the James Ossuary was

---

[52] Mike Licona, "First Person: Has the Family Tomb of Jesus Been Found?," *Baptist Press*, February 27, 2007, https://www.baptistpress.com/resource-library/news/first-person-has-the-family-tomb-of-jesus-been-found/.

[53] Goodacre, "Statistical Case."

[54] Zias, "Deconstructing."

[55] For examples of those who mention this, see Zias, "Deconstructing"; Chris Rosebrough, "Archaeological Identity Theft: The Lost Tomb of Jesus Fails to Make the Grade," *Extreme Theology*, February 26, 2007, https://www.extremetheology.com/2007/02/archeological_i.html.

[56] Laidlaw, "Christ's Tomb Found?"

photographed in the 1970s, it could not be from the Talpiot Tomb, which was discovered in 1980.[57]

- The dealer who supplied Oded Golan with the James Ossuary said that it came from Silwan, not Talpiot. The dirt found in the ossuary backs up that claim.[58] Plus, Silwan is within sight of the temple, as suggested by Eusebius.[59]
- According to ancient historian Eusebius (*Hist. eccl.* 2.23), James was buried at the same location where he was stoned, which was near the temple. This is not near the Talpiot location.[60]

Amos Kloner and Joe Zias disagree with James Tabor regarding the tenth ossuary. Kloner retrieved the tenth ossuary (now missing), and Zias catalogued it at the Rockefeller Museum while he was curator there. As the original scholars who did the work, they clarified the issue as follows:[61]

- The measurements of the tenth Talpiot ossuary are significantly different from that of the James Ossuary. The James Ossuary measures 50.5 cm × 25 cm × 30.5 cm, while the tenth ossuary measured 60 cm × 26 cm × 30 cm, with the latter measurements appearing in Kloner's original article.[62] So the tenth Talpiot ossuary is 20 percent longer than the James Ossuary.
- There was no name on the tenth ossuary—it was plain. So, it was not even photographed. Plain ossuaries without inscriptions or ornaments were then placed in the inner courtyard of the Rockefeller Museum while Zias was the curator there, and that is where the tenth box was taken. So, it was not the James Ossuary.
- Stephen Goranson of Duke University states that Tabor has known of the discrepancy between his view and the Kloner and Zias view at least since November 23, 2006, after complaining about Goranson's writing in the *Jerusalem Perspective*.[63]

---

[57] Laidlaw, "Christ's Tomb Found?"

[58] Witherington, "Jesus Tomb?"

[59] Witherington, "Problems Multiply."

[60] Witherington, "Jesus Tomb?"; Licona, "First Person."

[61] Kloner, "Tomb with Inscribed Ossuaries," 15–22; David Horovitz, "Kloner: A Great Story, but Nonsense," *Jerusalem Post*, February 27, 2007 , https://www.jpost.com/israel/kloner -a-great-story-but-nonsense; Zias, "Deconstructing"; personal emails from Joe Zias, March 1, 2007, and from Amos Kloner, March 3, 2007.

[62] Kloner, "Tomb with Inscribed Ossuaries" 21.

[63] Stephen Goranson as quoted by Mark Goodacre, *NT Blog*, February 27, 2007, 1–2.

- Tabor acknowledges straightforwardly: "I am not sure if the 10th ossuary is or is not the one we now know as the 'James ossuary.'" But he still thinks that when Kloner wrote his original article in 1996 that "he had nothing to go on but the registration number and dimensions, so he writes 'plain.'" If Kloner *did* see and remember the tenth ossuary, "that is for him to say."[64]
- So far, scholarship has sided firmly with the work of Kloner and Zias, and against the hypothesis that the tenth ossuary is that of James the brother of Jesus. Goodacre concludes: "At this point it looks highly unlikely that the James ossuary is the missing tenth box from the Talpiot tomb, unless the data we possess requires correction."[65] Jonathan Reed states: "I do not think Kloner would have missed that; I refuse to believe it."[66] Witherington concurs with the reports of Kloner and Zias, including some personal emails from the latter.[67] The almost uniform view is that the tenth ossuary was never missing or stolen; it has been accounted for since the beginning. But since it had no name on it and the dimensions are significantly different, it is very probably not the James Ossuary.

Do the patinas match on the Talpiot Tomb ossuaries and the James Ossuary?

- Zias charges that the film shows experts "scraping material from the ossuary, under the worst possible conditions." So, Zias concludes that the "experts" involved in this testing "have no expertise whatsoever with local materials"—one was reportedly an authority in auto crashes![68]
- Witherington says about the comparison of patinas: "This is not actually surprising at all since you can find terra rosa [*sic*] in various locales in and around Jerusalem."[69]

---

[64] Tabor comment from February 27, 2007 as quoted in Christopher Heard, "They're Baaaa-aaaack," February 25, 2007, http://www.heardworld.com/higgaion/?p=539. This URL is no longer active.

[65] Mark Goodacre, *NT Blog*, February 27, 2007, 2.

[66] Jonathan Reed, in *The Lost Tomb of Jesus: A Critical Look*, interview by Ted Koppel, Discovery Channel, aired March 4, 2007.

[67] Ben Witherington, "The Smoking Gun—Tenth Talpiot Ossuary Proved to Be Blank," *Ben Witherington* (blog), March 1, 2007, http://benwitherington.blogspot.com /2007/03/smoking-gun-tenth-talpiot-ossuary_9874.html.

[68] Zias, "Deconstructing."

[69] Witherington, "Problems Multiply."

- Ted Koppel reported, "We called Robert Genna at the Suffolk County Crime Lab and he said: 'The elemental composition of some of the samples we tested from the ossuaries are consistent with each other. But I would never say they are a match. . . . No scientist would ever say definitively that one ossuary came from the same tomb as another.'"[70]

The DNA testing

- A devastating problem for DNA testing is that multiple skeletons were often placed in the same ossuary. For instance, Joe Zias published the results of one tomb he investigated where fifteen ossuaries contained the remains of eighty-eight people![71] More crucially for our purposes, in his original article, investigating archaeologist Amos Kloner estimated that there were thirty-five different bodies associated with the Talpiot Tomb—seventeen in the ossuaries and eighteen outside the ossuaries.[72] Tabor disputes the presence of thirty-five people in the Talpiot Tomb, arguing that in the original report by Joseph Gath there were two or three people outside the ossuaries and "a dozen or so" inside the bone boxes.[73] But even without arguing the specifics, Tabor's total of fourteen to eighteen people still makes the point sufficiently well. Thus, Christopher Rollston rightly notes that, "because of the numbers of burials in the tombs, the practice of interring the skeletal remains of multiple people in a single ossuary, and the possibility of contamination of laboratory data, the notion that decisive data can be produced seems to me to be most difficult."[74] Indeed, without knowing whose bones we are testing, what good is DNA?
- Further, besides the presence of other persons in the same ossuaries, DNA testing could record the presence of anyone who came in contact with the bone boxes, including Joe Zias himself![75]

---

[70] Koppel, *Lost Tomb of Jesus.*
[71] Zias, "Deconstructing."
[72] Kloner, "Tomb with Inscribed Ossuaries," esp. notes 2, 22.
[73] Tabor, "Talpiot Jesus Tomb."
[74] Rollston, "Prosopography," note 29. Pfann agrees in "Improper Application of Statistics."
[75] Zias, "Deconstructing."

- Witherington states that the lack of a DNA control example is another huge issue—we need a sample from a member of Jesus's family. But without that sample, DNA may say that certain persons were related (although not this time!), but they could never say that they belonged to Jesus or anyone else in Jesus's family. But we do not have this family DNA evidence and never will.[76] Even Tabor agrees here: "Such tests, no matter what the results, could not 'prove' that this particular Jesus was the one who became known as Christ" but can only show relations between the persons buried in the tomb.[77]

- Carney Matheson, who performed the DNA test on the "Jesus" and "Mariamene" ossuaries, stated, "The only conclusions we made was that these two sets were not maternally related. To me it sounds like absolutely nothing."[78]

Conclusion of Critique Part 1

We have addressed here several aspects of the Talpiot hypothesis. In particular, we have responded to the claims regarding the commonality of the Talpiot Tomb names, the identification of an ossuary believed by a few to be that of Mary Magdalene, the question of the tenth ossuary, and the DNA testing. On each count, we have discovered no basis for the claims that this is the burial tomb of Jesus of Nazareth's family. The remainder of the claims will be addressed in the next section.

A Talpiot Critique Part 2: Statistical Argument and Other Problems

In the last section we argued that the Talpiot hypothesis falls substantially short on the issues of the incidence of family names, the identification of the Mariamene

---

[76] Witherington, "Jesus Tomb?"

[77] Tabor, *Jesus Dynasty*, 26, repeated on 27.

[78] Carney Matheson, in Christopher Mims, "Says Scholar Whose Work Was Used in the Upcoming Jesus Tomb Documentary: 'I Think It's Completely Mishandled. I Am Angry.'" *Scientific American*, March 2, 2007, http://blog.sciam.com/index.php?title=says _scholar_whose_work_was_used_ in_the&more=1&c=1&tb=1&pb=1. No longer accessible. Zias, "Deconstructing," concurs in this evaluation regarding the DNA testing.

ossuary as that of Mary Magdalene, the identification of the tenth ossuary as that of James the brother of Jesus, and the DNA testing.

Our chief subject here is to evaluate the statistical argument provided by those who support the Talpiot thesis, which they think shows to a high degree of likelihood (600:1 odds) that the Talpiot Tomb is the actual burial site of Jesus's family. Several other problems with the overall thesis also need to be mentioned, some of which are rarely discussed. Then we will view a number of scholarly conclusions to the Talpiot hypothesis.

Statistical Confirmation?

Statistics are based on the information provided. Adjustments to that information may translate into huge changes in the numbers. Mark Goodacre thinks that "the major part of the case that the Talpiot Tomb is Jesus's family tomb is based on the statistical claim."[79] If so, then this may be the most crucial portion of our discussion.

The statistician used in formulating the Talpiot hypothesis, Andrey Feuerverger of the University of Toronto, has said often that his "computations depend heavily on the assumptions that go into it." This is incredibly crucial, as he acknowledges: "Should even one of these assumptions not be satisfied then the results will not be statistically meaningful." For example, the identification of Mariamene with Mary Magdalene "drives the outcome of the computations substantially."[80] Similarly, Feuerverger reportedly told Ted Koppel: "I must work from the interpretations given to me, and the strength of the calculations are based on those assumptions." For example, regarding the Mariamene ossuary, "if for some reason one were to read it as just a regular form of the name Maria, in that case the calculation produced is not as impressive, and the statistical significance would wash out considerably."[81]

---

[79] Goodacre, "Statistical Case."

[80] Andrey Feuerverger, "Dear Statistical Colleagues," March 12, 2007, the quotations appear on 1, 2. Originally posted on Feuerverger's academic website at http://fisher.ustat .toronto.edu/andrey/OfficeHrs.txt. Unfortunately, this link no longer works.

[81] Andrey Feuerverger, in *The Lost Tomb of Jesus: A Critical Look*, interview with Ted Koppel, Discovery Channel, aired March 4, 2007.

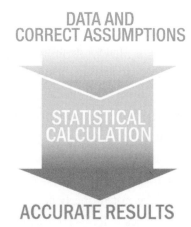
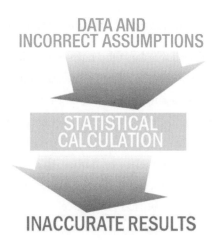

Designed by Doug Powell

Accordingly, Feuerverger now realizes that statistics cannot conclude whether or not the Talpiot family is that of Jesus of Nazareth. He states, "It is not in the purview of statistics to conclude whether or not this tombsite is that of the New Testament family." The reason for this is because "any such conclusion much more rightfully belongs to the purview of biblical historical scholars who are in a much better position to assess the assumptions entering into such computations." He concludes the matter: "I now believe that I should not assert any conclusions connecting this tomb with any hypothetical one of the NT family."[82] This indicates the ultimate importance of investigating these Talpiot Tomb assumptions. Since the assumptions feed the statistics, we must be sure that they are based on correct data.

Mathematician Joe D'Mello pointed out several problems with Feuerverger's computations and made key clarifications about what was being claimed. In particular, his chief point seems to be that slight changes in the interpretations or factual basis very quickly change the overall conclusions.[83]

Joseph Fitzmyer is typical of many when he argues that the Talpiot hypothesis contains far too "iffy" conditionals that basically all must be true to arrive at its conclusions. Further, too many rhetorical questions are meant to be answered positively when a negative answer will change the end result. As he concludes regarding this thesis: "Speculation is rife."[84]

---

[82] Feuerverger, "Dear Statistical Colleagues," 1.
[83] D'Mello, "Correct Interpretation."
[84] Fitzmyer, "Review of *The Jesus Family Tomb*."

Some Questionable Assumptions: General Issues

Virtually all scholars who have responded to the issues agree that the assumptions passed on to Feuerverger must be questioned very seriously, as can be seen below. Goodacre calls these assumptions a "fatal bias" that plagues the analysis from the beginning.[85]

Scholars have isolated several of the Talpiot hypothesis assumptions that they think need to be challenged. We will begin with four general concerns regarding the computed frequency of names, the number of persons who were often buried in the same ossuaries, the extended family nature of these rock tombs, and the several generations who buried their loved ones there. If these are not properly accounted for, as they were apparently not (see below), then the statistics will be seriously slanted.

As Tabor is very careful to point out, the first round of computations had nothing to do with the actual family of Jesus of Nazareth, but simply asked the frequency of these six or seven persons being altogether in the same family grouping.[86] We will dispute momentarily whether all these names existed as a single family under one roof, which it now seems they assuredly did not. But here we will simply point out that the odds of any group of six or seven people being together would be very improbable.

For example, what are the odds that a particular grouping of six or seven people were at my house last night watching a football game? Like the names in the Talpiot Tomb, most of these friends could have names that are among the most common in our society, but a couple of them could go by nicknames and one could include a "son of" designation. What are the odds that precisely these six or seven people and no others would be at my home, particularly if two or three of them have fairly distinctive names? We should also expect very high odds.

So, it would appear that the first round of the computation shows virtually nothing except that this half dozen or so people would not normally be all together at once! This is especially the case when a very similar cluster of Jewish names, including Mary, Martha, Matthew, Joseph, and Jesus, have been reported from a tomb on the Mount of Olives, as mentioned earlier.[87] Apparently the Talpiot cluster of names is not as rare as supposed.

---

[85] Goodacre, "Statistical Case."

[86] Tabor email, 2–3.

[87] "Dominus Flevit," 2 (downloaded on March 22, 2007); email from Michael S. Heiser, March 13, 2007.

Stephen Pfann says that the 600 to 1 probability that the Talpiot Tomb belonged to Jesus's family "is based upon a number of fallacies and a general misuse of statistics." To identify the family as being that of Jesus of Nazareth is "pure speculation." Most importantly, individual ossuaries "often contained the remains of more than one individual" (for example, the Caiaphas ossuary held the remains of several people).[88]

We have already recounted Zias's published results of a Jewish tomb where fifteen ossuaries contained the remains of eighty-eight different people! Accordingly, Zias thinks that the Talpiot hypothesis statistics were "rigged."[89] That multiple persons were buried specifically in the Talpiot ossuaries seems to be more than clear. Kloner estimated that seventeen individuals were buried in the ten ossuaries![90]

Further, as noted by Rollston, rock tombs held the remains of extended families, including one's uncles, aunts, cousins, and grandparents.[91] Witherington argues that we know that unrelated Christians were often buried together, so it is not necessary that all of the ossuaries from a particular site even be from just a single family.[92] After all, Matthew claims that Jesus was buried in a tomb belonging to Joseph of Arimathea (Matt 27:59–60), and the clear intent of all four Gospels is that Jesus was not interred in his own family tomb! Moreover, perhaps most crucially, Zias reminds us that these Jewish tombs usually held four to five generations of extended family members, and that is why stats "simply cannot be computed."[93] Witherington argues that the three languages found on the ossuaries in the Talpiot Tomb indicate that it was probably multigenerational.[94] We might add that that the large number of individuals inside the Talpiot Tomb—thirty-five people according to Kloner but only a third or so of that according to Tabor—is another indication that this tomb held far more than a single generational family. Most damaging of all, Kloner reported in his

---

[88] Stephen Pfann, "Improper Application of Statistics." Pfann also argues the following issues: most ancient Jewish tombs have already been looted, not all ossuaries have been saved even after being discovered, and Rahmani notes that only about 25 percent of ossuaries have names on them.

[89] Zias, "Deconstructing."

[90] Kloner, "Tomb with Inscribed Ossuaries," 22.

[91] Rollston, "Prosopography."

[92] Witherington, "Problems Multiply."

[93] Zias, "Deconstructing."

[94] Witherington, "Problems Multiply."

1996 report that this was also so in the Talpiot Tomb: "This burial cave was probably used for three or four generations."[95]

That Tabor plainly wants to argue otherwise on these points seems to be an indication of his realization that if the Talpiot Tomb indeed did contain the remains of several people in the individual ossuaries, plus an extended family of individuals over several generations, then this counts very heavily against his argument that the named ossuaries had to contain people who were directly related to each other and lived under one roof.[96] If they were not directly related, originating in the same household, then the probabilities of finding "the Jesus family" almost disappear. So, on these three general points, there is much to be lost from the Talpiot hypothesis, as we will see.

More Questionable Assumptions: Specific Issues

Besides these general concerns, scholars have also demarcated several more specific Talpiot hypothesis assumptions that they think are quite faulty. There is a remarkable amount of scholarly agreement here with regard to which theses are the most questionable. We will especially mention the assumptions regarding Mariamene, Jose, Matthew, Judah, and Jesus. Along with Mary and except for Judah, these are the individual persons who make up the Talpiot statistics.

With Mariamene there are at least two main issues: Was she the same person as Mary Magdalene? And was she married to Jesus? We argued earlier that there is very little chance that Mariamene was Mary Magdalene, and we won't repeat those arguments here. There is nothing that could really be called historical (or other) evidence for this identification. The suggested sources are not only very late, far after the time of Jesus, but they are not even clear that Mary Magdalene is this same individual. This is why Pfann says that the chief source "should be considered irrelevant to the discussion, being three centuries too late for consideration."[97]

Was Mariamene married to the Jesus in the Talpiot Tomb? Ted Koppel asked Carney Matheson, who performed the tests, about the conclusion that DNA revealed

---

[95] Kloner, "Tomb with Inscribed Ossuaries," 21.

[96] Tabor, "Talpiot Jesus Tomb."

[97] Pfann, "Improper Application of Statistics." For some of the scholars who agree that Mariamene is not Mary Magdalene, see Magness, "Tomb of Jesus"; Rollston, "Prosopography"; Goodacre, "Statistical Case"; Michael Barber, "7 Reasons Cameron's Theory is Sinking," February 27, 2007, 4; Rosebrough, "Archaeological Identity Theft."

that Jesus and Mariamene were probably married. Matheson replied: "There is a statement in the film that has been taken out of context. While marriage is a possibility, other relationships like father and daughter, paternal cousins, sister-in-law, or indeed two unrelated individuals [are also possible]. . . . My conclusion is that they are not maternally related. You cannot genetically test for marriage."[98] Goodacre concludes the matter as far as the vast majority of scholars are concerned: "Now given that no reputable historian of Christian origins seriously thinks that Jesus was married to Mary Magdalene (or anyone else, as far as we know), the presence of a Mariamne in the tomb can in no way be allowed to be a part of the statistical calculations here."[99]

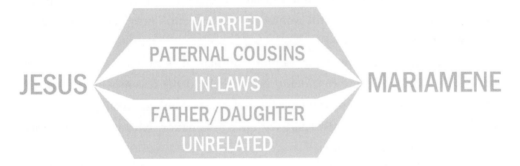

Designed by Doug Powell

Was Jose the brother of the Jesus buried in the Talpiot Tomb? Since we already have one Joseph in the tomb (Jesus's father), it is a far simpler view to hold that Jose is the familial nickname (perhaps given by his wife or other family members) for this same person rather than to suppose a second person of the same name.[100] Further, there is also some archaeological evidence for this view. L. Y. Rahmani, in the standard scholarly work on Jewish ossuaries that was used by Jacobovici and Pellegrino, said, "The similarity of this [Jose] ossuary and its inscription with that of Marya on No. 706, both from the same tomb, may indicate that these are the ossuaries of the parents of Yeshua (No. 704) and the grandparents of Yehuda (No. 702)."[101] But it

---

[98] Carney Matheson, in *The Lost Tomb of Jesus: A Critical Look*, interview by Ted Koppel, Discovery Channel, aired March 4, 2007.

[99] Goodacre, "Statistical Case."

[100] Rollston, "Prosopography."

[101] L. Y. Rahmani, *A Catalog of Jewish Ossuaries in the Collections of the State of Israel* (Jerusalem: Israel Antiquities Authority, 1994), no. 705.

seems that the only major reason to overlook Rahmani's sensible suggestion is that to claim that it is Jesus's of Nazareth's brother fits far better with the Talpiot hypothesis.

Initially, Jacobovici and Pellegrino thought that Matthew would be close to the family of Jesus of Nazareth because the name appears more than once in Luke's genealogy.[102] But to their credit, Feuerverger left it out of the second computation because the name is not explicitly mentioned in the Gospels as a family member.[103] Thus, although it did not figure in the statistical computation, most scholars thought that the Matthew ossuary shouldn't have entered the discussion at all, except as a negative factor (see below).

Judah the son of Jesus also did not figure as part of Feuerverger's statistics. Not only did most scholars reject the notion that this could be the son of Jesus, but also, like Matthew, many scholars still wanted to make Judah's presence in the tomb a negative factor (also see below).

What about the ossuary of the Talpiot man named "Jesus son of Joseph"? How rare is such a name? A few considerations are behind the reason why this ossuary name was virtually ignored by the Jewish scholars who worked on the Talpiot Tomb find. There is at least one other ossuary with this designation. Kloner noted that there were three or four such ossuaries.[104]

Using available listings of first-century names, estimates indicate that, during the time the ossuaries were used, Jerusalem would have contained approximately 1,008 men named Jesus, who also had a father named Joseph![105] Intriguingly, Pellegrino uses these same figures, including 7,200 men in Jerusalem named Jesus, 1,008 of whom would have had a Joseph for a father.[106] But Ingermanson points out a mathematical error in Pellegrino's figures, dropping his final figures from 2,500,000:1 all the way down to 31:1.[107] But as we will see, even this reduced figure is far too high.

---

[102] Jacobovici and Pellegrino, *Jesus Family Tomb*, 78.

[103] "Statistics Overview" from Andrey Feuerverger's analysis, Discovery Channel website. Article no longer available.

[104] Horovitz, "Kloner"; Witherington, "Jesus Tomb Show," 4.

[105] Randy Ingermanson, "Jesus Family Tomb: A Statistical Analysis of the 'Jesus Equation,'" *Randy Ingermanson: First Century Jewish Fiction* (blog), accessed October 31, 2023, https://www.ingermanson.com/mad-science/jesus-family-tomb/statistics/.

[106] Jacobovici and Pellegrino, *Jesus Family Tomb*, 75, also 77.

[107] Cf. Ingermanson, "Jesus Family Tomb: A Statistical Analysis," with Jacobovici and Pellegrino, *Jesus Family Tomb*, 82.

I think that we also need to add to this number in order to allow for other Jewish males with the same names from outside the city who could have, for whatever reason, been buried in Jerusalem. After all, Jesus was from Galilee, and the Talpiot hypothesis still places his tomb in this city. But it seems that this large number of men who were also named "Jesus son of Joseph" would change significantly the Talpiot statistics, as we will see below.

Many (if not most) researchers, however, think that there is more than these numbers alone. There are also important factors present here which should compute *negatively* against the computations that the Talpiot Tomb family is the same as Jesus of Nazareth's family. Ingermanson calls this the "not-Jesus factor."[108] Even Jacobovici and Pellegrino are well aware of this. They point out that if other names were present in the Talpiot Tomb, such as Jonah or Daniel, this "would have led us to question the entire assemblage" because these names would not fit in Jesus of Nazareth's family.[109] Feuerverger, too, acknowledges this factor, stating that there are no other "negatives" beyond those names that we already know from the tomb "that would in and of themselves invalidate 'the hypothesis' or that would appear to lessen its likelihood."[110] The difference, however, is that while Jacobovici, Pellegrino, and Feuerverger acknowledge this possibility, many scholars hold that there are *several "not-Jesus" factors that detract from the Talpiot statistics*. For example, Goodacre thinks that this is simply crucial to the equation, since "non-matches" with Jesus of Nazareth "contradict the literary record." When these negatives are ignored or treated as neutral, we have an "essential problem" and that is why the Talpiot case is "severely flawed."[111] Some of the problems have been alluded to immediately above. Here are the main ones, noted by many scholars.[112]

There is no early historical evidence that Jesus had a son. To invent such a person ("Judah" or whomever) and read the data that way is illegitimate. True, the Talpiot hypothesis, as we have just pointed out above, does not include Judah in its statistical computations. But that is the point: they thought that it was not a *positive* finding that

---

[108] Ingermanson, "Jesus Family Tomb: A Statistical Analysis."

[109] Jacobovici and Pellegrino, *Jesus Family Tomb*, 78.

[110] Feuerverger, "Dear Statistical Colleagues."

[111] Goodacre, "Statistical Case."

[112] Examples include Magness, "Tomb of Jesus"; Goodacre, "Statistical Case"; Witherington, "Jesus Tomb?"; Ingermanson, "Jesus Family Tomb: A Statistical Analysis"; Rosebrough, "Archaeological Identity Theft"; Barber, "7 Reasons," 1–2; cf. Rollston, "Prosopography."

related to their conclusion. But many scholars think that this is one of the facts that show that the Talpiot Tomb is *not* that of Jesus's family. In my opinion, Ingermanson places far too high the suggested chances against Jesus having a son.[113] But the "Judah factor" still militates against this being Jesus of Nazareth.

We could say almost the same thing about Matthew. He does not fit the Jesus family. And again, while we have already said that Matthew was not counted in the second Talpiot computation, it is actually worse than that. For this is another factor that, while possible, actually detracts from the Jesus of Nazareth supposition. As Witherington states, the Matthew reference is a liability, because even though "ancestors are irrelevant. . . . It's as simple as this: this is a family tomb and none of Jesus's brothers are Matthew."[114] Tabor objects to Judah being a negative factor, but only says that "if" such a son existed, this might help in some unexplained ways, without commenting further.[115]

Probably the case that bothers scholars the most is the *comparison between Mariamene and Mary Magdalene* because the case is so flimsy and is opposed by all of the early historical data. Not only must Mary Magdalene be taken out of the Talpiot computations, where she plays a very major role, but this too is seen as another negative factor that also detracts from the case that this may be Jesus of Nazareth.

Scholars conclude that this "not-Jesus factor" is very significant. Magness sums this up: "Taken individually, each of these points weakens the case for the identification of the Talpiot tomb as the tomb of Jesus and his family. Collectively these points are devastating, since the statistical analyses presented in the film are based on certain assumptions made about these names."[116] Goodacre also summarizes the matter: "The greater the number of non-matches, the less impressive the cluster becomes. Or, to put it another way, it stops being a cluster of striking names when the cluster is diluted with non-matches." Playing creatively on Jacobovici's use of the Beatles analogy and the significance of the name "Ringo,"[117] Goodacre illustrates the problem: "What we actually have is the equivalence of a tomb with the names John, Paul, George, Martin, Alan and Ziggy." Regarding the misuse of Mariamene, Matthew,

---

[113] See Ingermanson, "Jesus Family Tomb: A Statistical Analysis."
[114] Witherington, "Problems Multiply."
[115] Tabor, "Talpiot Jesus Tomb."
[116] Magness, "Tomb of Jesus."
[117] Mark Goodacre, quoted in Simcha Jacobovici, "Probability," *The Lost Tomb of Jesus*, https://www.jesusfamilytomb.com/evidence/probability.html.

and Judah, Goodacre concludes: "All data must be included. *You cannot cherry pick or manipulate your data before doing your statistical analysis.*"[118]

The Not-Jesus Factor	
Judah, Son of Jesus	No historical evidence Jesus had a son
Matthew	The list of Jesus's brothers does not include a Matthew
Mariamene and Mary Magdalene	No historical reasons to connect Mariamene and Mary Magdalene

Any of the three previous points damages the Talpiot hypothesis. But taken together they destroy this thesis since the statistical computations are based on the assumptions that these points militate against.

What Do the Reworked Statistics Look Like?

There is *strikingly little* that we can know from the Talpiot Tomb with regard to direct blood relations between the family members there. Two of the most crucial things to keep in mind about the nature of these Jewish burial tombs is that they were used for extended families, and that these families were buried there for three to five generations.

Assuming that the first name on the "son of Joseph" ossuary is indeed "Jesus," and that there was only one man buried in the tomb with the name of Jesus (unlike the two Marys), all we can know is that Joseph, Jesus, and Judah are related as father, son, and grandson, respectively. We cannot even know if one of the Marys is one of their mothers, or what relation Jose or Matthew were to the rest of the family. The others could be grandparents, cousins, aunts, uncles, adopted children, stepparents, previous children of the stepparents, or the spouses of many of these persons![119] Or the other names in the tomb could be people who all lived and died in this extended family during an earlier generation, perhaps before the Talpiot Jesus was even born!

So, we cannot state any known conclusions concerning Maria, Mariamene, Jose, or Matthew. So, quite contrary to the second computation of the Talpiot hypothesis

---

[118] Goodacre, "Statistical Case."

[119] See esp. Rollston, "Prosopography."

"Statistics Overview," we cannot use figures for Mariamene, Maria, or Jose. We simply do not know that information.

INCOMPATIBLE CLAIMS MADE BY THE TALPIOT ADVOCATES

600:1 IN FAVOR WITHOUT "NOT-JESUS" FACTORS	IN SPITE OF	1008:1 JERUSALEM MEN NAMED JESUS, SON OF JOSEPH

Designed by Doug Powell

As we just said, even Pellegrino (and apparently Jacobovici, too) acknowledges that the chances of there being a man named Jesus who also had a father named Joseph and who lived in Jerusalem during the era of the ossuaries is 1 in 79, and approximately 1,008 Jewish men living in Jerusalem probably had that relationship. Even if conceding all the other items mentioned above, there are, at best, only 1,008:1 odds that the Talpiot Tomb is the tomb of Jesus. Need we go any further on these grounds alone?

But unfortunately for the Talpiot hypothesis, to compute for the name Judah takes us even further away from the known family of Jesus of Nazareth. In fact, from what we know historically, if the Talpiot Jesus had a son named Judah, that would be more than enough to argue that he is indeed one of the 1,008 other men in Jerusalem who were named Jesus with a father named Joseph. For if we gave Jesus a 20 percent chance of having a son, which is probably a much higher percentage than most would grant, this alone would lower the probability to 1 in 5,000 that this is Jesus of Nazareth!

Probably no one has done more work on the statistics of the Talpiot Tomb than Randy Ingermanson. In his initial essay on the topic, he concluded that the odds are at least 10,000 to 1 that the Talpiot Tomb Jesus is not Jesus of Nazareth.[120] After his study, Rosebrough concluded that there was a 15,000:1 chance that all the major

---

[120] Ingermanson, "Jesus Family Tomb: A Statistical Analysis."

premises of the Talpiot hypothesis were true, from which Rosebrough derived the title of his essay "Archaeological Identity Theft"![121]

But Ingermanson went much further with a second study. Teaming up with Jay Cost, they used a very sophisticated application of Bayes' Theorem, a highly recognized means of using calculus in "improving an initial probability estimate in light of new information." They figured the problem in several ways, depending on how people answer the "fuzzy factors" where there are differences of opinion. For a typical historian, they arrived at a 1 in 19,000 chance that the Talpiot Tomb was that of Jesus. For a historian who leans toward this being Jesus's tomb, the chances are estimated at 1 in 1,100. For the historian who leans toward it not being Jesus's tomb, the odds drop all the way to 1 in 5,000,000![122]

Basically, the lesson of their study is that there are not enough realistic "fuzzy factors" to turn the odds in favor of the Talpiot Tomb being Jesus's burial place.[123] As Ingermanson concludes, "The article shows 5 different test cases that give estimates that would be computed by people with a wide range of different mindsets. The interesting thing is that, despite vast differences in assumptions, the final results are not terribly different."[124] Overall, their conclusions are absolutely devastating to the Talpiot hypothesis.[125]

TALPIOT ODDS AND BAYES' THEOREM

19,000:1 AGAINST	**1,100:1** AGAINST	**5,000,000:1** AGAINST
TYPICAL OPINION OF FUZZY FACTORS	SYMPATHETIC OPINION OF FUZZY FACTORS	UNSYMPATHETIC OPINION OF FUZZY FACTORS

Designed by Doug Powell

---

[121] Rosebrough, "Archaeological Identity Theft."

[122] Ingermanson, "Jesus Family Tomb: A Statistical Analysis.'"

[123] Ingermanson, "Jesus Family Tomb: Bayes Theorem and the Probability of Authenticity," *Randy Ingermanson: Bayes Theorem and the Probability of Authenticity* (blog), accessed October 31, 2023, https://www.ingermanson.com/mad-science/jesus-family-tomb/probability/.

[124] Personal email from Randy Ingermanson, March 26, 2007.

[125] Incredibly, in the article "Jesus Family Tomb: Bayes Theorem and the Probability of Authenticity," Ingermanson provides an Excel spreadsheet where interested readers can answer the same "fuzzy factors" and create their own odds!

Additional Problems

In the many critiques of the Talpiot hypothesis, there are a number of additional issues that ought to be mentioned. These tend to be somewhat less substantial, and a couple simply raise questions, but they should still be considered in any treatment of the subject.

Are there dating problems? Kloner wrote in his original article that the Talpiot Tomb could be dated from the end of the first century BCE until AD 70.[126] Of course, if the date is actually before about AD 30, this entire discussion is moot. On the other hand, Witherington argues for a post-70 date for the tomb, which is still possible because it is known that Jewish osslegium, or ossuary reburial, continued past 70 at least until 125 and the time of Bar Kokhba. Witherington finds potential indications of this conclusion in the following: (1) the tomb is not located in Old Jerusalem; (2) the appearance of three languages in the tomb, especially because early Christians and Jews usually did not speak Greek; (3) the ornamental marking outside the tomb "is meant to attract attention and draw people to the tomb," which is arguably the opposite of pre-70 times, when Christians were "beleaguered" and would not have wanted to show off where Jesus was buried![127]

Many scholars have mentioned that if Jesus's family had a family tomb, it would most likely be located in Nazareth, not Jerusalem.[128] For example, Alan Segal asks, "Why would Jesus's family have a tomb outside of Jerusalem if they were from Nazareth?"[129] Magness cites Rahmani's research and indicates that the custom was for Judean families to indicate ancestry by mentioning the father, "but in rock-cut tombs owned by non-Judean families . . . it was customary to indicate the deceased's place of origin" instead. At the very least, Magness notes that "we could expect that at least some of the ossuary inscriptions to reflect their Galilean origins." Further, if Jesus's family had owned their own tomb, Joseph would never have to have intervened.[130]

---

[126] Kloner, "Tomb with Inscribed Ossuaries," 21.

[127] Witherington, "Problems Multiply."

[128] Magness as quoted in Mims, "Special Report"; Witherington, "Jesus Tomb?"; Licona, "First Person."

[129] Alan Segal as quoted in Lisa Miller and Joanna Chen, "The Tomb of Jesus Christ?," *Newsweek*, March 5, 2007, 3.

[130] Magness, "Tomb of Jesus."

Likewise, some of these same scholars have added the point that Jesus's family was not wealthy and stone tombs are very expensive.[131] But Tabor countered this with the strong protest that wealthy followers of Jesus, such as Joseph of Arimathea or Lazarus (who also had a rock tomb), could have paid for the Jesus family tomb, just as Joseph did with his first burial, because of their "extraordinary devotion" to him.[132]

Zias seemed incensed by the Talpiot hypothesis interpretation of the symbols on the tomb. For example, the mysterious "X" marking on ossuaries are not Christian symbols, but simply an indication of which way the lid fits—it will not work in the reverse! Zias concludes, "Duh."[133]

As Witherington points out helpfully, Jesus was not called the son of Joseph by anyone who knew him intimately. This included his family members as well as his disciples.[134]

Although it would not necessarily refute any of the data, more than one scholar mentioned that the Talpiot Tomb claim was first voiced by the popular media instead of having the appeal made in the peer-reviewed literature. For example, Jodi Magness makes this point.[135]

Statistical studies fail to indicate that the Talpiot Tomb is the burial place of Jesus of Nazareth. Once again, every claim has been countered by many devastating critical responses. Scarcely has a thesis regarding the historical Jesus faced such a scholarly pummeling, especially in that the complaints have issued from those of various theological persuasions across the spectrum.

It is sufficient here to recall that both sides even acknowledge that there were likely more than 1,000 Jewish men in Jerusalem alone during the time of ossuary burials who were named "Jesus" and whose father was also named "Joseph." The auxiliary claims, along with several other problems, only move us even further away from the initial hypothesis. As Ingermanson has graphically argued above, the case against the Talpiot hypothesis is so decisive that it is almost a moot point how one answers

---

[131] Segal as quoted by Miller and Chen, "Tomb of Jesus Christ?," 3; Magness as quoted in Mims, "Special Report," 3; Licona, "First Person."

[132] James D. Tabor, "Two Burials of Jesus of Nazareth and the Talpiot Yeshua Tomb," *Bible History Daily*, March 14, 2007, https://www.biblicalarchaeology.org/daily/archaeology -today/biblical-archaeology-topics/two-burials-of-jesus-of-nazareth-and-the-talpiot -yeshua-tomb/.

[133] Zias, "Deconstructing."

[134] Witherington, "Problems Multiply."

[135] Magness, "Tomb of Jesus."

the relevant questions. The conclusion is still the same: this is not the tomb of Jesus of Nazareth.

The Resurrection of Jesus

Now we reach a huge question in the Talpiot Tomb saga. Given the claims of those who think that this is the family tomb of Jesus of Nazareth, how can we account for what history says happened on the first Easter? Answering this question is one of the most difficult for those who support the Talpiot thesis.

From the beginning, we need to be very clear when we address this topic with regard to our use of the New Testament and other ancient documents. It must be emphasized that the argument definitely does *not* assume that the Talpiot hypothesis must be mistaken just because it disagrees with the Bible, Christian tradition, or Christian beliefs. Unless there are firm reasons for believing these sources, this would be to reject the thesis for the wrong reasons.

Rather, we will take a different approach here. Almost exclusively, we will make use only of the established historical information generally held by the vast majority of scholars who study this topic. More crucially, when there is scholarly agreement about particular historical data, it is almost always because there are strong reasons for believing this information. This is especially the case when the specialists who agree about these facts disagree concerning what they do with the rest of Christian belief. While I will not be able to argue here how this historical basis is established, I have done so elsewhere in great detail.[136]

In other words, it is maintained here that the responses that are among the most difficult for the Talpiot claims are those that are drawn from accredited information that is approved by scholars precisely because they have strong reasons for doing so. Therefore, if these historical facts make it very difficult to accept the Talpiot hypothesis, then this will be a strong hurdle for the thesis to overcome without first disproving the widespread scholarly basis behind the objections.

---

[136] For just two examples of this approach as applied to the resurrection of Jesus, see Gary R. Habermas, *The Historical Jesus: Ancient Evidence for the Life of Christ* (Joplin, MO: College Press, 1996); Habermas with Michael R. Licona, *The Case for the Resurrection of Jesus* (Grand Rapids: Kregel, 2004). These and other texts may be consulted for much of the discussion in this chapter.

The Empty Tomb of Jesus

In all our ancient sources, friends and foes alike acknowledged that the tomb in which Jesus was buried was found empty shortly afterward. Our earliest source (1 Cor 15:4) states that the discovery of the vacated tomb of Jesus occurred just three days after the crucifixion. All four Gospels report that the women who visited Jesus's tomb discovered that it was open and empty. And it was reported that even the Jewish authorities thought that the tomb was empty.[137]

Why should anyone believe that this is actually what happened? Perhaps surprisingly, scholars have provided more than twenty reasons for the historicity of the empty tomb. The most frequently mentioned is the unanimous agreement that women were the first witnesses. In the patriarchal culture of first-century Palestine, women were unlikely to be asked to give important testimony. Generally, there was an inverse relation between the importance of a particular subject and whether or not a woman would be allowed to testify in court.

Given this scenario, why are the women listed by all our sources as the first witnesses to the empty tomb, unless it were true? Even further, why would we be told that the male disciples reacted by belittling the women and accusing them of spreading tales—basically gossip (see Luke 24:11)? These are examples of what scholars call the principle of embarrassment—that it is unlikely that authors will embarrass their heroes without very good reasons. But the texts clearly report these embarrassing accounts.

On the other hand, if you want to evidence something as important as the empty tomb, and you are as free with your sources as some scholars think, why not simply make up a story that says that the men found the empty tomb, so that their testimony would more readily be received? And even if you use the women, certainly do not make the later leaders of the church, the male disciples, criticize the women. That would mean that those who took Jesus's place were badly mistaken. But the disciples must be trusted for their wise counsel.

This is all backwards and a horrible way to establish your case—unless it is precisely what happened! These are some of the reasons why scholars take so seriously the "embarrassing" female testimony concerning finding the vacated tomb.

---

[137] Matt 28:11–15; Justin, *Dial.* 108; Tertullian, *Spect.* 30. Also, a Jewish writing from much later, the *Toledot Yeshu*, presents a similar account; see Habermas, *Historical Jesus*, 205–6; cf. Paul L. Maier, *In the Fullness of Time: A Historian Looks at Christmas, Easter, and the Early Church* (San Francisco: HarperCollins, 1991), 200–202.

Another reason to accept the empty tomb is that the city of Jerusalem should have been the very last place chosen for such a report if it were not so. Why? Both because the church was born in this city and there were many enemies who opposed the message. An afternoon walk to the tomb by either friend or foe could either verify or falsify the claim. If the tomb were not empty, how often could the claim have been disproven?

Some will object that the story of the women visiting the tomb does not surface until the Gospel of Mark, about thirty-five or forty years after the events. But we must not miss something important here. The predominant view of afterlife among the Jews of this day is clearly that of *bodily* resurrection.[138] So how could the disciples have gotten away with proclaiming that Jesus had risen and appeared to them after his death if the stone still remained in front of his tomb? Anyone who checked would disprove the entire enterprise in one easy step!

We will just mention one more argument for the empty tomb. Ancient historian Paul Maier reminds us, "Many facts from antiquity rest on just one ancient source, while two or three sources in agreement generally render the fact unimpeachable."[139] But the empty tomb is attested by between three and six independent sources, both in the Gospels and elsewhere.[140] This is simply excellent evidence by ancient standards.

So for these and many other reasons, that Jesus's burial tomb was empty very shortly afterwards is the best explanation for the data. How does the Talpiot hypothesis explain this data?

The Talpiot Tomb versus Jesus's Traditional Burial and Empty Tomb

According to the Talpiot hypothesis, Jesus of Nazareth died by crucifixion and was buried initially in a tomb, for perhaps a year, waiting for his flesh to rot. Then later,

---

[138] For many details on the Jewish view, see especially N. T. Wright, *The Resurrection of the Son of God*, vol. 3 of *Christian Origins and the Question of God* (Minneapolis: Fortress, 2003), chaps. 3–5.

[139] Maier, *In the Fullness of Time*, 197.

[140] When scholars count source attestation, they do not simply count the Gospels as four independent texts. They count what they perceive to be the number of different reports from which the various Gospel accounts were derived. On the empty tomb, depending on the scholar, we have anywhere from three to six very early sources. Besides the three to four sources that scholars think they can find in the Gospel texts at this point, we also have the potential early creedal statement in Acts 13:29–30, 35–37 and the implications of Paul's early creedal report in 1 Cor 15:3–5. This does not even count the later but still useful reports by Justin Martyr and Tertullian.

his bones would have been reburied in the Talpiot family tomb in the ossuary that bears his name.

According to James Tabor, a likely scenario would involve Jesus's original but temporary burial in a private tomb by Joseph of Arimathea, basically as the Gospels teach. But then someone, likely Joseph himself, would have moved the body quite soon afterward. This has nothing to do with "stealing" the body of Jesus. According to this view, Jesus's body was simply moved to a different tomb in an orderly fashion. Then, after the flesh had decayed, his bones would have been placed in the Talpiot ossuary.[141]

But this appears to involve a rather bizarre scenario that would never have been concocted unless one were trying specifically to bridge the two stories and make the Talpiot tomb the burial place of Jesus of Nazareth. It certainly does not make the best sense of what we know about Jesus's burial.

To begin, why would Joseph rebury the body in the same sort of tomb that Jesus's body had already been placed in? One could postulate that he simply wanted to keep the first one open for his own family or for other personal reasons, but the point we made above is that we would work with the data that are widely recognized by scholars, unless we have *strong reasons* for doing otherwise. But we clearly have *no* good reasons to think that Jesus's body was reburied within a day or so after his death but before the third burial in the ossuary, unless the entire point is to get Jesus's bones into the Talpiot tomb! There is simply no data that could establish this scenario.

Before moving on, one other issue needs to be mentioned. Biblical archaeologist Jodi Magness concludes that one can accept the explanation that Jesus was raised from the dead, or one can postulate that Jesus's body was reburied the most common way that it was done in first-century Judea: in a trench grave. This would involve placing the shrouded body in a rectangular opening in the earth. But "whatever explanation one prefers . . . his bones could not have been collected in an ossuary, at least not if we follow the Gospel accounts."[142]

So if the most common kind of reburial was employed, this would fail to account for the decay of the body, making its reburial a year or so later impossible. Jesus's flesh and bones would have been destroyed long before an ossuary burial would occur. There would be nothing left to rebury!

---

[141] Tabor, "Two Burials."
[142] Magness, "Tomb of Jesus."

Tabor is not sure whether or not Joseph would have told others about his reburial.[143] But on the one scenario, would Joseph, an honorable man who was just trying to do the best thing for Jesus, never have informed anyone of his decision? At the very least, it is highly unlikely that he moved Jesus's body by himself. So, no one witnessed the removal, especially when Joseph was not even trying to be secretive about it? And assuming that he got help, perhaps from more than one other person, what prevents them from sharing that incredibly important information? If everyone kept it hidden for some reason, especially if they never told anyone, including Jesus's mother and family, now the hypothesis seems to have migrated into some form of conspiracy and fraud. It becomes reminiscent of the old Egyptian stories that those who buried the pharaohs had to be killed so as not to divulge the whereabouts of the tombs!

So, because of these as well as other serious problems, let's suppose that Joseph told Jesus's family that he had moved the body. This seems most natural, after all, or even required, since if Jesus's bones showed up later in the family tomb, with his name clearly scratched on the outside of the ossuary, we can assume that many family members would have been quite aware of it!

It makes the most sense that Joseph would have informed them *before* he actually moved the body. After all, in any culture and time, would a man who appears to be virtually unknown to a family simply move their son's or brother's body and never tell them beforehand? This imposition would seem to be simply incredible!

But now it is very difficult to understand why the women, *including Jesus's mother Mary*, would go to the vacated tomb on Sunday morning and think it is significant that Jesus's body was no longer there! And even if Joseph straightened out the matter upon hearing of their mistake or at some time later, further serious problems would ensue, such as the rise of even their initial faith in the resurrection. But we will save some of these for the next portion of our discussion.

The empty tomb is such a problem for Tabor that when he gets to some of the sticky questions, presumably like these, he simply "punts" and says that we can say no more because of the theological nature of the Gospels. Not only is this assertion problematic in terms of the most recent New Testament studies, but by this time in the discussion Tabor has already borrowed from the Gospels whenever he wants to make the points he needs. For example, he assumes the general crucifixion and burial scenarios, the person of Joseph of Arimathea, the

---

[143] See Magness, "Tomb of Jesus."

time of the day and the hasty nature of Jesus's burial, the nature of the rock tomb and the stone rolled in front of it, and on and on.[144] But when these *exact same* sources destroy his hypothesis, he opts out of the process!

It must be noted here that perhaps the major problem so far for the Talpiot reburial hypothesis is that the evidence for the empty tomb is so strong. Indeed, Tabor concedes it, saying that it is too difficult to make sense of the data without this truth.[145] But as we have seen, the empty tomb alone plays havoc with the Talpiot thesis. The following problems have to be solved, without any evidence on their behalf:

- There is no known reason why Joseph had to rebury the body of Jesus within twenty-four hours.
- If Jesus's body were reburied the most common way—in a trench grave— there would be nothing left to place in the Talpiot Tomb ossuary. But what is the point of moving it to a very similar tomb?
- If Joseph never told anyone, how would he keep it from becoming known, especially given that he would presumably need help from others and that the process itself would likely gather attention?
- If Joseph did tell others, especially the family, why do Mary, the mother of Jesus, and others come to the tomb on Sunday morning and have no idea where Jesus's body was located?
- On what grounds do we accept the majority of the Gospel textual attestations to Jesus's death and burial, except when they clearly fail to support our beloved hypotheses?

The Resurrection Appearances of Jesus

We have said that whether they consider themselves liberal, moderate, or conservative, scholars often agree on a fair number of details from the life of Jesus and the beginning of the early church. For example, the vast majority of scholars today think, at the very least, that Jesus's disciples along with others thought that they had seen appearances of the risen Jesus.[146]

---

[144] Tabor, "Two Burials."
[145] Tabor, "Two Burials."
[146] For many details besides the sources already named, see Gary R. Habermas, "Experiences of the Risen Jesus: The Foundational Historical Issue in the Early Proclamation of the Resurrection," *Dialog: A Journal of Theology* 45 (2006): 288–97; Gary R. Habermas,

Why is this crucial fact conceded by virtually all scholars, even skeptics? There are many reasons, but here are several major ones. The starting point is almost always (1) Paul's eyewitness testimony that he had seen the risen Jesus, converting him from a life of persecuting Christian believers (1 Cor 9:1; 15:8–10). Equally important is that (2) this is set in the context of the early creedal material that Paul had received and passed on to others (1 Cor 15:3–7). Most critical scholars think that this information dates from immediately after the crucifixion and that Paul received it in the early to mid-30s from Peter and James the brother of Jesus during Paul's visit to Jerusalem (Gal 1:13–20).

Further (3) Paul took great care to check out his gospel message again with Peter, James the brother of Jesus, and John, and they confirmed his gospel, adding nothing (Gal 2:1–10). (4) Paul testified that the other apostles were teaching the same message that he was regarding the resurrection appearances of Jesus (1 Cor 15:11–14).

Other reasons also point to the disciples' conviction that they had seen the risen Jesus. (5) Many other creedal texts that date from the earliest period of Christianity also confirm these conclusions. (6) James the brother of Jesus was an unbelieving skeptic until he thought that he saw an appearance of the risen Jesus (1 Cor 15:7). (7) The disciples were willing to die specifically for their message of the resurrection of Jesus, which demonstrates that they were totally convinced it was true. (8) The empty tomb, discussed above, indicates that what happened to Jesus happened to his body, so this also points in the direction of actual appearances of the risen Jesus.[147]

These eight arguments are also accepted by most scholars, and they point quite strongly to the fact that we have been addressing: the earliest disciples were utterly convinced that they had witnessed appearances of the risen Jesus. Further, most scholars agree that alternative attempts to explain away the resurrection on natural grounds also fail. If this is so, then the disciples were correct about what they thought they had seen: appearances of the risen Jesus.

In other words, the evidence indicates that the disciples thought that Jesus was alive and that they had seen him. If natural events do not explain these experiences, then the resurrection appearances become the best explanation. So the experiences plus the absence of natural alternatives equals the resurrection appearances!

"Resurrection Research from 1975 to the Present: What Are Critical Scholars Saying?," *Journal for the Study of the Historical Jesus* 3 (2005): 135–53.

[147] For this list in a slightly different form, see Habermas, "Experiences of the Risen Jesus," 289–93.

We should mention once again that we are *not* saying that these facts are true simply because they are reported in the New Testament. If that were the basis for these events, then skeptical scholars who reject the inspiration or even the reliability of Scripture would presumably also reject these data. But virtually all scholars think that the disciples had real experiences that they thought were Jesus's resurrection appearances. It is rare to discover any scholars who deny this. That is because, as we said above, there are many reasons to accept these facts as historical. *That* is why so many scholars agree with them.

The Talpiot Tomb and the Risen Jesus

Therefore, we have to ask how the Talpiot Tomb hypothesis fares against these accredited historical data. It did not do a very good job of answering the burial data. How does it address the subject of the resurrection appearances? My contention is that it does an even poorer job here.

According to any burial scenario that we have mentioned above, Mary the mother of Jesus must have known, sooner or later, that Jesus had been reburied and later had his bones placed in an ossuary in the family tomb. Thus she would know that his body, at least, had *not* been raised from the dead. I argued above that it makes by far the most sense that if Joseph of Arimathea had reburied Jesus's body, then Jesus's family would necessarily have to have known where to find the bones in order to rebury them later in the family tomb. But it also makes the best sense that he informed them before he moved the body.

But if this was so, as we mentioned above, the women, including Mary and Mary Magdalene, would now have had no reason to go to the old tomb on Sunday morning to finish the burial, which had already been completed by Joseph. Nor would they be surprised to find the tomb empty. But now we encounter the next problem—what did the two Marys think when they and the other women saw Jesus? We might be reminded here that even very critical scholars take this claim very seriously.[148] Needless to say, the conviction of the appearance would collide with the knowledge that Jesus's body, at that very moment, lay dead in another tomb.

---

[148] Robert W. Funk and the Jesus Seminar, *The Acts of Jesus: The Search for the Authentic Deeds of Jesus* (New York: HarperCollins, 1998), 454; Helmut Koester, *Introduction to the New Testament* (Philadelphia: Fortress, 1982), 2:84.

Though it is unlikely that Joseph, a fairly obscure follower of Jesus, would decide on his own to move the body without telling the family and friends of Jesus, what if he did wait until later to inform them? This still does not dissolve the problem of the appearances to the women. Not only would they in all likelihood be present in the groups to which Jesus appeared (see Luke 24:33; John 20:17–18), but they are specifically mentioned as being present at the end of the forty days of Jesus's appearances right after the ascension (Acts 1:14). Even without these texts, to think that female disciples like the two Marys would not be present when Jesus appeared during this time is simply shortsighted.

The point is that there is absolutely no question from the texts we have that Jesus's mother Mary and Mary Magdalene were believers, thought they had also seen the risen Jesus and supported the efforts of the early church. Yet, if within a year or so (at the very longest) Jesus's bones would be reburied in the Talpiot Tomb, what would happen to their ongoing faith? And as we have said, it is much more likely that they knew that Jesus had been raised bodily from the dead without leaving any bones behind.

Every time they entered the family tomb in order to rebury a family member, they would be confronted with the reality of Jesus's horrible death by crucifixion. Perhaps they would even have to periodically move or step over Jesus's ossuary. Since the predominant Jewish view was resurrection of the body, with the ossuaries themselves being a pointer to this ongoing belief in the importance of the human bones, how could the women go on believing that Jesus had been raised from the dead? And then what becomes of their firm belief that they had seen him alive after his death?

With James the brother of Jesus we have a different twist to the problem. As the presumed head of the family after the death of Jesus, he too would have known where the family reburial tomb was located and that Jesus's name was displayed on the outside of the box. James would almost have had to repeatedly trip over, or at least pass by, his brother's bones to rebury additional family members during the intervening years before his own death. This is highly problematic given the critical scholarly view that James had been converted from skepticism by a resurrection appearance of Jesus, which is also a clear case of the principle of embarrassment mentioned above. He went from believing Jesus was deranged to a profound faith change.[149]

However, as a pious Jew, James knew that Jesus's "body" was still interred in the family tomb! How, then, could Jesus have been raised from the dead? After all, his

---

[149] Compare Mark 3:21 and John 7:5 with 1 Cor 15:7.

brother's bones were safe in the family tomb awaiting the resurrection! But there are additional problems in James's case that were not present for the Marys.

Given Jesus's reburial and then his interment in the ossuary, what would account for James's conversion from skepticism? And if James did not yet know that his brother's corpse had simply been moved, what about Jesus's appearance to him? And even if he had become a believer because of the resurrection appearance, as held by the majority of scholars, then why did he *keep* believing upon discovering the truth about his brother's body and bones? After all, a few years after Jesus's death, James is still the pastor of the church in Jerusalem (Gal 1:18–19; 2:1; Acts 15:13–21). And if James is the author of the epistle, written years after that, the Lord Jesus Christ is still described as "glorious" (Jas 2:1), waiting to come (5:7), and preparing to judge (5:9).

One last item about James should also be mentioned. If the recently discovered James Ossuary is authentic, it might actually work *against* the Talpiot Tomb hypothesis.[150] The ossuary designation of "James son of Joseph brother of Jesus" would arguably indicate that until his death, James was still identified with Christianity. This would confirm both the New Testament witness as well as the testimony of Josephus, who recorded James's martyrdom in Jerusalem (*Ant.* 20.9.1). Further, the ossuary inscription is a hint of Jesus's resurrection, for if James, for any reason, thought that Jesus had not been raised from the dead and was therefore less than the Lord, it would seem that he would no longer be so identified in his death.[151] But once again, this would seem to work against the Talpiot Tomb thesis.

We must move on now to one other very serious problem that the early conviction of resurrection appearances produces for the Talpiot hypothesis. Whenever Jesus's mother Mary, Mary Magdalene, and James found out about the reburial of Jesus's body, it would have to be no later than a year or so after the crucifixion, as occasioned by the burial of his bones in the Talpiot family tomb. But this would be only a year or so into the life of the Christian church. How could this information possibly stay hidden from the apostles and other early leaders? One would think that the effect on the faith of at least these three early leaders would be devastating!

But as soon as the secret leaked out, how would the early proclamation of the gospel—the deity, death, and resurrection of Jesus—be affected? The truth of Jesus's

---

[150] As noted above, this is disputed. See Hershel Shanks and Ben Witherington III, *The Brother of Jesus* (New York: HarperCollins, 2004).

[151] The epistle refers to Jesus as "Lord" and "Christ" (Jas 1:1; 2:1). See the thesis of Shanks and Witherington referenced in the prior note.

reburial would hit the movement right between the eyes at its very center! How would it affect Peter? How about John? How about others?

Then of course, what do we do with Paul's conversion, based on what he thought was a resurrection appearance of Jesus? With Jesus dead and with his body and bones already reburied by this time, does the Talpiot hypothesis reveal any new insights regarding Paul's conversion? It would seem that this subject is not even addressed. Therefore, a different approach is needed here. But it is far from clear that there is anything new to say about what changed Paul from a fearsome persecutor to a believer in Jesus Christ. But this change must be accounted for due to the central nature of Paul's experience and his early resurrection report. One thing to add is that, as a former Pharisee (Phil 3:5–6), it is even more clear that Paul believed in the resurrection of the body, as they did. This is further evidenced from his writings.[152]

Of course, the response might be that this is not a thesis about Paul. But since the Talpiot scenario does propose to be a fairly comprehensive contribution to the question of Christian origins and Jesus's resurrection in particular, we simply note that the issue of Paul's conversion is far from being solved in this manner. And as we have said, what happened to Paul is near the center of Christianity. The point is that by not addressing this question well, and thereby emphasizing its lack of response to Paul's conversion, the Talpiot hypothesis shows that it lacks explanatory power—a key ingredient of historical research. Therefore, it is weakened further.

However, all the evidence we have strongly opposes the Talpiot thesis here, and very firmly so. For example, during that initial meeting in Jerusalem mentioned above (Gal 1:18–20), perhaps six years after the crucifixion, Paul, Peter, and even James (who knew the truth about Jesus at least years earlier) met to discuss their shared Christian hope.[153] Fourteen years later, they all met again, this time along with John, in order to discuss the nature of the gospel, concerning which they agreed. The result was a renewed effort to continue their missionary effort with more zeal than ever (Gal 2:1–10).

There is not the slightest sign that any of them thought that they might be mistaken or were less than totally committed to the truth of this message. Indeed, very early first-century sources tell us that James, Paul, and Peter died as martyrs for the gospel that they preached, which included the central truth of Jesus's resurrection.[154]

---

[152] See Habermas and Licona, *Case for the Resurrection*, chap. 9.

[153] Jesus's bones should have been buried in the family tomb about five years earlier.

[154] For James's martyrdom, see Josephus, *Ant.* 20.9.1. For Peter's and Paul's martyrdom, see Clement of Rome, *Corinthians* 5.

This means, at the very least, that they believed their gospel message to the very end of their lives. This is simply devastating evidence against the Talpiot thesis.

We must add quickly here what we are *not* saying. We are not saying that those who hold to the Talpiot thesis will have nothing whatsoever to say. They will no doubt come up with some ideas that address a few of the many concerns raised in this appendix. But the key here is whether their scenarios are of the *what if* or *could be* types of "solutions," like what Tabor presents, or if their scenarios follow the historical evidence that we know.[155] Because as we have said, the evidence opposes them at virtually every turn. That is precisely why the almost-wholesale scholarly reaction is to reject their thesis.

One response that they have already made is to argue that Christians can still hold to a spiritual resurrection without believing that Jesus's body was actually raised from the dead. But the problems with such a scenario are simply immense. This presupposes that the Talpiot Tomb supposals are established when they are hardly even live options after everything is said and done. Further, this was not the view of the New Testament writers, and we must account for their teachings due to the powerful evidence in favor of them.[156]

From the beginning, the earliest proclamation was the unwavering belief that Jesus had appeared to his followers—that he was seen by them. Further, the latest indications are that the Greek words that they used always meant that it was the *body* that was raised, not the spirit alone. The words were used in this way by everyone—pagans, Jews, and Christians alike. So, the claim definitely was *not* that he was somehow spiritually alive. Rather, both individuals and groups claimed to have seen him, and this is hardly even questioned in the critical scholarly literature. The point is that we must account for the teachings themselves, not invent another scenario instead. Since the data we have supports this view, it simply must be addressed, not sidestepped. So, the spiritual resurrection claim fails from the outset.

Now we must summarize the issue here from this treatment above. We must *add* to the earlier list of burial problems for the Talpiot hypothesis, this time from the

---

[155] Especially in Tabor, "Two Burials."

[156] We must remember here what we said at the outset of this appendix. Our point is assuredly *not* that their view is wrong because the New Testament says so. The point is that with all the evidence we have in support of the historical facts that we are using here, those who subscribe to the Talpiot thesis are mistaken precisely because their hypothesis is refuted by that data at every turn. This is why virtually all scholars have reacted so strongly against their ideas.

known historical facts regarding the disciples' conviction that they had seen the risen Jesus, including their subsequent transformations and martyrdoms for the gospel message. Here is the other half of the major problems:

- Since the predominant Jewish view was that of bodily resurrection, further demonstrated specifically by the ossuary process itself and the particular word usage, knowing that Jesus's body and bones had never been raised would be an insurmountable barrier to the early resurrection faith.
- How could Jesus's mother Mary and Mary Magdalene reconcile their appearances of the risen Jesus with their knowledge that his body and bones had been reburied?
- How can we account for both James the brother of Jesus's conversion from skepticism as well as his work through the remainder of his life as pastor of the Jerusalem church when he also knew that Jesus's bones were in the family tomb?
- To presume that word of Jesus's reburial by Joseph and later interment in the ossuary never leaked out to the disciples is simply too much to suppose.
- The Talpiot thesis fails to address and account for Paul's conversion, which occurred after the supposed ossuary reburial.
- The preaching zeal of Jesus's chief apostles, followed by their recorded martyrdoms, indicate that they believed to the very end in spite of their knowledge of the reburials.

Conclusion

The Talpiot Tomb hypothesis fails on virtually every major claim that it makes. Scarcely has a view *ever* been confronted by more major refutations than this one. And seldom has the scholarly community—skeptical, liberal, moderate, and conservative alike—joined ranks and reacted with almost a single voice. In fact, a quick survey indicates that critical scholars seem to be leading the charge even more than their evangelical counterparts. "You are refuted by the known evidence" could be the clarion cry that has arisen time and again. The downright disgust with which several of these critical scholars have retorted has been surprising. In light of virtually all the facts that formulate the starting point for contemporary scholarship, there can be very little doubt that the Talpiot hypothesis was tried in the scholarly courts and found wanting!

A Final Question: A Spiritual Resurrection?

The Talpiot hypothesis does not rule out actual resurrection appearances of Jesus, except to argue that such events would not involve Jesus's exact same body that had been crucified. We will address two issues here: Could Jesus still have been raised from the dead? And what sort of resurrection appearances do the data most support?

Was Jesus Raised from the Dead?

We addressed this question in some detail in the latest discussion. Although brief, eight lines of evidence were suggested that are accepted by the vast majority of scholars. Additionally, many more detailed arguments were referenced in the notes.[157] These separate strands produce a tight, detailed historical argument for the resurrection. Such data have changed the contemporary critical view in the direction of this event. Truly, nothing of this nature exists in other religious literature.

Here we simply want to add an addendum to that discussion. All lines of evidence argue that Jesus's disciples thought that they had *seen* the risen Jesus. Virtually nothing from this time is more readily recognized by scholars. Although it would not be the traditional Christian answer, I simply want to make the point here that if Jesus was raised from the dead and appeared to his followers, either in a transformed body or even as a glorified spiritual being, *he would still actually have been raised from the dead*. Thus, the Talpiot hypothesis, *even if true*, decisively *fails* to disprove Jesus's resurrection. All the data show that Jesus was seen again after his death, and since natural theses have failed, the resurrection is strongly warranted.[158] But unfortunately for the Talpiot view, their position fails on its own merits, for dozens of reasons.

How Did Jesus Appear?

Even by postulating the prospect of a spiritual resurrection, the Talpiot hypothesis fails. Not only have its supporters not ruled out an actual resurrection, as just mentioned,

---

[157] For example, see the volume by Habermas and Licona, *Case for the Resurrection*.

[158] For the hallucination and other similar views, see Gary R. Habermas, "Explaining Away Jesus' Resurrection: The Recent Revival of Hallucination Theories," *Christian Research Journal* 23 (2001): 26–31, 47–49.

but an incredible amount of data point to Jesus being raised *bodily*, in the same body that was crucified, although there were definitely some incredibly wonderful changes.

Here we will be able only to list some of these arguments.[159] It is crucial to bear in mind that we are only asking about the *mode* of Jesus's appearance. The entire argument turns on what the early sources *taught* with regard to what was seen. Simply asked, did they think Jesus's raised body appeared? Or was he a disembodied, glorious spirit?[160]

Outlined Arguments for Jesus's Bodily Resurrection Appearances

1. The predominant Jewish view in the first-century AD was that of bodily resurrection, so this forms a helpful backdrop for our discussion.
2. Paul placed himself squarely in this traditional Jewish position by identifying with the Pharisees (Phil 3:4–6), a group that held to a bodily resurrection.[161]
3. N. T. Wright has shown in hundreds of pages of painstaking research that the chief terms for resurrection always signify a bodily event. In fact, for hundreds of years before and after Jesus, until about AD 200, regardless of whether pagans, Jews, or Christians used the terms, they always indicated bodily occurrences.[162]
4. As argued by Robert Gundry, the term "body" in the New Testament and other Jewish literature, and for Paul in particular, clearly refers to a physical organism. This is especially true of Paul's view of Jesus's resurrection appearances.[163]
5. For almost two centuries after Jesus, "spiritual body" never means an "immaterial body."[164]

---

[159] The sources in the previous chapter will also provide additional details for these points.

[160] Many of our points concern Paul's view, for it is by far the chief critical focus. That the Gospels teach bodily resurrection appearances is not challenged.

[161] In Acts 23:6–9, Luke reports that Paul claimed to still be a Pharisee, specifically identifying with their view of bodily resurrection.

[162] Wright, *Resurrection of the Son of God*, 32–552.

[163] Robert H. Gundry, *Sōma in Biblical Theology: With Emphasis on Pauline Anthropology* (Cambridge: Cambridge University Press, 1976), esp. chap. 13: "The Sōma in Death and Resurrection." Cf. Wright, *Resurrection of the Son of God*, 263–64. For one of the most careful and detailed studies of the relevant issues here, see John Granger Cook, *Empty Tomb, Resurrection, Apotheosis* (Tübingen: Mohr Siebeck, 2018), 1, 54–55, 591–93, 618, 623, plus numerous other considerations throughout this excellent text.

[164] Wright, *Resurrection of the Son of God*, 83; cf. Michael Licona, "The Risen Jesus: Casper or Corporeal?," in *Buried Hopes or Risen Savior: The Search for Jesus' Tomb*, ed. Charles L.

6. Paul answers the question by using a term in Phil 3:10–11 (cf. also 1 Cor 15:12) that signifies being raised out from the realm of the dead, specifically indicating that his body would be raised. In Phil 3:20–21, he asserts that Jesus would transform the believer's body to be like Jesus's glorious *body* (cf. also Rom 8:11).

7. Paul's sociology also indicates bodily resurrection. He always refers to the resurrection of the dead in the plural, indicating a corporate event; believers would be raised together. And the realm of resurrection is the transformed earth (Rom 8:18–23). These are very difficult concepts for glorified spirits!

8. Paul reports group appearances of Jesus (1 Cor 15:4–7; cf. the creedal statement in Acts 13:30–31), which are more indicative of bodily events.

9. Every Gospel resurrection account clearly describes a bodily appearance of Jesus, including the continuity of crucifixion scars and the offer to inspect his body.

10. An empty tomb strongly implies Jesus's bodily resurrection and appearances.

Quarles (Nashville: B& H, 2008); cf. Dale C. Allison Jr., *The Resurrection of Jesus: Apologetics, Polemics, History* (London: T&T Clark, 2021), 130–36; Wright, *Resurrection of the Son of God*, 349–53; Cook, *Empty Tomb, Resurrection, Apotheosis*, 591, Gundry, *Sōma in Biblical Theology*, 165–66.

PROVING NATURALISM
AND RELATED VIEWS?

O
ne of the most intriguing recent developments may pertain to how major naturalistic and similar-thinking researchers have critiqued their colleagues, hinting that there may be various sorts of deep fissures in their shared worldview perspectives, encompassing similarities among the varieties of materialism and other forms of atheism, for example. The history of philosophy and the history of ideas often involve infighting between somewhat like-minded schools of thought. Aristotelians argue with Platonists, while Freudians and cognitive behaviorists continue to hash out their theories and the meaning of empirical experiments.

But recent issues debated between species of naturalistic and related views often seem to go more deeply. When the various critiques are lined up side by side, the list grows to a rather impressive length. Instead of picking smaller items that might successfully convince one type of skeptic to move to just a slightly different emphasis, these recent deliberations seem to have more to do with the entire worldview not being able to explain the existence of some rather large and important ideas, such as being unable to substantiate naturalism along with like-minded positions, the seeming reality of free choices, or the existence of an immaterial portion of human thought processes that appears truly to have a real effect in the world, and so on.

For example, in a review of a new book by prominent "New Atheist" philosopher Daniel Dennett, equally prominent atheist philosopher Thomas Nagel charges Dennett with a very serious lapse. Nagel criticizes Dennett with casting scientific discussions according to his predetermined worldview without regard for whether the underlying position is accurate or correct. As Nagel complains: "And he asks us to do this because the reality of such phenomena is incompatible with the scientific materialism that in his view sets the outer bounds of reality." Hence, Dennett is blamed with making science appear to fit into his own preconceived materialistic mold, whether or not it actually does so. Driving home the point, Nagel adds regarding Dennett that "he is, in Aristotle's words, 'maintaining a thesis at all costs.'"[1]

This is a very serious charge. Nagel apparently thinks that, rather than following the available evidence wherever it might lead, Dennett prefers to craft and formulate his science in such a way that it appears to simply reaffirm his materialistic views, regardless of how misleading and inaccurate they may be! One may expect a theist to bring such a retort against a materialist or vice versa, but when a fellow who might be thought to share some similar ideas does so, it is more significant, since given the larger worldview picture, one might expect them to stand more or less shoulder to shoulder in the same corner of the ring.

But consider a comment regarding the power of worldviews from Harvard scientist Richard Lewontin:

> Our willingness to accept scientific claims that are against common sense is the key to an understanding of the real struggle between science and the supernatural. We take the side of science *in spite* of the patent absurdity of some of its constructs, *in spite* of its failure to fulfill many of its extravagant promises of health and life, *in spite* of the tolerance of the scientific community for unsubstantiated just-so stories, because we have a prior commitment, a commitment to materialism. It is not that the methods and institutions of science somehow compel us to accept a material explanation of the phenomenal world, but, on the contrary, that we are forced by our *a priori* adherence to material causes to create an apparatus of investigation and a set of concepts

---

[1] Thomas Nagel, "Is Consciousness an Illusion?," *New York Review*, March 9, 2017, https://www.nybooks.com/articles/2017/03/09/is-consciousness-an-illusion-dennett -evolution/, in a review of Daniel Dennett's book *From Bacteria to Bach and Back: The Evolution of Minds*.

that produce material explanations, no matter how counter-intuitive, no matter how mystifying to the uninitiated. Moreover, that materialism is absolute, for we cannot allow a Divine Foot in the door.[2]

This too is a radical comment. So, what is a proper answer? Are we all doomed to argue circularly from our predisposed, prior beliefs? Or, as scholars have done for centuries, perhaps it is largely a matter of comparing and contrasting arguments and ascertaining where the relevant evidence lies. No one is immune to personal bias or the force of our worldviews. Still, all we can do is conduct the most careful research possible, subject our views to peer review, lecturing widely, and interacting regularly with those with whom we disagree. Then others can judge who is exhibiting the best arguments.

Nagel comments further on the matter, drawing a few similar conclusions.[3] He also evaluates a book by leading Christian philosopher Alvin Plantinga regarding the comparing of evidence, showing that fruitful steps can still be taken, such as this theistic challenge to naturalism:

> I say this as someone who cannot imagine believing what he [Plantinga] believes. But even those who cannot accept the theist alternative should admit that Plantinga's criticisms of naturalism are directed at the deepest problem with that view—how it can account for the appearance, through the operation of the laws of physics and chemistry, of conscious beings like ourselves, capable of discovering those laws and understanding the universe that they govern. Defenders of naturalism have not ignored this problem, but I believe that so far, even with the aid of evolutionary theory, they have not proposed a credible solution.[4]

This is not a recent conclusion for Nagel either. He has been leveling it against naturalists and similar scholars for many years: "But the reasons against a purely

---

[2] Richard Lewontin, "Billions and Billions of Demons," *The New York Review*, January 9, 1997, https://www.nybooks.com/articles/1997/01/09/billions-and-billions-of-demons/, reviewing Carl Sagan's book *The Demon-Haunted World: Science as a Candle in the Dark.*

[3] Thomas Nagel, *Mind and Cosmos: Why the Materialist Neo-Darwinian Conception of Nature Is Almost Certainly False* (Oxford: Oxford University Press, 2012), 27.

[4] Thomas Nagel, "A Philosopher Defends Religion," *The New York Review*, September 27, 2012, https://www.nybooks.com/articles/2012/09/27/philosopher-defends-religion/, reviewing Alvin Plantinga's book *Where the Conflict Really Lies: Science, Religion, and Naturalism.*

physical theory of consciousness are strong enough to make it seem likely that a physical theory of the whole of reality is impossible."[5] Such a cross-over critique of Dennett and Plantinga can be valuable as a lesson on how to arrive at the most-evidenced positions in spite of our worldviews.

This comment by Nagel is also reminiscent of a much stronger concession made by Quentin Smith and published in a philosophy journal directed chiefly to naturalists and others of like mind. Smith remarked that philosophical theism had grown so strong in universities since the 1960s that, if an entire series of debates in the field of philosophy of religion took place between theistic philosophers and their naturalistic counterparts, even if moderated by naturalists, the theists would probably win every last debate![6]

The point here is that, as Nagel and Smith have argued, there are ways to break through biases of all sorts in order to ascertain who is presenting the better arguments. Books, journal articles, debates, dialogues, and friendly discussions are some ways to show this, especially where the events or articles are constructed in such a way that requires direct responses to questions that are designed to allow listeners and readers to ascertain where the best data lie.

Still other, rather shocking confessions have been pointed out by very influential naturalists and fellow thinkers. Besides those already mentioned here, Nagel and others have spoken out freely in favor of the contributions made by Intelligent Design theorists. This cuts to the heart of several weaknesses in these views, especially since very few topics are more anathema—no doubt due precisely to the deep threat that Intelligent Design may pose to their origins scenarios. John West quotes Nagel as such: "'The empirical arguments' offered by [Intelligent Design] proponents 'are of great interest in themselves.'" West adds, "It's the evidence that matters, and it's the evidence that demands a response."[7]

Another challenge is Michael Ruse's several published references to naturalism (or at least to certain versions or expressions of it along with similar stances) as actually being a religion, complete with its own dogma, highly rigid and inflexible pronouncements, and tendencies to simply pound the podium and issue constant

---

[5] Thomas Nagel, *What Does It All Mean? A Very Short Introduction to Philosophy* (Oxford: Oxford University Press, 1987), 36–37; cf. also Nagel, *Mind and Cosmos*, 37.

[6] Quentin Smith, "The Metaphilosophy of Naturalism," *Philo* 4 (2001): 195–215.

[7] John G. West, "Noted Atheist Philosopher Thomas Nagel: 'Defenders of Intelligent Design Deserve Our Gratitude,'" *Intelligent Design News*, August 22, 2012, 2.

"Amens!" and guffaws from the crowd instead of providing serious scholarly responses. Ruse remarks rather pointedly:

> I think that if, as I myself would, you extend the scope of [Darwinian] theory to an understanding of knowledge acquisition and justification and the same for morality—evolutionary epistemology and evolutionary ethics—then it can act as a religion substitute or alternative. It gives you a world picture that some people, starting with me, find entirely satisfying. I can't answer all of the questions—Why is there something rather than nothing? How does the conscious mind arise from the physical brain? Is there a purpose to it all? . . . I do nevertheless think that often Dawkins and company show the sociological characteristics of the religious.[8]

Intriguingly of late, though, it is widely proclaimed mostly by Dawkins and the "New Atheists" that religious individuals offer only faith while science offers "proof."[9] Well, the table has switched in the past few decades, with naturalists, materialists, and others too often providing too little, very shoddy, or virtually no scholarly comebacks at all. So what happened when Oxford University professor (with three earned doctorates) John Lennox debated Rich Dawkins twice? What about when William Lane Craig debated both Christopher Hitchens and Sam Harris on different occasions? Or

---

[8] Michael Ruse, "Is Darwinism a Religion?," *Huffington Post*, September 21, 2011, https://www.huffpost.com/entry/is-darwinism-a-religion_b_904828. Cf. Michael Ruse, "How Evolution Became a Religion, Creationists Correct?: Darwinians Wrongly Mix Science with Morality, Politics," *National Post Online*, May 13, 2000, http://www.nationalpost .com/artslife.asp?f=000513/288424.html. Cf. also Ruse's book, *Darwinism as Religion: What Literature Tells Us about Evolution* (Oxford: Oxford University Press, 2017).

[9] Such as Richard Dawkins, *The God Delusion* (Boston: Houghton Mifflin, 2006), 134; Christopher Hitchens, *God Is Not Great: How Religion Poisons Everything* (New York: Warner, 2007), 150, 202, 204; Sam Harris, *The End of Faith: Religion, Terror, and the Future of Reason* (New York: Norton, 2004), 23, 40. A host of theistic responses came quickly, most notably by scientists and philosophers such as John C. Lennox, *God's Undertaker: Has Science Buried God?* (Oxford: Lion Hudson, 2007); Peter S. Williams, *A Sceptic's Guide to Atheism* (Bucks: Authentic Media, 2009); James S. Spiegel, *The Making of an Atheist: How Immorality Leads to Unbelief* (Chicago: Moody, 2010); Dinesh D'Souza, *What's So Great about Christianity* (Washington, DC: Regnery, 2007); Alister McGrath and Joanna Collicutt McGrath, *The Dawkins Delusion? Atheist Fundamentalism and the Denial of the Divine* (Downers Grove, IL: InterVarsity, 2007). On the cover of the book by McGrath and McGrath, Michael Ruse amazingly quipped concerning Dawkins, "*The God Delusion* makes me embarrassed to be an atheist, and the McGrath's show why."

when Frank Turek debated Christopher Hitchens twice, and so many internet atheist comments complained that their fellow atheists brought the wrong defender and criticized Hitchens for doing an exceptionally poor job? By far the comments from both sides of the aisle thought the Christian theists got the best of the debates.

Still, the shrill mantra continues from atheists that religious persons cannot think while atheists are society's "brights," as Dawkins has been known to highlight.[10] But folks who know how to find the data can listen, read, and decide for themselves. Is this why, precisely as mentioned by atheist philosopher Quentin Smith above, he thinks that Christian philosophers would win *every single debate* on philosophy of religion matters against their secular counterparts, even with naturalist debate moderators? Smith obviously rejects the view that Christian philosophers do not think well.

Now, it needs to be added quickly that winning debates definitely does *not* indicate who speaks the truth. One thinker could simply be a better debater. That is just not how truth works. However, it may serve as one indicator of what is transpiring. When naturalists and those of similar positions do not respond well in written works where there is plenty of time to think through and develop one's position, or especially if they actually concede the victory to the theist and acknowledge that their earlier position can no longer be maintained after the conclusion of the give-and-take, these instances are far more significant than oral debates.[11] When fellow naturalists do the

---

[10] Dawkins, *God Delusion,* 380.

[11] For an example of how such written dialogues might determine an important issue, two intellectual "heavyweights" sporting diametrically opposed positions hammered out their respective views in a famous set of written challenges and responses. Oxford University atheist philosopher J. L. Mackie proposed in a 1955 article entitled "Evil and Omnipotence," *Mind* 64 (1955): 200–212, later reprinted in Louis P. Pojman, ed., *Philosophy of Religion: An Anthology* (Belmont, CA: Wadsworth, 1994), 185–92, that there was a *logical* problem for theists from the problem of evil which, if successful, would disprove theism. Mackie was challenged by Plantinga, who critiqued Mackie's argument point by point. The result of a protracted philosophical exchange was that Mackie actually conceded that Plantinga had sufficiently answered his objections here in Mackie's volume *The Miracle of Theism: Arguments for and against the Existence of God* (Oxford: Clarendon, 1982), 154. Later, another prominent atheist philosopher, William L. Rowe, likewise recognized that Mackie's logical objection from the problem of evil had failed: "No one, I think, has succeeded in establishing such an extravagant claim . . . there is a fairly compelling argument for the view that the existence of evil is logically consistent with the existence of the theistic God." Rowe's original essay was published as "The Problem of Evil and Some Varieties of Atheism," *American Philosophical Quarterly* 16 (1979): 335–41 and then was later

same regarding their system as a whole, that is also very significant. Other measures could add to or subtract from these conclusions.

Altogether, the many critiques of naturalism, materialism, atheism, and the like that have been published in recent years arguably provide evidence of a growing dissatisfaction with the perspective. But what causes a paradigm to begin to lose its luster? One popular notion is that new facts keep piling up until the older conceptions of reality can no longer handle a good many of these challenges, followed by the scientific teeter-totter flipping to the other side. But another popular, more relativistic conception is that over time enough influential individuals simply grow increasingly ready for change.

Historian and philosopher of science Thomas Kuhn argued that both developments can tip the scales away from prevailing views. One view "seems an attempt to force nature into the preformed and relatively inflexible box that the paradigm supplies . . . indeed, those that will not fit the box are often not seen at all."[12] One example was mentioned above with regard to Nagel's critique of Dennett's inability to squeeze everything into the naturalistic or materialistic mold.[13] For Kuhn, that is one of the features of a system that is suffering from significant stress.

In one of his scholarly volumes, C. S. Lewis mentions the other option: "When changes in the human mind produce a sufficient disrelish of the old Model and a sufficient hankering for some new one, phenomena to support the new one will obediently turn up." Perhaps a view "will die a violent death, ruthlessly smashed by an unprovoked assault of new facts." But Lewis still thinks that his initial option here is the more common one.[14]

Perhaps scholars are simply growing weary of the fundamental sterility of naturalism and related positions. But many scholars have argued that there are many indications of late that this position is opposed by too many serious problems and is currently doing a poor job of responding to them.

---

reproduced in William L. Rowe and William J. Wainwright, eds., *Philosophy of Religion: Selected Readings* (Fort Worth, TX: Harcourt Brace, 1998), 242. Cf. Ronald H. Nash's overview of this written dialogue in his text *Faith and Reason: Searching for a Rational Faith* (Grand Rapids: Zondervan Academic, 1988), 177–94.

[12] Thomas S. Kuhn, *The Structure of Scientific Revolutions*, 2nd ed. (Chicago: University of Chicago Press, 1970), 24, cf. 135.

[13] Nagel, "Is Consciousness an Illusion?"

[14] C. S. Lewis, *The Discarded Image: An Introduction to Medieval and Renaissance Literature* (Cambridge: Cambridge University Press, 1967), 221, 222–23, respectively.

For example, due to its dominance in the Western scholarly world today, perhaps naturalism has grown lax on its overall inability to show that it can even marshal the necessary data to argue that it is actually true. Debates with theists, such as those mentioned by Quentin Smith above, often appear to leave naturalists and other like-minded scholars with the short end of the stick when it comes to disproving the existence of God. The cause and birth of the universe is as large a problem as any, setting up a virtual war zone with studies in Intelligent Design. Nagel's decades of pounding fellow thinkers for their inability to indicate how consciousness and personhood can emerge from evolutionary beginnings is a major example.

Other potential weak points might concern where naturalism and related stances derive their notions of true beliefs, the personal perception and conviction of free will and making one's own decisions, or that all subjective states likewise must be derived from physical causation. What about Plantinga's charge (and C. S. Lewis's famous essay before that) that naturalism has severe epistemic issues in not knowing or recognizing the existence of truth, hence possessing no notion of "proof" or demonstration? Many sophisticated scholars have leveled these and still other serious criticisms at naturalism and sister views.[15]

---

[15] Robert C. Koons and George Bealer, eds., *The Waning of Materialism* (Oxford: Oxford University Press, 2010); Michael L. Peterson and Michael Ruse, *Science, Evolution, and Religion: A Debate about Atheism and Theism* (Oxford: Oxford University Press, 2017); C. Stephen Evans, *Natural Signs and Knowledge of God: A New Look at Theistic Arguments* (Oxford: Oxford University Press, 2010); Evans, *Why Christian Faith Still Makes Sense: A Response to Contemporary Challenges* (Grand Rapids: Baker Academic, 2015); Terence L. Nichols, *The Sacred Cosmos: Christian Faith and the Challenge of Naturalism* (Grand Rapids: Brazos, 2003). Many thanks to my former philosophy department colleague Thomas Provenzola, who shared these bibliographic sources immediately above. Another excellent critique, which J. P. Moreland (on the back cover of the text) calls, "The clearest and most penetrating exposition and critique of naturalism anywhere," is Stewart Goetz and Charles Taliaferro, *Naturalism, Interventions*, ed. Conor Cunningham and Peter Candler (Grand Rapids: Eerdmans, 2008), esp. chaps. 3–5; James Beilby, ed., *Naturalism Defeated? Essays on Plantinga's Evolutionary Argument against Naturalism* (Ithaca: Cornell University Press, 2002); Michael Dennett, "The Place of Life and Man in Nature: Defending the Anthropocentric Thesis," *BIO-Complexity* 2013 (2013): 1–15; Alvin Plantinga, "Dennett's Dangerous Idea," *Books and Culture* 2, no. 3 (1996): 16–18, 35; Phillip E. Johnson, "The Case against Naturalism," *Vision and Values* 4 (1996): 1–7; Richard Schlegel, "Is Science the Only Way to Truth?," *Zygon* 17 (1982): 343–59; R. F. Holland, *Against Empiricism: On Education, Epistemology, and Value* (Totowa, NJ: Littlefield, Adams, 1980); Gary R. Habermas, "Paradigm Shift: A Challenge to Naturalism," *Bibliotheca Sacra* 146 (1989): 437–50; Gregory E. Ganssle, "Metaphysical Naturalism Is Doomed (Sort of)" (paper

The most serious defense of naturalism and similar views has traditionally come from arguments regarding the existence of evil. But even here, many of the most influential philosophers exhibit a variety of significant disagreements among each other concerning the strength and application of these arguments, leading to impasses of one sort or another in the conclusions. Some like-minded scholars do think that the argument likely disproves theism, such as argued by Paul Draper.[16] Mackie's earlier thoughts were mentioned above, though he concluded that his argument from evil "may seem to be very modest." He further concluded, "We cannot, indeed, take the problem of evil as a conclusive disproof of traditional theism, because, as we have seen, there is some flexibility in its doctrines," though he considered his argument to be strong.[17]

Atheist William Rowe rejected Mackie's original deductive argument, going further and calling himself a "friendly atheist" because he concluded that "some theists are rationally justified in believing that the theistic God exists."[18] Much more recently, atheist philosopher Graham Oppy has argued against theses such as those by Draper, Mackie, Rowe, and other atheists.[19] Oppy thinks that the philosophical arguments *both* for and against God's existence are, on all sides, inconclusive in the end, especially from the perspective of neither side changing minds across the aisle.[20] Greg Ganssle has responded well to Oppy on a topic that is closer to the ones being raised in this volume.[21]

---

presented at the Evangelical Theological Society Annual Meeting, Nashville, TN, November 15–17, 2000).

[16] Paul Draper, "The Problem of Evil," in *The Oxford Handbook of Philosophical Theology*, ed. Thomas P. Flint and Michael C. Rea (Oxford: Oxford University Press, 2009), chap. 15; Draper, "Pain and Pleasure: An Evidential Problem for Theists," *Noûs* 23 (1989): 331–50.

[17] Mackie, *Miracle of Theism*, 176, also 172–76.

[18] Rowe, "Problem of Evil," 335–41, quotation on 340.

[19] Graham Oppy, "The Evidential Problem of Evil," in *A Companion to Philosophy of Religion*, ed. Charles Taliaferro, Paul Draper, and Philip L. Quinn, 2nd ed. (Oxford: Wiley-Blackwell, 2010).

[20] Graham Oppy, *Arguing about Gods* (Cambridge: Cambridge University Press, 2006), xv, plus sections 1.2 and 8.3. William Lane Craig responded to these ideas on several grounds in "Arguing Successfully about God: A Review Essay of Graham Oppy's *Arguing about Gods*," *Philosophia Christi* 10 (2008): 435–42, and also in Craig's upcoming second volume of his *Systematic Philosophical Theology*. Thanks to Bill Craig for highlighting some of these sources and ideas here on the problem of evil.

[21] Gregory E. Ganssle, review of *The Best Argument against God*, by Graham Oppy, *Philosophia Christi* 18 (2016): 503–6.

For many, perhaps even the best response to the problem of evil was written by Alvin Plantinga, for whom the bottom line regarding the problem of evil's force for the theist "is not that his beliefs are logically or probabilistically incompatible."[22] Rather, the remaining issues are more often of a personal, pastoral nature. Thus, Plantinga declared that the "Free Will Defense . . . solves the main philosophical problem of evil."[23]

Concerning the problem of evil, then, one insightful development has been the opposing viewpoints where influential thinkers, like those just mentioned, frequently oppose their own colleagues' viewpoints on whether and to what extent an argument demonstrates naturalism and related positions or disproves theism. Evil remains a serious problem across the board, perhaps for all positions, but it is not necessarily thought even by major naturalists, materialists, or other atheists to confirm or verify their positions or even to be determinative in its favor. Further, some of the naturalistic-type scholars do not think that evil refutes theism either. So, it must be insisted that the problem of indicating the truth of the atheistic view also remains a problem for a variety of reasons.

From various hints above among others, some philosophers assert that naturalistic and sister positions cannot be demonstrated to be true. For example, even materialist philosopher William G. Lycan treats materialism as lacking any strong reasons in its favor.[24] He concludes his essay by declaring, "nor have we seen any good argument for materialism."[25]

Similarly, philosopher Stephen Parrish asserted that "there are no good reasons for thinking that naturalism is true." He concludes his treatment with these words:

> Taking naturalism seriously, human beings are creatures randomly thrown up by a mindless process of evolution, bereft of free will, any sort of real or absolute value, an afterlife, and even, if one is consistent, rationality. . . . To sum up: it seems that the case against atheism and naturalism is overwhelming.[26]

---

[22] Alvin Plantinga, *God, Freedom, and Evil* (Grand Rapids: Eerdmans, 1977), 63.

[23] Plantinga, 64.

[24] William G. Lycan, "Redressing Substance Dualism," in *The Blackwell Companion to Substance Dualism*, ed. Jonathan J. Loose, Angus J. L. Menuge, and J. P. Moreland (Oxford: Wiley-Blackwell, 2018), 22.

[25] Lycan, 33. Thanks to J. P. Moreland for suggesting this example.

[26] Stephen E. Parrish, *Atheism? A Critical Analysis* (Eugene, OR: Wipf & Stock, 2019), 226.

APPENDIX 3

ISLAM AND THE RESURRECTION OF JESUS

From the time of the church's beginning, believers down through the centuries have offered many defenses of the central tenet of Christian apologetics: the historicity of Jesus's resurrection from the dead. It is not surprising, therefore, to find knowledgeable Muslim efforts that attempt to counter this essential message, usually by offering more general responses to these Christian approaches.

In this essay I will address what are perhaps the two most common sorts of Muslim critiques of the resurrection. Perhaps most frequently, the rather immediate response is to point out many apparent contradictions, conundrums, inconsistencies, and copyist errors in both the New Testament records themselves as well as in the thousands of existing Greek manuscripts. These objections also address what Christians think is the best and most commonly utilized of the contemporary translations.

The second path taken habitually by Muslim apologists is to directly address the historical center of the Christian gospel claim, both that Jesus died by Roman crucifixion and that he was raised from the dead and appeared in a bodily manner just a short time later. Though we will attempt to keep these two responses separate, these paths often coalesce for Muslims into a very similar or even the same point. We will respond to each of these Muslim critiques, supplying responses and suggestions.

The Minimal Facts Argument for Jesus's Resurrection

Though I will not be able to provide here anything beyond a very cursory description, I will be employing throughout what I have termed the minimal facts method of arguing for the resurrection of Jesus. I have elucidated, clarified, and explicated this methodology in much detail in literally dozens of readily available publications.[1]

Briefly, I have explained that the minimal facts argument makes use of only those historical facts that have two characteristics:

> Each event had to be established by more than adequate scholarly evidence, and usually by several critically-ascertained, independent lines of argumentation. Additionally, the vast majority of contemporary scholars in relevant fields had to acknowledge the historicity of the occurrence. Of the two criteria, I have always held that the first is by far the most crucial, especially since this initial requirement is the one that actually establishes the historicity of the event. Besides, the acclamation of scholarly opinion may be mistaken or it could change.[2]

This core collection of historical facts might be viewed as a species of the lowest common denominator approach. It builds a historical wall from the bottom up, adding facts to the structure like bricks, one at a time. The data are rarely disputed even by unbelieving scholars and are willingly acknowledged by essentially all critical scholars in germane areas of study.[3]

---

[1] Some of my publications on this argument include Gary R. Habermas, "The Minimal Facts Approach to the Resurrection of Jesus: The Role of Methodology as a Crucial Component in Establishing Historicity," *Southeastern Theological Review* 3 (2012): 15–26; *The Risen Jesus and Future Hope* (Lanham, MD: Rowman & Littlefield, 2003), chap. 1; Habermas with Michael R. Licona, *The Case for the Resurrection of Jesus* (Grand Rapids: Kregel, 2004).

[2] Habermas, "Minimal Facts Approach," 16.

[3] For an excellent example from a very recent dialogue, British New Testament specialist and self-described "agnostic unbeliever" James Crossley acknowledged the half dozen historical facts that I enumerated. Further, he freely commented that they were among the very strongest facts in the New Testament. See Gary Habermas and James Crossley, "Do the Minimal Facts Support the Resurrection?," July 31, 2015, in *Unbelievable*, produced by Premier Christian Radio, podcast, http://www.premierchristianradio.com/Shows/Saturday/Unbelievable/Episodes/Unbelievable-Do-the-minimal-facts-support-the-resurrection-Gary-Habermas-James-Crossley.

To avoid misunderstanding, the reliability and inspiration of Scripture are not at all being questioned here. For the record, I have also defended these latter positions on many occasions.[4] Rather, this method simply points out that, since the historical data that are utilized in the minimal facts argument are conceded by critics, the historicity of Jesus's resurrection should not be denied. It makes the point that even the *skeptic's* notion of an unreliable New Testament still recognizes and allows the existence of abundant data by which the facticity of the gospel message is established and follows. This approach is especially helpful, for example, when briefer discussions are required.

Philosopher Angus Menuge sums up the matter well: "Habermas's 'minimal facts' approach is not without its critics (some say it concedes too much to tendentious principles of biblical criticism), but it does explain why, over time, one skeptical alternative after another to the historical fact of the resurrection has been abandoned, leaving critics with shrinking cover to hide from Christ's claim on their life."[5]

In short, this approach actually concedes *no ground at all*, and certainly does not treat the skeptic's views as if they are in any way correct. It simply points out that even critical positions on the nature of the New Testament texts still do not preclude the establishment of the resurrection.

Contradictions and Discrepancies in the New Testament Accounts?

When responding to Christians, perhaps even the most popular tradition within Islamic apologetics is to discount the New Testament writings by pointing out what are considered to be highly corrupted textual copies as they were duplicated down through the ages. We are not referring so much here to the factual or other claims made by the individual authors themselves, but more commonly to the many acknowledged variant readings that have accumulated through the years during the copying process.

---

[4] Such as Habermas, *Risen Jesus*, chap. 10; Gary R. Habermas, "Jesus and the Inspiration of Scripture," *Areopagus Journal* 2, no. 1 (2002): 11–16; Habermas, "Recent Perspectives on the Reliability of the Scriptures," *Christian Research Journal* 28 (2005): 22–31.

[5] Angus Menuge, review of *Debating Christian Theism*, ed. J. P. Moreland, Chad Meister, and Khaldoun A. Sweis, *Philosophia Christi* 16 (2014): 451–56.

It has often been pointed out that the nature of this initial Muslim claim often sounds very odd indeed, especially to those who are acquainted with the actual particulars. Christians have acknowledged freely for over 200 years that there are many alternative readings in the New Testament. For example, Norman Geisler and William Nix in their standard textbook on this general subject, published by the conservative Moody Press, addressed this subject almost 50 years ago. These authors reported almost without comment that of the more than 5,000 Greek New Testament manuscripts that had been discovered up until that time, there were more than 200,000 variant readings in existence! The authors added the comment that "this figure will no doubt increase in the future as more manuscripts are discovered."[6]

Their prediction of course proved to be the case, as the number of newly discovered Greek manuscripts has grown to almost 6,000 with the number of variants being placed presently at some 200,000 to 300,000.[7] Some scholars have estimated an even higher number.

The point to be made clearly here is not only that the Muslim charges are largely already acknowledged by Christian scholars, at least in principle, but further that these variant numbers do not trouble Christian scholars at all due to these same variations paradoxically being among the best indicators that allow the texts to be reconstructed to a high degree. This general textual accuracy is even recognized by non-Christian scholars like Bart Ehrman as well as other skeptical New Testament specialists.[8]

But there are other aspects to these Muslim responses as well. The objections often indicate an almost complete misunderstanding of the subject altogether, even to an embarrassing degree, and in areas that have nothing to do with the truth of Christianity. One of the best examples of this tendency is manifest repeatedly in the writings of Ahmed Deedat, especially since he has more or less become the specific, influential pattern for other Muslim apologists.

For instance, in discussing what he terms "the extravagant and conflicting claims of the Jews and the Christians," an initial example provided by Deedat is his

---

[6] Norman L. Geisler and William E. Nix, *A General Introduction to the Bible* (Chicago: Moody, 1968), 360–67.

[7] Bart D. Ehrman, *The New Testament: A Historical Introduction to the Early Christian Writings* (Oxford: Oxford University Press, 2000), esp. 442–50.

[8] Ehrman, *New Testament*, 443, 447, 449. Cf. also Helmut Koester, *Introduction to the New Testament* (Philadelphia: Fortress, 1982), 2:15–21; John A. T. Robinson, *Can We Trust the New Testament?* (Grand Rapids: Eerdmans, 1977), 37–38, 41–42.

self-incriminating charge that the New International Version "unceremoniously expunged" the "According to" as the title of each Gospel, which he apparently views as a problem indicating that Christians changed their texts almost on a whim![9] Yet he seems to be unaware that these words as well as each of the four authors' names did not at all originally appear or circulate on any of the original Gospels! So how could it be any kind of a problem whatsoever? Who or what is this criticism aimed at?

Another instance of severe confusion is provided by Deedat when he states assuredly that "the Gospels, *any Christian scholar will confirm*, were first penned decades *and centuries* after Jesus."[10] Actually *not a single Christian scholar*, liberal or conservative, will date the initial writing of the Gospels to centuries after Jesus. There is an absolutely huge difference between the Gospels being written "decades" and "centuries" after Jesus! In factual terms, this is a totally mistaken statement. Could it possibly be the case that Deedat apparently thinks the 5,000 extant New Testament manuscripts represent "original" texts, as he actually calls them?[11] He seems to miss that the later texts are only copies of the originals.

These examples are not the only embarrassing claims. In another book, Deedat charges the early church with choosing just the four Gospels—Matthew, Mark, Luke, and John—"out of over four thousand differing manuscripts the Christians boast about." We are told that Christians chose these four Gospels because these volumes are the ones that supported "their prejudices."[12] Once again, like the problem above, Deedat is not only confusing the manuscript *copies* of these four texts but including copies of other New Testament books in his total as well, writings that are already found in the New Testament canon.

Finally, Deedat appears to think that new translations that differentiate from the King James Version are actually evidence of Christians continually corrupting the original writings. Here are a couple of Deedat's charges that he thinks follow from this point: when different translations change words like "virgin" in Isa 7:14 to "young woman" and "begotten Son" in John 3:16 becomes "only Son," these also betray textual corruptions![13] But as Norm Geisler and Abdul Saleeb point out, the Hebrew and

---

[9] Ahmed Deedat, *Crucifixion or Cruci-fiction?* (Jedda: Abul-Qasim, 1984), 6–7.

[10] Deedat, 64 (emphasis added).

[11] Deedat, 7.

[12] Ahmed Deedat, *Is the Bible God's Word?* (Chicago: Kazi, 1990), 24.

[13] Deedat, 7–11.

Greek terms here *have not changed one bit*, so nothing has been corrupted. These are simply translational choices in English for these foreign words.[14]

Blatant confusions like these only serve to indicate that Deedat is unaware of the Christian claims and nuances in the first place. Repeated charges that confuse original works with their own copies, and the same copies with new texts, are simply illegitimate critiques altogether.

There is also the claim that the authors of the original writings themselves or later Christians often contradicted themselves or each other, with several specific examples being given.[15] Many substantial and detailed responses have been made to this charge on a case-by-case basis, though many volumes of material cannot be duplicated here. Examples throughout the New Testament are available, even specifically directed to the Gospel accounts of Jesus's resurrection appearances.[16]

We will limit ourselves to one specific example that is far from a straw man argument. It may be the single most-common question of all with regard to the Gospel resurrection narratives. Namely, how many women discovered the empty tomb on the initial resurrection morning—who were they?

In Matthew's narrative, Mary Magdalene and another Mary made the walk to the tomb (Matt 28:1). Mark names two women named Mary and Salome (Mark 16:1). Luke also mentions two women named Mary and adds Joanna (Luke 24:10), while John names only Mary Magdalene (John 20:1).

Even leaving the list of names just like this by no means signifies the existence of a contradiction. Further, *each* Gospel contains additional caveats that clearly indicate that it was *not* the author's intention to be exhaustive in naming each of the women in attendance. For instance, when Luke identifies the women, beyond the three names mentioned, he plainly states that there were "other women with them" but without

---

[14] Norman L. Geisler and Abdul Saleeb, *Answering Islam: The Crescent in the Light of the Cross* (Grand Rapids: Baker, 1993), 301–2.

[15] Deedat also argues this way (*Crucifixion or Cruci-fiction?*, 6–7, 16, 19–21, 39–40, cf. 76).

[16] For both general as well as specific examples of these works, see Norman L. Geisler and Thomas Howe, *When Critics Ask: A Popular Handbook of Bible Difficulties* (Wheaton, IL: Victor, 1992); Gleason L. Archer Jr., *New International Encyclopedia of Bible Difficulties* (Grand Rapids: Zondervan, 1982); Craig L. Blomberg, *The Historical Reliability of the New Testament: Countering the Challenges to Evangelical Christian Beliefs* (Nashville: B&H, 2016); Peter J. Williams, *Can We Trust the Gospels?* (Wheaton, IL: Crossway, 2018); Steven L. Cox and Kendall H. Easley, eds., *Harmony of the Gospels* (Nashville: B&H, 2007); John Wenham, *The Easter Enigma: Are the Resurrection Accounts in Conflict?* (Grand Rapids: Zondervan, 1984).

naming any more (24:10). How much clearer could Luke be? Mark alone includes Salome along with the two named Mary, but while naming the same three women just several verses earlier during the burial account, he specifically states that there were several other women there as well (Mark 15:41).

Similarly, Matthew also names the women at the burial just a few verses earlier, and includes a third one, the unnamed mother of Zebedee's sons, James and John (Matt 27:56). But by not providing a proper name for this additional woman, he likewise indicates that it was not his purpose to identify all of them, or this could easily have been done. True, John mentions only Mary Magdalene by name, but when she goes to tell the disciples in the very next verse, she states that "we" do not know where Jesus's body was located (John 20:1–2). Why should she speak in the plural if she was the only one present?

That this may well be the most commonly raised objection in the Gospel burial and resurrection accounts is simply amazing. Each of the four writers either explicitly or implicitly acknowledges the presence of one or more additional, unnamed women. Combined with the normal rule of literary criticism not to blame an author for something that they never intended to do in the first place, there is no conflict between the lists of women from one Gospel account to the next.

Over the past century or so, there have also been many sophisticated responses from scholarly Muslim apologists. For example, Maulavi Sayid Amir Ali charges that Jesus never claimed to be a deity in any way. Rather, he was a great prophet whose story was changed by the Christian Gospel writers. Following our earlier point, he also contends that the crucifixion and resurrection accounts contain discrepancies.[17]

Another scholar, Mauliv Muhammad Ali, indicts the Gospel records for exaggerating their reports, including particularly Jesus's miracle claims, which he regards disdainfully as "clearly pure inventions or exaggerations made to compensate for the apparent failure" of Jesus's message to change his contemporaries, in spite of the Quran's recognition that Jesus performed miracles and was a prophet.[18]

In a surprising admission, Salih-ud-din Khuda Bukhsh freely acknowledges a number of problems in the Quran, such as Islam being an eclectic religion that borrowed

---

[17] Maulavi Saiyid Amir Ali, "Christianity from the Islâmic Standpoint," in *Christianity: Some Non-Christian Appraisals*, ed. David W. McKain (New York: McGraw-Hill, 1964), esp. 226–29, 232, 237.

[18] Mauliv Muhammad Ali, "Muhammad and Christ," in McKain, *Christianity*, particularly 279, 282, 287–88.

freely from other religious traditions, including Christianity, as well as reporting falsehoods. Nonetheless, Bukhsh still recounts Mohammed's rejecting the Gospel accounts of the crucifixion, though still holding that Jesus was a prophet. He concludes his essay by calling for greater cooperation between Muslims and Christians.[19]

Again, these challenges by Muslims or other scholars may be answered on a case-by-case basis, usually with surprisingly minimal effort. Still, it is at these points that the minimal facts argument is also very helpful, as it calls for using only those historical data that are freely recognized by critical scholars. Since these few facts admittedly meet the demands of historicity, the charges of discrepancies in disputed areas do not dislodge the force of the commonly held material. After all, if these well-grounded details are sufficient in themselves to establish the crucifixion and even the resurrection as historical events, then disagreements in other areas are simply beside the point of whether these events themselves occurred.

The Death and Resurrection of Jesus

Perhaps a fair place to begin here is to note that according to the teaching of the Quran and Islam as a whole, Jesus (or Isa) is a very important and lofty figure, one of the most exalted of the Muslim prophets.[20] The Quran often lists Jesus among other well-known Jewish prophets (QS 2:136; 6:86; 42:13). Jesus is also referred to as having been born of a virgin (3:47; 19:20–21) and as being the Jewish Messiah (3:45; 4:171; 5:75; cf. 6:90). He was also sinless (19:19) and performed miracles during his ministry (3:49; 5:110). Of course, he is not believed to be the Son of God in any sense of deity (4:171; 5:72; 19:35) and Allah alone is God (3:62–64; 4:171; 5:116–18) rather than there being a trinity of beings (4:171; 5:72–73, 116).

When it comes to the crucifixion, Muslims generally agree that Jesus did not die by crucifixion. However, several different options are chosen by various commentators as to what may have happened instead of the Gospel depictions. For example, Maulavi Ali points out that the orthodox Muslim position is that Jesus was "saved by divine

---

[19] Salih-ud-din Khuda Bukhsh, "A Mohammedan View of Christendom," in McKain, *Christianity*, 243–45, 254.

[20] According to QS 2:87, 136, 253; 3:45; 4:171; 5:111; 6:86, 90; 19:30; 42:13. Unless otherwise noted, Mohammed Marmaduke Pickthall's well-known volume is being used: *The Meaning of the Glorious Koran: An Explanatory Translation* (New York: New American Library, 1953).

agency . . . that [Jesus] was translated to heaven."[21] In his volume *Jesus in the Qur'an*, well-known comparative religions expert Geoffrey Parrinder seems to agree here, pointing out, "Traditional Islam has thought that Jesus was rapt to heaven, in a fleshly body, though the Qur'an does not say so."[22]

According to Bukhsh, another popular view is one that he ascribes to Mohammed's teaching that "Judas was substituted for Him and nailed to the cross, while the Christ himself ascended direct to heaven."[23] A recent English translation and commentary on the Quran at 4:157 comments, "It was Judas Iscariot, who sought to betray Jesus, who was arrested instead, and crucified instead of the Prophet Jesus, upon whom be peace."[24]

Deedat prefers to cite the Gospels except when he disagrees with them, so it is difficult to know precisely which option he holds. However, he is clear that, whatever happened, Jesus definitely did not die by crucifixion. Yet, Deedat seems to leave open the option as to whether Jesus was at least initially crucified without dying by this method of execution.[25] He concludes his small book with the affirmation of the bottom line: he believes the Quran (4:157) that Jesus did not die by crucifixion, but it only appeared that way.[26]

However, quite intriguingly, the very next verse in the Quran (4:158) states that Allah took Jesus up to himself. Similar teachings are affirmed elsewhere too. Allah caused Jesus to ascend to him (3:55). Jesus would die and be raised again (19:33–34). What do these intriguing texts indicate?

Parrinder cites Muslim scholar Baidāwi to point out that Muslim commentators have differed on the interpretation of these latter texts concerning Jesus ascending or being taken up to heaven. Some Muslims thought that Jesus was raised to heaven bodily, only to be sent back to earth seven days after this ascension in order to send out his disciples before being taken up to heaven again. Parrinder comments that the New Testament accounts of Jesus's ascension seem to be in view here. But he notes further that regarding the idea that Jesus returned to earth seven days later in order to send out his disciples, as in the Gospels, "then the parallel is rather with

---

[21] Ali, "Christianity from the Islâmic Standpoint," 231–32.

[22] Geoffrey Parrinder, *Jesus in the Qur'an* (Oxford: Oneworld, 1995), 122.

[23] Bukhsh, "Mohammedan View of Christendom," 244–45.

[24] *The Glorious Qur'an with English Translation and Commentary*, 18th ed. (Piscataway, NJ: Why Islam?, 2003), QS 4:157 plus comment.

[25] Deedat, *Crucifixion or Cruci-fiction?*, 31, 78.

[26] Deedat, 88.

the resurrection appearances of the Gospel." Parrinder continues: "These are not mentioned in the Qur'ān, but they are not denied, and they agree with the common interpretation."[27]

Going further, Parrinder cites Muslim authorities Bukhāri and Baidāwi, who note another traditional Muslim interpretation that Jesus will return someday to restore God's order in the world, citing texts concerning Jesus's exaltation and eschatological significance such as 3:45; 4:159; and especially the intriguing text in 43:61.[28] Incredibly, the English translation and commentary of the Quran mentioned earlier at 43:61 reads, "And (the second coming of Jesus shall be) a sign of the Hour." A textual note there indicates, "There is indication to Jesus's descension before the Day of Judgement."[29]

Parrinder is not alone in his hint that the Quranic teaching of Jesus's lack of death by crucifixion, followed by his potential return to commission his disciples in ministry and his ascension, seem to parallel the New Testament accounts of Jesus's appearances to his disciples after the crucifixion. After all, Jesus's commissioning of these men came after his resurrection and before his ascension (as in Matt 28:18–20; Luke 24:46–51; and Acts 1:1–11).

Another Muslim specialist, Donald Rickards, contends that the meaning of QS 4:157 is not to deny Jesus's death by crucifixion but to assert that such did not come from human hands. In the context of Allah's sovereignty, the verse points out that Jesus did die by crucifixion but by Allah's will rather than by human will. Further, Rickards points out that, in the Quran, Jesus (or Isa) predicted his own resurrection ahead of time (as in 19:33–34), with Allah confirming that Jesus's resurrection would occur (3:55; 4:158–59; 5:117).[30]

Granted, Rickard's interpretation is not the normal angle on this particular Quranic text, but it is intriguing nonetheless. Moreover, texts such as QS 19:33 that do refer to Jesus's death must also be explained. While the majority of commentators place his death in the end times after Jesus returns, the view that it happened at the crucifixion needs at least to be considered. Further, *whatever* is concluded regarding

---

[27] Parrinder, *Jesus in the Qur'an*, 122.

[28] Parrinder, 123–24.

[29] *Glorious Qur'an*, QS 43:61 and commentary on 493. For a more detailed note along these same lines, see QS 4:157 in this translation, plus the commentary afterward at 4:159.

[30] Donald R. Rickards, "The Contextualization of the Gospel in the World of Islam," *Liberty Baptist Theological Lecture Series* 1 (1984): 40–83, esp. 63–67.

Jesus's crucifixion, the issue of Jesus's resurrection and ascension are also keys here, especially given the various options among even Muslim interpreters.[31]

But it still must be noted that the Quran presents no strictly *historical* grounds for rejecting the Gospel's teaching of Jesus's crucifixion and subsequent resurrection. As many Muslim commentators usually report outright, their commitment to the position that Jesus did not die by crucifixion is almost always said to be their faith in their holy book.[32] In other words, holding their position is not due to there being such good evidence against this Christian teaching. Rather, it is their faith in a book that determines their position, even though the book was written almost exactly 600 years after the crucifixion event itself. But unless one grants total commitment to their holy texts, what is there to oppose the vast amount of evidence that favors the crucifixion?

Speaking historically, a document from 600 years after the earliest reported data is not usually counted as a historical document. Strangely enough, even the popular Muslim commentator Deedat concedes exactly that! He states, "The Christian objects, 'how can a man (Muhummed pbuh) a thousand miles away from the scene of a happening, and 600 years after the event, pronounce as to what transpired?'" Deedat's surprising and incredible answer is, "The Christian plea is valid. Their logic is good."[33]

Instead, Deedat's immediate response is to go to the Christian texts to attack them. This is an exceptionally common move on the part of Muslims. If one's own text has no historical provenance whatsoever, then let's question their texts! And right away, he opts to discuss contradictions in the Gospel texts, the very subject we addressed above.[34]

But we have seen that this tactic fails for at least three reasons. (1) These claims of contradiction regarding the New Testament texts can all be answered anyway. Many scholarly volumes and thousands of pages have shown that this is the case in both general as well as specific cases.

(2) Claimed contradictions and other such problems virtually never disprove events anyway. Ask any police officer, lawyer, physician, or journalist if conflicting stories indicate that a particular accident, crime, disease, or football game never

---

[31] *Glorious Qur'an*, QS 4:159, esp. the commentary on 102.

[32] Again, see Deedat, *Crucifixion or Cruci-fiction?*, 88.

[33] Deedat, 6.

[34] Deedat, 6; also, this same technique is found on 6–7, 16, 19–21, 39–40.

occurred. Highly trained professionals are experts at sorting out likely scenarios even in situations where the claims are far from unanimous.

(3) Finally, as pointed out above, using the minimal facts method bypasses this issue with claimed contradictions altogether because it utilizes *only* those facts which are exceptionally well established historically, to the point where virtually all critical scholars concede them. If they are sufficient to establish Jesus's death and resurrection, then the basic case for these events is shown to be true.

AUTHOR INDEX

855

SUBJECT INDEX

SCRIPTURE INDEX